THE GOSPELS AND THEIR RECEPTIONS

FESTSCHRIFT JOSEPH VERHEYDEN

BIBLIOTHECA
EPHEMERIDUM THEOLOGICARUM LOVANIENSIUM

EDITED BY THE BOARD OF
EPHEMERIDES THEOLOGICAE LOVANIENSES

Louis-Léon Christians – Henri Derroitte – Wim François – Éric Gaziaux
Joris Geldhof – Arnaud Join-Lambert – Johan Leemans
Olivier Riaudel (secretary) – Matthieu Richelle
Joseph Verheyden (general editor)

EDITORIAL STAFF

Rita Corstjens – Claire Timmermans

UNIVERSITÉ CATHOLIQUE DE LOUVAIN　　　　　　KU LEUVEN
LOUVAIN-LA-NEUVE　　　　　　　　　　　　　　LEUVEN

BIBLIOTHECA EPHEMERIDUM THEOLOGICARUM LOVANIENSIUM

CCCXXX

THE GOSPELS AND THEIR RECEPTIONS

FESTSCHRIFT JOSEPH VERHEYDEN

EDITED BY

HENK JAN DE JONGE – MARK GRUNDEKEN

JOHN KLOPPENBORG – CHRISTOPHER TUCKETT

PEETERS
LEUVEN – PARIS – BRISTOL, CT
2022

A catalogue record for this book is available from the Library of Congress.

ISBN 978-90-429-4876-1
eISBN 978-90-429-4877-8
D/2022/0602/49

*All rights reserved. Except in those cases expressly determined by law,
no part of this publication may be multiplied, saved in an automated data file
or made public in any way whatsoever
without the express prior written consent of the publishers.*

© 2022 – Peeters, Bondgenotenlaan 153, B-3000 Leuven (Belgium)

PREFACE

It was with great sadness that the editors of this volume learnt of the death of Professor Henk Jan de Jonge the day before Easter Day 2022. He was diagnosed with terminal cancer in early March and died in a hospice in Leiden on 16 April 2022. Henk Jan de Jonge had been the main driving force in initiating the production of this Festschrift: he had been involved in the planning of the volume, undertaken the first contacts with potential authors, as well as then undertaking the initial editing of all the essays as they were submitted, suggesting improvements, correcting errors and ensuring that the essays conformed to the correct style for the BETL series. He was just in the process of starting to read the first proofs when he became ill and was taken into hospital before being diagnosed. Everyone who has read Henk Jan de Jonge's work will know of his scholarship which was always honest, critical (in the best sense of the word) and open, covering a vast range of scholarly areas and subjects. His editorial work (over many years for journals and edited volumes) was invariably painstakingly detailed, insisting on the highest standards of accuracy. Above all, those of us who were privileged to know him personally will sorely miss a friend and colleague who enriched the lives of many people.

TABLE OF CONTENTS

Preface...	VII
Joseph Verheyden – A Portrait (Henk Jan DE JONGE – Mark GRUNDEKEN – John KLOPPENBORG – Christopher TUCKETT)	XIII
Academic Curriculum Vitae of Joseph Verheyden (°15 October 1957)...	XIX
Abbreviations	XXV
Bibliography of Joseph Verheyden 1979-2022	XXXI
Book Reviews Written by Joseph Verheyden 1982-2021.........	LXV

John S. KLOPPENBORG (Toronto, ON)
Plutarch Meets the Farrer Hypothesis..................... 1

Giovanni B. BAZZANA (Cambridge, MA)
The Language of Violence in the Sayings Gospel Q: An Initial Examination.. 21

Paul FOSTER (Edinburgh)
Are There Any Matthean Western Non-Interpolations? 45

Dietrich-Alex KOCH (Münster)
Das Markusevangelium als katechetisches Handbuch 71

Cilliers BREYTENBACH (Berlin)
Where Mark Did Not Follow LXX Versions: Pre-Markan Tradition in Mark 1,2; 4,12; 8,18; 9,48; 13,24-25; 15,34 97

Geert VAN OYEN (Louvain-la-Neuve)
La formule «σὺ εἶ» et la caractérisation narrative de Jésus chez Marc... 119

Henk Jan DE JONGE (Leiden)
The Baptism of Jesus by John the Baptist: A Bedrock Historical Datum?.. 139

Adela YARBRO COLLINS (New Haven, CT)
Messiah and Son of Man in Mark 8,27-33................. 151

Mark GRUNDEKEN (Freiburg i.Br.)
„Euer Heiland ruft und schreit!": Jesu Todesschrei in Mk 15,
34.37 171

Adelbert DENAUX (Leuven) – Albert HOGETERP (Bloemfontein – Elst)
The Author of Luke-Acts in a Bilingual Context............ 183

Uta POPLUTZ (Wuppertal)
Allusions to Education in Luke-Acts: Sidelights on Implicit
Conceptions of *Paideia* 209

Christopher TUCKETT (Oxford)
Luke and Ignatius 227

Andreas LINDEMANN (Bethel-Bielefeld)
„Ist das nicht Josephs Sohn?" (Lk 4,22): Jesu Familie in den
neutestamentlichen Evangelien 249

Daniel A. SMITH (London, ON)
"Why Do Doubts Arise in Your Hearts?" (Luke 24,38): Narrative as Apologetic in Gospel Resurrection Stories 273

Peter J. JUDGE (Rock Hill, SC)
Come and See – Once Again: The Call of the First Disciples
and Christology in John 1,35-51 295

Jörg FREY (Zürich)
Who Is Nathanael? Or: Who Can Nathanael Be for Readers of
John? Reception History and Biblical Scholarship in Dialogue.. 311

Christina M. KREINECKER (Leuven)
Mehrsprachigkeit am Kreuz: Papyrologische Anmerkungen zu
Joh 19,20 337

Reimund BIERINGER (Leuven)
Μαριάμ or Μαρία in John 20,16? A Plea for *docta ignorantia* 361

Jan VAN DER WATT (Nijmegen – Bloemfontein)
Tradition as Foundation in the Johannine Community........ 389

Thomas WITULSKI (Bielefeld)
Johanneisches Traditionsmaterial im Johannesevangelium, in
den Johannesbriefen und in den Ignatiusbriefen............. 411

Dan BATOVICI (Leuven)
The Reception of the *Gospel of Peter* in Late Antiquity 437

Jens SCHRÖTER (Berlin)
    Evangelientraditionen in der *Offenbarung des Petrus*   453

Korinna ZAMFIR (Cluj)
    Rereading Gospel Traditions in the *Acts of Thecla*: The Dilemma
    of the Beatitudes   479

Tobias NICKLAS (Regensburg)
    Der göttliche Lehrer und seine Schüler: Eine Erzählung über
    Passion, Ostern und die Anfänge der Kirche in Tertullians *Apolo-
    geticum*.   501

Francis WATSON (Durham)
    Negotiating the Passion Tradition: Athanasius and the Great
    Seth.   533

Sarah E. ROLLENS (Memphis, TN)
    Rethinking the Early Christian Mission   557

INDEXES
    Index Locorum.   579
    Index Auctorum   610

Photo: Flora Carrijn

JOSEPH VERHEYDEN – A PORTRAIT

On October 15, 2022, Joseph Verheyden, Professor of New Testament at the Faculty of Theology and Religious Studies of KU Leuven since 1994, will turn 65. The date mentioned is not the day on which Professor Verheyden *rude donabitur*, and still less the end of his scholarly career. It is simply his birthday and the day which colleagues and friends have chosen to pay homage to him because of his extraordinary merits in the field of the study of the New Testament and early Christian literature. This homage takes the form of the present academic Festschrift.

Professor Verheyden's scholarly achievements are indeed numerous and extremely varied. As a student of Professor Frans Neirynck (1927-2012), he was trained in pursuing research into the Synoptic Problem and thus became an expert in the study of the Synoptic Gospels and the sayings source Q. The methods he mastered were textual criticism, source criticism, redaction criticism, and tradition criticism. Already in his doctoral dissertation ("The Flight of the Christians to Pella", 1987) he extended his field of research to authors of the early church, especially Eusebius and Epiphanius.

The mere enumeration of the areas in which Verheyden has conducted research is astounding. Apart from the Synoptic Gospels and Q, he has published scholarly studies on John, Acts, the Pauline letters, and the Apocalypse; New Testament textual criticism, Old Testament pseudepigrapha (for instance, the *Ascension of Isaiah* and *1 Enoch*); ancient Christian apocrypha (*inter alia* the *Gospel of Peter*, the *Acts of Philip*, and the *Pseudo-Clementines*); the Apostolic Fathers (especially *1 Clement, Barnabas*, and the *Shepherd of Hermas*); the *Muratorian Fragment*; the formation of the New Testament canon; epigraphical evidence illustrating the New Testament; early Christian authors (including Irenaeus, Origen, Eustathius of Antioch, and Victor of Antioch); the reception of Old and New Testament traditions in patristic literature; the history of eastern Christianity; the history of New Testament scholarship; translating the Bible in early Christianity and in modern times; and other research areas could be added to this list.

The three main themes of Verheyden's research, however, are (1) the continuing defence and justification of the Two Source Theory with respect to the genesis of the Synoptic Gospels, including Markan priority and rejecting the hypothesis of Proto-Luke. (2) The relationship between Luke's Gospel and the Book of Acts, which Verheyden interprets in the sense that Luke, when writing his gospel, was already considering the idea of writing a continuation about what happened beyond the point where his gospel would stop: "Luke looks forward to Acts". To a certain extent, Luke and Acts can therefore be regarded as a two-volume work. (3) The reception of New Testament writings and traditions in later Christian authors and communities: which texts and traditions did they take up, how did they quote and interpret them, and in which contexts and with what intentions did they use them? The intended result of this research is a "patristic commentary" on the writings of the New Testament.

The bibliography of Verheyden's scholarly publications included in this volume gives an impression of the massive œuvre he has already produced. This œuvre will certainly grow in the years to come, for several of Verheyden's research projects will continue to bear fruit, some papers he has given at conferences have still to be prepared for publication, and the texts of several guest lectures he delivered at various universities still deserve to be published. It is to be hoped that one day we will see a volume, or rather some volumes, of his collected essays appear in print.

Verheyden's academic work is characterized by a strictly historical and literary-critical approach, a careful, contextual interpretation of texts, critical sense, methodical rigor, exhaustive knowledge of previous scholarly literature, the fair exchange of arguments with authors holding different opinions, a balanced judgement, and clarity in argumentation and presentation.

His published work comprises a great number of multi-author volumes he has edited, either alone or with one or more co-editors. This typifies his whole scholarly work: it shows his unrestrained readiness to serve the advancement of scholarship and the international community of researchers by helping teams of colleagues, individual scholars, and early career researchers to publish the results of their work. At the present moment, the number of books edited by Verheyden, alone or with others, is more than fifty, and still growing. We mention just four of them: *The Unity of Luke-Acts* (1999), *Prophets and Prophecy in Jewish and Early Christian Literature* (2010), *The Figure of Solomon in Jewish Christian and Islamic Tradition* (2013), and *Early Christian Communities between Ideal and Reality* (with M. Grundeken, 2015). (For details, see the bibliography.)

Quite a number of the research articles which Verheyden has published are of such a size and substance that they can rightly be considered short monographs. This applies, for instance, to his study on the date of the *Canon Muratori* (2001), which runs to no less than 70 pages. His article on the unity of Luke and Acts (1999) consists of 54 pages, that on Peter in the *Pseudo-Clementines* (2021) 51 pages, and his paper on the fate of the Matthean Peter in apocryphal literature (2011) numbers 49 pages. Of similar length are his articles on meals in the apocryphal acts (2017: 50 pages), the language of the Apocalypse of John (2017: 46 pages), and the number of disciples mentioned in Lk 10,1 (2005: also 46 pages).

Verheyden also promoted international research on the New Testament and related literature by his involvement as co-director and co-editor in such large-scale projects as *Documenta Q*, a critical survey of two centuries of research into Q (with John Kloppenborg and others; 2002-), and in two projects already alluded to above, the *Novum Testamentum Patristicum* (with Andreas Merkt, Tobias Nicklas, and others; 2007-), and the commentary on the New Testament based on information provided by ancient inscriptions (with Thomas Corsten and Markus Öhler; 2014-). Furthermore, in 2010 Verheyden founded the Leuven Centre for the Study of the Gospels and recruited a team of internationally reputed experts as members. Members of the Centre meet annually with other participants to study literary-critical and source-critical issues concerning the Gospels. The proceedings of the colloquia of the Centre have appeared in an impressive number of volumes edited by Verheyden in cooperation with other members of the Centre.

Since 1998, Verheyden has been a member of the editorial board of *Ephemerides Theologicae Lovanienses* (*ETL*), the Leuven journal of theology and canon law, and of the accompanying series "Bibliotheca Ephemeridum Theologicarum Lovaniensium" (BETL). In 2011, he became the editor in chief. In addition, he served on the editorial board of the international journal *New Testament Studies*, published by Cambridge University Press, from 2016 to 2019. Since 2016, he has been an editorial board member of the international quarterly *Novum Testamentum* and the series "Supplements to Novum Testamentum", published by Brill, Leiden. He acted also as executive editor of the *Journal of Eastern Christian Studies* from 2002 to 2015 and has been this journal's editor in chief since 2015; furthermore he has been executive editor of the series "Eastern Christian Studies" from 2005 to 2015 and its editor in chief since 2015. Both the *Journal* and the "Studies" are published by Peeters, Leuven. The series "Kommentare zur apokryphen Literatur" began to appear in 2010 under the shared editorship of Verheyden, Tobias Nicklas, and Christopher Tuckett, published by Vandenhoeck & Ruprecht, Göttingen. Verheyden has been, or is, a member of the editorial boards of several other scholarly periodicals (for details, see his curriculum vitae in this volume).

In view of the amount of work Verheyden has taken on as editor of journals, series, conference proceedings, and multi-author volumes of essays, one may wonder if any New Testament scholar has ever edited the writings of so many colleagues.

Verheyden's commitment to the furtherance of biblical scholarship is further exemplified by his role as Secretary and convener of the annual Colloquium Biblicum Lovaniense during the period 2001-2011. In 1998, he acted as President of the Colloquium. In 2012 he chaired the local committee which organized the General Meeting of the international Society of New Testament Studies (SNTS), which took place in Leuven that year. During the 2021 SNTS meeting, Verheyden was nominated as President of the Society for 2023-2024.

When in 2021, because of the COVID-19 pandemic, the venue that had originally been arranged for the 75th General Meeting of the SNTS became impossible, Jos Verheyden, together with Reimund Bieringer and Christina Kreinecker, took upon themselves to organize this meeting in a virtual, online form, technically arranged and supported from Leuven. They also offered to organize the 2022 SNTS General Meeting as an on-campus event in Leuven. At the moment of writing these lines it is still uncertain whether it will really take place on campus or online, or in a hybrid form.

In 2013, Verheyden was one of the founders of the Professor Frans Neirynck Foundation which aims to promote research and teaching in the field of theology and religious studies, in particular biblical studies, at KU Leuven. He also became its chair. The foundation organizes, *inter alia*, the annual Frans Neirynck Lecture in Leuven, delivered by leading New Testament scholars, and published in *ETL*.

Self-denial and readiness to serve other researchers are also reflected in the comprehensive bibliographies of recent work on the New Testament and early Christian literature which Verheyden compiled over the years with some Leuven colleagues and published in *ETL* or BETL. The same applies to the hundreds of book reviews he wrote for *ETL* and other journals; a complete list of his reviews published up to and including 2021 appears in this volume.

Verheyden is also an indefatigable conference participant. He attends more scholarly congresses, meetings, colloquia, and symposia of learned societies and expert groups than any colleague would be physically able to do. He not only attends them, but also enriches them with his lectures, papers, and responses. As a result, he has a dense and widespread network in academia; he knows more colleagues working in the fields of the New Testament, early Christian literature, and related disciplines all around the globe than anybody else. He used to fly so frequently back and forth between Europe and America, that – it is said – one day, on a return flight to Europe, when in the air his plane passed another plane heading to the US, he noticed himself behind a window of the other plane. And to think that he shuttled, and shuttles, much more often between the countries of Europe than between Europe and America … Unsurprisingly, since March 2020, when COVID-19 began to infect the world, Verheyden participated just as frequently in online video conferences as he did previously in live meetings.

One special way in which Verheyden has made a substantial impact on research of the New Testament and early Christian literature at Leuven is his active policy of devising research projects, applying to obtain funding for them from the Research Foundation of KU Leuven or the Research Foundation – Flanders, and, in the case of success, attracting able PhD students or postdocs to carry out the planned project. He has supervised 16 PhD students, and more will follow. His doctoral students, especially those from outside Belgium, tell us that there was no end to the helpfulness of Jos and his wife, Professor Flora Carrijn, in arranging their enrolment in the university, finding accommodation, and purchasing furniture for them. They depict Jos and Flora as lugging big shopping bags through the streets of Leuven to provide them with food, cutlery, and kitchen-ware. Flora has also made the photograph that serves as frontispiece to this volume.

The authors and editors of this volume of essays wish to congratulate Professor Verheyden both on his 65th birthday and on the impressive and important work he has accomplished as a scholar. We want to thank him for all the insights he has provided into the literature, history, and ideas of early Christianity. We also wish to congratulate Flora on this jubilee and to thank her for the backing she has continuously given to her husband. We wish them both many years to come with good health and a *varietas delectans* of *studiorum dulcedo* and *otium felix atque iucundum*.

Many more authors would have liked to participate in this tribute to Jos Verheyden. However, the practical constraint of the maximum page count of this volume inevitably imposed limitations on the number of authors involved. The honouree may nevertheless rest assured that numerous other colleagues share the admiration, respect, and sympathy for him which the authors and editors of this volume feel towards him.

Henk Jan DE JONGE
Mark GRUNDEKEN
John KLOPPENBORG
Christopher TUCKETT

ACADEMIC CURRICULUM VITAE OF JOSEPH VERHEYDEN
(° 15 OCTOBER 1957)

1. Academic titles and qualifications – administrative and managing tasks

Studies at KU Leuven
- BA Egyptology (1978), BA Islamic Studies (1980)
- MA Religious Studies (1979), MA Philosophy (1980), MA Languages and Culture of the Christian East (1983), MA and STL Theology (1985)
- Doctor in Theology (STD) (1987)

Academic and research career
- 1987-1989 Postdoctoral Research Fellow and 1989-2000 Senior Research Fellow at KU Leuven funded by the National Fund for Scientific Research of Belgium (NFWO)
- 1994-2000 Adjunct Professor ("Docent") of New Testament in the Faculty of Theology of KU Leuven (part time)
- 2000-2005 Associate Professor ("Hoofddocent")
- 2005-2009 Professor
- since 2009 Full Professor of New Testament in the Faculty of Theology and Religious Studies

Management and administration: membership in
- Advisory Board Interdisciplinary Centre for the Study of Religion, Faculty of Theology (2003-2012)
- Committee on IT Faculty of Theology (2003-2010)
- Head and Coordinator Research Unit Biblical Studies (2005-2008)
- Board of the Faculty of Theology (2005-2008)
- Board of the Institute of Eastern Christian Studies, Nijmegen (2005-2017)
- Expert Panel Theology, Philosophy and Religious Studies of the Flemish Research Foundation (FWO) (2006-2013; Chair 2012-2013)
- Advisory committee of the FWO for the restructuring of the experts panels (2007-2017)
- AKAST – Agentur für Qualitätssicherung und Akkreditierung kanonischer Studiengänge in Deutschland (2009- : member of the committee)
- Co-founder and chair of the Leuven Centre for the Study of the Gospels (LCSG) (2010-)

- Chair of the Frans Neirynck Foundation (2013-)
- Co-founder and co-chair of Polemikos: Centre for the Study of Religion and Polemics (2014-)
- Director of the Louvain Centre for Eastern and Oriental Christianity (LOCEOC) (2015-)
- President of Kosmoi: Interdisciplinary Centre for the Study of Religion (2015-2016)

Distinctions:
- Laureate of the Koninklijke Vlaamse Academie van België voor Wetenschappen en Kunsten – Royal Flemish Academy of Belgium for the Sciences and the Arts (19 December, 1987)
- Honorary Fellow of the Centre for Advanced Studies "Beyond Canon – Heterotopias of Religious Authority in Late Antique Christianity", Regensburg (27 July, 2020)

2. (Co-)supervisor of PhD projects

Completed: 16
In progress: 8

3. Ongoing and past research projects

- General editor, with P. Hoffmann (Bamberg), J.S. Kloppenborg (Toronto), and C. Heil (Graz), of the international research project *Documenta Q* (2003-)
- General editor, with A. Merkt and T. Nicklas (Regensburg), of the *Novum Testamentum Patristicum* (2007-)
- General editor, with M. Öhler and T. Corsten (Vienna), of the *Epigraphical Commentary on the NT* Project (2016-)
- *Social Structures and Functionaries in the Communities behind the Dead Sea Scrolls and behind New Testament Writings* (2003-2007; with F. García Martínez, Leuven) (funded by the KU Leuven Research Foundation)
- *Jesus and the Law in the Matthean Community: A Source- and Redaction-Critical Study of Matt 5,38-48* (2004-2008) (private funding)
- *From Text to Theology: Paul Ricoeur's Critical Hermeneutics and the Dialogue between Exegesis and Systematic Theology* (with T. Hettema, Leiden) (2006-2010) (funded by FWO)

- *The Kingdom of God and Human Responsibility: An Exegetical Study of Luke 19,12-27* (2006-2010)
- *De Bethsaida à Jéricho: L'identité du disciple en Marc 8,22–10,52* (2008-2012) (private funding)
- *In Search for the Implicit Community of the Shepherd of Hermas* (2008-2012) (funded by FWO)
- *"Aufklärung durch Philologie" : The Contribution of J.J. Wettstein to the Exegesis of the Acts of the Apostles* (2010-2014) (funded by FWO)
- *The History of the Reception of the Greek Versions of the Old Testament in the Byzantine Era, with a Study of the Commentary on Proverbs by Malachias Monachus* (2009-2015; sup.: Peter Van Deun; co-sup.: J. Verheyden) (funded by FWO)
- *Anti-Jewish Polemics in the Fourth Century: A Regional Approach* (2010-2011) (funded by FWO)
- *Lost (and Found): A Critical Study and Analysis of the History of Research on Lost Documents and Hypothetical Sources of Early Christianity* (2012-2016) (funded by FWO)
- *Hunting Ghosts: A Critical Study of the Concept of Docetism and Its Use in Ancient and Modern Discussions of Early Christian Christology and Soteriology* (2013-2017) (funded by FWO)
- *From Chaos to Order – the Creation of the World: New Perspectives on the Reception of Platonic Cosmogony in Greek Philosophical and Christian Tradition* (2012-2017; with G. Van Riel, J. Leemans, G. Roskam, P. Van Deun) (funded by the KU Leuven Research Foundation)
- *Longing for Perfection* (2017-2023; with G. Roskam, J. Leemans, P. Van Deun, G. Van Riel) (funded by the KU Leuven Research Foundation)
- *Epigraphical Commentary on 1 Thessalonians* (2019-2022; with M. Öhler and T. Corsten) (funded by the Austrian Research Foundation)

4. Member of the editorial or advisory board of journals and series

- *Ephemerides Theologicae Lovanienses* (Leuven): collaborator (1992-1997); member of the editorial board (1998-); editor in chief (2011-)
- *Bibliotheca Ephemeridum Theologicarum Lovaniensium* (Leuven): member of the editorial board and the executive board (2001-); editor in chief (2011-)
- *The Journal of Eastern Christian Studies* (Nijmegen – Leuven): executive editor (2002-2015); editor in chief (2016-)
- *Documenta Q* (Leuven): co-editor (2003-)

- *Eastern Christian Studies* (Nijmegen – Leuven): executive editor (2004-2015); editor in chief (2016)
- *Biblical Tools and Studies* (Leuven): co-editor (2005-)
- *Sacra Scripta* (Cluj-Napoca): member of the editorial board (2006-)
- *Review of Biblical Literature* (Atlanta, GA): member of the editorial board (2006-2014)
- *Novum Testamentum Patristicum* (Göttingen): co-editor (2008-)
- *Berliner Theologische Zeitschrift* (Berlin): member of the advisory board (2008-)
- *Society of Biblical Studies: Early Christian Literature* (Atlanta, GA), member of the editorial board (2009-2012)
- *Kommentare zur apokryphen Literatur* (Göttingen): co-editor (2010-)
- *Rivista Biblica*: member of the advisory board (2010-)
- *Adnotationes* (Turnhout): co-editor (2013-2017)
- *Neotestamentica* (Stellenbosch): member of the advisory board (2014-)
- *Digital Biblical Studies* (Leiden): member of the scientific committee (2015-)
- *Novum Testamentum* (Leiden): member of the editorial board (2016-)
- *Supplements to Novum Testamentum* (Leiden): member of the editorial board (2016-)
- *New Testament Studies* (Cambridge): member of the editorial board (2017-2019)

5. Membership of scholarly associations

- *Studiosorum Novi Testamenti Conventus* (1993-; president 2010)
- *Wetenschappelijk Comité Godsdienstgeschiedenis Koninklijke Vlaamse Academie van België voor Wetenschappen en Kunsten* (Scientific Committee for the History of Religions of the Flemish Royal Academy of Belgium for the Sciences and the Arts) (1993-2003)
- *Studiorum Novi Testamenti Societas – Society of New Testament Studies* (1994-): member of the *Committee* (1998-2000 and again 2012-2014; 2021- observer); co-chair (with J. Schröter) SNTS Seminar *Current Studies in the Synoptic Gospels* (2000-2004); co-chair (with C.M. Tuckett and T. Nicklas) SNTS Seminar *Apocryphal Gospels* (2008-2015); chair of the local team inviting SNTS to Leuven in 2012; keynote speaker SNTS Pretoria, 2017; chair of the local team inviting SNTS to Leuven in 2021 and 2022; Presidential Nominee for 2023/24.
- *Society of Biblical Literature* (1997-): co-chair of the SBL Q Section, 2003-2006 (with M. Debaufre-Johnson) and 2006-2009 (with P. Foster),

and member of the steering committee (2009-2013); member of the steering committees: Consultation: *Eusebius of Caesarea and the Creation of Christian Identity* (2008-2012); Seminar: *Digital Humanities in Biblical, Early Jewish and Christian Studies* (2013-2017); Consultation, then Seminar: *Early Exegesis of Genesis 1–3* (2015-2018)
- *European Association of Catholic Theology* (2004-2014)
- *Association pour l'étude de la littérature apocryphe chrétienne AELAC* (2004-)
- *Société belgo-luxembourgeoise d'Histoire des Religions (Liège) and International Association for the History of Religions* (2004-2008)
- *Wissenschaftliche Gesellschaft für Theologie* (Berlin) (2005-)
- *Catholic Biblical Association* (2006-)
- *Centre of Biblical Studies*, Babeş-Bolyai University Cluj-Napoca, Romania (2006-)
- *Association internationale d'études patristiques – International Association of Patristic Studies* (2006-)
- *Society for the Promotion of Byzantine Studies* (2008-)
- *LECTIO, Leuven Centre for the Study of the Transmission of Texts and Ideas in Antiquity, the Middle Ages, and the Renaissance* (2010-); member of the steering group (2017-)
- *BABEL, Belgian Association for the Study of Religions*: co-founder (2011-); president (2011-2015)
- *EASR, European Association for the Study of Religion*: member of the Committee (2014-2015); chair of the local team inviting EASR to Leuven in 2017; vice-president (2020-2022)
- *IAHR, International Association for the History of Religion*: member of the Committee (2014-2015)

- President of the *Colloquium Biblicum Lovaniense* XLVII, *The Unity of Luke-Acts* (1998)
- Secretary of the annual International *Colloquium Biblicum Lovaniense* (2001-2011)

ABBREVIATIONS

AASF	Annales Academiae Scientiarum Fennicae
AB	Anchor Bible
ABD	*The Anchor Bible Dictionary*, New York, Doubleday, 1992
ABG	Arbeiten zur Bibel und ihrer Geschichte
Aeg	*Aegyptus*
AELAC	Association pour l'étude de la littérature apocryphe chrétienne
AJEC	Ancient Judaism and Early Christianity
AnBib	Analecta Biblica
ANF	Ante-Nicene Fathers
ANRW	*Aufstieg und Niedergang der römischen Welt*
ANTC	Abingdon New Testament Commentaries
AOAT	Alter Orient und Altes Testament
APF	*Archiv für Papyrusforschung*
APF Beiheft	Beihefte zum Archiv für Papyrusforschung
ArBib	The Aramaic Bible
ASE	*Annali di storia dell'esegesi*
ATANT	Abhandlungen zur Theologie des Alten und Neuen Testaments
BASP	*Bulletin of the American Society of Papyrologists*
BBB	Bonner biblische Beiträge
BDAG	W. Bauer – F.W. Danker – W.F. Arndt – F.W. Gingrich (eds.), *A Greek-English Lexicon of the New Testament and Other Early Christian Literature*
BDF	F. Blass – A. Debrunner – R. Funk, *A Greek Grammar of the New Testament*
BDR	F. Blass – A. Debrunner – F. Rehkopf, *Grammatik des neutestamentlichen Griechisch*
BETL	Bibliotheca Ephemeridum Theologicarum Lovaniensium
BG	Codex Berolinensis Gnosticus (Berlin)
BGU	Ägyptische Urkunden aus den Königlichen Staatlichen Museen zu Berlin
BHT	Beiträge zur historischen Theologie
Bib	*Biblica*
BibInt	Biblical Interpretation Series
BJRL	*Bulletin of the John Rylands Library*
BL	Berichtigungsliste der griechischen Papyrusurkunden
BMSEC	Baylor Mohr Siebeck Studies in Early Christianity

BN	*Biblische Notizen*
BNTC	Black's New Testament Commentaries
BTB	*Biblical Theology Bulletin*
BTS	Biblical Tools and Studies
BTSt	Biblisch-Theologische Studien
BTZ	*Berliner Theologische Zeitschrift*
BZ	*Biblische Zeitschrift*
BZNW	Beihefte zur Zeitschrift für die neutestamentliche Wissenschaft
CahRB	Cahiers de la Revue biblique
CAL	*The Comprehensive Aramaic Lexicon*
CBET	Contributions to Biblical Exegesis & Theology
CBQ	*Catholic Biblical Quarterly*
CBR	*Currents in Biblical Research*
CCSA	Corpus Christianorum: Series Apocryphorum
CCSL	Corpus Christianorum: Series Latina
CdE	*Chronique d'Égypte*
CII	*Corpus Inscriptionum Iudaicarum*
CNT	Commentaire du Nouveau Testament
CNTTS	Center for New Testament Textual Studies
CPJ	*Corpus Papyrorum Judaicorum*
CRINT	Compendia Rerum Iudaicarum ad Novum Testamentum
CSCO	Corpus Scriptorum Christianorum Orientalium
CSEL	Corpus Scriptorum Ecclesiasticorum Latinorum
CUP	Cambridge University Press
DJD	Discoveries in the Judaean Desert
DNP	*Der Neue Pauly: Enzyklopädie der Antike*
DSD	*Dead Sea Discoveries*
EBib	Études bibliques
EKKNT	Evangelisch-katholischer Kommentar zum Neuen Testament
ETL	*Ephemerides Theologicae Lovanienses*
EWNT	*Exegetisches Wörterbuch zum Neuen Testament*
ExpTim	*Expository Times*
FB	Forschung zur Bibel
FKDG	Forschungen zur Kirchen- und Dogmengeschichte
FRLANT	Forschungen zur Religion und Literatur des Alten und Neuen Testaments
GCS	Die Griechischen Christlichen Schriftsteller der ersten drei Jahrhunderte
GNS	Good News Studies
GNT	Grundrisse zum Neuen Testament

HGV	Heidelberger Gesamtverzeichnis der griechischen Papyrusurkunden Ägyptens
HNT	Handbuch zum Neuen Testament
HNTC	Harper's New Testament Commentaries
HSCP	*Harvard Studies in Classical Philology*
HTKNT	Herders Theologischer Kommentar zum Neuen Testament
HTR	*Harvard Theological Review*
HTS	Harvard Theological Studies
HUT	Hermeneutische Untersuchungen zur Theologie
HvTSt	*Hervormde Teologiese Studies*
ICC	International Critical Commentary
ICP	Institut Catholique de Paris
IGLS	*Inscriptions grecques et latines de la Syrie*
IPM	Instrumenta Patristica et Mediaevalia
ISPCK	Indian Society for Promoting Christian Knowledge
JBL	*Journal of Biblical Literature*
JBTh	*Jahrbuch für biblische Theologie*
JEastCS	*Journal of Eastern Christian Studies*
JECS	*Journal of Early Christian Studies*
JEH	*Journal of Ecclesiastical History*
JHS	*Journal of Hellenic Studies*
JJS	*Journal of Jewish Studies*
JNES	*Journal of Near Eastern Studies*
JRS	*Journal of Roman Studies*
JSJ	*Journal for the Study of Judaism*
JSNT	*Journal for the Study of the New Testament*
JSNTSup	Journal for the Study of the New Testament Supplement Series
JSOTSup	Journal for the Study of the Old Testament Supplement Series
JSPSup	Journal for the Study of the Pseudepigrapha Supplement Series
JTS	*Journal of Theological Studies*
KAV	Kommentar zu den Apostolischen Vätern
KBL	L. Koehler – W. Baumgartner, *Lexicon in Veteris Testamenti libros*
KEK	Kritisch-exegetischer Kommentar über das Neue Testament
LCC	Library of Christian Classics
LCL	Loeb Classical Library
LDAB	Leuven Database of Ancient Books
LNTS	Library of New Testament Studies

LS	*Louvain Studies*
LSJ	H.G. Liddell – R. Scott – H.S. Jones, *A Greek-English Lexicon*
LUP	Leuven University Press
MBPF	Münchener Beiträge zur Papyrusforschung und antiken Rechtsgeschichte
MT	Masoretic Text
MTSR	*Method and Theory in the Study of Religion*
NA	Nestle-Aland, *Novum Testamentum Graece*
NHC	Nag Hammadi Codex, -dices
NHS	Nag Hammadi Studies
NIBCNT	New International Biblical Commentary on the New Testament
NICNT	New International Commentary on the New Testament
NIGTC	New International Greek Testament Commentary
NRSV	New Revised Standard Version
NT	*Novum Testamentum*
NTAbh	Neutestamentliche Abhandlungen
NTD	Das Neue Testament Deutsch
NTL	New Testament Library
NTOA	Novum Testamentum et Orbis Antiquus
NTS	*New Testament Studies*
NTTSD	New Testament Tools, Studies, and Documents
OBO	Orbis Biblicus et Orientalis
ÖBS	Österreichische biblische Studien
OECGT	Oxford Early Christian Gospel Texts
OECT	Oxford Early Christian Texts
ÖTBK	Ökumenischer Taschenbuchkommentar
OGIS	Orientis Graeci Inscriptiones Selectae
OLA	Orientalia Lovaniensia Analecta
OLZ	*Orientalistische Literaturzeitung*
OUP	Oxford University Press
PG	Patrologia Graeca
PL	Patrologia Latina
PO	Patrologia Orientalis
PS	Patrologia Syriaca
PSI	Papiri della Società Italiana
QD	Quaestiones Disputatae
RAC	*Reallexikon für Antike und Christentum*
RB	*Revue biblique*
RBL	*Review of Biblical Literature*

RBS	Resources for Biblical Study
REB	Revised English Bible
RGG	*Religion in Geschichte und Gegenwart*
RNT	Regensburger Neues Testament
RSV	Revised Standard Version
RTL	*Revue théologique de Louvain*
SANT	Studien zum Alten und Neuen Testament
SB	Sammelbuch griechischer Urkunden aus Ägypten
SBAB	Stuttgarter biblische Aufsatzbände
SBB	Stuttgarter biblische Beiträge
SBL	Society of Biblical Literature
SBLDS	Society of Biblical Literature Dissertation Series
SBLSP	Society of Biblical Literature Seminar Papers
SBLStBL	Society of Biblical Literature Studies in Biblical Literature
SBS	Stuttgarter Bibelstudien
SC	Sources chrétiennes
SHBC	Smyth & Helwys Bible Commentary
SNTA	Studiorum Novi Testamenti Auxilia
SNTS MS	Society for New Testament Studies Monograph Series
SP	Sacra Pagina
SPCK	Society for the Promotion of Christian Knowledge
STAC	Studien und Texte zu Antike und Christentum
STAR	Studies in Theology and Religion
STDJ	Studies on the Texts of the Desert of Judah
StUNT	Studien zur Umwelt des Neuen Testaments
SupplJSJ	Supplements to the Journal for the Study of Judaism
SupplNT	Supplements to Novum Testamentum
SupplVC	Supplements to Vigiliae Christianae
SupplVT	Supplements to Vetus Testamentum
TENTS	Texts and Editions for New Testament Study
THKNT	Theologischer Handkommentar zum Neuen Testament
TLZ	*Theologische Literaturzeitung*
TM	Trismegistos
TNTC	Tyndale New Testament Commentaries
TRE	*Theologische Realenzyklopädie*
TU	Texte und Untersuchungen
TvT	*Tijdschrift voor Theologie*
TWNT	*Theologisches Wörterbuch zum Neuen Testament*
TZ	*Theologische Zeitschrift*
UPZ	U. Wilcken, *Urkunden der Ptolemäerzeit*
UTB	Uni-Taschenbücher

VC	*Vigiliae Christianae*
WBC	Word Biblical Commentary
WMANT	Wissenschaftliche Monographien zum Alten und Neuen Testament
WUNT	Wissenschaftliche Untersuchungen zum Neuen Testament
ZAC	*Zeitschrift für Antikes Christentum*
ZBK NT	Zürcher Bibelkommentare: Neues Testament
ZKT	*Zeitschrift für katholische Theologie*
ZNW	*Zeitschrift für die neutestamentliche Wissenschaft*
ZPE	*Zeitschrift für Papyrologie und Epigraphik*
ZTK	*Zeitschrift für Theologie und Kirche*

BIBLIOGRAPHY JOSEPH VERHEYDEN 1979-2022

1979

De de Incarnatione *van Johannes Cassianus: Onderzoek naar de theologische fundering van het monachisme* (Licentiate's thesis Religious Studies), Leuven, 1979, In-4°, x-200 p. [unpublished].

1980

M. Foucault en F. Nietzsche: Fundamenten voor een nieuwe mens- en wereldopvatting (Licentiate's thesis Philosophy), Leuven, 1980, In-4°, ix-305 p. [unpublished].

1982

Ascensio Isaiae*: Inleiding en studie van AJ 4,13 en context* (Licentiate's thesis Humanities: Oriental Philology and History), Leuven, 1982, In-4°, xii-176 p. [unpublished].

Reviews: *ETL* 58 (1982) 158-159 (D. Judant); 159 (A. Paul); 172-173 (R. Gryson).

1983

Review: *ETL* 59 (1983) 363-364 (H. Guevara).

Chronicle: *ETL* 59 (1983) 414.

1984

Review: *ETL* 60 (1984) 157-160 (M. Pesce).

1985

De ondergang van de Joden in de Kerkgeschiedenis van Eusebius van Caesarea: Met een analyse van HE 3,5-10. I: *Tekst*. II: *Noten* (Licentiate's thesis Theology), Leuven, 1985, In-4°, xxviii-201 and 154 p. [unpublished; see 1987].

1986

"Alexandrijnse rijken door het oog van de naald", in *De Nieuwe Boodschap* (February 1986) 53-59; reprinted in *De Heraut* (February 1986) 50-56.

1987

De vlucht van de christenen naar Pella: Onderzoek van het getuigenis van Eusebius en Epiphanius. I: *Tekst*. II: *Bibliografie en noten* (Ph.D.

thesis, Faculty of Theology), Leuven, 1987, In-4°, XVI-377 and XLVIII-416 p. [cf. 1988].

"De vlucht van de christenen uit Jeruzalem in 70 na Chr.", in *V.B.S-Informatie* 18 (1987) 50-60.

1988

De vlucht van de christenen naar Pella: Onderzoek van het getuigenis van Eusebius en Epiphanius (Verhandelingen van de Koninklijke Academie voor Wetenschappen, Letteren en Schone Kunsten van België. Klasse der Letteren, Jaargang 50, 127), Brussel, Koninklijke Academie voor Wetenschappen, Letteren en Schone Kunsten, 1988, 285 p. [cf. 1987].

> Cf. J. WEHNERT, "Die Auswanderung der Jerusalemer Christen nach Pella – historisches Faktum oder theologische Konstruktion?", in *Zeitschrift für Kirchengeschichte* 102 (1991) 231-255.

"Mark 1,32-34 and 6,53-56: Tradition or Redaction?", in *ETL* 64 (1988) 415-428.

"De kindsheidverhalen in Matteüs: Preludium en programma", in W. WEREN et al. (eds.), *Geboorteverhalen van Jezus: Feit en fictie*, Boxtel, Katholieke Bijbelstichting; Brugge, Tabor, 1988, 61-74.

Collaboration: F. NEIRYNCK, *Q-Synopsis: The Double Tradition Passages in Greek* (SNTA, 13), Leuven, LUP – Peeters, 1988; ²1995 (revised edition with Appendix).

Review: *ETL* 64 (1988) 467 (R.G. Boling).

Chronicle: "R. Collins, The Thessalonian Correspondence: Colloquium Biblicum Lovaniense XXXVIII, 1988", in *TvT* 28 (1988) 393-394.

1989

"La Concordance des Pseudépigraphes", in *ETL* 65 (1989) 124-130.

"L'Ascension d'Isaïe et l'évangile de Matthieu: Examen de AI 3,13-18", in J.-M. SEVRIN (ed.), *The New Testament in Early Christianity – La réception des écrits néotestamentaires dans le christianisme primitif* (BETL, 86), Leuven, LUP – Peeters, 1989, 247-274.

"The Source(s) of Luke 21", in F. NEIRYNCK (ed.), *L'évangile de Luc – The Gospel of Luke* (BETL, 32), Leuven, LUP – Peeters, ²1989, 491-516.

1990

"The Flight of the Christians to Pella", in *ETL* 66 (1990) 368-384.

Review: *ETL* 66 (1990) 417-418 (R.E. Van Voorst).

1992

F. Neirynck – J. Verheyden – F. Van Segbroeck – G. Van Oyen – R. Corstjens, *The Gospel of Mark: A Cumulative Bibliography 1950-1990* (BETL, 102), Leuven, LUP – Peeters, 1992, XII-717 p.; (Collectanea Biblica et Religiosa Antiqua, 3), Brussel, Wetenschappelijk Comité voor Godsdienstwetenschappen. Koninklijke Academie voor Wetenschappen, Letteren en Schone Kunsten van België, 1992, XII-717 p.

F. Van Segbroeck – C.M. Tuckett – G. Van Belle – J. Verheyden (eds.), *The Four Gospels 1992: Festschrift Frans Neirynck* (BETL, 100A-C), Leuven, LUP – Peeters, 1992, 3 vols., XVIII-2668 p.

"Persecution and Eschatology: Mark 13,9-13", *ibid.*, 1041-1058.

"P. Gardner-Smith and 'The Turn of the Tide'", in A. Denaux (ed.), *John and the Synoptics* (BETL, 101), Leuven, LUP – Peeters, 1992, 423-452.

F. Neirynck – J. Verheyden, "Elenchus Bibliographicus *ETL* 1992. IV: Scriptura Sacra Novi Testamenti", in *ETL* 68 (1992) 234*-317*.

Review: *ETL* 68 (1992) 454-456 (C. Jacob).

1993

F. Neirynck – J. Verheyden, "Elenchus Bibliographicus *ETL* 1993. IV: Scriptura Sacra Novi Testamenti", in *ETL* 69 (1993) 225*-315*.

Reviews: *ETL* 69 (1993) 417-419 (M. Cimosa); 433-435 (J.L. Espinel Marcos).

1994

"Some Observations on the Gospel Text of Eusebius of Caesarea Illustrated from His Commentary on Isaiah", in A. Schoors – P. Van Deun (eds.), *Philohistor: Miscellanea in honorem Carlo Laga septuagenarii* (OLA, 60), Leuven, Peeters – Departement Oriëntalistiek, 1994, 35-70.

F. Neirynck – J. Verheyden, "Elenchus Bibliographicus *ETL* 1994. IV: Scriptura Sacra Novi Testamenti", in *ETL* 70 (1994) 245*-332*.

Reviews: *ETL* 70 (1994) 151-154 (C.T. Begg); 180-181 (D.N. Schowalter); 467-471 (M. Myllykoski); 471-475 (S. Byrskog); 478-479 (A. Dalbesio); 480-481 (V. Liberti); 481 (W. Kirchschläger); 482 (A. Gerhards); 482-483 (A. Quacquarelli); 484 (E. dal Covolo).

Reviews: *LS* 19 (1994) 75-77 (C.T. Begg); 77-78 (D.N. Schowalter); 376-377 (P.W. van der Horst); 377-378 (D.M. Frankfurter).

1995

"Les Pseudépigraphes d'Ancien Testament: Textes latins. À propos d'une Concordance", in *ETL* 71 (1995) 383-420.

F. NEIRYNCK – J. VERHEYDEN, "Elenchus Bibliographicus *ETL* 1995. IV: Scriptura Sacra Novi Testamenti", in *ETL* 71 (1995) 238*-318*.

Reviews: *ETL* 71 (1995) 227-230 (L. Bormann – K. Del Tredici – A. Standhartinger); 230-231 (E. Norelli); 231-232 (E. Manicardi); 232-233 (M. Adinolfi); 233-234 (L. Gianantoni); 234-237 (J. Ysebaert); 237-239 (I. Backus); 239 (S. Felici); 239-243 (J. Fontaine); 469-470 (S. Felici).

1996

"Origène et la Bible", in *ETL* 72 (1996) 165-180.

"Mark and Q", in *ETL* 72 (1996) 408-417.

"Origen on the Origin of 1 Cor 2,9", in R. BIERINGER (ed.), *The Corinthian Correspondence* (BETL, 125), Leuven, LUP – Peeters, 1996, 491-511.

F. NEIRYNCK – J. VERHEYDEN, "Elenchus Bibliographicus *ETL* 1996. IV: Scriptura Sacra Novi Testamenti", in *ETL* 72 (1996) 248*-322*.

Reviews: *ETL* 72 (1996) 240-241 (F. Noël); 241-245 (L. Bormann; P. Pilhofer); 245-246 (K. de Valerio); 246-247 (H.J. de Jonge – B.W.J. de Ruyter); 247-248 (M. Tardieu); 248-249 (E. Patlagean – A. Le Boulluec); 249-250 (R. Trevijano Etcheverría); 250-252 (Y.-M. Blanchard); 252-253 (J.J. Fernández Sangrador); 254-256 (J.L. Feiertag); 256-257 (P.-A. Jacob); 462-463 (E. Grünbeck); 463-465 (M.A.G. Haykin); 465-466 (A.-M. Malingrey).

Reviews: *LS* 21 (1996) 90-92 (C. Padilla); 289-291 (T.L. Brodie).

1997

"Supplementary Note on *LAB* 21,7-10", in *ETL* 73 (1997) 83.

"The New *Clavis Patrum Latinorum*", in *ETL* 73 (1997) 121-143.

"Describing the Parousia: The Cosmic Phenomena in Mk 13,24-25", in C.M. TUCKETT (ed.), *The Scriptures in the Gospels* (BETL, 131), Leuven, LUP – Peeters, 1997, 525-550.

F. NEIRYNCK – J. VERHEYDEN, "Elenchus Bibliographicus *ETL* 1997. IV: Scriptura Sacra Novi Testamenti", in *ETL* 73 (1997) 260*-336*.

Reviews: *ETL* 73 (1997) 184-185 (A. Schlatter); 185-187 (D.A. deSilva); 187-188 (L.M. McDonald); 188-191 (F.S. Jones); 191-192 (A. Mattioli); 192-194 (H.-J. Klauck); 194-196 (P.W. van der Horst); 196-197 (D. Ramos-

Lissón); 434-437 (L.H. Feldman – J.R. Levison); 437-438 (M. de Jonge – J. Tromp); 438-439 (J.T. Fitzgerald); 459-463 (E. Norelli); 463-466 (S.C. Mimouni); 466-468 (P. Evieux); 468-471 (J.-N. Guinot).

Reviews: *LS* 22 (1997) 93-95 (C.N. Jefford); 183-186 (S. Carruth); 385-386 (J. Alison); 388-389 (S.K. Roll).

1998

F. NEIRYNCK – J. VERHEYDEN – R. CORSTJENS, *The Gospel of Matthew and the Sayings Source Q: A Cumulative Bibliography 1950-1995* (BETL, 140A-B), 2 vols., Leuven, LUP – Peeters, 1998, 1-1000 + 1*-420* p.

"The Unity of Luke-Acts: Colloquium Biblicum Lovaniense XLVII (1998)", in *ETL* 74 (1998) 516-526; reprinted in *HvTSt* 55 (1999).

"Elenchus Bibliographicus *ETL* 1998. IV: Scriptura Sacra Novi Testamenti", in *ETL* 74 (1998) 267*-345*.

Reviews: *ETL* 74 (1998) 198-199 (G.D. Fee); 199-200 (V. Koperski); 200-203 (C. Landon); 203-204 (J.A. Fitzmyer); 204-205 (P.W. van der Horst); 205 (F.X. D'Sa); 205-206 (A. de Vogüé); 235 (G. Ginneberghe); 440 (D. Mendels); 441-442 (S.R. Llewelyn); 442-443 (G. Widengren – A. Hultgård – M. Philonenko); 443-444 (A. Borrell Viader – A. de la Fuente – A. Puig i Tàrrech); 444-445 (A. Mattioli); 445-446 (J.A. Francis); 446-448 (W.W. Reader); 448-449 (J.P. Tosaus Abadía; R. Trevijano Etcheverría); 451 (A. Milano); 452 (L. Pizzolato); 452-453 (M.-A. Calvet-Sébasti); 456 (M. Kertsch); 456-457 (G. Cremascoli); 458 (A. Dubreucq); 458-459 (G. de Martel); 503-504 (G. Canobbio).

Reviews: *LS* 23 (1998) 78 (J.A. Fitzmyer); 79-80 (F.J. Matera); 283-286 (S. Carruth – J.M. Robinson – C. Heil); 286-287 (A. Garsky *et al*.); 288 (T. Altizer); 288-289 (M. Hengel – A.M. Schwemer); 373-374 (G. Theissen – A. Merz); 377-378 (H. von Campenhausen); 378-379 (P. Blowers).

1999

(ed.), *The Unity of Luke-Acts* (BETL, 142), Leuven, LUP – Peeters, 1999, XXV-828 p.

"Introduction", *ibid*., XIII-XXV.

"The Unity of Luke-Acts: What Are We Up To?", *ibid*., 3-56.

"Elenchus Bibliographicus *ETL* 1999. IV: Scriptura Sacra Novi Testamenti", in *ETL* 75 (1999) 245*-318*.

Reviews: *ETL* 75 (1999) 201-202 (SBL 1998 Seminar Papers); 205-207 (E.E. Johnson – D. Hay); 207-208 (C.G. Kruse); 208-210 (B. Witherington);

211 (J. Reiling); 211-213 (M. Pascuzzi); 213-215 (P.W. Barnett); 215-217 (J.D.G. Dunn); 217-220 (J. Holmstrand); 221 (J.F. Kelly); 221-222 (L. Rizzerio); 230-231 (M. Krausgruber); 231-233 (C. Scholten); 233-235 (J.-C. Larchet); 250 (A. Linage); 444-445 (G. Ghiberti); 445-446 (F. Raurell); 446-447 (G. Benyik); 456-457 (L. Moraldi); 464-468 (R. Hoppe – U. Busse); 470-472 (J.A. Fitzmyer); 472-474 (W. Thüsing); 474-475 (G. O'Collins; F. Brambilla; J.D. Kingsbury); 475-476 (W. Weren); 482-486 (J.D.G. Dunn); 486-487 (J.L. Martyn); 488 (E. Verhoef); 488-491 (K. Backhaus); 492-495 (J.N. Bremmer; P.J. Lalleman); 495-497 (T. Silverstein – A. Hilhorst); 497-498 (M. Sachot); 498-500 (R.F. Hock – J.B. Chance – J. Perkins); 500-502 (G.G. Gamba); 502-504 (A.-L. Rey); 504 (P.W. van der Horst); 504-506 (A. de Vogüé).

Reviews: *LS* 24 (1999) 77-80 (C.M. Tuckett); 80-83 (C. Heil); 264-266 (J.B. Green); 266-268 (J. Painter); 373-377 (W.R. Farmer); 381-383 (J.E. Taylor).

Chronicle: "Fonds Albert en Mathilda Van Roey", in *ETL* 75 (1999) 75.

Chronicle: *ETL* 75 (1999) 258, 261.

Chronicle: "In memoriam O. Cullmann", in *ETL* 75 (1999) 566-567.

Chronicle: "In memoriam B. van Iersel", in *ETL* 75 (1999) 571-572.

Chronicle: *LS* 24 (1999) 361-363 (CBL 1999).

2000

Collaboration: A.-M. Denis et collaborateurs, avec le concours de J.-C. Haelewyck, *Introduction à la littérature religieuse judéo-hellénistique*, 2 vols., Turnhout, Brepols, 2000, XXI-1420 p. Esp. sections on "Écrits latins" (pp. 13-16, 121-123, 150, 260, 304-306, 349-429, 449-457, 496-497, 594-596, 629-630, 647-649, 668-670, 729-730, 761, 803-835, 865-870).

"Documenta Q: The Reconstruction of Q 22,38-30", in *ETL* 76 (2000) 404-432.

"Elenchus Bibliographicus *ETL* 2000. IV: Scriptura Sacra Novi Testamenti", in *ETL* 76 (2000) 151*-164* and 253*-331*.

Reviews: in *ETL* 76 (2000) 179-182 (R.F. Collins; J. Lambrecht); 182-184 (L.V. Rutgers et al.); 465-466 (G. Van Belle); 466-467 (J. Krasovec); 467 (A. Boud'hors); 473-475 (C. Lévy); 475-476 (K.P. Donfried – P. Richardson); 476 (R.N. Longenecker); 477-478 (A. Leinhäupl-Wilke – S. Lücking); 478-479 (E. Cothenet); 479-480 (P. Grelot); 480-481 (B.R. Gaventa; P. Richardson); 489-490 (S. Guijarro Oporto); 490-492

(V. Balabanski); 493-496 (B. Witherington); 496-497 (M. Gruber); 497-499 (J.H. Wray); 499-501 (I. Donégani); 501-502 (J. Kerner); 502-503 (I. Backus); 504-505 (H.R. Drobner); 505-506 (F. Bermejo Rubio); 506-507 (D.J. Bingham); 507-508 (W.J. Aerts – G.A.A. Kortekaas).

Review: *LS* 25 (2000) 277-279 (U. Schnelle); 379-380 (Ch. Seitz – K. Greene-McCreight); 380-381 (S. Garrett); 381-384 (C.K. Barrett).

Chronicle: "In memoriam Albert Van Roey", in *ETL* 76 (2000) 222-224.

Chronicle: *ETL* 76 (2000) 576-577.

2001

Collaboration: F. NEIRYNCK, *Q-Parallels: Q-Synopsis and IQP / CritEd Parallels* (SNTA, 20), Leuven, LUP – Peeters, 2001, 120 p.

"De christelijke gemeente in Korinte volgens de eerste brief van Clemens", in J. DELOBEL – H.J. DE JONGE – M. MENKEN – H. VAN DE SANDT (eds.), *Vroegchristelijke gemeenten tussen ideaal en werkelijkheid: Opstellen van leden van de Studiosorum Novi Testamenti Conventus*, Kampen, Kok, 2001, 68-83.

"The Conclusion of Q: Eschatology in Q 22,28-30", in A. LINDEMANN (ed.), *The Sayings Source Q and the Historical Jesus* (BETL, 158), Leuven, LUP – Peeters, 2001, 695-718.

"Elenchus Bibliographicus *ETL* 2001. IV: Scriptura Sacra Novi Testamenti", in *ETL* 77 (2001) 169*-181* and 272*-343*.

Reviews: *ETL* 77 (2001) 206-208 (W.S. Vorster); 208-209 (G. Leonardi; G. Segalla); 209-211 (F.J. Matera); 211-214 (J.Ma. Asgeirsson – K. De Troyer – M.W. Meyer); 217-218 (R.N. Longenecker); 219-220 (C.S. Keener); 224-226 (B. Chilton – C.A. Evans); 226-227 (G.-H. Baudry); 227-228 (W.A. Bienert – U. Kühneweg); 473-475 (F. Neirynck); 479-482 (D.E. Aune; G.K. Beale).

Reviews: *LS* 26 (2001) 89 (P. van Buren); 93 (J. Harrington).

2002

"Assessing Gospel Quotations in Justin Martyr", in A. DENAUX (ed.), *New Testament Textual Criticism and Exegesis: Festschrift J. Delobel* (BETL, 161), Leuven, LUP – Peeters, 2002, 361-377.

"Silent Witnesses / Mary Magdalene and the Women at the Tomb in the Gospel of Peter", in R. BIERINGER – V. KOPERSKI – B. LATAIRE (eds.), *Resurrection in the New Testament: Festschrift J. Lambrecht* (BETL, 165), Leuven, LUP – Peeters, 2002, 457-482.

"Elenchus Bibliographicus *ETL* 2002. IV: Scriptura Sacra Novi Testamenti", in *ETL* 78 (2002) 152*-166* and 274*-348*.

Reviews: *ETL* 78 (2002) 179-181 (J.-M. Auwers – A. Wénin); 181-182 (K. Koenen – R. Küschelm); 189-191 (A.-M. Denis); 191-192 (J.A. Fitzmyer); 192-193 (F.C. Holmgren); 193-194 (SBL 2000 Seminar Papers); 196-197 (D.G. Horrell); 197-198 (D.G.K. Taylor); 198-199 (W. Thüsing); 199-203 (J.D. Crossan); 203-205 (D. Marguerat – E. Norelli – J.-M. Poffet); 205-206 (H.-J. Klauck); 206-207 (J. Miler); 207-208 (J.C. Iwe); 208-209 (G. Van Oyen); 217 (P. Bossuyt); 217-218 (D. Marguerat); 218-219 (K. Scholtissek); 219-220 (J.D. Harvey); 220-221 (S. Hillert); 222-223 (S.K. Soderlund – N.T. Wright); 223 (M. Bachmann); 223-224 (K. Kuula); 224-225 (M.-E. Boismard); 225-227 (M. Barth – H. Blanke; J.A. Fitzmyer); 227-228 (B.L. Campbell; S.R. Bechtler); 228-230 (G. Giurisato); 230-231 (G. Glonner); 231-235 (D. Lührmann); 236-237 (A. Schneider); 237 (R. Roukema); 237-238 (H.J. Frede; R. Gryson); 238-239 (P. Descourtieux); 239-240 (G.-M. de Durand); 246-247 (U. Gantz); 248-249 (R. Etaix); 249-251 (G.-M. de Durand); 290 (K. Duchatelez).

Review: *International Journal of the Classical Tradition* 8 (2001-2002) 471-475 (D.L. Dungan).

Chronicle: "Institutum Iudaicum", in *ETL* 78 (2002) 283.

Chronicle: "International Conference on 'The Image of the Judeo-Christians in Ancient Jewish and Christian Literature' at UPFG, Brussels", in *ETL* 78 (2002) 283.

2003

"Grafverhalen in stereo", in *Schrift* 35/209 (2003) 169-174.

"The Canon Muratori: A Matter of Dispute", in J.-M. AUWERS – H.J. DE JONGE (eds.), *The Biblical Canons* (BETL, 163), Leuven, LUP – Peeters, 2003, 487-556.

"Epiphanius on the Ebionites (Pan. 30)", in P.J. TOMSON – D. LAMBERS-PETRY (eds.), *The Image of the Judaeo-Christians in Ancient Jewish and Christian Literature* (WUNT, 158), Tübingen, Mohr Siebeck, 2003, 182-208.

"The Fate of the Righteous and the Cursed at Qumran and in the Gospel of Matthew", in F. GARCÍA MARTÍNEZ (ed.), *Wisdom and Apocalypticism in the Dead Sea Scrolls and in the Biblical Tradition* (BETL, 168), Leuven, LUP – Peeters, 2003, 427-452.

"Elenchus Bibliographicus *ETL* 2003. IV: Scriptura Sacra Novi Testamenti", in *ETL* 79 (2003) 169*-187* and 290*-376*.

Review: *ETL* 79 (2003) 466-470 (H. van de Sandt – D. Flusser).

Chronicle: "International Conference on 'The Didache and Matthew' at Tilburg University", in *ETL* 79 (2003) 524-525.

Chronicle: "Walter Kasper Dr. honoris causa of the Catholic University of Leuven", in *JEastCS* 55 (2003) 137.

2004

"The Demonization of the Opponent in Early Christian Literature: The Case of the *Pseudo-Clementines*", in T.L. HETTEMA – A. VAN DER KOOIJ (eds.), *Religious Polemics in Context: Papers Presented to the Second International Conference of the Leiden Institute for the Study of Religions (LISOR) Held at Leiden, 27-28 April 2000* (STAR, 11), Assen, Van Gorcum, 2004, 330-359.

"The Greek Legend of the *Ascension of Isaiah*", in B. JANSSENS – B. ROOSEN – P. VAN DEUN (eds.), *Philomathestatos: Studies in Greek and Byzantine Texts Presented to Jacques Noret for His Sixty-Fifth Birthday* (OLA, 137), Leuven, Peeters – Departement Oosterse Studies, 2004, 671-700.

R. EBIED – H. TEULE, with the collaboration of P. HILL – J. VERHEYDEN (eds.), *Symposium Syriacum VIII*, in *JEastCS* 56 (2004), 356 p.

"Elenchus Bibliographicus *ETL* 2004. IV: Scriptura Sacra Novi Testamenti", in *ETL* 80 (2004) 156*-175* and 298*-392*.

2005

R. BIERINGER – G. VAN BELLE – J. VERHEYDEN (eds.), *Luke and His Readers: Festschrift A. Denaux* (BETL, 182), Leuven, LUP – Peeters, 2005, XXIX-470 p.

"How Many Were Sent according to Lk 10,1?", *ibid.*, 193-238.

J.M. ROBINSON, *The Sayings Gospel Q: Collected Essays*, ed. C. HEIL – J. VERHEYDEN (BETL, 189), Leuven, LUP – Peeters, 2005.

"Eschatology in the Didache and the Gospel of Matthew", in H. VAN DE SANDT (ed.), *Matthew and the Didache: Two Documents from the Same Jewish-Christian Milieu?*, Assen, Van Gorcum – Minneapolis, MN, Fortress, 2005, 193-215.

"The *Shepherd of Hermas* and the Writings that Later Formed the New Testament", in A.F. GREGORY – C.M. TUCKETT (eds.), *The Reception of the New Testament in the Apostolic Fathers*, Oxford, OUP, 2005, 293-329.

"Elenchus Bibliographicus *ETL* 2005. IV: Scriptura Sacra Novi Testamenti", in *ETL* 81 (2005) 166*-182* and 299*-386*.

Reviews: *JSJ* 36 (2005) 341-344 (M. de Jonge); 349-351 (L. Ginzberg).

Reviews: *JEastCS* 57 (2005) 186-188 (K. Ciggaar – H. Teule); 188-190 (H. Baum); 321-322 (G. Fossati); 323-324 (D. Motiuk); 324-325 (J. De Vocht); 328-329 (D. Donnelly – J. Famerée – A. Denaux); 329-330 (F. Enns – S. Holland – A.K. Riggs).

Supervision: J.-F. Baudoz (ICP) – J. Verheyden (supervisors): S. Savarimuthu, *A Community in Search of Its Identity: Mt. 21:28–22:14 in a Subaltern Perspective*. Ph.D. thesis ICP – KU Leuven. Published under the same title, Delhi, ISPCK, 2007.

2006

"The Shepherd of Hermas", in *ExpTim* 117 (2006) 397-401; reprinted in P. FOSTER (ed.), *The Writings of the Apostolic Fathers*, London – New York, T&T Clark, 2007, 63-71.

"Elenchus Bibliographicus *ETL* 2006. IV: Scriptura Sacra Novi Testamenti", in *ETL* 82 (2006) 179*-196* and 300*-387*.

Review: *Bib* 87 (2006) 439-442 (T.L. Brodie).

Reviews: *RBL* 8 (2006) 397-400 (M. Goodacre – N. Perrin; at TitleID=3619); 415-417 (D. Rhoads; cf. at TitleID=4556); J.A. Harrill (at TitleID=4981); G.A. Kennedy (at TitleID=4994); J.T. Fitzgerald – T.H. Olbricht – L.M. White (at TitleID=4997); M.J. Kruger (at TitleID=5035); S. Timpanaro (at TitleID=5058); F. Bovon (at TitleID=5121).

Review: *TvT* 46 (2006) 407 (A. Mastrocinque).

2007

"Evidence of 1 Enoch 10:4 in Matthew 22:13?", in A. HILHORST – E. PUECH – E. TIGCHELAAR (eds.), *Flores Florentino: Dead Sea Scrolls and Other Early Jewish Studies in Honour of Florentino García Martínez* (SupplJSJ, 122), Leiden – Boston, MA, Brill, 2007, 449-466.

"I. de la Potterie on John 19,13", in G. VAN BELLE (ed.), *The Death of Jesus in the Fourth Gospel* (BETL, 200), Leuven, LUP – Peeters, 2007, 817-837.

"Q 12:33-34: Evaluations", in S.R. JOHNSON (ed.), *Documenta Q: Q 12:33-34: Storing Up Treasures in Heaven*, Leuven – Paris – Dudley, MA, Peeters, 2007, pp. 16-17, 57-59, 105-107, 114, 117, 120-121, 127, 133, 138, 145, 152-153, 157, 162-163, 168, 172, 176, 182-183, 187, 195, 197-199.

"The Shepherd of Hermas", in P. FOSTER (ed.), *The Writings of the Apostolic Fathers*, London – New York, T&T Clark, 2007, 63-71; reprinted from *ExpTim* 117 (2006) 397-401.

"Some Reflections on Determining the Purpose of the 'Gospel of Peter'", in T.J. KRAUS – T. NICKLAS (eds.), *Das Evangelium nach Petrus: Text, Kontexte, Intertexte* (TU, 158), Berlin, De Gruyter, 2007, 281-299.

"Elenchus Bibliographicus *ETL* 2007. IV: Scriptura Sacra Novi Testamenti", in *ETL* 83 (2007) 158*-178* and 276*-353*.

Review: *JEH* 58 (2007) 293-294 (G. Aragione – E. Junod – E. Norelli).

Review: *JTS* 58 (2007) 629-632 (J. Nolland).

Reviews: *RBL* 9 (2007) 334-336 (L. Vaage; at TitleID=5273); 349-351 (R.A. Horsley; at TitleID=5736); 439-442 (P. Arzt-Grabner *et al.*; at TitleID=5454); R. Valantasis (at TitleID = 5177); D. Zeller (at TitleID= 5283); B.H. Gregg (at TitleID=5513); L.W. Hurtado (at TitleID=5643); G. Jossa (at TitleID=5749).

2008

J. VERHEYDEN – G. VAN BELLE – J. VAN DER WATT (eds.), *Miracles and Imagery in Luke and John: Festschrift U. Busse* (BETL, 218), Leuven, LUP – Peeters, 2008, XVIII-287 p.

IID., "Preface", *ibid.*, VII.

IID., "Ulrich Busse – a Portrait", *ibid.*, XIII-XIV.

H. TEULE – J. VERHEYDEN (eds.), *Heretics and Heresies in the Ancient Church and in Eastern Christianity: Studies in Honour of Adelbert Davids*, in *JEastCS* 60/1-4 (2008), 387 p.

"Epiphanius of Salamis on Beasts and Heretics: Some Introductory Comments", in *JEastCS* 60 (2008) 143-173; reprinted 2010.

"Een irenische dialoog met Wim Weren over geweld in Johannes 7:53–8:11", in *HvTSt* 64 (2008) 1787-1791.

K. ZAMFIR – J. VERHEYDEN, "Text-Critical and Intertextual Remarks on 1 Tim 2:8-10", in *NT* 50 (2008) 376-406.

"Jewish Christianity: A State of Affairs. Affinities and Differences with Respect to Matthew, James and the Didache", in H. VAN DE SANDT – J.K. ZANGENBERG (eds.), *Matthew, James, and Didache: Three Related Documents in Their Jewish and Christian Settings* (SBL Symposium Series, 45), Atlanta, GA, SBL, 2008, 123-135.

"Le jugement d'Israël dans la Source Q", in A. DETTWILER – D. MARGUERAT (eds.), *La source des paroles de Jésus (Q): Aux origines du christianisme* (Le monde de la Bible, 62), Genève, Labor et Fides, 2008, 191-219.

"Presenting Minor Characters in the Pseudo-Clementine Novel: The Case of Barnabas", in F. AMSLER – A. FREY (eds.), *Nouvelles intrigues pseudo-clémentines / Plots in the Pseudo-Clementine Romance* (Publications de l'Institut romand des sciences bibliques, 6), Prahins, Éditions du Zèbre, 2008, 249-257.

"The Violators of the Kingdom of God: Struggling with Q Polemics in Q 16,16-18", in H.W. HOLLANDER – J. TROMP – R. BUITENWERF (eds.), *Jesus, Paul, and Early Christianity: Studies in Honour of Henk Jan de Jonge* (SupplNT, 130), Leiden – Boston, MA, Brill, 2008, 397-415.

"Elenchus Bibliographicus *ETL* 2008. IV: Scriptura Sacra Novi Testamenti", in *ETL* 84 (2008) 143*-161* and 258*-331*.

Review: *ETL* 84 (2008) 238-240 (C. Focant).

Review: *JTS* 59 (2008) 295-297 (M. Hengel).

Review: *HvTSt* 64 (2008) 1096-1098 (M. Cromhout).

Review: *ExpTim* 119 (2008) 175 (C. Jefford).

Reviews: *RBL* 10 (2008) 29-36 (K. Erlemann *et al.*; at TitleID=5356, 5357, 5358, 5828).

Supervision: J. Thachuparamban, *Jesus and the Law in the Matthean Community: A Source- and Redaction-Critical Study of Mt 5,38-48*. Ph.D. thesis KU Leuven. Published under the same title, Delhi, ISPCK, 2011.

2009

T. NICKLAS – F.V. REITERER – J. VERHEYDEN (eds.), *The Human Body in Death and Resurrection* (Deuterocanonical and Cognate Literature: Yearbook 2009), Berlin – New York, De Gruyter, 2009, x-457 p.

"De samenhang in de werken van Lucas, of: hoe het evidente complex kan zijn", in *Schrift* 41/241 (2009) 3-8.

"Talkative Christians and Noisy Pagans in Corinth: Gongs and Cymbals in 1 Corinthians 13,1", in C.J. BELEZOS (ed.), *Saint Paul and Corinth: 1950 Years since the Writing of the Epistles to the Corinthians*, Athens, Psichogios Publications, 2009, 757-775.

"Text, NT", in K. DOOB SAKENFIELD (ed.), *The New Interpreter's Dictionary of the Bible*. Volume 5, Nashville, TN, Abingdon Press, 2009, 540-545.

"Traditions, Oral. B. New Testament", *ibid.*, 646-648.

"Elenchus Bibliographicus *ETL* 2009. IV: Scriptura Sacra Novi Testamenti", in *ETL* 85 (2009) 156*-175* and 279*-364*.

Supervision: J. Verheyden – Y.-M. Blanchard (ICP) (supervisors): P. Carbonaro, *Le roi et la loi dans la lettre d'Aristée à Philocrate*. Ph.D. thesis ICP – KU Leuven. Published under the title *La lettre d'Aristée et le mythe des âges du monde* (CahRB, 79), Pendé, Gabalda, 2012.

2010

T. Nicklas – A. Merkt – J. Verheyden (eds.), *Gelitten – Gestorben – Auferstanden: Passions- und Ostertraditionen im antiken Christentum* (WUNT, 2.273), Tübingen, Mohr Siebeck, 2010, XII-181 p.

T. Nicklas – J. Verheyden – E.M.M. Eynikel – F. García Martínez (eds.), *Other Worlds and Their Relation to This World: Early Jewish and Ancient Christian Traditions* (SupplJSJ, 143), Leiden – Boston, MA, Brill, 2010, XI-401 p.

Id., "Introduction", *ibid.*, IX-XI.

H. Teule – J. Verheyden (eds.), *Heresies and Heretics in the Ancient Church and in Eastern Christianity* (Eastern Christian Studies, 10), Leuven, Peeters, 2010, VIII-395 p.; reprint of *JEastCS* 60/1-4 (2008).

J. Verheyden – K. Zamfir – T. Nicklas (eds.), *Prophets and Prophecy in Jewish and Early Christian Literature* (WUNT, 2.286), Tübingen, Mohr Siebeck, 2010, VIII-348 p.

"Calling Jesus a Prophet, as seen by Luke", *ibid.*, 177-210.

P. Dschulnigg, *Studien zu Einleitungsfragen und zur Theologie und Exegese des Neuen Testaments: Gesammelte Aufsätze*, ed. B. Kowalski – R. Höffner – J. Verheyden (BTS, 9), Leuven, Peeters, 2010, XXI-601 p.

"Before Embarking on an Adventure: Some Preliminary Remarks on Writing the NTP Commentary on the *Gospel of Mark*", in J. Baun – A. Cameron – M. Edwards – M. Vinzent (eds.), *Studia Patristica 44: Papers Presented at the Fifteenth International Conference on Patristic Studies Held in Oxford 2007*, Leuven, Peeters, 2010, 145-156.

"Luke and Acts – The Early Years: Some Comments in the Margin of a Recent Monograph", in A.F. Gregory – C.K. Rowe (eds.), *Rethinking the Unity and Reception of Luke and Acts*, Columbia, SC, University of South Carolina Press, 2010, 97-118.

"Pain and Glory: Some Introductory Comments on the Rhetorical Qualities and Potential of the *Martyrs of Palestine* by Eusebius of Caesarea", in J. LEEMANS (ed.), *Martyrdom and Persecution in Late Antique Christianity: Festschrift B. Dehandschutter* (BETL, 241), Leuven – Paris – Walpole, MA, Peeters, 2010, 353-391.

"A Puzzling Hapax Legomenon – The Peacemakers of Matt 5,9", in E. BONS – D. GERBER – P. KEITH (eds.), *Bible et Paix: Mélanges offerts à Claude Coulot* (Lectio Divina, 233), Paris, Cerf, 2010, 97-109.

"Elenchus Bibliographicus *ETL* 2010. IV: Scriptura Sacra Novi Testamenti", in *ETL* 86 (2010) 167*-185* and 293*-382*.

Supervision: I. Migbisiegbe, *The Kingdom of God and Responsible Human Cooperation: An Exegetical Study of Luke 19,11-27*. Ph.D. thesis, KU Leuven.

2011

P. FOSTER – A. GREGORY – J.S. KLOPPENBORG – J. VERHEYDEN (eds.), *New Studies in the Synoptic Problem: Oxford Conference, April 2008. Essays in Honour of Christopher M. Tuckett* (BETL, 239), Leuven – Paris – Walpole, MA, Peeters, 2011, XXIV-828 p.

"Proto-Luke, and What Can Possibly Be Made of It", *ibid.*, 617-655.

J. VERHEYDEN – T.L. HETTEMA – P. VANDECASTEELE (eds.), *Paul Ricoeur: Poetics and Religion* (BETL, 240), Leuven – Paris – Walpole, MA, Peeters, 2011, XX-534 p.

J. VERHEYDEN – T. NICKLAS – A. MERKT (eds.), in cooperation with M. GRUNDEKEN, *Ancient Christian Interpretations of "Violent Texts" in the Apocalypse* (NTOA/StUNT, 92), Göttingen, Vandenhoeck & Ruprecht, 2011, 313 p.

J. VERHEYDEN (ed.), *Colloquium Biblicum Lovaniense – Journées Bibliques de Louvain – Bijbelse Studiedagen te Leuven 1-60 (1949-2011)*, Leuven – Paris – Walpole, MA, Peeters, 2011, 147 p.

"Preface", *ibid.*, 5-6.

W. WEREN – H. VAN DE SANDT – J. VERHEYDEN (eds.), *Life beyond Death in Matthew's Gospel: Religious Metaphor or Bodily Resurrection?* (BTS, 13), Leuven – Paris – Walpole, MA, Peeters, 2011, XVIII-284 p.

"The Great Escape: Some Comments on a Controversial Suggestion for Explaining Matt 28:2-4", *ibid.*, 201-216.

"Q 6:37-42: Evaluations", in L. YOUNGQUIST, in cooperation with T. KLAMPFL – S. CARRUTH – J.L. REED (eds.), *Documenta Q: Q 6:37-42: Not Judging – The Blind Leading the Blind – The Disciple and the Teacher – The Speck and the Beam*, Leuven – Paris – Walpole, MA, Peeters, 2011, pp. 20-21, 29-30, 39, 53-54, 90-92, 97, 112, 116, 121, 143-144, 210-213, 226, 232, 243-245, 250, 270-271, 293-294, 323-324, 337, 341-342, 352-353, 358-359, 367-368, 375, 381-382, 386, 392, 395, 398, 402-403, 406.

"A Son in Heaven, but no Father on Earth: A Note in the Margin of a 'Tale of Two Kings'", in *HvTSt/Theological Studies* 67/1 (2011) Art. # 928, 6 pages. DOI:10.4102/hts.v67i1.928.

"Creating Difference through Parallelism: Luke's Handling of the Traditions on John the Baptist and Jesus in the Infancy Narrative", in C. CLIVAZ – A. DETTWILER – L. DEVILLERS – E. NORELLI (eds.), *Infancy Gospels: Stories and Identities* (WUNT, 281), Tübingen, Mohr Siebeck, 2011, 137-160.

"Origen in the Making: Reading between (and behind) the Lines of Eusebius' 'Life of Origen' (*HE* 6)", in S. KACZMAREK – H. PIETRAS (eds.), *Origeniana Decima: Origen as Writer. Papers of the 10th International Origen Congress, University School of Philosophy and Education "Ignatianum", Krakow, Poland, 31 August – 4 September 2009* (BETL, 244), Leuven – Paris – Walpole, MA, Peeters, 2011, 713-725.

"Reading a New Testament Hapax within a Broader Context: The Case of ἀπο(ρ)ρίπτω (Acts 27:43)", in E. BONS – J. JOOSTEN (eds.), *Septuagint Vocabulary: Pre-History, Usage, Reception* (SBL Septuagint and Cognate Studies, 58), Atlanta, GA, SBL, 2011, 157-172.

"Rock and Stumbling Block: The Fate of Matthew's Peter", in D. SENIOR (ed.), *The Gospel of Matthew at the Crossroads of Early Christianity* (BETL, 243), Leuven – Paris – Walpole, MA, Peeters, 2011, 263-311.

"When Heaven Turns into Hell: The Vision of Dorotheus and the Strange World of Human Imagination", in W. AMELING (ed.), *Topographie des Jenseits: Studien zur Geschichte des Todes in Kaiserzeit und Spätantike* (Altertumswissenschaftliches Kolloquium, 21), Stuttgart, Steiner, 2011, 123-141.

J. VERHEYDEN *et al.* (eds.), "Elenchus Bibliographicus *ETL* 2011", in *ETL* 87 (2011) 968* p.

"Elenchus Bibliographicus *ETL* 2011. II: Historia Religionum", in *ETL* 87 (2011) 144*-174*.

"Elenchus Bibliographicus *ETL* 2011. IV: Scriptura Sacra Novi Testamenti", in *ETL* 87 (2011) 174*-195* and 323*-421*.

Review: *JEastCS* 63 (2011) 380-382 (C. Hall).

Review: *ETL* 87 (2011) 468-470 (C. Schnusenberg).

Review: *JEH* 62 (2011) 778-779 (A.-C. Jacobsen).

Supervision: I. Van Wiele, *De dag en het uur van het breken van het brood*. Ph.D. thesis KU Leuven.

2012

C. Clivaz – J. Meizoz – F. Vallotton – J. Verheyden (eds.), *Lire demain: Des manuscrits antiques à l'ère digitale*, Lausanne, Presses polytechniques et universitaires romandes, 2012, xix-192 p.

Iid., "Avant-propos: Des manuscrits antiques à l'ère digitale: Pratiques de lecture, échanges intellectuels et communication scientifique", *ibid.*, xi-xiv.

Iid. (eds.), *Reading Tomorrow: Des manuscrits antiques à l'ère digitale. From Ancient Manuscripts to the Digital Era* (e-book version), Lausanne, Presses polytechniques et universitaires romandes, 2012.

"Read, Write, and Correct: The Scribe and the Perfect Text", *ibid.*, 455-471.

J. Krans – J. Verheyden (eds.), *Patristic and Text-Critical Studies: The Collected Essays of William L. Petersen* (NTTSD, 40), Leiden – Boston, MA, Brill, 2012, xvi-617 p.

J. Verheyden (ed.), *Colloquium Biblicum Lovaniense – Journées Bibliques de Louvain – Bijbelse Studiedagen te Leuven 1-60 (1949-2011)*, Leuven – Paris – Walpole, MA, Peeters, 2012, 150 p.

"Preface", *ibid.*, 5-6.

"Justin's Text of the Gospels: Another Look at the Citations in *1Apol.* 15.1-8", in C.E. Hill – M.J. Kruger (eds.), *The Early Text of the New Testament*, Oxford, OUP, 2012, 313-335.

"Trouble at Bethsaida: Some Comments on the Interpretation and Location of Mark 8,22-26 within the Gospel", in G. Van Oyen – A. Wénin (eds.), *La surprise dans la Bible: Hommage à Camille Focant* (BETL, 247), Leuven – Paris – Walpole, MA, Peeters, 2012, 209-232.

"The Unity of Luke-Acts: One Work, One Author, One Purpose?", in S.A. Adams – M. Pahl (eds.), *Issues in Luke-Acts: Selected Essays* (Gorgias Handbooks, 26), Piscataway, NJ, Gorgias Press, 2012, 27-50.

J. Verheyden – M. Grundeken, "The Spirit Before the Letter: Dreams and Visions as the Legitimation of the *Shepherd of Hermas*. A Study of Vision 5", in B.J. Koet (ed.), *Dreams as Divine Communication in Christianity: From Hermas to Aquinas* (Studies in the History and Anthropology of Religion, 3), Leuven – Paris – Walpole, MA, Peeters, 2012, 23-56.

J. Verheyden et al. (eds.), "Elenchus Bibliographicus *ETL* 2012", in *ETL* 88 (2012) 957* p.

"Elenchus Bibliographicus *ETL* 2012. II: Historia Religionum", in *ETL* 88 (2012) 146*-180*.

"Elenchus Bibliographicus *ETL* 2012. IV: Scriptura Sacra Novi Testamenti", in *ETL* 88 (2012) 180*-204* and 321*-420*.

Review: *ETL* 88 (2012) 510-512 (D.-A. Koch).

Review: *Theologische Revue* 108 (2012) 297-299 (A. Puig i Tàrrech).

Reviews: *TvT* 52 (2012) 280 (M. Peppard); 280-281 (R. Zimmermann).

2013

(ed.), *The Figure of Solomon in Jewish, Christian and Islamic Tradition: King, Sage and Architect* (Themes in Biblical Narrative, 16), Leiden – Boston, MA, Brill, 2013, vi-274 p.

"Introduction", *ibid.*, 1-6.

"Josephus on Solomon", *ibid.*, 85-106.

B.J. Koet – S. Moyise – J. Verheyden (eds.), *The Scriptures of Israel in Jewish and Christian Tradition: Essays in Honour of Maarten J.J. Menken* (SupplNT, 148), Leiden – Boston, MA, Brill, 2013, xvii-475 p.

"A Cry for Help: A Note in the Margin of Acts 16:9", *ibid.*, 115-127.

T. Nicklas – A. Merkt – J. Verheyden (eds.), *Ancient Perspectives on Paul* (NTOA/StUNT, 102), Göttingen, Vandenhoeck & Ruprecht, 2013, 442 p.

P. Lanfranchi – J. Verheyden, "Jacob and Esau: Who Are They? The Use of Romans 9:10-13 in Anti-Jewish Literature of the First Centuries", *ibid.*, 297-316.

J.W. van Henten – J. Verheyden (eds.), *Early Christian Ethics in Interaction with Jewish and Greco-Roman Contexts* (STAR, 17), Leiden – Boston, MA, Brill, 2013, ix-306 p.

Iid., "Introduction", *ibid.*, 1-16.

"Lost (and Found): A Critical Study and Analysis of the History on Lost Documents and Hypothetical Sources of Early Christianity", in *Early Christianity* 4/3 (2013) 419-422.

"Some Comments on the Earliest Evidence for the Reception of the Book of Chronicles in Christian Tradition", in *The Review of Rabbinic Judaism* 16 (2013) 58-65.

"'Damn Paul ... and Leave It There': A Note on a Puzzling Formula", in P.-G. KLUMBIES – D.S. DU TOIT (eds.), *Paulus – Werk und Wirkung: Festschrift für Andreas Lindemann zum 70. Geburtstag*, Tübingen, Mohr Siebeck, 2013, 435-461.

"Dog. II. NT", in D.C. ALLISON *et al.* (eds.), *Encyclopedia of the Bible and Its Reception*. Volume 6, Berlin – New York, De Gruyter, 2013, 1034.

"Door, Doors. II. NT", *ibid.*, 1093-1094.

"The Early Church and 'the Other Gospels'", in J. SCHRÖTER (ed.), *The Apocryphal Gospels within the Context of Early Christian Theology* (BETL, 260), Leuven – Paris – Walpole, MA, Peeters, 2013, 477-506.

"The New Testament Canon", in J. CARLETON PAGET – J. SCHAPER (eds.), *The New Cambridge History of the Bible*. I: *From the Beginnings to 600*, Cambridge, CUP, 2013, 389-411.

"A Puzzling Chapter in the Reception History of the Gospels: Victor of Antioch and His So-called 'Commentary on *Mark*'", in M. VINZENT (ed.), *Studia Patristica 63: Papers Presented at the Sixteenth International Conference on Patristic Studies Held in Oxford 2011*, Leuven, Peeters, 2013, 17-27.

"Reading Matthew and Mark in the Middle Ages: The *Glossa Ordinaria*", in E.-M. BECKER – A. RUNESSON (eds.), *Mark and Matthew II: Comparative Readings. Reception History, Cultural Hermeneutics, and Theology* (WUNT, 304), Tübingen, Mohr Siebeck, 2013, 121-149.

"Talking Miracles – Celsus and Origen in Dispute: The Evidence of *Contra Celsum* I", in T. NICKLAS – J.E. SPITTLER (eds.), *Credible, Incredible: The Miraculous in the Ancient Mediterranean* (WUNT, 321), Tübingen, Mohr Siebeck, 2013, 251-282.

"Die zweite und dritte Missionsreise", in F.W. HORN (ed.), *Paulus Handbuch*, Tübingen, Mohr Siebeck, 2013, 109-116.

J. VERHEYDEN *et al.* (eds.), "Elenchus Bibliographicus *ETL* 2013", in *ETL* 89 (2013) 885* p.

"Elenchus Bibliographicus *ETL* 2013. II: Historia Religionum", in *ETL* 89 (2013) 155*-188*.

"Elenchus Bibliographicus *ETL* 2013. IV: Scriptura Sacra Novi Testamenti", in *ETL* 89 (2013) 188*-211* and 323*-415*.

Reviews: *ETL* 89 (2013) 425-426 (I. Singer); 426-427 (G.M. Beckman – T.R. Bryce – E.H. Cline); 427 (C.A. Eberhart); 427-428 (A. García-Moreno); 428-429 (S. Grosse); 430-431 (E. Bons – T. Legrand); 431-432

(J.-D. Causse – É. Cuvillier – A. Wénin); 432-433 (C. Stettler); 433-434 (M. Leuchter – J.M. Hutton); 439-440 (M. Thiessen); 446-448 (W. Loader); 448-450 (O. Wassmuth); 450-451 (M. Henze); 451-452 (J. Pastor – P. Stern – M. Mor); 453 (J. von Ehrenkrook); 454-456 (U. Busse; P. Hoffmann; R. Hoppe; D. Zeller); 456-457 (A. Lindemann); 457 (J.M. García Pérez); 458-459 (K.O. Sandnes); 459-460 (M. Bauspiess – C. Landmesser – F. Portenhauser); 460-461 (R.K. McIver); 461-463 (T. Holmén – S. Porter); 464-465 (R. Heyer); 465-466 (C. Focant); 466 (G.C. Bottini); 469 (C. Theobald); 470 (W.P. Atkinson); 472 (G. Haya-Prats); 472-473 (L. Barlet – C. Guillermain); 473-474 (C. Dionne); 474-475 (D.L. Eastman); 475-476 (J.P. Heil); 476-478 (P.-M. Beaude); 479-480 (K. Liljeström); 481-482 (A.J. Hultgren); 482-484 (R.N. Longenecker); 485-487 (Y. Redalié); 487 (E.F. Mason – K.B. McCruden); 488-489 (S. McKnight); 489-491 (J. Schlosser); 491-492 (K. Peter); 492-493 (N.F.H. O'Hear); 493-494 (M. Heimola); 494-495 (J.A. North – S.R.F. Price); 496 (C.A. Evans); 496-498 (A. Faivre); 498-499 (G. Aragione); 500-501 (J. O'Leary); 501-502 (F. Petit – L. Van Rompay – J.J.S. Weitenberg); 502-503 (G.J. Donker); 503-504 (J.-M. Garrigues); 504-505 (J.-M. Garrigues); 507-508 (R. Gryson); 513-514 (N. Hecquet-Noti); 514-517 (Archa Verbi 1-10); 518 (J.M. Davis – F.R.P. Akehurst – G. Gros).

Reviews: *JEastCS* 65 (2013) 275-276 (M. Zitnik); 276-278 (P. Wood); 278-279 (L.S.B. MacCoull); 279-280 (M. Heimgartner); 280-281 (P. Roelli); 281-282 (F. Armanios); 282-284 (V. Larin); 284-285 (C. Schiller – M. Grudule); 285-286 (S.M. Kenworthy); 286-287 (A. O'Mahony – J. Flannery); 287-288 (J.A. McGuckin).

Review: *JTS* 64 (2013) 232-234 (M. Gourgues).

Review: *LS* 37 (2013) 80-81 (I.C. Levy).

Supervision: M. Grundeken, *Community Building in the* Shepherd of Hermas: *A Critical Study of Some Key Aspects*. Ph.D. thesis KU Leuven. Published under the same title: (SupplVC, 131), Leiden, Brill, 2015.

Supervision: S.P. Mbumba Ntumba, *De Bethsaïda à Jéricho: L'identité du disciple en Mc 8,22–10,52*. Ph.D. thesis KU Leuven. Published under the title *Chrétien, qui es tu? Une manière de suivre le Christ en Mc 8,22–10,52*, Kinshasa, Médiaspaul, 2015.

2014

J.S. KLOPPENBORG – J. VERHEYDEN (eds.), *The Elijah-Elisha Narrative in the Composition of Luke* (LNTS, 493), London, Bloomsbury, 2014. Reprint 2015 (paperback), VIII-170 p.

"By Way of Epilogue: Looking Back at the Healing of Naaman and the Healing of the Centurion's Slave – in Response to John Shelton", *ibid.*, 153-160.

G. VAN BELLE – J. VERHEYDEN (eds.), *Christ and the Emperor: The Gospel Evidence* (BTS, 20), Leuven – Paris – Walpole, MA, Peeters, 2014, XXIX-428 p.

"Introduction: Christ and the Empire – An Appetizer", *ibid.*, IX-XXIX.

J. VERHEYDEN – G. VAN OYEN – M. LABAHN – R. BIERINGER (eds.), *Studies in the Gospel of John and Its Christology*: Festschrift Gilbert Van Belle (BETL, 265), Leuven – Paris – Walpole, MA, Peeters, 2014, XXXV-656 p.

ID., "Introduction", *ibid.*, XIII-XVI.

"A Good Way to End a Gospel? A Note in the Margin of John 21,25", *ibid.*, 567-593.

"The Devil in Person, the Devil in Disguise: Looking for King Sennacherib in Early Christian Literature", in I. KALIMI – S. RICHARDSON (eds.), *Sennacherib at the Gates of Jerusalem: Story, History and Historiography* (Culture and History of the Ancient Near East, 71), Leiden – Boston, MA, Brill, 2014, 389-431.

"A Jewish King in Egypt? A Note on the So-Called *History of Joseph*", in E. TIGCHELAAR (ed.), *Old Testament Pseudepigrapha and the Scriptures* (BETL, 270), Leuven – Paris – Walpole, MA, Peeters, 2014, 449-461.

"Q 13:34-35: Evaluations", in S.R. JOHNSON, in cooperation with M.G STEINHAUSER – R.L JOLLIFFE (eds.), *Documenta Q: Q 13:34-35: Judgment over Jerusalem*, Leuven – Paris – Walpole, MA, Peeters, 2014, pp. 163-167, 175-177, 182-184, 191-192, 197, 211-212, 224-225, 228-229, 243-244, 255-256.

Review: *ETL* 90 (2014) 176-178 (D. Zeller).

Review: *ExpTim* 125 (2014) 491-492 (W. Loader).

Review: *JEastCS* 66 (2014) 211-212 (D. Angelov – M. Saxby).

Review: *JEH* 65 (2014) 872 (V. Hovhannesian).

Reviews: *LS* 38 (2014) 382-383 (I.C. Levy – Ph.D.W. Kray – Th. Ryan); 383-385 (G. Vall).

Review: *Rivista Biblica* 62 (2014) 128-131 (S. de Vulpillières).

Review: *TLZ* 139 (2014) 1014-1015 (G. Aragione – R. Gounelle).

2015

A. GREGORY – C.M. TUCKETT (eds.), T. NICKLAS – J. VERHEYDEN (consulting editors), *The Oxford Handbook of Early Christian Apocrypha*, Oxford, OUP, 2015, XII-473 p.

J. VERHEYDEN – M. GRUNDEKEN (eds.), *Early Christian Communities between Ideal and Reality* (WUNT, 342), Tübingen, Mohr Siebeck, 2015, XIII-242 p.

IID., "Introduction", *ibid.*, VII-XIII.

G. VAN BELLE – J. VERHEYDEN (eds.), *Bultmann and the Gospels*, in *ETL* 91/3 (2015) 363-546.

IID., "Introduction", *ibid.*, 363-364.

"Ancient Christian Apocrypha", in *TLZ* 140/1-2 (2015) 141-147.

"Hermas and Bodmer: Another Look at the Text of *Vision* 1.3.4, 2.3.1, and 3.2.1 in *P. Bodm.* XXXVIII", in *Adamantius* 21 (2015) 144-154.

"Matthew's Building Blocks: Mark and Q – A Critical Look at a Recent Monograph", in *In die Skriflig/In luce verbi* 49/1 (2015) Art. # 1988, 10 p.

A. MERKT, in cooperation with T. NICKLAS – J. VERHEYDEN, "Das Novum Testamentum Patristicum (NTP): Ein Projekt zur Erforschung von Rezeption und Auslegung des Neuen Testamentes in frühchristlicher und spätantiker Zeit", in *Early Christianity* 6 (2015) 573-595.

T. NICKLAS – A. MERKT – J. VERHEYDEN (eds.), "The Pastoral Letters", in *Annali di Storia dell'Esegesi* 32/2 (2015) 285-392.

"Israel's Fate in the Apostolic Fathers: The Case of *1 Clement* and the *Epistle of Barnabas*", in M. TIWALD (ed.), *Q in Context I: The Separation between the Just and the Unjust in Early Judaism and in the Sayings Source* (BBB, 172), Bonn, Bonn University Press; Göttingen, V&R Unipress, 2015, 237-262.

"Matthew and the *Didache*: Some Comments on the Comments", in J.A. DRAPER – C.N. JEFFORD (eds.), *The Didache: A Missing Piece of the Puzzle in Early Christianity* (SBL Early Christianity and Its Literature, 14), Atlanta, GA, SBL, 2015, 409-425.

"On 'Rotten Stones' and a Couple of Other Marginalia in the *Shepherd of Hermas*", in D.M. GURTNER – J. HERNANDEZ JR. – P. FOSTER (eds.), *Studies on the Text of the New Testament and Early Christianity Essays in Honor of Michael W. Holmes* (NTTSD, 50), Leiden – Boston, MA, Brill, 2015, 578-593.

"Préface", in S.P. MBUMBA NTUMBA, *Chrétien, qui es tu? Une manière de suivre le Christ en Mc 8,22–10,52*, Kinshasa, Médiaspaul, 2015, 5-6.

"The Sibyl and the Bible, or How to Use Scripture before It Was Revealed", in R. GOUNELLE – B. MOUNIER (eds.), *La littérature apocryphe chrétienne et les Écritures juives* (Publications de l'Institut romand des sciences bibliques, 7), Lausanne, Éditions du Zèbre, 2015, 11-25.

"Strangers on the Walls: A Note on Paul's Escape from Damascus", in C. BREYTENBACH (ed.), *Paul and His Greco-Roman Context* (BETL, 277), Leuven – Paris – Bristol, CT, Peeters, 2015, 657-674.

Reviews: *JEastCS* 67 (2015) 395-396 (G. Gabra); 397-398 (T.M. van Lint – R. Meyer).

Review: *JTS* 66 (2015) 425-427 (M. Williams).

Review: *RBL* 2015 www.bookreviews.org/BookDetail.asp?TitleId=9753 (M.D. Litwa).

Chronicle: "Colloquium Biblicum Lovaniense LXIV: New Perspectives on the Book of Revelation", in *TvT* 55 (2015) 396.

Supervision: D. Batovici, *The Reception of Early Christian Apocrypha and of the Apostolic Fathers: Reassessing the Late-Antique Manuscript Tradition and the Patristic Witnesses*. Ph.D. thesis KU Leuven.

2016

T. CORSTEN – M. ÖHLER – J. VERHEYDEN (eds.), *Epigraphik und Neues Testament* (WUNT, 365), Tübingen, Mohr Siebeck, 2016, VIII-213 p.

IID., "Introduction", *ibid.*, 1-4.

M. LANG – J. VERHEYDEN (eds.), *Goldene Anfänge und Aufbrüche: Johann Jakob Wettstein und die Apostelgeschichte* (ABG, 57), Leipzig, Evangelische Verlagsanstalt, 2016, 463 p.

IID., "Vorwort", *ibid.*, 5-6.

J. VERHEYDEN – A. MERKT – T. NICKLAS (eds.), *"If Christ Has Not Been Raised ..." : Studies on the Reception of the Resurrection Stories and the Belief in the Resurrection in the Early Church* (NTOA/StUNT, 115), Göttingen, Vandenhoeck & Ruprecht, 2016, 229 p.

IID., "Introduction", *ibid.*, 7-9.

J. VERHEYDEN – G. VAN BELLE (eds.), *An Early Reader of Mark and Q* (BTS, 21), Leuven – Paris – Bristol, CT, Peeters, 2016, XII-300 p.

IID., "Preface", *ibid.*, IX-XI.

"Wettstein and We, or How to Use with Profit Ancient Sources", *ibid.*, 261-287.

C. CLIVAZ – P. DILLEY – D. HAMIDOVIC – M. POPOVIC – C.T. SCHROEDER – J. VERHEYDEN (eds.), *Digital Humanities in Ancient Jewish, Christian and Arabic Traditions*, in *Journal of Religion, Media and Digital Culture* 5/1 (2016) 1-278 (Special Issue).

"Clumsy Constructions? A Note on Parataxis, with an Eye on Mark and the Alexander Romance", in W.E. ARNAL – R.S. ASCOUGH – R.A. DERRENBACKER JR. – Ph.A. HARLAND (eds.), *Scribal Practices and Social Structures among Jesus Adherents: Essays in Honour of John S. Kloppenborg* (BETL, 285), Leuven – Paris – Bristol, CT, Peeters, 2016, 309-331.

"Origen on 'The Witch of Endor' (1Sam 28): Some Comments on an Intriguing Piece of Reception History", in W. DIETRICH in cooperation with C. EDENBURG – Ph. HUGO (eds.), *The Books of Samuel: Stories – History – Reception History* (BETL, 284), Leuven – Paris – Bristol, CT, Peeters, 2016, 589-598.

"Pessimism in All Its Glory: The Ascension of Isaiah on the Church in the Last Days", in J.N. BREMMER – Th. R. KARMANN – T. NICKLAS (eds.), *The Ascension of Isaiah* (Studies in Early Christian Apocrypha, 11), Leuven – Paris – Bristol, CT, Peeters, 2016, 305-346.

K. ZAMFIR – J. VERHEYDEN, "Reference-Text-Oriented Allusions", in B.J. OROPEZA – S. MOYISE (eds.), *Exploring Intertextuality: Diverse Strategies for New Testament Interpretations of Texts*, Eugene, OR, Cascade Books, 2016, 242-253.

Reviews: *ETL* 92 (2016) 695-697 (D. Gange – M. Ledger-Lomas); 710-712 (R. Bauckham – J.R. Davila – A. Panayotov); 715-716 (D.-A. Koch); 716-717 (V.K. Robbins); 717-719 (F. Watson); 721-723 (M. Theobald); 723-724 (C.M. Tuckett; J.S. Kloppenborg); 727-728 (J. Assaël – E. Cuvillier); 731-733 (G. Alberigo – A. Melloni).

Reviews: *JEastCS* 68 (2016) 403 (O. Artus); 403-404 (A.M. Silvas); 404-405 (S. Brock – B. Fitzgerald); 405-406 (P. Bruns – H.O. Luthe); 406-407 (K. Tolstaya).

Review: *JTS* 67 (2016) 296-298 (F. Szulc).

2017

A. BASTIT – J. VERHEYDEN (eds.), *Irénée de Lyon et les débuts de la Bible chrétienne: Actes de la journée du 1.VII.2014 à Lyon* (IPM, 77), Turnhout, Brepols, 2017, 502 p.

"Introduction", *ibid.*, 1-3.

"Four Gospels Indeed, but Where Is Mark? On Irenaeus' Use of the Gospel of Mark", *ibid.*, 169-204.

T. NICKLAS – C.R. MOSS – C.M. TUCKETT – J. VERHEYDEN (eds.), *The Other Side: Apocryphal Perspectives on Ancient Christian "Orthodoxies"* (NTOA/StUNT, 117), Göttingen, Vandenhoeck & Ruprecht, 2017, 269 p.

IID., "Foreword", *ibid.*, 11-12.

G. ROSKAM – J. VERHEYDEN (eds.), *Light on Creation: Ancient Commentators in Dialogue and Debate on the Origin of the World* (STAC, 104), Tübingen, Mohr Siebeck, 2017, X-314 p.

IID., "Preface", *ibid.*, v-vii.

J. VERHEYDEN – J.S. KLOPPENBORG (eds.), *Luke on Jesus, Paul and Christianity: What Did He Really Know?* (BTS, 29), Leuven – Paris – Bristol, CT, Peeters, 2017, XII-313 p.

IID., "Introduction", *ibid.*, IX-XI.

J. VERHEYDEN – T. NICKLAS – E. HERNITSCHECK (eds.), *Shadowy Characters and Fragmentary Evidence: The Search for Early Christian Groups and Movements* (WUNT, 388), Tübingen, Mohr Siebeck, 2017, IX-276 p.

IID., "Introduction", *ibid.*, 1-3.

"Eustathius of Antioch on 'The Witch of Endor' (1 Sam 28): A Critique of Origen and Exegetical Method", in *ETL* 93 (2017) 107-132.

"Objections to Luke A/B/C", in *Alpha* 1 (2017) 184-186.

"The Q-Recension Hypothesis: Some Reflections in Dialogue with Ulrich Luz", in *Sacra Scripta* 15 (2017) 194-211.

"'Authoritative Texts' and How to Handle Them: Some Reflections on an Ambiguous Concept and Its Use in Second-Century Christian Literature", in J. CARLETON PAGET – J. LIEU (eds.), *Christianity in the Second Century: Themes and Developments*, Cambridge, CUP, 2017, 188-199.

"Disqualifying the Opponent: The Catalogue of Vices in Matt 15:19 as Characterisation and Criticism", in R. ZIMMERMANN – S. JOUBERT (eds.), *Biblical Ethics and Application: Purview, Validity, and Relevance of Biblical Texts in Ethical Discourse* (WUNT, 384; Kontexte und Normen neutestamentlicher Ethik / Contexts and Norms of New Testament Ethics, 9), Tübingen, Mohr Siebeck, 2017, 91-104.

"Eating with Apostles: Eucharist and Table Fellowship in the Apocryphal Acts of the Apostles. The Evidence from the *Acts of John* and the *Acts of Thomas*", in D. HELLHOLM – D. SÄNGER (eds.), *The Eucharist – Its Origins and Contexts. Volume II: Patristic Traditions, Iconography* (WUNT, 376), Tübingen, Mohr Siebeck, 2017, 1011-1060.

"Jesus als Wanderprediger", in J. SCHRÖTER – C. JACOBI (eds.) unter Mitarbeit von L. NOGOSSEK, *Jesus Handbuch*, Tübingen, Mohr Siebeck, 2017, 262-272.

"Gründung einer Gemeinschaft: Ruf in die Nachfolge und die Bildung des Zwölferkreises", *ibid.*, 273-292.

"Strange and Unexpected: Some Comments on the Language and Imagery of the Apocalypse of John", in A. YARBRO COLLINS (ed.), *New Perspectives on the Book of Revelation* (BETL, 291), Leuven – Paris – Bristol, CT, Peeters, 2017, 161-206.

Review: *BN* 175 (2017) 159-160 (D. Roth – R. Zimmermann – M. Labahn).

Reviews: *ETL* 93 (2017) 387-390 (H.J. de Jonge); 537-538 (A.K. Marshak); 538-539 (M. Ebner); 539-540 (C. Heil); 540-541 (L. Oberlinner – F.R. Prostmeier); 541-542 (R.H. Gundry); 542-543 (S. Jöris); 549-551 (J.M. Lieu); 720-721 (J.J. Collins); 721-722 (E. Bons – P. Pouchelle); 728-729 (S.E. Porter – A.W. Pitts); 729-730 (U. Schnelle); 730-732 (J.D.G. Dunn); 732-733 (M. Reiser); 733-734 (M. Labahn – O. Lehtipuu); 737-738 (J.R. Harrison – L.L. Welborn); 738-739 (M. Navarro Puerto – M. Perroni); 739-741 (J.C. Poirier – J. Peterson); 741-742 (D. Chrupcala); 742-743 (C. Prieto); 743-744 (T. Esposito); 744-745 (J.W. Barker); 745-747 (D. Marguerat); 750-751 (C. Focant); 751-752 (S. Witetschek); 755-756 (H. Amirav); 756-757 (M. McNamara); 757-758 (J.A. Schroeder).

Reviews: *JEastCS* 69 (2017) 377-378 (M. Debié); 378-380 (H.H. Todt); 383-385 (M. Tamcke *et al.*); 385-386 (S.H. Griffith – S. Grebenstein).

Review: *ZAC* 21 (2017) 591-593 (Y.R. Kim).

Supervision: with J. Leemans, co-supervisor: D. Zaganas, *L'Hexaéméron d'Anastase le Sinaïte: Son authenticité, ses sources et son allégorisme*, Ph.D. thesis KU Leuven. Published under the title *L'Hexaemeron d'Anastase le Sinaïte: Son authenticité, ses sources et son exégèse allégorisante* (SupplVC, 172), Leiden – Boston, MA, Brill, 2022.

2018

P. LANFRANCHI – J. VERHEYDEN (eds.), *Jews and Christians in Antiquity: A Regional Perspective* (Interdisciplinary Studies in Ancient Culture and Religion, 18), Leuven – Paris – Bristol, CT, Peeters, 2018, VI-370 p.

IID., "Introduction", *ibid.*, 1-5.

J. Verheyden – R. Bieringer – J. Schröter – I. Jäger (eds.), *Docetism in the Early Church: The Quest for an Elusive Phenomenon* (WUNT, 402), Tübingen, Mohr Siebeck, 2018, xi-289 p.

Id., "Introduction", *ibid.*, 1-3.

J. Verheyden – J.S. Kloppenborg (eds.), *The Gospels and Their Stories in Anthropological Perspective* (WUNT, 409), Tübingen, Mohr Siebeck, 2018, viii-331 p.

Id., "Introduction", *ibid.*, 1-3.

J. Verheyden – M. Öhler – T. Corsten (eds.), *Epigraphical Evidence Illustrating Paul's Letter to the Colossians* (WUNT, 411), Tübingen, Mohr Siebeck, 2018, x-263 p.

Id., "Introduction", *ibid.*, ix-x.

S. Schulthess – H. Teule – J. Verheyden (eds.), *Arabica sunt, non leguntur ... Studies on the Arabic Versions of the Bible in Jewish, Christian and Islamic Tradition*, in *JEastCS* 70/1-2 (2018), 122 p.

Id., "Introduction", *ibid.*, 1-5.

J. Verheyden – J. Schröter (eds.), *Is There an "Apocalyptic" World View? Images of World and Cosmos, Future and Past in Late Antique Apocalyptic Writings*, in *ETL* 94/2 (2018) 205-316.

Id., "Introduction", *ibid.*, 205-206.

"Paul, Clement and the Corinthians", in J. Schröter – S. Butticaz – A. Dettwiler (eds.), *Receptions of Paul in Early Christianity: The Person of Paul and His Writings through the Eyes of His Early Interpreters* (BZNW, 234), Berlin – Boston, MA, De Gruyter, 2018, 555-578.

"The So-Called *Catena in Marcum* of Victor of Antioch: Throwing Light on *Mark* with a Not-So-Little Help from *Matthew* and *Luke*", in M. Vinzent (ed.), *Studia Patristica 91: Papers Presented at the Seventeenth International Conference on Patristic Studies Held in Oxford 2015*, vol. 17, Leuven – Paris – Bristol, CT, Peeters, 2018, 47-62.

Reviews: *ETL* 94 (2018) 326-327 (J.J. Collins *et al.*); 327-328 (S. Ashbrook Harvey *et al.*); 328-329 (K.J. Thomas – A.-A. Aghbar); 329-331 (B. Ritter); 331-332 (S. Yli-Karjanmaa); 332-334 (A. Abakuks); 324 (B. Pitre); 335-336 (M. Wolter); 336-337 (J. Barclay); 337-338 (M.J. Gorman); 341-342 (E.L. Vieyra); 342-343 (J.A. Marchal); 343 (V.K. Robbins – J.M. Potter); 346-348 (H. Seng – L.G. Soares Santopetre – C.O. Tommasi); 351-352 (H. Johannessen); 353-354 (I. Ramelli); 355 (S. Sardjveladze *et al.*); 355-356 (K.E. Børresen – A. Valerio); 356-357 (A. Merkt);

719-720 (F. Long – S. Dowling Long); 722-723 (D.P. Moessner); 723-724 (A. Gruca-Macaulay); 724-725 (P. Foster); 725-726 (R. Hoppe); 727 (N. DesRosiers – L.C. Vuong); 727-728 (P.F. Beatrice – B. Pouderon); 728-730 (E. Cattaneo); 732-733 (S. Labarre); 735-736 (S.M. Felch).

Reviews: *JEastCS* 70 (2018) 123 (K. Meiling); 123-124 (B. Llewellyn Ihssen); 125 (N. Miladinova); 126-127 (A. Kaldellis; J. Burke – R. Scott; D. Frendo – A. Fotiou; G. Betts – S. Gauntlett – T. Spilias; W. Mayer – S. Trzcionka); 127-128 (S.P. Brock); 128-129 (K. Smith); 132-133 (J.P. Monferrer-Sala); 133-134 (S. Stroumsa); 135-137 (E.G. Mathews Jr.); 138-139 (S.H. Rapp); 142-143 (P. Bartl); 143-144 (S.J. Koovayil); 144 (F. Hindi); 145 (C. Chaillot); 307-308 (M. Choat – M.C. Giorda); 308-309 (N. Kavvadas); 311-312 (M.R. Cosby); 323-324 (B. Groen); 324-325 (E. Rommen).

Review: *ExpTim* 129 (2018) 187 (B.D. Smith).

Review: *LS* 41 (2018) 441-442 (T. Burke – B. Landau).

Review: *Augustiniana* 68 (2018) 321-324 (A.S. Jacobs).

Supervision: with T. Nicklas, co-supervisor: E. Hernitscheck, *Much Ado about Almost Nothing: Eine Forschungsgeschichtliche Meta-Analyse zu apokryphen Evangelienfragmenten als Quellen des antiken Christentums*. Ph.D. thesis KU Leuven.

2019

D.J. BURN – G. MCDONALD – J. VERHEYDEN – P. DE MEY (eds.), *Music and Theology in the European Reformations* (Collection "Epitome musical"), Turnhout, Brepols, 2019, 500 p.

J. SCHRÖTER – T. NICKLAS – J. VERHEYDEN (eds.), *Gospels and Gospel Traditions in the Second Century: Experiments in Reception* (BZNW, 235), Berlin – Boston, MA, De Gruyter, 2019, XIV-368 p.

IID., "Introduction", *ibid.*, IX-XIII.

D. ZAGANAS – J. VERHEYDEN (eds.), *Studies on Anastasius of Sinai (with Particular Attention to the* Hexaemeron*)*, in *ETL* 95/3 (2019) 371-527.

IID., "Introduction", *ibid.*, 371-374.

"Mark, Gospel of. II. Christianity: A. Greek and Latin Patristics and Orthodox Christianity", in *Encyclopedia of the Bible and Its Reception*, 17, Berlin, De Gruyter, 2019, 927-929.

"Moses and Peter: Some Comments in the Margins of Christian Typology", in M. BODÓ – I. CSONTA – O. LUKÁCS – K. ZAMFIR (eds.), *Ünneplő ember a közösségben: Baráti köszöntőkötet Nóda Mózes tiszteletére*, Budapest, Szent István Társulat – Kolozsvár, Verbum, 2019, 387-400.

"The Reception History of the Gospel of Mark in the Early Church: Adventuring in Still Largely Unexplored Territory", in G. VAN OYEN (ed.), *Reading the Gospel of Mark in the Twenty-First Century: Method and Meaning* (BETL, 301), Leuven – Paris – Bristol, CT, Peeters, 2019, 395-428.

"Reward and Salvation: A Note on Mark 10:29-30", in D.S. DU TOIT – C. GERBER – C. ZIMMERMANN (eds.), *Soteria: Salvation in Early Christianity and Antiquity. Festschrift in Honour of Cilliers Breytenbach on the Occasion of His 65th Birthday* (SupplNT, 175), Leiden – Boston, MA, Brill, 2019, 155-165.

Reviews: *Apocrypha* 30 (2019) 209-211 (A. Mugridge); 211-212 (L.I. Lied – H. Lundhaug); 226-227 (H.W. Attridge – D.R. MacDonald – C.K. Rothschild); 239-241 (B. Gleede).

Review: *BN* 180 (2019) 136-138 (M. Hölscher).

Reviews: *ETL* 95 (2019) 343-344 (R. Bauckham); 344-345 (B.S. Crawford – M.P. Miller); 345-346 (J.N. Bremmer); 347-348 (C.K. Rothschild); 348-349 (J.-M. Auwers – R. Burnet – D. Luciani); 349-350 (T.S. de Bruyn – S.A. Cooper – D.G. Hunter); 359-360 (S. Reimann).

Review: *JEH* 70 (2019) 331-333 (M. Döhler).

Review: *TvT* 59 (2019) 174-178 (H. Teule – A. Brüning).

Supervision: J. Panthalanickel, *Luke's Strategy for the Salvation of the Rich: An Exegetical Analysis of Key Pericopes in the Gospel*. Ph.D. thesis KU Leuven.

2020

J.S. KLOPPENBORG – J. VERHEYDEN (eds.), *Theological and Theoretical Issues in the Synoptic Problem* (LNTS, 618), London – New York, T&T Clark, 2020, VIII-232 p.

IID., "Preface", *ibid.*, VI.

H. TEULE – J. VERHEYDEN (eds.), *Eastern and Oriental Christianity in the Diaspora* (Eastern Christian Studies, 30), Leuven – Paris – Bristol, CT, Peeters, 2020, X-227 p.

IID., "Introduction", *ibid.*, VII-X.

J. VERHEYDEN – D. MÜLLER (eds.), *Imagining Paganism through the Ages: Studies on the Use of the Labels "Pagan" and "Paganism" in*

Controversies (BETL, 312), Leuven – Paris – Bristol, CT, Peeters, 2020, XIV-343 p.

ID., "Introduction", *ibid.*, IX-XIV.

"Between Persiflage and Frustration: Another Look at the *Carmen contra paganos*", *ibid.*, 83-103.

"*Gentes*, *pagani*, and the 'Nijmegen School'", *ibid.*, 249-258.

"Gentiles and Pagans in the Vulgate: A Selective Survey of Relevant Vocabulary with a Few Comments", *ibid.*, 259-319.

B. GLEEDE – J. VERHEYDEN (eds.), *Zoroastrian Dualism in Jewish, Christian, and Manichaean Perspective*, in *ETL* 96/2 (2020) 193-419.

ID., "Introduction", *ibid.*, 193-198.

M. BAR-ASHER SIEGAL – M.B. DINKLER – T. NICKLAS – J. SCHRÖTER – J. VERHEYDEN (eds.), *Women in Biblical and Para-biblical Jewish and Christian Literature*, in *ETL* 96/3 (2020) 423-581.

"Attempting the Impossible? Ptolemy's *Letter to Flora* as Counter-Narrative", in F. WATSON – S. PARKHOUSE (eds.), *Telling the Christian Story Differently: Counter-Narratives from Nag Hammadi and Beyond* (The Reception of Jesus in the First Three Centuries, 4), London, Bloomsbury – T&T Clark, 2020, 95-120.

"*Didache*", in C. KEITH – H.K. BOND – C. JACOBI – J. SCHRÖTER (eds.), *The Reception of Jesus in the First Three Centuries.* Volume One: *From Paul to Josephus: Literary Receptions of Jesus in the First Century* CE, Volume editor H.K. BOND, London, Bloomsbury – T&T Clark, 2020, 337-362.

"Introducing 'Q' in French Catholic Scholarship at the Turn of the 19th and 20th Century: Alfred Loisy's *Évangiles synoptiques*", in M. TIWALD (ed.), *The Q Hypothesis Unveiled: Theological, Sociological, and Hermeneutical Issues behind the Sayings Source* (BWANT, 225), Stuttgart, Kohlhammer, 2020, 146-174.

"Polysemy and Repetition in Gregory of Nyssa's *Homilies on the Song of Songs*: Two Short Comments", in P. VAN HECKE (ed.), *The Song of Songs in Its Context: Words for Love, Love for Words* (BETL, 310), Leuven – Paris – Bristol, CT, Peeters, 2020, 577-592.

"Preface", in A. MORELLI – J. TYSSENS (eds.), *Quand une religion se termine… Facteurs politiques et sociaux de la disparition des religions* ("Religion et altérité"), Louvain-la-Neuve, EME Éditions (distributed by Éditions L'Harmattan, Paris), 2020, 5-7.

Interview for the documentary "The Passion of Jesus" for RMC Découverte (December 2019; broadcast in April 2020) https://vimeo.com/393657496/2e851cd592.

Review: *BN* 185 (2020) 147-148 (M.C. Hauck).

Reviews: *ETL* 96 (2020) 701-702 (T. Thatcher *et al.*); 705-706 (T.H. Lim); 706-707 (M. Gerhards); 708-709 (M. Ederer – B. Schmitz); 711-712 (N.L. Tilford); 716-717 (K. De Troyer – B. Schmitz); 719-720 (D. Jaillard – C. Nihan); 720-721 (A. Ercolani – P. Xella); 733-735 (J.L. Sumney); 737-739 (S. McKnight); 739-740 (R.F. Collins); 743 (J. Kügler); 746-748 (C. Bandt – F.X. Risch – B. Villani); 748-749 (P. Maraval); 749-750 (A. Canellis); 756-757 (M.E. Stone); 757-758 (J.A. Schroeder); 758-760 (A. Aniorté).

Reviews: *JEastCS* 72 (2020) 319 (B. Pouderon); 323-324 (C. dell'Osso); 24-325 (C.J. Stallman-Pacitti); 325-326 (E. Loosley Leeming); 326-327 (B. Neil – E. Anagnostou-Maoutides); 330-331 (J.-N. Mellon Saint-Laurent – K. Smith); 335-337 (A. Roeber).

Supervision: with H. Teule, co-supervisor: J. Fathi, *Apologie et mysticisme chez les chrétiens d'Orient: Recherches sur al-Kindī et Barhebraeus (vers 820 et 1280)*. Ph.D. thesis KU Leuven. Part of this work will be published under the title: *Le prince déchu: L'établissement de l'authenticité de l'*Apologie *d'al-Kindi et l'étude critique de la conclusion* (Orientalia Christiana Analecta), Roma, Pontificio Istituto Orientale, 2022 et *La colombe dans la voie de l'ascension de Barhebraeus: Étude et édition critique* (Série Patrimoine Arabe Chrétien), Beyrouth, CEDRAC, 2022. https://www.usj.edu.lb/publications/catalogue/periodique_dtls.htm?perid=130.

2021

P. D'HOINE – G. ROSKAM – S. SCHORN – J. VERHEYDEN (eds.), *Polemics and Networking in Graeco-Roman Antiquity* (Lectio: Studies in the Transmission of Texts & Ideas, 12), Turnhout, Brepols, 2021, 475 p.

IID., "Polemic, Networking and Their Interplay: Some Preliminary Comments", *ibid.*, 11-35.

J. SCHRÖTER – B.A. EDSALL – J. VERHEYDEN (eds.), *Jews and Christians – Parting Ways in the First Two Centuries CE? Reflections on the Gains and Losses of a Model* (BZNW, 253), Berlin – Boston, MA, De Gruyter, 2021, VI-409 p.

IID., "Introduction", *ibid.*, 1-10.

"Living Apart Together: Jews and Christians in Second-Century Rome – Re-visiting Some of the Actors Involved", *ibid.*, 307-345.

J. VERHEYDEN – T. NICKLAS (eds.), *Early Christian Commentators of the New Testament: Essays on Their Aims, Methods and Strategies* (BTS, 42), Leuven – Paris – Bristol, CT, Peeters, 2021, XIV-305 p.

IID., "Introduction", *ibid.*, IX-XII.

J. VERHEYDEN – J. SCHRÖTER – T. NICKLAS (eds.), *Texts in Context: Essays on Dating and Contextualising Christian Writings from the Second and Early Third Centuries* (BETL, 319), Leuven – Paris – Bristol, CT, 2021, VIII-319 p.

IID., "Introduction", *ibid.*, 1-4.

J.-M. SEVRIN, *Études sur l'Évangile selon Thomas et la littérature gnostique: Recueil d'articles*. Édité par P.-H. POIRIER – J. VERHEYDEN (BTS, 43), Leuven – Paris – Bristol, CT, Peeters, 2021, XIV-342 p.

P.-H. POIRIER – J. VERHEYDEN, "Avant-propos", *ibid.*, VII-IX.

"Obituary Note" [Paul Peeters], in *ETL* 97 (2021) i.

"All Mysteries Revealed? On the Interplay between Hiding and Revealing and the Dangers of Heavenly Journeys according to the *Ascension of Isaiah*", in I. DORFMANN-LAZAREV (ed.), *Apocryphal and Esoteric Sources in the Development of Christianity and Judaism: The Eastern Mediterranean, the Near East, and Beyond* (Texts and Studies in Eastern Christianity, 21), Leiden – Boston, MA, Brill, 2021, 70-87.

"Christian Inscriptions in a (Post-)Biblical World", in K.J. DELL (ed.), *The Biblical World. Second Edition*, London – New York, Routledge, 2021, 394-406.

"Dreams, Visions and the World-to-Come according to the *Shepherd of Hermas*", in J. SCHRÖTER – T. NICKLAS – A. PUIG I TÀRRECH (eds.), *Dreams, Visions, Imaginations: Jewish, Christian and Gnostic Views of the World to Come* (BZNW 247), Berlin – Boston, MA, De Gruyter, 2021, 215-234.

"The End of the Apostles: A Brief Response to Some Inspiring Essays", in M. VINZENT (ed.), *Studia Patristica 107: Papers Presented at the Eighteenth International Conference on Patristic Studies Held in Oxford 2019. Volume 4: Remembering Apostles as Martyrs*, ed. S. WITETSCHEK, Leuven – Paris – Bristol, CT, Peeters, 2021, 135-145.

"Fighting Paganism in the *Apocryphal Acts of the Apostles*: The Case of the *Acts of Philip*", in T. NICKLAS – J.E. SPITTLER – J.N. BREMMER (eds.),

The Apostles Peter, Paul, John, Thomas and Philip with Their Companions in Late Antiquity (Studies on Early Christian Apocrypha, 17), Leuven – Paris – Bristol, CT, Peeters, 2021, 295-313.

"Paul Peeters (8 October 1965 – 22 March 2021)", in M. VINZENT (ed.), *Studia Patristica 104: Papers Presented at the Eighteenth International Conference on Patristic Studies Held in Oxford 2019*. Volume 1: *Introduction – Historica*, Leuven – Paris – Bristol, CT, Peeters, 2021, 3.

"Peter in the Pseudo-Clementine Romance: Composed, Composite, and Complex. Revisiting the Evidence from *Homilies* 1–7", in J.M. LIEU (ed.), *Peter in the Early Church: Apostle – Missionary – Church Leader* (BETL, 325), Leuven – Paris – Bristol, CT, Peeters, 2021, 331-381.

D. BATOVICI – J. VERHEYDEN, "Digitizing the Ancient Versions of the Apostolic Fathers: Preliminary Considerations", in T. HUTCHINGS – C. CLIVAZ (eds.), *Digital Humanities and Christianity: An Introduction* (Introductions to Digital Humanities 4), Berlin, De Gruyter, 2021, 103-123. Doi: 10.1515/9783110574043-005.

"'En zij kwamen uit het Oosten': Wie waren de drie Wijzen echter precies en wat betekent hun verhaal nu voor ons?", in *Kerk en Leven*, 6 January, 2021, p. 10 (interview).

L. De Vocht, "Dringende oproep tot bekering" [Matt 12,38-42 par.], in *Tertio*, 3 February, 2021, 14-15 (interview).

Review: *Augustiniana* 71 (2021) 265-268 (T.J. Bauer – P. von Möllendorff).

Reviews: *ETL* 97 (2021) 520-522 (U. Schnelle); 529-530 (P. Roszak – J. Vijgen); 532-534 (G. Bray); 534-535 (M. Matheus); 535-537 (A. Lannoy – C. Bonnet – D. Praet).

Reviews: *JEastCS* 71 (2021) 129-130 (C. Gines Taylor); 130-132 (I. Bueno – C. Rouxpetel); 132-133 (A. Łajtar – J. van der Vliet); 133-135 (S. Schulthess).

Review: *LS* 44 (2021) 97-99 (W. Carter); 386-387 (A. Bausi – B. Reuddenbach – H. Wimmer).

Review: *Reading Religion AAR* 2021 (online) (M. Hengel – A.M. Schwemer).

Supervision: with H. Teule, co-supervisor: J.G.E.F. Valentin, *Evangelia Arabica: La version melkite du XIᵉ siècle (Kashouh jB): L'Évangile de Marc*. Ph.D. thesis KU Leuven.

Supervision: with B. ter Haar Romeny, co-supervisor: M. Pragt, *Lovers of Learning: The Reception of the Song of Songs in Two West Syrian Exegetical Collections (c. 600-900)*. Ph.D. thesis KU Leuven.

2022

J. VERHEYDEN – G. ROSKAM – G. VAN RIEL (eds.), *From Protology to Eschatology: Competing Views on the Origin and the End of the Cosmos in Platonism and Christian Thought* (STAC, 130), Tübingen, Mohr Siebeck, 2022, VII-262 p.

IID., "Introduction", *ibid.*, 1-6.

J. VERHEYDEN – J. SCHRÖTER – D.C. SIM (eds.), *The Composition, Theology, and Early Reception of Matthew's Gospel* (WUNT, 477), Tübingen, Mohr Siebeck, 2022, IX-379 p.

IID., "Introduction", *ibid.*, 1-5.

"Irenaeus and the Gospel of Matthew", *ibid.*, 289-320.

"From Jesus to the Second Century Apostolic Church", in J.J. COLLINS – G. HENS-PIAZZA – B. REID – D. SENIOR (eds.), *The Jerome Biblical Commentary for the Twenty-First Century*. Third Fully Revised Edition, London – New York – Sydney, Bloomsbury, T&T Clark, 2022, 1139-1153.

"Paul, Jerome and Galatians: Two Comments in the Margin of Martin Meiser's *Galater*", in S. KREUZER – W. KRAUS – M. KARRER – J. PERSCH (eds.), *Bibel und Patristik: Studien zur Exegese und Rezeption von Septuaginta und Neuen Testament. Festschrift für Martin Meiser*, Leiden, Brill Schöningh, 2022, 309-334.

Reviews: *ETL* 98 (2022) 166-168 (L. Junker); 169-171 (M. Quesnel); 171-172 (D.A. deSilva); 172-174 (S. McKnight); 175-176 (R. Hoppe); 176-178 (L.R. Zelyck); 178-180 (J.R. Harrison – L.L. Welborn); 186-187 (A. Bihler – F. Fritz); 187-188 (K. Herbers – A. Nehring – K. Steiner); 188-190 (D. Mondini – C. Jäggi – P.C. Claussen)

Supervision: Y. Matta (ICP) – J. Verheyden (supervisors): R.K. Fatchéoun, *Jésus prophète dans l'épître aux Hébreux: Étude exégétique d'He 3,1-6*. Ph.D. thesis ICP – KU Leuven.

Supervision: with H. Teule, co-supervisor: S. Noble, *The Kitāb al-Manfaʿa of ʿAbdallāh ibn al-Faḍl al-Anṭākī: Critical Edition, English Translation and Commentary*. Ph.D. thesis KU Leuven.

BOOK REVIEWS WRITTEN BY JOSEPH VERHEYDEN
1982-2021

Some titles included in this list have been slightly abridged. For reviews in the *Review of Biblical Literature* (*RBL*) which are mentioned here without page numbers, see the website www.sblcentral.org/home/rbl.

A. Abakuks, *The Synoptic Problem and Statistics* (2015), *ETL* 94 (2018) 332-334.
M. Adinolfi, *Il Verbo uscito dal silenzio* (1992), *ETL* 71 (1995) 232-233.
W.J. Aerts – G.A.A. Kortekaas, *Die Apokalypse des Pseudo-Methodius* (1998), *ETL* 76 (2000) 507-508.
A.-A. Aghbar, see K.J. Thomas – A.-A. Aghbar, *A Restless Search: A History of Persian Translations of the Bible* (2015).
F.R.P. Akehurst, see J.M. Davis – F.R.P. Akehurst – G. Gros, *Our Lady's Lawsuits in l'Advocacie Nostre Dame and La Chapellerie Nostre Dame de Baiex* (2011).
K. Akiyama, see T.H. Lim – K. Akiyama (eds.), *When Texts Are Canonized* (2017).
G. Alberigo – A. Melloni (eds.), *Conciliorum oecumenicorum generaliumque decreta: Editio critica* (2006-2013), *ETL* 92 (2016) 731-733.
J. Alison, *Raising Abel: The Recovery of the Eschatological Imagination* (1996), *LS* 22 (1997) 385-386.
T. Altizer, *The Contemporary Jesus* (1997), *LS* 23 (1998) 288.
H. Amirav, *Authority and Performance: Sociological Perspectives on the Council of Chalcedon (AD 451)* (2015), *ETL* 93 (2017) 755-756.
J.E. Amon, see A. Garsky – C. Heil – Th. Hieke – J.E. Amon – S. Carruth, *The Database of the International Q Project: Q 12:49-59. Children against Parents – Judging the Time – Settling out of Court* (1997).
E. Anagnostou-Maoutides, see B. Neil – E. Anagnostou-Maoutides (eds.), *Dreams, Memory and Imagination in Byzantium* (2018).
S.D. Anderson, see S. Carruth – A. Garsky – S.D. Anderson, *The Database of the International Q Project: Q 11:2b-4* (1996).
D. Angelov – M. Saxby (eds.), *Power and Subversion in Byzantium* (2013), *JEastCS* 66 (2014) 211-212.
A. Aniorté (ed.), *Commentaire des Psaumes attribué à Saint Bruno* (2017), *ETL* 96 (2020) 758-760.
G. Aragione, *Les chrétiens et la loi* (2011), *ETL* 89 (2013) 498-499.
G. Aragione – R. Gounelle (eds.), *"Soyez des changeurs avisés": Controverses exégétiques dans la littérature apocryphe chrétienne* (2013), *TLZ* 139 (2014) 1014-1015.
G. Aragione – E. Junod – E. Norelli (eds.), *Le canon du Nouveau Testament: Regards nouveaux sur l'histoire de sa formation* (2005), *JEH* 58 (2007) 293-294.
F. Armanios, *Coptic Christianity in Ottoman Egypt* (2011), *JEastCS* 65 (2013) 281-282.
O. Artus (ed.), *Loi et justice dans la littérature du Proche-Orient ancien* (2013), *JEastCS* 68 (2016) 403.
P. Arzt-Grabner et al., *1. Korinther* (2006), *RBL* 9 (2007) 439-442.

J.Ma. Asgeirsson – K. De Troyer – M.W. Meyer (eds.), *From Quest to Q: FS J.M. Robinson* (2000), *ETL* 77 (2000) 211-214.

S. Ashbrook Harvey – N.P. DesRosiers – S.L. Lander – J.Z. Pastis (eds.), *A Most Reliable Witness: Essays in Honor of R.S. Kraemer* (2015), *ETL* 94 (2018) 327-328.

J. Assaël – E. Cuvillier, *L'Epître de Jacques* (2013), *ETL* 92 (2016) 727-728.

W.P. Atkinson, *Baptism in the Spirit: Luke-Acts and the Dunn Debate* (2011), *ETL* 89 (2013) 470.

H.W. Attridge – D.R. MacDonald – C.K. Rothschild, *Delightful Acts: New Essays on Canonical and Non-canonical Acts* (2017), *Apocrypha* 30 (2019) 226-227.

D.E. Aune, *Revelation* (1997-1998), *ETL* 77 (2001) 479-482.

J.-M. Auwers – R. Burnet – D. Luciani (eds.), *L'antijudaïsme des Pères: Mythe et/ou réalité?* (2017), *ETL* 95 (2019) 348-349.

J.-M. Auwers – A. Wénin (eds.), *Lectures et relectures de la Bible* (1999), *ETL* 78 (2002) 179-181.

M. Bachmann, *Antijudaismus im Galaterbrief?* (1999), *ETL* 78 (2002) 223.

K. Backhaus, *Der neue Bund und das Werden der Kirche* (1996), *ETL* 75 (1999) 488-491.

I. Backus, *La patristique et les guerres de religion en France: Jacques de Billy* (1993), *ETL* 71 (1995) 237-239.

—, *Les sept visions et la fin des temps* (1997), *ETL* 76 (2000) 502-503.

V. Balabanski, *Eschatology in the Making* (1997), *ETL* 76 (2000) 490-492.

C. Bandt – F.X. Risch – B. Villani (eds.), *Die Prologtexte zu den Psalmen von Origenes und Eusebius* (2019), *ETL* 96 (2020) 746-748.

J.M.G. Barclay, *Paul and the Gift* (2015), *ETL* 94 (2018) 336-337.

J.W. Barker, *John's Use of Matthew* (2015), *ETL* 93 (2017) 744-745.

L. Barlet – C. Guillermain, *Le Beau Christ en Actes* (2011), *ETL* 89 (2013) 472-473.

P.W. Barnett, *The Second Epistle to the Corinthians* (1997), *ETL* 75 (1999) 213-215.

C.K. Barrett, *The Acts of the Apostles*, vol. 2 (1998), *LS* 25 (2000) 381-384.

M. Barth – H. Blanke, *The Letter to Philemon* (2000), *ETL* 78 (2002) 225-227.

P. Bartl (ed.), *Albania Sacra: Geistliche Visitationsberichte aus Albanien.* Vol. 3: *Diözese Sappa* (2014), *JEastCS* 70 (2018) 142-143.

A. Bastit, see E. Cattaneo, *Les misères dans l'Église ancienne: Textes patristiques du Ier au IIIe siècle* (trans. A. Bastit – C. Guignard) (2017).

R. Bauckham, *Jesus and the Eyewitnesses: The Gospels as Eyewitness Testimony* (2017), *ETL* 95 (2019) 343-344.

R. Bauckham – J.R. Davila – A. Panayotov (eds.), *Old Testament Pseudepigrapha: More Noncanonical Scriptures*, vol. 1 (2013), *ETL* 92 (2016) 710-712.

G.-H. Baudry, *La voie de la vie* (1999), *ETL* 77 (2001) 226-227.

D.R. Bauer, see U. Köpf – D.R. Bauer (eds.), *Kulturkontakte und Rezeptionsvorgänge in der Theologie des 12. und 13. Jahrhunderts* (2011).

T.J. Bauer – P. von Möllendorff, *Die Briefe des Ignatios von Antiochia: Motive, Strategien, Kontexte* (2018), *Augustiniana* 71 (2021) 265-268.

H. Baum, *Äthiopien und der Westen im Mittelalter* (2001), *JEastCS* 57 (2005) 188-190.

A. Bausi – B. Reuddenbach – H. Wimmer (eds.), *Canones: The Art of Harmony. The Canon Tables of the Four Gospels* (2020), *LS* 44 (2021) 386-387.

M. Bauspiess – C. Landmesser – F. Portenhauser (eds.), *Theologie und Wirklichkeit*: *Diskussionen der Bultmann-Schule* (2011), *ETL* 89 (2013) 459-460.

G.K. Beale, *The Book of Revelation* (1999), *ETL* 77 (2001) 479-482.

P.F. Beatrice – B. Pouderon, *Pascha nostrum Christus: Essays in Honour of R. Cantalamessa* (2016), *ETL* 94 (2018) 727-728.

P.-M. Beaude, *Saint Paul: L'œuvre de métamorphose* (2011), *ETL* 89 (2013) 476-478.

S.R. Bechtler, *Following in His Steps* (1998), *ETL* 78 (2002) 227-228.

G.M. Beckman – T.R. Bryce – E.H. Cline, *The Ahhiyawa Texts* (2011), *ETL* 89 (2013) 426-427.

C.T. Begg, *Josephus' Account of the Early Divided Monarchy (AJ 8,212-420): Rewriting the Bible* (1993), *ETL* 70 (1994) 151-154.

—, *Josephus' Account of the Early Divided Monarchy (AJ 8,212-420): Rewriting the Bible* (1993), *LS* 19 (1994) 75-77.

G. Benyik, *Ungarische Bibelübersetzungen* (1997), *ETL* 75 (1999) 446-447.

F. Bermejo Rubio, *La escisión imposible: Lectura del gnosticismo valentiniano* (1998), *ETL* 76 (2000) 505-506.

G. Betts – S. Gauntlett – T. Spilias (eds.), *Vitzentzos Kornaros,* Erotokritos (2017), *JEastCS* 70 (2018) 126-127.

W.A. Bienert – U. Kühneweg (eds.), *Origeniana septima* (1999), *ETL* 77 (2001) 227-228.

A. Bihler – F. Fritz (eds.), *Heiligkeiten: Konstruktionen, Funktionen und Transfer von Heiligkeitskonzepten im europäischen Früh- und Hochmittelalter* (2019), *ETL* 98 (2022) 186-187.

D.J. Bingham, *Irenaeus' Use of Matthew's Gospel* (1998), *ETL* 76 (2000) 506-507.

Y.-M. Blanchard, *Aux sources du canon: Le témoignage d'Irénée* (1993), *ETL* 72 (1999) 250-252.

H. Blanke, see M. Barth – H. Blanke, *The Letter to Philemon* (2000).

P. Blowers, *The Bible in Greek Christian Antiquity* (1997), *LS* 23 (1998) 378-379.

M.-E. Boismard, *L'énigme de la lettre aux Éphésiens* (1999), *ETL* 78 (2002) 224-225.

R.G. Boling, *The Early Biblical Community in Transjordan* (1988), *ETL* 64 (1988) 467.

C. Bonnet, see A. Lannoy – C. Bonnet – D. Praet (eds.), *"Mon cher Mithra …": La correspondance entre Franz Cumont et Alfred Loisy.* Vol. 1: *Introduction et Dossier épistolaire;* Vol. 2: *Commentaires et Annexes* (2019).

E. Bons – T. Legrand (eds.), *Le monothéisme biblique* (2011), *ETL* 89 (2013) 430-431.

E. Bons – P. Pouchelle (eds.), *The Psalms of Solomon: Language, History, Theology* (2015), *ETL* 93 (2017) 721-722.

M.E. Boring, see U. Schnelle, *The History and Theology of the New Testament Writings* (trans. M.E. Boring) (1998).

L. Bormann, *Philippi: Stadt und Christengemeinde zur Zeit des Paulus* (1995), *ETL* 72 (1996) 241-245.

L. Bormann – K. Del Tredici – A. Standhartinger (eds.), *Religious Propaganda and Missionary Competition in the New Testament: FS. D. Georgi* (1994), *ETL* 71 (1995) 227-230.

A. Borrell Viader – A. de la Fuente – A. Puig i Tàrrech (eds.), *La Bíblia i el Mediterrani* (1997), *ETL* 74 (1998) 443-444.
K.E. Børresen – A. Valerio (eds.), *The High Middle Ages* (Bible and Women 6.2) (2015), *ETL* 94 (2018) 355-356.
P. Bossuyt, *L'Esprit en Actes* (1998), *ETL* 78 (2002) 217.
G.C. Bottini, *Introduzione all'opera di Luca* (2011), *ETL* 89 (2013) 466.
A. Boud'hors, *Catalogue des fragments coptes de la Bibliothèque Nationale et Universitaire de Strasbourg* (1998), *ETL* 76 (2000) 467.
F. Bovon, *Studies in Early Christianity* (2005), *RBL* (2006).
F.G. Brambilla, *Il crocifisso risorto* (1998), *ETL* 75 (1999) 474-475.
R.L. Brawley, see M. Wolter, *Paul: An Outline of His Theology* (trans. R.L. Brawley) (2015).
G. Bray (ed.), *The Institution of a Christian Man: The Bishops' Book (1537), The King's Book (1543), Bishop Bonner's Book (1555)* (2018), *ETL* 97 (2021) 532-534.
J.N. Bremmer, *The Apocryphal Acts of John; Paul and Thecla; Peter* (1995-1998), *ETL* 75 (1999) 492-494.
—, *Maidens, Magic and Martyrs in Early Christianity: Collected Essays* (2017), *ETL* 95 (2019) 347-358.
S.P. Brock (ed.), *The Martyrs of Mount Ber'ain* (introd. P.C. Dilley) (2014), *JEastCS* 70 (2018) 127-128.
S.P. Brock – B. Fitzgerald (eds.), *Two Early Lives of Severus, Patriarch of Antiochia* (2013), *JEastCS* 68 (2016) 404-406.
T.L. Brodie, *The Gospel according to John: A Literary and Theological Commentary* (1993), *LS* 21 (1996) 289-292.
—, *The Quest for the Origin of John's Gospel* (1993), *LS* 21 (1996) 289-292.
—, *The Birthing of the New Testament: The Intertextual Development of the New Testament Writings* (2004), *Bib* 87 (2006) 439-442.
A. Brüning, see H. Teule – A. Brüning (eds.), *Handboek oosters christendom* (2018).
P. Bruns – H.O. Luthe (eds.), *Orientalia Christiana: Festschrift für Hubert Kaufhold zum 70. Geburtstag* (2013), *JEastCS* 68 (2016) 405-406.
T.R. Bryce, see G.M. Beckman – T.R. Bryce – E.H. Cline, *The Ahhiyawa Texts* (2011).
I. Bueno – C. Rouxpetel, *Les récits historiques entre Orient et Occident (XIe-XVe siècle)* (2019), *JEastCS* 71 (2021) 130-132.
J. Burke – R. Scott (eds.), *Byzantine Macedonia* (2017), *JEastCS* 70 (2018) 126-127.
T. Burke – B. Landau (eds.), *New Testament Apocrypha: More Noncanonical Scriptures*, vol. 1 (2016), *LS* 41 (2018) 441-442.
R. Burnet, see J.-M. Auwers – R. Burnet – D. Luciani (eds.), *L'antijudaïsme des Pères: Mythe et/ou réalité?* (2017).
U. Busse, see R. Hoppe – U. Busse (eds.), *Von Jesus zum Christus: FS P. Hoffmann* (1998).
—, *Jesus im Gespräch: Zur Bildrede in den Evangelien und der Apostelgeschichte* (2009), *ETL* 89 (2013) 454-455.
O. Bychkov, see M.B. Ingham – O. Bychkov (eds.), *John Duns Scotus, Philosopher: Proceedings of "The Quadruple Congress" on John Duns Scotus, Part 1* (2010).

S. Byrskog, *Jesus, the Only Teacher: Didactic Authority and Transmission* (1994), *ETL* 70 (1994) 471-475.
M.A. Calvet-Sébasti, *Grégoire de Nazianze* (1995), *ETL* 74 (1998) 452-453.
B.L. Campbell, *Honor, Shame and the Rhetoric of 1 Peter* (1998), *ETL* 78 (2002) 227-228.
H. von Campenhausen, *Ecclesiastical Authority and Spiritual Power* (1997), *LS* 23 (1998) 377-378.
A. Canellis (ed.), *Jérôme: Préfaces aux livres de la Bible. Textes latins, revus et corrigés* (2017), *ETL* 96 (2020) 749-750.
G. Canobbio, *I documenti dottrinali del magisterio* (1996), *ETL* 74 (1998) 503-504.
S. Carruth – A. Garsky – S.D. Anderson, *The Database of the International Q Project: Q 11:2b-4* (1996), *LS* 22 (1997) 183-186.
S. Carruth – J.M. Robinson – C. Heil, *The Database of the International Q Project: Q 4:1-13, 16. The Temptations of Jesus – Nazara* (1996), *LS* 23 (1998) 283-286.
S. Carruth, see A. Garsky – C. Heil – Th. Hieke – J.E. Amon – S. Carruth, *The Database of the International Q Project: Q 12:49-59. Children against Parents – Judging the Time – Settling out of Court* (1997).
W. Carter, *Mark* (2019), *LS* 44 (2021) 97-99.
E. Cattaneo, *Les misères dans l'Église ancienne: Textes patristiques du Ier au IIIe siècle* (trans. A. Bastit – C. Guignard) (2017), *ETL* 94 (2018) 728-730.
J.-D. Causse – É. Cuvillier – A. Wénin, *Divine Violence* (2011), *ETL* 89 (2013) 431-432.
C. Chaillot (ed.), *The Dialogue between the Eastern Orthodox and Oriental Orthodox Churches* (2016), *JEastCS* 70 (2018) 145.
J.B. Chance, see R.F. Hock – J.B. Chance – J. Perkins (eds.), *Ancient Fiction and Early Christian Narrative* (1998).
B. Chilton – C.A. Evans (eds.), *James the Just and Christian Origins* (1999), *ETL* 77 (2001) 224-226.
M. Choat – M.C. Giorda (eds.), *Writing and Communication in Early Egyptian Monasticism* (2017), *JEastCS* 70 (2018) 307-308.
L.D. Chrupcała, *Everyone Will See the Salvation of God: Studies in Lukan Theology* (2015), *ETL* 93 (2017) 741-742.
K. Ciggaar – H. Teule (eds.), *East and West in the Crusader States* (2003), *JEastCS* 57 (2005) 186-188.
M. Cimosa, *La letteratura intertestamentaria* (1992), *ETL* 69 (1993) 417-419.
P.C. Claussen, see D. Mondini – C. Jäggi – P.C. Claussen (eds.), *Die Kirchen der Stadt Rom im Mittelalter 1050-1300. Band 4: M–O: SS. Marcellino e Pietro bis S. Omobono* (2020).
E.H. Cline, see G.M. Beckman – T.R. Bryce – E.H. Cline, *The Ahhiyawa Texts* (2011).
J.J. Collins, *Apocalypse, Prophecy, and Pseudepigraphy: On Jewish Apocalyptic Literature* (2015), *ETL* 93 (2017) 720-721.
J.J. Collins – T.M. Lemos – S.M. Olyan (eds.), *Worship, Women, and War: Essays in Honor of S. Niditch* (2015), *ETL* 94 (2018) 326-327.
R.F. Collins, *First Corinthians* (1999), *ETL* 76 (2000) 179-182.
—, *Wealth, Wages, and the Wealthy: New Testament Insight for Preachers and Teachers* (2017), *ETL* 96 (2020) 739-740.

S.A. Cooper, see T.S. de Bruyn – S.A. Cooper – D.G. Hunter (eds.), *Ambrosiaster's Commentary on the Pauline Epistles: Romans* (2017).

M.R. Cosby, *Creation of History: The Transformation of Barnabas from Peacemaker to Warrior Saint* (2017), *JEastCS* 70 (2018) 311-312.

E. Cothenet, *Exégèse et liturgie* (1999), *ETL* 76 (2000) 478-479.

B.S. Crawford – M.P. Miller (eds.), *Redescribing the Gospel of Mark* (2017), *ETL* 95 (2019) 344-345.

G. Cremascoli – G. Leonardi (eds.), *La Bibbia nel medio evo* (1996), *ETL* 74 (1998) 456-457.

M. Cromhout, *Jesus and Identity: Reconstructing Judean Ethnicity in Q* (2007), *HvTSt* 64 (2008) 1096-1098.

R. Cross (ed.), *The Opera Theologica of John Duns Scotus: Proceedings of "The Quadruple Congress" on John Duns Scotus, Part 2* (2012), *ETL* 89 (2013) 514-517.

J.D. Crossan, *The Birth of Christianity* (1999), *ETL* 78 (2002) 199-203.

É. Cuvillier, see J.-D. Causse – É. Cuvillier – A. Wénin, *Divine Violence* (2011).

—, see J. Assaël – E. Cuvillier, *L'Epître de Jacques* (2013).

A. Dalbesio, *Quello che abbiamo udito e veduto: L'esperienza cristiana nella Prima lettera di Giovanni* (1990), *ETL* 70 (1994) 478-479.

E. dal Covolo, *I Severi e il cristianesimo* (1989), *ETL* 70 (1994) 484.

J.R. Davila, see R. Bauckham – J.R. Davila – A. Panayotov (eds.), *Old Testament Pseudepigrapha: More Noncanonical Scriptures*, vol. 1 (2013).

J.M. Davis – F.R.P. Akehurst – G. Gros, *Our Lady's Lawsuits in L'Advocacie Nostre Dame and La Chapellerie Nostre Dame de Baiex* (2011), *ETL* 89 (2013) 518.

M. Debié, *L'écriture de l'histoire en syriaque* (2015), *JEastCS* 69 (2017) 377-378.

T.S. de Bruyn – S.A. Cooper – D.G. Hunter (eds.), *Ambrosiaster's Commentary on the Pauline Epistles: Romans* (2017), *ETL* 95 (2019) 349-350.

G.-M. de Durand, *Hilaire de Poitiers* (1999), *ETL* 78 (2002) 239-240.

—, *Marc le Moine* (1999), *ETL* 78 (2002) 249-251.

H.J. de Jonge (ed.), *Opera Omnia Desiderii Erasmi Roterodami: Apologia contra Caranzam et quatuor apologiae contra Stunicam* (2015), *ETL* 93 (2017) 387-390.

H.J. de Jonge – B.W.J. de Ruyter (eds.), *Totdat hij komt: Een discussie over de wederkomst van Jezus Christus* (1995), *ETL* 72 (1996) 246-247.

M. de Jonge, *Pseudepigrapha of the Old Testament as Part of Christian Literature* (2003), *JSJ* 36 (2005) 341-344.

M. de Jonge – J. Tromp, *The Life of Adam and Eve and Related Literature* (1997), *ETL* 73 (1997) 437-438.

A. de la Fuente, see A. Borrell Viader – A. de la Fuente – A. Puig i Tàrrech (eds.), *La Bíblia i el Mediterrani* (1997).

C. dell'Osso, *Monoenergiti / Monoteliti der VII secolo in Oriente* (2017), *JEastCS* 72 (2020) 323-324.

K. Del Tredici, see L. Bormann – K. Del Tredici – A. Standhartinger (eds.), *Religious Propaganda and Missionary Competition in the New Testament: FS. D. Georgi* (1994).

G. de Martel (ed.), *Expositiones Pauli Epistolarum ad Rom., Gal. et Eph. e codice Avranches, Bibl. mun. 79* (1996), *ETL* 74 (1998) 458-459.

A. Denaux, see D. Donnelly – J. Famerée – A. Denaux (eds.), *The Holy Spirit, the Church, and Christian Unity* (2005).
A.-M. Denis, *Concordance latine des Pseudépigraphes* (1993), *ETL* 65 (1989) 124-130.
—, *Introduction à la littérature religieuse judéo-hellénistique* (2000), *ETL* 78 (2000) 189-191.
B.W.J. de Ruyter, see H.J. de Jonge – B.W.J. de Ruyter (eds.), *Totdat hij komt: Een discussie over de wederkomst van Jezus Christus* (1995).
P. Descourtieux, *Clément d'Alexandrie* (1999), *ETL* 78 (2002) 238-239.
D.A. deSilva, *Despising Shame: Honor Discourse and Community Maintenance in the Epistle to the Hebrews* (1996), *ETL* 73 (1997) 185-187.
—, *The Letter to the Galatians* (2018), *ETL* 98 (2022) 171-172.
N.P. DesRosiers – L.C. Vuong (eds.), *Religious Competition in the Greco-Roman World* (2016), *ETL* 94 (2018) 727.
N.P. DesRosiers, see S. Ashbrook Harvey – N.P. DesRosiers – S.L. Lander – J.Z. Pastis (eds.), *A Most Reliable Witness: Essays in Honor of R.S. Kraemer* (2015).
K. De Troyer, see J.Ma. Asgeirsson – K. De Troyer – M.W. Meyer (eds.), *From Quest to Q: FS J.M. Robinson* (2000).
K. De Troyer – B. Schmitz (eds.), *The Early Reception of the Book of Isaiah* (2019), *ETL* 96 (2020) 716-717.
K. de Valerio, *Altes Testament und Judentum im Frühwerk R. Bultmanns* (1994), *ETL* 72 (1996) 245-246.
J. De Vocht, *Father Delaere* (2005), *JEastCS* 57 (2005) 324-325.
A. de Vogüé, *De Saint Pachôme à Cassien* (1996), *ETL* 74 (1998) 205-206.
—, *Grégoire le Grand* (1998), *ETL* 75 (1999) 504-506.
S. de Vulpillières, *Nature et fonction des injonctions au silence dans l'évangile de Marc* (2010), *Rivista Biblica* 62 (2014) 128-131.
P.C. Dilley, see S.P. Brock (ed.), *The Martyrs of Mount Ber'ain* (introd. P.C. Dilley) (2014).
C. Dionne, *L'Evangile aux Juifs et aux païens: Le premier voyage missionnaire de Paul (Ac 13–14)* (2011), *ETL* 89 (2013) 473-474.
M. Döhler (ed.), *Acta Petri: Text, Übersetzung und Kommentar zu den Actus Vercellenses* (2017), *JEH* 70 (2019) 331-333.
I. Donégani, *À cause de la parole de Dieu* (1997), *ETL* 76 (2000) 499-501.
K.P. Donfried – P. Richardson (eds.), *Judaism and Christianity in First-Century Rome* (1998), *ETL* 76 (2000) 475-476.
G.J. Donker, *The Text of the Apostolos in Athanasius of Alexandria* (2011), *ETL* 89 (2013) 502-503.
D. Donnelly – J. Famerée – A. Denaux (eds.), *The Holy Spirit, the Church, and Christian Unity* (2005), *JEastCS* 57 (2005) 328-329.
S. Dowling Long, see F. Long – S. Dowling Long (eds.), *Reading the Sacred Scriptures: From Oral Tradition to Written Documents and Their Reception* (2018).
M. Dreyer – É. Mehl – M. Vollet (eds.), *La réception de Duns Scot. Die Rezeption des Duns Scotus. Scotism through the Centuries: Proceedings of "The Quadruple Congress" on John Duns Scotus, Part 4* (2013), *ETL* 89 (2013) 514-517.
H.R. Drobner, *Les Pères de l'Église* (1999), *ETL* 76 (2000) 504-505.

F. D'Sa (ed.), *Essays in Memory of G.R. Soares Prabhu* (1997), *ETL* 74 (1998) 205.
A. Dubreucq, *Jonas d'Orléans: Le métier de roi (De institutione regia)* (1995), *ETL* 74 (1998) 458.
K. Duchatelez, *Basilius de Grote* (1999), *ETL* 78 (2002) 290.
D.L. Dungan, *A History of the Synoptic Problem* (1999), *International Journal of the Classical Tradition* 8 (2001-2002) 471-475.
J.D.G. Dunn, *The Epistles to the Colossians and to Philemon* (1996), *ETL* 75 (1999) 215-217.
—, *The Theology of Paul the Apostle* (1998), *ETL* 75 (1999) 482-486.
—, *Neither Jew nor Greek: A Contested Identity* (2015), *ETL* 93 (2017) 730-732.
D.L. Eastman, *Paul the Martyr: The Cult of the Apostle in the Latin West* (2011), *ETL* 89 (2013) 474-475.
C.A. Eberhart (ed.), *Ritual and Metaphor: Sacrifice in the Bible* (2011), *ETL* 89 (2013) 427.
M. Ebner, *Inkarnation der Botschaft: Kultureller Horizont und theologischer Anspruch neutestamentlicher Texte* (2015), *ETL* 93 (2017) 538-539.
M. Ederer – B. Schmitz (eds.), *Exodus: Interpretation durch Rezeption* (2017), *ETL* 96 (2020) 708-709.
J. von Ehrenkrook, *Sculpting Idolatry in Flavian Rome* (2011), *ETL* 89 (2013) 453.
P. Elbert, see G. Haya-Prats, *Empowered Believers: The Holy Spirit in the Book of Acts* (ed. P. Elbert) (2011).
F. Enns – S. Holland – A.K. Riggs (eds.), *Seeking Cultures of Peace: A Peace Church Conversation* (2004), *JEastCS* 57 (2005) 329-330.
A. Ercolani – P. Xella (eds.), *Encyclopaedic Dictionary of Phoenician Culture.* Vol. 1. *Historical Characters* (2018), *ETL* 96 (2020) 720-721.
K. Erlemann – K.L. Noethlichs – K. Scherberich – J. Zangenberg (eds.), *Neues Testament und Antike Kultur*, 4 vols. (2004-2005), *RBL* 10 (2008) 29-36.
J.L. Espinel Marcos, *El pacifismo del Nuevo Testamento* (1992), *ETL* 69 (1993) 433-435.
T. Esposito, *Jesus' Meals with Pharisees and Their Liturgical Roots* (2015), *ETL* 93 (2017) 743-744.
R. Etaix, *Gregorius Magnus* (1999), *ETL* 78 (2002) 248-249.
C.A. Evans, see B. Chilton – C.A. Evans (eds.), *James the Just and Christian Origins* (1999).
— (ed.), *The World of Jesus and the Early Church* (2011), *ETL* 89 (2013) 496.
P. Evieux, *Isidore de Péluse* (1995), *ETL* 73 (1997) 466-468.
A. Faivre, *Chrétiens et églises: Des identités en construction* (2011), *ETL* 89 (2013) 496-498.
J. Famerée, see D. Donnelly – J. Famerée – A. Denaux (eds.), *The Holy Spirit, the Church, and Christian Unity* (2005).
W.R. Farmer, *The International Bible Commentary* (1998), *LS* 24 (1999) 373-377.
G.D. Fee, *Paul's Letter to the Philippians* (1995), *ETL* 74 (1998) 198-199.
J.L. Feiertag (ed.), *Questions d'un païen à un chrétien (Consultationes Zacchei christiani et Apollonii philosophi)*, 2 vols. (1994), *ETL* 72 (1999) 254-256.
S.M. Felch (ed.), *The Cambridge Companion to Literature and Religion* (2016), *ETL* 94 (2018) 735-736.
L.H. Feldman – J.R. Levison (eds.), *Josephus'* Contra Apionem: *Studies in Its Character and Context* (1996), *ETL* 73 (1997) 434-437.

S. Felici (ed.), *Esegesi e catechesi nei Padri (s. II-IV)* (1993), *ETL* 71 (1995) 239.
– (ed.), *Esegesi e catechesis nei Padri (s. IV-VII)* (1994), *ETL* 71 (1995) 469-470.
J.J. Fernández Sangrador, *Los orígenes de la comunidad cristiana de Alejandría* (1994), *ETL* 72 (1999) 252-253.
B. Fitzgerald, see S.P. Brock – B. Fitzgerald (eds.), *Two Early Lives of Severus, Patriarch of Antiochia* (2013).
J.T. Fitzgerald (ed.), *Greco-Roman Perspectives on Friendship* (1997), *ETL* 73 (1997) 438-439.
J.T. Fitzgerald – T.H. Olbricht – L.M. White (eds.), *Early Christianity and Classical Culture: Comparative Studies in Honor of A.J. Malherbe* (2003, paperback 2005), *RBL* (2006).
J.A. Fitzmyer, *The Biblical Commission* (1995), *ETL* 74 (1998) 203-204.
—, *The Semitic Background of the New Testament* (1997), *LS* 23 (1998) 78.
—, *To Advance the Gospel* (1998), *ETL* 75 (1999) 470-472.
—, *The Dead Sea Scrolls and Christian Origins* (2000), *ETL* 78 (2002) 191-192.
—, *The Letter to Philemon* (2000), *ETL* 78 (2002) 225-227.
J. Flannery, see A. O'Mahony – J. Flannery (eds.), *The Catholic Church in the Contemporary Middle East* (2010).
D. Flusser, see H. van de Sandt – D. Flusser, *The Didache* (2002).
C. Focant, *L'évangile selon Marc* (2004), *ETL* 84 (2008) 238-240.
—, *Marc, un évangile étonnant* (2006), *ETL* 84 (2008) 238-240.
—, *The Gospel according to Mark* (2012), *ETL* 89 (2013) 465-466.
—, *Les lettres aux Philippiens et à Philémon* (2015), *ETL* 93 (2017) 750-751.
J. Fontaine (ed.), *Ambroise de Milan: Hymnes* (1992), *ETL* 71 (1995) 239-243.
G. Fossati, *Aya Sofia Constantinople* (2003), *JEastCS* 57 (2005) 321-322.
P. Foster, *Colossians* (2016), *ETL* 94 (2018) 724-725.
A. Fotiou, see D. Frendo – A. Fotiou (eds.), *John Kaminiates, The Capture of Thessaloniki* (2017).
J.A. Francis, *Subversive Virtue: Asceticism and Authority in the Second-Century Pagan World* (1995), *ETL* 74 (1998) 445-446.
D.M. Frankfurter, *Elijah in Upper Egypt: The Apocalypse of Elijah and Early Egyptian Christianity* (1993), *LS* 19 (1994) 377-378.
H.J. Frede, *Kirchenschriftsteller* (1999), *ETL* 78 (2002) 237-238.
D. Frendo – A. Fotiou (eds.), *John Kaminiates, The Capture of Thessaloniki* (2017), *JEastCS* 70 (2018) 126-127.
F. Fritz, see A. Bihler – F. Fritz (eds.), *Heiligkeiten: Konstruktionen, Funktionen und Transfer von Heiligkeitskonzepten im europäischen Früh- und Hochmittelalter* (2019).
G. Gabra (ed.), *Coptic Civilization: Two Thousand Years of Christianity in Egypt* (2014), *JEastCS* 67 (2015) 395-396.
G.G. Gamba, *Petronio Arbitro e i cristiani* (1998), *ETL* 75 (1999) 500-502.
D. Gange – M. Ledger-Lomas (eds.), *Cities of God: The Bible and Archaeology in Nineteenth-Century Britain* (2013), *ETL* 92 (2016) 695-697.
U. Gantz, *Gregor von Nyssa* (1999), *ETL* 78 (2002) 246-247.
A. García-Moreno, *La neovulgata: Precedentes y actualidad* (^{2}2011), *ETL* 89 (2013) 427-428.
J.M. García Pérez, *Rastreando los orígenes: Lengua y exegesis en el Nuevo Testamento* (2011), *ETL* 89 (2013) 457.

S.R. Garrett, *The Temptations of Jesus in Mark's Gospel* (1998), *LS* 25 (2000) 380-381.
J.-M. Garrigues, *Deux martyrs de l'Église indivise: Saint Maxime le Confesseur et le pape saint Martin* (2011), *ETL* 89 (2013) 503-504.
—, *Le dessein divin* (2011), *ETL* 89 (2013) 504-505.
A. Garsky – C. Heil – Th. Hieke – J.E. Amon – S. Carruth, *The Database of the International Q Project: Q 12:49-59. Children against Parents – Judging the Time – Settling out of Court* (1997), *LS* 23 (1998) 286-287.
A. Garsky, see S. Carruth – A. Garsky – S.D. Anderson, *The Database of the International Q Project: Q 11:2b-4* (1996).
S. Gauntlett, see G. Betts – S. Gauntlett – T. Spilias (eds.), *Vitzentzos Kornaros, Erotokritos* (2017).
B.R. Gaventa, *Mary* (1999), *ETL* 76 (2000) 480-481.
A. Gerhards (ed.), *Die grössere Hoffnung der Christen: Eschatologische Vorstellungen im Wandel* (1990), *ETL* 70 (1994) 482.
M. Gerhards, *Protevangelium: Zur Frage der kanonischen Geltung des Alten Testaments und seiner christologischen Auslegung* (2017), *ETL* 96 (2020) 706-707.
G. Ghiberti – F. Mosetto, *L'interpretazione della Bibbia nella Chiesa* (1998), *ETL* 75 (1999) 444-445.
L. Gianantoni, *La paternità apostolica di Paolo* (1993), *ETL* 71 (1995) 233-234.
C. Gines Taylor, *Late Antique Images of the Virgin Annunciate Spinning: Allotting the Scarlet and the Purple* (2018), *JEastCS* 71 (2021) 129-130.
G. Ginneberghe, *Conseil international des associations de bibliothèques de théologie* (1996), *ETL* 74 (1998) 235.
L. Ginzberg, *Les légendes des Juifs* IV (2003), *JSJ* 36 (2005) 349-351.
M.C. Giorda, see M. Choat – M.C. Giorda (eds.), *Writing and Communication in Early Egyptian Monasticism* (2017).
G. Giurisato, *Struttura e teologia della Prima Lettera di Giovanni* (1998), *ETL* 78 (2002) 228-230.
B. Gleede, *Parabiblica Latina: Studien zu den griechisch-lateinischen Übersetzungen unter besonderer Berücksichtigung der apostolischen Väter* (2016), *Apocrypha* 30 (2019) 239-241.
G. Glonner, *Zur Bildersprache des Johannes von Patmos* (1999), *ETL* 78 (2002) 230-231.
M. Goodacre – N. Perrin (eds.), *Questioning Q: A Multidimensional Critique* (2004), *RBL* 8 (2006) 397-400.
M.J. Gorman, *Becoming the Gospel: Paul, Participation, and Mission* (2015), *ETL* 94 (2018) 337-338.
R. Gounelle, see G. Aragione – R. Gounelle (eds.), *"Soyez des changeurs avisés": Controverses exégétiques dans la littérature apocryphe chrétienne* (2013).
M. Gourgues, *Les deux Lettres à Timothée, La Lettre à Tite* (2009), *JTS* 64 (2013) 232-234. Doi:1093/jts/flt054.
S. Grebenstein, see S.H. Griffith – S. Grebenstein (eds.), *Christsein in der islamischen Welt: FS für M. Tamcke zum 60. Geburtstag* (2015).
J.B. Green, *The Gospel of Luke* (1998), *LS* 24 (1999) 264-266.
K. Greene-McCreight, see Ch. Seitz – K. Greene-McCreight (eds.), *Theological Exegesis: Essays in Honour of Brevard S. Childs* (1999).

B.H. Gregg, *The Historical Jesus and the Final Judgment Sayings in Q* (2006), *RBL* (2007).
P. Grelot, *Le mystère du Christ dans les Psaumes* (1998), *ETL* 76 (2000) 479-480.
S.H. Griffith – S. Grebenstein (eds.), *Christsein in der islamischen Welt: FS für M. Tamcke zum 60. Geburtstag* (2015), *JEastCS* 69 (2017) 385-386.
B. Groen, *De weg omhoog en de strijd om vrijheid: Nikos Kazantzakis, zijn Ascetica en de orthodoxe traditie* (2017), *JEastCS* 70 (2018) 323-324.
G. Gros, see J.M. Davis – F.R.P. Akehurst – G. Gros, *Our Lady's Lawsuits in L'Advocacie Nostre Dame and La Chapellerie Nostre Dame de Baiex* (2011).
S. Grosse, *Theologie des Kanons: Der christliche Kanon* (2011), *ETL* 89 (2013) 428-429.
M. Gruber, *Herrlichkeit in Schwachheit: 2 Kor. 2,14–6,13* (1998), *ETL* 76 (2000) 496-497.
A. Gruca-Macaulay, *Lydia as a Rhetorical Construct in Acts* (2016), *ETL* 94 (2018) 723-724.
M. Grudule, see C. Schiller – M. Grudule (eds.), *"Mach dich auf und werde licht": Zu Leben und Werk Ernst Glücks (1654-1705)* (2010).
E. Grünbeck, *Christologische Schriftargumentation und Bildersprache: Patristische Auslegung des 44. (45.) Psalms* (1994), *ETL* 72 (1996) 462-463.
R. Gryson, *Littérature arienne latine*. Vol. 1: *Débat de Maximinus avec Augustin: Scolies ariennes sur le concile d'Aquilée. Concordance et index* (1980), *ETL* 58 (1982) 172-173.
—, *Altlateinische Handschriften* (1999), *ETL* 78 (2002) 237-238.
— (ed.), *Tyconii Afri Expositio Apocalypseos* (2011), *ETL* 89 (2013) 507-508.
H. Guevara, *La resistencia judía contra Roma en la época de Jesús* (1981), *ETL* 59 (1983) 363-364.
C. Guignard, see E. Cattaneo, *Les misères dans l'Église ancienne: Textes patristiques du Ier au IIIe siècle* (trans. A. Bastit – C. Guignard) (2017).
S. Guijarro Oporto, *Fidelidades en conflict* (1998), *ETL* 76 (2000) 489-490.
C. Guillermain, see L. Barlet – C. Guillermain, *Le Beau Christ en Actes* (2011).
J.-N. Guinot, *L'exégèse de Théodoret de Cyr* (1995), *ETL* 73 (1997) 468-471.
R.H. Gundry, *Peter, False Disciple and Apostate according to Saint Matthew* (2015), *ETL* 93 (2017) 541-542.
C. Hall, *'Pancosmic' Church – Specific Românesc: Ecclesiological Themes in Nichifor Crainic's Writings 1922-1944* (2008), *JEastCS* 63 (2011) 380-382.
J.A. Harrill, *Slaves in the New Testament* (2005), *RBL* (2006).
D.J. Harrington, *Invitation to the Apocrypha* (1999), *LS* 26 (2001) 93.
J.R. Harrison – L.L. Welborn (eds.), *The First Urban Churches 1: Methodological Foundations* (2015), *ETL* 93 (2017) 737-738.
— (eds.), *The First Urban Churches 5: Colossae, Hierapolis, and Laodicea* (2019), *ETL* 98 (2022) 178-180.
J.D. Harvey, *Listening to the Text* (1998), *ETL* 78 (2002) 219-220.
M.C. Hauck, *Dynamis eis soterian: Eine Untersuchung zum semantischen Hintergrund eines neutestamentlichen Syntagmas* (2019), *BN* 185 (2020) 147-148.
D.M. Hay, see E.E. Johnson – D.M. Hay (eds.), *Pauline Theology*. Vol. 4: *Looking Back, Pressing On* (1997).
G. Haya-Prats, *Empowered Believers: The Holy Spirit in the Book of Acts* (ed. P. Elbert) (2011), *ETL* 89 (2013) 472.

M.A.G. Haykin, *The Spirit of God: The Exegesis of 1 and 2 Corinthians in the Fourth Century* (1994), *ETL* 72 (1996) 463-465.
N. Hecquet-Noti, *Avit de Vienne* (2011), *ETL* 89 (2013) 513-514.
C. Heil, see S. Carruth – J.M. Robinson – C. Heil, *The Database of the International Q Project: Q 4:1-13, 16. The Temptations of Jesus – Nazara* (1996).
—, see A. Garsky – C. Heil – Th. Hieke – J.E. Amon – S. Carruth, *The Database of the International Q Project: Q 12:49-59. Children against Parents – Judging the Time – Settling out of Court* (1997).
—, *The Database of the International Q Project: Q 12:8-12* (1998), *LS* 24 (1999) 80-83.
—, *Das Spruchevangelium Q und der historische Jesus* (2014), *ETL* 93 (2017) 539-540.
J.P. Heil, *The Letters of Paul as Rituals of Worship* (2012), *ETL* 89 (2013) 475-476.
M. Heimgartner, *Timotheus I., Ostsyrischer Patriarch* (2011), *JEastCS* 65 (2013) 279-280.
M. Heimola, *Christian Identity in the Gospel of Philip* (2011), *ETL* 89 (2013) 493-494.
M. Hengel, *Der unterschätzte Petrus: Zwei Studien* (2006), *JTS* 59 (2008) 295-297. http://doi.org/10.1093/jts/flm117.
M. Hengel – A.M. Schwemer, *Jesus and Judaism* (2019), *Reading Religion AAR* 2021 (online).
M. Henze, *Hazon Gabriel: New Readings of the Gabriel Revelation* (2011), *ETL* 89 (2013) 450-451.
K. Herbers – A. Nehring – K. Steiner (eds.), *Sakralität und Macht* (2019), *ETL* 98 (2022) 187-188.
R. Heyer (ed.), *Le voyage des paraboles* (2011), *ETL* 89 (2013) 464-465.
Th. Hieke, see A. Garsky – C. Heil – Th. Hieke – J.E. Amon – S. Carruth, *The Database of the International Q Project: Q 12:49-59. Children against Parents – Judging the Time – Settling out of Court* (1997).
A. Hilhorst, see T. Silverstein – A. Hilhorst, *Apocalypse of Paul: A New Critical Edition of Three Long Latin Versions* (1997).
S. Hillert, *Limited and Universal Salvation* (1999), *ETL* 78 (2002) 220-221.
F. Hindi, *L'identité des maronites et leur rôle dans l'établissement du Liban moderne selon Youakim Moubarak* (2016), *JEastCS* 70 (2018) 144.
R.F. Hock – J.B. Chance – J. Perkins (eds.), *Ancient Fiction and Early Christian Narrative* (1998), *ETL* 75 (1999) 498-500.
M. Hölscher, *Matthäus liest Q: Eine Studie am Beispiel von Mt. 11,2-19 und Q 7,18-35* (2017), *BN* 180 (2019) 136-138.
P. Hoffmann, *Jesus von Nazareth und die Kirche* (2009), *ETL* 89 (2013) 454.
S. Holland, see F. Enns – S. Holland – A.K. Riggs (eds.), *Seeking Cultures of Peace: A Peace Church Conversation* (2004).
T. Holmén – S. Porter (eds.), *Handbook for the Study of the Historical Jesus*, 4 vols. (2011), *ETL* 89 (2013) 461-463.
F.C. Holmgren, *The Old Testament and the Significance of Jesus* (1999), *ETL* 78 (2002) 192-193.
J. Holmstrand, *Markers and Meaning in Paul: 1 Thess., Phil. and Gal.* (1997), *ETL* 75 (1999) 217-220.
L. Honnefelder et al. (eds.), *Johannes Duns Scotus 1308-2008: Die philosophischen Perspektiven seines Werkes. Investigations into His Philosophy: Proceedings*

of *"The Quadruple Congress" on John Duns Scotus, Part 3* (2010), *ETL* 89 (2013) 514-517.
R. Hoppe, *Apostel – Gemeinde – Kirche* (2010), *ETL* 89 (2013) 454-456.
—, *Der erste Thessalonikerbrief: Kommentar* (2016), *ETL* 94 (2018) 725-726.
—, *Der zweite Thessalonikerbrief: Kommentar* (2019), *ETL* 98 (2022) 175-176.
R. Hoppe – U. Busse (eds.), *Von Jesus zum Christus: FS P. Hoffmann* (1998), *ETL* 75 (1999) 464-468.
D.G. Horrell, *Social Scientific Approaches to New Testament Interpretation* (1999), *ETL* 78 (2002) 196-197.
R.A. Horsley (ed.), *Oral Performance, Popular Tradition, and Hidden Transcript in Q* (2006), *RBL* 9 (2007).
V.S. Hovhannesian, *The Canon of the Bible and the Apocrypha in the Churches of the East* (2011), *JEH* 65 (2014) 872.
A. Hultgård, see G. Widengren – A. Hultgård – M. Philonenko, *Apocalyptique iranienne et dualisme qoumrânien* (1995).
A.J. Hultgren, *Paul's Letter to the Romans: A Commentary* (2011), *ETL* 89 (2013) 481-482.
D.G. Hunter, see T.S. de Bruyn – S.A. Cooper – D.G. Hunter (eds.), *Ambrosiaster's Commentary on the Pauline Epistles: Romans* (2017).
L.W. Hurtado, *The Earliest Christian Artifacts: Manuscripts and Christian Origins* (2006), *RBL* (2007).
J.M. Hutton, see M. Leuchter – J.M. Hutton (eds.), *Levites and Priests in History and Tradition* (2011).
M.B. Ingham – O. Bychkov (eds.), *John Duns Scotus, Philosopher: Proceedings of "The Quadruple Congress" on John Duns Scotus, Part 1* (2010), *ETL* 89 (2013) 514-517.
J.C. Iwe, *Jesus in the Synagogue of Capernaum* (1999), *ETL* 78 (2002) 207-208.
C. Jacob, *"Arkandisziplin", Allegorese, Mystagogie – Ambrosius von Mailand* (1990), *ETL* 68 (1992) 454-456.
P.-A. Jacob (ed.), *Honorat de Marseille: La vie d'Hilaire d'Arles* (1995), *ETL* 72 (1999) 256-257.
A.S. Jacobs, *Epiphanius of Cyprus: A Cultural Biography of Late Antiquity* (2016), *Augustiniana* 68 (2018) 321-324.
A.-C. Jacobsen (ed.), *Religion and Normativity: The Discursive Fight over Religious Texts in Antiquity* (2009), *JEH* 62 (2011) 778-779.
C. Jäggi, see D. Mondini – C. Jäggi – P.C. Claussen (eds.), *Die Kirchen der Stadt Rom im Mittelalter 1050-1300.* Band 4: *M–O: SS. Marcellino e Pietro bis S. Omobono* (2020).
D. Jaillard – C. Nihan (eds.), *Writing Laws in Antiquity / L'Écriture du droit dans l'Antiquité* (2017), *ETL* 96 (2020) 719-720.
C.N. Jefford (ed.), The *Didache* in *Context: Essays on Its Text, History and Transmission* (1997), *LS* 22 (1997) 93-95.
—, *The Apostolic Fathers and the New Testament* (2006), *ExpTim* 119 (2008) 175. https://doi.org/10.1177/00145246081190040302.
S. Jöris, *The Use and Function of* genea *in the Gospel of Mark: New Light on Mk 13;30* (2015), *ETL* 93 (2017) 542-543.
H. Johannessen, *The Demonic in the Political Thought of Eusebius of Caesarea* (2016), *ETL* 94 (2018) 351-352.
E.E. Johnson – D.M. Hay (eds.), *Pauline Theology.* Vol. 4: *Looking Back, Pressing On* (1997), *ETL* 75 (1999) 205-207.

F.S. Jones, *An Ancient Jewish Christian Source on the History of Christianity: Pseudo-Clementine Recognitions 1,27-71* (1995), ETL 73 (1997) 188-191.
G. Jossa, *Giudei o cristiani? I seguaci di Gesù in cerca di una propria identità* (2004), RBL 2007.
D. Judant, *Du christianisme au judaïsme: Les conversions au cours de l'histoire* (1981), ETL 58 (1982) 158-159.
L. Junker, *Das Scheidungslogion Q 16,18 und frühjüdische Reinheitsvorstellungen* (2019), ETL 98 (2022) 166-168.
E. Junod, see G. Aragione – E. Junod – E. Norelli (eds.), *Le canon du Nouveau Testament: Regards nouveaux sur l'histoire de sa formation* (2005).
A. Kaldellis, *Genesios on the Reigns of the Emperors* (2017), JEastCS 70 (2018) 126-127.
N. Kavvadas, *Jerusalem zwischen Aachen und Bagdad: Zur Existenzkrise des byzantinischen Christentums im Abbasidenreich* (2017), JEastCS 70 (2018) 308-309.
C.S. Keener, *A Commentary on the Gospel of Matthew* (1999), ETL 77 (2001) 219-220.
J.F. Kelly, *The World of the Early Christians* (1997), ETL 75 (1999) 221.
G.A. Kennedy (trans.), *Invention and Method: Two Rhetorical Treatises from the Hermogenic Corpus* (2005), RBL (2006).
S.M. Kenworthy, *The Heart of Russia: Trinity-Sergius, Monasticism, and Society after 1825* (2010), JEastCS 65 (2013) 285-286.
J. Kerner, *Die Ethik der Johannes-Apokalypse im Vergleich mit der des 4. Esra* (1998), ETL 76 (2000) 501-502.
M. Kertsch, *Exempla Chrysostomica: Zu Exegese, Stil und Bildersprache bei Joh. Chrysostomos* (1995), ETL 74 (1998) 456.
Y.R. Kim, *Epiphanius of Cyprus: Imagining an Orthodox World* (2015), ZAC 21 (2017) 591-593.
J.D. Kingsbury, *Matteo* (1998), ETL 75 (1999) 475.
W. Kirchschläger, *Die Anfänge der Kirche* (1990), ETL 70 (1994) 481.
H.-J. Klauck, *Die religiöse Umwelt des Urchristentums*, 2 vols. (1993-1995), ETL 73 (1997) 192-194.
—, *The Religious Context of Early Christianity* (2000), ETL 78 (2002) 205-206.
J. Kloppenborg, *Synoptic Problems: Collected Essays* (2014), ETL 92 (2016) 723-724.
D.-A. Koch, *Bilder aus der Welt des Urchristentums* (2009), ETL 88 (2012) 510-512.
—, *Geschichte des Urchristentums: Ein Lehrbuch* (2013), ETL 92 (2016) 715-716.
E. Koçlamazašvili, see S. Sardjveladze – T. Mgaloblisvili – E. Koçlamazašvili – S. Verhelst (eds.), *Jean de Bolnisi: Homélies des dimanches de carême* (2015).
K. Koenen – R. Kühschelm, *Zeitenwende: Perspektiven des Alten und Neuen Testaments* (1999), ETL 78 (2002) 181-182.
U. Köpf – D.R. Bauer (eds.), *Kulturkontakte und Rezeptionsvorgänge in der Theologie des 12. und 13. Jahrhunderts* (2011), ETL 89 (2013) 514-517.
S.J. Koovayil, *The Pneumatology of Jean Corbon's Theology of the Eucharist and Divinization* (2016), JEastCS 70 (2018) 143-144.
V. Koperski, *The Knowledge of Christ Jesus* (1996), ETL 74 (1998) 199-200.

G.A.A. Kortekaas, see W.J. Aerts – G.A.A. Kortekaas, *Die Apokalypse des Pseudo-Methodius* (1998).
J. Krasovec, *The Interpretation of the Bible* (1998), ETL 76 (2000) 466-467.
M. Krausgruber, *Die Regel des Eugippius* (1996), ETL 75 (1999) 230-231.
Ph.D.W. Kray, see I.C. Levy – Ph.D.W. Kray – Th. Ryan (eds.), *The Bible in Medieval Tradition: The Letter to the Romans* (2013).
M.J. Kruger, *The Gospel of the Savior: An Analysis of P. Oxy. 840* (2005), RBL (2006).
C.G. Kruse, *Paul, the Law, and Justification* (1997), ETL 75 (1999) 207-208.
J. Kügler, *Exegese zwischen Religionsgeschichte und Pastoral* (2017), ETL 96 (2020) 743.
U. Kühneweg, see W.A. Bienert – U. Kühneweg (eds.), *Origeniana septima* (1999).
R. Kühschelm, see K. Koenen – R. Kühschelm, *Zeitenwende: Perspektiven des Alten und Neuen Testaments* (1999).
K. Kuula, *The Law, the Covenant and God's Plan* (1999), ETL 78 (2002) 223-224.
M. Labahn – O. Lehtipuu (eds.), *People under Power: Early Jewish and Christian Responses to the Roman Empire* (2015), ETL 93 (2017) 733-734.
M. Labahn, see D.T. Roth – R. Zimmermann – M. Labahn (eds.), *Metaphor, Narrative, and Parables in Q* (2014).
S. Labarre, *Paulin de Périgueux: Vie de saint Martin. Prologue. Livres I-III* (2016), ETL 94 (2018) 732-733.
A. Łajtar – J. van der Vliet, *Empowering the Dead in Christian Nubia: The Texts from a Medieval Funerary Complex in Dongola* (2017), JEastCS 71 (2021) 132-133.
P.J. Lalleman, *The Acts of John* (1998), ETL 75 (1999) 494-495.
J. Lambrecht, *Second Corinthians* (1999), ETL 76 (2000) 179-182.
B. Landau, see T. Burke – B. Landau (eds.), *New Testament Apocrypha: More Noncanonical Scriptures*, vol. 1 (2016).
S.L. Lander, see S. Ashbrook Harvey – N.P. DesRosiers – S.L. Lander – J.Z. Pastis (eds.), *A Most Reliable Witness: Essays in Honor of R.S. Kraemer* (2015).
C. Landmesser, see M. Bauspiess – C. Landmesser – F. Portenhauser (eds.), *Theologie und Wirklichkeit: Diskussionen der Bultmann-Schule* (2011).
C. Landon, *A Text-Critical Study of the Epistle of James* (1996), ETL 74 (1998) 200-203.
A. Lannoy – C. Bonnet – D. Praet (eds.), *"Mon cher Mithra …": La correspondance entre Franz Cumont et Alfred Loisy*. Vol. 1: *Introduction et Dossier épistolaire*; Vol. 2: *Commentaires et Annexes* (2019), ETL 97 (2021) 535-537.
J.-C. Larchet, *La divinisation de l'homme selon St Maxime le Confesseur* (1996), ETL 75 (1999) 233-235.
V. Larin, *The Byzantine Hierarchical Divine Liturgy in Arsenij Suxanov's Proskinitarij* (2010), JEastCS 65 (2013) 282-284.
A. Le Boulluec, see E. Patlagean – A. Le Boulluec (eds.), *Les retours aux Écritures: Fondamentalismes présents et passés* (1993).
M. Ledger-Lomas, see D. Gange – M. Ledger-Lomas (eds.), *Cities of God: The Bible and Archaeology in Nineteenth-Century Britain* (2013).
Th. Legrand, see E. Bons – Th. Legrand (eds.), *Le monothéisme biblique* (2011).
O. Lehtipuu, see M. Labahn – O. Lehtipuu (eds.), *People under Power: Early Jewish and Christian Responses to the Roman Empire* (2015).

A. Leinhäupl-Wilke – S. Lücking (eds.), *Fremde Zeichen: Neutestamentliche Texte in der Konfrontation der Kulturen* (1998), *ETL* 76 (2000) 477-478.

T.M. Lemos, see J.J. Collins – T.M. Lemos – S.M. Olyan (eds.), *Worship, Women, and War: Essays in Honor of S. Niditch* (2015).

G. Leonardi, see G. Cremascoli – G. Leonardi (eds.), *La Bibbia nel medio evo* (1996).

—, *Vangelo secondo Marco* (1999), *ETL* 77 (2001) 208-209.

M. Leuchter – J.M. Hutton (eds.), *Levites and Priests in History and Tradition* (2011), *ETL* 89 (2013) 433-434.

J.R. Levison, see L.H. Feldman – J.R. Levison (eds.), *Josephus'* Contra Apionem: *Studies in Its Character and Context* (1996).

C. Lévy (ed.), *Philon d'Alexandrie et le language de la philosophie* (1998), *ETL* 76 (2000) 473-475.

I.C. Levy (ed.), *The Bible in Medieval Tradition: The Letter to the Galatians* (2011), *LS* 37 (2013) 80-81.

I.C. Levy – Ph.D.W. Kray – Th. Ryan (eds.), *The Bible in Medieval Tradition: The Letter to the Romans* (2013), *LS* 38 (2014) 382-383.

V. Liberti (ed.), *I laici nel Popolo di Dio: Esegesi biblica* (1990), *ETL* 70 (1994) 480-481.

L.I. Lied – H. Lundhaug (eds.), *Snapshots of Evolving Traditions: Jewish and Christian Manuscript Culture, Textual Fluidity, and New Philology* (2017), *Apocrypha* 30 (2019) 211-212.

J.M. Lieu, *Marcion and the Making of a Heretic: God and Scripture in the Second Century* (2015), *ETL* 93 (2017) 549-551.

K. Liljeström, *The Early Reception of Paul* (2011), *ETL* 89 (2013) 479-480.

T.H. Lim – K. Akiyama (eds.), *When Texts Are Canonized* (2017), *ETL* 96 (2020) 705-706.

A. Linage Conde *et al.*, *El santuario y el camarín de la Virgen de la Peña de Sepúlveda* (1996), *ETL* 75 (1999) 250.

A. Lindemann, *Glauben – Handeln – Verstehen*, Band 2 (2011), *ETL* 89 (2013) 456-457.

M.D. Litwa, *Iesus Deus: The Early Christian Depiction of Jesus as a Mediterranean God* (2014), *RBL* 2015.

S.R. Llewelyn, *New Documents Illustrating the New Testament* (1998), *ETL* 74 (1998) 441-442.

B. Llewelyn Ihssen, *John Moschos' Spiritual Meadow* (2014), *JEastCS* 70 (2018) 123-124.

W. Loader, *The Pseudepigrapha on Sexuality* (2011), *ETL* 89 (2013) 446-448.

—, *The New Testament on Sexuality* (2012), *ExpTim* 125 (2014) 491-492.

F. Long – S. Dowling Long (eds.), *Reading the Sacred Scriptures: From Oral Tradition to Written Documents and Their Reception* (2018), *ETL* 94 (2018) 719-720.

R.N. Longenecker, *Biblical Exegesis in the Apostolic Period* (1999), *ETL* 76 (2000) 476.

—, *The Challenge of Jesus' Parables* (2000), *ETL* 77 (2001) 217-218.

—, *Introducing Romans* (2011), *ETL* 89 (2013) 482-484.

E. Loosley Leeming, *Architecture and Asceticism: Cultural Interaction between Syria and Georgia in Late Antiquity* (2018), *JEastCS* 72 (2020) 325-326.

D. Luciani, see J.-M. Auwers – R. Burnet – D. Luciani (eds.), *L'antijudaïsme des Pères: Mythe et/ou réalité?* (2017).

S. Lücking, see A. Leinhäupl-Wilke – S. Lücking (eds.), *Fremde Zeichen: Neutestamentliche Texte in der Konfrontation der Kulturen* (1998).
D. Lührmann, *Fragmente apokryph gewordener Evangelien* (2000), ETL 78 (2002) 231-235.
H. Lundhaug, see L.I. Lied – H. Lundhaug (eds.), *Snapshots of Evolving Traditions: Jewish and Christian Manuscript Culture, Textual Fluidity, and New Philology* (2017).
H.O. Luthe, see P. Bruns – H.O. Luthe (eds.), *Orientalia Christiana: Festschrift für Hubert Kaufhold zum 70. Geburtstag* (2013).
L.S.B. MacCoull, *Documentary Christianity in Egypt: Sixth to Fourteenth Centuries* (2011), JEastCS 65 (2013) 278-279.
D.R. MacDonald, see H.W. Attridge – D.R. MacDonald – C.K. Rothschild, *Delightful Acts: New Essays on Canonical and Non-canonical Acts* (2017).
A.-M. Malingrey, *La littérature grecque chrétienne* (1996), ETL 72 (1996) 465-466.
E. Manicardi, *Teologia ed evangelizzazione: Saggi in onore di Mons. S. Zardoni* (1993), ETL 71 (1995) 231-232.
A. Manukyan, see M. Tamcke – A. Manukyan (eds.), *Herrnhüter in Kairo: Die Tagebücher 1769-1783* (2012); iid. – C. Mauder (eds.), *Die arabischen Briefe aus der Zeit der Herrnhüter Präsenz in Ägypten 1770-1783* (2012); iid. – K. Weiland (eds.), *Die Tagebücher J.H. Danckes aus Behnesse 1770-1772* (2013).
P. Maraval (ed.), *Grégoire de Nysse: Lettre canonique, Lettre sur la Pythonisse et six homélies pastorales* (2017), ETL 96 (2020) 748-749.
J.A. Marchal (ed.), *The People beside Paul: The Philippian Assembly and History from Below* (2015), ETL 94 (2018) 342-343.
D. Marguerat, *La première histoire du christianisme* (1999), ETL 78 (2002) 217-218.
—, *Les Actes des Apôtres 13–28* (2015), ETL 93 (2017) 745-747.
D. Marguerat – E. Norelli – J.-M. Poffet (eds.), *Jésus de Nazareth: Nouvelles approches d'une énigme* (1998), ETL 78 (2002) 203-205.
A.K. Marschak, *The Many Faces of Herod the Great* (2015), ETL 93 (2017) 537-538.
J.L. Martyn, *Theological Issues in the Letters of Paul* (1997), ETL 75 (1999) 486-487.
E.F. Mason – K.B. McCruden (eds.), *Reading the Epistle to the Hebrews: A Resource for Students* (2011), ETL 89 (2013) 487.
A. Mastrocinque, *From Jewish Magic to Gnosticism* (2005), TvT 46 (2006) 407.
F.J. Matera, *New Testament Ethics* (1997), LS 23 (1998) 79-80.
—, *New Testament Christology* (1999), ETL 77 (2001) 209-211.
M. Matheus (ed.), *Reformation in der Region: Personen und Erinnerungsorte* (2018), ETL 97 (2021) 534-535.
E.G. Matthews Jr., *On This Day: The Armenian Church Synaxarion: January, February, March; Armenian-English* (2014-2016), JEastCS 70 (2018) 135-137.
A. Mattioli, (FS for), *In spiritu et veritate* (1995), ETL 74 (1998) 444-445.
—, *Quel no del Giudaismo a Gesù: I motivi e le cause di un grande fatto storico* (1996), ETL 73 (1997) 191-192.
C. Mauder, see M. Tamcke – A. Manukyan – C. Mauder (eds.), *Die arabischen Briefe aus der Zeit der Herrnhüter Präsenz in Ägypten 1770-1783* (2012).

W. Mayer – S. Trzcionka (eds.), *Feast, Fast or Famine: Food and Drink in Byzantium* (2017), *JEastCS* 70 (2018) 126-127.

K.B. McCruden, see E.F. Mason – K.B. McCruden (eds.), *Reading the Epistle to the Hebrews: A Resource for Students* (2011).

L.M. McDonald, *The Formation of the Christian Biblical Canon* (1995), *ETL* 73 (1997) 187-188.

J.A. McGuckin (ed.), *The Encyclopedia of Eastern Orthodox Christianity* (2011), *JEastCS* 65 (2013) 287-288.

R.K. McIver, *Memory, Jesus, and the Synoptic Gospels* (2011), *ETL* 89 (2013) 460-461.

S. McKnight, *The Letter of James* (NICNT) (2011), *ETL* 89 (2013) 488-489.

—, *The Letter to Philemon* (ICC) (2017), *ETL* 96 (2020) 737-739.

—, *The Letter to the Colossians* (ICC) (2018), *ETL* 98 (2022) 172-174.

M. McNamara, *The Bible and the Apocrypha in the Early Irish Church (AD 600–1200)*, *ETL* 93 (2017) 756-757.

É. Mehl, see M. Dreyer – É. Mehl – M. Vollet (eds.), *La réception de Duns Scot. Die Rezeption des Duns Scotus. Scotism through the Centuries: Proceedings of "The Quadruple Congress" on John Duns Scotus, Part 4* (2013).

K. Meiling, *Julianus de Afvallige: Keuze uit zijn geschriften* (2016), *JEastCS* 70 (2018) 123.

J.-N. Mellon Saint-Laurent – K. Smith (eds.), *The History of Mar Behnam and Sarah: Martyrdom and Monasticism in Medieval Iraq* (2018), *JEastCS* 72 (2020) 330-331.

A. Melloni, see G. Alberigo – A. Melloni (eds.), *Conciliorum oecumenicorum generaliumque decreta: Editio critica* (2006-2013).

D. Mendels, *Identity, Religion and Historiography* (1998), *ETL* 74 (1998) 440.

M. Merino, see D. Ramos-Lissón – M. Merino – A. Viciano (eds.), *El diálogo fe – cultura en la antigüedad cristiana* (1996).

A. Merkt (ed.), *Metamorphosen des Todes: Bestattungskulturen und Jenseitsvorstellungen im Wandel – Vom alten Ägypten bis zum Friedwald der Gegenwart* (2016), *ETL* 94 (2018) 356-357.

A. Merz, see G. Theissen – A. Merz, *The Historical Jesus* (1998).

M.W. Meyer, see J.Ma. Asgeirsson – K. De Troyer – M.W. Meyer (eds.), *From Quest to Q: FS J.M. Robinson* (2000).

R. Meyer, see T.M. van Lint – R. Meyer (eds.), *Armenia: Masterpieces from an Enduring Culture* (2015).

T. Mgaloblisvili, see S. Sardjveladze – T. Mgaloblisvili – E. Koçlamazašvili – S. Verhelst (eds.), *Jean de Bolnisi: Homélies des dimanches de carême* (2015).

N. Miladinova, *The Panoplia Dogmatike by Euthymios Zyadenos: The First Edition Published in Greek in 1710* (2014), *JEastCS* 70 (2018) 125.

A. Milano, *Persona in teologia* (1996), *ETL* 74 (1998) 451.

J. Miler, *Les citations d'accomplissement dans l'évangile de Matthieu* (1999), *ETL* 78 (2002) 206-207.

M.P. Miller, see B.S. Crawford – M.P. Miller (eds.), *Redescribing the Gospel of Mark* (2017).

S.C. Mimouni, *Dormition et assomption de Marie: Histoire des traditions anciennes* (1995), *ETL* 73 (1997) 463-466.

D.P. Moessner, *Luke the Historian of Israel's Legacy, Theologian of Israel's 'Christ'* (2016), *ETL* 94 (2018) 722-723.

D. Mondini – C. Jäggi – P.C. Claussen (eds.), *Die Kirchen der Stadt Rom im Mittelalter 1050-1300*. Band 4: *M–O: SS. Marcellino e Pietro bis S. Omobono* (2020), *ETL* 98 (2022) 188-190.

J.P. Monferrer-Sala, *Scripta theologica arabica christiana: Andalusi Christian Arabic Fragments Preserved in Ms 83 (al-Maktabah al-Malikiyyah, Rabat)* (2016), *JEastCS* 70 (2018) 132-133.

M. Mor, see J. Pastor – P. Stern – M. Mor (eds.), *Flavius Josephus: Interpretation and History* (2011).

L. Moraldi, *Antichità Giudaiche di Guiseppe Flavio* (1998), *ETL* 75 (1999) 456-457.

F. Mosetto, see G. Ghiberti – F. Mosetto, *L'interpretazione della Bibbia nella Chiesa* (1998).

G. Most, see S. Timpanaro, *The Genesis of Lachmann's Method* (trans. G. Most) (2005).

D. Motiuk, *Eastern Christians in the New World* (2005), *JEastCS* 57 (2005) 323-324.

A. Mugridge, *Copying Early Christian Texts: A Study of Scribal Practice* (2016), *Apocrypha* 30 (2019) 209-211.

M. Myllykoski, *Die letzten Tage Jesu: Markus, Johannes, ihre Tradition und die historische Frage*, Band 2 (1994), *ETL* 70 (1994) 467-471.

M. Navarro Puerto – M. Perroni (eds.), *Gospels: Narrative and History* (2015), *ETL* 93 (2017) 738-739.

A. Nehring, see K. Herbers – A. Nehring – K. Steiner (eds.), *Sakralität und Macht* (2019).

B. Neil – E. Anagnostou-Maoutides (eds.), *Dreams, Memory and Imagination in Byzantium* (2018), *JEastCS* 72 (2020) 326-327.

F. Neirynck, *Evangelica III* (2001), *ETL* 77 (2001) 473-475.

H.P. Neuheuser (ed.), *Bischofsbild und Bischofssitz: Geistige und geistliche Impulse aus regionalen Zentren des Hochmittelalters* (2013), *ETL* 89 (2013) 514-517.

C. Nihan, see D. Jaillard – C. Nihan (eds.), *Writing Laws in Antiquity / L'Écriture du droit dans l'Antiquité* (2017).

F. Noël, *De compositie van het Lucasevangelie in zijn relatie tot Marcus* (1994), *ETL* 72 (1996) 240-241.

K.L. Noethlichs, see K. Erlemann – K.L. Noethlichs – K. Scherberich – J. Zangenberg (eds.), *Neues Testament und Antike Kultur*, 4 vols. (2004-2005).

J. Nolland, *The Gospel of Matthew* (2005), *JTS* 58 (2007) 629-632. https://doi.org/10.1093/jts/flm017.

E. Norelli, *L'Ascensione di Isaia* (1994), *ETL* 71 (1995) 230-231.

— et al. (eds.), *Ascensio Isaiae*. Vol. 1: *Textus*. Vol. 2: *Commentarius* (1995), *ETL* 73 (1997) 459-463.

E. Norelli, see D. Marguerat – E. Norelli – J.-M. Poffet (eds.), *Jésus de Nazareth: Nouvelles approches d'une énigme* (1998).

—, see G. Aragione – E. Junod – E. Norelli (eds.), *Le canon du Nouveau Testament: Regards nouveaux sur l'histoire de sa formation* (2005).

J.A. North – S.R.F. Price (eds.), *Religious History of the Roman Empire* (2011), *ETL* 89 (2013) 494-495.

L. Oberlinner – F.R. Prostmeier (eds.), *Jesus im Glaubenszeugnis des Neuen Testaments: Exegetische Reflexionen zum 100. Geburtstag von Anton Vögtle* (2015), *ETL* 93 (2017) 540-541.

G. O'Collins, *Cristologia* (1997), *ETL* 75 (1999) 474-475.
J. Odor, see T. Thatcher – J. Odor et al. (eds.), *The Dictionary of the Bible and Ancient Media* (2017).
N.F.H. O'Hear, *Contrasting Images of the Book of Revelation in Medieval and Early Modern Art* (2011), *ETL* 89 (2013) 492-493.
T.H. Olbricht, see J.T. Fitzgerald – T.H. Olbricht – L.M. White (eds.), *Early Christianity and Classical Culture: Comparative Studies in Honor of A.J. Malherbe* (2003, paperback 2005).
J.S. O'Leary, *Christianisme et philosophie chez Origène* (2011), *ETL* 89 (2013) 500-501.
M. Olszewski (ed.), *What Is "Theology" in the Middle Ages? Religious Cultures of Europe (11th-15th Centuries) as Reflected in Their Self-Understanding* (2007), *ETL* 89 (2013) 514-517.
—, *Dominican Theology at the Crossroads: A Critical Edition and Study of the Prologues to the Commentaries on Peter Lombard's Sentences by James of Metz and Hervaeus Natalis* (2010), *ETL* 89 (2013) 514-517.
S.M. Olyan, see J.J. Collins – T.M. Lemos – S.M. Olyan (eds.), *Worship, Women, and War: Essays in Honor of S. Niditch* (2015).
A. O'Mahony – J. Flannery (eds.), *The Catholic Church in the Contemporary Middle East* (2010), *JEastCS* 65 (2013) 286-287.
C. Padilla, *Los Milagros de la "Vida de Apolonio di Tiana": Morfología del realto de milagro y géneros afines* (1992), *LS* 21 (1996) 90-92.
J. Painter, *Just James: The Brother of Jesus in History and Tradition* (1997), *LS* 24 (1999) 266-269.
A. Panayotov, see R. Bauckham – J.R. Davila – A. Panayotov (eds.), *Old Testament Pseudepigrapha: More Noncanonical Scriptures*, vol. 1 (2013).
M. Pascuzzi, *Ethics, Ecclesiology and Church Discipline* (1997), *ETL* 75 (1999) 211-213.
J.Z. Pastis, see S. Ashbrook Harvey – N.P. DesRosiers – S.L. Lander – J.Z. Pastis (eds.), *A Most Reliable Witness: Essays in Honor of R.S. Kraemer* (2015).
J. Pastor – P. Stern – M. Mor (eds.), *Flavius Josephus: Interpretation and History* (2011), *ETL* 89 (2013) 451-452.
E. Patlagean – A. Le Boulluec (eds.), *Les retours aux Écritures: Fondamentalismes présents et passés* (1993), *ETL* 72 (1996) 248-249.
A. Paul, *Le monde des Juifs à l'heure de Jésus: Histoire politique* (1981), *ETL* 58 (1982) 159.
M. Peppard, *The Son of God in the Roman World* (2011), *TvT* 52 (2012) 280.
J. Perkins, see R.F. Hock – J.B. Chance – J. Perkins (eds.), *Ancient Fiction and Early Christian Narrative* (1998).
N. Perrin, see M. Goodacre – N. Perrin (eds.), *Questioning Q: A Multidimensional Critique* (2004).
M. Perroni, see M. Navarro Puerto – M. Perroni (eds.), *Gospels: Narrative and History* (2015).
M. Pesce (ed.), *Isaia, il Diletto e la Chiesa: Visione ed esegesi profetica Cristiano-primitiva nell'Ascensione di Isaia* (1983), *ETL* 60 (1984) 157-160.
K. Peter, *Apokalyptische Schrifttexte* (2011), *ETL* 89 (2013) 491-492.
J. Peterson, see J.C. Poirier – J. Peterson (eds.), *Marcan Priority without Q: Explorations in the Farrer Hypothesis* (2015).
F. Petit – L. Van Rompay – J.J.S. Weitenberg (eds.), *Eusèbe d'Emèse: Commentaire de la Genèse* (2011), *ETL* 89 (2013) 501-502.

M. Philonenko, see G. Widengren – A. Hultgård – M. Philonenko, *Apocalyptique iranienne et dualisme qoumrânien* (1995).
P. Pilhofer, *Philippi*. Band 1: *Die erste christliche Gemeinde Europas* (1995), *ETL* 72 (1996) 241-245.
B. Pitre, *Jesus and the Last Supper* (2015), *ETL* 94 (2018) 334.
A.W. Pitts, see S.E. Porter – A.W. Pitts, *Fundamentals of New Testament Textual Criticism* (2015).
L.F. Pizzolato, *Morir giovani: Il pensiero antico di fronte alla scandale della morte prematura* (1996), *ETL* 74 (1998) 452.
J.-M. Poffet, see D. Marguerat – E. Norelli – J.-M. Poffet (eds.), *Jésus de Nazareth: Nouvelles approches d'une énigme* (1998).
J.C. Poirier – J. Peterson (eds.), *Marcan Priority without Q: Explorations in the Farrer Hypothesis* (2015), *ETL* 93 (2017) 739-741.
F. Portenhauser, see M. Bauspiess – C. Landmesser – F. Portenhauser (eds.), *Theologie und Wirklichkeit*: *Diskussionen der Bultmann-Schule* (2011).
S.E. Porter – A.W. Pitts, *Fundamentals of New Testament Textual Criticism* (2015), *ETL* 93 (2017) 728-729.
J.M. Potter, see V.K. Robbins – J.M. Potter (eds.), *Jesus and Mary Reimagined in Early Christian Literature* (2015).
P. Pouchelle, see E. Bons – P. Pouchelle (eds.), *The Psalms of Solomon: Language, History, Theology* (2015).
B. Pouderon (ed.), see P.F. Beatrice – B. Pouderon, *Pascha nostrum Christus: Essays in Honour of R. Cantalamessa* (2016).
—, *Figures du premier Christianisme: Jésus appelé Christ, Jacques "frère du Seigneur", Marie dite Madeleine* (2018-2019), *JEastCS* 72 (2020) 319.
D. Praet, see A. Lannoy – C. Bonnet – D. Praet (eds.), *"Mon cher Mithra …": La correspondance entre Franz Cumont et Alfred Loisy*. Vol. 1: *Introduction et Dossier épistolaire*. Vol. 2: *Commentaires et Annexes* (2019).
S.R.F. Price, see J.A. North – S.R.F. Price (eds.), *Religious History of the Roman Empire* (2011).
C. Prieto, *Jésus thérapeute: Quels rapports entre ses miracles et la médecine antique?* (2015), *ETL* 93 (2017) 742-743.
F.R. Prostmeier, see L. Oberliner – F.R. Prostmeier (eds.), *Jesus im Glaubenszeugnis des Neuen Testaments: Exegetische Reflexionen zum 100. Geburtstag von Anton Vögtle* (2015).
A. Puig i Tàrrech, see A. Borrell Viader – A. de la Fuente – A. Puig i Tàrrech (eds.), *La Bíblia i el Mediterrani* (1997).
—, *Jesus, an Uncommon Journey* (2010), *Theologische Revue* 108 (2012) 297-299.
A. Quacquarelli (ed.), *Complementi interdisciplinari di patrologia* (1989), *ETL* 70 (1994) 482-483.
M. Quesnel, *La première épître aux Corinthiens* (2018), *ETL* 98 (2022) 169-171.
I.L.E. Ramelli, *Evagrius's* Kephalaia Gnostika: *A New Translation* (2015), *ETL* 94 (2018) 353-354.
D. Ramos-Lissón – M. Merino – A. Viciano (eds.), *El diálogo fe – cultura en la antigüedad cristiana* (1996), *ETL* 73 (1997) 196-197.
S.H. Rapp Jr., *The Sasanian World through Georgian Eyes: Caucasia and the Iranian Commonwealth in Late Antique Georgian Literature* (2014), *JEastCS* 70 (2018) 138-139.
F. Raurell, *I cappuccini e lo studio della Bibbia* (1997), *ETL* 75 (1999) 445-446.

W.W. Reader, *The Severed Hand and the Upright Corpse: The Declamations of M.A. Polemo* (1996), *ETL* 74 (1998) 446-448.
Y. Redalié, *La deuxième épître aux Thessaloniciens* (2011), *ETL* 89 (2013) 485-487.
J. Reiling, *De eerste brief van Paulus aan de Korintiërs* (1997), *ETL* 75 (1999) 211.
S. Reimann, *Die Entstehung des wissenschaftlichen Rassismus im 18. Jahrhundert* (2017), *ETL* 95 (2019) 359-360.
M. Reiser, *Kritische Geschichte der Jesus-Forschung: Von Kelsos und Origenes bis heute* (2015), *ETL* 93 (2017) 732-733.
B. Reuddenbach, see A. Bausi – B. Reuddenbach – H. Wimmer (eds.), *Canones: The Art of Harmony. The Canon Tables of the Four Gospels* (2020).
A.-L. Rey, *Centons homériques* (1998), *ETL* 75 (1999) 502-504.
D. Rhoads, *Reading Mark, Engaging the Gospel* (2004), *RBL* 8 (2006) 415-417.
P. Richardson, see K.P. Donfried – P. Richardson (eds.), *Judaism and Christianity in First-Century Rome* (1998).
—, *Herod the King of the Jews and Friend of the Romans* (1999), *ETL* 76 (2000) 480-481.
A.K. Riggs, see F. Enns – S. Holland – A.K. Riggs (eds.), *Seeking Cultures of Peace: A Peace Church Conversation* (2004).
F.X. Risch, see C. Bandt – F.X. Risch – B. Villani (eds.), *Die Prologtexte zu den Psalmen von Origenes und Eusebius* (2019).
B. Ritter, *Judeans in the Greek Cities of the Roman Empire* (2015), *ETL* 94 (2018) 329-331.
L. Rizzerio, *Clemente di Alessandria* (1996), *ETL* 75 (1999) 221-222.
V.K. Robbins, *Who Do People Say I Am? Rewriting Gospel in Emerging Christianity* (2013), *ETL* 92 (2016) 716-717.
V.K. Robbins – J.M. Potter (eds.), *Jesus and Mary Reimagined in Early Christian Literature* (2015), *ETL* 94 (2018) 343.
J.M. Robinson, see S. Carruth – J.M. Robinson – C. Heil, *The Database of the International Q Project: Q 4:1-13, 16. The Temptations of Jesus – Nazara* (1996).
A. Roeber, *Mixed Mariages: An Orthodox History* (2018), *JEastCS* 72 (2020) 335-337.
Ph. Roelli (ed.), *Marci Monachi opera ascetica: Florilegium et Sermones tres* (2009), *JEastCS* 65 (2013) 280-281.
S.K. Roll, *Towards the Origins of Christmas* (1995), *LS* 22 (1997) 388-389.
E. Rommen, *Being the Church: An Eastern Orthodox Understanding of Church Growth* (2017), *JEastCS* 70 (2018) 324-325.
P. Roszak – J. Vijgen (eds.), *Towards a Biblical Thomism: Thomas Aquinas and the Renewal of Biblical Theology* (2018), *ETL* 97 (2021) 529-530.
D.T. Roth – R. Zimmermann – M. Labahn (eds.), *Metaphor, Narrative, and Parables in Q* (2014), *BN* 175 (2017) 159-160.
C.K. Rothschild, *New Essays on the Apostolic Fathers* (2017), *ETL* 95 (2019) 347-348.
—, see H.W. Attridge – D.R. MacDonald – C.K. Rothschild, *Delightful Acts: New Essays on Canonical and Non-canonical Acts* (2017).
R. Roukema, *Gnosis and Faith in Early Christianity* (1999), *ETL* 78 (2002) 237.
C. Rouxpetel, see I. Bueno – C. Rouxpetel, *Les récits historiques entre Orient et Occident (XIe-XVe siècle)* (2019).

L.V. Rutgers et al. (eds.), *The Use of Sacred Books in the Ancient World* (1998), *ETL* 76 (2000) 182-184.
Th. Ryan, see I.C. Levy – Ph.D.W. Kray – Th. Ryan (eds.), *The Bible in Medieval Tradition: The Letter to the Romans* (2013).
M. Sachot, *L'invention du Christ* (1998), *ETL* 75 (1999) 497-498.
K.O. Sandnes, *The Gospel 'according to Homer and Vergil': Cento and Canon* (2011), *ETL* 89 (2013) 458-459.
S. Sardjveladze – T. Mgaloblisvili – E. Koçlamazašvili – S. Verhelst (eds.), *Jean de Bolnisi: Homélies des dimanches de carême* (2015), *ETL* 94 (2018) 355.
M. Saxby, see D. Angelov – M. Saxby (eds.), *Power and Subversion in Byzantium* (2013).
S.S. Schatzmann, see A. Schlatter, *Romans: The Righteousness of God* (trans. S.S. Schatzmann) (1995).
K. Scherberich, see K. Erlemann – K.L. Noethlichs – K. Scherberich – J. Zangenberg (eds.), *Neues Testament und Antike Kultur*, 4 vols. (2004-2005).
C. Schiller – M. Grudule (eds.), *"Mach dich auf und werde licht": Zu Leben und Werk Ernst Glücks (1654-1705)* (2010), *JEastCS* 65 (2013) 284-285.
A. Schlatter, *Romans: The Righteousness of God* (trans. S.S. Schatzmann) (1995), *ETL* 73 (1997) 184-185.
J. Schlosser, *La première épître de Pierre* (2011), *ETL* 89 (2013) 489-491.
B. Schmitz, see M. Ederer – B. Schmitz (eds.), *Exodus: Interpretation durch Rezeption* (2017).
—, see K. De Troyer – B. Schmitz (eds.), *The Early Reception of the Book of Isaiah* (2019).
A. Schneider, *Die Kirche als Geschöpf* (1999), *ETL* 78 (2002) 236-237.
U. Schnelle, *The History and Theology of the New Testament Writings* (trans. M.E. Boring) (1998), *LS* 25 (2000) 277-279.
—, *Die ersten 100 Jahre des Christentums: 30-130 n. Chr.* (2015), *ETL* 93 (2017) 729-730.
—, *Die getrennten Wege von Römern, Juden und Christen: Religionspolitik im 1. Jahrhundert n. Chr.* (2019), *ETL* 97 (2021) 520-522.
C.C. Schnusenberg, *The Mythological Traditions of Liturgical Drama: The Eucharist as Theater* (2010), *ETL* 87 (2011) 468-470.
C. Scholten, *Antike Naturphilosophie und christliche Kosmologie* (1995), *ETL* 75 (1999) 231-233.
K. Scholtissek, *Christologie in der Paulus-Schule* (1991), *ETL* 78 (2002) 218-219.
D.N. Schowalter, *The Emperor and the Gods: Images from the Time of Trajan* (1993), *ETL* 70 (1994) 180-181.
—, *The Emperor and the Gods: Images from the Time of Trajan* (1993), *LS* 19 (1994) 77-78.
J.A. Schroeder, *The Bible in Medieval Tradition: The Book of Genesis* (2015), *ETL* 93 (2017) 757-758.
—, *The Bible in Medieval Tradition: The Book of Jeremiah* (2017), *ETL* 96 (2020) 757-758.
S. Schulthess, *Les manuscrits arabes des lettres de Paul: État de la question et étude de cas (1 Corinthiens dans le Vat. Ar. 13)* (2019), *JEastCS* 71 (2021) 133-135.
A.M. Schwemer, see M. Hengel – A.M. Schwemer, *Jesus and Judaism* (2019).
R. Scott, see J. Burke – R. Scott (eds.), *Byzantine Macedonia* (2017).

G. Segalla, *Lettera ai Romani* (1999), *ETL* 77 (2001) 208-209.
Ch. Seitz – K. Greene-McCreight (eds.), *Theological Exegesis: Essays in Honour of Brevard S. Childs* (1999), *LS* 25 (2000) 379-380.
H. Seng – L.G. Soares Santopetre – C.O. Tommasi (eds.), *Formen und Nebenformen des Platonismus in der Spätantike* (2016), *ETL* 94 (2018) 346-348.
H.J. Sieben, *Anselm von Havelberg, Anticimenon, "Über die eine Kirche von Abel bis zum letzten Erwählten und von Ost bis West"* (2010), *ETL* 89 (2013) 514-517.
A.M. Silvas, *Basil of Caesarea: Questions of the Brothers. Syriac Text and English Translation* (2014), *JEastCS* 68 (2016) 403-404.
T. Silverstein – A. Hilhorst, *Apocalypse of Paul: A New Critical Edition of Three Long Latin Versions* (1997), *ETL* 75 (1999) 495-497.
I. Singer, *The Calm before the Storm: Selected Writings* (2011), *ETL* 89 (2013) 425-426.
B.D. Smith, *The Meaning of Jesus' Death: Reviewing the New Testament Interpretations* (2016), *ExpTim* 129 (2018) 187.
K. Smith, *The Martyrdom and History of Blessed Simeon Bar Sabba'e* (2014), *JEastCS* 70 (2018) 128-129.
—, see J.-N. Mellon Saint-Laurent – K. Smith (eds.), *The History of Mar Behnam and Sarah: Martyrdom and Monasticism in Medieval Iraq* (2018).
L.G. Soares Santopetre, see H. Seng – L.G. Soares Santopetre – C.O. Tommasi (eds.), *Formen und Nebenformen des Platonismus in der Spätantike* (2016).
Society of Biblical Literature 1998 Seminar Papers (1998), *ETL* 75 (1999) 201-202.
Society of Biblical Literature 2000 Seminar Papers (2000), *ETL* 78 (2002) 193-194.
S.K. Soderlund – N.T. Wright (eds.), *Romans and the People of God* (1999), *ETL* 78 (2002) 222-223.
T. Spilias, see G. Betts – S. Gauntlett – T. Spilias (eds.), *Vitzentzos Kornaros, Erotokritos* (2017).
C.J. Stallman-Pacitti, *The Life of Saint Pankratios of Taormina: Greek Text, English Translation and Commentary* (2018), *JEastCS* 72 (2020) 324-325.
A. Standhartinger, see L. Bormann – K. Del Tredici – A. Standhartinger (eds.), *Religious Propaganda and Missionary Competition in the New Testament: FS. D. Georgi* (1994).
K. Steiner, see K. Herbers – A. Nehring – K. Steiner (eds.), *Sakralität und Macht* (2019).
P. Stern, see J. Pastor – P. Stern – M. Mor (eds.), *Flavius Josephus: Interpretation and History* (2011).
Ch. Stettler, *Das letzte Gericht: Studien zur Endgerichtserwartung von den Schriftpropheten bis Jesus* (2011), *ETL* 89 (2013) 432-433.
M.E. Stone, *Uncovering Ancient Footprints: Armenian Inscriptions and the Pilgrimage Routes of the Sinai* (2017), *ETL* 96 (2020) 756-757.
S. Stroumsa, *Dāwūd al-Muqammaṣ: Twenty Chapters. An Edition of the Judeo-Arabic Text* (2016), *JEastCS* 70 (2018) 133-134.
J.L. Sumney, *Steward of God's Mysteries: Paul and Early Church Tradition* (2017), *ETL* 96 (2020) 733-735.
F. Szulc, *Le Fils de Dieu pour les Judéo-Chrétiens dans "Le Pasteur" d'Hermas* (2011), *JTS* 67 (2016) 296-298.

M. Tamcke – A. Manukyan (eds.), *Herrnhüter in Kairo: Die Tagebücher 1769-1783* (2012); iid. – C. Mauder (eds.), *Die arabischen Briefe aus der Zeit der Herrnhüter Präsenz in Ägypten 1770-1783* (2012); iid. – K. Weiland (eds.), *Die Tagebücher J.H. Danckes aus Behnesse 1770-1772* (2013); M. Tamcke – K. Weiland (eds.), *Herrnhüter in Behnesse: Die Diarien von C. Claussen (1782-1783), G.A. Roller (1775-1777) und G. Winiger (1775-1782)* (2014), *JEastCS* 69 (2017) 383-385.

M. Tardieu (ed.), *La formation des canons scripturaires* (1993), *ETL* 72 (1996) 247-248.

D.G.K. Taylor (ed.), *Studies in the Early Text of the Gospels and Acts* (1999), *ETL* 78 (2002) 197-198.

J.E. Taylor, *The Immerser: John the Baptist within Second Temple Judaism* (1997), *LS* 24 (1999) 381-383.

H. Teule – A. Brüning (eds.), *Handboek oosters christendom* (2018), *TvT* 59 (2019) 174-178.

H. Teule, see K. Ciggaar – H. Teule (eds.), *East and West in the Crusader States* (2003).

T. Thatcher – J. Odor *et al.* (eds.), *The Dictionary of the Bible and Ancient Media* (2017), *ETL* 96 (2020) 701-702.

G. Theissen – A. Merz, *The Historical Jesus* (1998), *LS* 23 (1998) 373-374.

C. Theobald, *Présences d'Évangile*, vol. 2 (2011), *ETL* 89 (2013) 469.

M. Theobald, *Jesus, Kirche und das Heil der Anderen* (2013), *ETL* 92 (2016) 721-723.

M. Thiessen, *Contesting Conversion: Genealogy, Circumcision, and Identity in Ancient Judaism and Christianity* (2011), *ETL* 89 (2013) 439-440.

K.J. Thomas – A.-A. Aghbar, *A Restless Search: A History of Persian Translations of the Bible* (2015), *ETL* 94 (2018) 328-329.

W. Thüsing, *Die neutestamentlichen Theologien und Jesus Christus* (1998), *ETL* 75 (1999) 472-474.

—, *Die neutestamentlichen Theologien und Jesus Christus*, Band 3 (1999), *ETL* 78 (2002) 198-199.

N.L. Tilford, *Sensing World, Sensing Wisdom: The Cognitive Foundation of Biblical Metaphors* (2017), *ETL* 96 (2020), 711-712.

S. Timpanaro, *The Genesis of Lachmann's Method* (trans. G. Most) (2005), *RBL* (2006).

H.H. Todt, *Petrus Martyr Anglerius, Legatio Babylonica: Die Gesandtschaft nach Babylon. Edition, Übersetzung und Kommentar* (2015), *JEastCS* 69 (2017) 378-380.

K. Tolstaya (ed.), *Orthodox Paradoxes: Heterogeneities and Complexities in Contemporary Russian Orthodoxy* (2014), *JEastCS* 68 (2016) 406-407.

C.O. Tommasi, see H. Seng – L.G. Soares Santopetre – C.O. Tommasi (eds.), *Formen und Nebenformen des Platonismus in der Spätantike* (2016).

J.P. Tosaus Abadía, *Cristo y el universe*: Estudio lingüístico y temático de Ef. 1,10b (1995), *ETL* 74 (1998) 448-449.

R. Trevijano Etcheverría, *Patrologia* (1994), *ETL* 72 (1996) 249-250.

—, *Origenes del cristianismo* (1995), *ETL* 74 (1998) 448-449.

J. Tromp, see M. de Jonge – J. Tromp, *The Life of Adam and Eve and Related Literature* (1997).

S. Trzcionka, see W. Mayer – S. Trzcionka (eds.), *Feast, Fast or Famine: Food and Drink in Byzantium* (2017).

C.M. Tuckett (ed.), *The Scriptures in the Gospels* (1997), *LS* 24 (1999) 77-80.
—, *From the Sayings to the Gospels* (2014), *ETL* 92 (2016) 723-724.
L. Vaage, *Religious Rivalries in the Early Roman Empire and the Rise of Christianity* (2006), *RBL* 9 (2007) 334-336.
R. Valantasis, *The New Q: A Fresh Translation with Commentary* (2005), *RBL* (2007).
A. Valerio, see K.E. Børresen – A. Valerio (eds.), *The High Middle Ages* (Bible and Women 6.2) (2015).
G. Vall, *Learning Christ: Ignatius of Antioch and the Mystery of Redemption* (2013), *LS* 38 (2014) 383-385.
G. Van Belle, *Index generalis (B)ETL 1982-1997* (2000), *ETL* 76 (2000) 465-466.
P.M. van Buren, *According to the Scriptures: The Origin of the Gospel and of the Church's Old Testament* (1998), *LS* 26 (2001) 89.
P.W. van der Horst, *Hellenism – Judaism – Christianity: Essays on Their Interaction* (1994), *LS* 19 (1994) 376-377.
—, *Bronnen voor de studie van de wereld van het vroege christendom*, 2 vols. (1997), *ETL* 73 (1997) 194-196.
—, *De woestijnvaders* (1998), *ETL* 75 (1999) 504.
– (ed.), *Aspects of Religious Contact and Conflict in the Ancient World* (1995), *ETL* 74 (1998) 204-205.
J. van der Vliet, see A. Łajtar – J. van der Vliet, *Empowering the Dead in Christian Nubia: The Texts from a Medieval Funerary Complex in Dongola* (2017).
H. van de Sandt – D. Flusser, *The Didache* (2002), *ETL* 79 (2003) 466-470.
T.M. van Lint – R. Meyer (eds.), *Armenia: Masterpieces from an Enduring Culture* (2015), *JEastCS* 67 (2015) 397-398.
G. Van Oyen, *The Interpretation of the Feeding Miracles in the Gospel of Mark* (1999), *ETL* 78 (2002) 208-209.
L. Van Rompay, see F. Petit – L. Van Rompay – J.J.S. Weitenberg (eds.), *Eusèbe d'Emèse: Commentaire de la Genèse* (2011).
R.E. Van Voorst, *The Ascents of James: History and Theology of a Jewish-Christian Community* (1989), *ETL* 66 (1990) 417-418.
S. Verhelst, see S. Sardjveladze – T. Mgaloblisvili – E. Koçlamazašvili – S. Verhelst (eds.), *Jean de Bolnisi: Homélies des dimanches de carême* (2015).
E. Verhoef, *De brieven aan de Tessalonicenzen* (1998), *ETL* 75 (1999) 488.
A. Viciano, see D. Ramos-Lissón – M. Merino – A. Viciano (eds.), *El diálogo fe – cultura en la antigüedad cristiana* (1996).
E.L. Vieyra, *L'Écriture dans la dynamique argumentative de 1 Corinthiens 1–4* (2016), *ETL* 94 (2018) 341-342.
B. Villani, see C. Bandt – F.X. Risch – B. Villani (eds.), *Die Prologtexte zu den Psalmen von Origenes und Eusebius* (2019).
M. Vollet, see M. Dreyer – É. Mehl – M. Vollet (eds.), *La réception de Duns Scot. Die Rezeption des Duns Scotus. Scotism through the Centuries: Proceedings of "The Quadruple Congress" on John Duns Scotus, Part 4* (2013).
W.S. Vorster, *Speaking of Jesus: Essays in Biblical Language* (1999), *ETL* 77 (2001) 206-208.
L.C. Vuong, see N.P. DesRosiers – L.C. Vuong (eds.), *Religious Competition in the Greco-Roman World* (2016).
O. Wassmuth, *Sibyllinische Orakel 1–2* (2011), *ETL* 89 (2013) 448-450.

F. Watson, *Gospel Writing: A Canonical Perspective* (2013), *ETL* 92 (2016) 717-719.
K. Weiland, see M. Tamcke – A. Manukyan – K. Weiland (eds.), *Die Tagebücher J.H. Danckes aus Behnesse 1770-1772* (2013); M. Tamcke – K. Weiland (eds.), *Herrnhüter in Behnesse: Die Diarien von C. Claussen (1782-1783), G.A. Roller (1775-1777) und G. Winiger (1775-1782)* (2014).
J.J.S. Weitenberg, see F. Petit – L. Van Rompay – J.J.S. Weitenberg (eds.), *Eusèbe d'Emèse: Commentaire de la Genèse* (2011).
L.L. Welborn, see J.R. Harrison – L.L. Welborn (eds.), *The First Urban Churches 1: Methodological Foundations* (2015).
—, see J.R. Harrison – L.L. Welborn (eds.), *The First Urban Churches 5: Colossae, Hierapolis, and Laodicea* (2019).
A. Wénin, see J.-M. Auwers – A. Wénin (eds.), *Lectures et relectures de la Bible* (1999).
—, see J.-D. Causse – É. Cuvillier – A. Wénin, *Divine Violence* (2011).
W. Weren, *Vensters op Jezus* (1998), *ETL* 75 (1999) 475-476.
L.M. White, see J.T. Fitzgerald – T.H. Olbricht – L.M. White (eds.), *Early Christianity and Classical Culture: Comparative Studies in Honor of A.J. Malherbe* (2003, paperback 2005).
G. Widengren – A. Hultgård – M. Philonenko, *Apocalyptique iranienne et dualisme qoumrânien* (1995), *ETL* 74 (1998) 442-443.
M. Williams, *The Doctrine of Salvation in the First Letter of Peter* (2011, paperback 2014), *JTS* 66 (2015) 425-427.
H. Wimmer, see A. Bausi – B. Reuddenbach – H. Wimmer (eds.), *Canones: The Art of Harmony. The Canon Tables of the Four Gospels* (2020).
S. Witetschek, *Thomas und Johannes – Johannes und Thomas: Das Verhältnis der Logien des Thomasevangeliums zum Johannesevangelium* (2015), *ETL* 93 (2017) 751-752.
B. Witherington, *Conflict and Community in Corinth* (1995), *ETL* 75 (1999) 208-210.
—, *The Acts of the Apostles* (1998), *ETL* 76 (2000) 493-496.
—, *Grace in Galatia* (1998), *ETL* 75 (1999) 208-210.
M. Wolter, *Paul: An Outline of His Theology* (trans. R.L. Brawley) (2015), *ETL* 94 (2018) 335-336.
Ph. Wood, *"We Have No King but Christ": Christian Political Thought in Greater Syria (c. 400-585)* (2010), *JEastCS* 65 (2013) 276-278.
J.H. Wray, *Rest as a Theological Metaphor in the Epistle to the Hebrews* (1998), *ETL* 76 (2000) 497-499.
N.T. Wright, see S.K. Soderlund – N.T. Wright (eds.), *Romans and the People of God* (1999).
P. Xella, see A. Ercolani – P. Xella (eds.), *Encyclopaedic Dictionary of Phoenician Culture*. Vol. 1: *Historical Characters* (2018).
S. Yli-Karjanmaa, *Reincarnation in Philo of Alexandria* (2015), *ETL* 94 (2018) 331-332.
J. Ysebaert, *Die Amtsterminologie im Neuen Testament* (1994), *ETL* 71 (1995) 234-237.
J. Zangenberg, see K. Erlemann – K.L. Noethlichs – K. Scherberich – J. Zangenberg (eds.), *Neues Testament und Antike Kultur*, 4 vols. (2004-2005).
D. Zeller, *Neues Testament und hellenistische Umwelt* (2006), *RBL* (2007).

—, *Der erste Brief an die Korinther* (2010), *ETL* 90 (2014) 176-178.
—, *Jesus – Logienquelle – Evangelien* (2012), *ETL* 89 (2013) 455-456.
L.R. Zelyck, *The* Egerton Gospel *(Egerton papyrus 2 + Papyrus Köln VI 255)* (2019), *ETL* 98 (2022) 176-178.
R. Zimmermann (ed.), *Hermeneutik der Gleichnisse Jesu* (2008), *TvT* 52 (2012) 280-281.
—, see D.T. Roth – R. Zimmermann – M. Labahn (eds.), *Metaphor, Narrative, and Parables in Q* (2014).
M. Zitnik, *Νῆψις: Christliche Nüchternheit nach Johannes Chrysostomus* (2011), *JEastCS* 65 (2013) 275-276.

PLUTARCH MEETS THE FARRER HYPOTHESIS

For more than half a century KU Leuven has been at the centre of the study of the Synoptic Gospels and in particular, the analysis of the Synoptic Problem. This has been due largely to the work of Frans Neirynck and now to that of his successor, Joseph Verheyden whom this volume honours. From his earliest publications on Mk 1,32-34 and on the infancy stories of Matthew[1], the Synoptics and the Synoptic Problem have always featured importantly among Verheyden's dauntingly broad range of scholarly competences, as his curriculum vitae will attest.

Each of the synoptic hypotheses that are in current discussion has entailments and implies a set of editorial policies on the part of the Synoptic evangelists. Accordingly, defenders of each of those hypotheses must offer a credible account of the many editorial alterations that are entailed in that hypothesis. Both the 2DH and the Farrer Hypothesis (FH) must account for how Matthew and Luke have *ex hypothesi* treated Mark. The 2DH must account *inter alia* for Matthew and Luke's differing uses of Q. The FH must render credible Luke's direct use of Matthew alongside Mark, while the Two Gospel Hypothesis must account for Mark's use of two predecessor gospels, his omission of much of the two predecessor gospels, and the alternating use of Matthew, then Luke. The Matthaean Posteriority Hypothesis must create a plausible scenario that accounts for Matthew's transformation of Luke and Mark. A survey of literature over the two centuries shows that scholars have promoted mutually exclusive hypotheses, often with the assertion that $x \to y$ is more 'credible' or 'likely' than $y \to x$. The debate often comes down to competing aesthetic imaginations.

One of the advances that has occurred recently is to insist on contextualizing the editorial transformations under discussion by appeal to material and culturally embedded practices of antiquity. This means positing editorial scenarios that accord with the ways in which other ancient authors manipulated and transformed their source materials, aware of the physical and technical constraints that ancient technologies imposed upon

---

1. *Mark 1,32-34 and 6,53-56: Tradition or Redaction?*, in *ETL* 64 (1988) 415-428; *De kindsheidverhalen in Matteüs: Preludium en programma*, in W. WEREN et al. (eds.), *Geboorteverhalen van Jezus: Feit en fictie*, Boxtel, Katholieke Bijbelstichting; Brugge, Tabor, 1988, 61-74.

those authors. This moves the debate from abstract suggestions about what *might* have been possible – the history of the Synoptic Problem is littered with brilliant conjectures about what ancient authors might have done – to scenarios that are probable, because they are attested elsewhere.

Several recent publications have addressed the issue of what I will call the technical feasibility of solutions to the Synoptic Problem. Robert Derrenbacker's study assessed synoptic hypotheses in the light of the constraints imposed on the ancient scribe: these included awareness of the realities created by the medium of scrolls or early codices written in *scripta continua* in relatively narrow columns; and the physical and cognitive limitations on editing that prevailed before the invention of a writing desk and the availability of large copy surfaces[2]. Close comparison of sources is now possible with a modern three- or four-column synopsis. But synoptic comparison and the cognitive revolution that it sparked was hardly possible before the creation of codex technologies at the time of Origen's *Hexapla* and Eusebius' *Chronicon*, which allowed for easy comparison of parallel accounts[3]. The studies of Alexander Damm and Duncan Reid viewed various synoptic hypotheses in the context of the norms of rhetorical performance, assessing the plausibility of various editorial scenarios against such rhetorical virtues of clarity and propriety[4]. A century after the appearance of the famous volume by William Sanday, the 2011 BETL volume, *New Studies in the Synoptic Problem*, offered comparative assessments of multiple issues in the Synoptic Problem[5], treating the Synoptic Problem not merely in abstract terms of what editorial transformations might have been theoretically possible but which were *likely*, given the physical constraints of copying and writing, the cognitive constraints of memory, and the cultural constraints of what constituted persuasive writing. In this essay honouring Verheyden I wish to continue these approaches by discussing the FH in the context of what

---

2. R.A. DERRENBACKER, *Ancient Compositional Practices and the Synoptic Problem* (BETL, 186), Leuven, LUP – Peeters, 2005. See also the earlier study of S.L. MATTILA, *A Question Too Often Neglected*, in *NTS* 41 (1995) 199-217, who assessed synoptic hypotheses in light of the editorial and compositional practices of Livy and Josephus.

3. See A. GRAFTON – M.H. WILLIAMS, *Christianity and the Transformation of the Book: Origen, Eusebius, and the Library of Caesarea*, Cambridge, MA, Harvard University Press, 2006.

4. A. DAMM, *Ancient Rhetoric and the Synoptic Problem: Clarifying Markan Priority* (BETL, 252), Leuven – Paris – Walpole, MA, Peeters, 2013; D. REID, *Miracle Tradition, Rhetoric and the Synoptic Problem* (BTS, 25), Leuven – Paris – Bristol, CT, Peeters, 2016.

5. P. FOSTER – A. GREGORY – J.S. KLOPPENBORG – J. VERHEYDEN (eds.), *New Studies in the Synoptic Problem: Oxford Conference, April 2008. Essays in Honour of Christopher M. Tuckett* (BETL, 239), Leuven – Paris – Walpole, MA, Peeters, 2011; W. SANDAY (ed.), *(Oxford) Studies in the Synoptic Problem*, Oxford, Clarendon, 1911.

is known of the editorial practices of another ancient author who used multiple sources, both predecessor histories and notebooks, in the composition of his *Lives* and *Moralia*, namely Plutarch.

I. Editing Mark and Matthew on the FH

On the 2DH, the principal sources for Matthew and Luke were a sayings source (Q) and Mark. Both Matthew and Luke used Mark and combined it with Q and other sayings and stories, but since they used these sources independently, they could only agree coincidentally in the particular ways that they fused Mark with Q. It should be very unlikely that Matthew and Luke would locate Q materials in the same way relative to the Markan narrative frame, or that the Markan elements that Matthew used to frame Q sayings would appear in Luke, and *vice versa*. And so it is. After the baptismal and temptation scenes (Mark 1,2-6.7-8.9-11.12-13; Q 3,2.7-9.16-17.[21-22]; 4,1-13) – where else could Matthew and Luke place these materials except in a Markan context[6]? – Matthew and Luke never agree in locating a Q saying in the same Markan context[7].

The Farrer hypothesis (FH) must also contend with the same literary fact that Matthew and Luke do not agree in combining the "Q"[8] and Markan materials in the same way. It does so by one of three types of explanations. First are explanations that have Luke consulting both Mark and Matthew directly. Luke preferred Mark's versions to their Matthaean counterparts in Lk 4,14-15; 4,31–6,19; 8,4–9,50 (with a number of omissions); 18,15–21,33 (again with numerous omissions); and 22,1–24,12 (with some notable transpositions), but he turned to Matthaean ("Q")

---

6. It should be noted that in spite of the fact that (on the 2DH and presumably the FH) Matthew and Luke chose to connect John's preaching with Mk 1,2-6, they did so differently, Matthew creating a new introduction, ἰδὼν δὲ πολλοὺς τῶν Φαρισαίων καὶ Σαδδουκαίων ἐρχομένους ἐπὶ τὸ βάπτισμα αὐτοῦ εἶπεν αὐτοῖς (3,7), while Luke adapted Mk 1,5 (καὶ ἐξεπορεύετο πρὸς αὐτὸν ... καὶ ἐβαπτίζοντο ὑπ' αὐτοῦ) in his ἔλεγεν οὖν τοῖς ἐκπορευομένοις ὄχλοις βαπτισθῆναι ὑπ' αὐτοῦ. The synopses of Aland and Huck-Greeven obscure this, but it is clearer in Boismard-Lamouille. See J.S. Kloppenborg, *Synopses and the Synoptic Problem*, in Foster – Gregory – Kloppenborg – Verheyden (eds.), *New Studies in the Synoptic Problem* (n. 5), 51-86, pp. 60-63.

7. See J.S. Kloppenborg, *Excavating Q: The History and Setting of the Sayings Gospel*, Minneapolis, MN, Fortress; Edinburgh, T&T Clark, 2000, pp. 29-32, and the discussion of various synoptic arrangements that either expose or hide this phenomenon in Kloppenborg, *Synopses* (n. 6).

8. I will use "Q" as a shorthand to denote the double tradition material. Of course, the FH does not posit a non-Markan source used by Matthew and Luke that is equivalent to the 2DH's Q.

materials in chaps. 3, 4, 6–7, and especially in the long section, Lk 9,51–18,14. Michael Goulder offered the most comprehensive account of how Luke proceeded, arguing that in the central section Luke first recruited sayings and stories from Matthew 7–12 and Matthew 16, but at 12,41 jumped to Matthew 24–25 and began working backwards through a scroll of Matthew[9]. Goodacre has also argued for direct usage of Matthew and Mark by Luke, but with the important qualification that Luke came to know and use Mark's gospel before learning about Matthew, with the result that Mark fundamentally controlled the shape of his composition. When he came to know the "Q" material from Matthew, he chose to locate it differently than Matthew had done rather than disturbing the Markan substructure, gathering most of it into the inaugural sermon (Lk 6,20b-49) and his travel narrative (Lk 9,51–18,14)[10].

Second, following Francis Watson's L/M hypothesis, Luke extracted the "Q" sayings from Matthew, placing them in a separate notebook and then later incorporated them into his new composition as he saw fit, but, as it turned out, consistently in ways different from Matthew's deployments[11]. Some of these sayings were incorporated into Luke in a Matthaean sequence (e.g., Lk 6,20-49), while Luke reserved others to be inserted later in his gospel. A more complex version of the notebook hypothesis has been advanced by John Poirier, who claims that Luke made extensive use of notebooks, first acquiring and recording the contents of his gospels on multiple wax tablets. In composing his gospel, this allowed him to include, omit, and transpose sayings and stories at will before reducing these preliminary drafts to a finished scroll[12].

---

9. M.D. GOULDER, *The Order of a Crank*, in C.M. TUCKETT (ed.), *Synoptic Studies: The Ampleforth Conferences of 1982 and 1983* (JSNTSup, 7), Sheffield, JSOT Press, 1984, 111-130, and in much greater detail, ID., *Luke: A New Paradigm* (JSNTSup, 20), Sheffield, JSOT Press, 1989, pp. 549 and following. This is not a thesis that has generally commended much assent: M.S. GOODACRE, *The Case against Q: Studies in Markan Priority and the Synoptic Problem*, Harrisburg, PA, Trinity Press International, 2002, p. 118, n. 23, treats it as "the most implausible element in Goulder's thesis on Luke's use of Matthew" and while J.C. POIRIER, *The Roll, the Codex, the Wax Tablet and the Synoptic Problem*, in *JSNT* 35 (2012) 3-30, pp. 12-13, argues that the backwards use of sources is technically feasible, he also regards Goulder's suggestions as "indefensible" when it comes to Luke.

10. GOODACRE, *Case against Q* (n. 9), chap. 4; ID., *Re-Walking the 'Way of the Lord': Luke's Use of Mark and His Reaction to Matthew*, in M. MÜLLER – J.T. NIELSEN (eds.), *Luke's Literary Creativity* (LNTS, 550), London, Bloomsbury T&T Clark, 2016, 26-43.

11. F. WATSON, *Gospel Writing: A Canonical Perspective*, Grand Rapids, MI, Eerdmans, 2013, pp. 168-216.

12. POIRIER, *The Roll, the Codex, the Wax Tablet* (n. 9), p. 21: "The evangelists *almost certainly* would have composed their Gospels with the aid of these tablets. This would have allowed them to refine their structure, phrasing and word choice with nearly as much ease as writers in the twenty-first century enjoy. Only after a complete set of tablets had been

None of these suggestions is impossible in the abstract. The first is in effect a hypothesis generated by the data it needs to explain (the non-agreement of Matthew and Luke in placing "Q" material) and as such is incapable of proof or disproof, since there is no independent way to determine which of the gospels first came to Luke's attention. The second and third are at least consistent with what is otherwise known of *some* other compositional procedures. There is good evidence of the existence of notebooks of sayings or anecdotes extracted from other sources and that some authors used notebooks in the process of composition. But as I will indicate below, ὑπόμνημα is a very broad term, ranging from short notes to penultimate drafts, and it is hardly the case that authors used ὑπομνήματα in the same way, if they used them at all. It is difficult, moreover, to evaluate the thesis of Poirier, since he has not worked out his theory in any detail.

On any of these explanations, the FH needs to provide a plausible accounting of how Luke, either in incorporating "Q" sayings directly from Matthew, or extracting them from Matthew only to use them later, came to avoid the editorial elements present in Matthew's versions and it must provide plausible reasons for Luke's editorial choices. That is, as Frans Neirynck has rightly insisted, the Synoptic Problem must be addressed not only at the level of general compositional scenarios but must consider individual texts. Many compositional scenarios are imaginable when one thinks in broad and abstract terms[13]. But the devil is in the details. Two pericopae epitomize this problem: Mt 17,19-20 ‖ Lk 17,5-6 ‖ Mk 9,28 and Mt 19,27-30 ‖ Lk 18,24-30 ‖ Mk 10,29-31.

1. *Lk 17,5-6 ‖ Mt 17,20*

Mt 17,20 occurs in the midst of a Markan context (Mk 9,14-29), the attempted exorcism of a boy by Jesus' disciples. Matthew dramatically reduces the story so that Mark's 270 words become 133[14], in the process

---

filled up would the new Gospel be 'published' by being transferred onto a roll or codex" (emphasis added). F.G. DOWNING, *Waxing Careless: Poirier, Derrenbacker and Downing*, in *JSNT* 35 (2013) 388-393, p. 391, points out that "*If* one were to imagine a close correlation between a fairly common papyrus column size *and* similar sized writing on wax, say, about 500 characters for each, then, on Poirier's figure, his Luke would seem to have needed around 180-200 tablets, or at least 60-70 for each one-third successive section of his Gospel – yes, 'a rather large stack' as Poirier allows, but without hazarding a figure".

13. See the criticism of Poirier offered by DOWNING, *Waxing Careless* (n. 12), p. 390: "How in detail wax tablets could have been used to the end indicated, and whether anyone (other than an imagined 'Farrerian Luke') ever did so use them, is left not only unevidenced, but unquestioned".

14. R. MORGENTHALER, *Statistische Synopse*, Zürich – Stuttgart, Gotthelf, 1971.

eliminating the lurid details of the boy's symptoms, but also the father's declaration of belief and his plea for Jesus to help his unbelief (βοήθει μου τῇ ἀπιστίᾳ, Mk 9,24). Both versions end with a responsive chria[15], the disciples asking why they were unable to perform the exorcism. Mark has Jesus respond with a bit of demonological lore about species of demons that are impossible to expel except by prayer. Matthew evidently regarded this answer as inadequate and so substituted the "Q" saying, ἀμὴν γὰρ λέγω ὑμῖν, ἐὰν ἔχητε πίστιν ὡς κόκκον σινάπεως, ἐρεῖτε τῷ ὄρει τούτῳ· μετάβα ἔνθεν ἐκεῖ, καὶ μεταβήσεται· καὶ οὐδὲν ἀδυνατήσει ὑμῖν (17,20). Matthew's point is not that certain types of demons need a stronger arsenal of weapons, but more generally, that faith, which the disciples evidently had in short supply[16], is overwhelmingly powerful. While Matthew excised Mark's saying, τοῦτο τὸ γένος ἐν οὐδενὶ δύναται ἐξελθεῖν, remnants of it remain in his peroration, καὶ οὐδὲν ἀδυνατήσει ὑμῖν.

On the FH, Luke has also condensed Mark's story, reducing the description of the boy's symptoms, omitting the father's pleas for faith, and dropping the demonological lore and Mark's comment on prayer. For Luke the story is one of Jesus' power in the face of unbelief. Luke has also transferred Mt 17,20b into a context of miscellaneous sayings on scandals (17,1-3a), forgiveness (17,3b-4), faith (17,5-6), and the appropriate conduct of household slaves (17,7-10). But in doing so he omitted any hint of Matthew's exorcistic context and dropped both ὀλιγοπιστία and Matthew's καὶ οὐδὲν ἀδυνατήσει ὑμῖν, adapted from Mark. Luke must also have changed Matthew's transplanting of a mountain into the uprooting of a mulberry tree.

It seems clear that whatever the original wording of Matthew's saying about faith in 17,20, he has assimilated it to Mk 11,23, which speaks of moving a mountain (τῷ ὄρει τούτῳ) into the sea. The FH must then assume that Luke not only dislodged the faith saying from its Markan context, but also changed ὄρος to συκάμινος, for reasons that seem beyond interpreters to suggest. In fact, most regard the Lukan συκάμινος as original, for precisely the reason that it is difficult to imagine a redactional change on Luke's part[17]. Moreover, by far the most common form

---

15. On types of chriae, see Theon, *Progymnasmata* §5 (p. 97 ed. SPENGEL).
16. The terms ὀλιγόπιστος and ὀλιγοπιστία are Matthaean, but also appear in Q (and Luke). See Mt 6,30 = Lk 12,28 (Q); Mt 8,26[R]; 14,31[R]; 16,8[R]; 17,30[R].
17. Thus, S. SCHULZ, *Q: Die Spruchquelle der Evangelisten*, Zürich, Theologischer Verlag Zürich, 1972, pp. 465-468; I.H. MARSHALL, *The Gospel of Luke: A Commentary on the Greek Text* (NIGTC), Exeter, Paternoster; Grand Rapids, MI, Eerdmans, 1978, p. 644; J.A. FITZMYER, *The Gospel according to Luke: A New Translation with Introduction and*

of the saying involves a mountain[18], not a tree, which would imply on the FH that Luke was moving *away*, not toward, the more common form of the saying. In any event, on the FH Luke has failed to take over a Markanism in Mt 17,20.

There is no evidence of Matthaean influence on Luke's formulation; Luke's framing of the saying with a request of the "apostles" to supply them with faith (πρόσθες ἡμῖν πίστιν, Lk 17,5) betrays the Lukan notion that πίστις can be removed (8,12) and supplied (17,5). If there is any influence on Luke's introductory request, it is perhaps a reminiscence of the father's plea in Mk 9,24, βοήθει μου τῇ ἀπιστίᾳ. But this is missing from Matthew's version[19].

Hence, if Luke used Mt 17,20, he has managed to detach all of the Markan features of the saying and substituted against both Mark and Matthew a mulberry tree in place of a mountain.

2. *Lk 22,28-30 ǁ Mt 19,28*

Like the saying about faith, Mt 19,28 appears in a wholly Markan context in Matthew, the story of the rich young man and Jesus' answer about wealth (Mt 19,16-30 ǁ Mk 10,17-31). Like the saying about faith, Jesus' answer also occurs in a responsive chria to the question of the disciples. (Luke turns this into a declarative [circumstantial] chria, in which unprompted, Jesus comments on the grief of the young man.) Then all the Synoptists have Peter boldly assert that they have "left all (their

---

Commentary, 2 vols. (AB, 28-28A), Garden City, NY, Doubleday, 1981-1985, p. 1142; R.H. GUNDRY, *Matthew: A Commentary on His Literary and Theological Art*, Grand Rapids, MI, Eerdmans, 1982, p. 352; F. BOVON, *Luke*. Vol. 2: *A Commentary on the Gospel of Luke 9:51–19:27* (Hermeneia), Minneapolis, MN, Fortress, 2013, p. 492; J. NOLLAND, *Luke* (WBC, 35A-C), Dallas, TX, Word, 1989-1993, vol. 2, p. 835; U. LUZ, *Matthew 8–20* (Hermeneia), Minneapolis, MN, Fortress, 2000, p. 407. Even F. HAHN, *Jesu Wort vom bergversetzenden Glauben*, in *ZNW* 73 (1985) 149-169, p. 158, who favours the Matthaean version of the saying as original, thinks that Luke was not responsible for the change, but relied on a pre-Lukan version of the saying, and preferred the removal of a tree because he regarded the removal of a mountain as "unwahrscheinlich".

NOLLAND, *Luke*, p. 835, also suggests that ταύτῃ is secondary in Luke, following 𝔓[75] ℵ D L 579 s sy[c] bo. Accordingly, ταύτῃ (A B W Θ Ψ λ φ), which makes little sense in Luke's context, is a textual assimilation to the Matthaean form.

18. Matthew's "mountain" is overwhelmingly preferred: *Acta Petri* 10; *Gospel of Thomas* 48; 106; Clement, *Strom.* 2.49.1; 5.2.6; Tertullian, *Fug.* 14.1; cf. 1 Cor 13,2, καὶ ἐὰν ἔχω πᾶσαν τὴν πίστιν ὥστε ὄρη μεθιστάναι.

19. A. PLUMMER, *A Critical and Exegetical Commentary on the Gospel according to S. Luke*, 5th ed. (ICC), Edinburgh, T&T Clark, 1922, p. 400, noted that the logic of Lk 17,5-6, especially the conditional, εἰ ἔχετε πίστιν ὡς κόκκον σινάπεως, ἐλέγετε ἂν …, implies that the apostles lack even the smallest portion of faith: "In the protasis the supposition is left open; in the apodosis it is implicitly denied". See BDF, §372 (1a).

possessions) and followed" (Mt 19,27 ‖ Mk 10,28 ‖ Lk 18,28), to which Jesus responds with an assurance of reward for those who have left family (Mark adds fields). Matthew, however, prefaces the Markan reward saying with ἀμὴν λέγω ὑμῖν ὅτι ὑμεῖς οἱ ἀκολουθήσαντές μοι ἐν τῇ παλιγγενεσίᾳ, ὅταν καθίσῃ ὁ υἱὸς τοῦ ἀνθρώπου ἐπὶ θρόνου δόξης αὐτοῦ, καθήσεσθε καὶ ὑμεῖς ἐπὶ δώδεκα θρόνους κρίνοντες τὰς δώδεκα φυλὰς τοῦ Ἰσραήλ (Mt 19,28).

Whether the pre-Matthaean saying had ἀκολουθέω or not, it is reasonable to assume that Matthew's οἱ ἀκολουθήσαντές μοι was appropriate to the context, which features ἀκολουθέω twice, at Mk 10,21 = Mt 19,21 and Mk 10,28 = Mt 19,27)[20]. But it is likely that Matthew added ὅταν καθίσῃ ὁ υἱὸς τοῦ ἀνθρώπου ἐπὶ θρόνου δόξης αὐτοῦ, anticipating Mt 25,31[21].

On the FH, Luke has removed the saying entirely from the context of a dialogue on following Jesus and abandoning wealth – even though the abandonment of wealth is a Lukan theme. He also deleted the image of the seated Son of Man coming in glory even though Acts 7,55 has a similar scene. Luke also connected the saying to another Markan story, the question of precedence (Mk 10,41-45), now relocated to the passion narrative. This relocation might account for some of the Lukan transformations: οἱ διαμεμενηκότες μετ' ἐμοῦ ἐν τοῖς πειρασμοῖς μου fits better the context of the passion narrative, which features πειρασμοί (22,40.46). Ἵνα ἔσθητε καὶ πίνητε ἐπὶ τῆς τραπέζης μου ἐν τῇ βασιλείᾳ μου (22,30) fits the Lukan meal scene and perhaps compensates for Luke's omission of Mk 14,25, perhaps deleted because in Luke's imagination Jesus did not forswear eating and drinking until the arrival of the kingdom, since he evidently ate and drank after the resurrection (Lk 24,30.35.42-43).

II. Source Utilization in Plutarch

Each of the compositional scenarios proposed by the FH can be assessed in relation to compositional practices attested elsewhere. We are of course at a disadvantage insofar as there are very few instances in which we have both an author's work and the source documents that he

---

20. Whether this is Matthaean redaction, or the grounds for the attraction of the saying to this Markan context is irrelevant for my purposes here. The IQP reconstructed Q with Matthew's οἱ ἀκολουθήσαντές μοι. See P. Hoffmann – S.H. Brandenburger – U. Brauner – T. Hieke, *Q 22:28-30: You Will Judge the Twelve Tribes of Israel*, in Documenta Q, Leuven, Peeters, 1998, pp. 191-195.

21. *Ibid.*, pp. 276-369.

used, which would allow us to see in detail the editing of the predecessor text by the later author. Alan Kirk's treatment of gnomologia offers some examples in which editorial practices can be deduced from micro-comparisons of gnomologia that used other sayings collections as their sources. Kirk's analysis has yielded models that make sense of Matthew's use of Q[22]. A papyrus fragment of the Ephoros (P.Oxy. III 1610 = FGrH 70 F 191), one of Diodorus of Sicily's sources, permits a micro-comparison of Diodorus with his source and an assessment of the degree to which verbatim copying or generous paraphrase were norms – it turns out that Diodorus engaged in both[23]. But when we want to inquire into kinds of editing presupposed by the FH, especially the rearrangement of sayings or whole episodes, Plutarch provides one of the best resources.

Christopher Pelling has shown that Plutarch, in composing the later Roman *Lives* of *Pompey*, *Cato*, *Crassus*, *Caesar*, *Brutus*, and *Antony*, worked with the same set of source materials, principally the *Historiae* of Asinius Pollio (76 BCE-4/5 CE), along with various other sources, including Livy, bits of oral tradition, and his own earlier works[24]. Although Asinius Pollio is no longer extant, it is possible to surmise a good deal of its contents by comparison of Plutarch with Appian's *Bellum civile* and Suetonius, who seem also to have used Pollio, and by noting the partially overlapping information Plutarch supplies in the related Roman *Lives*.

The contrast with two earlier *Lives*, *Lucullus* and *Cicero*, is marked, for it appears that Plutarch had relatively fewer source materials than he did in the later Roman biographies, with the result that details are missing in *Lucullus* and *Cicero* which Plutarch would surely have included had he known them. Moreover, when writing the Greek *Lives* Plutarch could rely on his extensive knowledge of Greek literature; but he learned Latin much later in life, and although he no doubt read histories of Rome in Greek, his knowledge of Latin sources was much more limited. By the time he composed *Pompey*, *Cato*, *Crassus*, *Caesar*, *Brutus*, and *Anthony*, Plutarch had read more widely and could offer more detail and correct earlier errors. For example, in *Cicero* the assassination of Julius Caesar

---

22. A. KIRK, *Q in Matthew: Ancient Media, Memory, and Early Scribal Transmission of the Jesus Tradition* (LNTS, 564), London, Bloomsbury T&T Clark, 2016.

23. J.S. KLOPPENBORG, *Variation in the Reproduction of the Double Tradition and an Oral Q?*, in *ETL* 83 (2007) 49-79. On the Ephoros fragment, see C.R. RUBINCAM, *A Note on Oxyrhynchus Papyrus 1610*, in *Phoenix* 30 (1976) 357-366.

24. C.B. PELLING, *Plutarch's Method of Work in the Roman Lives*, in *JHS* 99 (1979) 74-96. Pelling shows that Plutarch's sources sometimes overlapped with material also known to Appian, Suetonius, and Cassius Dio.

is mentioned in a single subordinate clause; the characters of Brutus and Cassius and their differing views of Caesar are not treated; and the assassination itself is attributed to the partisans of Brutus and Cassius[25]. But in *Caesar* the same events are narrated in richer detail (§§62–67), elaborating the distinct roles of Brutus and Cassius, describing the various omens given to Caesar, and narrating the assassination in great detail, including the direct participation of Brutus and Cassius. Cicero disappears from the account.

Perhaps more significantly, there are differences in the later *Lives* that are due to exigencies of each of these partially overlapping biographies. For example, *Anthony* (13–15), which focuses on Anthony's role, gives a streamlined and simpler account of Caesar's assassination, omitting the role of Lepidus and Cicero's proposal for an amnesty for the assassins (reported in *Cicero* 42.3). *Brutus* (7–19), however, parses many of the episodes summarized and compressed in *Anthony*, and whereas *Caesar* notes Cassius' hatred of Caesar only briefly, it is described in extensive detail in *Brutus*[26]. Although Plutarch composed *Anthony* and *Brutus* (and the other later Roman *Lives*) as part of a single project, likely with the same sources, his choices of what to include, and what to exclude from his sources in each biography were a function of the focus of each of the *Lives*[27].

In the later *Lives* Plutarch supplemented the account of Asinius Pollio with other materials. Some of these materials were drawn from an account that agrees substantially with one used by Appian in *Bellum civile*. But in other cases, Plutarch included anecdotes and personalia that do not appear to be typical of Appian or Pollio. Pelling comments:

> Some of this material may have been transmitted by Appian's source, and suppressed by Appian himself ... But one cannot believe that the source contained all these items. [Appian's] source seems elsewhere to have had less taste for personalia and anecdote than this material suggests; and, in particular, Appian's account of the senatorial debate of 17th March is too detailed and well informed to be reconciled with the errors and confusions of Plutarch's extraneous material. These mistakes surely come from elsewhere, and Plutarch has grafted them on to the more responsible version he found in the Pollio-source[28].

In spite of Plutarch's use of multiple sources, Pelling argues that Plutarch was mainly guided by Pollio's narrative, into which other materials were

---

25. *Cicero* 42.2: ὡς δ' οὖν ἐπέπρακτο τοῖς περὶ Βροῦτον καὶ Κάσσιον τὸ ἔργον.
26. PELLING, *Plutarch's Method* (n. 24), pp. 77-78.
27. This point is further elaborated in C.B. PELLING, *Plutarch's Adaptation of His Source Material*, in *JHS* 100 (1980) 127-139.
28. PELLING, *Plutarch's Method* (n. 24), p. 86.

inserted. But there is no evidence that Plutarch engaged in a thorough analysis and breakdown of his source materials and the reorganization of these materials into an independent narrative. Instead, his compositional methods were much the same as Livy's: Livy followed one source at a time, occasionally adding supplementary items, but not "to weave together a coherent and independent account of his own"[29].

Contradictions among the later *Lives* were due, Pelling argues, not to his use of multiple sources with divergent details, but more likely to Plutarch's faulty memory. For example, *Caesar* (66.4) attributes Anthony's delay in arriving at the curia on the day of the assassination to D. Brutus Albinus, but *Brutus* reports that it was C. Trebonius who had waylaid Anthony. In *Caesar* (22.3) Plutarch reports Caesar's killing of 400,000 barbarians in Gaul, but in *Cato* (51.1) and the *Comparison of Nicias and Crassus* (4.3) the number is 300,000. These variations, Pelling suggests, arose because his source, Pollio, was not to hand while he was composing the *Comparison* and *Cato*; Plutarch relied only on his memory[30].

Hence, the picture that emerges of Plutarch's composition of the later Roman *Lives* is of an author who used Pollio as his main guide, editing Pollio's account in accord with the focus of each of the biographies, and supplementing Pollio with a few other sources when those suited his literary purposes.

Pelling is more cautious in suggesting that Plutarch used ὑπομνήματα in the sense of notebooks[31] in the preliminary stages of composing the Roman *Lives*, as he admits to doing in the *Moralia* and perhaps in some of the Greek *Lives*[32]. For Pelling, Plutarch's relative haste in composing the later Roman *Lives* and his extensive use of the Pollio-source might have obviated the need for notebooks, or at best those ὑπομνήματα were simply brief notes on wax tablets. If Plutarch composed a ὑπόμνημα it

---

29. *Ibid.*, p. 92, citing T. LUCE, *Livy: The Composition of His History*, Princeton, NJ, Princeton University Press, 1977, p. 143.
30. PELLING, *Plutarch's Method* (n. 24), pp. 79, 93. Appian, *Bellum civile* (2.117) attributes Anthony's delay to Tribonius, thus agreeing with the account in *Brutus*.
31. The range of connotations for ὑπόμνημα is large, from brief notes, aide-mémoires, and notebooks, to rough drafts and *commentarii*. See F. MONTANARI, *Hypomnema*, in H. CANCIK – H. SCHNEIDER (eds.), *Brill's New Pauly*, http://dx.doi.org.myaccess.library.utoronto.ca/10.1163/1574-9347_bnp_e519990, 2006. On composing with notebooks, see J.P. SMALL, *Wax Tablets of the Mind: Cognitive Studies of Memory and Literacy in Classical Antiquity*, London – New York, Routledge, 1997, pp. 156-159.
32. See L. VAN DER STOCKT, *Compositional Methods in the Lives*, in M. BECK (ed.), *A Companion to Plutarch*, Oxford – Malden, MA, Blackwell, 2014, 321-332, who makes a strong case that for the composition of the *Moralia* and the Greek *Lives*, Plutarch used notebooks.

was more likely a penultimate draft of his work – the kind of work that Lucian describes in *Quomodo historia conscribenda sit* 48:

> When [the author] has collected all or most of the facts let him first make them into a kind of memorandum (ὑπόμνημά τι), a body of material as yet with no beauty or continuity. Then, after he has imposed an order (ἐπιθεὶς τὴν τάξιν), let him give it beauty and enhance it with the charms of expression, figure, and rhythm (trans. LCL adapted slightly).

This is not a matter of Poirier's multiple ὑπομνήματα that could be shuffled and rearranged at will, but a single draft that required polishing.

For the *Moralia*, however, Plutarch does admit to using ὑπομνήματα – presumably notebooks rather than the rough drafts described by Lucian. In *Tranq. an.* 464E-465A he states that he had composed this work in haste "from my notebooks which I happened to have made for my own use" (ἐκ τῶν ὑπομνημάτων ὧν ἐμαυτῷ πεποιημένος ἐτύγχανον).

Van der Stockt has collected fifty points in the Plutarchan corpus where Plutarch can be seen to be using ὑπομνήματα (notebooks). In order to identify the remnants of ὑπομνήματα he uses what he calls a "cluster method" – that is, passages in several essays in which the same constellation of citations and allusions appears. For example, in *Superst.* §5, *Quaest. conv.* 9.14 and *Suav. viv.* §§13–14 the same combination of an allusion to Pindar and references to Plato, *Tim.* 47D–48A and *Resp.* 519 appear (in different forms), suggesting that Plutarch's source is "a single unit; they show material that is basically identical, but modified in order to harmonize it with the varying contexts"[33]. Similarly, in both *Adul. amic.* 15–16 and *Tranq. an.* 12 Plutarch cites the examples of Megabyzus attempting to flatter Apelles (58D, 472A), the sprinter Crison deliberately losing a footrace to Alexander (58F, 472F), and a version of the Stoic maxim that the sage is not only prudent, just and brave, but an orator, poet, general, rich man, and king (58E, 472A)[34]. These agreements in illustrative material suggest that Plutarch had ὑπομνήματα containing collections of citations and anecdotes on a variety of topics that could be mobilized in his moral essays[35].

---

33. L. VAN DER STOCKT, *I Quote Therefore I Am: Plutarch's Technique of Hypomnemetic Composition*, unpublished paper presented at the International Conference of the Leuven Centre for the Study of the Gospels, *On Using Sources: Samples from Greco-Roman, Second Temple Judaism and Early Christian Literature*, Leuven, KU Leuven, 2019, p. 5.

34. See VAN DER STOCKT, *Compositional Methods* (n. 32), pp. 329-330. There are many other examples, e.g., *Alexander* 4.2 and *Quaest. conv.* 1.6, on which see E. MENSCHING, *Peripatetiker über Alexander*, in *Historia* 12 (1963) 274-282.

35. See also the striking agreement in sequence of topoi in *On Friendship and Flattery* §§5 and 6–8 (51BC and 51E–52F) and *On Having Many Friends* §§8–9 (96D–97B) pointing

III. Assessing the FH in the Light of Plutarch's Methods

Plutarch's compositional methods and his use of sources, either in the Roman or Greek *Lives* or the *Moralia*, are not necessarily representative or normative for compositional practices in general. But they do offer concrete examples of actual composition very close to Luke's time, against which to evaluate the proposals of the FH in regard to the two pericopae described above.

Fundamental to Goodacre's compositional scenario is the hypothesis that Mark had already become a foundational narrative for Luke before he came to know Matthew. And more than that, Goodacre argues that Luke adopted the Markan theme of the "Way of the Lord" – the movement from the wilderness, to Galilee and to Jerusalem, and the passion – as a key literary and theological structuring theme[36]. Luke's attraction to the Markan theme of going up on the road to Jerusalem (ἐν τῇ ὁδῷ ἀναβαίνοντες εἰς Ἱεροσόλυμα, Mk 10,32) is reflected in his use of ἡ ὁδός to describe the Jesus movement in Acts and at the multiple points at which Luke reminds the reader that Jesus was on his way to Jerusalem. That is not the way that Matthew structured his gospel. Goodacre points out that Matthew's redaction of Mark diminished the centrality of the themes of the "Way of the Lord"; it lacks a clearly delineated central section that functions as a transition between Galilee and Jerusalem; and Matthew's extensive use of the non-Markan material in the Galilean section of the gospel overloads the first part of his gospel with the consequence that it was impossible for Matthew to have a pivotal central section[37]. Luke, having invested in the Markan theme, could not take over the Matthaean material as it stood, since that would obscure the structure and theme he wished to promote. Instead, he relocated the non-Markan material into his central section, preserving and indeed expanding the central and transitional section.

Goodacre's scenario resembles in some ways Plutarch's approach to the later Roman *Lives*, where Plutarch is largely guided by Pollio's account. This does not mean for Plutarch that he could not conflate and combine episodes, relocate some materials, and even invert the chronological sequence of events. Pelling has shown that Plutarch engaged in

---

to the use of a notebook. See L. VAN DER STOCKT, *Semper duo, numquam tres? Plutarch's Popularphilosophie on Friendship and Virtue in* On Having Many Friends, in G. ROSKAM – L. VAN DER STOCKT (eds.), *Virtues for the People: Aspects of Plutarchan Ethics* (Plutarchea Hypomnemata), Leuven, LUP, 2011, 19-39, pp. 35-36.

36. GOODACRE, *Re-Walking* (n. 10), pp. 29-30.
37. *Ibid.*, p. 35.

abridgement, chronological compression (treating distinct episodes as belonging to the same period), chronological displacement, and the transfer of an item from one character to another[38]. Lukan examples of these kinds of transformations are not difficult to find: Luke abridges Markan scenes and leaves many out entirely. Chronological compression can be seen at Lk 19,45-46 (contrast Mk 11,12-14.15-17) where Luke eliminates an extraneous day. There are several examples of chronological displacement: Luke moves the stories of the imprisonment of the Baptist (3,19-20); Jesus' visit to Nazareth (4,16-30); the call of Peter (5,1-11); the anointing of Jesus by a woman (7,36-50); the question about greatness (22,24-30) and the tearing of the veil of the temple (23,44-48). He has also transferred speech from a Markan character to one of his own making (18,18-23, where a rich young man becomes one of the rulers). In most of these cases it is relatively easy to discern Luke's interest in stylistic economy and conciseness. Chronological displacements betray an interest arriving at a chronology that better accounts for certain developments than the Markan sequence[39]. Each of these transformations implies that Luke knew Mark well and could abbreviate, re-write, and reach forward or backward to shift materials to points in his narrative that better accomplished his purposes.

1. *Lk 17,5-6 || Mt 17,20*

The shifting of "Q" material offers a more difficult problem. That Luke was capable of relocating source elements is clear from how he edited Mark. What is far less clear is what he achieved by doing so. In the case of Lk 17,5-6, Goulder explains that in working backwards through Matthew, Luke had reached Mt 18,1-22 at his chap. 17 and so took over a warning about scandals (17,1-2 < Mt 18,6-7), then a saying on forgiveness (17,3-4 < Mt 18,15.22) – but skipping over Mt 18,10-15 which he had already used at 15,4-7. He then reached Mt 17,20 from which he took 17,6 (supplied with his own introduction in 17,5). But while he took over from Mt 17,20 the comparison of faith with a mustard seed, the συκάμινος was adapted from the συκῆ in Mt 21,21, but changed into a mulberry because it is bigger than a fig tree[40]. Continuing the backward journey

---

38. PELLING, *Plutarch's Adaptation* (n. 27), pp. 127-139.
39. For example, the transposition of the call of Peter to a point after Jesus' reputation spread and after several wonders (4,14-15.31-32.33-37.38-39.40-41) renders Peter's reaction in 5,1-11 more credible. The relocation of the arrest of the Baptist (3,19-20) to a point prior to Jesus' auto-baptism removes the Baptist from the scene, responding to the problem that Mt 3,15 solved in a very different way.
40. GOULDER, *Luke* (n. 9), pp. 641-642.

through Matthew, Goulder argues that Luke substituted the story of the ten lepers (17,11-19), prompted by the reference to Jesus "gathering in Galilee" (Mt 17,22) and by the healing in Mt 17,14-21, but created from elements in Mt 8,1-4.5-13, and Mt 11,5. This brought Luke back to Matthew 16, the very point from which he made "the great leap forward" to the end of Matthew and began working backwards[41].

Goulder's explanation seems needlessly complicated and raises several questions: if Luke had been satisfied to take over Mark in Lk 9,46-48 – in which Goulder also perceives "echoes" of Matthew's version[42] –, why did he not also keep Matthew's saying where it was? This is all the more important, because, as indicated above, *both* Matthew and Luke have ignored Mark's demonological explanation of the disciples' inability to perform an exorcism and shifted the emphasis to Jesus' power in the face of unbelief. Moreover, if he were interested in the spectacular results of faith as plainly he is in 17,6, the change of Matthew's ὄρος to a mulberry tree is odd. And as I have indicated above, Luke was evidently entirely uninfluenced by the one element that Matthew had adapted from Mark, καὶ οὐδὲν ἀδυνατήσει ὑμῖν, which, if Luke had been dependent upon Mt 17,20, would have been the fingerprint of Matthew's redaction. But it is absent from Lk 17,6.

Goodacre's general scenario of Luke's primary orientation to Mark seems a more cogent explanation of Luke's text than Goulder's theory of backwards redaction. Yet because Goodacre does not comment either on the relocation of 17,5-6 or the change in imagery, one can only speculate as to how he would deal with Luke's choices. That Luke failed to take over Mt 17,20 at Lk 9,37-43 might plausibly be the result of Luke's orientation to Mark: he either failed to notice Matthew's addition to Mark 9 or for some reason thought it superfluous, given his interests in Lk 9,37-43 in underscoring Jesus' ability to exorcize demons. This kind of account aligns with what we can observe in Plutarch: he omits details available to him when they do not contribute to his overall editorial strategy. Yet his explanation fails to account for two details. First, *at some point* Luke must have consulted Mt 17,14-21 in order to extract the "Q" saying. He then not only changed ὄρος to συκάμινος but also omitted the one sure sign of Matthaean redaction, καὶ οὐδὲν ἀδυνατήσει ὑμῖν.

Second, this explanation also fails to account for Luke's goals in 17,1-19, which is a rather miscellaneous collection of sayings extracted (*ex hypothesi*) from Mt 18,6-7; 18,15.22; 17,20 and two bits of *Sondergut* on scandals, forgiveness, faith, obedience, and the extraordinary reaction of a

---

41. *Ibid.*, p. 645.
42. *Ibid.*, p. 446.

Samaritan to healing. Since the collection is so miscellaneous, it is difficult to divine any editorial reasons for Luke's alterations of Mt 17,20[43].

Watson's scenario, of Luke first extracting from Matthew non-Markan sayings and placing them in a notebook is, as indicated above, not impossible. Plutarch (and others) certainly created notebooks from their readings, only to use these later in compiling their works. Watson suggests that Luke had extracted from Matthew several sets of sayings: five sets of sayings from Matthew 5–7 and used in Lk 6,20-49; 22 sayings from Matthew 5–12 redeployed at various points from Lk 11,2-4 to 17,33, and another collection extracted from Matthew 13–25 and used in multiple locations in Lk 10,23-24 to 22,29[44]. Conceding that Lk 17,1-19 is "disparate", he nonetheless thinks that sayings from Matthew 18 and 17,20 were combined with *Sondergut* material (17,1-10.11-19) into a block. He offers no reason for the combination, since there is no theme that runs through this collection. The one point worth considering is his suggestion that the Lukan introduction to the faith saying, πρόσθες ἡμῖν πίστιν, is an echo of Matthew's ὀλιγοπιστία in Mt 17,20. In that case, however, Luke has eliminated a term that he uses elsewhere (Lk 12,28). Watson's explanation of the supposed change from ὄρος to συκάμινος is that it betrays "Luke's tendency to differentiate himself from Matthew when dependent upon him"[45] – which, if there were such a tendency of Luke to disguise his sources, we would be hard pressed to account for the many Mt=Lk *verbatim* agreements.

The more general problem with the Lukan notebook theory – and this applies even more to Poirier – is that the kind of evidence that van der Stockt invoked to show that Plutarch used notebooks, namely configurations of sayings from different sources (e.g., Pindar, Plato) or configurations of the diverse illustrations and maxims that appear in several of Plutarch's essays in the same sequence, does not favour the FH any more than the 2DH. Luke's source for Lk 7,18-35 evidently contained an anecdote about John's question about the Coming One (7,18-23), Jesus comments about John (7,24-26), a citation combining and paraphrasing elements of Ex 23,30 and Mal 3,1 (Lk 7,27), a commendation of John (7,28), a question posed to the crowd comparing John with the Son of Man (7,31-34), and a Sophia saying (7,35). The sequence conforms exactly to that found in Mt 11,2-19. This datum, however, is precisely the same datum that the 2DH invokes in support of a pre-Matthaean, pre-Lukan

---

43. *Ibid.*, p. 643, describes 17,1-10 as a "rump of Matthaean logia with a Lucan parable tacked on".
44. WATSON, *Gospel Writing* (n. 11), pp. 185-187.
45. *Ibid.*, p. 212, n. 92.

notebook, namely Q. In order to support the kind of notebook that Watson has in mind, one would need independent evidence of a notebook with *Luke's* particular configuration of "Q" sayings, for example in Thomas. But as is clear from the table below, Thomas does not provide such evidence.

Mt	Lk	Thomas	
17,20	17,6	48, 106	faith as a mustard seed
18,3b-5	omit	22	entering the kingdom as children
18,6	17,2	—	better that a millstone …
18,7	17,1	—	inevitability of scandals
18,10-14	15,4-7	107	lost sheep
18,15-18	17,3	—	disciplinary procedures for sinning brother
18,19-20	omit	48	wherever two or three are gathered
18,21-22	17,4	—	if one sins seven times …
18,23-35	omit	—	parable of the unforgiving servant

The Mt-Lk agreements in non-Markan material certainly suggest the existence of a notebook, and the general agreement between Matthew and Luke in deploying most of these sayings in Matthew 18 and Luke 17 respectively suggests a common source. But the heterogeneous nature of Luke's deployment of these sayings, *versus* the organized nature of Matthew's in Mt 18,1-35 ought to suggest that Matthew's arrangement is posterior, not prior, to Luke's.

2. *Lk 22,28-30 || Mt 19,28*

Goulder recognizes that at 18,18-30 (the question of the ruler and Jesus' saying about rewards) Luke follows Mk 10,17-31 "without reference to Matthew … unless he has noted [22,30] down to use it at 22,30"[46]. When he comes to comment on Luke 22, he says nothing of the backwards use of the scroll of Matthew. Indeed, the location of Lk 22,29 does not smoothly fit Goulder's theory of Luke's backward progress through Matthew, since the last Matthaean materials he had used were in Matthew 17, 16 and 24, not Matthew 19[47].

Goulder's explanation of the presence of 22,28-30 in the transplanted Markan story of the question about greatness (Mk 10,41-45 || Lk 22,24-30) does not fare better, since as Goulder himself concedes,

> we have an uncomfortable combination of sources: the Twelve are discovered sitting round the banquet table of the age to come eating and drinking,

---

46. GOULDER, *Luke* (n. 9), p. 671.
47. According to GOULDER, *Crank* (n. 9), p. 130, and ID., *Luke* (n. 9), p. 666, Lk 17,11-19 was based on Mt 17,14-23 and 17,20–18,8 came from Mt 16,1-4, 16,25-28, and chapter 24.

and on thrones deciding the eternal fate of their fellow Jews, in the same half-sentence[48].

This clumsy use of sources of course demands an explanation on any source theory. But it seems obvious that the Matthaean setting of the Twelve thrones saying better fits the Markan context of a question about the eschatological rewards for temporal renunciation. On the principle of *lectio difficilior potior* Luke's version, not Matthew's, would seem to be the more original or to put it differently, since the "Q" saying is in both cases fused with a Markan chria, Matthew's version is the more satisfactory version, and hence the more edited.

Goodacre offers no comment on Lk 22,28-30, but one might surmise that he could argue that Luke's orientation to Mark caused him to pass over Matthew's editing of Mark in Mk 10,23-31 when he composed Lk 18,24-30 and only noticed Mt 19,29 when he came to know Matthew. But Goodacre's compositional scenario still encounters the objection that Matthew's deployment of the saying seems the more polished, and Luke's the clumsier. That would leave the explanation that for some reason Luke wanted to preserve the saying, in spite of its lack of fit, and could not use it in its Matthaean redactional location without disturbing the purity of the Markan account. This, however, *would* have been strong evidence of Luke's dependence on Matthew.

Lk 22,29 appears in Watson's second list of extracted sayings[49] but he offers no specific comment on the placement of 22,29 or the reasons for its extraction from Mt 19,29. His general theory is that Luke extracted non-Markan sayings from Matthew, and used some in Matthaean order, and others which he reserved for later use. His explanation of Luke's decisions is particularly unsatisfying: repeatedly, paraphrasing Luke, he simply declares that "it seemed good to him" as though it were an explanation of Luke's editorial decision[50]. As I have suggested elsewhere, this is not an argument; it simply renames the textual data (that is, that Luke's location of "Q" material differs from Matthew's) and turns it into an aesthetic preference in Luke's mind with the help of the source theory it presupposes[51].

The putative creation of a Lukan notebook of Matthaean sayings should also address the cognitive problem of whether an ancient author could engage in careful comparison of sources in order to create a "redaction-free"

---

48. GOULDER, *Luke* (n. 9), p. 732.
49. WATSON, *Gospel Writing* (n. 11), p. 187.
50. *Ibid.*, p. 169; similarly, p. 175, n. 32.
51. J.S. KLOPPENBORG, *Conceptual Stakes in the Synoptic Problem*, in H. OMERZU – M. MÜLLER (eds.), *Gospel Interpretation and the Q-Hypothesis* (International Studies on Christian Origins), London – New York, Bloomsbury, 2018, 13-42, pp. 22-24.

notebook. I have already noted a propos of Lk 17,6 that it lacks the redactional features of Mt 17,20. Likewise, Lk 22,29 lacks the use of ἀκολουθέω which, irrespective of whether it is a Matthaean redactional term or not, is clearly the verbal element that Matthew has used to connect the "Q" saying with its Markan context and Peter's declaration, ἠκολουθήκαμέν σοι (Mk 10,28 = Mt 19,27 = Lk 18,28). Watson avers that "there is no reason to doubt [Luke's] ability to discriminate between Markan and Matthean material"[52]. This is quite true on a scenario such as Goodacre's: if Luke were following Mark closely, this would almost automatically result in passing over the Matthaean additions to Mark. But when Watson explains further that "it does not take 'meticulous precision' to follow Mark in the first instance but to note the supplementary Matthean material and to find ways to reincorporate much of it at a later point relative to Mark"[53], he passes over the fact that Luke would have had to compare Mark with Matthew in order to produce a redaction-free extract. It is just this kind of micro-comparison that is unattested in Plutarch (who clearly used ὑπομνήματα) and which Pliny (*Ep.* 5.8.12) found burdensome (*onerosa collatio*)[54]. When ancient authors claimed to compare their sources, it was not at the level of sentence and phrase, but rather a broad comparison to determine which account was the more reliable[55].

Watson's theory of the putative relocation of Mt 19,29 by Luke also runs into Goulder's observation (quoted above) that Lk 22,24-30 is an "uncomfortable combination of sources". Of course, it is entirely possible that this combination "seemed good to Luke" – to invoke Watson's favourite explanation. But insofar as Luke's version seems a much poorer combination than Matthew's, his explanation is hardly persuasive.

IV. CONCLUSION

It is difficult to see either Goodacre's or Watson's account of Luke's use of Matthew (or a hypothetical Matthaean notebook) as in any way preferable to the 2DH version, according to which both Matthew and

---

52. WATSON, *Gospel Writing* (n. 11), p. 175.
53. *Ibid.* The allusion is to Streeter's criticism in B.H. STREETER, *The Four Gospels: A Study of Origins, Treating of the Manuscript Tradition, Sources, Authorship, and Dates*, London, Macmillan, 1924, p. 183.
54. See also LUCE, *Livy* (n. 29), pp. 142-143; MATTILA, *Question* (n. 2), pp. 206-207; K. OLSON, *Unpicking on the Farrer Theory*, in M. GOODACRE – N. PERRIN (eds.), *Questioning Q: A Multidimensional Critique*, Downers Grove, IL, InterVarsity, 2004, 125-150, p. 133; POIRIER, *The Roll, the Codex, the Wax Tablet* (n. 9), p. 9.
55. See DERRENBACKER, *Ancient Compositional Practices* (n. 2), pp. 54-76, on Arrian, Cassius Dio, and Philostratus.

Luke have used a "notebook" (Q)[56], combining it with Mark in two different ways (apart from the sayings fused with Mk 1,2-6.9-11.12-13). Two pericopae that present difficulties for the FH of course do not discredit the entire hypothesis: each of the hypotheses that vie for credibility has its own difficulties. But at least in the cases of Lk 17,6 and Lk 22,29 the simpler hypothesis would appear to be common and independent use of a pre-Matthaean and pre-Lukan notebook, Q.

University of Toronto John S. KLOPPENBORG
Trinity College/Larkin 311
6 Hoskin Avenue
Toronto ON M5S 1H8
Canada
john.kloppenborg@utoronto.ca

---

56. Ὑπόμνημα in Graeco-Egyptian papryi overwhelmingly means "memorandum" (report, declaration, complaint, petition, birth notice, trial protocol) rather than "notebook". There are, however, many examples of anthologies of sayings, anecdotes, and other materials, some used as school exercises, and others as resources for literary composition: TM 65709 = LDAB 6963: Chares, gnomic anthology, *sententiae* = Heidelberg, Institut für Papyrologie P. G434 (275-225 BCE); TM 131664 = LDAB 131664: Menander, *Sententiae* 467 and 652 = B. KRAMER, *Menandersentenzen auf einem Trierer Papyrus*, in *APF* 57 (2011) 261-266 (I BCE); TM 61304 = LDAB 2446: Menander, gnomic anthology, alphabetic *sententiae* = Wien, Nationalbibliothek G 19999 ab (I CE); TM 63288 = LDAB 4494: P.Oxy. XXXI 2606: anthology of prose citations = Oxford, Sackler Library, Papyrology Rooms, P.Oxy. 2606 (I-II CE); TM 59834 = LDAB 939: P.Oxy. XLV 3214: anthology of women in Euripides, Antiopa, Medea, Protesilaos, and Phoenix (II CE); TM 64097 = LDAB 5315: London, British Library, Add MS 37533: school notebook with conjugation tables, word lists, *gnomai* (III CE); TM 64564 = LDAB 5794: SB XXVI 16458: notebook of medical prescriptions (IV CE); TM 64120 = LDAB 5338: *ZPE* 49 (1982) 43-44: school exercise notebook with teacher's hand and pupil's copy (III CE); TM 64370 = LDAB 5592: schoolboy's notebook (alphabets, metrological exercise) = Paris, Bibliothèque Nationale, Cabinet des Médailles D 2563 (IV-V CE); TM 64976 = LDAB 6217: G. IOANNIDOU, *Catalogue of Greek and Latin Literary Papyri in Berlin: P. Berol. inv. 21101-21299, 21911* (Berliner Klassikertexte, 9), Mainz, von Zabern, 1996: list of words or *gnomai; monostichoi* (VI CE).

THE LANGUAGE OF VIOLENCE IN THE SAYINGS GOSPEL Q
AN INITIAL EXAMINATION

Violent language and imagery play a significant role in the Sayings Gospel Q, particularly when one takes into consideration the limited length of this writing as far as it can be reconstructed through a comparison of parallel passages in Matthew and Luke[1]. Such an observation is by no means a novelty in Q studies. The bulk of the traditional analyses that focused on this aspect of the Sayings Gospel have almost always tended to address this issue by historicizing it and by trying to find the "causes" of such a high degree of linguistic violence in the socio-historical context in which Q was arguably produced[2]. However, such a move – despite its undeniable attractiveness for reasons that would be too long to discuss here – raises other considerable problems.

On the one hand, it is not clear that Galilee (if we accept this geographical location as the place of origin of the Sayings Gospel) was significantly more "violent" in the first century CE than other Mediterranean regions or that it was under the pressure of a "spiral" of violence harsher than, for instance, Egypt or Asia Minor. From an exclusively historical-critical standpoint, this hypothesis suffers from the lack of evidence that characterizes any chronological or geographical segment of the ancient world, forcing one to rely – for this specific case – almost only on Josephus, whose testimony is notoriously ambiguous and problematic. Moreover, the very idea of a "spiral" of violence seems to suggest a teleological framework that should give pause to any historian. Finally (and arguably even more importantly for the purposes of the present discussion), to think that linguistic and cultural aspects of a given text might immediately reflect objective socio-historical conditions has become more and more problematic in the aftermath of the so-called "cultural turn".

---

1. I am happy to offer this essay to celebrate the career of Joseph Verheyden, who acted as a remarkably generous mentor for me when I was a young scholar entering the vast international field of New Testament studies from a very marginal position; it is also a pleasure to offer a study on Q, since Professor Verheyden shaped the study of the Sayings Gospel for my generation.
2. See a classic example of this attitude in R.A. HORSLEY, *Jesus and the Spiral of Violence: Popular Jewish Resistance in Roman Palestine*, San Francisco, CA, Harper & Row, 1987.

In light of these critical observations, it seems wise to address the issue of violent language and imagery in Q from a different perspective. It is worth looking at these phenomena not as features mechanistically produced in Q by the influence of external agents, but as a more or less conscious strategy through which the people who stood behind the composition of the Sayings Gospel advanced their literary interests, ideological stances, and theological programs.

The present treatment has two main goals, serving as initial observation to address the historical and interpretive questions that have just been sketched. At first, I will try to show that the language and imagery of violence occurring in the Sayings Gospel is profoundly (but obviously not exclusively) influenced by the quasi-technical bureaucratic jargon that is detectable also elsewhere and in conjunction with other topics and motifs in Q. Such an observation confirms the strength of those hypotheses that envisage a group or a circle of Galilean sub-elite village scribes as the most likely collectors and framers of the materials that were part of the Sayings Gospel[3].

One of the very few reliable and plentiful sources of information about the cultural interests and social practices of ancient individuals comparable (from a socio-cultural point of view) to those who stood behind Q is papyrological evidence, in particular its documentary components. From this source we know that a prominent task of Egyptian village scribes was the composition and managing of complaints addressed by royal and later imperial subjects to the higher echelons of the administrative machine. These complaints have a very stable formal structure, which remained mostly unchanged throughout the Hellenistic and Roman periods. Such a stable structure was filled out by the scribes using a repertoire of imagery and terminology that was equally formulaic in the ways in which it depicted criminal acts and their consequences. That the same linguistic tendencies are detectable in Q should give pause – as I have hinted already above – to those who are too quick to postulate a context of widespread violence as the environment in which the Sayings Gospel was put together.

The second goal of this contribution is to look more specifically at the ways in which Q deploys the imagery and language of violence. It is

---

3. See W.E. ARNAL, *Jesus and the Village Scribes: Galilean Conflicts and the Setting of Q*, Minneapolis, MN, Fortress, 2001, but also S.E. ROLLENS, *Framing Social Criticism in the Jesus Movement: The Ideological Project in the Sayings Gospel Q* (WUNT, 2.374), Tübingen, Mohr Siebeck, 2014, and G.B. BAZZANA, *Kingdom of Bureaucracy: The Political Theology of Village Scribes in the Sayings Gospel Q* (BETL, 274), Leuven – Paris – Bristol, CT, Peeters, 2015.

clear that the Sayings Gospel does not by any means restrict its use of violent language to those figures or situations that are cast in a negative light by the Q people. On the contrary, it is easy to show that violence is employed to describe both the activities of God and of the human characters who seem to be put on stage to provide a model of behavior for the Q readership. Such an observation could have important consequences for our understanding of Q's articulation of divine and human agencies in the context of the apocalyptic scenario against which one should arguably read the document.

I. THE LEGAL AND FORENSIC LANGUAGE OF VIOLENCE IN Q:
THE CASE OF Q 6,29-30

Before focusing in this section on an example of legal and forensic language in Q, it is worth stating that these occurrences – in Q as well as in Egyptian petitions, complaints, or other documentary genres – should not be taken into consideration as reliable and immediate indicators of an actual social situation. Frequently, in both the fields of papyrology and New Testament studies, evidence such as this has been used to estimate the amount of violence present in Egyptian or Galilean villages at the time when the texts were put into writing[4]. However, as shown by Benjamin Kelly in a recent monograph devoted to the theme of litigation in Roman Egypt[5], the very formulaic character of complaints and other documents of a similar type should invite scholars to change their methodological approach. Instead of being treated as "windows" that can give immediate access to a social "reality", these texts are best used as indicators of the type of social control that the authorities tried to impose on Egyptian society and of the ideological discourses that were deployed to bolster such control. Likewise, it must be judged methodologically dangerous to assume that the presence of violent imagery and phrases in the Sayings Gospel enables modern observers to conclude that Galilean society in the first century was torn apart by unusually sharp and strong conflicts and contrasts[6]. While the latter hypothesis should not be

---

4. A very influential example is D.W. HOBSON, *The Impact of Law in Village Life in Roman Egypt*, in EAD. – B. HALPERN (eds.), *Law, Politics, and Society in the Ancient Mediterranean World*, Sheffield, Sheffield Academic Press, 1993, 193-219.

5. B. KELLY, *Petitions, Litigation, and Social Control in Roman Egypt*, Oxford, OUP, 2011.

6. In recent years, this point has been strongly emphasized by M.H. JENSEN, *Herod Antipas in Galilee: The Literary and Archaeological Sources on the Reign of Herod*

dismissed out of hand and without further analysis, it is doubtful that it might be substantiated merely through an appeal to the presence of violent language in Q. On the contrary, in the following pages the language of the Sayings Gospel will be analyzed as a witness to the administrative discourse characteristic of the Q people and to its deployment of violent imagery and words for specific ideological purposes.

Given the limited space at my disposal here, I will examine in detail only a few sayings (Q 6,29-30), which are however usually considered representative of the use of violent imagery in the Sayings Gospel. These verses belong to the larger cluster Q 6,27-35 whose original order in Q is a matter of hot debate, but whose wording in turn is relatively undisputed. The sayings, coming immediately after the beatitudes, are usually understood as one of the most explicit (and disturbing) instances of the self-renouncing ethos that the Sayings Gospel requires from the followers of Jesus's teaching.

1. *Q 6,29a*

Q 6,29 has been reconstructed by the editors of the *Critical Edition of Q* as follows: "The one who slaps you on the cheek, offer him the other as well; and to the person wanting to take you to court and get your tunic, turn over to him the cloak as well"[7].

As far as the present treatment is concerned, it is worth starting the analysis by focusing on the two main problems entailed in the reconstruction of the most likely Q wording. By looking at Lk 6,29, one finds that the verb τύπτω is employed there to describe the act of "slapping" and that the order of "cloak" and "tunic" is the reverse of the one given above. Beginning with the first issue, one may note that the editors of the *Critical Edition of Q* preferred the verb that appears in Mt 5,39 (ῥαπίζω), but only with a relatively low degree of certainty (C). In this perspective, I think that a moderate case could be mounted in favor of τύπτω and for

---

Antipas and Its Socio-Economic Impact on Galilee (WUNT, 2.215), Tübingen, Mohr Siebeck, 2006. However, Jensen's conclusion that the "causes" behind the Jesus movement would then be only "religious" is equally problematic: see the observations in D.E. OAKMAN, *Jesus and the Peasants* (Matrix, 4), Eugene, OR, Cascade, 2008.

7. [Ὅστις] σε [ῥαπίζει] εἰς τὴν σιαγόνα [], στρέψον [αὐτῷ] καὶ τὴν ἄλλην, καὶ [τῷ θέλοντί σοι κριθῆναι καὶ] τὸν χιτῶνά σου [λαβεῖν, ἄφες αὐτῷ] καὶ τὸ ἱμάτιον, in J.M. ROBINSON – P. HOFFMANN – J.S. KLOPPENBORG (eds.), *The Critical Edition of Q* (Hermeneia Supplements), Philadelphia, PA, Augsburg Fortress, 2000. This Greek text is referred to here only for expediency's sake: this use does not carry any assumption with respect to its critical nature or its validity as a reconstruction of Q and I will offer my own alternative proposals when needed.

understanding the use of ῥαπίζω as the result of Matthean redactional intervention.

It is worth observing that a well-known parallel to the whole of Q 6,29-30 occurs in *Didache* 1.4[8]. The latter carries a form of Q 6,29a (δῷ ῥάπισμα) that looks closer to the Matthean than to the Lukan version. It is debated, however, whether one ought to conclude that *Didache* provides something more than a secondary development on the text of the canonical gospels. Admittedly, this was the position endorsed influentially by Helmut Köster in his seminal study of the "evangelical section" preserved in *Did*. 1.3b–2.1, which Köster considered a redactional addition to the original text of the church manual[9]. However, in more recent times, several scholars have tended to conclude that the gospel "quotations" in *Didache* and thus also verse 1.4 might be considered independent witnesses to the tradition that was included in the canonical writings. Indeed, while *Did*. 1.4 closely resembles Mt 5,39 and even presents the text of Mt 5,41 that is ostensibly absent from Luke, it is worth noting that, as far as Mt 5,40 is concerned, *Didache* omits the Matthean reference to the "judgment" and ends up with a text that is closer to Luke than to Matthew[10]. That being said, John Kloppenborg, in a recent re-examination of the issue, has concluded that *Did*. 1.4 does show knowledge of the Lukan and maybe even Matthean redaction of Q: on these grounds, the so-called "evangelical section" of *Didache* should be considered a creation postdating at the very least the writing of Luke[11]. In sum, given the still uncertain state of the evidence as far as *Didache* is concerned, it is probably safer to leave this parallel aside as it has been done in preparing the *Critical Edition of Q*.

---

8. Ἐάν τις σοι δῷ ῥάπισμα εἰς τὴν δεξιὰν σιαγόνα, στρέψον αὐτῷ καὶ τὴν ἄλλην, καὶ ἔσῃ τέλειος· ἐὰν ἀγγαρεύσῃ σέ τις μίλιον ἕν, ὕπαγε μετ' αὐτοῦ δύο· ἐὰν ἄρῃ τις τὸ ἱμάτιόν σου, δὸς αὐτῷ καὶ τὸν χιτῶνα· ἐὰν λάβῃ τις ἀπὸ σοῦ τὸ σόν, μὴ ἀπαίτει· οὐδὲ γὰρ δύνασαι. The Greek text is taken from B. EHRMAN (ed.), *The Apostolic Fathers* (LCL, 24), Cambridge, MA, Harvard University Press, 2003, vol. 1, pp. 418-419.

9. H. KÖSTER, *Synoptische Überlieferung bei den apostolischen Vätern* (TU, 65), Berlin, Akademie-Verlag, 1957.

10. Thus, one can read conclusions such as "für die ganze Perikope legt sich wieder die Vermutung nahe, dass wir eine der synoptischen Tradition parallele mündliche Überlieferung vor uns haben" (in K. NIEDERWIMMER, *Die Didache* [KAV, 1], Göttingen, Vandenhoeck & Ruprecht, 1989, p. 108), or "the divergences in the Didache from the canonical texts are significant and must be taken seriously as witnesses to an independent tradition" (so H. VAN DE SANDT – D. FLUSSER, in IID., *The Didache: Its Jewish Sources and Its Place in Early Judaism and Christianity* [CRINT, 3/5], Assen, Van Gorcum, 2002, p. 42).

11. J.S. KLOPPENBORG, *Use of the Synoptics or Q in Did. 1:3b–2:1*, in H. VAN DE SANDT (ed.), *Matthew and the Didache: Two Documents from the Same Jewish-Christian Milieu?*, Assen, Van Gorcum, 2005, 105-130.

However, there seem to be other arguments that can be invoked to support the originality of the Lukan τύπτω. First of all, while there is no doubt that the latter verb is a favorite of Luke[12], it is also routinely observed that terms connected to the lexical domain of the Matthean ῥαπίζω are used – to convey the image of slapping someone on the cheek – in a few Septuagint passages, the most important of which is certainly Is 50,6[13]. The latter verse is, from the very beginning of the Christian tradition of interpreting the Jewish scriptures christologically, one of the most important *testimonia* through which the followers of Jesus endeavored to make sense of Jesus's death by comparing it with the sufferings of the "righteous servant" of God announced by Isaiah. In this perspective, it is at the very least reasonable to imagine that Matthew might have modified the τύπτω he read in Q into ῥαπίζω to bring the text of the saying in line with the description of Jesus's sufferings and to present the same Jesus as the ideal embodiment of the virtues of patience and non-retaliation that are highlighted in Mt 5,39[14]. Indeed, Mt 26,67[15] offers a very tantalizing intertextual link that the Matthean redactor himself could have created to advance a specific interpretation of the sayings he collected in the Sermon on the Mount[16].

---

12. It is used 9 times in Luke-Acts, while only twice in Matthew and once in Mark.

13. Τὸν νῶτόν μου δέδωκα εἰς μάστιγας, τὰς δὲ σιαγόνας μου εἰς ῥαπίσματα, τὸ δὲ πρόσωπόν μου οὐκ ἀπέστρεψα ἀπὸ αἰσχύνης ἐμπτυσμάτων ("I have given my back to the flogs and my cheeks to the slaps, and I have not turned my face away from the shame of the spittings").

14. Paul HOFFMANN notes this much following Guelich ("die redaktionelle Rückkoppelung des Verhaltens Jesu in der Passion an die fünfte Antithese ist richtig beobachtet [vgl. auch den 'Widerstandsverzicht' in 26,52f mit 5,39a!]"), in *Tradition und Situation: Studien zur Jesusüberlieferung in der Logienquelle und den synoptischen Evangelien*, Münster, Aschendorff, 1995, p. 11, n. 41, but then inexplicably concludes that this cannot prove the redactional character of Mt 5,39b.

15. Τότε ἐνέπτυσαν εἰς τὸ πρόσωπον αὐτοῦ καὶ ἐκολάφισαν αὐτόν, οἱ δὲ ἐράπισαν ("Then they spat on his face and beat him, while others slapped"); the Matthean version of this verse too contains a significant modification of the original Mk 14,65, which has οἱ ὑπηρέται ῥαπίσμασιν αὐτὸν ἔλαβον ("the assistants beat him with slaps"). Kloppenborg's objection that the Matthean use of the verb would render meaningless the comparison with ῥάπισμα in the Septuagint does not seem too compelling to me, if one considers that Matthew might have needed a verb to substitute the τύπτω he read in Q. In this perspective, it is quite significant that ῥαπίζω occurs only in these two Matthean passages (besides Jn 18,22 and 19,3) in all the New Testament. It is worth noting that Matthew in turn, in the other scene of torture of Jesus, after Pilate's trial, in 27,30, employs the verb τύπτω, probably because there the soldiers beat Jesus with a stick (καὶ ἐμπτύσαντες εἰς αὐτὸν ἔλαβον τὸν κάλαμον καὶ ἔτυπτον εἰς τὴν κεφαλὴν αὐτοῦ, again dependent on Mk 15,19, which reads καὶ ἔτυπτον αὐτοῦ τὴν κεφαλὴν καλάμῳ καὶ ἐνέπτυον αὐτῷ, καὶ τιϑέντες τὰ γόνατα προσεκύνουν αὐτῷ).

16. Ronald A. PIPER too notes this connection and he even seems to dismiss the clearly unlikely idea that Matthew might have modified 26,67 on the basis of 5,39, but he too

An important reason that is usually invoked to exclude τύπτω as the original verb used in Q 6,29 is linked to the fact that most interpreters think that Luke reworked the two verses to have them look like events that may happen during a robbery. Indeed, τύπτω occurs in several Egyptian complaints relating physical aggressions and mostly dating to the Ptolemaic period[17]. Let us look at an instance that might also serve as an introduction to this type of papyrological evidence. P.Gur. 8 is a plea coming from Apollonias, a village in the Arsinoite nome, and dated to August 20th 210 BCE[18].

> (hand 2) (ἔτους) ιβ Ἐπεὶφ ι. ὑπ(όμνημα) Τεῷ βα(σιλικῷ) γρ(αμματεῖ).
> (hand 1) [Ἄ]μωσις κωμογραμματεὺς Ἀπολλωνιάδος Τεῷ χαίρειν.
> [το]ῦ δοθέντος ἡμῖν προσαγγέλματος παρ' Ἡράκωντος τοῦ προεστη-
> [κ]ότο[ς]
> [τ]ῶν Πειθολάου ὑποτέθεικά σοι τὸ ἀντίγραφον ὅπως εἰδῇς.
> (...) ἔρρωσο ιβ Ἐπεὶφ θ.
> [Π]ροσ[ά]γγελμα Ἀμώσει κωμογραμματεῖ κώμης Ἀπολλωνιάδος π[αρὰ]
> [Ἡ]ράκ[ω]ντος τοῦ προεστηκότος τῶν Πειθολάου. ἐπελθόντες [τῆι ...]
> [το]ῦ Ἐ[π]εὶφ ἐπὶ τὸν παράδεισον τοῦ προγεγραμμένου Πειθολάου
> ὄ[ντα]
> περὶ τὴν προγεγραμμένην κώμην Θεόφιλος Δωσιθέου Φιλιστίων [...]
> καὶ Τίμαιος Τελούφιος οἱ τρεῖς Ἰουδαῖοι τῆς ἐπιγονῆς ἐξετρύγησ[αν]
> ἀμ[π]έλους ι καὶ Ὥρου τοῦ φύλακος ἐκδραμόντος ἐπ' αὐτοὺς κακ[ο-
> ποιή-]
> σα[ν]τες αὐτὸν ἔτυπτον εἰς ὃ ἔτυχον μέρος τοῦ σώματος καὶ ἀφεί[λον-]
> το [ἀμ]πελουργικὸν δρέπανον. τυγχάνουσι δὲ οἱ προγεγραμμένοι
> λησ[ταὶ ἐν]
> Κε[ρ]κεοσίρει κατοικοῦντες εἰκάζω δὲ τὰ τετρυγημένα εἰς οἴνου
> με(τρητὰς) ς.
>
> (hand 2) The 12th year, 10th day of the month of Epeiph. Report handed to Teos, the royal scribe.

---

does not do anything with this observation ("The suggestion that Matthew is making a deliberate link with the passion narrative may imply a Matthean change in Matt 26.67 as plausibly as a change here [but cf. *rapisma* in Mark 14.65]", in *The Language of Violence and the Aphoristic Sayings in Q: A Study of Q 6:27-36*, in J.S. KLOPPENBORG (ed.), *Conflict and Invention: Literary, Rhetorical, and Social Studies on the Sayings Gospel Q*, Valley Forge, PA, Trinity Press International, 1995, 53-73, p. 68, n. 12. See also the similarly unconvincing argument of H. FLEDDERMANN, *Q: A Reconstruction and Commentary* (BTS, 1), Leuven – Paris – Dudley, MA, Peeters, 2005, p. 285.

17. Apart from the papyri that will be discussed below, the verb appears in the following documentary texts: P.Col. III 6 (257 BCE); P.Enteux. 80 (242 BCE); SB X 10271 (231 or 206 BCE); P.Köln VI 272 (second half of the III BCE); P.Hels. 2 (195-192 BCE); P.Grenf. I 38 (170 BCE); P.Diosk. 7 (153 BCE); P.Heid. VIII 416 (first half of II BCE); BGU VI 1247 (149-148 BCE); P.Ryl. II 68 (89 BCE); P.Wisc. 33 (II CE); P.Ryl. I 77 (late II CE).

18. The papyrus has been republished as C.Pap.Jud. I 21 and in J.S. KLOPPENBORG, *The Tenants in the Vineyard: Ideology, Economics, and Agrarian Conflict in Jewish Palestine* (WUNT, 195), Tübingen, Mohr Siebeck, 2006, pp. 455-456.

(hand 1) Amosis, the village scribe of Apollonias, greets Teos. Concerning the complaint handed to us by Herakon, the manager of the estates of Pitholaos, I submit to you this copy so that you may be informed. (...) Be well. The 12th year, Epeiph 9th. Complaint handed to Amosis, village scribe of the village of Apollonias, from Herakon, the manager in charge of the estates of Pitholaos. On the (...) of the month of Epeiph, coming into the orchard of the above mentioned Pitholaos, which is in the vicinity of the above mentioned village, Theophilos, son of Dositheos, Philistion, son of (...), and Timaeos, son of Telouphis, the three of them Judeans of the *epigone*[19], stole the grapes from 10 vines and, since the guardian Horos attacked them, they acted criminally and beat him in whatever part of the body they could and took away a pruning-knife for the vine. The above-mentioned bandits happen to be inhabitants of Kerkeosiris and I estimate the value of the stolen grapes at 6 metretas of wine.

This short document reveals several interesting data on the way in which petitions were presented in Ptolemaic Egypt. As one can immediately see, the text is actually written in two different hands and this is not the original complaint that Herakon handed to the village scribe of Apollonias, Amosis. On the contrary, this is a copy of the petition that Amosis himself (or one of the clerks working in his office in the village) prepared so that it could be sent up to his superior, the royal scribe of the Arsinoite nome, Teos. The second hand, which appears in the very first line of the document, is that of Teos (or of one of the clerks working in his office), who acknowledges to have received the communication of Amosis one day after the village scribe had prepared the copy of the original complaint. The papyrus beautifully shows the place occupied by an administrator as the village scribe in the workings of the bureaucratic apparatus. The κωμογραμματεύς had a jurisdiction whose extent is still matter of discussion among papyrologists, but he mostly played a role in passing up petitions[20]. Such a state of

---

19. Ethnic designations accompanied by the specification τῆς ἐπιγονῆς are quite common in the Ptolemaic era and characterize other groups beyond the Judeans (there are plenty of instances for "Persians" and some Greek sub-groups as "Cretans" or "Macedonians"). Quite probably this peculiar use originated in reference to the foreign mercenaries who settled in the Egyptian *chora* after Alexander's conquest and who accordingly enjoyed fiscal privileges. Later on, however, papyrological evidence shows that such designations became blurred (in keeping with the mobility and hybridity of the Egyptian society) and shifted from a primary ethnic meaning to an essentially socio-economic (or "occupational-status") one. On this still obscure issue see K. VANDORPE, *Persian Soldiers and Persians of the Epigone: Social Mobility of Soldiers-Herdsmen in Upper Egypt*, in *APF* 54 (2008) 87-108; C.A. LÀDA, *Who Were Those 'of the Epigone'?*, in *Akten des 21. internationalen Papyrologenkongresses, Berlin, 13.-19.8.1995* (APF, Beiheft 3), Stuttgart, Teubner, 1997, vol. 1, 563-569; J.F. OATES, *The Status Designation Πέρσης τῆς ἐπιγονῆς*, in *Yale Classical Studies* 18 (1963) 1-129.

20. See the discussion in L. CRISCUOLO, *Ricerche sul komogrammateus nell'Egitto tolemaico*, in *Aeg* 58 (1978) 3-101, pp. 83-86.

affairs explains the large number of these documents preserved in archives as that of Menches, the second-century BCE village scribe of Kerkeosiris, and – as far as the present argument is concerned – the rather good familiarity of the Q scribes with this legal terminology.

The petition itself describes a fairly unremarkable event: three men – possibly ethnic Judeans – have stolen grapes from the vineyard of an absentee landowner, Pitholaos. The cultivation of vines and the production of wine was a technically sophisticated and very lucrative activity in antiquity (a state of affairs mirrored in a number of gospel parables), so that commonly vineyards were walled and the produce was protected by guardsmen, as in the present case. The robbery resulted in the beating of the guard, Horos, but (interestingly enough) the petition filed by the manager Herakon requires primarily the apprehension of the thieves and the refunding of the financial loss, which the document estimates at 6 metretas of wine, a significant amount if one considers that the metreta was roughly the equivalent to 175 liters of liquid. This is in keeping with the lack of interest for criminal charges that is often noted – with puzzlement – for petitions and complaints of the Ptolemaic period. One last item worth mentioning is the final designation of the three perpetrators of the crime as λησταί, a word that is frequently employed in literary sources with the meaning of "bandits" or even "pirates". For instance, its repeated occurrence in Josephus's description of the unsettled state of the Land of Israel on the eve of the great revolt of 66 CE has led many to hypothesize the existence of an endemic state of "social unrest" in the region and to an endless critical discussion of the proper evaluation of such "social banditry"[21]. However, in petitions preserved on papyrus, the use of this and other similar phrases should be taken as primarily a rhetorical device employed by the author of the text in order to gain the sympathy of the addressee by casting the opponent in the worst possible light – after all, the theft of the grapes from 10 vines can hardly be qualified as an act of banditry or piracy[22]. The same is true for the amplifications of the lost values, which are very common in this type of documents.

---

21. See now the observations on this point in J.S. KLOPPENBORG, *Unsocial Bandits*, in Z. RODGERS (ed.), *A Wandering Galilean: Essays in Honour of Seán Freyne* (SupplJSJ, 132), Leiden, Brill, 2009, 451-484. For the routine use of terminology belonging to this semantic field in petitions, see B.C. MCGING, *Bandits, Real and Imagined in Greco-Roman Egypt*, in *BASP* 35 (1998) 159-183 (I owe this reference to John Kloppenborg).

22. The same can often apply to the recurring appearances of formulaic terms such as ὕβρις or βία to indicate "violence" in this type of documents. Obviously, this cannot exclude in principle that the events qualified as instances of "violence" were something more than the beating described in P.Gur. 8. For instance, βία occurs in P.Heid. VIII 416 (first half of the II century BCE), in which a witness narrates of an actual battle taking place

The survey of documentary papyri shows that τύπτω could be a very good fit for a Lukan redactional intervention designed to make Q 6,29-30 look like an instance of robbery. Nevertheless, the very same papyrological record tells us also that τύπτω is a verb routinely used to describe robberies in formulaic administrative writing such as complaints and petitions. Since the same exegetes, who ascribe to Luke the redactional goal to portray a robbery, tend also to see the original Q version as steeped in forensic or legal language, it is easy to argue that τύπτω would have worked in both contexts equally well.

2. *Q 6,29b*

The same ambiguity carries over to the second half of Q 6,29, which presents the well-known redaction-critical problem of the order of "cloak" and "tunic" which are in the opposite order in Matthew and Luke. It goes without saying that clothes were valuable items in antiquity much more than in our contemporary industrialized societies, in which their production and replacement has become relatively easy and cheap. On the contrary, it appears that, for Egyptian households, clothes constituted one of the most widespread and treasured forms of property[23]. As a consequence, it is fairly common to see that, when a petitioner lets an official know about a burglary or a robbery, the items that are almost always mentioned are clothes accompanied by an estimate of their value. It will suffice to give here one example, taken from SB VI 9068 [end of the third century BCE[24]], a complaint that comes from Moithymis, a village in the Memphite nome, and that contains an interesting association between a theft of clothes and the use of the verb τύπτω:

Δικαίῳ ἀρχιφυ(λακίτῃ) / Μοιθύμεως παρὰ / Πετοσίριος τοῦ / Θώτεως βασιλικοῦ / γεωργοῦ κώμης / Μοιθύμεως. / Τῇ κε τοῦ Παχὼν / περὶ ὥραν β ὀψέ, / ὄντος μου ἐν τῷ / ἱερῷ εἰσπηδή/σαντές τινες / εἰς τὴν οἰκίαν / μου ἐξέδυσαν / Θανοῦν τὴν / γυναῖκά μου ἱμάτιον / ἄξιον

---

around a barn in a village of the Herakleopolite nome and involving several men armed with sticks and stones.

23. "Kleidungsstücke jedweder Art stellten für das Gros der Bevölkerung im römischen Ägypten erhebliche Werte dar. (…) Die Entlohnung vor allem bei längerfristigen Arbeitsverhältnissen bestand z.T. aus Kleidung. Textilien wurden in Zeiten akuten Geldmangels zu Pfandleihern getragen", according to H.J. DREXHAGE, *Eigentumsdelikte im römischen Ägypten (1.-3. Jh. n. Chr.): Ein Beitrag zur Wirtschaftsgeschichte*, in ANRW 2.10.1 (1988) 952-1004, pp. 978-979. Cf. 2 Tim 4,13: "When you come, bring the cloak that I left with Carpus at Troas".

24. I follow here the dating suggested in BL 11,205, with reference to the discussion of the identity of Dikaios and of the other documents in which he is mentioned by Amphilochios Papathomas in P.Heid. VII 393, p. 45.

(δραχμῶν) σ / καὶ Αὔγχιν[α τ]ὴν / μητέρα αὐτῆς / ἱμάτιον ἄξιον (δραχμῶν) υ / καὶ Θερμουτ[άριον] / τὴν θυγατέρα / ὀθόνιον (δραχμῶν) ρ (γίνονται) (δραχμαὶ) ψ, / ταῖς τε μαχαίραις / ἔτυπτον αὐτὰς / ὥστε καινοπ[αθ-...]

To Dikaios, the chief of police of Moithymis, from Petosiris, son of Thotis, a royal farmer of the village of Moithymis. On the 25th of the month of Pachon, around the second hour of the night, while I was at the temple, some people, having broken into my house, undressed my wife, Thanous, of a tunic worth 200 drachmas, and her mother, Aunchis, of a tunic worth 400 drachmas, and the daughter Thermoutarios of a cloak worth 100 drachmas for a total of 700 drachmas. Moreover, they beat them with swords, so that (...).

The *archiphylakites* was an official whose presence is frequently attested at the village level in the Ptolemaic period. Being the commander of the police (*phylakites*) assigned to the village, the *archiphylakites* works normally in connection and usually in subordination to the village scribe and the komarch. As such, the chief of police often appears in papyrological evidence as the recipient and addressee of petitions as the one quoted here[25]. For the sake of the present argument, it is worth noting the monetary value attached to the stolen clothes by Petosiris. As observed before, the extent of the loss might be increased to serve Petosiris's interests as the victim of this crime, but, even factoring in this specific situation, the value of the stolen goods remains meaningful.

As for the case of τύπτω reviewed above, the mention of various pieces of clothing in Q 6,29b can fit both the description of a case of robbery (Lukan redaction) as well as a series of instructions cast in legal-administrative terminology (possible Q original). Here though, sorting out the relationship between the two versions is made easy by the Matthean reference to a judicial context, which – as widely recognized by exegetes – sits very well with the order tunic-cloak. It seems reasonable to conclude that the Sayings Gospel envisaged a situation in which one should be ready to concede to an opponent in trial even more than the maximum prescribed by the Torah[26]. Such a complex legal imagery has been simplified by Luke, who has reshaped the cluster of sayings into a more easily generalizable scene of a robbery[27].

---

25. For this administrative format, see now G. BAETENS, *A Survey of Petitions and Related Documents from Ptolemaic Egypt* (Trismegistos Online Publications Special Series, 5), Leuven, 2020, p. 199, n. 312.

26. Both Ex 22,25-26 and Dt 24,13 prescribe that a cloak taken as surety on a loan must be given back to the borrower before sunset. A similar attitude occurs in Q also elsewhere, e.g., in Q 12,58-59.

27. "Wegen dieser Generalisierung der Situation wird die Fassung vielfach Lk zugeschrieben" (HOFFMANN, *Tradition* [n. 14], p. 12, but see also PIPER, *Language of Violence* [n. 16], pp. 57-58). The same position in FLEDDERMANN, *Q* (n. 16), p. 286.

3. Mt 5,41

So far, the papyrological examples presented above have shown that the acts of violence evoked in Q 6,29 are described using the formulae and imagery that are common in the bureaucratic writing attested in documentary papyri. This hypothesis can be strengthened if one considers Mt 5,41 as part of the Sayings Gospel[28]. The verse is attested only in the Gospel of Matthew and thus, in principle, there should be no grounds for including it in the Sayings Gospel. However, the editors of the *Critical Edition of Q* have retained Mt 5,41 within their final text, even though the verse is enclosed within brackets signaling a low degree of certainty. Indeed, if one accepts the hypothesis that the Q text is here shaped by the technicalities of administrative language, Mt 5,41 is an exceptionally good candidate to be included in Q even if it is attested only by one witness.

It should suffice to look at the peculiar verb employed in Mt 5,41 (ἀγγαρεύω), which appears quite often in papyrological evidence and in meaningful contexts[29]. The term is of Persian origin and, as attested already by Herodotus, it was employed by the Achaemenid administration to indicate the royal postal service[30]. Early on, the words connected to this domain became part of regular use in Greek and, in the Hellenistic period as witnessed by papyrological evidence, ἀγγαρεύω was routinely used to express the act of requisitioning animals or boats not only for the simple delivery of official correspondence, but also for the all-important transportation of publicly owned grain or of notables travelling through the Egyptian *chora*. It is worth remarking, for the purposes of the present argument, that the terms became part of the technical terminology of royal administration, since they occur almost only in official documents both in the Ptolemaic and the early Roman periods[31].

It is quite probable that these compulsory services were paid, even though it is equally possible that the compensation was fixed at a level

---

28. Καὶ ὅστις σε ἀγγαρεύσει μίλιον ἕν, ὕπαγε μετ' αὐτοῦ δύο ("And the one who conscripts you for one mile, go with him for a second").

29. The present treatment will of course consider the verb (which is sometimes written as ἐγγαρεύω) and the noun connected to it (ἀγγαρεία). See also S.R. LLEWELYN, *New Documents Illustrating Early Christianity*. Vol. 7: *A Review of the Greek Inscriptions and Papyri Published in 1982-83*, Macquarie University, Ancient History Documentary Research Centre, 1994, pp. 58-87, and C. SPICQ, *Notes de lexicographie néo-testamentaire* (OBO, 22), Fribourg/CH, Éditions universitaires, 1982, vol. 1, pp. 31-33.

30. Herodotus, *Hist.* 3.126 and 8.98; the terminology is linked to the Persian empire also by Josephus, *Ant.* 11.203.

31. PSI IV 332 [257 BCE]; P.Cair.Zen. III 59509 [middle III BCE]; P.Petr. II 20 [218 BCE]; P.Köln VII 313 [186 BCE]; PSI XIV 1401 [118 BCE]; P.Tebt. I 5 [118 BCE]; P.Bingen 45 [33 BCE]; SB I 3924 [19 CE]; Chrest.Wilck. 439 [42 CE]; P.Ross.Georg. II 18 [139/140 CE]; P.Berl.Leihg. 2.43 [end of II CE].

largely below the market value. Moreover, as with other works accomplished as service (λειτουργίαι), the very structure of the system left significant spaces for mismanagements and abuses on the part of the local authorities that ultimately regulated the requisitions. Therefore, it cannot be surprising to see that the evolution of the language attached (and not only in modern Greek, but, for instance, in the Italian *angheria* as well) to these terms – and, in particular, to the noun ἀγγαρεία – the sense of the abusive acting of any superior authority over subjects and citizens. Thus, already in the second century BCE, papyrological evidence shows a series of interventions of Egyptian sovereigns striving to introduce some measure of order and regulation in this area. Chiefly, the means chosen for this type of official statements appears to have been the amnesty decree. Since those royal edicts were intended as ideological tools to showcase at best the sovereign's concern for the welfare of the subjects, it stands to reason that this provision as well – designed as it was to limit the burden unlawfully imposed by the administration – appeared in the same context[32]. The most interesting instance occurs in P.Tebt. I 5 [118 BCE], at the lines 178-187 and 252-254:

> Προστετάχασι δὲ μηδὲ τοὺς στρα(τηγοὺς) καὶ τοὺς
> ἄλλους τοὺς πρὸς ταῖς πραγματείαις ἕλκειν
> τινὰς τῶν κατοικούντων ἐν τῆι χώρᾳ
> εἰς λειτουργίας ἰδίας μηδὲ κτήνη αὐτῶν
> ἐγγαρεύειν ἐπί τι τῶν ἰδίων μηδὲ
> ἐπιρίπτειν μόσχους μηδὲ ἱερεῖα τρέφειν
> μηδὲ χῆνας μηδὲ ὄρνιθας μηδὲ οἰνικὰ
> ἢ σιτικὰ γενή(ματα) ἐπιρίπτειν τιμῆς μηδ' εἰς
> ἀνανεώσεις μηδὲ συναναγκάζειν ἔργα
> δωρεὰν συντελεῖν παρευρέσει μηδεμιᾷ. (…)
> Προστετάχασι δὲ μηθένα ἐγγαρεύειν
> πλοῖα κατὰ μηδεμίαν παρευρέσει
> εἰς τὰς ἰδίας χρείας.

[The sovereigns] have ordered that neither the *strategoi* nor any of the other officials force those who inhabit the country to perform private compulsory services and that they do not requisition their animals for private purposes and that they do not force them to feed calves or sacred animals or ducks or birds and that they do not force on them a price for wine or grain and that they do not force them to work for renewals and that they do not require them to perform works without compensation under any pretext. (…)
[The sovereigns] have ordered that no one's boats be requisitioned under any pretext for private necessities.

---

32. On Hellenistic royal amnesty decrees and their ideological significance, see also G.B. BAZZANA, *Basileia and Debt Relief: Forgiveness of Debts in the Lord's Prayer in the Light of Documentary Papyri*, in *CBQ* 73 (2011) 511-525.

The three sovereigns of Egypt, Ptolemy VIII, Cleopatra II, and Cleopatra III, who jointly issued the decree, had the primary political aim of restoring general trust in their government after a long period of internal dynastic dissensions and wars. Apart from the main act of forgiving crimes and remitting debts, one can see that one of the strategic goals is also that of limiting administrative abuses, in particular, in this case, avoiding the possibility that royal officers might derive personal advantages from the requisitioning either of privately owned animals or boats[33].

There is little doubt that the issue also remained contentious and problematic after the end of the Ptolemaic kingdom, since we have a series of edicts and pronouncements dating to the Roman time and addressing the same set of questions. The earliest instance appears in one of the two famous edicts that Germanicus issued during his controversial visit to Egypt in 19 CE[34]:

[Γερμανικὸς Καῖσαρ Σεβαστοῦ]
[υἱός, θεοῦ Σεβαστοῦ υἱωνός],
[ἀνθύπατος λέγει· εἰς τὴν ἐμὴν]
[παρουσίαν νῦν ἤδη ἀκούων]
ἀ[γγα]ρ[είας . . . . . . πλοίων]
καὶ κτηνῶν γείνεσθαι καὶ
ἐπισκηνώσεις καταλαμβά-
νεσθαι ξενίας πρὸς βίαν καὶ

---

33. As always, it is worth noting that this provision – as others contained in P.Tebt. I 5 – can hardly be considered unique or innovative; on the contrary, as happens often in the case of these very formulaic documents, it is clear that very similar clauses were repeated in the edicts periodically promulgated by all Egyptian sovereigns (a fact that, once again, signals the limited amount of control that the central authority could exercise on a bureaucratic structure that was theoretically designed to serve the king or the queen). The fragmentary P.Köln VII 313 [186 BCE], another amnesty decree, contains an almost identical provision limiting the requisitioning of private boats in column B, lines 5-9.

34. SB I 3924, lines 1-30; I take the text from the latest edition in J.H. OLIVER, *Greek Constitutions of Early Roman Emperors from Inscriptions and Papyri*, Philadelphia, PA, American Philosophical Society, 1989, nr. 16. Germanicus's visit to Egypt spurred controversies because the province had been forbidden to Roman political figures of senatorial rank since Augustus's conquest, probably for the fear that someone could establish in the newly acquired land the foundation for a coup against the reigning emperor (a fear proved very well founded by the events following Vespasian's visit to Alexandria in 69 CE). Germanicus was the nephew of Mark Antony and that generated even more awkwardness when he was received in the capital of Egypt as an emperor and a deity: the second edict (SB I 3924, lines 31-45) is the belated attempt to defuse these political tensions by ordering the Alexandrians to reserve such honors and acclamations only for the reigning emperor Tiberius. On this episode, see the narratives in Tacitus, *Ann.* 2.59–61, and Suetonius, *Tib.* 52, as well as the critical discussions in U. WILCKEN, *Zum Germanicus-Papyrus*, in *Hermes* 63 (1928) 48-65; M.P. CHARLESWORTH, *The Refusal of Divine Honours, and Augustan Formula*, in *Papers of the British School at Rome* 15 (1939) 1-10, and D.G. WEINGÄRTNER, *Die Ägyptenreise des Germanicus* (Papyrologische Texte und Abhandlungen, 11), Berlin, Habelt, 1969.

καταπλήσσεσθαι τοὺς ἰδιώτας,
ἀναγκαῖον ἡγησάμην δη-
λῶσαι, ὅτι οὔτε πλοῖον ὑπό τινος
ἢ ὑποζύγιον κατέχεσθαι βού-
λομαι, εἰ μὴ κατὰ τὴν Βαιβίου
τοῦ ἐμοῦ φίλου καὶ γραμματέως
προσταγήν, οὔτε ξενίας καταλαμ-
βάνεσθαι. Ἐὰν γὰρ δέῃ, αὐτὸς Βαίβιος
ἐκ τοῦ ἴσου καὶ δικαίου τὰς ξενίας
διαδώσει. καὶ ὑπὲρ τῶν ἀγγαρευ-
ομένων δὲ πλοίων ἢ ζευγῶν
ἀποδίδοσθαι τοὺς μισθοὺς κατὰ
τὴν ἐμὴν διαγραφὴν κελεύω.
Τοὺς δὲ ἀντιλέγοντας ἐπὶ τὸν
γραμματέα μου ἀνάγεσθαι βού-
λομ[αι, ὅ]ς ἢ αὐτὸς κωλύσει ἀδι-
κεῖσθαι τοὺς ἰδιώτας <ἢ> ἐμοὶ ἀναν-
γελεῖ. τὰ δὲ διὰ τῆς πόλεως διατρέ-
χοντα ὑποζύγια τοὺς ἀπαντῶν-
τας πρὸς βίαν περιαιρεῖσθαι κωλύω.
τοῦτο γὰρ ἤδη ὁμολογουμένης
λῃστείας ἐστὶν ἔργον.

Germanicus Caesar, son of Augustus, grandson of the god Augustus, consul, proclaims: as I hear now that, on the occasion of my visit, requisitions (…) of boats and animals have taken place and that guest-quarters for billeting are occupied illegally and that private citizens are beaten, I thought it necessary to make clear that I do not want that either boats or animals are appropriated by anyone or that any guest-quarter is occupied, unless following an order of Baebius, my friend and scribe[35]. If it will be needed, Baebius himself will assign lodgings with equity and justice. Moreover, I order that prices are paid for requisitioned boats and animals according to my decree and I want that those who oppose this be brought to my scribe, who either will himself forbid to treat the private citizens with injustice or will report to me. I forbid those who encounter beasts of burden moving through the city[36] from taking away their goods illegally, for this is a manifest act of banditry.

Germanicus's edict demonstrates very clearly some of the problems connected with the exceptional circumstances of his visit (παρουσία) to

---

35. For a possible identification of this figure, see M. HEIL, *Baebius und der erste Konsulat des Germanicus*, in *Klio* 77 (1995) 224-231, pp. 227-228.

36. The event presupposed here seems to refute the opinion of those who suggest that Luke omitted Mt 5,41 because a military requisition would have been impossible in a city and then incomprehensible for the mainly urban audience of the Third Gospel ("Lk könnte dieses Beispiel also ausgelassen haben, da es weder in seine städtische Gemeindesituation noch zur thematischen Ausrichtung seiner Bearbeitung passte", in HOFFMANN, *Tradition* [n. 14], p. 13).

the province. In this case, it is reasonable to imagine that, under the cover of the extraordinary requirements generated by the presence of such an important figure, official representatives – and even figures posing as such without legitimate authority – might have overstepped the boundaries of their roles or probably even committed actual crimes. What Germanicus tries to limit by putting everything under the direct supervision of his trusted Baebius are specifically requisitions of animals and boats for the purpose of transportation and of houses for the billeting of the significant number of people that must have travelled together with the designated heir to the imperial throne. The text uses the traditional Ptolemaic terminology (we encounter here both the noun ἀγγαρεία and the verb ἀγγαρεύω) when referring to the requisitions of means of transportation, but also the issue of billeting should be envisaged in precise continuity with pre-Roman times, as abuses and complaints on billeting as well occur repeatedly both in petitions and in the royal declarations that try to regulate it. For the purposes of the current analysis it is important to note that the unlawfulness of the requisition of boats or animals is evidenced at the terminological level by adding that these actions are performed "with violence" (πρὸς βίαν), a phrase that, at this stage, means simply "in violation of the law". We see also an occurrence of the already encountered "banditry" (λῃστεία) to label a behavior that is qualified as outside the boundaries of the acceptable or legal norm.

Quite apart from the extraordinary circumstances of Germanicus's presence in Egypt, it appears that the issue remained alive in the following years too, so much so that it required the regular intervention of provincial prefects acting in substantially the same way and in the same role as the Ptolemaic sovereigns who had previously tried to put order in the matter by means of their amnesty decrees. The earliest surviving instance is an edict promulgated in 42 CE by the prefect Lucius Aemilius Rectus and preserved on the verso of P.Lond. III 1171[37]:

Λεύκιος Αἰμίλλις Ῥῆκτος λέγει·
μηδενὶ ἐξέστω ἐνγαρεύειν τοὺς ἐπὶ τῆς χώρας
μηδὲ ἐφόδια ἢ ἄλλο τι δωρεὰν αἰτεῖν \ἄτερ τοῦ/ {ἄτερ}
ἐμο[ῦ] διπλώματος, λαμ[β]άνειν δὲ ἕκασ[το]ν τῶν
ἐχ[όν]των ἐμὸν δίπλωμα τὰ αὐτάρκη ἐπιτήδεια
τιμὴν ἀποδιδόντας αὐτῶν. ἐὰν δέ τις
μηνυθῇ ἢ τῶν στρατευομένων ἢ τῶν μαχαιροφόρω(ν)
ἢ ὅστις οὖν τῶν ὑπηρετῶν τῶ[ν ἐπὶ τ]αῖς δημοσ[ίαις]

---

37. The papyrus has been republished as ChrWilck 439; see L. MITTEIS – U. WILCKEN, *Grundzüge und Chrestomathie der Papyruskunde*. I. Band, 2. Hälfte: *Chrestomathie*, Leipzig – Berlin, Teubner, 1912; repr. Hildesheim, Olms, 1963, nr. 439.

χρείαις παρ[ὰ τ]ὸ ἐμὸν διάτα[γμ]α [π]εποιηκὼς ἢ βεβιασ-
μένος τινὰ τῶν ἀπὸ τῆς χώρας ἢ ἀργυρολογήσας,
κατὰ τούτου τῇ ἀνωτάτῳ χρήσομαι τιμωρίᾳ.
(ἔτους) β Τιβερίου Κλαυδίου Καίσαρος Σεβαστοῦ Αὐτοκράτορος
Γερμανικείου δ

Lucius Aemilius Rectus proclaims: No one is allowed to requisition those inhabiting the country nor is allowed to require travel provisions or anything else without payment unless in presence of a diploma of mine. In turn, all those who have a diploma of mine will take all the necessary goods by giving the payment for them. If a soldier or a policeman or anyone of the aides to the public officers will be charged with having acted against my order or with having exercised violence against one of the inhabitants of the country or with having extracted money, I will exact on this individual the most shameful punishment. In the second year of Tiberius Claudius Caesar Augustus Imperator Germanicus for the fourth time.

The edict of the prefect addresses the same issues encountered in Germanicus's decree, but with an interesting and much-discussed variant. The verb ἀγγαρεύω (which appears in the papyrus in the alternative spelling ἐνγαρεύω) is used at the very beginning of the document and its direct object is an ambiguous τοὺς ἐπὶ τῆς χώρας. The latter phrase has been the subject of a critical discussion because it might refer to animals requisitioned for transportation or to persons inhabiting the countryside of Egypt and forced to provide their physical labor by representatives of the imperial administration (as in the translation offered above)[38]. The first option is well attested, as we have seen above, for the Ptolemaic period, while the imposition of labor on actual human beings is designated by using the ἀγγαρεία terminology only in later documents, all dating to the Roman era[39].

This discussion might have some importance for the interpretation of Mt 5,41 and of this entire passage of the Sayings Gospel, if indeed the

---

38. See the discussion and the evidence presented in LLEWELYN, in *New Documents Illustrating Early Christianity*, 7 (n. 29), pp. 65-66.

39. Not long after the above-mentioned edict of Lucius Aemilius Rectus, another prefect, Cneus Virgilius Capito had to intervene on the same matter with another decree that has been preserved on an inscription, OGIS 665 (7th December 48 CE). There the prefect forbids illegal requisitions motivated as ἀνγαρεία and then goes on to state (lines 21-25): διὸ κελεύωι τοὺς διοδεύοντας διὰ τῶν νομῶν στρατιώτας καὶ ἱππεῖς καὶ [σ]τάτορας καὶ ἑκατοντάρχας καὶ χειλιάρχους καὶ τοὺς λοιποὺς ἅπαντας μηδὲν λαμβάνειν μηδὲ ἀνγαρεύειν εἰ μήι τινες ἐμὰ διπλώματα ἔχουσιν ("Therefore I order that all the soldiers, cavalrymen, statores, centurions, chiliarchs, and all the others who travel through the nomes do not take anything nor requisition unless they are in possession of my official letters"). The text reminds us that the problem of abuses in this area remained well alive notwithstanding repeated official interventions. Finally, it is worth noting that the prefect Capito attributed a responsibility in the control on these matters to local officials as, for instance, royal scribes, village scribes, and *topogrammateis* (lines 31-32).

verse was originally part of it. The New Testament contains another reference to ἀγγαρεία in Mk 15,21, where a man from Cyrene, Simon, is forced by the Roman soldiers to carry Jesus's cross to Golgotha[40]. There is no doubt that, in Mark's case, the text does not refer to the requisition of animals or boats, but to the forced labor of a man. This would count as an additional source confirming this particular use of the term in the second half of the first century CE, but technically without anticipating the first appearance that one encounters in Rectus's edict of 42 CE. It is, however, difficult to establish whether Mt 5,41 envisaged a case similar to that of Simon (conscription of an individual for direct physical work) or the requisition of privately owned animals for the purpose of transportation. The structure of the verse seems to support the first option, but one must reckon here with the potential metaphorical use of ἀγγαρεία and related terms.

Such uses are routinely exemplified in scholarly literature with reference to a famous passage from Epictetus's *Discourses* that is strikingly similar to Mt 5,41 and that will be mentioned again below. Papyrological evidence shows that metaphorical uses are much older and date back at least to the Ptolemaic time, when authors want to refer in a loose way to work that is compellingly required by a superior in an abusive fashion. An example can be found in P.Cair.Zen. III 59509 (middle of the third century BCE), a letter addressed to Zenon that contains a few lines of complaints for an alleged mistreatment[41]:

[Ζήνω]νι χαίρειν Σομοῆλ[ις φύλ]αξ ἐκ Φιλαδελφείας. κατεσπάρκα-
[μεν τὴ]ν τηνεῖ Ἀμανδε [...] ὑπάρχου\σιν/ οὖν σοι παρ' ἐμοῦ πυ(ροῦ) ἀρτ(άβαι) κ
[εἰς τὸ]ν σπόρον. ἀναφέρω [δέ σοι ταῦ]τα· καὶ μὴ ἀδικηθῶ ὑπὸ Ἐτεάρχου
[μήτε] κατὰ τοῦτο μήτε [κατ' ἄ]λλο μηθέν. ἐπέκλα[σεν γὰρ] μου
[...]ον ἀνγαρεύων δι[ὰ παντός. καλῶς ἂν οὖ]ν [ποιήσαις γρά]ψας
[μοι ἐ]πιστολὴν πρὸς αὐ[τόν, ἵνα] πρόγοιαν ἡ[μ]ῶν ποιῆτα[ι καὶ]
[μὴ] ἀδικώμεθα.

Somoelis, policeman from Philadelphia, greets Zenon. We have sowed the plot of *Amande*[...]. Therefore, I owe you 20 artabas of wheat for the sowing. I enter them into the account and I will not suffer injustice on this matter nor in anything else from Etearchos. For he called upon my [...],

---

40. Καὶ ἀγγαρεύουσιν παράγοντά τινα Σίμωνα Κυρηναῖον ἐρχόμενον ἀπ' ἀγροῦ, τὸν πατέρα Ἀλεξάνδρου καὶ Ῥούφου, ἵνα ἄρῃ τὸν σταυρὸν αὐτοῦ ("And they forced a certain Simon from Cyrene, the father of Alexander and Rufus, who was passing by on his way from the field, so that he may carry his cross"). Matthew – in the parallel verse 27,32 – has retained the verb, while Lk 23,26 has eliminated it (probably in order to minimize, as usual, the participation of the Roman authorities in Jesus's crucifixion).

41. Lines 1-7.

forcing him/it to work in every way. Therefore, you would do well if you were to write me a letter concerning him, so that you might provide for us and we might not suffer injustice.

The message's main contents are business matters, but among them the reader finds a sort of complaint, not in a formal sense (because Zenon does not have any official position), but in its essence, since Zenon is, in the Arsinoite nome, the closest collaborator of Apollonios, the *dioiketes* of all Egypt and therefore one of the most powerful men in the entire kingdom. In the present case, Somoelis asks Zenon for protection from the abusive requests of Etearchos. We do not know anything else about the issue between these two figures, but, as far as the present argument is concerned, it is important to note that Somoelis employs the term ἀγγαρεύω. Knowing whether Etearchos was a public official or not is of little import here, since the abuse for which Somoelis writes to Zenon might have been exactly the fact that Etearchos had required compulsory work without being formally allowed to do so. In relation to the interpretation of Mt 5,41, however, it might be helpful to clarify what is the object of the verb and then of the requisition. Unfortunately, the extreme left margin of the papyrus is badly damaged and the first letters of line 5 that are actually readable are *omicron* and *nu*, most probably the ending of a singular accusative masculine. In 1928, the first editor of the text, C.C. Edgar, proposed two possible conjectures for the lacuna: ὄνος ("ass") and υἱός ("son"). If the first option is taken as correct, then we have another instance of the Ptolemaic ἀγγαρεία, in which animals are requisitioned for the purpose of transportation. If the option "son" is preferred, then we would have an instance of forced labor, which would be quite unique in Ptolemaic Egypt, but might also be justified as a case of metaphorical use. Despite the fact that the verb καλέω does not seem to sit well with the option "ass" and despite the opinions expressed by some scholars[42], it is difficult to choose between the alternatives if one considers the regular use of ἀγγαρεία terminology in the Ptolemaic record.

How can this body of evidence help to establish whether the verse appeared in Q? In order to achieve this goal it is obviously quite important to explain why Luke might have deleted Mt 5,41, given the fact that the verse would fit rather well the administrative and legal uses that we have already seen in Q 6,29. An argument that is often advanced concerns the alleged inability of Luke's original audience – arguably located in an urban context in the Roman provinces of Asia or Greece – to understand the

---

42. Tcherikover, while republishing the papyrus in *CPJ*, 1 (1957), nr. 12, goes for the option "son", stating without further elaboration that this is the only possible one.

reference to a practice, the ἀγγαρεία, which would have been foreign to them. The above-mentioned papyrological evidence, however, shows – I think, compellingly – that the burden of ἀγγαρεία was felt and thus understood also in urban centers and even in provinces as was the case for Egypt, in which no military actions were usually taking place[43]. Moreover, Paul Hoffmann has already drawn attention to the use of the term in Epictetus (*Diatr.* 4.1.79), a passage demonstrating that the word could be used in a topical – metaphorical – way and be perfectly understandable[44]:

> Ὅλον τὸ σῶμα οὕτως ἔχειν σε δεῖ ὡς ὀνάριον ἐπισεσαγμένον, ἐφ' ὅσον ἂν οἷόν τε ᾖ, ἐφ' ὅσον ἂν διδῶται· ἂν δ' ἀγγαρεία ᾖ καὶ στρατιώτης ἐπιλάβηται, ἄφες, μὴ ἀντίτεινε μηδὲ γόγγυζε. εἰ δὲ μή, πληγὰς λαβὼν οὐδὲν ἧττον ἀπολεῖς καὶ τὸ ὀνάριον.
>
> You must keep all your body as a saddled ass, for how long it is possible or for how long it is allowed; if there is a requisition and a soldier takes it, let it go, do not resist and do not murmur. Otherwise, after having received a beating, you are going to lose the ass too.

This observation, however, also seems to undermine Hoffmann's own hypothesis that Luke eliminated Mt 5,41 from Q because it would not have been current any more in his context removed as it was from the harsh Roman domination that, according to Hoffmann, characterized the Land of Israel in the period immediately preceding the first Jewish war. At the very least, it seems clear that, if Epictetus's use of the image demonstrates its understandability, it ought to show its currency as well.

More than 30 years ago, Jürgen Sauer noted that a better explanation for Luke's omission is readily available not in the frankly vague historical context of Q, but in the very content of Mt 5,41. It is indeed well known that the author of Luke-Acts is much concerned with the need to portray the Roman government in a good light and in particular when it comes to its abuses and even persecution of the early Christ groups. Thus, the already mentioned fact that Lk 23,26 erases the ἀγγαρεία from the episode of Simon derives in part from Luke's general redactional strategy of minimizing Roman participation in Jesus's crucifixion. However, the same redactional tendency could have also been behind the case of Mt 5,41 with the additional benefit that, by eliminating the verse, Luke

---

43. While it is true that Egypt saw the presence of two legions (the III Cyrenaica and the XXII Deiotariana) throughout the first century CE, one should also consider that, for instance, the above-mentioned edict of Rufus does not limit the possibility of the ἀγγαρεία to soldiers alone.

44. HOFFMANN, *Tradition* (n. 14), p. 13, n. 51, quoting Dieter Zeller saying that "Lukas ihn weggelassen habe, weil Nötigung zum Mitgehen außerhalb Palästinas unverständlich gewesen sei …, leuchtet angesichts Epiktet, diss IV 1,49 [sic!] nicht ein". Then Hoffmann goes on to distinguish between "Unverständlichkeit" and "Inaktualität".

eliminated also an element that was quite difficult to square with the attempt to remodel the Q passage into the image of a robbery[45].

On these grounds, it is possible to suggest that Mt 5,41 was indeed part of the original form of this passage in the Sayings Gospel, as proposed by the editors of the *Critical Edition of Q*[46]. As stated above, the language and imagery of the saying fit quite well the context of Q 6,29 and would constitute a threefold display of offences or judicial-bureaucratic abuses that are easy to connect to the socio-cultural profile of local administrators in first-century Galilee. Moreover, if accepted as part of Q, the verse would offer a very interesting linguistic peculiarity, as the distance that has to be covered as compulsory service is expressed by using a Latin loanword (μίλιον), which is almost completely absent from Greek literature[47] and even from papyrological evidence for the period preceding the Roman conquest of the eastern Mediterranean. This occurrence would not be unique within the Sayings Gospel, since other similar phenomena have been pointed out in recent times[48]. These features, far from disproving the soundness of the Q hypothesis, underscore the exceptional relevance of the rediscovery of the Sayings Gospel, which enables historians to access one of the few surviving literary products of ancient sub-elites invested by the Romanization of the eastern Mediterranean.

4. *Q 6,30*

The reconstruction of Q 6,30 is far less controversial: the verse says that good moral behavior would be not to refuse to whoever asks and, in particular, not to deny whoever asks for a money loan[49]. Most probably, it contained an occurrence of the verb δανίζω, the *koine* form of the classic

---

45. J. SAUER, *Traditionsgeschichtliche Erwägungen zu den synoptischen und paulinischen Aussagen über Feindesliebe und Wiedervergeltungverzicht*, in ZNW 76 (1985) 1-28, p. 9.

46. See also the arguments deployed by O. ANDREJEVS, *Apocalypticism in the Synoptic Sayings Source* (WUNT, 2.499), Tübingen, Mohr Siebeck, 2019, p. 91, n. 10, against FLEDDERMANN, *Q* (n. 16), pp. 286-287. The verse would also meet the criterion 7a in P. VASSILIADIS, *The Nature and Extent of the Q Document*, in *NT* 20 (1978) 49-73, concerning "Sondergut" belonging to a larger section that has already been assigned to Q on other grounds (I owe this reference to John Kloppenborg).

47. The earliest occurrence of the term is in Strabo, *Geogr.* 7.7.4 (quoting a lost passage from Polybius discussing the equivalence between *milion* and *stadion* in establishing the length of the Via Egnatia), but then one has to wait until Plutarch to find another instance.

48. Marco Frenschkowski has recently drawn attention to the exceptional use of currency designations in Q (as, for instance, for the case of ἀσσάριον – another Latin loanword – in Q 12,6), but see also the remarks on οἰκετεία in BAZZANA, *Bureaucracy* (n. 3), pp. 96-104.

49. Τῷ αἰτοῦντί σε δός, καὶ [ἀπὸ] τ[οῦ δανι<ζομένου>, τὰ] σ[ὰ] μὴ ἀπ[αιτεῖ] ("To the one who asks of you, give; and from the one who borrows do not ask back what is yours").

Greek δανείζω[50]. This verb is regularly used in papyri that carry deeds of loan, which have survived in great number from the entire span of the Greco-Roman period.

In particular, the presence of this verse within the cluster Q 6,29+ Mt 5,41+Q 6,30 shows that these moral instructions can scarcely be connected with the lifestyle of early Christian "wandering radicals"[51]. The mention of the possibility of lending money makes much more sense for a group of village sub-elite than for itinerants renouncing all kin and economic ties[52]. The above-mentioned uncertainty about whether the ἀγγαρεία in Mt 5,41 concerns the requisition of animals for transportation or more direct compulsory work might have a certain bearing on the solution of this issue as well. If one takes the verse as a reference to forced labor (as in some of the Roman documents reviewed above and in the Markan verse mentioning Simon of Cyrene), the addition of Mt 5,41 to the cluster of sayings does not change much in the overall sense of the text, as it is shaped by Q 6,29. On the other hand, if Mt 5,41 envisages the requisition of animals for transportation, then it might be concluded that the verse envisages an audience of relatively propertied people, even if the extent of the envisaged possessions is limited to the ownership of an ox or a donkey.

The cluster of sayings is often taken as evidence of a particularly tense and violent climate that would have characterized the Galilean region – and, more in general, the entire Land of Israel – in the central decades of the first century CE. A chief example of this interpretive approach is Hoffmann's exegesis, in which the refusal of resistance to offences and abuses becomes a mirror of the Q people's disassociation from the military initiatives of

---

50. That Luke read δανίζω at this point in Q is demonstrated by the reappearance of the theme in the surely redactional 6,33-34, while the elimination from Lk 6,30 is consistent with the usual Lukan interest in transforming the Q passage into a scene of robbery (see HOFFMANN, *Tradition* [n. 14], pp. 14-15; SAUER, *Feindesliebe* [n. 45], p. 13; PIPER, *Language of Violence* [n. 16], p. 59).

51. The connection between this section of Q and the hypothetical wandering radicals was originally advanced by G. THEISSEN, *Gewaltverzicht und Feindesliebe (Mt 5,38-48/Lk 6,27-38) und deren sozialgeschichtlicher Hintergrund*, in ID., *Studien zur Soziologie des Urchristentums* (WUNT, 19), Tübingen, Mohr Siebeck, 1983, 160-197, but has been more recently revived, for instance, in M. EBNER, *Feindesliebe – ein Ratschlag zum Überleben? Sozial- und Religionsgeschichtliche Überlegungen zu Mt 5,38-47 par Lk 6,27-35*, in J.M. ASGEIRSSON – K. DE TROYER – M.W. MEYER (eds.), *From Quest to Q: Festschrift James M. Robinson* (BETL, 146), Leuven, LUP – Peeters, 2000, 119-142.

52. Other features of Q ethical instruction fit better this background than that proposed by Theissen: on the saying about "measuring out" in Q 6,38, see the insightful considerations of J.S. KLOPPENBORG, *Agrarian Discourse and the Sayings of Jesus: 'Measure for Measure' in Gospel Traditions and Agricultural Practices*, in B.W. LONGENECKER – K.D. LIEBENGOOD (eds.), *Engaging Economics: New Testament Scenarios and Early Christian Reception*, Grand Rapids, MI, Eerdmans, 2009, 104-127.

the zealots against Rome. We have already seen above – with reference to the discussions concerning Mt 5,41 – that such an approach yields at best contradictory results. In particular, since the cluster Q 6,29+Mt 5,41+ Q 6,30 followed immediately in Q after the last macarism of Q 6,23, it is often suggested that our sayings ought to be taken as concrete exemplifications of the motif of persecution mentioned in the last beatitude. However, the very structure of the cluster of sayings renders extremely problematic the "jump" from these brief fictional snippets to actual historical events. Already Jürgen Sauer noted that the order in which the sayings were organized in Q sketches a trajectory stretching from the very physical attack portrayed in Q 6,29a to the much less directly threatening invitation to give away one's own money to borrowers in Q 6,30b[53]. Others have repeatedly observed that this anti-climactic form of rhetorical argumentation might be considered typical of the Sayings Gospel[54]. Hence, it seems reasonable to conclude that the author(s) of Q liked to start a rhetorical pitch by calling on extreme and probably fictional instances, so that their conclusion might be a strengthened return to the more ordinary circumstances to which the entirety of the argument is directed. In the case of our cluster the reasoning begins with extreme instances of aggression and bureaucratic abuse, but then returns to the theme of releasing debts, a beloved and more realistic topic within the Sayings Gospel[55].

II. CONCLUSIONS

The preceding discussion has demonstrated – by way of a close examination of the cluster Q 6,29-30 – that much of the violent imagery and language occurring in the Sayings Gospel is linked to the representation of violent acts and behaviors in administrative and legal documents. This is not a surprising conclusion given that in all likelihood the authorship of Q should be posited within circles of Galilean village scribes. On the basis of these observations, it is worth repeating that the occurrence of violent

---

53. "Durch seinen Inhalt und seine betonte Schlußstellung mildert er [6:30] die Härte der vorangehenden Forderungen", in SAUER, *Feindesliebe* (n. 45), p. 15.
54. For a similar analysis of the beatitudes in Q, see ARNAL, *Jesus* (n. 3), pp. 136-145.
55. The ethical assumptions behind the larger Q section discussed here and its anticlimactic rhetorical structure are convincingly explained by A. KIRK, *Love Your Enemies, the Golden Rule, and Ancient Reciprocity (Luke 6:27-35)*, in *JBL* 122 (2003) 667-686; Kirk's explanation is much more plausible than the frankly fantastic image of debtors stripped naked and marching down the roads of their village with their friends and neighbors, now conscientized and joining them in "a victory parade" (so W. WINK, *Neither Passivity Nor Violence: Jesus' Third Way*, in D.J. LULL [ed.], *Society of Biblical Literature 1988 Seminar Papers* [SBLSP, 27], Atlanta, GA, Scholars, 1989, 210-224, p. 215).

language can scarcely reflect an immediate situation of social tensions or outright conflict in Galilee in the central decades of the first century CE. On the contrary, the use of violent imagery is the product of the literary and ideological imagination of the Q people and, as such, should be more profitably investigated by trying to understand what kind of agenda these sub-elite intellectuals were trying to advance by having recourse to it.

It seems that traditional examinations of violent imagery in the Sayings Gospel have more or less consistently tried to distance the Q people from the use of this very language. Thus, violent or abusive behaviors are usually ascribed only to characters that are portrayed as external to the Q people, as is the case for the above-discussed Q 6,29-30, in which one encounters actions that the Jesus followers are invited to suffer, but certainly not to perform on their own. Likewise, divine activities in Q should never be characterized in violent terms, but always cast in ways that might appear more positive, at least to the eyes of modern-day readers.

Unfortunately, such exegetical strategies cannot be supported through sound analysis of the text of the Sayings Gospel. In particular, several parables included in the Sayings Gospel show that violent and even sometimes morally objectionable behavior is attributed to figures that are almost impossible not to identify with God, as in the cases of the terrible punishment reserved for the untrustworthy slave in Q 12,46 or of the terrifying course of action taken by the master in the parable of the entrusted money[56]. Recently, John Kloppenborg has employed papyrological materials describing episodes of theft to illustrate that the same holds true for the parable of the thief (Q 12,39-40) with its dramatic and unsettling overtones[57].

In conclusion, this initial analysis opens new perspectives that call for further inquiry into the Q materials both in their socio-political configurations (in regard to the influence of royal ideologies as well as conceptions of slavery) and in their understanding of the complex interplay between divine and human agencies.

Harvard Divinity School   Giovanni B. BAZZANA
Divinity Hall 219
14 Divinity Avenue
02138 Cambridge, MA
USA
gbazzana@hds.harvard.edu

---

56. On these two texts in the context of Q, see now D.T. ROTH, *The Parables in Q* (LNTS, 582), London, T&T Clark, 2018, pp. 88-127.
57. J.S. KLOPPENBORG, *The Parable of the Burglar in Q: Insights from Papyrology*, in D.T. ROTH – R. ZIMMERMANN – M. LABAHN (eds.), *Metaphor, Narrative, and Parables in Q* (WUNT, 315), Tübingen, Mohr Siebeck, 2014, 287-306.

ARE THERE ANY MATTHEAN WESTERN NON-INTERPOLATIONS?

I. INTRODUCTION

In the second volume of their *The New Testament in the Original Greek*, Westcott and Hort coined the term "Western non-interpolations"[1]. This obviously cumbersome phraseology avoided, at least in part, speaking of the Alexandrian text as being interpolated at certain points. Westcott and Hort proposed the existence of a neutral text. According to their reasoning, this neutral text was in a relatively pristine state prior to later accretions and interpolations. Among the surviving manuscripts, those deemed as Alexandrian in character were viewed as best preserving the neutral text. Among the Alexandrian manuscripts, the primary witnesses were the great fourth-century codices, Sinaiticus (ℵ 01) and Vaticanus (B 03). Based upon the manuscripts known in their day, Westcott and Hort made the following assessment of the textual quality of Codex Sinaiticus and Codex Vaticanus respectively: "Of the two oldest MSS, ℵ is Pre-Syrian and largely neutral, but with considerable Western and Alexandrian elements, B is Pre-Syrian and almost wholly neutral, but with a limited Western element in the Pauline Epistles"[2]. Here Westcott and Hort used the term Syrian to denote what is now known as the Byzantine or Majority Text. By contrast, in relation to the so-called Western text, Westcott and Hort made the following observation.

> When Western readings generally are confronted with their ancient rivals in order to obtain a broad view of relations between the texts, it would be difficult for any textual critic to doubt that the Western not merely is a less pure text, but also owes most of its differences to a perilous confusion

---

1. B.F. WESTCOTT – F.J.A. HORT (eds.), *The New Testament in the Original Greek*, vol. 2, Cambridge – London – New York, Macmillan and Co., 1892, §§240-242, pp. 175-177. While the exact term "Western non-interpolation" is not used in the first volume containing the Greek text of the New Testament, Westcott and Hort come close to this terminology. They note cases of "[a] few very early interpolations in the Gospels, omitted by 'Western' documents alone (Luke xxii 19 f.; xxiv 3, 6, 12, 36, 40, 51, 52), or by 'Western' and 'Syrian' documents alone (Matt. xxvii 49), are inserted within double brackets ⟦ ⟧ in the body of the text". ID. (eds.), *The New Testament in the Original Greek*, vol. 1, Cambridge – London – New York, Macmillan and Co., 1890, p. 565.

2. WESTCOTT – HORT (eds.), *The New Testament in the Original Greek*, vol. 1 (n. 1), p. 551.

between transcription and reproduction, and even between the preservation of a record and its supposed improvement[3].

Thus, with the florid language of "perilous confusion", Westcott and Hort characterised the Western text as little more than a reckless paraphrase, and later they commented that those responsible for its formation had exercised a "dangerous type of license"[4]. For them, the Western text had been heavily polluted through expansionistic tendencies that resulted in wholesale deviations from the neutral text that they cherished and sought to reconstruct. This neutral text was seen as being most accessible through the early Alexandrian manuscripts that reproduced the neutral text most closely, but not perfectly. Unfortunately for their overall theory, there remained some contradictory evidence in the form of a small set of readings in the primary witness to the Western text of the gospels, Codex Bezae D 05, where shorter or non-expanded readings occurred. Westcott and Hort considered these readings to preserve the text of the earlier neutral text.

The implication was obvious, but somewhat troubling for their overall theory. The text form preserved in the chief Alexandrian manuscripts Codex Sinaiticus and Codex Vaticanus was not quite as "neutral" as Westcott and Hort might have wished. Instead of speaking of places where the Alexandrian text was interpolated, they chose instead to speak of places where the Western text was not interpolated, and thus emerged the cumbersome yet more palatable circumlocution of Western non-interpolations.

These Western non-interpolations were identified as a set of readings in the gospels where the Western text, primarily represented by Codex Bezae, preserved a shorter reading than the so-called neutral form of the text represented chiefly by Codex Vaticanus and Codex Sinaiticus. In this regard, Westcott and Hort identified twenty-seven variant readings where the Western text preserved the shorter reading in comparison with various other manuscripts. Under the influence of the dictum "the shorter reading is to be preferred", Westcott and Hort regarded these readings as having a greater claim to originality. The conceptual challenge for their theory was that the Alexandrian text, considered the best representative of the putative neutral text, was regarded as being the text form that most closely approximated the original text. By contrast, the Western text was an expansionistic and editorializing later form of the text, which moreover in places demonstrated notable theological tendencies. Therefore, the contrary idea that at places the Western text might preserve readings

---

3. *Ibid.*, p. 548.
4. *Ibid.*

that were earlier and thus closer to the neutral text than the Alexandrian was a challenge to their overall theory. While affirming the originality of these readings, Westcott and Hort saw them as aberrations from the more widespread expansionistic tendency of the Western text. Hence, they stated, "[t]o one small and peculiar class of Western readings, exclusively omissions, we shall ourselves have to call attention as having exceptional claims to adoption"[5]. Consequently, the larger theory was modified by formulating the hypothesis that the Alexandrian text was itself an edited text and in a few places contained expanded readings. Therefore, they accepted the originality of these Western non-interpolations, even though they were a proverbial "fly in the ointment" to the larger theory.

Among the twenty-seven shorter readings in Codex Bezae that were listed in this category, Westcott and Hort regarded nine of these as major Western non-interpolations. Of these nine, eight are found in the last three chapters of the Gospel of Luke (one in chapter 22 and seven in chapter 24). The remaining major Western non-interpolation they identified was located in the Gospel of Matthew, Mt 27,49. Of the remaining eighteen minor Western non-interpolations, six are in Matthew, three in Mark, seven in Luke, and two in John. The purpose of this study is to provide a focused consideration of the seven Matthean Western non-interpolations (one major, and six minor). These will be assessed individually. Then the results of those individual analyses will be brought together to assess the value of the theory of Western non-interpolations in relation to the Gospel of Matthew.

II. THE MAJOR MATTHEAN WESTERN NON-INTERPOLATION (MT 27,49)

At the broadest level, the textual variants found in the surviving manuscripts containing Mt 27,49 can be classified into two groups. On the one hand, there are those manuscripts that preserve the shorter reading. Based upon the misunderstanding that Jesus was calling for Elijah, this reading describes the mockery of the crowd's suggestion that they wait to see if Elijah comes to the rescue. On the other hand, a second group of manuscripts preserves a longer reading. That extended reading continues the verse with an additional narrative detail. It describes a further person taking a lance and piercing Jesus' side. This results in the effluxion of water and blood.

---

5. WESTCOTT – HORT (eds.), *The New Testament in the Original Greek*, vol. 2 (n. 1), §170, p. 121.

In the twenty-eighth edition of the Nestle-Aland Greek New Testament (NA[28]), the shorter reading is adopted as the base text as presented below. For convenience, this is placed in parallel with an English translation.

Mt 27,49 NA[28] Greek text	Mt 27,49
οἱ δὲ λοιποὶ ἔλεγον· ἄφες ἴδωμεν εἰ ἔρχεται Ἡλίας σώσων αὐτόν.	But the rest were saying, "Wait, let us see if Elijah comes to save him".

Westcott and Hort considered this example to be unusual among those readings that they classed as the major Western non-interpolations in two respects. First, it is the only major Western non-interpolation not found in Luke 22–24; and secondly, the shorter text also has support in the Byzantine text form (which they call the Syrian). Thus, they state, "[w]ith a singular peculiar exception (Matt. xxvii 49), in which the extraneous words are omitted by the Syrian as well as the Western text, the Western non-interpolations are confined to the last three chapters of St Luke"[6].

The NA[28] edition lists the following manuscripts as attesting the short form of the text: A D K W Δ Θ ƒ[1.13] 33 565 579 700 892 1241 1424 *l*844 𝔐 lat sy sa bo. Here the text printed in the NA[28] agrees with the Byzantine text form printed in the Robinson-Pierpont edition of the Greek New Testament[7]. By contrast, the longer form of the text is preserved in fewer manuscripts. Again, the longer form is presented in Greek with a parallel English translation.

Mt 27,49 Greek text longer form	Mt 27,49
οἱ δὲ λοιποὶ ἔλεγον· ἄφες ἴδωμεν εἰ ἔρχεται Ἡλίας σώσων αὐτόν. ἄλλος δὲ λαβὼν λόγχην ἔνυξεν αὐτοῦ τὴν πλευρὰν καὶ ἐξῆλθεν ὕδωρ καὶ αἷμα.	But the rest were saying, "Wait, let us see if Elijah comes to save him". But another taking a spear pierced his side and water and blood came out.

Again, according to the NA[28] apparatus, the manuscripts listed as attesting the longer reading are: ℵ B C L Γ vg[mss] mae. Strikingly, the first two witnesses listed, Codex Sinaiticus (ℵ 01) and Codex Vaticanus (B 03), are the two earliest manuscripts that are extant for this verse, both typically being dated to the fourth century. Moreover, the palimpsest majuscule C, Codex Ephraemi Rescriptus (C 04), is also relatively early being typically dated to the fifth century. The origin of the longer reading is no

---

6. *Ibid.*, §240, p. 175.
7. M.A. ROBINSON – W.G. PIERPONT (eds.), *The New Testament in the Original Greek: Byzantine Textform*, 2nd ed., Southborough, MA, Chilton Book Publishing, 2005, p. 98.

later than the earliest manuscripts that attest the shorter reading, which are Codex Alexandrinus (A 02) and Codex Bezae Cantabrigiensis (D 05). None of the extant papyri of the Gospel of Matthew preserves any portion of Mt 27,49. Therefore, the two manuscripts which are both the earliest surviving witnesses to Mt 27,49 and the earliest surviving witnesses to the complete text of the Gospel of Matthew, ℵ and B, and which are in general considered the best witnesses to the early text of the Gospel of Matthew, preserve the longer reading of Mt 27,49. However, despite the age of these witnesses, the assessment of their general superiority in preserving the text of the First Gospel, and the additional supporting witnesses C L Γ vg[mss] mae, the reading they preserve is widely rejected as a later expansion.

There are perhaps two principal reasons for rejecting the authenticity of the longer reading. The first is that the material in the second part of the longer text of Mt 27,49 has a close parallel with a tradition contained in Jn 19,34. The parallel between Mt 27,49 and Jn 19,34 is presented below. Alongside the noticeable similarities, the differences between the two traditions should also be noted.

Mt 27,49 Greek text longer form	Jn 19,34
οἱ δὲ λοιποὶ ἔλεγον· ἄφες ἴδωμεν εἰ ἔρχεται Ἠλίας σώσων αὐτόν. ἄλλος δὲ λαβὼν λόγχην ἔνυξεν αὐτοῦ τὴν πλευρὰν καὶ ἐξῆλθεν ὕδωρ καὶ αἷμα.	ἀλλ' εἷς τῶν στρατιωτῶν λόγχῃ αὐτοῦ τὴν πλευρὰν ἔνυξεν, καὶ ἐξῆλθεν εὐθὺς αἷμα καὶ ὕδωρ.
But the rest were saying, "Wait, let us see if Elijah comes to save him". But another taking a spear pierced his side and water and blood came out.	But one of the soldiers with a spear pierced his side, and immediately blood and water came out.

The longer reading is typically explained as being the result of the addition of the material found in Jn 19,34 being attached to Mt 27,49 due to a harmonistic tendency. Thus, Metzger states, "Although attested by ℵ B C L al the words ἄλλος δὲ λαβὼν λόγχην ἔνυξεν αὐτοῦ τὴν πλευράν, καὶ ἐξῆλθεν ὕδωρ καὶ αἷμα must be regarded as an early intrusion derived from a similar account in Jn 19.34"[8]. Metzger goes even further and offers an explanation of the possible process by which the material from Jn 19,34 worked its way into the Matthean text: "It is probable that the Johannine passage was written by some reader in the margin of Matthew

---

8. B.M. METZGER (ed.), *A Textual Commentary on the Greek New Testament*, 2nd ed., 2nd printing, Stuttgart – New York, Deutsche Bibelgesellschaft – United Bible Societies, 1998, p. 59.

from memory (there are several minor differences, such as the sequence of "water and blood"), and a later copyist awkwardly introduced it into the text"[9]. Metzger's description of this process as "probable" is perhaps too strong. It is, however, a possible explanation of the mechanism by which additional material became embedded in the Matthean narrative.

The majority of commentators likewise consider the longer reading to be later and due to the addition of material drawn from the Fourth Gospel. Luz sees this variant as reflecting the same tendency as exhibited in Mt 27,35. Consequently, he describes the longer reading in Mt 27,49 as "a witness for the early need of the churches to harmonize the texts of the Gospels especially in the account of Jesus' death"[10]. In the same vein and drawing on Metzger's suggestion, Nolland also sees the longer reading as due to the assimilation of Johannine material: "Though occasionally defended as original, this reading is widely recognised, despite its strong attestation, to be an intrusion of Johannine material, probably representing the early insertion of a marginal note"[11].

However, to varying degrees there are dissenting voices. With caution and due qualification, Davies and Allison make the following statement.

> ℵ B C L Γ 1010 *pc* vg[mss] mae add: "Another taking a lance stabbed his side and out came water and blood". This is customarily regarded as an interpolation from Jn 19.34. But in John the thrust follows the death cry, and inclusion would make Jesus scream because of the lance, a potential stumbling-block. We are almost moved to think the line original[12].

This does slightly appear to be wanting to have it both ways. Taken at face-value, Davies and Allison reject the longer reading. However, they make clear that they wavered in their decision-making process. By contrast, Comfort provides a strong statement in favour of the originality of the longer reading in Mt 27,49. He states that the longer reading should not be rejected and he brings together four reasons why it should be accepted as the authentic form of the Matthean text.

> However, the variant cannot be easily dismissed, for the following reasons: (1) The manuscript evidence for its inclusion is strong; indeed, the testimony of ℵ B C has far more often refuted that of A D W than vice versa in the

---

9. *Ibid.*, p. 59.
10. U. Luz, *Matthew 21–28* (Hermeneia), Minneapolis, MN, Fortress, 2005, pp. 541-542, n. 5.
11. J. Nolland, *The Gospel of Matthew* (NIGTC), Grand Rapids, MI, Eerdmans, 2005, p. 1201.
12. W.D. Davies – D.C. Allison, Jr., *A Critical and Exegetical Commentary on the Gospel according to Saint Matthew.* Vol. 3: *Commentary on Matthew XIX–XXVIII* (ICC), Edinburgh, T&T Clark, 1997, p. 627, n. 81.

NU text – why not here? The scribes of B (especially) and ℵ usually refrained from being gospel harmonists. (2) If it was taken from John 19:34, why was it not taken verbatim? As it is, the order of the last words in Matthew is "water and blood", whereas in John it is "blood and water", and there are four other words used in Matthew that do not appear in John (αλλος δε λαβων and εξηλθεν). (3) The reason scribes would want to delete it from the text is because the spearing (according to John) happened after Jesus' death, whereas here it occurs just before his death (see 27:50). Thus, the deletion was made in the interest of avoiding a discrepancy among the Gospels. Such harmonization was done full-scale in manuscripts like A D W. (4) Another reason for scribes to delete it is that it appears to present a jarring contradiction to what was just described: While many of the bystanders were waiting to see if Elijah would come and save Jesus, a Roman soldier (in complete opposition to this sentiment) lances Jesus with his spear. Therefore, the longer text should not be easily dismissed because, in fact, it is the harder reading and has excellent documentary support[13].

Without doubt Comfort has assembled the strongest reasons that have been brought forward in favour of the authenticity of the longer reading, and he has stated these reasons with particular clarity. However, there have also been rebuttals of each of these suggestions. In relation to the first reason, as Luz shows, there is another harmonistic reading from the Gospel of John in the immediate context with the longer reading of Mt 27,35 apparently incorporating material from Jn 19,24. As to the second reason, if the addition were made some time in the second or third century, then the water and the blood would have obvious echoes with baptism and eucharist. The change in order may be intended to reflect the usual order in which a person experienced these rites – baptism prior to receiving the eucharist. The third and fourth reasons are related. The obvious way to cope with these perceived problems would have been to move the tradition of the spear thrust to a slightly later point in the Matthean text[14]. Deletion was an unnecessary solution.

The second reason for adopting the shorter reading as the earlier form of the text is due to the decision to class the longer reading as a Western non-interpolation. That is, it is seen as one of the few places where the generally superior text preserved in the primary Alexandrian manuscripts

---

13. P.W. COMFORT, *New Testament Text and Translation Commentary: Commentary on the Variant Readings of the Ancient New Testament Manuscripts and How They Relate to the Major English Translations*, Carol Stream, IL, Tyndale House Publishers, 2008, p. 87.

14. This is also suggested by Metzger: "It might be thought that the words were omitted because they represent the piercing as preceding Jesus' death, whereas John makes it follow; but that difference would have only been a reason for moving the passage to a later position (perhaps at the close of ver. 50 or 54 or 56), or else there would have been some tampering with the passage in John, which is not the case". METZGER (ed.), *A Textual Commentary on the Greek New Testament* (n. 8), p. 59.

such and Vaticanus and Sinaiticus has been corrupted with a later expansionist text resulting in this case from harmonistic tendencies. Typically, this factor is not stated explicitly when commentators discuss the textual variants in Mt 27,49. However, the influence of Westcott and Hort's classification of the shorter reading as a Western non-interpolation has certainly exerted a "gravitational pull" on the discussion, and led to a weight of opinion that sees the longer reading as a harmonistic adaptation influenced by the Johannine tradition. Discussing the wider phenomenon of Western non-interpolations especially in regard to the seven major examples found in Luke 24, Martin makes the following observation that also contains a reference to Mt 27,49. He states, "[t]hree of these seven have some kind of relationship – most agree a literary relationship – to the end of the Fourth Gospel, as does the one non-Lukan reading, Matt 27:49b"[15]. Ehrman goes further than most scholars in suggesting that the incorporation of the longer reading into the text of Matthew was not motivated by mere harmonistic tendencies. He sees this as another piece of evidence supporting his larger thesis of the orthodox corruption of key New Testament texts. In particular, Mt 27,49b is regarded as a tradition incorporated from the Fourth Gospel to rebut docetic christological perspectives. Thus, Ehrman writes,

> The point should be clear that orthodox Christians found the Johannine tradition of Jesus' pierced side and the subsequent issuance of water and blood to be of some use in their debates with docetists. Moreover, when the tradition occurs *before* Jesus' death (as in Matthew) rather than *after* it (as in John), it suggests that Jesus really did suffer and shed blood while living, that his was a real body that bled, that his was a real and tangible death. In short, the change was not merely a harmonization but an orthodox corruption[16].

Ehrman discusses the theory of Western non-interpolations elsewhere in an excursus in his argument[17]. Ehrman draws attention to Hort's theory of Western non-interpolations that by the second century, when debates with docetists were live, the text had already split into a Western stream typically characterised by uncontrolled transcription and an early form of the Egyptian or Alexandrian text. This early form of the Alexandrian text, represented in third-century manuscripts such as $\mathfrak{P}^{75}$, was more controlled and better represented the so-called neutral text. However, it was not

---

15. M.W. MARTIN, *Defending the "Western Non-Interpolations": The Case for An Anti-Separationist Tendenz in the Longer Alexandrian Readings*, in *JBL* 124 (2005) 269-294, p. 273.
16. B.D. EHRMAN, *The Orthodox Corruption of Scripture: The Effect of Early Christological Controversies on the Text of the New Testament*, New York – Oxford, OUP, 1993, p. 195.
17. *Ibid.*, pp. 223-227.

entirely free of expansions and changes such as the harmonisation that is found in Mt 27,49b. Therefore, the shorter form of the text does in all probability represent the earliest recoverable form of the text.

This shorter form of Mt 27,49b of the text is one of the rare examples where the neutral (or earliest recoverable text) is better preserved in Codex Bezae than in the generally superior manuscripts Codex Sinaiticus and Codex Vaticanus. Whether this shorter reading should be labelled as a Western non-interpolation is debatable, and in the end relates in part at least to the definition of that term. Because the shorter form of Mt 27,49b is also preserved in the vast majority of Byzantine manuscripts it cannot be classed as an exclusively Western reading. However, it is precisely the combination of Western and Byzantine witnesses that makes the case for the shorter reading compelling, along with the reasons that can be adduced for motivating the longer harmonistic reading. So it might be more accurate to label this as a Byzantine-Western non-interpolation. Or to rid the discussion of such circumlocutions, it is a place where the Byzantine and Western texts preserve the earliest reading, and where the Alexandrian texts have been interpolated for theological reasons.

III. THE SIX MINOR MATTHEAN WESTERN NON-INTERPOLATIONS

Often comprising the omission of a short phrase or occasionally a whole verse, the minor Western interpolations are textual variants where Codex Bezae in combination with other witnesses preserves a shorter reading than the Alexandrian witnesses. Westcott and Hort describe these as "an intermediate class of Western omissions that may perhaps be non-interpolations"[18]. Among these they include the following six passages from the Gospel of Matthew: "Matt. (vi 15, 25;) ix 34; (xiii 33;) xxi 44; (xxiii 26;)"[19], where presumably the bracketed passages are less certain examples of Western non-interpolations than non-bracketed passages.

1. *Mt 6,15*

Drawing out the implications of the immediately preceding Matthean version of the Lord's Prayer (Mt 6,9-13), the evangelist specifies the consequences of not forgiving one's debtors that was mentioned in the prayer, ὡς καὶ ἡμεῖς ἀφήκαμεν τοῖς ὀφειλέταις ἡμῶν (Mt 6,12b). The

---

18. WESTCOTT – HORT (eds.), *The New Testament in the Original Greek*, vol. 2 (n. 1), §240, p. 176.
19. *Ibid.*

reason for Matthew expanding on this particular clause in Mt 6,14-15 is intriguing. Perhaps for some reason forgiveness (Mt 6,14-15), debt relief (Mt 6,12b), a tendency to hoard treasure (Mt 6,19-21), and focusing on material possessions (Mt 6,25-34) formed a set of interrelated problems at a community level. In this concatenation of related sayings, Matthew draws attention to mutuality of divine and human forgiveness. It is stated that practicing inter-human forgiveness guarantees divine forgiveness (Mt 6,14). Also the corollary is seen to follow: failure to practice inter-human forgiveness leads to the withdrawal of divine forgiveness. It is within the context of that second, negative formulation that a number of textual variants occur. The readings of various manuscripts and printed editions are helpfully viewed in parallel.

> ἐὰν δὲ μὴ ἀφῆτε τοῖς ἀνθρώποις τὰ παραπτώματα αὐτῶν, οὐδὲ ὁ πατὴρ ὑμῶν ἀφήσει τὰ παραπτώματα ὑμῶν (Β 03).
> ἐὰν δὲ μὴ ἀφῆτε τοῖς ἀνθρώποις, οὐδὲ ὁ πατὴρ ὑμῖν ἀφήσει τὰ παραπτώματα ὑμῶν (א 01).
> ἐὰν δὲ μὴ ἀφῆτε τοῖς ἀνθρώποις, οὐδὲ ὁ πατὴρ ὑμῶν ἀφήσει ὑμῖν τὰ παραπτώματα ὑμῶν (D 05).
> ἐὰν δὲ μὴ ἀφῆτε τοῖς ἀνθρώποις ᵀ, οὐδὲ ὁ πατὴρ ⸀ὑμῶν ἀφήσει⸁ τὰ παραπτώματα ὑμῶν (NA[28]).

There are two variation units in this verse. The second is the replacement of the two-word phrase ὑμῶν ἀφήσει supported by the majority of manuscripts with one of two alternatives. The genitive plural pronoun ὑμῶν is replaced by the dative plural form of the second person pronoun ὑμῖν, in א (01) and in some versional witnesses, c sy^c. A more pleonastic reading utilizing both the genitive and dative second person plural pronouns ὑμῶν ἀφήσει ὑμῖν occurs in the Greek manuscripts D (05) and the minuscule 1241, with further support in the versional witnesses it vg^cl sy^p.h. What is significant to note here is that D and supporting Western witnesses conflate and hence preserve an expansionistic text, which is understood to be the general behaviour of the Western text.

The first variation unit is where Westcott and Hort's minor Western non-interpolation is found. The variant relates to the inclusion or omission of the phrase τὰ παραπτώματα ὑμῶν after ἀνθρώποις, thereby producing a greater degree of parallelism with the second half of the verse, οὐδὲ ὁ πατὴρ ὑμῶν ἀφήσει τὰ παραπτώματα ὑμῶν (Mt 6,15b, as in B). The longer form of the text that includes the phrase τὰ παραπτώματα ὑμῶν after ἀνθρώποις is attested by an impressive array of witnesses: B K L W Δ Θ f^13 33 565 579 700 892^c 1241 1424 l844 l2211 𝔐 (b) f q sy^c.h sa bo^pt. By contrast, the shorter reading is attested in א D f^1 892* lat sy^p mae bo^pt. Here two things must be noted. The shorter reading is not solely Western in character, but is supported by the primary Alexandrian witness ℵ, f^1 with a distinctive character yet preserving a largely Byzantine text[20], 892* a secondary Alexandrian with Byzantine readings[21]. Furthermore, on the one hand, the longer reading can be seen as producing a greater degree of parallelism within Mt 6,15 itself:

ἐὰν δὲ μὴ ἀφῆτε τοῖς ἀνθρώποις τὰ παραπτώματα ὑμῶν,
οὐδὲ ὁ πατὴρ ὑμῶν ἀφήσει τὰ παραπτώματα ὑμῶν.

On the other hand, and producing an alternative claim of consistency on internal grounds, the shorter reading can be seen as producing a chiastic structure across the whole unit of Mt 6,14-15:

Ἐὰν γὰρ ἀφῆτε τοῖς ἀνθρώποις τὰ παραπτώματα αὐτῶν,	A
ἀφήσει καὶ ὑμῖν ὁ πατὴρ ὑμῶν ὁ οὐράνιος·	B
ἐὰν δὲ μὴ ἀφῆτε τοῖς ἀνθρώποις,	B´
οὐδὲ ὁ πατὴρ ὑμῶν ἀφήσει τὰ παραπτώματα ὑμῶν.	A´

Therefore, consideration of internal features produces competing claims that can be marshalled in support of either reading. It is difficult to determine any objective basis to judge between these two viewpoints.

Notwithstanding these internal arguments, the diversity of external support in favour of the shorter reading requires close consideration. The primary observation is that the shorter reading is not exclusively Western in character. It also receives support from Alexandrian manuscripts, both the primary Alexandrian ℵ, and the secondary Alexandrian 892*. Despite the fact that B 03 is generally considered to preserve the better text of the gospels in comparison with ℵ, here the editors of NA[28] have given more weight to the combination of a primary Alexandrian witness ℵ 01 in combination with D 05, the chief witness to the Western text, than to the primary Alexandrian witness B 03 in combination with the majority of Byzantine witnesses. It will be interesting to consult the text of the forthcoming *Editio Critica Maior* for Matthew when it appears. Perhaps the perceptible shift in favour of Byzantine readings seen in several of the fascicles that have already appeared might also result in a different printed text at this point. However, it is probably a misnomer to classify

---

20. Classed as category III by the Alands. K. ALAND – B. ALAND, *The Text of the New Testament: An Introduction to the Critical Editions and to the Theory and Practice of Modern Textual Criticism*, trans. E.F. Rhodes, 2nd rev. and enl. ed., Grand Rapids, MI, Eerdmans, 1989, p. 106.

21. The Alands (*ibid.*) classify 892 as a category II manuscript. That is, a manuscript of special quality, "but distinguished from manuscripts of category I by the presence of alien influences (particularly of the Byzantine text), and yet of importance for establishing the original text".

the shorter reading as a Western non-interpolation given the support across a variety of manuscripts that are not Western in character. Instead, the shorter reading (which has a strong claim to being the earliest recoverable form of the text of Mt 6,15) is best understood as a significant variant that finds support across a range of manuscripts, including those of the so-called Western cluster: D lat sy^p.

2. *Mt 6,25*

The text of Mt 6,25 catalogues a list of items about which individuals should not be troubled. Here the verse introduces the central emphasis of the passage, which is that focusing on items that are necessary for physical existence is viewed as a distraction from the life of discipleship and removes attention from the priority of seeking the kingdom (Mt 6,33). As Hagner eloquently states the matter,

> The passage, like the preceding one, stresses the importance of undistracted, absolute discipleship. ... The answer to this anxiety and all such debilitating anxiety is to be found in an absolute allegiance to the kingdom and the righteousness that is the natural expression of that kingdom[22].

As concrete examples, here Mt 6,25 lists a catalogue of the type of physical provisions that should not cause concern for followers of Jesus. The text in the NA[28] edition reads:

Διὰ τοῦτο λέγω ὑμῖν· μὴ μεριμνᾶτε τῇ ψυχῇ ὑμῶν τί φάγητε [ἢ τί πίητε], μηδὲ τῷ σώματι ὑμῶν τί ἐνδύσησθε. οὐχὶ ἡ ψυχὴ πλεῖόν ἐστιν τῆς τροφῆς καὶ τὸ σῶμα τοῦ ἐνδύματος;

The key textual variant concerns the phrase printed as [ἢ τί πίητε]. One variant involves the use of a different coordinating conjunction, thus reading καὶ τί πίητε. This variant reading occurs in the following manuscripts: K L N Γ Δ Θ 565 579 700 1241 1424 *l*844 𝔐 sy^{p.h}. The text printed in NA[28], albeit in brackets, is supported by the following witnesses: B W *f*^13 33 it sa^mss mae bo Or Hier^mss. A third reading omits the three-word phrase altogether, and is supported by the following manuscripts: ℵ *f*^1 892 *l*2211 a b ff^1 k l vg sy^c sa^mss.

In assessing the evidence surrounding these three variant readings, Metzger made the following comment.

> In favor of the shorter reading, lacking *ἢ τί πίητε*, is the possibility that the text was assimilated to ver. 31. The variation between *καί* and *ἤ* can also be taken as an indication of the secondary nature of the addition. On the other

---

22. D.A. Hagner, *Matthew 1–13* (WBC, 33A), Dallas, TX, Word, 1993, pp. 166-167.

hand, the similarity of the ending of *φάγητε* and *πίητε* may have occasioned a transcriptional oversight on the part of one or more copyists. To represent the balance of probabilities the Committee retained the words but enclosed them within square brackets[23].

Comfort makes similar points, but also adds the following observation. "The sense and poetic balance of the passage (τί φάγητε ... τί ἐνδύσησθε = 'what you eat ... what you are clothed with') are all better without ἢ τί πίητε ('or what you drink')"[24]. Admittedly, judgment about poetic balance and sense are subjective interpretations, but in combination with other observations about preference for the shorter reading this point may have corroborating value.

Therefore, the short reading omitting ἢ τί πίητε may have considerable weight in being regarded as the earliest recoverable form of the text of Mt 6,25. However, the larger question remains as to whether this shorter reading should be classed as a Western non-interpolation. Self-evidently, the major difficulties in classifying this omission as Western in character is the fact that the principal witness, Codex Bezae, is lacunose for Mt 6,20–9,2[25]. Consequently, in this primary witness to the Western text of Matthew there is no extant evidence as to whether the phrase ἢ τί πίητε was present or absent. Moreover, within the Greek manuscript tradition there is no Western textual witness to the shorter form of the text. The omission of the phrase, however, occurs in versional witnesses that represent the Western form of the text. This omission is most strongly supported in a range of Old Latin manuscripts a b ff[1] k l, the Vulgate vg, and the Curetonian Syriac sy[c]. The Old Latin manuscripts form the chief basis for viewing the omission as having support among manuscripts that are Western in character[26]. The text of the gospels in the Vulgate was itself a revision of the Old Latin undertaken by Jerome[27]. Furthermore, the Syriac text of the Curetonian Gospels is understood as being representative of

---

23. METZGER (ed.), *A Textual Commentary on the Greek New Testament* (n. 8), p. 15.
24. COMFORT, *New Testament Text and Translation Commentary* (n. 13), p. 16.
25. In relation to the text of Matthew in Codex Bezae D 05, Appendix I in NA[28] notes the following lacunae in Matthew: "vac. Mt 1,1-20; 6,20–9,2; 27,2-12". NA[28], p. 799.
26. In relation to Latin witnesses to the New Testament text, Houghton notes that while the notion of text-types is admittedly artificial, they can be useful. This is because each individual Latin manuscript is not an independent source for Greek readings but reflects a combination of various editorial interventions. Moreover, he states, "the concept of a text-type in Latin differs from the geographical text-types ('Alexandrian', 'Western' etc.) which used to be used to describe Greek tradition but now have fallen out of favour". H.A.G. HOUGHTON, *The Latin New Testament: A Guide to Its Early History, Texts, and Manuscripts*, Oxford, OUP, 2016, p. 150.
27. "Matthew was the first gospel to be revised by Jerome, and he makes a number of comments about readings known to him". *Ibid.*, p. 159.

the Western text. However, among the early versional evidence, the omission also occurs in Sahidic manuscripts sa[mss]. The Sahidic version is typically characterised as representing the Alexandrian form of the text.

Hence, while the omission is supported by Western versional evidence, within the Greek manuscript tradition support for the omission comes from other types of texts, ℵ f^1 892 *l*2211. Therefore, it is more accurate to describe the shorter reading as having varied support across a range of textual groups, including versions that are Western in character.

3. *Mt 9,34*

This variant is particularly interesting since the shorter form is supported only by witnesses that are usually classed as Western. The text as printed in the Nestle-Aland text is as follows:

|οἱ δὲ Φαρισαῖοι ἔλεγον· ἐν τῷ ἄρχοντι τῶν δαιμονίων ἐκβάλλει τὰ δαιμόνια.` (Mt 9,34, NA[28]).

The textual variant involves the absence of the whole verse in several manuscripts. The shorter reading is found in the following manuscripts: D a k sy[s]. It is also the reading preserved in the writings of Hilary of Poitiers (ca. 310 – ca. 367)[28]. The manuscripts that support the omission of this verse are appropriately described as Western in character. However, the majority of Old Latin manuscripts for which this portion of Matthew is extant and which are typically seen as reflecting a Western text do in fact preserve this verse. Therefore, the most accurate observation is that the omission is found in a subsection of the Western textual tradition.

Consequently, a decision about whether the omission of Mt 9,34 represents the earliest form of the text largely rests on an assessment of the internal consistency of the pericope. Metzger alludes to some of the internal factors when he comments "[a]ccording to several commentators (e.g. Allen, Klostermann, Zahn) the words here are an intrusion from 12.24 or from Lk 11.15. On the other hand, ..., the passage seems to be needed to prepare the reader for 10.25"[29]. Snodgrass provides a fuller explanation of reasons why the internal evidence favours the inclusion of Mt 9,34. He states,

> There is nothing gained by the addition of this verse, but it is easy to find a plausible motive for its omission. The statement plays no importance in this context, and the issue is dropped, thus leaving the charge unanswered.

---

28. In this regard his relevant work is his *In Evangelium Matthaei Commentarius*, typically dated prior to 356, when he went into exile in Phrygia.

29. METZGER (ed.), *A Textual Commentary on the Greek New Testament* (n. 8), p. 20.

In Matt 12:24-25; Mark 3:22-23; and Luke 11:14-15, the logic of the charge is refuted[30].

Comfort adds a little more in support of the originality of Mt 9,34 when he observes that "[p]erhaps it was excised because the previous verse provides a more positive ending to the pericope"[31].

There is a further argument that has not been suggested that also supports Mt 9,34 as being part of the earliest form of the text. The material in Mt 12,22-32 forms the stronger parallel with the account of the Beelzebul controversy (Mk 3,20-30//Lk 11,14-23). Hence, the material tradition in Mt 9,32-34 is a redactionally-created Matthean doublet, at least in regard to the climactic saying. This is a well-known compositional phenomenon in the First Gospel[32]. Furthermore, Matthew is partial to replicating high-impact concluding sayings even when they have been derived from source material. The classic example is the "weeping and gnashing of teeth" saying. The Q saying (Mt 8,12//Lk 13,28) occurs a total of six times in the Gospel of Matthew, with the evangelist redactionally replicating it five times (Mt 13,42.50; 22,13; 24,51; 25,30)[33]. Thus, Matthew has created the whole unit in Mt 9,32-34, providing a climactic saying drawn from Mk 3,22b. It mattered little to Matthew that the final saying was not rebutted in its immediate context, and that it might be considered somewhat ill-fitting. Matthew knew a response to this charge would be provided later in his gospel. This type of compositional activity is characteristically Matthean. Therefore, it seems entirely plausible that a later scribe, wishing not to leave this charge unanswered in the immediate context, excised Mt 9,34. Consequently, this scribal decision is seen in a handful of surviving manuscripts, D a k sy^s. These manuscripts are Western in character, but the omission is not found in the majority of Old Latin manuscripts. Therefore, it is sensible to conclude that this is an omission found only in a selection of Western manuscripts. It is unlikely to represent the earliest recoverable form of the Matthean text. Therefore, this omission does not preserve a form of the text that is likely to be original. Consequently, this variant does appear to be the earliest form of the text and thus should not be seen as being a Western non-interpolation.

---

30. K. SNODGRASS, *Western Non-Interpolations*, in *JBL* 91 (1972) 369-379, p. 376.
31. COMFORT, *New Testament Text and Translation Commentary* (n. 13), p. 27.
32. For a larger discussion of the Matthean doublets see P. FOSTER, *The Doublets in Matthew: What Are They Good for?*, in J. VERHEYDEN – G. VAN BELLE (eds.), *An Early Reader of Mark and Q* (BTS, 21), Leuven – Paris – Bristol, CT, Peeters, 2016, 109-138.
33. Davies and Allison succinctly comment, "Matthew has made this expression his own". W.D. DAVIES – D.C. ALLISON, *A Critical and Exegetical Commentary on the Gospel according to Saint Matthew*. Vol. 2: *Commentary on Matthew VIII–XVIII* (ICC), Edinburgh, T&T Clark, 1991, p. 31.

4. Mt 13,33

The textual variant in Mt 13,33 involves the final words in the opening clause. The NA[28] text prints the following as its reading: Ἄλλην παραβολὴν ⸂ἐλάλησεν αὐτοῖς⸃· (NA[28] Mt 13,33). Here the final two words ἐλάλησεν αὐτοῖς are replaced by a range of different readings in various manuscripts. Commencing with the printed text, the various readings are as follows:

ἐλάλησεν αὐτοῖς	B K N W Γ Δ 0242^{vid} f^1 33 565 579 700 892 1424 𝔐 lat sy^p bo
ἐλάλησεν αὐτοῖς λέγων	ℵ L Θ f^{13} h (l) q vg^{mss} sa^{ms} mae
παρέθηκεν αὐτοῖς λέγων	C 1241 sa^{mss}
omit	D d (k) sy$^{s.c}$

The reading ἐλάλησεν αὐτοῖς has strong external support spanning manuscripts that are classed as primary or secondary Alexandrian, multiple representatives of the Majority or Byzantine text, and the majority of Old Latin witnesses typically seen as Western in character. Among other versional evidence, the Peshitta (sy^p), which is typically seen as preserving a Western text form, attests this underlying form of the Greek text. Admittedly, the Syriac evidence is divided. One of the more expansive variants, ἐλάλησεν αὐτοῖς λέγων, again has a range of support from manuscripts with a variety of textual affinities.

The third variant, παρέθηκεν αὐτοῖς λέγων, conforms the speech reference to the form or words used to introduce the preceding parables in Mt 13,24.31. This conformity is observed by Nolland[34]. It is supported in two Greek manuscripts C 1241, as well as a range of Sahidic manuscripts. The final variant found in Codex Bezae (D 05) and Old Latin d is also apparently attested by the Old Latin manuscript k along with part of the Syriac tradition. It simply omits the words ἐλάλησεν αὐτοῖς, without anything in their place.

It is notable that, in their respective textual commentaries, both Metzger and Comfort provide no discussion of this variant. Presumably, they both felt it to be of limited significance as well as considering the printed text to be relatively secure. The tendency not to discuss this variant, or at least not to discuss the full range of variant readings, is also observed in the majority of commentaries that have text-critical notes. Since the variants do not greatly influence the sense of the passage, the various readings are

---

34. Nolland states the matter in the following manner: "παρέθηκεν αὐτοῖς λέγων ('he put [another parable] before them, saying') in C 1241 etc. sa^{mss} conforms the reading entirely to vv. 24 and 31". NOLLAND, *The Gospel of Matthew* (n. 11), p. 552.

not a focus of discussion. This same tendency is observed in certain editions of the Greek New Testament. For instance, the SBL edition records no variant readings at this point[35]. This is also the case with the UBS fourth edition[36]. However, describing the omission by D and other manuscripts, Snodgrass states, "[t]he internal evidence is not decisive: the words could have been omitted as unnecessary or could have been added for a smoother rendering. It seems to me, however, that the Western text is not characteristic of Matthew's style"[37].

The omission of the clause that refers to speech is characteristic of certain manuscripts that are typically deemed to be representatives of the Western form of the text, D d (k) sy$^{s.c}$. These manuscripts do include the principal textual witness to the Western text of the gospels, Codex Bezae (D 05). However, neither the totality or even the majority of representatives of the Western text, especially Early Latin witnesses, support this omission. Therefore, the omission is attested in a narrow section of the Western textual tradition. It is highly unlikely to represent the earliest recoverable reading for this variation unit in Mt 13,33, and hence should not be classed as a Western non-interpolation. The earliest recoverable form of the text is most likely to be the reading presented in the majority of printed Greek New Testaments, ἐλάλησεν αὐτοῖς. This reading is supported by a range of diverse and early manuscript attestation.

5. *Mt 21,44*

This variant is of far greater interest in terms of its size and range of attestation. Among the seven so-called Matthean Western non-interpolations, it is in fact the longest omission. This longer text contains an additional fifteen words, whereas the longer text in Mt 27,49b, which is classed as the only major Matthean Western non-interpolation, has an additional thirteen words. The reason for classing the longer omission in Mt 21,44 as a minor Western non-interpolation when the less extensive omission was classed as a major Western non-interpolation is not obvious. Several manuscripts omit the entirety of Mt 21,44. The manuscript support for inclusion or omission is as follows:

---

35. M.W. HOLMES (ed.), *The Greek New Testament SBL Edition*, Atlanta, GA, SBL, 2010, p. 33.
36. B. ALAND – K. ALAND – J. KARAVIDOPOULOS – C.M. MARTINI – B.M. METZGER (eds.), *The Greek New Testament*, United Bible Societies, 4th ed., 11th printing, Münster, Deutsche Bibelgesellschaft – United Bible Societies, 2006, p. 49.
37. SNODGRASS, *Western Non-Interpolations* (n. 30), p. 376.

καὶ ὁ πεσὼν ἐπὶ τὸν λίθον τοῦτον συνθλασθήσεται· ἐφ' ὃν δ' ἂν πέσῃ λικμήσει αὐτόν.
    ℵ B C K L W Z Δ (- καὶ Θ) 0102 $f^{1.13}$ 565 579 700 892 1241 1424 *l*844 𝔐 lat sy$^{c.p.h}$ co
omit   D 33 it sy^s Or Eus^{syr}

Among manuscripts that support the inclusion of Mt 21,44, it is important to note the minor variant in the ninth-century Codex Koridethi (Θ 038) with the omission of the initial καί. The inclusion of the verse is attested by the primary and early Alexandrian witnesses Codex Sinaiticus and Codex Vaticanus, both fourth century. This establishes the relative antiquity of the inclusion of the verse in early Greek manuscripts of Matthew. While the Vulgate attests the inclusion of the verse, this form of the Latin text is supported only by a limited range of Old Latin witnesses, as shown by the siglum, lat[38].

By contrast, the omission of this verse is supported by an impressive range of primarily Western witnesses. Representative of manuscripts typically seen as being Western in character, the verse is omitted by D it sy^s. The combination of Codex Bezae, the majority of the Old Latin manuscripts, and the Syriac Sinaiticus provide a combination of support for the omission of the verse in manuscripts that represent the Western text[39]. The verse also appears to be absent from the *Diatessaron*. Alongside this range of Western support for the omission of Mt 21,44, the verse is also omitted in the minuscule 33. This ninth-century minuscule 33 is described as category II. That is, it is a manuscript of special quality, "but distinguished from category I by the presence of alien influences (particularly of the Byzantine text)"[40].

Furthermore, and of potential importance, though not listed in the textual apparatus of NA[28] for Mt 21,44, is the late second-century manuscript 𝔓[104], also catalogued as P.Oxy. LXIV 4404[41]. This highly fragmentary and poorly

---

38. The siglum lat is defined as follows: "Agreement of only a part of the Old Latin with the Vulgate is indicated by the sign lat". ALAND – ALAND, *The Text of the New Testament* (n. 20), p. 250.

39. While Codex Bezae and the Old Latin tradition are seen as primary examples of the Western text, so also are several Syriac gospel texts. The palimpsest Codex Sinaiticus Syriacus or Syriac Sinaiticus dates from the late fourth century. It presumably represents, along with the Syriac Curetonian Gospels, an attempt to supplant and replace the *Diatessaron*. The Western text is seen as being reflected in much of this later Syriac New Testament tradition especially in the Peshitta, which itself was a revision of the earlier Old Syriac attested both by the Syriac Sinaiticus and the Curetonian Gospels.

40. ALAND – ALAND, *The Text of the New Testament* (n. 20), p. 106.

41. In the heading P.Oxy. LXIV 4404 is described as "Late Second Century". On the same page in the main text it is stated that "[t]he hand is clearly 'early', i.e. before c. 250". On the following page Thomas gives his fuller opinion in regard to the date of the text on this

preserved papyrus manuscript is written on both sides of a larger leaf of a papyrus codex. The fragment measures 7 × 5.2 cm. The text on the *recto* is largely legible. There are 110 legible letters on the *recto* and the text is readily identified as Mt 21,34-37. The *verso* is in a much poorer state of preservation with no single letter being complete. The image of the *verso* of P.Oxy. LXIV 4404 reveals the state of the problem.

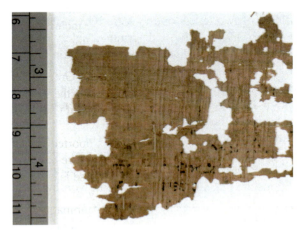

P.Oxy. LXIV 4404 *verso*

The *verso* has been identified as preserving traces of letters from Mt 21,43.45, but apparently not from Mt 21,44. This description of contents is presented in the *Kurzgefasste Liste*[42], reflecting the *editio princeps* of J. David Thomas[43]. Given the highly abraded nature of the *verso*, it appears no absolute conclusion can be drawn as to whether or not Mt 21,44 was present in the text of this manuscript. The reconstruction of the *verso* (↓) in the *editio princeps* is as follows:

"↓
14   ] δοθησετ[α]ι
     [εθνει ποιουν]τι τ[ο]υς καρ[που]ς
16   [αυτης και ακου]σα[]τες ο[ι

Scanty traces of 1 line"

papyrus fragment: "I should assign 4404 with some confidence to the second half of the second century, while not wishing to exclude altogether a slightly earlier or a slightly later date". Even with the later dating this fragment is at least a century earlier than any other surviving witnesses to this portion of the Gospel of Matthew. J.D. THOMAS, *Mt 21,34-37; 21,43-45 (?)*, in *The Oxyrhynchus Papyri* LXIV, London, Egypt Exploration Society, 1997, pp. 7-9, Pl. I and II.
  42. http://ntvmr.uni-muenster.de/liste (accessed 10 October 2020).
  43. THOMAS, *Mt 21,34-37; 21,43-45 (?)* (n. 41), pp. 7-9, Pl. II.

Here the reconstruction on lines 14-15 and the first word on line 16 reflects the ending of Mt 21,43 δοθήσεται ἔθνει ποιοῦντι τοὺς καρποὺς αὐτῆς. The remainder of line 16 reflects the beginning of Mt 21,45 καὶ ἀκούσαντες οἱ ἀρχιερεῖς. However, in the reconstruction, with the exception of one letter on line 15 (κ) and one letter on line 16 (ε), every other unbracketed letter, that is the letters for which there is a partial trace on the manuscript, is printed with an under-dot. This means that the editor could only be confident of two letters on the *verso*. Given that the omission of Mt 21,44 in P.Oxy. LXIV 4404 is determined solely by the remains of the six unbracketed letters on line 16, extreme caution must be exercised in relation to any conclusions that may be drawn[44]. The clearest letters on line 16 appear to be τες in ακου]σα[]τες. The three letters do not appear in that combination and order in any of Mt 21,44. Therefore, this is perhaps the strongest basis for the conclusion that Mt 21,44 is omitted in P.Oxy. LXIV 4404, the earliest witness to this portion of the Gospel of Matthew.

Of further significance for determining the earliest form of the Matthean text is the close parallel between Mt 21,44 and Lk 20,18. The parallel traditions are close but not identical in wording.

Mt 21,44	Lk 20,18
καὶ ὁ πεσὼν ἐπὶ τὸν λίθον τοῦτον συνθλασθήσεται· ἐφ' ὃν δ' ἂν πέσῃ λικμήσει αὐτόν.	πᾶς ὁ πεσὼν ἐπ' ἐκεῖνον τὸν λίθον συνθλασθήσεται· ἐφ' ὃν δ' ἂν πέσῃ, λικμήσει αὐτόν.

Here Matthew has added his own redactional concluding words of Jesus (Mt 21,43, not contained in Luke) to triple tradition material drawn from the Gospel of Mark (Mt 21,33-46//Mk 12,1-12//Lk 20,9-19). By contrast, Luke is responsible for the addition of Lk 20,18 to Markan material. Marshall sees the tradition in Lk 20,18 as based on scriptural material: Ps 118(117),22 "is followed by an OT allusion peculiar to Lk. from Dn. 2:34f., 45f"[45]. Furthermore, Fitzmyer notes that Luke has derived this parable (Mk 12,1-2//Lk 20,9-19) from Mark, "[a]part from v.18, which Luke has himself added (possibly derived from 'L' ..., or possibly Lucan composition – note its problematic presence in Matt 21:44 [bracketed])"[46]. Nolland favours viewing this additional Lukan verse as traditional in

---

44. Thomas expresses this point when he states, "[t]he readings suggested for ↓ are exceedingly tentative and this must be borne in mind when this papyrus is used for purposes of textual criticism". THOMAS, *Mt 21,34-37; 21,43-45 (?)* (n. 41), p. 7.

45. I.H. MARSHALL, *The Gospel of Luke: A Commentary on the Greek Text* (NIGTC), Grand Rapids, MI, Eerdmans, 1978, p. 726.

46. J.A. FITZMYER, *The Gospel according to Luke X–XXIV: A New Translation with Introduction and Commentary* (AB, 28A), New York, Doubleday, 1985, p. 1277.

origin. He states, "Luke is drawing on Christian tradition to elaborate his stone reference from Ps 118:22"[47].

Despite the widespread consensus among commentators dealing with the Gospel of Luke that Lk 20,18 is a Lukan addition to material derived from Mk 12,1-12, either stemming from redactional creativity or traditional material reflecting on the meaning of Ps 118(117),22, some textual commentaries when discussing Mt 21,44 have resisted the more obvious case for viewing this verse as an insertion due to assimilation towards the Lukan form of the parable. In this vein, the *Tyndale House Textual Commentary* makes the following observation:

> Matt. 21:44 has a near-exact parallel at Luke 20:18. If the verse were added as a harmonisation to the Lukan parallel by addition, we might expect to see closer alignment with the Lukan text here. In Luke, the parallel to Matt. 21:44 comes immediately after Jesus' quotation of Psalm 117:22 (LXX), but in Matthew, Jesus appears to conclude the discussion about the "stone which the builders rejected" with v. 43. After the LXX quotation, Jesus seems to conclude with a development marker, διὰ τοῦτο. Based on this feature of discourse, if v. 44 were added, we would expect it to have been added after v. 42, not at its present location after v. 43. Thus, the variation appears to be a stylistic omission. This kind of omission seems to be consistent with the earliest Latin version, which could also explain its absence in D05. Early witnesses, important later witnesses and the majority of manuscripts support the text[48].

The first point to make is that the alignment is actually remarkably close. The two differences are the replacement of Luke's initial πᾶς with the καί of Mt 21,44, and in place of Luke's demonstrative pronoun ἐκεῖνον, the Matthean parallel uses the near demonstrative pronoun τοῦτον with a slight change in word order. By contrast, when discussing Mt 23,14, the same editors see this as a later addition derived "from Mk 12:40 and Lk 20:47", even though the material "has been adjusted syntactically in order to fit Matthew's Gospel"[49]. In the case of Mt 23,14, the lack of exact parallelism is not considered a bar to harmonisation. Given the standard applied to Mt 23,14, then in regard to the example of Mt 21,44 where the parallelism is closer (but still not perfect), there is no reason to discount this verse as being a case of harmonisation through inclusion of Lk 20,18. As a concession, Metzger explains the reason the text was included in the printed editions: "While considering the verse to be an accretion to

---

47. J. NOLLAND, *Luke 18:35–24:53* (WBC, 35C), Dallas, TX, Word, 1993, p. 953.
48. E. HIXSON – D. JONGKIND (eds.), *Tyndale House Textual Commentary: A Textual Commentary on the Tyndale House Greek New Testament*, Wheaton, IL, Crossway; Cambridge, CUP, forthcoming, p. 65.
49. *Ibid.*, p. 70.

the text, yet because of the antiquity of the reading and its importance in the textual tradition, the Committee decided to retain it in the text, enclosed within square brackets"[50]. Here one wonders if double square brackets might have been more appropriate, or in common with Mt 23,14 that Mt 21,44 should be relegated to the apparatus.

The omission of this verse in predominantly Western witnesses such as D it sy[s], and the fact that the shorter form of the text omitting Mt 21,44 is likely original, make this verse one of the strongest candidates for application of the term Western non-interpolation in the Gospel of Matthew. Admittedly, support for the omission is not purely Western in character due to the omission being found in minuscule 33. Furthermore, if the challenging task of reconstructing the *verso* of the second-century fragment 𝔓[104]/P.Oxy. LXIV 4404 is correct in reading Mt 21,43 immediately followed by Mt 21,45, then this early Egyptian textual witness also affirms the shorter reading. Additionally, it may suggest that the assimilation of Lk 20,18 into the Matthean text of Mt 21,33-46 at Mt 21,44 occurred sometime between the late second century and prior to the middle of the fourth century, most likely at some stage in the third century.

Thus, it is possible to conclude that the majority of Western witnesses preserve a shorter and superior text at this point in regard to the omission of Mt 21,44. If one does not require such an omission to be exclusively Western (but is content with chiefly Western support of the shorter reading), then it is probably appropriate to classify the omission of Mt 21,44 as a Western non-interpolation. If, however, that label is deemed to be applicable only when exclusively Western witnesses preserve the shorter text, then it is still possible to affirm that the so-called Western text preserved an earlier form of the text at this point. Moreover, this shorter form of the text stands in contrast with the form preserved in the primary Alexandrians and those other manuscripts that contain Mt 21,44.

6. *Mt 23,26*

The variant in Mt 23,26 is on a much smaller scale than the omission of the entirety of Mt 21,44. Here it involves the omission of just three words. The NA[28] text is printed in the following form:

Φαρισαῖε τυφλέ, καθάρισον πρῶτον τὸ ἐντὸς τοῦ ποτηρίου ᵀ, ἵνα γένηται καὶ τὸ ἐκτὸς αὐτοῦ καθαρόν (NA[28] Mt 23,26).

---

50. METZGER (ed.), *A Textual Commentary on the Greek New Testament* (n. 8), p. 47.

After τοῦ ποτηρίου, several manuscripts add the words καὶ τῆς παροψίδος. The manuscript evidence is as follows:

καὶ τῆς παροψίδος	ℵ B C K L W Γ Δ 0102 0281 f^{13} 33 565 579 892 1241 1424 *l*844 𝔐 lat sy$^{p.h}$ co
omit	D Θ f^1 700 a e ff^2 r^1 sy^s Ir^{lat} Cl

The omission is supported by the following representatives of the Western textual tradition, Codex Bezae (D 05), part of the Old Latin tradition (a e ff^2 r^1) and the Syriac Sinaiticus (sy^s). Additional support for the omission is found in Codex Koridethi (Θ 038), family 1 manuscripts (f^1), and minuscule 700, an eleventh-century category III manuscript preserving a text of a somewhat distinctive and independent character[51]. While "[t]he weight of the external evidence appears to support the longer text"[52], the internal evidence can be construed in opposing ways. Thus, Snodgrass asks the following question, "[t]he internal evidence again is not decisive: were these words added to conform to the preceding verse or eliminated as repetitious and unnecessary?"[53].

Therefore, the context of the previous verse Mt 23,25 that introduces the fifth of Matthew's seven "woes" (with Mt 23,14 omitted as a later addition) is relevant to the determination of the earliest recoverable form of the text.

Mt 23,25	Mt 23,26
οὐαὶ ὑμῖν, γραμματεῖς καὶ Φαρισαῖοι ὑποκριταί, ὅτι καθαρίζετε τὸ ἔξωθεν τοῦ ποτηρίου καὶ τῆς παροψίδος, ἔσωθεν δὲ γέμουσιν ἐξ ἁρπαγῆς καὶ ἀκρασίας.	Φαρισαῖε τυφλέ, καθάρισον πρῶτον τὸ ἐντὸς τοῦ ποτηρίου [καὶ τῆς παροψίδος], ἵνα γένηται καὶ τὸ ἐκτὸς αὐτοῦ καθαρόν.

Structurally, the repetition of the phrase καὶ τῆς παροψίδος in Mt 23,26 does create a great balance and parallelism between the two verses. Yet, as Snodgrass points out, this could be a reason either for introducing the phrase, or alternatively the duplication of the three words might account for its omission. There may, however, be a further reason why a scribe may have chosen to omit the second occurrence of the phrase in Mt 23,25-26. It is possible that, after copying Mt 23,25, a scribe reflected on its contents and considered it natural to speak of the inside of a ποτήριον,

---

51. ALAND – ALAND (eds.), *The Text of the New Testament* (n. 20), p. 133.
52. METZGER (ed.), *A Textual Commentary on the Greek New Testament* (n. 8), p. 50.
53. SNODGRASS, *Western Non-Interpolations* (n. 30), p. 377.

but less natural to describe a παροψίς as having an inside. In the New Testament, the term παροψίς occurs only in this context. A wider survey of Greek literature, however, suggests that it refers to a food-serving utensil that is relatively flat – such as a platter or plate. The LSJ describes one meaning as being a "dish on which such meats are served"[54]. Similarly, it can denote "a small plate for a side dish"[55]. Given that these utensils tended to be much flatter than a ποτήριον with no pronounced inside (ἔσωθεν/ἐντός), a scribe might have thought that the reference to the inside of a παροψίς was logically incorrect.

Here the evidence is finely balanced[56]. However, the strength of the external evidence favours the inclusion of the three-word phrase καὶ τῆς παροψίδος, while on internal grounds it is possible to see the phrase omitted once a scribe had reflected on the logical problem of a παροψίς (a "plate") having an inside, or due to a more mechanical slip that caused the scribe to skip the second occurrence of the phrase. Therefore, on balance, it is probably best to see the longer reading as representing the earlier form of the text. Consequently, Mt 23,26 should not be classed as being a Western non-interpolation.

IV. Conclusions

The chief insight of this examination of the so-called Western non-interpolations as they occur in the Gospel of Matthew is that this set of seven variants must be treated individually and the different readings must be assessed on their own respective textual merits before making any decisions concerning an overarching theory to account for them as a group. Some of the shorter variant readings that are found among Mt 6,15.25; 9,34; 13,33; 21,44; 23,26 and 27,49 have a good claim to be seen as representing the earliest form of the text, while others do not. Yet, even among those where the shorter reading appears to be the earliest recoverable form of the text, not all of these have an equally strong claim to being distinctively Western in character.

---

54. LSJ, 1996, p. 1344.
55. H. Balz – G. Schneider (eds.), *Exegetical Dictionary of the New Testament*, 3 vols, Grand Rapids, MI, Eerdmans, 1991, vol. 3, p. 44.
56. The balanced nature of this textual choice is implied in the comments of the *Tyndale House Textual Commentary*. It is stated that, "If the shorter reading were original, the reading adopted as the text (καὶ τῆς παροψίδος) could have been added as a harmonisation to v. 25, where the phrase is uncontested. However, the text has the external support of a broad range of witnesses, including the earliest Greek manuscripts containing this passage". Hixson – Jongkind (eds.), *Tyndale House Textual Commentary* (n. 48), p. 70.

Among these seven variants it was judged that in the cases of Mt 9,34; 13,33 and 23,26 the longer reading appeared to have the better claim to represent the earliest recoverable form of the text. With the remaining four cases (Mt 6,15.25; 21,44; 27,49), these were instances where the shorter reading can plausibly be considered to represent the earliest recoverable stage of the text. However, in three of these cases (Mt 6,15.25; 27,49), the manuscript evidence in support of these shorter readings was far broader than primarily manuscripts that might be considered Western in character. So, while these might be "non-interpolations", or perhaps better, the earliest recoverable form of the text, they were not exclusively or chiefly Western in character. The one remaining variant Mt 21,44 did prove to be a case where the shorter reading was to be preferred and the manuscripts that support the shorter reading are primarily Western in character. One slightly strange decision on the part of Westcott and Hort was the decision to class Mt 27,49 as a major Western non-interpolation while Mt 21,44 was listed as a minor Western non-interpolation. The omission of the entirety of Mt 21,44 comprises an omission of fifteen Greek words, whereas the omission of Mt 27,49 is an omission of thirteen Greek words.

In the end, this analysis of the so-called seven Western non-interpolations in the Gospel of Matthew found that the evidence in support of the shorter readings was stronger in relation to four of these passages. However, only one of those four (Mt 21,44) was supported by predominantly Western manuscripts. The other three had support across manuscripts exhibiting a range of different texts. So are there any Western non-interpolations in the Gospel of Matthew? In part the answer is dependent on how exclusively Western the manuscript support should be before that label is applied. If it is felt that the preponderance of support should be Western, then perhaps only one of the seven passages, Mt 21,44, can be classified as a Western non-interpolation. However, one might legitimately ask if a single example warrants a category. If not, then at the very least and to their credit Westcott and Hort correctly identified a set of disparate variants where the shorter reading should be often regarded as the superior text. Here, to their credit reflecting the best practices of textual criticism, they followed the evidence and modified their overall theory to state that the Alexandrian text, while being the best representative of their putative neutral text, nonetheless was not itself free from early expansionistic tendency at a few points[57]. These preferred shorter

---

57. WESTCOTT – HORT (eds.), *The New Testament in the Original Greek*, vol. 1 (n. 1), pp. 548-562.

readings in the Gospel of Matthew all have Western support, but they also derive further support from various other non-Western manuscripts to various extents.

University of Edinburgh Paul FOSTER
The School of Divinity Mound Place
Edinburgh EH1 2LX
U.K.
paul.foster@ed.ac.uk

DAS MARKUSEVANGELIUM ALS KATECHETISCHES HANDBUCH

I. Fragestellung

Vor gut hundert Jahren begann mit drei nahezu zeitgleich veröffentlichten Untersuchungen im Bereich der neutestamentlichen Forschung in Deutschland die Phase der sog. „Formgeschichte"[1]. Dabei handelt es sich zum einen um das Werk von Karl Ludwig Schmidt „Der Rahmen der Geschichte Jesu", erschienen 1919. K.L. Schmidt zeigte, dass die Evangelien „kein Leben Jesu im Sinne einer sich entwickelnden Lebensgeschichte" bieten; auch sind sie „kein Aufriß der Geschichte Jesu, sondern nur Einzelgeschichten, Perikopen, die in ein Rahmenwerk gestellt sind"[2]. Der Untersuchung dieser Einzelgeschichten widmeten sich dann die ebenfalls 1919 veröffentlichte „Formgeschichte des Evangeliums" von Martin Dibelius[3] und die 1921 erschienene „Geschichte der synoptischen Tradition" von Rudolf Bultmann[4]. 1931 bzw. 1933 erlebten die Werke von Dibelius[5] und Bultmann[6] eine erheblich erweiterte Neuauflage.

---

1. Zu den Voraussetzungen vgl. die Hinweise bei K.L. Schmidt, *Formgeschichte*, in *RGG*² II (1928), Sp. 638-640; Schmidt, *ibid.*, Sp. 639, verweist ausdrücklich auf Johann Gottfried Herder als frühen Vorläufer und auf die Untersuchungen von Hermann Gunkel und Hugo Greßmann im Bereich des AT; zu Gunkel vgl. die umfassende Darstellung durch K. Hammann, *Hermann Gunkel: Eine Biographie*, Tübingen, Mohr Siebeck, 2014. Eine weitere Voraussetzung nennt Schmidt, *ibid.*, Sp. 638, also gleich zu Beginn: die von Franz Overbeck propagierte Unterscheidung zwischen der „christlichen Urliteratur" und der späteren patristischen Literatur. Diese Unterscheidung diente der „Formgeschichte" als Basis, die Evangelien als „Kleinliteratur" einzustufen (dazu s.u. Anm. 16).

2. K.L. Schmidt, *Der Rahmen der Geschichte Jesu: Literarkritische Untersuchungen zur ältesten Jesusüberlieferung*, Berlin, Trowitzsch, 1919 (Nachdruck: Darmstadt, Wissenschaftliche Buchgesellschaft, 1969), S. 317.

3. M. Dibelius, *Die Formgeschichte des Evangeliums*, Tübingen, J.C.B Mohr (Paul Siebeck), 1919, IV + 108 Seiten.

4. R. Bultmann, *Die Geschichte der synoptischen Tradition* (FRLANT, 29), Göttingen, Vandenhoeck & Ruprecht, 1921, 8* + 229 Seiten; Bultmanns Werk war ebenfalls bereits 1919 fertiggestellt, doch verzögerte sich die Drucklegung bis 1921; dazu vgl. K. Hammann, *Rudolf Bultmann: Eine Biographie*, Tübingen, Mohr Siebeck, ³2012, S. 102.

5. M. Dibelius, *Die Formgeschichte des Evangeliums*, 2. Aufl., Tübingen, J.C.B. Mohr (Paul Siebeck), 1933; IV + 315 Seiten; 3. durchgeseh. Aufl., hg. von G. Bornkamm, mit einem Nachtrag: G. Iber, *Neuere Literatur zur Formgeschichte*, S. 302-312; damit identisch: ⁴1961; ⁵1966; ⁶1971.

6. R. Bultmann, *Die Geschichte der synoptischen Tradition* (FRLANT, 29), Göttingen, Vandenhoeck & Ruprecht, 2. Aufl., 1931, 8* + 408 Seiten; 3. durchges. Aufl., 1957, 8* + 408 Seiten; damit identisch: ⁴1958; ⁵1961; ⁶1964; ⁷1967; ⁸1970; ⁹1979; 10. Aufl. 1995 (mit

Die „Formgeschichte", wie sie in den Werken von Dibelius und Bultmann entfaltet wird, macht mit der Einsicht Ernst, dass die Texte der Evangelien, und zwar auch die Einzeltexte, keinen direkten Zugriff auf den historischen Jesus ermöglichen, und sie zieht daraus die methodische Konsequenz: Es gilt danach zu fragen, unter welchen Bedingungen die Einzelperikopen der Evangelien geformt und tradiert wurden. Subjekt von Formung und Tradierung ist für diese neue Forschungsrichtung die „Gemeinde". Dabei ist für die „Formgeschichte" ein ausgesprochen antiindividualistischer Zug charakteristisch: „An diesem vorliterarischen Prozeß sind nicht einzelne bekannte Schriftstellerpersönlichkeiten beteiligt, sondern unbekannte unliterarische Menschen, deren Einzelerzählungen (‚kleine literarische Einheiten') von den Evangelisten gesammelt worden sind"[7]. Wichtig werden jetzt überindividuelle Faktoren, die Gattungen, die dem Einzelnen vorgegeben sind und in denen die Überlieferungen Gestalt gewinnen; ebenso wichtig sind die praktischen Bedürfnisse der Gemeinde, also die Verankerung der Einzelüberlieferungen im Leben der Gemeinde, der sog. „Sitz im Leben"[8].

Durch die Zuweisung der Einzelüberlieferungen zu bestimmten Gattungen sowie durch Strukturanalysen der jeweiligen Einzelstücke im Rahmen der betreffenden Gattung zielte die „Formgeschichte" auf die Erhellung des vorliterarischen Überlieferungsprozesses ab, eben auf eine „Geschichte der synoptischen Tradition". Erreicht werden sollte dieses Ziel mit zwei Mitteln:

a) Man untersuchte die Tendenzen der Textabänderungen vom Markusevangelium (MkEv) zu den späteren Evangelien und schloss daraus, dass analoge Beobachtungen auch Urteile über den vorliterarischen Prozess ermöglichten. Voraussetzung dafür war die Annahme, dass es auf dieser frühen Überlieferungsstufe keinen relevanten Unterschied zwischen mündlicher und schriftlicher Tradierung gab[9].

b) Man ging für den Ursprung einer Einzelüberlieferung grundsätzlich von ihrer möglichst einfachen Form aus. Einfachheit galt als Merkmal von Ursprünglichkeit[10].

---

einem Nachwort von Gerd THEISSEN [s. Anm. 8]), X + 452 Seiten; außerdem erschienen zwischen 1958 und 1979 Ergänzungshefte: 1958, 51 Seiten; ²1962, 56 Seiten = ³1966 (jeweils hg. von R. BULTMANN); ⁴1971 (hg. von G. THEISSEN und Ph. VIELHAUER), 125 Seiten = ⁵1979.

7. SCHMIDT, *Formgeschichte* (Anm. 1), Sp. 639.

8. Zu den dabei leitenden Grundannahmen der „Formgeschichte" vgl. auch G. THEISSEN, *Die Erforschung der synoptischen Tradition seit R. Bultmann: Ein Überblick über die formgeschichtliche Arbeit im 20. Jahrhundert*, in BULTMANN, *Geschichte*, 10. Aufl. (Anm. 6), S. IX-X, 409-452, bes. 409-411.

9. So BULTMANN, *Geschichte* (Anm. 6), S. 7.

10. Dies galt schon für die Gattungsanalysen von Gunkel, vgl. HAMMANN, *Hermann Gunkel* (Anm. 1), S. 176, der hervorhebt, dass für Gunkel die Gattungen „ursprünglich

Der andere überindividuelle Faktor, neben dem der Gattungen, war der „Sitz im Leben". Die Frage nach der schriftstellerischen Persönlichkeit des Autors wurde damit durch den Rekurs auf die Lebensvollzüge der Gemeinde ersetzt. Allerdings bleiben die Aussagen hierzu oft recht allgemein. M. Dibelius sieht die Predigt als Grundfunktion des Urchristentums, der er direkt die Gattung des „Paradigmas" zuordnet, während die Wundererzählungen („Novellen") der missionarischen Propaganda dienten[11]. Auch für R. Bultmann ist der „Sitz im Leben" „eine typische Situation oder Verhaltensweise im Leben einer Gemeinschaft"[12], er kann aber auch allgemeiner von den „im Leben der Gemeinde wirkenden Motiven" sprechen[13] und lehnt eine ausschließliche Zuordnung einer einzelnen Gattung zu einem einzelnen „Sitz im Leben" ab[14].

Antiindividualistisch ist auch die Sicht auf die Evangelisten, insbesondere auf Markus. „Die Verfasser sind nur zum geringsten Teil Schriftsteller, in der Hauptsache Sammler, Tradenten, Redaktoren"[15], und ihre Produkte, die Evangelien, sind zur unliterarischen „Kleinliteratur" zu rechnen[16]. Dass diese Sicht unzureichend ist, hat bereits die auf der „Formgeschichte" aufbauende sog. „Redaktionsgeschichte" gezeigt, die, ausgehend von der durch die Formgeschichte ermöglichten Unterscheidung zwischen Tradition und Redaktion, die „Redaktoren" als literarisch und theologisch ernst zu nehmende Autoren bestimmen konnte[17].

---

ihren Sitz im Volksleben hatten, zunächst nur in mündlicher Form existierten und vom Umfang her einfache, kleine Einheiten bildeten". Anfang der 30er Jahren erschien dann eine umfassende literatur- bzw. kulturwissenschaftliche Theorie dazu: A. JOLLES, *Einfache Formen*, (zuerst 1931), Tübingen, Niemeyer, [8]2006; zu einer neueren Darstellung des Problems (mit starkem Bezug auf Jolles) vgl. den Abschnitt „Das Problem der einfachen Formen" bei H. BAUSINGER, *Formen der „Volkspoesie"*, Berlin, E. Schmidt, 1968, S. 55-69.

11. DIBELIUS, *Formgeschichte* (Anm. 5), S. 93: „Die Predigt wirbt für das Heil und belegt, was sie sagt, durch ‚Paradigmen'. Die Novellen aber, von den Gemeinden erzählt, entfalten selbst werbende Kraft".
12. BULTMANN, *Geschichte* (Anm. 6), S. 4.
13. *Ibid.*, S. 5.
14. BULTMANN, *ibid*, S. 41, weist die Streitgespräche der „Apologetik und Polemik der palästinischen Gemeinde" zu, vgl. *ibid.*, S. 393: „Und so gewiß man etwa Wundergeschichten für Apologetik und Propaganda als Messiasbeweise benutzt haben wird, so wenig ist es möglich, ein spezielles Interesse als beherrschenden Faktor anzusehen".
15. DIBELIUS, *Formgeschichte* (Anm. 5), S. 2.
16. Vgl. *ibid.*, S. 2-3; damit greift Dibelius auf die von Franz Overbeck vertretene Unterscheidung zwischen der „christlichen Urliteratur" und der späteren patristischen Literatur zurück (s.o. Anm. 1).
17. Zur „Redaktionsgeschichte" vgl. O. MERK, *Redaktionsgeschichte/Redaktionskritik. II: Neues Testament*, in *TRE* 28 (1997) 378-384. Übrigens haben schon die Protagonisten der Formgeschichte faktisch wesentlich mehr über die Evangelisten zu sagen gewusst, als ihre Rolle lediglich als Sammler und Tradenten zu beschreiben. Dibelius und Bultmann fügen an ihre Analysen der Einzeltraditionen jeweils Darstellungen der Redaktionsarbeit der Evangelisten an, so DIBELIUS, *Formgeschichte* (Anm. 5), S. 219-234 (unter der

Seit längerem sind jedoch form- und redaktionsgeschichtlich orientierte Verfahrensweisen in erheblichem Umfang von linguistischen bzw. literaturwissenschaftlich ausgerichteten Auslegungsmodellen abgelöst worden, die bei aller inneren Differenziertheit durchgehend vom Primat der Synchronie ausgehen und damit vom vorliegenden Text, dessen Vorgeschichte nicht mehr Gegenstand des Interesses ist[18]. Allerdings meldet sich, jedenfalls bei einer stärker historischen Verankerung der neutestamentlichen Texte, insbesondere der Evangelien, die Frage von Schriftlichkeit und Mündlichkeit wieder zurück[19].

Für das Verhältnis von Mündlichkeit und Schriftlichkeit wird man allerdings feststellen müssen, dass die „Formgeschichte" die romantische Idee von Johann Gottfried Herders „Volkspoesie"[20] fortgeführt und deren unscharfe Bestimmung des Subjekts „Volk" beibehalten hat. Ebenso ist das Bild der Evangelisten als Sammler und Tradenten deutlich zeitgenössischen Konzepten verhaftet: Es entspricht in frappierender Weise dem landläufigen (allerdings verkürzten) Bild von den Gebrüdern Grimm als reinen Sammlern und Bewahrern von „Kinder- und Hausmärchen"[21]. Aber auch in zeitgenössischen Theoriekonzepten war der Autor lange nicht von eigenständigem Interesse. Im Mittelpunkt steht grundsätzlich

---

Überschrift „Sammlung"), der abschließend das MkEv als „Buch der geheimen Epiphanien" charakterisiert (S. 232), was einem reinen Sammelwerk sicher nicht entspricht; und BULTMANN, *Geschichte* (Anm. 6), S. 362-376, erörtert die „Redaktion des Erzählstoffes und die Komposition der Evangelien" und stellt für Mk 8,27-30 fest, dass hier – für den Leser – eine neue Epoche beginnt (S. 375), womit ja ansatzweise eine Gesamtstruktur des MkEv in den Blick kommt.

18. Charakteristisch ist, dass K. BERGER, *Formgeschichte des Neuen Testaments*, Heidelberg, Quelle & Meyer, 1984, sein Werk „Form*geschichte*" nennt, aber eine Geschichte der Gattungen der *schriftlich* existierenden neutestamentlichen Texte bietet und in Bezug auf seinen methodischen Ansatz erklärt: „Die Frage nach der mündlichen Vorgeschichte eines Stoffes oder Textes (z.B. als Tradition) ist von der Frage nach der Gattung und ihrer Geschichte prinzipiell zu trennen" (S. 12). THEISSEN, *Erforschung* (Anm. 8), interpretiert zwar die Exegese der 2. Hälfte des 20. Jh. als Wirkungsgeschichte der Ansätze der „Formgeschichte", doch räumt er rückblickend ein: Man könnte den Überblick über die neutestamentliche Forschung nach Bultmann und Dibelius auch „als Darstellung einer unumkehrbaren Erosion des formgeschichtlichen Konsenses konzipieren" (S. 452, Anm. 6).

19. Vgl. die verschieden gelagerten Beiträge in dem Sammelband von A. WEISSENRIEDER – R.B. COOTE (Hgg.), *The Interface of Orality and Writing: Speaking, Seeing, Writing in the Shaping of New Genres* (WUNT, 260), Tübingen, Mohr Siebeck, 2010.

20. Zur Bedeutung von J.G. Herder für die Entstehung des Konzepts der „Volkspoesie" bzw. „Volksdichtung" vgl. BAUSINGER, *Formen der „Volkspoesie"* (Anm. 10), S. 13-16.

21. Zur intensiven literarischen Gestaltung der Grimmschen Märchen vgl. BAUSINGER, *ibid.*, S. 162-179, und zusammenfassend H. RÖLLEKE, *Grimm, Jacob Ludwig Karl / Grimm, Wilhelm Karl. Kinder- und Hausmärchen*, in Kindlers Literaturlexikon, Bd. 6, Stuttgart, Metzler, 2009; Link: http://kll-aktuell.cedion.de/nxt/gateway.dll/kll/g/k0252500.xml?f= templates$fn=index.htm$3.0.

der Text, und provokativ wurde der „Tod des Autors im Text" proklamiert[22]. Immerhin ist in jüngster Zeit ein neues Interesse am Autor zu bemerken[23].

Ob der folgende Versuch – zumindest mittelbar – in diesen Kontext gehört, kann hier offen bleiben, jedenfalls soll gerade vom Bild des Autors her die Frage nach dem Verhältnis zwischen schriftlicher und mündlicher Überlieferung im Bereich der Synoptiker neu gestellt werden. Dabei kann es natürlich nicht um die Individualität des Verfassers gehen, sondern – und zwar speziell in Bezug auf Markus – um das Autorenprofil, das aus dem vorliegenden Werk erhoben werden kann. Die Untersuchung des Autorenprofils soll auf die Frage nach der Kompetenz des Autors konzentriert werden, und zwar in doppelter Hinsicht: a) welche Kompetenzen waren erforderlich, um ein Werk wie das Markusevangelium (MkEv) zu verfassen, und b) wie und wo konnte ein Autor im 1. Jh. n.Chr. diese Kompetenzen erwerben? Und schließlich c): Welche Rückschlüsse lässt das auf das „Milieu" des Autors, also frühchristliche Gemeinden der zweiten Hälfte des 1. Jh. n.Chr., zu?

II. Die literarische Gestalt des Markusevangeliums

Man kann das Markusevangelium als eine grundsätzlich biographisch ausgerichtete Großerzählung charakterisieren, die aus einer Vielzahl zumeist kürzerer Einzelerzählungen besteht. Diese narrativen Einzeleinheiten lassen sich in doppelter Hinsicht genauer beschreiben: a) hinsichtlich ihrer Länge und b) hinsichtlich ihrer Gattungen, wobei sich jeweils beide Aspekte in spezifischer Weise miteinander verbinden. Zum einen besteht das Markusevangelium aus zahlreichen kurzen narrativen Einheiten.

---

22. Vgl. den programmatischen Titel von R. Barthes, *La mort de l'auteur*, in *Œuvres complètes*, hg. von É. Marty, Paris, Seuil, 1994, 491-495; dazu vgl. aus systematisch-theologischer Sicht U.H.J. Körtner, *Autor. III. Systematisch-theologisch*, in *Lexikon der Bibelhermeneutik*, Berlin, De Gruyter, 2009, 61-62, und aus praktisch-theologischer Sicht: W. Engemann, *„Unser Text sagt…"*, in *ZTK* 93 (1996) 450-480, bes. S. 464-469. Zur Frage der Autorintention aus linguistischer Sicht vgl. auch J. Meibauer, *Autorintention. IV. Textlinguistisch*, in *Lexikon der Bibelhermeneutik*, S. 65-66. Im neutestamentlichen Bereich ist natürlich das Interesse am Autor Paulus nie erloschen, aber bei den Evangelisten erschöpft sich das Interesse am „Autor" meist in der Diskussion der altkirchlichen Nachrichten über die Verfasser.

23. Vgl. dazu (bezogen auf die moderne Person des Kommentators) E.-M. Becker, *Die Person des Kommentators als wissenschaftlicher ,persona'*, in Ead. – F.W. Horn – D.-A. Koch (Hgg.), *Der „Kritisch-exegetische Kommentar" in seiner Geschichte: H.A.W. Meyers KEK von seiner Gründung 1829 bis heute* (KEK, Sonderband), Göttingen, Vandenhoeck & Ruprecht, 2018, 70-82.

Die charakteristischen Gattungen sind hier die Wundererzählungen sowie Streit- und Schulgespräche. Hinzu kommen einige kürzere biographische Erzählungen (Taufe [Mk 1,9-11], Versuchung [1,12-13], Jüngerberufungen [1,16-20; 3,13-19], Verklärung [9,2-10]). Dreimal begegnen außerdem etwas umfangreichere Redeneinheiten (Mk 4; 7; 13), die jedoch narrativ gerahmt sind. Hiervon hebt sich in auffälliger Weise eine mittelgroße biographische Erzähleinheit ab, die Passionserzählung (Mk 14–15), die in sich in mehrere Einzelszenen gegliedert ist. Sie hat, allein schon durch ihren Umfang, aber natürlich auch durch ihre Stellung im Aufriss des Evangeliums, eine starke Prägekraft für das gesamte Werk. Aufs Ganze gesehen lässt sich für die einzelnen narrativen Bestandteile des Markusevangeliums ein geschicktes Gleichgewicht von vergleichbaren Erzählstrukturen (im Rahmen der jeweiligen Gattungen) und formaler und inhaltlicher Variation feststellen. Dies weist auf eine beachtliche darstellerische Kompetenz des Verfassers hin.

Blickt man nun auf das Gesamtwerk des Markusevangeliums, so stellt dieses keineswegs nur eine bloße Aneinanderreihung der in sich sehr vielgestaltigen Einzeleinheiten dar, vielmehr werden diese überlegt angeordnet und durch einen Gesamtrahmen zusammengehalten, der sich über das Ganze legt. Dies soll an zwei Punkten verdeutlicht werden:

1) Auf der Gesamtebene des Evangeliums ist zunächst eine klare geographische Strukturierung festzustellen, nämlich durch das Gegenüber von Galiläa (1,14–8,26) und Jerusalem (Kap. 11–15), dem sämtliche Einzeleinheiten zugeordnet sind. Der Übergang zwischen diesen beiden Schauplätzen wird sehr bewusst gestaltet: Ab 8,27 wird schrittweise Galiläa verlassen, und der „Weg", der den Rahmen für 8,27–10,52 bildet, ist, wie dann in 10,32 deutlich wird, der Weg nach Jerusalem. Hier liegt also erzählerisch die Peripetie des Gesamtwerkes. Wenn man aber neben der erzählerischen Gestalt des Markusevangeliums nach der inhaltlichen Gesamtgestaltung fragt, dann wird sofort wieder dieser Textabschnitt mit seinen inhaltlichen und gestalterischen Höhepunkten, dem Petrusbekenntnis (8,27–9,1) und den drei Leidens- und Auferstehungsankündigungen (8,31; 9,31; 10,32-34), in den Mittelpunkt rücken. Hier korrespondieren also geographische und inhaltliche Linienführung.

2) Ein Kabinettsstück eigener Art, an dem ebenfalls die gestalterische Kraft des Autors deutlich wird, ist der erste Unterabschnitt des Galiläateils, 1,14–3,6. Kennzeichnend für diesen Abschnitt ist die Zuordnung und Verschränkung von Wunder und Lehre. Zum einen gibt es zunächst eine Kette von drei, in sich durchaus unterschiedlich gestalteten Wundererzählungen; dabei handelt es sich um eine Exorzismuserzählung (1,21-28) und

zwei Krankheilungen (1,29-31; 1,40-45). Hinzu kommt als Summarium die generalisierende Heilungs- und Exorzismusszene von 1,32-34. Diesem Block von Wundertexten entspricht ab 2,13 ein Block von Einzelszenen, in denen Lehre vermittelt wird und die jeweils um das Thema „alt/neu" kreisen (vgl. das Logion 2,22): 2,13-17 (Zöllnergastmahl), 2,18-22 (Fastenfrage) und 2,23-28 (Sabbatfrage). Allerdings bleibt es nicht bei diesem Nebeneinander von Wunder und Lehre. Schon nach dem Wundersummarium 1,32-34 wird mit 1,35-39 eine Szene eingeschoben, die ausdrücklich formuliert, dass Jesu Aufgabe im Verkündigen *und* Dämonenaustreiben (in dieser Reihenfolge!) besteht, wobei sich „Verkündigen" und „Lehren" gegenseitig beleuchten und ergänzen, wie die Abfolge 1,21.22 (διδάσκειν) / 1,38-39 (κηρύσσειν) / 2,13 (διδάσκειν) zeigt[24].

Die Verschränkung von Wunder und Lehre in 1,14–3,6 greift aber noch wesentlich weiter: Am Anfang, in der Mitte und am Ende steht jeweils ein Wundertext, der so gestaltet ist, dass er in sich bereits eine Verbindung von Wunder und Lehre enthält. Dies gilt zum einen für 2,1-12, wo ihm Rahmen der Heilung eines Gelähmten die Frage nach der Vollmacht Jesu zur Sündenvergebung thematisiert wird. Dieser Text steht genau am Übergang von den Wunder- zu den Lehrtexten, hat also eine Scharnierfunktion für den ganzen Abschnitt. Untrennbar verbunden sind Wundertat und Lehre dann in dem Schlusstext des gesamten Abschnitts 1,14–3,6, in der Erzählung 3,1-5, in der die Heilung eines Kranken am Sabbat direkt den Konfliktfall bildet, der zu einer Grundsatzaussage über die Geltung des Sabbats führt. Diese Heilungs/Konfliktszene endet außerdem mit einem erzählerischen Coup, dem Todesbeschluss der Pharisäer und Herodianer in 3,6, der auf das Ende des Gesamtwerkes vorausweist und so Beginn und Ende miteinander verknüpft. Schließlich wird der gesamte Abschnitt, nach der biographischen Einleitung mit der Berufung der ersten vier Jünger (1,16-20), durch eine Exorzismuserzählung eröffnet, die zugleich eine Metareflexion zum Thema Lehre enthält. Diese Wundertat ist in einer Synagoge lokalisiert, also dem klassischen Ort der „Lehre", wobei der Erzähler vorweg referierend über Jesu Lehrtätigkeit sagt: „Er lehrte sie mit Vollmacht und nicht wie die Schriftgelehrten" (1,22). Dies wird nach der Wundertat durch die Zeugen in der Synagoge bestätigt, die eine „neue Lehre in Vollmacht" bestaunen.

Führt man sich die hier sichtbar werdende gestalterische Kraft vor Augen, so ergibt sich die Frage: Wo und wie konnte man im 1. Jh. n.Chr.

---

24. Vgl. die Aufnahme von καὶ ἐξελθόντες ἐκήρυξαν (Mk 6,12) durch καὶ ἀπήγγειλαν … πάντα ὅσα ἐποίησαν καὶ ὅσα *ἐδίδαξαν* in Mk 6,30 (Aussendung und die Rückkehr der Jünger).

eine derartige Kompetenz erwerben? Dabei sind die beiden Bereiche dieser Kompetenz zu beachten, die literarische und die inhaltliche.

III. DIE LITERARISCHE KOMPETENZ DES EVANGELISTEN MARKUS

Die literarische Kompetenz des Verfassers des Markusevangeliums betrifft sowohl die einzelnen narrativen Einheiten als auch die Gesamtstruktur des Evangeliums. Voraussetzung für die literarische Gestaltung des Werkes waren zunächst die Fähigkeiten, die im dreistufigen Bildungssystem des Hellenismus und der Kaiserzeit vermittelt wurden[25]. Das System war gegliedert in[26]:

a) den Elementarunterricht beim γραμματίστης; hier wurden die Grundlagen des Lesens, Schreibens und Rechnens vermittelt;

b) den sog. Grammatikunterricht, beim γραμματικός, der in die klassische Literatur einführte. Ziel dieses Unterrichts war die fehlerlose Wiedergabe der klassischen Texte aus Prosa und Dichtung. Das implizierte natürlich eine schon beachtliche Lektüre der entsprechenden Literatur. Parallel dazu wurden die Schüler auch an die Anfertigung eigener Texte herangeführt; dabei handelte es sich um einfache Übungstexte (*progymnasmata*), d.h. es ging um die Abfassung von Nacherzählungen, von Lehrszenen (Chrien) und Sentenzen sowie von kurzen thematischen Abhandlungen[27];

c) den Rhetorikunterricht beim ῥήτωρ. Die rhetorische Ausbildung war primär auf die Praxis der öffentlichen Rede, und zwar im politischen, juristischen und allgemein-gesellschaftlichen Bereich ausgerichtet. Dieser Zwecksetzung entsprachen die Standard-Genera, die *symbuleutische* (beratende) Rede, die *dikanische* Rede (Gerichtsrede) und die *epideiktische* Rede (Gelegenheits-/Festrede). Bestandteile des Unterrichts waren neben Vorlesungen die Klassikerlektüre[28] und die selbständige Abfassung von Texten, vor allem von Reden[29].

---

25. Hierzu sei exemplarisch verwiesen auf: H.-I. MARROU, *Geschichte der Erziehung im klassischen Altertum*, München, Deutscher Taschenbuch Verlag, [7]1977; W. LIEBESCHÜTZ, *Hochschule*, in *RAC* 15 (1991) 858-911; C. TORNAU, *Rhetorik*, in *RAC* 29 (2019) 1-94; K. VÖSSING, *Schule*, in *RAC* 29 (2019) 1160-1186; T. VEGGE, *Paulus und das antike Schulwesen: Schule und Bildung des Paulus* (BZNW, 134), Berlin, De Gruyter, 2006, S. 109-232.

26. Hierzu vgl. R. KANY, *Lehrer*, in *RAC* 22 (2008) 1091-1132, Sp. 1093-1101.

27. Quintilian, *Inst.* 1.9; 2.4.2-3; zur differenzierten Ausgestaltung der Aufgabenstellungen im Bereich der *progymnasmata* vgl. L. CALBOLI MONTEFUSCO, *Progymnasmata*, in *DNP* 10 (2001) 375-376; VEGGE, *Schulwesen* (Anm. 25), S. 121-138.

28. Dazu vgl. Quintilian, *Inst.* 2.5.

29. Vgl. Quintilian, *Inst.* 2.4.

Die Reden erforderten nicht nur die formale Beherrschung der jeweils charakteristischen Elemente der einzelnen Redegenera, es gehörte auch die Fähigkeit dazu, wichtige Bausteine einer Rede, wie die allgemein beliebten *exempla* oder auch die *narratio* (Erzählung), aktiv zu beherrschen, was durch praktische Übungen erreicht wurde[30]. Bei der *narratio* handelt es sich eigentlich um die Darstellung eines strittigen Rechtsfalls. Da aber die Rechtsfälle in der Regel Vorgänge betrafen, die eine z.T. erhebliche zeitliche Erstreckung aufweisen, ist die Bezeichnung der Darstellung als „Erzählung" durchaus berechtigt: Die Darstellung hatte durchweg narrative Struktur. „Narrativ" waren aber auch viele *exempla*[31] die häufig in der *argumentatio* zum Einsatz kamen. Von der *narratio* fordert Quintilian in weitgehendem Konsens mit seinen Vorgängern, dass sie „klar, kurz und wahrscheinlich" zu sein hat[32]. Ebenso wurde natürlich auch die Anfertigung der übrigen Teile der Rede wie *exordium*, *argumentatio* und *refutatio* eingeübt.

Die Rhetorikausbildung führte also bis zur Anfertigung eigener Texte, und zwar sowohl narrativer wie argumentativer Art. Zugleich zeigt die intensive Vermittlung von Dichtungs- und Prosatexten, dass die Anregungen des damaligen Bildungssystems über die rhetorische Zwecksetzung weit hinausgingen und sich so vielfältige Möglichkeiten individueller Aneignung und kreativer Anwendung eröffneten.

Vor diesem Hintergrund wird erkennbar, wie stark das Markusevangelium in die Welt der antiken Textproduktion eingebunden ist. Die Kompetenz für die Beherrschung narrativer Techniken konnte man somit in diesem Bildungssystem erwerben. Die markinischen Erzählungen entsprechen dabei durchaus den Anforderungen der Klarheit, der Kürze und der Glaubwürdigkeit – auch die Wundererzählungen entsprechen der Forderung der Glaubwürdigkeit, wenn an deren Ende die Zuschauer bezeugen: „So etwas haben wir noch nicht gesehen" (2,12).

Die Nähe zu den geläufigen Erzählgattungen und zugleich auch deren Abwandlung sind deutlich erkennbar. Die Nähe der Streit- und Schulgespräche zu den Chrien ist schon oft herausgestellt worden[33]. Zugleich erhalten die markinischen Chrien durch ihre szenische und inhaltliche

---

30. Zur *narratio* vgl. Quintilian, *Inst.* 4.2.
31. Dazu vgl. Quintilian, *Inst.* 5.11.
32. Quintilian, *Inst.* 4.2.31: *eam (i.e. narrationem) plerique scriptores … volunt esse lucidam, brevem, veri similem. neque enim refert, an pro lucida perspicuam, pro veri simili probabilem credibilemve dicamus* („von ihr [der Erzählung] fordern die meisten Fachschriftsteller …, sie solle klar, kurz und wahrscheinlich sein. Denn es macht keinen Unterschied, ob wir statt ‚klar' durchsichtig, statt ‚wahrscheinlich' einleuchtend oder glaubhaft sagen").
33. DIBELIUS, *Formgeschichte* (Anm. 5), S. 150-164.

Prägung (Schriftgelehrte und Pharisäer als Gesprächspartner, Gesetzesfragen als kontroverse Themen) ihr spezifisches Profil. Dies gilt in noch höherem Maße für die Wundererzählungen. Schon deren zahlenmäßig große Rolle ist auffällig, und innerhalb dieser Gruppe ist die hohe Zahl von Exorzismuserzählungen besonders hervorstechend. Im Vergleich zu den vielgestaltigen antiken Wundertexten lässt sich feststellen: Für alle gattungstypischen Einzelmerkmale (Darstellung der Krankheit, Bitte um Hilfe, Heilungsgestus, wunderwirkendes Wort, Demonstration der Heilung, Reaktion und Akklamation des Publikums) lassen sich Entsprechungen aufzeigen. An zwei Stellen wird aber ein vorgegebenes Motiv in charakteristischer Weise weiterentwickelt; dies gilt zum einen für die Äußerungen der Dämonen[34], die zum personalen Bekenntnis ausgebaut werden und nicht nur die Überlegenheit, sondern auch die Würde des Wundertäters (als „Heiliger Gottes" bzw. „Sohn Gottes") formulieren (1,24; 5,7, vgl. auch 3,11); in analoger Weise wird das Motiv vom Zutrauen zum Wundertäter (1,40; 5,28)[35] zur Aussage vom rettenden Glauben als Grund der Heilung weiterentwickelt (5,34; 10,52)[36].

Für die literarischen Großgattungen wie Biographie, Geschichtsschreibung oder auch die breite Palette der Fachliteratur (Geographie, Mechanik, Astronomie usw.) gab es keine mit den *progymnasmata* und der *narratio* vergleichbaren Lernprogramme. Hier waren die individuelle Kreativität und Gestaltungskraft die entscheidende Voraussetzung für den Erfolg. Im Ergebnis waren diese literarischen Erzeugnisse daher auch wesentlich individueller geprägt. Umgekehrt erwiesen sich die einzelnen Großgattungen, auch die Biographie, als ausgesprochen elastisch und boten erhebliche Variationsmöglichkeiten[37]. Wie stark Markus dabei die Gattung

---

34. Zu Beispielen für die Äußerung eines Dämons vgl. D.-A. KOCH, *Die Bedeutung der Wundererzählungen für die Christologie des Markusevangeliums* (BZNW, 42), Berlin, De Gruyter, 1975, S. 56, Anm. 7; personale Anreden, wie sie im MkEv vorliegen, sind jedoch extrem selten, vgl. KOCH, *ibid.*, S. 55, Anm. 4.

35. Vgl. dazu die Zusammenstellung bei G. THEISSEN, *Urchristliche Wundergeschichten: Ein Beitrag zur formgeschichtlichen Erforschung der synoptischen Evangelien* (StUNT, 8), Gütersloh, Gütersloher Verlagshaus Gerd Mohn, 1974, S. 64-65.

36. In 5,25-34 ist dies im Nebeneinander von V. 28 und V. 34 unübersehbar. Wie wichtig Mk das Thema ist, zeigt sich in der Fortsetzung: Vor dem Hintergrund von 5,25-34 bekommt die scheinbar beiläufige Bemerkung Jesu in 5,36: „Fürchte dich nicht, glaube nur" ein ganz anderes Gewicht; vgl. dazu KOCH, *Wundererzählungen* (Anm. 34), S. 139. Zusätzlich wird – im Rahmen des MkEv – der Dialog Jesu mit der blutflüssigen Frau von 5,33-34 und mit dem Vater in 5,36 durch den Dialog mit dem Vater des epileptischen Knabe in 9,22-44 ergänzt, der in dem Ausruf gipfelt: „Herr ich glaube, hilf meinem Unglauben".

37. Zur Biographie, deren Beginn im Hellenismus zu verorten ist, vgl. H. GÖRGEMANNS, *Biographie*, in *DNP* 2 (1997) 682-687; Vertreter der Einordnung des MkEv als Biographie betonen dabei regelmäßig die Variationsbreite antiker Biographien, die sich

„Biographie" umgestaltet hat, um sie seinem Darstellungsziel anzupassen, lässt sich erst im Zusammenhang mit der inhaltlichen Gesamtausrichtung seines Werkes erörtern.

IV. Das inhaltliche Profil des Markusevangeliums

Das Markusevangelium beschränkt sich nicht auf eine Darstellung der „Worte und Taten des Jesus von Nazareth", sondern erörtert auch explizit die Bedeutung seiner Person, und zwar indem ausdrücklich die Frage nach seiner Identität gestellt wird. Im Anschluss an die Wundertat der Sturmstillung stellen die geretteten Jünger die Frage, die man als Leitfrage des gesamten Markusevangeliums bezeichnen kann: „Wer ist dieser?" (4,41).

Auf der Metaebene des Buchbeginns wird bereits erkennbar, welche Antwort das Markusevangelium insgesamt geben will: Das Buch stellt sich selbst vor als εὐαγγέλιον von Jesus Christus, dem *Gottessohn* (1,1). Diese Antwort wird im Evangelium auf mehreren Ebenen in unterschiedlicher Weise entfaltet:

a) Auf der Ebene der göttlichen Legitimation wird Jesus zweimal vom Himmel her als Gottessohn identifiziert: Die Taufszene (1,9-11) gipfelt in der Aussage der „Stimme aus dem Himmel": „Du bist mein geliebter Sohn, an dem ich Wohlgefallen habe" (1,11). In der Szene der Verklärung (9,2-10) wird dies aufgenommen und im Blick auf die anwesenden Jünger ergänzt: „Dieser ist mein geliebter Sohn, auf ihn sollt ihr hören" (9,7). Beide Szenen sind bewusst platziert: die Taufe am Beginn des öffentlichen Wirkens Jesu überhaupt, und die Verklärung am Beginn

---

noch vergrößert, wenn man über die hellenistisch-paganen auch die jüdisch-hellenistischen Ausformungen einbezieht; vgl. THEISSEN, *Erforschung* (Anm. 8), S. 446-448; vgl. auch die Veröffentlichung von D. DORMEYER, *Das Markusevangelium als Idealbiographie von Jesus dem Nazarener* (SBB, 43), Stuttgart, Katholisches Bibelwerk, 1999, die schon im Titel die Generalthese des Buches enthält; vgl. deren Entfaltung S. 2-11. Gleichzeitig kann D. DORMEYER, *Formen/Gattungen III: Neues Testament*, in *RGG*[4] 3 (2000) 190-196, Sp. 195, formulieren: „Das Evangelium ist die originellste Gattung des Urchristentums". Die Gegenthese, die Zuordnung des MkEv zur Geschichtsschreibung wird von E.-M. BECKER, *Das Markus-Evangelium im Rahmen antiker Historiographie* (WUNT, 194), Tübingen, Mohr Siebeck, 2006, vertreten; vgl. EAD., *Der früheste Evangelist im Lichte der aktuellen Markusforschung: Eine Standortsbestimmung*, in EAD., *Der früheste Evangelist: Studien zum Markusevangelium* (WUNT, 380), Tübingen, Mohr Siebeck, 2017, 1-13; dort wird Mk als der früheste Evangelist charakterisiert, „der mit seiner Evangelienerzählung eine neue literarische Form, eine Gattung *sui generis*, schafft, die sich in den weiteren Rahmen der frühkaiserzeitlichen Historiographie einzeichnen lässt" (S. 8). – Einen kompakten Überblick über die neuere Diskussion zur Gattungsfrage des MkEv (einschließlich weiterer Vorschläge wie Aretalogie oder Roman) bietet U. SCHNELLE, *Einleitung in das Neue Testament* (UTB, 1380), Göttingen, Vandenhoeck & Ruprecht, [8]2017, S. 198-205.

des zweiten Teils des Markusevangeliums, der auf die Passion ausgerichtet ist.

b) Nicht göttlicher, aber doch übernatürlicher Herkunft ist das Wissen der Dämonen, die in Jesus den „Heiligen Gottes" (1,24), den „Gottessohn" (3,11) bzw. den „Sohn des höchsten Gottes" (5,7) erkennen.

c) Davon hebt sich das mangelnde bzw. begrenzte Verständnis der Menschen scharf ab. In der ersten Hälfte des Markusevangeliums sind es vor allem die Jünger, die trotz ihrer Nähe zu Jesus völlig ohne Verständnis sind. Auf die Sturmstillung reagieren sie mit der unverständigen Frage: „Wer ist dieser?" (4,41). Dem korrespondiert, dass in der zweiten Seegeschichte des Markusevangeliums, dem Seewandel (6,45-52), die Jünger Jesus nicht erkennen (6,49), was der Erzähler am Schluss mit der Feststellung kommentiert: „Sie waren nicht zum Verstand gekommen bei den Broten (d.h.: beim Wunder der Brotvermehrung 6,35-44), sondern ihr Herz war verhärtet"[38].

Am Beginn des zweiten Teils des Evangeliums wird die Frage nach der Person Jesu nochmals explizit gestellt, diesmal von Jesus selbst: „Wer sagen die Leute, dass ich sei?" (8,27). Nach drei unzureichenden Antworten gibt Petrus jetzt eine Antwort, die wenigstens in die richtige Richtung geht: „Du bist der Christus" (8,29). Diese Szene steht an der entscheidenden Peripetie des Evangeliums, dem Beginn des „Weges" (8,27: ἐν τῇ ὁδῷ) nach Jerusalem, d.h. zur Passion. Genau deswegen wird an dieses formal ja durchaus richtige Bekenntnis eine inhaltliche Präzisierung angefügt, nämlich die Ankündigung von Leiden und Auferstehung Jesu (8,31), die ausdrücklich als „notwendig" bezeichnet werden. Der anschließende Protest des Petrus (8,32) richtet sich dabei gegen die Notwendigkeit des Leidens, wie umgekehrt – nach der Zurückweisung dieses Protests (8,33) – die an die weitere Öffentlichkeit gerichtete ethische Belehrung von 8,34-37 die Leidensnachfolge zum Thema hat, und zwar mit dem bezeichnenden Stichwort des „Kreuz auf sich Nehmens" (8,34). Erst hier hat das *christos*-Bekenntnis seine endgültige Interpretation erfahren.

Im Verlauf des zweiten Teils setzt sich einerseits das mangelnde Verständnis der Jünger fort, so im Dialog nach der Verklärung (9,9-11) und im Zusammenhang der zweiten und dritten Leidens- und Auferstehungsankündigungen (9,30-32; 10,32-34). Der einzige, der etwas ahnt, ist ausgerechnet ein Blinder, der Jesus als „Sohn Davids" anruft (10,47-48).

---

38. Dem korrespondiert in Bezug auf den Bereich der Lehre das in 4,13 formulierte Unverständnis der Jünger angesichts der Parabelrede Jesu.

Die Frage nach der Identität Jesu begegnet dann letztmalig in der Passionsdarstellung, und zwar in doppelter Weise und jeweils an ausgesprochen exponierter Stelle: zum einen im Verhör durch den Hohen Rat, in dessen Verlauf der Hohe Priester Jesus fragt: „Bist du der Christus, der Sohn des Hochgelobten?" (14,61). Diese Frage ist vor dem Hintergrund des Petrusbekenntnisses von 8,29 zu lesen. Dort musste Markus den Zusammenhang zwischen christologischem Bekenntnis und Passion durch die Anfügung der Leidens- und Auferstehungsankündigung eigens herstellen, hier ist die Passionssituation so evident, dass das Selbstbekenntnis, das Jesus mit der bejahenden Antwort gibt (14,62), nicht missverstanden werden kann. Der zweite Ort, an dem die Frage nach der Identität Jesu beantwortet wird, ist das Kreuz selbst, wenn dort der römische Hauptmann sagt: „Wahrhaftig dieser Mensch war Gottes Sohn" (15,39) – und die Adressaten des MkEv sollen dies aufnehmen, aber in der Form: Wahrhaftig dieser Mensch *ist* Gottes Sohn.

Damit zeigt sich auch, wie Markus die Großgattung „Biographie" weiterentwickelt bzw. umgestaltet hat – hin zu einer Darstellung des irdischen Wirkens des jetzt erhöhten Gottessohns (vgl. 12,36). Dass hier nicht in üblicher Weise ein βίος erzählt wird, zeigt bereits der Buchbeginn, der keinem bisherigen literarischen Modell entspricht. In ihm wird vielmehr ein Begriff aus der mündlichen Verkündigung, nämlich εὐαγγέλιον, erstmals zur Bezeichnung eines schriftlichen Textes benutzt; und obwohl keines der auf Markus folgenden (und auf dem MkEv aufbauenden) „Evangelien" diesen Terminus als Buchbezeichnung aufgenommen hat, ist dieser Begriff zur Gattungsbestimmung geworden[39].

---

39. Dies erfolgte in der 1. Hälfte des 2. Jh. und ist bei Justin, *1 Apol.* 66, vorausgesetzt, wenn er den Text, aus dem im Vollzug der Eucharistie zitiert wird, zunächst als die ἀπομνημονεύματα („Erinnerungen") der Apostel bezeichnet und dann erklärend hinzufügt: ἃ καλεῖται εὐαγγέλια („die *euangelia* genannt werden"). Das bedeutet: 1. mit εὐαγγέλια ist ein schriftlicher Text gemeint; 2. mit der Bezeichnung ἀπομνημονεύματα wendet sich der Verfasser an Außenstehende, um ihnen so die innerchristliche Bezeichnung εὐαγγέλια zu erklären; zu Justin, *1 Apol.* 66 vgl. J. ULRICH, *Justin, Apologien* (Kommentare zu frühchristlichen Apologeten, 4/5), Freiburg i.Br., Herder, 2019, S. 509-510.
Die Verwendung von εὐαγγέλιον als Bezeichnung für einen schriftlichen Text liegt aber schon in *Did.* 15.3+4 vor, wenn dort zweimal eine ethische Mahnung mit dem Hinweis begründet wird: ὡς ἔχετε ἐν τῷ εὐαγγελίῳ („wie ihr es im Evangelium habt"). Gleiches gilt für *Did.* 8.2: In der Einleitung zum Vater-Unser-Gebet mit ὡς ἐκέλευσεν ὁ κύριος ἐν τῷ εὐαγγελίῳ αὐτοῦ („wie der Herr in seinem Evangelium befohlen hat") hat die Erwähnung des εὐαγγέλιον nur dann einen Sinn, wenn sie sich auf ein identifizierbares Buch bezieht; vgl. K. WENGST, *Didache (Apostellehre), Barnabasbrief, Zweiter Klemensbrief, Schrift an Diognet* (Schriften des Urchristentums, 2), Darmstadt, Wissenschaftliche Buchgesellschaft, 1984, S. 25-28. Für die *Didache* ist dabei die Nähe zum MtEv unübersehbar, obwohl Mt εὐαγγέλιον als Buchbezeichnung durch βίβλος γενέσεως ersetzt hat!

V. Die inhaltliche Kompetenz des Verfassers des Markusevangeliums

Führt man sich die intensive Gestaltung des MkEv vor Augen, dann ist zunächst festzustellen, dass sie sowohl die einzelnen kurzen Bestandteile des Evangeliums als auch das Werk als Ganzes betrifft – und dass beides aufs engste miteinander korrespondiert. Hier ist nicht ein fremdes Deutungskonzept über ein ganz anders ausgerichtetes Material gelegt worden, sondern beides, die Gestalt der Einzeleinheiten und die des Gesamtwerkes stammen aus einer Hand. Das setzt eine intensive und aktive Beschäftigung mit der Jesusüberlieferung seitens des Verfassers voraus, und es ist zu fragen, wo es im Urchristentum einen institutionellen Ort für eine solche Beschäftigung gab, einen Ort also, der dem Verfasser die Möglichkeit bot, eine derartige Kompetenz zu erwerben, denn einen Ort außerhalb des Bereichs der urchristlichen Gemeinden kann man mit Sicherheit ausschließen.

1. *Der institutionelle Ort der Jesustraditionen: Die Lehre im Urchristentum*

Schon Paulus schreibt wenige Jahre nach der Gründung der Gemeinde von Korinth an die dortige Gemeinde: „Und die einen hat Gott in der Gemeinde eingesetzt erstens als Apostel, zweitens als Propheten, drittens als Lehrer" (1 Kor 12,28a). Diese drei Funktionen sind bereits deutlich institutionalisiert – im Unterschied zu allen anderen „Charismen", die Paulus im Anschluss aufzählt (12,28b). Dabei ist klar, dass die vielfältigen Aufgaben, die in den im Aufbau (und weiterem Wachstum) befindlichen frühen Gemeinden bestanden, nur mit den personellen Ressourcen bewältigt werden konnten, die auch tatsächlich vorhanden waren. Gleichzeitig ist deutlich, dass mit „Apostel, Propheten und Lehrer" offenbar konstante Aufgaben beschrieben sind, die zur Bildung dieser relativ stabilen Ämter geführt haben. An der Spitze steht – in der geschichtlichen Situation der ersten Generation – der Apostel, der „den Herrn gesehen hat" (1 Kor 9,1, vgl. 15,8) und der, jedenfalls nach paulinischem Verständnis, in besonderer Weise mit der missionarischen und gemeindegründenden Funktion des Urchristentums verbunden ist. „Propheten" wird man – im Anschluss an 1 Kor 14 – am ehesten als vollmächtige Prediger bezeichnen können (vgl. 1 Kor 14,22-25).

Über die hier von Paulus ebenfalls erwähnten „Lehrer", die auch in Apg 13,1 für Antiochia neben den Propheten genannt werden, ist wesentlich weniger bekannt[40]. Das liegt sicher daran, dass deren Tätigkeit ganz

---

40. A.F. Zimmermann, *Die urchristlichen Lehrer: Studien zum Tradentenkreis der διδάσκαλοι im frühen Urchristentum* (WUNT, 2.12), Tübingen, Mohr Siebeck, 1984,

offensichtlich zu keinen Fragen Anlass gab oder gar Kontroversen hervorrief. Immerhin gibt Paulus in Gal 6,6 die Anweisung: „Derjenige, der über das ‚Wort' unterrichtet worden ist, gebe dem Unterrichtenden an allen Gütern Anteil". Das ist recht offen formuliert, schließt aber die Möglichkeit von finanziellen Leistungen ein[41]. Hierbei muss es sich um eine grundlegende und für die spätere Existenz des Unterrichteten wegweisende Unterweisung gehandelt haben. Insofern wird man die Anweisung von Gal 6,6 am ehesten auf diejenige Phase der Unterweisung beziehen können, die mit dem Eintritt in die Gemeinde, genauer gesagt: mit der Taufe verbunden war.

Insofern die Taufe „auf den Namen des Herrn Jesus"[42] erfolgte, war es notwendig, in Blick auf die rituell hergestellte Beziehung zu diesem κύριος, dessen Person zuvor dem Taufanwärter nahezubringen. Die Taufe als Basisritual der ständig wachsenden Urchristenheit führte, so muss man schlussfolgern, zu einem kontinuierlichen Bedarf an „Lehre" bzw. (in Anschluss an die Terminologie von Gal 6,6) an „Katechetik", und damit zu deren Institutionalisierung.

Zwar sind die direkten Belege für eine präbaptismale Unterweisung für das 1. Jh. n.Chr. selten, was jedoch kein Gegenbeweis ist. Ihr (weitgehendes) Fehlen in der Apostelgeschichte und im Matthäusevangelium ist aus der Zielsetzung der jeweiligen Schriften erklärbar[43]. Ein deutlicher

---

S. 92-113, hält 1 Kor 12,28a für ein paulinisches Zugeständnis an eine Petrus-Front, in deren Traditionsbereich (s. Apg 13,1) diese Trias institutionalisiert gewesen sei – aber eben nicht in den paulinischen Gemeinden (S. 106-113). Er nimmt vielmehr an, „dass sich in der Urgemeinde bald nach Jesu Tod und Auferstehung ein judaistisch-pharisäischer Kreis von διδάσκαλοι gebildet hat" (S. 218), der aber nicht lange Bestand gehabt habe. Diese Sicht hat sich mit Recht nicht durchgesetzt.

41. Dies ist in der Exegese umstritten, vgl. H. SCHLIER, *Der Brief an die Galater* (KEK, 7), Göttingen, Vandenhoeck & Ruprecht, (11/1)1951, S. 202-203; H.D. BETZ, *Der Galaterbrief* (Hermeneia; englisch: 1979), München, Kaiser, 1988, S. 517-520. Sicher ist nicht an eine direkte Bezahlung durch die Teilnehmer der christlichen Unterweisung gedacht, eher formuliert Paulus hier eine allgemeine ethische Maxime über das Verhältnis zwischen Unterweisendem und Unterwiesenen (Paulus vermeidet die Terminologie Lehrer/Schüler!), die auch – bei Bedarf – materielle Gemeinschaft einschließt.

42. Dazu vgl. die Studie von L. HARTMAN, *Auf den Namen des Herrn Jesus: Die Taufe in den neutestamentlichen Schriften* (SBS, 148), Stuttgart, Katholisches Bibelwerk, 1992.

43. Lk unterscheidet in der Apg nicht zwischen öffentlicher Missionsverkündigung (vorzugsweise durch Reden) und der Taufunterweisung. Er ist an der Bekehrung (möglichst vieler!) als direkter Folge der geistgewirkten Rede eines Apostels interessiert (exemplarisch: Apg 2,14-40/41). Katechetische Situationen werden ansatzweise in Apg 16,13-15 (die „gottesverehrende" Lydia) und etwas deutlicher in Apg 8,26-39 (der äthiopische Eunuch) sichtbar. – Auch die Nachordnung der „Lehre" nach der Taufe in Mt 28,19-20 berührt nicht die Frage nach der präbaptismalen Katechese: Für Mt ist die gesamte Verkündigung der Kirche „Lehre", Weitergabe dessen, was Jesus ihr „geboten hat", vgl. U. LUZ, *Das Evangelium nach Matthäus*. 4. Teilband: *Mt 26-28* (EKKNT, 1/4), Zürich, Benziger Verlag; Neukirchen-Vluyn, Neukirchener Verlag, 2002, S. 454-455.

Verweis auf eine feste Praxis der Taufunterweisung liegt dagegen in Hebr 6,1-2 vor, wenn dort zur „Anfangsunterweisung über Christus" die „Lehre über die Taufen"[44] selbst gehört – sie wird ja mit Sicherheit dem Taufakt vorausgegangen sein[45].

Bemerkenswert ist auch die Zuordnung von Taufe und Lehre in Röm 6. Thema ist die Taufe als Grund für die Befreiung der Adressaten von der Macht der Sünde: Aufgrund der in der Taufe hergestellten Christusgemeinschaft (6,2-5) können die Getauften der ἁμαρτία widerstehen. Dieser Existenzwandel bedeutet, dass es von denen, die zuvor „Diener der Sünde" waren, jetzt heißen kann: „Ihr seid dem Kern der Lehre gehorsam geworden, den ihr weitergegeben bekommen habt" (6,17)[46]. Mit diesem „Kern (oder auch: Extrakt) der Lehre" kann durchaus eine Kurzfassung der Lehre gemeint sein, die direkt im Taufvollzug Verwendung fand – aber eine solche Kurzfassung weist zurück auf das, was zuvor ausführlicher entfaltet wurde, also die präbaptismale Katechese.

2. *Zur Durchführung der Lehre*

Damit stellen sich zwei Fragen:

a) Wie wurde die „Lehre" durchgeführt, genauer gesagt: Wie wurde die Kenntnis der Person Jesu vermittelt?
b) Wer hat diese Aufgabe übernommen?

Zu a) Naheliegend war es, soweit vorhanden, konkrete Erinnerungen an das Wirken, die Lehre und das Geschick Jesu zum Gegenstand der Unterweisung zu machen. Dabei war dieses Wissen in den Gemeinden offenbar recht unterschiedlich. Legt man die recht geringe Verwendung von Jesustraditionen in den Paulusbriefen zugrunde, dann war auch das entsprechende Wissen in den von ihm gegründeten und geprägten Gemeinden recht begrenzt: Jedenfalls ist kein Grund ersichtlich, warum Paulus Jesusüberlieferungen absichtlich übergangen haben soll. Die

---

44. Zum Plural vgl. die Diskussion bei E. GRÄSSER, *An die Hebräer*. 1. Teilband: *Hebr 1–6* (EKKNT, 17/1), Zürich, Benziger Verlag; Neukirchen-Vluyn, Neukirchener Verlag, 1990, S. 341-342.
45. Als Inhalte der Taufunterweisung werden insgesamt drei Bereiche genannt: a) „Abkehr von den toten Werken" (nach Hebr 9,9-10.14 ist dies wohl auf den jüdischen Kult zu beziehen) und der „Glaube an Gott"; b) die „Lehre von den Taufen und der Handauflegung"; c) „Auferstehung und ewiges Gericht".
46. Zu diesem Verständnis von Röm 6,17 vgl. M. WOLTER, *Der Brief an die Römer*. Teilband 1: *Röm 1–8*, Ostfildern, Patmos; Neukirchen-Vluyn, Neukirchener Verlagsgesellschaft, 2014, S. 396-398. Der Bezug auf die Taufe ist aber auch dann gegeben, wenn man übersetzt „… der Gestalt der Lehre, der ihr übergeben wurdet", so E. LOHSE, *Der Brief an die Römer* (KEK, 4), Göttingen, Vandenhoeck & Ruprecht [15(1)]2003, S. 198, 201.

katechetischen Überlieferungen, die Paulus zitiert, beziehen sich auf Eckpunkte des Wirkens und Geschicks Jesu, auf Passion und Auferweckung (1 Kor 15,3b-5) und die Einsetzung des Herrenmahls (1 Kor 11,23-25). Anders als in den Texten des MkEv handelt es sich dabei um die knappe, in parallelen Zeilen angeordnete Darstellung von Vorgängen, aber nicht um narrative Stücke[47].

Die Debatte „Paulus und Jesus" wird zumeist als hermeneutische Frage geführt, und zwar als Frage nach dem Verhältnis der Botschaft Jesu zur Verkündigung des Paulus und dem Problem der Entstehung einer (expliziten) Christologie[48]. Diese Fragestellung ist völlig sachgemäß, doch erübrigt sich damit nicht die Rückfrage nach den möglichen historischen Gründen für die geringe Rolle der Jesusüberlieferungen bei Paulus. Hier wird man die realen Überlieferungswege der Jesuserinnerungen in den sich formierenden Gemeinden des Urchristentums berücksichtigen müssen. Dabei ist davon auszugehen, dass die primären Träger bzw. Vermittler der Jesuserinnerungen, die in personaler Kontinuität mit dem vorösterlichen Jesus standen, in den ersten Jahrzehnten des Urchristentums in Jerusalem ansässig waren. Hier hatte sich der Zwölferkreis vollständig niedergelassen, und mit der Mutter und den Brüdern Jesu war aus Galiläa maßgebliche Verstärkung gekommen[49]. Umgekehrt ist für Paulus festzustellen, dass seine tatsächlichen Kontakte zur Jerusalemer Urgemeinde ausgesprochen begrenzt waren. Abgesehen vom letzten Treffen, das die Überbringung der Kollekte für Jerusalem zum Ziel hatte[50], lassen sich nur zwei Besuche benennen. 1.) Der in Gal 1,18-19 erwähnte Besuch bei Petrus nach dem Ende seiner offenbar erfolglosen Arabienmission und seiner Flucht aus Damaskus (2 Kor 11,32-33; Apg 9,24-25)[51]. In diesen zwei Wochen hielt sich Paulus – ganz offensichtlich aus Sicherheitsgründen

---

47. Vgl. auch H. GREEVEN, *Propheten, Lehrer, Vorsteher bei Paulus: Zur Frage der „Ämter" im Urchristentum*, in *ZNW* 44 (1952/53) 1-43, S. 20-22, der in den διδάσκαλοι der paulinischen Gemeinden Träger des Traditionsgutes sieht.

48. Vgl. die seinerzeit grundlegende Darstellung von E. JÜNGEL, *Paulus und Jesus: Eine Untersuchung zur Präzisierung der Frage nach dem Ursprung der Christologie* (HUT, 2), Tübingen, Mohr Siebeck, 1967; zur neueren Debatte vgl. J. SCHRÖTER, *Jesus bei Paulus*, in F.W. HORN (Hg.), *Paulus Handbuch*, Tübingen, Mohr Siebeck, 2013, 284-285 (mit neuerer Literatur); ausführlicher: M. WOLTER, *Paulus: Ein Grundriss seiner Theologie*, Neukirchen-Vluyn, Neukirchener Verlag, 2011, S. 449-455 (§54: Paulus und Jesus).

49. Dies macht eine parallele stabile Gruppenbildung in Galiläa unwahrscheinlich, vgl. D.-A. KOCH, *Geschichte des Urchristentums: Ein Lehrbuch*, Göttingen, Vandenhoeck & Ruprecht, ²2014, S. 185-191.

50. Zur Kollektenreise vgl. KOCH, *ibid.*, S. 331-343; ID., *The Collection for Jerusalem: A Joint Action of Paul and Pauline Communities in Greece and Asia 53-56 AD*, in *ETL* 26 (2020) 603-622.

51. Ein früherer Besuch, nämlich unmittelbar nach seiner Bekehrung, wie er in Apg 9,26-30 dargestellt wird, ist historisch nicht zu sichern, da er klar den Angaben von Gal 1,17

– faktisch inkognito in Jerusalem auf und hatte über Petrus und Jakobus hinaus keinen Kontakt mit der Urgemeinde insgesamt[52]. 2.) Der zweite Besuch erfolgte im Rahmen des sog. Apostelkonzils (Apg 15; Gal 2,1-10); hier war Paulus neben (und nach!) Barnabas Vertreter der Gemeinde von Antiochia, um in Jerusalem eine Klärung des Problems der beschneidungsfreien Heidenmission zu erreichen. Das bedeutet, dass es einen kontinuierlichen Kontakt mit der Jerusalemer Gemeinde für Paulus nicht gegeben hat; und was er an katechetischen Jesusüberlieferungen kennt, geht offensichtlich auf seine Zeit in der antiochenischen Gemeinde zurück, in der diese Überlieferungen präsent waren.

Wenn man annimmt, dass der Verfasser des Markusevangeliums seine Kenntnis der Jesuserinnerungen innerhalb einer christlichen Gemeinde erworben hat – und eine Alternative dazu ist nicht erkennbar – dann ist zunächst festzustellen: In dieser Gemeinde war der Umfang der Jesuserinnerungen, die zur Verfügung standen, ungleich größer als in den paulinischen Gemeinden. Dann ist es aber auch eine naheliegende Annahme, dass diese Jesuserinnerungen in der „Lehre" Verwendung fanden, denn die Hauptaufgabe der Lehre bestand ja darin, Personen, die am Eintritt in die Gemeinde, und damit an der Taufe auf den Namen des Herrn Jesus, interessiert waren, Kenntnis dieses κύριος Ἰησοῦς zu vermitteln. Hier gab es einen festen institutionellen Ort für die Bewahrung und Weitergabe der Jesustraditionen, was natürlich deren Verwendung außerhalb der auf die Taufe ausgerichteten Lehre nicht ausschließt.

Zu b) Angesichts des kontinuierlichen Wachstums der christlichen Gemeinden war die Aufgabe der Lehre eine Dauerfunktion. Durchgeführt werden konnte diese Aufgabe natürlich nur durch Mitglieder der christlichen Gemeinden selbst, nicht durch externe Lehrkräfte. Doch gab es für diese Gemeindelehrer keine Möglichkeit, sich vor Beginn ihrer Tätigkeit auf ihre Aufgabe vorzubereiten. Ein christlicher Lehrer musste natürlich die Qualifikationen mitbringen, die das allgemeine Unterrichtssystem vermittelte, aber die konkreten inhaltlichen Kenntnisse und die Fähigkeit, diese zu vermitteln, musste er sich im Vollzug der Arbeit selbst aneignen.

Das bedeutete aber auch: Um diese Fähigkeiten zu erwerben, die der Verfasser des MkEv nach Ausweis seines Werkes zweifelsfrei besaß, war eine langjährige intensive Beschäftigung mit den Jesusüberlieferungen

---

widerspricht und umgekehrt dem Interesse des Lk an lückenloser Kontinuität in der Entwicklung des Urchristentums entspricht, vgl. KOCH, *Geschichte* (Anm. 49), S. 214-215.

52. Zu diesem Besuch vgl. D.-A. KOCH, *Paulus als Gast des Petrus in Jerusalem – Petrus als Gastgeber des Paulus*, in H. OMERZU – E.D. SCHMIDT (Hgg.), *Paulus und Petrus: Geschichte – Theologie – Rezeption. Festschrift für F.W. Horn* (ABG, 48), Leipzig, Evangelische Verlagsanstalt, 2016, 43-57.

erforderlich, und zwar zum einen zur inhaltlichen Profilierung der Einzeltraditionen und ihrer sprachlichen Gestaltung, und darüber hinaus erst recht zur schrittweisen Erarbeitung einer theologischen Gesamtkonzeption, die sich dann auch in der literarischen Gesamtkonzeption niederschlägt.

Im Blick auf den Verfasser des MkEv lässt sich feststellen:

1. Der Verfasser war ein urchristlicher Lehrer, der diese Tätigkeit im Rahmen einer christlichen Gemeinde für eine erhebliche Zeitspanne ausgeübt hat.

2. Für alle urchristlichen Lehrer in dieser Phase gilt, dass sie vor der Notwendigkeit standen, die Aufgabe des Lehrens ohne ausreichende Voraussetzungen zu übernehmen, so dass sie erst im Vollzug der Arbeit die Inhalte der Lehre entwickeln konnten.

3. Unter diesen Lehrern war der Verfasser des MkEv sicher eine herausragende Gestalt.

3. *Markus: Vom Lehrer zum katechetischen Schriftsteller*

Die Existenz des MkEv zeigt, dass ein einzelner urchristlicher Lehrer, von dem wir allenfalls den Namen kennen („Markus"), sich im Lauf seiner langjährigen Unterrichtstätigkeit eine hohe Kompetenz erworben hat und zu einem bestimmten Zeitpunkt dazu übergegangen ist, den Inhalt der mündlich vorgetragenen Lehre schriftlich niederzulegen. Um die Tragweite dieses Schritts abzuschätzen, ist kurz der Unterschied zwischen mündlicher und schriftlicher Vermittlung im Bereich der Lehre zu beleuchten:

a) Die unbestreitbaren Vorteile der mündlichen Vermittlung der Lehre sind unmittelbar mit ihrer personalen Kommunikation verbunden: Zum einen ermöglicht sie es, den Unterrichtsverlauf flexibel der jeweiligen Unterrichtssituation anzupassen. Das betrifft sowohl die Auswahl der Stoffe als auch das Tempo. Vor allem aber impliziert die direkte persönliche Vermittlung auch die Möglichkeit, Verständnisdefizite rasch zu erkennen und unmittelbar aufzufangen. Der grundsätzliche Nachteil direkter personal vermittelter Lehre besteht darin, dass sie gleichzeitig auch personal und räumlich begrenzt ist: Der Lehrer erreicht nur die Adressaten, die mit ihm zur gleichen Zeit am gleichen Ort leben und zur gleichen Christengemeinde gehören. Die Lehre, die an die Person des Lehrers gebunden ist, ist damit auch lokal begrenzt. Das gilt auch dann, wenn der Lehrer nach einiger Zeit seinen Wirkungsort wechselt – dann ist er zwar an einem neuen Ort tätig, aber wiederum nur an diesem[53].

---

53. Wanderlehrer sind aus *Did.* 11.1-2 und 13.2 bekannt. Zum Verhältnis von (wandernden) Aposteln, Propheten und Lehrern im Bereich der *Didache* vgl. K. NIEDERWIMMER, *Die Didache* (KAV, 1), Göttingen, Vandenhoeck & Ruprecht, 1989, S. 228:

b) Für die schriftliche Vermittlung gilt: Wenn der Inhalt der bislang mündlich vermittelten Lehre in Form eines Buches schriftlich fixiert und verbreitet wird, eröffnet sich natürlich eine ganz andere Reichweite: Die schriftlich verbreitete Lehre kann jetzt im Idealfall alle christlichen Gemeinden erreichen. Die räumliche Entgrenzung ist jedoch mit einem gravierenden Nachteil verbunden: Die Lehre wird jetzt nicht mehr personal vermittelt, der Lehrer kann den Lernerfolg nicht mehr beurteilen und konkreten Erfordernissen anpassen. Kurz: die Kommunikation ist von der Person des Lehrers abgelöst.

Ganz offensichtlich sind dem Verfasser die Nachteile bzw. Probleme der schriftlichen Vermittlung von Lehre bewusst. Jedenfalls ist feststellbar, dass er Sachverhalte, die ihm besonders wichtig sind, mehrfach anspricht und – leicht variierend – wiederholt. Am auffälligsten sind in dieser Hinsicht natürlich die drei Leidens- und Auferstehungsweissagungen (Mk 8,31; 9,31; 10,32-34), aber auch die verschiedenen Gottessohnproklamationen sind hier zu nennen. Vor allem aber: Markus musste das Gesamtverständnis der Person Jesu, das in der mündlichen Vermittlung anhand von Einzelüberlieferungen eher indirekt vermittelt wurde, jetzt auch explizit machen. Markus wusste, dass eine Gesamtdarstellung mehr ist als die bloße Aneinanderreihung von katechetischen Einzelstoffen.

4. Der Zweck der Verschriftlichung der Lehre

Geht man von einem insgesamt dynamischen, d.h. konkret: einem exponentiellen Wachstum der urchristlichen Gemeinden aus[54], dann wuchs in gleichem Maße auch der Bedarf an Lehre – und das heißt auch: der Bedarf an Lehrern. Neue Lehrer, die sich mit viel gutem Willen, aber wenig inhaltlichen Vorkenntnissen dieser Aufgabe zuwandten, benötigten Hilfestellung, und zwar in doppelter Hinsicht:

a) Sie benötigten Jesusüberlieferungen zu bestimmten Themen (Grundinformationen über die Person Jesu und seine Verkündigung; Grundorientierung in Fragen der christlichen Lebensführung);

b) darüber hinaus war es für sie erforderlich, ein Gesamtverständnis der Person Jesu zu gewinnen, um so einen Bezugsrahmen für die Einzelüberlieferungen zu haben. Beides lieferte das MkEv, und zwar nicht zufällig, weil es eben selbst aus der Lehre erwachsen war.

„Während zur Zeit des Didachisten mit Wander-*Aposteln* nicht mehr gerechnet wird, ist der wandernde *Prophet* nach wie vor eine der Gemeinde bekannte Gestalt. Neben ihn tritt jetzt der διδάσκαλος (von dem die alte Tradition 11,4-12 nichts gesagt hatte)".

54. Dazu vgl. KOCH, *Geschichte* (Anm. 49), S. 429-430.

Als Primäradressaten des MkEv sind daher die angehenden urchristlichen Lehrer zu identifizieren, was natürlich eine individuelle Lektüre durch andere Mitglieder christlicher Gemeinden nicht ausschließt. Das MkEv ist somit das Buch eines Lehrers für Lehrer, die sich in einem Prozess der Selbstqualifizierung befinden.

Für den Status des MkEv als eines schriftlichen Textes bedeutet das: Der Verfasser zielt darauf ab, dass die Primäradressaten, die Lehrer, dieses Buch zunächst selbst als schriftlichen Text rezipieren und damit die eigene theologische Selbstklärung voranbringen. Als Buch für Lehrer, die in der konkreten Pflicht stehen, Unterricht zu erteilen, ist es aber dafür gedacht, dass es dann als Handbuch für die zu erteilende Lehre benutzt wird. Damit wären auch die Nachteile der rein schriftlichen Vermittlung der Lehre wieder ausgeglichen: Der aus mündlicher Lehre hervorgegangene schriftliche Text würde wieder in mündliche Vermittlung überführt werden. Gleichwohl ist damit die Verschriftlichung nicht aufgehoben: In schriftlicher Form vorliegend bleibt der Text auch für dessen mündliche Umsetzung als Korrektiv dauerhaft präsent.

VI. Beobachtungen zur Rolle des Lehrens im Markusevangelium und im Prolog des Lukasevangeliums

1. *Die Rolle des Lehrens in der Darstellung des Wirkens Jesu im Markusevangelium*

Bestimmt man das MkEv in der vorgeschlagenen Weise als einen Text, der aus der Lehre heraus erwachsen ist und der zur Verwendung in der Lehre bestimmt war, erhält die Darstellung des Lehrens innerhalb des Werkes eine zusätzliche Bedeutung.

Es wurde schon zu Beginn darauf hingewiesen, dass Markus in dem besonders sorgfältig komponierten Abschnitt Mk 1,21–3,6 Jesus als Lehrer darstellt, der anders als das Gegenbild, die Schriftgelehrten, „in Vollmacht" lehrt (1,22), und dass Markus Jesu Verkündigung als „neue Lehre in Vollmacht" bezeichnet (1,27). Doch beschränkt sich das Thema des Lehrens nicht auf diesen Abschnitt. Charakteristisch für das MkEv ist die häufige Erwähnung des Lehrens, ohne dass damit ein bestimmter Inhalt verbunden wäre. Natürlich gibt es auch Verwendungen von διδάσκειν, die sich direkt auf bestimmte Lehrinhalte beziehen, so Mk 8,31; 9,31 (jeweils Leidens- und Auferstehungsankündigungen); 12,35 (Vollmachtsfrage). Wesentlich häufiger ist jedoch das absolute Vorkommen von διδάσκειν (1,21.22; 2,13; 4,1; 6,2.6.34; 10,1). „Worauf es Markus ankommt, ist nur die Tatsache, daß dieses Lehren in Vollmacht erfolgt"[55]. Besonders aufschlussreich ist dabei die redaktionelle Einleitung der Wunderüberlieferung von der Speisung der 5000 von 6,35-44: Vorangestellt ist die Aussage von 6,34, in der die zusammengeströmte Menge mit „Schafen, die keinen Hirten haben", verglichen wird, und genau auf diese Situation reagiert Jesus mit seinem Lehren: καὶ ἤρξατο διδάσκειν αὐτοὺς πολλά. Jesu intensives Lehren (πολλά) ist hier die Antwort auf die Orientierungslosigkeit der Menschen.

Charakteristisch für das MkEv ist schließlich die mehrfach begegnende esoterische Belehrung der Jünger, zumeist im „Haus" oder jedenfalls „allein", so in 4,10-20 (Parabelrede); 7,17-23 (Rein/Unrein); 9,28 (Exorzismus).

In diesen Erzählsituationen bildet sich natürlich nicht unmittelbar die Situation des Lehrens in einer urchristlichen Gemeinde ab. Der Lehrer, der hier als Autor den Text verantwortet, versteht sich auch nicht als Lehrer, der in eigener Autorität, oder gar „in Vollmacht" Lehre erteilen würde, sondern er vermittelt Lehre, deren Autorität in der Person dessen begründet ist, von dem in der Lehre gehandelt wird. Aber die hohe Bedeutung, die der Lehre aus der Sicht des Verfassers zukommt, ist ohne weiteres erkennbar. Zudem ist nicht zu übersehen, dass in der erzählten Welt des Evangeliums die Jünger, wenn auch in abgeleiteter Form, Anteil am Lehren Jesu bekommen (6,30).

2. *Evangelienstoffe als Inhalt der Katechese nach Lk 1,4*

In dem vieldiskutierten Prolog des Lukasevangeliums (LkEv), in Lk 1,1-4, gibt es am Schluss von 1,4 eine Bemerkung, die zumeist nicht im Vordergrund des Interesses steht. Der Verfasser formuliert hier in direkter Anrede an den Adressaten seines Buches das Ziel seines Werkes: Er habe es verfasst, ἵνα ἐπιγνῷς περὶ ὧν κατηχήθης λόγων τὴν ἀσφάλειαν („damit du die Zuverlässigkeit der Worte erkennst, in denen du unterrichtet worden bist")[56]. Mit den λόγοι von 1,4 nimmt Lk das absolute ὁ λόγος von 1,2 auf, wo von den Dienern „des" Wortes die Rede ist,

---

55. So zutreffend E. SCHWEIZER, *Die theologische Leistung des Markus*, in ID., *Beiträge zur Theologie des Neuen Testaments: Neutestamentliche Aufsätze (1955-1970)*, Zürich, Zwingli, 1970, 21-42, S. 25; so auch V. TROPPER, *Jesus Didáskalos: Studien zu Jesus als Lehrer bei den Synoptikern und im Rahmen der antiken Kultur- und Sozialgeschichte* (ÖBS, 42), Frankfurt a.M., Peter Lang, 2012; die Verfasserin stellt fest, „dass es dem Evangelisten auf den Akt des Lehrens überhaupt ankommt" (S. 21), und weist zutreffend darauf hin, dass das Sprachfeld διδαχή, διδάσκειν, usw. bei Mk signifikant häufiger erscheint als bei den übrigen Synoptikern (S. 17), während es in Q (fast) völlig fehlt (S. 34).

56. Den Hinweis auf Lk 1,4 verdanke ich Andreas Lindemann (Bielefeld).

womit in umfassender Weise die christliche Botschaft gemeint ist[57]. Am Übergang zu den Einzeltexten des LkEv, die sich dann an diesen Prolog einschließen, steht jetzt λόγοι im Plural: In den vielen λόγοι entfaltet sich die eine christliche Botschaft[58]. Mit diesen λόγοι sind die Jesusüberlieferungen gemeint, die Theophilos bereits kennt, also die Inhalte der Vorgänger, auf denen Lukas nach 1,1-2 aufbaut, somit auf jeden Fall auch der Inhalt des MkEv. Diese Inhalte will Lk dann seinerseits in zuverlässiger Weise weitergeben. Interessant ist hier, dass Lukas voraussetzt, dass Theophilos in der Evangelienüberlieferung bereits „unterrichtet worden ist". Dabei spricht die passivische Formulierung κατηχήθης (du bist unterrichtet worden) gegen eine reine Privatlektüre, also eine Art Selbststudium, sondern legt die Annahme einer personalen Vermittlung durch eine unterrichtende Person nahe. Hier ist also das MkEv als Grundlage für „katechetische" Belehrung vorausgesetzt[59].

VII. Der geographische und theologiegeschichtliche Ort des Markusevangeliums

Die Entstehung des MkEv ist nur erklärbar, wenn der Verfasser, und damit die Gemeinde, in der er als Katechet tätig war, einen breiten Zugang zur Jesusüberlieferung und d.h. auch: Kontakt zu deren Tradenten hatten[60]. Träger bzw. Vermittler der Jesusüberlieferungen waren die

---

57. So zutreffend M. Wolter, *Das Lukasevangelium* (HNT, 5), Tübingen, Mohr Siebeck, 2008, S. 63, mit Verweis auf Apg 4,4.29 u.ö.

58. Anders Wolter, *ibid.*, S. 67, der diesen Rückbezug nicht sieht.

59. Dabei ist es nicht von entscheidender Bedeutung, ob man hier κατηχεῖν allgemein als: (jmd. etwas) „mitteilen" versteht, oder bereits im speziellen Sinne als: (jemanden in religiöser Hinsicht) „unterrichten/unterweisen". Vor dem Hintergrund von Gal 6,6 ist jedenfalls ein spezielleres Verständnis zumindest möglich. Zu berücksichtigen ist, dass Lukas im Prolog scheinbar ganz neutral formuliert (vgl. Lk 1,1: διήγησιν περὶ τῶν πεπληροφορημένων ἐν ἡμῖν πραγμάτων / „die Erzählung von den Ereignissen, die in unserer Zeit abgeschlossen sind"), aber damit auf sehr spezielle Geschehnisse zielt. Ebenso kann κατηχεῖν zunächst neutral, aber eben auch mit spezifischem Inhalt gelesen werden. Auf jeden Fall ist die Übersetzung von ὧν κατηχήθης λόγων τὴν ἀσφάλειαν mit: „die Zuverlässigkeit dessen, was man dir gesagt hat" (so Wolter, *ibid.*, S. 57), zu beiläufig; zur Wortbedeutung vgl. G. Schneider, κατηχέω, in *EWNT* 2 (1981) 673-675.

60. Damit scheidet das immer wieder ins Spiel gebrachte Rom aus. Legt man den einzigen sicher in Rom im 1. Jh. n.Chr. entstandenen Text, den *1 Clem.*, zugrunde, dann ist nicht erkennbar, wie Markus in Rom Zugang zu Jesusüberlieferungen bekommen haben soll. Umgekehrt fehlt auch jede Rückwirkung des MkEv auf den *1 Clem*. Das sieht auch H. Lona, *Der erste Clemensbrief* (KAV, 2), Göttingen, Vandenhoeck & Ruprecht, 1998, S. 51, der (unter der Voraussetzung der Entstehung des MkEv im „lateinischen Sprachraum") überrascht konstatiert, „daß keine besondere Einwirkung des Markusevangeliums vorliegt, was ... doch zu erwarten wäre".

aus Galiläa nach Jerusalem übergesiedelten Jesusanhänger mit dem Zwölferkreis und der Familie Jesu an der Spitze. Diese Nähe zeigt sich auch in der Überschneidung der Überlieferungsbereiche von MkEv und Q. Geographisch kommt damit der Großraum Syrien einschließlich der phönizischen Küste in Betracht.

Innerhalb des Großraums Syrien scheiden Gemeinden mit deutlich judenchristlicher Prägung aus, und damit natürlich die Gemeinden im mehrheitlich jüdisch besiedelten Kernbereich Palästinas – sofern diese nach 70 n.Chr. noch existierten. Aufgrund der prinzipiell ablehnenden Haltung gegenüber der Sabbatpraxis (Mk 2–3) und den jüdischen Reinheitsgeboten (Mk 7) ist die Gemeinde des Markus als eine grundsätzlich „gesetzesfrei" lebende Gemeinde anzusprechen. Gleichzeitig sind auffällige Berührungen mit der Theologie des Paulus festzustellen[61], so in der Frage der Reinheitsgesetze (vgl. die Nähe von Mk 7,15.19 zu Röm 14,14.20), aber auch in der Verwendung des Leitbegriffs εὐαγγέλιον oder in der Rolle des Gottessohnchristologie und der Bedeutung der Passion[62]. In all diesen Punkten unterscheidet sich das MkEv zugleich deutlich von der Logienquelle. Umgekehrt fehlen aber auch charakteristische Themen der paulinischen Briefe, so die Weisheitstheologie von 1 Kor 1–4 oder die Rechtfertigungsbegrifflichkeit des Galater- und Römerbriefs.

Nähe und Distanz zur paulinischen Theologie sind nicht als Zufall zu bewerten und bedürfen einer gemeinsamen Erklärung. Dabei ist die Alternative zwischen einer direkten Abhängigkeit oder der völligen Unabhängigkeit des MkEv von Paulus zu einfach. Vielmehr sind beide als eigenständige Ausprägungen einer gemeinsamen theologischen Ausgangsbasis zu verstehen. Diese Ausgangsbasis kann in der Theologie der sog. „Hellenisten", also des Stephanuskreises, gesehen werden[63], dessen

---

61. Dazu vgl. die Aufsatzsammlungen von O. WISCHMEYER – D.C. SIM – I.J. ELMER (Hgg.), *Paul and Mark: Comparative Essays. Part I: Two Authors at the Beginnings of Christianity* (BZNW, 198), Berlin – Boston, MA, De Gruyter, 2014, und von E.-M. BECKER – T. ENGBERG-PEDERSEN – M. MÜLLER (Hgg.), *Mark and Paul: Comparative Essays. Part II: For and Against Pauline Influence on Mark* (BZNW, 199), Berlin – Boston, MA, De Gruyter, 2014.

62. Zum Vergleich von Markus mit Paulus im Bereich der Christologie s. U. SCHNELLE, *Paulinische und markinische Christologie im Vergleich*, in WISCHMEYER et al. (Hgg.), *Paul and Mark* (Anm. 61), 283-312; J. MARCUS, *Mark – Interpreter of Paul*, in BECKER et al. (Hgg.), *Paul and Mark* (Anm. 61), 29-49; zu εὐαγγέλιον vgl. A. LINDEMANN, *Das Evangelium bei Paulus und im Markusevangelium*, in WISCHMEYER et al. (Hgg.), *Paul and Mark*, 313-360.

63. Damit ist natürlich nicht ausgeschlossen, dass die hellenistisch-„antiochenische" Theologie zur Zeit des Markus inzwischen auch (!) paulinische Einflüsse aufwies, bzw. dass vorhandene Tendenzen durch paulinischen Einfluss verstärkt wurden. Doch ist das Modell einer direkten Umsetzung der paulinischen Theologie durch Markus zu einfach; so jedoch SCHNELLE, *Paulinische und markinische Christologie* (Anm. 62), S. 308: „Auch

Mitglieder nach ihrer Vertreibung aus Jerusalem im Küstenbereich von Syrien/Palästina (vgl. Apg 11,19) Gemeinden gründeten. Die Ausbreitung der „Hellenisten" reichte von Caesarea Maritima, wo Philippus als Gemeindeleiter tätig war (Apg 21,8-9), über Tyros und Sidon bis nach Antiochia am Orontes, wo Paulus seine theologische Prägung erhalten hat. Interne Indizien im MkEv weisen ebenfalls auf die phönizische Küste hin, wie die Hervorhebung von Tyros und Sidon (3,8; 7,24.31) zeigt. Vor allem aber ist bemerkenswert, dass die einzige Person, deren nichtjüdische Identität ausdrücklich erwähnt wird, die hilfesuchende Mutter von Mk 7,25-26 ist, deren Zugehörigkeit doppelt determiniert wird: Sie ist Ἑλληνίς, Συροφοινίκισσα τῷ γένει: „Griechin" – und näherhin „Syrophönizierin ihrer Herkunft nach". Das ist kaum als Zufall zu bewerten.

VIII. Ergebnis

Wenn es sich beim MkEv um eine Jesusdarstellung handelt, die aus der katechetischen Praxis entstanden und für die Verwendung in der Katechese bestimmt war, sind einige wichtige Schlussfolgerungen möglich:

a) Für das Verhältnis von Mündlichkeit und Schriftlichkeit: Mündlichkeit und Schriftlichkeit sind nicht als starres Gegenüber zu bestimmen, sondern die mündliche Durchformung der Jesusüberlieferung ist Voraussetzung für deren schriftliche Darstellung, wie umgekehrt der Bedarf der mündlichen Lehre letztlich als Grund für die Abfassung des MkEv anzusehen ist. Die Verschriftlichung zielt auf erneute mündliche Umsetzung, jetzt aber mit dem schriftlichen Text als Bezugspunkt.

b) Die Funktion als katechetisches Handbuch erklärt die weite Verbreitung, die für das MkEv anzunehmen ist. Diese manifestiert sich nicht nur in der Tatsache, dass Matthäus und Lukas sich zu einer eigenen Jesusdarstellung herausgefordert fühlten und dabei das MkEv zur Grundlage nahmen. Die weite Verbreitung zeigt sich darin, dass das MkEv –

---

wenn eine direkte Bezugnahme auf paulinische Briefe durch Markus nicht nachzuweisen ist, legt sich aus den genannten Übereinstimmungen eine Kenntnis und eigenständige Verarbeitung paulinischer Gedanken durch den ältesten Evangelisten nahe. Sie könnte in Rom erfolgt sein, wo beide mit einem nicht allzu großen zeitlichen Abstand wirkten und Markus seine Kenntnis paulinischer Theologie wahrscheinlich erwarb". Einen anderen Akzent setzt in Bezug auf die Verwendung von εὐαγγέλιον LINDEMANN, *Das Evangelium* (Anm. 62), S. 355: „In die synoptische Tradition wurde das Wort εὐαγγέλιον offensichtlich erst vom Verfasser des MkEv eingeführt. Dass er dabei von Paulus direkt abhängig ist, lässt sich nicht zeigen; aber zweifellos weist auch das MkEv den bei Paulus belegten Gebrauch des Wortes als ‚die frohe Botschaft' auf".

anders als die Logienquelle – trotz seiner umfangreichen Rezeption im MtEv und LkEv als eigenständiger Text weiterhin erhalten geblieben ist[64] und der Gattung „Evangelium" ihren Namen gegeben hat.

c) Als eigenständige Ausprägung der „hellenistischen" Theologie hat das MkEv sicher zur Verstärkung der gesetzesfreien Tendenzen im Urchristentum beigetragen.

Nicolaistraße 4	Dietrich-Alex KOCH
DE-48161 Münster/W.	Westfälische Wilhelms-Universität
Deutschland	
dakoch@uni-muenster.de	

---

64. Zur weiteren Rezeption des MkEv vgl. den Beitrag des Jubilars: J. VERHEYDEN, *The Reception History of the Gospel of Mark in the Early Church*, in G. VAN OYEN (Hg.), *Reading the Gospel of Mark in the Twenty-First Century: Method and Meaning* (BETL, 301), Leuven – Paris – Bristol, CT, Peeters, 2019, 395-428, S. 403-404.

WHERE MARK DID NOT FOLLOW LXX VERSIONS

PRE-MARKAN TRADITION
IN MARK 1,2; 4,12; 8,18; 9,48; 13,24-25; 15,34

Narrative analysis of the Gospel according to Mark is the order of the day[1]. However, as I have argued on many occasions during the *Colloquium Biblicum Lovaniense*, from 2001 to 2012 under the friendly guidance of Joseph Verheyden as secretary[2], one should not give up the quest for pre-Markan tradition. Comparing parallel tradition between Mark and early Christian letters, overlaps between Mark and those sayings in Luke and Matthew attributed to Q, and comparing Mark's citations with what is written in the Pentateuch, in the Prophets and in the Psalms, are secure ways of discerning pre-Markan tradition, without returning to the pitfalls of traditional Redaction Criticism[3]. In dealing with Mark's references to what has been written, one has to distinguish between at least two possible scenarios. In dictating his prior oral performances to a scribe, Mark could have consulted a Greek scroll when quoting scriptural passages. It is also conceivable that Mark quoted from memory. In this essay, I will argue that in a few cases Mark drew on pre-Markan uses of key biblical texts and that these cases shed some light on the dark images one can have of the early phase of pre-Markan tradition.

The Gospel according to Mark often quotes what has been written (1,2-3; 7,6-7; 11,17; 12,10-11; 14,27), what Moses said, allowed or wrote (7,10; 10,4; 12,19.26), or central texts from the Torah (10,6-8; 12,29-30.31.32-33) or Psalms (12,10-11.36)[4]. There is consensus among scholars that in such cases the text of Mark follows "the" LXX. To be

---

1. See G. VAN OYEN (ed.), *Reading the Gospel of Mark in the Twenty-First Century: Method and Meaning* (BETL, 301), Leuven – Paris – Bristol, CT, Peeters, 2019.
2. J. VERHEYDEN (ed.), *Colloquium Biblicum Lovaniense 1-60*, Leuven – Paris – Walpole, MA, Peeters, 2011.
3. C. BREYTENBACH, *The Gospel according to Mark as Episodic Narrative* (SupplNT, 182), Leiden, Brill, 2021, pp. 66-105, 404-497.
4. For quotations and/or allusions in these texts, see *ibid.*, pp. 246-273, 433-467. Three times the author uses γέγραπται (9,12.13; 14,21) without quoting a text. On the differentiation between quotation, allusion and "free allusion" in Mark, see M. MEISER, *Die Funktion der Septuaginta-Zitate im Markusevangelium*, in W. KRAUS – S. KREUZER (eds.), *Die Septuaginta – Text, Wirkung, Rezeption. 4. Internationale Fachtagung veranstaltet von Septuaginta Deutsch (LXX.D), Wuppertal 19.-22. Juli 2012* (WUNT, 325), Tübingen, Mohr Siebeck, 2014, 517-543, pp. 520-522.

precise, the text of Mark transmitted in ℵ, A and B, follows the text of the LXX as attested in those manuscripts[5]. In six cases, the texts he presents differ considerably from that of the LXX (1,2; 4,12; 8,18; 9,48; 13,24-25 and 15,34). Of these texts only the first one is marked as a quotation[6]. These six cases will be the object of our analysis. How does the wording of these texts in Mark differ from the text transmitted in the LXX? Do these deviations from the LXX indicate that Mark's reception of the biblical texts was influenced by the Hebrew text (HT)[7] or an Aramaic version of the text?

I. Mark 1,2(-3)

Following Codex Vaticanus (B, which has a *spatium* before verse 4: ΤΡΙΒΟΥΣΑΥΤΟΥ ΕΓΕΝΕΤΟΙΩΑΝΝΗΣ), Origen, and Basil the Great, we put the full stop after αὐτοῦ, taking verses 1-3 as one period[8]. Mark conflated three passages from Scripture. By attributing all of them to Isaiah, he programmatically illustrated the importance of the Isaiah scroll as intertext

---

5. In this essay, "LXX" refers to these manuscripts. As a rule, the variant readings in the Göttingen editions and for α', ϑ' and σ', Origen's Hexapla have been compared and deviations noted. The use of the term LXX to refer to the Greek translations of the HT (Hebrew Text) is problematic, but indispensable. See G.J. Steyn, *Which LXX Are We Talking about in New Testament Scholarship? Two Examples from Hebrews*, in M. Karrer – W. Kraus (eds.), *Die Septuaginta – Texte, Kontexte, Lebenswelten* (WUNT, 219), Tübingen, Mohr Siebeck, 2008, 297-307; Id., *A Comparison of the Septuagint Textual Form in the Torah Quotations Common to Philo of Alexandria and the Gospels of Mark and Matthew*, in M.K.H. Peters (ed.), *XIV Congress of the IOSCS, Helsinki 2010* (SBL Septuagint and Cognate Studies, 59), Atlanta, GA, SBL, 2013, 605-624. For a summary of research on Mark's use of the LXX, see Meiser, *Funktion* (n. 4), pp. 518-520; for a discussion of those cases where Mark drew on the LXX for the cited pre-text and the text-critical differences between later versions of the text of Mark and versions of the LXX, see *ibid.*, p. 522 (Mk 1,2b.3), pp. 527-528 (7,6-7.10), p. 530 (10,7), pp. 532-536 (11,17; 12,10-11.29-30.35-37).

6. On ἵνα as introduction to the citation in Mk 4,12, see below. On the identification of quotations, see H.F. Plett, *The Poetics of Quotation*, in J.S. Petöfi – T. Olivi (eds.), *Von der verbalen Konstitution zur symbolischen Bedeutung* (Papiere zur Textlinguistik, 62), Hamburg, Buske, 1988, 313-334, p. 315. He argues that the most obvious feature is "intertextual repetition: a pre-text is reproduced in a subsequent text". The quotation has a "segmental character" because the pre-text "is not reproduced entirely, but only partially". The quotation cannot stand alone, it depends on the context of the focus text into which it is integrated.

7. In this essay "HT" refers to the consonantal text of Codex Leningradensis. The DSS have only parallels to Isaiah (see E. Ulrich, *The Biblical Qumran Scrolls: Transcriptions and Textual Variants* [SupplVT, 134], Leiden, Brill, 2010), which have been compared to the HT. Differences other than *matres lectionis* are noted in the tables.

8. See C. Breytenbach, *Mark's Use of τὸ εὐαγγέλιον*, in R.M. Calhoun et al. (eds.), *Paul, the Corpus Paulinum, and Their Reception*, Leiden, Brill, forthcoming [2022].

to understand his narrative⁹. The latter part of the quotation in Mk 1,3 is indeed from the prophet. Mark followed a Greek text as we have it transmitted in manuscripts ℵ, A and B. Only one change is significant¹⁰. He replaced the possessive genitives τοῦ θεοῦ ἡμῶν with the genitive pronoun αὐτοῦ, which refers back to κυρίου. Correlated by καθώς to verse 1, there can be little doubt that κύριος and thus αὐτοῦ (as well as σου in 1,2) refer back to Ἰησοῦ Χριστοῦ [υἱοῦ θεοῦ] in the first line. Such minor changes to fit a quotation from the pre-text in the LXX into the context of the Markan focus text is on a par with the normal procedure of the evangelist.

The same applies to the procedure of combining two or more quotations under one introduction¹¹. Because of the word order and ἀποστέλλω, the first part of the quotation in Mk 1,2b is from Ex 23,20 rather than from 32,34 or Mal 3,1, but the second part in 1,2c is probably from Mal 3,1. Mk 1,2b repeats Ex 23,20a¹², the only difference being that verse 2b does not have καί and probably not the emphatic ἐγώ¹³. Nevertheless, ἀποστέλλω is first person singular, with or without the emphatic ἐγώ. After the (erroneous)¹⁴ introduction in 1,2a, the *vox Dei* speaks through the prophet Isaiah. God will send his messenger. In the next verse, the audience hears what this messenger will say and do. In Mk 1,4, the narrator identifies him with John the Baptizer and says what he does.

Mk 1,2c, however, deviates from Ex^LXX 23,20. The Hebrew text of Ex 23,20b reads: לשמרך בדרך. The Masora vocalised לִשְׁמָרְךָ בַּדָּרֶךְ – an infinitive construct with 2nd person suffix, if it is assumed that the Hebrew *Vorlage* of the LXX translator (ἵνα φυλάξῃ σε ἐν τῇ ὁδῷ – "in order to guard [שָׁמַר] you on your way")¹⁵ read identically to the MT. The

---

9. See M.D. HOOKER, *Isaiah in Mark's Gospel*, in S. MOYISE – M.J.J. MENKEN (eds.), *Isaiah in the New Testament*, London, T&T Clark, 2005, 35-49; D.P. MOESSNER, *Mark's Mysterious "Beginning" (1:1-3) as the Hermeneutical Code to Mark's "Messianic Secret"*, in R.M. CALHOUN – D.P. MOESSNER – T. NICKLAS (eds.), *Modern and Ancient Literary Criticism of the Gospels: Continuing the Debate on Gospel Genre(s)* (WUNT, 451), Tübingen, Mohr Siebeck, 2020, 243-271, pp. 250-252.

10. See Table 1 at the end of this section.

11. See Mk 7,10; 11,9-10.17; 12,19.29-31; 13,24-25; 14,62 and BREYTENBACH, *Episodic Narrative* (n. 3), 433-455, pp. 444-446, 453.

12. The differences to Mal 3,1 are more substantial. Mk 1,2b could lack the emphatic ἐγώ (see next note) and does not have the intensive ἐξαποστέλλω of Mal 3,1, but has – like Ex 23,20 – πρὸ προσώπου σου as an adverbial phrase to ἀποστέλλω. In Mal 3,1 πρὸ προσώπου μου qualifies the second verb.

13. The attestation of ἐγώ is strong: ℵ A L W f^1.13 33 etc. NA²⁸ opted to delete it like B D Θ 28* etc.

14. As Porphyry noted (see Jerome, *Comm. Matt.* 3.2 [PL 26, 29]), Matthew corrected Mark by omitting Mk 1,2.

15. See KBL, *s.v.* qal 1. On the interpretation of Ex 23,20 in the Targumim, see S. PELLEGRINI, *Elia – Wegbereiter des Gottessohnes: Eine textsemiotische Studie zum*

final relative clause[16] Mk 1,2c reads: ὃς κατασκευάσει τὴν ὁδόν σου. The future indicative of κατασκευάζω ("to prepare")[17], κατασκευάσει, can hardly translate שמר. It is thus more likely that in 1,2c Mark drew on Mal 3,1 as pre-text[18]. Here the LXX also has the future tense, but from the verb ἐπιβλέπω. The difference between κατασκευάσει in Mk 1,2c and ἐπιβλέψεται of Mal[LXX] 3,1 can be explained[19]. The Hebrew text of Mal 3,1b reads: ופנה־דרך לפני. The Masora vocalised: וּפִנָּה־דֶרֶךְ לְפָנָי. Here Mark's version reflects their understanding, which reads the ו as final and took פנה as pi'el פִּנָּה, meaning with the direct object "to clear (the way)"[20]. The LXX took the verb as qal (פָּנָה, "to turn to")[21], and translated with ἐπιβλέψεται ("he will look carefully upon")[22]. Mark thus used the pre-text Ex 23,20 in verse 2b and merged it in verse 2c with a translation of Mal[HT] 3,1, which deviated from the LXX. He refrained from repeating πρὸ προσώπου μου from Mal 3,1 in verse 2c, since the phrase already occurs in verse 2b, which uses it like Ex[LXX] 23,20 with the pronoun σου. Referring back to σου in verse 2b, verse 2c uses the second person σου instead of the μου from Mal 3,1.

That Mark followed his own understanding of the Hebrew text in 1,2c rather than the LXX is highly significant, because he normally followed the readings of the LXX. He did exactly that in verses 2b and 3. However, verse 2c is closer to the Hebrew text. This is even more significant, since Mk 1,2b-c has a close parallel in Mt[Q] 11,10//Lk[Q] 7,27. Matthew and Luke also combined Ex[LXX] 23,20 and Mal 3,1. Their texts also have ὃς κατασκευάσει τὴν ὁδόν σου as translation for ופנה־דרך לפני. Both end with ἔμπροσθέν σου, translating לפני, but applying it to Jesus and thus using σου, and not the first person as in Mal 3,1. It is thus highly likely that Mark and the Q-tradition both used a common tradition in which a combination of Ex 23,20 and Mal 3,1 was applied to John the Baptist and

---

Markusevangelium (Herders Biblische Studien, 26), Freiburg i.Br., Herder, 2000, pp. 193-194.

16. See BDR, §378₁.
17. See LSJ, *s.v.* 3.
18. See A. RESCH, *Aussercanonische Paralleltexte zu den Evangelien. Zweiter Theil: Paralleltexte zu Lucas*, Leipzig, Hinrichs, 1895, p. 114; later H.B. SWETE, *The Gospel according to St Mark*, London, Macmillan, 1902, pp. 2-3; E. LOHMEYER, *Das Evangelium des Markus* (KEK, I/2), Göttingen, Vandenhoeck & Ruprecht, 1937, p. 11; details in J. MARCUS, *The Way of the Lord: Christological Exegesis of the Old Testament in the Gospel of Mark*, Louisville, KY, Westminster, 1992, p. 13.
19. ϑ' ἑτοιμάσει. σ' ἀποσκευάσει.
20. See KBL, *s.v.* pi. 3.
21. See KBL, *s.v.* qal 1.
22. According to LSJ, *s.v.* 2, the verb means "look well at, observe".

Jesus. Mk 1,2 reflects a pre-Markan use of Scripture, which the evangelist inherited from tradition[23].

Mark and Mt^Q 11,10//Lk^Q 7,27 have the merged citation Ex^LXX 23,20 and Mal 3,1 in common, showing that their versions drew on a tradition influenced by the Hebrew text of Mal 3,1. Only the second quotation Mk 1,3 comes from Is 40,3. It is a parallelism. The version of Mark (and the parallel passage in Mt 3,3) does not agree with that in the LXX. Lk 3,4-6 quotes Is 40,3-5 according to the LXX. All three versions have a change compared to the LXX and the HT. τοῦ θεοῦ ἡμῶν is replaced with αὐτοῦ. As a result, the reference to κυρίου has become indistinct. In the Isaiah text (LXX) τοῦ θεοῦ ἡμῶν renders לאלהינו (Is 40,3). In Mark the text is related to Jesus, who is here called κύριος and is taken up again with αὐτοῦ. The verbs κατασκευάζειν, ἑτοιμάζειν and ποιεῖν + εὐθύς, all of which have ὁδόν or τρίβους as an object, show that the preparation of the way of the Lord was already announced in Scripture. The Isaiah quotation (40,3) now describes the messenger. A voice calls out from where all new beginnings come from: the desert. The messenger is thus assigned to the prophetic tradition of renewal. What does the prophetic voice of the messenger call out? The way of the "Lord", i.e., the way of the one who is superior to the messenger, should be made ready, his paths should be straightened. This gives the messenger a clear preparatory function in relation to the "Lord", a function that Isaiah already foretold. With the "Lord", Jesus Christ, the Son of God, is meant (see verse 1 and verses 9-11)[24]. Who the messenger sent by God is remains open until verse 4.

To summarise: Mark quotes Is 40,3 as what is written in Scripture, but introduces it with a combination of Ex 23,20 and Mal 3,1 that was already connected with the mission of John the Baptist and his relation to Jesus, as one can see in Lk^Q 7,27//Mt^Q 11,10. Mark probably did not know Q, but he drew on an old tradition combining Ex 23,20 and Mal 3,1 also attested by the Q-tradition and included it to show his audience that as it is written in the prophet Isaiah, God sent John the Baptizer as messenger to prepare the way of Jesus Christ, the Son of God[25]. Recapping on 1,2-3,

---

23. This was already noticed by RESCH, *Paralleltexte* (n. 18), p. 114.

24. See also H.-J. KLAUCK, *Vorspiel im Himmel? Erzähltechnik und Theologie im Markusprolog*, Neukirchen-Vluyn, Neukirchener Verlag, 1997, pp. 31-33.

25. There is more evidence that a translation of Mal 3,1 different from the LXX influenced emerging Christian texts. When Gabriel announces John's birth to Zacharias, Luke uses the combination of ἑτοιμάζω from Is 40,3 and the non-Septuagintal κατασκευάζω from Mal 3,1. John will go before the Lord with the spirit and power of Elijah to turn the hearts of fathers to their children, and the disobedient to the insight of the righteous, "to make ready for the Lord a people that is restituted" (ἑτοιμάσαι κυρίῳ λαὸν κατεσκευασμένον, Lk 1,17).

the evangelist developed this theme further in 9,11-13, drawing an analogy between John the Baptist as Elijah returned and the Son of Man.

Mk 1,2	Ex 23,20		Q	
	HT	LXX	Mt 11,10	Lk 7,27
καθὼς γέγραπται ἐν τῷ Ἠσαΐᾳ τῷ προφήτῃ·			οὗτός ἐστιν περὶ οὗ γέγραπται·	οὗτός ἐστιν περὶ οὗ γέγραπται·
ἰδοὺ ἀποστέλλω τὸν ἄγγελόν μου πρὸ προσώπου σου,	הִנֵּה אָנֹכִי שֹׁלֵחַ מַלְאָךְ לְפָנֶיךָ לִשְׁמָרְךָ בַּדָּרֶךְ וְלַהֲבִיאֲךָ אֶל־הַמָּקוֹם אֲשֶׁר הֲכִנֹתִי׃	Καὶ ἰδοὺ ἐγὼ ἀποστέλλω τὸν ἄγγελόν μου πρὸ προσώπου σου, ἵνα φυλάξῃ σε ἐν τῇ ὁδῷ, ὅπως εἰσαγάγῃ σε εἰς τὴν γῆν, ἣν ἡτοίμασά σοι.	ἰδοὺ ἐγὼ ἀποστέλλω τὸν ἄγγελόν μου πρὸ προσώπου σου,	ἰδοὺ ἀποστέλλω τὸν ἄγγελόν μου πρὸ προσώπου σου,
	Mal 3,1				
	HT	LXX		
ὃς κατασκευάσει τὴν ὁδόν σου·	הִנְנִי שֹׁלֵחַ מַלְאָכִי וּפִנָּה־דֶרֶךְ לְפָנָי	ἰδοὺ ἐγὼ ἐξαποστέλλω τὸν ἄγγελόν μου, καὶ ἐπιβλέψεται ὁδὸν πρὸ προσώπου μου,....	ὃς κατασκευάσει τὴν ὁδόν σου ἔμπροσθέν σου.	ὃς κατασκευάσει τὴν ὁδόν σου ἔμπροσθέν σου.
Mk 1,3	Is^LXX 40,3		Mt 3,3	Lk 3,4
			οὗτος γάρ ἐστιν ὁ ῥηθεὶς διὰ Ἠσαΐου τοῦ προφήτου λέγοντος·	ὡς γέγραπται ἐν βίβλῳ λόγων Ἠσαΐου τοῦ προφήτου·
φωνὴ βοῶντος ἐν τῇ ἐρήμῳ· ἑτοιμάσατε τὴν ὁδὸν κυρίου, εὐθείας ποιεῖτε τὰς τρίβους αὐτοῦ.	φωνὴ βοῶντος ἐν τῇ ἐρήμῳ Ἑτοιμάσατε τὴν ὁδὸν κυρίου, εὐθείας ποιεῖτε τὰς τρίβους τοῦ θεοῦ ἡμῶν·		φωνὴ βοῶντος ἐν τῇ ἐρήμῳ· ἑτοιμάσατε τὴν ὁδὸν κυρίου, εὐθείας ποιεῖτε τὰς τρίβους αὐτοῦ.	φωνὴ βοῶντος ἐν τῇ ἐρήμῳ· ἑτοιμάσατε τὴν ὁδὸν κυρίου, εὐθείας ποιεῖτε τὰς τρίβους αὐτοῦ.

Table 1

II. Mark 4,12

In Mk 4,12 the narrator lets Jesus repeat so much of Is 6,9 and 10b that one could regard it as quotation, even though he did not introduce it as such[26]. He rather lets Jesus continue his direct speech, introducing the

---

26. See Table 2 at the end of this section. For H.A.W. MEYER, *Kritisch exegetisches Handbuch über die Evangelien des Markus und Lukas*, Göttingen, Vandenhoeck & Ruprecht, 1864, p. 54, Mk 4,12 is expressed "in Erinnerung von" Is 6,9-10. According to SWETE, *Mark* (n. 18), p. 77, it is "an adaptation" of Is^LXX 6,10. B. WEISS, *Die Evangelien des*

pre-text with a ἵνα in verse 12a. This ἵνα, to which I shall return, depends on the preceding ἐν παραβολαῖς τὰ πάντα γίνεται and determines the subjunctives in verse 12b. A glance at Is 6,9 shows that ἵνα cannot be part of a quotation from the HT and the LXX. The recurrence of the pre-text Is 6,9-10 in the focus text Mk 4,12b-c is only partial. Nevertheless, enough of Is 6,9-10 is re-aligned to allow us to speak of a quoted text[27]. Repeating Is 6,9-10, Mark omitted 6,10a and the first part of 10b, which means that in Mk 4,12c, μήποτε connects μὴ ἴδωσιν ... μὴ συνιῶσιν to ἐπιστρέψωσιν and ἀφεθῇ, and not as in Is[LXX] 6,10b, the verbs ἐπαχύνθη, ἤκουσαν and ἐκάμμυσαν in 10a with ἴδωσιν, ἀκούσωσιν, συνῶσιν, ἐπιστρέψωσιν and ἰάσομαι in 10b[28]. *Mutatis mutandis*, this also applies to the Hebrew and the Aramaic versions of Is 6,9-10. The function of neither μήποτε nor פן or דלמא in Is 6,10 can be transferred to Mk 4,12c to clarify the function of μήποτε in the new construction in the focus text in Greek. Its role depends on the Greek syntax in the abbreviated quotation on the lips of the main character Jesus.

Connected by ἵνα to τὰ πάντα γίνεται, the abbreviated quotation in Mk 4,12bα commences with a participle (βλέποντες), followed by two third person subjunctives, the first one in the present (βλέπωσιν), the second negated in the aorist (μὴ ἴδωσιν). Still dependent on τὰ πάντα γίνεται ἵνα ..., verse 12bβ repeats the pattern (ἀκούοντες ἀκούωσιν καὶ μὴ συνιῶσιν). However, Mk 4,12 first mentions the clause about "looking and not seeing" and only then that on "hearing and not understanding", contrary to Is 6,9, where the clause on "hearing and not understanding" comes first and only then that on "looking and not seeing". Mark thus inverts the order of the clauses: he makes that on "looking" precede that on "hearing". This inversion indicates that Mark was "quoting" from memory. Mk 4,3-31 is an appeal to hear and to listen in order to understand. Further scrutiny reveals that Mark did not remember the text as attested in the major LXX manuscripts of Is 6,9.10b.

Following normal praxis in the LXX, Is[LXX] 6,9 translated the imperatives/ iussives שמעו and ראו with future indicatives (ἀκούσετε and βλέψετε) and the negated imperfects/futures תבינו and תדעו with aorist subjunctives

---

Markus und Lukas (KEK, 1/2⁹), Göttingen, Vandenhoeck & Ruprecht, 1901, p. 62, classifies it as "Anspielung"; E. KLOSTERMANN, *Markusevangelium* (HNT, 3), Tübingen, J.C.B. Mohr (Paul Siebeck), 1936, p. 41, assumes that Mark altered the LXX version of Is 6,9-10 "wenig", but he concludes by noticing "entsprechender dem hebr. וְרָפָא לוֹ: καὶ ἀφεθῇ αὐτοῖς". LOHMEYER, *Markus* (n. 18), p. 84, "ziemlich frei nach" Is[LXX] 6,9-10. For A. YARBRO COLLINS, *Mark: A Commentary* (Hermeneia), Minneapolis, MN, Fortress, 2007, p. 249, Mark "alludes to Isa 6:9-10".

27. See PLETT, *Poetics* (n. 6), pp. 314-315.
28. Is 6,10 is quoted in 1QH[a] XV 5-6 (VII 2-3).

(συνῆτε and ἴδητε)²⁹. The absolute infinitives שמוע and ראו that emphasise the commands to hear and to see are rendered respectively with the dative ἀκοῇ and the participle βλέποντες³⁰: "By listening, you will listen, looking, you will look". The latter way, rendering the infinitive absolute with a participle, occurs in Mk 4,12b, where the participles βλέποντες and ἀκούοντες in lieu of the infinitives absolute are strengthening the subjunctives βλέπωσιν and ἀκούωσιν. The latter function as imperatives³¹, but deviating from the HT and the LXX, they were rephrased as general commands in the third person plural. Who is meant in Mark? The third person takes up those outside (ἐκείνοις ... τοῖς ἔξω) from verse 11: "Look! They will see ... Hear! They will listen".

Even though Mk 4,12c and the LXX both have ἐπιστρέψωσιν for שב, Mark hardly re-aligned a pre-text from Is 6,9 if he followed a version identical to the HT or the known LXX versions. In the last phrase ורפא לו, the LXX translated רפא as qal with ἰάσομαι (to heal), changing the subject from לבב (heart) to the first person³², rendering, "and I shall heal them" (καὶ ἰάσομαι αὐτούς). Mark has ἀφεθῇ αὐτοῖς, a passive, and the third person dative, which refers to those outside.

T.W. Manson first suggested that Mk 4,12 rather followed the oral translation of the Hebrew into Aramaic, as reflected later in *Tg. Is.*³³. Verse 9b of Isaiah starts with a relative clause (די), referring back to עמא הדין (this people)³⁴. It renders the imperatives and infinitives absolute in the HT with the verbs as participles, making assertions in the third person: these people, "who hear definitely but do not comprehend (מסתכלין in etpaal), and see really but do not understand (ידעין in peal)". In meaning, Mark's ἐπιστρέφω in verse 12c corresponds to תוב "to turn back"³⁵ used by *Tg. Is.* in peal in 6,10. Like ἀφίημι in Mk 4,12c, the etpeel of the verb שבק in *Tg. Is.* 6,10 can mean "to forgive" and designate "to

---

29. See BDR, §362; M. ZERWICK, *Biblical Greek* (Subsidia Biblica, 41), Roma, Gregorian & Biblical Press, 2014, §280.
30. For the rendering of the Hebrew absolute infinitive by the dative or participle, see BDR, §422; ZERWICK, *Greek* (n. 29), §§60-61 and 369.
31. See BDR, §§364 and 387(a).
32. Note that in ἐπιστρέψωσιν, the LXX also changed the subject to the plural. In the HT, the singular subject of שב is, as in לבב, יבין.
33. T.W. MANSON, *The Teaching of Jesus: Studies in Its Form and Content*, Cambridge, CUP, 1931, pp. 77-78. Followed by J. JEREMIAS, *Die Gleichnisse Jesu* (ATANT, 11), Zürich, Zwingli, 1947, p. 9; V. TAYLOR, *The Gospel according to St. Mark*, London, MacMillan, 1952, p. 256; E. SCHWEIZER, *Das Evangelium nach Markus* (NTD, 1), Göttingen, Vandenhoeck & Ruprecht, 1978, p. 46.
34. With a preformative verbal form, ד can also be "so that, in order to". See *The Comprehensive Aramaic Lexicon* (= CAL; http://cal.huc.edu), *s.v.* dy 2.
35. See CAL, *s.v.* twb G 2.

forgive sin"[36]. The sentence starting with דלמא in *Tg. Is.* 6,10 thus ends: "lest ... they turn back and it be forgiven to them". Mark's dative pronoun αὐτοῖς corresponds to להון in *Tg. Is.* There can be little doubt that the truncated reception of Is 6,9-10 in Mk 4,12 is closer to the text attested by *Tg. Is.* than to any of the Old Greek or Hebrew versions.

Mk 4,12	Is 6,9-10		
NA[28]	TGM[37]	LXX	MT[38]
ἵνα	ואמר איזיל ותימר לעמא הדין	καὶ εἶπε Πορεύθητι καὶ εἶπον τῷ λαῷ τούτῳ	וַיֹּאמֶר לֵךְ וְאָמַרְתָּ לָעָם הַזֶּה
βλέποντες βλέπωσιν καὶ μὴ ἴδωσιν, καὶ ἀκούοντες ἀκούωσιν καὶ μὴ συνιῶσιν,	דשמעין משמע ולא מסתכלין וחזן מחזא ולא ידעין:	Ἀκοῇ ἀκούσετε καὶ οὐ μὴ συνῆτε καὶ βλέποντες βλέψετε καὶ οὐ μὴ ἴδητε·	שִׁמְעוּ שָׁמוֹעַ וְאַל־תָּבִינוּ [1QIsa^a ועל] וּרְאוּ רָאוֹ וְאַל־תֵּדָעוּ: [1QIsa^a ראו ראו ועל]
	[10] טפיש לביה דעמא הדין ואודנוהי יקר ועינוהי טמטים	[10]ἐπαχύνθη γὰρ ἡ καρδία τοῦ λαοῦ τούτου, καὶ τοῖς ὠσὶν αὐτῶν βαρέως ἤκουσαν καὶ τοὺς ὀφθαλμοὺς αὐτῶν ἐκάμμυσαν,	[10] הַשְׁמֵן לֵב־הָעָם הַזֶּה [1QIsa^a השם] וְאָזְנָיו הַכְבֵּד וְעֵינָיו הָשַׁע
μήποτε ἐπιστρέψωσιν καὶ ἀφεθῇ αὐτοῖς.	דלמא יחזון בעיניהון ובאודניהון ישמעון ובליבהון יסתכלון ויתובון וישתביק להון	μήποτε ἴδωσι τοῖς ὀφθαλμοῖς καὶ τοῖς ὠσὶν ἀκούσωσι καὶ τῇ καρδίᾳ συνῶσι καὶ ἐπιστρέψωσι καὶ ἰάσομαι αὐτούς.	פֶּן יִרְאֶה בְעֵינָיו וּבְאָזְנָיו יִשְׁמָע וּלְבָבוֹ יָבִין [1QIsa^a ישמעו בלבבו] וְשָׁב וְרָפָא לוֹ:

Table 2

Several allusions to and quotations of Is 6,9-10 show that Matthew and Luke-Acts also quoted the text[39]. However, it is Mark that mediated a

---

36. 11QTgJob (11Q10) Col. XXXVIII,2; Targumim, see CAL (n. 34), s.v. šbq Gt 2.
37. "And he said, 'Go, and speak to this people that hear indeed, but do not understand, and see indeed, but do not perceive. [10]Make the heart of this people dull, and their ears heavy and shut their eyes; lest they see with their eyes and hear with their ears, and understand with their hearts, and repent and it be forgiven them'" (text CAL; trans. B.D. CHILTON, *The Isaiah Targum: Introduction, Translation, Apparatus and Notes* [ArBib, 11], Edinburgh, T&T Clark, 1987, p. 15).
38. On the variant readings in 1QIsa^a, see C.A. EVANS, *To See and Not Perceive: Isaiah 6.9-10 in Early Jewish and Christian Interpretation* (JSOTSup, 64), Sheffield, Sheffield Academic Press, 1989, pp. 53-60.
39. See J. GNILKA, *Die Verstockung Israels: Isaias 6,9-10 in der Theologie der Synoptiker* (SANT, 3), München, Kösel, 1961; D.E. HARTLEY, *The Wisdom Background and Parabolic Implications of Isaiah 6:9-10 in the Synoptics* (Studies in Biblical Literature,

reception analogous to *Tg. Is.* When Manson claims that the closeness of Mk 4,12 to the Targum "stamps the saying as Palestinian in origin" one can agree, without concluding that it "thus creates a strong presumption in favour of its authenticity"[40]. What can be inferred from the evidence is that Mark had put a version of Is 6,9-10 on the lips of Jesus, which was moulded in a community where a version of Is 6,9-10 close to the one later attested in *Tg. Is.* was "in the ears". In direct speech, the Markan Jesus makes a statement: for those outside, those who do not belong to the group with him, everything happens in parables. Connecting the words adapted from Is 6,9-10 with ἵνα, the Markan Jesus explains what it means that everything happens to them in parables[41]: "Listening, they should listen, but not understand! Hearing, they should hear, but not perceive!". In Mark's truncated text, μήποτε introduces a new utterance[42], expressing doubt about the future actions of those outside and the consequence[43]: "Perhaps they will turn around and it will be forgiven them".

In composing chapter 4, the evangelist took up three strands of tradition. Firstly, three "parables" which explain the theme of the coming kingdom of God in terms of metaphors. The source domain of the metaphors is the agricultural experience of rural communities living off the land, in, e.g., the plain of Gennesaret, and the metaphors range from sowing to harvesting. From the tradition parallel to Mk 4,3-8 in *Gos. Thom.* 9 and that corresponding to Mk 4,30-32 in Lk^Q 13,18-19//Mt^Q 13,31-32, it is clear that these two parables were part of the oral pre-Markan tradition. Secondly, the same applies to the sayings to the disciples in Mk 4,21-25. They all reflect the poetic structure typical of Semitic parallelism and all have equivalents in the so-called sayings source Q[44]. Thirdly, Mark took up Is 6,9-10 as an explanation by the followers of Jesus why his addressees did not accept his message[45]. Mark's deviation from the text of the LXX

---

100), New York, Peter Lang, 2006 (*non vidi*). For the reception of Is 6,9-10 in Paul, Mark, Matthew, Luke-Acts, John and the Fathers, see Evans, *To See and Not Perceive* (n. 38), pp. 81-135, 147-162.

40. Manson, *Teaching* (n. 33), p. 77.

41. See BDR, §456$_2$; P. Lampe, *Die markinische Deutung des Gleichnisses vom Sämann: Markus 4 $_{10-12}$*, in *ZNW* 65 (1974) 140-150, pp. 141-143; Mk 9,12.

42. Neither פֶּן in Is 6,10 nor דִלְמָא in *Tg. Is.* 6,10 can clarify the function of μήποτε in the shortened text of Mk 4,12c. See above, in the body of the text after n. 28.

43. See BDR, §370.3; Lampe, *Deutung* (n. 41), pp. 143-144.

44. See F. Neirynck, *Q-Parallels: Q-Synopsis and IQP/CritEdParallels* (SNTA, 20), Leuven, Peeters, 2001, on Lk^Q 11,33//Mt^Q 5,15 parallel to Mk 4,21; Lk^Q 12,2//Mt^Q 10,26 to Mk 4,22; Lk^Q 6,38//Mt^Q 7,2 to Mk 4,24; Lk^Q 19,29//Mt^Q 25,29 to Mk 4,25.

45. In Rom 11,8 Paul developed an analogous argument, drawing on Dt^{LXX} 29,3 and Is 29,10. See M. Wolter, *Der Brief an die Römer. 2. Teilband: Röm 6–9* (EKKNT, 6/2), Göttingen, Vandenhoeck & Ruprecht, 2019, pp. 154-155.

is caused by the reception of the oral version of Is 6,9-10 as transmitted in an Aramaic speaking community.

This is not the place to put Mk 4,12 into the context of the speech at the lake in chapter 4, which is essentially an exhortation to listen correctly to the message about Jesus as mediator of the mysterious advent of God's royal rule[46]. Nevertheless, it is clear that the recourse to the prophet played a crucial role in the composition of the speech the Markan Jesus, sitting in the boat, gave to the multitude on the shore.

III. MARK 8,18

Mark used βλέπω and ἀκούω in 4,12 with Is 6,9-10 as pre-text. These verbs are repeated in Mk 8,18, but the occurrence of ὀφθαλμοί and ὦτα makes it likely that he cites part of Jer 5,21[47]. In Jer 5,21, the LXX, MT, and *Tg. Jer.* make statements and have the verbs in the third person. Mark, however, lets Jesus question the disciples, and had to change from the third to the second person plural. Mark's deviation from the LXX, where the dative is rendered by a particle, is more substantial. He correctly rendered the plural nouns עין and אזן, both followed by ל and a pronominal suffix, by means of the accusatives ὀφθαλμούς and ὦτα and a concessive participle ἔχοντες.

If Mark deviates from the manuscripts of LXX here, because he used a version of Jer 5,21 closer to the HT and more familiar to him, then we can assume that he used two traditional elements to compose the episode 8,14-21: the saying in 8,15, which has its parallels in Lk^Q 12,1//Mt^Q 16,6 and the versions of Jer 5,21 as reflected in the Hebrew (or Aramaic)[48]. Integrating the two episodes on Jesus' feeding of the multitude (6,35-44; 8,1-10), the narrative section 6,32–8,21 develops the theme of the growing

---

46. For my view, see C. BREYTENBACH, *Nachfolge und Zukunftserwartung nach Markus* (ATANT, 71), Zürich, Theologischer Verlag Zürich, 1984, pp. 176-190.

47. See Table 3 at the end of this section. Jer 5,21 is also quoted in *1 En.* 101,6. Some commentators opt for a reoccurrence of Is 6,9 (since WEISS, *Evangelien* [n. 26], p. 127), many for a combination of Jer 5,21 and Ez 12,2, altering the LXX (first SWETE, *Mark* [n. 18], p. 171; LOHMEYER, *Markus* [n. 18], p. 158; lately M.E. BORING, *Mark: A Commentary* [NTL], Louisville, KY, Westminster, John Knox, 2006, p. 227). More recently for Jer 5,21 only: D. LÜHRMANN, *Das Markusevangelium* (HNT, 3), Tübingen, Mohr Siebeck, 1987, p. 138; YARBRO COLLINS, *Mark* (n. 26), p. 387. TAYLOR, *Mark* (n. 33), p. 367, combines all three. MEYER (*Handbuch* [n. 26], p. 104) referred to interesting, but very early and hardly relevant, *sententiae* in Xenophon (*Anabasis* 3.1.27) and Demosthenes (*In Aristogitonem* 1.89.5).

48. The translation of Jer 5,21 in Lk^Q 12,1//Mt^Q 16,6 is less precise than that of Mark, nevertheless, this is the pre-text, rather than Ez 12,2, which has two additional constructive infinitives in the relative clause.

failure of Jesus' disciples to understand who he is because of the hardness of their hearts (6,52) and culminates in the episode 8,14-21[49].

Mk 8,18	Jer 5,21		
	LXX	MT	TGM[50]
	ἀκούσατε δὴ ταῦτα, λαὸς μωρὸς καὶ ἀκάρδιος,	שִׁמְעוּ־נָא זֹאת עַם סָכָל וְאֵין לֵב	שמעו כען דא עמא טפשא ולית ליה לב
ὀφθαλμοὺς ἔχοντες οὐ βλέπετε καὶ ὦτα ἔχοντες οὐκ ἀκούετε;	ὀφθαλμοὶ αὐτοῖς καὶ οὐ βλέπουσιν, ὦτα αὐτοῖς καὶ οὐκ ἀκούουσι.	עֵינַיִם לָהֶם וְלֹא יִרְאוּ אָזְנַיִם לָהֶם וְלֹא יִשְׁמָעוּ׃	דעינין להון ולא חזן אודנין להון ולא שמעין

Table 3

IV. Mark 9,48

In the narrative sequence Mk 9,30–10,31, four sections follow the second announcement of Jesus' passion and resurrection in 9,30-32. After teaching his disciples about servitude, humility (9,33-37), tolerance toward others acting in his name (9,38-41), and the responsibility towards the children (9,42), the Markan Jesus warns against wrong action (9,43. 45.47.48). This section closes with a citation from Is 66,24[51], where the phrase "for their worm shall not die and their fire not be quenched" explains why it is still possible to see the corpses of those who sinned against the Lord. Introducing Mk 9,48 with ὅπου, the Markan Jesus describes the γέεννα he mentioned in 9,43, 45, and 47, by using this phrase from Is 66,24.

Gehenna is the Graecized form of the Aramaic גֵיהִנָּם[52]. By using the present indicatives τελευτᾷ and σβέννυται, Mk 9,48 deviates from the LXX versions with their future tenses τελευτήσει (A, however, reads τελευτᾷ) and σβεσθήσεται. This is noteworthy, because Mark normally kept to the future tense of the pre-text when he cited the LXX[53]. This leads us to note another detail. Neither the LXX nor the HT explicitly indicates that Gehenna is the place of the everlasting worms and the inextinguishable

---

49. On the composition of this episode, see Breytenbach, *Nachfolge* (n. 46), pp. 191-206.
50. "Hear this now. O stupid people who have no understanding: who have eyes, but do not see; who have ears, but do not hear" (text CAL; trans. R. Hayward, *The Targum of Jeremiah: Introduction, Translation, Apparatus and Notes* [ArBib, 12], Edinburgh, T&T Clark, 1987, p. 64).
51. See Table 4 at the end of this section. Is 66,24 is also quoted in *1 En.* 27,2-3.
52. See BDAG, *s.v.* with reference to Dalman.
53. This is the case with καταλείψει and ἔσονται in 10,7-8; ἀγαπήσεις in 12,30 and 31, and the passives προσκολληθήσεται in 10,7 and κληθήσεται in 11,17.

fire. *Tg. Is.* 66,24 however, adds the phrase "and there will be lawsuits for the wicked in Gehenna" (בגיהנם).

Mark had put the phrase from the last verse of the Book of Isaiah on the lips of Jesus ending the three warnings. He selected this verse, because in the oral tradition translating the Hebrew text of Is 66,24 into Aramaic, the verse was associated with Gehenna. It served Mark's purpose to underline the urgency of the warnings by describing the everlasting horrors of Gehenna[54].

Mk 9,47-49	Is 66,24		
καλόν σέ ἐστιν μονόφθαλμον εἰσελθεῖν εἰς τὴν βασιλείαν τοῦ θεοῦ ἢ δύο ὀφθαλμοὺς ἔχοντα βληθῆναι εἰς τὴν γέενναν,	LXX	MT	*Tg. Is.*[55]
[48] ὅπου ὁ σκώληξ αὐτῶν οὐ τελευτᾷ καὶ τὸ πῦρ οὐ σβέννυται.	ὁ γὰρ σκώληξ αὐτῶν οὐ τελευτήσει, καὶ τὸ πῦρ αὐτῶν οὐ σβεσθήσεται,	כִּי תוֹלַעְתָּם לֹא תָמוּת וְאִשָּׁם [ואשהמה] 1QIsa^a לֹא תִכְבֶּה	[...] ארי נשמתהון לא ימותן ואשתהון לא תטפי ויהון מידדנין רשיעיא בגיהנם
[49e] Πᾶς γὰρ πυρὶ ἁλισθήσεται.	καὶ ἔσονται εἰς ὅρασιν πάσῃ σαρκί.	וְהָיוּ דֵרָאוֹן לְכָל־בָּשָׂר: [הבשר] 1QIsa^a	עד דיימרון עליהון צדיקיא מיסת חזינא:

Table 4

V. MARK 13,24-25

"In those days, after the tribulation" (Mk 13,24a), there will be a return to the chaos, before God created light (Gen 1,14-18). In 13,24b-25 Mark drew on Is 13,10 and 34,4 to depict a cosmic catastrophe[56]. Verse 24b is only seemingly close to the LXX[57]. "Whereas the passage in the prophet follows the order stars-sun-moon, the sequence in Mark is sun-moon-stars,

---

54. See also C. FOCANT, *The Gospel according to Mark: A Commentary*, Eugene, OR, Pickwick, 2012, p. 394.

55. "For their breaths will not die and their fire shall not be quenched, and the wicked shall be judged in Gehenna until the righteous will say concerning them, 'We have seen enough'" (trans. CHILTON, *Isaiah* [n. 37], p. 128).

56. See Table 5 at the end of this section. For earlier research on these verses, see J. VERHEYDEN, *Describing the Parousia: The Cosmic Phenomena in Mk 13,24-25*, in C.M. TUCKETT (ed.), *The Scriptures in the Gospels* (BETL, 131), Leuven, LUP – Peeters, 1997, 520-550, pp. 520-534.

57. D.S. DU TOIT, *Der abwesende Herr: Strategien im Markusevangelium zur Bewältigung der Abwesenheit des Auferstandenen* (WMANT, 111), Neukirchen-Vluyn, Neukirchener Verlag, 2006, pp. 222-223, sees Is^LXX 13,9-13 als "primärer Intertext". For the differences between Mk 13,24b-25 and the LXX, see VERHEYDEN, *Describing the Parousia* (n. 56), pp. 534-540.

and the intermediate element (καὶ ὁ Ὠρίων ... οὐ δώσουσι) is lacking"[58]. In Mk 13,24bα ὁ ἥλιος is the logical subject of σκοτισθήσεται: "The sun will be darkened". In the LXX ὁ ἥλιος is part of the genitive absolute: "It will be dark when the sun rises". Mk 13,24bα is closer to the HT: "The sun is dark in its rise". Mk 13,24bβ translates אורו with τὸ φέγγος αὐτῆς (her radiance), Is 13,10 with τὸ φῶς αὐτῆς. Τὸ φέγγος also occurs in Jl[LXX] 2,10, but as translation of נגה. On the basis that Jl 2,10 also mentions ἥλιος in the nominative, followed by συσκοτάζω (intransitive "to become dark" or "to lose light")[59], has the order sun-moon-stars, and mentions that the heaven will be shaken (σεισθήσεται), Joseph Verheyden suggested that influence of Jl[LXX] 2,10 might have caused the differences between Mk 13,24 and Is[LXX] 13,10[60].

In the case of Mk 13,25b, Swete suggested dependence on the Hebrew[61]. The Hebrew phrase that the whole army of heaven will melt away, is lacking in the LXX[62], but does occur in α' and θ'[63]. In an inversion typical for oral/aural transmission, Mark then had put the phrase rendering צבא השמים (or as in *Tg. Is.* חילי שמיא) with αἱ δυνάμεις αἱ ἐν τοῖς οὐρανοῖς at the end of verse 25. Without any introduction that this is a quotation, the Markan Jesus thus says that the powers that are in heaven[64] will be shaken (σαλευθήσονται).

But what happened to Is 34,4b? The evangelist saved the motif of the falling leaves and the withered fruit on the fig tree for Mk 13,28. The sign that the end is near will come in spring, when the branch of the fig tree becomes tender. In autumn, the leaves of the vine and the withered figs falling, the end will come (13,24-25), when an unidentified "they" will see the Son of Man coming in the clouds (13,26). The motif of the withered fruit on the fig tree not only serves as a bridge to the parable of the branches of the fig tree softening in spring (13,28) as a sign of the imminent destruction of the temple. Mark used it also to frame the episode

---

58. VERHEYDEN, *Describing the Parousia* (n. 56), p. 534.
59. T. MURAOKA, *A Greek-English Lexicon of the Septuagint*, Leuven – Paris – Walpole, MA, Peeters, 2009, *s.v.*
60. VERHEYDEN, *Describing the Parousia* (n. 56), pp. 539-540.
61. SWETE, *Mark* (n. 18), p. 311, already noted that αἱ δυνάμεις αἱ ἐν τοῖς οὐρανοῖς in Mk 13,25b are the צְבָא הַשָּׁמַיִם of Is 34,4. VERHEYDEN, *Describing the Parousia* (n. 56), pp. 356 and 538, acknowledges that Mk 13,25b does not go back to Is[LXX] 34,4a, and opts for a text form close or identical to θ'.
62. For the numerous other differences with the LXX, see DU TOIT, *Herr* (n. 57), p. 222.
63. In the variants, the logical subject of τακήσομαι alternates between στρατιά (α') and δυνάμεις (θ', sing. in σ'). See VERHEYDEN, *Describing the Parousia* (n. 56), pp. 536-538, for the details, including Eusebius' commentary on Isaiah.
64. For L. HARTMAN, *Mark for the Nations: A Text and Reader-orientated Commentary*, Eugene, OR, Pickwick, 2010, p. 548, the "angels, planets, weather-gods".

about Jesus expelling the merchants from the temple during his first visit (11,12-14.[15-19].20).

In Mk 11,17, the narrator introduces Jesus' speech and Jesus introduces the citation with γέγραπται ὅτι. This is the normal way in which Mark follows the LXX. With the words ὑμεῖς δὲ πεποιήκατε αὐτόν the Markan Jesus combines the LXX version of Is 56,7 with the motif of the misuse of the temple as a cave of perpetrators of violence from Jer[LXX] 7,11 (σπήλαιον ληστῶν). When Mark introduces what is written, he often uses the same compositional technique: combining two different pretexts from the LXX with a few of his own words, he presents them as part of one coherent speech of Jesus[65].

The rare "mix" in Mk 13,24-25 that Joseph Verheyden discussed with great precision does not fit the normal pattern we find in 11,17. In the light of the findings in sections II, IV and VI of this essay, I would rather propose that Mk 13,25 preserved a version of Is 34,4a that was transmitted orally and reveals closeness to the Hebrew or Aramaic. This could be another case where he does not follow the LXX.

Mk 13,24	Is 13,10	
Ἀλλ' ἐν ἐκείναις ταῖς ἡμέραις μετὰ τὴν θλῖψιν ἐκείνην	LXX	MT
ὁ ἥλιος σκοτισθήσεται, καὶ ἡ σελήνη οὐ δώσει τὸ φέγγος αὐτῆς,	οἱ γὰρ ἀστέρες τοῦ οὐρανοῦ καὶ ὁ Ὠρίων καὶ πᾶς ὁ κόσμος τοῦ οὐρανοῦ τὸ φῶς οὐ δώσουσι, καὶ σκοτισθήσεται τοῦ ἡλίου ἀνατέλλοντος καὶ ἡ σελήνη οὐ δώσει τὸ φῶς αὐτῆς.	כִּי־כוֹכְבֵי הַשָּׁמַיִם וּכְסִילֵיהֶם לֹא יָהֵלּוּ אוֹרָם חָשַׁךְ הַשֶּׁמֶשׁ בְּצֵאתוֹ וְיָרֵחַ לֹא־יַגִּיהַ אוֹרוֹ׃ [1QIsa[b] יגה]
Mk 13,25	Is 34,4	
	LXX	MT
καὶ αἱ δυνάμεις αἱ ἐν τοῖς οὐρανοῖς σαλευθήσονται.	καὶ ἑλιγήσεται ὁ οὐρανὸς ὡς βιβλίον,	וְנָמַקּוּ כָּל־צְבָא הַשָּׁמַיִם [1QIsa[a] והעמקים יתבקעו וכול צבא] [חשמים יפולו] וְנָגֹלּוּ כַסֵּפֶר הַשָּׁמָיִם
καὶ οἱ ἀστέρες ἔσονται ἐκ τοῦ οὐρανοῦ πίπτοντες,	καὶ πάντα τὰ ἄστρα πεσεῖται	וְכָל־צְבָאָם יִבּוֹל
Cf. Mk 11,20 and 13,28	ὡς φύλλα ἐξ ἀμπέλου καὶ ὡς πίπτει φύλλα ἀπὸ συκῆς.	כִּנְבֹל עָלֶה מִגֶּפֶן וּכְנֹבֶלֶת מִתְּאֵנָה׃ [1QIsa[a] מגופן ... מן תראה]

Table 5

65. See the examples in BREYTENBACH, *Episodic Narrative* (n. 3), pp. 437 (Mk 7,10), 422 (10,7-8), 477 (12,19), 453, and 481-486 (12,29-31).

VI. Mark 15,34 and the Allusions in 15,24 and 29-30

In the passion narrative that Mark knew, Jesus died after uttering the words of Ps 22,2 in Aramaic[66]. From a comparison between the different versions of Ps 22(21),2, it is evident that the Markan Jesus utters the words of the Psalm in Aramaic in 15,34. He addresses God in Aramaic with אלהי אלהי, "my God, my God". Mark transcribed ελωι with the omega for the dark $\bar{a}$ (qamets khatuf) and vocalised למה ("why") Aramaic as לְמָה[67].

Mark himself translated the words into Greek and did not use the text of the LXX. His translation differs from our known LXX versions, which have an extra phrase with an aorist imperative πρόσχες μοι: "(My God, my God), attend to me!". Only then the question introduced by ἵνα τί ("why") follows. Closer to the Aramaic, Mark used εἰς τί ("for what")[68] with focus on the purpose of Jesus' death. "For what purpose did you leave me?".

Mk 15,34a	Ps 22,2	Mk 15,34b	Ps 21,2	Ps 22,2
ἐβόησεν ὁ Ἰησοῦς φωνῇ μεγάλῃ·	MT	ὅ ἐστιν μεθερμηνευόμενον·	LXX	TG. PS.[69]
ελωι ελωι	אֵלִי אֵלִי	ὁ θεός μου ὁ θεός μου,	Ὁ θεὸς ὁ θεός μου, πρόσχες μοι·	אלהי אלהי
λεμα σαβαχθανι;	לָמָה עֲזַבְתָּנִי	εἰς τί ἐγκατέλιπές με;	ἵνα τί ἐγκατέλιπές με;	מה מטול שבקתני

Table 6.1

---

66. See Table 6.1-6.3 in this section. A. Suhl, *Die Funktion der alttestamentlichen Zitate und Anspielungen im Markusevangelium*, Gütersloh, Gerd Mohn – Gütersloher Verlagshaus, 1965, pp. 26-45, discussed the earlier research on the reception of Psalm 22 in the Markan passion narrative. For more recent research, see S. Ahearne-Kroll, *The Psalms of Lament in Mark's Passion: Jesus' Davidic Suffering* (SNTS MS, 142), Cambridge, CUP, 2007, pp. 71-77, 191-212.

67. See G. Dalman, *Die Worte Jesu*, Band 1, Leipzig, Hinrichs, 1930, pp. 42-43; followed by Swete, *Mark* (n. 18), p. 385. *Tg. Ps.* 22,2 has "what" (מה) "because" (מטול, cf. CAL, *s.v.*), and the peal verb שבק "to leave" (cf. CAL, *s.v.*) with first person suffix: "because of what did you leave me".

68. See BDR, §12.3; Focant, *Mark* (n. 54), p. 646. α': ἰσχυρέ μου, ἰσχυρέ μου. σ' and θ': ὁ θεός μου, ὁ θεός μου. On the LXX version of Psalm 21, see E. Bons, *Die Septuaginta-Version von Psalm 22*, in D. Sänger (ed.), *Psalm 22 und die Passionsgeschichten der Evangelien*, Neukirchen-Vluyn, Neukirchener Verlag, 2008, 12-32.

69. "My God, my God, why have you forsaken me? (Why are you so) far from my deliverance, (from) the words of my cry?" (text CAL; trans. D.M. Stec, *The Targum of Psalms: Introduction, Translation, Apparatus and Notes* [ArBib, 169], Edinburgh, T&T Clark, 2004, pp. 57-58).

A close reading of the episode of the crucifixion reveals that the action is depicted against the backdrop of Psalm 22. From ancient sources on crucifixion, we know that in some cases those convicted were crucified naked[70]. In line with Jesus' final cry in the words of Ps 22,2, more elements of the Psalm were used to show that the death of Jesus is foreshadowed in the Psalm. In the Psalm (see also Jn 22,19), the clothes are distributed, and the casting of the dice is confined to the garment which is not divided. Taking up these two motifs from the Psalm, Mark conflated the two actions. Dramatically the narrator tells in the historical present: "and they (*sc.* the Roman soldiers) crucify him and distribute (διαμερίζονται) his clothes by throwing (βάλλοντες) the lot over them (*sc.* the clothes), who should pick up what". Ps 22,19 forms the backdrop of the narrative but is not cited.

Mk 15,24	Ps (21)22,19		
	LXX	MT	TG. PS.[71]
Καὶ σταυροῦσιν αὐτὸν			
καὶ διαμερίζονται τὰ ἱμάτια αὐτοῦ,	διεμερίσαντο τὰ ἱμάτιά μου ἑαυτοῖς	יְחַלְּקוּ בְגָדַי לָהֶם	מפלגין לבושי להון
βάλλοντες κλῆρον ἐπ' αὐτὰ τίς τί ἄρῃ.	καὶ ἐπὶ τὸν ἱματισμόν μου ἔβαλον κλῆρον.	וְעַל־לְבוּשִׁי יַפִּילוּ גוֹרָל׃	ועלוי פתאגאי ירמון עדבין:

Table 6.2

It was common to jeer at those who were crucified. Again, the narrator depicts two actions in a way reminiscent of Ps 22,8-9. The passers-by are like the onlookers in Ps 22,8. They blasphemed Jesus, shaking their heads. The motif in the Psalm, that the Lord will help the one suffering, returns inverted in Mk 15,30. The passers-by mocked Jesus by telling him to save himself and descend from the cross. Deviating from the Psalm, the narrator knows that God will not save Jesus. He will abandon him. The final cry of 15,34 is implied in the exhortation in 15,30 that Jesus should save himself. Working backwards from the traditional citation from Ps 22,2 in Mk 15,34, the narrator tells about the crucifixion

---

70. D.W. CHAPMAN – E.J. SCHNABEL, *The Trial and Crucifixion of Jesus: Text and Commentary* (WUNT, 344), Tübingen, Mohr Siebeck, 2015, p. 287; J.G. COOK, *Crucifixion in the Mediterranean World* (WUNT, 327), Tübingen, Mohr Siebeck, 2014 (2nd ed., 2019), pp. xxvii-xxviii, 192-193, 427. Did the executioners have the right to appropriate the clothes of the executed? See the reference to the late *Digesta Iustiniani* 48.20.6 by M. DIBELIUS, *Die Formgeschichte des Evangeliums*, Tübingen, J.C.B. Mohr (Paul Siebeck), 1933, p. 188.

71. "They divide my clothes among them, and for my garments they cast lots" (trans. STEC, *Psalms* [n. 69], p. 59).

with Ps 22,8-9 and 19 resounding in his text. Since there are no signs that the Greek of the LXX influenced the episode directly and it is undisputable that verse 34 draws on the Aramaic, it is possible that some of the details in the episode on Jesus' crucifixion and death were told in the colours of Psalm 22 (and 69) even before the passion narrative was translated into Greek[72].

Mk 15,29-30	Ps (21)22,8-9		
	LXX	MT	TG. PS.[73]
Καὶ οἱ παραπορευόμενοι	πάντες οἱ θεωροῦντές με	כָּל־רֹאַי יַלְעִגוּ לִי	לי כל דחמין
ἐβλασφήμουν αὐτὸν κινοῦντες τὰς κεφαλὰς αὐτῶν	ἐξεμυκτήρισάν με, ἐλάλησαν ἐν χείλεσιν, ἐκίνησαν κεφαλήν	יַפְטִירוּ בְשָׂפָה יָנִיעוּ רֹאשׁ׃	ירהבון עלי מתגריך״מתנדדיך״ בסיפוותהון יטלטלון״ומטלטליך״ ברישהון:
καὶ λέγοντες· οὐὰ ὁ καταλύων τὸν ναὸν καὶ οἰκοδομῶν ἐν τρισὶν ἡμέραις,			
[30] σῶσον σεαυτὸν καταβὰς ἀπὸ τοῦ σταυροῦ.	Ἤλπισεν ἐπὶ κύριον, ῥυσάσθω αὐτόν· σωσάτω αὐτόν, ὅτι θέλει αὐτόν.	גֹּל אֶל־יְהוָה יְפַלְּטֵהוּ יַצִּילֵהוּ כִּי חָפֵץ בּוֹ׃	ישבח קדם ושזביה פצא יתיה יהוה מטול דאיתרעי ביה:

Table 6.3

VII. CONCLUSION

Our investigation has shown that there are cases where Mark deviated from his normal procedure to quote the LXX – in such cases often introducing the text from the LXX with a "quotation formula" – and did not use a LXX version we know: 1,2; 4,12; 8,18; 9,48; 13,24-25 and 15,34.

---

72. Restricting ourselves to citations, we skip the possible allusions to Ps 69,10 and 22 in Mk 15,32, 26 and 36, and to Is 53,12 in Mk 14,27. As early as 1918 Martin Dibelius argued that early Christian "teachers" reading the Psalms in the light of Jesus' crucifixion, brought the motif in verse 24 into the narrative. See M. DIBELIUS, *Die alttestamentlichen Motive in der Leidensgeschichte des Petrus- und des Johannesevangeliums*, in ID., *Botschaft und Geschichte: Gesammelte Aufsätze. Erster Band: Zur Evangelienforschung*, Tübingen, J.C.B. Mohr (Paul Siebeck), 1953, 221-247, p. 229. For the other motifs illustrating Jesus' passion that are in accordance with Scripture, see DIBELIUS, *Formgeschichte* (n. 70), pp. 187-189.

73. "All who see me mock at me, they instigate evil with their lips, they shake their heads. [9] I sang before the LORD, and he rescued me; he delivered me, because he took delight in me" (trans. STEC, *Psalms* [n. 69], p. 58).

In some of the latter cases he merged pre-texts (Ex 23,20 and Mal 3,1 in Mk 1,2; Is 13,10; 34,4a and Jl 2,10 in Mk 13,24-25) and inverted the word order (in 1,2; 4,12 and 13,24-25). In some instances, he used Greek words that are closer translations of the Hebrew or Aramaic known to us than the words our LXX manuscripts preferred (1,2; 4,12; 8,18; 13,25b; 15,34).

In the case of 1,2, Mark follows a conflation of Ex 23,20 with a translation of the reading of Mal 3,1 as attested in Codex Leningradensis. A similar word choice occurs also in Mt^Q 11,10//Lk^Q 7,27. Under the premise that Mark did not know Q, the conflated citation must reach back into the stages of the synoptic tradition when followers of Jesus, who drew on the Hebrew of Mal 3,1, began depicting the role of John the Baptist as forerunner of Jesus with the help of Ex 23,20 and Mal 3,1.

Mk 4,12 uses Is 6,9-10 to explain why Jesus' audience did not understand him. The text is closest to *Tg. Is*. In Mk 8,18, Jesus questions the disciples. Those who ought to have seen and heard correctly did not. Using Jer 5,21 to warn them against hardness of heart, the Markan focus text shows more similarity to the HT. It seems that those who transmitted the traditions about Jesus found the answers why Jesus' preaching and his deeds were misunderstood by his contemporaries and his followers in their Aramaic and Hebrew texts of the prophets. This explains why the pre-text as focussed in the Gospel according to Mark, still shows remainders of Is 6,9-10 and Jer 5,21 in those Aramaic or Hebrew versions accessible to us.

With its connection to Gehenna, *Tg. Is*. 66,24 cited in Mk 9,48, could have closed the list of warnings in Mk 9,43, 45 and 47 even before it was translated into Greek.

Mk 13,24-25 uses a conflation of Is 13,10; 34,4 and Jl 2,10, in which the recurrence of Is 34,4 in Mk 13,25b is closer to the HT as attested by Leningradensis or 1QIsa^a. The motif of the withered figs from Is 34,4 seems to have played a seminal role in the composition of Mk 13,24-30 and 11,15-21.

The last utterance of the Markan Jesus in the Aramaic version of Ps 22,2 led early Christian narrators to tell more details of Jesus' passion in the language of the Psalm. It cannot be excluded that the allusions in Mk 15,24 and 29 reach back to a stage before the passion narrative was told in Greek.

In the current discourse, the narrator (1,2-3) and the main character Jesus (4,12; 8,18; 13,24-25 and 15,34) used these pre-texts as the focal points to develop key narrative themes that go beyond one specific episode: the relation between John the Baptist and Jesus (1,2-3), the reaction of those outside (4,12) and the disciples (8,18) on Jesus' message, the sign when the temple will be destroyed and the end will come (13,24-25), for what purpose God deserted Jesus (15,34). These cases have four traits in common. (1) None of the texts cited was quoted in the non-Christian Jewish literature of the second temple. Their use has been introduced through the text of Mark. (2) With the exception of Mk 1,2-3, where the introductory formula in 1,2a applies to 1,3 and not to 1,2b and c, Mark did not mark the recurrence of the pre-texts from the prophets Isaiah and Jeremiah or Psalm 22 as citations from or allusions to what is written. (3) All citations are closer to the HT or its Aramaic translations documented in the later Targumim than to the LXX. (4) The themes expressed with the help of the pre-texts are overarching, they go beyond the episode in which they occur[74]. These four characteristics are of great importance, since the uniform style of Mark makes it almost impossible to discern pre-Markan tradition from the final narrative[75].

These few cases allow us to formulate hypotheses about pre-Markan tradition behind some of Mark's narratives. In the light of the evidence presented above, I suggest that at a stage when the Hebrew text of what is written and its Aramaic translations still influenced the choice of words, the followers of Jesus used these texts to interpret difficult and contradictory experiences. They aligned John the Baptist and Jesus, interpreted the lack of understanding for Jesus' message by the people and his close followers, envisaged the expected return of Jesus as Son of Man and explained his death in the language of the texts discussed above. These texts were not particularly popular; they were chosen because they facilitated the understanding of contradicting and difficult memories about Jesus. Without being specifically marked as part of what is written, these texts were instrumental to evoke overarching narrative themes connecting episodes. Such themes were developed during the early stages of oral performances of the larger narrative that would later become the Gospel according to Mark[76]. It is possible that some of the allusions to Scripture in Mark's text have a similar pre-history. In an allusion, however, where insufficient elements of a pre-text are repeated, the linguistic

---

74. The citations from the LXX – some consisting of two combined texts – in Mk 7,6-7; 10,4.6-7.19; 12,19.26.29-30.32-33.36 function within the episode in which they are cited; see BREYTENBACH, *Episodic Narrative* (n. 3), pp. 433-467. The functions of Ps^{LXX} 109,1 and Ps^{LXX} 117,22-23 in respectively Mk 12,36 and 14,62 and in 8,31 and 12,10-11 are more complex; see *ibid.*, pp. 246-273.

75. For other ways to discern what was before Mark, see the introduction and notes 3 and 4.

76. On Mark's written text and preceding oral performances, see BREYTENBACH, *Episodic Narrative* (n. 3), pp. 468-479.

evidence does not allow us to put forward a convincing argument, since the basis of comparison between the pre-text and its reception in the focus text alluding to the pre-text is too narrow[77].

Institut für Christentum und Antike Cilliers BREYTENBACH
Theologische Fakultät
Humboldt-Universität zu Berlin
cilliers.breytenbach@hu-berlin.de

New Testament and Ancient Studies
Stellenbosch University
South Africa

---

77. For example, 6,34; 13,27; 14,34.62. For valuable suggestions and corrections, I thank Jimmie Loader, Johannes Renz, David du Toit, Gert Steyn, and last but not least, Anamika Wehen.

LA FORMULE «ΣΥ ΕΙ» ET LA CARACTÉRISATION NARRATIVE DE JÉSUS CHEZ MARC

Dire qu'aux yeux de la majorité des exégètes l'identité de Jésus est le thème principal de l'évangile selon Marc revient à enfoncer une porte ouverte. Mais justement le fait que cette idée soit acceptée sans aucune discussion, comme un axiome, risque de réduire l'interprétation de l'évangile à une lecture christologique qui ne tient pas assez compte de la complexité et de la génialité du récit. La pensée classique généralement acceptée est simple: la véritable identité de Jésus consiste à être Fils de Dieu et Christ et, par une «intrigue de révélation», cette identité est dévoilée lentement, si pas pour les personnages, au moins pour les lecteurs[1]. L'hypothèse de cette contribution est plutôt que le jeu entre les différentes opinions sur l'identité de Jésus et la manière de les présenter enrichit et complique cette ligne de pensée. Cette approche d'une «caractérisation complexe» n'est en rien nouvelle et elle peut être présentée sous différents angles[2]. Très concrètement nous allons analyser l'intrigue créée par les cinq occurrences de la formule σὺ εἶ («tu es …») utilisée pour «identifier» Jésus. La formule introduit cinq perspectives différentes

---

1. Voir, p. ex., ces deux passages qui se lisent sur l'internet: «Autant de paroles et de gestes énigmatiques qui suscitent l'étonnement: ‹Qui est-il donc?›. La question traverse les siècles. Aujourd'hui encore tous ceux qui admirent l'homme Jésus ne sont pas forcément prêts à le reconnaître comme ‹Christ› ou à le déclarer ‹Fils de Dieu›. D'ailleurs, que signifient ces formules? C'est tout l'enjeu du récit de Marc» (https://www.bible-service.net/extranet/current/pages/261.html); «Au cœur de l'évangile de Luc (mais aussi chez Matthieu et Marc), on trouve cette question adressée par Jésus à ses disciples: ‹Qui dîtes-vous que je suis?›. Avant que Jésus ne meure et ne ressuscite, il s'agit pour les disciples de reconnaître en lui le Fils de Dieu, le Messie. C'est Pierre qui sera le premier disciple à confesser Jésus comme étant le Christ. Cette reconnaissance est bien présentée comme une confession de foi: ce n'est pas une connaissance qui lui aurait été donnée d'acquérir, mais sa foi en cet homme qui s'exprime. Aussitôt cette confession de foi prononcée, Jésus les met en demeure: il inscrit ce titre messianique dans la perspective de sa mort et de sa résurrection. En faisant cela, on peut entendre que Jésus comprend sa mission comme étant encore à accomplir, jusqu'au bout. Il n'en demeure pas moins (et ce, quelque soient les diverses interprétations), que l'identité de Jésus reste le fil conducteur des évangiles. Leurs auteurs témoignent de son identité messianique pour leurs auditeurs, leurs lecteurs soient amenés eux aussi à reconnaître en lui le Fils de Dieu» (https://www.theovie.org/Croire-et-comprendre-aujourd-hui/Les-gros-mots-de-la-theologie/Incarnation/Textes-bibliques/L-identite-de-Jesus).

2. Voir S.P. AHEARNE-KROLL, *The Scripturally Complex Presentation of Jesus in the Gospel of Mark*, dans S.E. MYERS (éd.), *Portraits of Jesus* (WUNT, 2.321), Tübingen, Mohr Siebeck, 2012, 45-67, pp. 45-47 (avec référence à E. Malbon et d'autres).

sur Jésus dans cinq contextes différents disséminés dans l'ensemble de l'évangile. La voix céleste (1,11), les démons (3,11) et Pierre (8,29) se prononcent par des phrases affirmatives; le grand-prêtre (14,61) et Pilate (15,2) posent une question. La rhétorique autour de cette formule σὺ εἶ est ainsi renforcée par la riche alternance de déclarations et d'interrogations et par les réactions diverses de la part de Jésus. En parcourant les cinq références, nous allons découvrir comment l'expression σὺ εἶ peut contribuer à une meilleure compréhension du personnage de Jésus dans le récit, une compréhension interactive entre le récit et le lecteur. Avant d'entreprendre l'exégèse des cinq passages, nous nous arrêtons brièvement sur la question de ce que sont l'identité et la caractérisation de Jésus.

I. L'IDENTITÉ OU LA CARACTÉRISATION DE JÉSUS?

Notre première réflexion n'est pas – à proprement parler – exégétique, mais il est nécessaire de se demander ce que signifie «l'identité de Jésus». Identité est l'un de ces mots communs, utilisé par tout un chacun, sans que l'on sache précisément le définir. On pourrait dire que l'identité indique ce qui est propre et unique à quelqu'un ou à quelque chose. Mais ensuite, comment l'expliquer concrètement? Qu'est-ce que l'identité de l'enseignement catholique? L'identité des Flamands? L'identité de l'Europe? Qu'est-ce que «mon identité», qui suis-je? Quelle est l'identité d'un proche que je suis censé connaître? Parlons-nous d'une identité philosophique, sociale, psychologique, nationale, culturelle, religieuse? L'identité peut-elle changer ou évoluer? Comment l'identité de quelqu'un se construit-elle: par lui-même, par son histoire, par son environnement, par l'opinion des autres? Quelles sont les interactions symboliques ou non dites qui jouent un rôle dans la formation d'une identité? Il n'y a pas moyen d'approfondir ici toutes ces questions avant de s'interroger sur l'identité de Jésus[3]. Mais elles forcent l'exégète à préciser ce qu'il/elle veut dire par «identité de Jésus dans l'évangile selon Marc» et elles montrent qu'il est simplement impossible de définir de manière exhaustive la question de l'identité. Toute réponse ne peut être que partielle.

---

3. La littérature sur la question de l'identité abonde. B. GAVENTA – R.B. HAYS (éds), *Seeking the Identity of Jesus: A Pilgrimage*, Grand Rapids, MI, Eerdmans, 2008, en particulier les articles de R.W. JENSON, *Identity, Jesus and Exegesis* (43-59) et de J. MARCUS, *Identity and Ambiguity in Markan Christology* (133-147); l'ouvrage de base est toujours celui de H.W. FREI, *The Identity of Jesus. Expanded and Updated Edition: The Hermeneutical Bases of Dogmatic Theology*, Eugene, OR, Wipf & Stock, 2013 (version originale de 1975, basée sur des articles de 1967).

La notion d'identité dans l'exégèse est fort liée à l'apparition de la critique rédactionnelle qui cherchait à découvrir les idées christologiques de chaque évangile. Elle part d'une clarté presqu'objective de ce que c'est qu'être le Christ ou le Fils de Dieu. L'interprétation exégétique s'accompagne d'une conviction théologique que Marc avait une idée claire et nette de qui était Jésus. On a l'impression que cela correspond à la théologie encore confiante des années 1960-1980. Tout est basé et concentré sur la foi en Jésus Christ. C'est aussi l'époque des grandes œuvres christologiques[4]. L'hypothèse «classique» de ce que c'est l'identité d'une personne part de l'idée qu'elle peut être définie par une expression ou par un titre, le cas échéant «Fils de Dieu» (ou tout autre titre christologique)[5].

Mais c'est justement cette exégèse rédactionnelle qui, à la suite de l'étude originale de W. Wrede sur le secret messianique (1901), a découvert que l'identité de Jésus en Marc n'est pas du tout évidente mais complexe. Cette idée sera renforcée par l'analyse narrative. Au lieu de se fixer sur la seule «intention» de l'évangéliste rédacteur, la narratologie, à partir de 1970, va plutôt accentuer toutes les relations, les perspectives, les interactions, et les controverses qui jouent autour de la figure de Jésus dans le récit. Ainsi, l'usage du terme «caractérisation» au lieu d'identité aide à comprendre la différence entre exégèse historico-critique et narratologie[6]. On entre en tant que lecteur dans la dynamique intérieure du récit. On essaie de comprendre ou de vivre différentes opinions à propos d'un personnage. Cette approche est seulement possible si on tient aussi compte des émotions qui surgissent à la lecture du texte[7]. La caractérisation

---

4. E. SCHILLEBEECKX, *Jesus: An Experiment in Christology*, London, Collins, 1979 (original en néerlandais, 1973); H. KÜNG, *Christ Sein*, München – Zürich, Piper, 1976 (voir la section B sur Jésus Christ); C. DUQUOC, *Messianisme de Jésus et discrétion de Dieu: Essais sur les limites de la christologie*, Genève, Labor et Fides, 1984.

5. C. KEITH, *The Markan Portrayal of Jesus' Identity*, in *Leaven: A Journal of Christian Ministry* 19 (2011) 20-24, présente une analyse de cinq versets avec leur titre christologique: 1,1 (Fils de Dieu), 8,29 (le Christ), 15,16-32 (le Roi des Juifs), 15,39 (un/le Fils de Dieu), pour terminer avec la tension entre les femmes et le lecteur en 16,8. Voir aussi C.M. TUCKETT, *Christology and the New Testament: Jesus and His Earliest Followers*, Louisville, KY, Westminster John Knox, 2001, pp. 109-118 («Chapter Six: Mark»): Seigneur, Messie, Fils de l'homme, Fils de Dieu. Pour une présentation du débat autour d'une christologie «haute» ou «basse», voir D. JOHANSSON, *The Identity of Jesus in the Gospel of Mark: Past and Present Proposals*, dans *CBR* 9 (2011) 364-393.

6. C.W. SKINNER – M.R. HAUGE (éds), *Character Studies and the Gospel of Mark* (LNTS, 483), London – New York, Bloomsbury T&T Clark, 2014; S. FINNERN – J. RÜGGEMEIER, *Methoden der neutestamentlichen Exegese: Ein Lehr- und Arbeitsbuch* (UTB, 4212), Tübingen, Francke, 2016, pp. 195-210 («Figurenanalyse»).

7. K. OATLEY, *A Taxonomy of the Emotions of Literary Response and a Theory of Identification in Fictional Narrative*, in *Poetics* 23 (1994) 53-74.

d'un personnage n'est pas neutre. Elle se construit à travers les réseaux du personnage dans le récit et elle part d'une représentation mentale dans l'esprit du lecteur. L'enjeu global pour la théologie d'une lecture de l'«identité narrative de Jésus» a bien été illustré par A. Gesché dans un article de 1998[8]. Comprendre qu'il s'agit dans les évangiles d'une identité narrative de Jésus est une condition nécessaire pour éviter qu'une lecture soit historicisante soit théologisante du personnage de Jésus. Voici deux citations qui illustrent ce point:

> «… la théorie de l'identité narrative, faite à la fois sur le plan exégétique, philosophique et théologique […] par son caractère activant et dynamique (c'est la nature même de son processus), […] se trouve très exactement au mitan du binôme figé et exclusif [à savoir le Jésus de l'histoire et le Christ de la foi] qui maintenait la pensée christologique dans une véritable anxiété conceptuelle» (p. 348). «Mais c'est aussi et surtout l'identité dogmatique qui se trouve mieux posée d'être passée d'abord par l'identité narrative. Car l'énoncé dogmatique, livré à lui-même, finit, il faut bien le dire, par ne plus rien vouloir dire (ou risquer de ne plus rien vouloir dire). Parce que, figé, fait d'assurances lasses et répétitives, on n'en comprend plus le sens» (p. 352).

II. Marc 1,11: la perspective de Dieu

καὶ φωνὴ ἐγένετο ἐκ τῶν οὐρανῶν· **Σὺ εἶ ὁ υἱός μου ὁ ἀγαπητός**, ἐν σοὶ εὐδόκησα (Marc 1,11)

L'expression σὺ εἶ se rencontre pour la première fois lors du baptême de Jésus. Après avoir entendu l'opinion du Baptiste sur Jésus (1,7: ὁ ἰσχυρότερός μου), une autre voix se prononce sur le protagoniste: Σὺ εἶ ὁ υἱός μου ὁ ἀγαπητός, ἐν σοὶ εὐδόκησα (1,11). Elle est anonyme et elle passe par l'Écriture, mais la mise en scène des cieux qui se déchirent, l'Esprit qui descend et la citation de Ps 2,7 ne permet aucune ambiguïté: c'est Dieu qui parle à son fils, David dans le psaume, Jésus dans l'évangile. Ces paroles se caractérisent de plusieurs manières. Premièrement, la citation mixte du v. 11. Les discussions sur la cohérence entre les possibles contextes vétérotestamentaires dans la combinaison des citations ou allusions sont innombrables. La citation du Ps 2,7 (σὺ εἶ ὁ υἱός μου) qui attribue à Jésus en tant que Messie le titre de fils davidique est combiné avec Gn 22,2 (ὁ ἀγαπητός) et Is 42,1 (ἐν σοὶ εὐδόκησα)[9], deux

---

8. A. Gesché, *Pour une identité narrative de Jésus*, dans *RTL* 30 (1998) 153-179, 336-356. Pour l'importance de cette approche dans l'exégèse, voir E.S. Malbon, *Mark's Jesus: Characterization as Narrative Christology*, Waco, TX, Baylor University Press, 2009, chapitre 1: «Characterization of Jesus as Narrative Christology» (pp. 1-19).

9. On pense aussi à Sg 2,13-18 (v. 18: ὁ δίκαιος υἱὸς θεοῦ).

citations qui ajoutent l'idée de la souffrance de Jésus et de l'amour préférentiel de Dieu. Ainsi, les paroles de la voix créent dès le début de l'évangile une ouverture vers plusieurs interprétations sur ce qui est propre à Jésus dans la perspective de Dieu. Le plus discutable est la référence sacrificielle à Isaac[10], mais elle ne peut pas être exclue de l'interprétation. Les différents contextes vétérotestamentaires rendent presqu'impossible de déterminer avec certitude l'intention précise de Marc. C'est le lecteur qui choisira et qui fournira les arguments. Ce qui est incontestable est l'accent sur le fait qu'il y ait une relation d'amour et de joie («belovedness and pleasingness»)[11].

Une deuxième particularité qui nous intéresse encore plus, est que la voix s'adresse directement à Jésus à la deuxième personne. La construction du Ps 2,7 LXX (υἱός μου εἶ σύ) est inversée pour mettre l'accent sur la personne de Jésus. Plusieurs auteurs ont indiqué que seul Jésus entend la voix et que l'expérience du sens du baptême se déroule dans l'intimité entre le Père et le fils. Aucun autre personnage ne semble être présent ou entendre la voix. Après la voix qui crie dans le désert et appelle à préparer le chemin du Seigneur (1,3: φωνὴ βοῶντος ἐν τῇ ἐρήμῳ), cette deuxième voix – cette fois-ci des cieux (φωνὴ … ἐκ τῶν οὐρανῶν) – indique le fils comme roi et prophète messianique. Au niveau rhétorique de l'intrigue cette reconnaissance par la voix céleste est un élément parmi d'autres qui montre la place unique qu'occupe cet être humain qu'est Jésus. Le narrateur (1,1), les prophètes (1,2-3) et Jean Baptiste (1,4-8) ont parlé de lui dans un sens positif. En tant que lecteur, nous ne pouvons pas oublier que nous nous trouvons dans le prologue de l'évangile. Le narrateur prépare le cadre de l'annonce de l'évangile *par* Jésus à partir de 1,14. Dans le prologue, il donne des arguments qui justifient que Jésus parlera et agira avec autorité.

Pour plusieurs raisons, il est difficile de considérer l'expression «mon fils bien-aimé» comme un titre christologique. C'est une expression qui ouvre vers le récit qui suivra. D'abord, c'est Dieu qui parle et il n'a pas besoin de «confesser» qui est Jésus; ensuite, il parle de «mon» fils; puis, les ajouts de «bien-aimé» et «il m'a plu de te choisir» font partie

---

10. G. GUTTENBERGER, *Das Evangelium nach Markus* (ZBK NT, 2), Zürich, Theologischer Verlag Zürich, 2018, p. 42: «weist nicht auf Gen 22»; R.H. GUNDRY, *Mark: A Commentary on His Apology for the Cross*, Grand Rapids, MI, Eerdmans, 1993, p. 52. Pour une opinion différente, voir AHEARNE-KROLL, *The Scripturally Complex Presentation* (n. 2), pp. 4-5: «Genesis 22 should be read alongside Mark's story of Jesus, starting with the baptism» (p. 5).

11. GUNDRY, *Mark* (n. 10), p. 53; compare MALBON, *Mark's Jesus* (n. 8), p. 79: «what the Markan Jesus does and says is pleasing to (God)».

de l'épithète. La formulation des paroles renforce l'intimité de la relation entre le Père et le fils: φωνή en début de phrase (diff. 9,7), σύ comme premier mot de la citation, l'ajout de l'article ὁ devant υἱός, la construction avec répétition de l'article ὁ υἱός μου ὁ ἀγαπητός[12]. Cette interprétation auditive de Jésus qui est seulement entendu par les lecteurs de l'évangile est très importante pour interpréter le reste de l'évangile qui donnera du contenu aux paroles de la voix. Pourquoi la voix dit-elle que Jésus est le fils bien-aimé et comment se réalisera le programme impliqué par cette actualisation du Ps 2?

L'importance de cette première phrase initiée par σὺ εἶ se situe d'abord au niveau de l'intrigue et notamment de la communication entre les personnages, ici le Père et le fils. Jésus apprend au moment du baptême, de manière auditive, que Dieu l'aime de façon unique. Il est caractérisé dès le début par les premières paroles qu'il entend: Dieu le considère comme son fils et trouve de la joie dans son élection. Tout au long de l'évangile, le fils conservera ce mystère entre lui et Dieu. Il est à noter qu'il n'y a pas de réaction de la part de Jésus. Le deuxième niveau de communication qui intervient est celui entre texte et lecteurs. Ces derniers reçoivent une première perspective sur Jésus de la part de Dieu, une perspective qui explique la position du narrateur exprimée en 1,1, mais qui prépare aussi le programme de l'évangile en lien avec les citations de l'AT. L'appellation «fils» en soi reçoit son sens final dans les paroles et les actions de Jésus. Dans son interprétation globale du prologue, le commentaire sur Marc de John Donahue et Daniel Harrington va encore plus loin. Les auteurs résument bien l'intention d'une christologie qui ne se limite pas aux titres donnés à Jésus, mais qui reçoit son sens profond au moment où les lecteurs comprennent le message de Jésus[13]. Tout le récit est orienté vers les actions et les paroles de Jésus. Robert Gundry note aussi ces deux niveaux de communication quand il dit que les paroles du v. 11 ont un double but: (1) augmenter la conscience de Jésus, et (2) informer l'auditoire de Marc d'une interprétation correcte des paroles, actes, crucifixion et résurrection de Jésus[14]. Les personnages du récit ne sont

---

12. Pour les détails, voir GUNDRY, *Mark* (n. 10), p. 49.

13. J. DONAHUE – D.J. HARRINGTON, *The Gospel of Mark* (SP, 2), Collegeville, MN, Liturgical Press, 2002, pp. 66-67: «The function of Mark's Gospel was not to *prove* that Jesus was ‹the Son of God›, nor was it simply to offer biographical information about Jesus. Rather, it was to engage the readers in the unfolding story of Jesus ‹from Nazareth of Galilee› (1:9), so that they too might be caught up by his message (1:14-15) and be challenged to believe that neither demonic powers nor brutal rulers can ultimately triumph over Jesus or over them».

14. GUNDRY, *Mark* (n. 10), p. 49. Voir aussi p. 50: «The question whether Jesus was God's Son before the baptism does not come into view. As an omniscient narrator Mark

pas mis au courant de cette communication secrète et privée. Le lecteur accompagnera les différents personnages entourant Jésus et il verra comment ils entreront en relation avec lui. «Indeed, much of the plot of Mark revolves around how the secret of Jesus' identity comes to be known. In short, if Jesus looked like any other man, how did anyone know that he was the Son of God?"[15]. C'est une distinction extrêmement importante pour comprendre la rhétorique de l'évangile. Les personnages ne savent pas que Jésus est caractérisé par la voix comme fils bien-aimé. C'est par ses paroles et ses actes qu'ils devront le découvrir. Les lecteurs savent qu'il est le fils bien-aimé mais ils seront surpris par ce que le fils va faire et dire.

Jésus ne donne aucune réaction à ce qu'il entend. Ne rien dire revient à consentir. Par la voix, le narrateur montre que l'enseignement et les miracles de Jésus viennent de Dieu: «on this attribution the Markan Jesus would agree»[16]. Et dans la perspective de Dieu qui appelle Jésus son fils, celui-ci devient le protagoniste dans la continuation de l'action de Dieu dans l'histoire humaine[17].

III. Marc 3,11: la perspective des démons

Καὶ τὰ πνεύματα τὰ ἀκάθαρτα, ὅταν αὐτὸν ἐθεώρουν, προσέπιπτον αὐτῷ καὶ ἔκραζον λέγοντες ὅτι **σὺ εἶ ὁ υἱὸς τοῦ θεοῦ** (Marc 3,11)

La deuxième occurrence de σὺ εἶ se situe dans un contexte très différent. Après une «première journée à Capharnaüm» (1,21-45) et cinq récits de conflits (2,1–3,6), un sommaire rédactionnel sur les foules qui viennent de partout et sur les guérisons et exorcismes (3,7-12) s'achève par une brève citation en discours direct par les démons: «Tu es le fils de Dieu». Les démons savent qui est Jésus (1,24 «le saint de Dieu»; cf. 1,34b), mais en 3,11 ils utilisent explicitement le titre Fils de Dieu (et cela à plusieurs reprises: ὅταν suivi de l'imparfait dans le sommaire). Deux questions indissociables se posent. (1) Qu'est-ce que les démons veulent dire quand ils appellent Jésus «fils de Dieu»? (2) Pourquoi en 3,12 Jésus

---

is simply telling his audience of Jesus' true identity, as already indicated by Mark in v. 1 but now as acknowledged by none other than God, and is setting the stage for Jesus' exercise of divine power».

15. R.A. Culpepper, *Mark* (SHBC, 20), Macon, GA, Smyth and Helwys, 2007, p. 49.
16. Malbon, *Mark's Jesus* (n. 8), p. 76.
17. *Ibid.*, pp. 76-77: «In recognizing Jesus as ‹my Son›, [God] is continuing God's action in human history for the people of God and designating Jesus for a role in that activity».

les rabrouait pour qu'ils ne le fassent pas connaître? Une distinction entre tradition et rédaction n'est pas utile dans notre méthodologie. Nous ne pouvons répondre à ces deux questions qu'en distinguant entre les différents niveaux de communication déjà mentionnés dans la réflexion sur 1,11.

Le sens de ce que disent les démons dépend de la perspective qu'ont ceux qui l'entendent: Jésus ou le lecteur. Nous savons que Jésus refuse les paroles des démons (v. 12; cf. 1,25.34), mais nous ne savons pas pourquoi. Différentes options se présentent. Gundry pense que les démons disent la vérité sur la divinité de Jésus mais que celui-ci leur interdit de parler parce qu'il risque d'être écrasé par la foule[18]. Mais selon Focant, les démons sont «un type d'acteur [qui] n'est pas crédible» et «les mots utilisés ... ne sont pas adaptés à ce qui est connu de Jésus à ce moment du récit, ni peut-être à ce que la foule peut comprendre»[19]. S'agit-il d'une confession de foi (peu probable), d'une tentative d'être plus fort que Jésus, d'une ironie ou d'une moquerie ...? Le texte de Marc ne nous permet pas de donner une réponse définitive au niveau de la communication entre Jésus et les démons. Pourquoi Jésus interdit-il de proclamer? Parce qu'il pense qu'ils ont raison, mais que c'est trop tôt pour le dire publiquement ou parce qu'il pense qu'ils ont tort? La seule chose que nous pouvons dire est que la réaction de Jésus qui leur interdit de le faire connaître, montre qu'une proclamation de leur part ne fait pas partie du programme de la venue du Royaume de Dieu telle que Jésus la conçoit. Une analyse précise du sommaire montre aussi qu'il n'est pas dit que d'autres personnes sont présentes lors des exorcismes. Le fait que, pour le narrateur, la présence ou la réaction d'autres personnages à ce conflit n'a aucune importance pour la continuation de l'intrigue, montre que l'essentiel du message se situe dans la communication entre le texte et le lecteur.

Le lecteur se trouve alors dans une situation extrêmement difficile. Il sait que le narrateur proclame le commencement de l'évangile de Jésus Christ *Fils de Dieu* et il entend maintenant que le fils ne souhaite pas que l'on proclame qui il est. Apparemment, cela fait partie de la caractérisation

---

18. GUNDRY, *Mark* (n. 10), pp. 157, 159. La péricope est intitulée «Jesus' magnetism» et selon l'auteur le sujet du passage n'est pas la proclamation de l'identité du Fils de Dieu mais le fait que Jésus attire des foules. Voir aussi R.T. FRANCE, *The Gospel of Mark* (NIGTC), Grand Rapids, MI, Eerdmans; Carlisle, Paternoster, 2002, p. 155: «... the motive for silencing the demons is not simply that they are undesirable witnesses, but that the truth they declare is not to be divulged».

19. C. FOCANT, *L'évangile selon Marc* (Commentaire biblique: Nouveau Testament, 2), Paris, Cerf, 2001, p. 140.

de Jésus de réagir différemment selon les personnages qui le reconnaissent. Le message pour le lecteur est clair: par la caractérisation de Jésus il comprend que l'identité – si on peut utiliser le mot – n'est pas déterminée par un simple titre hors de son contexte. C'est dans les circonstances spécifiques d'un dialogue et par la réaction de Jésus que l'on comprend surtout comment il ne veut pas être perçu. Il est clair que le cœur du message se trouve là: les exorcismes proprement dits ne sont pas racontés! La rencontre entre les démons et Jésus montre la profondeur du gouffre entre les deux royaumes, celui de Dieu et celui du Satan.

Nous découvrons donc une sorte de clé de lecture: Jésus refuse d'être identifié par un titre «christologique» si le personnage qui parle à Jésus en utilisant l'expression σὺ εἶ n'a pas l'intention de contribuer à la diffusion positive de la bonne nouvelle de la venue du Royaume de Dieu. On peut douter de la sincérité des paroles des démons. Au niveau de l'intrigue, les démons ne confessent pas la vraie identité de Jésus avec l'intention de s'engager dans son projet. Le geste de la prosternation des démons n'y ajoute rien: elle peut être hypocrite. Des expressions identiques peuvent donc être utilisées dans un autre sens. Il est aussi intéressant de constater ce qui n'est pas raconté. Jésus ne fait aucun effort pour éduquer les démons ou leur faire comprendre ce qu'est le Royaume de Dieu. Le narrateur accroît ainsi le caractère mystérieux du personnage de Jésus. La tension narrative augmente: y aura-t-il, dans le récit, des personnages qui seront capables de dire qui est Jésus et est-ce que Jésus accueillera positivement leurs paroles?

IV. MARC 8,29: LA PERSPECTIVE DES DISCIPLES

καὶ αὐτὸς ἐπηρώτα αὐτούς· ὑμεῖς δὲ τίνα με λέγετε εἶναι; ἀποκριθεὶς ὁ Πέτρος λέγει αὐτῷ· **σὺ εἶ ὁ χριστός** (Marc 8,29)

Nous rencontrons ici un troisième cas de figure introduit par σὺ εἶ, celui d'un disciple qui reconnaît par une formule qui est Jésus. Avec la «confession» de Pierre nous atteignons la première instance de l'usage de χριστός dans Marc après le titre (1,1). La courte phrase σὺ εἶ ὁ χριστός est en discours direct et fait partie d'un dialogue entre Jésus et les disciples dont Pierre est le porte-parole. Une nouveauté par rapport aux cas précédents est que Jésus pose une question aux disciples pour savoir qui il est selon eux. En reprenant dans sa réponse le même mot qu'en 1,1, la parole de Pierre pourrait être considérée comme le point culminant de la première partie de l'évangile. La voix de Pierre semble être en symphonie avec la voix du narrateur. Mais l'enthousiasme de cette pensée est très vite contrarié par la suite. Certes, la «confession» est un écho de l'ouverture de l'évangile, mais en reprenant le mot χριστός, Pierre ne met pas une fin au «commencement de la bonne nouvelle». Pierre et Jésus comprennent le mot de manière différente. Si la phrase introduite par σὺ εἶ est parfois considérée comme un point culminant du récit, elle l'est par sa dimension ambivalente qui donne à penser plutôt que par sa justesse. En effet, elle crée l'opportunité pour le narrateur d'introduire par la voix de Jésus la deuxième partie de l'évangile qui mettra en exergue le thème de la souffrance du Messie. La confession de Pierre et le commandement sévère de Jésus de ne parler de lui à personne font une unité avec la première annonce de sa mort et de sa résurrection qui est suivie par un refus intentionnel de la part de Pierre d'accepter cet élément du message de Jésus. S'il est encore possible de croire que les démons sont de mauvaise foi, il n'est guère envisageable de penser que Pierre n'est pas sincère. Mais sa sincérité cache son ignorance.

Si le lecteur se posait déjà des questions par rapport au refus de Jésus de la reconnaissance par les démons, il est encore plus troublé par la réprimande de Jésus envers Pierre. Le narrateur avait appelé Jésus le Christ (1,1) et quand il y a un personnage important, Pierre, qui l'affirme, il est critiqué par Jésus. De nouveau, la question se pose de savoir si Jésus commande le silence parce que Pierre a raison ou parce qu'il a tort? Ou veut-il éviter de courir à nouveau le risque de ne pas être compris de façon correcte? Au niveau de l'intrigue du récit, Jésus ne s'oppose pas à l'expression mais à l'usage que Pierre en fait, ignorant la «nécessité» de la passion comme complément indispensable pour comprendre le message de Jésus. C'est cela qui devient clair dans la réaction de Jésus qui commence à parler «ouvertement» de sa passion (8,32). Pierre refuse d'accepter. Nous constatons donc, de nouveau, que l'usage d'un titre ne suffit pas pour assurer une vision juste sur «l'identité» de Jésus. Le dialogue entre Jésus et Pierre (et les autres disciples) en 8,27-33 illustre bien qu'appeler Jésus le Christ implique aussi d'intégrer son message et la passion qu'il subira. La caractérisation de Jésus est tellement liée au message qu'il proclame que la question de son identité ne se détermine pas par l'usage d'un «simple» titre. Cela deviendra péniblement visible par la suite de l'évangile car le disciple qui l'appelle le Christ ne sera pas du tout capable de le suivre jusqu'au bout, à Jérusalem. Au contraire, il niera trois fois connaître Jésus (14,68: ὁ δὲ ἠρνήσατο λέγων· οὔτε οἶδα οὔτε ἐπίσταμαι σὺ τί λέγεις). Dans la perspective de la fin de la présence active de Pierre dans le récit, on comprend mieux pourquoi Jésus l'appelle «Satan» en 8,33. Par son ignorance et son opposition au contenu du message de Jésus (8,27-33) et par son refus déterminé d'être du côté du Nazaréen de Galilée (14,66-72) Pierre semble plutôt appartenir au groupe des opposants de Jésus. C'est le sens de la réprimande de Jésus en 8,33: «tes vues ne sont pas celles de Dieu, mais celles des hommes».

La fonction de ce petit dialogue au centre de l'évangile ne se limite pas à une meilleure compréhension de l'intrigue ou des relations entre les personnages. Le lecteur aussi est concerné par cette scène. S'il a bien écouté le récit, une fois de plus il est mieux informé sur Jésus que les disciples. En fait, les disciples ne pouvaient pas savoir avant 8,31 que Jésus devrait souffrir et mourir. Bien que le récit qui précède contienne beaucoup d'informations sur sa passion et sa mort, cette information se trouve au niveau de la communication entre le narrateur et le lecteur/ auditeur. Ainsi, par exemple, le verset 3,6 («les pharisiens tinrent aussitôt conseil avec les Hérodiens contre Jésus sur les moyens de le faire périr») est une information importante dont dispose le lecteur mais pas les disciples. Cela vaut aussi pour la petite parenthèse après la mention du nom de Judas Iscarioth: «celui-là qui le livra» (3,18). Ces deux exemples de commentaire direct de la part du narrateur pourraient être complétés par un exemple de commentaire indirect. La construction en sandwich ABA' de la mission des disciples (A), la mort de Jean Baptiste (B) et le retour des disciples (A') contient au centre une anticipation de la mort violente de Jésus (et des disciples!). Mais ce récit de la mort de Jean Baptiste – un flashback dans le temps - est seulement raconté à ceux qui entendent l'évangile et pas aux disciples.

Le lecteur de l'évangile de Marc doit néanmoins rester prudent, car il est souvent pris à contrepied par le narrateur. Son avance concernant l'identité de Jésus n'implique pas automatiquement qu'il est meilleur disciple! Le mécanisme herméneutique de 8,27-33 fonctionne dans un double sens. Premièrement, les disciples dans le récit sont mis au courant «ouvertement» d'une nouvelle information sur le destin de Jésus: il devra souffrir et mourir et il ressuscitera. De cette manière, les disciples comme Pierre sont mis sur un pied d'égalité avec le lecteur. Ils disposent maintenant de la même information. Deuxièmement, le lecteur qui est déjà (partiellement) au courant de ce qui va se passer avec Jésus est maintenant aussi assimilé aux disciples. Ce qui sera dit aux disciples sera aussi dit au lecteur. Ce qui sera fait par les disciples deviendra aussi un acte miroir de ce que le lecteur pourra faire. En d'autres termes, le lecteur est mis devant les mêmes choix que les disciples: va-t-il suivre Jésus jusqu'à la fin quand il entend le message concernant la passion? La transition d'une approche narratologique qui parle du narrateur impliqué vers une lecture pragmatique de l'évangile qui envisage des lecteurs réels est bien formulée par M. Strauss: «Like Peter, all of us need to hear Jesus' rebuke of our self-promoting perceptions of the Messiah and submit ourselves to his authority and lordship»[20].

V. Marc 14,61: la question du grand-prêtre

πάλιν ὁ ἀρχιερεὺς ἐπηρώτα αὐτὸν καὶ λέγει αὐτῷ· **σὺ εἶ ὁ χριστὸς ὁ υἱὸς τοῦ εὐλογητοῦ;**
ὁ δὲ Ἰησοῦς εἶπεν· ἐγώ εἰμι, ... (Marc 14,61)

Les deux dernières occurrences de σὺ εἶ se trouvent à une distance assez courte l'une de l'autre. Elles introduisent une question du grand-prêtre (14,61) et une autre de Pilate (15,2). L'évangile de Marc contient plus de 110 questions[21]. Plus de la moitié de ces questions sont posées par Jésus. Nous venons de lire la question qui se trouve au cœur de l'évangile: «Et vous, qui dites-vous que je suis?» (8,29), Jésus lui-même mettant ainsi au centre le thème de son identité, annoncé déjà par le narrateur dès le premier verset de l'évangile «de Jésus Christ, Fils de Dieu» (1,1). Cette question de Jésus n'est pas surprenante et elle tient une place logique dans l'intrigue. D'une part, d'autres personnages avaient déjà manifesté leur étonnement et leur curiosité en posant des questions concernant l'identité (1,24; 5,7; 6,3), l'enseignement (1,27; 2,7; 6,2b) et les actes de Jésus (2,16; 4,41; 6,2c) ou en exprimant leurs opinions sur son identité (6,14-16). D'autre part, Jésus lui-même avait déjà questionné les disciples à différentes occasions (4,13.21.30.40; 6,38; 7,18.19; 8,5.18-21). Ici, au cœur du récit de la Passion nous avons les deux instances où des personnages interrogent Jésus en utilisant la formule σὺ εἶ.

La question du grand-prêtre «Es-tu le Christ, le fils du Béni?»[22] fait partie de l'interrogatoire au Sanhédrin. Elle est la deuxième question posée par le grand-prêtre[23]. À la première question sur les accusations contre

---

20. M.L. Strauss, *Mark* (Exegetical Commentary on the New Testament, 2), Grand Rapids, MI, Zondervan, 2014, p. 366.
21. G. Van Oyen, *Questions in the Gospel of Mark: Two Examples (Mk 1,24; 16,3)*, in B. Koet – A. van Wieringen (éds.), *Asking Questions in Biblical Texts* (CBET), Leuven – Paris – Bristol, CT, Peeters, à paraître.
22. Le terme «fils du Béni» dans la bouche du grand-prêtre est généralement considéré comme équivalent à Fils de Dieu selon la coutume juive. Pour l'idée que Fils du Béni est un «case of restrictive apposition» après «Christ», voir J. Marcus, *Mark 8–16: A New Translation with Introduction and Commentary* (AB, 27A), New Haven, CT – London, Yale University Press, 2009, p. 1005.
23. Pour être précis, il faut dire que la première question en 14,60 pourrait être interprétée comme une double question, exemple du style de Marc (p. ex. 1,24; 2,7; 2,8; 4,21; 4,41; 6,3; etc.): «καὶ ἀναστὰς ὁ ἀρχιερεὺς εἰς μέσον ἐπηρώτησεν τὸν Ἰησοῦν λέγων· οὐκ ἀποκρίνῃ οὐδέν[;] τί οὗτοί σου καταμαρτυροῦσιν;». Voir Focant, *Marc* (n. 19), pp. 551-552.

Jésus, celui-ci n'avait pas répondu (14,60). La deuxième contient deux titres qui font écho avec certains versets que nous avons déjà rencontrés (1,1; 3,11; 8,29; voir aussi 1,24; 5,7) et prolonge ainsi l'arche tendue autour du titre «Christ» à partir de 1,1 en passant par 8,29 jusqu'à 14,61 (et 15,32). Elle est aussi une étape dans l'autre arche créée par «Fils de Dieu» (1,1; 1,24; 3,11; 5,7; 14,61; 15,39). À cette question – à première vue inattendue à ce moment de l'intrigue, mais peut-être suite logique de ce qui précède[24] – Jésus répond en deux temps (14,62). En effet, «Je (le) suis» (ἐγώ εἰμι) est suivi par «et vous verrez *le Fils de l'homme* (Dn 7,13) *siégeant à la droite du Tout-Puissant* (Ps 110,1) et *venant avec les nuées du ciel* (Dn 7,13)» (καὶ ὄψεσθε τὸν υἱὸν τοῦ ἀνθρώπου ἐκ δεξιῶν καθήμενον τῆς δυνάμεως καὶ ἐρχόμενον μετὰ τῶν νεφελῶν τοῦ οὐρανοῦ). À la citation mixte de l'AT de la voix des cieux qui a appelé Jésus «fils» (1,9) correspond ainsi une citation mixte de l'AT prononcée par le fils Jésus (Dn 7,13 et Ps 110,1). Avant d'examiner le sens de la réponse de Jésus, qui nous aidera à interpréter la question, regardons de plus près la question elle-même.

Grammaticalement, la phrase σὺ εἶ ὁ χριστὸς ὁ υἱὸς τοῦ εὐλογητοῦ est une phrase affirmative dont la première partie (σὺ εἶ ὁ χριστός) correspond littéralement aux paroles de Pierre en 8,29. La longue introduction avec les deux verbes principaux (indicatif imparfait ἐπηρώτα αὐτόν et indicatif présent historique λέγει αὐτῷ)[25] joue sur l'ambiguïté de deux sens (interrogatif et affirmatif)[26]. Jésus n'avait jamais dit auparavant qu'il était le Christ et le sujet n'a pas été abordé dans les accusations qui précèdent (mais voir note 24). Pourquoi le grand-prêtre veut-il savoir si Jésus est le Christ? Avec Focant, on peut dire que le grand-prêtre interroge Jésus «sur son identité, ce que souligne l'usage emphatique du pronom personnel: ‹*Toi* (*su*), es-tu...?›»[27]. Dans le contexte d'accusation, la question n'est pas neutre ou simplement informative. Elle cherche à trouver une raison pour éliminer Jésus. Dans ce sens, on pourrait ajouter

---

24. MARCUS, *Mark* (n. 22), pp. 1005, 1015-1016, voit dans le πάλιν une indication que la deuxième question est une reprise plus forte encore de la première sur les accusations que Jésus aurait dit qu'il allait reconstruire le temple. Voir aussi FOCANT, *Marc* (n. 19), p. 552: en se basant sur des textes de Qumrân, il conclut que «puisque Jésus est accusé de vouloir bâtir un autre temple non fait de main d'homme et qu'il ne répond pas, il est logique que le grand-prêtre lui pose la question sous une autre forme».

25. La combinaison des deux verbes n'est pas exceptionnelle en Mc, mais dans les autres cas il s'agit d'un verbe principal suivi d'un participe de λέγω (8,27; 9,11; 12,18; 14,60; 15,4). Remarquons, en effet, que la première question (14,60) était introduite par les mêmes verbes.

26. La solution est bien formulée par C.C. BLACK, *Mark* (ANTC), Nashville, TN, Abingdon, 2011, p. 307: «In Greek this clause is formulated as a *declaration*; only the context (14:60) suggests that it is put as a question».

27. FOCANT, *Marc* (n. 19), p. 552.

qu'elle contient «a note of scorn and incredulity»[28]. En effet, pour Culpepper il y a probablement du sarcasme dans la question quand l'accent est mis sur le pronom personnel «*tu* es...»[29]: pour le grand-prêtre, il est impossible que le prisonnier livré devant lui soit le Christ Fils de Dieu! Il ne s'attendait donc probablement pas à une réponse positive de la part de Jésus. Quoiqu'il en soit, ce qui se manifeste de toute manière c'est un antagonisme entre deux points de vue sur les représentations du modèle du Christ. Dans la perspective des autorités, il n'y a pas d'espace pour un Messie qui souffre[30]. Cette opposition à un Messie souffrant implique, selon nous, au moins deux autres refus. Premièrement, celui qui refuse un Christ souffrant refuse aussi la conception et la manière de vivre qu'il a manifestées. La passion de Jésus ne peut pas être isolée de sa vie: c'est à cause de sa proclamation du Royaume de Dieu et de l'appel à la conversion pour devenir «l'esclave de tous» (10,44) qu'il doit être éliminé. Une fois encore, la formule σὺ εἶ suivie d'un titre concerne beaucoup plus que le titre en soi. Celui qui reconnaît que Jésus est le Christ s'engage à comprendre son message et à le suivre jusqu'au bout. Comme le dit correctement Malbon, parce que le titre «Christ» n'est jamais défini de manière nette et distincte, «it is the Markan narrative as a whole that must provide whatever clarity there is»[31]. Deuxièmement, le décalage entre les deux manières de comprendre le titre «Christ» implique aussi une représentation diamétralement opposée du personnage de Dieu. En effet, l'annonce de la proximité du Royaume de Dieu tel qu'il se manifeste dans la vie de Jésus représente un Dieu qui respecte chaque personne en tant qu'individu et qui diffère de la représentation du Dieu des autorités, liée à la lettre de la Loi, au pouvoir du temple, aux coutumes de pureté et au respect inconditionnel pour le sabbat plutôt que pour l'homme[32]. La question du grand-prêtre ne fonctionne pas comme

---

28. CULPEPPER, *Mark* (n. 15), p. 519.
29. Il n'y a pas de σύ, par exemple, en 14,70. BLACK, *Mark* (n. 26), p. 307: «This is a crucial, deeply ironic statement». GUNDRY, *Mark* (n. 10), p. 908, refuse une interprétation ironique à cause de la réponse de Jésus qui suit («Je le suis»). Mais est-ce que c'est vraiment un contre-argument? Jésus «corrige» sa réponse lui-même par une deuxième partie (comme nous allons voir).
30. MALBON, *Mark's Jesus* (n. 8), p. 115: «Although there was no unified expectation of a messiah (Christ) in first-century Judaism, suffering and death were not part of any of the various expectations. Mark's Gospel is dealing with this conflict in a most dramatic way in the direct speech of the high priest and the Markan Jesus».
31. *Ibid.*, p. 171.
32. Pour plus de détails sur la nouveauté de l'image de Dieu apportée par le récit de Marc, voir G. VAN OYEN, *Du secret messianique au mystère divin: Le sens de la narratologie*, dans ID. (éd.), *Reading the Gospel of Mark in the Twenty-First Century: Method and Meaning* (BETL, 301), Leuven – Paris – Bristol, CT, Peeters, 2019, 9-37.

un soutien au projet de Jésus. Au contraire, par elle il veut arrêter la réalisation de la venue du Royaume.

Différemment de 8,27-29, l'ordre «question de Jésus – réponse des disciples» est inversé en «question du grand-prêtre – réponse de Jésus». Une réponse de Jésus à une question (ou à une affirmation) sur sa messianité est assez exceptionnelle. Tandis qu'il a manifesté jusqu'ici le désir d'éviter d'être appelé Christ ou Fils de Dieu, en 14,62 il semble accepter les deux titres à la fois. Il est difficile de nier que Jésus donne ici une réponse positive «sobre» et qu'il «confirme sans réserve qu'il est bien le Messie, le Fils du Béni»[33]. En effet, dans tout le récit précédent, jamais quelqu'un n'a été aussi proche de prononcer qui Jésus est. Il a fallu attendre jusqu'à la passion, parce que Jésus n'a pas caché que la passion est la condition nécessaire pour que l'on comprenne qui il est et ce qu'il proclame. Mais dans cette réaction positive de la part de Jésus, il reste néanmoins une sorte de voile de mystère qui invite le lecteur au travail. Jésus répond par des citations vétérotestamentaires. Et pour bien pouvoir évaluer la réponse, il importe de lire les deux phrases de la réponse ensemble comme une unité qui s'ouvre à plusieurs sens[34]. Voici quelques éléments de réflexion.

D'abord, «Je le suis» (ἐγώ εἰμι; cf. 6,50) peut être une parole de Jésus lui-même mais aussi une citation intentionnelle de l'AT (Ex 3,14). Dans ce cas, une autre couche de sens se surimprime. Jésus n'affirme pas seulement, au moment où il est dans la crise de sa passion, qu'il est le Christ, mais il est soutenu par la voix divine qui a déjà parlé lors du baptême[35]. On retrouve donc le même mécanisme: Jésus ne s'oppose pas au titre, mais à l'usage du titre qui ne lui rend pas l'honneur pour les bonnes raisons. En acceptant le titre par l'utilisation de la citation, Jésus semble dire en même temps que l'honneur appartient à Dieu. Cela implique aussi que la réaction du grand-prêtre qui dit que Jésus blasphème est une réaction contre la représentation de Dieu par Jésus telle que Marc la présente.

Deuxièmement, l'ironie que nous avons déjà mentionnée pourrait être poussée plus loin encore. Au moins deux possibilités de lecture se présentent. Si la question du grand-prêtre est ironique («Toi? le fils de Dieu?

---

33. FOCANT, *Marc* (n. 19), p. 552.
34. MALBON, *Mark's Jesus* (n. 8), p. 171, parle de «layers of meaning» qui ne sont pas nécessairement des alternatives opposées.
35. MALBON, *ibid.*, p. 170, renvoie à Elizabeth Shively selon qui les paroles de Jésus pendant son interrogation sont inspirées par l'Esprit Saint (voir Mc 13,11); E. SHIVELY, *The Story Matters: Solving the Problem of the Parables in Mark 3:23-27*, dans E.S. MALBON (éd.), *Between Author and Audience in Mark: Narration, Characterization, Interpretation* (New Testament Monographs, 23), Sheffield, Sheffield Phoenix, 2009, 122-144, p. 138.

Impossible!») la réponse de Jésus peut être affirmative: «Je le suis vraiment, en effet, même si tu penses que ce n'est pas ainsi». Si la question du grand-prêtre est sincère et s'il veut vraiment objectivement savoir ce que Jésus va répondre en pensant qu'il est le Christ glorieux, la réponse de Jésus peut être ironique: «Je le suis, mais tu as tort». Dans la première lecture, Jésus dit: Je suis qui tu ne penses pas que je suis. Dans la deuxième lecture, il affirme: Je ne suis pas qui tu penses que je suis. Le lecteur est toujours invité à une réflexion qui va au-delà du titre.

Troisièmement, la deuxième partie de la réponse sur la venue du Fils de l'homme est un «correctif» (Focant), «immediately deflecting the focus elsewhere» (Malbon)[36]. Même si on admet que Jésus devant le grand-prêtre accepte les titres Christ et Fils de Dieu, il les réinterprète une dernière fois[37]. L'importance et l'originalité de cette quatrième occurrence de l'expression σὺ εἶ tiennent dans le fait qu'il s'agit d'un dialogue entre le grand-prêtre, représentant du pouvoir religieux, et Jésus, dans un contexte de jugement. Celui qui souffre et qui est jugé (Jésus) annonce le jugement du juge (grand-prêtre). L'expression «Fils de l'homme» synthétise ainsi l'aspect de souffrance (8,31; 9,31; 10,31) et l'aspect eschatologique (13,26.30). La caractérisation narrative de Jésus par le dialogue avec le grand-prêtre est une critique très forte envers le pouvoir religieux qui s'oppose à la venue du Royaume de Dieu et à ses conséquences. Le langage eschatologique dans la bouche de Jésus a un impact concret pour le présent. Il critique tous ceux qui pensent pouvoir juger et punir les autres tandis que le seul juge est Dieu (voir en particulier Mc 9,42-50)[38].

VI. Marc 15,2: l'interrogation par Pilate

Καὶ ἐπηρώτησεν αὐτὸν ὁ Πιλᾶτος· **σὺ εἶ ὁ βασιλεὺς τῶν Ἰουδαίων;** ὁ δὲ ἀποκριθεὶς αὐτῷ λέγει· σὺ λέγεις (Marc 15,2)

La dernière occurrence de σὺ εἶ introduit une question posée par un nouveau personnage dans le récit, Pilate: «Es-tu le roi des Juifs?». La question ouvre l'interrogatoire de Jésus (vv. 2-5). Apparemment, Pilate aime les questions car chaque fois qu'il parle en Mc il pose des questions (15,2.4.9.12.14). La question en 15,2 – de nouveau une phrase affirmative introduite par le verbe ἐπηρώτησεν – avec la réponse de Jésus (σὺ

---

36. Focant, *Marc* (n. 19), p. 552; Malbon, *Mark's Jesus* (n. 8), p. 171.
37. Voir l'analyse fine dans Malbon, *Mark's Jesus* (n. 8), pp. 208-210.
38. G. Van Oyen, *Réflexions sur la rétribution dans les évangiles synoptiques*, dans S. Ramon – R. Burnet – E. Pastore (éds), *Repenser la rétribution / Rethinking Retribution* (BETL), Leuven – Paris – Bristol, CT, Peeters, à paraître.

λέγεις) fait incliner le registre du niveau religieux au niveau politique, ce qui ne veut pas dire que religion et politique soient séparées. Au contraire, si Pilate a appris que Jésus est le Messie[39], il en tire les implications pour son rôle dans la société et la politique. Et on lit aussi que les grands-prêtres continuent à jouer leur rôle d'accusateur durant le procès devant Pilate (v. 3). Mais, comme c'était le cas avec le grand-prêtre, le dialogue (question de Pilate et réponse de Jésus) se prête à plusieurs interprétations par son contenu, par le profil de l'interrogateur et par la forme énigmatique de la réponse de Jésus.

Quand on compare le cas présent aux quatre σὺ εἶ précédents, on constate que le contenu est différent. Tandis que les autres titres reprenaient tous des mots utilisés par le narrateur ou par d'autres personnages, le titre ὁ βασιλεὺς τῶν Ἰουδαίων n'a pas encore été utilisé dans l'évangile (mais voir plus loin 15,9.12.18.26). L'interprétation de la question de Pilate dépend donc de l'interprétation globale de la royauté de Jésus dans Mc. Est-ce que le titre Roi des Juifs[40] s'applique correctement à Jésus? Ou est-ce que l'évangile se distancie de ce titre? Si on pense que Jésus est présenté comme un Christ-Roi – et qu'il y a une christologie «royale» dans l'évangile – on pourrait penser à une réponse de la part de Jésus qui affirme au moins partiellement ce que Pilate dit. Si tel n'est pas le cas, la réponse de Jésus devrait être interprétée de manière négative. Malbon représente la deuxième hypothèse. Elle pense que le titre Roi des Juifs ne correspond pas à ce que Jésus pense de lui-même ni à ce que le narrateur veut communiquer aux lecteurs[41]. La réponse de Jésus «C'est toi qui le dis» est donc «positive enough to seal his death but noncommittal enough to disvalue the discourse»[42]. Un grand nombre d'exégètes, bien connus par Malbon[43], pensent différemment et voient en Jésus le messie royal, le «bon» roi contre les «mauvais» rois (comme Pilate, Hérode et d'autres). Le texte n'est pas univoque, mais il y a sûrement une position différente de la part du narrateur par rapport au titre «Roi des Juifs» et les autres titres.

---

39. Plusieurs exégètes pensent sur la base de 15,1 qu'il a été informé par les membres du Sanhédrin. Voir 15,12.
40. Ici prononcé par un Romain. Cf. Roi d'Israel pour les juifs.
41. MALBON, *Mark's Jesus* (n. 8), p. 119: «Thus if ‹King of the Jews› is to be applied in a positive way to Jesus, it must be seen as in tension with what the Markan Jesus says (as are ‹Christ› and ‹Son of God› to some extent […]) as well as not confirmed by the narrator (as ‹Christ› and ‹Son of God› are) or by (God) – as ‹Son› is»; p. 120: «The leadership the Markan Jesus teaches and manifests does not fit into the type of the ‹king›, and the metaphor is not redeemed».
42. *Ibid.*, p. 172.
43. Voir les références en *Mark's Jesus* (n. 8), p. 119, n. 131.

Une dernière question est celle de savoir si la question de Pilate est ironique, voir sarcastique. Le «tu» emphatique, qui pourrait aller dans le même sens que la question du grand-prêtre, peut suggérer que Pilate se moque de Jésus. Van Iersel comprend la question de cette manière et la réponse de Jésus qui reprend le «tu» (σὺ λέγεις, au présent) est encore plus négative qu'une simple négation[44]. Comme Jésus remet la responsabilité de l'usage et de l'interprétation du titre «Roi des Juifs» à Pilate, le narrateur demande au lecteur lui-même de chercher la réponse à cette question comme à d'autres[45]. Et on voit très bien comment les commentateurs sur l'évangile oscillent entre une acceptation positive de la part de Jésus, une négation absolue, ou une réponse ambiguë[46]. Avec cette remarque, nous atteignons déjà à un élément de la conclusion de cette contribution.

VII. Conclusion

L'analyse des cinq références σὺ εἶ dans l'évangile selon Marc a montré que ces passages se prêtent bien pour illustrer comment la caractérisation de Jésus se construit au travers d'une prise de position de Jésus envers des personnages qui cherchent à lui donner des «titres». La réaction de Jésus (silence, ordre de se taire, refus, réaction ambivalente) sont des indices que pour Jésus le plus important n'est pas de le reconnaître par un titre. À l'exception de 1,11 (où «fils» n'est pas vraiment un titre), sa réaction met toujours en question la validité des intentions de l'usage des titres. Ceux qui recourent à un titre (démons, Pierre, grand-prêtre, Pilate) sont invités à réfléchir sur les raisons pour lesquelles ils le font. Si ce ne sont pas les titres qui sont au centre, comment pourrions-nous formuler de manière positive les réactions de Jésus? Premièrement, il me

---

44. B.M.F. van Iersel, *Mark: A Reader-Response Commentary* (JSNTSup, 164), Sheffield, Sheffield Academic Press, 1998, p. 459: «The question sounds rather sarcastic. If the reader were asked whether Jesus is, or considers himself, the king of the Jews, he or she would give a firm negative answer. This is borne out by Jesus' reply. He intimates that the terms in which the question is put are the questioner's and indirectly those of the ones who accuse him of kingly pretensions. With this Jesus has given an answer that sounds more negative than an outright denial». Beaucoup d'autres auteurs vont dans le même sens. Par exemple, Marcus, *Mark 8–16* (n. 22), p. 1033: «The portrayal of the bound Jesus prepares for the sarcastic tone of Pilate's initial question».

45. Van Iersel, *Marcus* (n. 44), p. 459: «Pilate's question concerns Jesus' identity and, as such, challenges the readers to seek an answer for themselves, as has been the case with similar questions earlier in the book (8.27; 14.61)».

46. Voir l'article de J. Schwiebert, *Jesus's Question to Pilate in Mark 15:2*, in *JBL* 136 (2017) 937-947, pour les différents points de vue.

semble qu'il demande aux interlocuteurs un changement d'attitude selon les normes de l'annonce du Royaume de Dieu. Cette attitude qui correspond au Royaume est vécue par Jésus lui-même. Il montre ce que signifie «se convertir et croire à l'évangile» (1,15). C'est donc plutôt par l'orthopraxie que par l'orthodoxie que l'on comprend l'identité de Jésus. Par ses actes, ses paroles et son destin, il révèle ce que veut dire être fils de Dieu. Seulement, si on ne suit pas son programme, on a tort de l'appeler et de l'identifier par un titre. L'identité de Jésus se crée par le dialogue. Deuxièmement, par sa critique contre un faux usage des titres – que ce soit intentionnel ou pas – Jésus (1,11) renvoie à Dieu, celui qui l'a reconnu comme fils plutôt qu'au fils lui-même. C'est ce que Malbon appelle une «christologie déflectrice» («deflective Christology»)[47]. Ainsi, en proclamant la bonne nouvelle de la venue du Royaume, il ne montre pas seulement, par sa vie, comment ce Royaume se construit, mais il se détache complètement de l'honneur qu'il pourrait recevoir. Cette prise de distance est un appel à ses interlocuteurs: celui qui entre dans le Royaume ne le fait pas pour sa propre gloire mais pour montrer au monde une image de Dieu au service de «ces petits qui croient» (9,42). Dans ses répliques aux phrases σὺ εἶ Jésus parle toujours de manière énigmatique. Son attitude ou sa réponse disent quelque chose mais créent aussi un vide; vide qui est sans doute plus important que ce qui est affirmé. Il demande une réponse de la part des interlocuteurs dans le récit et des lecteurs qui entendent ou lisent le texte. Chaque individu est mis devant sa responsabilité de répondre aux ouvertures créées par les réponses de Jésus: «σὺ εἶ …». C'est seulement en devenant un personnage du récit que le lecteur comprendra mieux l'enjeu de sa propre situation vis-à-vis de Jésus.

Nous avons commencé ce parcours par une réflexion sur l'identité narrative. J'aimerais terminer par un extrait du livre de Jean-Pierre Sonnet, *«Lorsque ton fils te demandera…»*[48], qui reprend le même thème mais qui, j'espère, après notre analyse des cinq versets σὺ εἶ se comprend dans toute sa profondeur. Dans la petite section sur l'identité narrative[49] il montre comment l'évangile de Marc par son intrigue autour de l'identité de Jésus s'ouvre à une réflexion du lecteur sur sa propre identité. Les deux quêtes – comprendre Jésus et se comprendre soi-même – sont inséparables.

---

47. «Déflectrice» en français veut dire «servant à modifier la direction d'un courant gazeux, liquide, électrique». Malbon veut dire que l'honneur donné à Jésus n'est pas seulement refusé par celui-ci, mais aussi redirigé vers Dieu.
48. J.-P. Sonnet, *«Lorsque ton fils te demandera…»: De génération en génération l'histoire biblique à raconter* (Le livre et le rouleau, 47), Namur – Paris, Lessius, 2014.
49. *Ibid.*, pp. 25-27; les citations qui suivent se trouvent aux pages 26-27.

Comme le sait le lecteur depuis le premier verset de l'évangile de Marc, Jésus est le Messie et fils de Dieu […], mais ce lecteur a besoin de tout le récit pour comprendre *comment* Jésus l'est – à la manière du fils de l'homme et du serviteur souffrant. Le récit biblique se méfie des reconnaissances prématurées […]. [L']accès à son identité n'est possible qu'à celui qui entre dans un cheminement à sa suite – cheminement qui, pour le lecteur, prendra la forme des tours et des détours de l'histoire racontée. […] Les deux titres initiaux – Christ et fils de Dieu – ont été ainsi revisités et reconfigurés de l'intérieur au long de l'intrigue, notamment dans son étape pascale.

Le *qui?* de Jésus dans son mystère personnel est ainsi révélé en même temps que protégé par le récit. Ce qui est vrai du Dieu du buisson ardent («je serai qui je serai»), ce qui est vrai du Christ de l'évangile, est également vrai de nous-mêmes. Entrer dans le dynamisme du récit biblique, dans l'articulation de l'intrigue et de ses personnages, c'est découvrir combien nous sommes nous-mêmes des êtres dont l'identité est narrative.

Erasme Ruelensvest 101   Geert VAN OYEN
BE-3001 Heverlee
Belgique
geert.vanoyen@uclouvain.be

THE BAPTISM OF JESUS BY JOHN THE BAPTIST

A BEDROCK HISTORICAL DATUM?

Mk 1,9 relates that Jesus "came from Nazareth of Galilee and was baptized by John in the Jordan"[1]. In recent studies on the historical Jesus it has become customary to state that Jesus' baptism by John is one of the certain, or even most certain events in Jesus' earthly ministry. John P. Meier concludes his discussion of the historicity of Jesus' baptism by stating that we may take this event "as the firm historical starting point for any treatment of Jesus' public ministry"[2]. James Dunn states: "This is one of the most securely grounded facts in all the history of Jesus"[3]. Jens Schröter says that the meeting between Jesus and John, including Jesus' baptism by John, is "the first historically ascertained event of Jesus' life"[4].

Many earlier New Testament scholars were no less convinced of the historical reliability of Mk 1,9. Dibelius and Bultmann considered the account of Jesus' baptism by John in Mk 1,9 an old, trustworthy tradition (not of course the legendary sequel with the opening of the heavens, the descending of the Spirit and the voice from heaven, vv. 10-11)[5]. Käsemann wrote: "The baptism of Jesus by John belongs to the indubitable events of the historical life of Jesus"[6].

Authors of monographs on John the Baptist also have a firm belief in the historicity of Jesus' baptism by John. Carl Kraeling remarked: "Here

---

1. I assume here without discussion the Two Document Hypothesis, Markan priority, the dependence of John on Mark, Luke and Matthew, and the mutual independence of Mark and Q. I am aware that these theories are debated.

2. J.P. MEIER, *A Marginal Jew: Rethinking the Historical Jesus*. Vol. 2: *Mentor, Message, and Miracles*, New York, Doubleday, 1994, p. 105.

3. J.D.G. DUNN, *Jesus Remembered* (Christianity in the Making, 1), Grand Rapids, MI – Cambridge, Eerdmans, 2003, p. 350.

4. J. SCHRÖTER, *Jesus von Nazaret* (Biblische Gestalten, 15), Leipzig, Evangelische Verlagsanstalt, ⁶2017, p. 151.

5. M. DIBELIUS, *Die urchristliche Überlieferung von Johannes dem Täufer* (FRLANT, 15), Göttingen, Vandenhoeck & Ruprecht, 1911, pp. 63-66. R. BULTMANN, *Jesus* (Die Unsterblichen, 1), Berlin, Deutsche Bibliothek, 1926, p. 26; ID., *Die Geschichte der synoptischen Tradition*, Göttingen, Vandenhoeck & Ruprecht, ⁴1958, p. 263; ID., *Theologie des Neuen Testaments*, Tübingen, Mohr (Siebeck), ⁵1965, pp. 28, 41.

6. E. KÄSEMANN, *Zum Thema der urchristlichen Apokalyptik*, in *ZTK* 59 (1962) 257-284, p. 260. J. SCHNIEWIND, *Das Evangelium nach Markus* (NTD, 1), Göttingen, Vandenhoeck & Ruprecht, ⁸1958, p. 11: "Dass Jesus von Johannes getauft wurde, ist sicherste Überlieferung".

we are on the most solid historical ground"[7]. According to Charles Scobie, Jesus' baptism by John is one "of the best attested facts of the New Testament"; it is an "undeniable fact"[8]. Jürgen Becker notices that it can be said "with historical certainty" that John baptized Jesus[9]. Josef Ernst calls what Mk 1,9 says about Jesus' baptism by John "credible historical information"[10]. At present, the greatest authority on the historical figure of John the Baptist is the Munich New Testament scholar Knut Backhaus. In two recent studies on John, persuasive on many points, he comes to speak about the historicity of Jesus' baptism by John. In one of these Backhaus says: "The tradition that Jesus has been baptized by John is most reliable"[11]. In the other he writes that Jesus' baptism "can be considered a certainty"[12].

Scholars who have doubted or dismissed the historicity of Jesus' baptism by John are rather rare. One of them was the Berlin historian Eduard Meyer[13]. In his view, the episode of Jesus' baptism (Mk 1,9-11) is so closely connected with the "mythical" story of his temptation (1,12-13) that the baptism cannot be considered to belong to the historical element of the gospel. Ernst Haenchen rejected the historical authenticity of the episode of Jesus' baptism by John, mainly on account of the discrepancy between John's image of God – severe, demanding and wrathful – and that of Jesus, for whom God was hard but merciful. In view of this and other theological differences, Jesus can neither have been a disciple of John, nor have been baptized by him[14]. Morton Enslin went so far as to argue that the paths of Jesus and John never crossed. The reason why John

---

7. C.H. KRAELING, *John the Baptist*, New York – London, Scribner, 1951, p. 131.
8. C.H.H. SCOBIE, *John the Baptist*, Philadelphia, PA, Fortress, 1964, pp. 142-143. W. WINK, *John the Baptist in the Gospel Tradition* (SNTS MS, 7), Cambridge, CUP, 1968, takes the historicity of Jesus' baptism by John for granted; see, e.g., p. 107.
9. J. BECKER, *Johannes der Täufer und Jesus von Nazareth* (Biblische Studien, 63), Neukirchen-Vluyn, Neukirchener Verlag, 1972, p. 15.
10. J. ERNST, *Johannes der Täufer* (BZNW, 53), Berlin, De Gruyter, 1989, p. 17. A. VÖGTLE, *Offenbarungsgeschehen und Wirkungsgeschichte*, Freiburg i.Br. – Basel – Wien, Herder, 1985, p. 83: "ein historisch unanfechtbares Faktum".
11. K. BACKHAUS, *Echoes from the Wilderness: The Historical John the Baptist*, in T. HOLMÉN – S.E. PORTER (eds.), *Handbook for the Study of the Historical Jesus*. Vol. 2: *The Study of Jesus*, Leiden, Brill, 2011, 1747-1785, p. 1782.
12. K. BACKHAUS, *Jesus und Johannes der Täufer*, in J. SCHRÖTER – C. JACOBI (eds.), *Jesus Handbuch*, Tübingen, Mohr Siebeck, 2017, 245-252, p. 250: "Als sicher kann gelten, dass Jesus sich ... von Johannes im Jordan taufen ließ (Mk 1,9-11)".
13. E. MEYER, *Ursprung und Anfänge des Christentums*. Bd. 2: *Die Entwicklung des Judentums und Jesus von Nazareth*, Stuttgart – Berlin, Cotta, 1921, p. 406.
14. E. HAENCHEN, *Der Weg Jesu*, Berlin, Töpelmann, 1966, pp. 51-63. Haenchen's thesis is that the story of Jesus' baptism originated as a retrojection of the early Christian baptism into Jesus' life.

was incorporated in the life of Jesus was twofold: (1) the rivalry between the disciples of Jesus and John after both had died, and (2) the need to answer the criticism of those who said that Jesus could not be God's final envoy since Elijah had not come, as Mal 4,5 (and 3,1) had foretold[15]. Thus, John obtained the role of Elijah.

However, a majority of New Testament interpreters would still agree with Lars Hartman's judgement: "That Jesus was baptized by John is historically certain"[16]. But is it really? That is what the present essay intends to re-examine.

I. The Redactional Character of Mk 1,9-11

Let us begin by asking if Mk 1,9-11 preserves traces of older tradition. Καὶ ἐγένετο in v. 9 clearly is Mark's editorial opening of the new pericope. In itself καὶ ἐγένετο with finite verb is a current idiom (cf. 4,4), but in 1,9 its specific literary function is to link the episode of Jesus' baptism to the account of John's activity in the wilderness (vv. 4-8). Ἐν ἐκείναις ταῖς ἡμέραις reoccurs in 13,17 and 13,24, and the singular ἐν ἐκείνῃ τῇ ἡμέρᾳ in 4,35. It may be considered part of Mark's narrative style. The words ἦλθεν Ἰησοῦς ... καὶ ἐβαπτίσθη εἰς τὸν Ἰορδάνην ὑπὸ Ἰωάννου resume and specify v. 5; the result is a typical instance of "duality in Mark"[17]. Finally, Mark as narrator inserted ἀπὸ Ναζαρὲτ τῆς Γαλιλαίας to give his readers at least a minimum of biographical information about Jesus, whom he introduces here for the first time[18]. Apart from the fact that the proper names Jesus, Nazareth and Galilee derive from tradition current in the Jesus movement, the text of Mk 1,9 looks very redactional and gives no cause to suppose that it is based on older tradition.

---

15. M.S. Enslin, *John and Jesus*, in *ZNW* 66 (1975) 1-18. In the same vein as Enslin: F. Katz, *Hat Johannes der Täufer Jesus getauft?*, in P. Müller – C. Gerber – T. Knöppler (eds.), *"… was ihr auf dem Weg verhandelt habt"*, Neukirchen-Vluyn, Neukirchener Verlag, 2001, 27-36.

16. L. Hartman, *Baptism*, in D.N. Freedman (ed.), *ABD*, vol. 1, New York, Doubleday, 1992, 583-594, p. 584. Cf. J. Gnilka, *Das Evangelium nach Markus*, 1. Teilband: *Mk 1–8,26* (EKKNT, 2/1), Zürich, Benziger Verlag; Neukirchen-Vluyn, Neukirchener Verlag, 1978, p. 51: "Die Taufe Jesu gehört nach der überwiegenden Meinung der Forschung zu den historisch gesichertsten Daten des Lebens Jesu"; J. Marcus, *Jesus' Baptismal Vision*, in *NTS* 41 (1995) 512-521, p. 512: "The fact of the baptism itself, therefore, is a bedrock historical datum"; D.-A. Koch, *Geschichte des Urchristentums*, Göttingen, Vandenhoeck & Ruprecht, 2013, p. 143: "… die historisch sichere Taufe Jesu durch den Täufer".

17. F. Neirynck, *Duality in Mark* (BETL, 31), Leuven, Peeters, ²1988, pp. 96, 139.

18. Gnilka, *Markus* (n. 16), who takes vv. 9-11 as on the whole traditional, but regards τῆς Γαλιλαίας in particular as a redactional insertion by Mark.

It is true that it is difficult to tell what may be hidden behind a narrator's editorial text, but in any case Mk 1,9 does not invite us to assume such underlying tradition.

The same applies to vv. 10-11. Καὶ εὐθύς is generally considered a characteristic of Mark's style[19]. Ἀναβαίνων ἐκ (v. 10) and καταβαῖνον εἰς (v. 10) form a specific type of Markan duality: the repeated use of cognate verbs in the same context[20]. Τοῦ ὕδατος (v. 10) duplicates ὕδατι (v. 8). As for εἶδεν, the fact that only Jesus sees the heavens ripped apart coheres with Mark's messianic secret motif and thus reflects Markan theology and redaction[21]. Mark is probably also responsible for the use of the violent verb σχίζεσθαι (v. 10), which Matthew and Luke replace by the more common and less vehement ἀνοίγεσθαι. Σχίζεσθαι reappears in Mk 15,38 τὸ καταπέτασμα τοῦ ναοῦ ἐσχίσθη. Mark's use of the verb in 1,10 and 15,38 is sometimes seen as intentional and redactional[22]. The words τοὺς οὐρανούς (v. 10) and τῶν οὐρανῶν (v. 11) show again a form of duplication which Mark liked so much[23]. Similarly, τὸ πνεῦμα (v. 10) duplicates πνεύματι ἁγίῳ (v. 8). The use of εἰς pro ἐπί (v. 10) may not be typical of Mark, but is well attested in his gospel: 13,3 καθημένου ... εἰς τὸ ὄρος; 13,16 ὁ εἰς τὸν ἀγρόν. The agreements between v. 11 καὶ φωνὴ ἐγένετο ἐκ τῶν οὐρανῶν· σὺ εἶ ὁ υἱός μου ὁ ἀγαπητός and 9,7 καὶ ἐγένετο φωνὴ ἐκ τῆς νεφέλης· οὗτός ἐστιν ὁ υἱός μου ὁ ἀγαπητός cannot be coincidental. The most obvious explanation is that they are due to Mark as narrator and redactor, the more so since the term Son of God applied to Jesus is of paramount importance for Mark as the expression most adequately describing who Jesus is[24]. In at least 1,1; 3,11 and 15,39 the term "Son of God" is certainly redactional[25]. Mark makes God speak here in language borrowed from Ps 2,7 LXX, Υἱός μου εἶ σύ, but changes the word order from subject complement – copula – subject to subject – copula – subject complement, and adds the article ὁ

---

19. F. Neirynck, *The Redactional Text of Mark*, in Id. (ed.), *Evangelica* (BETL, 60), Leuven, LUP – Peeters, 1991, 618-636, p. 621.

20. Neirynck, *Duality* (n. 17), p. 77.

21. H. Greeven, περιστερά, in *TWNT*, 6, Stuttgart, Kohlhammer, 1965, 63-72, p. 67, n. 57; J. Marcus, *Mark 1–8: A New Translation with Introduction and Commentary* (AB, 27), Garden City, NY, Doubleday, 2000, p. 164.

22. S. O'Connell, *Beyond Power – Jesus and the Spirit in Mark*, in G. Van Oyen (ed.), *Reading the Gospel of Mark in the Twenty-First Century: Method and Meaning* (BETL, 301), Leuven – Paris – Bristol, CT, Peeters, 2019, 679-690, p. 681.

23. Neirynck, *Duality* (n. 17), p. 139.

24. C.M. Tuckett, *Christology and the New Testament*, Edinburgh, Edinburgh University Press, 2011, p. 114.

25. Gnilka, *Markus* (n. 16), p. 60.

before υἱός. The same word order and the article occur in 9,7 (see above). The words ἐν σοὶ εὐδόκησα rather seem to echo Is 42,1[26].

The absolute use of τὸ πνεῦμα (v. 10) and the christological use of Ps 2,7 are no doubt pre-Markan tradition[27]. But in vv. 9-11, there is no indication that the baptismal story as such derives from tradition. With this story, Mark intends to reveal to his readers, right at the beginning of his book, what he considers the true identity of Jesus: Jesus is the Son of God, bearer of God's Spirit, the source of his unique authority, which God himself has bestowed on him[28].

II. Arguments Used in Support of the Story's Historicity

The ground most frequently adduced to defend the historicity of Mark's account of Jesus' baptism, is the argument of embarrassment: followers of Jesus would never have devised a story which depicts Jesus as dependent on, and subordinate to, John and as accepting a "baptism for the forgiveness of sins" (vv. 4-5) as if he was a sinner[29].

It is true that the later evangelists try to soften or to eliminate features in the story of the baptism which might seem to give an undesirable image of Jesus[30]. In the Gospel of John, the whole event is even suppressed. However, as Morna Hooker has observed, Mark is apparently unembarrassed by the problems raised by this story which troubled later writers[31]. In Mark's story, there is still nothing to be found of any embarrassment[32]. One reason for this is that for Mark Jesus' baptism in

---

26. A. Yarbro Collins, *Mark: A Commentary* (Hermeneia), Minneapolis, MN, Fortress, 2007, p. 150.

27. For Ps 2,7, see Heb 1,5; 5,5 and Acts 13,33, but interpreted there as referring to Jesus' resurrection and exaltation, not to his appearance in the world.

28. M. de Jonge, *Christology in Context*, Philadelphia, PA, Westminster, 1988, p. 56.

29. See, e.g., Meier, *Marginal Jew* (n. 2), pp. 101-103; Schröter, *Jesus* (n. 4), pp. 149-150.

30. M. Goodacre, *The Synoptic Problem: John the Baptist and Jesus*, in A.B. McGowan – K.H. Richards (eds.), *Method and Meaning: Essays on New Testament Interpretation in Honor of H.W. Attridge* (RBS, 67), Atlanta, GA, Society of Biblical Literature, 2011, 177-192, pp. 181-183.

31. M.D. Hooker, *The Gospel according to St Mark* (BNTC), London, Black, 1991, p. 44. Similarly, V. Taylor, *The Gospel according to St Mark*, London, MacMillan, ²1966, p. 159: "The Markan narrative antedates these difficulties, which are not even felt by the Evangelist. ... The difficulty has not occurred to him. ... No sense of embarrassment is present in the Markan account".

32. K. Backhaus, *Die "Jüngerkreise" des Täufers Johannes*, Paderborn, Schöningh, 1991, p. 47. Backhaus does assume that Mk 1,9 is based on tradition.

itself was not that important[33]. He mentions it only in passing in a passage which primarily intends to inform the readers who Jesus really was: the one on whom the Spirit had descended and whom God himself had acclaimed as his Son. Mark wanted to make it clear right at the beginning of his book that Jesus was indisputably the Son of God because God had declared him to be so. Mark was so focused on this identification of Jesus as the Son of God that he seems to have remained unaware of any trouble the baptismal scene might provoke. In other words, if one assumes that Mk 1,9-11 gives an embarrassing picture of Jesus, one judges Mark by standards of later christologies. Such a judgement is anachronistic.

Furthermore, once Mark had decided to present John in his book as Jesus' forerunner (as tradition had already done before him, witness Q), it was a quite natural step for him to let John and Jesus meet by the beginning of Jesus' public career and – since John was known as baptizer – to have John baptize Jesus. Mark seems to narrate this episode entirely naively without being conscious of any possible objections his story could evoke against the christologically low image of Jesus it presents. But neither did Mark need to fear such objections since he had already made John say that Jesus would be more powerful and a much greater authority than he, John, was (vv. 7-8).

In sum, the argument of embarrassment is not really applicable in this case.

Another argument often used to support the historicity of Jesus' baptism is the argument from multiple attestation[34]. According to this line of reasoning, a version of the account of Jesus' baptism would have been part of Q: Q 3,21-22. This version is reconstructed from the minor agreements of Mt 3,16-17 and Lk 3,21b-22 against Mk 1,9-11. The agreements include the absence of ἐν ἐκείναις ταῖς ἡμέραις (Mk 1,9); the use of the passive participle βαπτισθε- instead of the finite verb ἐβαπτίσθη in Mk 1,9; the verb ἀνοίγεσθαι instead of σχίζεσθαι in Mk 1,10; and ἐπ'αὐτόν instead of εἰς αὐτόν in Mk 1,10. The details can be found in several editions of Q[35].

---

33. HAENCHEN, *Weg Jesu* (n. 14), pp. 51-52.
34. MEIER, *Marginal Jew* (n. 2), pp. 103-105.
35. E.g., J.M. ROBINSON – P. HOFFMANN – J.S. KLOPPENBORG (eds.), *The Critical Edition of Q*, Minneapolis, MN, Fortress; Leuven, Peeters, 2000, pp. 18-21. Q 3,21-22 is included here with a D rating, that is, with a very high degree of doubt. A footnote mentions that one of the editors, Kloppenborg, does not regard the passage as part of Q. Cf. P. HOFFMANN – C. HEIL (eds.), *Die Spruchquelle Q*, Darmstadt, Wissenschaftliche Buchgesellschaft; Leuven, Peeters, 2002, pp. 34-35; a note on p. 118 reports how scholars involved in the study of Q assessed the (un)certainty of the presence of the passage in Q.

However, several scholars have argued that the baptismal story should be excluded from Q since the agreements of Matthew and Luke against Mk 1,9-11 can easily and satisfactorily be explained as the result of Matthaean and Lukan redaction of Mark in accordance with their editorial habits[36]. Since this argumentation is based on more verifiable evidence than the theory which keeps open the possibility that Q contained the baptismal story, it seems to be preferable not to regard this story as part of Q.

Yet, in favour of a Q 3,21-22 pericope, James Robinson, followed by Meier, has suggested that Q requires a story, preceding that of the temptations, in which Jesus is acclaimed as Son of God because otherwise the devil's address in Q 4,1-13, "if you are God's Son", would be meaningless[37]. But this argument is not persuasive: the story of the temptation is quite comprehensible without a preceding acclamation of Jesus as God's Son, for the term Son of God was certainly current also outside the process of the synoptic tradition. Moreover, as Christopher Tuckett has pointed out, in Q 4,3 and 4,9 "Son of God" is perhaps not even a christological term, for it lacks the article before υἱός and may simply mean "a son of God"[38]. On the other hand, it is not abnormal for a subject complement to lack the article. Be this as it may, Q does not require the account of Jesus' baptism.

The argument of multiple attestation has also been used by appeal to some passages in Jn 1,29-34[39]. But John cannot be regarded anymore as independent of Mark[40]. He was likely familiar with both Mark and

---

36. See, e.g., J. KLOPPENBORG, *The Formation of Q*, Philadelphia, PA, Fortress, 1987, pp. 84-85; F. NEIRYNCK, *The Minor Agreements and Q*, in R.A. PIPER (ed.), *The Gospel behind the Gospels* (SupplNT, 75), Leiden, Brill, 1995, 49-72, pp. 65-67; reprinted in F. NEIRYNCK, *Evangelica III* (BETL, 150), Leuven, LUP – Peeters, 2001, 245-266, pp. 260-261; J.S. KLOPPENBORG, *Excavating Q*, Edinburgh, T&T Clark, 2000, p. 93; F. NEIRYNCK, *The Reconstruction of Q*, in A. LINDEMANN (ed.), *The Sayings Source Q and the Historical Jesus* (BETL, 158), Leuven, LUP – Peeters, 2001, 53-93, pp. 78-82.

37. J.M. ROBINSON, *The Sayings Source Q*, in F. VAN SEGBROECK – C.M. TUCKETT – G. VAN BELLE – J. VERHEYDEN (eds.), *The Four Gospels 1992* (BETL, 100), Leuven, LUP – Peeters, 1992, vol. 1, 361-388, p. 384; MEIER, *Marginal Jew* (n. 2), p. 103. This view has been contested by NEIRYNCK, *The Minor Agreements and Q*, 2001 (n. 36), p. 260; and KLOPPENBORG, *Excavating Q* (n. 36), p. 93.

38. C.M. TUCKETT, *The Temptation Narrative in Q*, in VAN SEGBROECK et al. (eds.), *The Four Gospels 1992* (n. 37), vol. 1, 479-507, pp. 495-496.

39. MEIER, *Marginal Jew* (n. 2), pp. 103-104; BACKHAUS, *Jüngerkreise* (n. 32), p. 47.

40. R. KIEFFER, *Jean et Marc*, in A. DENAUX (ed.), *John and the Synoptics* (BETL, 101), Leuven, LUP – Peeters, 1992, 109-125; F. NEIRYNCK, *John and the Synoptics 1975-1990*, ibid., 3-62; D.-A. KOCH, *Der Täufer als Zeuge des Offenbarers*, in VAN SEGBROECK et al. (eds.), *The Four Gospels 1992* (n. 37), vol. 3, 1963-1984; G. VAN BELLE, *The Two Johannine Colophons and John's Rereading of Mark 1,7-8*, in VAN OYEN (ed.), *Reading* (n. 22), 781-798.

Luke[41], probably also with Matthew. Jn 1,34 seems to reflect Mark's editorial use of Ps 2,7 in the context of the baptismal scene (Mk 1,11), not as adumbrating Jesus' exaltation as in Heb 1,5; 5,5, nor as prediction of his resuscitation by God as in Acts 13,33. John also follows Mark's redactional word order subject – copula – subject complement, and Mark's addition of the article ὁ before υἱός: οὗτός ἐστιν ὁ υἱὸς τοῦ θεοῦ (Jn 1,34). Consequently, it is not safe to treat John as an independent witness to the baptism episode.

Neither can 1 Jn 5,6, "he has come through water and blood", be used as independent testimony to the account of Jesus' baptism, as Meier suggests[42]. Meier is probably right in taking "water" here as a reference to Jesus' baptism, but when 1 John originated, the idea that Jesus had been baptized was probably already widespread, thanks to the gospels and preaching about him.

All in all, the historicity of Mark's story of Jesus' baptism is supported neither by the argument of embarrassment nor by that of multiple attestation.

III. THE CHRISTOLOGICAL ROLE OF JOHN THE BAPTIST IN MK 9,11-13 AND 1,1-11

An important impediment to the recognition of the historicity of Mark's account of Jesus' baptism by John is a passage in Mark's gospel itself: 9,11-13. The interpretation of this passage is beset with difficulties, but so much is clear that it reflects an attempt to answer Jewish objections that Jesus could not be the definitive inaugurator of God's reign because Elijah had not yet returned[43]. It remains unclear whether such objections were really raised by Jewish opponents of the Jesus movement, or were just part of the preventive apologetics produced within the circle of followers of Jesus to justify their recognition of Jesus as God's final envoy. This question does not need to be answered here[44]. But whatever the answer may be, in Mk 9,12-13 the evangelist assures his readers that it cannot be objected against the acceptance of Jesus as God's definitive eschatological agent that Elijah has not yet appeared, since "Elijah *has* come", no doubt in the person of John the Baptist.

---

41. C.K. BARRETT, *The Gospel according to St John*, London, SPCK, ²1978, p. 15.
42. MEIER, *Marginal Jew* (n. 2), pp. 104-105.
43. HOOKER, *Mark* (n. 31), p. 221.
44. JUSTIN, *Dialogue with Trypho* 49, cannot settle the question.

The important part of Mk 9,11-13 is that it shows that the evangelist uses the prophecy of Mal 4,5 (3,22-23 LXX) to underpin his claim that Jesus was the definitive eschatological agent of God. The purport of Mk 9,11-13 is clearly christological. John the Baptist is enrolled in Jesus' biography to bring out the latter's unique function as God's final envoy. True, in this pericope, Mark does not call Jesus the Christ or the Son of God, but the Son of man (v. 12). This is properly the title used to designate the one who will descend from heaven to act as judge or saviour at the final judgement (13,26; 14,62). But Mark often allows his Christ and his Son of God, that is Jesus, to designate himself as the "Son of man", especially in passages about his suffering, death and resurrection, as in 8,31; 9,31; 10,32-34 and here in 9,12. In other instances the term "Son of man" just stresses Jesus' special authority[45].

If the conclusion is correct that the intention behind Mk 9,11-13 is christological, the question presents itself unavoidably whether Mark's use of Mal 3,1 in Mk 1,2 and his introduction of John the Baptist in 1,4-7 are not equally inspired by christological motives. It is not difficult to see that this question has to be answered affirmatively. The christological purpose becomes clear in 1,11, where the evangelist makes God declare Jesus his Son. Since it is God who says this, the designation of Jesus as God's Son is unquestionably true and certain. Yet Mark takes the trouble of preparing God's proclamation of Jesus as his Son by explaining that Jesus had come in the way Mal 3,1 had foresaid the Lord would appear, namely preceded by a messenger preparing the way before him. Mark thus clearly uses Malachi's messenger (in his view John the Baptist) to make sure that Jesus is the messianic figure, "the Son of God", indicated and acclaimed by God.

The advantage of Mal 3,1 over Mal 4,5 for Mark is that it describes the "messenger" announced by the prophet more clearly as a "forerunner" than Mal 4,5 does. It helps Mark to present the tandem John the Baptist – Jesus as prophesied long ago and foreseen in God's plan for Israel.

It should be noticed here that Mark was not the first to use (a) the combination John the Baptist – Jesus (with the one preparing the way for the other) and (b) Mal 3,1 as prophetic announcement of the appearance of the two and their mutual relationship. Mark took both elements over from tradition about Jesus, witness Q 7,27 which says: "He [John the Baptist] is the one about whom it is written: 'See, I am sending my messenger ahead of you, who will prepare your way before you' [Mal 3,1]".

---

45. DE JONGE, *Christology* (n. 28), p. 59.

But the main thing to realize at this point is that everything Mark tells his readers from 1,1 to 1,11 serves his intention to establish beyond doubt that Jesus is the Son of God. It is in the interest of this theological and christological purpose that Mark appeals to Malachi's prophecy about the forerunner and the one coming after him, and to Isaiah's prophecy about the voice in the desert[46]. In the interest of the same goal Mark uses the combination of the figures of John the Baptist and Jesus, a construct he knew from tradition transmitted by followers of Jesus, witness Q 7,27 and perhaps 7,33-34. In the same interest he tells in a few words how Jesus met John and was baptized by him, a story concluded by the divine voice acclaiming Jesus as the Son of God. The baptism is thus mentioned to enable the divine voice to acclaim Jesus as the Son of God. The story of the baptism has a christological function, just as the whole of 1,1-11. What can we say then about the origin of this story?

IV. MARK'S MOTIVES FOR MENTIONING JESUS' BAPTISM

In his opening section 1,1-11, Mark intends to identify Jesus immediately as the Son of God. He attains this goal by reporting what the voice from heaven said. This voice concludes the scene of Jesus' baptism. Narratologically, the baptism itself (1,9) is only a corollary of the account of God's revelatory interventions: the descent of the Spirit and the divine voice. In itself the baptism is of relatively little importance here; it is told in surprisingly few words: ἦλθεν Ἰησοῦς ἀπὸ Ναζαρὲτ τῆς Γαλιλαίας καὶ ἐβαπτίσθη εἰς τὸν Ἰορδάνην ὑπὸ Ἰωάννου. Obviously, the baptism is just mentioned here to provide a locale for the appearance of the Spirit and the sounding of the heavenly voice.

Why did Mark mention the baptism at all? Could he not have had God speak to Jesus without mentioning the baptism? He certainly could, but he had a good reason to tell his story the way he did. For in this way he could bring the two persons whom Malachi and Isaiah had announced, the forerunner and the one for whom he prepared the way, together in *one* scene[47]. Mark's baptismal episode thus can be viewed as an actualization or materialization of the prophecies quoted in 1,2-3. Strictly speaking, Mark could have made John and Jesus meet personally without an account of

---

46. On the quotations in 1,2-3, see S. MOYSE, *Composite Citations in the Gospel of Mark*, in S.A. ADAMS – S.M. EHORN (eds.), *Composite Citations in Antiquity*. Vol. 2: *New Testament Uses* (LNTS, 593), London, Bloomsbury, 2018, 16-33.

47. In the canonical gospel tradition, Jesus' baptism is the only scene in which Jesus and John the Baptist meet.

the baptism. But once Mark had conceived the idea of bringing John and Jesus together in one scene, it was an obvious step to let the Baptist do what he was famous for, baptizing, and to let him baptize Jesus.

Using Old Testament passages to produce or to give shape to stories about Jesus, is a practice which shows up repeatedly in the Gospel of Mark. Notorious cases in point are Jesus' riding on a colt at the entry in Jerusalem (Mk 11,2.7-10), inspired by Zech 9,9; the flight of the disciples (Mk 14,50), adumbrated in Zech 13,7 (see Mk 14,27) and the division of Jesus' clothes by casting lots (Mk 15,24) in accordance with Ps 22,19. Much in Mark's gospel is told ἵνα πληρωθῶσιν αἱ γραφαί (Mk 14,49). Similarly, the baptismal scene in Mk 1,9 can be seen as an implementation of the prophecies on the forerunner preparing the way of the Lord quoted in Mk 1,2-3.

V. THE HISTORICITY OF THE STORY OF JESUS' BAPTISM. CONCLUSION

If this is approximately how Mark came to compose the story about Jesus' baptism, what about its historical authenticity?

One should realize that there is no evidence for Jesus' baptism either in Q, or in Paul, or in Josephus[48]. Mk 1,9 is the only independent source at our disposal. One should also bear in mind that Mark's mention of the baptism was just a corollary of his attempt to bring John and Jesus together in one scene and to make God's voice sound in the context of that encounter. What mattered most to Mark was that, somewhere near the beginning of his gospel, God would declare Jesus his Son, "Son of God" being a key christological term for Mark. Finally, one should take into account that Mk 1,9-11 is strongly redactional: the story as *story* shows no traces of being grounded in tradition. It is likely to be a composition by the evangelist, due to his literary creativity and christological ideas.

How "certain" is such a story, historically speaking? The least one can say is that Jesus' baptism cannot be called "historically certain" or

---

48. Josephus deals with Jesus and John, in this order, in separate sections of *Ant.* 18.63-64 and 116-119. J. TROMP, *John the Baptist according to Flavius Josephus, and His Incorporation in the Christian Tradition*, in A. HOUTMAN – A. DE JONG – M. MISSET-VAN DE WEG (eds.), *Empsychoi Logoi – Religious Innovations in Antiquity* (AJEC, 73), Leiden, Brill, 2008, 135-149, argues that Jesus and John probably never met since according to Josephus John's public activity would have been posterior to that of Jesus. In my view, however, Josephus' account does not exclude the possibility that John's and Jesus' ministries overlapped during some time. Nor is Josephus' discussion of Jesus and John necessarily incompatible with the order in which John and Jesus appear in the gospels. But it is true that in Josephus there is no connection whatsoever between Jesus and John.

a "bedrock historical datum" or "one of the most certain facts of Jesus' life". As we have seen, there are good reasons to doubt the historicity of the story: its redactional character, its typically Markan-theological, christological objective, and the lack of any other attestation. The historicity is not supported by the argument of embarrassment, nor does the silence of Q, Paul and Josephus on the event inspire confidence in the plausibility of the story.

On the other hand, theoretically, the possibility cannot be ruled out that Jesus and John did meet and John did baptize Jesus. It is possible. But Mark's note on Jesus' baptism in 1,9 does not raise the possibility to the level of probability, let alone certainty. One cannot go further than concluding: *non liquet*. This may be a disappointing result, but it is better to have less history than more that is not ascertained and possibly illusory.

Henk Jan DE JONGE †

MESSIAH AND SON OF MAN IN MARK 8,27-33

The focus of this study is the question how the substitution of the label "Son of Man" in Mk 8,31 for the label "Messiah" in 8,29 can best be explained. The essay takes as a premise that the written texts of Second Temple Jewish writers and texts from early writers of the Christ-movement are not cut off from the oral tradition of the people. Such writers draw upon oral traditions and transform them in creative ways. Their works are then (re)oralized by being read to gatherings of people and being used by those who teach or proclaim to them. Another premise of the study is that "title" and "label" are interchangeable terms that are appropriate for the epithets "Messiah", "Son of Man", "Son of God", and "Son of David"[1]. The essay begins with a selective summary of research on certain key issues related to its focal question. It then continues with further discussion leading to a proposed answer to that question.

I. Peter's Confession as a Turning Point in the Narrative of Mark

The passage Mk 8,27–10,45 is the middle section of Mark, in which Jesus teaches the disciples that the Son of Man must suffer and that discipleship involves faithful suffering[2]. Julius Wellhausen already argued that the confession of Peter was intended to be a turning point in the gospel. This is shown by the change of mood that it brings about and especially by the following account of the transfiguration; for the latter is an underlining and a heavenly authentication of the confession of Peter[3]. Although Wellhausen does not say so explicitly in this context, his view of the transfiguration is based on the understanding that "Son

---

1. The term "title" is used here for a social role, not an office. See the discussion in M.V. Novenson, *Names, Titles, and Other Possibilities*, in Id., *Christ among the Messiahs: Christ Language in Paul and Messiah Language in Ancient Judaism*, New York, OUP, 2012, pp. 64-97. He defines χριστός in Paul's letters as honorific (*ibid.*, pp. 87-97).
2. A. Yarbro Collins, *Mark: A Commentary* (Hermeneia), Minneapolis, MN, Fortress, 2007, p. 397.
3. J. Wellhausen, *Das Evangelium Marci*, 2nd ed., Berlin, Georg Reimer, 1909, p. 65; trans. is mine. A similar position is taken by W. Wrede, *The Messianic Secret*, trans. J.C.G. Greig, Cambridge, James Clarke, 1971, p. 14.

of God" in Mark is a royal title that the evangelist uses for Jesus as the Messiah[4].

Norman Perrin has referred to 8,27–9,1 as "the watershed of the Gospel"[5]. Augustine Stock argues that Peter's confession is a recognition scene, like those in Greek drama[6]. Mary Ann Tolbert concludes that Peter's identification of Jesus as "'the Christ' (8,27-30) ... easily qualifies as the central turning point of the story (*peripeteia*), because at that point the momentum turns in a different direction"[7].

II. THE STATUS OF PETER'S CONFESSION IN MARK

The status of Peter's confession has been interpreted in at least three different ways.

1. *Conflation of "Messiah" and "Son of Man"*

The two labels in Mark of course designate the same person: Jesus of Nazareth. They each, however, were used in different ways before Mark was written and have quite different connotations in Mark. At least two scholars, nevertheless, have conflated the two beginning right from the point of the confession of Peter. In his interpretation of 8,31, the first passion prediction, which uses the label "Son of Man", H.B. Swete comments, "The Christ must suffer"[8]. Similarly, Vincent Taylor comments on 8,27-33 in the section of his Introduction on "The Literary Structure of the Gospel" with the words, "The confession of Peter and the strong rebuke addressed to him are linked together by a prophecy of Messianic suffering"[9].

2. *Peter's Confession Is Right*

Christopher Bryan comments on 8,29, "We know that Peter is right, for Mark has told us so from the beginning (1:1)"[10]. Larry Hurtado takes

---

4. This view is highly probable; YARBRO COLLINS, *Mark* (n. 2), pp. 65-67, 213-214, 426, 767. See section V.1 below on the "Son of God" in Mark.
5. N. PERRIN, *What Is Redaction Criticism?* (Guides to Biblical Scholarship), Philadelphia, PA, Fortress, 1969, p. 52.
6. He refers to 8,27-30; A. STOCK, *Call to Discipleship: A Literary Study of Mark's Gospel* (GNS, 1), Wilmington, DE, Michael Glazier, 1982, p. 32; cf. pp. 64-65.
7. M.A. TOLBERT, *Sowing the Gospel: Mark's World in Literary-Historical Perspective*, Minneapolis, MN, Fortress, 1989, p. 114.
8. H.B. SWETE, *Commentary on Mark*, Grand Rapids, MI, Kregel, 1977, p. 178.
9. V. TAYLOR, *The Gospel according to St. Mark*, 2nd ed., Grand Rapids, MI, Baker Book House, 1966, p. 98.
10. C. BRYAN, *A Preface to Mark: Notes on the Gospel and Its Literary and Cultural Settings*, New York, OUP, 1993, p. 99.

a similar position, remarking that Peter "acclaims Jesus as Christ (or Messiah) … the same title given to Jesus at the beginning of Mark (1:1)"[11]. In his view, "Peter's use of the title displays some recognition of Jesus' true significance", but subsequent passages show that he is not the Messiah of popular expectation[12].

Norman Perrin argues the same point from the passage itself. Perrin rightly infers from the command not to speak about him to anyone (v. 30) that Jesus, as a character in the narrative, accepts Peter's identification of him as the Messiah[13]. Stock argues that "The contrast between Peter and the 'others', as well as the importance the title 'Christ' assumes later in the story, suggest that Peter is correct … Jesus' injunction to silence follows from the untimeliness of the confession rather than its truth"[14].

Christopher Tuckett takes a more restrained view. Since Peter's confession is preceded by the two-stage healing of the blind man at Bethsaida (8,22-26), "it may be then that Mark wishes to imply that Peter only comes to a true insight of who Jesus is gradually, and at this point in the narrative, with his confession of Jesus as the Messiah, has only reached an intermediate stage"[15]. Tuckett does, however, affirm that "Messiah" is a christological category that "is clearly one that Mark does not regard negatively"[16].

3. Peter's Confession Rejected or Its Status Ambivalent

Kirsten Marie Hartvigsen defines Peter's confession linguistically as an "assertive point"[17]. Although his claim would remind members of the audience of the phrase "Jesus Messiah" in 1,1 and his "assertive point distinguishes itself from the claims of other characters", the status of his statement is ambivalent because "Jesus neither confirms nor rejects this assertive point"[18].

According to Richard Horsley, Peter acclaims Jesus as the Messiah, "but Mark in effect rejects the acclamation"[19]. Although the apparent

---

11. L.W. HURTADO, *Mark* (NIBCNT, 2), Peabody, MA, Hendrickson, 1989, p. 135.
12. *Ibid.*
13. PERRIN, *What Is Redaction Criticism* (n. 5), p. 41.
14. STOCK, *Call to Discipleship* (n. 6), p. 134. J. MARCUS takes a similar position: *Mark 8–16: A New Translation with Introduction and Commentary* (AB, 27A), New Haven, CT, Yale University Press, 2009, p. 612.
15. C.M. TUCKETT, *Christology and the New Testament: Jesus and His Earliest Followers*, Louisville, KY, Westminster John Knox, 2001, p. 111.
16. *Ibid.*
17. K.M. HARTVIGSEN, *Prepare the Way of the Lord: Towards a Cognitive Poetic Analysis of Audience Involvement with Characters and Events in the Markan World* (BZNW, 180), Berlin, De Gruyter, 2012, p. 311.
18. *Ibid.*, p. 312.
19. R.A. HORSLEY, *Hearing the Whole Story: The Politics of Plot in Mark's Gospel*, Louisville, KY, Westminster John Knox, 2001, p. 250. He also argues with regard to

affirmation of Jesus as Messiah in 1,1 is part of the first sentence of the gospel (the *incipit*), Horsley refers to it as the "superscript" and argues that it was not part of the original, presumably oral, story, "but was added later in the manuscript tradition"[20]. Sherman Johnson argues that Jesus rejects the label "Messiah" in Peter's confession but may accept it in 14,62[21]. James Williams concludes that Peter's answer, "You are the Messiah", is inadequate for Mark unless it includes "the suffering and death of God's chosen one"[22].

III. MARK REINTERPRETS PETER'S CONFESSION

So too, the possibility that Mark reinterprets the tradition has been proposed in various ways.

1. *False versus True Christology*

Perrin took a position on the significance of Peter's confession and Jesus' response in Mark that was based on scholarship influential in the 1960s. For example, Leander Keck argued that the Markan summary in 3,7-12 introduces a cycle of miracle stories that presented Jesus as a θεῖος ἀνήρ[23]. He argued further that Mark included these stories in order to subordinate their glorifying Christology to the theology of the cross[24]. Another scholar who made an impact on Perrin's work was Theodore J. Weeden[25]. Weeden accepted the argument of other scholars that there is a "polemic against the disciples" in Mark. He argued that the polemic

---

Peter's confession that, "in the subsequent narrative sequence Mark is either rejecting or strongly qualifying what that declaration would appear to signify" (*ibid.*, p. 251).

20. *Ibid.*, p. 250.

21. S.E. JOHNSON, *A Commentary on the Gospel according to St. Mark* (HNTC), Peabody, MA, Hendrickson, 1960, p. 149.

22. J.G. WILLIAMS, *Gospel against Parable: Mark's Language of Mystery* (Bible and Literature Series), Decatur, GA, Almond Press, 1985, p. 70.

23. R. BULTMANN had earlier used the idea of the θεῖος ἀνήρ to understand the Hellenistic kerygma of the early church and the Synoptic Gospels: *Theology of the New Testament*, 2 vols., New York, Scribner's Sons, 1951-1953, vol. 1, pp. 130-131; see the discussion in M. BOTNER, *What Has Mark's Christ to Do with David's Son? A History of Interpretation*, in *CBR* 16 (2017) 50-70, p. 55.

24. L.E. KECK, *Mark 3:7-12 and Mark's Christology*, in *JBL* 84 (1965) 341-358; cited by N. PERRIN, *The Christology of Mark: A Study in Methodology*, in ID., *A Modern Pilgrimage in New Testament Christology*, Philadelphia, PA, Fortress, 1974, 104-121, pp. 106, 112.

25. T.J. WEEDEN, *The Heresy that Necessitated Mark's Gospel*, in *ZNW* 59 (1968) 145-158; ID., *Mark – Traditions in Conflict*, Philadelphia, PA, Fortress, 1971. Both works are cited by PERRIN, *Christology of Mark* (n. 24), p. 110, n. 16.

was aimed at their ϑεῖος ἀνήρ Christology, which was "inherent in a large section of Markan material"[26]. The alleged Christology of the disciples was criticized in favor of Mark's theology of the cross[27].

The influence of the views of Keck and Weeden on Perrin's interpretation of Mark is clear. He concludes that Mark presented Jesus as a divine man in 1,1–8,29, "so that the reader of his Gospel is left with only one possible conclusion: Peter confesses Jesus as a 'divine man' or a 'divine man-Messiah'"[28]. He continues, "Peter confesses Jesus as the Messiah and goes on to interpret this messiahship in terms of a 'divine man' Christology", referring to Peter's rebuke of Jesus, presumably for speaking of the necessity for the Son of Man to suffer[29]. In turn Jesus rejects "this understanding of Christology in the most explicit terms possible" in 8,33. Perrin then infers that "Mark presents a false understanding of Christology on the lips of Peter, a true understanding on the lips of Jesus ... The purpose of this schematization of the disciples' misunderstanding of Jesus in Mark's Gospel is to press for an acceptance of a suffering servant Christology in the church for which Mark is writing"[30].

2. *A New Definition of "Messiah"*

Stock argues that in the Caesarea Philippi incident, the tension between Peter's correct confession of Jesus as the Messiah and Jesus' prediction of his death show that, "At this point in the Gospel, Mark seems to be leading the reader to arrive at a new definition of messiahship ... Jesus is the Messiah but a Crucified Messiah"[31]. Furthermore, "The [suffering] Son of Man sayings had served to correct the popular view of the Messiah by bringing it into focus in terms of Jesus' passion and death"[32]. The Son of Man sayings in 13,26 and 14,62 in turn "inform the reader that Jesus' death as Messiah will be vindicated when he returns in power and glory"[33].

---

26. WEEDEN, *Heresy* (n. 25), p. 10.
27. *Ibid.*; *Mark – Traditions in Conflict* (n. 25), pp. 162-163.
28. PERRIN, *What Is Redaction Criticism?* (n. 5), p. 55.
29. *Ibid.*, p. 56.
30. *Ibid.* He infers the "suffering servant Christology" from Mk 10,45, which he sees as the climax of the section 8,27–10,52; see N. PERRIN, *The Son of Man in the Synoptic Tradition*, in ID., *A Modern Pilgrimage* (n. 24), 57-83, p. 81; cf. p. 77.
31. STOCK, *Call to Discipleship* (n. 6), p. 135. WELLHAUSEN takes a similar position; Peter had imagined the Messiah in a way different from suffering and dying: *Evangelium Marci* (n. 3), p. 66.
32. STOCK, *Call to Discipleship* (n. 6), p. 177.
33. *Ibid.*

IV. Analysis and Appraisal

1. *Peter's Confession as a Turning Point*

Peter's confession and its immediate aftermath is indeed a turning point in the Gospel of Mark. Wellhausen and Tolbert describe it best. Although there is opposition to Jesus already in the first half of the gospel, the mood created by the narrative changes significantly after this scene, as Wellhausen suggested. The narrative begins to emphasize the suffering that Jesus and his disciples must face. Stock's interpretation of Peter's confession as a recognition scene is appropriate, since he has been acting, in a sense, incognito since he began to call disciples, to teach, heal, and exorcise. Tolbert's term *peripeteia* is better, however, since it describes well the change in the kinds of activities that are primary for Jesus in the second half, as well as a change in the direction of his movements (toward Jerusalem and thus suffering and death).

2. *The False Christology of the θεῖος ἀνήρ*

The use of the phrase θεῖος ἀνήρ in the scholarship reviewed above is a misuse of the phrase as it was employed by Ludwig Bieler[34]. He did not use it as a fixed concept related to a label that could be applied to most traditional holy or charismatic persons in antiquity. He used it as an umbrella term in his search for the ancient roots of the medieval saints. In any case, the idea that there was an early Christian "divine-man Christology" has fallen from favor due in large part to critical studies of its use[35].

3. *The Term "Messiah" in the Milieu of Mark*

The status of the label "Messiah" in Mark should be seen in terms of the milieu of the gospel. First of all, the label is an important part of the tradition that the author inherited. For example, already in the letters of Paul the term χριστός is used of Jesus frequently and without explanation.

---

34. L. BIELER, *Θεῖος ἀνήρ, Das Bild des "göttlichen Menschen" in Spätantike und Frühchristentum*, 2 vols., Wien, O. Höfels, 1935-1936.
35. D.L. TIEDE, *The Charismatic Figure as Miracle Worker* (SBLDS, 1), Missoula, MT, Society of Biblical Literature, 1972; C.R. HOLLADAY, *Theios Aner in Hellenistic Judaism: A Critique of the Use of This Category in New Testament Christology* (SBLDS, 40), Missoula, MT, Scholars, 1977; B. BLACKBURN, *Theios Aner and the Markan Miracle Traditions: A Critique of the Theios Aner Concept as an Interpretative Background of the Miracle Traditions Used by Mark* (WUNT, 2.40), Tübingen, Mohr Siebeck, 1991.

The reason for this must be that proclamation of Jesus as the Messiah of Israel and the nations was part of the preaching and teaching that Paul imparted to the communities he founded[36]. The earliest audiences of the Gospel of Mark probably understood the phrase τοῦ εὐαγγελίου Ἰησοῦ Χριστοῦ in the opening sentence as "the good news about Jesus [as the] Messiah"[37].

In the milieu of Mark there were certain things that the Messiah was expected to do, for example, to defeat the enemies of Israel and drive them out of the land. The *Psalms of Solomon* call upon God to raise up for the people of Israel the predestined king, the son of David, who will "shatter unrighteous rulers; and purify Jerusalem of the nations that trample it down in destruction"[38]. According to the Dead Sea Scrolls, the Messiah of Israel "is the scepter who will smite the nations, slay the wicked with the breath of his lips, and restore the Davidic dynasty. Hence his role in the eschatological war"[39].

This idea of a militant Messiah was a live issue around the time that Mark was written. In 66 CE Menahem, a son or grandson of Judas the Galilean, who had led an uprising against the Romans after the death of Herod (the Great), seized arms from Masada and entered Jerusalem like a king to direct the siege of the palace[40]. He was apparently a messianic pretender and was killed after a short time by a rival[41]. The most prominent messianic leader in the first Jewish war with Rome was Simon son of Gioras. He was recognized by many of the rebels, including people of high social status, as having an apparently messianic role[42]. He was executed in the triumph of Vespasian and Titus in Rome[43].

After the war hopes for a militant Messiah did not disappear. According to the *Syriac Apocalypse of Baruch*, when the Messiah comes "he will call all the nations together". He will destroy the nations that have

---

36. A. YARBRO COLLINS, *Jesus as Messiah and Son of God in the Letters of Paul*, in EAD. – J.J. COLLINS, *King and Messiah as Son of God: Divine, Human, and Angelic Messianic Figures in Biblical and Related Literature*, Grand Rapids, MI, Eerdmans, 2008, 101-122.

37. YARBRO COLLINS, *Mark* (n. 2), pp. 130-132.

38. *Pss. Sol.* 17,21-22; trans. S.P. BROCK (modified), in H.F.D. SPARKS (ed.), *The Apocryphal Old Testament*, Oxford, Clarendon, 1984, 649-682, p. 678.

39. J.J. COLLINS, *The Scepter and the Star: Messianism in Light of the Dead Sea Scrolls*, 2nd ed., Grand Rapids, MI, Eerdmans, 2010, p. 77.

40. Josephus, *J.W.* 2.430-434.

41. Josephus, *J.W.* 2.441-448. Another apparent messianic pretender was John of Gischala (*J.W.* 4.389-395). See the discussion of these messianic figures in YARBRO COLLINS, *Mark* (n. 2), pp. 604-605.

42. Josephus, *J.W.* 4.510.

43. Josephus, *J.W.* 7.154.

exploited Israel and spare the ones that have not[44]. *4 Ezra* describes the coming of the hoped for Messiah in two symbolic visions. In the first of these the Messiah appears in the form of a lion and reproves the eagle representing the Roman empire. Thereafter the eagle is burned[45]. In the second vision Ezra sees "something like the figure of a man come up out of the heart of the sea, who flew with the clouds of heaven". An enormous crowd gathers to make war against him. A stream of fire comes from his mouth and burns them up, and only ashes remain[46]. This "messianic man" is an interpretation and application of the one like a son of man in Dan 7,13-14 and also of the "war-like Davidic messiah"[47]. A suffering and dying *Messiah* had been an unheard-of possibility before the death of Jesus.

The label "Messiah", therefore, in the context of these traditions and events in the milieu of Mark called to mind a militant Messiah who would destroy the Roman empire or at least put an end to its power over the people of God. He would then reign over Israel or over all people in a new age of peace. Such events were not part of the narrative of Mark. They were not even mentioned as major events of the eschatological future. The risen Christ returns to judge his own (Mk 8,34). Those who are not ashamed of him in this generation will enter into "life", that is, into the kingdom of God, rather than into the fire of Gehenna[48]. When the risen Jesus returns, moreover, he does not destroy or even judge his enemies but rather sends angels to gather his elect (13,26-27). Judging on the basis of 14,62, the point of his return with regard to his enemies is to be vindicated, to show them that he indeed is the heavenly Son of Man.

Furthermore, if the label "Messiah" were not reinterpreted, Mark would open the door to the possibility of a leader of the revolt against Rome being acclaimed as Messiah. If Mark had used such language, for example, the gospel could be seen as validating the claim of those who saw Simon son of Gioras as a rival to Jesus for the role of Messiah in spite of his execution by the Romans. The author of Mark had to redefine the concept "Messiah" in order to preclude the expectation of the perpetration of violence by the Messiah and to exclude the apparent rivals to Jesus for that role.

---

44. *2 Bar.* 72; trans. R.H. CHARLES – L.H. BROCKINGTON, in SPARKS (ed.), *Apocryphal Old Testament* (n. 38), 835-895, p. 884.
45. *4 Ezra* 11,36–12,36; M.E. STONE, *Fourth Ezra* (Hermeneia), Minneapolis, MN, Fortress, 1990, pp. 343-371.
46. *4 Ezra* 13,3-11; trans. STONE, *Fourth Ezra* (n. 45), pp. 381-382.
47. COLLINS, *Scepter and the Star* (n. 39), p. 78.
48. Mk 9,42-48.

4. Why Choose the Label "Son of Man" in Relation to Suffering?

a) The Origin of the Son of Man Sayings

The best explanation of the origin of the Son of Man sayings of the synoptic tradition is one that maintains continuity in the history of their tradition and use while allowing for change and development. That explanation is that the historical Jesus referred in his teaching to the "one like a son of man" in Dan 7,13-14 as one who would come in the future[49]. It is unwarranted to rule out the possibility that he identified that figure with himself. It seems more likely, however, that he spoke about a third agent of God, who would succeed John the Baptist and himself. In any case, the disciples of Jesus identified him with that figure when they experienced him as risen from the dead. If Jesus did refer to Dan 7,13-14, it is likely that he used a definite form of the Aramaic phrase, meaning something like "that Son of Man", that is, the one in Daniel 7[50]. That practice was adopted when Jesus was identified with that figure in Aramaic and, *mutatis mutandis*, when the Greek label "the Son of Man" was applied to Jesus[51].

Ps 110,1 was apparently the oldest text used to explicate the resurrection of Jesus, and it did so in terms of his exaltation to the right hand of God[52]. This interpretation was soon elaborated by combining the allusion to Ps 110,1 with allusions to Zech 12,10-12 and Dan 7,13[53]. Thus, the earliest Son of Man saying is of the apocalyptic type: the expectation that the Son of Man will come on the clouds of heaven[54].

b) The Significance of the "Son of Man" in the Milieu of Mark

We have already seen that *4 Ezra* 13 portrays the Messiah by alluding to Dan 7,13-14: a mysterious man from the sea appears and destroys his enemies. In the eagle and lion vision of *4 Ezra* 11–12, the lion is said to be the Davidic Messiah. This implies that he is a human being. In chapter 13,

---

49. A. YARBRO COLLINS, *The Origin of the Designation of Jesus as Son of Man*, in *HTR* 80 (1987) 391-407.
50. The definite form in Hebrew is בן האדם; in Aramaic: בר אנשא or בר נשא. Analogous language is used in the *Similitudes of Enoch* (*1 En.* 37–71) to link its messianic figure to Dan 7,13-14. See section on the origin of the suffering Son of Man sayings (IV.4.c) below.
51. YARBRO COLLINS, *Origin* (n. 49), pp. 404-405.
52. PERRIN, *The Son of Man in the Synoptic Tradition* (n. 30), pp. 58-59.
53. *Ibid.*, p. 59.
54. *Ibid.* It is not possible to reconstruct any Son of Man sayings spoken by the historical Jesus with any degree of probability, but his references would probably have been of the apocalyptic type.

however, he seems to be a heavenly figure whom God has reserved for many ages. The *Similitudes of Enoch* (*1 En.* 37–71) also allude to Dan 7,13-14 in referring to a heavenly figure as "that Son of Man"[55]. He is also called the Messiah, the Chosen One, and the Righteous One[56].

These two apocalyptic works agree in their interpretation of the "one like a son of man" in Daniel 7 as the Messiah. A number of rabbinic passages take the same position[57]. No text in the milieu of Mark interprets the "one like a son of man" as a collective symbol[58].

c) The Origin of the Suffering Son of Man Sayings

For the purposes of this study, the next question to be addressed is the origin of the suffering Son of Man sayings. Morna Hooker and Christopher Tuckett argue that the idea of the Son of Man suffering comes from Daniel 7 itself[59]. Tuckett takes the position that the "one like a son of man" is "some kind of representative of the 'saints of the Most High'"[60]. The people of the "holy ones of the Most High" (angels) are "the Jews suffering persecution under Antiochus Epiphanes because of loyalty to their Jewish faith and practice". Although "the 'son of man' figure in Daniel 7 is not explicitly said to be a suffering figure", the context implies, in his view, "that the scene of vindication and triumph which it paints is one of triumph out of suffering"[61]. The problem with this conclusion is that the "one like a son of man" is a heavenly being, not a symbolic representative. This heavenly being is portrayed as putting an end to the suffering of the people, not as sharing it.

Taking his starting point in the history of early Christian tradition, Perrin concludes that Mark inherited a tradition that used the verb παραδιδόναι and the label "Son of Man" in connection with the passion of Jesus[62]. He cites two examples of sayings embodying this tradition, which

---

55. *1 En.* 46,1-2.3; 62,5.7.9.14; 63,11; 69,26.27.29; 70,1; 71,17; the translation and significance of 71,14 are contested.
56. *1 En.* 38,2; 53,6 (Righteous One); *1 En.* 39,6; 40,5; 45,3.4; 49,2.4; 51,3.5a; 52,6.9; 53,6; 55,4; 61,5.8.10; 62,1 (Chosen One); *1 En.* 48,10; 52,4 (Anointed One/Messiah). On "that son of man" and all these terms as various labels for the same redeemer figure, see G.W.E. NICKELSBURG – J.C. VANDERKAM, *1 Enoch 2: A Commentary on the Book of Enoch Chapters 37–82* (Hermeneia), Minneapolis, MN, Fortress, 2012, pp. 113-123.
57. COLLINS, *Scepter and the Star* (n. 39), p. 211, n. 88; J.J. COLLINS, *Daniel: A Commentary on the Book of Daniel* (Hermeneia), Minneapolis, MN, Fortress, 1993, p. 307.
58. COLLINS, *Scepter and the Star* (n. 39), p. 211; ID., *Daniel* (n. 57), p. 306.
59. TUCKETT, *Christology and the New Testament* (n. 15), pp. 112-113; he refers (p. 117, n. 5) to M.D. HOOKER, *The Son of Man in Mark*, London, SPCK, 1967.
60. TUCKETT, *Christology and the New Testament* (n. 15), p. 112.
61. *Ibid.*, pp. 112-113.
62. PERRIN, *The Son of Man in the Synoptic Tradition* (n. 30), p. 79.

he declares are "both certainly pre-Markan". These are Mk 14,21 and 14,41[63]. Mk 14,21ab may be traditional and fits the type of saying Perrin identified[64]. The situation is more complicated with 14,41. The saying in question, v. 41c, "Look, the Son of Man is about to be handed over into the hands of sinners", could well be a Markan composition based on the second and third passion predictions (9,31; 10,32-34) to fit the present context and to point to the imminent fulfillment of those predictions[65]. The saying in Mk 14,21 could also be a Markan composition. If not, the question would remain why an early Christian tradent would have connected the glorious "one like a son of man" in Dan 7,13-14 with suffering and death.

It is striking how often the verb παραδιδόναι appears in Mark in connection with arrest, suffering, and death. This usage is like that of a leitmotif in music, repeated at key moments, emphasizing thereby an idea or event. The verb applies primarily to Jesus but also expresses the fate of John the Baptist in the past and the destiny of the disciples in the future[66]. It is probably not a coincidence that this verb occurs twice in the Greek version of the poem about God's servant in Is 52,13–53,12: "The Lord has handed him over for our sins" (Is 53,6b LXX) and "He will distribute the spoils of the mighty because he [literally "his life" or "soul"] was handed over to death ... and he bore the sins of many, and on account of their sins he was handed over" (53,12 LXX)[67].

This theme in Mark and its apparent relation to Isaiah 53 suggest that the author of Mark is the one who first connected the Son of Man with suffering and death. The hypothesis that the evangelist created that connection is interesting in light of the evidence that he was bilingual. He included some Aramaic sayings and terms in his narrative[68]. Before discussing that hypothesis further, it should be emphasized that the earliest Son of Man sayings are the apocalyptic ones and that ὁ υἱὸς τοῦ ἀνθρώπου (the Son of Man) is always a title of Jesus in Mark. At the same time, however, if the evangelist was bilingual, he would be aware of the idiom in Hebrew

---

63. *Ibid.*, p. 76.
64. YARBRO COLLINS, *Origin* (n. 49), p. 401. The statement at the end of this verse, "it would be better for him if that man had not been born" is probably an elaboration composed by the evangelist using a separate tradition; YARBRO COLLINS, *Mark* (n. 2), p. 652.
65. YARBRO COLLINS, *Mark* (n. 2), p. 682.
66. Mk 1,14 (John the Baptist); 3,19; 9,31; 10,33; 14,10.11.18.21.41.42.44; 15,1.10.15 (Jesus); 13,9.11.12 (disciples).
67. Trans. is mine.
68. Mk 5,41; 7,34; 11,9-10; 14,32.36; 15,22.34. Note the play on presupposed Aramaic words in which a bystander misunderstands "Eloi" (my God) to be a calling out to Elijah in 15,35-36.

and Aramaic in which "a son of man" meant "a man" or "man" in general. These indefinite forms are בן אדם in Hebrew and בר נשה in Aramaic.

The author of Mark did not speak about a suffering Messiah for the reasons cited above in section IV.3. Furthermore, the idea of a suffering Messiah seemed absurd, since the term "Messiah" had a regular and strong connotation of victory. It would also be a problem to attribute suffering and death to the glorious Son of Man of Dan 7,13-14. The evangelist, however, could draw upon the Aramaic idiom and use the similar Greek phrase meaning "the Son of Man" on the lips of Jesus to talk about his suffering. The idiom would resonate behind the Greek title for the evangelist and those in his audience who were also bilingual. If a definite form was used[69], the evangelist had Jesus talk about "the man" who must suffer, meaning himself. This way of speaking is analogous to Paul's use of the phrase οἶδα ἄνθρωπον ἐν Χριστῷ ("I know a man in Christ") in 2 Cor 12,2 to speak of his own ascent to heaven.

V. How Does the "Son of God" Label Relate to "Messiah" and "Son of Man"?

1. *The "Son of God" in Mark*

In the received text of Mark, the theme of Jesus as "Son of God" begins in the opening sentence. The majority of Greek manuscripts include the words υιου του θεου in the opening titular sentence. Those words, however, may not have been in the earliest recoverable text of the gospel[70]. This conclusion does not lessen the importance of the Son of God theme in Mark.

In chapter 1 Jesus is portrayed narratively as the Son of God at the time of his baptism, when the voice from heaven addresses him, "You are my beloved son; I take delight in you" (1,11). This declaration alludes to two passages from scripture. The first is Ps 2,7, in which God says to the king of Israel, "You are my son", and the second is Is 42,1, "Behold my servant, whom I uphold, my chosen, in whom my soul delights"[71]. This pairing is significant and seems to foreshadow the

---

69. The definite form of the phrase in Hebrew is בן האדם; there are two definite forms in Aramaic: בר אנשא and בר נשא.

70. A. YARBRO COLLINS, *Establishing the Text: Mark 1:1*, in T. FORNBERG – D. HELLHOLM (eds.), *Texts and Contexts: Biblical Texts in Their Textual and Situational Contexts. Essays in Honor of Lars Hartman*, Oslo, Scandinavian University Press, 1995, 111-127.

71. J. MARCUS, *The Way of the Lord: Christological Exegesis of the Old Testament in the Gospel of Mark*, Louisville, KY, Westminster John Knox, 1992, pp. 50-53; A. YARBRO

portrayal of Jesus in the gospel both as the Messiah and as the suffering Son of Man, the latter theme, with the refrain of "being handed over", evoking the suffering of the servant of God in Isaiah 53[72].

The interpretation of the allusion to Ps 2,7 here as messianic is supported indirectly by a text from the Dead Sea Scrolls which interprets 2 Sam 7,14, where God, referring to David's offspring, says, "I [will be] his father and he shall be my son". The interpretation is, "He is the Branch of David who shall arise with the Interpreter of the Law [to rule] in Zion [at the end] of days"[73]. The Branch of David is the Davidic Messiah[74]. In addition, it is likely that "son of God" and "son of the Most High" in a controversial Aramaic fragment from the Dead Sea Scrolls refers to the Davidic Messiah[75]. In the Gospel of Mark, therefore, the divine voice at the baptism of Jesus suggests to members of the audience of Mark familiar with the messianic reading of Psalm 2 that Jesus is the Davidic Messiah or the Messiah of Israel.

Jesus is also presented as Son of God in the Markan summary of 3,7-12. In that passage the unclean spirits prostrate themselves before Jesus and acclaim him as "Son of God" (3,11). The obeisance of the unclean spirits fits the implication that the label "Son of God" means Messiah, the anointed king. In response, Jesus forbids them to make him known (3,12), just as he sternly instructed the disciples in 8,30 to tell no one "about him", that is, that he is the Messiah. Thus this part of the summary belongs to the theme of the messianic secret in Mark. Judging from the first passion prediction, which follows the command to silence, the messiahship of Jesus must be kept secret until the predicted suffering has begun its predestined actualization.

The divine voice speaks once again at the transfiguration of Jesus, this time from a cloud (3,7). The overshadowing cloud is a theophanic element, indicating the presence of God[76]. Both here and in 1,11 the voice designates Jesus as God's beloved son. Only Jesus heard the voice the first time,

---

COLLINS, *Mark and His Readers: The Son of God among Jews*, in *HTR* 92 (1999) 393-408, p. 394.

72. See section IV.4.c above on the origin of the suffering Son of Man sayings.
73. 4QFlorilegium (4Q174) frgs. 1 col. I, 21, 2, lines 11-12; trans. COLLINS, *Scepter and the Star* (n. 39), p. 185.
74. 4QPatriarchal Blessings (4Q252 = 4QpGen) col. V, lines 3-4; COLLINS, *Scepter and the Star* (n. 39), p. 185.
75. 4QAramaic Apocalypse (4Q246) 2.1; trans. G. VERMES, *Complete Dead Sea Scrolls in English*, rev. ed., London, Penguin Books, 2003, p. 618; F. GARCÍA MARTÍNEZ – E.J.C. TIGCHELAAR (eds.), *The Dead Sea Scrolls Study Edition*, 2 vols., Leiden, Brill, 1997-1998, vol. 1, p. 495; COLLINS, *Scepter and the Star* (n. 39), pp. 154-164.
76. YARBRO COLLINS, *Mark* (n. 2), p. 425.

and only three disciples hear it the second time. The limitation to three disciples indicates that Jesus' identity is still a secret. The secrecy motif confirms the view that "beloved son" (Son of God) here identifies Jesus as the Messiah. On one level, the use of the "Son of God" label, a royal title, confirms Peter's confession of Jesus as the Messiah. On another level, "listen to *him*" exhorts the disciples to understand and accept the first passion prediction[77].

The parable of the wicked tenants implies that Jesus is the Son of God (12,1-12). The Markan Jesus narrates this parable after the chief priests, the scribes, and the elders question his authority (11,27-33). The story he tells of a man planting a vineyard evokes the poem about God and his vineyard in Is 5,1-7. According to Isaiah, the vineyard is the house of Israel (5,7). In the allegory attributed to Jesus, the owner, who represents God, lets the vineyard out to tenants and then sends servants to collect the fruit. Finally, he sends his beloved son. The expression "beloved son" calls to mind the words of the heavenly voice in the scenes of the baptism and transfiguration. According to Isaiah, God looked for justice and righteousness from his vineyard, but found only bloodshed and a cry (5,7). In the allegory in Mark, the servants are analogous to the prophets who called for justice. The beloved son clearly has a status higher and greater than that of the prophets. The trope in which the vineyard is the "house of Israel" suggests that Jesus, like Solomon, the son of David, beloved by God (2 Sam 7,15), is a king in the line of David, whose patrimony is the house of Israel. The shocking outcome of the story is due to the reinterpretation of messianic kingship in Mark, so that the heir to kingship does not go to collect his property by force but allows himself to be killed[78].

The dialogue between the High Priest and Jesus at the trial before the Sanhedrin (the Judean Council) is very important for understanding the relationship of the labels "Son of God", "Messiah", and "Son of Man" to one another in Mark[79]. It is striking first of all that the High Priest uses "the Messiah" and "the Son of the Blessed (Son of God)" as synonyms. The explanatory relationship of "the Son of the Blessed" to "the Messiah" makes clear that, for Mark, "Son of God" is a royal messianic label. This inference is confirmed by the strongly affirmative response of Jesus to the statement of the High Priest: ἐγώ εἰμι. This scene is indeed

---

77. *Ibid.*, p. 426.
78. This paragraph is based on YARBRO COLLINS, *Son of God among Jews* (n. 71), p. 402.
79. Mk 14,61-62.

"the unveiling of the messianic secret"[80]. The reason that the secret may now be revealed is that the suffering of Jesus as Son of Man is already underway.

As in the scene at Caesarea Philippi, Jesus affirms that he is the Messiah, there implicitly, here explicitly. In both cases he goes on to speak about the Son of Man. In 14,62 he declares that "you" (plural) will see the Son of Man seated at the right hand of the Power. This statement inserts the label "Son of Man" into the evocation of Ps 110,1, a text used early in the Christ-movement to express the exaltation of Jesus from death to the right hand of God. The High Priest and members of the Sanhedrin may not be meant to see such a scene directly in the future but to infer it from the fulfillment of the second part of Jesus' statement, "(you will see the Son of Man) coming with the clouds of heaven". This is surely meant to describe a motion from heaven to earth[81] so that Jesus may be vindicated in the sight of those who did not accept his messiahship.

The climax of the theme of Jesus as the "Son of God" in Mark is the remark of the centurion in 15,39[82]. Immediately before his statement is the announcement that, at the death of Jesus, "the curtain of the sanctuary was split in two from top to bottom" (15,38). This omen evokes the splitting of the heavens at the baptism of Jesus (1,10)[83]. At the baptism, "You are my beloved son" alludes to Ps 2,7, a royal psalm. As we have seen, "Son of God" in Mark is primarily a royal and messianic label. Secrecy surrounds the label "Son of God" as it does the label "Messiah", as we have also seen. Thus from the point of view of the production of the narrative and of the expectations of the earliest readers, "God's son" in 15,39 is also a messianic label.

The messianic secret, namely, that Jesus is Son of God and the Messiah, could be unveiled at the trial before the Sanhedrin because his suffering was already underway. Mark places the centurion's acclamation of Jesus as God's son immediately following the death of Jesus to make a narratively rhetorical point. Jesus may be recognized as Son of God only as one who suffers and dies. This is the final step in the redefinition of "Messiah" and "Son of God" and its climactic actualization[84].

---

80. PERRIN, *Christology of Mark* (n. 24), p. 108.
81. N. PERRIN, *Mark 14:62: The End Product of a Christian Pesher Tradition?*, in ID., *A Modern Pilgrimage* (n. 24), 11-17.
82. YARBRO COLLINS, *Mark* (n. 2), p. 764.
83. The verb σχίζειν is used in both 1,10 and 15,38.
84. On the relation of the centurion's phrase υἱὸς θεοῦ to the imperial phrases θεοῦ υἱός and *divi filius*, see YARBRO COLLINS, *Mark* (n. 2), pp. 767-768. The use of this phrase confirms the inference that Jesus is being acclaimed here as a ruler or king.

2. *Does Mark Reject the Label "Son of David"?*

As we have seen, the *Psalms of Solomon* and texts from the Dead Sea Scrolls express expectation of a Messiah who will be a son of David and will restore the Davidic dynasty[85]. In the account of the healing of his blindness, Bartimaeus acclaims Jesus as "the Son of David" twice[86]. This label is analogous to that used by Peter ("Messiah"). The son of Timaeus is not rebuked or corrected; rather his acclamation of Jesus as Son of David seems to be accepted[87]. This could be because Jesus is about to enter Jerusalem, suffer, and die. The acclamation is now timely.

When Jesus approaches Jerusalem, the crowd blesses "the coming kingdom of our father David" (11,10). There is no rebuke or correction of the crowd's acclamation. On the contrary, the Markan Jesus seems to have evoked it by riding a donkey as he approaches the city. He does not ride a mule to evoke the narrative about Solomon's succession to the throne of David (1 Kgs 1,33). Rather he rides a donkey alluding both to the royal tradition of Gen 49,11 and the humility (or the gentle and benign exercise of power) of Zech 9,9[88].

A key passage for understanding how Mark reinterprets the notion of "Son of David", and thus of "Messiah" as well, is 12,35-37[89]. The Markan Jesus poses a problem for those listening to his teaching in the temple precinct. He asks how the Messiah can be the Son of David in light of Ps 110,1. This verse, as we have seen, was probably the first passage of scripture used to interpret the vindication of Jesus as exaltation to heaven to a seat on the right hand of God. Ironically, much of the rest of the psalm depicts a warlike king who will defeat his enemies with shattering violence. Jesus focuses, however, on a different point. He reads the first verse on the assumption that David is the author of the psalm. The opening verse states, "The Lord said to my Lord, sit at my right hand". "The Lord" is presumably God enthroned in heaven. "My Lord" is read as referring to the Messiah, that is, to the Messiah of Israel, the Davidic Messiah. Jesus poses an apparently insoluble problem: If the Messiah is David's son, why does he call him "Lord"?

This conundrum appears to shed light on one of the reasons why the label "Son of Man" in 8,31 is substituted for "the Messiah" in 8,29. The

---

85. See the section on "The Term Messiah in the milieu of Mark" (IV.3) and "The Son of God in Mark" (V.1) above.
86. Mk 10,47.48.
87. YARBRO COLLINS, *Mark* (n. 2), p. 510.
88. *Ibid.*, p. 518.
89. For a history of scholarship on this passage, see BOTNER, *What Has Mark's Christ to Do with David's Son?* (n. 23), pp. 50-70.

evangelist suggests there and here that Jesus' messiahship will not be exercised during his earthly life. He will not be a human warrior-king. If he were, David would hardly address him as "my Lord". Rather he will be a heavenly Messiah, comparable to and probably identified with the "one like a son of man" in Dan 7,13-14. Thus, even if Jesus is a descendant of David, he will be much greater than David when he is exalted to heaven. Paul solves a similar problem by saying that Jesus was "born from the seed of David according to the flesh" (Rom 1,3). Moreover, Jesus will exercise his messiahship after his death, beginning with his exaltation. As Son of Man he will also return so that he can publicly be vindicated and gather his elect.

The conundrum and its solution, however, do not appear to mean that Jesus, as Messiah, is not the Son of David. The acclamations of Peter, Bartimaeus, and the crowd entering Jerusalem with Jesus can be affirmed as long as it is understood that Jesus, as Son of Man, will suffer, die, rise from the dead, and thereafter enter into his glory. This is the perspective from which to read the trial and crucifixion of Jesus.

3. *Jesus as King in the Passion Narrative*

When reading chapter 15 of Mark, it is important to remember that the Markan Jesus accepted the identity of the "Messiah" and "Son of the Blessed (Son of God)" in 14,61-62. His going on to speak of himself as "Son of Man" does not eliminate those other aspects of his identity.

When Jesus is handed over to Pilate, he asks Jesus, "Are you the king of the Jews?". Jesus' answer, "You say (so)", is ambiguous[90]. The reason is probably not that Jesus as a character in the narrative (and the author of the gospel) is rejecting the label "king"[91]. It is rather because the label "king of the Jews" is too narrow. As the "one like a son of man", Jesus' kingship will be over "all peoples, nations, and languages" (Dan 7,14).

Some soldiers then mock Jesus as a king (15,16-20). They are mistaken in limiting his kingship to "the Jews" but not in challenging his claim to be a king. In this scene the author makes use of dramatic irony, expecting his audience to understand that, in spite of this mocking rejection, Jesus actually is a king (designate)[92].

---

90. Mk 15,2.
91. Contra E.S. MALBON, *Mark's Jesus: Characterization as Narrative Christology*, Waco, TX, Baylor University Press, 2009, p. 121; see the discussion in BOTNER, *What Has Mark's Christ to Do with David's Son?* (n. 23), pp. 60-61.
92. YARBRO COLLINS, *Mark* (n. 2), p. 726.

The inscription on the cross, "the king of the Jews" is once again too narrow. It is also closer to a legal or political label that the Romans would recognize, since it could be translated "king of the Judeans". Besides being a charge against Jesus, it also mocks the helpless would-be king hanging on a cross.

The mocking of the chief priests and the scribes is more to the point: "let the Messiah, the king of Israel, come down now from the cross, in order that we may see and believe" (15,32). Here there is a shift from outsider language (king of the Jews) to insider language (Messiah, king of Israel). The use of the insider terms by opponents of Jesus does not indicate that the character of Jesus and the evangelist are rejecting these labels. The ironic character of this part of the narrative allows for these titles to be appropriate in spite of their use in mockery.

4. *The Label "Son of Man"*

If "Messiah" and "Son of David" normally refer to the earthly Messiah as a king, and usually as a warrior, the label "Son of Man" refers to a heavenly Messiah. An example of the latter usage is, as we have seen, the *Similitudes of Enoch* (*1 En.* 37–71). In the *Similitudes* God's primary agent is a heavenly being known under various names: "the Righteous One", "the Chosen One", "the Son of Man", and the Lord's "Anointed One" ("Messiah"). This heavenly being "is the embodiment of three parallel figures of high status celebrated in Israel's religious tradition. Transformed in a significant way, these figures are: (a) the Davidic king ..., (b) Second Isaiah's Servant of Yhwh and *Chosen One*, the *Righteous One* ..., and (c) the heavenly "'one like a *son of man*'"[93]. The label "Son of God" is not actually used of this figure in the *Similitudes*, but it would be appropriate under the rubric of "the Davidic king", a role that this heavenly Son of Man has absorbed and transformed.

4 Ezra was written in Hebrew, translated into Greek, but best preserved in Latin. In the account of the messianic man from the sea, the Most High, who interprets the dream-vision for Ezra, refers to the redeemer figure as "my Son" (13,32). The Latin word *filius* here may translate the Greek υἱός or παῖς, which in turn may have translated Hebrew בן or עבד. So it is difficult to determine whether the original phrase was "my Son" or "my Servant"[94].

---

93. Nickelsburg – VanderKam, *1 Enoch 2* (n. 56), p. 44.
94. See the discussion in Stone, *Fourth Ezra* (n. 45), pp. 207-208.

In Mark the Son of Man is portrayed as the Son of God: "when [the Son of Man] comes *in the glory of his Father* with the holy angels" (8,38). In this setting, he is coming to judge his followers on the basis of whether they were "ashamed" of him or not. The Son of Man in the *Similitudes* is also presented as the agent of God in the eschatological judgment[95]. In each case, both being Son of God and being Judge probably come from the merging of the role of the Davidic Messiah with that of the Son of Man.

VI. Conclusion

The introductory sentence of the gospel speaks of Jesus as the Messiah (1,1). This observation makes clear that the author of Mark has inherited a tradition that affirms Jesus in that role. Since the letters of Paul are the only surviving writings in the Christ-movement that are older than Mark, they are the most reliable way of discerning what "Messiah" meant among Christ-confessors prior to Mark[96]. In his study of "Christ language" in Paul, Matthew Novenson concludes that Paul's "scriptural source texts are overwhelmingly associated with the house of David ... Paul shows a particular affinity for passages that envision the Davidic king ruling over the Gentile nations"[97]. It is thus likely that the earliest audiences of Mark understood the term χριστός in 1,1 in terms of the Davidic Messiah.

It is also likely that Peter's confession of Jesus as the Messiah would have been understood by early audiences of Mark as referring to the Davidic Messiah. In addition to the emphasis on the house of David in Paul's letters, the *Psalms of Solomon* 17, messianic passages in the Dead Sea Scrolls, *2 Baruch*, and the vision about the eagle and the lion in *4 Ezra* all present a militant Messiah who would destroy the Roman empire or at least put an end to its power over the people of God. He would then reign over Israel or over all people in a new age of peace. Even the vision of the messianic man from the sea in *4 Ezra* 13 has features of a warlike Davidic Messiah in addition to those of the "one like a son of man" in Dan 7,13-14. If traditions like these were associated

---

95. *1 En.* 62,1-9.
96. The word χριστός does not occur in the concordance to Q in J.M. Robinson – P. Hoffmann – J.S. Kloppenborg (eds.), *The Critical Edition of Q* (Hermeneia), Minneapolis, MN, Fortress; Leuven, Peeters, 2000.
97. Novenson, *Christ among the Messiahs* (n. 1), p. 173.

with Peter's confession, this circumstance would explain Peter's rebuke of Jesus' prediction of suffering in 8,32.

The reinterpretation of the label "Messiah" in the narrative of Mark begins with the prediction of suffering in 8,31, not of Jesus as Messiah, but Jesus as the Son of Man. The explicit attribution of suffering to the Messiah would have been a textual move harshly contradictory to the expectations of the audience. Attributing suffering to the glorious "one like a son of man" in Dan 7,13-14 would also be unexpected.

Language about the Son of Man, however, was more easily expanded. The evangelist had already added to the apocalyptic role of the Son of Man the role of Son of Man on earth exercising authority by forgiving sins (2,10) and over the Sabbath (2,28). As Tuckett has argued, these sayings present Jesus the Son of Man as "one who is arousing hostility and opposition", opposition that will lead to the cross[98]. These sayings prepared the way for the suffering Son of Man sayings that begin to appear in 8,31.

Another reason that the Son of Man language was flexible is that "son of man" is an idiom in Hebrew and Aramaic. If the evangelist was bilingual, as seems likely, the indefinite "a son of man" could be understood as "a man", and "the son of man" as "the man" or "that man". Sensitivity to the idiom would have allowed the evangelist to create suffering Son of Man sayings in which Jesus, as a character in the narrative, talked about his own coming suffering as that of "the man" or "that man", as Paul talked about "a man in Christ" who ascended to Paradise.

The creation of the idea that the Son of Man could suffer opened the way for him to be portrayed as the suffering servant of God in the poem of Isaiah 53 in its Greek version. This portrayal is reflected in the sayings about the Son of Man being "handed over" and coming to serve and to give his life as a ransom for many[99].

102 Leetes Island Road	Adela YARBRO COLLINS
Guilford, CT 06437	
USA	
adela.collins@yale.edu	

---

98. TUCKETT, *Christology and the New Testament* (n. 15), p. 113.
99. The sayings about the Son of Man being handed over are 9,31; 10,33; 14,21.41; the saying about the Son of Man coming to serve and to give his life is 10,45.

„EUER HEILAND RUFT UND SCHREIT!"

JESU TODESSCHREI IN MK 15,34.37

Meinem Doktorvater in Dankbarkeit gewidmet

Die Erzählung von Jesu Todesschrei in der ältesten uns überlieferten Passionsgeschichte (Mk 15,34.37) ist aus mehreren Gründen ein exegetisches Problem[1]. Zuerst ist es narrativ gesehen auffällig, dass ein Gekreuzigter kurz vor seinem Tod schreit, da der Tod bei einer Kreuzigung durch Erschöpfung eintritt[2]. Dies ist ein Indiz, dass das Erzählelement kein biographischer Endpunkt ist, sondern einem theologischen Ziel dient.

Eine andere exegetische Frage ist, ob Mk 15,34.37 aussagt, dass Jesus am Kreuz *einmal* oder *zweimal* schrie. In Mk 15,34 steht: ἐβόησεν ὁ Ἰησοῦς φωνῇ μεγάλῃ („Jesus schrie mit lauter Stimme"), gefolgt von einem Zitat[3]

---

1. Nach M. PETZOLDT, *Freue dich, erlöste Schar, BWV 30*, in ID., *Bach-Kommentar: Theologisch-musikwissenschaftliche Kommentierung der geistlichen Vokalwerke Johann Sebastian Bachs. Band 3: Fest- und Kasualkantaten, Passionen* (Schriftenreihe der Internationalen Bachakademie Stuttgart, 14), Kassel, Bärenreiter; Stuttgart, Internationale Bachakademie Stuttgart, 2018, 150-173, S. 157, spiele der Satz „Euer Heiland ruft und schreit!" in der Arie „Kommt, ihr angefochtenen Sünder" der Bachkantate „Freue dich, erlöste Schar" auf die Stimme Johannes des Täufers an: „Die Stimme des Täufers hat die Vollmacht des Heilandes". Es ist zwar so, dass im vorangehenden Rezitativ „Der Herold kömmt und meldt den König an" sowie im folgenden Choral „Eine Stimme läßt sich hören" der Johannesruf gemeint ist, die Arie weist aber meines Erachtens auf Jesu Rufen beziehungsweise Schreien am Kreuz hin (ein Kernthema der Kantate ist das durch Christus beziehungsweise durch Christi Tod gebrachte Heil). Deswegen wurde das Bachzitat für den Titel dieses Aufsatzes gewählt.
2. Vgl. dazu u. a. E. LOHMEYER, *Das Evangelium des Markus* (KEK, 2), Göttingen, Vandenhoeck & Ruprecht, [16]1963, S. 346.
3. In Mk 15,34 wird Ps 22,2a auf Aramäisch (mit hebräischem Einfluss, vgl. ελωι) in griechischer Umschrift wiedergegeben und ins Griechische übersetzt, wobei die griechische Übersetzung der Septuaginta nahesteht, damit aber nicht genau übereinstimmt (Mk hat zweimal [ὁ θεός] *μου*, liest πρόσχες μοι nicht und hat εἰς τί statt ἵνα τί). Verwendet wurden A. RAHLFS – R. HANHART (Hgg.), *Septuaginta: Id est Vetus Testamentum graece iuxta* LXX *interpretes*, Stuttgart, Deutsche Bibelgesellschaft, [2]2006, und NESTLE-ALAND (Hgg.), *Novum Testamentum Graece: Griechisch-Deutsch*, 28. Aufl., Stuttgart, Deutsche Bibelgesellschaft – Katholische Bibelanstalt, [2]2013. Die Übersetzungen in diesem Aufsatz sind meine eigenen. Nach M. STOWASSER, *„Mein Gott, mein Gott, warum hast du mich verlassen?" (Mk 15,34): Beobachtungen zum Kontextbezug von Ps 22,2 als Sterbewort Jesu im Markusevangelium*, in BZ 58 (2014) 161-185, S. 163, orientiere Mk sich bei seinen Zitaten und Anspielungen in erster Linie an der Septuaginta,

aus Ps 22,2 („Mein Gott, mein Gott, wozu[4] hast du mich verlassen?"). In Mk 15,37 heißt es dann: ὁ δὲ Ἰησοῦς ἀφεὶς φωνὴν μεγάλην ἐξέπνευσεν. Die Frage ist, ob V. 37 einen zweiten Schrei erwähnt oder den Schrei des V. 34 wieder aufnimmt. Letzteres halte ich für wahrscheinlicher. Jesu Schrei mit wörtlicher Rede (V. 34) lässt sich erklären als eine auf Ps 22 basierte Ausfüllung des von Mk aus seiner Tradition übernommenen wortlosen Schreis (V. 37)[5]. Nach der (vermutlich redaktionellen[6]) Verspottungsszene (VV. 35-36) nimmt Mk in V. 37 den Schrei des V. 34 wieder auf: „Jesus war aber, nachdem er laut geschrien hatte, gestorben"[7]. Dabei gibt δέ („aber") den Gegensatz zwischen der Erwartung der

---

der hebräische Text sei erst sekundär zu berücksichtigen. Bezüglich Mk 15,34 spekuliert er, Mk basiere möglicherweise auf einer verlorenen griechischen Version oder einer unbekannten Variante der Septuaginta-Überlieferung (S. 180, Anm. 66). Dem Beitrag von C. BREYTENBACH im vorliegenden Sammelband zufolge, ist in Mk 15,34 die Septuaginta nicht verwendet.

4. Nach H.-U. RÜEGGER – A. HÄMMIG, „Mein gott: varzuo hastu mich gelassen?" Philologische Annäherung an eine theologische Frage (Mk 15,34), in ZNW 102 (2011) 40-58, sollte εἰς τί in Mk 15,34 nicht mit „warum", sondern mit „wozu" übersetzt werden. In diesem Zusammenhang kommentiert P.-G. KLUMBIES, Narrative Kreuzestheologie bei Markus und Lukas, in ID. (Hg.), Das Markusevangelium als Erzählung (WUNT, 408), Tübingen, Mohr Siebeck, 2018, 93-110, S. 102: „Das Erfassen des finalen Charakters (d. h., ‚wozu', MG) anstelle der kausalen Zuweisung (d. h., ‚warum', MG) lässt eine Sinnperspektive erkennen. Der Erzähler eröffnet der glaubenden Leserschaft einen Horizont. Mag auch der sterbende Jesus selbst keine Antwort mehr auf seine Frage vernommen haben, die Leserschaft des achten Jahrzehnts weiß, wozu dieses Sterben sinnvoll war. ... Sie weiß um dessen soteriologische Bedeutung".

5. Vgl. u. a. H. CONZELMANN – A. LINDEMANN, Arbeitsbuch zum Neuen Testament (UTB, 52), Tübingen, Mohr Siebeck, [13]2000, S. 504: „Jesu verzweifelter Gebetsruf in V. 34 mit den Worten von Ps 22,2 ist vermutlich eine christologisch reflektierte Ausfüllung seines wortlosen Todesschreis (V. 37)", und A. YARBRO COLLINS, Mark: A Commentary (Hermeneia), Minneapolis, MN, Fortress, 2007, S. 753: „Jesus' cry of abandonment in v. 34 is probably a secondary elaboration of the wordless or unreported cry in v. 37. ... The evangelist was not content to describe Jesus' death with a wordless cry, as his source did". Dass es in V. 37 um denselben Schrei als in V. 34 geht, verteidigt neulich mit guten Gründen auch M.H. DE LANG, One Cry or Two? Mark's Composition of Mark 15:34-37, in Journal of Biblical Text Research 45 (2019) 235-253.

6. Vgl. dazu u. a. E. KLOSTERMANN, Das Markusevangelium (HNT, 3), Tübingen, Mohr Siebeck, [4]1950, S. 165.

7. Für die Übersetzung eines Aorists (hier ἐξέπνευσεν) als Plusquamperfekt vgl. bes. A.T. ROBERTSON, A Grammar of the Greek New Testament in the Light of Historical Research, Nashville, TN, Broadman, [4]1934, S. 840-841. Für die Interpretation des ἐξέπνευσεν im Sinne von „sterben" vgl. u. a. M.E. BORING, Mark: A Commentary (NTL), Louisville, KY, Westminster John Knox, 2006, S. 431, der (zu Recht) das Verb als Synonym von ἀπέθανεν sieht. Anders u. a. J.E. AGUILAR CHIU, A Theological Reading of ἐξέπνευσεν in Mark 15:37, 39, in CBQ 78 (2016) 682-705, der meint, ἐξέπνευσεν in Mk 15,37.39 alludiere Jesu Gabe des Geistes (πνεῦμα, vgl. Mk 1,8) als Offenbarungsvermittler (vgl. z. B. das Bekenntnis des Zenturios in Mk 15,39). Seine Interpretation beruht aber (im Grunde) weitgehend auf Paulus: „from the Christian point of view, it is only because of the Spirit that one can confess the divinity of Jesus (see 1 Cor 12:3)"

Spötter, „Lasst uns sehen, ob Elija kommt, um ihn herunterzuholen!" (V. 36), und dem Verlauf der Dinge an: *Jesus war aber gestorben*[8]. Wenn V. 37 als Wiederaufnahme des V. 34 gesehen wird, dann zeigen sich in Mk 15,34-37 drei typisch markinische Phänomene: *Dualität* als Merkmal des redaktionell-markinischen Stils[9], *Sandwich-Konstruktion* (nach dem Schema A-B-A') als markinisches Erzählprinzip[10] und die *Doppelung* einer vorgegebenen Tradition in indirekter Rede mit einer Verdeutlichung in direkter Rede[11]. Mk 15,34.37 besagt also, dass Jesus am Kreuz *einmal* schrie (anders Mt 27,46.50: s. πάλιν in V. 50)[12]. Jetzt ist die Frage, worin die *Funktion* dieser Erzählsequenz im Mk besteht[13].

(S. 689). Diese Bemerkung ist schon deswegen problematisch, weil Mk Jesus nicht als „göttlich" bezeichnet. Nach KLUMBIES, *Kreuzestheologie* (Anm. 4), S. 103-104, gebe ἐξέπνευσεν an, dass „das Pneuma im Moment des Todes Jesu entweicht", da die Szene auf die Taufperikope in Mk 1,9-11 Bezug nehme (vgl. φωνή, πνεῦμα, σχίζω und die Richtungsangabe „von oben nach unten").

8. Gegen u. a. M. FLOWERS, *The Bystanders at the Cross and Their Expectations about Elijah*, in *CBQ* 80 (2018) 448-469, der meint, die Worte der Umstehenden in Mk 15,35-36 seien ernsthaft gemeint, das heißt, die Umstehenden denken oder hoffen, dass Elija kommen wird, um Jesus als den Messias zu salben und anzukündigen. Die Dabeistehenden sind aber wahrscheinlich als Gegner gemeint. Vgl. dazu die Verhöhnungen Jesu im Kontext der Markuspassion (vgl. Mk 14,65; 15,16-20.29-32) sowie die Anspielung in Mk 15,36 an Ps 68,22 LXX (vgl. bes. die Kombination von ἐπότιζεν bzw. ἐπότισαν und ὄξος), wo es um die Quälerei eines leidenden Gerechten durch seine Feinde geht: „Sie gaben mir Galle zu essen und für meinen Durst Essig zu trinken (ἐπότισάν με ὄξος)". Jesu Tod durchkreuzt die von seinen Gegnern geplante Quälerei.

9. Vgl. dazu bes. F. NEIRYNCK, *Duality in Mark: Contributions to the Study of the Markan Redaction* (BETL, 31), Leuven, LUP – Peeters, ²1988, S. 112-113.

10. Vgl. dazu bes. J.R. EDWARDS, *Markan Sandwiches: The Significance of Interpolations in Markan Narratives*, in *NT* 31 (1989) 193-216.

11. Vgl. bes. D. LÜHRMANN, *Das Markusevangelium* (HNT, 3), Tübingen, Mohr Siebeck, 1987, S. 244 (zu Mk 14,35-36).

12. Vgl. u. a. D. DORMEYER, *Die Passion Jesu als Verhaltensmodell: Literarische und theologische Analyse der Traditions- und Redaktionsgeschichte der Markuspassion* (NTAbh, 11), Münster, Aschendorff, 1974, S. 204: „ἀφείς (d. h., in Mk 15,37, MG) greift auf V 34 zurück. Es hat also nur einen Schrei gegeben". Anders u. a. M.-J. LAGRANGE, *Évangile selon saint Marc* (EBib, 7), Paris, Lecoffre, ⁴1947, S. 433-434, 436, der meint, Jesus schrie (tatsächlich) zweimal. Auf die Zwei-Quellen-Hypothese (im Hinblick auf Mk 15,34.37 par. Mt 27,46.50) ist hier nicht weiter einzugehen.

13. Die Frage ist, was die Erzählung von Jesu Todesschrei, historisch-kritisch betrachtet, aussagen will. Jesu Todesschrei ist ein exegetisches Problem, das um eine Erklärung fragt. Bei meinem Deutungsversuch ohne Anspruch auf endgültige Wahrheit (nach G. VAN OYEN – P. VAN CAPPELLEN, *Mark 15,34 and the Sitz im Leben of the Real Reader*, in *ETL* 91 [2015] 569-599, werde die Interpretation von Jesu letzten Worten vor seinem Tod in Mk 15,34 durch den Sitz im Leben der individuellen Exeget*innen geprägt) gehe ich vom Text und nicht von einer unterstellten historischen Situation aus.

I. Ps 22 als literarischer Hintergrund von Mk 15,20b-41

Auf die Übereinstimmungen zwischen der Markuspassion und Ps 22 (21 LXX) hat die Forschung ausführlich hingewiesen[14]. Deswegen beschränke ich mich beim folgenden Vergleich auf einige wesentliche Berührungspunkte zwischen Ps 22 und der Erzählung von Jesu Kreuzestod in Mk 15,20b-41[15]. Die Erzählung in Mk 15,24 über die Verteilung von Jesu Kleidern und dem Werfen des Loses findet eine Entsprechung im Parallelismus Ps 21,19 LXX: „Sie verteilten meine Kleider unter sich und sie warfen das Los um mein Gewand"[16]. Das Kopfschütteln als Ausdruck des Hohnes in Mk 15,29 entspricht Ps 21,8 LXX: „Alle, die mich sahen, verspotteten mich …, sie schüttelten den Kopf"[17]. Mittels des Rettungsmotivs, das in Mk 15,30-32.36 mehrfach aufgegriffen ist, klingt Ps 21,9 LXX an: „Er hoffte auf den Herrn, er errette ihn; er rette ihn, denn er hat Gefallen an ihm"[18]. Mk 15,34 bringt bekanntlich ein Zitat aus Ps 21,2 LXX: „Gott, mein Gott …: Warum hast du mich verlassen?"[19]. Schließlich formt das Bekenntnis des Zenturios, der in Mk 15,39 bekennt, dass der Mensch Jesus Gottes Sohn war, einen möglichen Berührungspunkt mit Ps 21,28 LXX: „Es werden gedenken und sich zum Herrn

---

14. Rezent u. a. J. FREY, *Vom Sinn-Raum der Schrift zur erfüllten Prophetie: Zur Psalmenrezeption in den Passionserzählungen der Evangelien*, in *JBTh* 32 (2017) 101-127, S. 106-112, und B. JANOWSKI, *„Mein Gott, mein Gott, wozu hast du mich verlassen?": Zur Rezeption der Psalmen in der Markuspassion*, in *ZTK* 116 (2019) 371-401, S. 387-391, 396-397. Vgl. auch u. a. CONZELMANN – LINDEMANN, *Arbeitsbuch* (Anm. 5), S. 504: „In Mk 15,24b-32 gibt es zahlreiche Erzählelemente, die sich alttestamentlichen Bezügen verdanken (vor allem aus Ps 22 und Ps 69), und die insofern unhistorisch sind", und J. GNILKA, *Das Evangelium nach Markus. 2. Teilband: Mk 8,27–16,20* (EKKNT, 2/2), Neukirchen-Vluyn, Neukirchener Verlag; Düsseldorf – Zürich, Benziger Verlag, ⁶2008, S. 311: „Der Grundbericht (d. h., der vormarkinische, vom Verfasser des Mk in Mk 15,20b-41 überarbeitete Bericht, MG) erweist sich als durch Motive bzw. Zitate aus den Psalmen vom leidenden Gerechten, insbesondere aus Psalm 22, geprägt. Dies bedeutet, daß schon er interpretierte Geschichte bietet und nicht als reiner Geschichtsbericht aufzufassen ist".
15. Vgl. dazu u. a. (kritisch) STOWASSER, *Beobachtungen* (Anm. 3), S. 177-182, der nur wenige Berührungspunkte für überzeugend hält.
16. Vgl. in Mk 15,24 διαμερίζονται τὰ ἱμάτια αὐτοῦ βάλλοντες κλῆρον ἐπ' αὐτά mit dem, was in Ps 21,19 LXX steht: διεμερίσαντο τὰ ἱμάτιά μου ἑαυτοῖς καὶ ἐπὶ τὸν ἱματισμόν μου ἔβαλον κλῆρον.
17. Vgl. in Mk 15,29 κινοῦντες τὰς κεφαλὰς αὐτῶν mit dem, was in Ps 21,8 LXX steht: πάντες οἱ θεωροῦντές με ἐξεμυκτήρισάν με, … ἐκίνησαν κεφαλήν.
18. Es geht hier um das Rettungsmotiv. In Ps 21,9 LXX steht: Ἤλπισεν ἐπὶ κύριον, ῥυσάσθω αὐτόν· σωσάτω αὐτόν, ὅτι θέλει αὐτόν.
19. Vgl. in Mk 15,34 ὁ θεός μου ὁ θεός μου, εἰς τί ἐγκατέλιπές με mit dem, was in Ps 21,2 LXX steht: Ὁ θεὸς ὁ θεός μου, πρόσχες μοι· ἵνα τί ἐγκατέλιπές με.

bekehren alle Enden der Erde und sich vor deinem Angesicht niederwerfen alle Stämme der Völker"[20].

Aus diesem kurzen Vergleich ergibt sich, dass Mk 15,20b-41 in erheblichem Maße durch Motive aus Ps 22 geprägt wird[21]. Da Ps 22 sich als wichtiger literarischer Hintergrund von Mk 15,20b-41 erweist, liegt es nahe, anzunehmen, dass der *ganze* Psalm (und nicht nur V. 2 und dessen unmittelbarer Kontext) berücksichtigt werden muss, um zu einem adäquaten Verständnis von Jesu Todesschrei zu kommen[22]. Im Hinblick auf Jesu Schrei sind von Ps 22 vor allem VV. 2-3, 6 und 25 relevant. In Ps 21,2-3 LXX steht: „Gott, mein Gott, achte auf mich: Warum hast du mich verlassen? … Mein Gott, des Tages werde ich schreien (κεκράξομαι), du wirst aber nicht zuhören …", in V. 6: „Zu dir (d. h., Gott) schrien (ἐκέκραξαν) sie (d. h., ‚unsere Väter', V. 5) und wurden gerettet; auf dich hofften sie und wurden nicht zuschanden" und in V. 25: „Denn er (d. h., Gott) hat nicht verachtet, und hat keinen Widerwillen empfunden gegen das Gebet des Armen und sein Angesicht nicht von mir abgewendet; und als ich zu ihm schrie (ἐν τῷ κεκραγέναι με), erhörte er mich" (V. 25)[23]. Vor dem Hintergrund von Ps 22,2-3.6.25 bringt Jesu Todesschrei in Mk 15,34.37 Jesu Gottverlassenheit und zugleich dessen Gottvertrauen zum Ausdruck.

II. Jesu Gottverlassenheit und Gottvertrauen

Die Idee, dass in der Erzählung von Jesu Kreuzestod dessen *Gottverlassenheit* ernst genommen und dessen *Gottvertrauen* hervorgehoben wird, ist in der Mk-Forschung weitverbreitet. Dahingegen bildet die

---

20. Es geht hier um das Bekehrungsmotiv. In Ps 21,28 LXX steht: μνησθήσονται καὶ ἐπιστραφήσονται πρὸς κύριον πάντα τὰ πέρατα τῆς γῆς καὶ προσκυνήσουσιν ἐνώπιόν σου πᾶσαι αἱ πατριαὶ τῶν ἐθνῶν. Anders u. a. N. EUBANK, *Dying with Power: Mark 15,39 from Ancient to Modern Interpretation*, in *Bib* 95 (2014) 247-268, nach dem die Worte des Zenturios „sarkastisch" gemeint seien. Eine sarkastische Verwendung von υἱὸς θεοῦ ist aber im Kontext des Mk unwahrscheinlich (vgl. bes. Mk 1,11 und 9,7).
21. Damit ist nicht gesagt, dass keine anderen alttestamentlichen Texte im Hintergrund stehen.
22. Vgl. u. a. B. STANDAERT, *Évangile selon Marc: Commentaire*. Troisième partie: *Marc 11,1 à 16,20* (EBib, 61), Pendé, Gabalda, 2010, S. 1139-1142. Anders u. a. STOWASSER, *Beobachtungen* (Anm. 3), S. 177-185: Da Mk nur aus der ersten Hälfte des Ps 22 (21 LXX), aus dem „Klageteil", zitiere, nehme die markinische Darstellung nur Bezug auf den unmittelbaren Kontext des Psalmzitats, nämlich auf V. 3, und nicht auf den weiteren Kontext des Psalms.
23. In der Septuaginta wird für das Schreien also andere Terminologie verwendet als in Mk 15,34.37: κεκράξομαι (Ps 21,3 LXX), ἐκέκραξαν (V. 6) und ἐν τῷ κεκραγέναι (V. 25).

Auffassung, dass gerade Jesu Todesschrei die Gottverlassenheit und das Gottvertrauen miteinander verbindet, eine Ausnahme[24]. Die gezielte

24. Dass die genannte Auffassung nicht gängig ist, zeigen u. a. (hier alphabetisch geordnet) S.P. AHEARNE-KROLL, *The Psalms of Lament in Mark's Passion: Jesus' Davidic Suffering* (SNTS MS, 142), Cambridge, CUP, 2007, S. 205-210; BORING, *Mark* (Anm. 7), S. 430-431; C. BREYTENBACH, *Narrating the Death of Jesus in Mark: Utterances of the Main Character, Jesus*, in ZNW 105 (2014) 153-168, S. 167; W.S. CAMPBELL, „Why Did You Abandon Me?": Abandonment Christology in Mark's Gospel, in G. VAN OYEN – T. SHEPHERD (Hgg.), *The Trial and Death of Jesus: Essays on the Passion Narrative in Mark* (CBET, 45), Leuven – Paris – Dudley, MA, Peeters, 2006, 99-117, S. 113-117; R.A. COLE, *The Gospel according to Mark: An Introduction and Commentary* (TNTC, 2), Leicester, Inter-Varsity; Grand Rapids, MI, Eerdmans, ²1989, S. 320-323; YARBRO COLLINS, *Mark* (Anm. 5), S. 753-755, 759; E.P. GOULD, *A Critical and Exegetical Commentary on the Gospel according to St. Mark* (ICC), Edinburgh, T&T Clark, ²1983, S. 294-295; W. GRUNDMANN, *Das Evangelium nach Markus* (THKNT, 2), Berlin, Evangelische Verlagsanstalt, ⁹1984, S. 434-436; R.H. GUNDRY, *Mark: A Commentary on His Apology for the Cross*, Grand Rapids, MI, Eerdmans, 1993, S. 965-970; M.D. HOOKER, *A Commentary on the Gospel according to St Mark* (BNTC), London, Black, 1991, S. 375-377; KLOSTERMANN, *Markusevangelium* (Anm. 6), S. 165-167; LOHMEYER, *Markus* (Anm. 2), S. 344-346; LÜHRMANN, *Markusevangelium* (Anm. 11), S. 263-264; J. MARCUS, *Mark 8–16: A New Translation with Introduction and Commentary* (AB, 27A), New Haven, CT – London, Yale University Press, 2009, S. 1063-1066; W. SCHENK, *Der Passionsbericht nach Markus: Untersuchungen zur Überlieferungsgeschichte der Passionstraditionen*, Gütersloh, Mohn, 1974, S. 43-45; L. SCHENKE, *Das Markusevangelium: Literarische Eigenart – Text und Kommentierung*, Stuttgart, Kohlhammer, 2005, S. 344-346: R. SCHNACKENBURG, *Das Evangelium nach Markus*, Teil 2 (Geistliche Schriftlesung: Erläuterungen zum Neuen Testament für die geistliche Lesung, 2), Düsseldorf, Patmos, ³1984, S. 307-311; E. SCHWEIZER, *Das Evangelium nach Markus* (NTD, 1), Göttingen, Vandenhoeck & Ruprecht, ⁶1983, S. 192-195; STOWASSER, *Beobachtungen* (Anm. 3), *passim*; und B. WITHERINGTON, *The Gospel of Mark: A Socio-Rhetorical Commentary*, Grand Rapids, MI – Cambridge, Eerdmans, 2001, S. 398-399. Vgl. dazu noch W. FRITZEN, *Von Gott verlassen? Das Markusevangelium als Kommunikationsangebot für bedrängte Christen*, Stuttgart, Kohlhammer, 2008, *passim*, der meint, ganz Evangelium nach Mk sei eine Antwort auf die Frage des Mk 15,34. Die Botschaft des Mk sei: Gott ist für Christusgläubige, wie er an Jesus gezeigt hat, verborgen da. Fritzen zufolge (S. 341-348), nehmen die markinischen Anspielungen auf Ps 22 nur Bezug auf die Klageelemente des Psalms, nicht auf die Vertrauensbekenntnisse (VV. 4-6.10-12.20-22), das Danklied (VV. 23-27) oder den Lobpreis (VV. 28-32). Andere meinen dagegen, dass die hoffnungsvollen Elemente des Psalms wohl mitzuhören seien, vgl. u. a. LAGRANGE, *Marc* (Anm. 12), S. 434; R. PESCH, *Das Markusevangelium. Teil 2: Kommentar zu Kap. 8,27–16,20* (HTKNT, 2), Freiburg i.Br., Herder, ²1980, S. 494-495 (dessen Behauptung, Jesus habe den ganzen Psalm gebetet, bleibt aber spekulativ); GNILKA, *Markus* (Anm. 14), S. 321-323; J. ERNST, *Das Evangelium nach Markus* (RNT), Regensburg, Pustet, 1981, S. 471-473; J.R. DONAHUE – D.J. HARRINGTON, *The Gospel of Mark* (SP, 2), Collegeville, MN, Liturgical Press, 2002, S. 450-451; P. DSCHULNIGG, *Das Markusevangelium* (Theologischer Kommentar zum Neuen Testament, 2), Stuttgart, Kohlhammer, 2007, S. 399-402; STANDAERT, *Marc* (Anm. 22), S. 1139-1142; T. NICKLAS, *Die Gottverlassenheit des Gottessohns: Funktionen von Psalm 22/21 LXX in frühchristlichen Auseinandersetzungen mit der Passion Jesu*, in W. EISELE – C. SCHAEFER – H.-U. WEIDEMANN (Hgg.), *Aneignung durch Transformation: Beiträge zur Analyse von Überlieferungsprozessen im frühen Christentum. Festschrift für Michael Theobald* (Herders Biblische Studien, 74), Freiburg i.Br., Herder, 2013, 395-415, S. 396-398, 414-415; V. AUVINEN, „Eloi, eloi, lema sabakthani" *(Mark 15:34) – A Cry of Despair or Trust?*,

Verbundenheit von „Gottverlassenheit" und „Gottvertrauen" in Mk 15,34.37 wird erkennbar, wenn diese Verse konsequent in Verbindung mit Ps 22,2-3.6.25 gesehen werden: Ps 22,2-3 bringt das Element der Gottverlassenheit, die hoffnungsvollen Hilferufe des Ps 22,6.25 das Element des Gottvertrauens ein.

Gegen diese Auslegung von Jesu Schrei in Mk 15,34.37 könnte eingebracht werden, dass das Gottvertrauen beim Todesschrei Jesu implizit bleibt[25]. Dies ist zwar so; dem Einwand könnte aber Folgendes entgegengesetzt werden: Programmatisch für die markinische Passionserzählung ist die Vorstellung, dass Jesus weiß, was geschehen wird: Der Menschensohn muss leiden, getötet werden und nach drei Tagen auferstehen (vgl. bes. Mk 8,31; 9,31; 10,32-34). Entsprechend dieser Perspektive auf die Gestalt Jesu scheint es folgerichtig anzunehmen, dass Jesus nach Mk nicht in Verzweiflung starb[26], sondern mit dem Vertrauen, dass Gott ihn retten würde.

Dazu kommt, dass in der frühesten Rezeptionsgeschichte des Mk, nämlich bei Mt, Jesu Gottvertrauen bei seinem Sterben explizit gemacht wird. Mt verbindet das Rettungsmotiv des Mk 15,30-32.36 mit Ps 22,9: In Mt 27,43a sagen die Hohepriester, Schriftgelehrten und Ältesten mit

---

in S. BYRSKOG – T. HÄGERLAND (Hgg.), *The Mission of Jesus: Second Nordic Symposium on the Historical Jesus, Lund, 7-10 October 2012* (WUNT, 2.391), Tübingen, Mohr Siebeck, 2015, 203-219, S. 219; und T. HIEKE, *Literatur setzt Literatur voraus: Das Alte Testament im Markusevangelium*, in ID. (Hg.), *Studien zum Alten Testament im Neuen Testament* (SBAB, 67), Stuttgart, Katholisches Bibelwerk, 2018, 31-36, S. 35-36. Anders JANOWSKI, *Rezeption der Psalmen* (Anm. 14), S. 395, 397-400, der meint, Jesu Schrei bringe weder Verzweiflung noch Rettungsgewissheit zum Ausdruck, sondern sei ein Versuch, wieder Vertrauen aufzubauen, wobei die Hoffnung auf mögliche Veränderung betont werde. Dass in Ps 22 das Syntagma φωνὴ μεγάλη (vgl. Mk 15,34.37) nicht verwendet wird, scheint mir nicht entscheidend zu sein, da Ps 22 sowieso das „Rückgrat" des Mk 15,20b-41 formt (s. o.). Gegen J. SCHREIBER, *Der Kreuzigungsbericht des Markusevangeliums: Mk 15,20b-41: Eine traditionsgeschichtliche und methodenkritische Untersuchung nach William Wrede (1859-1906)* (BZNW, 48), Berlin, De Gruyter, 1986, S. 296-299. Nach DORMEYER, *Passion* (Anm. 12), S. 200, bezeichne die Wendung βοάω φωνὴν μεγάλην in der Septuaginta „das flehende Gebet des bedrängten Gerechten". Ausführlich zur (theologischen) Rezeptionsgeschichte des Mk 15,34 F. BIGAOUETTE, *Le cri de déréliction de Jésus en croix: Densité existentielle et salvifique* (Cogitatio Fidei, 236), Paris, Cerf, 2004, *passim*.

25. Vgl. GUNDRY, *Mark* (Anm. 24), S. 967 (zu Mk 15,34): „[N]ot even a Jewish audience – much less Mark's Gentile audience – would hear the cry as pointing to a later salvific passage. The substitution of trustful and triumphant statements in Luke 23:46; John 19:30 reacts against the despairing cry in Mark 15:34 par. Matt 27:46. It does not interpret that cry in the light of later verses in Psalm 22, for then phraseology would have been drawn from them".

26. Ähnlich u. a. GNILKA, *Markus* (Anm. 14), S. 322. Anders u. a. A. BEDENBENDER, *Der gescheiterte Messias* (Arbeiten zur Bibel und ihrer Umwelt, 5), Leipzig, Evangelische Verlagsanstalt, 2019, S. 120: „Am Ende verzweifelt Jesus an seiner Isolation, selbst von Gott glaubt er sich verlassen (Mk 15,34)".

einem Zitat aus Ps 22,9: „*Er* (d. h., Jesus) *vertraut auf Gott* (πέποιθεν ἐπὶ τὸν θεόν)[27]; *der erlöse ihn nun, wenn er Gefallen an ihm hat*". In Mt 27,43a sind diese Worte zwar spottend gemeint, die Botschaft von Jesu Auferweckung (Mt 28,6-7) wird indessen den scheinbar berechtigten Zweifel, der sich in diesem Spott artikuliert, beseitigen. Mt *ex*pliziert, was bei Mk *im*pliziert wird: Jesus vertraut im Sterben auf den rettenden Gott.

Wird Jesu Todesschrei in Mk 15,34.37 von Ps 22 her ausgelegt, dann ist er kein (bloßer) Schmerzensschrei[28], Siegesschrei[29], Protestschrei[30], Gerichtsruf[31], apokalyptisches Endzeichen[32], Kundgabe von Jesu Tod an die Welt[33] oder Ähnliches, sondern der Hilferuf eines leidenden Gerechten[34]. Der Ausdruck „leidender Gerechter" wird hier verwendet im Sinne von dem in der alttestamentlichen und hellenistisch-jüdischen Literatur entwickelten und in der frühchristlichen Literatur verwendeten Motiv eines Frommen, der wegen seiner Gerechtigkeit und seines Gehorsams gegenüber Gott von Feinden geplagt und erniedrigt wird, dennoch weiterhin auf Gott vertraut und schließlich (während seines Lebens oder nach seinem Tod) von Gott gerettet wird[35]. In der frühchristlichen Literatur vor Mk

---

27. πέποιθεν ist meines Erachtens ein präsentisches Perfekt. Vgl. BDR, [18]2001, S. 279-280 (§341).
28. Vgl. u. a. GOULD, *Mark* (Anm. 24), S. 295: „The final cry of his agony, with which he expired".
29. Vgl. u. a. GRUNDMANN, *Markus* (Anm. 24), S. 435; COLE, *Mark* (Anm. 24), S. 323; SCHNACKENBURG, *Markus* (Anm. 24), S. 310.
30. Vgl. u. a. WITHERINGTON, *Mark* (Anm. 24), S. 399 (als Option: „a cry of ... defiance").
31. Vgl. u. a. SCHENK, *Passionsbericht* (Anm. 24), S. 43-45; SCHREIBER, *Kreuzigungsbericht* (Anm. 24), S. 294-302 (Gerichts- und Siegesschrei).
32. Vgl. u. a. W. POPKES, *Christus traditus: Eine Untersuchung zum Begriff der Dahingabe im Neuen Testament* (ATANT, 49), Zürich, Zwingli, 1967, S. 231-232, Anm. 656.
33. Vgl. u. a. GNILKA, *Markus* (Anm. 14), S. 323 (vgl. dazu auch POPKES, *Christus* [Anm. 32], S. 232, Anm. 656).
34. Anders u. a. S.P. AHEARNE-KROLL, *Challenging the Divine: LXX Psalm 21 in the Passion Narrative of the Gospel of Mark*, in VAN OYEN – SHEPHERD (Hgg.), *Trial* (Anm. 24), 119-148, S. 143, der Ps 21 LXX und Mk 15,34.37 nicht im Sinne der Rehabilitation eines unschuldig leidenden Gerechten interpretiert: „Jesus' cry can be viewed as expressing the outrage, abandonment and/or incomprehension of a chosen royal figure, just as the psalm [d. h., Ps 21 LXX, MG] does. And it could be seen as the final attempt of Jesus to convince God to save him from his suffering".
35. Zur markinischen Darstellung Jesu als leidenden Gerechten vgl. bes. M. DE JONGE, *Christology in Context: The Earliest Christian Response to Jesus*, Philadelphia, PA, Westminster, 1988, S. 61-62, 176-179. Zur Tradition des leidenden Gerechten vgl. u. a. auch L. RUPPERT, *Der leidende Gerechte: Eine motivgeschichtliche Untersuchung zum Alten Testament und zwischentestamentlichen Judentum* (FB, 5), Würzburg, Echter; Stuttgart, Katholisches Bibelwerk, 1972; ID., *Jesus als der leidende Gerechte? Der Weg Jesu im Lichte eines alt- und zwischentestamentlichen Motivs* (SBS, 59), Stuttgart, Katholisches Bibelwerk, 1972; und K.T. KLEINKNECHT, *Der leidende Gerechtfertigte: Die alttestamenlich-jüdische*

finden wir dieses Motiv, auf Jesus angewendet, unter anderem im Philipperbrief, in dem Paulus schreibt, dass Jesus Gott gehorsam war bis zu seinem Kreuzestod und dass „Gott ihn *deswegen* erhöht hat" (Phil 2,9).

III. DER MEHRFACHE ZWECK DER ERZÄHLUNG VON JESU TODESSCHREI

Wenn Mk mit Jesu Todesschrei in der Tat aussagen will, dass Jesus nur scheinbar in Gottverlassenheit am Kreuz verschied, sondern vielmehr voll Gottvertrauen starb, dann dient dies meines Erachtens mehreren Zwecken. Erstens wird Jesus durch die Verknüpfung der Erzählung von seinem Sterben mit Ps 22 dargestellt als leidender Gerechter, der nach seinem Tod von Gott ins Recht gesetzt wurde. Direkt nach Jesu Kreuzestod hatte diese Vorstellung zum Ziel, auszusagen, dass Jesu Tod kein Fiasko war, sondern das vorgesehene Schicksal eines leidenden Gerechten, der letztlich von Gott erhöht wurde. Man war keinem Versager gefolgt und tat es auch jetzt nicht.

Zur Zeit der Abfassung des Mk diente die Darstellung Jesu als leidenden Gerechten womöglich auch dem Zweck, darzulegen, dass Jesus und seine Nachfolger*innen keine Aufrührer*innen waren[36]. Kurz nach der Niederschlagung des Jüdischen Aufstands (66-70) und der Einnahme Jerusalems durch Titus (70)[37] war es für Jesu Nachfolger*innen geboten deutlich zu machen, dass sie keine Aufrührer*innen waren[38]. Der Verfasser des Mk schreibt, dass Jesus ein leidender Gerechter war, um zu begründen, dass Jesus und seine Nachfolger*innen nicht als (potenzielle) Unruhestifter*innen gesehen werden sollen: Mk zufolge, ist Jesus kein Revolutionär gewesen,

---

Tradition vom „leidenden Gerechten" und ihre Rezeption bei Paulus (WUNT, 2.13), Tübingen, Mohr Siebeck, 1984. Vgl. rezent D. FRICKER – N. SIFFER, *La figure biblique du juste et ses enjeux théologiques dans le Nouveau Testament* (CahRB, 97), Leuven – Paris – Bristol, CT, Peeters, 2020.

36. Vgl. zu diesem Zweck des Mk bes. H.J. DE JONGE, *Plight, Ethos and Theology in Mark*, in J. FLEBBE – M. KONRADT (Hgg.), *Ethos und Theologie im Neuen Testament: Festschrift für Michael Wolter*, Neukirchen-Vluyn, Neukirchener Theologie, 2016, 59-81.

37. Die in Mk 13,2 von Jesus angekündigte Tempelzerstörung halte ich für ein *vaticinium ex eventu*. Für die Datierung des Mk in oder kurz nach dem Jahr 70 vgl. bes. DE JONGE, *Plight* (Anm. 36), S. 63-65.

38. Vgl. bes. H.N. ROSKAM, *The Purpose of the Gospel of Mark in Its Historical and Social Context* (SupplNT, 114), Leiden – Boston, MA, Brill, 2004, *passim*. Roskam verortet Mk in Galiläa. Vgl. dazu auch DE JONGE, *Plight* (Anm. 36), der zudem einen kurzen Überblick bietet von galiläischen Orten, wo um 70 n. Chr. subversive (anti-römische) jüdische Gruppierungen aktiv waren (S. 67-68) sowie von (gemäßigten) Juden, die in den Sechziger- und Siebzigerjahren gegen Dissidenten auftraten, um zu verhindern, dass die römischen Autoritäten jene für Unruhestifter halten und ihre (eventuellen) Strafmaßnahmen gegen alle jüdischen Menschen richten würden (S. 75-76).

er wollte Israel nicht von der römischen Macht befreien, er stellte keinen weltlichen, politischen Machtanspruch[39] und auch seine Nachfolger*innen bilden keine Gefahr für die politischen Autoritäten.

Historisch gesehen ist es plausibel, dass Jesus als politisch verdächtig vorgestellter Jude[40] unter der Herrschaft des Kaisers Tiberius (14-37) auf Befehl des römischen Präfekten von Judäa Pontius Pilatus (26-36) durch Kreuzigung hingerichtet wurde[41]. Vor dem Hintergrund, dass im Römischen Reich die Kreuzigung als eine der schmählichsten Hinrichtungsarten galt, die auch zur Aufrechterhaltung der öffentlichen Ordnung gegen Schwerverbrecher oder Aufrührer verhängt wurde[42], zeigen sich im Mk (und in anderen frühchristlichen Schriften) „apologetische" Tendenzen. Eine solche Tendenz ist die Betonung der Schuldlosigkeit Jesu: Jesus wurde zwar gekreuzigt, war aber ein unschuldig leidender Gerechter (vgl. z. B. Mk 15,20b-41 unter Berücksichtigung des Ps 22). Eine andere Tendenz ist die Entlastung der römischen Autoritäten: Es wird zum Beispiel betont, dass Pilatus (ein Römer) bei Jesus kein Verbrechen finden konnte (vgl. Mk 15,14). Ziel dieser Tendenzen ist es, Jesus und seine Nachfolger*innen als nicht-subversiv vorzustellen[43].

Jesu Schrei am Kreuz dient angesichts Ps 22 also einerseits dem Zweck, hervorzuheben, dass Jesus zwar wie ein Kapitalverbrecher gekreuzigt wurde, in Wirklichkeit aber ein unschuldig leidender Gerechter war, der nach seinem Tod von Gott rehabilitiert wurde. Dementsprechend seien Jesu

---

39. Zur „depolitisierenden" Botschaft des Mk vgl. rezent C. BREYTENBACH, „Wie geschrieben ist" und das Leiden des Christus: Die theologische Leistung des Markus, in ID. (Hg.), The Gospel according to Mark as Episodic Narrative (SupplNT, 182), Leiden – Boston, MA, Brill, 2021, 358-373, S. 366, der meint, Mk interpretiere die (jüdische) Messias-Erwartung so um, dass seine Rezipient*innen Jesus trotz seines Kreuzestodes stets als den Christus sehen können: „Er ist König Israels, der Gesalbte, aber nicht in einem politischen Sinne, sondern als ein Leidender".

40. Vgl. u. a. CONZELMANN – LINDEMANN, Arbeitsbuch (Anm. 5), S. 508, und rezent BREYTENBACH, Leiden des Christus (Anm. 39), S. 361-362, nach dem man Jesus für einen „Usurpator" (d. h., für einen Aufständischen mit dem Anspruch, König zu sein) hielte.

41. Vgl. außer den frühchristlichen Passionserzählungen bes. Tacitus, Ann. 15.44.2-3. Verwendet wurde die Edition P.C. Tacitus, Annalen: Lateinisch-deutsch, hg. E. HELLER (Sammlung Tusculum), Mannheim, Artemis & Winkler, [6]2010, S. 748.

42. Vgl. dazu u. a. GNILKA, Markus (Anm. 14), S. 319.

43. Einem ähnlichen Zweck könnte auch das „Messiasgeheimnis" dienen. Wenn Mk Jesus mehrmals sagen lässt, seine messianische Würde solle bis zur Auferstehung des Menschensohnes geheim gehalten werden (vgl. bes. Mk 9,9-10), so dient diese Forderung vermutlich dazu hervorzuheben, dass erst im Licht von Kreuz und Osterglauben deutlich werden wird, was „Messianität" beinhaltet. Damit betont die markinische Gemeinde in ihrem Glauben, dass Jesus zwar der Messias war, aber keine weltlich-politischen Ambitionen hatte. Vgl. dazu bes. DE JONGE, Plight (Anm. 36), S. 78-79. So betrachtet hängt der Zweck des Messiasgeheimnisses mit dem Zweck des Motivs der passio iusti zusammen.

Nachfolger*innen weder Anhänger*innen eines Versagers (und damit selbst auch keine Versager*innen) noch Anhänger*innen eines Unruhestifters (und damit selbst auch keine Unruhestifter*innen).

Andererseits dient die Vorstellung, dass Jesus, in scheinbarer Gottverlassenheit, in Gottvertrauen starb, vermutlich dem Zweck, die Rezipient*innen des Mk zu ermutigen, in ihrem Leiden (vgl. z. B. Mk 8,34-38 über die „Leidensnachfolge")[44] auf Gott zu vertrauen. Jesu Todesschrei in Mk 15,34.37 ist der Hilferuf eines leidenden Gerechten, der von Gott erhört wird (vgl. bes. Ps 22,6.25)[45]. Jesu Schrei am Kreuz bringt unter Berücksichtigung des Ps 22 im Hinblick auf die Rezipient*innen des Mk also auch zum Ausdruck, dass Gott dem Gerechten, der ihm treu ist, treu bleibt[46]. So betrachtet sollten die Rezipient*innen des Mk am Geschick Jesu lernen, dass Gott, auch wenn er fern scheint, sie nicht verlässt[47].

Zum Schluss sind die letzten Worte Jesu im Mk die narrative Fassung des alten jüdischen Bekenntnisses zur Treue Gottes. Sie sind, in narrativer Performanz, Ausdruck des jüdischen Gottesglaubens: Gott ist treu! Der Verfasser des Mk kommt an dieser Stelle nicht über (früh)jüdische Bekenntnisaussagen hinaus. In der Darstellung Jesu Sterbens macht er für Jesusanhänger*innen die Anschlussfähigkeit der christlichen mit der jüdischen Glaubenstradition gewissermaßen als das unverbrüchliche und daher bindende Erbe fest. Dies bietet uns nicht nur einen Einblick in das

---

44. Nach C.M. TUCKETT, *Gospels and Communities: Was Mark Writing for a Suffering Community?*, in R. BUITENWERF – H.W. HOLLANDER – J. TROMP (Hgg.), *Jesus, Paul, and Early Christianity: Studies in Honour of Henk Jan de Jonge* (SupplNT, 130), Leiden – Boston, MA, Brill, 2008, 377-396, S. 384-394, richte Mk sich nicht an *verfolgte* Christusgläubige, sondern er *warne* seine Rezipient*innen vor Unterdrückung und Verfolgung. Nach DE JONGE, *Plight* (Anm. 36), S. 72-74, zeigen hingegen Mk 4,17, 8,34-38, 10,29-30 und 13,9-13, dass die Rezipient*innen des Mk von Unterdrückung und Verfolgung durch Juden oder politische Autoritäten betroffen waren.

45. Anders GNILKA, *Markus* (Anm. 14), S. 323, der meint, Jesu Schrei in Mk 15,37 sei *nicht* „der Hilferuf des Gerechten wie in Vers 34".

46. In Mk 15,20b-41 dient Ps 22 also nicht zum Nachweis, dass Jesus die Erfüllung alttestamentlicher Messiaserwartungen ist. Gegen B. ADAMCZEWSKI, *The Gospel of Mark: A Hypertextual Commentary* (European Studies in Theology, Philosophy and History of Religions, 8), Frankfurt a.M., Peter Lang, 2014, S. 189: „By referring to the Aramaic and Greek versions of Ps 22[21]:2 as having predicted that Jesus would be forsaken by God, Mark clearly demonstrated the Pauline idea that Jesus' shameful, apparently ungodly death on the cross in fact occurred in full agreement with the Jewish Scriptures (1 Cor 15:3)". Vgl. FREY, *Sinn-Raum* (Anm. 14), S. 109-110, nach dem es dem Verfasser des Mk nicht um die Erfüllung der Schrift, sondern um die Charakterisierung Jesu im Sinn-Raum der Schrift als des leidenden Gerechten gehe.

47. Vgl. SCHENKE, *Markusevangelium* (Anm. 24), S. 345. Ähnlich, dennoch anders, R.A. CULPEPPER, *Mark* (SHBC), Macon, GA, Smyth & Helwys, 2007, S. 558: „[in] Mark 15:34 … two Markan themes … culminate …: (1) the abandonment of Jesus, the righteous sufferer, and (2) the assurance of God's presence with the persecuted community".

Profil des Verfassers des Mk, sondern auch in das geistig-kulturelle Milieu der markinischen Gemeinde.

IV. Fazit

Jesu Schrei am Kreuz in Mk 15,34 lässt sich plausibel erklären als eine auf Ps 22 basierte Ausfüllung des von Mk aus seiner Tradition übernommenen wortlosen Todesschreis (V. 37) und V. 37 im Kontext der markinischen Erzählung als Wiederaufnahme des V. 34. Mk 15,34.37 bringt also zum Ausdruck, dass Jesus am Kreuz *einmal* laut schrie.

Da Ps 22 (21 LXX) sich als wichtiger literarischer und theologischer Hintergrund der Erzählung von Jesu Kreuzestod Mk 15,20b-41 erweist (vgl. z. B. Mk 15,24 mit Ps 21,19 LXX; V. 29 mit Ps 21,8 LXX; VV. 30-32.36 mit Ps 21,9 LXX; V. 34 mit Ps 21,2 LXX und V. 39 mit Ps 21,28 LXX), liegt es nahe, anzunehmen, dass der *ganze* Psalm berücksichtigt werden muss, um zu einem adäquaten Verständnis Jesu Todesschreis zu kommen. Wird Jesu Schrei vor dem Hintergrund von Ps 22,2-3.6.25 ausgelegt, dann bringt Mk damit zum Ausdruck, dass Jesus – in scheinbarer Gottverlassenheit – in Gottvertrauen starb.

Die Verknüpfung Jesu Todesschreis mit Ps 22 dient einem mehrfachen Zweck. Erstens wird Jesus damit dargestellt als unschuldig leidender Gerechter, der von Gott ins Recht gesetzt wurde, mit dem Ziel, hervorzuheben, dass Jesus weder ein Versager noch ein Aufrührer war und dass auch seine Nachfolger*innen keine Versager*innen oder Aufrührer*innen sind. Zweitens dient die Verbindung dazu, die Rezipient*innen des Mk zu ermutigen, in ihrem Leiden Jesu Vorbild zu folgen (vgl. bes. Mk 8,34-38) und ihr Gottvertrauen nicht aufzugeben. Drittens sorgt die Verbindung dafür, dass Jesu Sterben und damit das christliche Bekenntnis fest in der jüdischen Glaubenstradition verankert wird. Eine weiterführende Frage, die sich aufdrängt, ist, ob Jesu Schrei nicht bereits in der vormarkinischen Tradition als Hilferuf des leidenden Gerechten galt.

Albert-Ludwigs-Universität Freiburg   Mark Grundeken
Theologische Fakultät
Lehrstuhl für Neutestamentliche Literatur und Exegese
Platz der Universität 3
DE-79085 Freiburg i.Br.
Deutschland
mark.grundeken@theol.uni-freiburg.de

THE AUTHOR OF LUKE-ACTS IN A BILINGUAL CONTEXT

I. Introduction

Bilingualism was widespread in the ancient world[1], in particular in the first-century CE Eastern Mediterranean world of emerging Christianity[2]. The narrative of Acts repeatedly implies a bilingual environment of contacts between Greek and Semitic languages as the habitat of the early missionary Jesus movement in the Syro-Palestinian regions. Acts contains crucial references to a Semitic native language of inhabitants of Jerusalem, as illustrated by the name Ἀκελδαμάχ and its Greek rendering χωρίον αἵματος, "field of blood" (Acts 1,19)[3], the references to Ἑβραῖοι and Ἑλληνισταί in the Jerusalem church (Acts 6,1), to Ἰουδαῖοι and Ἑλληνισταί as part of the movement in Syrian Antioch (Acts 11,19-20), and to Paul speaking τῇ Ἑβραΐδι διαλέκτῳ to a Jerusalemite audience (Acts 21,40; 22,2), after having addressed a Roman tribune in Greek (Acts 21,37)[4].

This article will focus on the author of Luke-Acts in a bilingual context. The evidence of Acts noted above mainly concerns "external" indications, which merit attention in their own right. Yet the study of bilingualism is further illuminated by text-internal indications of Graeco-Semitic language contact behind a Semitized register of Greek in the narrative of Acts. In this regard, traces of Graeco-Semitic bilingualism should be delimited

---

1. See J.N. Adams – M. Janse – S. Swain (eds.), *Bilingualism in Ancient Society: Language Contact and the Written Word*, Oxford, OUP, 2002; T.V. Evans – D.D. Obbink (eds.), *The Language of the Papyri*, Oxford, OUP, 2010, contains no less than 6 out of 17 papers devoted to the bilingual theme of "Language Contact" (pp. 185-284). Cf. A. Mullen – P. James (eds.), *Multilingualism in the Graeco-Roman Worlds*, Cambridge, CUP, 2012; O. Elder – A. Mullen, *The Language of Roman Letters: Bilingual Epistolography from Cicero to Fronto*, Cambridge, CUP, 2019.

2. See recently S.-I. Lee, *Jesus and Gospel Traditions in Bilingual Context: A Study in the Interdirectionality of Language* (BZNW, 186), Berlin, De Gruyter, 2012; M. Janse, *Bilingualism, Diglossia and Literacy in First-Century Jewish Palestine*, in G.K. Giannakis et al. (eds.), *Encyclopedia of Ancient Greek Language and Linguistics*, Brill online, 2013; See J.M. Watt, *Some Implications of Bilingualism for New Testament Exegesis*, in S.E. Porter – A.W. Pitts (eds.), *The Language of the New Testament* (Linguistic Biblical Studies, 6), Leiden, Brill, 2013, 9-27.

3. Cf. ἀγρὸς αἵματος in Mt 27,8. BDAG, ³2000, p. 35, s.v. Ἀκελδαμάχ, mentions Aramaic חֲקֵל דְּמָא as referential background for this un-Greek name.

4. In section II below, we will go into detail about the meaning of Ἑβραῖοι, Ἑλληνισταί, τῇ Ἑβραΐδι διαλέκτῳ.

from very early borrowings incorporated in the Greek language[5]. We will focus here on the Book of Acts, because we have already published a systematic investigation of Semitisms in Luke's gospel[6]. There we surveyed arguments for and against bilingualism as the possible context of Luke's Greek, concluding that there are no *a priori* grounds against taking bilingualism into consideration[7].

The sections of our study here discuss characterizations of the author of Luke-Acts, the study of Lukan bilingualism, and Jerusalem and Antioch as urban milieus of Graeco-Semitic bilingualism (section II); Semitisms in Acts in retrospect, since their study by M. Wilcox in 1965, with select examples in comparative respect (section III); a preliminary survey of Semitisms in Acts (section IV); and finally we turn to an evaluation of the distribution of Semitisms along the compositional forms of Acts before giving our conclusions (section V).

II. REFLECTIONS ON LUKE-ACTS AND BILINGUALISM

1. *Scholarly Perspectives on Luke-Acts and Bilingualism*

a) Characterizations of the Author of Luke-Acts

The author of Luke-Acts has often been described as a Greek-speaking gentile Christian writing for gentiles[8]. Various commentators have held that Luke, supposedly a gentile Christian, would have been an outsider to Palestinian milieus, in view of the lack of a Lukan counterpart to Mk 7,1–8,10[9]. The recent representation of the state of scholarship by M. Kitchen reflects this view: "Scholars have long recognised that the Third Gospel was composed at least ten years after the destruction of

---

5. See É. MASSON, *Recherches sur les plus anciens emprunts sémitiques en Grec* (Études et commentaires, 67), Paris, Klincksieck, 1967.
6. A. HOGETERP – A. DENAUX, *Semitisms in Luke's Greek: A Descriptive Analysis of Lexical and Syntactical Domains of Semitic Language Influence in Luke's Gospel* (WUNT, 401), Tübingen, Mohr Siebeck, 2018.
7. *Ibid.*, pp. 44-48.
8. Cf., e.g., H.F.D. SPARKS, *The Semitisms of St. Luke's Gospel*, in *JTS* 44 (1943) 129-138, p. 132; W. SCHMITHALS, *Das Evangelium nach Lukas* (ZBK NT), Zürich, Theologischer Verlag Zürich, 1980, p. 9; B.D. EHRMAN, *The New Testament: A Historical Introduction to the Early Christian Writings*, New York, OUP, ²2000, p. 105, on Luke as "a kind of Greco-Roman biography", "written by a Greek-speaking Christian somewhere outside of Palestine".
9. See our discussion in HOGETERP – DENAUX, *Semitisms in Luke's Greek* (n. 6), p. 44, with reference to commentaries by J. Kremer, G. Petzke, and J. Ernst; yet our own diachronic survey of Luke in Synoptic perspective has yielded a different picture; see pp. 478-494.

Jerusalem around 70 CE and there remains a strong assumption that it is a Gospel written by a Gentile for a Gentile readership"[10].

Yet there are more and more exceptions to this supposed trend in Lukan scholarship. J.A. Fitzmyer already held a slightly different identification of Luke: "I regard Luke as a Gentile Christian, not, however, as a Greek, but as a non-Jewish Semite, a native of Antioch, where he was well educated in a Hellenistic atmosphere and culture"[11]. The fact that the precise affiliation of the author of Luke-Acts is not a closed discussion is illustrated by the following observation of W. Radl: "Er (= Lk) ist offenbar in der hellenistischen Kultur zu Hause. Nicht entschieden ist damit aber die Frage, ob er Juden- oder Heidenchrist ist". Radl concludes: "Sollte es sich dennoch um einen Heidenchristen handeln, dann um einen Hellenisten, der in einmaliger Weise griechische Bildung und jüdische Frömmigkeit, die hellenistische Kultur und die biblische Tradition in seiner Person vereinigt hat"[12].

A different direction has been proposed by J. Jervell: "Sein Griechisch ist das eines Juden, geprägt von der hellenistischen Synagoge". This is a rather exceptional viewpoint, which will not be followed here, but his view on Luke's Greek still merits attention: "das Griechisch eines zweisprachigen Juden [hat] eine Reihe semitischer Elemente ..., nicht nur im Vokabular, sondern vor allem stilistisch und syntaktisch"[13].

Early church traditions on Luke as a doctor coming from Syrian Antioch have regularly been drawn into characterizations of Luke as an author from a bilingual background[14]. For instance, R.H. Connolly wrote in the

---

10. M. KITCHEN, *The Good News of Restoration: Reading Luke-Acts Then and Now*, in *Pacifica* 23 (2010) 157-172, p. 159, and n. 7 referring to J.T. SANDERS, *The Jews in Luke-Acts*, Minneapolis, MN, Fortress, 1987; C. EVANS, *Luke* (NIBCNT), Peabody, MA, Hendrickson, 1990, p. 3; L.T. JOHNSON, *The Writings of the New Testament: An Interpretation*, rev. ed., London, SCM, 1999, p. 219; C. MOUNT, *Pauline Christianity: Luke-Acts and the Legacy of Paul*, Leiden, Brill, 2002, p. 50; B.R. GAVENTA, *The Acts of the Apostles*, Nashville, TN, Abingdon, 2003, p. 50; while yet arguing *contra*: J.A. FITZMYER, *The Gospel according to Luke I–IX: A New Translation with Introduction and Commentary* (AB, 28), Garden City, NY, Doubleday, 1981, pp. 45, 57-59; P.F. ESLER, *Community and Gospel in Luke-Acts: The Social and Political Motivations of Lucan Theology*, Cambridge, CUP, 1987, p. 31; M. SALMON, *Insider or Outsider? Luke's Relationship with Judaism*, in J.B. TYSON (ed.), *Luke-Acts and the Jewish People: Eight Critical Perspectives*, Minneapolis, MN, Fortress, 1988, 76-82; P.J. ACHTEMEIER – J.B. GREEN – M.M. THOMPSON (eds.), *Introducing the New Testament*, Grand Rapids, MI, Eerdmans, 2001, pp. 149-154; R. STRELAN, *Luke the Priest: The Authority of the Author of the Third Gospel*, Aldershot, Ashgate, 2008, pp. 110-113.

11. FITZMYER, *Luke I–IX* (n. 10), p. 42.

12. W. RADL, *Das Evangelium nach Lukas: Kommentar. Erster Teil: 1,1–9,50*, Freiburg i.Br., Herder, 2003, p. 6.

13. J. JERVELL, *Die Apostelgeschichte* (KEK, 3), Göttingen, Vandenhoeck & Ruprecht, [17]1998, p. 73, and n. 123.

14. For a survey of early Christian traditions, cf. C.K. BARRETT, *A Critical and Exegetical Commentary on the Acts of the Apostles. Vol. 1: Preliminary Introduction and Commentary on Acts 1–14* (ICC), London, T&T Clark, 1994, pp. 30-48.

early twentieth century: "if he [Luke] was 'a Syrian of Antioch', as the Prologue [an ancient prologue to Luke, followed by Eusebius *Hist. eccl.* 3.4 and Jerome *Vir. ill.* 7] states, the chances are that he was bilingual, and that his second language was Syriac"[15]. J.A. Fitzmyer wrote about the source of Aramaic interference in Luke's gospel that it "could be Luke's origin in Syrian Antioch, where he lived as an *incola*, speaking the Aramaic dialect of the indigenous natives of that country, though he was also educated in the good Hellenistic culture of that town"[16]. More recently, H. Klein also took early Christian tradition into account in the description of Luke as a Syrian bilingual, at home in Aramaic as well as Greek, including the Semitizing register of LXX Greek[17]. While arguments with reference to early church traditions are of a secondary nature, possible connections between evidence for a bilingual context to Acts and early Christian tradition will be discussed below.

b) Linguistic Perspectives

There is a longstanding implicit recognition of bilingualism behind the gospels and Acts, even though it has not constituted a central focus of investigation until relatively recently[18]. In his critique of older Semitic source hypotheses and in defence of Luke as a "septuagintalizer", H.F.D. Sparks made a passing reference to a bilingual speech situation as "the Semitic-Greek *patois* current among so many of his (Luke's) co-religionists"[19]. In his subsequent article on Semitisms in Acts, Sparks again left room for the idea that "some Semitisms, of course, are attributable directly to his Aramaic-speaking informants; some, too, to the unconscious influence upon him of the Semitic-Greek *patois* current among so many of his co-religionists; but most, I believe, are his own 'septuagintalisms'"[20]. More generally, G.H.R. Horsley addressed the phenomenon of bilingualism, distinguishing productive from receptive bilingualism, while he rightly criticized the notion of "Jewish Greek" as a fiction[21].

Our study of Semitisms in Luke's gospel has indicated that biblical Hebraisms from LXX Greek greatly influence the style of Luke's narrative

---

15. R.H. CONNOLLY, *Syriacisms in St Luke*, in *JTS* 37 (1936) 374-385, p. 375.
16. FITZMYER, *Luke I–IX* (n. 10), pp. 116-117.
17. H. KLEIN, *Lukasstudien* (FRLANT, 209), Göttingen, Vandenhoeck & Ruprecht, 2005, p. 37.
18. The study by LEE, *Jesus and Gospel Traditions in Bilingual Context* (n. 2), is a recent exception.
19. SPARKS, *The Semitisms of St. Luke's Gospel* (n. 8), p. 131.
20. H.F.D. SPARKS, *The Semitisms of Acts*, in *JTS* 1 (1950) 16-28, p. 26.
21. G.H.R. HORSLEY, *The Fiction of 'Jewish Greek'*, in ID., *New Documents Illustrating Early Christianity*. Vol. 5: *Linguistic Essays*, Northride, N.S.W., Macquarie University, 1989, 5-40, pp. 24, 32.

framework, but there are more varying influences at play in the words of Jesus and the poetic wording of the Lukan infancy hymns. These varying influences also include non-Septuagintal Hebrew and Aramaic backgrounds[22].

The Book of Acts has further been categorized along patterns of literary code-switching between standard Koine, Semitized, and midrange registers of Greek by J.M. Watt[23]. According to the statistical investigation of a Pentateuchal variety of Greek (posited at 100 in a LXX-index) by G. Walser, the Book of Acts (60) arguably ranks less close to the Greek of the ancient synagogue than Luke (86), but both are relatively closer to a Pentateuchal variety of Greek than the standard Koine of, for instance, Epictetus (19) and Dio Chrysostom (-22)[24].

In what follows, we turn to Jerusalem and Syrian Antioch as urban milieus of Graeco-Semitic bilingualism, considering the narrative of Acts and contextual evidence, in order to set the scene for the survey of types of Semitisms in Acts and for addressing the question of their bearing on Graeco-Semitic bilingualism.

2. *Urban Milieus of Graeco-Semitic Bilingualism*

a) Jerusalem

i) Ἑβραῖοι and Ἑλληνισταί

Acts 6,1 mentions the co-existence of Ἑβραῖοι and Ἑλληνισταί in the Jerusalem church. Ἑβραῖοι is a well-attested term in ancient literature, referring to language[25], ancestral lineage (cf. Phil 3,5 ἐκ γένους Ἰσραήλ, φυλῆς Βενιαμίν, Ἑβραῖος ἐξ Ἑβραίων)[26], ethnic allegiance[27],

---

22. HOGETERP – DENAUX, *Semitisms in Luke's Greek* (n. 6), pp. 494-499.
23. J.M. WATT, *Code-Switching in Luke and Acts* (Berkeley Insights in Linguistics and Semiotics, 31), New York, Peter Lang, 1997.
24. G. WALSER, *The Greek of the Ancient Synagogue: An Investigation on the Greek of the Septuagint, Pseudepigrapha and the New Testament* (Studia Graeca et Latina Lundensia, 8), Stockholm, Almqvist & Wiksell, 2001, p. 164.
25. Cf. Ἑβραίων with διάλεκτος in Aristobulus, *Fragmenta* frg. 2a, l. 3; Josephus, *Ant.* 1.33, 1.36, 2.278, 5.121, 5.336; *Ag. Ap.* 1.167; with γλῶττα/γλῶσσα in Philo, *Conf.* 68; *Abr.* 27, 57; Josephus, *Ant.* 1.34, 1.333, 3.291, 5.201 (twice), 5.323, 6.22, 6.302, 7.67, 9.290, 18.228. See also τῇ Ἑβραΐδι φωνῇ in *4 Macc* 12,7; 16,15. Note the Jewish self-identification with Ἑβραῖοι in Josephus, *Ant.* 3.32, κατὰ τὴν ἡμετέραν διάλεκτον.
26. Cf. Josephus, *Ant.* 1.146, on Heber (Ἕβερ), grandson of Arpaxad as forefather of the Hebrews, ἀφ' οὗ τοὺς Ἰουδαίους Ἑβραίους ἀρχῆθεν ἐκάλουν; Philo, *Joseph* 43, ἡμεῖς οἱ Ἑβραίων ἀπόγονοι. On Jews called Ἑβραῖοι as descendants of Abraham, see Cornelius Alexander Polyhistor, *Fragmenta* frg. 4, l. 4; Josephus, *Ant.* 14.255 (cited decree of Pergamum); Aelius Herodianus, *De prosodia catholica* 3.1, p. 32, ll. 25-26.
27. Ἑβραίων occurs with various ethnic terms: γένος, in Ezek. Trag., *Exagoge* ll. 12, 43, 155; Philo, *Migr.* 20; *QE* 2 frg. 2, l. 4; Josephus, *Ant.* 2.225, 4.127, 4.201, 5.93, 5.298,

and religious identity[28]. Thus, Ἑβραῖοι may encompass an ethno-linguistic sense, including the use of a Semitic language, native and/or through cultural education[29]. In view of Jerusalemite settings of a Semitic native tongue (τῇ ἰδίᾳ διαλέκτῳ αὐτῶν Ἀκελδαμάχ, Acts 1,19; τῇ Ἑβραΐδι διαλέκτῳ, Acts 21,40; 22,2; see further discussion below), it stands to reason that the term Ἑβραῖοι also denotes a Semitic-speaking capacity in Acts 6,1.

Ἑλληνιστής is a rare term in Greek, for it does not occur either in other literary texts in κοινή Greek or in documentary texts before late antiquity[30], and as such it could be called a Lukan neologism. The term Ἑλληνιστής has been taken, on the basis of the cognate verb ἑλληνίζειν, to refer to people speaking κοινή Greek over against non-Greek languages or Attic Greek, and its possibly varying senses in Acts 6,1, 9,29, and 11,20 have led C.K. Barrett to conclude that "Luke had no

---

10.183; *J.W.* 5.443; Appian, *Civil Wars* 2.10.71; ἔθνος in *Ant.* 4.308, 7.356, 8.120; λαός in Ezek. Trag., *Exagoge* l. 107; Josephus, *Ant.* 5.342, 6.210, 7.53, 8.38, 8.173, 8.335, 8.341, 10.155; κοινόν in *Ant.* 6.17; πλῆθος in *Ant.* 6.369; πολιτεία in *4 Macc* 17,9. The ethnic allegiance denoted by Ἑβραῖοι is not restricted to the biblical past of Israel, but also occurs, e.g., in 2 Macc 7,31; 11,13; 15,37; *4 Macc* 4,11; 5,2; 8,2; 9,6.18; 17,9; Plutarch, *Antonius* 27.4; Pausanias, *Graeciae descriptio* 1.5.5. Cf. 2 Cor 11,22 on Ἑβραῖοι, Ἰσραηλῖται, and σπέρμα Ἀβραάμ in a negative rhetorical context as terms of boasting about pedigree.

28. ὁ θεὸς τῶν Ἑβραίων, LXX Ex 3,18; 5,3; 7,16; 9,1.13; 10,3; ὁ τῶν Ἑβραίων θεός, Josephus, *Ant.* 9.20; *T. Jos.* 12,3; cf. *Jub.* 12,26 on Hebrew as the "tongue of creation". Note also late antique evidence for synagogues "of the Hebrews": [συν]αγωγὴ Ἑβρ[αίων], *CII* 1 no. 718 (Corinth); [τ]ῇ ἁγιοτ[άτῃ σ]υναγωγῇ τῶν Ἑβραίων, *CII* II no. 754 (Lydia – Philadelphia, 3rd-4th c. CE).

29. *Pace* BARRETT, *Acts 1–14* (n. 14), p. 308, whose view that "Ἑβραῖος does not have a primarily linguistic connotation" does not sufficiently take into account the early Jewish evidence cited in note 25 above.

30. A search in the online Thesaurus Linguae Graecae (henceforth: TLG) yields 111 hits, starting with Acts 6,1; 9,29 (11,20 Ἑλληνιστάς standard text NA[28] vs. Ἕλληνας 𝔓[74] ℵ[2] A D*) as the earliest literary attestation of Ἑλληνιστής, followed by the 3rd c. CE *Testament of Solomon* (rec. A and B, mss. H I L P Q), 3rd-4th c. CE *Passiones Philetaeri et Eubioti*, a 4th c. CE letter of emperor Julian, Basilius (4th c. CE) citing Acts 6,1, and other late antique literature. The one documentary attestation of Ἑλληνιστής is also from late antiquity: P.Kellis I 66 (300-325 CE), ll. 20-21: ἑλληνιστὴς γὰρ γέγονεν καὶ ἀναγνώστης συναγκτικός [with a sore or hoarse throat]. TLG search of the related verb ἑλληνίζειν yields 120 pre-300 CE results which usually denote the act of "speaking Greek" or "expressing oneself in Greek", in view of the frequent co-occurrence with terms such as φωνή and διάλεκτος. This act of speaking Greek can be qualified in various ways: κακῶς, "badly" (Strabo, *Geogr.* 14.2.28, ll. 63, 65); ἀκριβέστερον, "more accurately" (Plutarch, *Adv. Col.* 1116e, l. 3) or ἀκριβῶς, "accurately" (Dio Chrystostom, *2 Serv. lib.* [*Or. 15*] §15; Galen, *In Hippocratis librum iii epidemiarum commentarii iii*, KÜHN, vol. 17a, p. 625, l. 53); καλῶς, "well" (Appian, *Samnitica* 7.4, l. 3); φαύλως, "badly" (Rufus, Med., *De corporis humani appellationibus* 133, l. 3). The substantivized πάντες οἱ ἑλληνίζοντες typically means "all who speak Greek" in Dio Chrysostom, *Borysth.* (*Or.* 36), §19.

precise understanding of a party of 'Hellenists' in the primitive church"[31]. This is probably right, and it should be added that the very rendering as "Hellenists" could be misleading if it is taken to stand for a homogeneous group. If Ἑλληνισταί can appear in various localities in Acts 6,1-5 and 11,20[32], it may rather be an umbrella term referring to a heterogeneous group of followers of Jesus, who had a Greek-speaking orientation in common over against a Semitic-speaking capacity. In Acts 6,1, a reference to Greek-speaking Jews may stand to reason, in view of the inclusion of Nicolaos, an Antiochian proselyte, and Stephen, among the ranks of the appointed seven among the Ἑλληνισταί. That is, Stephen's speech (Acts 7,2-53) comprises various identifications with the ancestral narrative of Judaism[33], even though his vision of worshipping God ultimately opposed the priestly establishment in its antagonism with the movement of followers of the crucified and risen Jesus (Acts 7,47-53).

In sum, the ethno-linguistic references to Ἑβραῖοι and Ἑλληνισταί, i.e., Aramaic (and/or Hebrew) and Greek-speaking Jewish[34] Christians in the Jerusalem community in Acts 6,1, introduce a setting of Graeco-Semitic bilingual contacts. This is an uneasy setting of tensions (γογγυσμός, Acts 6,1) within the movement, which could yet be resolved, and strained relations with the surrounding environment followed by a scattering of the Jerusalem church, except for the apostles (Acts 8,1), i.e., the twelve among the Hebrews (Acts 1,2.26; 6,1-2).

ii) *τῇ Ἑβραΐδι διαλέκτῳ*

The narrative of Acts also relates bilingual activity of the apostle Paul in Jerusalem, speaking Greek (Acts 21,37) as well as τῇ Ἑβραΐδι διαλέκτῳ (Acts 21,40; 22,2), strongly implying that the latter, Semitic tongue would best serve him to address the crowds in Jerusalem and actually get them to listen to him.

---

31. BARRETT, *Acts 1–14* (n. 14), pp. 308-309, at 309, also with comparative references to Lucian, Sextus Empiricus, Posidippus, Dio Cassius, and Chrysostom. Cf. Josephus, *Ant.* 1.128-129, on Hellenized forms (ἐξελληνισάντων, ἡλλήνισται) of toponyms.
32. See Acts 6,5 on seven appointed men among the Ἑλληνισταί, with various names including one Nicolaus, a proselyte of Antioch, while the standard text of Acts 11,20 refers to contacts with Ἑλληνισταί on the part of some men of Cyprus and Cyrene who came to Antioch.
33. Cf. τῷ πατρὶ ἡμῶν Ἀβραάμ, Acts 7,2; διαθήκη περιτομῆς, Acts 7,8; οἱ πατέρες ἡμῶν, Acts 7,11.12.38.
34. Cf. E. HAENCHEN, *Die Apostelgeschichte* (KEK, 3), Göttingen, Vandenhoeck & Ruprecht, [14]1965, pp. 213-214; JERVELL, *Die Apostelgeschichte* (n. 13), p. 216.

Yet what does ἡ Ἑβραΐς διάλεκτος precisely mean? It is rendered "in the Hebrew language" in translation[35], but it has been noted about Acts 21,40, 22,2, and 26,14 on the other hand, that these passages "refer to the Aramaic spoken at the time in Palestine"[36]. In recent years, the hypothesis that Hebrew was also spoken to some extent in first-century CE Judaea has been taken up[37], but it is widely held that Aramaic was most common next to Greek in first-century CE Palestine[38]. Even studies of the relatively few Hebrew documentary texts from the desert of Judah from the time of Bar Kokhba have subscribed to this view[39]. In one document of 140 CE the idiom reportedly contains "a mixture of Hebrew and Aramaic elements"[40]. Josephus sometimes has an Aramaic term (עֲצַרְתָּא) in mind, when referring to Hebrews: Ἑβραῖοι ἀσαρθὰ καλοῦσι (Ant. 3.252). Yet in Hebrew, the term would be עֲצֶרֶת, standing for the "concluding feast of the Passover festival, i.e., the Feast of Weeks, Pentecost"[41].

R. Buth and C. Pierce recently critiqued previous lexicographical identifications of the word group Ἑβραΐς, Ἑβραϊστί, Ἑβραϊκή, arguing that "there is no methodologically sound support for the meaning 'Aramaic

---

35. RSV Acts 21,40; 22,2; cf. J.A. FITZMYER, *The Acts of the Apostles: A New Translation with Introduction and Commentary* (AB, 31), New York, Doubleday, 1998, p. 34, "in Hebrew".

36. BDAG, ³2000, p. 270, *s.v.* Ἑβραΐς. Cf. HOGETERP – DENAUX, *Semitisms in Luke's Greek* (n. 6), pp. 2 and 44, n. 135, on τῇ Ἑβραΐδι διαλέκτῳ as Aramaic, yet with reference to the Hebrew alphabet over against Greek.

37. See the contributions in R. BUTH – R.S. NOTLEY (eds.), *The Language Environment of First Century Judaea* (Jerusalem Studies in the Synoptic Gospels, 2), Leiden, Brill, 2014.

38. Cf. HOGETERP – DENAUX, *Semitisms in Luke's Greek* (n. 6), pp. 23-24, n. 189, with further literature, and p. 51, n. 186, on documentary evidence for Aramaic as majority language over against a more restricted use of Hebrew.

39. See H. ESHEL, *On the Use of the Hebrew Language in Economic Documents from the Judaean Desert*, in R.S. NOTLEY – M. TURNAGE – B. BECKER (eds.), *Jesus' Last Week* (Jerusalem Studies in the Synoptic Gospels, 1; Jewish and Christian Perspectives, 11), Leiden, Brill, 2006, 245-258, p. 245, on Aramaic as the most common documentary language in legal texts from the Judaean desert and from quotations in the Mishnah; G.W. NEBE, *Die hebräische Sprache der Naḥal Ḥever Dokumente 5/6Ḥev 44-46*, in T. MURAOKA – J.F. ELWOLDE (eds.), *The Hebrew of the Dead Sea Scrolls and Ben Sira* (STDJ, 26), Leiden, Brill, 1997, 150-157, pp. 154-155, on Hebrew as the language of halakha, theological schools, and law, albeit with many Aramaisms, next to Aramaic and Greek as legal language.

40. E. ESHEL – H. ESHEL (ז״ל) – A. YARDENI, *A Document from "Year 4 of the Destruction of the House of Israel"*, in *DSD* 18 (2011) 1-28, p. 5.

41. M. JASTROW, *A Dictionary of the Targumim, the Talmud Babli and Yerushalmi, and the Midrashic Literature*, London, Luzac; New York, Putman, 1903, p. 1103. Cf. I. ELBOGEN, *Jewish Liturgy: A Comprehensive History*, trans. R.P. Scheindlin, Philadelphia, PA, Jewish Publication Society of America; New York, Jewish Theological Seminary of America, 1993, p. 111, with reference to עצרת (Pentecost), in Aramaic עצרתא, being among the "three pilgrim festivals".

language'"[42]. They probably have a case to insist that scholarship should not categorically deny the possibility that Hebrew may also be in view with the word group Ἑβραΐς, Ἑβραϊστί, Ἑβραϊκή. Yet their discussion of divergent interpretations of this word group by A. Pelletier (Aramaic) and J.M. Grintz (Hebrew), with ἀσαρθά (*Ant.* 3.252) as a test case, leaves possible that this particular word has an Aramaic form[43], while yet being among the vocabulary of Ἑβραῖοι, "Hebrews". If we turn to the language use of the inhabitants of Jerusalem, Buth and Pierce infer from *The Letter of Aristeas* §11 that "the Jews in Jerusalem were speaking a language different than Aramaic (Συριακή)", rather Hebrew[44]. But does this passage refer to spoken language? According to B.G. Wright, the whole discourse of *Aristeas* §§1-11 "presumably is referring throughout to the written form of these languages", since *Aristeas* §3 also stated that the Jewish law had been written in "Hebrew letters"[45]. Buth and Pierce further turn to Josephus' *Antiquities* 11.159, supposing that the language use, Ἑβραϊστί, presumably "speaking Hebrew, rather than Aramaic", fits the conversation about the condition of Jerusalem[46]. Yet this concerns the time of Nehemiah, as part of Josephus' *Biblical Antiquities*, not first-century CE Jerusalem which is the setting we have in view for Acts 21,40, 22,2, and 26,14.

If we turn to the evidence of Acts, the first word related to the Jerusalemites' own language, τῇ ἰδίᾳ διαλέκτῳ αὐτῶν, admittedly stems from an Aramaic language background, Ἀκελδαμάχ (חֲקֵל דְּמָא) in Acts 1,19, as Buth and Pierce also concede[47]. There is no clear-cut Hebrew equivalent for this[48], but a noun qualified by "blood" would end on דמים(ה)- or דם- in biblical Hebrew[49], while biblical Hebrew does comprise the word

---

42. R. BUTH – C. PIERCE, Hebraisti in Ancient Texts: Does Ἑβραϊστί Ever Mean 'Aramaic'?, in BUTH – NOTLEY (eds.), *Language Environment* (n. 37), 66-109.
43. *Ibid.*, pp. 80-81; cf. p. 87 on ἀσαρθά as stemming "from an intermediate Aramaic form עצרתא".
44. *Ibid.*, p. 84.
45. B.G. WRIGHT, *The Letter of Aristeas: 'Aristeas to Philocrates' or 'On the Translation of the Law of the Jews'* (Commentaries on Early Jewish Literature), Berlin, De Gruyter, 2015, p. 112.
46. BUTH – PIERCE, Hebraisti in Ancient Texts (n. 42), p. 90.
47. *Ibid.*, pp. 77-78. We do not need to be concerned with their discussion of "The Use of Ἑβραϊστί with Alleged 'Aramaic' Names" (pp. 99-108), since this is a lengthy digression on toponyms in John, rather than directly relating to the expression τῇ Ἑβραΐδι διαλέκτῳ in Acts 21,40; 22,2; 26,14.
48. All examples for חֲקֵל denoting "(marked out) field" in JASTROW, *Dictionary* (n. 41), p. 497, come from Targumic Aramaic. On the study of specific Targumic Aramaic contexts to Ἀκελδαμάχ, cf. H.P. RÜGER, *Zum Problem der Sprache Jesu*, in ZNW 59 (1968) 113-122, pp. 116-118.
49. Cf. איש־דמים in MT 2 Sam 16,8 and Ps 5,7; איש הדמים in MT 2 Sam 1 6,7; אנשי דמים in MT Ps 26,9 and Prov 29,10; שפך־דם in MT 1 Kgs 18,28.

חֶלְקָה denoting "plot of land, field" in the narrative about king Ahab's bloodshed of Naboth and his sons (2 Kgs 9,26 MT). The word Ἀκελδαμάχ thereby clearly stems from Aramaic, not from Hebrew. Thus, when Paul comes to speak to a Jerusalemite audience τῇ Ἑβραΐδι διαλέκτῳ in Acts 21,40 and 22,2, it should stand to reason that he made himself understood in their own language.

If Hebrew and Aramaic were in close language contact around the turn of the common era, as some evidence may suggest (n. 40 above), this may leave some ambiguity[50]. Yet when turning from the Lukan Paul to Graeco-Semitic bilingualism in the apostle's own words, such as ἀββὰ ὁ πατήρ (Rom 8,15; Gal 4,6) and μαράνα θά (1 Cor 16,22), Aramaic backgrounds again turn up[51]. If the speech of the Lukan Paul indeed addresses an "open-air crowd"[52] (Acts 21,40, λαός; Acts 22,1, ἄνδρες ἀδελφοὶ καὶ πατέρες) rather than, for instance, a smaller circle of priests and scribes[53], it stands to reason that he uses a language most widely understood by that audience. This could well be Aramaic, in light of Acts 1,19 and the diverse nature of pre-70 CE Jerusalemite documentary evidence of Aramaic[54].

In view of ethnic associations with Ἑβραῖοι (n. 27 above), the expression τῇ Ἑβραΐδι διαλέκτῳ could be understood as "the Hebrews' language",

---

50. H.M. COTTON et al. (eds.), *Corpus Inscriptionum Iudaeae/Palaestinae*. Vol. 1: *Jerusalem. 1. 1-704* (= CIIP I/1), Berlin, De Gruyter, 2010, include various bilingual and Semitic inscriptions of pre-70 CE Jerusalem, which are often designated as "Hebrew/Aramaic", usually consisting of a few words. Among inscriptions in Aramaic, those more extensive than only a few words are nos. 25 (2 lines, 8 words), 55 (7 lines, 26 words), 83 (2 lines, 9 words), 93 (2 lines, 7 words), 225 (10 words), 287 (2 lines, 10 words), 375 (2 lines, 6 words), 381 (3 lines, 6 words), 392 (4 lines, 35 words), 407 (2 lines, 8 words), 439 (4 lines, ca. 14 words), 460 (4 lines, 11 words), 602 (4 lines, 8 words), 605 (3 lines, 14 words), 620 (2 columns, ca. 45 words), and 621 (5 lines, ca. 12 words). Among inscriptions in Hebrew, the more extensive ones are nos. 137 (3 lines, 20 words) and 693 (2 columns, ca. 70 words).

51. Cf. W.C. VAN UNNIK, *Aramaisms in Paul*, in ID., *Sparsa Collecta: The Collected Essays of W.C. van Unnik*. Vol. 1: *Evangelia – Paulina – Acta* (SupplNT, 29), Leiden, Brill, 1973, 129-143. For Aramaic אַבָּא behind ἀββά, cf. BDAG, ³2000, p. 1, whereas the Hebrew appellation of God as "Father" would be אָב (Ps 68,6; cf. the vocative אבינו in rabbinic Hebrew, ELBOGEN, *Jewish Liturgy* [n. 41], p. 178). For Aramaic מָרְנָא תָא behind μαράνα θά, cf. BDAG, ³2000, p. 616, whereas Hebrew for "our Lord" would be אדונינו (cf. אדוני, "Lord", in 4Q504 [*4QWords of the Luminaries*ᵃ] frg. 8r, l. 1; frg. 4, l. 14; frg. 5, col. ii+3, col. 1, l. 3; frg. 3, col. Ii, l. 5; frgs. 1-2, col. Ii, l. 7; frgs. 1-2, col. vi, ll. 3 and 10), while biblical Hebrew also uses the verb אָתָה, "to come" (cf. Is 21,12).

52. FITZMYER, *The Acts of the Apostles* (n. 35), p. 704.

53. COTTON et al. (eds.), CIIP I/1 (n. 50), include Hebrew (הכהן, p. 77, no. 32) and Aramaic (כהנה, p. 99, no. 55; p. 453, no. 434) terms for "priest" and a Hebrew "scribe" (הספר, p. 128, no. 86) among funerary inscriptions.

54. COTTON et al. (eds.), *ibid.*, include religious, public, funerary inscriptions (ossuaries), ostraca, jar fragments, and a stone weight among Aramaic inscriptional evidence.

which also encompasses Aramaic as spoken language, next to Hebrew as the language of biblical tradition[55].

b) Syrian Antioch

i) Ἰουδαῖοι and Ἑλληνισταί

The attention for a bicultural composition of the early church shifts from Ἑβραῖοι and Ἑλληνισταί in Jerusalem (Acts 6,1) to Ἰουδαῖοι and Ἑλληνισταί[56] in Antioch (Acts 11,19-20). Syrian Antioch was reportedly the place where followers were first called Christians (Acts 11,19-26). The shift in terms in Acts 11,19-20 may reflect a slightly different situation, since the ethno-linguistic composition of the Jewish community in Syrian Antioch would not have been identical with that in Jerusalem. In fact, Josephus states that most Syrian Jews, Ἰουδαῖοι, lived in Antioch who also attracted many Greeks, Ἕλληνες, to their religious ceremonies (*J.W.* 7.43-45). The term "Hebrews" would rather suggest a geographical orientation toward the ancestral lands of the Jews, i.e., the land of Israel[57].

Nevertheless, the narrative of Acts also indicates various links between Jerusalem and Antioch. Acts 6,5 refers to one Nicolaus, a proselyte of Antioch. Barnabas is mentioned as the delegate from the church of Jerusalem to Antioch (Acts 11,22), who had previously been characterized in Acts 4,36 as a Levite, a native of Cyprus, whose very surname would derive from Semitic onomastics[58]. Acts 11,27 refers to prophets coming from Jerusalem to Antioch. Acts 15 reflects on the tight relations between the Jerusalem church and the Jesus movement in Antioch, while also dwelling on the influence of the party of the Pharisees (Acts 15,5).

---

55. According to Origen, *Letter to Africanus* (ANF) §6, Hebrews, Ἑβραῖοι, could have recourse to φωνῇ τῇ Συριακῇ, presumably (Syrian) Aramaic, instead of the Hebrew, ἀντὶ τῆς Ἑβραΐδος, if a Hebrew word for Greek terms was not known in Scripture.

56. Ἕλληνας according to a variant reading of Acts 11,20 $\mathfrak{P}^{74}$ ℵ² A D*, but Ἑλληνιστάς in Acts 11,20 B D² E L Ψ 81 323 614 945 1241 1505 1739 Majority Text, is the standard text in NA²⁸ and defended as the greater "transcriptional probability" by BARRETT, *Acts 1–14* (n. 14), p. 551, while FITZMYER, *The Acts of the Apostles* (n. 35), p. 476, paradoxically adopts Ἕλληνας as reading in Acts 11,20, even though he regards Ἑλληνιστάς as *lectio difficilior*. It is beyond the scope of this paper to go more deeply into this problem.

57. Cf. Ex 40,15 on the "land of the Hebrews". In his *Biblical Antiquities*, Josephus often refers to the land of the Hebrews, ἡ τῶν Ἑβραίων χώρα (*Ant.* 6.106, 6.245, 6.281, 7.53, 7.219, 7.297, 7.303, 7.337, 8.132, 8.255, 8.353). Pausanias, *Graeciae descriptio* 1.5.5 even differentiates Ἑβραῖοι from Syria, referring to Hadrian's reducing "the Hebrews beyond Syria, who had rebelled", while associating the "land of the Hebrews", ἡ Ἑβραίων γῆ/χώρα, with Joppa (4.35.9), the river Jordan, lake Tiberias, the Dead Sea (5.7.4), and Jerusalem (8.16.4-5).

58. Barnabas is called an ἀνὴρ Ἑβραῖος in the Pseudo-Clementine *Homilies* 1.9.1, i.e., as one of the Ἑβραῖοι.

ii) *Evidence of Bilingualism*

Several types of evidence suggest the presence of a bilingual Graeco-Semitic urban milieu in Syrian Antioch[59]. In the course of his narrative about Mark Antony's military campaign in the East, Plutarch refers to one Alexander of Antioch whose ability to speak Parthian (Παρθιστί) and Syrian, i.e., (Syrian) Aramaic (Συριστί)[60], next to Greek, illustrates Antiochian bilingualism (*Antonius* 46.2)[61]. Inscriptional evidence of 73-74 CE regarding non-Greek appellations for city quarters (Βαγαδάτης, Φαρνάκης, Δαμασαφέρνης) in Syrian Antioch further suggests ethno-linguistic diversity[62].

The broader regional context of Syria also yields varying indications for Aramaic as spoken language next to Greek, ranging from documentary to literary evidence. Documentary evidence from the early Roman period includes pagan inscriptions of which the Greek (Ζεὺς Μάδβαχος) comprises Aramaic interference (מדבחא, "altar")[63]. There are also various examples of Aramaic/Nabataean, Palmyrene, and bilingual Semitic-Greek inscriptions on epitaphs in early Roman Syria[64]. Literary evidence comes from an epigram of Meleager of Gadara, with σαλαμ as transliterated Aramaic (שלם) for a Syrian greeting, and from Josephus' narrative about Roman soldiers of Syrian origin recognizing Aramaic spoken by Jews of Gamala (*J.W.* 4.38)[65]. Further, Strabo twice cites Posidonius, a Greek native of Syria, regarding the habit of Syrians to call themselves

---

59. This paragraph partly draws on HOGETERP – DENAUX, *Semitisms in Luke's Greek* (n. 6), pp. 52-53.
60. Συριστί renders אֲרָמִית in LXX Greek (LXX 4 Kgdms 18,26; 2 Esd 4,7; Is 36,11; Dan LXX, Th 2,4).
61. N.J. ANDRADE, *Syrian Identity in the Greco-Roman World*, Cambridge, CUP, 2013, pp. 148-149, discusses Plutarch's *Antony* 46.2 as "an intriguing example of Syrian bilingualism", referring to two languages "that characterized the Syrian *ethnos*, whose members spoke Greek, Aramaic, both, or even more".
62. D. FEISSEL, *Deux listes de quartiers d'Antioche astreints au creusement d'un canal (73-74 après J.-C.)*, in *Syria* 62 (1985) 77-103, pp. 98-99, on Persian backgrounds of these names on the double inscription (A 32, A 33, B 33).
63. IGLS ii 465-475, quoted in D.G.K. TAYLOR, *Bilingualism and Diglossia in Late Antique Syria and Mesopotamia*, in ADAMS – JANSE – SWAIN (eds.), *Bilingualism in Ancient Society* (n. 1), 298-331, pp. 307-311, with further examples of Aramaic interference.
64. See L. DE JONG, *The Archaeology of Death in Roman Syria: Burial, Commemoration, and Empire*, Cambridge, CUP, 2017, pp. 105-106, with tables referring to the sites of Apamea, Baalbek, Beirut, Bosra, Deb'aal, Dura-Europos, Hama, Hauran, Homs, Jebleh, Limestone Plateau, Palmyra, and Tyre, at p. 106: "The chronological distribution suggests that Semitic and bilingual Semitic-Greek inscriptions often belong to the earliest group of the 1st c. BCE and CE".
65. Literary examples from K. BEYER, *The Aramaic Language: Its Distribution and Subdivisions*, trans. J.F. Healey, Göttingen, Vandenhoeck & Ruprecht, 1986, p. 35, n. 45.

"Arameans", Ἀραμ(μ)αῖοι (*Geography* 1.2.34 and 16.4.27), thereby implying their identification with Aramaic as a "shared ancestral language"[66].

In sum, the literary and documentary evidence supports the idea that emerging Christianity had a linguistic setting in Syrian Antioch among Graeco-Semitic bilingual milieus.

III. REVISITING SEMITISMS IN ACTS

1. *Semitisms in Retrospect since Wilcox*

Inasmuch as the study of Semitisms in Acts was once bound up with the search for Aramaic backgrounds of the gospels and Acts[67], it has yielded much ground to hypotheses regarding the influence of Septuagintal Greek on the Greek of Acts[68]. The study *The Semitisms of Acts* published by M. Wilcox in 1965[69] broke away from older Semitic source hypotheses[70]. However, his study did not receive uniform scholarly support. The following statement of J.A. Fitzmyer in 1998, who cites an article by E. Richard (1980), may be revealing in this regard: "Of Wilcox's data, Richard has written: 'In not one single instance is his evidence persuasive' ('The Old Testament in Acts', 340). To which I say,

---

66. See further N.J. ANDRADE, *Assyrians, Syrians and the Greek Language in the Late Hellenistic and Roman Imperial Periods*, in *JNES* 73 (2014) 299-317, p. 304, with further attention for the complexities of ancient Syrian ethnic identity, encompassing both Greek-speaking and Aramaic-speaking inhabitants.

67. For the old hypothesis on Semitic sources behind Acts 1–15 through the subjective discernment of "mistranslations" from Semitic originals, see C.C. TORREY, *The Composition and Date of Acts* (HTS, 1), Cambridge, MA, Harvard University Press, 1916. For early criticisms of Torrey's theory, see G.A. BARTON, *Prof. Torrey's Theory of the Aramaic Origin of the Gospels and the First Half of the Acts of the Apostles*, in *JTS* 36 (1935) 357-373; H.J. CADBURY, *Luke – Translator or Author?*, in *The American Journal of Theology* 24 (1920) 436-455.

68. Cf., e.g., C.S. KEENER, *Acts* (New Cambridge Bible Commentary), Cambridge, CUP, 2020, pp. 97-98: "Some have noted a distinctly Semitic character to the language of Acts 1–15, though few today follow C.C. Torrey's thesis of a continuous Aramaic source behind it. Luke's Semitisms may sometimes recall his sources but probably often recall Septuagintal style in exclusively Jewish settings".

69. M. WILCOX, *The Semitisms of Acts*, Oxford, Clarendon, 1965. The subject of Semitisms in the New Testament was also more broadly surveyed by M. WILCOX in *Semitisms in the New Testament*, in *ANRW* 2.25.2 (1984) 978-1029, and in *Semiticisms in the NT*, in D.N. FREEDMAN et al. (eds.), *ABD*. Vol. 5: *O-Sh*, New York, Doubleday, 1992, 1081-1086.

70. WILCOX, *The Semitisms of Acts* (n. 69), p. 181, stated that "these little knots of Semitic material surviving unrevised" in Acts "do not permit us to argue in favor of translation of Aramaic or Hebrew sources by Luke".

'Amen!'"[71]. Yet E. Richard focused on 24 biblical citations in Acts, covering only part of Wilcox's book (chapter 2, pp. 20-55), but not its totality, which also surveys issues such as the Septuagint and Lukan diction (chapter 3, pp. 56-86), residual lexical Semitisms (chapter 4, pp. 87-111), and other Semitic elements (chapter 5, pp. 112-156) in Acts[72]. As such, intertextual use of the Septuagint for a Semitized variety of Greek and bilingual competence do not necessarily exclude one another[73]. Wilcox's study did not only meet with negative criticism; more positive critical appraisal came from, e.g., H.-Fr. Weiss (1967)[74], D.F. Payne (1970)[75], and R.A. Martin (1987)[76].

In what follows, we will provide some select examples of Semitisms in Acts with a comparative view to Wilcox's chapters 4–5 and subsequent scholarship, in order to give a glimpse of Semitisms which have not been maintained and those which are still on the table today.

2. *Select Examples of Residual Lexical Semitisms*

a) ἐκλέγεσθαι ἐν in Acts 15,7

In the Greek of Acts, the object of ἐκλέγεσθαι is usually in the accusative case (Acts 1,24; 6,5; 13,17; 15,22.25), but in Acts 15,7 ἐκλέγεσθαι ἐν, "to choose among", is actually without a direct object[77]. It has

---

71. FITZMYER, *The Acts of the Apostles* (n. 35), p. 116. This concerns an article by E. RICHARD, *The Old Testament in Acts: Wilcox's Semitisms in Retrospect*, in *CBQ* 42 (1980) 330-341.
72. RICHARD, *The Old Testament in Acts* (n. 71), on citations in Acts 13,22; 13,11; Eph 4,8; Acts 7,3.5.10; 7,4.32; 2,40; 7,16; 8,32; 3,22 & 7,37; 3,13 & 7,32; 5,30 & 10,39; 20,32 & 26,18; 7,33; 7,26.41; 2,24; 15,16; 13,47, at p. 331, focusing on "Semitisms via Wilcox's analysis of OT quotations (his chapter two)".
73. Cf. H. KLEIN, *Lukasstudien* (FRLANT, 209), Göttingen, Vandenhoeck & Ruprecht, 2005, p. 37. Note that among the "Septuagintalisms" in WILCOX, *The Semitisms of Acts* (n. 69), pp. 58-68, there are items, e.g., ἐκ κοιλίας μητρός, which we did not maintain; HOGETERP – DENAUX, *Semitisms in Luke's Greek* (n. 6), p. 216.
74. H.Fr. WEISS, *Review: Wilcox, Max, The Semitisms of Acts*, in *OLZ* 11/12 (1967) 575-578, p. 578, who thanked Wilcox for his avoiding generalizing conclusions about Semitisms in Acts: "weitaus schwieriger (...), als daß es sich durch die Alternative 'Übersetzungsgriechisch' – 'Septuaginta-Biblizismus' des Lukas lösen ließe".
75. D.F. PAYNE, *Semitisms in the Book of Acts*, in W.W. GASQUE – R.P. MARTIN (eds.), *Apostolic History and the Gospel: Biblical and Historical Essays Presented to F.F. Bruce*, Exeter, Paternoster, 1970, 134-150, p. 135, on Wilcox's book as "an adequate discussion" of Semitisms in Acts.
76. R.A. MARTIN, *Syntax Criticism of the Synoptic Gospels* (Studies in the Bible and Early Christianity, 10), Lewiston, NY – Queenston, Ont., Mellen, 1987, 2-4, p. 2, on M. Wilcox as well as H.F.D. Sparks having provided "detailed studies" regarding multicausal backgrounds to Semitisms in the gospels and Acts.
77. Cf. BDAG, ³2000, p. 305, *s.v.* ἐκλέγομαι 2.c.γ, with infinitive following this verb. On this odd Greek construction, cf. D. MARGUERAT, *Les Actes des apôtres (13–28)* (CNT,

been stressed by M. Wilcox and D.F. Payne that ἐκλέγεσθαι ἐν is relatively rare in LXX Greek, while it closely approximates the Hebrew בָּחַר בְּ[78]. H. Conzelmann considered ἐκλέγεσθαι ἐν to be derived from "a prototype (…) in the LXX (there used for בָּחַר בְּ, 'he chose')", and J.A. Fitzmyer considered it a "Septuagintism", referring to 1 Sam 16,10; 1 Kgs 8,16.44; 11,32; 2 Chr 6,5.34[79]. It should be added that the combination of the verb ἐκλέγεσθαι with an object in the accusative case is more usual in LXX Greek, occurring there 81 times[80], while its combination with ἐν occurs 13 times, rendering Hebrew בחר ב (LXX 1 Kgdms 16,9.10; 3 Kgdms 8,16.44; 11,32; 1 Chr 28,4.5; 2 Chr 6,5 [twice]; 6,6.34; 7,12; 2 Esd 19,7). Thus ἐκλέγεσθαι ἐν is the more Hebraizing variety of LXX Greek. TLG search yields no clear parallel for this usage in pre-300 CE texts apart from early Jewish and Christian literature. Further, the Hebrew form בחר ב is not impossible in Aramaic, as illustrated by Qumran Aramaic as partly reconstructed in 4Q544 frg. 1, l. 12: [במן מננא אנת]ה בחר לאשתלטה, "which of us do you choose to be ruled?"[81]. Thus, the usage of ἐκλέγεσθαι ἐν may fit the Jewish setting of Peter's speech (Acts 15,7-11) who was one of the Ἑβραῖοι.

b) ἐπὶ τὸ αὐτό in Acts 1,15; 2,1.44.47

The phrase (εἶναι) ἐπὶ τὸ αὐτό, "(to be) all together" (as a community) recurs in Luke's Greek (Lk 17,35; Acts 1,15; 2,1.44; cf. Acts 2,47,

---

deuxième série 5b), Geneva, Labor et Fides, 2015, p. 93, n. 27, "construire un indicatif (ἐξελέξατο) avec un infinitif (ἀκοῦσαι sans τοῦ) et un accusatif du sujet (τὰ ἔθνη) n'est pas grec et unique dans le NT".

78. WILCOX, *The Semitisms of Acts* (n. 69), pp. 92-93; p. 93, on ἐκλέγεσθαι ἐν as a "Hebraism"; PAYNE, *Semitisms in the Book of Acts* (n. 75), pp. 143-144; p. 143, "we ought not to class it as a Septuagintalism".

79. H. CONZELMANN, *A Commentary on the Acts of the Apostles*, trans. J. Limburg – A.T. Kraabel – D.H. Juel (Hermeneia), Philadelphia, PA, Fortress, 1987, p. 116; FITZMYER, *The Acts of the Apostles* (n. 35), p. 547. Cf. F.C. CONYBEARE – S.G. STOCK, *Grammar of Septuagint Greek*, Boston, MA, Ginn and Company, 1905, §98, p. 88, on Hebrew influence behind prepositions after verbs.

80. Lxx Gen 13,11; Num 16,5.7; 17,5(20); Dt 1,33; 4,37; 7,7; 10,15; 12,5.11.14.21.26; 14,2.24.25; 16,6; 17,8.15; 18,5.6; 26,2; 30,19; Josh 9,27; 24,22; Judg 10,14; 1 Kgdms 2,28; 8,18; 10,24; 12,13; 13,2; 16,8; 17,8.40; 2 Kgdms 6,21; 19,38(39); 24,14; 3 Kgdms 3,8; 11,13.34; 14,21; 18,23.25; 4 Kgdms 23,27; 1 Chr 15,2; 21,10; 2 Chr 7,16; 33,7; 35,19; 2 Esd 11,9; Job 29,25; Ps 32(33),12; 46(47),4; 64(65),4; 77(78),67.68.70; 104(105),26; 131(132),13; 134(135),4; Jl 2,16; Zech 3,3(2); Is 7,15.16; 14,1; 40,20; 41,8.9.24; 43,10; 44,1.2.13; 49,7; 56,4; 58,5.6; 65,12; 66,3.4; Ez 20,38.

81. Text and translation by F. GARCÍA MARTÍNEZ – E.J.C. TIGCHELAAR, *The Dead Sea Scrolls Study Edition*. Vol. 2 *(4Q274–11Q31)*, Leiden, Brill; Grand Rapids, MI, Eerdmans, 2000, pp. 1088-1089. On the subject of Hebraisms in Qumran Aramaic, cf. C. STADEL, *Hebraismen in den aramäischen Texten vom Toten Meer* (Schriften der Hochschule für jüdische Studien Heidelberg, 11), Heidelberg, Universitätsverlag Winter, 2008.

προστιθέναι ἐπὶ τὸ αὐτό). Regarding its identification as a Semitism, M. Wilcox argued beyond parallels in LXX Greek for understanding this phrase as a Hebraism against specific communal connotations in Qumran Hebrew, such as להיות ליחד (1QS V 2) paralleling εἶναι ἐπὶ τὸ αὐτό, and בהאספם ליחד (1QS V 7) and להוסיף ליחד (1QS VI 14) paralleling προστιθέναι ἐπὶ τὸ αὐτό[82]. Other scholars have been more reserved in their evaluation. J.A. Fitzmyer noted LXX parallels to the sense of "together" and other Greek parallels to a spatial sense "in one place", while C.K. Barrett reviewed varying ideas about ἐπὶ τὸ αὐτό, including "an ordinary Greek expression, very common in the LXX"[83]. It should be added that it appears difficult to maintain a purely linguistic identification of ἐπὶ τὸ αὐτό as a Semitism beyond its evaluation as a cultural expression for communal gathering in Jewish milieus, since there are also many general Greek parallels to ἐπὶ τὸ αὐτό. That is, this phrase recurs in documentary Greek of Oxyrhynchus papyri, where it may signify something like "grand total" or "all together"[84], as well as in literary Greek[85]. This is not to deny that there was a "living Hebrew tradition"[86] parallel to εἶναι ἐπὶ τὸ αὐτό in the specific setting of a community of goods, as illustrated in 1QS[87].

---

82. WILCOX, *The Semitisms of Acts* (n. 69), pp. 93-100, esp. 96-99, who also referred to 1QHᵃ. Cf. M. BLACK, *An Aramaic Approach to the Gospels and Acts*, Oxford, Clarendon, ³1967 (= BLACK, *AAGA*³), p. 10, n. 4; PAYNE, *Semitisms in the Book of Acts* (n. 75), pp. 142-144, esp. 144, on "Septuagintal parallels bearing a different connotation from the Acts usage", 149; D. MARGUERAT, *Les Actes des apôtres (1–12)* (CNT, deuxième série, 5a), Geneva, Labor et Fides, 2007, p. 59, n. 9.
83. FITZMYER, *The Acts of the Apostles* (n. 35), pp. 222, 238; BARRETT, *Acts 1–14* (n. 14), pp. 172-173.
84. Cf. P.Oxy. LVII 3904 (99 CE), l. 1 ἐπὶ τὸ α(ὐτὸ) ἄρο(υραι) γ; P.Oxy. LVII 3905 (99 CE), l. 27 ἐπ(ὶ) τ[ὸ][αὐ]τ(ὸ) (ἄρουραι) ζ; P.Oxy. LVII 3909 (99 CE), l. 5 ἐπὶ τὸ αὐτὸ ἀρο(ύρας) γ; P.Oxy. LXII 4336 (169-173 CE), l. 32 ἐ(πὶ τὸ αὐτὸ) (δραχμαὶ) ρπ; P.Oxy. LXVI 4526 (69-70 CE), l. 25 ἐπὶ τὸ αὐτὸ (δραχμαὶ) ψνβ; P.Oxy. LXXII 4857 (118 CE), ll. 10-11 ἐπὶ τὸ αὐτὸ (πυροῦ) (ἀρτάβαι) η; P.Oxy. LXXII 4869 (123 CE), ἐπὶ τὸ α(ὐτὸ) (ἀρτάβαι) ιη, "grand total 18 artabas" (HGV 114249 translation); P.Oxy. LXXII 4876 (135 CE), l. 12 ἐπὶ τὸ α(ὐτὸ) (ἀρτάβαι) ιε; P.Oxy. LXXII 4878 (135 CE), ll. 8-9 ἐπὶ τὸ α(ὐτὸ) πυρο(ῦ) ἀρτάβ(αι) εἴκοσι ἑπτά; P.Oxy. LXXII 4882 (153 CE), l. 9 ἐπ(ὶ τὸ αὐτὸ) (ἀρτάβαι) κζ; P.Oxy. LXXII 4884 (157 CE), ll. 8-9 ἐπὶ τὸ (αὐτὸ) ἀρτάβ(αι) ἑκατὸν τεσσαράκοντα ἕξ.
85. TLG search yields various classical Greek parallels for ἐπὶ τὸ αὐτό: Thucydides 1.792, 6.104.1; Plato, *Respublica* 462c, 464d; Democritus, *Fragmenta* frg. 128, l. 6; Aristotle, *De caelo* 271a, *Eth. nic.* 1125b, *Hist. an.* 617a, 706a, ll. 28, 32, 707a, *Mem. rem.* 453a, *Phys.* 199b, 262a; Theophrastus, *Characters* 7.2.
86. PAYNE, *Semitisms in the Book of Acts* (n. 75), p. 143.
87. For a broader cultural comparison between Lukan and Qumran perspectives, cf. A. HOGETERP, *Immaterial Wealth in Luke between Wisdom and Apocalypticism: Luke's Jesus Tradition in Light of 4QInstruction*, in *Early Christianity* 4 (2013) 41-63.

c) γνωστὸν ἔστω with dative in Acts 2,14; 4,10; 13,38; 28,28

M. Wilcox identified constructions with γνωστόν, in particular γνωστὸν ἔστω τινι ὅτι in the speeches of Acts, as Semitic idiom, in view of parallels in biblical Aramaic יְדִיעַ לֶהֱוֵא ל (Ezra 4,12.13; 5,8; Dan 3,18) as well as a second century CE Hebrew letter, שידע יהי לך ש[88]. C.K. Barrett affirmed this interpretation of M. Wilcox[89], but other commentators have emphasized a biblical style, thereby referring to LXX Greek parallels[90]. It should be added that TLG search yields only one literary Greek parallel outside Jewish and Christian literature before 300 CE: Aeneas Tact., *Poliorcetica* (4th c. BCE) 27.4, l. 3: τοῦτο δ' ἔστω γνωστὸν ὅτι. Yet it is definitely not a stock phrase in ancient Greek oratory, where it does not occur. In ancient literary Greek, ἴστε[91], εὖ ἴστε[92] or ἴστε δή[93] would be more common expressions to convey the sense of "be well assured/ know then/know for certain (that)"[94]. On the other hand, γνωστὸν ὑμῖν ἔστω ὅτι further occurs in *Greek Enoch* 98,12, while 4Q550 (*4QJews at the Persian Court ar*), frg. 1, line 7: ידיע להוא לכון די, constitutes an Aramaic parallel[95].

In sum, the identification of γνωστὸν ἔστω as Semitic idiom depends on stylistic grounds. Even though parallels from LXX Greek affirm the impression of a biblical style, these stem from a biblical Aramaic background. Therefore, γνωστὸν ἔστω cannot be called a Septuagintal Hebraism, but early Jewish and LXX Greek mainly deriving from an Aramaic background.

---

88. WILCOX, *The Semitisms of Acts* (n. 69), pp. 90-91, esp. 91, n. 1, with reference to DJD 2 (1961), pp. 155ff.
89. BARRETT, *Acts 1–14* (n. 14), p. 134.
90. FITZMYER, *The Acts of the Apostles* (n. 35), p. 251, rejected an "Aramaism" in view of LXX parallels (Dan 3,18; 1 Esd 2,18; 6,8; 2 Esd 4,12-13; 5,8) and a Hebrew background in LXX Ez 36,32, γνωστὸν ἔσται; MARGUERAT, *Les Actes des apôtres (1–12)* (n. 82), p. 87 and n. 15.
91. Demosthenes, *De Chersoneso* §11; Appian, *Civil Wars* 1.11.101.
92. Antiphon, *De caede Herodis* §§73, 93; Xenophon, *Hellenica* 3.5.11, 5.1.14, 5.1.16, 5.1.17, 6.1.15, 6.4.24, 6.5.44, 7.1.44, ll. 8, 12, 7.3.7, 7.4.40; *Anabasis* 1.7.3, 6.1.29, 6.1.32; *Cyropaedia* 2.2.27, 2.3.3, 3.3.44, 4.2.37, 7.1.22, 8.5.24; Dionysius of Halicarnassus, *Ant. rom.* 5.10.7; Josephus, *J.W.* 1.379; Plutarch, *Brutus* 50.8; Cassius Dio, *Hist. rom.* 14.57.5, 50.30.2.
93. Dionysius of Halicarnassus, *Ant. rom.* 3.29.5, 4.77.2, 10.10.3.
94. In a classical Greek register, this sense would further be conveyed by ἐπίστασθε (Herodotus 8.144), by εὖ ἐπίστασθε (Xenophon, *Hellenica* 3.5.15, 4.2.3; *Anabasis* 3.1.36; Aeschines, *In Timarchum* 192) or by εὖ ἐπίστω (Sophocles, *Electra* 616; *Oedipus Tyrannus* 658; *Philoctetes* 1239; Xenophon, *Hellenica* 5.4.35).
95. É. PUECH, *Qumrân grotte 4. XXVII: Textes araméens. Deuxième partie: 4Q550– 4Q575a, 4Q580–4Q587 et appendices* (DJD, 37), Oxford, Clarendon, 2009, p. 12.

3. Select Examples of Other Semitic Elements in Acts

a) The Impersonal Plural in Acts 3,2; 19,19b

M. Wilcox identified the impersonal use of third person plural active verbs to denote a passive voice as a Semitism in Acts 3,2 (ἐτίθουν) and 19,19b (συνεψήφισαν, εὗρον), thereby referring to longstanding scholarship on this subject[96]. This identification of a Semitism is further affirmed by C.K. Barrett[97]. We can be brief about this identification of a Semitism, since we already affirmed it as such after extensive discussion in *Semitisms in Luke's Greek*[98].

b) The Proleptic Pronoun

The use of αὐτός as a proleptic pronoun before a noun was identified as an Aramaism by M. Wilcox, with reference to ἐν αὐταῖς δὲ ταῖς ἡμέραις in Acts 11,27 (B) and to (ἐν) αὐτῇ τῇ ὥρᾳ in Lukan Greek[99]. However, in our study on Semitisms in Luke's Greek, we noted many general Greek parallels to ἐν αὐτῇ τῇ ἡμέρᾳ, which renders this identification of a Semitism difficult to maintain, since this would amount to special pleading[100].

c) ῥήματα λαλεῖν εἰς (κατά) in Acts 6,11(.13)

Denoting an adversative sense of "speaking words against", this Greek phrase has been interpreted as a Semitism, "probably Aramaic in origin", by M. Black, which was corroborated by M. Wilcox[101]. In our discussion of Semitisms in Luke's Greek, we added Semitic, in particular Aramaic evidence behind the idiomatic expression, εἰπεῖν λόγον εἰς + acc. (Lk 12,10a) / λαλεῖν ῥήματα βλάσφημα εἰς + acc. (Acts 6,11)[102]. The more common Greek use of the preposition κατά to denote an adversative sense is exemplified by λαλῶν ῥήματα κατά in Acts 6,13.

---

96. WILCOX, *The Semitisms of Acts* (n. 69), pp. 127-128, referring to Wellhausen, Moulton – Howard, and M. Black. See also the translation of a passive voice in Acts 19,19b by FITZMYER, *The Acts of the Apostles* (n. 35), p. 651.

97. BARRETT, *Acts 1–14* (n. 14), p. 179.

98. HOGETERP – DENAUX, *Semitisms in Luke's Greek* (n. 6), pp. 430-433.

99. WILCOX, *The Semitisms of Acts* (n. 69), pp. 128-130, referred to Wellhausen and retrojected ἐν αὐταῖς δὲ ταῖς ἡμέραις to Aramaic בהון (ב)יומיא on p. 130, n. 2.

100. HOGETERP – DENAUX, *Semitisms in Luke's Greek* (n. 6), pp. 459-462; see p. 460.

101. BLACK, *AAGA*³ (n. 82), p. 195; WILCOX, *The Semitisms of Acts* (n. 69), p. 134. Wilcox (pp. 135-136) adds the more problematic discussion of ἀντιλέγειν, which he situates eventually between Koine and LXX Greek.

102. HOGETERP – DENAUX, *Semitisms in Luke's Greek* (n. 6), pp. 176-179; cf. Dan 7,25; CD-A V 12-13, ותועבה הם מדברים בם; 4Q541 9 i 5, שגיאן מלין עלוהי יאמרון; and 4Q550 7+7a 2, כול אנש די ימר מלה[בא]ישה על.

IV. A Preliminary Survey of Semitisms in Acts

Having set the stage with a brief retrospect on Semitisms in Acts since the study by M. Wilcox, it is time to outline a preliminary survey of the types of Semitisms[103], which we also categorized in our study on Semitisms in Luke's Greek: Septuagintal Hebraisms; Hebraistic language from biblical tradition; Aramaisms; Semitisms of mixed background.

1. *Septuagintal Hebraisms*

Septuagintal vocabulary includes the noun σάββατον, "sabbath"[104]; the temporal expressions ἡμέραι with proper name (Acts 7,45) and ἐν ταῖς ἡμέραις ἐκείναις, "in those days" (Acts 2,18; 7,41; 9,37), analogously with biblical Hebrew בַּיָּמִים הָהֵם; καὶ ἰδού, "and behold", analogously with biblical Hebrew וְהִנֵּה[105]; and *figurae etymologicae*, i.e., verbs combined with their nominal equivalents[106].

Septuagintal Hebraisms of syntax include prepositions, verbal syntax, and Hebraistic word order. Prepositions include ἐνώπιον, parallel to biblical Hebrew לִפְנֵי, in theocentric contexts (Acts 2,25 [LXX Ps 15,8]; Acts 4,19; 7,46; 10,31.33; 27,35) and in combination with the verbs παριστάναι (Acts 4,10) and ἱστάναι (Acts 6,6; 10,30)[107]; and πρὸ προσώπου (לִפְנֵי) in a temporal sense (Acts 13,24)[108]. Significant examples of Septuagintal influence on verbal syntax are (a) the inchoative use of participles before finite main verbs, such as ἀναστάς[109] and

---

103. It is beyond the scope of this paper to aim at a definitive assessment of Semitisms in Acts, for that would merit a book-length treatment. Our preliminary survey is mainly based on Hogeterp – Denaux, *Semitisms in Luke's Greek* (n. 6). In-depth study of the periphrastic imperfect in Acts is deferred to another occasion; cf. Wilcox, *The Semitisms of Acts* (n. 69), pp. 123-124; see p. 124: "little real weight can be put upon the evidence".
104. Acts 1,12; 13,14.27.42.44; 15,21; 16,13; 17,2; 18,4. Hogeterp – Denaux, *Semitisms in Luke's Greek* (n. 6), pp. 83-89, esp. p. 83.
105. Acts 1,10; 5,28; 8,27; 10,30; 11,11; 12,7; 16,1; 27,24. Hogeterp – Denaux, *Semitisms in Luke's Greek* (n. 6), pp. 203-212.
106. Acts 2,17 (LXX Jl 3,1); Acts 5,28; 13,41 (LXX Hab 1,5); Acts 19,4; 23,14. Hogeterp – Denaux, *Semitisms in Luke's Greek* (n. 6), pp. 191-198, esp. 191.
107. Cf. Hogeterp – Denaux, *Semitisms in Luke's Greek* (n. 6), pp. 230-243, esp. 239-242. Cf. Acts 6,5; 9,15; 19,9.19.
108. Cf. Hogeterp – Denaux, *Semitisms in Luke's Greek* (n. 6), pp. 252-254. As compared with Lk 7,27, 9,52, and 10,1, where πρὸ προσώπου denotes "before, ahead of", it has a purely temporal sense of "before, prior to" in Acts 13,24. The temporal sense of πρὸ προσώπου has been connected with LXX Mal 3,1 by Fitzmyer, *The Acts of the Apostles* (n. 35), p. 513. See also BDR, ¹⁷1990, §217 ("Hebraisierende Umschreibungen präpositionaler Begriffe").
109. Acts 5,6; 8,27; 9,11.39; 10,20.23; 14,20; 22,10. Hogeterp – Denaux, *Semitisms in Luke's Greek* (n. 6), pp. 377-381, with a biblical Hebrew background in the use of the verb קוּם.

ἀποκριθείς[110]; (b) uses of the articular infinitive in sub-clauses, such as temporal ἐν τῷ + infinitive[111] and the consecutive or telic use of τοῦ + infinitive[112]; (c) the adverbial use of an indicative form of προστιθέναι with the infinitive (Acts 12,3)[113]; (d) sentence constructions with ἐγένετο δέ, usually asyndetically followed by an infinitive, except for the syndetic construction with a finite verb in Acts 5,7[114]; (e) lack of the copula εἰμί in verbless clauses following (καὶ) ἰδού[115]. The Hebraistic word order of an unmarked verb-subject sequence recurs many times in the Greek of Acts[116], of which 20 directly relate to intertextuality with the Septuagint in the form of citation or allusion[117].

2. Hebraistic Language from Biblical Tradition

Hebraistic vocabulary includes the use of ἄνθρωπος signifying τις (Acts 10,28)[118] and the adnominal genitive (τὰ πετεινὰ τοῦ οὐρανοῦ, Acts 10,12; 11,6)[119]. We already noted ἐκλέγεσθαι ἐν in Acts 15,7 (section III.2.a above). A further case in point concerns πιστεύειν εἰς with accusative (Acts 10,43; 14,23; 19,4), which was identified as a calque on biblical Hebrew, בְּ הֶאֱמִין[120], by J.H. Moulton –

---

110. Acts 4,19; 5,29; 8,24.34; 19,15; 25,9. HOGETERP – DENAUX, *Semitisms in Luke's Greek* (n. 6), pp. 381-388, with a biblical Hebrew background in the use of the verb ענה.
111. Acts 2,1; 3,26; 4,30; 8,6; 9,3; 11,15; 19,1. Cf. HOGETERP – DENAUX, *Semitisms in Luke's Greek* (n. 6), pp. 363-376.
112. Present inf.: Acts 3,2.12; 7,19; 13,47; 15,20; 20,3.30; 21,12; 27,1; aor. inf.: Acts 5,31; 9,15; 10,25; 18,10; 23,20; 26,18. Cf. HOGETERP – DENAUX, *Semitisms in Luke's Greek* (n. 6), pp. 344-362.
113. Cf. HOGETERP – DENAUX, *Semitisms in Luke's Greek* (n. 6), pp. 397-401.
114. Acts 4,5; 5,7; 9,32.37.43; 11,26; 14,1; 16,16; 19,1; 22,6.17-18; 28,8.17. Of these sentence constructions one is paratactic (+ καί + finite main verb: Acts 5,7), while the other 12 are followed by an infinitive as main verb. According to FITZMYER, *The Acts of the Apostles* (n. 35), p. 115, Acts 9,19 would constitute another example, but this is problematic, as his translation, "Saul stayed some days with the disciples in Damascus" (p. 16), also strongly suggests that ἐγένετο here means "stayed". Since there is no other verb to accompany μετὰ τῶν ἐν Δαμασκῷ μαθητῶν in Acts 9,19, ἐγένετο should be excluded as a sentence construction with ἐγένετο δέ.
115. Acts 5,9; 8,36; 9,10; 10,19; 13,11. Cf. HOGETERP – DENAUX, *Semitisms in Luke's Greek* (n. 6), pp. 415-430; see pp. 428-429.
116. Cf. WILCOX, *The Semitisms of Acts* (n. 69), pp. 112-114, acknowledged the influence of the LXX. For exact attestations totalling 346, distributed across Acts, 180 occurring in Acts 1–14, cf. HOGETERP – DENAUX, *Semitisms in Luke's Greek* (n. 6), pp. 450-451.
117. Acts 2,20c.26a.b.34b; 3,22.25c; 4,25b.26a; 7,6b.7a.18a.37b.49c; 8,33c; 13,33c.41c; 15,17a.b.c; 28,27a.
118. Cf. HOGETERP – DENAUX, *Semitisms in Luke's Greek* (n. 6), pp. 64-68.
119. Cf. *ibid.*, p. 201.
120. בְּ הֶאֱמִין occurs in MT Gen 15,6; Ex 14,31; 19,9; Num 14,11; 20,12; Dt 1,32; 28,66; 1 Sam 27,12; 2 Kgs 17,14; Jer 12,6; Jon 3,5; Mic 7,5; Ps 78,22.32; 106,12; 119,66; Prov 26,25; Job 4,18; 15,15.31; 24,22; 39,12; 2 Chr 20,20 (twice). לְ הֶאֱמִין occurs

W.F. Howard[121]. An alternative form is לְהַאֲמִין[122]. Yet LXX Greek most usually renders πιστεύειν with a dative, thereby conforming with Koine Greek target language. That is, TLG search yields no literary parallel for πιστεύειν εἰς in Graeco-Roman literature without reference to the synagogue before 300 CE, where πιστεύειν is usually followed by a dative, an infinitive or ὅτι. Examination of Greek papyri renders a similar result (usually πιστεύειν with a dative)[123].

3. Aramaisms

Vocabulary which derives from Aramaic idiom includes onomastics, such as toponyms, Ἀκελδαμάχ (Acts 1,19)[124], and proper names that incorporate the Aramaic word for "son" (בר), such as Βαρθολομαῖος (Acts 1,13)[125], Βαριησοῦς (Acts 13,6)[126], Βαρναβᾶς[127], and Βαρσα(β)βᾶς (Acts 1,23; 15,22)[128]. The word בר is the Aramaic counterpart of the Hebrew בן. Another proper name from an Aramaic origin is Ταβιθά (Acts 9,36.40)[129]. We already noted λαλεῖν ῥήματα βλάσφημα εἰς in an adversative sense (Acts 6,11; see section III.3.c above). The noun word group ὁ υἱὸς τοῦ ἀνθρώπου (Acts 7,56) derives from Jesus tradition, of which the wording and semantic usage, possibly as circumlocution, may be paralleled by בר נש(א) in Aramaic[130].

In syntactical respect, it is a far more complicated matter to discern any Aramaic influence. Yet the use of third person plural active verbs

---

in MT Gen 45,26; Ex 4,1; 4,8 (twice); 4,9; Dt 9,23; 1 Kgs 10,7; 2 Chr 9,6; 32,15; Ps 106,24; Prov 14,15; Is 43,10; 53,1; Jer 40,14.
121. J.H. MOULTON – W.F. HOWARD, *A Grammar of New Testament Greek*. Vol. 2: *Accidence and Word Formation*, Edinburgh, T&T Clark, 1919-1929, pp. 462-463.
122. MT Gen 45,26; Ex 4,1.8.9; Dt 9,23; 1 Kgs 10,7; Is 43,10; 53,1; Jer 40,14; Ps 106,24; Prov 14,15; 2 Chr 9,6; 32,15.
123. www.papyri.info yields few exceptions of πιστεύειν εἰς occurring in late antique Christian letters (P.Lond. VI 1929, l. 14; PSI III 238, l. 4; cf. BGU III 874, ll. 10-11, not securely dated, 323-642 CE).
124. Cf. WILCOX, *The Semitisms of Acts* (n. 69), pp. 87-89; BDAG, ³2000, p. 35, חֲקֵל דְּמָא.
125. BDAG, ³2000, p. 167, בַּר תַּלְמַי.
126. Cf. WILCOX, *The Semitisms of Acts* (n. 69), p. 89; BDAG, ³2000, p. 167, בַּר יֵשׁוּעַ.
127. Acts 4,36; 9,27; 11,22.30; 12,25; 13,1.2.7.43.46.50; 14,12.14.20; 15,2.12.22.25. 35.36.37.39. Cf. BARRETT, *Acts 1–14* (n. 14), pp. 258-259, on the etymology בר נבי with further bibliography; FITZMYER, *The Acts of the Apostles* (n. 35), pp. 320-321; BDAG, ³2000, p. 167: "ברנבו?"; MARGUERAT, *Les Actes des apôtres (1–12)* (n. 82), p. 171, "Du point de vue du sens, c'est toutefois le substrat araméen *bar-nebouah* ('fils de la prophétie') qui est le plus proche".
128. BDAG, ³2000, p. 167: "בַּר שַׁבָּא or בַּר סָאבָּא".
129. Cf. WILCOX, *The Semitisms of Acts* (n. 69), pp. 109-110, טביתא; BDAG, ³2000, p. 987, "טָבִיתָא, also טְבִיתָא".
130. Cf. HOGETERP – DENAUX, *Semitisms in Luke's Greek* (n. 6), pp. 122-137.

denoting a passive voice (Acts 3,2; 19,19) may reflect an Aramaic-speaking bilingual background (cf. section III.3.a above), or, in the words of H.F.D. Sparks, it may have been part of "the Semitic-Greek *patois*" of many of Luke's co-religionists (cf. section II.1.b above).

4. *Semitisms of Mixed Backgrounds*

Lexical Semitisms of mixed backgrounds include nouns, such as πάσχα (Acts 12,4), σάββατον denoting "week" (Acts 20,7), and σατανᾶς (Acts 5,3; 26,18)[131]; and noun word groups, such as υἱός as a noun of relationship, exemplified by υἱὲ διαβόλου (Acts 13,10), υἱὸς παρακλήσεως (Acts 4,36), and οἱ υἱοὶ τῶν προφητῶν καὶ τῆς διαθήκης (Acts 3,25)[132]. Another set of noun word groups is that of nouns qualified by a "Hebraic" genitive of quality[133]: ῥήματα βλασφημίας (Acts 6,11 א* D), φλογὶ πυρός (Acts 7,30), χολὴ πικρίας (Acts 8,23), σκεῦος ἐκλογῆς (Acts 9,15). The idiom γνωστὸν ἔστω with dative (Acts 2,14; 4,10; 13,38; 28,28) has already been noted (section III.2.c above).

Syntactical Semitisms of mixed backgrounds include the use of ἰδού as particle that indicates time (Acts 11,11)[134]; the complex preposition κατὰ πρόσωπον with genitive in Peter's speech (Acts 3,13)[135]; the resumptive pronoun following a relative pronoun (Acts 1,3; 12,4; 15,17)[136]; the ordinal use of the cardinal numeral εἷς in the phrase ἐν τῇ μιᾷ τῶν σαββάτων (Acts 20,7)[137]; and temporal parataxis in Acts 1,10, with a protasis in the clause with a periphrastic imperfect, καὶ ὡς ἀτενίζοντες ἦσαν (...) (Acts 1,10a), and an apodotic καί starting with καὶ ἰδού (Acts 1,10b)[138].

V. EVALUATION AND CONCLUSIONS

It remains to be seen how Semitisms are distributed along the compositional forms of Acts.

---

131. *Ibid.*, pp. 80-83, 83-89, 89-93.
132. For the Lukan οἱ υἱοὶ τῶν προφητῶν, cf. LXX 3 Kgdms 21,35; 4 Kgdms 2,3.5.7.15; 4,38 (twice); 5,22; 6,1; 9,1; Tob^AB 4,12; 4Q481a (4QapocrElisha) 2 4. For the Lukan οἱ υἱοὶ ... τῆς διαθήκης, cf. LXX Ez 30,5; Hebrew בני ברית in 4Q284 4 2, 4Q385b 4-5, 4Q501 2 and 7, 4Q503 7-9 3. Cf. HOGETERP – DENAUX, *Semitisms in Luke's Greek* (n. 6), pp. 112-113.
133. MOULTON – HOWARD, *Accidence* (n. 121), p. 440; BDR, ¹⁷1990, §165.
134. HOGETERP – DENAUX, *Semitisms in Luke's Greek* (n. 6), pp. 224-226.
135. *Ibid.*, pp. 247-252.
136. *Ibid.*, pp. 254-264.
137. *Ibid.*, pp. 293-295.
138. *Ibid.*, pp. 433-448, esp. 440-443.

The Acts of the Apostles consist of several compositional forms, such as narratives, i.e., the narrative framework of Acts; summaries[139]; the so-called "we" passages (Acts 16,10-17; 20,5–21,18; 27,1–28,16); and speeches, reportedly "almost a third of Acts"[140]. The "we" passages are a hybrid category to be sure, since they also contain speech materials (Acts 20,18-35; 27,21-26). Yet they are interesting in their own right, since they may be informative about the narrator as a narrative character[141].

In the narratives of Acts, Semitic idiom includes Aramaic proper names which M. Wilcox related to an Aramaic milieu, such as Βαριησοῦς, Βαρναβᾶς, and Ταβιθά (see section IV.3 above); nouns, such as πάσχα (Acts 12,4), σάββατον denoting sabbath[142], and σατανᾶς (Acts 5,3); πιστεύειν εἰς with accusative (Acts 14,23; 19,4); the stylistic use of καὶ ἰδού, "and behold"[143]; and *figurae etymologicae*[144]. Examples of Semitic syntax include the resumptive pronoun after the relative pronoun (Acts 1,3; 12,4), syndetic sentence construction with ἐγένετο δέ (Acts 5,7), the inchoative use of ἀναστάς[145], the use of a temporal subclause with ἐν τῷ + infinitive (Acts 2,1; 4,30), the periphrastic imperfect (ἀτενίζοντες ἦσαν (Acts 1,10), and a Hebraistic word order, that is, unmarked verb-subject order.

In the summaries of Acts, we further encounter syntactical Semitisms, such as the periphrastic imperfect ἦσαν προσκαρτεροῦντες (Acts 1,14; 2,42)[146] and a Hebraistic verb-subject order (Acts 2,43a; 4,33; 5,12b.13b. 16a; 6,7b).

In the speeches of Acts, Semitic idiom includes Aramaic onomastics, such as Ἀκελδαμάχ (Acts 1,19); Semitic nouns, such as σάββατον meaning sabbath (Acts 13,27; 15,21) and σατανᾶς (Acts 26,18); noun word groups, οἱ υἱοὶ τῶν προφητῶν καὶ τῆς διαθήκης (Acts 3,25); verbs with prepositions, such as ἐκλέγεσθαι ἐν (Acts 15,7) and πιστεύειν εἰς with

---

139. FITZMYER, *The Acts of the Apostles* (n. 35), p. 97, distinguishes "major summaries" in Acts 2,42-47; 4,32-35; 5,12-16 from "minor summaries" in Acts 1,14; 6,7; 9,31; 12,24; 16,5; 19,20; and 28,30-31.
140. *Ibid.*, p. 103. At p. 104, Fitzmyer distinguishes 28 speeches in Acts 1,4-5.7-8; 1,16-22; 2,14b-36.38.39; 3,12b-26; 4,8b-12.19b-20; 5,29b-32; 5,35b-39; 6,2b-4; 7,2-53; 10,34b-43; 11,5-17; 13,16b-41; 14,15-17; 15,7b-11; 15,13b-21; 17,22-31; 18,14b-15; 19,25b-27; 19,35b-40; 20,18b-35; 22,1.3-21; 24,2b-8; 24,10b-21; 25,8.10b-11; 25,14c-21.24-27; 26,2-23.25-27.29; 27,21-26; 28,17c-20.25b-28.
141. Cf. W.S. CAMPBELL, *The "We" Passages in the Acts of the Apostles: The Narrator as Narrative Character* (SBLStBL, 14), Atlanta, GA, Society of Biblical Literature, 2007.
142. Acts 1,12; 13,14.42.44; 17,2; 18,4.
143. Acts 1,10; 5,28; 8,27; 10,30.
144. Acts 4,17 E sy[hmg] (gig h mae); Acts 5,28; 23,14. Cf. MOULTON – HOWARD, *Accidence* (n. 121), p. 443.
145. Acts 5,6; 8,27; 9,11.39; 10,20.23; 14,20; 15,7a.
146. Cf. HOGETERP – DENAUX, *Semitisms in Luke's Greek* (n. 6), pp. 401-415, esp. 402.

acc. (Acts 10,43); and *figurae etymologicae*[147]. Examples of Semitic syntax include ἰδού as a particle that indicates time (Acts 11,11); the predicative use of the preposition εἰς in γίνεσθαι εἰς (Acts 5,36)[148]; the use of complex prepositions with πρόσωπον, such as ἀπὸ προσώπου (Acts 3,20; 7,45) and πρὸ προσώπου in a temporal sense (Acts 13,24)[149]; the resumptive pronoun in Acts 15,17; the inchoative use of ἀναστάς (Acts 22,10); the consecutive or telic use of τοῦ with infinitive (Acts 15,20); the temporal use of ἐν τῷ with infinitive (Acts 3,26); and a Hebraistic verb-subject order.

In the "we" passages of Acts (16,10-17; 20,5–21,18; 27,1–28,16), Semitic idiom includes the use of σάββατον to denote both "sabbath" (Acts 16,13) and "week" (Acts 20,7). Examples of Semitic syntax include the ordinal use of the cardinal numeral in the phrase ἐν τῇ μιᾷ τῶν σαββάτων (Acts 20,7) and sentence construction with ἐγένετο δέ (Acts 16,16; 28,8.17).

Having broadly surveyed the presence of Semitisms among the compositional forms of Acts, it should be noted that their distribution is not as uneven as sometimes supposed with regard to a somewhat more Semitic character of the language of Acts 1–15 in contradistinction to that in the second half of Acts (cf. nn. 67-68 above). For instance, sentence constructions with ἐγένετο δέ are part of narratives (Acts 4,5; 5,7; 9,32.37.43; 11,26; 14,1; 19,1), "we" passages (Acts 16,16; 28,8.17), and speeches (Acts 22,6.17-18) alike.

Next to Semitic vocabulary and syntax, Jewish cultural expressions also recur in various compositional forms: in the narratives, σαββάτου ἔχον ὁδόν, a sabbath day's journey away (Acts 1,12), ἡ ἡμέρα τῆς πεντηκοστῆς (Acts 2,1), ἡμέραι τῶν ἀζύμων (Acts 12,3); in the speeches, "Moses ... is read" (Acts 15,21; cf. 2 Cor 3,15); and in the "we" passages, προσευχή (Acts 16,13.16), σεβομένη τὸν θεόν (Acts 16,14), τὰς ἡμέρας τῶν ἀζύμων (Acts 20,6).

---

147. ὁράσεις ὁρᾶν (Acts 2,17); ἐνυπνίοις ἐνυπνιάζεσθαι (Acts 2,17) (cit. LXX); ὅρκῳ ὤμοσεν (Acts 2,30). Cf. MOULTON – HOWARD, *Accidence* (n. 121), p. 443.
148. MOULTON – HOWARD, *Accidence* (n. 121), pp. 462-463; BDR, [17]1990, §157.5; BARRETT, *Acts 1–14* (n. 14), p. 294. The use of the Greek preposition εἰς is thereby compared with that of ל.
149. Cf. HOGETERP – DENAUX, *Semitisms in Luke's Greek* (n. 6), pp. 252-254. As compared with Lk 7,27, 9,52, and 10,1, where πρὸ προσώπου denotes "before, ahead of", it has a purely temporal sense of "before, prior to" in Acts 13,24. The temporal sense of πρὸ προσώπου has been connected with LXX Mal 3,1 by FITZMYER, *The Acts of the Apostles* (n. 35), p. 513. See also BDR, [17]1990, §217 ("Hebraisierende Umschreibungen präpositionaler Begriffe").

Finally, we may highlight some implications of the foregoing examination concerning the author of Luke-Acts in a bilingual context. First, some observations are in place regarding the conceptual orbit of bilingualism in Acts. Certain Semitisms, such as the onomastics, inform us about local colours of the Semitic, viz. Aramaic milieus of those who carried the gospel traditions forward. Other Semitisms may be assigned to thematic clusters, such as the language of Jewish tradition with its religious calendar, or the language of faith (e.g., ἐκλέγεσθαι ἐν, πιστεύειν εἰς, σκεῦος ἐκλογῆς). Second, the study of Semitisms in Acts as taken up by M. Wilcox is less outdated in certain respects than it would appear to some (see section III.1 above). The composite character of the Semitisms, which we categorized into various types (section IV above), still leaves room for certain Aramaic influences[150]. Third, the receptive bilingual competence of the author of Luke-Acts suggests that the literary position of this work may also be situated "in a cross-cultural context between the worlds of pagan Hellenism, Jewish Hellenism and Judaism"[151].

Engelendalelaan 89   Adelbert DENAUX
BE-8310 Brugge
Belgium
adelbert.denaux@theo.kuleuven.be
Faculty of Theology and Religious Studies
KU Leuven
Dean em. Tilburg School of Catholic Theology

Stationsdwarsstraat 9   Albert HOGETERP
NL-6662 AZ Elst
The Netherlands
ahogeterp@hotmail.com
Bloemfontein
South Africa
Department of Old and New Testament Studies
University of the Free State

---

150. *Contra* FITZMYER, *The Acts of the Apostles* (n. 35), p. 116.
151. HOGETERP – DENAUX, *Semitisms in Luke's Greek* (n. 6), p. 515.

ALLUSIONS TO EDUCATION IN LUKE-ACTS

SIDELIGHTS ON IMPLICIT CONCEPTIONS OF *PAIDEIA*

I. INTRODUCTION

The Greek lexeme παιδεία means "education" or "schooling" and derives from the verb παιδεύω, which contains the root word παῖς[1]. The verb παιδεύω means literally "to be together with a child" or "to be concerned with a child intensively or professionally"[2]. The substantive παιδεία is found for the first time in the works of the tragedian Aeschylus, but there it still has the same meaning as τροφή, which means simply the rearing of children, but thereby also has a rather "physical" character[3]. Subsequently, since the time of the first Sophists[4] at the latest in the fifth century BC, παιδεία was understood on the one hand as the process of intellectual and ethical schooling and education[5] and, on the other, as the result of the educational process in the sense of training, formal schooling, or insight[6]. Thus, one can understand the Sophists in a certain sense as

---

1. Dedicated to Jos Verheyden, a role model of education and intellect, in gratitude; cf. U. POPLUTZ, *Bildungs-Allusionen im lukanischen Doppelwerk: Streiflichter impliziter* paideia-*Konzepte*, in *JBTh* 35 (2020) 135-152.
2. The verbal ending -ευω contained in παιδεύω is a description of a state, cf. D. FÜRST – S. WIBBING, παιδεύω κτλ., in L. COENEN – K. HAACKER (eds.), *Theologisches Begriffslexikon zum Neuen Testament*, vol. 1, Wuppertal – Neukirchen, Neukirchener Verlag, 1997, 409-412, p. 409. On the numerous meanings and attestation of the derivatives, LSJ, 1286-1289.
3. Aesch., *Sept.* 18. On the concept of education in the Greco-Roman context, see also B. ORTH, *Lehrkunst im frühen Christentum: Die Bildungsdimension didaktischer Prinzipien in der hellenistisch-römischen Literatur und im lukanischen Doppelwerk* (Beiträge zur Erziehungswissenschaft und biblischen Bildung, 7), Frankfurt a.M., Lang, 2002, pp. 75-78. The volume by J. CHRISTES – R. KLEIN – C. LÜTH (eds.), *Handbuch der Erziehung und Bildung in der Antike*, Darmstadt, Wissenschaftliche Buchgesellschaft, 2006, is also comprehensive and very informative.
4. The Sophist program consisted primarily of techniques of argumentation and the education in rhetorical expression, and served the formation of the individual. In a certain sense, one can characterize this as an early form of "Aufklärungspädagogik", as R. KOERRENZ, *Pädagogik, II. Geschichte*, in *RGG⁴* 6 (2003) 776-781, p. 777, suggests. The Sophists certainly were the first to consider *all* human beings, irrespective of their social background, as capable of education and schooling. There was, however, one restriction: they demanded an honorarium for their services.
5. The word παίδευσις has the same meaning, cf., e.g., Aristoph., *Nub.* 961; Thuc. 2.39.1.
6. Cf., e.g., Democr. 180; Plat., *Prot.* 327d; *Gorg.* 470e; *Resp.* 378e; Aristot., *Pol.* 1338a30; cf. G. BERTRAM, παιδεύω κτλ., in *TWNT* 5 (1954) 596-624, pp. 596-597; FÜRST –

the "first pedagogical movement"[7]. They distinguished three factors as important when considering the process of instruction: aptitude, educational content and drill[8]. As far as content was concerned, the Sophists, to be sure, drew on traditional elementary education in gymnastics, music, reading, writing and arithmetic, but to this traditional curriculum they added grammar, rhetoric, dialectics, geometry, astronomy and harmony[9]. The educational system was further developed by, among others, Isocrates (436-338 BC), who aspired to the ideal of a selfless intellectual education of a rhetorical-humanist character in which good thinking was intended to go hand in hand with expressing oneself well and with good behavior[10]; this type of education was intended to be transferrable to all professions and situations of life and was understood as political education[11]. Plato (428-347 BC), on the other hand, distanced himself from the prevailing rhetoric that Isocrates advocated because it was not linked with any ethics. With the Πολιτεία he then presented his main pedagogical work. On the development of the ancient *paideia* concept as a whole, one may say:

> dass die *paideia* spätestens seit Platon wie eine Ellipse zwei Brennpunkte in sich beschließt: einerseits den Bereich der Erziehung im engeren Sinn mit dem Erwerb von Wissen, Können und Haltung, andererseits die Formung des Erwachsenen, die den Gebildeten als einen Menschen ausweist, der Probleme als solche zu erkennen und Behauptungen adäquat zu beurteilen vermag[12].

WIBBING, παιδεύω κτλ. (n. 2), p. 409; J. CHRISTES, *Bildung*, in *DNP* 2 (1996) 663-673, p. 663. On the history of education, H.-I. MARROU, *Geschichte der Erziehung im klassischen Altertum*, ed. R. HARDER, Freiburg i.Br., Herder, 1957, is still worth reading. The most recent analysis is offered by C. AUFFARTH, *Henri-Irénée Marrous* Geschichte der Erziehung im klassischen Altertum: *Der Klassiker kontrastiert mit Werner Jaegers* Paideia, in P. GEMEINHARDT (ed.), *Was ist Bildung in der Vormoderne?* (Seraphim, 4), Tübingen, Mohr Siebeck, 2019, 39-66.

7. M.A. RITTER, *Pädagogik*, in *Lexikon der Alten Welt* (1965) 2188-2192, p. 2189.
8. Cf. C. LÜTH, *Einführung: Griechenland*, in CHRISTES et al. (eds.), *Handbuch* (n. 3), p. 12.
9. *Ibid.*, p. 15.
10. Cf. *ibid.*, p. 12.
11. See on this W. STEIDLE, *Redekunst und Bildung bei Isokrates*, in H.-T. JOHANN (ed.), *Erziehung und Bildung in der heidnischen und christlichen Antike* (Wege der Forschung, 377), Darmstadt, Wissenschaftliche Buchgesellschaft, 1976, 170-226.
12. S. VOLLENWEIDER, *Bildungsfreunde oder Bildungsverächter? Überlegungen zum Stellenwert der Bildung im frühen Christentum*, in GEMEINHARDT (ed.), *Was ist Bildung in der Vormoderne?* (n. 6), 283-304, p. 287 ("that the *paideia* since Plato at the latest comprises an ellipse with two foci within it: on the one hand the area of education in the narrower sense with the acquisition of knowledge, ability and attitude, and on the other the formation of the adult person that identifies the person so educated as a human being who is able to recognize problems as such and to judge assertions adequately").

In this view, *paideia* is to be understood as a kind of "shaping of the entire human existence"[13] and is not to be restricted only to a school education.

In the New Testament, the word group associated with the lexeme *paideia* appears twenty-four times in all[14]. Strikingly, Luke is the only evangelist who makes use of these "educational terms" (Lk 23,16.22; Acts 7,22; 22,3). To be sure, the instances where they occur do not allow us to determine immediately the Lukan educational concept standing behind them, but they can nevertheless be a starting point and a legitimate reason for pursuing a specific Lukan claim for education underlying the passages at issue. For, while Jesus and his disciples in all probability had a rather distant relationship to higher education[15], and their teaching corresponded to the simplicity and rustic nature of the imagery they used (as, for example, in their parables and figurative language)[16], the synoptic evangelists each in their own way altered and modified this form of

13. Cf. P. GEMEINHARDT, *Wege und Umwege zum Selbst: Bildung und Religion im frühen Christentum*, in J. RÜPKE – G.D. WOOLF (eds.), *Religious Dimensions of the Self in the Second Century CE* (STAC, 76), Tübingen, Mohr Siebeck, 2013, 259-277, p. 260 (*verbatim*: "Formgebung der ganzen menschlichen Existenz").

14. The substantive παιδεία is found in Eph 6,4; 2 Tim 3,16 as well as in Heb 12,5.7.8.11; forms of παιδεύω are found in Lk 23,16.22 (beat, discipline); Acts 7,22; 22,3 (instruct, educate); cf. also 1 Cor 11,32; 2 Cor 6,9; 1 Tim 1,20; 2 Tim 2,25; Tit 2,12; Heb 12,6.7.10; Rev 3,19; παιδευτής in Rom 2,20 and Heb 12,9; παιδαγωγός in Gal 3,24.25; 1 Cor 4,15.

15. R. RIESNER, *Jesus als Lehrer: Eine Untersuchung zum Ursprung der Evangelien-Überlieferung* (WUNT, 2.7), Tübingen, Mohr Siebeck, ³1988, assesses the educational level of Jesus more optimistically; this is due to his basic thesis that the teaching of Jesus has been transmitted quite reliably in the oral process from the historical Jesus up to the Synoptic Gospels.

16. CHRISTES, *Bildung* (n. 6), p. 671: "Jesus und seine Jünger standen der ant[iken Bildung] fern. Die 'Fischersprache' der Bibel und *rusticitas* und *simplicitas* der Christen – überwiegend einfacher Leute – blieben lange geschmäht. Erst im Verlauf des 2. Jh. traten vermehrt Personen mit höherer B[ildung] dem Christentum bei. Die Aufwertungsversuche der frühesten Apologeten vermochten niemanden zu beeindrucken". Recently, however, several scholars have argued that the first Christian generations were of a reasonably educated level. The strongest advocate of this view is probably Thomas Söding, who labels Christianity as a "religion of education" and, consequently, has to interpret the fact that pagan authors held the earliest followers of Jesus, women and men, in contempt because of their lack of education as pure polemic; cf. T. SÖDING, *Das Christentum als Bildungsreligion: Der Impuls des Neuen Testaments*, Freiburg i.Br., Herder, 2016. U. SCHNELLE, *Das frühe Christentum und die Bildung*, in *NTS* 61 (2015) 113-143, is equally optimistic. This view has been criticized by VOLLENWEIDER, *Bildungsfreunde* (n. 12), p. 285: "Die heutigen Anwälte eines bildungsfreundlichen Urchristentums arbeiten mit einem sehr großzügig entworfenen Bildungsverständnis. Was immer in den frühchristlichen Schriften an Lehren und Lernen, an Textproduktion und Textrezeption in Erscheinung tritt, wird unter diesem Label verhandelt. Das ist natürlich möglich. Aber die Kehrseite dieser Sprachregelung besteht darin, dass die Kategorie selber nicht mehr wirklich griffig ist". On Jesus' level of education, see also C. HEIL, *Analphabet oder Rabbi? Zum Bildungsniveau Jesu*, in ID.

teaching in the last decades of the first century AD in order to make it comprehensible and attractive for their congregations or for a wider "Christian" readership. As a matter of course, in doing so they used the existing genres of the Hellenistic-Roman culture as a medium. Luke's self-understanding stands out especially in this context[17]: as a scripturally- and historically-educated Christian author writing for an audience that is obviously educated to a certain degree and has a certain measure of wealth[18], he has an interest in presenting faith in Christ as attractive also for groups of people in the Roman Empire who belong to higher intellectual and social circles. In the first two centuries, Christian women and men did not develop their own school system, nor a genuine program of education[19]; they rather formed a sub-culture under the umbrella of the Hellenistic-Roman majority culture and were influenced by the prevailing educational system, especially in the urban milieu[20]. However, as early as the middle of the second century Christianity was no longer a religion of just lower-class uncultured people, at least in certain places[21].

(ed.), *Das Spruchevangelium Q und der historische Jesus* (SBAB, 58), Stuttgart, Katholisches Bibelwerk, 2014, 265-291.

17. Cf. K. BACKHAUS, *Die Apostelgeschichte: Anspruch und Aktualität: Eine Hinführung*, in ID., *Die Entgrenzung des Heils: Gesammelte Studien zur Apostelgeschichte* (WUNT, 422), Tübingen, Mohr Siebeck, 2019, 1-19, p. 9: "Lukas ist bereits als Christ von der paganen Mehrheitskultur so geprägt, dass er sie – kritisch und selbstbewusst – nicht als Fremdes wahrnimmt: Er ist Zeitgenosse, weil ihm nichts anderes übrigbleibt, aber er ist im Neuen Testament der wachste Zeitgenosse".

18. Cf. VOLLENWEIDER, *Bildungsfreunde* (n. 12), p. 291.

19. This is connected, of course, with the fact that the acute imminent eschatological expectation, which influenced the first Christian women and men, rendered any kind of educational program as theoretically and practically obsolete.

20. On this, VOLLENWEIDER, *Bildungsfreunde* (n. 12), p. 289: "Es ist hinlänglich bekannt, wie ungemein stark die Gravitationskraft der hellenistisch-römischen Bildung die Menschen der damaligen globalisierten Mittelmeerwelt, insbesondere ihre urbanen Eliten, bestimmt hat. Wir können im Frühchristentum des ersten und zweiten Jahrhunderts eine ganze Palette von Bildungsphänomenen beobachten, von denen sich einige gelegentlich und indirekt auf das Bildungssystem der Mehrheitskultur beziehen […]".

21. Cf. GEMEINHARDT, *Wege* (n. 13), p. 261, with reference to Just., *2 Apol.* 10.8, who speaks of the fact that, along with artisans (χειροτέχναι) and ordinary people (παντελῶς ἰδιῶται), philosophers (φιλόσοφοι) and literarily educated people (φιλόλογοι) also belonged to the Christian congregation. For this reason, it may be assumed that the proportion of the elite in early Christian communities corresponded approximately to that in the rest of society. On this ambiguity, A. MERKT, *"Eine Religion von törichten Weibern und ungebildeten Handwerkern": Ideologie und Realität eines Klischees zum frühen Christentum*, in F.R. PROSTMEIER (ed.), *Frühchristentum und Kultur* (Kommentar zu frühchristlichen Apologeten, Erg.-Bd. 2), Freiburg i.Br., Herder, 2007, 293-309, p. 303: "Ja, das frühe Christentum war eine Religion der Unterschichten – aber eben nicht nur. Und ebenso sehr stimmt: das frühe Christentum war eine Religion der Mittel- und Oberschichten – aber eben nicht nur. Die dürftige Quellenlage erlaubt es uns nicht, die genauen Anteile der einzelnen Stände in den christlichen Gemeinden zu bestimmen".

With his two-volume work, Luke represents a special landmark on this path. The way he, as a Christian writer and historian, takes up certain educational concepts and educational discourses and sublimely integrates them into his theological design is illuminated in the following by considering selected passages in his gospel and Acts.

II. Competence: Jesus *Didaskalos*

In the Gospel of Luke, Jesus is frequently referred to as a διδάσκαλος (teacher)[22], but also as an ἐπιστάτης (overseer, master)[23], while the Greek transliterations of the Hebrew ῥαββί (my master) and ῥαββουνί (my master) do not occur in Luke[24].

Already in the infancy narrative, Jesus is presented as teaching. The special intelligence and talent of the twelve-year-old emerge[25] when, in the temple in Jerusalem, he discusses with the scribes in such a way that they "are beside themselves" with amazement and ecstasy (Lk 2,41-51a; v. 47: ἐξίστημι) – a reaction with which the people in the course of the narrative also respond to Jesus' miracles[26]. Jesus is depicted here as on a par with the διδάσκαλοι, since he engages them not only as one who questions them and learns from them (Lk 2,46), but also as one who

---

22. Lk 7,40; 8,49; 9,38; 10,25; 11,45; 12,13; 18,18; 19,39; 20,21.28.39; 21,7; 22,11; John the Baptist (3,12) and the scribes (2,46) also are designated as διδάσκαλοι.

23. Lk 5,5; 8,24.45; 9,33.49; 17,13; this designation of Jesus is found in the New Testament exclusively in Luke; Luke in 8,24 and 9,49 replaces διδάσκαλε from the Gospel of Mark with ἐπιστάτα.

24. On the statistical data in detail, see V. TROPPER, *Jesus Didáskalos: Studien zu Jesus als Lehrer bei den Synoptikern und im Rahmen der antiken Kultur- und Sozialgeschichte* (ÖBS, 42), Frankfurt a.M., Peter Lang, 2012, pp. 17-35. Luke, in general, foregoes using Hebrew-Aramaic terms, either because his readership was no longer familiar with them, or to raise the level of his style.

25. On the other hand, J.R. BACKES, *Die Nazoräerschule: Bildung und Identität bei Lukas*, in ID. – E. BRÜNENBERG-BUSSWOLDER – P. VAN DEN HEEDE (eds.), *Orientierung an der Schrift: Kirche, Ethik und Bildung im Diskurs* (BTSt, 170), Göttingen, Vandenhoeck & Ruprecht, 2017, 173-188, pp. 174-175, is wrong in my opinion when he says: "Jesus ist als Schüler bereits Lehrer, wenn er als Zwölfjähriger im Tempel zu Jerusalem den Schriftexperten zuhört, sie befragt und zum allgemeinen Erstaunen ihre Fragen beantworten kann". It is nowhere said here that Jesus instructs his listeners; Luke rather emphasizes his particular intelligence and talent. See B. VAN IERSEL, *The Finding of Jesus in the Temple: Some Observations on the Original Form of Luke ii 41-51a*, in *NT* 4 (1960) 161-173, p. 166: "In Luke ii 47 Jesus does not act as διδάσκαλος, but on the contrary as a disciple, who 'sits, listens and asks questions'"; R.E. BROWN, *The Birth of the Messiah: A Commentary on the Infancy Narratives in Matthew and Luke*, London, Geoffrey Chapman, 1977, p. 474.

26. Cf. Lk 5,26; 8,56; see also the reaction in Acts 2,7.12; 3,10; 8,9.11.13; 10,10.45f.; 12,16.

understands them and gives them answers (Lk 2,47)[27]. The fact that the scribes in this passage are explicitly designated with the title διδάσκαλοι, which elsewhere in the Gospel of Luke is reserved almost exclusively for Jesus[28], conveys a sublime message: in spite of his youth – a narrative setting unique for the gospels – Jesus is not the classic type of student who follows certain teachers and must go through an apprenticeship in order to become a teacher himself; rather he is "blessed" from the very beginning with a special wisdom (σοφία) (cf. Lk 2,40.52) to which the scribes in the temple, who are anything but credulous, independently bear witness. Without a personal connection to the student Jesus, the διδάσκαλοι who, on the basis of their profession, certainly can be considered to be the most reliable "consultants", show their enthusiasm for his early display of understanding together with "all those who heard him"[29]. Thus, Jesus' outstanding talent is quasi-officially confirmed.

The circumstances in which this scene takes place is probably also typical for contemporary teaching situations: the temple area which Luke has in mind here is probably the colonnaded hall (στοά) of Solomon, in which the school of the apostles is later situated[30]. At the same time, however, the account deviates from every known standard: while normally *one* teacher gathers around himself several students who sit "at his feet" (cf. Acts 22,3), Jesus is found alone "in the midst" (Lk 2,46) of several teachers and demonstrates his wisdom to them in conversation[31].

---

27. Cf. N. KRÜCKEMEIER, *Der zwölfjährige Jesus im Tempel (Lk 2.40-52) und die biografische Literatur der hellenistischen Antike*, in *NTS* 50 (2004) 307-319, p. 313.

28. See note 22.

29. Along with σοφία, Jesus also has σύνεσις (*synesis, insight, power of judgement, understanding*), which in the Septuagint is frequently an insight nurtured by religious faith. Cf. F. BOVON, *Das Evangelium nach Lukas*. 1. Teilband: *Lk 1,1–9,50* (EKKNT, 3/1), Zürich, Benziger Verlag; Neukirchen-Vluyn, Neukirchener Verlag, 1989, pp. 157-158. According to Is 11,2 LXX, σοφία and σύνεσις are the first features of the promised Prince of Peace, who is the bearer of God's Spirit (Is 11,1-9), cf. TROPPER, *Jesus* (n. 24), p. 131.

30. See Acts 3,11; 5,12.21.25; also Lk 11,31. H.J. DE JONGE, *Sonship, Wisdom, Infancy: Luke II. 41-51a*, in *NTS* 24 (1978) 317-354, p. 329: "Colonnades were the most usual locale for secondary and higher education in the time of Luke. *Gymnasia* consisted, according to the architectural tradition of the period, simply of four colonnades around a square courtyard, and many philosophers besides the Stoics taught their pupils in colonnades which offered protection from the sun. Furthermore, a colonnade named after Solomon, who was famous for his wisdom (Luke xi. 31), must have been, for Luke, a peculiarly appropriate place for instruction". Cf. B. HEININGER, *Familienkonflikte: Der zwölfjährige Jesus im Tempel (Lk 2,41-52)*, in C.G. MÜLLER (ed.), *"Licht zur Erleuchtung der Heiden und Herrlichkeit für dein Volk Israel": Studien zum lukanischen Doppelwerk. FS J. Zmijewski* (BBB, 151), Hamburg, Philo & Philo Fine Arts, 2005, 49-72, p. 64.

31. This corresponds to 1 Sam 10,10-11, where Saul is seen "in the midst" of the prophets (ἐν μέσῳ αὐτῶν) and all who knew him before wonder whether he, too, has now become a prophet; cf. M. WOLTER, *Das Lukasevangelium* (HNT, 5), Tübingen, Mohr

In this way, Luke installs an independent jury that is as large as possible and that certifies, as it were, Jesus' extraordinary talent.

The pericope illustrates in an anecdotal-narrative way the two summary framing verses Lk 2,40 and 2,52, which are inspired by 1 Sam 2,21.26[32]:

> And the child grew and became strong, filled with wisdom, and the grace of God was upon him (Lk 2,40).
> And Jesus increased in wisdom and in age and in grace with God and human beings (Lk 2,52).

Both summaries emphasize that Jesus at the age of twelve is, to be sure, no longer a (small) child, but that his development is neither physically nor spiritually nor intellectually at an end[33]. While Lk 2,40 emphasizes the phase of physical growth, Lk 2,52 has in view his progression in wisdom and his mental development[34]: Jesus becomes wiser and more esteemed with increasing age, but already as a child has a remarkable talent at his disposal. But σοφία and χάρις are not only traditional attributes of men of God[35]; they are also found as motifs in episodes from childhood portrayed in Hellenistic biographical literature. Luke was clearly aware of these conventions; he applies them to his protagonists and also uses them in his Jesus biography[36]. This seems to indicate that Luke knows Hellenistic biographical literature and has read certain childhood accounts. It should not be supposed that he had available a written catalogue of biographical motifs, which he inserted into his narrative about the young Jesus in the temple one after another and which he then

---

Siebeck, 2008, p. 148. On the training situation in this context, see C.S. KEENER, *Acts: An Exegetical Commentary*. Vol. 3: *15:1–23:35*, Grand Rapids, MI, Baker Publishing Group, 2014, pp. 3220-3222; see also T. VEGGE, *Paulus und das antike Schulwesen: Schule und Bildung des Paulus* (BZNW, 134), Berlin, De Gruyter, 2006.

32. On this complex of themes, see especially R.D. AUS, *The Child Jesus in the Temple (Luke 2:42-51a), and Judaic Traditions on the Child Samuel in the Temple (1 Samuel 1–3)*, in ID. (ed.), *Samuel, Saul and Jesus: Three Early Palestinian Jewish Christian Gospel Haggadoth* (South Florida Studies in the History of Judaism, 105), Atlanta, GA, Scholars, 1994, 1-64.

33. Cf. DE JONGE, *Sonship* (n. 30), pp. 319-322. In Lk 2,43, Jesus is designated as παῖς. While a boy of twelve years of age was still considered a child for two or three years more, a girl at the age of twelve found herself on the threshold of becoming an adult, and therewith at a marriageable age. Luke knew this and for this reason – in contrast to Mark (5,42) – pointedly affixes the age of Jairus' daughter to the narrative about her healing (in Lk 8,42) and thereby makes plain the special tragedy of the situation, cf. *ibid.*, p. 320.

34. Cf. BOVON, *Lukas* (n. 29), p. 162.

35. Cf. WOLTER, *Lukas* (n. 31), p. 147; examples are given by H. CONZELMANN, χάρις κτλ., in *TWNT* 9 (1973) 366.

36. On the basic discussion, see R.A. BURRIDGE, *What Are the Gospels? A Comparison with Graeco-Roman Biography*, Grand Rapids, MI, Eerdmans, ²2004.

ticked off from his list[37]. Rather he casually takes up certain topoi from literary tradition in order to portray Jesus' extraordinary characteristics. Precisely in going beyond the conventional and familiar, he can sharpen Jesus' profile narratively.

In Greek biographical literature, not only rulers and politicians such as Cyrus, Solon and Themistocles, are depicted as amazingly intelligent while still children, but also philosophers such as Apollonius of Tyana and Pythagoras, as well as orators such as Cicero and poets such as Homer[38]. However, the clearest parallels are found in the *Vita Augusti* by Nicholas of Damascus (ca. 20 BC), the *Vita Apollonii* by Flavius Philostratus (ca. 200 AD) and the *Vita Pythagorica* by Iamblichus (ca. 300 AD)[39]. Although the texts are temporally relatively distant from each other, they do show numerous common motifs that apparently belonged to the standard set of motifs typical of this genre. They can be listed here only in summary form: a) all four authors (including Luke) give the *juvenile age* of their protagonists quite precisely; b) all youths undertake a *journey*, during which some of them attach themselves to various teachers and give proof of their intellectual strength; c) this journey leads Augustus, Apollonius, Pythagoras and Jesus to the *temple*, among other places, where the public receives a sample of their sayings and the outstanding wisdom of the youths is demonstrated. This σοφία now encompasses two dimensions: an intellectual one and a religious or liturgical one[40]; d) all four youths, finally, *excite* and amaze the people who become cognizant of their wisdom; in various ways, *teachers*, too, play a role[41].

Luke endows Jesus of Nazareth with traditional and familiar attributes borrowed from biographies – which were devoted exclusively to prominent personalities such as rulers or philosophers – especially from the

---

37. Cf. Krückemeier, *Jesus* (n. 27), p. 316, *verbatim*: "Dabei hat er nicht etwa einen schriftlichen Katalog inhaltlicher Motive vor Augen, von denen er nun eines nach dem anderen in seine Erzählung vom jungen Jesus im Tempel einbaut und abhakt".

38. Cf. de Jonge, *Sonship* (n. 30), pp. 339-342.

39. See on this the fine analysis by Krückemeier, *Jesus* (n. 27), pp. 307-319, to which I am indebted in the following. There are, of course, still further parallels from antiquity, also from the Jewish sphere, cf. W. Radl, *Der Ursprung Jesu: Traditionsgeschichtliche Untersuchungen zu Lukas 1–2* (Herder's Biblical Studies, 7), Freiburg i.Br., Herder, 1996, pp. 248-251.

40. Krückemeier, *Jesus* (n. 27), p. 311: "Diese σοφία schließt nun zweierlei Dimensionen in sich ein: eine intellektuelle und eine religiöse bzw. liturgische Dimension". The intellectual dimension is shown in the fact that the protagonists make public speeches or give wise answers to the questions posed to them. The liturgical-religious component is expressed in the fact that the episodes frequently take place in a temple, and that the special proximity of the youths to God is pointed at.

41. Cf. *ibid.*, pp. 312-313.

section dealing with these persons' youth. Thus, Luke shows that already as a boy Jesus possessed astonishing wisdom and that the grace of God lived in him. But in addition to this, he also states that Jesus "became strong" (ἐκραταιοῦτο, Lk 2,40). This "becoming strong", which is a divinely-wrought process, implies a claim to sovereignty[42]. Moreover, the childhood episode in Lk 2,42-51 carries special weight because here we find the first words spoken by Jesus in Luke's two-volume work (Lk 2,49) and Jesus thus, for the first time, becomes his own interpreter, after only others had spoken about him up to this point[43]. At his baptism, he is then endowed further with the Spirit (Lk 3,21-22) and proclaimed as the Son of God. The passage is marked by a motif that is already found in the birth narrative: the messiahship of Jesus[44]. Such a motif is not found among the Hellenistic writers; here, Luke rather follows impulses from Jewish literature.

In Luke's view, then, Jesus obtained his competence as a teacher already in his childhood or youth and his words continued to overwhelm the people, as, for instance, at his inaugural sermon in Nazareth (Lk 4,16-30; see v. 22: "... and all were amazed at the words of grace [ἐπὶ τοῖς λόγοις τῆς χάριτος] that came from his mouth ...")[45] or during his subsequent stay in Capernaum (Lk 4,31-37, see v. 32: "they were beside themselves at his teaching, for he spoke with authority [ἐν ἐξουσίᾳ]"); also, during his later confrontation in the temple, Jesus' answers are so startling that they even silence his duplicitous questioners (Lk 20,26)[46]. In the Emmaus narrative, finally, Jesus is designated as a prophet (cf. Lk 7,16) who is "mighty in deed and word" (Lk 24,19), a phrase which summarizes his effective performance in public (his miracles and teaching).

III. Deepening: Grace, Wisdom and Power

Not only Jesus himself is filled with grace, wisdom and the Spirit, he also promises his disciples that the Holy Spirit will support them when they stand before worldly courts (Lk 12,11-12) as well as a "mouth and wisdom" (στόμα καὶ σοφία, Lk 21,15). The gifts of the Spirit and wisdom

---

42. Cf. W. Michaelis, κράτος κτλ., in *TWNT* 3 (1950) 905-914. In the New Testament, the word κράτος usually refers to the ruling power of God; see, e.g., Lk 1,51.
43. Cf. Wolter, *Lukas* (n. 31), p. 146.
44. Krückemeier, *Jesus* (n. 27), p. 318.
45. This amazement concerns not only the family origins of Jesus ("Is this not a son of Joseph?"), but also implicitly the modest educational milieu from which he comes. The reaction to Peter and John in Acts 4,13 reflects a similar amazement.
46. Cf. Radl, *Ursprung* (n. 39), pp. 262-263.

will result in speech of such a power that – as already with Jesus in Lk 20,26 – all their opponents must admit defeat of their arguments: "they can neither withstand (ἀντιστῆναι) nor contradict (ἀντιλέγειν)" (Lk 21,15)[47]. In other words: the disciples are promised the charisma of persuasive speech – especially in a hostile environment[48].

This promise is fulfilled in the figure of Stephen: "they were unable to withstand (ἀντιστῆναι) the wisdom and the Spirit with which he spoke" (Acts 6,10)[49]. In the context of the Stephen episode, it is then, significantly, also said that he was filled with grace (χάρις) and power (δύναμις; Acts 6,8)[50]. In this way, Luke deliberately constructs a correspondence between Jesus and Stephen. The fact that Luke mentions χάρις and σοφία here as particular gifts of the Spirit and that he creates analogies between the Lord and the disciples, not just in the fate they undergo, but also in their outstanding attributes, may be taken as reflecting Luke's editorial intention[51].

These attributes have a decidedly intellectual character. This appears from Stephen's speech in Acts 7 – incidentally, the longest speech of all in Acts – where reference is made to Joseph and Moses, among others, for whom grace and wisdom likewise are attested:

> He freed him [sc. Joseph] from all his afflictions, and he gave him grace (χάρις) and wisdom (σοφία) in the sight of Pharaoh, king of Egypt, and he made him leader of Egypt and over his entire house (Acts 7,10).

Joseph, the descendant of Abraham living in a foreign land, is blessed by God with the wisdom of the interpretation of dreams and can be understood as the prototype of the (suffering) righteous one[52], out of

---

47. How Luke imagines a pneumatically-inspired defense is shown in Acts 4,8-12, where Peter, filled with the Holy Spirit, delivers an apologetic speech; cf. WOLTER, *Lukas* (n. 31), p. 446.

48. Cf. K. ERLEMANN, *Lizenz zum Reden: Die lk. Apostel zwischen Geist und Rhetorik*, in A. VON DOBBELER – K. ERLEMANN – R. HEILIGENTHAL (eds.), *Religionsgeschichte des Neuen Testaments: FS K. Berger*, Tübingen, Francke, 2000, 79-91, p. 81.

49. The gifts of the Spirit and wisdom have qualified Stephen and the other members of the group of seven as deacons (Acts 6,3); cf. ERLEMANN, *Lizenz* (n. 48), p. 82; J. ZMIJEWSKI, *Die Apostelgeschichte* (RNT), Regensburg, Pustet, 1994, p. 300.

50. E. HAENCHEN, *Die Apostelgeschichte* (KEK, 3), Göttingen, Vandenhoeck & Ruprecht, ⁷1977, p. 163: "Die neben der χάρις genannte δύναμις entspricht der πίστις von V. 5".

51. Cf. ERLEMANN, *Lizenz* (n. 48), p. 82: "Es darf als redaktionelle Absicht des Lukas gewertet werden, dass er χάρις und σοφία als besondere Pneumagaben nennt und dass er den Herrn und die Jünger nicht nur in ihrem Schicksal, sondern auch in ihren herausragenden Merkmalen analogisiert". It should be noticed that, apart from Jesus himself, Stephen and his colleagues belonging to the group of seven are the only followers of Jesus to whom Luke attributes σοφία; he does not ascribe it to the other disciples (cf. Acts 6,3.10).

52. Vgl. R. PESCH, *Die Apostelgeschichte (Apg 1–12)* (EKKNT, 5/1), Düsseldorf, Benziger Verlag; Neukirchen-Vluyn, Neukirchener Verlag, ³2005, p. 250.

whose suffering a rich blessing flows for those belonging to him precisely because of his compelling wisdom[53]. Luke characterizes Joseph in such a way that he becomes an analogy and almost a type of Stephen, the man "full of grace and power" (Acts 6,8) and "wisdom" (Acts 6,3.10) – and ultimately also of Jesus[54]: they are all three suffering righteous ones endowed with extraordinary wisdom.

As for Moses, Stephen in his speech says about him that he enjoyed an education in Egypt[55]:

> And Moses was educated in all the wisdom of the Egyptians (ἐπαιδεύθη Μωϋσῆς [ἐν] πάσῃ σοφίᾳ Αἰγυπτίων), and he was powerful (δυνατός) in his words and deeds (Acts 7,22).

This education in the diaspora is depicted without reservation as something positive; this is evident from the fact that, according to Luke, its result was that Moses "was powerful in his words and acts". In Luke's days, this was in no way a matter of course[56]. Josephus, for example, affirms that the wisdom of all the peoples had its origin in the Jewish law and that the Greek philosophers up to Plato made use of this blueprint[57]. Similarly, Artapanos of Alexandria makes Moses the teacher of the Egyptians[58]. Luke seems to signalize his esteem for the pagan education that, in his view, Stephen and his Hellenistic colleagues enjoyed[59]. Luke's readers will have taken notice of this with approval and will have been able to interpret it as an appreciative recognition of themselves and of their own pagan or Jewish diaspora past.

The characterization of Moses as "powerful in his words and deeds" takes up the characterization of Jesus in Lk 24,19 and is repeated with slight variation when Apollos' rhetorical abilities are mentioned in Acts 18,24. The interesting part of this is that Stephen, or rather Luke, attests Moses' empowerment *before* the burning bush scene (Acts 7,30), in clear deviation from the biblical narrative. Ex 4,10 emphasizes that Moses was not exactly eloquent and considered this as a great deficit[60]:

---

53. Cf. ZMIJEWSKI, *Apostelgeschichte* (n. 49), p. 310.
54. Luke here expands Gen 41,33.39 by adding the attribute of wisdom, cf. ZMIJEWSKI, *Apostelgeschichte* (n. 49), p. 317; K. KLIESCH, *Das heilsgeschichtliche Credo in den Reden der Apostelgeschichte* (BBB, 44), Köln – Bonn, Hanstein, 1975, p. 156.
55. See also Philo, *Mos.* 1.20-23; Josephus, *Ant.* 2.232-237.
56. Cf. C.S. KEENER, *Acts: An Exegetical Commentary*. Vol. 2: *3:1–14:28*, Grand Rapids, MI, Baker Academic, 2013, pp. 1385-1386.
57. Josephus, *C. Ap.* 2.257, 280-281.
58. Artapanos 3.6-8; cf. PESCH, *Apostelgeschichte* (n. 52), p. 252.
59. Cf. KEENER, *Acts* (n. 56), p. 1387. This is clear from the well-composed speech and the historical narrative that Luke puts into the mouth of Stephen.
60. Cf. *ibid.*

> But Moses said to the Lord: Lord, I am not a man of words, neither in the past nor even now that you have spoken to your servant; I am slow of speech and slow of tongue (Ex 4,10).

Josephus (and along with him Sir 45,3) omits this apparent weakness on the part of Moses and makes him into a highly-gifted person from a very early age who was not only "of impressive appearance", but also "possessed the gift of having an influence upon the masses through his natural eloquence"[61]. Keener is certainly right in his judgement: "Indeed, Josephus makes Moses into a Hellenistic orator (3.14-23)"[62]. The Lukan image of Moses ("powerful in his words") is in agreement with that of Josephus; Luke presents Moses as having had an education in the entirety of Egyptian wisdom, which recalls Jesus' increasing wisdom in Lk 2,40.52. Jesus, though, does not need instruction, he has the advantage of the fullness of the Spirit over Moses (Lk 4,1)[63].

Grace (χάρις) and wisdom (σοφία) irrefutably play a prominent role in the history of Hellenistic thought and ideas, to which we can merely refer here[64]. Striving for σοφία is seen as the highest goal not only in early Jewish speculation about wisdom, but also in the Greco-Roman environment. For Philo, χάρις, σοφία and perfection are closely connected[65]. While χάρις is the endowment of the human being through creation[66], only the pious person can recognize it as such.

For Quintilian, the Roman rhetorician and contemporary of Luke, wisdom and rhetoric were originally two sides of the same coin, which, however, had been carelessly torn apart over the course of time:

> These two disciplines, as Cicero very clearly argues, were once so closely joined by nature and united in function, that philosophers and orators were taken to be the same (*ut idem sapientes atque eloquentes haberentur*). The

---

61. Josephus, *Ant.* 3.13. See also *Ant.* 2.230: "The age of the boy, though, remained behind his intelligence and sagacity, for he was so developed in wisdom and education in the Spirit that he would have done honor to one at an advanced age".

62. KEENER, *Acts* (n. 56), p. 1387. In Acts, Luke also makes Paul, who himself recognizes his "weakness, fear and trembling" (1 Cor 2,3), into a brilliant speaker.

63. Cf. ZMIJEWSKI, *Apostelgeschichte* (n. 49), p. 319; the formulation "filled with the Holy Spirit" (πλήρης πνεύματος ἁγίου, Lk 4,1) is found also in reference to the circle of the seven from Jerusalem (Acts 6,3.5), Stephen (Acts 7,55) and Barnabas (11,24).

64. Cf. ERLEMANN, *Lizenz* (n. 48), pp. 82-83; further instances may be found in U. WILCKENS, σοφία κτλ., in *TWNT* 7 (1964) 498-503; in detail: D. ZELLER, *Charis bei Philon und Paulus* (SBS, 142), Stuttgart, Katholisches Bibelwerk, 1990.

65. Cf. *ibid.*, pp. 33-128.130. On the whole subject, E. FRÜCHTEL, *Philon und die Vorbereitung der christlichen Paideia und Seelenleitung*, in PROSTMEIER (ed.), *Frühchristentum* (n. 21), 19-33, is most instructive.

66. CONZELMANN, χάρις (n. 35), p. 380 (*verbatim*: "die Ausstattung des Menschen durch die Schöpfung").

subject then split into two, and it came about, through failure of art, that there were thought to be more arts than one[67].

If philosophy and rhetoric are the same in regard to their origins, then the only good speaker is the one who also is a good man (*vir bonus*) and a philosopher[68]. The *gratia varietatis*, the art of diversified speaking, is the mark of the professional rhetor – it implies graceful speech and its aesthetic embellishment –[69], while *sapienta* (wisdom) is rather the name for the side concerned with content. In Greco-Roman thought, σοφία is a designation for the ideal of education *per se*[70].

If one considers the Lukan conception of σοφία against this background, it becomes clear how unmistakably the author of Luke-Acts picks up the thread of the traditional range of meanings of the term in order to make the main Christian characters of his narrative compatible for educated (Jewish-)Hellenistic circles. The fathers in the history of Israel had already distinguished themselves through wisdom and grace (bestowal of favor), which gave them the ability of explaining Scripture or also interpreting dreams (Joseph). Jesus and Stephen continue this line seamlessly[71]. In Hellenistic literature, rulers, miracle workers and philosophers were blessed with the gift of persuasive speech that manifested itself, in part, at a youthful age; Jesus and Stephen, too, possess this charismatic gift enabling them to outdo their opponents in argument.

Along with σοφία, the πνεῦμα now appears as an attribute of the Lukan Jesus and Stephen: speaking wisdom is decidedly a gift from God[72]. To be sure, χάρις, too, has the aspect of being a gift of grace, a bestowal of favor – mediated through a higher power or a divinity – but it is, in the Septuagint, for instance, *not* a theological concept[73].

---

67. Quint., *Inst.* 1.13; cf. ERLEMANN, *Lizenz* (n. 48), pp. 82-83; further instances in WILCKENS, σοφία (n. 64); in more detail, ZELLER, *Charis* (n. 64).

68. Quint., *Inst.* 1, Pr. 18: "So let our orator be the sort of man who can truly be called 'wise', not only perfect in morals (for in my view that is not enough, though some people think otherwise) but also in knowledge and in his general capacity for speaking".

69. Cf., for example, Quint., *Inst.* 9.4.43; 8.3.52; also 8.3.3: *sublimitas profecto et magnificentia et nitor et auctoritas expressit illum fragorem*. "It was, after all, the sublimity and the splendor, the elegance and the authoritative manner that evoked that storm of applause".

70. Cf. ERLEMANN, *Lizenz* (n. 48), p. 83.

71. The parallelism between Jesus and Stephen shining through again and again becomes also clear in the fact that Stephen, under comparable circumstances, dies like Jesus (cf. Lk 23,46; Acts 7,59-60); see on this K. BACKHAUS, *Mose und der Mos Maiorum: Das Alter des Judentums als Argument für die Attraktivität des Christentums in der Apostelgeschichte*, in ID., *Entgrenzung* (n. 17), 257-282, p. 274.

72. Cf. WILCKENS, σοφία (n. 64), p. 515.

73. Cf. CONZELMANN, χάρις (n. 35), p. 379, for the evidence.

IV. Amplification: The Art of ΠΑΡΡΗΣΙΑ

The charismatic and efficacious speech of the chief protagonists in Acts can be delineated more precisely by considering the concept of παρρησία (plain, fearless speech)[74]. The term occurs five times and generally in pivotal passages (Acts 2,29; 4,13.29.31; 28,31). The prominent significance that Luke attaches to παρρησία appears from the fact that it is the next-to-last word in Luke-Acts: in spite of his house arrest, Paul can proclaim the sovereignty of God and the teaching about Jesus Christ the Lord in the center of the world at that time, in Rome, "in all openness, unhindered" (μετὰ πάσης παρρησίας ἀκωλύτως).

In Acts, παρρησία and παρρησιάζεσθαι are connected quite closely with the λαλεῖν and διδάσκειν of the apostles (4,29.31; 9,27-28; 18,25-26)[75]. The forum before which παρρησία comes into play is always the popular public and the political-judicial authorities[76]. Thus, it would appear that this concept too has an affinity with Hellenistic παιδεία and rhetoric[77]. In point of fact: bold, fearless and plain speech was an important goal for a philosopher of the first century[78]. However, he regularly got into difficulty through it if a humorless emperor sat in his audience. "Several famous philosophers in the later first century, especially under Nero and the Flavian dynasty, faced death or exile for their endless moral prattling. [...] As Epictetus said before he was exiled by Domitian, 'Tyranny hates wisdom' (*Discourses* 1.29.10). The mark of a true philosopher therefore was a determination to speak out with *parrhēsia* without regard for the consequences"[79].

In Quintilian's view (to take him once again as an authority), παρρησία (Latin *licentia*) is much more than just a rhetorical device chosen for reasons of flattery; it attempts to contain the risk of negative reactions

---

74. Cf. M. Becker, *Lukas und Dion von Prusa: Das lukanische Doppelwerk im Kontext paganer Bildungsdiskurse* (Studies in Cultural Contexts of the Bible, 3), Paderborn, Schöningh, 2020, pp. 112-120; W.C. van Unnik, *The Christian's Freedom of Speech in the New Testament*, in Id., *Sparsa collecta: Collected Essays*, 2 (SupplNT, 30), Leiden, Brill, 1980, 269-289, pp. 279-283.
75. Cf. H. Schlier, παρρησία, παρρησιάζομαι, in *TWNT* 5 (1954) 869-884, p. 880.
76. It is in general either the Jews (Acts 2,29; 9,27f.; 13,46; 18,26; 19,8), the Jewish authorities (Acts 4,13; 26,26) or the Jews and the people (Acts 14,2-3; together with the political representatives Acts 4,29.31), cf. Schlier, παρρησία (n. 75), p. 880.
77. Cf. Erlemann, *Lizenz* (n. 48), p. 84.
78. Musonius defines παρρησία quite generally as the "non-concealment of what one thinks" (Muson., *Diatr.* 9.48.14-15).
79. S. Mason, *Flavius Josephus and the New Testament*, Peabody, MA, Hendrickson, ²1993, pp. 219-220.

through a certain well-considered mixture of praise and reproach[80]. Rather all speech should basically show παρρησία:

> The same may be said of Free Speech (*oratio libera*), which Cornificius calls licence (*licentia*), and the Greeks *parrhesia*. For what is less 'figured' (*figuratum*) than true freedom (*vera libertas*)? Yet flattery (*adulatio*) is often concealed under this cover[81].

Παρρησία is thus not just a rhetorical figure; it rather focuses on the truth and mentions it without flattery or timidity. Technique and virtue blend together here[82]. In early Jewish wisdom literature, on the other hand, παρρησία is above all a quality of the just and wise person[83], but can also be the mode of expression of Wisdom itself[84], or of God[85].

A key passage for understanding the Lukan concept of παρρησία – but also for comprehending the theme of education that interests us in this contribution – is Acts 4,1-22. Here it is said that Peter and John, because of their impressive sermon in the temple, are brought before the Synedrion. In the situation of his interrogation, Peter, now "filled with the Holy Spirit", speaks with all παρρησία (Acts 4,8-13.29), a boldness which even outruns Jesus' promise in Lk 12,12 (see also 21,12-15). Plain, fearless speech is thus attributed here to pneumatic inspiration.

The reaction leaves nothing to be desired and fits in with the already-known series of reactions that follow upon Spirit-filled words and deeds:

> But as they saw the fearlessness (παρρησία) of Peter and John and realized that they were illiterate and uneducated people, they were astonished. It became clear to them that they belonged to Jesus. And since they saw the

---

80. Of course, παρρησία is also a rhetorical stylistic device (see, for instance, Cic., *Or.* 3.205: *vox quaedam libera*; for further examples, see SCHLIER, *παρρησία* [n. 75], pp. 869-872). Quintilian, though, campaigns for a deeper understanding that goes beyond παρρησία as pure ornamentation *(ornatus)*; this fits generally with his criticism of modern orators, whose style in his view is too extravagant and opulent and is geared alone toward the pleasure of the uneducated crowd (cf. Quint., *Inst.* 10.1.43); see on this F. KÜHNERT, *Quintilians Stellung zu der Beredsamkeit seiner Zeit*, in *Listy Filologické/Folia Philologica* 87 (1964) 33-50, p. 36: "Quintilian tadelt also an den modernen Rednern im allgemeinen, dass sie nur auf den Beifall der Menge, nicht aber auf den Nutzen und den Sieg der von ihnen vertretenen Sache bedacht sind, dass sie ihre Redekunst prahlerisch zur Schau stellen, dass sie mit ihrer Beredsamkeit, die schlaff und verweichlicht ist, nur dem Genuss und Vergnügen der Zuhörer dienen".
81. Quint., *Inst.* 9.2.27-28.
82. Cf. ERLEMANN, *Lizenz* (n. 48), p. 85.
83. Cf. Prov 13,5; 20,9; Wis 5,1; *4 Macc* 10,5; SCHLIER, *παρρησία* (n. 75), p. 874: "Der δίκαιος, nicht der ἀσεβής, hat παρρησία. Dabei ist der δίκαιος zugleich der σοφός, so dass die hellenistische Auffassung, die dem Philosophen Parrhesie zuschreibt, hier in einer der jüdischen Orientierung am Gesetz entsprechenden Umwandlung wiederkehrt".
84. Prov 1,20.
85. Cf. Ps 93,1 LXX.

man who had been healed standing before them, they could say nothing in answer to them (Acts 4,13-14).

The interesting part of this passage is the fact that the astonishment of the members of the Synedrion at the rhetorical abilities of Peter and John has to do with the low level of the apostles' education. Luke considers this lack of education positively here, unlike what he does usually. When Luke elsewhere in his writings comes to speak about the educational level of people portrayed by him, then for the most part he underscores what is positive to it and expresses his appreciation[86]. Here, on the other hand, the members of the Synedrion show themselves astonished at the apostles' eloquence and παρρησία because these stand in contradiction to their modest educational background: Peter and John are called illiterates (ἀγράμματος) and uneducated (ἰδιῶται). Along with Matthias Becker, I assume that this reference to the apostles' lack of education is not meant as a (historical) statement about the socio-cultural background of the apostles; it is rather to be understood as a means to differentiate true *paideia* from the useless abundance of too much learning[87]. One can illustrate this by referring to the self-dramatization of Dion of Prusa: the reference-point of Dion's philosophical ideal is not the highly-educated philosophers making use of a comprehensive general education, but rather such rudimentarily educated personalities as Socrates and Diogenes. Dion considers himself to be "far removed" even from these[88]. With his critique of education, Dion joins the ranks of certain circles of the Cynic, Stoic, Epicurean and Sceptic schools of thought. Seneca, for instance, can ask:

> We might even make the statement that it is possible to attain wisdom without the 'liberal studies' (*sine liberalibus studiis*); for although virtue is a thing that must be learned, yet it is not learned by means of these studies. What reason have I, however, for supposing that one who is ignorant of letters will never be a wise man, since wisdom is not to be found in letters? (Sen., *Ep.* 88.32)[89].

There is every reason not to rule out the possibility that pagan-educated readers of Luke who were familiar with this kind of educational critique

---

86. Cf. BECKER, *Lukas* (n. 74), p. 615, with reference to Acts 7,22; 22,3; 18,24–19,1; Jesus, in Luke, also is never designated as a carpenter (Mk 6,3) or as a son of a carpenter (Mt 13,55).
87. See (also on the following) *ibid.*, pp. 615-616.
88. Dion, *Or.* 72.16: "Just so, though each of us has the garb of Socrates and Diogenes, in intellect we are far from being like those famous men, or from living as they did, or from uttering such noble thoughts. Therefore, for no other reason than because of our personal appearance, we, like the owls, collect a great company of those who in truth are birds, being fools ourselves besides being annoyed by others of like folly".
89. Translation by R.M. GUMMERE (LCL, 1920).

were able to see the analogy between Acts 4,13 and the connection made in Cynic-Stoic philosophy between the lack of linguistic-literary education and the true pursuit of virtue and wisdom[90]. In that case, one message conveyed by this text would be that being a Christian makes no special demands on one's education; Christianity rather appeals to all social classes. In addition to this it becomes clear that free, plain speech is a divine gift that transcends every kind of human schooling: it simply cannot be acquired in schools of rhetoric, but rather is – like χάρις and σοφία – a gift of the Holy Spirit[91]. All of these gifts enable those who have received them to impart their message in such a persuasive manner that they astonish those who hear them.

V. Result: Implicit *Paideia* Allusions

The remarks presented here, which intentionally did not focus on the apostle Paul's educational biography (Acts 22,3) or his speech on the Areopagus (Acts 17,16-34), but rather on pronounced allusions to (rhetorical) educational concepts and discourses, show how subtly Luke integrates his affinity for education in his narrative. The starting point was the image of the twelve-year-old Jesus in the temple, who, blessed with wisdom (Lk 2,40.52), displays such extraordinary abilities in the understanding of Scripture that the διδάσκαλοι present are amazed at his wisdom. This unique episode of Jesus' youth can be fitted into the context of ancient biographies concerned with the precocious intelligence of famous personalities. The intended readers with a pagan and/or Jewish education could understand the episode against this background of the ancient biography. However, Luke's readers could also recognize the feature in which it deviates from usual youth biographies: the σοφία with which Jesus is blessed is conceived as independent of any kind of human παιδεία whatsoever – it is exclusively due to God, the source and giver of all wisdom.

Being filled with grace, wisdom and the Spirit, Jesus promises his disciples the charisma of persuasive speech, which is realized particularly in Stephen where Luke, over long stretches of the text of Acts 6–7, draws analogies between him and Jesus. In Stephen's speech he points out that Moses had received schooling in the Egyptian diaspora – and even before the scene with the burning bush. This schooling is interpreted positively

---

90. With Becker, *Lukas* (n. 74), p. 621.
91. Cf. Erlemann, *Lizenz* (n. 48), p. 87.

so that potential readers with an analogous *paideia* experience could appreciate their schooling positively. Charismatic speech is a fruit of the endowment with wisdom (σοφία) and grace (χάρις). In the case of Stephen – as already in the case of Jesus – the πνεῦμα is an additional factor of primary importance.

The striking and efficacious speech that Jesus and the apostles display culminates in παρρησία, which the chief protagonists display in public, but also and above all before political-judicial audiences. Παρρησία, plain speech, is also a rhetorical stylistic device, but according to Quintilian, it should be orientated towards the truth. In early Jewish literature it is a quality of the righteous and wise person. The remark made by the Jewish leaders in Acts 4,13, which seems to deny the apostles Peter and John any education at all, may at first glance be somewhat irritating, but can be understood as corresponding to a well-known educational discourse: the Christian message makes no specific demands on people's education, but can be spread by every believer. Plain speech is not acquired in schools; rather it is a divine gift, granted to women and men without their agency, just as is the gift of wisdom and grace.

Chair of Biblical Theology Uta POPLUTZ
(New Testament Exegesis)
Faculty of Humanities
Bergische Universität Wuppertal
Gaußstraße 20
DE-42119 Wuppertal
Germany
poplutz@uni-wuppertal.de

LUKE AND IGNATIUS

I. Introduction

Trying to locate early Christian texts in their original historical contexts can be at times an almost impossibly complex task. Yet such a task is vital if we are to interpret these texts in a historically responsible way. The task can involve considering a text on its own (asking where and when it is most appropriately placed within early Christian history); but part of the task can involve questions about the relationship between different texts. Thus if text A uses, or presupposes, text B, then B must pre-date A. At the very least, this may impose some restrictions on the possible date of B (though these will be dependent on our ability to date A).

These considerations are particularly relevant in relation to the Gospel of Luke. Luke-Acts was for many years confidently dated to the 80s (or perhaps 90s) of the first century CE. However, a number of scholars are now advancing the theory that Luke-Acts (perhaps especially Acts) is to be dated to the early (or even mid-)second century[1]. The reasons for this are varied, including the possibility that Luke presupposes knowledge of Josephus' *Antiquities*, as well as the Pauline letters[2]; but a contributory factor is also the claim that Luke's work was not known by other early Christian authors[3]. Such a theory could have many implications, one of which is to question the traditional Two Source theory as the solution to the Synoptic Problem: if Luke is to be dated into the second century, it may be more difficult to claim that Luke did not know Matthew's gospel (since Matthew was becoming widely disseminated and known);

---

1. Notably R. Pervo, *Dating Acts: Between the Evangelists and the Apologists*, Sonoma, CA, Polebridge, 2006, who is now followed by several others. See the survey in A.F. Gregory, *Acts and Christian Beginnings: A Review Essay*, in *JSNT* 39 (2016) 97-115.

2. See S. Mason, *Josephus and the New Testament*, Peabody, MA, Hendrickson, 1992, pp. 185-225; also in more detail, Id., *Josephus: A Source for Luke-Acts?*, paper presented at the Symposium *On Using Sources* arranged under the auspices of the Leuven Centre for the Study of the Gospels, KU Leuven, 2019.

3. The comprehensive study of A.F. Gregory, *The Reception of Luke and Acts in the Period before Irenaeus* (WUNT, 2.169), Tübingen, Mohr Siebeck, 2003, finds no evidence of the reception of Luke or Acts prior to the middle of the second century. See also his conclusion on p. 353 with possible implications (though cautiously expressed) about the date of Luke and Acts on the basis of his findings.

hence a theory positing the existence of a Q source to explain the agreements between Matthew and Luke becomes more implausible[4].

This essay seeks to test one tiny aspect of this theory about the date of Luke-Acts by examining once again the possible link between Luke and Ignatius. The argument here will be that Ignatius presupposes some knowledge (direct or indirect) of Luke's gospel. This may not, of itself, tell us very much since the date of Ignatius' letters is now hotly disputed (see below). Nevertheless, it may help in the complex business of trying to fit together some pieces from the massive jigsaw made up of texts and fragments of texts which survive from early Christianity.

Many recent discussions of a possible relationship between Ignatius and Luke have concluded Ignatius does not presuppose Luke's gospel: at most there are just a very few common traditions which they share but the links lie at the pre-Lukan and pre-Ignatian stages of the tradition[5].

---

4. See J.C. POIRIER, *Introduction: Why the Farrer Hypothesis? Why Now?*, in ID. – J. PETERSON (eds.), *Markan Priority without Q: Explorations in the Farrer Hypothesis* (LNTS, 455), London, T&T Clark, 2015, 1-15, pp. 12-13; M. MÜLLER, *Acts as Biblical Rewriting of the Gospels and Paul's Letters*, in ID. – J.T. NIELSEN (eds.), *Luke's Literary Creativity* (LNTS, 550), London, Bloomsbury T&T Clark, 2016, 96-117; cf. too S. MATTHEWS, *Does Dating Luke-Acts into the Second Century Affect the Q-Hypothesis?*, in M. MÜLLER – H. OMERZU (eds.), *Gospel Interpretation and the Q-Hypothesis* (LNTS, 573), London, T&T Clark, 2018, 244-265 (though she answers the question of her title negatively).

It was the issue of the implications for the study of the Q hypothesis that led me to this topic. This area is one in which Jos Verheyden has had a long-standing interest throughout his scholarly career and where he has made significant contributions to the debates. He has also done important work on the Lukan writings. This small essay is then offered here with thanks for his many contributions, and for his friendship over many years.

5. See e.g. H. KÖSTER, *Synoptische Überlieferung bei den apostolischen Vätern* (TU, 65), Berlin, Akademie-Verlag, 1957, pp. 44-56; É. MASSAUX, *Influence de l'Évangile de saint Matthieu sur la littérature chrétienne avant saint Irénée* (BETL, 75), Leuven, LUP – Peeters, 1986, pp. 108-111; H. PAULSEN, *Studien zur Theologie des Ignatius von Antiochien*, Göttingen, Vandenhoeck & Ruprecht, 1978, pp. 39-41; ID., *Die Briefe des Ignatius von Antiochia und der Brief des Polykarp von Smyrna* (HNT, 18), Tübingen, Mohr Siebeck, 1985, pp. 92-93; D.A. HAGNER, *The Sayings of Jesus in the Apostolic Fathers and Justin Martyr*, in D. WENHAM (ed.), *Gospel Perspectives 5: The Jesus Tradition outside the Gospels*, Sheffield, JSOT Press, 1984, 233-268, p. 239; W.R. SCHOEDEL, *Ignatius of Antioch* (Hermeneia), Philadelphia, PA, Fortress, 1985, pp. 9, 222-223, 226-227, 262; GREGORY, *Reception* (n. 3), pp. 70-75; A.J. BELLINZONI, *The Gospel of Luke in the Apostolic Fathers: An Overview*, in A.F. GREGORY – C.M. TUCKETT (eds.), *The New Testament and the Apostolic Fathers*. Vol. 2: *Trajectories through the New Testament and the Apostolic Fathers*, Oxford, OUP, 2005, 45-68, pp. 57-58; P. FOSTER, *The Epistles of Ignatius of Antioch and the Writings That Later Formed the New Testament*, in A.F. GREGORY – C.M. TUCKETT (eds.), *The New Testament and the Apostolic Fathers*. Vol. 1: *The Reception of the New Testament in the Apostolic Fathers*, Oxford, OUP, 2005, 159-186, p. 182; ID., *Ignatius and the Gospels*, in J. SCHRÖTER – T. NICKLAS – J. VERHEYDEN (eds.), *Gospels and Gospel Traditions in the Second Century* (BZNW, 235), Berlin, De Gruyter, 2019, 81-106, p. 101; A. LINDEMANN, *The Apostolic Fathers and the Synoptic Problem*, in P. FOSTER et al. (eds.), *New Studies in the Synoptic Problem* (BETL, 239), Leuven – Paris – Walpole, MA,

It is probably now rather a minority view which would argue that Ignatius might derive one (or more) tradition(s), directly or indirectly, from Luke's gospel itself[6].

It should however be noted that any claim that Ignatius "knew" Luke or "used" Luke will go far beyond the evidence at hand. It is well known that Ignatius rarely if ever *cites* any writer or text. He mostly just alludes to traditions which appear in other texts[7]. The most we might be able to show is that Ignatius displays parallels with Luke and agrees with Luke in elements which may be due to Luke's redactional or compositional activity. This would then exclude the possibility that the Luke-Ignatius agreements in question are due to common traditions shared by the two writers. If such instances can be established, they would show that by the time Ignatius wrote, the tradition which he used had already gone through the stage of Luke's writing his gospel[8]. Whether Ignatius derived the tradition *directly* from Luke cannot however be shown on this basis. It may well be that Ignatius was dependent on oral tradition secondary to the writing of Luke (via a process of "secondary orality") rather than actually using a text of Luke's gospel itself. Nor do such instances say anything, one way or the other, about Ignatius' views about what kind of authority the text of Luke's gospel might have had. But if such agreements can be shown to exist, they do show that Ignatius presupposes that the tradition he used had already been used and redacted by Luke, and hence Ignatius post-dates Luke.

The evidence for a possible link between Luke and Ignatius is limited in extent. Two texts in Ignatius – *Smyrn.* 3.2 and *Pol.* 2.1 – and parallel

---

Peeters, 2011, 689-719, pp. 703-708; S.E. YOUNG, *Jesus Tradition in the Apostolic Fathers* (WUNT, 2.311), Tübingen, Mohr Siebeck, 2011, pp. 229-232.

6. This is usually argued for the parallel between Ign. *Smyrn.* 3.2 and Lk 24,39: see C. MAURER, *Ein umstrittenes Zitat bei Ignatius von Antiochen (Smyrn. 3.2)*, in *Jahrbuch der Gesellschaft für die Geschichte des Protestantismus in Österreich* 67 (1951) 165-170; F. NEIRYNCK, *Luc 24,36-43: Un récit lucanien*, in ID., *Evangelica II 1982-1991: Collected Essays* (BETL, 99), Leuven, LUP – Peeters, 1991, 205-226; P. VIELHAUER, *Jewish Christian Gospels*, in E. HENNECKE (ed.), *New Testament Apocrypha*, vol. 1, London, SCM, 1963, pp. 129-130; D.A. SMITH, *Revisiting the Empty Tomb: The Early History of Easter*, Minneapolis, MN, Fortress, 2010, p. 110.

7. See M.W. MITCHELL, *In the Footsteps of Paul: Scriptural and Apostolic Authority in Ignatius of Antioch*, in *JECS* 14 (2006) 27-45, who points out that this is the case even in relation to the Pauline corpus where the case for Ignatius' knowledge of prior texts (especially 1 Corinthians) is strongest: even here Ignatius does not *quote* Paul, but uses his vocabulary freely. Mitchell argues convincingly that the "authority" here is not the Pauline letter qua text but Paul qua authoritative person.

8. The importance of redactional material reappearing in another text as a strong indicator of dependence is emphasized by KÖSTER, *Synoptische Überlieferung* (n. 5), p. 3, and many others following him.

texts in Luke will be examined here. It will be argued that in these two instances, Ignatius agrees with elements in Luke which may derive from Luke's editorial work. As will be noted briefly at the end, there are other parallels between Ignatius and Luke where it is not possible to argue so clearly that the Lukan version of the parallel is redactional. Nevertheless, these other instances may give some subsidiary support to the theory that Ignatius presupposes Luke's gospel and certainly they call into question the value of an argument to the effect that any one instance of possible use of Luke by Ignatius is improbable because there are no other examples of possible use of Luke[9].

II. IGN. *SMYRN*. 3.2//LUKE 24,39

In *Smyrn.* 3.2, as part of his argument that Jesus was really "in the flesh" (ἐν σαρκί) after the resurrection (as well as before), Ignatius cites a saying of Jesus: "Reach out, touch me and see that I am not a bodiless demon" (Λάβετε ψηλαφήσατέ με καὶ ἴδετε ὅτι οὐκ εἰμὶ δαιμόνιον ἀσώματον)[10], a saying which is close to Lk 24,39, where Jesus in a resurrection appearance responds to the concern of the disciples that he might be a πνεῦμα by saying "Touch me and see; for a πνεῦμα does not have flesh and bones as you see that I have" (ψηλαφήσατέ με καὶ ἴδετε, ὅτι πνεῦμα σάρκα καὶ ὀστέα οὐκ ἔχει καθὼς ἐμὲ θεωρεῖτε ἔχοντα).

It is widely recognised that the two sayings are close to each other. The main difference is in the wording of what is denied: in Luke, Jesus denies that he is a πνεῦμα; in Ignatius, he denies that he is a "bodiless demon" (δαιμόνιον ἀσώματον). Nevertheless, the introductory words of Jesus' invitation to touch him and see are identical in the two versions (ψηλαφήσατέ με καὶ ἴδετε ὅτι).

1. *The "Afterlife" of Ign.* Smyrn. *3.2*

I consider first the "afterlife" of Ignatius' version of the saying. This version of the saying was evidently known and discussed[11]. Eusebius

---

9. So e.g. *ibid.*, p. 45 (after discussing *Pol.* 2.1, but *before* any discussion of what is widely regarded as the strongest piece of evidence for a possible Luke-Ignatius relationship, viz. Ign. *Smyrn.* 3.2//Lk 24,39); also SCHOEDEL, *Ignatius of Antioch* (n. 5), p. 226 (on *Smyrn.* 3.2: dependence on Luke is unlikely because there is no other clear example).
10. ET from Ehrman's LCL edition.
11. See VIELHAUER, *Jewish Christian Gospels* (n. 6), pp. 128-129; A.F.J. KLIJN, *Jewish-Christian Gospel Tradition*, Leiden, Brill, 1992, pp. 121-123; A.F. GREGORY, *The Gospel*

(*Hist. eccl.* 3.36.11) knows the saying as recorded by Ignatius, but says that he does not know its source:

> He [Ignatius] also wrote to the Smyrneans quoting words from I know not what source and discoursing thus about Christ: "For I know and believe that he was in the flesh also after the resurrection, and when he came to those with Peter he said to them, 'Take, handle me and see that I am not a bodiless demon'".

Jerome too knows the saying as coming from Ignatius, and attributes it to the *Gospel of the Hebrews*:

> Ignatius ... wrote ... to the Smyrneans, and separately to Polycarp ... in which letter he offers the following testimony about the gospel that has recently been translated by me, concerning the person of Christ, saying (*dicens*): "Truly I both saw him after the resurrection in the flesh and I believe that it was he; and when he came to Peter and to those with Peter, he said to them: 'Look, touch me and see that I am not a bodiless demon (*daemonium incorporale*)'. And immediately they touched him and they believed" (*Vir. ill.* 16; also *Comm. Isa.* 65, prol.).

However, Jerome is almost certainly dependent on Eusebius: he mistakenly claims that the saying comes from Ignatius' letter to Polycarp (perhaps misreading Eusebius who has a reference to Ignatius' letter to Polycarp just before his note about the saying from *Smyrneans*); and he also follows Eusebius in apparently attributing Ignatius' introduction to the Jesus logion to the source, possibly too changing Eusebius' "I know" (οἶδα) to "I saw" (*vidi*)[12], failing then to recognise these as the words of Ignatius himself. Hence it is widely agreed that Jerome's attribution of the saying to the *Gospel of the Hebrews* is mistaken[13].

---

according to the Hebrews and the Gospel of the Ebionites, Oxford, OUP, 2017, pp. 275-279.

12. The situation is however complicated by textual variants in the texts of both Ignatius and Eusebius. A correction in one MS of Eusebius (codex Laurentianus) has εἶδον for οἶδα; and one mediaeval Latin MS of Ignatius has *vidi* for οἶδα. See P.F. BEATRICE, *The "Gospel according to the Hebrews" in the Apostolic Fathers*, in *NT* 48 (2006) 147-195, pp. 156-158. Thus KLIJN, *Jewish-Christian Gospel Tradition* (n. 11), p. 123, claims that Eusebius' text as used by Jerome had εἶδον; Beatrice claims that εἶδον was the original text of Ignatius, preserved by the later MS tradition of Eusebius. However, the MS evidence for "I saw" in either Ignatius or in Eusebius is extremely tenuous (*pace* Beatrice) and it seems easier to assume that Jerome has indeed made a mistake at this point.

13. Gregory thus includes this under the heading "spurious patristic witnesses" (to *Gos. Hebr.*); also J. FREY, *Die Fragmente judenchristlicher Evangelien*, in C. MARKSCHIES – J. SCHRÖTER (eds.), *Antike christliche Apokryphen in deutscher Übersetzung*. Bd. 1: *Evangelien und Verwandtes*, Teilbd. 1, Tübingen, Mohr Siebeck, 2012, 560-592, p. 585. Beatrice mounts a vigorous defence of Jerome's accuracy in attributing the citation to the *Gospel of the Hebrews* (though see the detailed rejoinder of M.W. MITCHELL, *Bodiless Demons and Written Gospels: Reflections on "'The Gospel according to the Hebrews' in the*

Origen too knows the saying, but attributes it to an apocryphal "Teaching of Peter" (*Princ., praef.* 8). Precisely what text Origen might have had in mind is uncertain. This part of Origen's text survives only in Rufinus' Latin translation and the words here (*doctrina Petri*) might refer to a work known to exist (but not extant) from elsewhere called the κήρυγμα Πέτρου, or they could refer to another work known as the διδασκαλία Πέτρου[14]. But how much weight can be placed on this seems very uncertain[15].

In summary it seems likely that the patristic evidence tells us little about the origin of the saying in Ignatius. Speculations about a non-canonical source probably simply arose because of the difference in wording from Luke.

2. *Ign.* Smyrn. *3.2 Compared with Lk 24,39*

I now consider the versions of the saying in Luke and Ignatius, looking not only at the saying itself but also the context in which the saying is placed in the two texts:

Luke 24	Ignatius, *Smyrn.* 3
[33] Καὶ ἀναστάντες αὐτῇ τῇ ὥρᾳ ὑπέστρεψαν εἰς Ἰερουσαλὴμ καὶ εὗρον ἠθροισμένους τοὺς ἕνδεκα καὶ τοὺς σὺν αὐτοῖς, [34] λέγοντας ὅτι ὄντως ἠγέρθη ὁ κύριος καὶ ὤφθη Σίμωνι. [35] καὶ αὐτοὶ ἐξηγοῦντο τὰ ἐν τῇ ὁδῷ καὶ ὡς ἐγνώσθη αὐτοῖς ἐν τῇ κλάσει τοῦ ἄρτου.	

Apostolic Fathers", in *NT* 52 [2010] 221-240). Beatrice argues that the whole section here, including the introduction (he takes the subject of the introductory *dicens* as the "testimony", not Ignatius), is from the *Gospel of the Hebrews*, with the "I" of "I saw" as the apostle Matthew. The theory is fairly speculative; not least of the difficulties is why the sequel is in the third person, not the first person: presumably the reference to those "with Peter" encompasses all the eleven (perhaps more), including Matthew: why then does the text say that Jesus "said to *them* ... and *they* touched him" (not that Jesus "said to us ... and we touched him")?

14. See W. SCHNEEMELCHER, *The Kerygma Petrou*, in E. HENNECKE (ed.), *New Testament Apocrypha*, vol. 2, London, Lutterworth, 1965, 94-102, pp. 97-98.

15. HAGNER, *Sayings* (n. 5), p. 239, uses these patristic attributions of the saying as virtually the sole argument to reject any direct link between Ignatius and Luke; but this seems somewhat optimistic (bearing in mind too that the patristic evidence is by no means unitary). GREGORY, *Reception* (n. 3), p. 73, links the claim of Origen with the note in Ign. *Smyrn.* 3.2 that Jesus came to "those who were *with Peter*" to suggest a specifically Petrine source (or a source linked with the name of Peter) here. But the note about Peter in Ignatius may be better explained in another way: see below.

³⁶ Ταῦτα δὲ αὐτῶν λαλούντων αὐτὸς ἔστη ἐν μέσῳ αὐτῶν καὶ λέγει αὐτοῖς· εἰρήνη ὑμῖν. ³⁷ πτοηθέντες δὲ καὶ ἔμφοβοι γενόμενοι ἐδόκουν πνεῦμα θεωρεῖν. ³⁸ καὶ εἶπεν αὐτοῖς· τί τεταραγμένοι ἐστὲ καὶ διὰ τί διαλογισμοὶ ἀναβαίνουσιν ἐν τῇ καρδίᾳ ὑμῶν; ³⁹ ἴδετε τὰς χεῖράς μου καὶ τοὺς πόδας μου ὅτι ἐγώ εἰμι αὐτός· **ψηλαφήσατέ με καὶ ἴδετε, ὅτι** πνεῦμα σάρκα καὶ ὀστέα οὐκ ἔχει καθὼς ἐμὲ θεωρεῖτε ἔχοντα. ⁴⁰ καὶ τοῦτο εἰπὼν ἔδειξεν αὐτοῖς τὰς χεῖρας καὶ τοὺς πόδας. ⁴¹ ἔτι δὲ ἀπιστούντων αὐτῶν ἀπὸ τῆς χαρᾶς καὶ θαυμαζόντων εἶπεν αὐτοῖς· ἔχετέ τι βρώσιμον ἐνθάδε; ⁴² οἱ δὲ ἐπέδωκαν αὐτῷ ἰχθύος ὀπτοῦ μέρος· ⁴³ καὶ λαβὼν ἐνώπιον αὐτῶν ἔφαγεν.	² καὶ ὅτε πρὸς τοὺς περὶ Πέτρον, ἦλθεν ἔφη αὐτοῖς· λάβετε, **ψηλαφήσατέ με καὶ ἴδετε, ὅτι** οὐκ εἰμὶ δαιμόνιον ἀσώματον. καὶ εὐθὺς αὐτοῦ ἥψαντο καὶ ἐπίστευσαν, κραθέντες τῇ σαρκὶ αὐτοῦ καὶ τῷ πνεύματι. διὰ τοῦτο καὶ θανάτου κατεφρόνησαν, ηὑρέθησαν δὲ ὑπὲρ θάνατον. ³ μετὰ δὲ τὴν ἀνάστασιν συνέφαγεν αὐτοῖς καὶ συνέπιεν ὡς σαρκικός, καίπερ πνευματικῶς ἡνωμένος τῷ πατρί.

Clearly the two texts display significant differences. And *if* Ignatius presupposes Luke's gospel in any way, it is clear that he is not *quoting* Luke (see above). But despite the differences between Ignatius and Luke, there are significant areas of agreement[16].

– There is verbatim agreement in the words ψηλαφήσατέ με καὶ ἴδετε ὅτι.

– In both texts, the saying refutes the notion that Jesus' physical body is in any way illusory (though in different words in relation to what is denied: see above).

– In both texts, the proof of Jesus' claim is provided by the offer to "touch" him and "see". (In Luke the offer is not explicitly taken up; in Ignatius it is.)

– Both texts conclude with a note that Jesus "ate" with the disciples.

– The setting in both is the same. In Ignatius, Jesus comes to "those who were around Peter" and spoke to them. In Luke, there is no reference to Peter in v. 39; however, the story here is very closely linked

---

16. Set out clearly and fully by KÖSTER, *Synoptische Überlieferung* (n. 5), p. 46, even though Köster himself discounts these and argues that Ignatius and Luke are independent of each other.

(in Luke's narrative) with the previous story in that the appearance of Jesus takes place while "they" were still speaking – and in the context, "they" are the two disciples who had been on the road to Emmaus who have come back to Jerusalem, met with the eleven "and those with them" (who must then include Peter) who have said that Jesus had already appeared to "Simon" (= Peter). In Luke, the audience is thus quite a wide group, including the eleven, but also "those with them" (v. 33) and the disciples from the Emmaus story[17]. On any showing this group includes Peter, and Peter had been singled out for mention as someone to whom Jesus had already appeared (probably in an initial resurrection appearance, cf. 1 Cor 15,5). From a perspective which was focused on Peter, this group could then easily be described as "those who were around Peter". There is thus certainly no discrepancy between Luke and Ignatius in this respect, and the two settings are perfectly consistent with each other[18].

The most obvious difference between the two versions is the different forms of what is denied: Luke's (implicit) denial that Jesus is a πνεῦμα contrasts with Ignatius' language that Jesus is "not a bodiless demon". It is here that more detailed arguments for the independence of Luke and Ignatius (if given at all) are developed. Two claims are often made: (i) there is no clear reason why Ignatius would have changed Luke's language if he had known it; and (ii) Ignatius seems to echo the words of Jesus he cites in his earlier charge that his opponents (who claim that Jesus only appeared to suffer) are equally "bodiless and demonic" (Ign. *Smyrn.* 2: ἀσωμάτοις καὶ δαιμονικοῖς); this charge seems to arise from the language of 3.2 (Jesus is not a "bodiless demon"), suggesting that the latter was already present in Ignatius' tradition and he echoed it in this earlier charge against his opponents[19]. I discuss each argument in turn.

---

17. Hence the suggestion that Luke uses the resurrection appearances in the flesh to bolster the authority of the Twelve as the sole witnesses of the resurrection (cf. S. MATTHEWS, *Fleshly Resurrection, Authority Claims, and the Scriptural Practices of Lukan Christianity*, in *JBL* 136 [2017] 163-183) seems unconvincing.

18. KÖSTER, *Synoptische Überlieferung* (n. 5), p. 45, lists this as one of the differences between the texts; but any difference is in wording, not in substance. Hence too the suggestion that Ignatius got this tradition from a specifically Petrine source (cf. above) seems otiose. There is nothing peculiarly Petrine about the story in Ignatius, and nothing to suggest that Peter played a significant role, other than as a member of the wider group of Jesus followers.

19. For (i), see KÖSTER, *Synoptische Überlieferung* (n. 5), pp. 47-48; SCHOEDEL, *Ignatius of Antioch* (n. 5), p. 226; GREGORY, *Reception* (n. 3), p. 72. (Schoedel also argues that, if Ignatius has known the Lukan wording, this would have suited his argument better: I cannot follow the logic of this.) For (ii), see KÖSTER, *Synoptische Überlieferung* (n. 5),

Why might Ignatius have changed the wording of Luke's version if he had known it? Gregory writes that "it is difficult to see why Ignatius would have substituted δαιμόνιον ἀσώματον for the Lukan πνεῦμα and σάρξ, for elsewhere Ignatius uses σαρκικός τε καὶ πνευματικός of Jesus"[20]. However, such a change of Luke's wording by Ignatius is by no means difficult to envisage. Luke's account here clearly implies that Jesus is *not* a πνεῦμα: Jesus invites the disciples to touch him and realise that a πνεῦμα does not have flesh and bones as Jesus manifestly (in the story) does. But Ignatius elsewhere clearly implies that Jesus *is* certainly πνευματικός and associated positively with πνεῦμα[21]. Precisely because of this, Ignatius would have found the Lukan wording here difficult to accept. Hence a change to have Jesus say that he is not a "bodiless demon" rather than not a πνεῦμα is entirely comprehensible as a secondary alteration made by Ignatius. The assertion that Jesus is not "bodiless" is entirely fitting with his polemic against his "opponents" here[22]. Whether Jesus might be a "demon" raises the issue of the relationship between the words Ignatius ascribes to Jesus here in 3.2 and the description of his opponents as δαιμονικοί just before this.

The claim that Ignatius' attack on his opponents in *Smyrn.* 2 as "bodiless and demonic" derives from Jesus' words about not being a "bodiless demon", with the inference drawn that the wording of the latter must have pre-dated Ignatius in a tradition which he took over and which then provided the source of his language in the earlier passage, is also debatable. In a recent article, Travis Proctor has shown very well how the language of Ignatius' invective in *Smyrn.* 2 gains considerable rhetorical power by labelling his opponents as δαιμονικός[23]. Although in earlier classical writers, a δαίμων or δαιμόνιον might be regarded positively[24], later writers generally, and early Christians uniformly, regarded δαίμονες

---

p. 48; SCHOEDEL, *Ignatius of Antioch*, p. 227; YOUNG, *Jesus Tradition* (n. 5), p. 230, and others.

20. GREGORY, *Reception* (n. 3), p. 72. He adds "and the expression σὰρξ καὶ πνεῦμα is one of which he is fond", though why this is relevant is not clear.

21. As indeed Gregory himself says ("Ignatius uses ... πνευματικός *of Jesus*": see above). Cf. Ign. *Eph.* 7.2; *Magn.* 1.2; 13.1; *Smyrn.* 12.2.

22. I do not discuss here the vexed question of the identity of Ignatius' "opponents", and/or whether they form a unitary group throughout his letters. See the discussion in the recent essay of J.W. MARSHALL, *The Object of Ignatius' Wrath and Jewish Angelic Mediators*, in *JEH* 56 (2005) 1-23, and the plausible hypothesis that they may indeed have been a unitary group throughout the letters, regarding Jesus as an angelic figure.

23. See T.W. PROCTOR, *Bodiless Docetists and the Daimonic Jesus: Daimonological Discourse and Anti-Docetic Polemic in Ignatius' Letter to the Smyrneans*, in *Archiv für Religionsgeschichte* 14 (2013) 183-204.

24. *Ibid.*, p. 193, referring to e.g. Hesiod, Plato.

negatively as evil[25]. Further, "demons" were often regarded as constituted by πνεῦμα, thus being "pneumatic"[26]. The claim that the opponents were "bodiless" might have been regarded by the opponents themselves as relatively harmless, or indeed taken positively: if they believed that Jesus' resurrected (and perhaps earthly) body was somewhat unreal, then his risen life would have been "bodiless" and his followers too would have been happy to share in such a bodiless existence[27]. However, for Ignatius, the claim that these people are "bodiless" would be the very opposite of positive: for he claims that Christians must unite with the "flesh and spirit" of Jesus[28]. By denying the reality of the "flesh" of Jesus, and focusing solely on a "bodiless" existence, they are excluding themselves from any share in full resurrection life. Further, Ignatius immediately damns such ideas by saying that the opponents are not only bodiless but "bodiless – and demonic!"[29]. This further claim has considerable rhetorical power, casting the opponents in the category of the demonic and hence irredeemably evil. This claim is linked closely with the saying of Jesus which follows almost immediately in 3.2, that he is "not a bodiless δαίμων". The claims of the opponents (about bodiless existence) are thus said to be nothing to do with Jesus himself: such claims are "demonic" and Jesus is *not* a "demon". Moreover, they are shown here to be absurd: if they imply the demonic nature of Jesus, then this would be neither accepted, nor asserted, by any Christian. The words placed on Jesus' lips here by Ignatius are thus a *reductio ad absurdum*: manifestly Jesus is not a "demon" (since, in the world view of early Christians, demons are regarded negatively and evil: see above)[30].

---

25. *Ibid.*, p. 194: "*Daimons* are almost exclusively evil within early Christian literature, and carried increasingly sinister undertones within 'pagan' Greek literature at the time when Ignatius' letters would have been composed and initially interpreted".

26. Whether this meant that a demon was "bodiless" is less clear: see the discussion in G.A. SMITH, *How Thin Is a Demon?*, in *JECS* 16 (2008) 479-512, arguing that demons were regularly thought to have physical substance of some sort. (I am grateful to Professor John Kloppenborg for this reference.)

27. Cf. Marcion, *Acts of John* 93, the Ophites of Iren. *Epid.* 1.30.13: see PROCTOR, *Bodiless Docetists* (n. 23), pp. 190-191.

28. Cf. *Magn.* 1.2; *Smyrn.* 1.1; 3.2; 12.2; 13.2.

29. For this as the force of the καὶ δαιμονικοῖς, see PROCTOR, *Bodiless Docetists* (n. 23), pp. 184, 198; also SCHOEDEL, *Ignatius of Antioch* (n. 5), p. 226. Thus being "bodiless" and "demonic" may be originally separate categories: cf. too n. 26 above.

30. Cf. PROCTOR, *Bodiless Docetists* (n. 23), p. 194: "*Smyrn.* 3.2 is an interpretive absurdity, in that it insinuates that Ignatius' opponents equated Jesus with a 'daimon'. This would have been a most unlikely Christology due to the pervasiveness of apocalyptic daimonology in early Christianity". Also p. 195: "Ignatius' insinuation that his opponents describe the bodiless Jesus as daimonic, then, constructs a conflate Christology that twists positive bodiless terminology ('pneumatic') into its sinister counterpart. In sum, Ignatius'

The logic of this is that the reference to the opponents as "demonic" in *Smyrn.* 2 and the denial by Jesus that he is a "bodiless demon" in 3.2 are linked inextricably together. Further, given the uniformly negative view of "demons" in early Christianity, it is difficult to see how any early Christian would have seriously entertained the notion that Jesus might have been a δαίμων using that specific terminology. The "demon" language in both contexts is thus inextricably linked with Ignatius' polemic. As a result, it is very hard to envisage the saying in 3.2 having some independent existence with this wording prior to Ignatius. Hence rather than the saying in *Smyrn.* 3.2 existing prior to Ignatius in precisely this form and then providing the impetus and the terminology for the earlier invective in *Smyrn.* 2, it is much more likely that the specific language of demon/demonic is due to Ignatius himself, developing his arsenal of arguments to use against his opponents[31]. The saying about Jesus being not a bodiless demon thus probably originates with Ignatius himself.

In conclusion, neither of the two main arguments often deployed to support a traditional (i.e. pre-Ignatian) origin of Ignatius' form of the saying of Jesus denying that he is a bodiless demon are fully convincing. There are very good reasons why Ignatius would have wanted to change the form of the saying in Luke where Jesus denies that he is a πνεῦμα; and rather than the wording of Ignatius' attack on his opponents for being "bodiless and demonic" in *Smyrn.* 2 being inspired by a pre-existing saying about Jesus not being a "bodiless demon", the language of both sayings may well be due to Ignatius himself. Thus Ignatius himself is responsible for the wording of the Jesus saying in *Smyrn.* 3.2, and he could easily have redacted the form of the saying in Lk 24,39 for his own rhetorical and theological purposes.

Is there though any evidence to suggest that Ignatius is dependent on the *Lukan* form of the tradition, rather than on an independent version? The fact that Ignatius' version is very "Ignatian" tells us nothing on its own about the nature of the tradition which might lie behind the saying

---

'daimonic' terminology functions as a rhetorical absurdity that distorts 'heretical' Christologies into the indefensible belief in a 'daimonic Jesus'". Also, the fact that "bodiless demon" may be something of an oxymoron (cf. n. 26 above) may add to the absurdity.

31. YOUNG, *Jesus Tradition* (n. 5), pp. 231-232, also sees Ignatius' language as later than that of Luke, and determined by anti-docetic polemic; but he ascribes it to the "wider Christian community" in which such polemic was taking place. But why then distinguish between Ignatius himself and the "wider community"? Ignatius was undoubtedly part of a wider community, but his language here could just as easily be his own (and Ignatius does not appeal to the views in any "wider community" to attack his opponents).

here[32]. A possible indication that Ignatius is indeed presupposing Luke's version of the tradition may however be shown by a consideration of the slightly wider context of the saying in both Luke and Ignatius.

As noted earlier, Ignatius and Luke both agree in following the saying about "touch and see" (that Jesus is not a πνεῦμα/bodiless demon) with a note about Jesus "eating", albeit in slightly different form: in Luke Jesus asks for something to eat and they give him a piece of fish which he proceeds to "eat" (Lk 24,42-43); in Ignatius there is the more general statement that "after his resurrection he [Jesus] ate and drank with them as a fleshly being" (Ign. *Smyrn.* 3.3). The significance of this in the present context is that the reference to Jesus eating here may be due to Luke's redaction of the tradition; Ignatius' agreement with Luke in this detail of the structuring of material at this point may therefore show that Ignatius presupposes Luke's redactional activity and hence presupposes Luke's finished gospel. To show this requires a consideration of the broader Lukan narrative.

The story which Luke tells of the appearance of Jesus to the disciples, which occupies the extended section in Lk 24,36-50, is highly complex. In terms of its origins, and parallels, it raises many critical issues which have generated considerable discussion in recent years. In particular the questions of the relationship of the section (and indeed the whole of Luke 24) with John, and with the gospel text presupposed by Marcion, have been intensively debated[33]. I leave those issues aside for the purposes of this essay and focus solely on the text of Luke on its own.

Even without considering any source-critical questions, the Lukan text poses a number of problems. Luke 24 is an extremely long chapter, and traditional critical scholarship divides the material up into a number of different "pericopes"; however, it should be noted that such a division

---

32. NEIRYNCK, *Luc 24,36-43* (n. 6), pp. 213-219, argues that the whole of Lk 24,36-43 was a Lukan creation, and hence the agreement of Ignatius with Luke shows that Ignatius presupposes Luke's finished gospel. However, the arguments are rather general and not fully persuasive. E.g., Neirynck refers to the parallel structure between the appearance of Jesus in Luke 24 and the appearance of the angel in Lk 1,28-30: a greeting (1,28; 24,36) followed by a note of perplexity (1,29; 24,37) and then a response by the angel/Jesus (1,30; 24,38). But the structure is still fairly general and e.g. the responses of the angel in Luke 1 and Jesus in Luke 24 are rather different in substance. Neirynck also seeks to show that much of the vocabulary of the section can be shown to be Lukan: this is undeniable with Lukan vocabulary to be seen in the use of e.g. εἰρήνη (v. 36), διαλογισμοί (v. 38), ἐνθάδε (v. 41), ἐπέδωκαν (v. 42); but these instances cannot of themselves show that the substance of the tradition is a Lukan creation *de novo*.

33. For the relationship with John, see e.g. NEIRYNCK, *Luc 24,36-43* (n. 6), and others discussed there; for Marcion, see D.A. SMITH, *Marcion's Gospel and the Resurrected Jesus of Canonical Luke 24*, in *ZAC* 21 (2017) 41-62, and the survey of different scholarly views.

is rather artificial, and potentially misleading, at least in relation to the chronology and geography which Luke's own story line provides. Traditionally the story after v. 12 is divided into at least three pericopes which are often treated separately: the appearance of Jesus on the road to Emmaus (vv. 13-35), the appearance to the disciples (vv. 36-43), and the teaching of Jesus to the disciples and his departure from them (vv. 44-50)[34]. Yet we should note that, for Luke, the three stories form one, almost seamless, whole. The Emmaus story leads straight into the story of the appearance in vv. 36-43, and with no break at all in the personnel involved between v. 35 and v. 36 (so that the two disciples on the Emmaus road *are* included in the group who see and hear Jesus in vv. 36-43: see above). And the teaching of Jesus in vv. 44-49 follows on without a break from v. 43.

The account of the appearance of Jesus to the disciples focuses on the issue of whether Jesus is a πνεῦμα. What exactly the disciples may have had in mind is debated[35]. In the usual line of interpretation of the story, Jesus gives two responses to the suggestion to reject any idea that he is πνεῦμα: first, Jesus invites them to see his hands and feet and then to touch him to verify that he really does have flesh and bones (v. 39). Luke then (perhaps) says that Jesus does then show them his hands and feet

---

34. Even if the last two are not always placed in different pericopes, there is very often a clear break marked between v. 43 and v. 44 by e.g. a new paragraph starting at v. 44.

35. See the survey of possibilities in D.A. SMITH, *Seeing a Pneuma(tic Body): The Apologetic Interests of Luke 24.36-43*, in *CBQ* 72 (2010) 752-772. I find Smith's suggestion that the Lukan Jesus is here criticising Paul and Pauline ideas somewhat difficult if only because there is no hint elsewhere in Luke-Acts that Luke is critical of Paul in any way: indeed precisely the opposite – Paul is the hero of the whole of the second half of Acts with no suggestion that his ideas about resurrection might be a little suspect. Smith does not include in his survey the possibility that the disciples in Luke might have regarded Jesus as an angelic figure. Yet the idea of a dead person returning as a divine messenger is not unprecedented (cf. Abraham in Lk 16,19-31); so too Luke may have sometimes used "spirit" and "angel" interchangeably: cf. Acts 23,7, where the claim that the Sadducees say that there is "neither resurrection nor angel nor spirit" while the Pharisees accept "both" (τὰ ἀμφότερα) may imply that Luke regarded "angel" and "spirit" here as virtually synonymous. The notion that the risen Jesus might have been (like) an angel was clearly widespread (cf. the negative comments in Heb 1–2; *Gospel of Thomas* 13, and more positive references in *Hermas* and other writings: see the survey in MARSHALL, *Object* [n. 22], pp. 12-18); and for the terminology where "spirit" is used for a person who has died but is still alive in some form in a heavenly context, see e.g. Heb 12,23; 1 Pet 3,19; *1 En.* 22. The Emmaus story also has a well-known parallel in the story of the angel Raphael in the book of Tobit: and it may well be that Luke, by juxtaposing the Emmaus story with the account in Lk 24,36-39, wants to suppress firmly any notion that the risen Jesus was an angelic (or angelomorphic) figure: see e.g. C.H.T. FLETCHER-LOUIS, *Luke-Acts: Angels, Christology and Soteriology* (WUNT, 2.94), Tübingen, Mohr Siebeck, 1997, pp. 62-70; D.R. CATCHPOLE, *Resurrection People: Studies in the Resurrection Narratives of the Gospels*, London, Darton, Longman and Todd, 2000, pp. 85-135.

(v. 40)[36]. However, the disciples' reaction appears to be somewhat ambiguous: they are still "unbelieving" (ἀπιστούντων), though this may be mitigated slightly by the fact that it is said to be "from joy" (ἀπὸ τῆς χαρᾶς)[37]. Thus the disciples' reaction appears to be slightly negative, and not 100% positive. According a widely held line of interpretation, Jesus then gives a further response to the disciples' concerns in vv. 41-43: he asks for something to eat, they give him some fish and he eats it before their eyes (v. 43: ἐνώπιον αὐτῶν). This, it is often said, is then the clear definitive evidence that Jesus is a fully fleshly being, eating as well as having flesh and bones: the disciples are now fully convinced of the reality of Jesus' resurrection body as fully human (and fleshly) and Jesus has succeeded in correcting their prior, incorrect understanding of him[38].

However, if this is the way Luke intended the story to be read, it is very surprising that he is completely silent about any reaction of the disciples after Jesus eats the fish. If this were the moment that the "penny dropped" for them, as if Jesus' eating were the final definitive proof, one would surely expect some note by the narrator to the effect that the disciples have lost their unbelief of just two verses earlier and are now convinced by Jesus' further action of eating with their minds set on the right track[39]. Also Luke gives no explanation of why or how the fact that Jesus ate something showed that his body was real and fleshly[40]. In fact

36. However, the verse is a "Western non-interpolation", missing in D and related MSS. Part of the problem of the verse, if it is part of Luke's original text, is that it is somewhat redundant, adding very little to what has already been said. The parallel in John (cf. Jn 20,20) raises issues about the possible relationship between Luke and John which would extend this essay beyond its allotted space.

37. However positive one could take the language of being "unbelieving" (or "disbelieving") and "marvelling" here (cf. M. WOLTER, *Das Lukasevangelium* [HNT, 5], Tübingen, Mohr Siebeck, 2008, pp. 790-791, with classical parallels), it remains the case that for Luke, ἀπιστέω and ἄπιστος are always used in a negative sense (cf. Lk 24,11; 9,41; 12,46). Contrast Ignatius' own unambiguous affirmation that, having touched Jesus, the disciples "believed" (ἐπίστευσαν).

38. See e.g. NEIRYNCK, *Luc 24,36-43* (n. 6), pp. 224-225; J.A. FITZMYER, *The Gospel according to Luke X–XXIV: A New Translation with Introduction and Commentary* (AB, 28A), New York, Doubleday, 1985, p. 577; FLETCHER-LOUIS, *Luke-Acts* (n. 35), pp. 64-65; WOLTER, *Lukasevangelium* (n. 37), p. 790.

39. See R.J. DILLON, *From Eye-Witnesses to Ministers of the Word: Tradition and Composition in Luke 24* (AnBib, 82), Roma, Biblical Institute, 1978, pp. 166-167.

40. Many claim there was a widespread assumption that angels do not eat, and that this is presupposed here: hence Jesus' eating something shows that he is not an angel. But would Luke's readers have known this? In fact the situation is not quite so clear-cut: there are famous instances in the Hebrew Bible itself where angels do eat (cf. Gen 18,8; 19,3; also as late as Tob 6,5). It is true that many later commentators seek to evade the force of the Genesis texts and argue that the angels did not really eat; also Tob 12,19 claims that the angel only appeared to eat and Tobit and Tobias only saw a vision. See the survey in D. GOODMAN, *Do Angels Eat?*, in *JJS* 37 (1986) 160-175. However, the fact remains that the stories of angels eating are firmly present in Jewish scriptural tradition. So would a

Jesus goes on immediately to give them important teaching, and Luke says that "he opened their minds to understand the scriptures" (v. 45). This suggests that their intellectual understanding was still in some way deficient, even by the end of v. 43. It might be of course that their understanding of the nature of Jesus' resurrection body was full and complete by the time of v. 43, and that in vv. 44, 46 Jesus now gives teaching on a new topic, viz. how all that has happened is in line with scripture. Yet still the lack of any mention of a response by the disciples to Jesus' eating the fish remains. Thus even if the deficient understanding of the disciples (requiring Jesus to "open their minds" in v. 45) relates only to the topics of the later teaching, it is still the case that the possible demonstration in Jesus' eating the fish is not necessarily the persuasive knockdown argument it is sometimes said to be. After Jesus has explained things to the disciples (vv. 46-47), charged them to be witnesses (v. 48), and promised that they will receive "power from on high" (v. 49), Jesus disappears from their sight and they "worship" Jesus and return to Jerusalem "with great joy" (v. 52): here seems to be the positive counterpart to the somewhat muted, and slightly negative earlier reaction of the disciples in v. 41: whereas earlier they were "unbelieving" because of (or almost in spite of) their joy, now their joy is unqualified and complete[41]. It seems therefore more likely that, insofar as the earlier attempt by Jesus to put right the deficient and/or wrong understanding of the disciples was not entirely successful, what corrects things is not just the eating of the fish by Jesus, but rather the whole section of the story where Jesus eats fish *and* gives important teaching to the disciples, as well as giving them the charge to go and preach about repentance and forgiveness and promising them the power to enable them to do so.

How does Jesus' eating fish contribute to this? As we have seen, if it is intended to be a final argument convincing the disciples that they were wrong in their understanding, it may have only partial success (since Jesus "opens their minds" in v. 45); and nothing is said by the narrator suggesting that Jesus succeeded in convincing them by eating, where he had only (at best) half succeeded by inviting them to touch him. All this suggests that the eating may not be related to the issue of Jesus' body being fleshly at all. Rather, it may have a quite different function.

The small incident may rather set up a context where Jesus and the disciples are now *having a meal together*. The language can be taken as

---

reader of Luke who was not so well versed in contemporary Jewish traditions have deduced that Jesus could not be an angel from the fact that he ate something?

41. See DILLON, *Eye-Witnesses* (n. 39), p. 188; J. NOLLAND, *Luke 18:35–24:53* (WBC, 35C), Waco, TX, Word, 1993, pp. 1214-1215.

implying that Jesus alone eats the fish[42]. However, it can also be taken as implying that the food is shared and eaten by all[43]. The meal may not be intended to be "eucharistic"[44]; but the Eucharist in Luke is one of a series of stories where Jesus provides important teaching, especially about repentance and forgiveness, in the context of a meal. Indeed this linking of teaching with a meal context seems to be particularly characteristic of Luke[45]. Hence the narrative sequence here, with a reference to Jesus eating, thereby indicating a meal context, and leading on to further key teaching by Jesus (on repentance and forgiveness: cf. v. 47) and instructions for the disciples, looks to be Lukan through and through[46]. Thus the sequence here – the "touch me and see" account, the eating of the fish implying a meal context, and then further teaching by Jesus – looks very much as if it is a Lukan compositional creation.

If we now reconsider the evidence from Ignatius in the light of this analysis of Luke, Ignatius' agreements with Luke gain in significance. For Ignatius agrees with Luke not only in the verbal agreements in the "touch me and see" saying, but also in the sequence whereby this incident is followed by a reference to eating together (Lk 24,42-43; Ign. Smyrn. 3.3). Yet it is this which may well be due to Luke's redactional or compositional activity, creating this narrative sequence. Ignatius has

---

42. And indeed it is taken this way by those who argue that the purpose of the small story is to convince the disciples that Jesus' body is real and fleshly.

43. For other examples of one person (or some people) eating ἐνώπιον others, but clearly in context implying a shared meal, see e.g. 2 Sam 11,43; 1 Kgs 1,25; Lk 13,26, and see CATCHPOLE, *Resurrection People* (n. 35), p. 101. In any case, the story would be more than a little artificial if it assumed that just one portion of fish had been prepared – by a large group of people who were not expecting a special visitor – and this was then given to Jesus alone to eat! (Cf. too NEIRYNCK, *Luc 24,36-43* [n. 6], p. 225, for the fact that the story presupposes things that are not said [though he argues that what is not said here is a positive reaction by the disciples].)

44. See CATCHPOLE, *Resurrection People* (n. 35), p. 131. It is "fish" (not bread or wine) that is eaten; and there are no verbal echoes of the Last Supper where Jesus "blessed", "broke" and "gave" bread to the others, as e.g. in v. 30 where eucharistic echoes are widely acknowledged.

45. See *ibid.*, pp. 131-134; see variously Lk 5,29-32; 7,36-50; 15,2.3-10.11-32 (esp. v. 23); 14,1-14.15-24. The reference to the meal is redactional in 5,29 (cf. Mk 2,15); the other references may well be redactional too (though they occur in Q or "L" contexts so that one cannot be certain).

46. This may be further supported by the strong structural parallels, involving common motifs, between Lk 24,36-53 and Acts 1,1-14 (on which, see H.J. DE JONGE, *The Chronology of the Ascension Stories in Luke and Acts*, in *NTS* 59 [2013] 151-171, pp. 163-165). The brief indication of a meal context provided by the note about Jesus eating is then the parallel to the meal context implied in the συναλιζόμενος in Acts 1,4 (for this as referring to eating together, see *ibid.*, p. 162, n. 34); this would add further support to the interpretation of the note about Jesus' eating as primarily a reference to a common meal, not as a proof of Jesus' fleshly body.

exactly the same sequence. Yet Ignatius has nothing of the broader Lukan context where the eating motif is integrally related (for Luke) to Jesus' teaching which follows and which forms the key part of the sequel. Thus in Luke we have a coherent, and characteristically Lukan, sequence; in Ignatius we see what seem to be simply vestiges of this original Lukan scheme. All this suggests strongly that Ignatius presupposes the Lukan account, betraying knowledge of the Lukan sequence here which is not simply traditional but part of Luke's narrative compositional activity using the materials he has. With individual traditions, it is always possible to argue that agreement between two accounts may be due to dependence on a common tradition; but the agreement here in the sequencing of the two traditions seems to be a case where Ignatius is presupposing not just common tradition(s) he might share with Luke, but also Luke's compositional activity.

As noted earlier, Ignatius may not know Luke's gospel as such. He is certainly not "quoting" Luke at all. But the evidence here does suggest that Ignatius presupposes Luke's finished gospel and his version of the Jesus tradition he uses here implies that Luke's narrative sequence here, which was created by Luke, was already in existence.

III. IGN. *POL.* 2.1//LUKE 6,32

The parallel between Ign. *Pol.* 2.1 and Lk 6,32 is rarely noted in discussions of the possible relationship between Luke and Ignatius, and is equally rarely noted in commentaries[47]. Nevertheless, there may be a significant overlap in wording:

Lk 6,32	Ign, *Pol.* 2.1
καὶ εἰ ἀγαπᾶτε τοὺς ἀγαπῶντας ὑμᾶς, ποία ὑμῖν χάρις ἐστίν; ...	Καλοὺς μαθητὰς ἐὰν φιλῇς χάρις σοι οὐκ ἔστιν

47. GREGORY, *Reception* (n. 3), p. 70, mentions it in a footnote, but does not discuss it in detail in his discussion of Ignatius (he refers to his discussion of the parallel in *2 Clem.* 13.4, though he does not mention the text of Ignatius there [pp. 134-135]). Foster does not mention the parallel explicitly in either of his two essays; nor does Young (though he does not claim to provide a comprehensive treatment of possible evidence from Ignatius, focusing only on the one saying in *Smyrn.* 3.2). SCHOEDEL, *Ignatius of Antioch* (n. 5), p. 262, simply states that the similarity between the texts "suggests an indebtedness to common tradition", but without any detailed analysis; PAULSEN, *Briefe* (n. 5), p. 102, simply has "Vgl. Lk 6,32". Only KÖSTER, *Synoptische Überlieferung* (n. 5), p. 45, provides any detailed discussion. It is though noted in (some) editions of the Apostolic Fathers (though obviously without comment): see e.g. F.X. FUNK – K. BIHLMEYER – W. SCHNEEMELCHER (eds.), *Die apostolischen Väter*, Tübingen, Mohr Siebeck, 1956, ³1970, p. 111.

In one way Ignatius' wording is quite different from Luke's, despite the general similarity in content. Ignatius has "good disciples" as the potential object of love by the hearer; Luke has "those who love you". Ignatius uses φιλέω for "love", Luke uses ἀγαπάω[48]. Nevertheless, it may be noteworthy that both versions use the construction with χάρις in the apodosis. The significance of this lies in the fact that, in the synoptic tradition, Luke's use of χάρις here is widely recognised as redactional compared with Matthew's parallel using μισθός: Luke has probably redacted the Q saying to bring it into line with the vocabulary of a Hellenistic reciprocity ethic[49]. Hence Ignatius here appears to betray knowledge of Luke's redactional activity in reworking this saying about reciprocity. Thus Ignatius again presupposes Luke's editing of the tradition. This is not to say that Ignatius is *citing* Luke's gospel: manifestly he is not; but it does mean that he is to be placed at a point in a trajectory which is later than Luke, after the time when the saying absorbed this element of Lukan editorial activity.

Köster recognises that Ignatius may display here an agreement with LkR activity; but he does not follow his own methodology (of taking the presence of synoptic redactional material in another text as clear evidence of dependence), claiming instead that the two versions are independent[50]. He argues that sayings about love of enemies circulated with many variations in early Christianity so that one cannot deduce literary dependence between any two versions. This may be so; but one is not here arguing that Ignatius' version is due to "literary dependence" ("literarische Abhängigkeit") on Luke – only that Ignatius' version of the saying is here shown to be post-Lukan[51]. Köster also claims that this is the only specific link between Ignatius and Luke and hence one cannot easily, and perhaps then should not, deduce anything about Ignatius' knowledge of Luke from this one example. However, this assertion is made by Köster at the end of his discussion of this text before he has

---

48. φιλέω is also used in some readings of *Did.* 1.3 (P.Oxy. 1739 and *Apos. Con.*) in a saying very similar to this. But whether one can deduce from this the existence of a variant form of the saying is doubtful: the two verbs are all but synonyms.

49. See C.M. TUCKETT, *Synoptic Tradition in the Didache*, in J.-M. SEVRIN (ed.), *The New Testament in Early Christianity* (BETL, 86), Leuven, LUP – Peeters, 1989, 197-230, pp. 220-224 (on a similar parallel between Lk 6,32 and *Did.* 1.3) with further references; also J.M. ROBINSON – P. HOFFMANN – J.S. KLOPPENBORG (eds.), *The Critical Edition of Q*, Minneapolis, MN, Fortress; Leuven, Peeters, 2000, p. 68 (taking Matthew's wording at this point as closest to Q).

50. KÖSTER, *Synoptische Überlieferung* (n. 5), p. 45.

51. As noted earlier, no claim is being made here that Ignatius used Luke directly as a source – only that his version in these parallels presupposes Luke's editing of the same material and hence that Ignatius post-dates Luke.

given any consideration to the parallel between Ign. *Smyrn.* 3.2 and Luke 24[52]. If one takes seriously the possibility that the latter parallel may also be due to Ignatius presupposing Luke's gospel, then the parallel here may not be quite so isolated.

IV. OTHER PARALLELS

One other possible example of Ignatius presupposing Luke's gospel occurs in *Smyrn.* 1.2. Here Ignatius says that Jesus' death on the cross occurred "under Pontius Pilate and the tetrarch Herod". The involvement of Herod along with Pilate in the passion story is attested in Lk 23,6-12, but not in the other canonical gospels. Insofar as the possible parallel is discussed in detail it is usually attributed to common tradition (or a common passion tradition). Köster, and following him Schoedel, appeals to the interpretation of the "kings of the earth" of Ps 2,2 as Herod and Pilate in Acts 4,25-28 as evidence for an earlier tradition in pre-Lukan Christianity which had linked Pilate and Herod in relation to Jesus' passion[53]. But the Acts speeches might be regarded today as owing rather more to Luke's own creativity and hence may not provide clear evidence of earlier traditions. Herod and Pilate are also linked in the passion narrative in the *Gospel of Peter*, but that gospel is probably also dependent on the canonical gospels and hence this detail there may well derive from Luke[54]. Whether the introduction of Herod into the passion narrative is due to Luke himself or is based on a pre-Lukan tradition in Luke 23 is very difficult to say. Hence one cannot argue here that this detail clearly shows a link between Ignatius and Luke's redactional activity. A link between Ignatius and "L" material does not necessarily show a link between Ignatius and Luke. Nevertheless, the evidence may give some subsidiary support to the possibility that Ignatius presupposes Luke's finished gospel.

---

52. KÖSTER, *Synoptische Überlieferung* (n. 5), p. 46. His discussion of the "touch me and see" passage follows immediately after his discussion of the love saying. But to claim that there is just one example of Ignatius possibly knowing Luke, and then to make deductions from its alleged uniqueness, prejudges the whole issue if one does not consider all the possible evidence first. See n. 8 above.

53. *Ibid.*, pp. 26-27; SCHOEDEL, *Ignatius of Antioch* (n. 5), pp. 222-223. Köster's treatment also seems to be part of his "divide and conquer" approach: his discussion of this parallel occurs under the heading "Kerygmatische Überlieferung" (p. 26) and the example is then dismissed well before discussing "Besondere Verwandtschaft mit einem Evangelium" (p. 44).

54. Cf. P. FOSTER, *The Gospel of Peter*, Leiden, Brill, 2010, pp. 119-147.

Some further subsidiary support may be provided by the possible parallel between Ign. *Eph.* 1.2 and Lk 14,26.27(//Mt 10,37.38)[55]:

Ign. *Eph.* 1.2	Lk 14,26.27	Mt 10,37.38
... δυνηθῶ μαθητὴς εἶναι	... οὐ δύναται εἶναί μου μαθητής	... οὐκ ἔστιν μου ἄξιος

The verbal agreement is relatively slight, though the context in both Ignatius and the gospels is that of suffering for one's Christian commitment. In the gospels, the words provide the conclusion of the Q sayings about hating one's family and cross-bearing. The wording is quite different in Matthew. It is however uncertain whether Luke or Matthew preserves the Q wording more accurately, and hence it is difficult to know if the Lukan version is LkR[56]. The parallel is clearly not close, but Ignatius' wording does align with the Lukan version over against Matthew. However, the fact that Luke's version is not clearly redactional means that one cannot exclude the possibility that Ignatius might link with the tradition underlying Luke (Q?), rather than with Luke's gospel itself. On its own, the parallel is probably too slight to bear very much weight in the overall argument. However, it may provide another instance to show that possible examples of Ignatius presupposing Luke's gospel are by no means isolated.

Finally, two other pieces of evidence may be noted very briefly here, though they probably cannot contribute anything of great significance to this debate. Thus at a few points, Ignatius has parallels to texts which appear in both Luke and Matthew. The two closest are perhaps Ign. *Eph.* 14.2// Lk 6,44//Mt 12,33 and Ign. *Eph.* 11.1//Lk 3,7//Mt 3,7.

Ign. *Eph.* 14.2	Lk 6,44	Mt 12,33
φανερὸν τὸ δένδρον ἀπὸ τοῦ καρποῦ αὐτοῦ	ἕκαστον γὰρ δένδρον ἐκ τοῦ ἰδίου καρποῦ γινώσκεται	ἐκ γὰρ τοῦ καρποῦ τὸ δένδρον γινώσκεται.

Ign. *Eph.* 11.1	Lk 3,7	Mt 3,7
ἢ γὰρ τὴν μέλλουσαν ὀργὴν φοβηθῶμεν	τίς ὑπέδειξεν ὑμῖν φυγεῖν ἀπὸ τῆς μελλούσης ὀργῆς;	τίς ὑπέδειξεν ὑμῖν φυγεῖν ἀπὸ τῆς μελλούσης ὀργῆς;

---

55. I am grateful to Professor Henk Jan de Jonge for drawing my attention to this possible parallel.
56. ROBINSON – HOFFMANN – KLOPPENBORG, *Critical Edition* (n. 49), p. 452, take Luke's wording here as more likely that of Q.

The parallels are not close (the second in particular consists only of the phrase "coming wrath"); and in both instances, Luke's version is all but identical with Matthew's so that it is impossible to determine if Ignatius shows knowledge of the specifically Lukan version of the tradition. Thus these cases cannot show very much in relation to the issue of the relationship between Ignatius and Luke. It is highly likely that Ignatius presupposes Matthew's finished gospel[57]; hence any verbal similarity here could be due to familiarity with Matthew (or even with Q) rather than with Luke.

V. CONCLUSION

The evidence examined here suggests that there is strong evidence that, in a couple of instances, Ignatius has parallels to Lukan traditions, and shows agreement with Lukan redactional or compositional features. This implies that Ignatius probably presupposes Luke's finished gospel and not simply earlier tradition(s) which he shares with Luke. Other evidence is ambiguous but is at least consistent with this result.

The issue of whether Ignatius presupposes Luke's gospel is part of a broader issue concerning the reception of Luke by early Christian writers. As noted at the start, it is widely held that there is no evidence that Luke's gospel was known by a swathe of early Christian authors. However, such a claim may need some reassessment. I have argued here that Ignatius presupposes (possibly knows) Luke's gospel. I have also argued elsewhere that Luke may be presupposed by the *Didache*, and not only in the section *Did.* 1.3–2.1 (which is widely regarded as a later addition to an earlier form of the *Didache*)[58], as well as by the author of *2 Clement*[59], and possibly too by the author of James[60].

How much help this all is in actually dating Luke with any confidence is not so certain, since many of these texts are themselves of uncertain date. So too with Ignatius, what was at one time regarded as a very firm

---

57. See FOSTER, *Epistles of Ignatius* (n. 5), pp. 174-175, especially on the parallel between Ign. *Smyrn.* 1.1 (ἵνα πληρωθῇ πᾶσα δικαιοσύνη ὑπ' αὐτοῦ) and Mt 3,15, arguing against Köster.

58. TUCKETT, *Synoptic Tradition in the Didache* (n. 49), pp. 212-214 (on *Did.* 16.1// Lk 12,35).

59. C.M. TUCKETT, *2 Clement*, Oxford, OUP, 2012, p. 238 (on *2 Clem.* 13.4//Lk 6,32).

60. C.M. TUCKETT, *James and Q*, in W.E. ARNAL *et al.* (eds.), *Scribal Practices and Social Structures among Jesus Adherents: Essays in Honour of John S. Kloppenborg* (BETL, 285), Leuven – Paris – Bristol, CT, Peeters, 2016, 233-250.

date for Ignatius is now much debated[61]. Thus to say that Luke pre-dates Ignatius may not prove very much about the date of Luke in absolute terms. Nevertheless, the widespread view that Luke is unknown among early Christian writers may need some qualification.

1 Wallingford Road, Cholsey   Christopher TUCKETT
Wallingford OX10 9LQ
UK
christopher.tuckett@theology.ox.ac.uk

---

61. The traditional date is some time in the period ca. 110-117 CE. For arguments that the letters are all pseudonymous and come from ca. 160 CE, see e.g. R.M. HÜBNER, *Thesen zur Echtheit und Datierung der sieben Briefe des Ignatius von Antiochien*, in ZAC 1 (1997) 44-72, and T. LECHNER, *Ignatius adversus Valentinianos? Chronologische und theologiegeschichtliche Studien zu den Briefen des Ignatius von Antiochien* (SupplVC, 47), Leiden, Brill, 1999. For responses, see e.g. A. LINDEMANN, *Antwort auf die 'Thesen zur Echtheit und Datierung der sieben Briefe des Ignatius von Antiochien'*, in ZAC 1 (1997) 185-194; M.J. EDWARDS, *Ignatius and the Second Century: An Answer to R. Hübner*, in ZAC 1 (1997) 214-226. For a date in between the two extremes, see T.D. BARNES, *The Date of Ignatius*, in ExpTim 120 (2008) 119-130 (Ignatius writes against Ptolemaeus); cf. also P. FOSTER, *The Writings of the Apostolic Fathers*, London, T&T Clark, 2007, pp. 84-89, for a survey (and suggesting a date ca. 125-150 CE).

„IST DAS NICHT JOSEPHS SOHN?" (LK 4,22)

JESU FAMILIE IN DEN NEUTESTAMENTLICHEN EVANGELIEN

Der christliche Glaube sieht Jesus als den Gesalbten („Christus") und als „Sohn Gottes", sogar als den präexistenten λόγος, aber zugleich versteht er Jesus als Menschen, der in einem bestimmten historischen Kontext lebte. Die Rede von der Inkarnation bringt das in besonderer Weise zum Ausdruck, lange bevor in der altkirchlichen Dogmatik die „Zwei-Naturen-Lehre" entwickelt wurde[1]. Die neutestamentlichen Evangelien sprechen auf jeweils ihre Weise vom irdischen Leben Jesu[2], und dazu gehört seine Zugehörigkeit zu einer Familie[3]. In der folgenden Darstellung soll versucht werden, die in den Evangelien gezeichneten unterschiedlichen Bilder der Familie Jesu auf ihre möglichen christologischen Implikationen und Konsequenzen hin zu befragen.

I. Jesus und seine Familie bei Markus, Matthäus und Johannes

1. *Jesu Familie bei Markus*

Das Markusevangelium beginnt nach der Eröffnungsaussage (1,1) mit dem durch ein Schriftzitat eingeleiteten Bericht über das Auftreten Johannes des Täufers, der das „Kommen" eines „Stärkeren" ansagt (1,7-8); und „es geschah in jenen Tagen", dass Jesus „kam" aus Nazareth in Galiläa[4] und sich taufen ließ (1,9-11). Damit ist Jesus als handelnde Person eingeführt, erst später erfährt man etwas über seine Herkunft. Nach

---

1. Zur „Zwei-Naturen-Lehre" vgl. U.H.J. Körtner, *Dogmatik* (Lehrwerk Evangelische Theologie, 5), Studienausgabe, Leipzig, Evangelische Verlagsanstalt, 2020, S. 411-417; zur Inkarnationsvorstellung *ibid.*, S. 523-530.
2. Das gilt unabhängig davon, ob man sie der Gattung nach eher als biographische oder eher als historiographische Schriften einordnet. Zur Diskussion vgl. E.-M. Becker, *Das Markus-Evangelium im Rahmen antiker Historiographie* (WUNT, 194), Tübingen, Mohr Siebeck, 2006, S. 99-100.
3. „Familie" wird im Folgenden verstanden als eine Gemeinschaft von Eltern und Kindern, ohne nähere Definition; vgl. D. Dettinger, *Neues Leben in der alten Welt: Der Beitrag frühchristlicher Schriften des späten ersten Jahrhunderts zum Diskurs über familiäre Strukturen in der griechisch-römischen Welt* (ABG, 59), Leipzig, Evangelische Verlagsanstalt, 2017, S. 95-105 (Haus und Familie im Frühjudentum).
4. Der Hinweis auf Nazareth in 1,9a ist von Bedeutung, nachdem in 1,5 von Judäa und von Jerusalem gesprochen worden war; Jesus ging, „aus Nazareth kommend", an den

Aktivitäten an verschiedenen Orten in Galiläa (1,14–3,12) kommt Jesus nach der Berufung der „Zwölf, die er auch Apostel nannte" (3,13-19)[5], „ins Haus" (εἰς οἶκον, 3,20a)[6], und in diesem Zusammenhang heißt es, dass οἱ παρ' αὐτοῦ ihn „ergreifen wollten"[7], weil sie meinten (ἔλεγον), er sei von Sinnen (3,21). Möglicherweise ist an Jesu (Familien-)Angehörige zu denken[8], die (in Nazareth?[9]) von seinem Tun gehört hatten und sich deshalb zum Eingreifen veranlasst sahen[10]. Von Angehörigen Jesu war aber bis dahin nicht die Rede gewesen – es baut sich also eine gewisse Spannung auf, von welchen Personen in 3,21 gesprochen wird[11]. Dann aber „kommen" Jesu Mutter und οἱ ἀδελφοὶ αὐτοῦ und fragen nach Jesus (V. 31-32). „An der Zusammengehörigkeit von V. 20f. und 31-35 scheint man nicht zweifeln zu dürfen", meint R. Bultmann, denn V. 20-21 verlangen eine Fortsetzung; es ist anzunehmen, „daß V. 20f.

Jordan; der Ortsname Ναζαρέτ begegnet im MkEv nur hier. Jesus kam also aus einem relativ weit entfernten Ort.

5. Zum Kreis der „Zwölf" s. J. VERHEYDEN, *Gründung einer Gemeinschaft: Ruf in die Nachfolge und die Bildung des Zwölferkreises*, in J. SCHRÖTER – C. JACOBI (Hgg.), *Jesus Handbuch*, Tübingen, Mohr Siebeck, 2017, 273-292, S. 283-292.

6. A. YARBRO COLLINS, *Mark: A Commentary* (Hermeneia), Minneapolis, MN, Fortress, 2007, S. 226: εἰς οἶκον „is idiomatic for ‚(going) home'". Gemeint ist aber möglicherweise das in 2,1 erwähnte Haus in Kafarnaum, denn ähnlich wie in 2,2 kommt wieder (πάλιν) eine große Volksmenge zusammen (3,20b).

7. Gehören 3,20 und 3,21 zusammen, oder schließt im Gegenteil 3,20 die vorangegangene Szene und wird in 3,21 das Folgende eingeleitet? Das lässt sich nicht eindeutig sagen; dazu J.D. CROSSAN, *Mark and the Relatives of Jesus*, in *NT* 15 (1973) 81-113, S. 83-84.

8. So etwa J. GNILKA, *Das Evangelium nach Markus. 1. Teilband: Mk 1–8,26* (EKKNT, 2/1), Zürich, Benziger Verlag; Neukirchen-Vluyn, Neukirchener Verlag, 1978, S. 148: „Da es Markus um eine Vorbereitung des Geschehens 3,31ff geht, können nur die Verwandten gemeint sein. Sie brachen von ihrem Heimatort [!] auf, um Jesus zurückzuholen".

9. So B.M.F. VAN IERSEL, *Mark: A Reader-Response Commentary* (JSNTSup, 164), Sheffield, Sheffield Academic Press, 1998, S. 169: „This is the first time that the relatives of Jesus are mentioned. The story does not say where they live, but as Jesus is from Nazareth in Galilee (1.9), the reader presumes that they set out from there to stop Jesus continuing his activities. This is exactly the opposite of what the public wants. The motive for their action is that they believe Jesus to be out of his mind (ἐξέστη). With this piece of information on Jesus' family the narrator takes the readers for a moment away from the house where Jesus is staying".

10. Dazu J. LAMBRECHT, *The Relatives of Jesus in Mark*, in *NT* 16 (1974) 241-258, S. 252. Vgl. B. WITHERINGTON III, *The Gospel of Mark: A Socio-Rhetorical Commentary*, Grand Rapids, MI, Eerdmans, 2001, S. 155. B. BOSENIUS, *Der literarische Raum des Markusevangeliums* (WMANT, 140), Neukirchen-Vluyn, Neukirchener Verlag, 2014, S. 289: Von 3,20 her ist „zu vermuten, dass die Verwandten Jesu die Befürchtung hegen, dieser sei aufgrund des engen Kontaktes, den er in seinen Exorzismen zu den Dämonen hatte, in der Zwischenzeit selbst von einem bösen Geist besessen – und somit verrückt geworden".

11. Absolut gebrauchtes οἱ παρ' αὐτοῦ ist selten – in der Regel wird zuvor eine Bezugsperson genannt.

und V. 31-35 durch V. 22-30 getrennt sind"[12]. Als οἱ παρ' αὐτοῦ erweisen sich also offenbar die dann in V. 31 explizit genannten Personen[13], die Jesus zunächst völlig missverstehen (V. 21) und dann Kontakt zu ihm suchen, dabei aber „draußen" stehen bleiben und ihn rufen lassen[14]. Jesus sagt sich geradezu von ihnen los und konstituiert in seinen an den ὄχλος gerichteten Worten seine nach ganz anderen Kriterien gebildete neue Familie (3,33-35)[15].

Abgesehen von einem kurzen Besuch im Land der Gerasener (5,1-20) hält sich Jesus weiterhin in Galiläa auf und kommt (6,1-6) εἰς τὴν πατρίδα αὐτοῦ (V. 1)[16]. Als er dort in der Synagoge lehrt, erstaunen die Hörer über seine Weisheit und über αἱ δυνάμεις τοιαῦται, „die durch seine Hände geschehen" (V. 2b)[17], fragen dann aber (V. 3a): „Ist dies nicht der Zimmermann[18], Sohn der Maria, Bruder des Jakobus ... und sind nicht auch seine Schwestern hier bei uns"? Der Erzähler ergänzt (V. 3b), dass sie an Jesus „Anstoß" nahmen[19]; der Besuch endet mit einem Fehlschlag (6,5.6a). Jesu Mutter und seine Geschwister werden in dieser Szene namentlich genannt, treten aber nicht in Erscheinung[20]; im

---

12. R. BULTMANN, *Die Geschichte der synoptischen Tradition* (FRLANT, 29), Göttingen, Vandenhoeck & Ruprecht, ²1931, S. 28. Der redaktionelle Charakter von V. 20 ist „deutlich; das ἀκούσαντες V. 21 hat an ihm keinen rechten Rückhalt" (*ibid.*). „Natürlich kann das Motiv von V. 21 nicht einfach aus dem Logion V. 35 herausgesponnen sein, sondern beruht offenbar auf guter alter Tradition" (S. 29). Zu V. 22-30 und der Q-Parallele Lk 11,14-23/Mt 12,22-30 BULTMANN, *ibid.*, S. 10-12.

13. Ein Stück Auslegungsgeschichte zeigt die von den Codices D und W (sowie it) bezeugte Korrektur: ἀκούσαντες (D: ὅτε ἤκουσαν) περὶ αὐτοῦ οἱ γραμματεῖς καὶ οἱ λοιποὶ ἐξῆλθον ... So wird vermieden, dass an Jesu Verwandte gedacht sein könnte; zugleich wird zwischen οἱ γραμματεῖς (V. 21) und οἱ γραμματεῖς οἱ ἀπὸ Ἱεροσολύμων καταβάντες (V. 22) differenziert.

14. Anders S.C. BARTON, *Discipleship and Family Ties in Mark and Matthew* (JSNTSup, 164), Sheffield, Sheffield Academic Press, 1998, S. 75: „Since the accusations by both the relatives of Jesus and by the scribes are formally parallel, it appears that Mark is placing Jesus' relatives in the same category as the hostile scribes". CROSSAN, *Mark* (Anm. 7), S. 97: „They are in the most complete isolation, not just from the official disciples but from the crowd itself".

15. YARBRO COLLINS, *Mark* (Anm. 6), S. 235: „The story was preserved, if not composed, because of the ongoing importance of the tension between doing God's will and family ties". Jesus „rejects his family because they try to prevent him from continuing his work as God's agent".

16. Der Name der Stadt wird nicht genannt.

17. Solche Taten hatte Jesus in Nazareth gar nicht vollbracht; es wird also auf das Wissen angespielt, das die Leser nach der Lektüre von Mk 1–5 haben.

18. Auf die genaue Bedeutung der Berufsbezeichnung ὁ τέκτων kommt es hier nicht an; jedenfalls kennen die Bewohner Nazareths Jesus auch als erwachsenen Menschen.

19. Jesus reagiert mit der Sentenz οὐκ ἔστιν προφήτης ἄτιμος εἰ μὴ ἐν τῇ πατρίδι αὐτοῦ καὶ ἐν τοῖς συγγενεῦσιν αὐτοῦ [!] καὶ ἐν τῇ οἰκίᾳ αὐτοῦ (V. 4).

20. LAMBRECHT, *Relatives* (Anm. 10), S. 253: „In vi 3 nothing suggests that the relatives belong to those who take offense at Jesus".

weiteren Verlauf des MkEv wird von ihnen nicht mehr die Rede sein[21]. Ob das Fehlen eines Hinweises auf Jesu Vater anzeigt, dass die Aussage der Himmelsstimme σὺ εἶ ὁ υἱός μου ὁ ἀγαπητός, ἐν σοὶ εὐδόκησα (1,11) in einem (auch) biologisch zu verstehenden Sinn aufzufassen ist, lässt sich nicht sagen[22]. Die Erwähnung der Geschwister impliziert jedenfalls, dass Jesu Mutter verheiratet war. Das MkEv setzt voraus, dass Jesus Teil einer Familie ist, aber für die mk Christologie ist dies nahezu bedeutungslos.

2. Das Bild der Familie Jesu bei Matthäus

Das Matthäusevangelium als βίβλος γενέσεως Ἰησοῦ Χριστοῦ υἱοῦ Δαυὶδ υἱοῦ Ἀβραάμ (1,1)[23] beschreibt in 1,2-16 Jesu Ahnenreihe von Abraham über David[24] bis zu Joseph, der nicht als Vater Jesu vorgestellt wird, sondern als (Ehe-)Mann der Maria, „aus der Jesus geboren wurde, der Christus genannt wird" (1,16). Die Reihe der γενεαί umfasst dann aber auch Christus (ἕως τοῦ Χριστοῦ, V. 17).

In 1,18 folgt unvermittelt die an die Leserinnen und Leser gerichtete Ankündigung der Geburt Jesu Christi[25] als Information über die Schwangerschaft der Maria ἐκ πνεύματος ἁγίου[26]. Der Erzähler weiß (und teilt den Lesern mit), dass Joseph als ἀνὴρ ... δίκαιος ὤν sie heimlich verlassen will (V. 19.20a)[27]. Da erscheint der ἄγγελος κυρίου dem Joseph im Traum und ermutigt ihn, seine schwangere Frau „anzunehmen", und so erfährt Joseph, was sich ereignet hat (V. 20b). Überdies (V. 21a) wird ihm (und den Lesern) mitgeteilt, dass das künftige Kind ein Sohn ist, dem

---

21. J. MARCUS, *Mark 1–8: A New Translation with Introduction and Commentary* (AB, 27), New York, Doubleday, 2000, S. 279-280: Das MkEv ist „the harshest of all the Gospels in its depiction of Jesus' relation to his family"; das sei bis zu einem gewissen Grad historisch, aber vor allem spiegelten sich hier „experiences of familial alienation and persecution common among early Christians" wider.

22. BARTON, *Discipleship* (Anm. 14), S. 88-89: „The omission is consistent with Mark's positive lack of interest in Joseph generally (3.31-5), since for Mark, Jesus is the Son of God". CROSSAN, *Mark* (Anm. 7), S. 102, hält es für möglich, dass erst Mk in seiner Textredaktion die Nennung des Vaters Jesu durch die der Mutter ersetzt hat.

23. M. KONRADT, *Das Evangelium nach Matthäus* (NTD, 1), Göttingen, Vandenhoeck & Ruprecht, 2015, S. 26: Die Wendung βίβλος γενέσεως Ἰησοῦ Χριστοῦ bezieht sich vermutlich auf das ganze Buch, auch wenn dann die Bedeutung des Begriffs γένεσις, der in 1,18 wieder begegnet, nicht ganz klar zu bestimmen ist.

24. David wird ausdrücklich „Sohn Abrahams" genannt, die Bezeichnung Jesu Christi als „Sohn Davids" ist also nicht in erster Linie auf seine Messianität zu beziehen.

25. Hier ist γένεσις allein auf das „Werden" Jesu bezogen.

26. KONRADT, *Evangelium nach Matthäus* (Anm. 23), S. 36-67: „Im Vergleich zum Alexander- oder Augustusmythos fällt dabei auf, dass jegliche geschlechtliche Andeutung zum Zeugungsakt fehlt".

27. Impliziert ist offenbar, dass Joseph die Schwangerschaft auf einen Bruch des Eheversprechens zurückführt; wenn er Maria verlässt, erschiene sie als die von ihm Betrogene.

er den Namen Ἰησοῦς geben soll[28]; die Erläuterung (V. 21b: αὐτὸς γὰρ σώσει τὸν λαὸν αὐτοῦ ἀπὸ τῶν ἁμαρτιῶν αὐτῶν) bezieht sich auf den hebräischen Namen יְהוֹשֻׁעַ, Matthäus setzt voraus, dass die Textrezipienten die Etymologie verstehen. Die als „Reflexionszitat" formulierte Aussage in V. 22.23 unterbricht die erzählte Handlung; durch das Zitat von Jes 7,14 LXX mit dem zuvor nicht verwendeten Begriff παρθένος erweisen sich die vorangegangenen Aussagen (V. 18b: ἐν γαστρὶ ἔχουσα, V. 21aα: τέξεται δὲ υἱόν, V. 21aβ: καὶ καλέσεις τὸ ὄνομα αὐτοῦ …) als genaue Erfüllung des prophetischen Wortes[29]. Schließlich (V. 24) wird notiert, dass Joseph alles tat, was ihm der Engel des Herrn aufgetragen hatte[30]. Erst in V. 25 wird ausdrücklich von Maria gesprochen, aber aus der Perspektive des Joseph: καὶ οὐκ ἐγίνωσκεν αὐτὴν ἕως οὗ ἔτεκεν (Maria) υἱόν· καὶ ἐκάλεσεν τὸ ὄνομα αὐτοῦ Ἰησοῦν[31]. Eine Ortsangabe fehlt.

Als Jesus dann in der Zeit des Königs Herodes in Bethlehem in Judäa geboren wird[32], kommen μάγοι ἀπὸ ἀνατολῶν nach Jerusalem und fragen nach dem Ort der Geburt des βασιλεὺς τῶν Ἰουδαίων, dessen „Stern" sie gesehen haben und den sie verehren wollen (2,1)[33]. Herodes „und ganz Jerusalem mit ihm" erhalten durch genaue Lektüre der Schrift die den Lesern bereits bekannte Antwort: „In Bethlehem in Judäa" (2,5, mit dem Zitat des biblischen Belegtexts Micha 5,1.3[34]). Der Stern leitet die μάγοι

---

28. D.L. BARTLETT, *Adoption in the Bible*, in M.J. BUNGE – T.E. FRETHEIM – B.R. GAVENTA (Hgg.), *The Child in the Bible*, Grand Rapids, MI – Cambridge, Eerdmans, 2008, 375-398, S. 386-387: Jesus wird von Joseph adoptiert. „It is this adoption that makes possible the claim that Jesus is not only Son of God but also (still) son of David, Messiah, through his adoptive father. In this sense Joseph follows the pattern both of Old Testament and of first-century Greco-Roman adoption: he claims Jesus for his own and by claiming him makes him part of his patrilineal family – son of Joseph, son of David".

29. Einige Handschriften (so Codex D) haben entsprechend dem LXX-Text korrigiert, καλέσεις statt καλέσουσιν.

30. In V. 25a wird gesagt, dass das Paar bis zur Geburt Jesu keinen Geschlechtsverkehr hatte. Dazu H. RÄISÄNEN, *Die Mutter Jesu im Neuen Testament* (AASF, 158), Helsinki, Suomalainen Tiedeakatemia, 1969, S. 72: „Anders als die Mütter der Theogamieerzählungen bleibt Maria auch nach der Empfängnis unberührte Jungfrau. Matthäus betont die Jungfrauschaft der Maria jedoch ausschliesslich im Zusammenhang mit der Geburt des Kindes. Die Bedeutung dieser Jungfrauschaft besteht darin, dass *das Wort Gottes sich erfüllt*. Nach der Geburt heisst Maria μήτηρ". Die Aussage ist ganz aus der Perspektive Josephs formuliert (οὐκ ἐγίνωσκεν αὐτὴν …).

31. Gemäß 1,21 ist das Subjekt zu ἐκάλεσεν τὸ ὄνομα αὐτοῦ Ἰησοῦν wieder Joseph.

32. Die Einleitung τοῦ δὲ Ἰησοῦ γεννηθέντος ἐν Βηθλέεμ τῆς Ἰουδαίας … erinnert an 1,18 (τοῦ δὲ Ἰησοῦ Χριστοῦ ἡ γένεσις οὕτως ἦν).

33. Vgl. T. HOLTMANN, *Die Magier vom Osten und der Stern: Mt 2,1-12 im Kontext frühchristlicher Traditionen* (Marburger Theologische Studien, 87), Marburg, Elwert, 2005, vor allem S. 239-242.

34. Die Szene ist nicht frei von Ironie, Micha 5 müsste eigentlich bekannt sein. Die Änderung von Micha 5,1 in Mt 2,6a (σὺ Βηθλέεμ, γῆ Ἰούδα, οὐδαμῶς ἐλαχίστη εἶ ἐν

dorthin, wo das Kind war (2,9), und „sie gingen in das Haus und sahen das Kind mit Maria, seiner Mutter und huldigten ihm (προσεκύνησαν αὐτῷ) und brachten Geschenke" (2,11). Joseph wird nicht erwähnt.

Aber auf die Notiz über die Heimreise der μάγοι folgt erneut eine Traumerscheinung des ἄγγελος κυρίου für Joseph, der beauftragt wird, mit „dem Kind und seiner Mutter" nach Ägypten zu fliehen (2,13). Dort bleibt er (ἦν ἐκεῖ) bis zum Tode des Herodes[35], damit die Verheißung erfüllt wird[36]: ἐξ Αἰγύπτου ἐκάλεσα τὸν υἱόν μου[37]. In Ägypten erscheint der ἄγγελος κυρίου dem Joseph nochmals (V. 19), jetzt mit der Weisung, er solle „das Kind und seine Mutter" nehmen und εἰς γῆν Ἰσραήλ reisen. Ἰσραήλ bezeichnet im NT sonst nicht das Land im geographischen Sinne[38], in Verbindung mit dem Hosea-Zitat (V. 15) wird die Rückkehr nach „Israel" als ein heilsgeschichtliches Ereignis erwiesen (V. 20a.21). Weil in Judäa der Herodes-Sohn Archelaus regiert, fürchtet sich Joseph, dorthin zu gehen; er zieht nach einer weiteren Anweisung κατ' ὄναρ schließlich εἰς τὰ μέρη τῆς Γαλιλαίας (V. 22[39]) und nimmt Wohnung „in einer Stadt namens Nazareth" (V. 23), wofür nochmals eine (fiktive) biblische Verheißung angeführt wird (Ναζωραῖος κληθήσεται)[40]. Joseph wird in Mt 1–2 nicht als „Vater" Jesu bezeichnet; aber er wird, ganz anders als im MkEv, ausführlich erwähnt als der stets umsichtig und erfolgreich für „das Kind und seine Mutter"[41] handelnde Mann, während

τοῖς ἡγεμόσιν Ἰούδα) gegenüber dem LXX-Text (... ὀλιγοστὸς εἶ τοῦ εἶναι ἐν χιλιάσιν Ἰούδα) verdankt sich dem heilsgeschichtlichen Interesse des Matthäus.

35. In 2,15a (καὶ ἦν ἐκεῖ ...) wird nicht ausdrücklich von der Familie gesprochen, deren Anwesenheit ist aber natürlich vorausgesetzt.

36. Die Einleitung des Reflexionszitats in 2,15 entspricht der in 1,23 (ἵνα πληρωθῇ τὸ ῥηθὲν ὑπὸ κυρίου διὰ τοῦ προφήτου λέγοντος).

37. Hos 11,1 nimmt auf den Exodus Bezug. Das Zitat in Mt 2,15 weicht vom LXX-Text ab (διότι νήπιος Ἰσραὴλ καὶ ἐγὼ ἠγάπησα αὐτὸν καὶ ἐξ Αἰγύπτου μετεκάλεσα τὰ τέκνα αὐτοῦ); die LXX-Fassung hat den hebräischen Text קָרָאתִי לִבְנִי ad sensum geändert. Die Ägypten-Episode in Mt 2,13-15 dient dazu, dieses Schriftzitat in das erzählte Geschehen einzubringen. KONRADT, Evangelium nach Matthäus (Anm. 23), S. 33: „Die Ausgestaltung des Erzählzyklus in Mt 1–2" verdankt sich „im Wesentlichen dem Evangelisten selbst bzw. seinem Kreis".

38. Vgl. A. LINDEMANN, Israel und sein ‚Land' im Neuen Testament, in ID., Glauben, Handeln, Verstehen: Studien zur Auslegung des Neuen Testaments. Band II (WUNT, 282), Tübingen, Mohr Siebeck, 2011, 149-189.

39. Die Tatsache, dass auch in Galiläa ein Sohn des Herodes (Herodes Antipas) als Fürst herrscht, spielt in diesem Zusammenhang keine Rolle.

40. Die ungenaue Quellenangabe (ὅπως πληρωθῇ τὸ ῥηθὲν διὰ τῶν προφητῶν) deutet an, dass es eine entsprechende prophetische Aussage nicht gibt. Bethlehem als Geburtsort verdankt sich der in 2,6 zitierten biblischen Tradition; Nazareth ist mit Jesus fest verbunden und „bedarf" deshalb ebenfalls eines Schriftbelegs.

41. So die konstant verwendete Formulierung; vgl. E. NELLESSEN, Das Kind und seine Mutter: Struktur und Verkündigung des 2. Kapitels im Matthäusevangelium (SBS, 39), Stuttgart, Katholisches Bibelwerk, 1969.

die Mutter ganz passiv bleibt; man kann also geradezu von einem traditionellen „Familienbild" sprechen.

In 3,1-12 tritt unvermittelt Ἰωάννης ὁ βαπτιστής auf, als wäre er den Adressaten des MtEv bereits bekannt. Ähnlich wie im MkEv kommt Jesus aus Galiläa[42] an den Jordan, um sich taufen zu lassen. Nach der Taufe und der Versuchung kehrt er nach Galiläa zurück[43] und verlässt dann τὴν Ναζαρά (!), um in Kafarnaum[44] zu wohnen.

Von Jesu Mutter und von seinen zuvor nicht erwähnten Geschwistern wird im Anschluss an Jesu Worte über die Rückkehr des unreinen Geistes in einen Menschen (Mt 12,43-45/Lk 11,24-26 Q) gesprochen. Die Szene Mt 12,46-50 entspricht Mk 3,31-35, die Notiz in Mk 3,21 war übergangen worden. Gegenüber der Mk-Vorlage ist die kritische Tendenz abgeschwächt, denn es heißt jetzt ausdrücklich, dass seine Mutter und seine Brüder, die „draußen" stehen, mit ihm *reden* wollen (ζητοῦντες αὐτῷ λαλῆσαι); die Reaktion Jesu ist aber unverändert.

Ebenso wie in Mk 6 löst bei Jesu Besuch in seiner πατρίς (Mt 13,54-58) sein Lehren in der Synagoge Erstaunen aus[45]; jetzt fragen die Anwesenden ausdrücklich: „Ist er nicht der Sohn des Zimmermanns?" (13,55a[46]), und dazu sprechen sie auch, ebenso wie in Mk 6,3b, von Jesu Mutter und seinen Geschwistern (13,55b.56) – die Familienverhältnisse sind in Nazareth also bekannt. Auf der Ebene des MtEv ist die Aussage der Bewohner natürlich falsch – Jesus ist nicht ὁ τοῦ τέκτονος υἱός, aber das können sie nicht wissen. Danach ist von Jesu Familie nicht mehr die Rede, schon in seinem Wort über den Propheten in seiner πατρίς und in seiner οἰκία fehlt der Hinweis auf die συγγενεῖς (13,57, anders Mk 6,4).

Grundlegend über Markus hinausgehend erzählt Matthäus in den beiden Eingangskapiteln von Jesu Zeugung ἐκ πνεύματος ἁγίου, von seiner Geburt in dem biblisch verheißenen Ort Bethlehem und von seiner Bewahrung in Ägypten. Nach der Ankunft der Familie in Nazareth ist Jesus im MtEv aber kaum anders als in der Mk-Vorlage ein Mensch, der in familiären Zusammenhängen steht, die für sein Wirken nicht von Bedeutung sind.

---

42. Anders als in Mk 1,9 wird Nazareth dabei nicht erwähnt.
43. Auf die bemerkenswerten Änderungen der beiden Szenen in Mt 3,13-17 bzw. Mt 4,1-11 gegenüber Mk 1,9-11 und 1,12-13 ist hier nicht einzugehen.
44. Die genaue geographische Beschreibung in 4,13 dient der Vorbereitung auf das lange Reflexionszitat in 4,15-16.
45. Die Gleichnisrede Mt 13 geht unmittelbar voraus (13,53); so ist sie auf der Textebene ein Beleg für Jesu σοφία.
46. Einige Handschriften haben in Mk 6,3 entsprechend Mt 13,55 korrigiert (… τοῦ τέκτονος υἱός;).

3. *Jesus und seine Familie bei Johannes*

Das Johannesevangelium[47] spricht im Prolog explizit von „Inkarnation" – der λόγος, der „im Anfang bei Gott war" (1,1-2), wurde „Fleisch" und „wohnte unter uns und wir sahen seine δόξα" (1,14)[48]; von Jesu Geburt wird nicht gesprochen[49], sondern Jesus wird ganz unvermittelt eingeführt, als Johannes ihn „kommen" sieht (1,29). Jesus beruft Philippus (1,43), der seinerseits den Nathanael über Jesu Herkunft informiert: „Den, von dem Mose geschrieben hat im Gesetz und die Propheten, haben wir gefunden, Jesus, den Sohn Josephs, aus Nazareth" (1,45) – Jesu Bezeichnung als υἱὸς τοῦ Ἰωσήφ konkretisiert die Aussage in 1,14. Nathanaels Reaktion deutet an, dass Jesu Abstammung von Joseph und seine Herkunft aus Nazareth zur biblischen Verheißung in Spannung stehen. Die Herkunft Jesu aus Galiläa statt aus Bethlehem wird in 7,40-44 nochmals thematisiert, wobei nicht angedeutet wird, die auf die Schrift bezogene rhetorische Frage in V. 42[50] könne auf einem Irrtum basieren.

Jesu Mutter, deren Name im JohEv nicht genannt wird, wird in 2,1b erstmals erwähnt – sie ist bei der Hochzeit zu Kana[51] unvermittelt anwesend, Jesus und seine Jünger waren „eingeladen" (V. 2). Als der Wein zur Neige geht, ergreift die Mutter die Initiative (V. 3), überlässt ihm dann aber nach seiner abwehrenden Reaktion (V. 4) das weitere Handeln (V. 5, vgl. V. 6-10). Im Anschluss an das in V. 11 als ἀρχὴ τῶν σημείων charakterisierte Ereignis ziehen alle, auch die bisher nicht erwähnten Brüder (V. 12a), nach Kafarnaum, „und dort blieben sie einige Tage" (V. 12b[52]).

---

47. Die Frage, ob das JohEv eine literarische Bekanntschaft mit den synoptischen Evangelien, insbesondere mit dem MkEv, voraussetzt, kann hier unerörtert bleiben.

48. ἐσκήνωσεν meint nicht, der inkarnierte λόγος habe nur vorübergehend ἐν ἡμῖν gelebt.

49. μονογενής (1,14.18; vgl. 3,16.18) bezieht sich nicht auf die „Zeugung", sondern meint „einzigartig". R. BULTMANN, *Das Evangelium des Johannes* (KEK, 2), Göttingen, Vandenhoeck & Ruprecht, [18]1964, S. 40: „Der Offenbarer ist nichts als ein Mensch". *Ibid.*, Anm. 2: „Damit erübrigen sich alle Fragen, wie es bei dem ἐγένετο zugegangen sei, oder seit wann sich der Logos mit dem Menschen Jesus vereinigt habe". H. THYEN, *Das Johannesevangelium* (HNT, 6), Tübingen, Mohr Siebeck, [2]2015, S. 95: μονογενής hat „keinerlei sexuelle Konnotation und keine unmittelbare Verbindung mit dem Verbum γεννᾶν".

50. Bethlehem als Herkunftsort wird im JohEv explizit dementiert, im MkEv wird Bethlehem nicht erwähnt.

51. Die Frage, ob die Erzählung auf eine bestimmte im JohEv verarbeitete („Semeia"-) Quelle zurückgeht, kann hier unberücksichtigt bleiben.

52. … καὶ ἐκεῖ ἔμειναν οὐ πολλὰς ἡμέρας. Einige Handschriften, darunter 𝔓[66c] und A, lesen statt ἔμειναν den Singular ἔμεινεν, womit offenbar schon V. 13 vorbereitet werden soll.

Offenbar allein geht Jesus dann zum Passa nach Jerusalem (2,13), wo es zur „Tempelreinigung" kommt (2,14-16)[53].

Später wird Jesus von seinen Brüdern aufgefordert, von Galiläa nach Judäa zu gehen ἵνα καὶ οἱ μαθηταί σου θεωρήσουσιν σοῦ τὰ ἔργα ἃ ποιεῖς (7,3); der Erzähler führt diese Aufforderung darauf zurück, dass die Brüder „nicht an ihn glaubten" (V. 5). Jesus bleibt in Galiläa (V. 6-9), doch dann gehen die Brüder „und dann auch er hinauf" (V. 10), aber Jesus hält sich zunächst verborgen[54]. Die Brüder werden im JohEv nicht mehr erwähnt.

Jesu Mutter ist unvermittelt wieder anwesend bei Jesu Kreuzigung. Dass Jesus sie seinem „Lieblingsjünger" anvertraut (19,25-27), hat möglicherweise symbolischen Sinn[55]; vielleicht gibt es eine heilsgeschichtliche Perspektive[56] oder es steht jüdisches Familienrecht im Hintergrund[57]. Eine eindeutige Auslegung ist nicht möglich.

Das JohEv weiß von Joseph als dem Vater Jesu, auch wenn er nicht als handelnde Person auftritt, sondern nur andere von ihm sprechen. Als Jesus nach der Speisung der Fünftausend von sich sagt ἐγώ εἰμι ὁ ἄρτος ὁ καταβὰς ἐκ τοῦ οὐρανοῦ (6,41), reagieren οἱ Ἰουδαῖοι mit der empörten Feststellung (6,42): „Ist dieser nicht Jesus, der Sohn Josephs?! Kennen wir nicht seinen Vater und seine Mutter? Wieso sagt er nun: Ich bin aus dem Himmel herabgestiegen"? Es wird deutlich, dass Jesus für das

---

53. Die Aktion Jesu geschieht also, nicht anders als in den synoptischen Evangelien, bei seinem ersten Aufenthalt in der Stadt; auch im JohEv sind die Jünger nicht beteiligt, rechtfertigen aber Jesu Aktion nachträglich (2,17). Als handelnde Personen treten sie erst wieder in 3,22 auf.

54. Der Widerspruch in V. 10 kann ausgeglichen werden, da Jesus „trotz des öffentlichen Lehrens der verhüllte Offenbarer bleibt und sein Wirken nicht im Sinne der Aufforderung von V. 3f. den Charakter des κρυπτόν verliert" (BULTMANN, *Evangelium des Johannes* [Anm. 49], S. 221).

55. So *ibid.*, S. 521: „Die Mutter Jesu stellt das Juden-Christentum dar, das den Anstoß des Kreuzes überwindet, das durch den Lieblingsjünger repräsentierte Heidenchristentum wird angewiesen, jenes als seine Mutter … zu ehren", das sich seinerseits „in die große kirchliche Gemeinschaft eingegliedert" wissen soll.

56. R.E. BROWN, *The Gospel according to John XIII–XXI: A New Translation with Introduction and Commentary* (AB, 29A), New York, Doubleday, 1966, S. 926: „[T]he Johannine picture of Jesus' mother becoming the mother of the Beloved Disciple seems to evoke the OT themes of Lady Zion's giving birth to a new people in the messianic age, and of Eve and her offspring. This imagery flows over into the imagery of the Church who brings forth children modeled after Jesus, and the relationship of loving care that must bind the children to their mother".

57. J. ZUMSTEIN, *Das Johannesevangelium* (KEK, 2), Göttingen, Vandenhoeck & Ruprecht, 2016, S. 723-724: Jesus stellt „seine Mutter unter den Schutz des Lieblingsjüngers. Dieser hat nun den Auftrag, für die Mutter Jesu die Rolle zu übernehmen, die bisher Jesus spielte. In Abwesenheit des Sohnes ist also der Lieblingsjünger sein Repräsentant". Man wird aber kaum sagen können, dass Jesus im JohEv am Schicksal seiner Mutter interessiert gewesen wäre.

JohEv „der Sohn Gottes" ist (3,16-18) und Gott Jesu „Vater" ist (3,35; 4,21.23 u.ö.). Der in 1,14 eingeführte Gedanke der Inkarnation ist für die Christologie des JohEv bedeutsam, aber dieser Gedanke wird nur in ganz abstrakter Weise erzählerisch realisiert, insofern Jesus Eltern und Geschwister hat und zu einer menschlich-irdischen Familie gehört. Das JohEv bietet kein „Familienbild", das sich grundsätzlich von den entsprechenden Aussagen im MkEv und im MtEv unterscheidet.

II. Jesus und seine Familie bei Lukas

Der Evangelist Lukas beginnt seine διήγησις „ganz vorn" (1,3)[58], indem er zuerst von der wunderbaren Geburt des Sohnes von Zacharias und Elisabeth erzählt, der Jesu Vorgänger sein wird (1,5-25.57-80)[59]. Die Geschichte Jesu wird eingeleitet mit der Entsendung des ἄγγελος Γαβριήλ nach Nazareth zu einer mit Joseph, einem Mann ἐξ οἴκου Δαυίδ, „verlobten" Jungfrau (παρθένος)[60], die Maria heißt (1,26-27). Als sie von dem Engel erfährt, sie werde schwanger werden und einen Sohn gebären, den sie Jesus nennen soll (1,31)[61], ist sie überrascht (1,34), woraufhin ihr der Engel ankündigt, dass das Wunder der späten Schwangerschaft der Elisabeth noch überboten werden wird[62]. Wie sich die Leser das „Kommen" des Heiligen Geistes und das Wirken der δύναμις Gottes (V. 35.36) konkret vorstellen sollen, sagt Lukas nicht[63]. Nach einem

---

58. In Lk 1,1-4 scheint Kritik an den „vielen Vorgängern" auf, die eine solche Arbeit wie die hier beschriebene nicht geleistet haben.

59. Die Parallelität zwischen den beiden Geburtsankündigungen (und dann auch Geburten) ist programmatisch; vgl. P. Böhlemann, *Jesus und der Täufer: Schlüssel zur Theologie und Ethik des Lukas* (SNTS MS, 99), Cambridge, CUP, 1997, S. 10-44.

60. M. Wolter, *Das Lukasevangelium* (HNT, 5), Tübingen, Mohr Siebeck, 2008, S. 87: Lukas hat diese Information „aus der Überlieferung übernommen", wie die Übereinstimmung mit Mt 1,18 zeigt. Von der Verlobung wird gesprochen, weil man „die aus der Jesustradition überkommene Information, derzufolge Josef als Vater Jesu (Lk 3,23; 4,22; Joh 1,45; 6,42) und Ehemann Marias (Mt 1,16) bekannt war, mit der Vorstellung der Geburt Jesu von einer Jungfrau ausgleichen musste".

61. Ihm gelten große Verheißungen, zu denen auch gehört, dass Gott ihm geben wird τὸν θρόνον Δαυὶδ τοῦ πατρὸς αὐτοῦ (1,32-33). Ist damit auf 1,27 angespielt? Für Joseph, obwohl „aus dem Hause Davids", gilt eine solche Verheißung ja offenbar nicht.

62. Wolter, *Lukasevangelium* (Anm. 60), S. 92: Die Frage in V. 34b bekommt „einen guten Sinn als indirekte Information für die Leser, dass Maria ihren Sohn nicht auf dem üblichen Wege empfangen wird", und so liefert Gabriel in V. 35 die erbetene Erklärung.

63. Von einer geschlechtlichen Beziehung zwischen Gott bzw. dem Heiligen Geist und Maria wird nicht gesprochen; es klingt nicht einmal an, wann die Schwangerschaft der Maria beginnt. Dazu M. Wolter, *Wann wurde Maria schwanger? Eine vernachlässigte Frage und ihre Bedeutung für das Verständnis der lukanischen Vorgeschichte*, in Id., *Theologie und Ethos im frühen Christentum: Studien zu Jesus, Paulus und Lukas* (WUNT,

Besuch der Maria bei Elisabeth (1,39-45.56) und ihrem „Magnifikat" (1,46-55) bringt Elisabeth ihren Sohn zur Welt, der den Namen Johannes erhält (1,57-66); dem Lobgesang seines Vaters Zacharias (1,67-79) folgt die Notiz, dass „das Kindlein heranwuchs und an Geist zunahm", während es sich ἐν ταῖς ἐρήμοις aufhielt (1,80).

Mit der auf 1,80 bezogenen Zeitangabe ἐγένετο δὲ ἐν ταῖς ἡμέραις ἐκείναις (2,1a)[64] ändert sich die Szene: Caesar Augustus gab den Befehl (δόγμα) zu einer ἀπογραφή in der ganzen οἰκουμένη (2,1b)[65]. Weil dazu jeder „in seine Stadt" ging (2,3)[66], reiste auch Joseph von Galiläa nach Judäa „in die Stadt Davids, die Bethlehem heißt", denn – so heißt es betont am Ende – er stammte „aus dem Haus und Familiengeschlecht Davids" (2,4[67]); begleitet wird er von der als ἐμνηστευμένη αὐτῷ vorgestellten Maria, die schwanger ist (2,5)[68]. Dass diese Schwangerschaft ungewöhnlich sein könnte, wird nicht angedeutet; es gibt insbesondere keinen Rückverweis auf Marias Begegnung mit dem Engel Gabriel[69]. Dass der Weg von Nazareth nach Bethlehem für Maria womöglich überaus beschwerlich ist, wird nicht gesagt. In Bethlehem erfolgt, nicht unbedingt gleich nach dem Eintreffen in dieser Stadt, die Geburt (2,6); die Dauer der Schwangerschaft weist offenbar keine Besonderheiten auf[70].

236), Tübingen, Mohr Siebeck, 2009, S. 336-354. Lukas setze keineswegs voraus, dass Maria schwanger ist, als sie Elisabeth besucht.

64. 2,1 könnte sogar so verstanden werden, dass sich das Folgende erst während der ἀνάδειξις des Johannes abspielt (1,80 ... ἕως ἡμέρας ἀναδείξεως αὐτοῦ πρὸς τὸν Ἰσραήλ); jedenfalls wird über den zeitlichen Abstand nichts gesagt.

65. Lukas setzt das Wissen der Leser voraus, dass die ἀπογραφή ein *census* ist, durch den die Steuerkraft einer Region ermittelt wird. Vgl. den Exkurs bei H. KLEIN, *Das Lukasevangelium* (KEK, 1/3), Göttingen, Vandenhoeck & Ruprecht, 2006, S. 131-133. Der *census* im Jahre 6 n.Chr. hatte zur Entstehung des Zelotismus geführt (vgl. Apg 5,37); in Lk 2 wird er kommentarlos als ein ohne Weiteres akzeptierter Verwaltungsvorgang dargestellt. BULTMANN, *Geschichte* (Anm. 12), S. 323, hält die Verbindung des *census* mit der Überlieferung von Jesu Geburt und der Hirtenverkündigung für redaktionell lk; es sei eine vermutlich im „hellenistischen Christentum" entstandene „christliche Legende" (S. 325).

66. Über die Frage der praktischen Durchführbarkeit einer solchen als „weltweit" gedachten Aktion macht sich der Erzähler keine Gedanken. WOLTER, *Lukasevangelium* (Anm. 60), S. 122: „Sein Ziel ist es, zwei unterschiedliche Überlieferungen – dass Jesus in Bethlehem geboren wurde und dass er aus Nazareth stammte – miteinander in Einklang zu bringen".

67. Das war schon in 1,27 erwähnt worden, ohne dass daran jetzt erinnert wird.

68. Die schon in 1,27 erwähnte „Verlobung" war eine verbindliche Beziehung.

69. WOLTER, *Lukasevangelium* (Anm. 60), S. 125, meint, die Information in 2,5 korrespondiere „in spannungsvoller Weise mit Marias Kennzeichnung als Jungfrau in 1,27. Erst jetzt erfahren die Leser, dass die Ankündigung Gabriels in 1,31 sich erfüllt hat".

70. Vgl. WOLTER, *Wann wurde Maria schwanger?* (Anm. 63), S. 348: Lukas legt den Lesern nahe, den Beginn der Schwangerschaft Marias „in die Zeit des Heranwachsens und des Wüstenaufenthalts des Johannes vor dessen öffentlichem Auftreten zu datieren. Im Ablauf des lukanischen Erzählgefüges wird Maria demnach erst in 1,80 schwanger".

Maria bringt einen Sohn zur Welt, ihren Erstgeborenen (2,7)[71]; sie wickelt ihn in Windeln (ἐσπαργάνωσεν αὐτόν), wie es mütterlicher Fürsorge entspricht[72]. In 2,1-7a wird also, ungeachtet der in Lk 1 erfolgten Ankündigung einer wunderbaren Schwangerschaft, ein „normales" Ehepaar vorgestellt, das der Geburt eines Kindes entgegensieht; die in 2,1-3 erwähnte staatliche Anordnung führt zwar dazu, dass die Geburt mit besonderen äußeren Umständen verbunden, im Übrigen aber alltäglich ist.

Auffallend ist allerdings (2,7b), dass eine Futterkrippe als Kinderbett des Säuglings dient; die Formulierung ἀνέκλινεν αὐτὸν ἐν φάτνῃ legt die Annahme nahe, dass das Kind nicht nur für einen kurzen Augenblick dort „hingelegt" wurde, sondern dass die φάτνη während des im Folgenden dargestellten Aufenthalts in Bethlehem diese besondere Funktion hat. Die Begründung (διότι οὐκ ἦν αὐτοῖς τόπος ἐν τῷ καταλύματι) ist nicht eindeutig zu verstehen: Wenn gemeint ist, dass „sie", die Eltern und das Kind, überhaupt keinen Platz in der Herberge hatten[73], so wäre φάτνη ein gesondertes Gebäude („Stall")[74]; aber die Wendung ἐν τῷ καταλύματι spricht eher dafür, dass die Eltern in der Herberge untergebracht sind[75]

---

71. Mit πρωτότοκος wird angedeutet, dass später weitere Kinder folgen. Auch wenn das Wort die Funktion haben kann, jemanden in besonderer Weise bildhaft herauszuheben (vgl. Ex 4,22 LXX in der Beziehung Gottes zu Israel: υἱὸς πρωτότοκός μου Ἰσραήλ, als Übersetzung von בְּנִי בְכֹרִי יִשְׂרָאֵל, so ist in Lk 2,7 πρωτότοκος nicht im Sinne von μονογενής zu verstehen (vgl. W. MICHAELIS, πρῶτος κτλ., in *TWNT* 6 [1959] 877).

72. In Hiob 38,9 sagt Gott von der Erschaffung des Meeres: „Ich habe ihm ein Gewölk (νέφος) als Gewand gegeben, mit einer Nebelwolke (ὀμίχλη) habe ich es in Windeln gewickelt (ἐσπαργάνωσα)". In Sap 7,4 sagt König Salomo von sich: „In Windeln und mit großer Fürsorge wurde ich aufgezogen (ἐν σπαργάνοις ἀνετράφην καὶ φροντίσιν)", und so begann das Leben aller Könige (7,5). In Ez 16,4 wird die „verkehrte" Geburt Jerusalems geschildert („... du wurdest nicht mit Salz abgerieben und nicht in Windeln gewickelt (σπαργάνοις οὐκ ἐσπαργανώθης)". WOLTER, *Lukasevangelium* (Anm. 60), S. 126: Es geht nicht darum, „die Niedrigkeit Jesu gegenüber dem imperialen Anspruch des römischen Caesars zu akzentuieren".

73. κατάλυμα ist ein vorübergehend genutzter Aufenthaltsort (Mk 14,14 par Lk 22,11). KLEIN, *Lukasevangelium* (Anm. 65), S. 134: κατάλυμα bezeichnet „den Übernachtungsort oder Gästeraum (22,11) für Leute, die von auswärts kommen (1 Sam 1,18 LXX), nicht die ‚Herberge', die πανδοχεῖον (10,34) heißt". Die Eltern „wohnen entweder im κατάλυμα, das erhöht ist, wo aber kein Platz mehr für das Baby ist, während unten, im selben Raum, wo die Tiere hausen, in der Krippe Platz dafür ist, oder in einem Nebenraum eines Hauses, der nur für die Tiere vorhanden war" (S. 134-135).

74. Das wäre grundsätzlich möglich, ist hier aber wenig wahrscheinlich; vgl. M. HENGEL, φάτνη, in *TWNT* 9 (1973) 51-57.

75. WOLTER, *Lukasevangelium* (Anm. 60), S. 126: „[V.] 7d will nicht sagen, dass Jesu Eltern obdachlos waren". Anders W. RADL, *Das Evangelium nach Lukas: Kommentar. Erster Teil: 1,1–9,50*, Freiburg i.Br. – Basel – Wien, Herder, 2003, S. 112: Es müsste „eigentlich" heißen: „Die Herberge war überfüllt – so mußten sie in einen Stall ausweichen – dort legte sie das Kind in eine Krippe. Oder umgekehrt: Sie legte das Kind in eine Krippe; sie hatten nämlich in einen Stall ausweichen müssen, ‚weil in der Herberge kein Platz für sie war'". Der Text gibt zu solchen Konstruktionen keinen Anlass.

und dass hier die φάτνη („Futterkrippe") als das für das Kind geeignete Bett zu denken ist[76].

In 2,8 wechselt die Szene: An einem nicht weit entfernten Ort[77] gehen Hirten ihrer nächtlichen Arbeit nach[78], als plötzlich der ἄγγελος κυρίου[79] bei ihnen ist (ἐπέστη αὐτοῖς, V. 9a) und die δόξα κυρίου die Hirten umstrahlt, die deshalb in große Furcht geraten (V. 9b). Die Reaktion des Engels: μὴ φοβεῖσθε (V. 10a) und seine Freudenbotschaft: εὐαγγελίζομαι ὑμῖν χαρὰν μεγάλην ... (V. 10b-12) sind die erste wörtliche Rede in der in 2,1 begonnenen Erzählung. Adressaten sind die Hirten, aber die Botschaft wird ganz Israel gelten (ἔσται παντὶ τῷ λαῷ) – angesichts des in V. 1 eröffneten Horizonts (πᾶσαν τὴν οἰκουμένην) könnte sogar die Menschheit im Blick sein[80]. Die Botschaft lautet: ἐτέχθη ὑμῖν σήμερον σωτὴρ ὅς ἐστιν χριστὸς κύριος ἐν πόλει Δαυίδ (V. 11). Die verwendeten Titel stehen in direktem Bezug zur jüdischen Tradition[81], ebenso der

---

76. WOLTER, *Lukasevangelium* (Anm. 60), S. 126: Die für den Futtertrog gegebene Begründung erweist diesen „als Lösung eines Problems, das seine *Eltern* hatten (οὐκ ἦν αὐτοῖς)". „Eine φάτνη konnte sich innerhalb oder außerhalb des Hauses befinden (letzteres ist in Lk 13,15 vorausgesetzt), sie konnte beweglich, als Nische in die Hauswand eingelassen, aus Lehm geformt oder in den Felsen gehauen sein". F. BOVON, *Das Evangelium nach Lukas*. 1. Teilband: *Lk 1,1–9,50* (EKKNT, 3/I), Zürich, Benziger Verlag; Neukirchen-Vluyn, Neukirchener Verlag, 1989, S. 127: Die Krippe war „wahrscheinlich ... aus Stein ... etwa in die Wand einer Höhle oder eines Felsens gehauen, oder aus Lehm; Holz war zu teuer". Hat der Erzähler solche Erwägungen angestellt?

77. M. WOLTER, *Die Hirten in der Weihnachtsgeschichte (Lk 2,8-20)*, in ID., *Theologie und Ethos* (Anm. 63), 355-372, S. 362-363: „Kein Leser denkt, wenn ihm in einer Erzählung Hirten begegnen, die sich in der Nacht auf dem freien Feld befinden und ihre Herde bewachen, an David – auch wenn sie dies alles in der Nähe von Bethlehem tun".

78. Impliziert die Angabe τῆς νυκτός an dieser Stelle zugleich die nächtliche Geburt des Kindes?

79. Zahlreiche Handschriften lesen καὶ ἰδοὺ ἄγγελος κυρίου ..., um das nun beginnende Neue hervorzuheben; auf der Textebene ist der ἄγγελος κυρίου bekannt (1,11-13; vgl. 1,26-38), denn Gabriel und der ἄγγελος κυρίου dürften identisch sein.

80. WOLTER, *Lukasevangelium* (Anm. 60), S. 128: Die Hirten werden „einerseits zu Empfängern einer Israel geltenden Heilsproklamation", andererseits repräsentieren sie „auf Grund der mit ihnen verknüpften *aurea-aetas*-Semantik aber auch die Hoffnungen der gesamten Menschheit auf universalen Frieden".

81. σωτήρ ist ein auch politisch gebrauchter Titel; vgl. M. KARRER, *Jesus, der Retter (Sôtêr): Zur Aufnahme eines hellenistischen Prädikats im Neuen Testament*, in ZNW 93 (2002) 153-176. Vgl. T. JANTSCH, *Jesus, der Retter: Die Soteriologie des lukanischen Doppelwerks* (WUNT, 381), Tübingen, Mohr Siebeck, 2017, S. 149-164: Der Titel σωτήρ bezieht sich üblicherweise auf die Vergangenheit, doch schwingt mit, „dass ein solches rettendes Handeln für die Zukunft erwartet wird"; Lukas „aktiviert" diese Erwartung: „Von diesem Herrn soll zukünftiges Rettungshandeln erwartet werden" (*ibid.*, S. 161-162). χριστός („Messias") bezeichnet den von einigen Gruppen im zeitgenössischen Judentum erwarteten Heilbringer und Befreier. WOLTER, *Lukasevangelium* (Anm. 60), S. 128: Lukas setzt nicht „einen gezielten Kontrapunkt gegen die kaiserlichen σωτήρ-Prädikationen", sondern diese Bezeichnung „nominalisiert ... an dieser Stelle nicht mehr als die Funktion Jesu". *Ibid.*, S. 129: Offenbar sind an dieser Stelle χριστός und κύριος

Hinweis auf die „Stadt Davids"[82]; dabei ist die Botschaft „aktuell" – der σωτήρ wurde *heute* (σήμερον) geboren; der dann folgende Verweis auf das σημεῖον (V. 12) fordert die Hirten dazu auf, der Botschaft nachzugehen: Der *heute* geborene σωτήρ ist selbstverständlich ein in Windeln gewickelter Säugling[83], aber ungewöhnlich ist die Futterkrippe, und sie ist deshalb das eigentliche „Zeichen"[84]; die Hirten werden das Kind nicht suchen, sondern sie werden es finden (εὑρήσετε). Das plötzlich anwesende πλῆθος στρατιᾶς οὐρανίου stimmt dazu einen Lobgesang an, der über die aktuelle Situation weit hinausweist (V. 14). Danach kehren die Engel in den Himmel zurück (V. 15a), während die Hirten beschließen, nach Bethlehem zu gehen[85], um zu sehen τὸ ῥῆμα τοῦτο τὸ γεγονὸς ὃ ὁ κύριος ἐγνώρισεν ἡμῖν (V. 15b)[86]. Und sie gingen „eilends" (ἦλθαν σπεύσαντες) und fanden (ἀνεῦραν)[87] Maria und Joseph und τὸ βρέφος κείμενον ἐν τῇ φάτνῃ (V. 16)[88]. Das Ziel des Weges war der Säugling, aber die Eltern werden jetzt zuerst genannt[89], da sie als Erste wahrgenommen wurden[90]. Es herrscht also wieder „Normalität", nicht anders als vor dem Kommen der Engel zu den Hirten.

Jetzt berichten die Hirten (ἐγνώρισαν[91]), was ihnen über dieses Kind gesagt worden war (V. 17); da die Leser das kennen, braucht Näheres nicht gesagt zu werden. Bei der Schilderung der Reaktion (V. 18: πάντες

„gleichgeordnete titulare Bezeichnungen", ähnlich wie in Apg 2,36 (καὶ κύριον αὐτὸν καὶ χριστὸν ἐποίησεν ὁ θεός).

82. Als πόλις Δαυίδ gilt eigentlich Jerusalem bzw. Zion (2 Regn 5,7.9; 6,10.12.16 u.ö.); vgl. aber 1 Regn 20,6 (... εἰς Βηθλεὲμ τὴν πόλιν αὐτοῦ, sc. Davids).

83. βρέφος in Lk 1,41.44 für das noch ungeborene Kind (Johannes); in Lk 18,15 ersetzt der Evangelist durch βρέφη das unspezifische παιδία aus Mk 10,13.

84. Vgl. dazu J. KÜGLER, *Die Windeln Jesu als Zeichen: Religionsgeschichtliche Anmerkungen zu ΣΠΑΡΓΑΝΩ in Lk 2*, in BN 77 (1995) 20-28, S. 28, der aus den Angaben zu dem „Zeichen" folgert: „In Jesus ist ein Kyrios *sui generis* zur Welt gekommen".

85. Der Aspekt der erzählerischen Plausibilität tritt zurück; das Schicksal der Herde spielt keine Rolle, ebensowenig die Frage, wie die Hirten in der Nacht in Bethlehem jene Futterkrippe finden können.

86. τὸ ῥῆμα bezieht sich nicht nur auf „das Wort" des Engels, sondern zugleich auf das darin ausgesagte Geschehen; in der Wendung ὃ ὁ κύριος ἐγνώρισεν ἡμῖν ist ὁ κύριος offenbar Gottesprädikat – die Botschaft des Engels kam von Gott.

87. Jetzt verwendet Lukas wie auch in Apg 21,4 das Verb ἀνευρίσκειν, damit vielleicht auf ein besonders intensives Suchen verweisend.

88. Die Windeln haben für die Erzählung ihren Dienst getan und werden nicht mehr erwähnt.

89. Maria und Joseph werden namentlich genannt; dass sie die Eltern des neugeborenen Kindes sind, ist vorausgesetzt.

90. KLEIN, *Lukasevangelium* (Anm. 65), S. 140: „Für die Hirten sind aber nicht die Eltern, sondern nur das Kind in der Krippe entscheidend, weil es das Zeichen ist, das der Engel angab. Darum wird es am Ende genannt".

91. In 2,17 wird das Verb γνωρίζειν aus V. 15 wiederholt.

οἱ ἀκούσαντες ...)⁹² ist entweder an einen größeren Kreis von Anwesenden zu denken, oder der Blick des Erzählers reicht schon über die akute Erzählsituation hinaus; dass Maria „dies alles in besonderer Weise durchdenkt" (V. 19), entspricht ihrer Rolle als Mutter. W.C. van Unnik betont aber die Differenz: Die ἀκούσαντες (V. 18) waren „verwundert" (ἐθαύμασαν), während hingegen Maria den ῥήματα „nicht ratlos gegenüberstand, sondern ihre genaue Bedeutung entdeckte"⁹³. Dass sich Maria an die an sie gerichteten Worte des Engels Gabriel „erinnert" hätte, wird allerdings nicht angedeutet⁹⁴.

Ebenso wie die Geburtserzählung (2,1-7) weist auch das in 2,16-19 gezeichnete Bild des in der Futterkrippe liegenden neugeborenen Sohnes der Maria und des Joseph keinerlei Herrlichkeitszüge auf; von all dem, was „der Engel des Herrn" und die „himmlischen Heerscharen" gesagt hatten (2,8-15), ist dem Kind nichts anzusehen⁹⁵. Die Leserinnen und Leser waren Zeugen, die jetzt anwesenden Personen, insbesondere auch die Eltern, hören davon aber nur aus dem Munde der Hirten. Abschließend (V. 20) folgt die Notiz über die Rückkehr der Hirten und über ihr Verkündigen.

92. Vgl. 2,33: καὶ ἦν ὁ πατὴρ αὐτοῦ καὶ ἡ μήτηρ θαυμάζοντες ἐπὶ τοῖς λαλουμένοις περὶ αὐτοῦ.
93. W.C. VAN UNNIK, *Die rechte Bedeutung des Wortes treffen, Lukas ii 19*, in *Sparsa Collecta: The Collected Essays of W.C. van Unnik*. Part One: *Evangelica – Paulina – Acta* (SupplNT, 29), Leiden, Brill, 1973, 72-91, S. 88. Nach VAN UNNIK, *ibid.*, S. 85-86, bedeutet συμβάλλω „im Zusammenhang mit Dingen, die durch ihre Vieldeutigkeit dunkel sind, ‚die richtige Bedeutung treffen'"; man könne geradezu von einem terminus technicus sprechen. „Eine Übersetzung mit ‚erwägen', ‚bedenken' ist sowohl durch die Bedeutung des griechischen Wortes, als auch durch den Textzusammenhang, in dem es zu finden ist, ausgeschlossen". VAN UNNIK meint sogar, Maria sei hier „prophetisch tätig"; aber er macht zugleich darauf aufmerksam, dass Lukas nicht sagt, wie Marias „richtige Auslegung" der gehörten ῥήματα lautete (S. 90).
94. Anders RADL, *Lukas* (Anm. 75), S. 119: Maria ist „nach allem, was sie in Nazaret und im Haus der Elisabet erfahren hat, in der Lage, um die Bedeutung der Geschehnisse zu wissen". Ähnlich WOLTER, *Lukasevangelium* (Anm. 60), S. 132: Maria kann „nicht einfach unter diejenigen subsumiert werden, die sich über das von den Hirten Gesagte nur ‚wundern' können". „Auf Grund der Ankündigung Gabriels weiß Maria mehr als diejenigen, die nur den Bericht der Hirten kennen und die sich darum nur wundern können". Vgl. aber BOVON, *Lk 1,1–9,50* (Anm. 76), S. 131: συμβάλλουσα ἐν τῇ καρδίᾳ αὐτῆς verweist „nicht auf eine logische und intellektuelle Deutung des Geschehens", die Deutung ereignet sich „nicht in ihrem Intellekt (νοῦς), sondern im Organ des Willens und des Gefühls". In der ansonsten analog formulierten Aussage in 2,51b fehlt συμβάλλουσα.
95. NELLESSEN, *Kind* (Anm. 41), S. 109: Ein Eingehen auf die einzigartigen Umstände der Empfängnis und Geburt Jesu empfahl sich nur dort, „wo die Anfänge des menschlichen Lebens Jesu überhaupt zum Gegenstand einer erzählenden Darstellung gemacht wurden". Dies erkläre, warum z.B. bei Paulus davon nicht die Rede ist. Aber man muss umgekehrt fragen, warum Matthäus und Lukas überhaupt von Jesu Geburt und frühester Kindheit erzählen – offenbar doch, um Jesus als Menschen zu zeigen und nicht, um die Jungfrauengeburt ins Zentrum zu stellen.

„Er"[96] wurde am achten Tag beschnitten und erhielt dabei den Namen „Jesus" (2,21a)[97]; dazu wird auf die entsprechende Ansage des Engels Gabriel vor Beginn der Schwangerschaft der Maria (1,31) verwiesen, wobei die Aussage unpersönlich im Passiv formuliert ist (τὸ κληθὲν ὑπὸ τοῦ ἀγγέλου, 2,21b) – es wird nicht gesagt, Maria habe sich daran erinnert[98]. Die in 2,22-52 folgenden Szenen sind mit Ortswechseln verbunden[99]. Als die Eltern der Tora folgend in Jerusalem ein Opfer darbringen[100], begegnen sie im Tempel einem Mann namens Simeon (V. 25-35)[101], der das neugeborene Kind preist als φῶς εἰς ἀποκάλυψιν ἐθνῶν καὶ δόξαν λαοῦ σου Ἰσραήλ (V. 32). Der Erzähler merkt an, dass sich „sein Vater und seine Mutter"[102] darüber wunderten (θαυμάζοντες, V. 33)[103], was an V. 18 erinnert, aber gerade deshalb überraschend ist. An Maria gerichtet sagt Simeon, es komme durch Jesu Wirken in Israel zu Konflikten (... εἰς σημεῖον ἀντιλεγόμενον, V. 34)[104] – die als „Schwert" auch durch sie „hindurchgehen" werden (V. 35a)[105] – , damit „die Gedanken aus vielen Herzen offenbar werden" (V. 35b). Die Worte Simeons bleiben ohne eine Reaktion der Eltern bzw. der Mutter. In V. 36-38a wird die Prophetin

---

96. Codex D und viele andere Handschriften lesen τὸ παιδίον anstelle von αὐτόν.

97. Beschneidung und Namengebung sind üblicherweise nicht miteinander verbunden.

98. Ganz anders die Namengebung des Johannes in 1,59-66.

99. Auf die Frage nach dem möglichen Verhältnis von „Tradition" und lk Redaktion ist hier nicht einzugehen; im Ganzen wird das Urteil von KLEIN, *Lukasevangelium* (Anm. 65), S. 143, zu Lk 2,(21)22-40 zutreffen: „In seiner jetzigen Gestalt ist der Abschnitt von Lk sprachlich überarbeitet". Ähnlich zu 2,41-52: „In ihrer jetzigen Form ist die Erzählung von Lukas gestaltet" (S. 152).

100. Ermöglicht V. 22a einen Rückschluss auf die Dauer des Aufenthalts in Bethlehem? Die Mutter darf das Haus erst vierzig Tage nach der Geburt des Sohnes verlassen (vgl. WOLTER, *Lukasevangelium* [Anm. 60], S. 134-135), aber hat Lukas dies wirklich im Blick? Die Formulierung καθαρισμοῦ αὐτῶν ist nicht korrekt, nach Lev 12 gilt nach der Geburt nur die Mutter als unrein.

101. Besonders betont wird mit Blick auf Simeon das Wirken des πνεῦμα (V. 25-27).

102. Viele Handschriften lesen Ἰωσήφ anstelle von ὁ πατὴρ αὐτοῦ, was sich natürlich späterer Korrektur verdankt.

103. Die Formulierung ἦν ὁ πατὴρ αὐτοῦ καὶ ἡ μήτηρ θαυμάζοντες ist sprachlich hart. Hieß es womöglich ursprünglich ἦν ὁ πατὴρ αὐτοῦ θαυμάζων und wurde dann ἡ μήτηρ ergänzt und dementsprechend die Pluralwendung θαυμάζοντες korrigiert, ohne dass ἦν zu ἦσαν korrigiert wurde?

104. WOLTER, *Lukasevangelium* (Anm. 60), S. 142: „Simeon kündigt an, dass Jesus Israel durcheinanderbringen und so etwas wie einen Paradigmenwechsel herbeiführen wird, insofern er selbst nämlich zum Kriterium über die Zuweisung von Heil und Unheil (dafür stehen die Metaphern ‚Aufstehen' und ‚Fallen') wird". Nach RADL, *Lukas* (Anm. 75), S. 130, Anm. 482, scheinen Simeons Aussagen über Jesus „den Vater jetzt und später nichts anzugehen". Aber Joseph ist natürlich als anwesend gedacht.

105. Der Sinn der Parenthese V. 35a ist schwer zu entschlüsseln; WOLTER, *Lukasevangelium* (Anm. 60), S. 142-143: Man wird „nicht mehr sagen können, als dass Simeon Maria hier leidvolle Erfahrungen ankündigt".

Hanna ausführlich vorgestellt, deren Botschaft in V. 38b knapp referiert wird[106]. Angesichts Jesu und dessen Familie sprechen der Prophet und die Prophetin von der Hoffnung und Erwartung Israels[107]; die Eltern kommentieren das nicht, sondern kehren „nach Galiläa in ihre Stadt Nazareth" zurück (V. 39), womit ihr in V. 4 begonnener Aufenthalt in der Fremde sein Ende findet. Abschließend (V. 40) notiert der Erzähler die erfreuliche Entwicklung des Kindes (vgl. 1,80)[108].

In 2,41 setzt die Schilderung des Lebens einer offensichtlich „durchschnittlichen" jüdischen Familie neu ein. Jesu Eltern[109] gingen jährlich zum Passa nach Jerusalem, und Jesus ging im Alter von zwölf Jahren[110] erstmals mit ihnen[111]. Auf dem Rückweg wird er von den Eltern vermisst, und als sie ihn nach drei Tagen der Suche[112] im Tempel finden, sitzt er dort inmitten der Lehrer[113], die er hört und befragt (V. 46). Henk Jan de Jonge meint, Lukas wolle durch diesen besonderen Ort die besondere Weisheit Jesu herausstellen: „There, and not in some Galilean village synagogue, was where Luke wanted Jesus to excel"[114]. Michael Wolter

---

106. WOLTER, *Lukasevangelium* (Anm. 60), S. 143: Lukas „liefert lediglich einen summarischen Redebericht, in dem nur gesagt wird, *dass* sie über Jesus spricht; *was* sie über ihn sagt, bleibt unerwähnt und der Imagination der Leser überlassen".

107. *Ibid.*: „Lukas sagt auch nicht, dass Hanna mit Jesus und seinen Eltern zusammentrifft". Aber man soll sicher implizit annehmen, dass es zu einer Begegnung kommt.

108. In 1,80 war von Johannes gesagt worden: τὸ δὲ παιδίον ηὔξανεν καὶ ἐκραταιοῦτο πνεύματι, in 2,40 heißt es von Jesus: τὸ δὲ παιδίον ηὔξανεν καὶ ἐκραταιοῦτο πληρούμενον σοφίᾳ, καὶ χάρις θεοῦ ἦν ἐπ' αὐτό. Dass Jesus hinsichtlich des πνεῦμα „wächst", kann Lukas nicht sagen.

109. Einige Minuskeln sowie die Itala lesen statt οἱ γονεῖς αὐτοῦ die Namen „Joseph und Maria".

110. H.J. DE JONGE, *Sonship, Wisdom, Infancy: Luke II. 41-51a*, in NTS 24 (1978) 317-354, S. 317-324: Lukas betont, dass Jesus noch ein Kind war. „In 47, mention is made of the intelligence which Jesus displayed … Luke presents Jesus as still immature, not fully developed either spiritually or rationally, in order to make his wisdom appear all the more clearly". Dazu gehört insbesondere auch der in der Antike verbreitete Gedanke, dass die besondere Begabung des späteren „Helden" schon früh sichtbar wurde (S. 339-342).

111. Der Zeitraum zwischen Lk 2,39 und 2,42 wird in der „Kindheitserzählung des Thomas" durch etliche Erzählungen gefüllt.

112. Wie in V. 42 heißt es einleitend καὶ ἐγένετο, das Suchen wird stark betont, ohne dass den „drei Tagen" besondere Bedeutung zukommt (vgl. DE JONGE, *Sonship* [Anm. 110], S. 324-327).

113. Der Begriff διδάσκαλος wird im LkEv sonst nur für Jesus gebraucht. D.D. SYLVA, *The Cryptic Clause* en tois tou patros mou dei einai me *in Lk 2,49b*, in ZNW 78 (1987) 132-140, S. 136-137, Anm. 15: „the fact that in subsequent chapters in the Lukan narrative Jesus is presented as condemning many views of the Jewish teachers makes it highly unlikely that Luke would present Jesus as a student of Jewish teachers". Aber gesagt wird einfach, dass Jesus als (heranwachsendes) Kind *Lehrern* begegnet und, trotz des Ortes, nicht Priestern.

114. DE JONGE, *Sonship* (Anm. 110), S. 330, vergleicht dies mit dem Auftritt des Paulus auf dem Areopag.

nennt die dargestellte Situation „in höchstem Maße konstruiert und unrealistisch ..., denn normalerweise versammelt *ein* Lehrer eine Mehrzahl von Schülern um sich und nicht umgekehrt"; offenbar solle „das Gefälle zwischen Lehrenden und Lernendem" eingeebnet werden[115]. Der Erzähler notiert zwar (V. 47), dass alle außer sich gerieten über seinen Verstand und seine Antworten[116], aber das bedeutet wohl nicht, dass sich damit das Bild „wandelt" und „die Lehrer, die bisher seine Fragen beantwortet haben, ... nun zu Hörenden und, wie der Schluß von V. 47 zeigt, zu Fragenden" werden[117] – Lehrer, die einen Schüler etwas fragen, werden dadurch nicht zu Lernenden. Bei diesem Anblick erregen sich die Eltern (ἐξεπλάγησαν), und, der Situation entsprechend, sagt die Mutter[118]: „Kind, warum hast du uns das angetan? Sieh, dein Vater und ich[119] haben dich mit Schmerzen[120] gesucht" (ἐζητοῦμέν σε, V. 48). In seiner als Gegenfrage formulierten Antwort (V. 49) kommt erstmals im LkEv Jesus selbst zu Wort[121]: „Was suchtet ihr mich? (τί ὅτι ἐζητεῖτέ με;) Wusstet ihr nicht, dass ich bei dem sein muss, was zu meinem Vater gehört?"[122].

115. WOLTER, *Lukasevangelium* (Anm. 60), S. 148. Schüler sitzen überdies „zu Füßen" der Lehrer, nicht in ihrer Mitte. Aber hier muss m.E. kein Gegensatz bestehen.
116. Nichts spricht dafür, dass V. 47 „sekundär" gegenüber dem Kontext ist; dass es im Tempel ein hörendes Publikum gibt, ist realistisch. V. 47 ist, ebenso wie der ganze Abschnitt V. 41-52 redaktionell lk (vgl. DE JONGE, *Sonship* [Anm. 110], S. 342-348).
117. So RADL, *Lukas* (Anm. 75), S. 139. I.H. MARSHALL, *The Gospel of Luke: A Commentary on the Greek Text* (NIGTC), Grand Rapids, MI, Eerdmans, 1978, S. 128: „Jesus appears as a pupil who astonishes his teachers by the understanding of the law apparent in his questions and answers to their counter-questions; there is no thought of his precociously teaching the experts".
118. Dass die Mutter besonders besorgt ist, entspricht vermutlich einfach der Erfahrung, wie sie der Erzähler kennt. Anders BOVON, *Lk 1,1–9,50* (Anm. 76), S. 158-159: „Daß die Mutter und nicht der Vater spricht, liegt an der marianischen Perspektive der lukanischen Vorgeschichte wie an der literarischen Absicht des Verfassers, im Dialog ein Gegenüber der zwei Väter anschaulich zu machen". Ähnlich KLEIN, *Lukasevangelium* (Anm. 65), S. 155: „Daß Maria diese Vorwürfe vorbringt, bringt nach Lk zum Ausdruck, daß sie wirklich die Mutter, Josef hingegen nur der rechtliche Vater ist".
119. DE JONGE, *Sonship* (Anm. 110), S. 330-331: Die Reihenfolge ὁ πατήρ σου καὶ ἐγώ ist im Griechischen ungewöhnlich, ἐγώ wird üblicherweise vorangestellt; Lukas kam es offenbar darauf an, das Wort πατήρ als Thema von V. 48.49 stark zu betonen. „Luke does not play off one father against the other. He puts both parents in a position far beneath that of God. Luke lets the child Jesus indicate the limits to the authority and claims which his parents had over him ... Jesus was not dependent on men in his life and actions but was guided by the will of God" (S. 331).
120. Die Formulierung ὀδυνώμενοι ist sehr stark, vgl. Lk 16,24-25 (von den Schmerzen im Feuer des Hades).
121. BOVON, *Lk 1,1–9,50* (Anm. 76), S. 159: „Im Gedächtnis der lukanischen Gemeinde ist Jesus nicht nur als Sohn des göttlichen Vaters aufgetreten, sondern auch völlig menschlich als mündig werdender Knabe".
122. Zu der kaum übersetzbaren Wendung in V. 49b (οὐκ ᾔδειτε ὅτι ἐν τοῖς τοῦ πατρός μου δεῖ εἶναί με;) s. die Analyse von DE JONGE, *Sonship* (Anm. 110), S. 331-335: „It seems justified to conclude that Luke uses an enigmatic turn of phrase with two

Von Jesu Gottessohnschaft war seit der Ankündigung seiner wunderbaren Geburt nicht mehr gesprochen worden, sondern Joseph und Maria wurden ohne weiteres als Jesu Eltern beschrieben. Jesu Worte widersprechen dem nicht, sondern Lukas zeigt, dass Jesus als der Sohn Josephs und der Maria der Sohn Gottes ist. Leserinnen und Leser wissen das; die Eltern dagegen „verstanden nicht, was er ihnen gesagt hatte" (οὐ συνῆκαν τὸ ῥῆμα ὃ ἐλάλησεν αὐτοῖς, V. 50) – diese Notiz des Erzählers geht über das bisher schon mehrfach notierte Nicht-Verstehen (2,18.19; 2,33) deutlich hinaus[123]. An der Beziehung zwischen Jesus und seinen Eltern wird sich nichts ändern, und so endet der in V. 42 eröffnete „Reisebericht" mit der Rückkehr der Familie nach Nazareth und der Feststellung, dass „er ihnen ständig gehorsam war" (V. 51a)[124]. In V. 51b wird abermals gesagt, dass seine Mutter alles, was sie bisher erfahren hatte, „in ihrem Herzen bedachte"[125]; von Jesu Vater wird erst wieder in 4,22 gesprochen[126]. Der Prozess des Heranreifens Jesu ging weiter (V. 52: προέκοπτεν ἐν τῇ σοφίᾳ καὶ ἡλικίᾳ[127]). Nach Wolter fällt „die Jugendbiographie Jesu in

---

meanings. The first, which in spite of its unusual wording impresses itself on the reader of the Greek text, is ‚I must be in the house of my Father, i.e. the temple'. The second is ‚I must be about my Father's business'" (S. 335). Anders SYLVA, *Cryptic Clause* (Anm. 113), S. 136: Die lk Wendung „prefigures Jesus' teaching ministry in the temple during his final days in Jerusalem, as is recorded in Lk 19,45–21,38. [V.] 49b should be translated as ‚do you not know that I must be concerned with my father's words in the temple?'".

123. RADL, *Lukas* (Anm. 75), S. 141: „Bei Maria, die (nach 1,35.43; 2,19) um Jesu Identität weiß, verwundert das [sc. Nichtverstehen] zunächst. Aber es handelt sich wohl um ein Standardmotiv im Zusammenhang mit rätselhaften Offenbarungsworten, das deren Offenbarungscharakter – paradoxerweise – gerade unterstreichen soll. Im übrigen gilt auch für Maria Lk 10,22: ‚Niemand kennt den Sohn außer dem Vater'". Aber von einem „Standardmotiv" wird man angesichts der geschilderten Situation kaum sprechen können. WOLTER, *Lukasevangelium* (Anm. 60), S. 150: Dass Jesu Eltern mit Unverständnis reagieren, lässt „die Tragik der Situation deutlich zutage treten"; Wolter verweist auf das angesichts der Leiden- und Auferstehungsansage wahrzunehmende Unverständnis der Jünger (Lk 18,34), das dann durch den Auferstandenen „beseitigt" werde (24,45), „und dasselbe gilt ganz offensichtlich auch von Maria (vgl. Apg 1,14)". Aber Apg 1,14 lässt kaum etwas über Maria erkennen.

124. WOLTER, *Lukasevangelium* (Anm. 60), S. 151: Diese Notiz „will Jesus in den Bereich der menschlichen Normalität zurückholen, nachdem ein extrem außeralltäglicher Vorgang berichtet wurde".

125. Die Wendung ἡ μήτηρ αὐτοῦ διετήρει πάντα τὰ ῥήματα ἐν τῇ καρδίᾳ αὐτῆς wiederholt V. 19a ohne das erläuternde Partizip συμβάλλουσα. Dazu BOVON, *Lk 1,1–9,50* (Anm. 76), S. 162, Anm. 54: „Das Motiv des Interpretierens kann hier in 2,51 nicht wieder aufgenommen werden, da nach 2,50 weder Maria noch Josef die Aussage Jesu begriffen hatten". Das spricht dafür, die Bedeutung des συμβάλλουσα in 2,19 nicht allzu hoch einzuschätzen.

126. Missverständlich KLEIN, *Lukasevangelium* (Anm. 65), S. 156, Anm. 51: „In dem αὐτῶν ist Joseph zum letzten Mal im Evangelium genannt".

127. Der Artikel bei σοφίᾳ (ἐν τῇ) fehlt in den Handschriften fast durchgängig, nur der Sinaiticus und L lesen ihn; aber der Rückbezug auf V. 40 ist deutlich – die schon erwähnte σοφία Jesu nahm weiter zu.

den lk Summarien nicht aus dem Rahmen konventioneller Biographien überdurchschnittlich begabter Jugendlicher" heraus[128].

Für das in 1,5–2,52 geschilderte Geschehen besaß Lukas offensichtlich keine literarische Vorlage. Das ändert sich in Lk 3: Im Zusammenhang des in 3,1-2 genau datierten öffentlichen Auftretens des Johannes in der Wüste (vgl. 1,80) und seiner Inhaftierung (3,3-20, vgl. Mk 1,4-8.14a) erwähnt Lukas die Taufe Jesu (3,21f.) in Anlehnung an Mk 1,9-11[129]. In 3,23-38 folgt eine genealogische Übersicht; ähnlich wie die Parallele Mt 1,2-16 scheint sie durch die einleitende Notiz ὢν υἱός, ὡς ἐνομίζετο, Ἰωσὴφ τοῦ Ἡλί (V. 23)[130] ihren Sinn zu verfehlen[131], aber durch V. 38 (... τοῦ Ἀδὰμ τοῦ θεοῦ) wird das richtige Verstehen hergestellt[132].

In 4,14-15 notiert Lukas Jesu Lehrtätigkeit in Galiläa (vgl. Mk 1,14-15). Jesus kommt nach Ναζαρά[133], wo er aufgewachsen war (4,16a; vgl. 2,51)[134], liest im Gottesdienst[135] den Text Jes 61,1.2/58,6 LXX (V. 18-19) und sagt dazu dann (V. 20): σήμερον πεπλήρωται ἡ γραφὴ αὕτη ἐν τοῖς ὠσὶν ὑμῶν (V. 21). Die Anwesenden, die „sehr viel weniger ablehnend" reagieren als in Mk 6,3[136], erstaunen[137] ἐπὶ τοῖς λόγοις τῆς χάριτος. Sie verweisen in einer rhetorischen Frage auf Jesu Abstammung

---

128. WOLTER, *Lukasevangelium* (Anm. 60), S. 151.
129. Wer Jesus tauft, wird nicht gesagt, Jesus und sein Vorläufer begegnen einander nicht einmal bei Jesu Taufe.
130. WOLTER, *Lukasevangelium* (Anm. 60), S. 172: ὡς ἐνομίζετο „verweist auf die merkwürdigen Umstände, die mit dem Beginn von Marias Schwangerschaft einhergingen (vgl. 1,34). Obwohl Jesus nach lk Verständnis nicht der leibliche, sondern ... der soziale Sohn Josefs war, ist Josef der Vermittler von Jesu genealogischer Identität ..., die nun entfaltet wird".
131. Die Angabe αὐτὸς ἦν Ἰησοῦς ἀρχόμενος ὡσεὶ ἐτῶν τριάκοντα ist nach 2,42 der zweite Hinweis auf Jesu Lebensalter. ὡς ἐνομίζετο muss nicht eine nur „soziale" Vaterschaft Josephs aussagen, denn die Geschlechterfolge gilt auch dann, wenn Joseph Jesu „leiblicher" Vater ist.
132. WOLTER, *Lukasevangelium* (Anm. 60), S. 174: Ein Geschlechtsregister, „dass die Reihe der Vorfahren bis auf Gott als den Erschaffer des ersten Menschen zurückführt", ist analogielos.
133. Diese Ortsbezeichnung sonst nur noch in Mt 4,13.
134. Lukas hat die Szene aus Mk 6,1-6a übernommen, aber chronologisch an einen viel früheren Ort versetzt. Der in Mk 6,1 gebrauchte Begriff πατρίς wird zunächst vermieden, aber Jesus verwendet ihn dann in 4,24. Ungeachtet der in Lk 1–2 entwickelten Vorstellung von Jesu Geburt in Bethlehem gilt Nazareth als Ort der Herkunft Jesu, in 4,16 ganz präzise (οὗ ἦν τεθραμμένος).
135. 4,16b: ἀνέστη ἀναγνῶναι. Es wird nicht gesagt, Jesus sei zu dieser Lesung aufgefordert worden.
136. WOLTER, *Lukasevangelium* (Anm. 60), S. 193.
137. RADL, *Lukas* (Anm. 75), S. 260: „Es ist eine durchweg positive Reaktion". WOLTER, *Lukasevangelium* (Anm. 60), S. 194: Lukas beschreibt „eine kognitive Dissonanz zwischen der *Rolle*, in der Jesus den Synagogenbesuchern gegenübertritt, und dem *Status*, der ihm in dem Ort seiner Kindheit und Jugend zugewiesen wird". Da ihn hier alle nur als den „Sohn Josefs" kennen, beschränkt sich ihre Reaktion „auf ein Staunen über die Wohlgestalt der Worte Jesu". Wolter übersetzt λόγοι τῆς χάριτος mit „gefällige Worte".

(οὐχὶ υἱός ἐστιν Ἰωσὴφ οὗτος; V. 22) und sprechen damit, anders als in Mk 6,3, in ganz traditioneller Weise von seiner familiären Herkunft. Im Übrigen wird Jesu Familie nicht erwähnt; in Jesu Wort über den Propheten in seiner πατρίς (4,24) fehlen, abweichend von Mk 6,4, die συγγενεῖς. Dann nimmt die Nazareth-Szene eine dramatische Wendung, bis hin zu einer tödlichen Bedrohung Jesu (V. 29); aber er verlässt den Ort unbehelligt (V. 30).

In Lk 8,19-21 wird analog zu Mk 3 unvermittelt von Jesu Mutter und erstmals auch von seinen Geschwistern gesprochen. Die befremdliche Aussage in Mk 3,21 wird übergangen, aber in 8,19-21 folgt Lukas der Vorlage Mk 3,31-35, allerdings modifiziert: Jesu Mutter und seine Brüder können nicht zu ihm gelangen διὰ τὸν ὄχλον[138], und als man Jesus sagt, dass sie „draußen stehen und dich sehen wollen", reagiert er zurückhaltend[139]; einen innerfamiliären Konflikt lassen seine Worte nicht erkennen[140]. Weitere Erwähnungen der Familie Jesu gibt es im LkEv nicht[141].

In Apg 1,13.14a werden elf Männer namentlich genannt, die sich σὺν γυναιξίν[142] nach Jesu Himmelfahrt einmütig zum Gebet versammeln; in V. 14b wird ergänzt: καὶ Μαριὰμ τῇ μητρὶ τοῦ Ἰησοῦ[143] καὶ τοῖς ἀδελφοῖς αὐτοῦ. Die Mutter Jesu und seine Geschwister sind offenbar einfach „anwesend", Näheres über sie wird nicht gesagt[144]. Ein erstmals in 12,17

---

138. Jesus spricht in der Stadt vor einer großen Zuhörerschar (8,4, συνιόντος δὲ ὄχλου πολλοῦ …).
139. Die kritische Frage Mk 4,33 (τίς ἐστιν ἡ μήτηρ μου καὶ οἱ ἀδελφοί μου;) übernimmt Lukas nicht; er orientiert sich in 8,21 (μήτηρ μου καὶ ἀδελφοί μου οὗτοί εἰσιν οἱ τὸν λόγον τοῦ θεοῦ ἀκούοντες καὶ ποιοῦντες) an Mk 3,34b.35a. Dazu RADL, *Lukas* (Anm. 75), S. 537: „Die Blutsverwandten sind damit nicht ausgeschlossen. Im Gegenteil: Gerade von der Mutter Jesu (und damit auch von seinen Brüdern) gilt, daß sie das genannte Kriterium erfüllen". Gibt es für diese Auslegung einen Beleg?
140. H. CONZELMANN, *Die Mitte der Zeit: Studien zur Theologie des Lukas* (BHT, 17), Tübingen, Mohr Siebeck, ⁵1964, S. 29: Anders als in Mk 3,21 wollen die Verwandten Jesus nicht „ins Privatleben zurückholen", aber sie wollen ihn „sehen", nicht anders als bald danach Herodes (9,9). „Sie wollen Wunder vorgeführt haben, sie wollen ihn nach Nazareth holen, damit er dort als an dem gebührenden Orte wirke".
141. In Lk 11,27-28 bezieht sich der von einer unbekannten Frau ausgerufene Makarismus auf Jesu Mutter; Jesu Reaktion (μενοῦν ...) stellt eine Richtigstellung dar. WOLTER, *Lukasevangelium* (Anm. 60), S. 422: Nur auf der Textoberfläche gilt der Lobpreis der Mutter, tatsächlich aber bezieht er sich auf Jesus.
142. Codex D ergänzt τέκνοις. Um welche Frauen es sich handelt, sagt Lukas nicht.
143. Die Formulierung Μαριὰμ τῇ μητρὶ τοῦ Ἰησοῦ nimmt darauf Bezug, dass in Lk 24,10 von Maria Magdalena und von Μαρία ἡ Ἰακώβου gesprochen worden war; die Mutter Jesu wird in der Apg nur hier erwähnt. BOVON, *Lk 1,1–9,50* (Anm. 76), S. 419, schreibt zu Lk 8,21, Maria werde „erst nach Ostern dem Kreis der Jünger Jesu angehören, nicht wegen ihrer Mutterschaft, sondern wegen ihres dort (Lk 1,38; 2.19.51) beschriebenen Glaubens", aber davon spricht der Text nicht.
144. Der Ursprung dieser Überlieferung lässt sich nicht aufhellen; s. C.K. BARRETT, *The Acts of the Apostles I* (ICC), Edinburgh, T&T Clark, 1994, S. 89-90: „Luke either has no information, or is not concerned to provide information, about Mary in the

erwähnter Mann namens Jakobus[145] hält beim „Apostelkonzil" die entscheidende Rede (15,13-21) und spielt beim letzten Aufenthalt des Paulus in Jerusalem eine wichtige Rolle (21,18-25); dass er ein Bruder Jesu ist, wird in der Apg nicht einmal angedeutet[146].

Das von Lukas mit besonderer Intensität gezeichnete Bild der Familie Jesu ist nahezu ausschließlich auf die Beziehung zwischen Jesus und seinen Eltern konzentriert. Darin liegt der besondere christologische Akzent der lukanischen Perspektive dessen, was als „Inkarnation" bezeichnet werden kann, ohne dass es dafür im LkEv eine begriffliche Entsprechung gibt.

III. Jesu Familie in den Evangelien: Perspektiven für die Christologie

Die Evangelien sprechen vom Leben des Menschen Jesus von der Glaubensgewissheit her, dass Jesus starb und von Gott auferweckt und „erhöht" wurde. Im MkEv begegnet Jesus als erwachsener Mann, der Mutter und Geschwister hat, die sich ihm gegenüber ablehnend (3,20) oder jedenfalls sehr distanziert verhalten (3,31-35); das Wirken Jesu bleibt davon unberührt. Das MtEv betont die außergewöhnlichen Umstände der Schwangerschaft der Maria, während Jesu Geburt lediglich am Rande erwähnt wird; hervorgehoben wird die besondere Beziehung zwischen Joseph und Maria und dabei insbesondere das fürsorgliche Handeln Josephs als des Ehemanns der Mutter Jesu, nicht aber als dessen Vater. Die in Mt 1 und 2 geschilderten Ereignisse spielen für das Jesusbild im übrigen Verlauf des MtEv keine Rolle mehr. Das JohEv spricht von der „Inkarnation" (ὁ λόγος σὰρξ ἐγένετο), die aber lediglich konstatiert, nicht „erzählt" wird. Jesu Mutter und seine Geschwister treten auf, und man weiß in Jesu Umfeld auch von seinem Vater; aber für das Jesusbild, also für die „Christologie" des JohEv, hat dies nur geringe Bedeutung.

---

post-resurrection period … The earthly family of Jesus is now taken up into his spiritual family".

145. Er wird nicht näher vorgestellt, im Unterschied zu Jakobus Zebedäi (12,2).

146. Paulus traf während seines Besuchs bei Kephas in Jerusalem dort auch Jakobus, „den Bruder des Herrn" (Gal 1,19); die in 1 Kor 15,7 zitierte Formel ὤφθη Ἰακώβῳ und die in Gal 2,9 offenbar zitierte „Konzilsvereinbarung" nennen Jakobus ohne weiteres Attribut. Paulus erwähnt auch Brüder Jesu, ohne Namennennung (1 Kor 9,5). Von Jesu Mutter spricht Paulus nur in Gal 4,4 (… γενόμενον ἐκ γυναικός), von seinem irdischen Vater nirgends.

Lukas dagegen entwirft eine eindringliche Vorstellung von Jesu Familie: Der in 1,35 als υἱὸς θεοῦ angekündigte Sohn der Maria wird als *vere homo* vorgestellt, indem seine Geburt als ein alltägliches Ereignis geschildert wird, dessen besondere Bedeutung nur durch das allein den Hirten zuteil werdende Erscheinen himmlischer Personen (2,10-14) sowie durch die Prophezeiungen des Simeon und der Hanna (2,25-38) sichtbar gemacht wird, ohne dass den Eltern Jesu ein umfassendes Verstehen gegeben ist. Damit hebt Lukas Geburt und Kindheit Jesu aus dem Unbekannten und möglicherweise Mythischen oder Sagenhaften ins Licht des Menschlichen: Jesus wurde in einem konkreten geographischen Raum geboren, und er wuchs dort heran – in einer konkreten historischen Zeit und in einer konkreten Familie. Auch wenn die entsprechenden Schilderungen legendarisch sind, dienen sie doch dazu, das Menschsein Jesu christologisch zu reflektieren. Im LkEv hat das Bild von Jesus als dem Sohn Gottes, dessen Vater Joseph und dessen Mutter Maria ist, eine besondere Akzentuierung erhalten, die dem späteren dogmatischen *vere Deus vere homo* nahe kommt.

An der Rehwiese 38	Andreas LINDEMANN
DE-33617 Bielefeld	
Deutschland	
lindemann.bethel@t-online.de	

"WHY DO DOUBTS ARISE IN YOUR HEARTS?" (LUKE 24,38)

NARRATIVE AS APOLOGETIC IN GOSPEL RESURRECTION STORIES

When the risen Jesus appears to the Eleven and others in Luke 24, he reproves them, saying, "Why are you troubled, and why do doubts (διαλογισμοί) arise in your hearts?" (v. 38)[1]. Within the context, this reproof does not address the disciples' initial failure to believe the report of the women (vv. 10-11) or their failure to recognize Jesus when he appears to them (vv. 15-16), but rather their faulty conceptualization of his embodied risen presence (vv. 37-43). For when Jesus speaks, he invites them to see his hands and feet, and to touch and handle him; and he addresses their mistaken view that he is (a) spirit/pneuma and thus not embodied with flesh and bones (πνεῦμα σάρκα καὶ ὀστέα οὐκ ἔχει καθὼς ἐμὲ θεωρεῖτε ἔχοντα, v. 39). This language is the opposite of that found in Paul's discussion of resurrection bodies as spiritual (πνευματικός, 1 Cor 15,35-57) and of the inability of "flesh and blood" (σάρξ καὶ αἷμα) to inherit the kingdom of God (v. 50). A good case can be made that Luke's precise language, and the risen Jesus' physical demonstrations (see also vv. 41-43), were intended to correct a Pauline view of the resurrection body and to assert a particular kind of authority for Luke's

---

* It is my great honour to contribute this essay in gratitude for the outstanding contributions which Prof. Joseph Verheyden has made to our field, the study of early Christian literature, and for his friendship and support.

1. The topic of resurrection is well represented in Prof. Verheyden's extensive bibliography: see J. VERHEYDEN, *L'Ascension d'Isaïe et l'évangile de Matthieu: Examen de AI 3,13-18*, in J.-M. SEVRIN (ed.), *The New Testament in Early Christianity – La réception des écrits néotestamentaires dans le christianisme primitif* (BETL, 86), Leuven, LUP, 1989, 247-274; ID., *Silent Witnesses: Mary Magdalene and the Women at the Tomb in the Gospel of Peter*, in R. BIERINGER – V. KOPERSKI – B. LATAIRE (eds.), *Resurrection in the New Testament: Festschrift J. Lambrecht* (BETL, 165), Leuven, LUP – Peeters, 2002, 457-482; T. NICKLAS – F.V. REITERER – J. VERHEYDEN (eds.), *The Human Body in Death and Resurrection* (Deuterocanonical and Cognate Literature. Yearbook), Berlin – New York, De Gruyter, 2009; T. NICKLAS – A. MERKT – J. VERHEYDEN (eds.), *Gelitten – Gestorben – Auferstanden: Passions- und Ostertraditionen im antiken Christentum* (WUNT, 2.273), Tübingen, Mohr Siebeck, 2010; W. WEREN – H. VAN DE SANDT – J. VERHEYDEN (eds.), *Life beyond Death in Matthew's Gospel: Religious Metaphor or Bodily Reality?* (BTS, 13), Leuven – Paris – Walpole, MA, Peeters, 2011; J. VERHEYDEN – A. MERKT – T. NICKLAS (eds.), *"If Christ Has Not Been Raised ...": Studies on the Reception of the Resurrection Stories and the Belief in the Resurrection in the Early Church* (NTOA/StUNT, 115), Göttingen, Vandenhoeck & Ruprecht, 2016.

Twelve[2]. It is interesting that the narrative depicts the "pneumatic" view as something originating within the movement, and not as an outsider misunderstanding of Jesus' resurrection and appearances. Among the canonical gospels, this is a particular interest of the Gospel of Luke: other appearance stories do not theorize the embodied risen presence of Jesus so explicitly (e.g., Mt 28,16-20).

The point here is to illustrate that these narratives afford us access primarily to the literary and theological purposes of their authors, which are often or even usually directed to answering doubts or disputes (διαλογισμοί) of one kind or another about the resurrection of Jesus. Attempts to go behind these texts to earlier traditions, or even to historical events or experiences, are problematic. The story of the discovery of the empty tomb shows significant development from its earliest form (Mk 16,1-8) to its later ones, whose various additions and alterations display the theological and editorial concerns of their authors[3]. The appearance stories as well are highly stylized and stereotypical, as scholars have long recognized, with a high degree of conformity both to one another and also to other known appearance or vision reports[4]. This suggests a significant amount of assimilation at the literary or pre-literary level. The resurrection narratives display secondary features including theological development, apologetic intervention, scriptural influence, and polemical intent, in keeping with the broader interests of the evangelists in their own historical and religious contexts. One can discern apologetic tendencies in many, if not most, of the narrative developments in both the empty tomb story and the

---

2. On these two points, see D.A. SMITH, *Seeing a Pneuma(tic Body): The Apologetic Interests of Luke 24,36-43*, in *CBQ* 72 (2010) 752-772; and S. MATTHEWS, *Fleshly Resurrection, Authority Claims, and the Scriptural Practices of Lukan Christianity*, in *JBL* 136 (2017) 163-183.

3. See D.A. SMITH, *Revisiting the Empty Tomb: The Early History of Easter*, Minneapolis, MN, Fortress, 2010; D.C. ALLISON, JR., *The Resurrection of Jesus: Apologetics, Polemics, History*, London, Bloomsbury T&T Clark, 2021, pp. 116-166. See also M. GOODACRE, *How Empty Was the Tomb?*, in *JSNT* 44 (2021) 123-148, arguing that "empty tomb" is a misnomer as most of the sources presuppose a large elite tomb holding multiple bodies (e.g., Mk 16,5-6).

4. See R. BULTMANN, *The History of the Synoptic Tradition*, trans. J. Marsh, Oxford, Blackwell, 1963², pp. 285-291; C.H. DODD, *The Appearances of the Risen Christ: An Essay in Form-Criticism of the Gospels*, in D.E. NINEHAM (ed.), *Studies in the Gospels: Essays in Memory of R.H. Lightfoot*, Oxford, Blackwell, 1955, 9-35; see also K. BERGER, *Visionsberichte: Formgeschichtliche Bemerkungen über pagane hellenistische Texte und ihre frühchristlichen Analogien*, in ID. – F. VOUGA – M. WOLTER – D. ZELLER (eds.), *Studien und Texte zur Formgeschichte* (Texte und Arbeiten zum neutestamentlichen Zeitalter, 7), Tübingen, Francke, 1992, 177-225; J. HARTENSTEIN, *Geschichten von der Erscheinung des Auferstandenen in nichtkanonischen Schriften und die Entwicklung der Ostertradition*, in NICKLAS – MERKT – VERHEYDEN (eds.), *Gelitten – Gestorben – Auferstanden* (n. 1), 123-142.

appearance stories, refining or defining matters that were the subject of debates internal or external to the early Christian movements.

Some interpreters, such as N.T. Wright, downplay the stereotypical features and secondary developments in (canonical) gospel resurrection stories in order to claim that the appearance stories primarily reflect "genuinely early oral tradition"[5]. Wright contends that because the appearance stories lack "developed elements" such as the "theology and exegesis" of Paul's letters, they must be "chronologically as well as logically prior to the developed discussions of the resurrection which we find in Paul and many subsequent writers", and that "stories as earth-shattering as this, stories as community-forming as this, once told, are not easily modified"[6]. Wright presupposes that the "traditions" provide reliable access, if not to the "events", at least to "what several different people thought had happened", which is important in answering the kinds of historical questions Wright wants to answer[7]. Many other authors similarly view these texts as providing more or less direct access to the resurrection appearances as "events"[8]. Once the stereotypical features and secondary developments are considered, however, certainty about the original traditions concerning the resurrection appearances seems possible only at the most basic level, such as what Paul handed on: "he appeared (ὤφθη) to Cephas, then to the Twelve" (1 Cor 15,5; cf. Lk 24,34).

The focus of this paper, however, is not the original shape, function, or genuineness of early traditions concerning the resurrection of Jesus; instead, this paper analyses the narrative developments evident in our texts and the apologetic motivations or effects of these developments. In the case of the empty tomb story, it can be taken for granted that Mk 16,1-8 is our earliest surviving textual source, and moreover, that it stands at the beginning of a trajectory of textual developments that sought to efface its more problematic aspects. With the appearance stories, however, we do not have as firm and fixed a starting point. The earliest textual source for the appearances is 1 Cor 15,5-8 (i.e., the tradition Paul cites), which provides no narrative structure and no substantial information about how the

---

5. N.T. WRIGHT, *The Resurrection of the Son of God*. Vol. 3: *Christian Origins and the Question of God*, London, SPCK, 2003, pp. 597-598, 611-612.

6. *Ibid.*, pp. 611-612.

7. *Ibid.*, pp. 613-614.

8. See for example M.R. LICONA, *The Resurrection of Jesus: A New Historiographical Approach*, Downers Grove, IL, IVP Academic, 2010. For the appearance stories as sources of "residue" of visionary experiences, see P.F. CRAFFERT, *Re-Visioning Jesus' Resurrection: The Resurrection Stories in a Neuroanthropological Perspective*, in J. VERHEYDEN – J.S. KLOPPENBORG (eds.), *The Gospels and Their Stories in Anthropological Perspective* (WUNT, 409), Tübingen, Mohr Siebeck, 2018, 251-280.

appearances were received or understood[9]. However, there is a basic shared structure in the appearance stories, somewhat along these lines: setting; appearance; greeting; recognition; commissioning[10]. Our focus will be how individual texts uniquely fill out this basic structure and what that can tell us about their apologetic or theological interests (as with Lk 24,36-43 above)[11].

I. The Trouble with the Tomb

Mk 16,1-8 is the earliest and only independent witness to the story of the discovery of the empty tomb. There is strong internal evidence that the story was not a Markan creation[12]. There are also good grounds for thinking that v. 8 was the original conclusion of Mark's gospel: our earliest text-critical evidence shows that Mark was being circulated, read, and copied with ἐφοβοῦντο γάρ (v. 8) as its final clause[13]. As it stands, the Markan story contains several problems and ambiguities that successive retellings, whether directly or indirectly dependent on Mark, sought to remedy; and in most cases, strong evidence of a "traditional" origin of these improvements is lacking. But not all narrative developments in the story address Mark's shortcomings. Some, as we will see, also address external apologetic concerns.

The author of Mark seems aware of one possible problem with the empty tomb story: it is open to the interpretation that the women, here "Mary Magdalene, Mary the [mother] of James, and Salome" (v. 1), simply arrived at the wrong place. Although Mark is not consistent in the

---

9. As is well known, there is considerable scepticism whether the original concept – let alone the originating experience(s) – can be recovered from the term ὤφθη, even in a first-person report like that of Paul himself (1 Cor 15,8; cf. Gal 1,15-17). See H.J. de Jonge, *Visionary Experience and the Historical Origins of Christianity*, in Bieringer – Koperski – Lataire (eds.), *Resurrection in the New Testament* (n. 1), 35-53, pp. 43-46.

10. Dodd, *Appearances of the Risen Christ* (n. 4), p. 11. See also Allison, *Resurrection of Jesus* (n. 3), pp. 60-61: setting; appearance; doubt; commissioning; promise of support (for the appearance to the Twelve).

11. The topic is worthy of a longer and more comprehensive treatment than can be managed here. For reasons of space, the paper cannot address a further apologetic tendency in the resurrection stories, which is to authorize certain figures and/or legitimize certain teachings.

12. J. Marcus, *Mark 8–16: A New Translation with Introduction and Commentary* (AB, 27A), New Haven, CT, Yale University Press, 2009, p. 1083; Allison, *Resurrection of Jesus* (n. 3), pp. 117-119. See also Smith, *Revisiting the Empty Tomb* (n. 3), pp. 77-78.

13. ℵ B *et al.* The Shorter Ending and the Longer Ending (Ps.-Mk 16,9-20) are acknowledged to be secondary, but some scholars have proposed that the original ending is now lost. For an overview of the issues, see Marcus, *Mark 8–16* (n. 12), pp. 1088-1096.

naming of the "other Mary" (cf. Mk 15,40.47; see also Mt 27,61; 28,1), the text specifies that two of the women mentioned in Mk 16,1 "saw where he was put" (Mk 15,47) and then returned to the same place on the first day of the week[14]. That said, Mk 16,1-8 leaves many questions unanswered for its reader/hearer. Who rolled the stone away, and why (v. 4)? Who was the young man in the tomb, and why did he speak so authoritatively about what had happened to Jesus – and to his body (vv. 5-7)? If the women fled in fear and told no one, how did the story come to be known (v. 8)? And finally, if Jesus was raised from the dead, why did he not appear immediately to his followers[15]?

The question of who removed the stone, if unanswered, could allow the suspicion that disciples or sympathizers – or even opponents – opened the tomb and removed the body, in the former case to support a resurrection claim (Mt 27,62-66; *Gos. Pet.* 8.29-33)[16], or in the latter to transport it to a more permanent resting place in keeping with a dishonourable burial[17]. Matthew's solution, which is to have an angel roll the stone away (Mt 28,2), is one piece of a major narrative intervention which interposes scenes focusing on the Jewish leadership and the guard at the tomb with scenes focusing on Jesus and the disciples. The guard at the tomb allows Matthew, first, to guarantee that the reader knows the disciples did not steal the body, but secondly, to explain the origin of the body-theft rumour, "disseminated among Jews to this very day" (Mt 28,15), as a false narrative created by those who knew the truth (vv. 11-15; see also Justin, *Dial.* 108; Origen, *Cels.* 1.51). Many scholars, including Ulrich Luz, who sees a high degree of "fictionality" in Mt 27,62-66 and 28,11-15, nevertheless think Matthew created the story based on a tradition according to which the tomb was watched, if not guarded[18]. Although this is possible, it is by no means necessary: Luz

---

14. A. YARBRO COLLINS, *Mark: A Commentary* (Hermeneia), Minneapolis, MN, Fortress, 2007, p. 779; MARCUS, *Mark 8–16* (n. 12), p. 1060.

15. This last question is perhaps more about the narrative purposes of Mark, for the text alludes to an appearance to take place in Galilee (Mk 16,7). Yet early interpreters of Mark evidently found a mere allusion to be insufficient (e.g., Mt 28,9-10).

16. Ancient Mediterranean literature provides many examples of stories in which people contrived to hide bodily remains to produce the conclusion that the person in question had been transported into the divine realm (not resurrected). See SMITH, *Revisiting the Empty Tomb* (n. 3), pp. 47-61.

17. The latter issue is not an explicit concern in our texts, but there are hints that Jesus' opponents may have arranged for a (shameful?) burial in Acts 13,27-29; *Gos. Pet.* 6.21; Justin, *Dial.* 97.1.

18. U. LUZ, *Fictionality and Loyalty to Tradition in Matthew's Gospel in the Light of Greek Literature*, in ID., *Studies in Matthew*, Grand Rapids, MI, Eerdmans, 2005, 54-79, pp. 58-59. Luz supposes that Matthew was familiar with an earlier "community tradition"

himself observes that "the style and wording are largely Matthean"[19]. In any case, the presence of the guard also requires that the tomb be opened, hence the angel. The *Gospel of Peter* follows Matthew in some of these details, except that the stone rolls away by itself (*Gos. Pet.* 9.37) to allow "two men" (δύο ἄνδρας, v. 36; νεανίσκοι, v. 37) who descend from heaven to enter the tomb and assist Jesus in his rising, in full view of the centurion, the soldiers, and the elders (10.38-42)[20]. Although the culpability of the witnesses is thereby heightened, no false report is spread by either the Jewish leadership or Pilate and the Romans in the *Gospel of Peter*: here they opt to remain silent about the resurrection (11.45-49).

Neither Luke nor John explains who rolled away the stone, but both add a new feature: grave clothes in the tomb, discovered not by the women, but by apostles who inspect the tomb later and confirm the women's story (Lk 24,12, ὀθόνια; Jn 20,3-10, ὀθόνια and σουδάριον)[21]. Luke and John show no evidence that the body-theft rumour was a concern, but later Christian authors take the empty linen wrappings as proof that the disciples did not steal the body (e.g., John Chrysostom, *Hom. Ioh.* 85.4; Theodore of Mopsuestia, *Comm. Ioh.* 7)[22]. On the other hand, given the emphasis in Luke and John on the tangibility and robust embodiedness of the risen Jesus (Lk 24,36-43; Jn 20,24-28), the grave clothes were more likely intended to restrict the interpretation of the resurrection appearances along such lines. When Jesus appears in Luke, as explained

---

that attempted to refute the body-theft rumour by claiming that the tomb had been guarded. See also W.J.C. WEREN, *"His Disciples Stole Him Away" (Mt 28,13): A Rival Interpretation of Jesus' Resurrection*, in BIERINGER – KOPERSKI – LATAIRE (eds.), *Resurrection in the New Testament* (n. 1), 147-163, pp. 156-162.

19. U. LUZ, *Matthew 21–28: A Commentary* (Hermeneia), Minneapolis, MN, Fortress, 2005, p. 609.

20. Text from P. FOSTER, *The Gospel of Peter: Introduction, Critical Edition and Commentary* (TENTS, 4), Leiden, Brill, 2010. For the direct dependence of the *Gospel of Peter* on Matthew, see *ibid.*, pp. 132-137. A similar description of the resurrection is found in *Mart. Isa.* 3.14-19, in which angels (the angel of the Holy Spirit and Michael) open the tomb and carry the Beloved out on their shoulders.

21. Because Lk 24,12 is absent from certain Western witnesses (D it), and because it displays verbatim parallels with Jn 20,5 (καὶ παρακύψας βλέπει τὰ ὀθόνια), it is sometimes supposed that it was a scribal addition to canonical Luke derived from John. There are good grounds, however, for considering the verse original to Luke: see F. NEIRYNCK, *Once More Luke 24,12*, in *ETL* 70 (1992) 319-340; ID., *Luke 24,12: An Anti-Docetic Interpolation?*, in A. DENAUX (ed.), *New Testament Textual Criticism and Exegesis: Festschrift J. Delobel* (BETL, 161), Leuven, LUP – Peeters, 2002, 145-158; see also SMITH, *Revisiting the Empty Tomb* (n. 3), pp. 115-118.

22. See ALLISON, *Resurrection of Jesus* (n. 3), pp. 152-153, nn. 213-214. The idea that Jesus' body had been moved seems more a dramatic device in John: it is the fear of Mary Magdalene (Jn 20,2.13.15), who, although she peers into the tomb, does not notice the grave clothes (vv. 11-12; cf. vv. 6-7).

above, he does not appear as the spirit (πνεῦμα, vv. 37.39) of one whose body still lies in a tomb, but as one risen from the dead and out of the tomb in a flesh-and-bones body (v. 39). A similar emphasis is also found in the *Gospel of the Hebrews*, in which Jesus hands the grave clothes to the servant of the priest as he exits the tomb (*Gos. Heb.* fr. 7; Jerome, *Vir. ill.* 2)[23].

Mark's mysterious "young man" (νεανίσκος, Mk 16,5) is promoted in various ways in later versions of the story. As already noted, in Matthew an angel descends from heaven to roll away the stone (Mt 28,2), while in Luke two angelic figures (called "men in dazzling clothing", Lk 24,4) address the frightened women (vv. 5-8). In *Gos. Pet.* 11.44, a "certain man" descends from heaven and enters the tomb to await the women's arrival (he later is called νεανίσκος, 13.55). In the *Martyrdom of Isaiah*, they are identified as "the angel of the Holy Spirit and Michael", who both open the tomb and assist the Beloved in rising (3.16-18; there is no mention of the women). In John, the appearance of the angels is downplayed: their exchange with Mary Magdalene is very brief (Jn 20,13), but they do take up symbolically meaningful positions "one at the head and one at the feet, where the body of Jesus had lain" (v. 12)[24]. This diminished angelophany should probably be understood in relation to how certain texts rectify Mark's failure to describe an appearance of the risen Jesus at or near the tomb: as the encounters between Jesus and the women become increasingly more complex (Mt 28,9-10; Jn 20,14-18; *Ep. Apos.* 9.1–11.1), the angelophany becomes less so, to the point where it is entirely absent in the *Epistle of the Apostles*[25]. In any case, the promotion of Mark's "young man" in various ways to an angelic figure (or figures) addresses the problem of his insight and authority, and it also makes the tomb of Jesus more explicitly the site of divine revelation.

Mark's troubling conclusion to the story, that the women "told no one, for they were afraid" (Mk 16,8), while open to various interpretations, creates a narrative difficulty that is straightforwardly addressed by many sources: they did, in fact, go off to tell the disciples (see Mt 28,8; Mk [SE];

---

23. Numbered fr. 5 in J. FREY, *Die Fragmente des Hebräerevangeliums*, in C. MARKSCHIES – J. SCHRÖTER (eds.), *Antike christliche Apokryphen in deutscher Übersetzung*. Bd. 1: *Evangelien und Verwandtes*, Teilbd. 1, Tübingen, Mohr Siebeck, 2012, 593-606.

24. See R.E. BROWN, *The Gospel according to John XIII–XXI: A New Translation with Introduction and Commentary* (AB, 29A), Garden City, NY, Doubleday, 1970, p. 989, who mentions (but does not endorse) as a "proposed symbolism" an allusion to the cherubim on the mercy-seat (Ex 25,17-22). I am not aware of an ancient commentator who notices this allusion.

25. *Ibid.*, p. 999; see also F. WATSON, *An Apostolic Gospel: The 'Epistula Apostolorum' in Literary Context* (SNTS MS, 179), Cambridge, CUP, 2020, p. 112: "angels only have a genuine role in the Easter traditions where the risen Jesus himself is absent".

cf. Ps.-Mk 16,9-11; *Ep. Apos.* 10.1-9), even when the angels do not commission them with the news of the resurrection. In John, although the angels do not commission Mary Magdalene to tell the disciples (Jn 20,13), Jesus does, and she complies (vv. 17-18); in Luke, by contrast, the angels tell the women not to tell but to "remember" (Lk 24,6b-8), and although they do report to the Eleven, it is important for Luke that women are not directly commissioned with the news of Jesus' rising[26].

There are also noticeable tendencies to improve the status of the tomb in which Jesus was put, and (eventually) to add the language of ritual mourning to the burial and tomb stories[27]. These two tendencies are related and may ultimately derive from a memory that Jesus' burial was a shameful one[28]. Raymond Brown noted that several expected features of an honourable burial – preparing the body according to prescribed rituals, including washing, and placing it in a family tomb – are absent from Mark's description[29]. Others suggest that Mk 16,1 implies that the women wanted to supplement the "abbreviated" (but not dishonourable) burial carried out by Joseph of Arimathea[30]. Interestingly, despite the efforts to improve the tomb in which Jesus was put by making it new and unused, or even Joseph's own tomb (Mt 27,60; Lk 23,53; Jn 19,41; *Gos. Pet.* 6.24), and to improve the burial itself with spices for anointing (Mk 16,1; Lk 24,1; Jn 19,39-40), "mourning" and "washing" language are absent from the canonical accounts (but cf. *Gos. Pet.* 6.24; 12.50-52; *Ep. Apos.* 9.3)[31]. The canonical gospels, then, "embellish and glamourize the burial of Jesus", without explicitly claiming it was an honourable one[32]. This set of narrative improvements probably results from sensitivity about the burial of Jesus, and not to specifically apologetic concerns.

Gospel writers after Mark correct, as it were, its lack of resurrection appearances not only by narrating encounters with the risen Jesus, but also by introducing aspects of the appearance traditions into the tomb

---

26. See, among others, MATTHEWS, *Fleshly Resurrection* (n. 2), pp. 169-170.
27. There is also a tendency to enhance the allegiance of Joseph of Arimathea to Jesus and his movement: compare Mk 15,43 with Mt 27,57; Lk 23,50-51; Jn 19,38.
28. See R.E. BROWN, *The Burial of Jesus (Mark 15,42-47)*, in *CBQ* 50 (1988) 233-245; B.R. MCCANE, *Roll Back the Stone: Death and Burial in the World of Jesus*, Harrisburg, PA, Trinity Press International, 2003, pp. 89-108.
29. BROWN, *Burial of Jesus* (n. 28), pp. 242-245; cf. MARCUS, *Mark 8–16* (n. 12), pp. 1074-1075.
30. MARCUS, *Mark 8–16* (n. 12), p. 1082.
31. See further D.A. SMITH, *"Look, the Place Where They Put Him" (Mark 16,6): The Space of Jesus' Tomb in Early Christian Memory*, in *HTS Teologiese Studies/Theological Studies* 70.1 (2014), Art. # 2741; http://dx.doi.org/10.4102/hts.v70i1.2741.
32. MCCANE, *Roll Back the Stone* (n. 28), pp. 101-104 (citation from p. 101).

story itself. The risen Jesus appears at or near the tomb in both Mt 28,9-10 (although the location is not clear) and Jn 20,14-18. The implication is that when Jesus appears, he appears as one who was raised bodily out of the tomb, thus narrativizing the claim that "He was raised, he is not here" (Mk 16,6, etc.)[33]. Furthermore, in Lk 24,12 and Jn 20,3-10, Peter (and in John, the Beloved Disciple) go to the tomb to inspect it themselves. Although some scholars propose that these scenes were intended to corroborate the women's story of the empty tomb for readers, because women's testimony was considered suspect or inferior in the ancient world[34], it seems more likely that the intention was to position a primary witness of the resurrection, Peter (and in John, the Beloved Disciple), at the tomb to control how the appearances were to be interpreted. In Luke, the proclamation of the resurrection originates with Peter (Lk 24,34: "the Lord indeed was raised, and he appeared to Simon"), and if Peter saw the tomb and the grave clothes empty, Jesus' risen presence as experienced by him must have been embodied. Luke also takes the authoritative word about the empty tomb, and the first announcement of the resurrection, away from women, and gives both to male apostolic figures[35].

To sum up: many narrative developments in the empty tomb story seem to be apologetically motivated. Matthew's additional materials about the guarding of the tomb, and the collusion of Jewish leaders and Roman soldiers to invent the body-theft rumour, were intended to refute rival interpretations of Christian claims about an empty tomb. (Whether Matthew would have been read by such outsiders, or whether they would have been convinced, is entirely another question.) This would also address potential insider concerns about the veracity of Jesus' resurrection. The promotion of Mark's "young man" in the tomb to an angel or angels both removes suspicions about his identity or insight while at the same time authenticating the interpretation of the missing body as a more clearly divine message. The addition of empty grave clothes excludes the possibility that the women had entered the wrong tomb, while at the same time restricting the interpretation of the resurrection appearances: Jesus was raised out of the tomb (and out of the grave clothes) in a tangible body, and when he appeared, it was this body that his followers saw, and not

---

33. SMITH, *Revisiting the Empty Tomb* (n. 3), p. 131 (on Matthew).
34. See, e.g., F. BOVON, *Luke*. Vol. 3: *A Commentary on the Gospel of Luke 19,28–24,53* (Hermeneia), Minneapolis, MN, Fortress, 2012, p. 353: "the fragile testimony of the women received a more reliable confirmation through a man". For literature on women's testimony in early Jewish culture, see SMITH, *Revisiting the Empty Tomb* (n. 3), p. 230, n. 5.
35. SMITH, *Revisiting the Empty Tomb* (n. 3), p. 113.

his spirit or daimon[36]. Having primary apostolic witnesses of the risen Jesus also inspect the tomb would address similar questions, whether internal or external, about the nature of the resurrection appearances.

II. Resurrection and Exaltation

M. David Litwa defines resurrection, in the stories about Jesus, as "the revivification of his own body after a genuine death to an immortal transformed state", or "postmortem immortalization"[37]. In other words, our texts describe Jesus' resurrection not as a return to "the same sort of life that humans presently experience", but to restored life in an immortal and incorruptible body (cf. 1 Cor 15,42-45) which, for ancients, would have required his translation (or assumption), that is, his exaltation to the divine realm[38]. A careful reading of the resurrection narratives show that they are not only interested in questions about Jesus' body (concerning which, see the following section), but also in the process itself, although they do not narrate the resurrection directly (cf. *Gos. Pet.* 10.38-42)[39]. Because of this lack of direct narration, readers must, at least in the gospel stories, pay attention to textual clues which align Jesus' resurrection with ideas about translation (or assumption) and apotheosis in both Jewish and Greco-Roman sources – or to direct statements about his resurrection as exaltation (cf. Lk 24,26). These clues would have been evident to ancient readers and would have led them to conclude that Jesus' resurrection was not the resuscitation of someone nearly or recently dead (e.g., Mk 5,35-43) nor the return to life of a "revenant", that is, a reanimated corpse (e.g., Phlegon of Tralles, *Mirab.* 1), but something else[40].

---

36. Compare Lk 24,39 (ψηλαφήσατέ με καὶ ἴδετε, ὅτι πνεῦμα σάρκα καὶ ὀστέα οὐκ ἔχει καθὼς ἐμὲ θεωρεῖτε ἔχοντα) with Ignatius, *Smyrn.* 3.2 (λάβετε, ψηλαφήσατέ με καὶ ἴδετε, ὅτι οὐκ εἰμὶ δαιμόνιον ἀσώματον). For more on this parallel, see pp. 289-290 below.
37. M.D. Litwa, *Iesus Deus: The Early Christian Depiction of Jesus as a Mediterranean God*, Minneapolis, MN, Fortress, 2014, p. 144.
38. The citation is from Wright, *Resurrection* (n. 5), p. 83. Litwa, *Iesus Deus* (n. 37), pp. 149-151, rightly takes Wright to task setting up a "superficial comparison" (*ibid.*, p. 151), but does not note that Wright elsewhere in the same book describes Jesus' risen body as "transphysical", meaning "still robustly physical but also significantly different from the present one" (i.e., immortal and incorruptible; but also capable of appearing and disappearing, etc.): see Wright, *Resurrection* (n. 5), pp. 477-478. Allison, *Resurrection of Jesus* (n. 3), pp. 229-230, explains that the "transphysicality" to which Wright points is "less unexpected than he implies", given ancient ideas about the capabilities of angels.
39. The correlation, more common in later Christian literature (e.g., Rufinus, *Symb.* 29), between the descent to Hades and the resurrection of Jesus in the tomb, is already present in *Gos. Pet.* 10.42.
40. See D. Felton, *Haunted Greece and Rome: Ghost Stories from Classical Antiquity*, Austin, TX, University of Texas Press, 1999, pp. 25-29, who notes that ancient Greek

In an earlier study, I argued that two core traditions about Jesus' *post-mortem* vindication and its results – which I called the disappearance tradition (cf. Mk 16,1-8) and the appearance tradition (cf. 1 Cor 15,5-8) – gradually converged as the resurrection narratives continued to develop after Mark. Admittedly, delineating these two "traditions" as "distinct"[41] was artificial, but it allowed me to highlight the fact that motifs and ideas typically associated with assumption (or translation) had a profound influence on both the conceptualization and narration of Jesus' resurrection. Assumption may be defined as the bodily removal of a human person (before, at, or after death) from earth to the divine realm, with apotheosis or exaltation as the result. Assumption stories usually describe the perspective of earth-bound observers, sometimes emphasize the means by which the person is taken away or carried up, and always stress the disappearance of the body or bodily remains (e.g., 2 Kgs 2,11-12). Although it is often held that assumption happens only to the living in the Tanakh and early Jewish literature, assumption and exaltation/deification after death is not unknown in Jewish sources and quite common in Greco-Roman ones[42]. Several recent studies have highlighted the importance of this category for understanding the resurrection of Jesus[43], and it appears that our authors sometimes used motifs and concepts connected with assumption to narrate Jesus' resurrection and its after-effects.

Mk 16,1-8 focuses not on the restored presence of the risen Jesus, but his absence from the tomb: "he has been raised, he is not here; look, the place where they laid him" (v. 6). Although the text shows knowledge

---

sources do not have distinct terminology for "revenants" but use standard "ghost" language, despite robustly embodied descriptions.

41. Q 13,34-35 predicts the speaker's disappearance and reappearance ("you will not see me until you say", οὐ μὴ ἴδητέ με ἕως [[ἥξει ὅτε]] εἴπητε, v. 35) in a manner suggestive of the typical correlation between assumption (disappearance; cf. 2 Kgs 2,12 LXX, καὶ οὐκ εἶδεν αὐτὸν ἔτι) and eschatological function; but nowhere does Q apply "resurrection" language to Jesus individually. Meanwhile, Paul can speak about resurrection appearances without any reference to an empty tomb, i.e., the disappearance of Jesus' body (1 Cor 15,4-8). See SMITH, *Revisiting the Empty Tomb* (n. 3), pp. 27-45 (on Paul), 63-81 (on Q).

42. See D.A. SMITH, *The Post-Mortem Vindication of Jesus in the Sayings Gospel Q* (LNTS, 338), London, T&T Clark, 2006, pp. 49-94; ID., *Revisiting the Empty Tomb* (n. 3), pp. 53-60; J.G. COOK, *Empty Tomb, Resurrection, Apotheosis* (WUNT, 410), Tübingen, Mohr Siebeck, 2018, pp. 322-412.

43. Besides my own work and LITWA, *Iesus Deus* (n. 37), pp. 141-179, see also D.Ø. ENDSJØ, *Greek Resurrection Beliefs and the Success of Christianity*, New York, Palgrave Macmillan, 2009; R.C. MILLER, *Resurrection and Reception in Early Christianity* (Routledge Studies in Religion, 44), New York, Routledge, 2015. See also, much earlier (1924), E. BICKERMANN, *Das leere Grab*, in P. HOFFMANN (ed.), *Zur neutestamentlichen Überlieferung von der Auferstehung Jesu* (Wege der Forschung, 522), Darmstadt, Wissenschaftliche Buchgesellschaft, 1988, 271-284; see also G. LÜDEMANN, *The Resurrection of Jesus: History, Experience, Theology*, Minneapolis, MN, Fortress, 1994, pp. 120-121.

of a resurrection appearance in Galilee (v. 7), none is narrated in Mark until the addition of the Longer Ending (Ps.-Mk 16,9, etc.) sometime in the second century. This focus on Jesus' absence is not only a problem of discipleship (cf. Mk 2,19-20), but it also is an important narrative clue. A missing body, an unsuccessful search, witnesses overcome with fear and amazement, and a theological interpretation: although this is a resurrection story, Mark uses motifs consistent with assumption stories (here only the after-effects), which are often correlated with apotheosis or immortalization, and in the Jewish tradition, preservation in the divine realm for a special eschatological function[44]. "What the women do not see – the body of Jesus – also points to God's decisive act. It signifies that God has taken the dead Jesus away to await his return as Son of Humankind, and this means rescue from death, restoration to life, and exaltation in heaven"[45]. An appearance of Jesus would temporarily restore his presence, and potentially authorize and commission certain select followers, but here Mark focuses on Jesus' long absence before his return as the Son of Humankind (Mk 13,3-27).

In Matthew, this combination of resurrection language and assumption motifs remains important. When the angel descends to roll away the stone in Mt 28,2, it is not to allow the risen or rising Jesus out of the tomb (cf. *Gos. Pet.* 9.37–10.40; *Mart. Isa.* 3.16b-19), but to show that he is already risen and gone: "he is not here, for he was raised" (Mt 28,6)[46]. While some think the idea here is that Jesus' risen body has unique, divine capabilities[47], so that he could have left the tomb despite the stone, an ancient reader would probably have concluded from the missing body that Jesus had been taken away into the divine realm[48]. Matthew therefore

---

44. G. HAUFE, *Entrückung und eschatologische Funktion im Spätjudentum*, in *Zeitschrift für Religions- und Geistesgeschichte* 13 (1961) 105-113. For typical narrative motifs in assumption/disappearance stories, see SMITH, *Revisiting the Empty Tomb* (n. 3), pp. 49-60.

45. SMITH, *Revisiting the Empty Tomb* (n. 3), p. 94.

46. LUZ, *Matthew 21–28* (n. 19), p. 596; see also (e.g.) Origen, *Cels.* 5.58, implicitly as least. Most commentators prefer not to decide whether the stone was rolled away to effect the resurrection, to let Jesus out, or to show that Jesus had risen from a sealed tomb. See, e.g., C.F. EVANS, *Resurrection and the New Testament* (Studies in Biblical Theology, 2.12), London, SCM, 1970, p. 86; W.D. DAVIES – D.C. ALLISON, JR., *A Critical and Exegetical Commentary on the Gospel according to Saint Matthew*. Vol. 3: *Commentary on Matthew XIX–XXVIII* (ICC), Edinburgh, T&T Clark, 1997, p. 665.

47. M. KONRADT, *Das Evangelium nach Matthäus* (NTD, 1), Göttingen, Vandenhoeck & Ruprecht, 2015, p. 454; cf. R.H. GUNDRY, *Matthew: A Commentary on His Handbook for a Mixed Church under Persecution*, Grand Rapids, MI, Eerdmans, ²1994, p. 587, who suggests that the angel rolls away the stone to let Jesus out, "though he remains unobserved for the time being".

48. SMITH, *Revisiting the Empty Tomb* (n. 3), p. 123; ENDSJØ, *Greek Resurrection Beliefs* (n. 43), p. 167; MILLER, *Resurrection and Reception* (n. 43), pp. 169-170, 193, n. 69.

intensifies what we have already noted in Mark: the introduction of the angel who rolls away the stone excludes any other possible interpretation of the missing body. Jesus' exalted status is clear in the second resurrection appearance in Matthew, where he claims, using language drawn from Dan 7,14a (Theodotion), that "all authority has been given to me in heaven and upon earth" (Mt 28,18b), commissioning the Eleven to "make disciples of all nations" (v. 19)[49]. Christopher Evans has observed that an ascension after this scene "would be unthinkable" for Jesus is already exalted[50]. If, as suggested above, an ancient reader would have inferred that Jesus rose out of the tomb into the divine realm, then when Jesus appears to the Eleven, he appears from that divine realm into which he was raised.

Many scholars see Luke-Acts as separating Jesus' exaltation from his resurrection, that is, "historicizing" the exaltation by narrating it as "the Ascension" (Lk 24,50-53; Acts 1,6-11; see also Ps.-Mk 16,19)[51]. But things are not so simple. As is well known, Luke-Acts has two ascension accounts, apparently separated by forty days (Acts 1,3). However, if the ascension historicizes the exaltation, the problem remains that Luke also seems to indicate that the two coincide (Lk 24,26; Acts 2,32-33; cf. Acts 5,30-31). Most scholars do not attempt to solve the chronological problem but allow that the two stories serve distinct purposes at the end of Luke and at the beginning of Acts[52]. However, Henk Jan de Jonge offers a convincing solution to the chronological problem. He proposes that Acts 1,3 provides a "flash forward" to the appearances during the forty days, but 1,4-14 recapitulates – with different details – the events narrated in Lk 24,36-49.50-53[53]. The two accounts, then, describe the same ascension on the day of Jesus' resurrection (see also *Barn.* 15.9). A straightforward reading of Lk 24,26 ("Was it not necessary that the Messiah

---

49. See also the vision of "the One like a Son of Humankind" in Rev 1,9-20, which also draws on Daniel 7 and seems to correlate exaltation with resurrection (vv. 17-18).

50. EVANS, *Resurrection and the New Testament* (n. 46), p. 83.

51. The idea that Luke "historicized" Jesus' exaltation in the ascension stories originates with G. LOHFINK, *Die Himmelfahrt Jesu: Untersuchungen zu den Himmelfahrts- und Erhöhungstexten bei Lukas* (SANT, 26), München, Kösel, 1971, pp. 272-275. For the ascension/exaltation as a "second stage of after-death experience" for Jesus (i.e., following his resurrection), see C.R. HOLLADAY, *Acts: A Commentary* (NTL), Louisville, KY, Westminster John Knox, 2016, p. 105; see also COOK, *Empty Tomb, Resurrection, Apotheosis* (n. 42), pp. 617-618 (taking ὑψωθείς in Acts 2,33 to refer to Jesus' ascension).

52. See the survey in H.J. DE JONGE, *The Chronology of the Ascension Stories in Luke and Acts*, in *NTS* 59 (2013) 151-171, pp. 152-158.

53. *Ibid.*, p. 165 (summary). For a different solution, which still sees exaltation as coinciding with resurrection in Luke-Acts, see A.W. ZWIEP, *The Ascension of the Messiah in Lukan Christology* (SupplNT, 87), Leiden, Brill, 1997.

should suffer these things and enter into his glory?") allows the conclusion, with respect to the relationship between resurrection and exaltation in Luke, that "the tomb is empty because Jesus is in heaven", and that "when Jesus appears after his resurrection ... he appears from heaven"[54]. What is missing in Luke is any further narrative indication, such as we saw in Matthew, that Jesus' resurrection involved his translation or assumption from the tomb – unless, that is, we consider the grave clothes (τὰ ὀθόνια, Lk 24,12) evidence that Jesus disappeared from the tomb, leaving them behind, in keeping with ancient ideas about assumption[55]. More to the point, Luke has the risen Jesus himself affirm that his resurrection also meant his exaltation (Lk 24,26; cf. Acts 2,32-33).

In John, the grave clothes still refute the possibility that the body was removed, but the possible implication that Jesus was raised and translated (which was just suggested for Luke) seems unlikely here, because the risen Jesus is not in heaven but in the garden (Jn 20,14-18). He tells Mary Magdalene, "I have not yet gone up to the Father" (v. 17). The relationship between resurrection and exaltation is also less clear, for the descent-ascent christological schema (Jn 3,13) of the Fourth Gospel aligns Jesus' glorification with his death and/or return to the Father (e.g., 17,1-5). It is likely that in John Jesus' death, resurrection, and ascension cannot be clearly separated from one another or from his glorification/exaltation[56]. Another issue is how Jesus' first resurrection appearance, to Mary Magdalene (Jn 20,14-18), relates to his "going up to the Father" (v. 17) and how that relates to his glorification/exaltation. Jn 7,39 states that "as yet there was no Spirit, because Jesus was not yet glorified", and in Jn 20,22 Jesus breathes on the disciples and says, "Receive the Holy Spirit". On this basis, one might suppose that Jesus' "glorification" is his return to the Father, that is, his ascension, perhaps separated from his resurrection, but this is not entirely clear. In any case, as Brown and others have observed, the present tense ἀναβαίνω πρὸς τὸν πατέρα μου κτλ. (20,17b)

---

54. DE JONGE, *Chronology of the Ascension Stories* (n. 52), p. 167. See similarly J.A. FITZMYER, *The Gospel according to Luke X–XXIV: A New Translation with Introduction and Commentary* (AB, 28A), Garden City, NY, Doubleday, 1985, pp. 1588-1589.

55. On this possibility in Jn 20,6, see C.K. BARRETT, *The Gospel according to St. John: An Introduction with Commentary and Notes on the Greek Text*, Philadelphia, PA, Westminster, ²1978, p. 563: "Here however it seems that the body had in some way disappeared from, or passed through, the cloths and left them lying as they were".

56. BROWN, *Gospel according to John XIII–XXI* (n. 24), pp. 1013-1014. See also O. LEHTIPUU, "*I Have Not Yet Ascended to the Father*": *On Resurrection, Bodies, and Resurrection Bodies*, in R. BIERINGER – B. BAERT – K. DEMASURE (eds.), *Noli Me Tangere in Interdisciplinary Perspective: Textual, Iconographic, and Contemporary Interpretations* (BETL, 283), Leuven – Paris – Bristol, CT, Peeters, 2016, 43-59, pp. 56-59.

"means that Jesus is already in the process of ascending"[57]. There may even be the implication that he is in a liminal bodily state until he returns to the Father, as suggested already by Origen (*Comm. Ioh.* 6.37: Jesus required a purification that only his return to the Father could bring about)[58]. The narrative developments in the resurrection stories of the Fourth Gospel bring the risen and appearing Jesus into close proximity to the tomb, but also evoke larger Johannine themes concerning Jesus' glorification.

The *Gospel of Peter* displays a descent-ascent Christology similar to that of the Fourth Gospel, and likewise associates Jesus' ascension closely with his resurrection. Although the *Gospel of Peter* narrates the rising of Jesus, it stops short of describing his ascension (*Gos. Pet.* 10.39-42). Later, however, the young man tells the women, "He has risen and gone to the place from whence he was sent" (13.56; see, similarly, *Apocryphon of John* [*Secret Book of John*], NHC II.1.5-12). Paul Foster sees this as a tendency to "collapse the temporal distance between [the resurrection and the ascension], in contrast to the portrayal in Matthew and Luke-Acts"[59]. As discussed above, however, in Matthew the ascension is not narrated, and it can be inferred that Jesus was translated into heaven when he was raised from the dead; in Luke-Acts, the same scenario is possible. In any case, it seems that the *Gospel of Peter* makes much more concrete what is only alluded to or implied in the canonical gospels: that Jesus' resurrection also entails his glorification (accomplished through ascension/assumption).

In contrast, Ps.-Mk 16,19 more clearly separates resurrection and exaltation, by combining ascension and session[60]. The *Epistle of the Apostles* has a similar approach: Jesus' risen body is the same as before his death, but apparently immortal (*Ep. Apos.* 21.1-3); and he "remains with his feet firmly on the ground for between two or three hours, ... and he then ascends through the heavens to take his place at the right hand of the

---

57. Brown, *Gospel according to John XIII–XXI* (n. 24), p. 994.
58. M.R. D'Angelo, *A Critical Note: John 20,17 and Apocalypse of Moses 31*, in *JTS* 41 (1990) 529-536. D'Angelo reviews several references to this verse in the works of Origen, and a possible parallel in *Apoc. Mos.* 31 (μηδείς μου ἅψηται, concerning the body of Adam before its removal to God's presence; cf. μή μου ἅπτου, Jn 20,17). "Origen clearly sees the command of Jesus to Mary as drawing attention to the ambiguous character of Jesus' being when he encounters Mary in the garden" (*ibid.*, p. 534). So also Smith, *Revisiting the Empty Tomb* (n. 3), pp. 147-148; Lehtipuu, *I Have Not Yet Ascended* (n. 56), pp. 51-52.
59. Foster, *Gospel of Peter* (n. 20), p. 493.
60. J.A. Kelhoffer, *Miracle and Mission: The Authentication of Missionaries and Their Message in the Longer Ending of Mark* (WUNT, 2.112), Tübingen, Mohr Siebeck, 2000, pp. 228-230.

Father who sent him" (*Ep. Apos.* 11.6-8; 51.1-4)[61]. Meanwhile, several of the Nag Hammadi writings depict Jesus appearing after his resurrection in a glorified state, from heaven (*Apocryphon of John* [*Secret Book of John*]; *Letter of Peter to Philip*; *Sophia of Jesus Christ*).

III. Embodied States and Modes of Seeing

Paul provides a detailed but not unambiguous account of resurrection bodies which can safely be assumed to provide a glimpse into how he also thought about the risen body of Jesus (1 Cor 15,35-57; cf. v. 45; also vv. 20-22). In 1 Cor 15,42-49, Paul contrasts the regular human body, which he calls "soulish" (τὸ σῶμα ψυχικόν), with the resurrection body, which he calls "spiritual" (τὸ σῶμα πνευματικόν, v. 44). Furthermore, "the first Adam became a living being (εἰς ψυχὴν ζῶσαν), the last Adam, a life-giving spirit" (πνεῦμα ζῳοποιοῦν, v. 45). Paul also states that "flesh and blood cannot inherit the kingdom of God" (v. 50). Whether all this means that Paul, unlike some of our gospel authors, thought that Jesus' risen body was "spirit" and not "flesh and blood" (cf. "flesh and bones", Lk 24,39), and indeed whether he would have thought Jesus left an empty tomb, are not our problems to solve here[62]. It is important to note, however, that he did introduce an ambiguity that occasioned debate and disagreement that is evident in later Christian texts, particularly about whether "resurrection" is really "the resurrection of the flesh" (a term which does not occur in the New Testament)[63]. This internal debate, well underway in the second century, had an obvious effect on how stories about the resurrection appearances were read and were written. For this reason, we are justified in examining the representations of the risen Jesus in early Christian texts for their apologetic interests.

Consequently, although there are a few exceptions, most of our sources are quite circumspect – or even, as with Luke, quite explicit – in how they represent the risen body of Jesus and/or the experience of those to whom he appears. Matthew, for example, does not theorize the risen body of Jesus in his appearance stories (Mt 28,9-10.16-20). The women

---

61. Watson, *An Apostolic Gospel* (n. 25), p. 121.
62. For an overview and literature, see most recently Cook, *Empty Tomb, Resurrection, Apotheosis* (n. 42), pp. 570-593; see also D.B. Martin, *The Corinthian Body*, New Haven, CT, Yale University Press, 1995, pp. 104-136; Smith, *Revisiting the Empty Tomb* (n. 3), pp. 35-42.
63. See O. Lehtipuu, *Debates over the Resurrection of the Dead: Constructing Early Christian Identity* (Oxford Early Christian Studies), Oxford, OUP, 2015.

do hold onto Jesus' feet (v. 9), but this seems to emphasize the appropriateness of worship, not the tangibility of Jesus' risen body[64]. In the appearance to the Eleven, seeing Jesus occasions doubt, but this is not oriented to questions about Jesus' risen body as in Lk 24,36-43: rather, Matthew highlights the ambivalence of their reaction (see also Mt 14,28-33; 28,7)[65].

Luke's risen Jesus, as already seen, gives a definitive statement on the composition of his body: "Handle me and see", he tells Peter and the others, "for a spirit does not have flesh and bones as you see that I have" (Lk 24,39). Any further misgivings (v. 41) are dispelled when Jesus eats a piece of broiled fish in their presence (vv. 42-43). Although there seems to be good support for the view that Luke is responding to a Pauline or post-Pauline view, because of the linguistic parallels[66], the issue here is not merely whether resurrection bodies are tangible or whether Jesus' resurrection really happened. In Luke-Acts, the Twelve male apostles are authorized and commissioned by the risen Jesus, receiving insight into the true meaning (or mind[67]) of the Scriptures (vv. 44-49; cf. Acts 1,21-26). It is important that their connection to him is based on flesh-and-bones encounters over the forty days, during which the Twelve ate and drank with him (Acts 1,3). "References to eating with the resurrected Jesus pertain to apostolic privilege, with the final such reference [viz., Acts 10,40b-41] underscoring the exclusive nature of that privilege", even if Luke 24 includes others beyond the Twelve[68].

In Ignatius of Antioch's *Letter to the Smyrnaeans*, we read a statement from the risen Jesus similar to that found in Lk 24,39:

> For I both know and believe that he was in the flesh even after the resurrection. And when he came to those of Peter's group, he said to them, "Take, handle me and see that [ψηλαφήσατέ με καὶ ἴδετε ὅτι: cf. Lk 24,39] I am not a bodiless demon". And immediately they touched and believed, having been mixed with his flesh and spirit. And after the resurrection, he ate and drank with them as a fleshly [being] even though [he was] spiritually united with the Father (Ign. *Smyrn.* 3.1-3)[69].

---

64. Luz, *Matthew 21–28* (n. 19), p. 607.
65. *Ibid.*, pp. 622-623.
66. Smith, *Seeing a Pneumatic Body* (n. 2), pp. 765-771.
67. M. Bates, *Closed-Minded Hermeneutics? A Proposed Alternative Translation for Luke 24,45*, in *JBL* 129 (2010) 537-557.
68. Matthews, *Fleshly Resurrection* (n. 2), p. 182.
69. A similar saying is reported in Jerome, *Vir. ill.* 16 (on Ignatius), but (incorrectly?) attributed to the *Gospel of the Hebrews*. For a detailed discussion of the parallel between Lk 24,39 and Ign. *Smyrn.* 3.2, see in the present volume C.M. Tuckett, *Luke and Ignatius*, especially the section "I. Ign. *Smyrn.* 3.2//Luke 24,39".

Although the fleshly character of Jesus' resurrection is affirmed (3.1), "flesh and bones" is not part of Jesus' statement about his body. Instead, "flesh and spirit" are the locus of union between Jesus and the apostles, and although eating and drinking is mentioned here, touch is what occasions this union. This relates to Ignatius' views, expressed elsewhere, that there is a fleshly component to the spiritual union underpinning the ecclesial hierarchy[70]. As with Luke, the fleshly composition of Jesus' risen body is important to exclusionary authority claims, which illustrates that there is more at stake here than questions about the veracity of Jesus' resurrection.

Along these lines, but making a more concerted case for the resurrection of the flesh, is the *Epistle of the Apostles*[71]. There, as mentioned above, Jesus appears to the women and then to the apostles in a body that is indistinguishable from his pre-resurrection body: the reader assumes that Jesus walks with the women when they go to meet the apostles (*Ep. Apos.* 11.1-2), and "there is no episodic appearing and disappearing"[72]. Further, Jesus invites Peter and Thomas to probe his wounds (as in Jn 20,26-29) and asks Andrew to inspect his feet to ensure they are in contact with the ground: "For it is written in the prophet, 'As for the appearance of a demon, its foot is not in contact with the ground'" (11.6-8, citation v. 8)[73]. There is a clear correlation between the resurrection of Jesus and the future resurrection of believers: "as my Father raised me from the dead, so you too will rise" (21.1), "so that you who were born in flesh might be raised in your flesh as in a second birth" (21.3). In this resurrection, "there is no eating or drinking and no anxiety or grief and no corruption for those who are above" (19.13). Clearly, then, there is an apologetic interest in the depiction of the risen Jesus' embodied state in the *Epistle of the Apostles*: it supports the idea of the resurrection of the flesh.

In the Fourth Gospel, Jesus does not issue any definitive pronouncements about his risen body such as he does in Luke. Touching Jesus' risen body is also at issue in the Fourth Gospel, although here the meaning is not as unambiguous as in Luke, Ignatius, and the *Epistle of the Apostles*. Jesus prohibits Mary from touching him (or: asks him to stop touching him), but perhaps, as seen above, the problem was the liminal state of

70. See also Ign. *Eph.* 5.1 (for mixing language) and *Magn.* 13.2 (for the fleshly/spiritual union). For a fuller discussion, see D.A. SMITH, *Marcion's Gospel and the Resurrected Jesus of Canonical Luke 24*, in *ZAC* 21 (2017) 41-62, pp. 54-59.

71. For the risen Jesus' exposition on the resurrection of the flesh, see *Ep. Apos.* 19.17–26.6.

72. WATSON, *An Apostolic Gospel* (n. 25), p. 126.

73. Trans. WATSON, *An Apostolic Gospel* (n. 25), here and below. Watson mentions an opposing view in *Acts John* 93.10-13, in which John claims he never did see Jesus' footprints (*ibid.*, pp. 116-117).

Jesus' body, post-resurrection but pre-ascension (Jn 20,14-18; μή μου ἅπτου, v. 17)[74]. Later, of course, Jesus invites Thomas to probe his wounds, but the reader does not learn whether he does: Thomas only confesses Jesus as "my Lord and my God" (vv. 26-29; v. 28). For Thomas at least, the issue is identifying the one seen by the others as Jesus himself (see v. 25), whereas for Mary, this was not in question once she heard Jesus speak her name and turned toward him (v. 16). For the narrator, it is important at the conclusion of the gospel that Jesus asserts that those who believe in him without seeing – unlike Thomas – are blessed (v. 29; cf. vv. 30-31). In John 21, Jesus appears for "the third time" (21,1-14; v. 14) but his identity is not immediately clear to the disciples, until the Beloved Disciple recognizes him and Peter swims to meet him (v. 7). The miraculous catch of fish sets up a breakfast scene in which Jesus serves but does not eat, and the remainder of the story addresses Peter's commission to "feed my sheep" and "follow me" (vv. 15-19) – with more hints about the rivalry between the two apostolic figures (vv. 20-23). In all this, there is no deep speculation about the composition of Jesus' body nor about the mode in which he was seen by the disciples: the various commissionings, as in Matthew, seem to be more important (Mary, 20,17-18; the disciples, 20,21-23; Peter, 21,15-19; and by implication, the Beloved Disciple, 21,24).

In many appearance stories, Jesus is usually not immediately recognized by his followers, such as in the Emmaus Road encounter (Lk 24,13-15). Mark's Longer Ending briefly summarizes this story as follows: "after this, he appeared in another form (ἐφανερώθη ἐν ἑτέρᾳ μορφῇ) to two of them walking, as they were journeying in the country" (Ps.-Mk 16,12). Although Luke emphasizes that Cleopas and the other disciple "were prevented from recognizing him" (Lk 24,16), the Longer Ending of Mark seems to indicate a kind of polymorphic Christology. Paul Foster defines this trend as a way of reflecting on Jesus' post-resurrection state (in addition to supporting so-called docetic Christologies): "Changed physical state demonstrates both lack of constraint by the mortal body and transcendence over the earthly realm"[75]. Examples in the canonical gospels include instances when Jesus appears to his followers suddenly inside locked rooms, but in those instances, Jesus is eventually recognized and

---

74. Among many contributions to this question, see H.W. ATTRIDGE, *"Don't Be Touching Me": Recent Feminist Scholarship on Mary Magdalene*, in A.-J. LEVINE – M. BLICKENSTAFF (eds.), *A Feminist Companion to John*, 2 vols., London – New York, Sheffield Academic Press, 2003, vol. 2, 140-166.

75. P. FOSTER, *Polymorphic Christology: Its Origins and Development in Early Christianity*, in *JTS* 58 (2007) 66-99, p. 71.

does not appear in a different form (he even bears his wounds: Lk 24,39.41, etc.). Foster suggests that the brief descriptor ἐν ἑτέρᾳ μορφῇ in Ps.-Mk 16,12 indicates "a certain domestication" of the idea of a polymorphic risen Jesus in the second century[76]. Other significant examples of this include: the enormous height of the rising Jesus in *Gos. Pet.* 10.40; his successive appearances as a youth, an old man, and a servant in the *Apocryphon of John* (NHC II.1.31–2.9); and his appearance as a pearl-merchant in *Acts of Peter and the Twelve Apostles* (NHC VI.2.10–3.11; cf. 9.1-19). In different ways these texts emphasize the transcendent character of Jesus' risen presence.

Finally, many of our texts also stress the glorious and luminous character of Jesus' resurrection appearances as well as their visionary character. Both are evident in Rev 1,9-20, in which the risen Jesus (cf. v. 18) appears as "one like the Son of Humankind" (v. 13)[77]. In the *Gospel of Mary*, Jesus appears to Mary Magdalene and although the encounter itself is not described, Mary tells the others, "I saw the Lord in a vision and I said to him, 'Lord, I saw you today in a vision'" (BG 8502 10.10-13)[78]. The text evidently does not have a resurrection of the flesh in view since everything material will dissolve (7.1-9). Other texts that emphasize the visionary character of the resurrection appearances and their luminous nature likewise do not have a bodily or fleshly resurrection in view. In the *Sophia of Jesus Christ*, the Saviour appears "after he rose from the dead", but "not in his previous form but in the invisible spirit; and his likeness resembles a great angel of light" (NHC III.90.15–91.24)[79]. It was these and other texts that led James Robinson to conclude that there were two trajectories in conceptualizing or visualizing the risen Jesus in early Christianity: one corporeal and non-luminous, one luminous and non-corporeal, and both ultimately traceable back to Paul's originating concept of a "spiritual body" (1 Cor 15,44; cf. vv. 40-41) which was also "the body of his glory" (Phil 3,21), that is, both corporeal and luminous[80].

76. *Ibid.*
77. On the visionary character of this encounter (despite its Danielic textual inspiration), and the similarities to the appearance to Mary Magdalene in the Fourth Gospel, see M.R. D'ANGELO, *"I Have Seen the Lord": Mary Magdalen as Visionary, Early Christian Prophecy, and the Context of John 20,14-18*, in D. GOOD (ed.), *Mariam, the Magdalen, and the Mother*, Bloomington, IN, Indiana University Press, 2005, 95-122.
78. Trans. G.W. MACRAE – R.McL. WILSON, in J.M. ROBINSON (ed.), *The Nag Hammadi Library in English*, Leiden, Brill, 1977, p. 472.
79. See also *Ap. John* NHC II.1.30-32; *Ep. Pet. Phil.* NHC VIII.134.9-18 (here Jesus seems to be invoked: 133.17–134.9); *Pist. Soph.* 1.2.
80. J.M. ROBINSON, *Jesus – From Easter to Valentinus (or to the Apostles' Creed)*, in *JBL* 101 (1982) 5-37.

IV. Conclusion

In a well-known passage in his *First Apology*, Justin insisted that in speaking about Jesus Christ – born without sexual union, crucified and killed, raised, and gone up into heaven (ἀνεληλυθέναι εἰς τὸν οὐρανόν) – Christians "do not bring anything new in comparison with those who among you are called Sons of Zeus" (*1 Apol.* 21.1). Justin's tactic here was to concede the comparisons at first, but to disallow them in the end because, in fact, what had happened to Jesus was true while the analogous claims about other figures were not (τὸ ἀληθὲς λέγομεν, 23.1; cf. Origen, *Cels.* 2.55-56). The authors of gospel stories about Jesus' resurrection – the discovery of the empty tomb and the appearances of the risen Jesus to his followers – made their apologetic adjustments not by asserting the uniqueness of Jesus, but by refining the work of their predecessors, by adding details to remove suspicion, by aligning their narratives with widely accepted theological paradigms, and by defining the nature of Jesus' body or the mode of his appearing. While the representative nature of this survey precludes a definitive and universal conclusion, it does seem to be the case that many or even most of the developments in the empty tomb and appearance stories were intended to answer (or forestall) questions originating either internally or externally concerning Jesus' resurrection, and to refine and define its meaning and significance.

Huron University College Daniel A. Smith
1349 Western Rd.
London, ON
Canada, N6G 1H3
dsmith89@huron.uwo.ca

COME AND SEE – ONCE AGAIN

THE CALL OF THE FIRST DISCIPLES AND CHRISTOLOGY
IN JOHN 1,35-51

It is a great pleasure to offer these pages in honor of Professor Joseph Verheyden on the occasion of his sixty-fifth birthday. We worked together for a number of years with Professor Frans Neirynck as we grew into the profession. At the same time, our families grew together, and we and our children maintain joyful friendships to this day. All who know Jos know that his energy and enthusiasm for contributing to our world of learning will not grind to a halt now that he is of pensionable age. His wide range of interests and knowledge, his contributions through writing, editing, publishing, innumerable conference organization, attendance, and presentations, and all in his congenial and respectful manner, put us in awe. It is a joy to celebrate him.

A number of years ago, I wrote about the call of the first disciples in the Gospel of John and indicated that the exchange between Jesus and his initial followers (Jn 1,35-51) was an opening that prepared readers to understand who Jesus was and what he meant as they entered into the gospel's story[1]. In a word, the passage concludes the first chapter of the Fourth Gospel, which as a whole sets the stage for what is quite likely the key emphasis of the whole work: Christology[2].

I. Setting the Scene

The first chapter of John opens with a poetic prologue (1,1-18) that informs the audience in lofty terms that Jesus is the very Word – the

---

1. P.J. Judge, *Come and See: The First Disciples and Christology in the Fourth Gospel*, in J. Verheyden – G. Van Oyen – M. Labahn – R. Bieringer (eds.), *Studies in the Gospel of John and Its Christology: Festschrift Gilbert Van Belle* (BETL, 265), Leuven – Paris – Walpole, MA, Peeters, 2014, 61-69. Scripture quotations are taken from the NRSV unless noted otherwise.

2. F.J. Matera, *New Testament Christology*, Louisville, KY, Westminster John Knox, 1999, p. 215: "One could argue that [the Fourth Gospel] is preeminently a work of Christology since Jesus is the focal point of its many signs and discourses. The Gospel presents Jesus, and Jesus presents himself, as one who has come from heaven to reveal himself as the one sent by the Father".

self-expression of God – who has become flesh and dwelt among us and thus made the unseen God known to humans. This is followed by the testimony of John the Baptizer (1,19-34), who denies any identification as the Messiah/Christ (ὁ χριστός), Elijah, or the prophet (presumably, the "prophet like me" promised by Moses in Dt 18,15). All these are messianic (one might say, "christological") titles in accord with traditional Jewish expectations. The Baptist claims that one is coming after him whose sandal he is not worthy to untie and "the next day" points to Jesus coming toward him and declares him to be the "Lamb of God who takes away the sin of the world" (1,29). He further claims that he witnessed the Spirit (of God) descend on Jesus and remain on him, proof to John that "this is the Son of God" (1,34).

On "the next day", John again declares that Jesus is the Lamb of God in the hearing of two of his disciples and they follow Jesus, who turns to them and asks, "What do you seek?" (τί ζητεῖτε;) (1,38 RSV). They address him as Rabbi and ask in return, "Where are you staying?" (ποῦ μένεις;). Jesus replies with the invitation, "come and see" (1,39). They follow and stay with him. One of the two, Andrew, finds his brother Simon and declares, "We have found the Messiah" and brings him to Jesus, who promises that he will be called Peter.

On "the next day", Jesus finds Philip in Galilee and invites him to "Follow me" (1,43). Philip, in turn, finds Nathanael and exclaims, "We have found him about whom Moses in the law and also the prophets wrote, Jesus son of Joseph from Nazareth". Nathanael expresses some doubt about what good could come from Nazareth (ironically, Nathanael is from the obscure town of Cana), but Philip invites him to "Come and see" (1,46). Jesus sees Nathanael coming and recognizes him as the one he had seen sitting under a fig tree before Philip even called him and declares he is an Israelite "in whom there is no deceit" (1,47). Nathanael, marveling at Jesus' apparently miraculous knowledge of him, exclaims Jesus as Rabbi, Son of God, and King of Israel. Thus far, these early disciples have attached titles to Jesus that are rather consistent with Jewish messianic expectations.

Jesus finishes off this sequence of events by saying that he, Nathanael, will see greater things, and then, to at least the group of characters in the narrative and, in a sense, outwardly as if turning to the audience, he says, "Very truly, I tell you, you (both pronouns in the plural) will see heaven opened and the angels of God ascending and descending upon the Son of Man" (1,51). Here he introduces another title, a bit ambiguous but with some messianic implications, and an image of a new connection between the realm of God and that of humans. Jn 1,51 partially quotes

Gen 28,12, depicting Jacob's vision of a ladder stretching between heaven and earth upon which "the angels of God were ascending and descending", but gives it a new twist: the vehicle of communication between God and humans is now none other than Jesus himself.

Thus, while the characters in the narrative become acquainted with Jesus and his significance in ways that are quite rooted in traditional Jewish ways of thinking about the Messiah, the audience of the gospel has been clued in from the very beginning, in the prologue, about who Jesus really is in a way that suggests taking these titles the first disciples use to a new level. And while Jesus' invitation to "come and see" in response to his first followers' query about where he stays or remains is quite understandable on the surface level of the narrative, it can readily be understood by the reader as a "provocative statement" that, following upon his initial question, "What do you seek?", has an existential power for the gospel's readers that points to "the establishment of a discipleship associated with the unique revelation of God by Jesus Christ, the word of God"[3]. In other words, for the reader, who has been informed by the prologue about Jesus' identity, the invitation to "come and see" is an invitation to enter upon a journey to fully comprehend the Christology of John's message[4].

II. CHRISTOLOGY DOWNPLAYED

Recently, Toan Do authored a chapter in a very engaging book on ethics in the Johannine literature in which he questions the importance of the emphasis on Christology that interpreters draw from the invitation to "come and see"[5]. He wonders: "Is Christology a sufficient response to the come-and-see invitation, especially in the case of Philip's invitation to Nathanael?"[6]. His concern reaches beyond christological exclamations

---

3. F.J. MOLONEY, *The First Days of Jesus and the Role of the Disciples: A Study of John 1:19-51*, in ID., *Johannine Studies 1975-2017* (WUNT, 372), Tübingen, Mohr Siebeck, 2017, 307-330, p. 323.

4. See also R. CHENNATTU, *On Becoming Disciples (John 1:35–51): Insights from the Fourth Gospel*, in *Salesianum* 63 (2001) 465-496, p. 489; and B. BYRNE, *Life Abounding: A Reading of John's Gospel*, Collegeville, MN, Liturgical Press, 2014, pp. 45-46.

5. T. DO, *The Johannine Request to "Come and See" and the Ethic of Love*, in S. BROWN – C. SKINNER (eds.), *Johannine Ethics: The Moral World of the Gospel and Epistles of John*, Minneapolis, MN, Fortress, 2017, 177-196; p. 178. He makes explicit reference to my article *Come and See* (n. 1).

6. *Ibid.*, p. 178. One wonders whether it is appropriate to characterize Christology as a "response". Is it not rather a theological concept that arises out of our understanding of

made by the characters in the narrative to "*the way in which* the proclaimers achieve their faith in Jesus"[7]. He prefers to emphasize how disciples truly live out their discipleship to Jesus (rather than simply professing it) by adhering to his command to "love one another" (Jn 13,34) and in so doing demonstrate their love for him (Jn 14,15). This is borne out as a chief concern of the Johannine letters as well[8]. Thus, for Toan Do,

> [i]n the course of the invitees' response to the come-and-see invitation (i.e., coming to, seeing, knowing, remaining with, and believing in Jesus), **Christology is downplayed** not only by John but also by the subsequent Johannine authors, who experienced the challenge of *living* their christological *confessions*[9].

Toan Do sets out to make his case in three steps. First, he demonstrates how Jn 1,19-51 "pervasively alludes" to Christology by listing the christologically suggestive titles which the Baptist refuses and then those that he and the first disciples ascribe to Jesus. By the end of the chapter the reader has encountered a series of titles that are "replete with allusive christological significance" and contribute to the narrative development of "John's exalted Christology"[10]. But, he asks, "Can each character understand what these titles mean without short-sighted failure? Why does John fill this narrative of Jn 1,19-51 with repeated titles attributed to Jesus, had these indeed not presented major challenges to the proclaimers?". For the gospel, proclamation of faith in Jesus with these titles is important for discipleship, but the epistles stress the importance of acting on one's belief, he says. In his view, then, Christology by itself became the "issue that eventually divided the Johannine communities"[11].

Second, Toan Do examines the four instances of "come and see" in the Fourth Gospel – 1,39.46 (in our passage); 4,29 (the Samaritan woman's invitation to her villagers); and 11,34 (the villagers of Bethany in response to Jesus' "where have you laid [Lazarus]") – as typical examples of Johannine repetition and variation and concludes that they are "without much Christology" and "scholarly emphasis on Christology in John's narrative of Jesus's invitation to the Baptist's two disciples may be untenable. The narratives surrounding these invitations raise critical questions

---

a work or collection of works, in this case the Gospel of John with its plot, portrayal of Jesus' character, his words and works?

7. *Ibid.*, italics original.
8. *Ibid.* See, for instance, 1 Jn 2,3-6.
9. *Ibid.*, p. 179, italics original, bold added.
10. *Ibid.*, pp. 180-183.
11. *Ibid.*, p. 183.

to a possible exaggeration of christological emphasis"[12]. He says that all four instances "expect a similar outcome, namely, the narrative figures (the disciples and respective villagers) in the stories eventually come to Jesus and *allegedly* believe in him"[13]. I think we can discount the last occurrence since it has nothing to do with the Bethany villagers possibly believing in Jesus; they are simply pointing out Lazarus' grave to him. Be that as it may, the general conclusion is that these instances "show either the characters' misunderstanding or their inadequate faith in Jesus" and "Despite the trend of scholars focusing on Jesus's come-and-see invitation as the fundamental and principal key to Johannine Christology, the overall narrative scheme demonstrates that such an invitation is more likely a Johannine stylistic repetition"[14]. There are a number of problems with the analysis of each of these passages but my basic question is: even if the expression is typical of the evangelist's habit of repetition and variation why can it not also carry significance for the gospel's Christology?

Third and finally, Toan Do lays emphasis on an ethic of love that overshadows christological confessions. Having concluded that the characters in each of the pericopes where "come and see" occurs have "misunderstood Jesus and his role", Toan Do turns to John 14 and the exchange between Jesus and two of his disciples, Thomas and Philip. With rather stringent, negative language he contends that Thomas' statement and question, "Lord, we do not know where you are going. How can we know the way?" (14,5) is a "denial" that "negates the disciples' knowledge of Jesus"[15]. Similarly, Philip's request that Jesus "show us the Father and we will be satisfied" (14,8) "betrays any possibility that they might have known or believed in Jesus". He continues:

> Such a portrayal of ignorance echoes John's deep sense of irony in 1:35-51, in which he describes how the disciples (Andrew, Philip, and Nathanael) have inadequately confessed Jesus with various titles. Any argument in favor of the disciples' christological confessions of Jesus in 1:35-51 is therefore challenged by this dialogue in 14:1-14 between Jesus and Thomas and Philip[16].

The contention is, rather, that we should look to Jesus' words in 14,15: "If you love me, you will keep my commandments" for what really matters. Christological confessions of faith in Jesus are not of prime importance;

---

12. *Ibid.*, pp. 184-185.
13. *Ibid.*, p. 184.
14. *Ibid.*, p. 191.
15. *Ibid.*, p. 192.
16. *Ibid.*, p. 193.

rather it is acting out one's love for Jesus. This is why the evangelist portrays the "disciple whom Jesus loved" at the foot of the cross when "Jesus's prominent disciple Peter has deserted him"[17]. The "climax of faith" therefore lies not in christological confessions but in one's love for Jesus. This carries over into the epistles where Christology has become a cause of division in the Johannine communities so much so that the command to love Jesus and one another "is the author's only and single appeal" to those members who have not strayed. "Many christological elements that scholars have detected in John's invitations (1:39,46; 4:29; 11:34) have in reality been replaced by Jesus's love command"[18].

The upshot of all this appears to be that Christology in the Fourth Gospel has taken a back seat to ethical behavior; in fact, Christology "may not be as serious a problem as is sometimes suggested". "The different Johannine 'parties' may not, in fact, have differed radically in their Christology [!]. But their lives, their relationships with one another, and their 'ethics' did not reflect their christological beliefs"[19]. What true disciples are really invited to "come and see" is an ethic of love, exemplified by Jesus in the Gospel of John and urged by the author(s) of the Johannine letters.

III. An Opening to an Evolving Understanding

No one would object to the notion that ethical behavior should be consistent with beliefs, but is it necessary to insist on such a separation between confessions of faith and actions? Is not belief a foundation for action so that the two are intimately connected? One does not need to be preferred over the other. A genuine ethic should flow from a commitment of faith. In the case of the Gospel of John, truly knowing Jesus, what he means and what he offers, should lead to loving him and obeying his commandment to love one another. The disciples in the narrative are on a journey to learn this and they are presented in a fairly positive light by the end of the story. Genuine discipleship is epitomized, of course, in the Beloved Disciple. The main concern here, however, is to probe further the scene in the programmatic first chapter of the gospel, especially Jesus' initial question (v. 38) and invitation (v. 39)[20].

---

17. *Ibid.*
18. *Ibid.*, p. 194.
19. *Ibid.*, p. 196.
20. Note Byrne's use of the word programmatic for these verses, Byrne, *Life Abounding* (n. 4), pp. 45-46. I would extend this idea and characterize the entire chapter 1 as

We can agree with Francis Moloney in his general perspective that the first disciples' encounter with Jesus must be interpreted and understood in light of what the reader has been aware of in both the prologue and the witness of John the Baptist (1,1-34)[21]. As mentioned above, the reader has been clued in on exactly who Jesus is and what he means to those who accept him so that when we enter the scene along with the disciples, as it were, we readers are quite prepared to grasp deeper nuances in the encounter with Jesus.

When the two disciples left the Baptist and followed Jesus, he turned and "gazed upon those following"[22]. The verb translated in the NRSV as "saw" (θεάομαι) is the same as that found in 1,14: "we have seen his glory" (NRSV; RSV has "we have *beheld* his glory"). While the word can simply mean physical sight[23], it frequently carries a deeper, more perceptive connotation[24].

Here Jesus gazes on the two and "transforms this encounter into an epiphany"[25]. His gaze provides the context with which the depth of the question he will ask can be understood[26]. Jesus' question, τί ζητεῖτε; "what are you looking for?" (NRSV) has obvious meaning on the surface level of the narrative, but it carries a deeper significance for the two disciples and especially for the reader, perhaps rendered with more nuance in the RSV, "What do you seek?"[27]. Raymond Brown could write:

> Jesus' first words in the Fourth Gospel are a question that he addresses to everyone who would follow him ... more than a banal request about their

---

programmatic of the gospel, beginning with the prologue of course. See also CHENNATTU, *Becoming Disciples* (n. 4), p. 472, on the "bridge-building character" of this call scene: it brings to a close the ministry of the Baptist and sets Jesus' mission in motion, and it prepares the reader for the revelation of Jesus' δόξα in 2,11, which fulfills the promise of 1,51 and is elaborated even more through the remainder of the gospel.

21. MOLONEY, *First Days* (n. 3). See also ID., *The Gospel of John* (SP, 4), Collegeville, MN, Liturgical Press, 1998, pp. 48-63.

22. F.J. MOLONEY, *Belief in the Word: Reading John 1–4*, Minneapolis, MN, Fortress, 1993, p. 67.

23. R.E. BROWN, *The Gospel according to John I–XII: A New Translation with Introduction and Commentary* (AB, 29), Garden City, NY, Doubleday, 1966, p. 74; but see Appendix I, p. 502.

24. BDAG, pp. 445-446: 1) to have an intent look at something, to take something in with one's eyes, with implication one is esp. impressed, *see, look at, behold*; 3) to perceive something above and beyond what is merely seen with the eye, *see, behold, perceive*. The verb occurs in Jn 1,14.32.38; 4,35; 6,5; 11,45; 1 Jn 1,1; 4,12.14. Cognate θεωρέω occurs in John 24 times and once in 1 John, with a similar range of meaning.

25. M.J. BUCKLEY, *What Do You Seek? The Questions of Jesus as Challenge and Promise*, Grand Rapids, MI, Eerdmans, 2016, p. 14.

26. *Ibid.*, p. 15.

27. So also MOLONEY, *Belief in the Word* (n. 22), p. 67.

reason for walking after him. This question touches on the basic need of [humans] that causes [them] to turn to God...[28].

R. Allen Culpepper says that at this deeper level Jesus' question "is one of the great existential questions of life: what are you searching for?"[29]. More recently, Brendan Byrne observed, "Little in the Fourth Gospel operates simply on one level. Beneath the ordinary and everyday, there runs a deeper level of meaning of which the ordinary is often a symbol. The question asks the disciples – and through them all readers of the gospel – concerning their deepest desires. What are you really looking for? What do you want out of life?". For Byrne, it is important to note "the programmatic nature of Jesus' initial question"[30]. This question sets the agenda for the whole gospel. Buckley notes:

> Above all it is crucial to recognize both in this Gospel and in the total life of the Christian, that it is Christ who asks the question. ... In his gaze, the first event of discipleship, human beings can gain the quiet courage to hear and respond to the searching quality of the foundational question: "What are you looking for? What do you seek?"[31].

It is worth noting that Jesus asks the two disciples *what* they are seeking and not *whom*. The neuter τί is clearly the best attested reading and makes sense in our reading of this question as programmatic for the gospel and a deeply existential question posed to both the characters in the narrative and readers. The variant masculine/feminine accusative

---

28. BROWN, *John* (n. 23), p. 78.
29. R.A. CULPEPPER, *The Gospel and Letters of John* (Interpreting Biblical Texts), Nashville, TN, Abingdon, 1998, p. 122.
30. BYRNE, *Life Abounding* (n. 4), p. 45. See also JUDGE, *Come and See* (n. 1), p. 61, n. 2; p. 62, n. 4, for a partial list of those who interpret the question in this way. Cf. recently J. BEUTLER, *A Commentary on the Gospel of John*, trans. M. Tait, Grand Rapids, MI, Eerdmans, 2017, p. 65; D.C. ESTES, *The Questions of Jesus in John: Logic, Rhetoric and Persuasive Discourse* (BibInt, 115), Leiden, Brill, 2012, p. 105; p. 107: "Jesus' question is also persuasive to the reader; as a sequence question, it asks the reader to reflect on what the reader is desiring in his or her life. Due to the mild rhetorical quality, pushing the question toward reflection, the implied reader understands an answer may not be immediately forthcoming but the question will linger in the reader's mind. John's persuasive use of interrogatives within the Fourth Gospel engages characters and readers alike to build from this opening point of reflection"; and M.M. THOMPSON, *John: A Commentary* (NTL), Louisville, KY, Westminster John Knox, 2015, p. 49: "'What are you looking for?' urges them to move from sight to insight. It has its parallel in the double meaning of the word 'follow' ... quite literally ... walking behind Jesus. But to follow Jesus is to be his disciple". See also earlier CHENNATTU, *Becoming Disciples* (n. 4), pp. 476-477; and J.F. MCHUGH, *A Critical and Exegetical Commentary on John 1–4* (ICC), London, T&T Clark, 2009, p. 150: "The first words uttered by Jesus in the Fourth Gospel address with matchless lucidity the primordial existential question of 'the world'".
31. BUCKLEY, *What Do You Seek?* (n. 25), p. 22.

singular τίνα (whom?) in the ninth century Codex Θ could be seen as no more than a corruption of the text in harmonization with Jesus' question to those who would arrest him in Jn 18,4.7 or Jesus' question to Mary Magdalene in 20,15. However, given the christological emphasis of John 1 thus far and recognition by readers that what is likely *the* major theme of the gospel is knowing who Jesus is, believing in him, and so establishing a lasting relationship with him, this textual variant is intelligible in that it "suggests that this text was understood in antiquity in terms of a theology of discipleship"[32].

Moreover, aside from the variant, this "first and foundational" question is repeated by Jesus at the aforementioned "two pivotal junctures of the Gospel ... [which] underlines its preeminence and thematic seriousness for anyone contemplating the Gospel narrative"[33]. Thus, in Jesus' first appearance and words at the beginning of the gospel, at the beginning of his passion, and in his first resurrection appearance, Jesus puts this crucial question with the verb ζητεῖν / "to seek" that involves recognizing him and what he is about[34].

The two disciples respond to Jesus' opening question with a question of their own: ῥαββί ... ποῦ μένεις; / "Rabbi ... where are you staying?". This, of course, has the surface meaning of a query about location; they are requesting to come to wherever Jesus is residing (whether temporarily or more regularly) for instruction. But, as I have written in my earlier piece, a deeper significance is present here. It is hard to miss the significance of the verb μένω in John – it occurs 40 times in the gospel alone and 27 times in the letters[35].

---

32. CHENNATTU, *Becoming Disciples* (n. 4), p. 477. See also BROWN, *John* (n. 23), p. 74; and R.F. COLLINS, *The Search for Jesus*, in ID., *These Things Have Been Written: Studies in the Fourth Gospel* (Louvain Theological & Pastoral Monographs, 2), Leuven, Peeters, 1990, 94-127, pp. 102-103.

33. BUCKLEY, *What Do You Seek?* (n. 25), p. 16.

34. See also MCHUGH'S very suggestive observation, *John 1–4* (n. 30), p. 150: "In this question to the first would-be disciples, we encounter for the first time in this Gospel the verb ζητεῖν. Its last occurrence comes in the first words spoken by the risen Jesus, at 20.15: τίνα ζητεῖς; If we exclude from consideration ch. 21, this is the final question asked by Jesus in John's gospel, and it is put to his last disciple (Mary Magdalen). The narratives it introduces in ch. 20 bring to an end the quest initiated at 1.38. The two questions thus make a perfect *inclusio*, embracing the entire Gospel".

35. This verb is translated in John by the NRSV variously with "stay" (see also 1,39; 4,40 bis; 7,9; 11,6) and otherwise elsewhere in the Fourth Gospel variously as "remain" (1,32.33.39; 7,9; 9,41; 10,40; 11,54; 12,24.34.46; 21,22.23), "endure" (3,36; 6,27), "abide" (5,38; 6,56; 14,17; 15,4 ter.5.6.7 bis.9.10), "continue" (8,31) "have a place" (8,35 bis); "dwell" (14,10); "am still with" (14,25), "last" (15,16), and "left" (19,31). Interestingly, the word is translated "stay" in its first occurrence in 1,39 and as "remain" the second time.

Certainly, there are instances where the literal sense of staying in a location is all that is intended (for instance, 2,12; 7,9; 11,6) but elsewhere it is "so characteristic of John's theology"[36] that it is used much more frequently to characterize Jesus' intimate relationship with the Father or with those who believe in him, and the abiding of the Spirit with Jesus and/or the disciples[37].

The reader has been informed already in the prologue about where Jesus dwells: he is the Word made flesh who "made his home among us" (1,14 REB for ἐσκήνωσεν ἐν ἡμῖν) but he is also the Son who is "close to the Father's heart" (1,18 NRSV; εἰς τὸν κόλπον τοῦ πατρός literally "in the bosom of the Father")[38]. In the verses just before the pericope of the first disciples following Jesus, John the Baptist witnesses that he saw the Spirit descend and remain upon Jesus (μένον ἐπ' αὐτόν 1,32-33)[39]. So with μένειν in mind the reader is prepared to hear the disciples' question with nuance; it opens a quest for what will be learned more fully as the gospel unfolds. Barrett concludes that in John "[n]othing is more important than to know where Jesus abides and may be found"[40]. Brown also notes "the answer of the disciples must be interpreted on the same theological level" as Jesus' question[41]. Discipleship is defined by this notion of abiding with or in Jesus just as he abides with or in the Father. This is most emphatically proclaimed in the remarkable repetition of μένειν in the metaphor of the vine and branches in Jn 15,4 (3×).5.6.7 (2×).9.10. And it is stated in other terms in Jesus' prayer for mutual indwelling of the Father, himself, and his disciples in 17,20-23 and that the disciples "may be with me where I am" (17,24). "The concept of 'remaining' or 'abiding' and 'remaining/abiding with' can safely be said to be a key to understanding the message of the Fourth Gospel about who Jesus is and what discipleship is; about what disciples truly seek and what Jesus has to offer"[42].

Jesus invites the two then to "come and see", a "provocative statement" that together with his opening question to them is powerful for the reader[43].

---

36. C.K. BARRETT, *The Gospel according to John: An Introduction with Commentary and Notes on the Greek Text*, London, SPCK, ²1978, p. 181.
37. JUDGE, *Come and See* (n. 1), p. 67.
38. BYRNE, *Life Abounding* (n. 4), p. 46.
39. D.A. LEE, *Abiding in the Fourth Gospel: A Case-Study in Feminist Biblical Theology*, in *Pacifica* 10 (1997) 123-136, p. 127; and BEUTLER, *John* (n. 30), p. 65.
40. BARRETT, *The Gospel according to John* (n. 36), p. 181.
41. BROWN, *John* (n. 23), p. 78; this is the continuation of the final sentence quoted above; see at n. 28.
42. JUDGE, *Come and See* (n. 1), p. 67.
43. MOLONEY, *First Days* (n. 3), p. 323.

Chennattu translates "come and you shall see", placing a future emphasis on the invitation as a promise of what is to unfold for these two as disciples[44]. McHugh, on the other hand, refuses this translation but states that "*see* hovers between a future (with *you will* not so much suppressed as understood) and an imperative"[45]. In any case, Jesus' invitation is rather proleptic or, as Byrne says, it

> is also operative on two levels and programmatic. ... On a deeper level they are being invited to embark upon a life of discipleship that will involve 'seeing' where he truly lives: 'ever in the bosom of the Father' (1:18). In other words, they – and all readers of the gospel – are being invited to go on the journey that will enable them to make their own the affirmation in the Prologue: 'we have seen his glory, glory as of an only son of the Father, full of grace and truth' (1:14c-e)[46].

With this, the scene is set for the unfolding of a discipleship based on the revelation of the unseen God by Jesus, the Word made flesh[47]. The disciples go with Jesus and abide with him. "These disciples did what all are bidden to do"[48]. They set out on a journey of discipleship with Jesus that is a never-ending process of discovery of just who he is and what he offers[49].

As the scene progresses, one of the two, Andrew, brings his brother Simon/Peter to Jesus and the next day Jesus calls Philip who in turn brings Nathanael to Jesus. They give several titles to Jesus – "Rabbi", "Messiah", "him about whom Moses in the law and also the prophets wrote", "Son of God", "King of Israel". There is some truth to the assertion of Moloney, followed by Toan Do, that these titles reflect traditional Jewish messianic expectations and for that reason are inadequate as they stand; the disciples in the narrative do not yet fully grasp who Jesus is[50]. Yet Toan Do also says the various titles in Jn 1,20-51 are

---

44. CHENNATTU, *Becoming Disciples* (n. 4), pp. 478, 489. Likewise, the New American Bible (and the revision of 2011), the New International Version, and the New American Standard Version.

45. MCHUGH, *John 1–4* (n. 30), p. 151.

46. BYRNE, *Life Abounding* (n. 4), p. 46. See also R.F. COLLINS, *John and His Witness* (Zacchaeus Studies: NT), Collegeville, MN, Liturgical Press, 1991, p. 44: Jesus' "invitation is not that the disciples should come to visit some Bedouin's tent or a roadside inn; it is that they should come to perceive that Jesus abides with the Father and the Father with him. It is that they should come to experience the mutual indwelling with Jesus which is the essence of the Christian life".

47. Cf. MOLONEY, *First Days* (n. 3), p. 323.

48. BARRETT, *The Gospel according to John* (n. 36), p. 181.

49. CHENNATTU, *Becoming Disciples* (n. 4), p. 490.

50. MOLONEY, *John* (n. 21), pp. 54-56; ID., *Belief in the Word* (n. 22), pp. 67-68; ID., *First Days* (n. 3), pp. 323-324; DO, *Come and See* (n. 5), *passim*.

"replete with allusive christological significance"[51]. I think the inherent tension here helps us grasp the proleptic nature of this call narrative.

In the narrative world, the characters themselves appear not to fully grasp who Jesus is. Their encounter with Jesus is disappointing to the reader who knows from the prologue exactly who Jesus is and what he has come to reveal and offer. Their use of these traditional titles is stuck in old categories that the reader knows must be transcended; Jesus must be understood and embraced at a much higher level[52]. Yet, the disciples' use of these titles is not completely wrong, either[53]. Some occur later as the gospel unfolds and gain nuance that does indeed transcend their traditional significance in Judaism.

The disciples call Jesus "Rabbi" and the narrator specifically explains "which translated means Teacher (διδάσκαλος)" (1,38). Jesus does not reject this title here or elsewhere in the gospel. In fact, Jesus embraces the title and uses it to refer to himself in his instruction to his disciples after the Footwashing: "You call me Teacher (διδάσκαλος) and Lord (κύριος) – and you are right, for that is what I am. So if I, your Lord and Teacher, have washed your feet, you also ought to wash one another's feet" (13,13-14). Later, Mary Magdalene calls him ῥαββουνί when she recognizes the risen Jesus in the garden (20,16; again, the narrator explains, "which means Teacher").

Andrew refers to Jesus as the Messiah (τὸν Μεσσίαν) and we are told it is translated Christ (χριστός 1,41), which is the first title (translated by the NRSV Messiah, 1,20) that John the Baptist eschews as he begins his witness. In Jesus' encounter with the Samaritan woman she says to him, "I know that Messiah is coming (who is called Christ)". Jesus replies, "I am he, the one who is speaking to you" (4,25-26). Jesus clearly accepts the title. Last but far from least, when the narrator expresses the purpose for the gospel we are told "these are written so that you may come to believe that Jesus is the Messiah (ὁ χριστός), the Son of God" (20,31 NRSV).

That title "Son of God" is one of those exclaimed by Nathanael (1,49) as he meets Jesus. In its traditional Jewish messianic usage, this term would have referred to an adoptive relationship between God and king (for example, 2 Sam 7,14 or Ps 2,7). It could indeed represent a misunderstanding by Nathanael in the narrative, an understanding that must be transcended as the gospel narrative develops. In fact, the reader has already heard John

---

51. Do, *Come and See* (n. 5), p. 182.
52. MOLONEY, *First Days* (n. 3), pp. 322-323.
53. G.R. BEASLEY-MURRAY, *John* (WBC, 36), Nashville, TN – London, ²1999, p. 30: "All these are valid confessions of faith, and they are especially pertinent for the Church's witness to the synagogue. *But they have to be filled with greater meaning than they have in Judaism*" (italics added).

the Baptist utter "a profound Johannine truth" that "this [one on whom he saw the Spirit descend and remain] is the Son of God" (1,34), recalling what is proclaimed in the prologue[54]. By the time we come to Jn 20,31 the term's full christological meaning is clear, with Jesus having referred to himself on numerous occasions as the Son of God.

Nathanael's calling Jesus "King of Israel", too, fits the traditional Messiah-King figure in Israel's expectations and from that perspective can be considered an inadequate confession on the part of one of the first disciples. This title will be transcended as well when the reader comes to the exchange between Jesus and Pilate in 18,33-38, especially v. 36 when Jesus acknowledges a kingship but "not of this world". The irony is played out with the crown of thorns and purple cloak, the mock hailing of the soldiers (19,2-5), Pilate's declaration "Here is your King" (19,14), and the inscription on the cross and the dispute over it between Pilate and the chief priests. Nathanael's title for Jesus misses the mark when he utters it, but the journey through the gospel confirms just what kind of king Jesus is[55].

Thus, strictly on the level of the narrative, the disciples' apprehension of Jesus and the titles they give him are "disappointing" to the audience who realize Jesus is much more than the Messiah/Christ of Jewish expectations. Their titles for Jesus lack "the transcendent, more-than-human sense that will emerge as the narrative unfolds (and of which we who have read the Prologue are already aware [1:18])"[56]. Nonetheless, they bear the seeds of a full christological understanding of Jesus in John. On another level, therefore, they prompt the reader likewise to embark on a journey of grasping more fully what has been learned about Jesus in John 1.

IV. Jesus as Wisdom

It is useful here to recall a motif suggested by M.-É. Boismard and mentioned favorably by Raymond Brown in his commentary: Jesus as divine Wisdom. He points to several verses in Wisdom 6 that may be drawn as parallels to this episode in Jn 1,35-51[57]:

> Wis 6,12: "Wisdom is ... easily *seen* (θεωρεῖται LXX; NRSV has *discerned*) by those who love her and *found* by those who *look for* (τῶν ζητούντων; NRSV, seek) her".

---

54. MOLONEY, *First Days* (n. 3), p. 327.
55. Cf. BYRNE, *Life Abounding* (n. 4), p. 49.
56. *Ibid.*
57. BROWN, *John* (n. 23), p. 79, with reference to M-É. BOISMARD, *Du baptême à Cana (Jean 1.19–2.11)*, Paris, Cerf, 1956, pp. 78-80. Translations from Wisdom are Brown's.

6,13: "She anticipates those who desire her by first making herself known to them" (just as Jesus takes the initiative, Brown adds).

6,16: "She makes her rounds seeking those worthy of her and graciously appears to them as they are on their way" (see Jn 1,43).

Brown could also look to Prov 1,20-28: Wisdom cries out in the streets for followers but some refuse. On the other hand, "whoever finds me finds life" (Prov 8,35).

More recently, McHugh insists likewise that the call of the first two disciples (Jn 1,35-40) "must be read in the light of the Prologue" where the first verse "exhibits the close relationship, even identity, between the Logos in John and the concept of Wisdom in Prov 8, especially the work of creation (8,22-31)" followed closely by Prov 8,35, quoted above. Following this, is the description of Wisdom building her house and extending the invitation to the simple, "Come, eat of my bread and drink of the wine I have mixed. Lay aside immaturity, and live, and walk in the way of insight" (9,1-6)[58].

Finally, in the newly published commentary on John by Mary Coloe in the Wisdom Commentary series, great emphasis is laid throughout on linking Jesus with Woman Wisdom. On the present passage, Coloe calls attention to Wis 10,10, which recounts Jacob's flight from Esau and his dream at Bethel: "When a righteous man fled from his brother's wrath, she [Wisdom] guided him on straight paths; she showed him the kingdom of God and gave him knowledge of holy things; she prospered him in his labors, and increased the fruit of his soil". Coloe sees in Jesus' final saying to all in Jn 1,51 with its reference to Jacob's vision at Beth-el, the "house of God", a recollection of 1,14 with its reference to the incarnation of the Word now dwelling among us. Jesus is now the tabernacle, the "house of God" among the people of God. Jesus/Sophia is the revealer of holy things. She concludes: "Jesus has acted as Wisdom incarnate in inviting disciples to her lodgings and promising that she will reveal to Jacob/Israel's children the very dwelling of God"[59].

V. Conclusion

The calling of the first disciples in Jn 1,35-51 is an invitation to the characters within the story to "come and see" who Jesus is and what it means to "abide" with him. Their responses to him may seem superficial

---

58. McHugh, *John 1–4* (n. 30), p. 151.

59. M.L. Coloe, *John 1–10* (Wisdom Commentary, 44a), Collegeville, MN, Liturgical Press, 2021, pp. 46-47.

and reflect old categories of messianic thinking but they are invited to expand and transcend those categories and the titles they use. For the gospel's audience, who have already been told who Jesus is, it is an invitation to grow more fully in their understanding of exactly what it means to know and believe in the Word made flesh. For both disciples and audience it is the beginning of a journey that will unfold to fully grasp the Christology of John's good news. And, of course, it will eventually involve living what they have understood.

We can embrace Brown's conclusion that we "cannot treat John i 35-51 simply as a historical narrative". It should be obvious that the disciples in the story did not gain insight into who Jesus is in just two or three days. Rather, we should see here that the evangelist has placed in the mouths of the disciples "a synopsis of the gradual increase of understanding that took place throughout the ministry of Jesus and after the resurrection. John has used the occasion of the call of the disciples to summarize discipleship in its whole development"[60].

What does it mean to follow Jesus? Disciples and audience alike are invited to "come and see"!

Winthrop University Peter J. JUDGE
Home: 1739 Rue de Ville
Rock Hill, SC 29732
USA
judgep@winthrop.edu

---

60. BROWN, *John* (n. 23), p. 78.

WHO IS NATHANAEL? OR: WHO CAN NATHANAEL BE FOR READERS OF JOHN?

RECEPTION HISTORY AND BIBLICAL SCHOLARSHIP IN DIALOGUE

Who is Nathanael? Or – if he ever was – who *was* Nathanael? This question already points to the core problem. It touches on not only key issues of the Fourth Gospel, aspects of its historical reference and scriptural background, its symbolic overtones, its narrative strategy, and its position towards and rhetorical appeal to "Israelites", "Judeans", or Jews. The quest for Nathanael also provides glimpses into the reception history of the Gospel of John, because the riddle of this literary character in John 1 has caused numerous combinations and speculations that can only show how differently the gospel material was adopted, combined with other data, and creatively developed.

In the present contribution, honoring a scholar and friend, whose learning equally includes New Testament exegesis and Patristics, I will first present a few considerations about reception history and its exegetical function, which is, of course, inspired by my own scholarly background and from the projects with which I am involved. I will, then, present some selective glimpses into the various ways the figure of Nathanael was identified, commented upon, and creatively developed in exegetical reception. My approach in this section will not be a strictly historical one. Instead, I attempt to systematize and explain various types of reception to gain access to the function of Nathanael according to various perspectives.

A final section will briefly sketch my own ideas of an exegetical understanding of this narrative figure and its function in the text of John. The question answered in the end might not be "Who is, or was, Nathanael?", but rather "Who can Nathanael be for readers of the Fourth Gospel?".

I. Reception History between *NTP* and *EKK*

Biblical reception history is a relatively new discipline which can only be done with a mutual interchange between exegetes and specialists of other fields. There are various paradigms and projects focusing on the reception history of the Bible, some of them with a more exegetical focus, such as the commentary series *Evangelisch-katholischer Kommentar*

(EKK), in which I have been commissioned to write the commentary on the Gospel of John[1], others with the focus on particular areas of biblical reception, such as the *Novum Testamentum Patristicum (NTP)*, where Jos Verheyden is involved[2]. What I will present in the following does not follow the requirements of the *NTP*. It is by no means a complete survey, neither of the reception of Nathanael in antiquity nor in any later period or area of reception. After all, the pursuit of comprehensiveness has been the death of many projects, and a complete collection of all data might overlook other aspects which are relevant to the understanding of biblical texts.

Biblical Reception History[3] has significantly developed over the course of recent decades. As we can see in the *Encyclopedia of the Bible and Its Reception*, where I was involved in the project's initial conceptualization and now serve as an area editor for Johannine Literature, the areas that deserve consideration are almost unlimited. They include not only all periods of Christianity until the present, but also philosophy, literature in various languages, arts, music, film, popular culture, etc. Thus, reception history has become a vast scholarly field in which experts from various specializations join (or work alongside each other) to assemble a huge amount of knowledge about the theological or cultural reception of books, texts, persons, or motifs of the Bible. But even in this giant project, only a selection of reception perspectives can be presented which is, admittedly, often determined by the limited fields of expertise of potential authors. Who, as an expert in literature, will equally be able to cover German literature from the Middle Ages to the present, as well as English, French, or Russian literature? And who, as an exegete, can be more than an amateurish observer in those other fields?

---

1. On my own exegetical decisions regarding the commentary, see J. FREY, *Approaches to the Interpretation of John*, in ID., *The Glory of the Crucified One: Christology and Theology in the Gospel of John* (BMSEC, 6), Waco, TX, Baylor University Press, 2018, pp. 3-36; for a sample study on a significant Johannine passage with references to reception history, see J. FREY, *Das prototypische Zeichen (Joh 2,1-11)*, in R.A. CULPEPPER – J. FREY (eds.), *The Opening of John's Narrative (John 1:19–2:22): Historical, Literary, and Theological Readings from the Colloquium Ioanneum in Ephesus* (WUNT, 385), Tübingen, Mohr Siebeck, 2017, 165-216.

2. On the *NTP*, see A. MERKT (in collaboration with T. NICKLAS and J. VERHEYDEN), *Das Novum Testamentum Patristicum (NTP): Ein Projekt zur Erforschung von Rezeption und Auslegung des Neuen Testaments in frühchristlicher und spätantiker Zeit*, in *Early Christianity* 6 (2015) 573-595.

3. For a recent systematic reflection, cf. R. BURNET, *Exegesis and History of Reception: Reading the New Testament Today with the Readers of the Past* (WUNT, 455), Tübingen, Mohr Siebeck, 2021.

As a biblical exegete, I am not merely interested in the documentation of the vast relevance of the Bible for both "Western" culture, and worldwide culture more broadly. I also want to see how the data from the reception history (of any given period) can help shed light on the difficulties, ambiguities, or the semantic potential of the biblical text. This is in accord with the hermeneutical reflections inspired by the German philosopher Hans-Georg Gadamer[4]. Reception History, or *Wirkungsgeschichte*, as hermeneutically understood in line with Gadamer, is not a continuation of the historicist quest for "objective" data[5]. While former studies on the history of biblical interpretation, at least in a Protestant context, were often meant as an act of critically distancing modern, "reasonable" exegesis from the biases and prejudices of former dogmatic approaches[6], others studied the history of interpretation in order to connect their own understanding with the tradition of the church. In light of Gadamer's reflection on the understanding of history, *Wirkungsgeschichte* can only be done as an expression of the hermeneutic awareness of the historical contingency of the interpreter's own point of view. This implies that the reception-historical perspective influences the interpretation itself: it is brought into dialogue with voices from the past, with readers and users of the same biblical text. Such a perspective is an expression of the awareness that our own interpretation is necessarily skewed by our own perspective and implies a certain degree of subjectivity. As such, a comprehensive understanding of a text will never be complete[7]. This has been aptly phrased in two theses by Moysés Mayordomo:

> "1. Wirkungsgeschichte sucht in der Betrachtung von historischen Rezeptionszeugnissen nicht diese zu überwinden, sondern das Bewusstsein für die eigene Geschichtlichkeit und damit auch Subjektivität der Auslegung zu schärfen.
> 2. Wirkungsgeschichte vollzieht sich im Bewusstsein sowohl der eigenen Endlichkeit als auch der allgemeinen Unabgeschlossenheit von Verstehen".

---

4. See the fundamental work on the understanding of history: H.-G. GADAMER, *Hermeneutik I: Wahrheit und Methode* (Gesammelte Werke, 1), Tübingen, Mohr Siebeck, 1986 (originally 1960); on Gadamer's understanding of *Wirkungsgeschichte* and its hermeneutical relevance, see P. STUHLMACHER, *Vom Verstehen des Neuen Testaments: Eine Hermeneutik* (GNT, 6), Göttingen, Vandenhoeck & Ruprecht, 1979, pp. 197-200, and U. LUZ, *Theologische Hermeneutik des Neuen Testaments*, Neukirchen-Vluyn, Neukirchener Verlag, 2014, pp. 362-372.

5. A recent discussion is provided in M. MAYORDOMO, *Was heisst und zu welchem Ende studiert man Wirkungsgeschichte?*, in *TZ* 72 (2016) 42-67.

6. See the examples presented *ibid.*, pp. 45-47, the commentary on Revelation by R.H. Charles and the *opus magnum* on the parables of Jesus by A. Jülicher, who both mention the history of exegesis mostly with the intention of overcoming former viewpoints or, rather, with a joyous tone celebrating the fact that the former viewpoints have now been overcome.

7. Thus MAYORDOMO, *Wirkungsgeschichte* (n. 5), p. 64.

When studying *Wirkungsgeschichte* of New Testament texts, motifs, and figures, my approach follows the framework of the *EKK* project. This commentary series was founded in the late 1960s, in the period after the Second Vatican Council, as a deliberately ecumenical cooperation, and it is still developed in a programmatic dialogue between Protestant and Roman Catholic scholars[8]. In the early period, stimulated by the "biblical awakening" of Roman Catholic theology, New Testament exegetes felt the enthusiasm of mutual understanding their viewpoints as shaped from the tradition of their respective denominations, and the investigation and reflection of the history of interpretation was an important tool for an exegetical dialogue. A unique historic moment in this ecumenical dialogue in NT exegesis was the mutual exchange between Eduard Schweizer and Rudolf Schnackenburg on the ecclesiological view of the Deutero-pauline Epistles (Colossians and Ephesians), where the Reformed dialogue partner was even given the opportunity to supplement his colleague's commentary with a dissenting intervention[9].

Although the exegetical and ecumenical climate has changed during the last fifty years, the *EKK* series is still dedicated to a close connection of exegesis and *Wirkungsgeschichte*. The most commendable and advanced example has been presented by Ulrich Luz in his monumental commentary on Matthew[10]. Luz has also presented further reflections on the hermeneutical function of *Wirkungsgeschichte* or impact of historical exegesis in programmatic articles[11] and in the summary of his book *Theologische Hermeneutik*[12]. Of course, the approaches to *Wirkungsgeschichte* differ from author to author and from writing to writing, and some authors have tried to avoid the task, while others never finished their work due to the overabundance of reception-historical data. Over time, the shape and understanding of reception history has also changed, from a mere focus on the denominational differences between the exegetical traditions to a much wider perception of the impact of biblical texts on Christian liturgy,

---

8. Thus, every author has his or her dialogue partner ("*syzygos*") representing the other side. My Roman Catholic dialogue partner is Michael Theobald.

9. Cf. the "Anmerkung des Evangelischen Partners" (i.e., Eduard Schweizer) in R. SCHNACKENBURG, *Der Brief an die Epheser* (EKKNT, 10), Zürich, Benziger Verlag; Neukirchen-Vluyn, Neukirchener Verlag, 1982, pp. 195-196.

10. U. LUZ, *Das Evangelium nach Matthäus*, 4 vols. (EKKNT, I/1-4), Neukirchen-Vluyn, Neukirchener Verlag; Düsseldorf, Benziger Verlag, 1985-2002.

11. U. LUZ, *Wirkungsgeschichtliche Exegese: Ein programmatischer Arbeitsbericht mit Beispielen aus der Bergpredigtexegese*, in BTZ 2 (1985) 18-32; ID., *Die Bedeutung der Kirchenväter für die Auslegung der Bibel*, in ID., *Theologische Aufsätze* (WUNT, 414), Tübingen, Mohr Siebeck, 2018, 275-294; ID., *Wirkungsgeschichtliche Hermeneutik und kirchliche Auslegung der Schrift*, ibid., 299-318; ID., *Textauslegung und Ikonographie*, ibid., 319-342.

12. LUZ, *Theologische Hermeneutik* (n. 4), pp. 397-409.

piety, and culture; visual arts, poetry, and literature; and even modern popular culture and worldwide Christianity. With such a widening of the scope, the task became even more impossible, as no biblical exegete is equally well-versed in catacomb iconography, Eastern Orthodox liturgy, medieval passion plays, Dostoyevski's novels, Bach's music, and contemporary Bible films. All these media, however, contribute to the whole of the reception history of a biblical text and may also point to its potentials and problems. They reveal the questions "normal" readers pose when reading a biblical story, the variety of use and misuse of biblical texts, and the numerous interactions between the Bible and the wider culture, even in our widely secularized time. Of course, such a daring attempt to look at various and diverse areas of Christian or cultural history implies all the pitfalls of dilettantism. But if the broader view gives additional insights, and maybe insights that work with the magnifying glass could not provide, such an approach is also justified, at least as long it is practiced in dialogue with other scholars who know more about all those other fields than an individual exegete.

The only chance of not failing in light of such a broad perspective of reception history is being radically eclectic, drawing on material that has already been analyzed and presented by specialists, looking for the exchange with experts in various fields, and, most importantly, considering what the diverse receptions and effects of biblical traditions can mean for the understanding of the text. My hope is that the inclusion of material from at least some of the areas mentioned will finally give new insights into the semantic potentials and dangers of the biblical texts and open new dialogues for their understanding and relevance.

II. THE IDENTITY OF NATHANAEL IN RECEPTION-HISTORICAL PERSPECTIVES

With these considerations in mind, we turn to Nathanael. Here, the range of receptions is not as wide as for other Johannine figures, such as Nicodemus[13], Lazarus[14], or Thomas[15], thus the task is more limited. What

---

13. On Nicodemus, see my essay J. FREY, *Die Figur des Nikodemus zwischen literarischer Ambivalenz und pluriformer Rezeption* in ID. – N. UEBERSCHAER (eds.), *Johannes lesen und verstehen: Im Gespräch mit Jean Zumstein* (BTSt, 186), Göttingen, Vandenhoeck & Ruprecht, 2021, 69-105.

14. On Lazarus, see the important study by J. KREMER, *Lazarus*, Stuttgart, Katholisches Bibelwerk, 1985.

15. On Thomas, see G.W. MOST, *Doubting Thomas*, Cambridge, MA, Harvard University Press, 2007, and also B. SCHLIESSER, *To Touch or Not to Touch: Doubting and Touching in John 20:24-29*, in *Early Christianity* 8 (2017) 69-93.

I can present here are selected and systematized glimpses into the reception and interpretation history, with the aim of disclosing aspects of the dynamics and the creative potential of the biblical text[16].

Nathanael is the literary figure of a disciple of Jesus only mentioned in the Gospel of John. He is unknown to the Synoptics – at least under this name. In John, he appears only in the scene of the calling of the disciples in Jn 1,45-51, and he is mentioned again in the final chapter, which is possibly added secondarily to the gospel, in a list of disciples. Only there, it is added that he was "from Cana in Galilee" (Jn 21,2), the place where Jesus performed two of his miracles, most notably the wine miracle at the wedding which is narrated immediately after the presentation of Nathanael in Jn 2,1-11. This last mention not only suggests that Nathanael is present at the third appearance of the Risen One in Jn 21,1-14, but also that he belongs to the group of disciples accompanying Jesus during his entire ministry.

1. *The Difference between the Calling Accounts*

Unlike the Synoptic accounts of the calling of the disciples in Mk 1,16-20 parr. and Mk 3,13-19 parr., the Johannine calling account in Jn 1,35-51 only mentions five disciples: Andrew and his unknown companion, Peter, Philip, and Nathanael. The circle of the Twelve, instead, is only of marginal relevance in John. In various aspects, the Johannine calling account strikingly differs from its Synoptic counterpart, the call of the two pairs of brothers, Peter and Andrew and John and James, at the shore of the lake (Mk 1,16-20). It is located at a different place, namely the baptism place of John, called "Bethany beyond the Jordan" (Jn 1,28), dubbed "Bethabara" by later interpreters since Origen[17]. Furthermore, the calling scene is designed quite differently, in four consecutive calling scenes. Three of them do not present a direct "charismatic" call by Jesus, only the call of Philip in the third scene (Jn 1,43-44) matches the Synoptic pattern. The other three follow a structure according to which a person first hears the testimony of another one that points him to Jesus, and, in

---

16. I am particularly indebted to U. HOLZMEISTER, *Nathanael fuitne idem ac S. Bartholomaeus Apostolus?*, in *Bib* 21 (1940) 38-49, and R. STICHEL, *Nathanael unter dem Feigenbaum: Die Geschichte eines biblischen Erzählstoffes in Literatur und Kunst der byzantischen Welt*, Wiesbaden – Stuttgart, Steiner, 1985.

17. On the history of this identification, see now J. DOCHHORN, *Βηθαβαρά in Joh 1,28: Eine Variante und ihre religionsgeschichtlichen Hintergründe*, in J. FREY – T. NICKLAS (eds.), *Antik-christliche Johannesrezeption* (History of Biblical Exegesis), Tübingen, Mohr Siebeck, 2022 (in press).

following the testimony, comes to a personal encounter with Jesus that actually leads to faith or discipleship (Jn 1,38-39.42.47-50). In the second and fourth scene, Peter and Nathanael are directly addressed by Jesus, or even given a name, and thus come to discipleship or utter a confession.

a) Questions for the Readers

The scene with Nathanael in Jn 1,45-50 is the most detailed calling scene, and functions as the climax of the whole passage. It directly follows the calling of Philip in 1,43-44, with a new constellation of characters: Philip "finds" Nathanael whose relation to Philip or the others is not clarified and he points him to Jesus (Jn 1,45), just as Andrew did before with his brother Simon (Jn 1,41). A small dialogue emerges. Nathanael questions that Jesus could be the Messiah because he comes from Nazareth, which is not mentioned in the Scriptures as the origin of the Messiah. Upon the invitation "come and see" (Jn 1,46; cf. 1,39) Nathanael follows in spite of his doubts, and Jesus directly addresses him with a surprising statement: he is called "truly an Israelite in whom there is no deceit" (Jn 1,47). Nathanael wonders how Jesus could say this without even knowing him before, and Jesus's answer is that he had seen him before sitting under the fig tree before Philip called him. These words immediately lead Nathanael to a full confession of faith: he calls Jesus "King of Israel" and "Son of God", i.e., the Messiah (Jn 1,49). His skepticism is overcome by Jesus himself, his words, or his enigmatic knowledge. In any case, Nathanael is presented as a disciple, and he is promised that he will see even greater things in the future.

Structurally, this scene is parallel to the second scene with the calling of Peter (Jn 1,41-42). In both scenes, it is a pronouncement of Jesus that makes Peter or Nathanael disciples. But while Peter is completely passive in his calling, Nathanael is active. He expresses his doubt, argues on the basis of his scriptural knowledge, follows the call to come and meet Jesus, and also poses a question to Jesus before his resistance is finally overwhelmed. Both Philip's testimony and Nathanael's confession underline, in accord with the Baptist's words (1,32), that Jesus is made known in "Israel". Nathanael is an Israelite who encounters the Messiah and King of Israel.

For readers, this narrative prompts numerous questions: what is alluded to by "truly an Israelite with no deceit"? Is this a contrasting allusion to Jacob, the deceiver? And what is meant by "sitting under the fig tree"? Is there a particular scriptural background behind the scene? And what did Jesus see? Is it just a glimpse from afar, or a miraculous "television" that convinces Nathanael of Jesus's miraculous powers?

Is Jesus's word a divine introspection, or an eschatological promise? Does it allude to a wider view of scriptural expectations? And how is Nathanael related to Jacob? And what does this mean? We will have to return to these issues later.

b) Historical Questions and Harmonizing Suggestions

On a more basic level, the differences between the Johannine and the Synoptic calling accounts have struck interpreters from the very beginning. Interpreters in antiquity were already puzzled by the contradictions between John and the Synoptics.

The predominant interpretive approach was to harmonize the narratives, using the chronological note in Jn 3,24[18]. If the events narrated in Jn 1,19–4,3 (or 4,42) actually happened before the imprisonment of John the Baptist, which is briefly mentioned in Mk 1,14, the Johannine calling scene could be an initial encounter between Jesus and the disciples, which did not immediately make them part of a close circle around Jesus. Only later, after the imprisonment of the Baptizer, did Jesus call those disciples (and others) again to become the circle of the Twelve. And while interpreters from antiquity[19] until modernity[20] wondered how the disciples could follow Jesus's call (according to the Synoptics) so immediately without any reservation, leaving everything behind, such a step of obedience could appear more conceivable if the disciples had come to know Jesus earlier.

These chronological aspects cannot be discussed further in the present context. But it is clear that the differences between the Synoptic lists of Jesus's disciples and the Johannine calling scene in John 1 demand a decision about how the disciples mentioned are related. Peter, Andrew, and Philip are also part of all the Synoptic lists, and the unknown companion of Andrew was mostly identified with the Beloved Disciple from

---

18. See the explanation in Eusebius, *Hist. eccl.* 3.24.11-12 and also Theodore of Mopsuestia, in *Ioh.* 2 (on Jn 3,24), cf. H. MERKEL, *Die Widersprüche zwischen den Evangelien: Ihre polemische und apologetische Behandlung in der Alten Kirche bis Augustin* (WUNT, 130), Tübingen, Mohr Siebeck, 1971, p. 185.

19. Cf. Epiphanius, *Pan.* 51.7.7-9 and John Chrysostom, *Hom. in Matt.* 14 (PG 57, 218-219); see MERKEL, *Widersprüche* (n. 18), p. 195.

20. Thus, e.g., F. LÜCKE, *Commentar über die Schriften des Evangelisten Johannes. 1. Theil: Allgemeine Untersuchungen über das Evangelium des Johannes und Auslegung von Kap. I – IV*, 3rd ed., Bonn, Weber, 1840, p. 555, who refers to a marginal note in the Philoxeniana on Jn 3,36; but cf. also modern commentators who are interested in the historical validity of both the Synoptics and John, thus, e.g., C.L. BLOMBERG, *The Historical Reliability of John's Gospel*, Downers Grove, IL, InterVarsity, 2001, p. 80, and C.S. KEENER, *The Gospel of John: A Commentary*, 2 vols., Peabody, MA, Hendrickson, 2005, vol. 1, p. 466.

Jn 13,23 and considered to be John the son of Zebedee. But what about Nathanael? Is he one of the Twelve? Is he an apostle, or not? Who is this Nathanael?

2. *Who Is Nathanael? An Apostle or Not?*

Under the presupposition that John and the Synoptics are both historically valid testimonies, there must be a connection, and we can discover different kinds of reasoning in the various attempts at a solution.

a) An Apostle or One of the Closest Disciples

In writings from the second century, which are probably dependent on John and not yet concerned with harmonization, we find Nathanael among the closest disciples of Jesus, together with his colleagues from John and other traditions. Here, the number twelve is not (yet) normative.

One of the earliest testimonies is the list of disciples presented by Papias of Hierapolis, an author from Asia Minor (about 130 CE) who probably draws on John and thus even prefers John's narrative sequence over Mark[21]. In his account of the authorities[22] whose traditions he had followed and collected in his earlier years, Papias presents a list of disciples which has many overlaps with the list of disciples from John 1 as well as with the list from John 21[23]:

John 1	Papias	John 21
Andrew	Andrew	
1 unknown disciple		
Peter	Peter	Peter
Philip	Philip	
	Thomas	Thomas
	James and John (2 sons of Zebedee)	
Nathanael	Matthew	Nathanael
		2 sons of Zebedee
	2 "*presbyteroi*" (Aristion and John)	2 unknown disciples

Papias follows the list from John 1 with Andrew at the beginning. He omits the unknown disciple, so Peter follows Andrew, and then comes

---

21. On the testimonies of Papias, see M. HENGEL, *Die johanneische Frage: Ein Lösungsversuch, mit einem Anhang zur Apokalypse von Jörg Frey* (WUNT, 67), Tübingen, Mohr Siebeck, 1994, pp. 75-95; on the verdict about Mark from a "Johannine" perspective, see M. HENGEL, *Die vier Evangelien und das eine Evangelium von Jesus Christus* (WUNT, 224), Tübingen, Mohr Siebeck, 2007, pp. 123-124.
22. Eusebius, *Hist. eccl.* 3.39.4.
23. See also the table in HENGEL, *Die johanneische Frage* (n. 21), p. 81.

Philip. So far this is in accord with John 1. Papias then mentions Thomas who is also most prominent in John, then the two sons of Zebedee (which implies that he probably does not identify the unknown disciple from John 1 with John the son of Zebedee). As the last one of the series of "apostles", before mentioning two more recent "elders", Aristion and the *presbyteros* John, he mentions Matthew. Is Matthew mentioned here simply because he was another important tradition-bearer? Or is he mentioned in this "Johannine" list instead and in place of Nathanael? As Papias's list mentions no other disciple from the Twelve, and also no disciple who is not mentioned in John, the mention of Matthew seems to indicate that Papias considered Nathanael to be Matthew, possibly because of the meaning of the name (with נְתַנְאֵל = מַתִּתְיָה = gift of God/JHWH). There is no need to follow the speculative idea that the author of John already wanted to distance himself from the Gospel of Matthew as his "opposite" by concealing the name of its author in a different (and symbolic) form[24]. To be clear, neither Papias nor John draws on a firm list of twelve disciples, but if Papias draws on the Johannine data, as I think is probable, and if the parallel is not accidental, Papias considered Nathanael one of the closest disciples of Jesus, or even one of the Twelve, namely Matthew.

A second testimony from the second century is the *Epistula Apostolorum*[25], which is opened by a list of eleven disciples authorizing the present "letter": John, Thomas, Peter, Andrew, James, Philip, Bartholomew, Matthew, Nathanael, Judas the Zealot, Cephas. The list has some oddities, such as the doubling of Peter and Cephas. In the first place, there is John, followed by Thomas. The mention of John and Thomas first, along with the first six names as a whole indicate that the Johannine tradition is the most influential one. After those six disciples, Bartholomew, Matthew, and Nathanael are mentioned. At least this list – in its Ethiopic textual form which may or may not be the form of the second century – shows that Nathanael is included in the circle of eleven disciples, but – importantly – he is not identical with Matthew, nor with Bartholomew. In these early lists of disciples, inspired by John and not (yet) aligned with the Synoptic lists, the number of disciples is still not necessarily twelve and Nathanael appears among the circle of disciples.

On the other hand, in a list of disciples which is probably independent of John, as reported by Epiphanius from the so-called "Gospel of the

---

24. Thus the reasoning *ibid.*, pp. 82-83.
25. *Ep. Apost.* 2 (13); see now the new translation and discussion by F. WATSON, *An Apostolic Gospel: The "Epistula Apostolorum" in Literary Context* (SNTS MS, 179), Cambridge, CUP, 2020.

Ebionites"[26], Nathanael is not mentioned at all. This is conceivable, as he is only known from John.

This insertion of Nathanael into the circle of Jesus's disciples is also attested in the church order edited by Schermann in 1914[27], where the sequence is John, Matthew, Peter, Andrew, Philip, Simon, James, Nathanael, Thomas, Cephas, Bartholomew, and Judas son of James. The same is true for the Syriac *Didascalia Apostolorum*, where the list is as follows: John, Matthew, Peter, Andrew, Philip, Simeon, James, Nathanael, Judas son of James, Thomas, Cephas, Bartholomew[28]. Here, Nathanael is part of a list of the Twelve.

The tradition that Nathanael was one of the Twelve or one of the apostles, has been preserved in the later period: Nathanael is explicitly called an apostle in some liturgical books of the Eastern church, the synaxarion from Constantinople on the 22nd of April, the *Menologion Basilii* on the same day, and the Syriac martyrologium of Rabban Sliba on the 21st of April[29]. Possibly more sources could be found that represent the same tradition and consider Nathanael an apostle, but being comprehensive is not our concern here.

b) Not an Apostle – But a Jewish Scribe

A very different view decisively excludes Nathanael from the circle of the apostles because he is missing in the lists of the Twelve from the Synoptics and Acts. Based on the idea of a basic harmony of the gospels as developed in the early church and finally established in Augustine's *De consensu evangelistarum*, the Synoptic lists give the true information about the circle of disciples which cannot be questioned by the incomplete lists in John 1 or John 21. Thus, for Augustine, Nathanael cannot be an apostle since he is not listed among the Twelve:

> *Ecce vere Israelita, in quo dolus non est. Magnum testimonium! hoc nec Andreae dictum, nec Petro dictum, nec Philippo, quod dictum est de Nathanaele: Ecce vere Israelita, in quo dolus non est. ...* Non solum primus

---

26. Epiphanius, *Pan.* 30.13.2-3; on this list see also J. FREY, *Die Fragmente des Ebionäerevangeliums*, in C. MARKSCHIES – J. SCHRÖTER, *Antike christliche Apokryphen in deutscher Übersetzung*. Bd. 1: *Evangelien und Verwandtes*, Teilbd. 1, Tübingen, Mohr Siebeck, 2012, 607-620, p. 617.

27. T. SCHERMANN, *Die allgemeine Kirchenordnung, frühchristliche Liturgien und kirchliche Überlieferung*. 1. Teil: *Die allgemeine Kirchenordnung des 2. Jahrhunderts*, Paderborn, Schöningh, 1914, p. 12; cf. the same group in slightly different sequence in A. VON HARNACK, *Die Lehre der Zwölf Apostel nebst Untersuchungen zur ältesten Geschichte der Kirchenverfassung und des Kirchenrechts* (TU, II/1-2), Leipzig, Hinrichs, 1884, p. 225.

28. A. VÖÖBUS, *Die Didascalia Apostolorum in Syriac* (CSCO, 402/I), Turnhout, Brepols, 1979, pp. 30-31.

29. HOLZMEISTER, *Nathanael* (n. 16), p. 35.

non invenitur in Apostolis, sed nec medius, nec ultimus inter duodecim Nathanael est, *cui tantum testimonium perhibuit Filius Dei, dicens, Ecce vere Israelita, in quo dolus non est*[30].

"Behold, truly an Israelite in whom there is no deceit". Great testimony! This is said neither to Andrew nor to Peter nor to Philip, what is said to Nathanael: "Behold, truly an Israelite in whom there is no deceit." ... *Not only is he not found to be first among the apostles, but neither in the middle nor the last one among the Twelve is Nathanael*, to whom the Son of God bore such great witness, saying: "Behold, truly an Israelite in whom there is no deceit".

In a sermon on John 21, Augustine briefly says: *Nathanael inter Apostolos fuit et Apostolus non fuit* ("Nathanael was among the apostles, but he was not an apostle")[31].

What is the reason for such a verdict? Of course, there are the Synoptic lists of the Twelve where Nathanael is not included. But there may be also a hint in the word of Jesus that he is "Truly an Israelite" which Augustine repeats three times in the passage quoted. Unlike Simon Peter[32], he does not get a new name that expresses his new identity as the rock of the church. He only receives a word which describes him: He is an Israelite (i.e., a Jew), and this seems to imply that he is not a "Christian". Even if he is a good Israelite and a knowledgeable reader of the Scriptures, he cannot be an apostle. Interestingly, Augustine adds an argument about his education:

> *Intelligere enim debemus ipsum Nathanaelem eruditum et peritum Legis fuisse: propterea noluit illum Dominus inter discipulos ponere; quia idiotas elegit, unde confunderet mundum*[33].
>
> For we have to understand that Nathanael himself was educated and skilled in the law. Therefore the Lord did not want to place him among the disciples. For he elected the uneducated, to confound the world.

From Nathanael's argument in Jn 1,46, Augustine concludes that he was learned in the Jewish Scriptures. Thus, the main reason for his exclusion from the circle of the apostles is that education might lead to arrogance, and Jesus did not call a learned rhetor, but rather illiterate people (cf. 1 Cor 1,26-28). A similar verdict is expressed by Jerome and Gregory the Great[34], and Augustine's view was followed by numerous

---

30. Augustine, *Tract. eu. Jo.* VII 16.2–17.1 (PL 35, 1445-1446).
31. Augustine, *Sermo de feria 3 Paschae*, in G. MORIN (ed.), *Sancti Augustini sermones post Maurinos reperti* (Miscellanea Agostiniana; Testi e studi, 1), Roma, Typographia Polyglotta Vaticana, 1930, p. 187.
32. On the word of Jesus to Simon, Augustine elaborates in *Tract. eu. Jo.* VII 14.
33. Augustine, in *Tract. eu. Jo.* VII 17.2 (PL 35, 1446).
34. Jerome, *Comm. Eph.* 2.12 (PS 26, 471D) and Gregory the Great, *Moralia in Job* 33.15 (PL 76, 693D; CCSL, 134B, 1702,32-33, ed. ADRIAEN): *Nec tamen Dominus Nathanaelem in sorte praedicantium numerat*.

medieval interpreters, including Hugh of Saint-Cher, Albertus Magnus, and Thomas Aquinas[35].

The idea that Nathanael was a scribe, however, can be traced back to earlier interpreters. In his commentary on the Diatessaron, Ephrem states that Nathanael was called "a scribe of Israel"[36]. Moreover, he is praised as a good scribe, unlike those Pharisees and scribes who interpreted the Scriptures according to their own pleasure[37]. Similarly, Chrysostom in his homilies on John says that Nathanael was "an exact man, and one who viewed all things with truth" (ὁ Ναθαναὴλ ἀκριβὴς ἦν, καὶ πάντα διεσκεμμένος μετὰ ἀληθείας), and that "Nathanael had considered the writings of the prophets more than Philip"[38]. In a Syriac list of seventy-two disciples, Nathanael is mentioned as "Nathanael the scribe" (Ναθαναηλ ὁ γραμματεύς)[39]. In another Syriac list of the names of the disciples, he is even called "chief of the scribes"[40]. Therefore Tjitze Baarda assumes that there was an earlier Syriac tradition about Nathanael the scribe that could already be used by Ephrem. Such a tradition could easily develop from Jn 1,45 where Philip explicitly refers to Moses and the prophets, and Nathanael enters an argument with him about Nazareth, thus demonstrating his own deeper reasoning in the Scriptures. A later tradition, preserved in the Armenian synaxarion even develops the idea that from the law and the prophets Nathanael expressed strong rejections against the Jews, so that he finally died (as a martyr) because of them[41].

c) A Disciple not from the Twelve, But from a Wider Circle

As already mentioned, other interpreters locate Nathanael within a wider circle of disciples, e.g., the seventy disciples from Lk 10,1. Thus, Epiphanius, in his *Panarion* narrates that Jesus on his way to Emmaus appeared to Nathanael and Klopas. Thus, Nathanael is identified with the

---

35. See the passages mentioned in HOLZMEISTER, *Nathanael* (n. 16), p. 31.
36. Ephrem, *Comm. in Diatessaron*, on Jn 1,47; see T. BAARDA, *Nathanael, "the Scribe of Israel": John 1:47 in Ephraem's Commentary on the Diatessaron*, in ETL 72 (1995) 321-336.
37. BAARDA, *Nathanael* (n. 36), p. 336, suggests that the idea came from an exegetical tradition, not from the text of the Diatessaron. See the texts in L. LELOIR, *Le témoignage d'Éphrem sur le Diatessaron* (CSCO, 227), Leuven, Peeters, 1962, pp. 20 and 111 (cf. BAARDA, *Nathanael* [n. 36], p. 323).
38. John Chrysostom., *Hom. in Jo.* 20 (PG 59, 125).
39. T. SCHERMANN, *Prophetarum vitae fabulosae, indices apostolorum discipulorumque Domini, Dorotheo Ephiphanio, Hippolyto aliisque vindicata*, Leipzig, Teubner, 1907, pp. 171-177 (175,8-9); see also another list, *ibid.*, p. 183,14-15.
40. *Ibid.*, 218-221; 219,21-22; cf. BAARDA, *Nathanael* (n. 36), p. 334.
41. G. BAYAN (ed.), *Le synaxaire arménien de Ter Israel* (PO, 21), Paris, Firmin-Didot, 1930, p. 276 (1320).

unnamed companion of Klopas (Lk 24,18)[42]. Some lists presenting the names of the seventy (or seventy-two) disciples mention Nathanael[43], partly as preacher for the Hauran region in Syria[44].

Other possibilities of identification, such as with the disciple Matthias elected in Acts 1, were not suggested in antiquity. Of course, John's Nathanael could fit the criteria for apostleship mentioned in Acts 1, being with Jesus from the very beginning, and being a witness to his resurrection. But the first author to suggest such an identification is the nineteenth-century scholar Adolf Hilgenfeld[45].

d) Simon Kananaios and Simon son of Klopas

An identification with one of the other members of the Twelve is suggested in various texts. A first possibility is the identification with Simon the Zealot (Lk 6,15; Acts 1,13), who in Mt 10,4 and Mk 3,18 is also called Σίμων ὁ Καναναῖος. As the linguistic background of this form, which is the Aramaic קַנְאָן (= "zealot" = Greek ζηλωτής), was unknown to later authors, they mixed it up with "from Cana", suggesting that Simon "from Cana" is actually Nathanael. This identification is attested in some synaxaria from the Eastern church, in Greek, Arabic, and Ethiopic. Nathanael is thus added to the celebration of Simon Kananaios on May 10 or 11[46].

In the Ethiopian synaxarion, however, there is also a salutation to Nathanael, "the new apostle" added at the feast of Simon son of Klopas[47],

---

42. Epiphanius, *Pan.* 22.6.5.
43. Thus the Armenian synaxarion on April 9th, see BAYAN (ed.) *Le synaxaire arménien* (n. 41), pp. 272-279, where lists of the twelve apostles, of the seventy-two apostles, of female apostles (!), and of forty martyrs are compiled.
44. T. SCHERMANN, *Propheten- und Apostellegenden nebst Jüngerkatalogen des Dorotheus und verwandter Texte* (TU, 31/3), Leipzig, Teubner, 1907, pp. 302-303 and 342-343; also in the Syriac *Book of the Bee*, compiled by Solomon of Bosra (thirteenth century): E.A.W. BUDGE (ed.), *The Book of the Bee* (Anecdota Oxoniensia, I/2), Oxford, OUP, 1886, p. 110; cf. HOLZMEISTER, *Nathanael* (n. 16), p. 33.
45. A. HILGENFELD, *Novum Testamentum extra canonem receptum*, Leipzig, Weigel, 1866, pars 4, p. 105: *ille propter nominis significationem Matthiae in Judae proditoris locum substituto (Act. I, 23 sq.) respondere videtur*.
46. See the references in HOLZMEISTER, *Nathanael* (n. 16), p. 35; H. DELEHAYE (ed.), *Synaxarium ecclesiae Constantinopolitanae e codice Sirmondiano*, Propylaeum ad Acta sanctorum Novembris, Bruxelles, Société des Bollandistes, 1902, p. 671, ll. 11-12; R. BASSET (ed.), *Le Synaxaire arabe jacobite* (PO, 16), Paris, Firmin-Didot, 1922, pp. 185-424 (pp. 384-385 [1026-1027]); E.A.W. BUDGE (ed.), *The Book of the Saints of the Ethiopian Church: A Translation of the Ethiopic Synaxarium Made from Manuscripts Oriental 660 and 661 in the British Museum* (4 vols.), Cambridge, CUP, 1928, vol. III, p. 890 (on 15 Genbôt = 20 May).
47. BUDGE, *The Book of the Saints* (n. 46), vol. 4, p. 1099; cf. I. GUIDI (ed.), *Le synaxaire éthiopien: Les mois de Sanè, Hamlè et Nahasè II* (PO, 7), pp. 204-454 (297-298); cf. further references in HOLZMEISTER, *Nathanael* (n. 16), p. 36.

who according to Hegesippus was the successor of James as bishop of Jerusalem[48]. If Klopas was considered a brother of Joseph, this Simon would be a cousin of Jesus, so Nathanael could even become a relative of Jesus. But this identification, which is chronologically quite implausible, may be due to a confusion of the two Simons.

e) Bartholomew

Most influential was, however, the identification with one particular apostle from the lists of the Twelve, Bartholomew[49]. If there was knowledge that the name Βαρθολομαῖος could also be interpreted as "the son of Tholomaios", a connection with another name was quite easy. Moreover, Bartholomew occurs in the Synoptic lists of the disciples (Mt 10,3; Mk 3,18; Lk 6,14) directly after Philip. And when Bartholomew is placed after Thomas in Acts 1,13, this is in accord with Jn 21,2 where Nathanael is placed immediately after Thomas. Thus, scriptural reasoning could lead to the identification of Nathanael and Bartholomew. However, this identification, which became quite common in later times, seems to be unknown in ancient interpreters such as Origen, Chrysostom, Theodore, Cyril, as well as in Bede and Alcuin[50]. It is, therefore, impossible to state that Augustine and Gregory the Great implicitly reject this interpretation[51].

The identification does not appear before the ninth century, when the Nestorian bishop Ishodad of Merw[52] in a brief remark mentions "Nathanael or also Bartholomew". From there, we could assume that the identification originated in the Syriac region, but two centuries later, it can be found in the Greek author Nicetas Paphlagon (tenth century) as an already developed tradition that now influences traditions about the apostle Bartholomew[53]. Furthermore, in his commentary from the twelfth century, Rupert of Deutz explains the identification from the connection with Philip in the other gospels and from a rendering of the Aramaic name Βαρθολομαῖος as *filius suspendentis aquas* ("son of the one who

---

48. Eusebius, *Hist. eccl.* 3.11.1-2.
49. Mt 10,3; Mk 3,18; Lk 6,14; in Acts 1,13 he is listed after Thomas, in the seventh position. Since Bartholomew is a patronym (son of Talmai), the possibility remained open to speculate about his own name.
50. Thus HOLZMEISTER, *Nathanael* (n. 16), pp. 38-39, with detailed references.
51. Thus the suggestion by C. MARKSCHIES, *Bartholomaeustraditionen/Bartholomaeusevangelium*, in ID. – SCHRÖTER (eds.), *Antike christliche Apokryphen* I/1 (n. 26), 696-701, p. 696. However, the extant apocryphal texts about Bartholomew do not provide enough evidence for such a conclusion.
52. M.D. GIBSON (ed.), *The Commentaries of Isho'dad of Merw* (Horae Semiticae, 5-7), Cambridge, CUP, 1922, vol. 5, p. 123, and vol. 7, p. 223.
53. See the next paragraph below.

removes the waters") which is linked with the wine miracle performed at Cana, the place where Nathanael is from. Therefore, he concludes briefly: *Fortassis ergo hic ipse Nathanael qui erat a Cana Galilaeae, Bartholomaeus est*[54].

3. *The Legendary Transfer of Jn 1,51 to Bartholomew*

The Greek testimony deserves further consideration. In a eulogy on St. Bartholomew[55], the Byzantine author Nicetas Paphlagon not only mentions, as a matter of course, that Jesus called Bartholomew (!) a true Israelite[56]. When narrating Bartholomew's martyrdom by means of crucifixion, he also recounts that the heavens opened, and angels descended and ascended on him to provide him a heavenly welcome[57].

> Καὶ ὃς εὐθύμως προσῄει τῷ ξύλῳ, μετὰ πλείστης ὅσης προσηλοῦτο χαρᾶς· ἐντεῦθεν ἄγγελοι μὲν οὐρανόθεν ἐπ' αὐτὸν καταβαίνοντες καὶ ἀναβαίνοντες, ὑπερφυεστάτην ἀνάβασιν ᾠδοποίουν. Διηνέῳκτο δὲ ὁ οὐρανὸς ἄνωθεν αὐτῷ, καὶ πᾶσαι δὲ τῶν οὐρανίων Δυνάμεων ἱεραρχίαι, πρὸς ὑποδοχὴν καὶ δεξίωσιν τῷ φιλτάτῳ τοῦ Κυρίου παρεσκευάζοντο μαθητῇ.
>
> And when he went to the cross with cheerful mind, he was nailed with the utmost joy, then angels from heaven descending upon him and ascending provided him the most honorable way to ascend. The heaven opened over him and all the orders of heavenly powers were prepared to receive and welcome the beloved disciple of the Lord.

This means that the word of Jesus from Jn 1,51 is now read as a personal promise to Nathanael-Bartholomew and considered fulfilled in his own biography, his martyrdom. The identification caused the idea of the narrative fulfilment of the promise from Jn 1,51.

There is a vague parallel in the apocryphal *Questions of Bartholomew* (1.6) where the disciple talks to the Risen Christ and narrates that when Jesus was crucified, he saw angels descend from heaven and venerate Jesus. Yet, this is not the pattern presented in Jn 1,51, because the angels only descend to venerate Jesus: so the double movement of descent and ascent is missing. Thus, in my view, this passage and some other passages in this text (1,21.24-27) cannot confirm an identification of Bartholomew with Nathanael[58]. Nor is there any further support in the Coptic *Book of*

---

54. Rupert of Deutz, *Comm. Joh.* 1.50 (PL 169, 273 A).
55. Nicetas Paphlagon, *Oratio in laudem S. Bartholomaei apostoli* (PG 105, 195-214).
56. *Ibid.*, p. 201C.
57. *Ibid.*, p. 209D.
58. MARKSCHIES, *Bartholomaeustraditionen* (n. 51), p. 696, interprets this as "ein deutlicher Bezug auf die Verheißung an Nathanael"; he refers to the hints to this passage

Bartholomew on Resurrection (fol. 15-16)[59] where the Risen One utters blessings on his disciples in the sequence Andrew – James – John – Philip – Thomas – Bartholomew – Matthew – James son of Alphaeus – Simon Zelotes – [Judas] son of James – Thaddaeus – Matthias[60]. The list follows Acts 1,13 (with Peter missing at the beginning, where he is replaced by Andrew). Here, nothing suggests that Bartholomew functions as Nathanael, and despite the dense presence of angels in this book, there is, as far as I can see, no clear allusion to Jn 1,51.

Thus the issue of the sources for the interesting transfer of the promise of Jn 1,51 to the martyrdom of Bartholomew is, in my view, still unsolved. Of course, the identification of Nathanael with Bartholomew can be earlier than the ninth century, but it was hardly widespread, because in that case we should expect some more explicit mentions before that time.

4. *A Creative Legendary Development: Nathanael under the Fig Tree*

One question, however, remained unsolved in all these identifications: why did Nathanael believe so quickly at Jesus's statement that he had seen him under the fig tree? Here, another apocryphal tradition that can be traced in Eastern Christianity – most densely in Slavonic and Russian literature and iconography – provides a most interesting and creative answer. The reasoning is that Jesus must have told Nathanael something he could not know from others, some secret knowledge, an event of his childhood or family tradition. This is the reasoning behind the tradition that Nathanael, as a child, had been hidden under a fig tree, and so survived the infanticide under Herod. I can only mention some of the testimonies which are more thoroughly analyzed in two studies by Rainer Stichel[61].

The tradition is first perceptible in the apocryphal *History of the Blessed Virgin*, a summary of earlier infancy stories with the focus on

---

and to the Coptic *Book of Bartholomew* in J.-D. KAESTLI, *L'évangile de Barthélemy d'après deux écrits apocryphes*, in *Apocryphes: Collection de poche de l'AELAC*, Turnhout, Brepols, 1993, p. 16.

59. E.A.W. BUDGE, *Coptic Apocrypha in the Dialect of Upper Egypt*, London, Longman, 1913; cf. M. WESTERHOFF, *Auferstehung und Jenseits im koptischen Buch der Auferstehung Jesu Christi, unseres Herrn* (Orientalia Biblica et Christiana, 11), Wiesbaden, Harrassowitz, 1999, and, on the genre, A. SUCIU, *The Book of Bartholomaios: A Coptic Apostolic Memoir*, in *Apocrypha* 26 (2015) 211-237.

60. See the translation in BUDGE, *Coptic Apocrypha* (n. 59), pp. 203-204.

61. STICHEL, *Nathanael* (n. 16); on the iconography, see also R. STICHEL, *Die Geburt Christi in der russischen Ikonenmalerei*, Stuttgart, Steiner, 1990.

the life of Mary, transmitted in Syriac and Arabic[62]. There, after the narrative of a miracle of the twelve-year-old Jesus, the story of Nathanael is inserted: "Now when war broke out against the children, and they were about to be slain by Herod, the mother of Nathaniel took him, and set him up in a fig-tree, and she covered him with the leaves thereof"[63]. Then, the story from Jn 1,45-49 is narrated, but with a different closure: "And Nathaniel went and told his mother everything which Jesus had narrated unto him; and his mother said unto him, 'Verily, my son, this is the Messiah for Whom creation waiteth'"[64]. Here, the mother of Nathanael knows that Jesus told the secret truth, and confirms to him the identity of Jesus as the Messiah.

In the Syriac *Book of the Bee* (thirteenth century), there is an addition to the story about the killing of Zacharias and the protection of the young John (the Baptist) from Herod's infanticide. Here, it is Nathanael's father who put him under the fig tree so that he was rescued from persecution[65]. In the Arabic compilation *The Lamp of the Darkness* by the Coptic priest Abu'l Barakat, the story is narrated in more detail, with the variation that Nathanael's mother had informed him about the secret of his early life, so that he could believe immediately upon Jesus's word[66]. The story is also included in the Coptic synaxarion (in Arabic), in connection with Simon the Zealot (who is identified with Nathanael there). Here, a further legendary explanation is given: as a young man, Nathanael had a fight with a pagan, in which he wounded and killed his adversary and then buried him under a fig tree. Again, only the Savior knows and tells him the dark secret of his life[67]. The plurality of stories shows the creativity of narrators with respect to Jn 1,47-48.

---

62. Cf. E.A.W. BUDGE, *The History of the Blessed Virgin Mary and the History of the Likeness of Christ* (Luzac's Semitic Text and Translation Series, 5), London, Luzac, 1899, pp. 82-83.

63. *Ibid.*, pp. 82-83. In the Arabic Infancy Gospel, this narrative seems to be associated with Nicodemus, see. E. PROVERA, *Il Vangelo arabo dell'infanzia secondo il Ms. Laurenziano or. (n. 387)*, Jerusalem, Franciscan Printing Press, 1973, pp. 27 and 123; cf. STICHEL, *Nathanael* (n. 16), p. 34.

64. BUDGE, *The History* (n. 62), p. 83.

65. Solomon of Bosra, *Book of the Bee* (n. 44), p. 48; BUDGE, *Book of the Bee* (n. 44), p. 86.

66. On this work, see G. GRAF, *Geschichte der christlich arabischen Literatur*, vol. 2 (Studi e Testi, 133), Città del Vaticano, Biblioteca Apostolica Vaticana, 1947, pp. 439-442; text in F. HAASE, *Apostel und Evangelisten in orientalischen Überlieferungen* (NTAbh, IX/1-3), Münster, Aschendorff, 1922, pp. 299-300; cf. STICHEL, *Nathanael* (n. 16), pp. 34-35.

67. J. FORGET, *Synaxarium Alexandrinum II* (CSCO, Script. Arab. ser., 3), Beirut, Typographeum Catholicum; Paris – Poussielgue – Leipzig, Harrassowitz, 1905.

The legend is also linked to the pilgrimage to the Holy Land. In an eleventh-century adaptation of the text of the *vita* of Willibald, Bishop of Eichstätt, who had travelled to the Holy Land in 751 CE, when Willibald comes from Bethlehem to Teqoa, the place of the memory of the infanticide, there is a note that Nathanael had been hidden there by his mother under the fig tree[68]. Here, Nathanael is not in Cana, but in Teqoa.

But wherever he was, how could Jesus "see" him? The Old Russian version goes further in its explanations. While the child Jesus is in Egypt with his family, Nathanael is in Bethsaida. But even as a child and at this great distance Jesus sees Nathanael and sends his angel to protect him[69].

There is also another version of the Nathanael legend in the Old Russian tradition: in the Slavonic translation of the synaxarion called "Prolog", Nathanael is presented as the guardian of a vineyard, who was sitting under a fig tree and provided Joseph with a hiding place when he asked for a place to hide Jesus and his mother from Herod's executioners. So, when Jesus later tells Nathanael that he saw him under the fig tree, he reminds him of that earlier encounter, with the result that Nathanael believes and follows Jesus[70].

I cannot further detail the narrative creativity of these Russian traditions which deserve to be considered more thoroughly. Their origins are hard to determine. Stichel's bold suggestion that the narrative originates in a Greek milieu in the East, even in the pre-Johannine period[71], and was later suppressed or censored, cannot be confirmed. The legendary development is, instead, to be explained as a creative reasoning based on Jn 1,45-50, especially 1,48.

Yet, one reference to iconography and art history cannot be omitted. The legendary scene with Nathanael as a child under the fig tree found its way into the composition of Russian nativity icons, where among the numerous scenes of the nativity, not only John (the Baptist) but also a second child, under a tree, is hidden from the soldiers of Herod[72]. So Nathanael's story becomes a part of the commemoration of Christmas, and he is brought in close connection with Christ himself.

---

68. *Nathanahel sub ficu a matre absconsus evasit, ideoque sibi dictum est a Domino, quia: Cum esses sub ficu, novi te*. Cf. O. HOLDER-EGGER, *Vitae Willibaldi et Wynnebaldi auctore sanctimoniali Heidenheimensi* (Monumenta Germaniae historica. Scriptores, 15/1), Hannover, Hahn, 1887, pp. 80-117; here p. 99. Cf. STICHEL, *Nathanael* (n. 16), pp. 45-46.
69. See the Old Russian text with German translation in STICHEL, *Nathanael* (n. 16), p. 45.
70. Text and translation *ibid.*, pp. 87-88.
71. *Ibid.*, p. 58.
72. Cf. STICHEL, *Geburt* (n. 61), pp. 134-139.

5. *The Reasoning behind the Various Options and the Potentials of the Text(s)*

The variety of interpretive options not only of the identification of him, but also of legendary developments of the tradition about Nathanael, could be interpreted as a mere sign of the arbitrary character of reception. After the "death of the author" (R. Barthes), texts are free and recipients can do with them what they want. But this is not the whole truth in the reception of the Bible, where biblical texts are not only continued, combined, and reconceptualized; the reception of the Bible also attempts to fill lacunae and solve open questions therein[73]. There is a certain reasoning that undergirds the various options in the reception history.

a) When John is read without the need of harmonizing it with the Synoptics, Nathanael is clearly a disciple from the very beginning until the end of Jesus's ministry. He is an "apostle", although this is not the Johannine terminology used for the disciples. Papias and the *Epistula Apostolorum* are testimonies of this early, pre-harmonistic reading.

b) Further questions arose when the harmony of the gospels determined the reading. Now, the list of the Twelve provided the framework. Although they are not completely identical, they could easily be harmonized (with Mt 10,3 as the most influential list). Now interpreters had to decide whether Nathanael was actually one of those Twelve or a disciple from a wider circle. The latter option is chosen when Nathanael is identified with the companion of Klopas from the Emmaus story. There are not so many narrative figures in the Bible that could be an option to be included in the lists of the seventy, thus the lists of the seventy or seventy-two disciples[74] are filled by later and also legendary figures. But probably the later lists of the seventy already presuppose Nathanael's identification with one of the Twelve.

c) For interpreters who identified Nathanael as one of the Twelve, different considerations can be determined. While the choice of Simon Kananaios results from a linguistic misunderstanding, the identification of Nathanael with Bartholomew is a smart biblical option: in the Synoptic

---

73. This is a common feature of the composition of "para-Scriptural" texts, see J. FREY, *From Canonical to Apocryphal Texts: The Quest for Processes of "Apocryphication" in Early Jewish and Early Christian Literature*, in ID. – C. CLIVAZ – T. NICKLAS (eds.), *Between Canonical and Apocryphal Texts: Processes of Reception, Rewriting, and Interpretation in Early Judaism and Early Christianity* (WUNT, 419), Tübingen, Mohr Siebeck, 2019, 1-43, pp. 12-14.

74. The first list is by Ps.-Hippolytus, *On the Seventy Apostles of Christ*; see also Solomon of Bosra, *Book of the Bee* (n. 44).

lists, this disciple appears after Philip, in Acts 1,13 after Thomas, as in Jn 21,2. Moreover, interpreters knew that Bartholomaios could simply be a patronym (i.e., son of Tholomaios or Talmaj), so it was easy to supply the "real" name of this disciple. This identification is possible, although there is nothing in the Johannine or Synoptic texts that speaks in favor of it. In any case, it is more thoughtful than any of the other numerous suggestions adduced by modern exegetes against the "Catholic" identification with Bartholomew.

d) Once the identification is established, the motifs can be transferred to the lives of the various figures, especially Simon Kananaios and Bartholomew, and the place of such legendary developments is the commemoration of the saints in the church, thus the elements occur in calendric texts, in menologia, or in synaxaria.

e) A striking riddle in the Johannine pericope, however, is still unsolved by those identifications: the question why Nathanael believes so quickly upon Jesus's word about the fig tree. Whereas modern interpreters could refer to the idea that Jesus was deliberately presented as a figure with miraculous knowledge, as a "theios aner" or the Messiah bestowed with divine wisdom, readers of all periods were puzzled by Nathanael's sudden confession of faith. The legendary expansions seek to account for this by a "natural", psychologically plausible explanation: Jesus had told Nathanael a secret that others did not know, and his identity is confirmed when Nathanael remembers that secret or is told this secret by his mother. The motif of the threatened newborn child could bring him in even closer connection with the infancy stories, which even has an impact on iconography.

Thus, narrative creativity and biblical reasoning are connected, and the stories finally point to a lacuna within the biblical text. Reception history develops in steady dialogue with the ongoing reading of the Bible, and it can help to reveal problems in the texts that are insufficiently solved by the theories of critical exegesis.

III. Who Can Nathanael Be for Readers of John?

With these reception-historical interpretations in mind, we can return to exegetical considerations. Who is Nathanael? Or who was he? And who can he be for readers of the gospel? Any identification with other known persons is speculative. He is an individual literary figure that cannot be harmonized with synoptic disciples and – like very much in John – carries symbolic overtones. Whether there is a factual disciple of Jesus behind him or whether the figure is fictitiously introduced, must remain open. What can readers find in this figure[75]?

1. Various Symbolic Overtones

Symbolic overtones of the figure must be determined independently of any identification. Nathanael is mentioned only in 1,45-49 and then only again in the final chapter (Jn 21,2) in the group of disciples, and from there, his presence in the whole Johannine narrative can be presupposed. It remains open whether he and Philip are considered disciples of John the Baptist, and how Philip (from Bethsaida) could know and thus find Nathanael (from Cana), but these lacunae in the narrative only stimulate the reader's imagination. As the figure is active in only one scene, it is impossible to discover any character development. For our image of Nathanael, we can only draw on his interaction with Jesus and on the scriptural references or allusions in the scene. The following elements can be noted: an Israelite, sitting under the fig tree, no guile (δόλος), the argument against a Messiah from Nazareth, the confession about Jesus as the King of Israel, and the Jacob typology. With varying degrees of clarity, we can articulate a few perspectives:

a) Nathanael is an "Israelite", that is, a member of the people of God, Israel. He is also a Ἰουδαῖος. But he is set apart from the Ἰουδαῖοι in John by the term Ἰσραηλίτης, which occurs only here. This is reinforced by ἀληθῶς: the difference is ultimately shown in the fact that he, unlike many other Ἰουδαῖοι, comes to faith in Jesus.

It is obvious that many later receptions were not interested in this motif, as there was no real encounter with Israelites or Jews any longer.

b) As an Israelite "sitting under the fig tree" (which was, according to rabbinic texts, a popular place for the study of Scripture), Nathanael may already be knowledgeable of the Scriptures. However, the rabbinic parallels are all late and not very helpful. But Nathanael's scriptural knowledge is also evident without those parallels: he points to the tension between Jesus's origin from Nazareth and the scriptural traditions about the origins of the Messiah. He searches the Scriptures (like the Ἰουδαῖοι

---

75. For a detailed exegesis of the text, I must refer to my commentary which is scheduled for 2023/24. See the important hints in C.R. KOESTER, *Messianic Exegesis and the Call of Nathanael (John 1.45-51)*, in *JSNT* 39 (1990) 23-34; J.A. STEIGER, *Nathanael – ein Israelit, an dem kein Falsch ist: Das hermeneutische Phänomen der Intertestamentarizität aufgezeigt an Joh 1,45-51*, in *BTZ* 9 (1992) 50-73; T. NICKLAS, *"Unter dem Feigenbaum": Die Rolle des Lesers im Dialog zwischen Jesus und Nathanael (Joh 1.45-50)*, in *NTS* 46 (2000) 193-203.

in Jn 5,39-40), but (unlike them) he comes to Jesus in response to Philip's invitation, he sees him, and believes. The personal encounter leads him to profess Jesus as Messiah, "King of Israel". It is not without reason that authors such as Ephrem, Chrysostom, and Augustine considered him a scribe, learned in the Scriptures. Yet the word ἀληθῶς was often used to contrast him against other Jews (e.g., the Pharisees).

c) With the attribute "no guile" and the Jacob typology in v. 51, Nathanael is placed into a typological relationship with Jacob. Unlike the cunning deceiver[76], Nathanael is "without deceit", but like Jacob (and Simon in Jn 1,42) he is given a name: Jacob became "Israel" (Gen 32,29; 35,10), now Nathanael is called truly an "Israelite without deceit". He bears this predicate ascribed to him (like "Cephas", the rock), as a person whose skepticism was overcome.

d) The play with δόλος opens another avenue of scriptural allusions, especially when "sitting under the fig tree" is read as an image of eschatological hope[77]. If Jesus's "seeing" is not only a miraculous view from a distance, but a foresight of the eschatological redemption, Nathanael becomes a cipher of the redemption of Israel, which comes through the Messiah and "King of Israel", who functions as a "placeholder of the rest of Israel"[78]. He is an Israelite believing in Jesus, "given by God" himself.

From there, Nathanael appears to be a serious reader of the Scriptures who is initially skeptical of the testimony of the Messiah and whose skepticism is then overcome by Jesus. The brief encounter with Jesus is a condensed account of the journey from skepticism to confession. Furthermore, he is an "Israelite" (i.e., a Jew), but he is positively distinguished from the Ἰουδαῖοι. As an "Israelite without deceit" he becomes a counterpart to Jacob the father of the Israelites. The Jacob-motif will then be strengthened again, albeit somewhat differently, in Jn 1,51.

2. *A Role Model for Jewish Readers of John*

Is Nathanael, therefore, a "role model" for Jewish readers of John? Here, numerous issues of John's relationship with contemporary Judaism or with groups of Jewish Jesus followers are at stake. How Jewish or anti-Jewish is the Gospel of John? In recent research, this issue was

---

76. Cf. Gen 27,35-36 LXX; Gen 32,24-29.
77. On this, see STEIGER, *Nathanael* (n. 75), pp. 52-57.
78. STEIGER, *Nathanael* (n. 75), p. 52, yet in John, a hope for "all Israel" (as in Romans 11) cannot be found.

turned into a rhetorical issue. It was the Jewish Johannine scholar Adele Reinhartz who, after a long journey of "Befriending the Beloved Disciple"[79], now states that John is thoroughly Jewish but at the same time anti-Jewish in its rhetoric: it urges readers to affiliate with Jesus and the group of believers, but it also inspires them to disaffiliate with the groups of the Ἰουδαῖοι, or the Pharisees[80]. Thus, Reinhartz states negatively that there is no positive role model for Jewish readers of John, as the rhetoric of the book urges them to disaffiliate with the Ἰουδαῖοι and come to a clear confession of Christ.

Whereas I follow Adele Reinhartz in most of her rhetorical observations[81], I do not follow her in her final negative verdict. It is not true that there are absolutely no positive role models for Jewish readers of John. Like Jesus himself, all the disciples are, and stay, Jewish, but for most of them, this is not explicitly noted. Nathanael is an exception. He is explicitly called an Israelite, knowledgeable in the Scriptures, and he comes to a high, fully sufficient confession (Jn 1,49). Jesus is the Messiah, the King of Israel, the Son of God. Another potential role model is Nicodemus (Jn 3,1-10), who though quite blind in the beginning, provides Jesus with a royal burial at the end of the gospel (Jn 19,39-40)[82].

3. *Exegesis and Reception History*

Who can Nathanael be for readers of John? Asked this way, the question permits a variety of answers. For Jewish readers, he could probably be a role model, a cipher of the redemption for Israelites. For other, later readers, he could be a role model for anyone following the invitation to come and see Jesus, for abandoning their skepticism in view of Jesus's word, or for the process of coming to faith through the testimony of others and through a personal encounter with Jesus.

Numerous other issues could be linked with this figure. Exegetically, they are not altogether justified. But even the utmost creativity in the development of legends like that of Nathanael under the fig tree show the fertile potentials of the biblical text. The reasoning behind the creative

---

79. See her early monograph A. REINHARTZ, *Befriending the Beloved Disciple: A Jewish Reading of the Gospel of John*, New York, Continuum, 2001.

80. A. REINHARTZ, *Cast Out of the Covenant: Jews and Anti-Judaism in the Gospel of John*, Lanham, MD, Lexington, 2018.

81. Cf. J. FREY, *"John within Judaism?" Textual, Historical, and Hermeneutical Considerations*, in J. SCHRÖTER – B.A. EDSALL – J. VERHEYDEN (eds.), *Jews and Christians – Parting Ways in the First Two Centuries CE? Reflections on the Gains and Losses of a Model* (BZNW, 253), Berlin – Boston, MA, De Gruyter, 2021, 185-215.

82. Cf. FREY, *Die Figur des Nikodemus* (n. 13).

moves may point us to questions that can be posed by any reader of the texts. Thus, reception history can create exegetical awareness for readers, and can sometimes even lead to a more nuanced understanding of the texts themselves.

Theologische Fakultät Jörg FREY
Kirchgasse 9
CH-8001 Zürich
Switzerland
Jörg.frey@theol.uzh.ch

MEHRSPRACHIGKEIT AM KREUZ

PAPYROLOGISCHE ANMERKUNGEN ZU JOH 19,20

Zu einem der vielen Unterschiede zwischen dem Johannesevangelium und den synoptischen Evangelien zählt in den Passionsberichten die Kreuzesaufschrift, der τίτλος (vom lateinischen Wort *titulus*). Nur im Johannesevangelium (Joh 19,20) findet sich der Hinweis, dass diese in drei Sprachen verfasst gewesen sei, nämlich auf Aramäisch, Latein und Griechisch (Ἑβραϊστί, Ῥωμαϊστί, Ἑλληνιστί)[1]. Selbst wenn die biblischen Handschriften in der Reihenfolge dieser Sprachen uneins sind, an der Auswahl der erwähnten Sprachen ändert eine nicht zuletzt im Mehrheitstext bezeugte Reihenfolge „Aramäisch, Griechisch und Latein", wie sie auch die lateinischen Zeugen lesen, nichts. Die explizite Erwähnung dieser mehrsprachigen Kennzeichnung ist aus mehrfacher Hinsicht interessant, wird sie doch der Erzählung gemäß in Joh 19,22 von Pilatus selbst in Auftrag gegeben: „Was ich habe schreiben lassen, habe ich schreiben lassen" (ὃ γέγραφα, γέγραφα). Anders erweist sich die Darstellung bei den Synoptikern. Mk 15,26 und Lk 23,38 erwähnen an dieser Stelle eine ἐπιγραφή mit der griechischen Bezeichnung, geben aber weder die Sprache an noch, ob es sich ihrem Verständnis nach um mehr als eine gehandelt hat. Auch wer für diese Aufschrift verantwortlich gewesen sein soll, wird nicht erörtert, es wird lediglich deskriptiv festgehalten, dass es eine solche gab. Davon weicht Mt 27,37 insofern ab, als er der Aufschrift keinen eigenen Namen gibt, dafür aber auf den Ort verweist, wo der Kreuzigungsgrund befestigt war (ἐπάνω τῆς κεφαλῆς αὐτοῦ,

---

* Der vorliegende Beitrag wurde im Rahmen des Projektes „New Testament in Translation" (KU Leuven Internal Fonds 3H190608) verfasst. Er baut wesentlich auf den Untersuchungen des FWF-Projekts zum Papyrologischen Kommentar zu den Passionsberichten (2008-2011) sowie meiner philologischen Dissertation (Salzburg 2010) auf. Die Abkürzungen der Papyruseditionen folgen der von J.F. OATES und W.H. WILLIS begründeten *Checklist of Editions of Greek, Latin, Demotic and Coptic Papyri, Ostraca and Tablets*, die in ihrer aktuellen Form online publiziert ist (<https://papyri.info/docs/checklist>). Die zusätzliche Angabe „BL" verweist auf die *Berichtigungsliste der Griechischen Papyrusurkunden* (13 Bände, diverse Verlage, 1922-2017).

1. Der erweiternde Zusatz „mit griechischen, römischen und hebräischen Buchstaben", der in einer Reihe von bedeutenden Majuskeln, Minuskeln und alten Übersetzungen in Lk 23,38 steht, lässt sich durch den Einfluss der Parallelüberlieferung erklären. Vgl. zur Stelle Institut für Neutestamentliche Textforschung Münster/Westfalen unter der Leitung von H. STRUTWOLF (Hg.), *Nestle-Aland, Novum Testamentum Graece*, 28., revidierte Auflage, Münster, Deutsche Bibelgesellschaft – Katholische Bibelanstalt, 2012.

„über seinem Kopf")[2]. Ebenso wie Mk und Lk schweigt Mt über die involvierte(n) Sprache(n). Im Gegensatz zu ihnen gibt er aber sehr wohl die Akteure an, die den Kreuzigungsgrund über dem Kreuz anbringen, nämlich „sie", die „Soldaten des Statthalters", wie sie seit Mt 27,27 Akteure des Geschehens sind. Die Kette der aktiven Handlungen, die mit der Verspottung begonnen hat und zu der in weiterer Folge das Zwingen Simons von Kyrene zum Kreuztragen, das Reichen des Wein-Galle-Gemisches, die Kreuzigung selbst und das Verteilen der Kleider gehört, findet nun mit dem Aufbringen des Kreuzigungsgrundes seinen Abschluss (Mt 27,27-37). So gesehen kann Mt mit seiner Darstellung der Soldaten des Pilatus als der Scharniertext zur Johannespassion gesehen werden, in der Pilatus für den τίτλος direkt verantwortlich gemacht wird[3].

Die im Johannesevangelium angeführte Dreisprachigkeit deckt auf einen ersten Blick sowohl die Sprache Roms und damit die Sprache der Machthaber (Latein), die römische Verwaltungssprache im hellenisierten Osten (Griechisch) und die Sprache der einheimischen Bevölkerung Judäas (Aramäisch) ab. Auf einen zweiten Blick lassen sich aber viele Fragen stellen, wie etwa die nach der Intention dieser Erwähnung. Gab es in den johanneischen Gemeinden eine Diskussion darüber? Folgt die Erwähnung der Sprachen lediglich der Erzähllogik des Textes, dass wirklich jeder und jede, die am Kreuz vorbeikam, die Möglichkeit hatte, zu verstehen, wer hier gekreuzigt war? Im Folgenden soll der Frage nachgegangen werden, wie üblich es im antiken Alltag war, Sprachen als solche zu kennzeichnen und explizit in Texten anzuführen. Denn wie auch im Text des Johannesevangeliums ist es nicht die Aufschrift selbst, die erhalten ist, sondern die Erwähnung einer solchen. In diesem Sinn sind die primären Vergleichstexte für den johanneischen Text ebenfalls solche, die über eine Mehrsprachigkeit berichten, nicht diese als Artefakt selbst bezeugen[4].

---

2. Umgekehrt ist der Text der Aufschrift in Joh 19,19 näher an Mt 27,37, wie auch J. VERHEYDEN, *I. de la Potterie on John 19,13*, in G. VAN BELLE (Hg.), *The Death of Jesus in the Fourth Gospel* (BETL, 200), Leuven, LUP – Peeters, 2007, 817-837, S. 829-830, festhält.

3. Für weitere Ausführungen, dass Joh 19,20-22 gegenüber dem synoptischen Befund sekundär ist, vgl. u.a. F. SCHLERITT, *Der vorjohanneische Passionsbericht: Eine historisch-kritische und theologische Untersuchung zu Joh 2,13-22; 11,47–14,31 und 18,1–20,29* (BZNW, 154), Berlin, De Gruyter, 2007, S. 429-432, und M. LANG, *Johannes und die Synoptiker: Eine redaktionsgeschichtliche Analyse von Joh 18–20 vor dem markinischen und lukanischen Hintergrund* (FRLANT, 182), Göttingen, Vandenhoeck & Ruprecht, 1999, S. 214-219.

4. Die Untersuchung mehrsprachiger Inschriften zur Zeit der Erzählung und zur Zeit ihrer Abfassung fällt in das Terrain anderer, wie z.B. T. CORSTEN – M. ÖHLER – J. VERHEYDEN (Hgg.), *Epigraphik und Neues Testament* (WUNT, 365), Tübingen, Mohr Siebeck, 2016.

Als Quellenmaterial werden dafür in diesem Beitrag nicht-christliche dokumentarische Alltagstexte, wie sie auf Papyrus, Ostraka und Holztäfelchen aus dem 3. vorchristlichen bis 3. nachchristlichen Jahrhundert erhalten geblieben sind, herangezogen[5]; eine Sichtung literarischer Texte wäre gesondert durchzuführen.

Im Folgenden werden zunächst solche Beispiele aus dem antiken Alltag angeführt, in denen mehrsprachige Schilder erwähnt werden (I), sodann solche, in denen die in Joh 19,20 angeführten Sprachen explizit erwähnt werden, und zwar in chronologischer Reihenfolge der papyrologischen Belege, also Aramäisch (II), Griechisch (III) und Latein (IV). Im Anschluss daran werden Texte besprochen, die eine explizite Verwendung einer Sprache oder Schrift aufweisen oder begründen (V). Vor dem Fazit steht noch ein kurzer, für das Passionsgeschehen nicht unwesentlicher Blick in die belegte Sprachverwendung römischer Truppen (VI). Ziel dieses Beitrages ist es, anhand der tatsächlich erhaltenen Alltagstexte einen Eindruck zu gewinnen, wie üblich oder unüblich der explizite Ausweis von drei Sprachen der antiken Leserschaft erschienen sein mag.

I. Erwähnungen von mehrsprachigen Tafeln in dokumentarischen Texten

Wie in der neutestamentlichen Wissenschaft bekannt, finden sich in den dokumentarischen Texten keine expliziten Hinweise auf Kreuzesaufschriften, geschweige denn mehrsprachige. Die Frage, ob es solche überhaupt gegeben hat, lässt sich hier also weder stellen noch beantworten[6]. Erwähnt werden mehrsprachige Tafeln jedoch in anderen Kontexten, und zwar bereits in ptolemäischer Zeit, allerdings keine dreisprachigen. Dennoch lassen sich aus den folgenden Beispielen Rückschlüsse auf die Intention der mehrsprachigen Beschriftung ziehen, die auch für die johanneische Darstellung relevant sein können.

---

5. Vgl. zu dieser Vorgangsweise P. ARZT-GRABNER, *Philemon* (Papyrologische Kommentare zum Neuen Testament, 1), Göttingen, Vandenhoeck & Ruprecht, 2003, S. 43-56.
6. Vgl. E. BAMMEL, *The* titulus, in ID. – C.F.D. MOULE (Hgg.), *Jesus and the Politics of His Day*, Cambridge, CUP, 1984, 353-364. Auch in den literarischen Texten ist ein eindeutiges Aufbringen von Schuldgründen am Kreuz nicht belegt, wenngleich die Bekanntgabe des Grundes für die Todesstrafe durchaus erwähnt wird; vgl. zusammenfassend zur römischen Praxis N. FÖRSTER, *Der Titulus Crucis: Demütigung der Judäer und Proklamation des Messias*, in *NT* 56 (2014) 113-133, S. 113-119. Zu Erwähnungen von Kreuzigungen in antiken Texten siehe J.G. COOK, *Crucifixion in the Mediterranean World* (WUNT, 327), Tübingen, Mohr Siebeck, 2014 (mit Hinweisen zu Kreuzesaufschriften auf den S. 110, 180 und 427).

Aus dem 2. Jahrhundert v.Chr. ist der amtliche Brief P.Genova III 92 (29. August – 27. September 165 v.Chr.) erhalten. Darin wird der Auftrag erteilt, einen königlichen Erlass, der dem Schreiben beigefügt ist, in allen Dörfern auf Griechisch und auf Demotisch bekannt zu machen. Auf dem Fragment A des Textes heißt es in den Zeilen 4-7 (mit BL X S. 279): μεταλαβόν[τ]ες | [?].ν τὸ ὑποτεταγμένον πρόσταγμα το[ῖ]ς | τε Ἑλληνικοῖς καὶ ἐνχωρίοις γράμμασ[ι] | ἔκθετε κατὰ κώμην („empfangt und veröffentlicht von Dorf zu Dorf den angefügten Erlass in griechischer und einheimischer Schrift"). Ein weiterer königlicher Erlass, und zwar einer, der den Fang bestimmter heiliger Fische verbietet, soll ebenfalls auf Griechisch und Demotisch verfasst und an den wichtigsten Orten veröffentlicht werden, wie P.Yale I 56,6-8 (100 v.Chr.) berichtet: τὸ ὑπ[ο]τετ[α]γμέν[ον πρόσταγμα] | [? μεταγρα]φὲν τοῖς Ἑλληνικοῖς καὶ ἐγχω[ρίοις γράμμασιν] | [ἐν τοῖς ἐπ]ισημοτάτοις τόποις. Es handelt sich bei diesen beiden Texten um einen von höchster Instanz kommenden Erlass. Insofern Pilatus in Judäa für den römischen Kaiser die Verwaltung übernimmt, lässt sich hier durchaus ein Vergleich zur Johannesstelle ziehen. Der Grund für die Mehrsprachigkeit ist zwar – wie auch im Johannesevangelium – nicht explizit erwähnt, doch lässt sich gerade aus dem Fischfangverbot im zweiten Beispiel annehmen, dass die Zweisprachigkeit pragmatische Gründe hat und die Umsetzung des Verbots unterstützen soll. Je mehr Menschen das Verbot verstehen, umso mehr können sich auch daran halten[7].

Auch im persönlichen Bereich werden mehrsprachige Tafeln erwähnt. So bittet ein gewisser Petesis den König in UPZ I 108 (nach 21. Oktober 99 v.Chr.) in persönlicher Angelegenheit erneut um Hilfe. Schon länger waren er und sein Haus gewalttätigen Übergriffen ausgesetzt gewesen, sodass er in einem früheren Schreiben um eine schriftliche Verordnung ersucht hat, ein Betretungsverbot für sein Haus zu verhängen. Dieser Bitte um Schutz gegen gewaltsames Eindringen wurde, wie Petesis erwähnt, stattgegeben und in Folge wurde eine weiße Tafel (λεύκωμα), die übliche Form für die „Publikation von Erlassen"[8], mit den entsprechenden Anweisungen an seiner Tür angebracht. Diese Tafel war sowohl auf Griechisch als auch auf Demotisch verfasst, wie es in den Zeilen

---

7. Bei einem erwähnten zweisprachigen Verbot legen sich natürlich Vergleiche zu Josephus' Darstellung von in der Mauer eingelassenen Betretungsverboten des Jerusalemer Tempels nahe, die auf Griechisch und Latein verfasst gewesen sein sollen (*B.J.* 5.194). Anders als in den vorliegenden Beispielen wird bei Josephus die Sprache des Landes, Aramäisch, aber nicht erwähnt.

8. U. WILCKEN in L. MITTEIS – U. WILCKEN, *Grundzüge und Chrestomathie der Papyruskunde*, I. Band, 1. Hälfte, Leipzig – Berlin, Teubner, 1912, S. XXXII.

29-30 heißt: προτεθέντος δὲ καὶ πρὸ τῆς οἰκίας μ[ου] | ἐγ λευκώμα(τι) τοῖς τε Ἑλληνικοῖς καὶ ἐνχω(ρίοις) γράμμασιν τοῦ προγράμμα(τος) („nachdem aber auch vor meinem Haus auf einer weißen Tafel in griechischer und einheimischer Schrift der öffentliche Anschlag[9] angebracht worden ist"). Trotz dieser zweisprachigen Anordnung sei sein Haus nun vom Beamten Numenios geplündert worden. Dagegen erhebt Petesis mit dem vorliegenden Schreiben Einspruch und bittet den König um Hilfe. Zwar erwähnt auch dieser Text nicht explizit, warum die Anweisungen zweisprachig erfolgt sind, doch lässt sich auch hier die Pragmatik der Verständlichkeit möglichst vieler vermuten. Darüber hinaus lässt die Zweisprachigkeit aber auch den erneuten Angriff auf das eigene Heim als noch größeres Unrecht erscheinen als zuvor, für Ausreden gibt es für den Angeklagten weniger Spielraum. Dieser Gedanke lässt sich in Erweiterung auch für die Erzähllogik im Johannesevangelium anwenden: trotz dreisprachiger Aufschrift nicht zu wissen, dass mit Jesus der „König der Juden" gekreuzigt ist, fällt schwer.

Wie bereits eingangs erwähnt, liegt der Vergleichswert der dokumentarischen Texte mit dem biblischen Befund an dieser Stelle darin, dass in beiden Texten über solche mehrsprachigen Tafeln gesprochen wird. Die Frage, ob es solche Tafeln auch wirklich gegeben hat – Funde von λευκώματα sind selbstverständlich zahlreich – und in welchem Kontext diese mehrsprachig waren, ist an die Epigraphik und Archäologie zu stellen[10].

II. EXPLIZITE ERWÄHNUNGEN DES ARAMÄISCHEN IN DOKUMENTARISCHEN TEXTEN

Das in Joh 19,20 verwendete Wort Ἑβραιστί ist bisher nur ein einziges Mal in den dokumentarischen Papyri belegt, und zwar im Privatbrief P.Yadin II 52 (September – Oktober 135 n.Chr.), der aus Judäa und den letzten Tagen des Bar-Kochba-Aufstandes stammt. Darin ersucht ein gewisser Sumaios angesichts eines bevorstehenden jüdischen Festes, wahrscheinlich des Laubhüttenfestes, dringend um die Rücksendung

---

9. Zur Bedeutung von πρόγραμμα im vorliegenden Kontext vgl. U. WILCKEN, *Urkunden der Ptolemäerzeit (ältere Funde). Band I: Papyri aus Unterägypten*, Berlin – Leipzig, De Gruyter, 1927, S. 457.

10. Dass es natürlich auch auf Inschriften Erwähnungen von Mehrsprachigkeit geben kann, zeigt etwa die Inschrift auf einer Kalksteinstele aus Herakleopolis, C.Ord.Ptol. 75-76 (12. April 41 v.Chr.). Dort wird vom Königspaar in den Zeilen 5-6 bestimmt, dass das nachfolgende πρόσταγμα in griechischer und einheimischer Schrift geschrieben und verbreitet werden soll: τοῖς τε Ἑλληνικοῖς | καὶ ἐνχωρίοις γράμμασι.

eines gewissen Agrippa. Dieser war offensichtlich mit dem Auftrag beschäftigt, Holz und Obst zu besorgen. Gegen Ende des Textes findet sich eine explizite Begründung, warum der Brief auf Griechisch verfasst wurde. In den Zeilen 11-15 heißt es: ἐγράφη | δ[ὲ] Ἑληνεστὶ (l. Ἑλληνιστὶ) διὰ | τ[ὸ ἡ]μᾶς μὴ εὑρη|κ[έ]ναι Ἑβραεστὶ (l. Ἑβραιστὶ) | ἐ[γγρ]άψασθαι („[der Brief] ist aber auf Griechisch geschrieben, weil wir keine Möglichkeit gefunden haben, dass [er] Hebräisch geschrieben wird"). Mit „Hebräisch" ist hier wohl die Schrift gemeint, wie sie auch für das Aramäische verwendet wird, nicht die Sprache selbst[11]. Bewusst wird in diesem Beitrag die passive Form des Verbes γράφω übersetzt, falls die Rekonstruktion zutreffend ist, und nicht mit einer aktiven Konstruktion, wie etwa Cotton dies tut, wenn sie die relevante Passage folgendermaßen übersetzt: „because of our inability (= we are unable) to write Hebrew (or Aramaic)". Die passive Übersetzung entspricht der üblichen antiken Praxis, dass Briefe diktiert, also „geschrieben werden". Dass dies auch im vorliegenden Fall zutrifft, zeigt der in den Zeilen 20-21 von zweiter Hand geschriebene Schlussgruß des Sumaios, der also selbst durchaus der griechischen Schrift mächtig ist. Es legt sich nahe, dass weder der Schreiber des Briefes noch der Verfasser Sumaios in hebräischer Schrift schreiben konnten. Zwar ist es wohlbekannt, dass die Fähigkeit eine Sprache zu sprechen unabhängig von der Fähigkeit ist, diese auch schreiben zu können, doch scheint dies gerade im judäischen Kontext und einem Griechisch schreibenden Sumaios zusätzlich erklärungsbedürftig. Cotton erläutert dazu plausibel: „If Soumaios is a Nabataean, which seems very likely, he would have no problem with Aramaic except for the script [...], for Nabataean Aramaic is written differently from Jewish Aramaic"[12].

Es legt sich nahe, dass auch in Joh 19,20 die hebräische Schrift und sprachlich das Aramäische gemeint ist. Im Umkehrschluss ist damit ein weiterer Beleg aus den dokumentarischen Papyri erwähnenswert, in dem

---

11. Vgl. ausführlich zur Diskussion um Aramäisch und Hebräisch, die beide in der erhaltenen Korrespondenz um Bar Kochba belegt sind, sowie zu den möglichen Leseweisen der entsprechenden Verse H.M. COTTON in P.Yadin II S. 357-360; weiters S.D. CHARLESWORTH, *Recognizing Greek Literacy in Early Roman Documents from the Judaean Desert*, in *BASP* 51 (2014) 161-189, S. 185, und klassisch J. FITZMYER, *The Languages of Palestine in the First Century* A.D., in *CBQ* 32 (1970) 501-531, S. 528-531, sowie J. BARR, *Which Language Did Jesus Speak? Some Remarks of a Semitist*, in *BJRL* 53 (1970) 9-29.

12. H.M. COTTON in P.Yadin II S. 359. Vgl. außerdem S.E. PORTER, *The Greek Papyri of the Judaean Desert and the World of the Roman East*, in ID. – C.A. EVANS (Hgg.), *The Scrolls and the Scriptures: Qumran Fifty Years After* (JSPSup, 26; Roehampton Institute London Papers, 3), Sheffield, Sheffield Academic Press, 1997, 219-316, S. 298-316.

das Wort Συριστί vorkommt. Dieses kann nämlich sowohl die syrische als auch die aramäische Sprache meinen[13]. Wie auch in den literarischen Belegen ist diese Verwendung im dokumentarischen Bereich selten[14]. Lediglich einmal und bereits im 3. Jahrhundert v.Chr. findet sich ein Beispiel, und zwar das Testament P.Petr.² I 14 (238-237 v.Chr.). Dort wird in den Zeilen 15-16 ein gewisser Apollonios erwähnt, „der auf Syrisch auch Jonathas gerufen wird" (ὃς καὶ Συριστὶ Ἰωναθᾶς | [καλεῖται]). Dieser Text ist für das Neue Testament insofern von Interesse, als er die auch für Paulus (alias Saulus) zutreffende, dokumentarisch weit bezeugte Praxis belegt, in unterschiedlichen Sprach- und Herkunftskontexten mit unterschiedlichen Namen bekannt zu sein. Für die in Joh 19,20 erwähnte Mehrsprachigkeit dient der Papyrus zumindest insofern als wertvoller Hinweis, als die gleichzeitige Präsenz mehrerer Sprachwirklichkeiten – wie in vielen anderen Texten auch – bezeugt wird, auf die auch die johanneische Erzählung verweist.

Als kurzes Zwischenfazit kann also festgehalten werden, dass die explizite und namentliche Erwähnung der hebräischen Schrift und der aramäischen Sprache in den dokumentarischen Texten äußerst selten ist. Dies mag u.a. mit der papyrologischen Fundsituation zu tun haben, da aufgrund klimatischer Verhältnisse nach wie vor die meisten erhaltenen und edierten Texte aus dem ägyptischen Bereich stammen, in der die hebräische Schrift wohl selbst in den dort belegten jüdischen Kreisen aufgrund der Hellenisierung eine untergeordnete Rolle im täglichen Leben gespielt haben dürfe. Doch darf dies angesichts der zahlreichen aus der judäischen Wüste erhaltenen aramäischen und nabatäischen Dokumente auch nicht überbewertet werden[15]. Vielmehr scheint es, dass in den erhaltenen Texten eine Erwähnung der Sprache nicht nötig war, sei es, weil diese ohnehin für Sender und Senderinnen sowie Adressaten und Adressatinnen der Texte offensichtlich war, sei es, weil angesichts des Inhalts kein Grund für einen expliziten Verweis auf die Sprache gegeben war.

---

13. Vgl. u.a. B. ROCHETTE, *Le SB VIII 9843 et la position du grec en Palestine aux deux premiers siècles après J.-C.*, in *APF* 44 (1998) 42-46, S. 44.

14. Vgl. M. ZUGMANN, *„Hellenisten" in der Apostelgeschichte: Historische und exegetische Untersuchungen zu Apg 6,1; 9,29; 11,20* (WUNT, 2.264), Tübingen, Mohr Siebeck, 2009, S. 59-60.

15. Vgl. u.a. H.M. COTTON – W.E.H. COCKLE – F.G.B. MILLAR, *The Papyrology of the Roman Near East, A Survey*, in *JRS* 95 (1995) 214-235.

III. EXPLIZITE ERWÄHNUNGEN DES GRIECHISCHEN IN DOKUMENTARISCHEN TEXTEN

Das Wort Ἑλλενιστί findet sich in dokumentarischen Texten an unterschiedlichen Stellen belegt. Bereits im 3. Jahrhundert v.Chr. wird es in der Sammlung von Gesetzen P.Rev. (259-258 v.Chr.) in Zeile 1 der Kolumne LXXXVI möglicherweise gemeinsam mit [Αἰγυπτ]ιστί erwähnt, der Kontext bleibt aber unklar. Hinweise auf Übersetzungen aus dem Demotischen ins Griechische finden sich im ägyptischen Kontext nicht nur in den Belegen der vorchristlichen Jahrhunderte, sondern auch noch in römischer Zeit. Denn gerade in Rechtsangelegenheiten war das Demotische in der römischen Verwaltung nicht mehr zulässig, demotische Urkunden mussten also, wo nötig, ins Griechische übersetzt werden[16]. Doch findet sich das Wort Ἑλληνιστί auch in anderem Zusammenhang, wie etwa im Steckbrief P.Oxy. LI 3617 (mit BL XII 151; 3. Jh. n.Chr.). Dort dient es als Identifikationsmerkmal eines ägyptischen Sklaven, der des Griechischen nicht mächtig ist, wie es in Zeile 3 heißt: Ἑλληνιστί μὴ εἰδώς. Die Mehrzahl der Belege findet sich aber im Kontext von Übersetzungen. So sind mehrere ägyptische Kaufverträge erhalten geblieben, in denen die Übersetzung aus dem Demotischen ins Griechische deutlich ausgewiesen ist. Zudem findet sich regelmäßig der Hinweis, dass die Übersetzung „soweit möglich" (κατὰ δύναμιν oder κατὰ τὸ δυνατόν) erfolgt sei (siehe dazu unten). Zu diesen Beispielen zählen u.a. UPZ II 175a (5. Jänner 145 v.Chr.), UPZ II 177 (30. Jänner 136 v.Chr.), BGU III 1002 (24. Juni 55 v.Chr.), CPR XV 1 (29. August – 27. September 3 v.Chr.) sowie CPR XV 2, 3 und 4 und SB I 5231 und 5275 (alle 21. November 11 n.Chr.). Weitere Übersetzungen von Verträgen sind in den Prozessakten P.Giss. I 36 (nach 9. November 134 v.Chr.) und P.Tor.Choach. 12 (11. Dezember 117 v.Chr.) erwähnt, auch hier findet sich der einschränkende Übersetzungshinweis „soweit möglich".

Die lokale Sprache und Schrift kann auch ohne namentliche Benennung ausgewiesen sein, wie etwa in der Formulierung ἐνχωρία γράμματα für

---

16. Siehe u.a. F. FEDER, *Der Einfluß des Griechischen auf das Ägyptische in ptolemäisch-römischer Zeit*, in T. SCHNEIDER – F. BREYER – O. KAELIN – C. KNIGGE (Hgg.), *Das Ägyptische und die Sprachen Vorderasiens, Nordafrikas und der Ägäis: Akten des Basler Kolloquiums zum ägyptisch-nichtsemitischen Sprachkontakt, Basel, 9.-11. Juli 2003* (AOAT, 310), Münster, Ugarit-Verlag, 2004, 509-521, S. 516-519; R. MAIRS, *Hermēneis in the Documentary Record from Hellenistic and Roman Egypt: Interpreters, Translators and Mediators in a Bilingual Society*, in *Journal of Ancient History* 8 (2020) 50-102, S. 55-58; S. TORALLAS TOVAR, *Linguistic Identity in Graeco-Roman Egypt*, in A. PAPACONSTANTINOU (Hg.), *The Multilingual Experience in Egypt, from the Ptolemies to the Abbasids*, Farnham, Ashgate, 2010, 17-43, S. 25-28.

das Demotische in ptolemäischer Zeit[17]. So steht in der bereits erwähnten Gesetzessammlung P.Rev. (259-258 v.Chr.) in Kolumne IX, dass bestimmte Verträge innerhalb von zehn Tagen sowohl „mit griechischen als auch mit den regionalen Buchstaben" (Zeilen 4-5) geschrieben werden sollen. Erwähnenswert ist weiters UPZ II 218 (131-130 v.Chr.), wo vom Verkauf eines königlichen Hügels berichtet wird. Diesem Verkauf geht der Auftrag des Vizethebarchen Dionysios voran, einen Bericht über Lage- und Besitzfragen anzufertigen. Der Bericht selbst wurde vom zuständigen Dorfschreiber namens Imuthes auf Demotisch angefertigt und vom Bezirksschreiber Pchorchonsis ins Griechische übersetzt. Die namentliche Nennung des Übersetzers ist in dokumentarischen Texten äußerst selten, umso bemerkenswerter ist hier der explizite Hinweis des Pchorchonsis in den Zeilen 11-13 der Kolumne II: πεπόηται (l. πεποίηται) τ[ὴν ἀναφορὰν γεγραμμένην] | τοῖς ἐνχωρίοις γρά[μμασιν, ἣν μεθερμηνεύ]ǀσαντες Ἑλληνιστί („er [der Dorfschreiber] hat den Bericht gemacht, der mit einheimischen Buchstaben geschrieben ist und den wir auf Griechisch übersetzt haben"). Eine Kopie dieses griechischen Berichtes ist, wenn auch nur fragmentarisch erhalten, dem Schreiben angefügt[18].

---

17. Zur demotisch-griechischen Zweisprachigkeit und den dazu erhaltenen Texten siehe u.a. W. PEREMANS, *Über die Zweisprachigkeit im ptolemäischen Ägypten*, in H. BRAUNERT (Hg.), *Studien zur Papyrologie und antiken Wirtschaftsgeschichte: Friedrich Oertel zum achtzigsten Geburtstag gewidmet*, Bonn, Rudolf Habelt Verlag, 1964, 49-60; B. ROCHETTE, *Sur le bilinguisme dans l'Égypte gréco-romaine*, in *CdE* 71 (1996) 153-168, S. 154-159; P. FEWSTER, *Bilingualism in Roman Egypt*, in J.N. ADAMS – M. JANSE – S. SWAIN (Hgg.), *Bilingualism in Ancient Society, Language Contact and the Written Text*, Oxford, OUP, 2002, 220-245; D.J. THOMPSON, *Literacy and Power in Ptolemaic Egypt*, in A. BOWMAN – G. WOOLF (Hgg.), *Literacy and Power in the Ancient World*, Cambridge, CUP, 1994, 67-83; W. CLARYSSE, *Bilingual Texts and Collaboration between Demoticists and Papyrologists*, in *Atti del XVII Congresso Internazionale di Papirologia (Napoli, 19-26 maggio 1983)*, Band 3, Napoli, Centro Internazionale per lo Studio dei Papiri Ercolanesi, 1984, 1345-1353.

18. Für weitere Beispiele und Überlegungen zu Übersetzern und Übersetzerinnen vgl. R. MAIRS, *κατὰ τὸ δυνατόν: Demotic-Greek Translation in the Archive of the Theban Choachytes*, in J. CROMWELL – E. GROSSMAN (Hgg.), *Scribal Repertoires in Egypt from the New Kingdom to the Early Islamic Period* (Oxford Studies in Ancient Documents), Oxford, OUP, 2018, 211-226, S. 216-218; EAD., *Interpreters and Translators in Hellenistic and Roman Egypt*, in P. SCHUBERT (Hg.), *Actes du 26ᵉ Congrès international de papyrologie, Genève, 16-21 août 2010* (Recherches et rencontres, 30), Genf, Librairie Droz, 2012, 457-462, S. 460-461. Die im administrativen Bereich weit verbreitete Anonymität der übersetzenden Person gilt indes nicht im Bereich literarischer Werke; dort werden Übersetzungen durchaus ausgewiesen und stellen mitunter einen freien Umgang mit der Vorlage dar, wie etwa in christlicher Zeit im Fall der lateinischen Übersetzung des Origenes durch Rufin, vgl. C.M. KREINECKER, *Rufinus' Translation of Origen's Commentary on Romans*, in H.A.G. HOUGHTON (Hg.), *Commentaries, Catenae and Biblical Tradition: Papers from the Ninth Birmingham Colloquium on the Textual Criticism of the New Testament in Association with the COMPAUL Project*, Piscataway, NJ, Gorgias, 2016, 227-251, mit der dort zitierten Literatur.

Die hier angeführten Beispiele sind insofern für Joh 19,20 relevant, als sie die Praxis belegen, die lokale Sprache einer hellenisierten Region und später Provinz ins Griechische zu übertragen, auch wenn es sich hier nicht um Aramäisch, sondern um Demotisch handelt. Gerade diese Texte aus dem ptolemäischen Kontext und nach der Machtübernahme 30 v.Chr. aus dem römischen Kontext bieten auch für die Situation in Judäa eine Vergleichsbasis. Sie zeigen vor allem, dass es im Alltag zumindest ein Nebeneinander der Sprache(n) vor Ort und der griechischen Verwaltungssprache gegeben haben dürfte, möglicherweise mit einer Dominanz der örtlichen Sprache zumindest in den Dörfern und ländlichen Gegenden[19]. Das Griechische hingegen war insbesondere für offizielle Akten nötig. Die Situation verschiebt sich in römischer Zeit, wie die nun folgenden Beispiele zeigen, unter denen auch die expliziten Hinweise auf das Griechische im Zusammenhang mit Übersetzungen aus der lateinischen Sprache angeführt werden.

IV. EXPLIZITE ERWÄHNUNGEN DES LATEINISCHEN IN DOKUMENTARISCHEN TEXTEN

Das Adverb Ῥωμαϊστί als solches ist zwar bisher nicht in den edierten dokumentarischen Papyri belegt, wohl aber finden sich explizite Erwähnungen der lateinischen Sprache. Dass die ältesten erhaltenen Belege für derartige Erwähnungen aus dem 2. Jahrhundert n.Chr. stammen, verwundert nicht. Denn die überhaupt ältesten Papyrustexte auf Latein selbst stammen aus der römischen Kaiserzeit. Als ältester lateinischer Alltagstext gilt der in der Wiener Papyrussammlung aufbewahrte Privatbrief

---

19. Ob es sich um ein Mit- oder Nebeneinander handelt, ist eine Frage der Interpretation, doch ist deutlich, dass vernakulare Sprachen auch in römischer Zeit nicht verschwinden, vgl. J. CLACKSON, *Language Maintenance and Language Shift in the Mediterranean World during the Roman Empire*, in A.P. MULLEN – P. JAMES (Hgg.), *Multilingualism in the Graeco-Roman Worlds*, Cambridge, CUP, 2012, 36-57, S. 47-50, und TORALLAS TOVAR, *Linguistic Identity* (Anm. 16). M. DEPAUW, *Language Use, Literacy, and Bilingualism*, in C. RIGGS (Hg.), *The Oxford Handbook of Roman Egypt*, Oxford, OUP, 2012, 493-506, S. 498, hält dazu für das römische Ägypten fest: „The progressive disappearance of the indigenous scripts from the written record could have led to the assumption that the ancient Egyptian language was disappearing quickly, like so many local languages in the Roman provinces. Linguistic interference in Greek is only one of the arguments to suggest that the indigenous language was spoken by a large majority of the population, even under Roman rule. […] But no doubt the crucial evidence is the emergence of Coptic in the third and fourth centuries". Vgl. auch S. TORALLAS TOVAR – M. VIERROS, *Languages, Scripts, Literature, and Bridges between Cultures*, in K. VANDORPE (Hg.), *A Companion to Greco-Roman and Late Antique Egypt* (Blackwell Companions to the Ancient World), Hoboken, NJ, Wiley Blackwell, 2019, 485-499, S. 488-489.

SB XX 15139 eines gewissen Diaconus an Macedo, der auf den Zeitraum 5 bis 2 v.Chr. datiert wird und aus dem „Freigelassenenmilieu" stammt[20]. Bemerkenswert im Zusammenhang mit der Sprachverwendung ist an diesem Brief nicht zuletzt, dass das Datum am Ende in Zeile 16, der 27. Epeiph (17. Juli), auf Griechisch geschrieben ist, wie dies auch in anderen lateinischen Papyri der Fall ist. Gerade in den östlichen römischen Provinzen ist die Verwendung der lateinischen Sprache der römischen Elite vorbehalten; die breite Masse der Bevölkerung wird in der landesüblichen Sprache und nicht zuletzt in der für die allgemeine Administration und Kommunikation vorgesehenen *lingua franca*, dem Griechischen, verkehrt haben. Dies belegen nicht nur tausende griechische Papyrusfunde aus der römischen Verwaltung und zudem griechische Texte aus der Wüste Judäas, sondern eindrücklich auch jene Papyri aus Ägypten, die eine griechische Übersetzung aus dem Lateinischen aufweisen[21].

1. *Lateinische Texte nach dem* ius civile

Dass ein Text überhaupt auf Latein verfasst wurde, ist außerhalb des militärischen Kontextes vor allem für solche Dokumente belegt, die nach dem römischen Recht (*ius civile*) auf Latein sein mussten[22]. Dies ist u.a. für römische Testamente, Vormundschaftsbestellungen und Ansuchen um die offizielle Zuerkennung einer rechtmäßigen Erbschaft, sogenannte *agnitiones bonorum possessionis*, der Fall.

---

20. J. KRAMER, *Vulgärlateinische Alltagsdokumente auf Papyri, Ostraka, Täfelchen und Inschriften* (APF Beiheft, 23), Berlin, De Gruyter, 2007, S. 39-46 (Zitat auf S. 41). Gesammelte Darstellungen lateinischer Dokumente finden sich z.B. in C.Epist.Lat. I-III, Ch.L.A. und C.Pap.Lat. (für diese Abkürzungen, s. Anm. *). Vgl. auch C.M. KREINECKER, *2. Thessaloniker* (Papyrologische Kommentare zum Neuen Testament, 3), Göttingen, Vandenhoeck & Ruprecht, 2010, S. 19-31.
21. Vgl. TORALLAS TOVAR – VIERROS, *Languages* (Anm. 19), S. 488: „Thus, in the Roman Period, the use of Greek in administration was pervasive". Für einen Überblick zu griechisch-lateinischen Dokumenten vgl. MAIRS, *Documentary Record* (Anm. 16), S. 10-15.
22. Vgl. A. STEIN, *Untersuchungen zur Geschichte und Verwaltung Aegyptens unter roemischer Herrschaft*, Stuttgart, J.B. Metzlersche Buchhandlung, 1915, S. 140-151 und 171. Für eine Auflistung weiterer Beispiele vgl. H. HALLA-AHO, *Bilingualism in Action: Observations on Document Type, Language Choice and Greek Interference in Latin Documents and Letters on Papyri*, in M.-H. MARGANNE – B. ROCHETTE (Hgg.), *Bilinguisme et digraphisme dans le monde gréco-romain: L'apport des papyrus latins: Actes de la Table Ronde internationale (Liège, 12-13 mai 2011)*, Liège, Presses Universitaires de Liège, 2013, 169-181, S. 170-173. Für Beispiele von schriftlichen Übersetzungen sowohl lateinischer als auch aramäischer Textpassagen vgl. P. ARZT-GRABNER – R.E. KRITZER, in P. ARZT-GRABNER – R.E. KRITZER – A. PAPATHOMAS – F. WINTER, *1. Korinther* (Papyrologische Kommentare zum Neuen Testament, 2), Göttingen, Vandenhoeck & Ruprecht, 2006, S. 179 und 406-409.

a) Ansuchen um Zuerkennung einer rechtmäßigen Erbschaft

Sowohl der lateinische Text als auch die griechische Übersetzung einer *agnitio bonorum possessionis* ist mit SB I 1010 (15. September 249 n.Chr.; hauptsächlich Latein) und SB VI 9298 (14. September 249 n.Chr.; Griechisch) erhalten geblieben. Die Notwendigkeit einer griechischen Übersetzung lässt Rückschlüsse auf die Sprachfähigkeit der Antragssteller und Antragsstellerinnen zu, liegt es doch nahe, dass der offiziell notwendige lateinische Text nicht verständlich war und für den Eigengebrauch, eventuell das eigene Familienarchiv, eine verständliche griechische Version nötig war. Die *agnitio* ist an den Präfekten Ägyptens, Aurelius Appius Sabinus, gerichtet, und zwar vom noch minderjährigen Marcus Aurelius Chaeremon, auch Didymos genannt, der mit seinem Vater Marcus Aurelius Chaeremon, alias Zoilus, als Rechtsbeistand agiert. Die entscheidende Formulierung des Ansuchens lautet in den Zeilen 4-7: *rogo domine des mihi bonorum possessi*[*o*]*ṇẹm matris meae Aureliae Hammoṇịllae Heraclaṣ* | [..] *cịvitatis Oxyrynchitarum ex ea parte edicti quae* (l. *qua*) | [*legi*]*timis heredibus · b*(*onorum*) *p*(*ossessionem*) *daturum te polliceris* („ich ersuche dich, Herr, dass du mir den Besitz der Güter meiner Mutter, Aurelia Hammonilla, Tochter des Heraclas, gibst … [aus] der Stadt Oxyrhynchos, aus dem Teil des Edikts, durch den du versprichst, dass du den rechtmäßigen Erben den Besitz der Güter geben wirst"). Der Hinweis auf die Gesetzesbestimmung, auf die sich der Antragssteller bezieht, ist für diese Schreiben üblich. Es folgen Datum in Latein und Unterschrift des Marcus Aurelius Chaeremon von zweiter Hand auf Griechisch. In weiterer Folge stehen ein Eingangsvermerk und die bestätigende Anerkennung des Ansuchens jeweils von anderer Hand geschrieben, schließlich bereits darunter beginnend die griechische Übersetzung von einer fünften Hand. Der Papyrus bricht dort allerdings bei der Nennung des Vaters des Antragsstellers ab.

Aus der auf SB VI 9298 (mit BL VII 207 und VIII 343) erhaltenen griechischen Übersetzung der lateinischen *agnitio* lassen sich aber interessante Beobachtungen zur Übersetzungstechnik und den sprachlichen Herausforderungen, mit denen sich die übersetzende Person konfrontiert sah, ableiten. So lässt sich etwa anhand des korrekten griechischen Genitivs des Namens Heraclas – Ἡρακλᾶ in SB VI 9298,12 – überlegen, ob die lateinische Form *Heraclas* in SB I 1010,5 eher darauf zurückzuführen ist, dass der Schreiber des Textes den Nominativ als indeklinabel verstand oder möglicherweise doch Probleme hatte, einen entsprechenden lateinischen Genitiv zu formulieren. Im Vergleich mit anderen erhalten gebliebenen Übersetzungen solcher *agnitiones* lässt sich darüber hinaus vermuten, dass es keine standardisierte griechische Übersetzung solcher

Texte gab, vielleicht aber eine Tendenz zu bestimmten Formulierungen. Denn die lateinische Wendung *rogo domine* wird zwar im vorliegenden Fall mit δέομαι, κύριε (SB VI 9298,9) übersetzt, in der Mehrzahl der Fälle steht allerdings ἐρωτῶ, κύριε, und zwar dem Lateinischen entsprechend ohne Akkusativ der Person[23].

Ein weiteres Beispiel für eine *agnitio bonorum possessionis* mit lateinischer Übersetzung findet sich mit P.Oxy. IX 1201 (24. September 258 n.Chr.). Der lateinische Text lautet in den Zeilen 1-3 mit BL VII 136: *Mussio Aemiliano v(ices) a(genti) praef(ecti) Aeg(ypti) | ab Aurelio Heudaemone. | rogo domine des mihi b(onorum) p(ossesionem) | [Catilli] i̯ V̯a̯ri̯a̯ni̯ patris mei* („an Mussius Aemilianus, den Vizepräfekten Ägyptens, von Aurelius Eudaimon. Ich ersuche, Herr, gib mir den Besitz der Güter meines Vaters Catillius Varianus"). Danach ist der Text unlesbar, doch lässt sich aufgrund der formelhaften Wendungen dieser rechtlichen Texte der weitere Inhalt rekonstruieren, also die Erwähnung der Gesetzesbestimmung. Wieder lesbar sind dann auf Griechisch und von zweiter Hand Datum und Unterschrift des Schreibers sowie in Zeile 11 von dritter Hand der lateinische Hinweis *ex edicto: legi* („aus dem Edikt: ich habe es gelesen"). Dann folgen auf Griechisch der Verweis auf das Edikt mit Abschnittsangabe und schließlich die Übersetzung, eingeleitet mit ἑρμηνεία τῶν Ῥωμαικῶν in Zeile 12.

Derartige explizite Hinweise darauf, dass der in einem Papyrus stehende Text eine Übersetzung ist, sind auch an anderen Stellen in dokumentarischen Papyri belegt. In der Mehrzahl der Fälle ist dabei die lateinische Vorlage erst gar nicht Teil des Textes, sodass es sich bei den griechischen Texten entweder um eine Kopie einer anderweitig vorliegenden Übersetzung handelt oder um eine Übersetzung anhand eines lateinischen Textes, der auf einem anderen und heute nicht erhalten gebliebenen Blatt gestanden haben muss. Darüber hinaus finden sich

---

23. Zur engen Anlehnung der griechischen Formulierung an die lateinische Vorgabe bei den Wörtern des Bittens *rogo* und *oro* vgl. E. DICKEY, *Latin Influence and Greek Request Formulae*, in T.V. EVANS – D.D. OBBINK (Hgg.), *The Language of the Papyri*, Oxford, OUP, 2010, 208-220. Weitere Beispiele für ἐρωτῶ, κύριε sind P.Oxy. XLIII 3108,7 (ca. 240 n.Chr.); IX 1201,15 (24. September 258 n.Chr.) mit lateinischem Text; PSI X 1101,5-6 (Jänner – Februar 271 n.Chr.); vgl. dazu R. HAENSCH, *Die Bearbeitungsweisen von Petitionen in der Provinz Aegyptus*, in *ZPE* 100 (1994) 487-546, S. 529 mit Anm. 22; weiters H. KRELLER, *Erbrechtliche Untersuchungen auf Grund der gräko-ägyptischen Papyrusurkunden*, Leipzig, Teubner, 1919 (Nachdruck Aalen, Scientia Verlag, 1970), S. 124-126; M. AMELOTTI, *Le forme classiche di testamento: Il testamento romano attraverso la prassi documentale*, Band 1 (Studi e testi di papirologia, 1), Firenze, Le Monnier, 1966, S. 60; R. KATZOFF, *The Provincial Edict in Egypt*, in *Tijdschrift voor rechtsgeschiedenis* 37 (1969) 415-437, S. 418; KREINECKER, *2. Thessaloniker* (Anm. 20), S. 76-86.

auch lediglich Erwähnungen von Übersetzungen, wie etwa die griechische Version einer Kopie der *agnitio* einer gewissen Aurelia Thermuthion in der Deklaration P.Oxy. XIX 2231 (1. Jänner 241 n.Chr.) in den Zeilen 26-28: ἀντίγραφον [ἑ]ρμη|νευθὲν Ἑλληνικοῖς γράμ|μασι κατὰ τ[ὸ] δυνατόν („in griechischer Sprache übersetzte Kopie, soweit es geht").

b) Anträge auf Vormundschaft

Explizite Übersetzungen aus dem Lateinischen finden sich auch bei Anträgen um Vormundschaft, so etwa in P.Oxy. XXXIV 2710 (17. Mai 261 n.Chr.), wo der griechische Text in Zeile 2 mit ἑρμηνεία τῶν Ῥω[μαικ]ῶν („Übersetzung des Lateinischen") beginnt. Davor könnten Buchstabenreste auf den ursprünglich vorhandenen lateinischen Text verweisen. Besser erhalten ist hier P.Oxy. XII 1466 (21. Mai 245 n.Chr.). Dort heißt es im Lateinischen in den Zeilen 1-2 (mit Ch.L.A. 1361): *Valerio Firmo praef(ecto) Aeg(ypti) ab Aurelia Arsinoe. rogo, domine, [des mihi auctorem e lege Iulia et Titia et ex s(enatus) c(onsulto) Aurel(ium)]* | *Erminum* („an den Präfekten Ägyptens, Valerius Firmus, von Aurelia Arsinoe. Ich bitte, Herr, gib mir aus der *lex Iulia et Titia* und dem Senatsbeschluss als Vormund Aurelius Erminus"). Die griechische Übersetzung beginnt in Zeile 3, wiederum eingeleitet mit dem Hinweis ἑρμηνεία τῶν Ῥω[μαικῶν]. Die Übersetzung selbst lautet dann in den Zeilen 4-5: Οὐαλερίῳ Φίρμῳ ἐπάρχῳ Αἰγύπτου πα[ρὰ Αὐρηλίας Ἀρσινόης. ἐρωτῶ, κύριε, δοῦναί μοι] | κύριον ἐπιγραφόμενον κατὰ νόμον Ἰούλιον κ[αὶ Τίτιον κατὰ δόγμα συγκλήτου Αὐρήλιον Ἑρμεῖνον] („an Valerius Firmus, Eparch von Ägypten, von Aurelia Arsinoe. Ich ersuche, Herr, mir als Kyrios Aurelius Hermeinos zu geben gemäß dem geschriebenen Iulianischen und Titianischen Gesetz"). Das lateinische *rogo* wird auch hier mit ἐρωτῶ übersetzt. Wie schon in den oben erwähnten Beispielen zu *agnitiones* finden sich auch in diesem Text Datumsangaben, Unterschriften und die Antwort auf das Ansuchen ausschließlich auf Griechisch verfasst.

c) Römische Testamente

Die griechische Übersetzung eines nach römischem Recht abgefassten Testaments findet sich in P.Diog. 9 (186-210 n.Chr.?). Gleich zu Beginn in Zeile 1 ist die Übersetzung als solche, wie nun schon mehrfach gesehen, ausgewiesen: ἀντί[γρ(αφον)] διαθήκ[η]ς Ῥ[ω]μαικῆς ἑρμηνευθείσης κατὰ τὸ [δυνατόν] („Kopie eines römischen Testaments, übersetzt soweit möglich"). Erwähnungen von Übersetzungen römischer Testamente finden sich in der Quittung BGU VII 1662 (29. September

182 n.Chr.) in Zeile 7: Ῥωμ[α]ι[κῇ διαθή]κῃ .... μεθηρμηνευμένης (l. μεθηρμηνευμένη) Ἑλληνιστὶ κατὰ τὸ δυνα[τόν] und in P.Lips. I 9 (13. Mai 233 n.Chr.) in Zeile 14 (mit BL I 204). Selten und daher besonders erwähnenswert ist der Hinweis am Ende des Testaments BGU I 326 (21. Februar 194 n.Chr.). Dort meldet sich nämlich in den Zeilen 22-23 der Kolumne II (mit BL VIII 23) der Übersetzer selbst zu Wort: Γάιος Λούκκιος Γεμινι[ανὸ]ς νομικὸς Ῥωμαικὸς ἡρμήνευσα τὸ προκείμενον ἀντίγραφον καί ἐστιν σύμφωlνον τῇ αὐθεντικῇ διαθήκῃ („ich, Gaius Lucius Geminianus, rechtmäßiger römischer Beisitzer, habe die vorliegende Kopie übersetzt und sie ist wortgetreu dem ursprünglichen Testament"). Wie bereits bei den Beispielen aus ptolemäischer Zeit festgestellt, ist eine derartige Identifikation des Übersetzers äußerst selten belegt[24].

2. Weitere Belege und Übersetzungen „soweit möglich"

Neben den angeführten Beispielen aus dem *ius civile* gibt es auf Papyrus noch weitere Beispiele für griechische Übersetzungen aus dem Lateinischen. Erwähnenswert ist der Brief BGU I 140 (4.-29. August 119 n.Chr.), mit dem Kaiser Hadrian zum Rechtsstatus von (illegalen) Soldatenkindern Stellung nimmt. Gleich zu Beginn des Briefes wird in den Zeilen 1-2 (mit BL XII 10) darauf hingewiesen, dass es sich um eine Übersetzung handelt: ἀν[τί]γρα(φον) ἐπιστ[ολ(ῆς)] τοῦ κυρίου με]θηρμ[ην]ευμένης [κατὰ τὸ δυνατ]όν („Kopie eines Briefes des Herrn, übersetzt soweit möglich"). Ein kaiserliches Reskript auf Griechisch ist in der Petition P.Harr. I 67 (ca. 150 n.Chr.?) enthalten. Dass es sich dabei um eine Übersetzung handelt, weist der Text in Kolumne II Zeile 11 aus: ἑρμηνεία Ῥωμα[ι]κῶν κατὰ τὸ δυνατόν.

Als Zwischenbeobachtung lässt sich festhalten, dass viele explizite Erwähnungen einer Übersetzung vor allem im rechtlichen Kontext den Zusatz κατὰ τὸ δυνατόν („soweit möglich") aufweisen, und zwar nicht nur im griechisch-lateinischen Bereich, sondern auch bereits im demotisch-griechischen, wie die oben angeführten Beispiele zeigen[25]. Während sich aus linguistischer Perspektive ein solcher Hinweis als das ehrliche Eingestehen jeder übersetzenden Person deuten ließe, dass perfekte Übersetzungen nun einmal nicht möglich sind, so handelt es sich in den vorliegenden Fällen doch eher um eine rechtliche Absicherung, um nicht für

---

24. Vgl. oben Anm. 18.
25. Vgl. dazu auch MAIRS, κατὰ τὸ δυνατόν (Anm. 18); EAD., *Interpreters* (Anm. 18), S. 460.

etwaige Unstimmigkeiten und Streitigkeiten, die aus übersetzungsbedingten Unterschieden in den Texten entstehen könnten, zur Verantwortung gezogen und rechtlich belangt werden zu können[26].

V. HINWEISE AUF GRÜNDE FÜR EXPLIZITEN SPRACH- UND SCHRIFTGEBRAUCH

In Joh 19,20 wird, wie eingangs erwähnt, kein Grund dafür genannt, warum die Kreuzesaufschrift in drei Sprachen, geschweige denn in den drei genannten, verfasst wird. Diese Beobachtung scheint vor dem papyrologischen Befund nicht ungewöhnlich, denn auch dort werden Gründe für eine bestimmte Sprach- oder Schriftwahl eher selten angeführt. Neben dem bereits erwähnten Brief P.Yadin II 52 (September – Oktober 135 n.Chr.) aus Judäa finden sich explizite Hinweise eher dort, wo innerhalb eines Textes zu einer anderen Sprache oder Schrift gewechselt wird. Das Beispiel der Geschwister Marepsemis und Tamarres aus der ersten Hälfte des 1. Jahrhunderts n.Chr. ist dabei besonders aufschlussreich. Diese vereinbaren in P.Tebt. II 383 (11. Juli 46 n.Chr.) ihr gemeinsames Eigentum zu teilen. Da Marepsemis selbst nicht schreiben kann, unterschreibt an seiner Stelle der Schreiber Psoiphis. Für Tamarres und ihren Vormund, in diesem Fall ihr Ehemann Psenkebkis, unterschreibt ein anderer Schreiber mit dem Namen Marepsemis. Die Begründung, die dafür in den Zeilen 57-58 angeführt wird, ist aufschlussreich: ἔγραψεν ὑπὲρ αὐτῶν Μαρεψῆμις διὰ τὸ [τὸν μὲν Ψεν]κῆβκιν Ἐγυπτυτια (l. Αἰγύπτια) γράφιν (l. γράφειν) τὴν τὲ (l. δὲ) ἄλ<λ>ην μὴ ε[ἰδέναι γράμ(ματα)] („Marepsemis hat für sie geschrieben, weil Psenkebkis die ägyptische Schrift, die andere keine Schrift kennt"). Es ist also nicht so, dass Psenkebkis gar nicht schreiben könnte, er kann es bloß nicht mit griechischen Buchstaben. Wie zum Beweis unterschreibt Psenkebkis dann in Zeile 59 mit seinem eigenen Namen auf Demotisch. Psenkebkis' demotische Unterschrift ist auch im Darlehensvertrag SB XII 11041 (20-21 n.Chr.) in Zeile 10 erhalten geblieben. Auch dort weist der Schreiber Marepsemis explizit darauf hin, dass Psenkebkis nur auf Ägyptisch schreiben könne (Zeilen 8-9: [διὰ τὸ τὸν μὲν] | Ψενκῆβκιν Αἰγύπτια γρ[άφειν]), während

---

26. „It is a formula, in the same way as the rest of the introduction to a translation [...]. The possible advantages [...] are evident: the translator is absolved of responsibility for any mistakes, and all concerned are assured that the contents of the translation have been transmitted in good faith", so MAIRS, κατὰ τὸ δυνατόν (Anm. 18), S. 216. Vgl. auch die S. 219-224 mit Beispielen für Übersetzungsfehler zwischen Demotisch und Griechisch.

der Vertragspartner, ein gewisser Marres, gar nicht schreiben kann[27]. Derartige Hinweise sind auch in anderen Texten erhalten, wie etwa im Hauskaufvertrag P.Dime III 29 (23. November 55 n.Chr.), in dem ein gewisser Apynchis in Zeile 7 auf Demotisch unterschreibt, der Rest des Textes aber auf Griechisch von einem Schreiber abgefasst wird, „weil er [= Apynchis] die griechische Schrift nicht kann, sondern Ägyptisch schreibt", wie es in Zeile 6 heißt: [διὰ τὸ μὴ εἰδέναι αὐτὸν] γράμματα [Ἑλλ]ηνικά, ἀλλὰ Αἰγύπτια γράφει[28].

Erwähnenswert sind diese Beispiele insbesondere, weil sie den Unterschied zwischen der Unfähigkeit zu schreiben (Analphabetismus) und der Unfähigkeit in einer bestimmten Schrift (und Sprache) zu schreiben, deutlich machen. Die hier angeführten Hinweise, dass jemand nur in einer bestimmten Schrift schreiben könne und daher einen Schreiber nötig habe, ist also klar von der sogenannten ἀγράμματος-Formel zu unterscheiden, die in den offiziellen Texten weit verbreitet ist[29]. Die Unkenntnis einer Schrift besagt indes noch nicht die Unkenntnis einer Sprache. Dies wird eindrücklich auch durch jene Papyri illustriert, in denen lateinischer Text mit griechischen Buchstaben und griechischer Text mit lateinischen Buchstaben geschrieben wird. Der erste Fall ist häufiger belegt und verweist darauf, dass die griechische Schrift im Mittelmeerraum, nicht zuletzt aufgrund der Hellenisierung seit dem 4. Jahrhundert v.Chr., weit verbreitet und gängiger war als die lateinische. Auch im römischen Bereich waren die griechische Sprache und Schrift nicht nur in der Oberschicht als Bildungssprache anerkannt, auch von zahlreichen Sklaven und Sklavinnen in Rom ist davon auszugehen, dass sie aus dem Osten kommend – wenn überhaupt – eher eine griechische als eine lateinische Bildung besaßen.

---

27. Vgl. J.G. KEENAN, *Two Papyri from the University of California Collection*, in E. KIESSLING – H.-A. RUPPRECHT (Hgg.), *Akten des XIII. Internationalen Papyrologenkongresses. Marburg/Lahn, 2.-6. August 1971* (MBPF, 66), München, Beck, 1974, 207-214, S. 211-214.

28. Ähnliche Beispiele finden sich im Kaufvertrag P.Gen. I² 30 (20. Juni 142 n.Chr.); im Darlehensvertrag P.Vind.Worp 10 (143-144 n.Chr.) und im Hauskaufvertrag P.Vind. Tand. 26 (28. November – 27. Dezember 143 n.Chr.). Kein expliziter Grund findet sich im nur in wenigen Zeilen erhaltenen Vertrag P.Tebt. III.2 980 (30. Oktober 153 v.Chr.) erwähnt, in dem die Unterzeichnung „in einheimischer Schrift" (Zeilen 5-6: τοῖς ἐν|χωρίοις γράμμασιν) erfolgt und der entsprechende demotische Text auf die griechische Erklärung folgt.

29. H.C. YOUTIE, *Agrammatos: An Aspect of Greek Society in Egypt*, in *HSCP* 75 (1971) 161-176; ID., *„Because They Do Not Know Letters"*, in *ZPE* 19 (1975) 101-108; ID., *ΥΠΟΓΡΑΦΕΥΣ: The Social Impact of Illiteracy in Graeco-Roman Egypt*, in *ZPE* 17 (1975) 201-221; A.E. HANSON, *Ancient Illiteracy*, in M. BEARD – A.K. BOWMAN – M. CORBIER – T. CORNELL (Hgg.), *Literacy in the Roman World* (Journal of Roman Archaeology. Supplement, 3), Ann Arbor, MI, University of Michigan, 1991, 159-198.

Berühmt ist in diesem Zusammenhang der lateinische Sklavenkaufvertrag SB III 6304 (ca. 151 n.Chr.) aus Ravenna, in dem alle Beteiligten (Käufer, Verkäufer und Bürge) zwar griechische Muttersprachler sein dürften, aber dennoch auf Latein schreiben, allerdings mit Gräzismen. Der Käufer Aischines Flavianus muss jedoch seinen Teil in den Zeilen 1-11 mit griechischen Buchstaben schreiben. Ein kurzer Auszug soll hier zur Illustration genügen (Zeilen 3-7): Αἰσχίνης Αἰσχίνου Φλαουιανὸς Μιλήσιος σκρίἰψι μὴ ἀκκηπίσσε ἃ Τίτῳ Μεμμίῳ Μοντανῷ | μίλιτε πεντήρῳ Αὐγίστι δηναρίους σεσκένἰτους βιγέντι κίνκυε πρέτιουμ πουέλλαι Μαρ|μαριαῖ βετράνε. Mit lateinischen Buchstaben sieht dies in orthographisch korrigierter Transkription so aus: *Aeschines Aeschinu Flavianus Milesius scripsi me accepisse a Tito Memmio Montano milite pentero Augusti denarios sescentos vigenti quinque pretium puellae Marmariae veteranae* („Ich, Aischines Flavianus aus Milet, Sohn des Aischines, habe geschrieben, dass ich von Titus Memmius Montanus, Soldat auf einem Fünfruderer des Augustus, sechshundertundfünfundzwanzig Denare als Preis für das altgediente Sklavenmädchen aus Marmaria bekommen habe")[30].

Der umgekehrte Fall, in dem Griechisch mit lateinischen Buchstaben geschrieben wird, findet sich z.B. in den Anweisungen eines Bankiers aus Oxyrhynchos, P.Oxy. XXXVI 2772 (28. April 11 n.Chr.?), oder im Antrag auf Überführung von Kleinvieh, P.Oxy. II 244 (2. Februar 23 n.Chr.). Das letztgenannte Beispiel ist dabei besonders aufschlussreich, denn Unterschrift und Datum sind in diesem Text auf Latein verfasst, lediglich das griechische Wort ἐπιδέδοκα („ich habe vorgelegt") wird in Zeile 16 mit lateinischen Buchstaben geschrieben (*epid*[*e*]*doca*). Dies verweist darauf, dass es sich beim Schreiber Cerinthus, dem Sklaven einer gewissen Antonia, um einen griechischen Muttersprachler handeln dürfte. J.N. Adams geht davon aus, dass er als Sklave eines Römers zwar Latein gelernt hat, nicht aber die lateinische Entsprechung für den griechischen fachsprachlichen Begriff kennt[31].

Diese Beobachtungen zum abwechselnden Schriftgebrauch sind hier der Vollständigkeit halber angeführt, für Joh 19,20 lässt sich daraus nicht ableiten, wie die jeweiligen Sprachen auf einer Kreuzesaufschrift in der Vorstellung des Verfassers und seiner Leser und Leserinnen ausgesehen haben könnten. Doch liefern derartige papyrologische Beobachtungen

---

30. Siehe KRAMER, *Alltagsdokumente* (Anm. 20), S. 129-131; J.N. ADAMS, *Bilingualism and the Latin Language*, Cambridge, CUP, 2003, S. 53-63; ID., *The Regional Diversification of Latin, 200 BC – AD 600*, Cambridge, CUP, 2007, S. 626-628. Für weitere Beispiele vgl. KREINECKER, *2. Thessaloniker* (Anm. 20), S. 19-31.
31. Siehe dazu ausführlich ADAMS, *Bilingualism* (Anm. 30), S. 306-307.

wichtige Belege, um sich des Unterschiedes zwischen Sprache und Schrift bewusst zu sein. Dies ist in Joh 19,20 insbesondere für die Verwendung von „Hebräisch" relevant, insofern es sich hier auch mit dem papyrologischen Befund begründet durchaus plausibel um die hebräische Schrift und damit die aramäische Sprache handeln kann.

VI. Kurze Beobachtungen zum Sprach- und Schriftgebrauch im römischen Heer

Zusätzlich zu den bisher angeführten Beispielen lohnt sich für die Erzählwelt der neutestamentlichen Passionsberichte mit den dort erwähnten römischen Soldaten abschließend ein kurzer Blick auf den Sprach- und Schriftgebrauch des römischen Heeres. Dabei sind es wiederum die expliziten Erwähnungen von Sprachen, die im Folgenden untersucht werden. Dass Latein im römischen Heer einen besonderen Stellenwert hatte, ist unbestritten. Der papyrologische Befund belegt dies eindrücklich, da neben den offiziellen Texten auch private Texte auf Latein aus dem militärischen Kontext und den Römerlagern des Imperiums erhalten geblieben sind. Ähnlich dem *ius civile* finden sich auch im militärischen Bereich Texte, die stets auf Latein verfasst sind, wie etwa Entlassungszertifikate (Militärdiplome), die auf Täfelchen erhalten sind[32]. Daneben ist aber auch das Griechische im Alltagsleben des Militärs als Verkehrssprache in Gebrauch. Dies scheint sogar notwendig, weil römische Soldaten aufgrund ihrer zahlreichen zivilen Aufgaben auch mit der jeweiligen Zivilbevölkerung vor Ort in Kontakt kamen[33]. In den edierten dokumentarischen Texten finden sich auch Beispiele für die bisher angeführten Phänomene, wie etwa, dass Latein mit griechischen Buchstaben geschrieben wurde. So werden die Listen von Kranken auf O.Claud. II 191 und 192 (beide 138 – ca. 154 n.Chr.) zwar auf Latein geführt, aber mit griechischen Buchstaben geschrieben. Auch Texte, in denen zwei Sprachen verwendet werden, sind zu finden. Eine bemerkenswerte Mischung aus Sprachen und Schriften steht in den Wacheinteilungen O.Claud. II 309-336 (alle Mitte 2. Jh. n.Chr.).

---

32. Vgl. Adams, *Bilingualism* (Anm. 30), S. 614, und Stein, *Untersuchungen* (Anm. 22), S. 176-177.
33. Zu den zivilen Aufgaben des römischen Heeres vgl. B. Palme, *Zivile Aufgaben der Armee im kaiserzeitlichen Ägypten*, in A. Kolb (Hg.), *Herrschaftsstrukturen und Herrschaftspraxis: Konzepte, Prinzipien und Strategien der Administration im römischen Kaiserreich: Akten der Tagung an der Universität Zürich, 18.-20. 10. 2004*, Berlin, Akademie Verlag, 2006, 299-328.

Die Einteilungen erfolgen nach demselben Schema[34]: zunächst werden unter dem Tagesdatum, geschrieben mit den griechischen Zahlenwerten, acht Namen von Soldaten auf Griechisch angeführt. Vor diese Namen werden dann von zweiter Hand entweder die römischen Zahlen von eins bis vier oder entsprechend die Zahlen mit griechischen Buchstaben geschrieben, die vermutlich die Reihenfolge der Wache angeben. Darunter folgt mit griechischen Buchstaben, aber auf Latein zunächst der Hinweis σίγνεν (für *signum*) und danach das Passwort selbst. Unter den erhaltenen Passwörtern finden sich neben Namen von Gottheiten wie *Vesta, Mars* und *Minerva* auch Propagandaworte wie *concordia, pietas, victori(a), fortuna* sowie die Wendung *salus imperatoris* jeweils mit griechischen Buchstaben.

Die griechische Sprache findet sich darüber hinaus insbesondere in der Verwaltung des Heeres belegt, wie die griechische Bestellanforderung P.Flor. II 278 (nach 24. September 203 n.Chr.) und griechische Empfangsbestätigungen, z.B. P.Oxy. IV 735 (4. September 205 n.Chr.), deutlich machen. Überhaupt scheint das Griechische für Empfangsbestätigungen im militärischen Kontext üblicher als das Lateinische[35]. Dieser Eindruck wird durch viele sprachliche Fehler im Griechischen verstärkt, die den Verfasser eindeutig als lateinischen Muttersprachler ausweisen. In Rom. Mil.Rec. 76 (5) (9.-13. Jänner 179 n.Chr.) findet sich so z.B. eine lateinische Beeinflussung gleich zu Beginn bei der Fallverwendung. Während im Lateinischen die Angabe der jeweiligen Truppe (*turma*) im Genitiv oder im Ablativ erfolgt, ist die griechische Entsprechung der Genitiv. Der Schreiber des vorliegenden Textes dürfte aber in Zeile 1 mit der Formulierung εἴλης οὐατρανα Γαλιγα τούρμα an den lateinischen Ablativ gedacht haben, obwohl der Satz noch korrekt mit dem griechischen Genitiv begonnen wurde. Korrekt müsste es ἴλης οὐετρανῆς Γαλλικῆς τούρμης lauten, also „[Soldat] der *ala Veterana Gallica*, der Truppe von N.N.". Anhand solcher und vieler weiterer Fehler in den erhaltenen Empfangsbestätigungen resümiert J.N. Adams: „Clearly some writers were familiar with Latin morphology, and they could not prevent themselves from lapsing occasionally into Latin inflections even when writing Greek. They could no doubt have used Latin instead; and on that assumption it becomes clear that in this unit there was a policy, [...] that Greek should be used for all such receipts"[36]. Derartige Beispiele machen deutlich,

---

34. Vgl. A. BÜLOW-JACOBSEN, in J. BINGEN *et al.* (Hgg.), *Mons Claudianus*, vol. 2, Kairo, Institut Français d'Archéologie Orientale, 1997, S. 166.
35. So R.O. FINK in Rom.Mil.Rec. S. 284 (für die Abkürzung, s. Anm. *).
36. ADAMS, *Bilingualism* (Anm. 30), S. 602.

dass Latein keineswegs die einzige offizielle Sprache in der Verwaltung des römischen Heeres war[37].

Diese Beobachtungen sind für die Auslegung von Joh 19,20 und den Sprachgebrauch in der römischen Verwaltung in den östlichen Provinzen insofern belangreich, als sie allzu selbstsicheren, voreiligen Annahmen Einhalt gebieten können, die Kommunikation der Soldaten hätte selbstverständlich immer auf Latein erfolgen müssen. Natürlich können die hier vorgebrachten Beispiele weder die eine noch die andere Sprachverwendung in Judäa, geschweige denn in konkreten Einzelfällen beweisen. Was die vorhandene Beleglage allerdings sehr wohl zulässt, sind Überlegungen, wie sehr die antike Adressatenschaft der Evangelien mit den römischen Gegebenheiten vertraut war und dementsprechend den Darstellungen der neutestamentlichen Passionsberichte mit differenziertem Alltagswissen begegnet ist.

VII. ABSCHLIESSENDE BEMERKUNGEN

Dieser Beitrag hat ausgehend von der Erwähnung in Joh 19,20, die Kreuzesaufschrift sei in drei Sprachen verfasst gewesen, antike Alltagstexte daraufhin befragt, ob mehrsprachige Aufschriften erwähnt werden und in welchen Kontexten die Verwendung von Sprachen, insbesondere die drei im Johannesevangelium genannten, explizit ausgewiesen wird. Die papyrologischen Belege zeigen, dass eine Dreisprachigkeit als solche bei Übersetzungen nicht explizit erwähnt wird. Dreisprachige Texte selbst sind in den Papyri selten und bestehen meist aus einer Zusammensetzung verschiedener Textteile in unterschiedlichen Sprachen, nicht aus drei Versionen desselben Textes in drei Sprachen[38]. Die Notwendigkeit in einer mehrsprachigen Welt, Texte in die eine oder andere Sprache zu übersetzen, steht indes auch für das Römische Imperium und seine Provinzen außer Frage und wird von zahlreichen expliziten papyrologischen Beispielen für Zweisprachigkeit belegt.

---

37. Für zahlreiche weitere Beispiele des gegenseitigen Einflusses zwischen Griechisch und Latein im militärischen Kontext und darüber hinaus siehe ADAMS, *Bilingualism* (Anm. 30), S. 617-623; J. KRAMER, *Die Wiener Liste von Soldaten der III. und XXII. Legion (P. Vindob. L 2)*, in *ZPE* 97 (1993) 147-158; ID., *Alltagsdokumente* (Anm. 20), S. 90-92 und 94-101; HALLA-AHO, *Bilingualism* (Anm. 22), S. 173-178.

38. Auf Griechisch, Aramäisch und Nabatäisch sind so z.B. P.Yadin I 14 und 15 (beide 11. oder 12. Oktober 125 n.Chr.), P.Hever 64 (9. November 129 n.Chr.), P. Yadin I 20 (19. Juni 130 n.Chr.) und P. Yadin I 21 und 22 (beide 11. September 130 n.Chr.) erhalten.

Die eingangs gestellte Frage, wie üblich oder unüblich der antiken Leserschaft der explizite Hinweis auf drei Sprachen erschienen sein mag, lässt sich angesichts der papyrologischen Belege mit Nuancen beantworten. Der Hinweis auf mehrere Sprachen selbst ist papyrologisch insbesondere im Kontext von Übersetzungen gegeben. Dem scheint auch die Darstellung in Joh 19,20 Rechnung zu tragen, selbst wenn der Text lediglich in einer Sprache, nämlich der Erzählsprache Griechisch steht und die Übersetzung als solche nicht erwähnt wird, wie dies an anderen Stellen im Johannesevangelium der Fall ist[39]. Daraus lässt sich indes keine eindeutige Aussage über die dem Evangelisten und seiner Adressatenschaft vor Augen stehende Ausgangs- und Zielsprache treffen. Der papyrologische Befund wäre hier um mehrsprachige, darunter auch dreisprachige, Inschriften zu ergänzen, die den Lesern und Leserinnen möglicherweise bekannt waren. Es könnte also dennoch sein, dass der Autor des Johannesevangeliums hier auf eine tatsächliche Realität der Adressaten und Adressatinnen in den Provinzen anspielt.

Ein Grund für die Mehrsprachigkeit wird in Joh 19,20 nicht genannt. Im Vergleich mit den Papyri lassen sich indirekte Beobachtungen anführen, vor allem pragmatische Gründe legen sich nahe: je mehr Sprachen verwendet werden, umso größer ist die Wahrscheinlichkeit, dass der Text auch von möglichst vielen verstanden wird. Dies scheint gerade bei den oben im Text angeführten Verboten (Fischfang, Hausbetretungsverbot) plausibel. Im Licht des Johannesevangeliums könnte damit über die eigentliche Erzählung eine Anspielung auf die Verbreitung des Christusglaubens gegeben sein, denn zumindest ist durch die drei erwähnten Sprachen erzähltechnisch das gesamte Judentum, der gesamte hellenistische Raum und die römische Herrschaft eingeschlossen: sie alle werden darüber „informiert" – sollten es zumindest in einer Sprache verstehen können, dass Jesus ein König ist. Nicht notwendig kerygmatisch erweist sich diese Verbreitung allerdings, wenn man abseits der Erzähllogik den Unterschied zwischen den Formulierungen „König der Juden" aus römischer Perspektive und „König Israels" aus jüdischer Perspektive bedenkt[40].

---

39. So steht in Joh 1,38 ῥαββί, ὃ λέγεται μεθερμηνευόμενον διδάσκαλε („Rabbi, das heißt übersetzt ‚Lehrer'") und in Joh 1,41 heißt es εὑρήκαμεν τὸν Μεσσίαν, ὅ ἐστιν μεθερμηνευόμενον χριστός („wir haben den Messias gefunden, das ist übersetzt ‚Christus'").

40. Vgl. u.a. R. BROWN, *The Death of the Messiah: From Gethsemane to the Grave* (The Anchor Bible Reference Library), New York – London – Toronto – Sydney – Auckland, Doubleday, 1994, S. 962-968. Zur Darstellung Jesu als *Caesar* vgl. L.J. HUNT, *Jesus Caesar: A Roman Reading of the Johannine Trial Narrative* (WUNT, 2.506), Tübingen, Mohr Siebeck, 2019, S. 187-210 (und S. 289-296 zur Darstellung in Joh 19,20).

Für Joh 19,20 belangreich ist außerdem der aus den Papyri an mehreren Stellen deutliche Unterschied zwischen Schrift und Sprache. Dass ein Name sowohl die Schrift als auch die damit geschriebenen Sprachen bezeichnen kann, wird nicht zuletzt bei den wenigen Beispielen zu Ἑβραϊστί und Συριστί deutlich. Dasselbe gilt, wie die oben angeführten Beispiele zeigen, für explizite Hinweise auf die „Buchstaben" (γράμματα), seien es einheimische, griechische oder lateinische. Auch sie können sowohl die Schrift als auch die Sprache meinen. Darüber hinaus liefern Papyri selbst den Hinweis darauf, dass man eine Sprache auch mit anderen Buchstaben schreiben kann, wie etwa das Lateinische mit griechischen Buchstaben. Damit lässt sich noch einmal auf die mögliche Erzählintention in der Johannespassion verweisen, dass möglichst viele den Text am Kreuz zur Kenntnis nehmen sollen. Denn wenn die Unkenntnis einer Schrift nicht notwendigerweise die Unkenntnis einer Sprache bedeutet, erhöht sich mit einer dreifachen Beschriftung des Kreuzes in der Erzähllogik die Chance, dass noch mehr Menschen den Text verstehen können. Immerhin heißt es in Joh 19,20 ja explizit, dass aufgrund der Lage viele Juden vorbeikamen und das Schild zur Kenntnis nahmen. Möglicherweise ist hier ein Hinweis enthalten, dass sowohl die Aramäisch sprechenden als auch die Griechisch sprechenden Juden und Jüdinnen der Diaspora den Text zur Kenntnis nehmen konnten. Denn eines ist vom papyrologischen Befund her deutlich: mehrere Sprachen braucht es dort, wo eben nicht vorausgesetzt ist, dass alle Menschen dieselbe Sprache verstehen. So gesehen scheint es naheliegend, dass dem Verfasser für seine Passionserzählung eine Wirklichkeit vor Augen stand, in der eben nicht alle Griechisch – geschweige denn Latein oder Aramäisch – konnten und daher mehrere Sprachen nötig waren.

Wie der Befund aus Ägypten zeigt, wird es in den römischen Provinzen durchaus üblich gewesen sein, auf Übersetzungen zwischen der einheimischen Sprache und der Verkehrssprache Griechisch zu stoßen. Interessant ist für Joh 19,20, dass dies vor allem in rechtlichen Kontexten geschieht, zwischen Demotisch und Griechisch insbesondere bei Verträgen. Doch auch Übersetzungen ins Griechische aus dem Lateinischen sind vor allem im rechtlich relevanten Kontext belegt. Dort, wo es offiziell wird und möglicherweise rechtliche Konsequenzen mit bestimmten Formulierungen in einer Übersetzung verbunden sind, findet sich daher auch der absichernde Hinweis, dass eine Übersetzung mit Vorbehalt, eben „soweit möglich" erfolgt. Hier bietet sich zumindest in der Erzähllogik ein Anknüpfungspunkt mit Joh 19,20. Denn wenn insbesondere dem Lateinischen dieser „Hauch" des Offiziellen und Rechtlichen anhaftet, dann wird auch dem Hinweis in den Evangelien, dass es sich bei der Kreuzesaufschrift um den „Grund" für die römische Kreuzigung handelt, zumindest in der Erzählung (und unabhängig von der historischen Frage nach Kreuzigungsgründen) zusätzliches, offizielles Gewicht verliehen.

Eine weitere Gemeinsamkeit des Bibeltextes mit dem Befund der papyrologischen Texte ist darüber hinaus, dass die Person, die die eigentliche Übersetzung angefertigt hat, im Regelfall und mit einigen Ausnahmen nicht namentlich angeführt ist. Auch in Joh 19,20 wird davon auszugehen sein, dass Pilatus in der Vorstellung der Erzählung weder die Tafel selbst beschrieben (kausativ-intransitive Verbalkonstruktion) noch den darauf geschriebenen Text selbst übersetzt hat.

Noch einmal sei abschließend betont, dass die dokumentarischen Texte nicht dazu verwendet werden können, einen bestimmten historischen Verlauf der Passion Jesu zu belegen. Sie geben keine Auskunft über die Sprachverwendung zwischen Pilatus, den Soldaten, Einzelpersonen und der Bevölkerung vor Ort. Vielmehr zeigen die erhaltenen Alltagstexte eine Bandbreite an Möglichkeiten, die für die johanneische Passionserzählung zusätzliche Tiefe und Interpretationsmöglichkeiten eröffnen.

KU Leuven   Christina M. KREINECKER
Faculty of Theology and Religious Studies
Sint-Michielsstraat 4/3101
BE-3000 Leuven
Belgium
christina.kreinecker@kuleuven.be

ΜΑΡΙΑΜ OR ΜΑΡΙΑ IN JOHN 20,16?

A PLEA FOR *DOCTA IGNORANTIA*

I. Introduction

In a recent article on Jn 20,16, Michael Peppard discusses the text-critical problem of the name which Jesus uses in his address to the woman he meets at the tomb, namely Μαριαμ or Μαρια[1]. Peppard opts for Μαριαμ as the "oldest and most reliable reading"[2]. He laments the "paucity of scholarly attention to this feature of such a famous story"[3]. He suggests two reasons for this lack of attention, the first being that modern translations do not distinguish when the Greek text uses Μαριάμ or Μαρία and render both forms with the same name, for instance, "Mary" in English. According to Peppard, the second reason is a likely "subconscious misogynist bias"[4] which he claims resulted in much more scholarly attention for ραββουνι in Jn 20,16 than for Μαριάμ. In order to make up for this, suggesting that it is now "Mary Magdalene's turn" for attention, Peppard complements his text-critical discussion with a section in which he proposes four possible interpretations of the meaning of the name Μαριάμ in 20,16.

In this contribution, we shall enter into critical dialogue with the views proposed by Peppard, after having analysed the position of J. Duncan M. Derrett on the same issue. In a second part, we shall undertake our own investigation of the text-critical problem of the readings Μαριαμ and Μαρια in Jn 20,16 and the possible theological implications. It is a great honour to offer this study to my Leuven colleague Professor Joseph Verheyden on the occasion of his 65th birthday.

II. A Critical Dialogue with J. Duncan M. Derrett and Michael Peppard

Some basic ingredients of the positions of Derrett and Peppard have long been known and controversially discussed in biblical scholarship. Before we turn to their specific contributions, we shall give a brief and selective overview of what their predecessors said on the subject.

---

1. M.P. Peppard, *Mary Magdalene's Turn: Text Criticism and Reception History of John 20,16*, in *ETL* 96 (2020) 563-581, pp. 567-569.
2. *Ibid.*, p. 568.
3. *Ibid.*
4. *Ibid.*, p. 569.

1. *Highlights of the Discussion that Preceded Derrett's and Peppard's Studies*

The oldest codices[5] of the Greek text of the NT attest to the variation Μαριαμ and Μαρια no matter to which "Mary" they refer. In some of them, Μαριαμ is more frequent (e.g., ℵ01) and in others Μαρια (e.g., D05). In older studies, scholars claimed that Μαριαμ was reserved for the mother of Jesus, whereas the other Marys in the NT were referred to as Μαρια[6]. This is the case, for instance, in codex E07, in the text of Stephanus of 1550 and in the Byzantine textual tradition[7]. But looking at earlier manuscripts we realise that things are more complicated.

First of all, the name Μαριαμ does not fit in any paradigm of the Greek declensions and is usually considered as indeclinable[8]. This is certainly the case in the LXX and Philo[9]. It is, however, generally agreed with regard to the New Testament occurrences that the genitive Μαριας is not only used as the genitive of Μαρια, but also of Μαριαμ[10]. In the oldest manuscripts, we find no instances where a form that can grammatically be identified as a genitive reads Μαριαμ. A certain amount of ambiguity remains, as it is not always clear whether Μαριας is intended as the genitive of Μαρια or Μαριαμ (see Mk 6,3; cf. also Mt 1,16.18.20 and 2,11). The situation is also somewhat ambiguous concerning the dative. In Lk 2,5 the oldest codices except D read Μαριαμ where a dative is required because of the preposition σύν. In Mk 16,9, the dative Μαρια seems to be used as the dative of Μαρια in A D E, since in these manuscripts Mary Magdalene is referred to as Μαρια in the preceding references to her in 15,40.47 and 16,1 (cf., however, C which reads Μαριαμ in 16,9 even though all the other references to Mary Magdalene that precede have Μαρια). However, in Acts 1,14 both ℵ and A clearly use

---

5. In this essay, when we use the expression "oldest codices" we include ℵ A B C D05 and E07.

6. See, for instance, O. BARDENHEWER, *Der Name Maria: Geschichte der Deutung desselben* (Biblische Studien, 1/1), Freiburg i. Br., Herder, 1895, pp. 8-10.

7. See M.A. ROBINSON – W.G. PIERPONT (eds.), *The New Testament in the Original Greek: Byzantine Textform 200*, Southborough, MA, Chilton Books, 2005.

8. F.J.A. HORT, *Notes on Orthography*, in B.F. WESTCOTT – F.J.A. HORT, *The New Testament in the Original Greek: Introduction, Appendix*, Cambridge – London, Macmillan, 1882, Appendix, 141-173, p. 156; A.T. ROBERTSON, *A Grammar of the Greek New Testament in the Light of Historical Research*, Nashville, TN, Broadman, ⁴1923, repr. 1934, p. 259.

9. See the use of Μαριαμ as an indeclinable noun in the LXX where it occurs in the nominative, dative and accusative. Similarly, in the works of Philo, only the form Μαριάμ occurs. It is used as a genitive in *Leg* 1.76, 2.66 and *Contempl.* 87.

10. Cf. J.H. MOULTON – W.F. HOWARD, *A Grammar of New Testament Greek*. Vol. 2: *Accidence and Word-Formation*, Edinburgh, T&T Clark, 1929, p. 144: "In the gen. Μαρίας stands 'virtually without variation' (WH) for all the women so named". The reference "WH" is to HORT, *Notes on Orthography* (n. 8), p. 156.

Μαρια as the dative of Μαριαμ since in the gospels these two codices refer to the mother of Jesus as Μαριαμ. In the case of the accusative, the textual tradition distinguishes between Μαριαν as the accusative of Μαρια and Μαριαμ as the accusative of Μαριαμ. We can summarise the declension of Μαριαμ and Μαρια as follows:

case	Μαριαμ	Μαρια
nom.	Μαριαμ	Μαρια
voc.	Μαριαμ	Μαρια
gen.	Μαριας	Μαριας
dat.	Μαριαμ and Μαρια	Μαρια
acc.	Μαριαμ	Μαριαν

Table 1: Declension of Μαριαμ and Μαρια

A second factor that has made recent scholars more cautious is the fact that the oldest codices hardly ever refer to one Mary exclusively with Μαριαμ or exclusively with Μαρια. The following chart is intended to illustrate this. In general, we count the genitive Μαριας with either Μαριαμ or Μαρια if the context allows a clear association. We list the genitive Μαριας of Mk 6,3 separately since this is the only reference to the mother of Jesus by name in the Gospel of Mark. We only list the four Marys that are referred to more than once in the New Testament[11].

Marys	ℵ01	A02	B03	C04	D05	E07
the mother of Jesus Mk 6,3	Μαριαμ 18 Μαριας 1 Μαρια 0	Μαριαμ 13 Μαριας 2 Μαρια 0	Μαριαμ 13 Μαριας 1 Μαρια 5	Μαριαμ 13 Μαριας 1 Μαρια 1	Μαριαμ 7 Μαριας 1 Μαρια 11	Μαριαμ 17 Μαριας 1 Μαρια 0
Mary Magdalene	Μαριαμ 8 Μαρια 5	Μαριαμ 2 Μαρια 13	Μαριαμ 4 Μαρια 9	Μαριαμ 4 Μαρια 3	Μαριαμ 0 Μαρια 13	Μαριαμ 0 Μαρια 12
the mother of James (and Joseph/Joses)	Μαριαμ 0 Μαρια 7	Μαριαμ 1 Μαρια 6	Μαριαμ 1 Μαρια 6	Μαριαμ 2 Μαρια 5	Μαριαμ 1 Μαρια 5	Μαριαμ 0 Μαρια 7
Mary of Bethany	Μαριαμ 1 Μαρια 10	Μαριαμ 1 Μαρια 10	Μαριαμ 10 Μαρια 1	Μαριαμ 2 Μαρια 4	Μαριαμ 4 Μαρια 7	Μαριαμ 0 Μαρια 9

Table 2: Overview of the uses of Μαριαμ and Μαρια for respectively the same Mary in the NT gospels (see also below Appendix)[12]

11. There are three Marys in the New Testament who are only mentioned once: Mary of Clopas in Jn 19,15, Mary, the mother of John Mark in Acts 12,12 and Mary in Rom 16,6.
12. See below, pp. 386-388.

As we can see, manuscripts of the New Testament gospels regularly refer to the same woman with both Μαριαμ and Μαρια in different parts of the same book with no obvious reason being detectable for the variations[13]. This differs from the LXX and Philo where Μαριάμ is found exclusively (6×)[14] and also from Josephus who uses Μαριάμμη (47× in *A.J.* and 25× in *B.J.*)[15]. Μαρία occurs only once, but in reference to a different person (*B.J.* 6.201).

The most widespread explanation of the parallel use of Μαριάμ, Μαρία and Μαριάμμη is that Μαριάμ is the Greek transcription of the Hebrew name מרים and that Μαρία and Μαριάμμη are attempts to Graecise the name[16]. Since Greek nouns in the nominative singular cannot end in -μ[17], the action of Graecising Μαριάμ had two options, namely making it into a first declension noun ending in -α by dropping the μ or to make it into a first declension noun ending in -η by adding -μη. The discovery of inscriptions with the Hebrew name מריה raised questions as to whether Μαρία is truly the Graecised or Hellenised form of Μαριάμ. In 1960, BDF §53 concludes: "It is no longer correct to say that Μαρία is a Hellenized form since Jerusalem inscriptions have מריה"[18]. Μαρία could thus simply be the transcription of the Hebrew form מריה which is

---

13. Cf. MOULTON – HOWARD, *A Grammar of New Testament Greek* (n. 10), p. 145, who with regard to the representation of the name of Mary Magdalene in the manuscripts, state: "it will be clear, however, that there are great inconsistencies, and a rule seems unattainable".

14. P. BORGEN – K. FUGLSETH – R. SKARSTEN, *The Philo Index: A Complete Greek Word Index to the Writings of Philo of Alexandria* (UniTrel Studieserie, 25), Dragvoll – Trondheim, Religionsvitenskapelig Institutt, 1997, p. 193, *s.v.* Μαριάμ: *Leg.* 1.76, *Leg.* 2.66, *Leg.* 3.103, *Agr.* 80, 81, *Contempl.* 87.

15. However, no one seems to have investigated this question in the extant manuscripts of these text corpora to see whether there are any variations.

16. F. BLASS, *Grammatik des neutestamentlichen Griechisch*, Göttingen, Vandenhoeck & Ruprecht, ²1902 (= ³1911), §10.2, p. 31: "teils zu Μαρία hellenisiert". This reference to an alleged Hellenisation was still found in the eleventh edition in 1961. Cf. also ROBERTSON, *Grammar of the Greek New Testament* (n. 8), p. 259: "In the Aramaic as in the Hebrew probably all were called Μαριάμ. Μαρία is merely the Hellenized form of Μαριάμ".

17. The explanation for this is that in Indo-European the nominative singular of nouns ended in -s, -ā, -os, -is, or -us, but never in -m. See C.D. BUCK, *Comparative Grammar of Greek and Latin*, Chicago, IL, University of Chicago Press, 1933, repr. 1959, p. 172.

18. This passage obviously influenced the formulation in R.E. BROWN, *The Gospel according to John XIII–XXI: A New Translation with Introduction and Commentary* (AB, 29A), Garden City, NY, Doubleday, 1970, pp. 990-991: "… in Jesus' time *Mryh* also appears in inscriptions, so that it is no longer correct to claim that *Maria* is necessarily a Hellenized form (BDF, §53³)". The German text expresses a bit more hesitation. See BDR (¹⁷1990), §53, n. 12: "Ob mit Μαρία eine Hellenisierung vorliegt, ist nunmehr unsicher mit Bezug auf die Form מריה in den Inschriften von Jerusalem". We were unable to verify in which German edition this statement appeared for the first time.

seen as a development of מרים. E.Y. Kutscher to whose work BD and BDF refer for support concludes his linguistic analysis saying that "מריה, Μαρια arose through backformation"[19] from מרים. It seems difficult to know whether there is a difference in meaning between מרים and מריה[20].

We now turn to the representation of the name of Mary Magdalene in the five passages where she is mentioned in John: 19,25; 20,1.11.16.18. Where John's text speaks of Mary Magdalene, the editions of Erasmus (*Novum Instrumentum omne*, 1516[21]), Stephanus (1550), Bengel (1734), Griesbach (1774; ²1796) and Wettstein (1751) all read Μαρια. Scholars obtained easier access to Codex Vaticanus in the first published edition of 1857/1859 and the facsimile edition of 1868/1872. The edition of Tregelles of 1857-1879[22] obviously was one of the first to opt for the readings of Codex Vaticanus, namely Μαρια in Jn 19,25; 20,1.11 and Μαριαμ in 20,16.18. The same readings were chosen in the edition by Westcott-Hort of 1881[23] which exerted much influence in exegetical scholarship of the subsequent years because it "was one of the key texts used in the creation of the original Nestle text"[24].

Since then, some scholars have discussed the readings of the name of Mary Magdalene text-critically, but above all semantically, in some cases theologically. From a text-critical point of view, the authority of Codex Vaticanus is mostly followed blindly in scholarly discussions. As for the meaning of Μαριάμ, it is usually assumed without further discussion that it corresponds to the Hebrew or more precisely Aramaic form of the name in agreement with the Magdalene's immediate reply ραββουνι

---

19. E.Y. KUTSCHER, *The Language of the 'Genesis Apocryphon': A Preliminary Study*, in C. RABIN – Y. YADIN (eds.), *Aspects of the Dead Sea Scrolls* (Scripta Hierosolymitana, 4), Jerusalem, Hebrew University Magnes Press, 1958, 1-35, p. 24, n. 118.

20. It is unclear what the following suggestion of BROWN, *John*, vol. 2 (n. 18), p. 991, is based on: "'Maria' may have been an informal designation for women named 'Mariam'".

21. In the five passages at issue, all later editions of Erasmus (1519, 1521, 1527, 1535) too read Μαρία; see A.J. BROWN (ed.), *Opera omnia Desiderii Erasmi Roterodami*, vol. VI-2, Amsterdam, Elsevier, 2001, critical apparatus *ad locos*.

22. S.P. TREGELLES, *The Greek New Testament, Edited from Ancient Authorities, with the Latin Version of Jerome, from the Codex Amiatinus*, London, Bagster – Stewart, 1857, p. 237.

23. B.F. WESTCOTT – F.J.A. HORT, *The New Testament in the Original Greek: Text*, Cambridge – London, Macmillan, 1881. See also HORT, *Notes on Orthography* (n. 8), p. 156, and B.F. WESTCOTT, *The Gospel according to St. John: The Authorized Version with Introduction and Notes*, repr. Grand Rapids, MI, Eerdmans, 1958, p. 292, at Jn 20,16: "Jesus 'called her by name', *Mary* (Μαριάμ); and in that direct personal address awakes the true self".

24. M.W. HOLMES, *The Greek New Testament: SBL Edition*, Atlanta, GA, SBL; Bellingham, WA, Logos Bible Software, 2010, Introduction, p. ix. See the first edition of E. NESTLE (ed.), *Novum Testamentum Graece*, Stuttgart, Württembergische Bibelanstalt, 1898.

where a parenthesis specifies the language as Ἑβραϊστί (20,16). The meaning is then sought in the postulated linguistic correspondence Μαριάμ – ραββουνι which is interpreted as recourse to the "original [Hebrew/Aramaic] language" in an otherwise Greek text. The effects of this are interpreted as realism[25], authenticity[26] or intimacy[27]. We note, however, that most recent commentaries are completely silent as to the Greek form of the name for "Mary" in 20,16[28] or, as in the case of Brown, discourage the above-mentioned conclusions and plead ignorance in the matter[29].

In this first subsection of the present study we have given some background information on the exegetical issues connected to the name of Mary Magdalene in the New Testament. It became clear that the issues related to this name and especially to the form of the name in Jn 20,16 have been discussed for over a hundred and fifty years. It seems that in the past thirty years many interpreters have either not been aware of the problem of the variation in Mary Magdalene's name in John, or they have reached the conclusion that it is insignificant for the interpretation of Jn 20,16. In what follows we shall discuss the positions of two notable exceptions.

2. *The Typological Interpretation of J. Duncan M. Derrett: Mariam as the New Miriam*

Some thirty years ago J. Duncan M. Derrett devoted a short study to the question of the form of the name in Jn 20,16[30]. He discussed the

25. S. VAN TILBORG, *Johannes: Belichting van het bijbelboek*, Boxtel, KBS; Leuven, VBS; Brugge, Tabor, 1988, p. 218: "... het uitwisselen van de namen, Mariam, Rabboeni, in het Hebreeuws dat een touch van realisme bewerkt".

26. A. TASCHL-ERBER, *Maria von Magdala – Erste Apostolin? Joh 20,1-18: Tradition und Relecture* (Herders Biblische Studien, 51), Freiburg i.Br. – Basel – Wien, Herder, 2007, p. 136: "Die aramäischen Worte (vgl. auch die Namensform Μαριάμ) sollen der Szene möglichste Authentizität verleihen".

27. F.J. MOLONEY, *The Gospel of John* (SP, 4), Collegeville, MN, Liturgical Press, 1998, p. 528: "The name Jesus calls Mary and her response are Greek transliterations of Aramaic, although the narrator explains that it is Hebrew. There is a level of intimacy implied by the recourse to an original language in both the naming and the response".

28. This applies, e.g., to the commentaries of J. Becker, J. Beutler, H. Ridderbos, R. Schnackenburg, U. Schnelle, H. Thyen, M.M. Thompson and J. Zumstein. A favourable exception is C.K. BARRETT, *The Gospel according to St John*, London, SPCK, ²1978, p. 564, at Jn 20,16: "Μαριάμ. The name alone is sufficient to convince Mary of the identity of the speaker. The good shepherd calls his own sheep by name and they recognize his voice (10.3)".

29. BROWN, *John*, vol. 2 (n. 18), pp. 990-991.

30. J.D.M. DERRETT, *Miriam and the Resurrection (John 20,16)*, in *Bibbia e Oriente* 33 (1991) 211-219, reprinted in *Downside Review* 111 (1993) 174-186 and in ID., *Miriam and the Resurrection (John 20,16)*, in ID., *Studies in the New Testament*. Vol. 6: *Jesus*

text-critical and the theological dimensions of the topic. In the text-critical discussion, Derrett briefly alludes to the external attestation stating that the reading Μαριαμ in Jn 20,16 is "supported by one papyrus, six uncial manuscripts, and supporting minuscules"[31]. Following Westcott and Hort[32], Derrett finds it particularly significant that both Codex Sinaiticus and Codex Vaticanus read Μαριαμ in Jn 20,16 as we can see in the statement that concludes his text-critical discussion: "But six uncials including *both* Sinaiticus and *B* raise a presumption of accuracy. And all *reliable* evidence points to Mary Magdalene being in reality the *only Mariam* in John, and only at 20, 16 with, possibly, 20, 18"[33]. Derrett can only claim Mary Magdalene to be "the *only Mariam* in John" because he argues that Mary of Bethany and Mary of Clopas are referred to as Μαρια in the strongest textual witnesses. However, one problem of Derrett's argument is that some of the uncial witnesses to which he refers not only read Μαριαμ in 20,16.18 but also in 20,11 (cf. 𝔓[66]) or in all the references to Mary Magdalene in John (cf. ℵ). Derrett tries to solve this problem by explaining their use of Μαριαμ as due to "the tendency to harmonize"[34]. But to overcome Derrett's exclusive reliance on numbers and implicitly on age, the external evidence needs to be subjected to a much more thorough review. We shall examine the external evidence for the use of Mary's names once again in section III of this essay.

Turning to internal criticism we see in Derrett's presentation a few arguments of intrinsic probability even though he does not use this terminology. First, he claims that by not mentioning the name of the mother of Jesus, the fourth evangelist prepares for the focus on Mary Magdalene as the new prophetess Miriam[35]. The problem here is that Derrett underestimates the importance of Mary of Bethany in the Gospel of John whose name occurs nine times compared to the five occurrences of Mary Magdalene's name. When Derrett claims "John ... reserves the name 'Mary' for Mary Magdalene"[36], he obviously does not respect the evidence. A second argument of internal evidence in favour of the reading Μαριαμ in 20,16 is its overtone of formality which it shares with ραββουνι. Pointing to ὑμεῖς φωνεῖτέ με· ὁ διδάσκαλος, καί· ὁ κύριος, καὶ καλῶς

---

among Biblical Exegetes, Leiden, Brill, 1995, pp. 160-172. In this essay, we quote from the publication in *Downside Review*.
31. *Ibid.*, p. 177.
32. See Derrett's own reference to this on pp. 176-177.
33. *Ibid.*, p. 178.
34. *Ibid.*, p. 177.
35. See *ibid.*, p. 176.
36. *Ibid.*

λέγετε· εἰμὶ γάρ (Jn 13,13), Derrett holds that Jesus' relationship with his disciples is characterised by a certain formality which he also perceives in Mary's address: ραββουνι. This results in Derrett's question: "If Mary replies to Jesus in a formal style worthy of being called 'in Hebrew', how will this affect the one startling word Jesus utters to her, 'Mary'?"[37]. Here, Derrett's *a priori* is that ραββουνι expresses formality. Others have claimed that ραββουνι expresses familiarity and that the dialogue Μαριαμ – ραββουνι is not devoid of a certain intimacy[38]. I conclude that the internal argument in favour of the reading Μαριαμ is rather weak in every respect.

Derrett starts his theological interpretation of Μαριαμ in Jn 20,16 with a general (unsubstantiated) claim: "All Maries and Miriams recall Miriam (*Miryam*), the sister of Moses"[39]. He does not seem to realise that with this claim he undermines his text-critical discussion. In fact, if all Marys (I suppose in the New Testament) recalled the biblical "Miriam", then this would be true, even if the preferred reading in Jn 20,16 was Μαρια. Subsequently, Derrett starts describing the parallels he postulates between Miriam and Mary Magdalene focusing on Ex 2,3-8. He compares Moses in a basket with a cover on the Nile to the tomb from which the stone had been removed. He sees a parallel between Moses being rescued from the Nile and Jesus being raised from the dead. The role of Miriam was to watch the basket, wait, report, and to "act as intermediary"[40]. In a daring comparison Derrett says about Mary Magdalene: "So a Miriam was required to report on the movement of the body of the Second Redeemer, from a tomb from which the cover had already been removed"[41]. Derrett also focuses on Miriam as a prophetess according to Ex 15,20-21 and Num 12,2. Since in Derrett's opinion the evangelist put the name Μαριάμ into Jesus' mouth when he addressed Mary Magdalene, Derrett concludes: "According to John, Jesus, in effect, reminds the Magdalene that she was a Miriam and therefore a prophetess (Exodus 15,20-21)"[42].

---

37. *Ibid.*, p. 175. Cf. p. 177: "Jesus, therefore, places weight on that pedantic form, and if Mary replies to Jesus in a formal form, that will emphasize the fact".

38. For a study of the different proposed meanings of ραββουνι in Jn 20,16, see R. BIERINGER, *'Ραββουνί in John 20,16 and Its Implications for Our Understanding of the Relationship between Mary Magdalene and Jesus*, in ID. – B. BAERT – K. DEMASURE (eds.), *Noli me tangere in Interdisciplinary Perspective: Textual, Iconographic and Contemporary Interpretations* (BETL, 283), Leuven – Paris – Bristol, CT, Peeters, 2016, 3-42, pp. 19 and 31.

39. DERRETT, *Miriam* (n. 30), p. 179.

40. *Ibid.*, p. 180.

41. *Ibid.*

42. *Ibid.*, p. 181.

Derrett is convinced that Mary's role even goes beyond that of Miriam. In Num 12,5c-8b a distinction is introduced between, on the one hand, Aaron and Miriam who are prophets to whom God relates through visions and dreams and, on the other, Moses to whom God relates face to face. In John 20, however, Derrett sees Mary as being raised to the level of Moses when he summarises his position as follows: "Now Jesus will visit God, improving on Moses's achievement, leaving his 'Miriam' with no insignificant role, for she had spoken to him face to face as Moses spoke with Yahweh"[43].

It seems rather farfetched to compare the role of the sister of Moses in Ex 2,3-8 to that of Mary Magdalene at the empty tomb. First, we note that in Ex 2,3-8 the name of Moses' sister is not mentioned[44]. Second, the two scenes, Ex 2,3-8 and Jn 20,1-18, and the roles of "Moses' sister" and Mary Magdalene are so different that a few vague similarities cannot make us forget that. Third, it is hard to believe that the name Μαριάμ alone can conjure up a transfer of Miriam's role as prophetess to Mary Magdalene. It is true that Jesus leaves Mary "with no insignificant role", but Derrett makes no attempt to demonstrate that this role is conceived in John as a prophetic role. All things considered, it is not surprising that Derrett's position seems to have had relatively little impact on the discussion of the text and interpretation of Jn 20,16[45]. Michael Peppard, whose position we shall analyse next, shares Derrett's text-critical conclusion but leaves no doubt that he does not follow his theological interpretation[46].

3. *The Cosmological Interpretation of Michael Peppard: Mary Magdalene's Authorization for Resurrection Ministry*

In 2020, Michael Peppard published a study of Jn 20,16 in which the name of Mary Magdalene plays a central role[47]. In it he says:

> ... the three oldest Greek manuscripts ($\mathfrak{P}^{66*}$, B, ℵ) and the Sahidic Coptic are the most consistent in their naming patterns for Mary of Bethany. For

---

43. *Ibid.*, p. 182.
44. On the basis of the biblical passages on "Miriam", it is rather problematic to assume that she was the sister of Moses. See R.J. BURNS, *Miriam*, in *ABD*, vol. 4, 869-870, p. 870: "There is little doubt that the view of Miriam as sister of Moses and Aaron is the product of a long history of tradition. The three leaders are presented together without kinship terminology in Numbers 12 and Mic. 6:4 (...)".
45. See, however, S. RUSCHMANN, *Maria von Magdala im Johannesevangelium: Jüngerin – Zeugin – Lebensbotin* (NTAbh, NF 40), Münster, Aschendorff, 2002, p. 89.
46. PEPPARD, *Mary Magdalene's Turn* (n. 1), pp. 567-568, n. 15.
47. *Ibid.*, pp. 567-574.

this reason, it is striking that three of these ($\mathfrak{P}^{66*}$, B, Copt^{sa}) contain a name change in the account of Mary Magdalene ... Why, if these three manuscripts were careful to standardize the name of Mary of Bethany, would they present the name of Mary Magdalene in two different forms? Did they sense the significance of Mary's being called by name, called *Mariam*, in 20,16? Did they sense that her name turned from *Maria* to *Mariam* at this pivotal moment[48]?

However, Peppard's text-critical argument is not completely correct and, as a result, his conclusion based on this argument, namely that Mary Magdalene's name is changed in 20,16, remains inconclusive. It is true that, in John, Codex ℵ always refers to Mary of Bethany as Μαρια and to Mary Magdalene as Μαριαμ. But although B refers to Mary of Bethany as Μαριαμ, 11,20 is the one exception where it uses Μαρια. In view of this exception, I doubt that we can speak of standardisation. If the change in the form of the name is deemed significant in the B reading of 20,16, why not postulate a significance also for the change in the form of the name in the B reading of 11,20, albeit in the opposite direction? Moreover, the $\mathfrak{P}^{66}$ readings of the name of Mary of Bethany do not support the claim of standardisation beyond reasonable doubt. In most occurrences, the $\mathfrak{P}^{66}$ reading is indeed Μαρια. But in 11,20 there is a lacuna in the manuscript. The editors of N^{28} and CNTTS list the reading Μαρια as "*ut videtur*", thus indicating that the reading is not certain. More importantly, in 11,32 $\mathfrak{P}^{66*}$ reads Μαρια while $\mathfrak{P}^{66c}$ reads Μαριαμ. It is only possible to speak of a standardisation of the name if one privileges $\mathfrak{P}^{66*}$. But no reasons are given why one should prefer the reading of the *prima manus* here. Moreover, it is crucial for Peppard's theory that $\mathfrak{P}^{66}$ reads Μαρια in 20,11, because only then is there potentially a so-called "name change" from Μαρια in 20,11 to Μαριαμ in 20,16. But in 20,11 someone added a μ in superscript position at the end of the *prima manus*' Μαρια. It is not clear on what basis Peppard opts for the *prima manus* reading. Finally, Peppard never explicitly admits that the reading of the name as Μαριαμ in 20,16 which he proposes for $\mathfrak{P}^{66}$ is not at all certain due to the fact that the papyrus is fragmentary in John 20 and any reconstruction is highly uncertain[49]. It is true that, in his Fig. 1, Peppard records the $\mathfrak{P}^{66*}$ reading in 20,16 (and equally in 19,25) as [ ] thus admitting that no text is extant there. But he does not draw the unavoidable conclusion that $\mathfrak{P}^{66*}$ is not an unambiguous witness to his position.

---

48. *Ibid.*, p. 568.
49. See below, p. 378.

Peppard summarises his text-critical conclusion as follows: "By the principles of text criticism, the version with the name change is the oldest and most reliable reading as acknowledged by Nestle-Aland, the UBS edition, and the recent SBL edition"[50]. Here it is not clear which "principles of text criticism" he is referring to. Moreover, it should not be forgotten that "oldest and most reliable" does not automatically mean that this is the "original" reading. It is, however, beyond doubt that in the next section of his study, Peppard treats it as the words dictated and intended by the evangelist. But the limited and uncertain text-critical evidence and considerations adduced by Peppard by no means result in a convincing argument. Finally, it also seems questionable to us to speak of a "name change", as Peppard frequently does without any critical reflection. Afterwards we will examine this *a priori* critically.

In section III of his contribution, Peppard discusses four different possibilities of what the supposed name change might mean. As mentioned above, Peppard assumes that the codex B readings of the name in 20,11.16.18 stem from the evangelist himself. According to his first explanation, Μαριάμ is a "marker of ethnic identity"[51]. This view is based on the problematic assumption that "the name Mariam is more a Semitic version of the name than Maria"[52]. As many others do, Peppard reads 20,16 in light of 10,1-16 and in particular 10,4: ὅταν τὰ ἴδια πάντα ἐκβάλῃ, ἔμπροσθεν αὐτῶν πορεύεται καὶ τὰ πρόβατα αὐτῷ ἀκολουθεῖ, ὅτι οἴδασιν τὴν φωνὴν αὐτοῦ. However, he suggests that φωνή in this verse does not mean "voice" but "language" and concludes: "When Jesus was a stranger asking her [Mary Magdalene] questions in Greek, she did not know his φωνή, but when he spoke her name in the language she knew [i.e., Hebrew], she turned and recognized her shepherd"[53]. It is doubtful whether φωνή really means "language" in 10,4-5. LSJ lists a few instances outside the bible where φωνή is used in the meaning "language". Focusing on the Greek bible, BDAG only sees this meaning in 1 Cor 14,10-11 and 2 Pet 2,16. However, in both cases the interpretation with "language" is debatable. In the case of 1 Cor 14,10-11 both the interpretation of φωνή as "voice" and the interpretation as "language" is defended by various commentators. In 2 Pet 2,16 there is a contrast between the speechlessness of donkeys in general and the speaking of Balaam's donkey with a human voice. The emphasis is not on which

---

50. PEPPARD, *Mary Magdalene's Turn* (n. 1), p. 568.
51. *Ibid.*, pp. 569-570.
52. *Ibid.*, p. 570. This view has been called into question in scholarship for many years. See above, notes 15, 17.
53. *Ibid.*

language the donkey speaks (Greek or Hebrew?) but on the fact that an animal that normally does not speak (ἄφωνον) is said to speak like a human person (ἐν ἀνθρώπου φωνῇ). But even if one accepted the meaning "language" for φωνή in Jn 10,4-5 and even if one agreed that "Mariam is more a Semitic version of the name", Peppard's line of reasoning would remain problematic in view of the context. In fact, in Jn 20,15 Mary Magdalene is portrayed as answering in Greek to a question that Jesus had posed to her in Greek. Moreover, in 20,13 Mary Magdalene is portrayed as speaking with the angels in Greek. So Peppard's argument can work, if he is suggesting that before 20,16 the Magdalene hears and understands Greek spoken, but ultimately does not understand, and that this lack of understanding only comes to an end when Jesus addresses her with the Hebrew form of her name. But is Μαριάμ really intended as the Hebrew form of the name and is there anything else in the context that suggests that it is the utterance in the Hebrew language that opens her eyes? It should not be overlooked that in the text itself the adverb Ἑβραϊστί is only used with the Magdalene's answer ραββουνι and it remains an open question whether Ἑβραϊστί is to be understood implicitly as qualifying Jesus' address as well.

Peppard's second attempt to explain the postulated name change is equally open to discussion. He suggests interpreting 20,16 in light of "the pattern of recognition scenes between separated lovers in ancient novels"[54]. He admits that "the role of the name change is difficult to understand"[55]. Finally, he settles for the following explanation: "just as Adam's first act upon seeing Eve was to name her (Gen 2,23), so too the new Adam names the first woman to participate in the new creation"[56]. Thus, the explanation is not found in ancient novels on romantic love, but in the book of Genesis. Peppard obviously overlooked that in Gen 2,23 Eve is named for the first time; this is far from being a name change. Most importantly, the question Peppard fails to answer is why, when "the new Adam names the first woman", the form of the name Μαριάμ would be more appropriate than Μαρία. In sum, the whole argument is not convincing.

In his third explanation of the so-called name change, Peppard refers to parallels with other name changes in the bible. Jn 20,16 is then interpreted as "a change in her status, a status imagined both in terms of her relationship to Jesus and to the other disciples"[57]. He first compares the

---

54. *Ibid.*
55. *Ibid.*, p. 571.
56. *Ibid.*, p. 572.
57. *Ibid.*

name change to the change from Ἀβραμ to Ἀβρααμ and concludes from the claimed parallel: "Like Abraham, Mariam Magdalene is commissioned to gather a new people, a renewed ἔθνος, with spiritual siblings united under God as father"[58]. But one should not overlook that in Gen 17,1-8 the name change from Ἀβραμ to Ἀβρααμ is a change within the same language with a change of meaning. This is not the case in Peppard's understanding of the supposed change from Μαρία to Μαριάμ.

Subsequently, Peppard compares the postulated name change of Peter in Jn 1,42 to Mary's in 20,16. "Like Mary, Peter is given an Aramaic name (Cephas) by Jesus (1,42)"[59]. It is questionable whether the two verses can really be considered parallel with regard to the names. Concerning the verb form κληθήσῃ in 1,42 we need to ask what its precise meaning is and whether it is to be understood as a real future or as an equivalent of an imperative. Does this verb suggest a name change or the addition of a nickname? In view of the fact that in the Gospel of John this person is mostly referred to as Σίμων Πέτρος, one might be more inclined to assume the latter. Jesus' statement in 1,42 also leaves us wondering when this nickname will be given to Simon. All this demonstrates that caution is needed when one tries to use 1,42 to interpret 20,16. While in 1,42 two names are paralleled explicitly, this is not the case in the Codex B readings of 20,11-18. As we said above, the Hellenistic character of the name Μαρία has been called into question with the consequence that the claim that there is a name change from a Greek name to an Aramaic name is problematic. It goes too far, therefore, to base the following claim on the supposed name change: "... what Peter was for Christ's original mission, Mary Magdalene was for Christ's resurrected mission"[60].

Finally, Peppard adds a fourth way of explaining what he understands as a name change in Jn 20,16. He expresses his view succinctly as follows: "When Jesus pronounced her name as Mariam, he was declaring her divinely appointed name and calling her forward to salvation"[61]. He finds support for this salvific understanding of the supposed name change in Is 43,1: "I have called you by name, you are mine"[62]. However, nothing in this Isaiah text refers to a name change. It would make no difference whether the Magdalene would be called by name as Μαριάμ or Μαρία.

---

58. *Ibid.*, p. 573.
59. *Ibid.*
60. *Ibid.*
61. *Ibid.*
62. Cited from PEPPARD, *ibid.*, pp. 573-574.

The second Isaiah text that Peppard quotes to sustain his position is Is 62,1-2[63] where one of the promises is "you shall be called by a new name". He also points to the parallel in Rev 2,17. In my opinion, the references to these two passages are problematic. In Is 62,2 someone is "called by a new name that the mouth of the Lord will give". In Jn 20,16 Jesus would then have to be the one who gives the Magdalene a new name. However, I do not think that the supposed shift from the alleged Greek/Graecised version of a name (Μαρία) to its corresponding Hebrew version (Μαριάμ) would qualify for what Isaiah has in mind as a "new name" given by God. The Magdalene does not receive a new name, but at most a variant of the same name. In Rev 2,17 we hear about "a new name that no one knows except the one who receives it". There is nothing in Jn 20,16-18 that would point to such secrecy. The Codex B readings which Peppard presupposes for his hypothetical proposals give the name Μαριάμ not only in the intimate dialogue between Jesus and the Magdalene, but also in 20,18 in the mouth of the narrator.

The alleged parallel of Jn 20,16 with the calling of the name Λάζαρε in 11,43 is no less problematic. Peppard calls 20,16 "a spiritual version of Lazarus' calling by name"[64]. But Lazarus is called by his one and only name[65], not by a new name nor by a different form of his name. The contexts of the name callings in 11,43 and 20,16 are quite different. Lazarus is presented as literally dead, even with a smell, and he is called by name in a call to come out of the tomb back to life. The Magdalene is not presented as (literally) dead, but as standing outside Jesus' empty tomb looking for his dead body. Even if one were to accept the interpretive option that the evangelist wants to present the Magdalene as spiritually dead and that Jesus calls her back to real life by calling her name, this would not require a new name, as the case of Lazarus proves. Peppard takes Jn 5,25 as his hermeneutical key: "the dead will hear the voice of the Son of God, and those who hear will live". This verse certainly applies to Lazarus, but, as we just saw above, it is much more problematic to apply it to the Magdalene in 20,16. In light of John 10, Peppard considers "Mary's calling by name ... an embodiment of that shepherd and sheep metaphor". But again, there is nothing about the calling by name in 10,4-5 that points to a name change[66].

---

63. Peppard mistakenly refers to Is 61,1-2.
64. *Ibid.*, p. 574.
65. I note that in the earliest witnesses which I checked there are no different versions of the name of Lazarus.
66. It is noteworthy that in his first hypothetical explanation, Peppard claimed that φωνή in Jn 10,4-5 should be understood as "language"; see above, pp. 371-372. Here he has obviously returned to the common interpretation of φωνή as "voice".

Peppard synthesises his fourth hypothetical explanation as follows: "Mary hovers at the door of the tomb, like at a sheep gate between death and life, but because she 'listens to his voice' and 'belongs' to the shepherd, she 'turns' from Maria to Mariam at a pivotal moment in John's cosmological tale"[67]. This synthesis brings to light the weak points of Peppard's position. His aim is to give the alleged name change of the Magdalene in Jn 20,16 a theological meaning. However, in John, listening to the voice of the shepherd or the Son of God and being called to life has nothing to do with a name change or with a "new name". The presentation of the different forms of the name of the Magdalene in the Codex B readings of 20,11.16.18 can hardly qualify as the giving of a new name similar to that mentioned in Is 62,2 or Rev 2,17. Finally, we would point out that Peppard makes no effort in this section to explain why in his hypothesis the (form of the) name Μαριάμ would have a deeper theological and more specifically salvific meaning than Μαρία. He only claims the "that" but does not expound the "what" of his hypothesis. Peppard comments that the four interpretations he offers are "plausible" and adds that "the third and fourth options do have the most explanatory power"[68]. As I have set out above, I consider all four options logically problematic and equally unconvincing.

Summarizing what I have argued in this section: neither the text-critical nor the theological interpretations of Derrett and Peppard are convincing. There are limitations in their presentation and interpretation of the textual evidence concerning the name of the Magdalene in the Gospel of John and concerning the name of all the Marys in the New Testament. There are also problems with their assumptions concerning the differences between Μαρία and Μαριάμ in the New Testament manuscript tradition. As a result, their attempts to give theological meaning to the name Μαριάμ and to the supposed name change from Μαρία to Μαριάμ between Jn 20,11 and 20,16 are based on questionable foundations. In section III of this contribution, I will present an alternative approach.

III. Μαρία and Μαριάμ: An Alternative Approach

In reaction to the positions which I critically analysed above, I will now develop an alternative approach which will proceed in two steps. The first will consist of an external text-critical discussion of the *variae*

---

67. PEPPARD, *Mary Magdalene's Turn* (n. 1), p. 574.
68. *Ibid.*

lectiones Μαρια and Μαριαμ in the textual tradition of the Gospel of John. In a second step, taking into account the text-critical analysis, I will investigate by way of internal criticism which meaning(s) the name or names of the Magdalene might have in the context of John 20.

1. *Text-Critical Analysis of the Occurrences of Μαρια and Μαριαμ in John*

As stated above[69], the textual transmission of the name Μαριάμ/Μαρία in the New Testament is rather complex. In the various textual witnesses, none of the Marys in the New Testament (the mother of Jesus, Mary of Clopas, Mary of James and Joses/Joseph, Mary Magdalene, Mary of Bethany, Mary of Rome) is consistently referred to by Μαριάμ or Μαρία. In the table below, we focus on how the Magdalene's name appears in some major codices in the Synoptics.

	Mt 27,56	Mt 27,61	Mt 28,1	Mk 15,40	Mk 15,47	Mk 16,1	[Mk 16,9]	Lk 8,2	Lk 24,10
ℵ01	*vac ᶜΜαρια	Μαριαμ	Μαριαμ	Μαρια	Μαρια	*vac ᶜΜαρια	–	Μαρια	Μαριαμ
A02	Μαρια	Μαρια	Μαρια	Μαρια	Μαρια	Μαρια	Μαριᾳ	Μαριαμ	Μαρια
B03	Μαρια	Μαριαμ	Μαρια	Μαριαμ	Μαρια	Μαρια	–	Μαρια	Μαρια
D05	Μαρια	Μαρια	Μαρια	Μαρια	Μαρια	Μαρια	–	Μαρια	Μαρια
E07	Μαρια	Μαρια	Μαρια	Μαρια	Μαρια	Μαρια	–	Μαρια	Μαρια

Table 3: The Form of the Name of the Magdalene in the Synoptic Gospels[70]

I note that in Codex ℵ the Magdalene is referred to as Μαριαμ in Mt 27,61 and 28,1, as Μαρια in Mark[71], and once as Μαρια (8,2) and once as Μαριαμ (24,10) in Luke. Codex A calls the Magdalene always Μαρια except in Lk 8,2 where she is called Μαριαμ. Similarly, Codex B always calls the Magdalene Μαρια with the exception of Mk 15,40 and Mt 27,61, where she is called Μαριαμ. Codices D and E always call her Μαρια.

The situation is even more confusing with regard to the five occurrences of the name Μαριαμ/Μαρια in the Gospel of John, as illustrated by the table below:

---

69. See above, pp. 362-364.
70. Based on https://manuscripts.csntm.org/ (accessed on 27 October 2021).
71. Note that in the *prima manus* a longer portion of the text at the end of 15,47 and the beginning of 16,1 is missing due to parablepsis. In the corrector's addition, the name appears as Μαρια.

mss	19,25	20,1	20,11	20,16	20,18
𝔓⁵	vac	vac	vac	[Μαρια]	vac
𝔓⁶⁰	[Μαρια]	vac	vac	vac	vac
𝔓⁶⁶	Μαρι̣[α]	[Μαρια]	*Μαρια ᶜΜαριαμ	Μα̣[ρια]	Μαριαμ
𝔓⁶⁶ ⁷²	ᵛⁱᵈ Μαρια	ᵛⁱᵈ Μαρια	*ᵛⁱᵈ Μαρια ᶜᵛⁱᵈ Μαριαμ	ᵛⁱᵈ Μαριαμ	Μαριαμ
𝔓⁶⁶ ⁷³		[Μαρια]	Μαριαμ	Μα̣[ριαμ]	Μαριαμ
ℵ01	Μαριαμ	Μαριαμ	Μαριαμ	Μαριαμ	Μαριαμ
A02	Μαρια	Μαριαμ	Μαρια	Μαρια	Μαρια
B03	Μαρια	Μαρια	Μαρια	Μαριαμ	Μαριαμ
C04	vac	vac	vac	vac	vac
D05	Μαριαˢᵘᵖ	Μαριαˢᵘᵖ	Μαριαˢᵘᵖ	Μαρια	Μαρια
E07	Μαρια	Μαρια	Μαρια	Μαρια	Μαρια
G011	vac	Μαρια	Μαρια	Μαρια	Μαρια
H013	Μαρια	Μαρια	Μαρια	vac	vac
K017	Μαρια	Μαρια	Μαρια	Μαρια	Μαρια
L019	Μαριαμ	Μαριαμ	Μαρια	Μαριαμ	Μαριαμ
M021	Μαρια	Μαρια	Μαρια	Μαρια	Μαρια
N022	Μαρια	Μαρια	Μαρια	Μαριαμ	Μαρια
S028	Μαρια	Μαρια	Μαρια	Μαρια	Μαρια
U030	Μαρια	Μαρια	Μαρια	Μαρια	Μαρια
W032	Μαρια	Μαριαμ	Μαρια	Μαριαμ	Μαρια
Y034	Μαρια	Μαρια	Μαρια	Μαρια	Μαρια
Δ037	vac	Μαρια	Μαρια	Μαρια	Μαρια
Θ038	Μαρια	Μαρια	Μαρια	Μαρια	Μαρια
Λ039	Μαρια	Μαρια	Μαρια	Μαρια	Μαρια
Π041	*Μαρια ᶜΜαριαμ	Μαρια	Μαρια	Μαριαμ	Μαρια
Ψ044	Μαριαμ	Μαρια	Μαριαμ	Μαρια	Μαρια
Ω045	Μαρια	Μαρια	Μαρια	Μαρια	Μαρια
1	Μαριαμ	Μαριαμ	Μαριαμ	Μαριαμ	Μαριαμ

72. The readings of 𝔓⁶⁶ according to the online critical apparatus of the Center for New Testament Textual Studies (CNTTS).

73. The readings of 𝔓⁶⁶ according to V. MARTIN – J.W.B. BARNS, *Papyrus Bodmer II Supplément: Evangile de Jean Chap. 14–21*, Nouvelle édition augmentée et corrigée avec reproduction photographique complète du manuscrit (chap. 1–21), Geneva, Bibliotheca Bodmeriana, 1962, p. [145].

13	Μαρια	Μαρια	Μαρια	Μαρια	Μαρια
22	Μαρια	Μαρια	Μαρια	Μαρια	Μαρια
33	Μαριαμ	Μαριαμ	Μαριαμ	Μαριαμ	Μαριαμ
118	Μαρια[sup]	Μαρια[sup]	Μαρια[sup]	Μαρια[sup]	Μαρια[sup]
565	Μαριαμ	Μαριαμ	Μαριαμ	Μαριαμ	Μαριαμ
579	Μαρια	Μαριαμ	Μαρια	vac	vac
1582	Μαριαμ	Μαριαμ	Μαριαμ	Μαριαμ	Μαριαμ
f^1	Μαριαμ	Μαριαμ	Μαριαμ	Μαριαμ	Μαριαμ
f^{13}	Μαρια	Μαρια	Μαρια	Μαρια	Μαρια

Table 4: The Form of the Name of the Magdalene in the Gospel of John[74]

We can see clearly that there are many witnesses in which Μαρια occurs consistently (majuscules: D05[sup] E K M S U Y Θ Λ Ω; minuscules: 13 22 118 f^{13}). There are significantly fewer witnesses which read consistently Μαριαμ (ℵ 1[75] 33[76] 565 1582 cf. f^1). There are also cases where both Μαρια and Μαριαμ appear in the same witness and many different combinations occur. In codex A02, Μαριαμ is found in 20,1 and Μαρια in all the other places. The opposite is true in codex L019 where Μαριαμ occurs in all places except one, namely in 20,11. In codex W032, Μαριαμ occurs in 20,1 and 20,16 and in codex Ψ044 Μαριαμ is attested in 19,25 and 20,11. Codex B03 is the only Greek[77] witness where Μαριαμ occurs only in 20,16 and 18, while the other readings in John are Μαρια. As we saw, Derrett and Peppard claim that 𝔓[66], too, attests this reading. It is, however, impossible to know which form of the name 𝔓[66] originally read in 20,16 due to the fragmentary nature of the papyrus in this part. The name occurs in the middle of the line, only the first letter μ and part of the second letter α is still legible and in the remainder of the line only the two letters αφ of the following word στραφεισα are extant. In 𝔓[66] the spaces between the letters are of varying length anyhow and the right margin is uneven. As a result, it is impossible to reconstruct the text with the precision of one letter difference, as some have undertaken with opposite results[78].

---

74. Based on the "International Greek New Testament Project's online electronic edition of John", see http://itseeweb.bham.ac.uk/iohannes/transcriptions/index.html (accessed on 27 October 2021).
75. 19,25 uncertain?
76. In 19,25 the ending is illegible.
77. Cf. Coptic sa.
78. It is not surprising that the reconstructions differ. As Table 4 illustrates, in 20,16 the Bodmer transcription is Μα[ριαμ]. See MARTIN – BARNS, *Papyrus Bodmer II*

Finally, it should be noted that, in the manuscripts listed in Table 4 above, there is one witness that reads Μαριαμ only in 20,16 and Μαρια everywhere else, namely N022. This is also the case in Π041 if we follow the *prima manus* which reads Μαρια in 19,25 while the corrector changed it to Μαριαμ.

All these observations raise the question on what authority or on the basis of what reasoning one might consider the Codex B readings as the stronger readings that preserve the earliest attainable text. This seems to happen only on account of the generally recognised high quality of the manuscript. But as we saw above, even this codex has variations between Μαρια and Μαριαμ in Matthew and in Mark for which it seems impossible to find an explanation. The reliability of Codex B is further undermined when we examine the way this witness represents the name of Mary of Bethany.

John	case	ℵ01	A02	B03	C04	D05	E07
11,1	G	Μαριας	Μαριας	Μαριας	vac	Μαριας	Μαριας
11,2	N	Μαρια	Μαρια	Μαριαμ	vac	Μαρια	Μαρια
11,19	A	Μαριαν	Μαριαν	Μαριαμ	* Μαριαμ c Μαριαν	Μαριαμ	Μαριαν
11,20	N	Μαρια	Μαρια	Μαρια	Μαρια	Μαρια	Μαρια
11,28	A	Μαριαν	Μαριαμ	Μαριαμ	Μαριαμ	Μαριαμ	Μαριαν
11,31	A	Μαριαν	Μαριαν	Μαριαμ	* Μαριαμ c Μαριαν	Μαριαμ	Μαριαν
11,32	N	Μαρια	Μαρια	Μαριαμ	* Μαριαμ c Μαρια	Μαρια	* Μαριαμ c Μαρια
11,45	A/D	Μαριαν	την Μαριᾶ	Μαριαμ	τη Μαριαμ	Μαριαμ	Μαριαν
12,3	N	Μαρια	Μαρια	Μαριαμ	vac	Μαρια	Μαρια

Table 5: The Form of the Name of Mary of Bethany in the Gospel of John[79]

The name of Mary of Bethany occurs almost twice as often in John as the name of the Magdalene. The variations between Μαριαμ and Μαρια are analogous. Codex ℵ, which represents the name of the Magdalene consistently as Μαριαμ, always refers to Mary of Bethany as Μαρια (if

---

Supplément: Evangile de Jean Chap. 14–21 (n. 73), p. [145]. The Birmingham reconstruction, however, is Μα̣[ρια]. See http://itseeweb.bham.ac.uk/iohannes/transcriptions/index.html?witness=P66&language=greek#K20V16 (accessed on 22 October 2021).

79. Based on the "International Greek New Testament Project's online electronic edition of John", see http://itseeweb.bham.ac.uk/iohannes/transcriptions/index.html (accessed on 27 October 2021).

we count the genitive Μαριας as the genitive of Μαρια). Codex E07 which always refers to the Magdalene as Μαρια, also uses this form of the name for Mary of Bethany, except in 11,32 where the *prima manus* reads Μαριαμ, changed by a corrector into Μαρια. In Codex A, Mary of Bethany is always Μαρια, except in 11,28 where it reads Μαριαμ. Similarly, the same codex refers to the Magdalene as Μαρια with one exception, 20,1 where her name is Μαριαμ. Codex D05 which consistently presents the Magdalene as Μαρια almost alternatingly uses Μαρια and Μαριαμ for Mary of Bethany. In the six extant occurrences of the name of Mary of Bethany in Codex C04 a corrector has changed the reading Μαριαμ of the *prima manus* into Μαριαν in 11,19 and 32. But no changes were made to the occurrences of Μαριαμ in 11,28 and 45. Codex B consistently represents the name of Mary of Bethany as Μαριαμ, except in 11,20. It is impossible to find an explanation for this exception as there is nothing different or particular about the content of this verse in comparison with the other occurrences of the name of Mary of Bethany. The representation of the name of Mary of Bethany in the Gospel of John as Μαριαμ and Μαρια respectively is confusing to say the least. There is only one verse, namely 11,20 where all the major codices we checked read Μαρια[80], there is none where they all read Μαριαμ. Even though all read the genitive Μαριας in 11,1, in some witnesses this form seems to be used as the genitive of Μαρια and in others as the genitive of Μαριαμ. In Codex C04 (and to a lesser degree in Codex E07) we see correctors at work who obviously attempt to harmonise the forms of the name. There are no instances where one could easily interpret variations in the transmission of the name as intended to convey a particular meaning.

On the basis of my text-critical examination I conclude that I find no support for opting for the codex B readings of the Magdalene's name in John. The Codex B constellation with Μαριαμ only in 20,16 and 18 has been demonstrated to be a singular reading in the Greek textual tradition. One cannot escape the conclusion that the witnesses reading Μαριαμ in all the Johannine references to the Magdalene (ℵ01 1 33 565 1582) as well as those that read Μαρια consistently (D05 E07 K017 et al.) reflect secondary harmonisations. However, among the witnesses that in mentioning the name of the Magdalene use a mixture of Μαριαμ and Μαρια, we have not discovered any constellation that occurs more than once. Consequently, there does not seem to be any rhyme or reason why one witness might

---

80. It is noteworthy that NA[26-28], in spite of its obvious aim to harmonise, nevertheless opted for the reading Μαριαμ in 11,20, even though its earliest witnesses are the ninth-century manuscripts Θ 33 and 565.

be considered more trustworthy than any other. This leads us to serious doubt about the choice for the Codex B readings in the Nestle tradition.

2. *Semantic Analysis of* Μαρια *and* Μαριαμ *in John*

In this second part of the section in which we present our alternative approach (III), we turn to the internal criticism of the textual transmission of Mary Magdalene's name in the Gospel of John. We ask which form of the Magdalene's name the scribes and the fourth evangelist are likely to have written in Jn 20,16 and 18.

a) Transcriptional Probability

On the basis of the evidence which we examined in the previous subsection (III.1), an interpreter needs to choose between two possibilities. *Either* each single book originally called each separate Mary consistently by the same name, Μαριάμ or Μαρία, so that one and the same Mary had one and the same name all through the book; *or* each book originally called one or another Mary by both names, and copyists tried to harmonise this original inconsistency into consistency. In what follows we opt for the latter possibility.

We distinguish three reasons which may have prompted the process of harmonisation. First, it is the normal practice to refer to the same person by the same (form of the) name throughout a text. Rare exceptions are the result of phonetics, especially when certain letters or letter combinations can reflect the same pronunciation (e.g., Ηλειας next to Ηλιας and Ισαιας next to Ησαιας). However, these exceptions are of a different kind than the Μαριαμ/Μαρια variations.

Second, the process of harmonisation may have been fueled by the tendency to assimilate the form of the name to the form of the name with which copyists were acquainted in their own cultural context. As stated above, it is too simplistic to consider Μαριάμ as the Hebrew form of the name and Μαρία as the Graecised form. However, the very fact that the name of מרים, who is presented as the sister of Aaron, is represented as Μαριάμ in the LXX and in Philo would inescapably result in the general perception that Μαριάμ is closer to the Hebrew biblical tradition than Μαρία. Even if the derivation of מריה from מרים is correct[81], it should not be overlooked that מריה is less frequent than מרים and that Μαρία corresponds more closely to Greek (and Latin) linguistic patterns than Μαριάμ. It is therefore not surprising that manuscripts copied in later

81. See above, pp. 364-365.

Byzantine or in Latin contexts tend to assimilate the different forms to Μαρία and "Maria". The Vulgate uses "Maria" as the nominative for all the biblical Marys, including the sister of Aaron, and "Mariam" occurs as the accusative of "Maria"[82].

Third, one can observe a tendency among the scribes to use the different forms of the name to distinguish the different Marys in John and in the Synoptics. This is above all the case for the three Marys whose names occur most frequently in the New Testament.

Mss	mother of Jesus in Matthew	mother of Jesus in Luke	Mary of Bethany in John	Mary Magdalene in John
ℵ01	Μαριαμ	Μαριαμ	Μαρια	Μαριαμ
A02	vac	Μαριαμ	(Μαριαμ)	(Μαριαμ)
B03	mixed	(Μαριαμ)[83]	(Μαριαμ)	mixed
D05	Μαριαμ	Μαρια	mixed	Μαρια
E07	Μαριαμ	Μαριαμ	Μαρια	Μαρια

Table 6: The Tendency to Distinguish the Marys by the Use of Μαριαμ or Μαρια

This table illustrates that in none of the early codices listed are all the three Marys referred to as only Μαριαμ[84] or as only Μαρια. Codex ℵ01 calls all the Marys Μαριαμ except Mary of Bethany. Codex E07 calls the mother of Jesus in Matthew and Luke Μαριαμ and the other two Marys Μαρια. Codex D05 refers to the mother of Jesus in Matthew as Μαριαμ and in Luke as Μαρια. The same codex refers to Mary Magdalene in John as Μαρια. In Codex B03, none of the three Marys is always referred to by the same form of the name.

We conclude this section by observing that among the five early manuscripts reviewed in this section, Codex B03 is the least advanced in the process of scribal harmonisation of the forms of the names for the three Marys most frequently mentioned in the New Testament. This is an additional warning against attaching too much significance to the occurrence of Μαριαμ in Jn 20,16 and 18.

---

82. A detailed study of the way the name "Maria" is rendered in the Latin biblical tradition (Old Latin and Vulgate) would be important, but exceeds the scope of this study.

83. Parentheses are used to indicate that there is one exception; if there is more than one exception, we use the qualifier "mixed".

84. Codex A02 uses mostly Μαριαμ when referring to the three Marys, but for Mary of Bethany and Mary Magdalene there are exceptions and the passages of Matthew that refer to the mother of Jesus are not extant.

b) Intrinsic Probability

In this subsection we will deal with the question how the fourth evangelist is most likely to have represented the name of the Magdalene in John 20. We will mainly concentrate here on variations in names in the Gospel of John.

The first point to discuss is the phenomenon of naming children at birth. This occurs in the Gospel of Luke with regard to John (the Baptist) and in Matthew and Luke with regard to Jesus. In the Gospel of John there are no traces of this procedure of naming persons at birth. The second point is the giving of additional names to persons at a later stage. This usually happens in order to distinguish different people who have the same name. This is often effected by adding a reference to an important family relation (wife of, daughter of, son of, mother of, father of) as in "Mary of Clopas" in 19,25 or by mentioning the place of origin as in the case of Philip who "was from Bethsaida" (1,44). In some cases, the identifiers become part of the name and it often becomes impossible to know their exact meaning. Some cases in point in John are "Judas Iscariot"[85] in 6,71; 12,4; 13,2.26, with its counterpart "Judas (not Iscariot)" in 14,22, and Mary "Magdalene". The name Θωμᾶς ὁ λεγόμενος Δίδυμος occurs in 11,16; 20,24 and 21,2. In this case Δίδυμος is the Greek translation of the Hebrew word which is transcribed in Θωμᾶς, but the expression ὁ λεγόμενος suggests that Δίδυμος was a second name as in the case of Ἰησοῦς ὁ λεγόμενος Χριστός (Mt 1,16; 27,17.22) and Ἰησοῦς ὁ λεγόμενος Ἰοῦστος (Acts 1,23). In light of these parallels, Θωμᾶς ὁ λεγόμενος Δίδυμος seems to mean "Thomas who is also known under the name Didymus". Besides, a second name may also be given to indicate that the person concerned receives a new mission or a new task. In John this seems to be the case when Jesus says to Simon: σὺ κληθήσῃ Κηφᾶς, ὃ ἑρμηνεύεται Πέτρος (1,42). In the Gospel of John, he is often called by his double name "Simon Peter". However, none of the examples mentioned so far corresponds to Μαριάμ/Μαρία.

There is also the phenomenon of the Hellenisation of Hebrew names. A good synthesis is found in Blass-Debrunner:

> Semitic names of the NT period are far more susceptible to Hellenization. Often the same name, if it belongs to a person of the NT period, is Grecized, and not Grecized if it designates a person of a former age or is used of a NT person in a formal manner[86].

---

85. The form of "Iscariot" in the Greek manuscript tradition is extremely complex.
86. BDF, §53².

One illustration of this may be the name Ἰακώβ/Ἰάκωβος. The Synoptics use Ἰακώβ for the patriarch and Ἰάκωβος for the son of Zebedee who follows Jesus. In John, only the name Ἰακώβ occurs (4,5.6.12). I have not discovered any other example of this phenomenon in John. This would only be the case if in the Gospel of John Μαριάμ was used for the sister of Aaron and Μαρία for Mary Magdalene. But this is not the case. Μαριάμ and Μαρία are used for the same person. Another possibility would be if Μαριάμ was the formal form of the name and Μαρία the informal form of the same name. But this would be the only instance of this phenomenon in the Fourth Gospel. Moreover, it would be difficult to demonstrate that the formal/informal distinction can account for all the variations of the readings Μαριαμ and Μαρια in the manuscripts of the New Testament. In fact, there are no other examples of a personal name of one and the same person which occurs in the same manuscripts in two different forms in different places. The only exception is the name of John which occurs as Ἰωαννης and as Ἰωανης. However, Ἰωαννης and Ἰωανης are just orthographical variants of the same name[87]; this case is not analogous to that of Μαριαμ and Μαρια.

As we have seen above, Peppard and other scholars claim that a real name change from Μαρία to Μαριάμ takes place in Jn 20,16 in comparison with 20,11. They see this confirmed in the fact that in 20,18, the only other instance where the Magdalene is mentioned by name, she is again called Μαριάμ. A clear example of a name change occurs in Gen 17,5, explicitly announced and clearly marked by an explanation of the new name. Before 17,5 the man involved is called Ἄβραμ and from 17,5 onwards his name is Ἀβρααμ. If a name change takes place in Jn 20,16, it would be something entirely implicit; any reference to the meaning of the new name would be lacking.

Finally, we see one other possible reason why the names Μαριάμ and Μαρία might have been used side by side for one person: different variants of the same name could be used for different levels of closeness in relationships or for cross-cultural communication. An example of the first possibility might be found in Paul's use of the name Πρίσκα in his letters, different from the same person's name Πρίσκιλλα in Acts 18. But it remains unclear whether there is really a difference in sentimental value between the two names; perhaps Πρίσκα is just an abridged, convenient form of Πρίσκιλλα. Moreover, if Μαριάμ and Μαρία were used on different levels of closeness, then it remains remarkable that the random way these two forms of the name are used in the manuscripts does

---

87. BDR, §40.

not reflect such different shades of meaning at all. The same applies to the second possibility: if Μαριάμ and Μαρία were names facilitating the cross-cultural communication between people belonging to different cultural contexts, helping them to pronounce or to remember the name more easily, the random nature of their occurrence in the manuscripts would be counterproductive for this goal.

In sum, it seems obvious that the variation of Μαριάμ and Μαρία in John does not correspond to any of the discussed phenomena related to naming or the use of names, whether in general or in the Gospel of John.

IV. Conclusion

On the basis of our text-critical analysis of Μαριαμ and Μαρια in the New Testament and in the Gospel of John in particular, it seems very difficult to defend the Codex B readings of Mary Magdalene's name as reflecting the earliest attainable text. If I were to make a critical edition of the Greek text of the Gospel of John, on the basis of this study, I would be at a complete loss as to how to establish the name of Mary Magdalene in the Gospel of John. Furthermore, from the point of view of internal criticism, it seems very difficult to ascertain that the variation between Μαριάμ and Μαρία intends to express a difference in theological or other meaning. Therefore, I plead for *docta ignorantia* in this matter.

Katholieke Universiteit Leuven Reimund BIERINGER
Faculty of Theology and Religious Studies
St.-Michielsstraat 4/3101
BE-3000 Leuven
Belgium
reimund.bieringer@kuleuven.be

APPENDIX

Μαριαμ and Μαρια in New Testament Manuscripts and Editions

NT	case	ℵ01	A02	B03	C04	D05	E07	Steph 1550	N²⁸ 2012
Matt 1,16	G	Μαριας	vac	Μαριας	Μαριας	Μαριας	Μαριας	Μαριας	Μαριας
1,18	G	Μαριας	vac	Μαριας	Μαριας	Μαριας	Μαριας	Μαριας	Μαριας
1,20	A	Μαριαμ	vac	Μαριαν	Μαριαμ	Μαριαμ	Μαριαμ	Μαριαμ	Μαριαν
2,11	G	Μαριας	vac	Μαριας	Μαριας	Μαριας	Μαριας	Μαριας	Μαριας
13,55	N	Μαριαμ	vac	Μαριαμ	Μαρια	Μαριαμ	Μαριαμ	Μαριαμ	Μαριαμ
27,56	N	ℵ* vac ℵᶜ Μαρια	Μαρια	Μαριαμ	C* Μαριαμ Cᶜ Μαρια	Μαρια	Μαρια	Μαρια	Μαρια
27,56	N	Μαρια	Μαρια	Μαρια	Μαριαμ	Μαρια	Μαρια	Μαρια	Μαρια
27,61	N	Μαριαμ	Μαρια	Μαριαμ	Μαριαμ	Μαρια	Μαρια	Μαρια	Μαριαμ
27,61	N	Μαρια	Μαριαμ	Μαριαμ	Μαριαμ	Μαριαμ	Μαρια	Μαρια	Μαρια
28,1	N	Μαριαμ	Μαρια	Μαρια	Μαριαμ	Μαρια	Μαρια	Μαρια	Μαριαμ
28,1	N	Μαρια	Μαρια	Μαρια	Μαρια	Μαρια	Μαρια	Μαρια	Μαρια
Mark 6,3	G	Μαριας	Μαριας	Μαριας	Μαριας	Μαριας	Μαριας	Μαριας	Μαριας
15,40	N	Μαρια	Μαρια	Μαριαμ	Μαριαμ	Μαρια	Μαρια	Μαρια	Μαρια
15,40	N	Μαρια	Μαρια	Μαρια	Μαρια	Μαρια	Μαρια	Μαρια	Μαρια
15,47	N	Μαρια	Μαρια	Μαρια	Μαρια	Μαρια	Μαρια	Μαρια	Μαρια
15,47	N	Μαρια	Μαρια	Μαρια	Μαρια	Μαρια	Μαρια	Μαρια	Μαρια
16,1	N	Μαρια	Μαρια	Μαρια	Μαρια	Μαρια	Μαρια	Μαρια	Μαρια
16,1	N	Μαρια	Μαρια	Μαρια	Μαρια	Μαρια	Μαρια	Μαρια	Μαρια

ΜΑΡΙΑΜ OR ΜΑΡΙΑ IN JOHN 20,16?

	D							
[16,9]	vac	vac	Μαρια	vac	Μαριαμ	Μαρια	Μαρια	Μαρια
Luke 1,27	N	Μαριαμ	Μαριαμ	Μαριαμ	Μαριαμ	Μαριαμ	Μαριαμ	Μαριαμ
1,30	V	Μαριαμ	Μαριαμ	Μαριαμ	Μαριαμ	Μαριαμ	Μαριαμ	Μαριαμ
1,34	N	Μαριαμ	Μαριαμ	Μαριαμ	C* Μαρια / Cᶜ Μαριαμ	D* Μαρια / Dᶜ Μαριαμ	Μαριαμ	Μαριαμ
1,38	N	Μαριαμ	Μαριαμ	Μαριαμ	C* Μαρια / Cᶜ Μαριαμ	Μαρια	Μαριαμ	Μαριαμ
1,39	N	Μαριαμ	Μαριαμ	Μαριαμ	Μαριαμαμ	Μαρια	Μαριαμ	Μαριαμ
1,41	G	Μαριας	Μαριας	Μαριας	Μαριας	Μαριας	Μαριας	Μαριας
1,46	N	Μαριαμ	Μαριαμ	Μαριαμ	C* Μαρια / Cᶜ Μαριαμ	Μαρια	Μαριαμ	Μαριαμ
1,56	N	Μαριαμ	Μαριαμ	Μαριαμ	Μαριαμ	Μαρια	Μαριαμ	Μαριαμ
2,5	D	Μαριαμ	Μαριαμ	Μαριαμ	Μαριαμ	Μαρια	Μαριαμ	Μαριαμ
2,16	A	Μαριαμ	Μαριαμ	Μαριαμ	vac	Μαριαν	Μαριαμ	Μαριαμ
2,19	N	א* Μαρια / אᶜ Μαριαμ	Μαρια	Μαρια	vac	Μαρια	Μαριαμ	Μαριαμ
2,34	A	Μαριαμ	Μαριαμ	Μαριαμ	vac	Μαριαν	Μαριαμ	Μαριαμ
8,2	N	Μαρια	Μαριαμ	Μαρια	vac	Μαρια	Μαρια	Μαρια
10,39	N	Μαριαμ	Μαρια	B* Μαρια / Bᶜ Μαριαμ	C* Μαριαμ / Cᶜ Μαρια	Μαρια	Μαρια	Μαρια
10,42	N	Μαρια	Μαρια	Μαριαμ	Μαρια	Μαρια	Μαρια	Μαρια
24,10	N	Μαριαμ	Μαρια	Μαρια	?	Μαρια	Μαρια	Μαρια
24,10	N	Μαρια	Μαρια	Μαρια	Μαρια	Μαρια	Μαρια	Μαρια
John 11,1	G	Μαριας	Μαριας	Μαριας	vac	Μαριας	Μαριας	Μαριας
11,2	N	Μαρια	Μαρια	Μαριαμ	vac	Μαρια	Μαρια	Μαριαμ

NT	case	ℵ01	A02	B03	C04	D05	E07	Steph 1550	N[28] 2012
11,19	A	Μαριαν	Μαριαν	Μαριαμ	Μαριαμ	Μαριαμ	Μαριαν	Μαριαν	Μαριαμ
11,20	N	Μαρια	Μαρια	Μαρια	Μαρια	Μαρια	Μαρια	Μαρια	Μαριαμ
11,28	A	Μαριαν	Μαριαμ	Μαριαμ	Μαριαμ	Μαριαμ	Μαριαν	Μαριαν	Μαριαμ
11,31	A	Μαριαν	Μαριαν	Μαριαμ	C* Μαριαμ C^c Μαριαν	Μαριαμ	Μαριαν	Μαριαν	Μαριαμ
11,32	N	Μαρια	Μαρια	Μαριαμ	C* Μαριαμ C^c Μαρια	Μαρια	E* Μαριαμ E^c Μαρια	Μαρια	Μαριαμ
11,45	A	Μαριαν	Μαριαν	Μαριαμ	C* Μαριαμ C^c Μαριαν	Μαριαμ	Μαριαν	Μαριαν	Μαριαμ
12,3	N	Μαρια	Μαρια	Μαριαμ	vac	Μαρια	Μαρια	Μαρια	Μαριαμ
19,25	N	Μαριαμ	Μαρια	Μαρια		D^sup Μαρια	Μαρια	Μαρια	Μαρια
19,25	N	Μαριαμ	Μαρια	Μαρια		D^sup Μαρια	Μαρια	Μαρια	Μαρια
20,1	N	Μαριαμ	Μαριαμ	Μαρια		D^sup Μαρια	Μαρια	Μαρια	Μαρια
20,11	N	Μαριαμ	Μαρια	Μαρια		Μαρια	Μαρια	Μαρια	Μαρια
20,16	V	Μαριαμ	Μαρια	Μαριαμ		Μαρια	Μαρια	Μαρια	Μαριαμ
20,18	N	Μαριαμ	Μαρια	Μαριαμ	Μαρια	Μαρια	Μαρια	Μαρια	Μαριαμ
Acts 1,14	D	Μαρια	Μαρια	Μαριαμ		Μαρια	E08 Μαριαμ	Μαρια	Μαριαμ
12,12	G	Μαριας	Μαριας	Μαριας		Μαριας	E08 Μαριας	Μαριας	Μαριας
Rom 16,6	A	Μαριαμ	Μαριαν	Μαριαν	Μαριαν	D06 Μαριαμ	?	Μαριαμ	Μαριαν

TRADITION AS FOUNDATION IN THE JOHANNINE COMMUNITY

The Gospel of John states in 20,30-31 that the presence of the resurrected Son of God is continued in what is written in the gospel, thus suggesting that the gospel should serve as a traditional basis for the ethos of the Johannine group[1]. It offers a body of existing, shared knowledge that is implicitly or explicitly part of the social know-how of the Johannine group ("canon of institutionalized actions"[2] or "ethos") and is passed on from generation to generation, thus forming a constitutive part of the identity[3] of this group[4]. 1 John, which was written at the end of the first century as a situation oriented document, stands in this tradition, reflecting the language and theology of the gospel, in spite of differences between these two writings. In this article the aim is to explore the nature and extent of what may be called traditional, shared knowledge in 1 John, also considering the possible influence of the reservoir of knowledge (tradition) offered in the gospel.

This essay is offered in honour of my friend and colleague, Jos Verheyden, in acknowledgement and appreciation of his huge contribution to the study of the New Testament and early Christianity.

I. REFERENCES TO TRADITION IN 1 JOHN

For a relatively short letter, 1 John is rich in material related to existing knowledge[5]. Tradition functions as common ground for determining what

---

1. Cf. J.G. VAN DER WATT, *A Grammar of the Ethics of John: Reading John from an Ethical Perspective*, vol. 1 (WUNT, 431), Tübingen, Mohr Siebeck, 2019, pp. 39-44.
2. M. WOLTER, *Theologie und Ethos im frühen Christentum* (WUNT, 236), Tübingen, Mohr Siebeck, 2009, p. 127.
3. On the importance of ancestry in determining identity in ancient times, see Aristotle (*Rhet.* 1.5.5, 1360b), Plato (*Menex.* 237) and Quintilian (*Inst.* 5.10.24); B.J. MALINA – J.H. NEYREY, *Portraits of Paul: An Archaeology of Ancient Personality*, Louisville, KY, Westminster John Knox, 1996, pp. 23-26, 159.
4. Cf. T. SCHMELLER, *Neutestamentliches Gruppenethos*, in J. BEUTLER (ed.), *Der neue Mensch in Christus* (QD, 190), Freiburg i.Br. – Basel – Wien, Herder, 2001, 220-234; WOLTER, *Theologie und Ethos* (n. 2), pp. 133-136. Works by G. THEISSEN, *Soziologie der Jesusbewegung* (Theologische Existenz Heute, 194), München, Kaiser, [5]1988; F.R. PROSTMEIER, *Handlungsmodelle im ersten Petrusbrief* (FB, 63), Würzburg, Echter, 1990; and R. HEILIGENTHAL, *Werke als Zeichen* (WUNT, 2.9), Tübingen, Mohr Siebeck, 1983, might also be mentioned here.
5. C. BENNEMA, *Christ, the Spirit and the Knowledge of God: A Study in Johannine Epistemology*, in M. HEALY – R. PARRY (eds.), *The Bible and Epistemology: Biblical*

is acceptable and what not within a particular group, based on their accepted identity within their particular group. People often take their tradition seriously in dealing with novel situations, allowing for both a conservative as well as a creative element. This was especially true of ancient group-orientated societies. Tradition may be referred to in a document in different ways, for instance, through the use of phrases like "you/we know that ...", "you have heard ..."[6]. References to what was heard, taught or known also suggests a common traditional frame of knowledge. Terms related to traditional knowledge, as well as increasing or confirming that knowledge, include, for instance, οἶδα, γινώσκω, φανερόω, ἀκούω, γράφω, μαρτυρέω, ἀγγέλλω and derivatives[7]. This is also the case in 1 John, where these terms refer to areas of knowledge that cover a large spectrum of life, from knowing God and Jesus (1 Jn 1,1.3.5; 2,20-21; 5,20; 2 Jn 1), receiving identity as part of the group through salvation (1 Jn 3,5.14-15; 5,13.18.19), acting accordingly in love (1 Jn 2,29; 3,11; 4,16; 2 Jn 6) and following commandments (1 Jn 2,7), to unfolding eschatological realities while they wait for the return of Jesus (eschatology) (1 Jn 2,18; 3,2; 4,3).

Edwards also refers to the importance of terms like "'antichrist', 'Chrism' and 'God's seed' in 1 John that are introduced without explanation, presuming that the readers are familiar with them", thus suggesting traditional material[8]. In the letter the authenticity and authority of this tradition is also increased by linking it (implicitly or explicitly) to the Johannine concept of truth, which refers to what is authentically divine[9].

Already in the Prologue of 1 John (1,1-4) clear indications are found of the importance of tradition in the letter, based on direct eyewitness experiences that are proclaimed by the author. These eyewitness accounts go back to "the beginning"[10] when the (metaphorically expressed) Life and the Word of life were physically experienced on earth in the person of the Son, the One who reveals the divine reality on earth. Life eternal

Soundings on the Knowledge of God, Milton Keynes, Paternoster, 2007, 107-133, remarks on p. 129: "Looking at the *Sitz im Leben* of the Johannine church(es), we may learn *why* John puts so much emphasis on knowledge".

6. Cf., for instance, 1 Jn 2,29; 3,5.13-15; 4,16; 5,18-20.

7. Cf. J.M. LIEU, *The Theology of the Johannine Epistles* (NT Theology), Cambridge, CUP, 1991, p. 102; R. SCHNACKENBURG, *The Moral Teaching of the New Testament*, London, Burns & Oates, 1982, pp. 324-325.

8. R.B. EDWARDS, *The Johannine Epistles* (Sheffield NT Guides), Sheffield, Sheffield Academic Press, 2001, p. 40.

9. Cf. 1 Jn 1,6.10; 2,4.21. Cf. VAN DER WATT, *Grammar* (n. 1), pp. 344-359.

10. The phrase Ὃ ἦν ἀπ' ἀρχῆς in 1 Jn 1,1 most probably refers to the beginning of the ministry of Jesus. Cf. M.J.J. MENKEN, *1, 2 en 3 Johannes* (Tekst en toelichting), Kampen, Kok, 2010, p. 52.

is thus revealed or manifested (ἡ ζωὴ ἐφανερώθη, 1,2) and was physically experienced from the very "beginning". The reference to "the beginning" (1,1) establishes the authority of this information, forming the starting point of this tradition[11]. This formed the fixed message the author *proclaimed* and *witnessed* about as eyewitness basis for the Johannine tradition[12].

What follows is a discussion of some of the basic ways in which the author of 1 John deals with the concept of tradition.

II. WHAT DID THE COMMUNITY ACTUALLY KNOW (ΟΙΔΑ AND ΓΙΝΩΣΚΩ)?

The two verbs οἶδα and γινώσκω are used by the author *inter alia* to refer to what was known in the group[13]. Klauck correctly remarks that the phrase "you know" brings "vorgegebene Glaubenstraditionen ins Spiel"[14], while Malherbe noted that an indication that "content is traditional and not new is indicated by such phrases as 'as you know'…; related to this feature is its general applicability …; since what is advised is already known, the exhorter disavows the need for further instruction, but merely reminds his listeners of what they already know … He similarly compliments them for what they are already doing and encourages them to continue …"[15]. Although Painter opines that "the two verbs seem to be used without difference in meaning"[16], closer scrutiny shows that they are rhetorically also used in different ways, although in the end

---

11. In ancient times older information was usually preferred and was regarded as more authoritative.
12. Cf. the words in the phrase in 1 Jn 1,2: μαρτυροῦμεν καὶ ἀπαγγέλλομεν.
13. The verb οἶδα is used 15 times in 1 John and once in 3 John, mostly with ὅτι to refer to something the people know (i.e., οἶδα ὅτι …). This is the favorite way John refers to existing knowledge. The word γινώσκω is used in two ways: i) referring to knowledge of something – a person knows another object, very similar to οἶδα; ii) with the phrase ἐν τούτῳ (γινώσκομεν) ὅτι … linking two aspects usually in a pattern that you know the one thing because of the other. See also MENKEN, *1, 2 en 3 Johannes* (n. 10), p. 57.
14. H.-J. KLAUCK, *Der erste Johannesbrief* (EKKNT, 23/1), Zürich, Benziger Verlag; Neukirchen-Vluyn, Neukirchener Verlag, 1991, p. 185.
15. Cf. A.J. MALHERBE, *Moral Exhortation: A Greco-Roman Sourcebook*, Philadelphia, PA, Westminster, 1986, p. 125.
16. J. PAINTER, *1, 2, and 3 John* (SP, 18), Collegeville, MN, Liturgical Press, 2002, p. 223. In 1 Jn 2,29 these words are used without apparent difference in meaning (ἐὰν εἰδῆτε ὅτι δίκαιός ἐστιν, γινώσκετε ὅτι …), but in 1 Jn 5,20 the two verbs are used together in the same context, the one (οἴδαμεν) emphasizing facts that are known and the other (γινώσκωμεν) that a person is known, which might point to a semantically differentiated use of the words. Cf. also I. DE LA POTTERIE, *Oida et ginōskō, les deux modes de la connaissance dans le quatrième évangile*, in *Bib* 40 (1959) 709-725.

they emphasize the same thing, namely, sharing existing knowledge, i.e., traditional knowledge.

In light of the use of the two terms οἶδα and γινώσκω in 1 John[17], what the group knew, i.e., what might be considered as their tradition material, could be summarized as follows[18]:

Examples of verses	Content
1,3; 2,24	They have heard the message from the beginning and are therefore solidly *embedded in the eyewitness tradition* that was revealed by, and deals with, Jesus.
1,4-5; 2,13-14; 3,1.6; 4,7; 5,20	The group was intimately aware of *their relationship and co-operation* (κοινωνία) *with and knowledge of the Father and the Son*; they knew God and Christ. Jesus also gave them the insight that they know the true God, are in the true God and are in the light (*Immanenz*).
3,14-15; 5,13.18.19	They are acutely aware of their new *identity* as children of God, having passed from death to life by being *born of God* and receiving *eternal life*.
2,20-21; 5,20	The birth of God places them squarely within the framework of the *truth*; they know the truth since God is the truth.
3,11; 4,16	They know the *love* of God that they must reciprocate by *miming the love of Jesus*.
2,7	They know the *commandments*, especially of mutual love. They are also aware of the new christological framework of the commandments, i.e., the new commandment that also reflects the old commandment.
2,29	They know that Jesus, as their moral example, is *righteous* hence they must be *righteous*.
1,8; 3,5; 5,18	They knew that Jesus conquered and *took away their sin*; evil has no grip on the child of God. They may live a *conquering life* since sin was dealt with and will be dealt with through the blood of Christ.
5,15	They know that *God listens* to them and so that *they could ask* from him according to his will.
2,18; 3,2; 4,3	They were conscious of *eschatological realities*. They have heard about the coming of the antichrist in the last days. They also knew that Jesus is coming again and then believers will be like him. They shared in the tradition of early Jewish and Christian apocalyptical expectations.

17. DE LA POTTERIE, *Oida et ginōskō* (n. 16).
18. The table summarizes only contexts where the two terms in question are used and is not comprehensive.

The table above shows that the author covered a wide spectrum of Christian life in what might be regarded as traditional material. The impression is thus created that the group is well versed in the tradition and its structure, ranging from the birth of a person, his identity, behaviour, to what is to be expected in the future, with emphases on being born to life, being saved from sin, acting like Jesus, receiving what is needed through prayer, suggesting rather fixed borders for what might be called their "tradition"[19]. This confirms an established set of knowledge, i.e., a rather established tradition, outlining a strong sense of identity and self-awareness by the group, in contrast to sparse, loose or unrelated information that would point to a weak tradition in its initial stages.

The repetition of the phrase "we know that ..." in 5,18.19 and 20[20] poses the question whether the author wants to *remind* the addressees of what they have in common in their tradition, or whether he wants to *establish* the common tradition in this way, or both. These remarks do not really seem to convey any novel knowledge, although some of the phrases are not formulated in precisely the same way in the rest of the letter. This re-affirmation of what is already known seems to favour the idea that the author wants to confirm their shared tradition.

It should however be noted that these two verbs rarely refer to knowledge of love *per se*, although connections between their existing knowledge and love are not absent (like in 3,14; 4,7)[21]. The people in the group in the first place know who God is, what Jesus did, who they are. The use of these verbs focuses more on identity than on behaviour.

It should be noted that all the above-mentioned aspects are well attested in the Gospel of John, implying knowledge and acceptance by the addressees of the content of the gospel[22].

III. What Did They Hear (ἈΚΟΥΩ)?

Related to what they know is what they actually *heard* (ἀκούω), assuming shared accepted knowledge, something to which the author

---

19. I can therefore not concur with Lieu, *Johannine Epistles* (n. 7), p. 105, who argues that the actual expressed content of the tradition "is surprisingly meagre, neither is there any interest in the process of transmission or present authentication". The missionary references, though not in focus, as well as the strong argument in 1,1-6 argues against the point Lieu makes.

20. 1 Jn 5,18: Οἴδαμεν ὅτι; 5,19: οἴδαμεν ὅτι; 5,20: οἴδαμεν δὲ ὅτι.

21. This is most probably because love is a key problem with the addressees as well as the schismatics.

22. These include aspects like birth and life, love, truth, commandments, prayer, *Immanenz*, etc. Cf. R.E. Brown, *The Epistles of John: A New Translation with Introduction and Commentary* (AB, 30), Garden City, NY, Doubleday, 1982, pp. 19-30.

consistently refers. The content of what they heard partially overlaps with what they know, but with some differences.

a) They heard about the Word of Life from the *beginning* (1,1.3; cf. also 2,24)
b) They heard an old commandment from the *beginning* (2,7)
c) They heard that they should love one another from the *beginning* (3,11)
d) They heard the message that *God is light* (1,5)
e) They heard about the *antichrist that is coming* (2,18; 4,3)

On the basis of what is heard *from the beginning* (a-c above), the author proclaims and writes (1,1-5), confirming that his message is grounded in the tradition of the historical Jesus (1,1.3). This is the "original" message they heard, which in ancient times suggested authenticity. What was heard concerns the Word of life, Jesus and the commandment to love one another, thus echoing similar ideas in the gospel tradition[23].

IV. The Author Writes, Proclaims and Witnesses

Another way in which the author usually confirms shared knowledge is when he notes that he "writes" for a specific purpose or reason (phrases including ὅτι or ἵνα)[24]. These references serve as a reminder of what is known and are thus related to their tradition. He similarly uses the phrase ταῦτα γράφω (I write *these things*) where ταῦτα not only refers to the immediate context[25], but often implicitly refers to the broader contents of the letter[26]. For instance, 5,13 states, "I write these things to you who believe in the name of the Son of God, that you may know that you have eternal life". This refers to what was previously stated in 5,10-12 and to God giving eternal life through his Son (for instance, 1 Jn 4,9), echoing the essence of the gospel message on this matter (for instance, Jn 3,16; 20,31), thus reaffirming the tradition.

---

23. When the author refers to what the Johannine group had heard (or what was proclaimed to them) some emphasis falls on what is expected in terms of their behaviour: they should obey the commandment to love one another, based on their knowledge of Jesus as life and God as light. Again, this reflects the tradition about Jesus and echoes what is proclaimed in the gospel.

24. Cf. 1 Jn 1,4; 2,1.12.13.14.21; 5,13.

25. 1 Jn 2,7-8 and 2 John 5 are the only passages where there is reference to what the author writes – he writes them a command they had from the beginning, although it is new.

26. Cf. 1 Jn 1,4; 2,1.26; 5,13.

The author of the gospel, too, writes about things that both he and the addressees are aware of as part of the tradition – they know the Father and the Son (14,7-11), their sins are dealt with (1,29) and they should not sin any more[27], they are in conflict with, but victorious over evil (10,28-29; 12,31), they know the truth (3,21; 8,32; 18,37), they know the commandments from the beginning (13,34; 14,15.21; 15,12.17). This has the rhetorical effect of cognitive cohesion between author and addressees, sharing in this common knowledge. Similarly, 1 Jn 2,13-14 describes the identity of the addressees as those who know God and whose sins are forgiven, in contrast to the antichrists.

Related, but not so prominent as the references to the "author writing to the addressees", are the few references to his proclamation and witness – ἀγγέλλω and derivatives and μαρτυρέω –, two concepts that are often used in combination. This proclamation and witness indeed relate to some basic and well-known elements of the Johannine message, namely, to his witness to the life (Jesus, 1 Jn 1,2-3), that they must love one another (3,11), or that the Father sent his Son (4,14), as well as to the light (1,5). This obviously serves to confirm the eyewitness tradition of which the author is the witness.

V. STATEMENTS

The author presents himself as the bearer of the eyewitness tradition by making statements in a variety of ways to argue his points. In many cases these statements are simply assumed to be true[28], while in other cases they are argued elsewhere in the letter, or seem to suggest common beliefs. These statements often serve as anchor points for his arguments and are presented as "fixed" and accepted information within the circle he represents.

A few examples of the numerous occurrences in the letter will suffice to illustrate the diversity of these statements as far as content and rhetoric are concerned.

- *Absolute statements as base for further argumentation*: The statement that "God is light", for instance, serves as a basic truth for the ethical arguments that follow (1,5-10). There is no motivation for the truth of this

---

27. Cf. T. MORGAN, *Popular Morality in the Early Roman Empire*, Cambridge, CUP, 2007, p. 162, for informative material on the views of some ancient moral philosophers.

28. As a *gnomê* or *sententia*; G.L. PARSENIOS, *First, Second, and Third John* (Paideia: Commentaries on the NT), Grand Rapids, MI, Baker, 2014, pp. 16-20.

statement – it is simply stated as truth that forms part of the accepted knowledge the author represents[29].

- *Statements logically linked to one another*: Conceptual logic holds statements together and is based on shared knowledge, often echoing the gospel tradition (the *underlined* phrases below, for instance, echo shared gospel tradition). 1 Jn 3,7-10 may serve as a compact example:

  3,7: *Imperative*: Do not let anyone deceive you.
  Statement: He who does what is right is righteous like Jesus.
  3,8: *Statement*: He who sins is of the *devil*[30].
  Reason (ὅτι): The *devil* sins[31] from the beginning.
  Statement: For this purpose Jesus came, to destroy the works of the *devil*[32].
  3,9: *Statement*: He who is *born* of God[33] does not sin.
  Reason (ὅτι): Because God's *seed* remains in him
  Statement: He cannot sin.
  Reason (ὅτι): He is *born* of God[34].
  3,10: *Statement*: By this it is evident who are the *children* of God[35] and of the devil[36]: Those who do not practice righteousness and do not love their brothers[37] are not of God.

  The argument is developed in a logical and systematic way, starting with the devil and sin, moving to Jesus destroying the works of the devil, making it possible for those who are born of God not to sin, but to practice righteousness and love. This illustrates how the author develops his argument by combining what is known in the Johannine (gospel) tradition with his own additional material.

- *Statements motivated*: The statement, "God is love" in 4,8.16 is motivated by God sending his Son. This is, of course, a basic idea within the Johannine (gospel) tradition[38]. Linking a statement to a commonly shared motivation to support the validity of the statement frequently occurs in 1 John. The author remarks in 3,8 that he who sins is of the devil with the motivation that the devil sins from the beginning, while in 5,3 commandments should be kept *because* that is what love of God requires.

  Closely related to the above, are *statements that are motivated by or based on (reflecting on) dogma*: In 3,13 a statement is motivated by the development of remarks reflecting what was commonly accepted, namely that believers have eternal life and love their fellow-believers[39]:

---

29. Cf. also 1 Jn 2,15-17; 3,7.22; 4,8.19; 5,4.17.
30. Cf. Jn 8,44.
31. Cf. Jn 8,44.
32. Cf. Jn 1,29; 12,31; 16,11.
33. Cf. Jn 1,12-13; 3,3.5.
34. Cf. Jn 1,12-13; 3,3.5.
35. Cf. Jn 20,17.
36. Cf. Jn 8,44.
37. Cf. Jn 13,34-35; 15,12.
38. Cf. Jn 3,16; 4,34; 5,23.30, etc.
39. Cf. also 1 Jn 4,7-10.19.21; 5,1-2; 3 Jn 4-8.

3,13: *Statement*: do not be surprised if the <u>world hates you</u>[40].
     Tradition: We know we passed from <u>death to life</u>[41].
     Reason (ὅτι): We <u>love our brothers</u>[42].

A further example is found in 2,1-2, where the salvific significance of Jesus is simply spelled out: Jesus is the *Paraclete*, the atonement for the sins of the world. These remarks are dogmatic remarks that are not motivated, but simply stated. Rhetorically, it seems that they formed part of an accepted and shared set of "truths" about Jesus that need no further clarification. These "truths" are then used to explain other concepts, like how sin is dealt with, as is done in 2,1-2.

These examples illustrate that the author combines (gospel) tradition with his own directives and statements, also adding reasons for doing so. In this way his message is embedded in tradition and thus gains more authority. This suggests a living tradition that was interpreted, leading to conclusions and statements that logically echo this tradition (conservative element), but was simultaneously applied to the challenges of a new situation (creative element). Describing the identity or motivating the ethical behaviour of the group is by no means a stagnant repetition of tradition, but a reflective process in which tradition serves as the basis and final control for the application and development of the views of the author in his current situation.

VI. AUTHORITY AND THE TRADITIONAL MESSAGE

It is noteworthy that the author is hesitant to identify himself as an authoritative figure in the letter, not even at the beginning, and even if he does refer to himself, he identifies himself as part of the eyewitness group adhering to the traditional message they have from the beginning. There is very little evidence that he appeals to personal authority to influence his addressees. However, in his language he shows awareness of considerable authority. Many of his statements seem to be absolute or at least reflect absolute facts, as was clear even from the remarks above. It seems that what he says or the statements he makes are based on solid, accepted and undeniable truths, i.e., solid and accepted tradition. What seems to happen is that he "hides" behind the authority of the tradition,

---

40. Cf. Jn 15,18–16,4.
41. Cf. Jn 11,25-26.
42. Cf. Jn 13,34-35.

allowing the tradition to speak authoritatively for itself. He just conveys the authoritative tradition as the one who writes, witnesses and proclaims that tradition. The focus remains on the authority that is inherently part of the tradition itself.

In 5,9-12 reference is made to the witness of God concerning his Son (5,10): "he who does not believe God has made him a liar, because he has not believed *the testimony that God has given of his Son*". God's testimony is that his Son brings life, which overlaps with the basic traditional message the author is witnessing about, underlining that it is true (cf. 1,2; 4,14). What the author testifies about is confirmed by the testimony of God himself, illustrating where the source of all authority lies. To disbelieve this (his) message is to make God a liar (5,10). This elevates the proclamation and witness of the author to a considerable level of authority, since it is in line with the testimony of God himself.

VII. THE ROLE OF THE SPIRIT IN PRESERVING THE TRADITION WITHIN THE JOHANNINE GROUP

As is the case in the gospel, the Holy Spirit has a very specific role to play in 1 John[43], which is especially linked to the tradition of the group[44]. Olsson summarizes the role of the Spirit aptly: "The letter recipients are to abide in the teaching which the Spirit has given and continues to give them (2.27), and also in that which they have heard from the beginning (2.24). Only by so doing can they abide in the Son and in the Father. The Spirit and the truth, that is, the tradition passed on from Jesus as interpreted by the Johannine 'fathers', cannot be separated without serious consequences", however, "the author seems to be describing more the result of the Spirit's activity than the Spirit's activity as such"[45].

1. *The Work of the Spirit of Truth*

The word πνεῦμα is used in the following verses, showing the particular foci of the activities of the Spirit in 1 John:

---

43. Cf. U.C. VON WAHLDE, *The Johannine Commandments: 1 John and the Struggle for the Johannine Tradition* (Theological Inquiries), Mahwah, NJ, Paulist, 1990; B. OLSSON, *Deus semper maior? On God in the Johannine Writings*, in J. NISSEN – S. PEDERSEN (eds.), *New Readings in John: Literary and Theological Perspectives* (JSNTSup, 182), Sheffield, Sheffield Academic Press, 1999, 143-171, pp. 156-157.
44. References to the Spirit are found in the second part of the letter (3,24; 4,1.2.3.6.13; 5,6.8) and show a consistent and interrelated pattern of use.
45. OLSSON, *Deus semper maior?* (n. 43), p. 157.

Verse	What is said
3,24	Now he who keeps his *commandments abides in him, and he in him*. And by this we know that he *abides in us, by the Spirit* whom he has given us.
4,1	Beloved, do not believe *every spirit*, but *test the spirits*, whether they are of God.
4,2	By this you know the *Spirit of God*, every *spirit* that *confesses* that Jesus Christ has come in the flesh is of God.
4,3	and every *spirit* that does *not confess* that Jesus Christ has come in the flesh is not of God. And this is the *spirit* of the *antichrist*.
4,6	We are of God. He who knows God hears us; he who is not of God does not hear us. By this we know the *spirit of truth* and the *spirit of error*.
4,13	By this we know that we *abide in him, and he in us*, because he has given us of his *Spirit*.
5,6	And it is the *Spirit* who *bears witness*, because the *Spirit is truth*.
5,8	And there are three that bear witness on earth: the *Spirit*, the water and the blood; and these three agree as one.

The above table shows that the Spirit is especially involved in the *correct confession* about the person of Jesus[46], in contrast to what the false spirits (i.e., those not of God, 4,1) confess or do not confess (4,1-3)[47]. The confession of Jesus is described as the primary focus of the work of the Spirit. This view echoes the function of the Paraclete, the Spirit of truth, in the gospel[48]. The test for distinguishing between false spirits, i.e., the spirit of the antichrist (4,3), and the Spirit of God (who is of God) indeed lies with the correct confession, i.e., the tradition about Jesus that is related to the baptism and death of Jesus (5,6-9), dealing with the salvific earthly mission of Jesus as Christ and human, who brings eternal life to this world (cf. Jn 20,30-31)[49]. Since the Spirit works within the framework of the confessed tradition about the mission of Jesus, he is

---

46. Cf. also B.F. WESTCOTT, *The Epistles of St. John: The Greek Text with Notes and Essays*, London – New York, Macmillan, ⁴1902, p. 79.
47. Cf. PAINTER, *1, 2, and 3 John* (n. 16), p. 258; MENKEN, *1, 2 en 3 Johannes* (n. 10), p. 77; R. SCHNACKENBURG, *Johannesbriefe* (HTKNT), Freiburg i.Br., Herder, 1984, pp. 210-211.
48. Cf. SCHNACKENBURG, *Johannesbriefe* (n. 47), pp. 210-211; VAN DER WATT, *Grammar* (n. 1), pp. 251-256.
49. OLSSON, *Deus semper maior?* (n. 43), p. 156, notes that if the idea of the presence of the Spirit goes back to the covenant ideas in Jeremiah 31 and Ezekiel 36, the idea of revelation and prophecy is predominant (cf. also Jl 2,28-29; Is 60,1). See also MENKEN, *1, 2 en 3 Johannes* (n. 10), p. 91.

identified as the true Spirit or Spirit of truth (5,6). Klauck[50] even interprets the evidence of the witness of the Spirit more specifically in terms of keeping the double commandment of faith and love (3,24), two cornerstones of the tradition.

2. Anointing in 2,18-28

The discussion in 1 Jn 2,18-28 might be of some help in understanding the dynamics of the Spirit in relation to the Johannine tradition. Here the author addresses the problem of schism within the community[51], distinguishing the Johannine group from the antichrists with the following statement: "But you have an anointing (ὑμεῖς χρῖσμα ἔχετε) of the Holy One, and all of you have knowledge" (2,20). He continues by pointing out that the Johannine group knows the truth, resulting in their correct confession of the Son, illustrating their union with the Father (2,22-23).

In 2,27 the author deals with the concept of anointing: "but the anointing which you received from him abides in you[52], and you have no need that any one should teach you; as his anointing teaches you about everything, and is true, and is no lie, just as it has taught you, abide in him". In the latter case the anointing is personified: "it" teaches, making any other teaching unnecessary[53]. Apart from that, the union (*Immanenz*) of believers with God (being in or having God) is consistently linked to the anointing and the knowledge resulting from that union[54]. This knowledge is the knowledge they heard from the beginning (2,24) and is thus linked to the tradition within which the group finds themselves. By having this "anointing" believers can detect and even understand the errors of the secessionists, because of the spiritual insight resulting from the "anointing"[55]. Based on their tradition they can distinguish between right and wrong.

The question now is: what exactly is intended by the term "anointing"? It is not directly clear from the passage and several possibilities

---

50. KLAUCK, *Johannesbrief* (n. 14), p. 225.
51. See 1 Jn 2,18-19.21-22.26.
52. The phrase "remaining in them" emphasizes the permanence of the "anointing" among them; cf. S.S. SMALLEY, *1, 2, 3 John* (WBC, 51), Dallas, TX, Word, 1984, p. 124.
53. D.L. AKIN, *1, 2, 3 John* (New American Commentary, 38), Nashville, TN, B&H Publishing Group, 2001, p. 125, opines, "Additional revelation was not needed; indeed, it could be deadly. Spiritual illumination of the received traditions was the pattern they should follow".
54. 1 Jn 2,23-24.27-28.
55. SMALLEY, *1, 2, 3 John* (n. 52), p. 105; I.H. MARSHALL, *The Epistles of John* (NICNT), Grand Rapids, MI, Eerdmans, 1978, p. 153.

are proposed[56]. In 2,20 it seems to refer to an act (of anointing)[57] or it may also refer to an object (like the oil) which might then symbolically[58] refer to the Spirit[59]. It might also remind the reader of baptism[60]. The gift of the Spirit is, of course, often associated with baptism[61], but Smalley[62] points out that there is no evidence of people being anointed during baptism in the first century. One should therefore be careful not to associate anointment too quickly with baptism[63].

Several commentators read "anointing" as a parallel expression for *Spirit*[64]. It is argued that anointing in the Old Testament is often associated

---

56. BDAG, *ad loc.*, distinguishes between two views: "*anointing* (so lit. Ex 29:7) 1J 2:20, 27a, b, usu. taken to mean anointing w. the Holy Spirit (differently Rtzst., Mysterienrel '27, 396f, who thinks of the 'formal equation of the baptismal proclamation w. the χρῖσμα')". These two views may also be combined. LSJ, 1940, repr. 1968, *ad loc.*, point out that in classical Greek the word is used to refer to anything that was smeared on. It may also be used in the sense of an assignment (see J.P. LOUW – E.A. NIDA, *Greek-English Lexicon of the New Testament, Based on Semantic Domains*, New York, United Bible Societies, 1996, *ad loc.*). BROWN, *Epistles of John* (n. 22), pp. 342-347, and G. STRECKER, *Die Johannesbriefe* (KEK, 14), Göttingen, Vandenhoeck & Ruprecht, 1989, pp. 126-128, provide a good overview of positions taken in this regard. Cf. also KLAUCK, *Johannesbrief* (n. 14), pp. 156-158. The occurrences in the LXX usually concern kings, priests and prophets being anointed. In the church fathers the anointment at baptism is often referred to.

57. Cf. R. BULTMANN, *The Johannine Epistles: A Commentary on the Johannine Epistles* (Hermeneia), Philadelphia, PA, Fortress, 1973, p. 37, against WESTCOTT, *Epistles of St. John* (n. 46), p. 73.

58. C. HAAS – M. DE JONGE – J.L. SWELLENGREBEL, *1 John: A Translator's Handbook on the Letters of John*, New York, United Bible Societies, 1972, p. 66, remark: "The New Testament probably does not use it with reference to the actual performance of the rite, but in a comparable metaphorical or symbolical sense". Cf. LIEU, *Johannine Epistles* (n. 7), pp. 29-30; PAINTER, *1, 2, and 3 John* (n. 16), p. 198, MARSHALL, *The Epistles of John* (n. 55), p. 153.

59. Cf. LIEU, *Johannine Epistles* (n. 7), p. 29. HAAS *et al.*, *1 John* (n. 58), p. 65, distinguish between the possibilities in the following way: "The noun 'anointing' occurs only here and v. 27 in the New Testament. It may refer, (1) to an object, 'the means of anointing', that is, 'anointing oil' (cp. Ex. 29.7; 30.25), or (2) to an event, either (2a) 'the (act of) anointing', or (2b) 'the (result of) being anointed'. Meanings (1) and (2b) are both possible here". MENKEN, *1, 2 en 3 Johannes* (n. 10) p. 49, favours the idea that "anointing" refers to the result of the action in this instance.

60. LIEU, *Johannine Epistles* (n. 7), p. 30, rejects this notion.

61. See Mk 1,10; Lk 4,18; Acts 10,38 – this might refer to the baptism of Jesus –, Lk 3,21-22. Cf. also 2 Cor 1,21-22. KLAUCK, *Johannesbrief* (n. 14), p. 157, supports this idea strongly. Cf. also T.F. JOHNSON, *1, 2, and 3 John*, Grand Rapids, MI, Baker, 1995, p. 57; PAINTER, *1, 2, and 3 John* (n. 16), p. 198; MENKEN, *1, 2 en 3 Johannes* (n. 10), p. 49.

62. SMALLEY, *1, 2, 3 John* (n. 52), p. 106.

63. Cf. also MARSHALL, *Epistles of John* (n. 55), pp. 153-154.

64. WESTCOTT, *Epistles of St. John* (n. 46), p. 73; HAAS *et al.*, *1 John* (n. 58), p. 65; MARSHALL, *Epistles of John* (n. 55), p. 153; SCHNACKENBURG, *Johannesbriefe* (n. 47), p. 210; KLAUCK, *Johannesbrief* (n. 14), p. 157; JOHNSON, *1, 2, and 3 John* (n. 61), pp. 57-58; S.J. KISTEMAKER, *Exposition of James and the Epistles of John*, Grand Rapids, MI, Baker, 2001, p. 279, to mention but a few.

with the presence of the Spirit[65], while in two cases in the New Testament Jesus was anointed with the Spirit[66]. The association of "anointing" with the Spirit is also supported by the personification of "anointing" in 2,27, namely, that the Spirit *teaches* believers everything. This sounds like an echo of a similar view in the gospel, namely, that the Spirit will lead the disciples in the truth[67]. Smalley is therefore convinced that there are good grounds for accepting that "anointing" refers to "God's indwelling Spirit acting as teacher and guide in all matters of truth"[68].

Some scholars, however, are of the opinion that the "anointing" refers to the *word of God*, i.e., "the teaching of the Christian gospel itself"[69] that also indwells in a person, enabling him to teach. Gnostics argued that anointing equalled initiation into supernatural knowledge, which could serve as a parallel to receiving the word of God[70]. Apart from this there is evidence elsewhere in the Johannine literature that the word remains in the believer[71]. This is further borne out in this context where it is said that what they have heard from the beginning remains in them – this might refer to the word of God. Smalley mentions the view of Dodd in this regard: "Thus Dodd concludes that χρῖσμα, in vv. 20 and 27, 'which confers knowledge of God, and is also a prophylactic against the poison of false teaching, is the Word of God, that is, the Gospel, or the revelation of God in Christ, as communicated in the rule of faith to catechumens, and confessed in Baptism'"[72].

Several scholars sensibly argue that perhaps the concept of "anointing" includes both these latter views. "John is deliberately using the idea of χρῖσμα to signify *both* the Spirit and the word of God. The faithful, that is to say, are those who have (inwardly) received the gospel of truth, and made it their own *through* the activity of the Spirit (cf. 1 Thess 1,5-6); thereby they possess the antidote to heresy"[73].

---

65. Cf. 1 Sam 16,13 or Is 61,1.
66. Lk 4,18; Acts 10,38.
67. Jn 15,26; 16,8-15. For further discussion, cf. SCHNACKENBURG, *Johannesbriefe* (n. 47), pp. 151-154; SMALLEY, *1, 2, 3 John* (n. 52), pp. 107, 126; MENKEN, *1, 2 en 3 Johannes* (n. 10), p. 49.
68. SMALLEY, *1, 2, 3 John* (n. 52), p. 106.
69. Cf. I. DE LA POTTERIE, *L'onction du chrétien par la foi*, in *Bib* 40 (1959) 12-69; HAAS et al., *1 John* (n. 58), p. 65; SMALLEY, *1, 2, 3 John* (n. 52), 106; LIEU, *Johannine Epistles* (n. 7), p. 35; KLAUCK, *Johannesbrief* (n. 14), p. 157; KISTEMAKER, *Epistles of John* (n. 64), p. 279; MENKEN, *1, 2 en 3 Johannes* (n. 10), p. 49.
70. SMALLEY, *1, 2, 3 John* (n. 52), p. 106.
71. 1 Jn 1,10; 2,14; 2 John 2; Jn 5,38; 15,7.
72. SMALLEY, *1, 2, 3 John* (n. 52), p. 107.
73. *Ibid.* HAAS et al., *1 John* (n. 58), p. 66, are of the same opinion: "The two do not exclude one another, for the Gospel cannot give true knowledge unless through the Spirit,

For our purposes there is no need to distinguish between these two options, since both strongly emphasize the importance of the tradition within the Johannine group. Their identity, who they are, what they believe and should believe is deeply embedded in the Johannine tradition and the χρῖσμα has a role in this process. Olsson aptly remarks: "The author ... would link teaching from the Spirit closely together with the tradition. What is required is *both* the Spirit *and* the truth ...; the Spirit does not operate independently"[74].

These considerations in 2,18-28, read with the remarks about the Spirit in 4,1-4, show that the Spirit works within a well-defined traditional framework, outlined by the authenticity of the confessions linked to the Jesus tradition[75]. The Spirit confirms what is known, as Akin puts it: "Additional revelation was not needed ... Spiritual illumination of the received traditions was the pattern they should follow"[76]. This implies that the remark that they need not be taught anything is confirming and protecting the borders of their tradition, perhaps against the (gnostically inclined) secessionists who claim their own special knowledge[77].

VIII. Does the Eschatology in 1 John Reflect Johannine Tradition?

It is widely accepted that there are differences between the gospel and 1 John when it comes to eschatological views. The main emphasis in the gospel is on realizing eschatology[78], a concept also true of the birth and eternal life passages in 1 John. However, sections in 1 John, like 1 Jn 2,28–3,4, focus on a futuristic eschatological view, implying that the eschatology of 1 John is also based on a cosmological drama with apocalyptic traits[79].

---

and the Spirit is to be tested by the Gospel". Cf. MARSHALL, *Epistles of John* (n. 55), p. 154.

74. OLSSON, *Deus semper maior?* (n. 43), p. 157.
75. Cf. WESTCOTT, *Epistles of St. John* (n. 46), p. 79.
76. AKIN, *1, 2, 3 John* (n. 53), p. 125.
77. Cf. R.E. BROWN, *The Community of the Beloved Disciple: The Life, Loves, and Hates of an Individual Church in New Testament Times*, New York, Paulist, 1979, p. 142; SCHNACKENBURG, *Johannesbriefe* (n. 47), p. 162; SMALLEY, *1, 2, 3 John* (n. 52), p. 126; JOHNSON, *1, 2, and 3 John* (n. 61), p. 58.
78. The concept of realized eschatology (having eternal life) in the gospel is often favoured, although the idea of realizing eschatology (i.e., the eschatological process is not yet finished but is unfolding, realizing itself, culminating in the resurrection on the final day – Jn 6,39-40.44) is gaining in acceptance.
79. Cf. BULTMANN, *Johannine Epistles* (n. 57), pp. 35-36; STRECKER, *Johannesbriefe* (n. 56), pp. 62-63. MENKEN, *1, 2 en 3 Johannes* (n. 10), pp. 47-48, sees early Christian traditions as the foundation of the Johannine ideas here.

The letter describes two opposing spiritual powers that stand in conflict in this world, namely, the divine and evil, God and the devil, but this conflict will be (is) resolved with the (final) conflict and judgment. The negative situation in the present age will change to an ideal one in the future according to the hope of the believers (3,1-3). But this will only happen after the escalating presence of evil in the last hour in the form of the antichrist, deception and false prophets (2,18-19). This process has already started (2,18-19). Reference is made to the apocalyptic last hour that arrived with the appearance of antichrists (2,18-22), as well as the destruction of the works of the devil (sin) by Jesus (3,8).

The events surrounding the schismatics are interpreted within a realizing eschatological framework, i.e., they prove themselves to be dead and do not have eternal life like the believers (cf. 3,11-18), since their behaviour as antichrists are evil, murderous and false. The apocalyptic antichrists are indeed as real as the schismatics[80]. Although the conflict itself is not described in any detail, as for instance in the Apocalypse of John, the use of certain concepts within the arguments implies an underlying presence of such an apocalyptic conflict.

Although some elements of this apocalyptic view are found in the gospel too (for instance, the conflict between God and the devil, the devil being conquered), the apocalyptic view is more developed in 1 John. This suggests that in 1 John the more traditional Christian eschatological view is foregrounded, but in synergy with the typical Johannine realizing eschatology: believers already have eternal life (3,14-18; 5,11-13). Thus, the author of 1 John combines Christian traditional material (apocalyptic future events) with material that is normally associated with Johannine tradition (eternal life). This synergy is, for instance, evident in his treatment of the concept of antichrist (2,18-19; 4,3), identifying the presence of the antichrist(s) and thus the presence of the apocalyptic last hour (2,18) as "now"[81], the "last hour" being an apocalyptic expression associated with

---

80. The secessionists were declared antichrists who in certain respects deviated from this set of traditional knowledge (1 Jn 2,18-27), not knowing God (1 Jn 4,6) and were therefore no longer regarded as part of the Johannine group, no longer sharing the identity of the Johannine group. Although they continued to proclaim Christ in their own way, it is not done within the confines of the tradition of the eyewitness group in the letter. B.J. MALINA – J.H. NEYREY, *Conflict in Luke-Acts: Labeling and Deviance Theory*, in J.H. NEYREY (ed.), *The Social World of Luke-Acts: Models for Interpretation*, Peabody, MA, Hendrickson, 1991, 97-124, p. 100, call this "negative labelling", "Negative labels, in fact, are accusations of *deviance*. Behaviour is deviant when it violates the sense of order or the set of classification which people perceive to structure their world" (cf. also B.J. MALINA – R.L. ROHRBAUGH, *Social-science Commentary on the Gospel of John*, Minneapolis, MN, Fortress, 1998, p. 33).

81. Cf. 1 Jn 2,18.22; 4,3; 2 John 7; see also 2 Thess 2,1-12; Revelation 12–13. Although the term antichrist is not specifically used in Revelation or Thessalonians, there might

the final eschatological events[82]. The phrase "last hour" occurs only here in the New Testament, but the absence of an article (ἐσχάτη ὥρα) might suggest that it might have been a general and well-known phrase[83], although Bultmann suggests that the phrase might stem from Jewish apocalyptic[84]. It seems to refer to the period of escalating evil before the final *parousia* and final judgment[85], meaning that the "community's own story is being played out in the immediate context of apocalyptic events of the end time"[86], as can be seen from the several references in 1 John to the *parousia* or return of Jesus (2,28; 3,2)[87].

Lieu, however, is a bit sceptical about the role of future hope as a motivating factor within the schism. She remarks: "Faced with schism and perhaps with hostility, 1 John does not take refuge from the present in the hopes of the future. It is easy to see what it does do as a retreat into tradition, a turning in on itself"[88]. The tradition forms the safe haven for the Johannine group in this situation. However, the author does not exclude the hope in the future (cf. 3,1-3). Lieu is correct that a reason for defining and motivating the group lies in their tradition and history with Jesus. It might be more accurate to say that the past (the Jesus tradition) and future (the hope that is part of this tradition) merge in the present (focusing on the present situation), obviously with the main emphasis on the Jesus tradition. The tradition indeed also carries the promise of the future.

The way the author combines typically Johannine traditional material with more general Christian traditional material illustrates the living interpretative tradition of the Johannine group. It was by no means a stagnant repetition of tradition, but a lively application of the tradition to their challenging situation. In 1 John a crisis with the schismatics prompted the view that the last hour is now and the antichrist(s) are here,

---

be a conceptual link, as BULTMANN, *Johannine Epistles* (n. 57), p. 36, suggests. Cf. also STRECKER, *Johannesbriefe* (n. 56), p. 214; SMALLEY, *1, 2, 3 John* (n. 52), pp. 98-100. MARSHALL, *Epistles of John* (n. 55), p. 151, however, warns against an apocalyptic over-interpretation of these passages in 1 John.

82. KLAUCK, *Johannesbrief* (n. 14), p. 234; BROWN, *Epistles of John* (n. 22), p. 497; SMALLEY, *1, 2, 3 John* (n. 52), p. 101; MARSHALL, *Epistles of John* (n. 55), p. 148.
83. Cf. HAAS et al., *1 John* (n. 58), p. 61; SMALLEY, *1, 2, 3 John* (n. 52), p. 95.
84. BULTMANN, *Johannine Epistles* (n. 57), p. 36.
85. Cf. SMALLEY, *1, 2, 3 John* (n. 52), p. 95. BROWN, *Epistles of John* (n. 22), p. 381, argues that because the term *parousia* is not explained in the text, it points to "a Johannine apocalyptic tradition". KLAUCK, *Johannesbrief* (n. 14), p. 174, shows that the idea of the *parousia* is an apocalyptic *topos*. It will lead to the final judgment at which point believers will not shrink from him in shame because of their righteous behaviour (2,28-29).
86. STRECKER, *Johannesbriefe* (n. 56), p. 63.
87. Cf. KLAUCK, *Johannesbrief* (n. 14), pp. 174, 181.
88. LIEU, *Johannine Epistles* (n. 7), p. 90.

thus drawing on end time apocalyptic ideas to interpret their current situation. The author indeed finds solace in both the Johannine and more general Christian tradition. What happened with schismatics was expected, at least according to the tradition. In spite of these apocalyptic events being realized among them, the traditional future hope is not abandoned, but clearly defined – when Jesus comes again, believers will be like him.

IX. THE OBJECTIVE NATURE OF THE JOHANNINE VIEWS

The debate whether there are values that might be deemed universally true (objective) or whether values are always dependent on particular situations or societies (subjective), is as old as Western philosophy, dating back to the debates of the Sophists or Socrates[89]. These debates show that identity, ethics and tradition cannot be separated. Reflections on identity and behaviour are always embedded in and argued from some or other theoretical framework, as part of the accepted tradition of a particular group.

For example, discussions about ethics in the Western philosophical tradition represent numerous different subjective perspectives. The Sophists, for instance, relativized ethics as a cultural phenomenon while philosophers like Socrates, Plato and Aristotle *inter alios* focused on what lies behind human behaviour in the form of virtue in order to live a good and virtuous life on a rational basis. Emphases later shifted, for instance, among the Stoics, from the virtuous ethical agent to the question of which deeds express moral virtue. Stoics valued contemplation as part of the good life, being able to reflect rationally on theoretical truths[90]. Open and diverse discussions about different aspects from different perspectives related to behaviour (for instance, virtue, the benefit of the society, religious views, etc.) were part and parcel of ethical reflections from the very beginning and indeed produced a variety of views, not to mention the diversity of views we know today.

In line with this tendency, Johannine tradition functions within the confines of the particular *religious* convictions of the Johannine group, based on their faith in the Father and the Son, giving it a subjective character (i.e., theoretically it does not depart from reason, social responsibilities, the

---

89. Cf. VAN DER WATT, *Grammar* (n. 1), pp. 20-21, 57-59.
90. Cf. Diogenes Laertius (7.130) as evidence that Stoics believed that the best life is not theoretical or practical, but rational.

necessity for virtue, etc.). However, their tradition also claims that their theological (religious) conviction is solidly based on the revelatory presence of the pre-existent, true God[91]. The divine reality represented by this God is transcendental, suggesting a pre-existent and objective reality outside this relative, worldly, human reality, thus claiming objectivity (universal truth) for the Johannine theological system[92].

X. Some Concluding Remarks

Both the identity and the behaviour of the Johannine group are firmly grounded in the eyewitness tradition the group preserved and observed from the beginning, based on the physical presence of the "Word of life" (1,1-4). In this "Word of life", identified as Jesus the Son, the divine and human realities are merged. Johannine tradition thus offers a new symbolic universe where the transcendental reality becomes the central and dominating reality of believers in this world. As children of God who are in the light, they must live according to the requirements of the light in the family of God (1,5-7). This new reality is described, preserved and could be known in the tradition of the Johannine group. This formed the foundation of their identity, implying that once this tradition is rejected, as was the case with the schismatics, this identity is lost and this obviously affected their behaviour.

Within the Johannine group a synergy exists between tradition, identity and ethics. It is based on the revelation of God through Christ, characterizing it as revelatory and not self-conceived. Who they as Christians are and how they should behave is not to be determined by human decision, but is to be understood through the God-given message as it is expressed in and "prescribed" by their eyewitness tradition. If somebody does not live within the confines of this tradition, he or she is not of God and his or her actions are not according to the truth or God's will. This is also the reason why an appeal might be made to the objectivity (truth) of the tradition. Truth is from God, the creator, who transcends human subjectivity.

The author of 1 John sees himself as part of an ongoing process of transmitting the tradition that started and was revealed at the beginning

---

91. Cf. Jn 1,1-4; 17,3. This creator God is the God referred to as the Light or Love in 1 John.
92. It might be argued that this is also subjective, since it is based on the set of beliefs of the Johannine group. However, from the perspective of the author, it lies within the objective transcendental world.

(Ὃ ἦν ἀπ' ἀρχῆς, 1,1) when Jesus was heard, seen and touched[93], which refers to the remembered Jesus of the gospel. This knowledge is further applied to their living spirituality in this world. If they were simply told: "Behave as is expected of you", the Johannine believers would at least have had some idea of what is expected of them, by recalling existing ethical knowledge, i.e., their tradition. Their tradition served as source for their everyday life.

The shared traditional knowledge in the first letter includes a comprehensive body of knowledge covering a wide spectrum of Christian life, from the knowledge of the transcendental reality, to salvation, ethics and even eschatology[94]. Klauck correctly remarks that by referring to what the group knows, the author brings "vorgegebene Glaubenstraditionen ins Spiel"[95] that lead to and constitute the fellowship with the Father and the Son[96]. The traditional message becomes a "Bindemittel zwischen Christus und den Glaubenden"[97]. This suggests the presence of a rather fixed tradition within the Johannine group, but does not suggest a stagnant tradition that defies application in novel situations, to the contrary.

It is remarkable that the author does not identify himself as an authoritative figure in the letter as was often the case in ancient letters, thus establishing the authoritative basis for his message. He rather presents himself as the anonymous carrier of the traditional eyewitness message. Real authority was seated in the tradition as such and not in him as the messenger. He apparently foresees that the group might listen because of the truth of the tradition that was revealed and not because of who he is.

What is the core of this Johannine tradition? In the formation of the Johannine tradition, the gospel as such represents the development over the larger part of the first century[98], while the letters were most probably written at the end of the first century as situation oriented documents. The close link between the language and ideas became apparent in the discussions above. In spite of differences, the author of 1 John confirmed the tradition represented in the gospel and encouraged the addressees to

---

93. See, for instance, SCHNACKENBURG, *Johannesbriefe* (n. 47), pp. 52-58; BROWN, *Epistles of John* (n. 22), pp. 162-174; STRECKER, *Johannesbriefe* (n. 56), pp. 62-72; KLAUCK, *Johannesbrief* (n. 14), pp. 73-74; PAINTER, *1, 2, and 3 John* (n. 16), pp. 129-131; MENKEN, *1, 2 en 3 Johannes* (n. 10), pp. 21-25.
94. Cf. BENNEMA, *Christ, the Spirit* (n. 5), pp. 110-112.
95. KLAUCK, *Johannesbrief* (n. 14), p. 185.
96. Cf. 1 Jn 2,24; PAINTER, *1, 2, and 3 John* (n. 16), p. 201; MENKEN, *1, 2 en 3 Johannes* (n. 10), p. 52.
97. SCHNACKENBURG, *Johannesbriefe* (n. 47), p. 159.
98. This includes the oral period that started in the first part of the first century and formed the roots of what was eventually written down.

abide by this tradition which they heard from the beginning (thus including the gospel)[99]. The traditional eyewitness message was indeed seen as something that was inherently part of the essential identity of the Johannine group, which should be witnessed from generation to generation. The author's frequent references to the apocalyptic future also confirm that the gospel was not his only source of shared information; he also developed his message with reference to more general Christian convictions. This leaves one with the picture, not of an isolated, closed, Johannine group, but of a group that was aware of and open to broader Christian views and traditions. The traditional water of the gospel, as well as that of wider Christianity, also flows in the traditional stream of 1 John.

79 Greenway Jan VAN DER WATT
Greenside 2193
Randburg
South Africa
Jgvdw100@gmail.com

---

[99]. Support for this view is common in scholarship, as is evident from the work of scholars like C.M. TUCKETT, *Christology and the New Testament: Jesus and His Earliest Followers*, Edinburgh, Edinburgh University Press, 2001, p. 173, and BROWN, *Epistles of John* (n. 22), pp. 19-30.

JOHANNEISCHES TRADITIONSMATERIAL IM JOHANNESEVANGELIUM, IN DEN JOHANNESBRIEFEN UND IN DEN IGNATIUSBRIEFEN

In der gegenwärtigen Forschung scheint weitgehende Einigkeit darüber zu herrschen, dass der antiochenische Bischof Ignatius in den sieben von ihm überlieferten Briefen[1] das neutestamentliche Joh[2] nicht zitiert habe, dass sich darüber hinaus auch eine wie auch immer zu definierende andersgeartete literarische Abhängigkeit zwischen den Ignatianen und dem vierten Evangelium nicht wahrscheinlich machen lasse[3]. Damit ist freilich keinesfalls von vornherein ausgeschlossen, dass sowohl der Verfasserkreis des Joh als auch Ignatius in ihren jeweiligen Schriften gleiches oder ähnliches Traditionsmaterial verarbeitet haben, dass zwischen ihnen bzw. ihren jeweiligen Werken somit also eine traditionsgeschichtliche Abhängigkeit bestehe[4]; vielmehr lässt der etwa von E. von der Goltz vorgelegte Aufweis nicht unerheblicher sprachlicher Berührungen zwischen dem Joh und den johanneischen Schriften einer- und den Ignatiusbriefen andererseits[5] eine

---

1. Zur Datierung der Briefe vgl. H. LÖHR, *Die Briefe des Ignatius von Antiochien*, in W. PRATSCHER (Hg.), *Die Apostolischen Väter* (UTB, 3272), Göttingen, Vandenhoeck & Ruprecht, 2009, 104-129, S. 108-109; Löhr bilanziert: „Man ist so für die Datierung der Ignatianen im Wesentlichen auf das Verhältnis zu Polyk sowie auf die Einordnung in die christliche Theologiegeschichte des 2. Jh. n.Chr. verwiesen". Zur Diskussion der möglichen Echtheit dieser Briefe vgl. S. 107, zu ihrem – augenscheinlichen – kleinasiatischen Abfassungsort vgl. S. 109-111.

2. Zum Zeitpunkt der Abfassung des Joh und der drei Johannesbriefe vgl. – unabhängig von der dort vertretenen zeitlichen Reihenfolge der einzelnen Schriften – U. SCHNELLE, *Einleitung in das Neue Testament* (UTB, 1830), Göttingen, Vandenhoeck & Ruprecht, ⁹2017, S. 524, 529, 537-540, 555-557; Schnelle verortet die Entstehung der johanneischen Literatur insgesamt in Ephesus. Somit ergibt sich eine zumindest lokale Koinzidenz zwischen den Ignatianen, dem Joh und den Johannesbriefen, die allein schon die in der vorliegenden Studie verhandelte Fragestellung rechtfertigt.

3. Vgl. hierzu zusammenfassend H. PAULSEN, *Studien zur Theologie des Ignatius von Antiochien* (FKDG, 29), Göttingen, Vandenhoeck & Ruprecht, 1978, S. 37: „Läßt man einmal alle stützenden Argumente beiseite und beschränkt sich auf das Problem der literarischen Abhängigkeit, so läßt sich kein einziges wörtliches Zitat aufzeigen. Und selbst wenn man auf absolute verbale Kongruenz nicht viel geben will, so läßt sich auch dann literarische Dependenz gegenüber dem Johannesevangelium nicht beweisen".

4. Vgl. hierzu wiederum PAULSEN, *ibid.*, S. 37: „Über eine traditionsgeschichtliche Verwandtschaft in Sprache und Theologie ist damit [d.h. mit der Negation einer unmittelbaren literarischen Dependenz zwischen dem Joh und den Ignatiusbriefen] durchaus noch kein Urteil gefällt".

5. Vgl. hierzu E. VON DER GOLTZ, *Ignatius von Antiochien als Christ und Theologe* (TU, 12,3), Leipzig, Hinrichs, 1894, S. 196-203, darüber hinaus C.E. HILL, *The Johannine Corpus in the Early Church*, Oxford, OUP, 2004, S. 427-446.

solche traditionsgeschichtliche Abhängigkeit mehr als wahrscheinlich erscheinen[6]. Im Rahmen der vorliegenden Studie soll es nun nicht primär darum gehen, eine solche traditionsgeschichtliche Abhängigkeit erneut nachzuweisen – dass eine solche bestehe, wird angesichts der gegenwärtigen Forschungslage, wenn auch in unterschiedlichem Umfang[7], als gegeben angenommen[8], so dass es zureichend scheinen will, im Rahmen der folgenden Ausführungen lediglich *en passant* darauf zu verweisen bzw. diese Frage dann zu diskutieren, wenn sie für die entsprechenden Darlegungen von unmittelbarem Interesse ist –, sondern darum, dieselbe näher in den Blick zu nehmen. Anhand der jeweiligen semantischen und systematisch-theologischen Verwendung des Begriffs φῶς im Johannesevangelium, in den übrigen johanneischen Schriften und schließlich in den Ignatiusbriefen soll paradigmatisch untersucht werden, ob und in welcher Weise sich die bei Ignatius nachweisbare Verarbeitung johanneischen Traditionsmaterials in die aus dem Joh und den Johannesbriefen ableitbare, den johanneischen Kreis in seiner Gesamtheit prägende theologische Systematik einordnen lässt. Lässt sich im Blick auf diese Forschungsfrage ein positives Ergebnis formulieren, muss es in einem zweiten Schritt zumindest im Ansatz darum gehen, diesen nachgewiesenen systematisch-theologischen Zusammenhang mit den historischen Verhältnissen und Entwicklungen innerhalb des in der römischen Provinz Asia im zweiten nachchristlichen Jahrhundert sich ausbreitenden Christentums zu korrelieren.

---

6. Vgl. hierzu etwa VON DER GOLTZ, *Ignatius* (Anm. 5), S. 143: „Bei Ign. müssen wir mit Sicherheit bei der Annahme völliger literarischer Unabhängigkeit, aber starker geistiger Verwandtschaft stehen bleiben"; ähnlich auch T. ZAHN, *Geschichte des neutestamentlichen Kanons I/2*, Erlangen – Leipzig, Deichert, 1889, S. 903: „Ignatius citirt das 4. Ev. ebensowenig als irgendeine andere Schrift des NT's; aber er zeigt sich nicht nur selbst mit demselben sehr vertraut, sondern setzt auch die gleiche Vertrautheit bei den Gemeinden voraus, an die er schreibt". In diesem Sinne auch, wenn auch etwas weniger eindeutig, L. WEHR, *Arznei der Unsterblichkeit: Die Eucharistie bei Ignatius von Antiochien und im Johannesevangelium* (NTAbh, NF 18), Münster, Aschendorff, 1987, S. 36: „Zusammenfassend kann also festgehalten werden: Bei Ign findet sich kein einziges vollständiges wörtliches Zitat aus dem Joh. Die vorhandenen Parallelen sind nicht so groß, daß sie eine Abhängigkeit ausreichend begründen könnten. Viel wahrscheinlicher ist es, daß sie sich aus dem gleichen geistigen Hintergrund erklären". Was genau mit diesem „gleichen geistigen Hintergrund" gemeint sein könnte, lässt Wehr freilich offen.
7. Vgl. hierzu etwa T. NAGEL, *Die Rezeption des Johannesevangeliums im 2. Jahrhundert* (ABG, 2), Leipzig, Evangelische Verlagsanstalt, 2000, S. 207-251.
8. Vgl. hierzu auch A. BRENT, *Ignatius and Polycarp: The Transformation of New Testament Traditions in the Context of Mystery Cults*, in A. GREGORY – C. TUCKETT (Hgg.), *The New Testament and the Apostolic Fathers*. Vol. 2: *Trajectories through the New Testament and the Apostolic Fathers*, Oxford, OUP, 2005, 325-349, S. 325: „Those letters [d.h. die Briefe des Ignatius], however, also, make some references, and some tantalizing allusions, to the world of the writer of the Apocalypse, as they do to that of the Fourth Gospel and the Johannine Epistles".

I. Der Begriff ΦΩΣ κτλ.[9]
Joh 1,4-5.9a; 3,20-21; 8,12a.b.c; 12,35.36a.46[10] und
Ign. Phld. 2.1aα

1. *Der Begriff φῶς κτλ. bei Joh*

In Joh 1,4-5 wird der um das dessen universale Geltung untermauernde Genitivattribut τῶν ἀνθρώπων[11] ergänzte Terminus φῶς nicht, wie etwa in Joh 1,9a, unmittelbar auf die Figur des – später dann in der Gestalt Jesu inkarnierten – λόγος[12], sondern, im Rahmen eines sich aus Joh 1,1-3 ergebenden schöpfungstheologischen Kontextes[13], auf das – wiederum schöpfungstheologisch zu interpretierende[14] – Heilsgut der ζωή bezogen:

---

9. Dass dem Begriff φῶς bzw. den mit demselben konstruierten entsprechenden Syntagmata und den durch jene repräsentierten theologischen Inhalten in der johanneischen Tradition offensichtlich eine große Bedeutung zugekommen sind, bestätigt allein schon der Sachverhalt, dass von den insgesamt 73 für diesen Terminus im Neuen Testament nachweisbaren Belegen insgesamt 29, also beinahe die Hälfte, auf die johanneischen Schriften (23 Belege im Joh, 6 im 1 Joh) entfallen; vgl. hierzu H. Ritt, φῶς, in *EWNT*² III, 1071-1075, Sp. 1072.

10. Die Belege Joh 9,5 – hier begegnet, vergleichbar mit Joh 8,12, das Syntagma φῶς τοῦ κόσμου – und Joh 11,9-10 – hier tritt, wie in Joh 8,12 das Syntagma τὸ φῶς τοῦ κόσμου in Erscheinung – werden in der vorliegenden Studie nicht diskutiert, da sie über den Hinweis auf die Gestalt des inkarnierten λόγος als des φῶς τοῦ κόσμου kaum Relevantes zum Verständnis des φῶς-Begriffs im Joh beitragen können. In einer umfassenden monographischen Darstellung werden diese Belege dann aber selbstverständlich zu berücksichtigen sein. Dies gilt auch im Blick auf die relevanten synoptischen Belege für den Begriff φῶς, die hier nur am Rande berücksichtigt werden können.

11. Vgl. hierzu J. Zumstein, *Das Johannesevangelium* (KEK, 2), Göttingen, Vandenhoeck & Ruprecht, 2016, S. 77: „Die Benutzung des Begriffs ‚Mensch' im Plural (τῶν ἀνθρώπων) betont, dass dieses Licht nicht einem kleinen Kreis der Auserwählten vorbehalten ist, sondern allen angeboten wird". Vgl. hierzu auch M. Theobald, *Das Evangelium nach Johannes: Kapitel 1–12* (RNT), Regensburg, Pustet, 2009, S. 115.

12. Diese – keinesfalls unerhebliche – Differenz notiert R. Bultmann, *Das Evangelium des Johannes* (KEK, 2), Göttingen, Vandenhoeck & Ruprecht, ²¹1986, S. 31.

13. Vgl. hierzu Zumstein, *Johannesevangelium* (Anm. 11), S. 77.

14. J. Becker, *Das Evangelium nach Johannes*. Bd. 1: *Kapitel 1–10* (ÖTBK, 4/1), Gütersloh, Mohn; Würzburg, Echter, ³1991, S. 73 führt im Blick auf die hier erwähnte ζωή aus, dass hier „nicht einfach nur allgemein vom Leben, sondern im qualifizierten Sinn vom eigentlichen Leben gesprochen" werde. Dies sei „dadurch angezeigt, daß ‚Leben' und ‚Licht' miteinander verbunden ... [seien]". Becker zufolge könne sich „Leben ... verfehlen oder erfüllt sein: Es kann scheitern, versagen, ins Böse pervertieren oder heilvoll, gut, vollkommen sein. Dabei werden Lebensverfehlung und Lebenserfüllung vom Logos her definiert. Insofern er Leben und Licht ist, ist der Lebenssinn das schöpfungsgemäße Leben unter dem Logos bzw. Gott. So stehen sich Gottlosigkeit und logosgemäßes Menschsein gegenüber" (S. 73). Aufgrund des in Joh 1,1-3 Ausgeführten einerseits, angesichts des das Substantiv φῶς näher bestimmenden und jenem damit eine universale Geltung zuschreibenden Genitivattributes τῶν ἀνθρώπων andererseits lässt sich jedoch kaum wahrscheinlich machen, dass es in Joh 1,4 schon um den Gedanken der Gottlosigkeit, somit also eine pessimistisch-anthropologische Perspektive gehe. Eine solche Perspektive einzuführen,

ἐν αὐτῷ [d.h. ἐν λόγῳ] ζωὴ ἦν, καὶ ἡ ζωὴ ἦν <u>τὸ φῶς τῶν ἀνθρώπων</u>. Dabei wird die ἐν λόγῳ zu verortende ζωή hier – und dies indiziert die Verwendung des wesentlich eine ontologische Relation definierenden Prädikates ἦν – unmittelbar mit dem φῶς τῶν ἀνθρώπων identifiziert: Das Leben war das Licht „für die Menschen", das Leben – und damit natürlich auch der λόγος als dessen Träger – erleuchtete die Menschheit in ihrer Gesamtheit und ermöglichte der Menschheit in ihrer Gesamtheit damit ihre das σκότος ἐπάνω τῆς ἀβύσσου (Gen 1,2b) überwindende Lichtwerdung. Das bedeutet zunächst: Dem Terminus φῶς bzw. dem Syntagma φῶς τῶν ἀνθρώπων eignet in Joh 1,4b im Blick auf seine semantische und zugleich auch theologische Substanz, somit also substantial, eine universal-anthropologische, damit also in das Kosmologische hinein geweitete, und zugleich soteriologische, die universale menschliche Lebensfähigkeit und -möglichkeit widerspiegelnde Konnotation[15], wobei keinesfalls übersehen werden darf, dass in Joh 1,4b nicht der Begriff des κόσμος, sondern derjenige des ἄνθρωπος begegnet.

Diese kosmologisch-soteriologische, ins Anthropologische ausgreifende semantische Substanz wird ergänzt um ein in Joh 1,4 jedoch – zunächst nur – bestenfalls implizit wahrnehmbares und die Christologie betreffendes semantisches Akzidenz: Der – und dies dürfte hier im Hintergrund stehen, auch wenn die Inkarnation selbst im weiteren Verlauf des Joh erstmalig in Joh 1,14 explizit thematisiert wird – mit der geschichtlichen Person Jesu als dessen Inkarnation identifizierte Logos zeichnet als dauerhafter[16] Spender[17] dieser ζωή, somit als Spender eben des φῶς τῶν ἀνθρώπων, erantwortlich für die Herstellung dieser universalen menschlichen Lebensfähigkeit und -möglichkeit[18]. Damit gewinnt die substantiale

---

hieße Joh 1,4 nicht mehr in protologischem (vgl. hierzu u. S. 414-416), sondern schon in eschatologischem Sinne zu interpretieren, eine Interpretation, die in Sonderheit angesichts der Ausführungen in Joh 1,1-3 jedoch kaum plausibilisiert zu werden vermag.

15. Vgl. hierzu etwa RITT, φῶς (Anm. 9), Sp. 1073: „Der Prolog (*Joh* 1,1-18) ... drückt die Heilswirklichkeit, die dem Glaubenden durch Christus geschenkt ist, durch die Begriffe ‚Leben' und *Licht* aus (V. 4)". Das dem Begriff φῶς zugeordnete Genitivattribut τῶν ἀνθρώπων zeigt allerdings an, dass es zumindest in Joh 1,4 nicht nur um die Christen gehen kann, sondern die gesamte Menschheit in den Blick genommen wird.

16. Zu diesem Imperfekt vgl. ZUMSTEIN, *Johannesevangelium* (Anm. 11), S. 77: „Das Imperfekt ‚war' (ἦν) betont, dass sich das Leben nicht vorübergehend, sondern dauerhaft im Logos befindet".

17. Vgl. hierzu ZUMSTEIN, *ibid.*, S. 77: „Gleichzeitig bedeutet dies, dass das Leben kein Gut ist, das sich der Mensch durch seine Arbeit oder seine Verdienste erwerben könnte. Das Leben ist das Eigentum Gottes. Es kann und darf nur als Geschenk Gottes bzw. des Logos empfangen werden". Vgl. in diesem Sinne auch THEOBALD, *Johannes* (Anm. 11), S. 114.

18. Vgl. hierzu ZUMSTEIN, *Johannesevangelium* (Anm. 11), S. 77: „Umgekehrt ist der Logos nur in dem Masse Logos, in dem er den Menschen Leben gibt". Zumstein verweist

kosmologisch-soteriologische Akzentuierung des Begriffs Joh 1,4 zugleich resultativen Charakter: Die soteriologische Wirksamkeit des φῶς bzw. φῶς τῶν ἀνθρώπων ergibt sich aus dessen Verortung ἐν λόγῳ. Dies heißt seinerseits wiederum, dass der zunächst lediglich implizit erkennbaren christologischen Konnotation derselben, wiewohl lediglich akzidential konstruiert, kausativer Charakter zukommt: Der λόγος wird wirksam eben als der Spender, der „Anzünder" dieses φῶς τῶν ἀνθρώπων – und damit natürlich zugleich auch der ζωή. Der Sachverhalt, dass sowohl die Ausführungen zur Verortung der ζωή in Joh 1,4a als auch diejenigen zur näheren ontologischen Charakterisierung derselben in Joh 1,4b im Imperfekt formuliert sind, indiziert in Sonderheit vor dem Hintergrund der Darlegungen in Joh 1,1-3, dass es sich bei dieser in diesem Vers implizit thematisierten und einen entsprechenden Zustand generierenden Aktivität des schöpferischen „Anzündens" des Lichtes „für die Menschen", d.h. dieser schöpferischen Stiftung der zuständlich, d.h. ständig sich vollziehenden Potentialität universaler menschlicher Existenz, um eine grundlegend und erstmalig in der – protologischen und damit vorgeschichtlichen[19] – Vergangenheit beginnende Handlung handelt.

Das in diesem Vers verwendete Imperfekt bezeichnet einerseits einen Zustand[20], in diesem Fall die Kontinuität der durch den λόγος gespendeten ζωή als dem φῶς τῶν ἀνθρώπων[21], andererseits aber auch eine Handlung, nämlich diejenige der jeweiligen Realisierung von Leben, die zu einem Zeitpunkt der Vergangenheit ihren Anfang nahm[22]. Letztlich transportieren die beiden Imperfekte in Joh 1,4 somit nachgerade einen

in diesem Zusammenhang auf Prov 8,35-36 und die dort niedergelegten Aussagen der σοφία (S. 77, Anm. 62).

19. Vgl. hierzu BULTMANN, *Johannes* (Anm. 12), S. 6, der seine Ausführungen zu Joh 1,1-4, nicht jedoch diejenigen zu Joh 1,5-13 mit dem Titel „Das vorgeschichtliche Sein des Logos" überschreibt, um die Darstellung in Joh 1,5-13 dann mit dem Titel „Der Logos als Offenbarer in der Geschichte" zu versehen (S. 26). Mit Joh 1,5 verlässt die Darstellung die protologische Dimension von Wirklichkeit und taucht in die – als temporal und zugleich als spatial zu charakterisierende – eschatologische Dimension ein. Anders hier H. THYEN, *Das Johannesevangelium* (HNT, 6), Tübingen, Mohr Siebeck, ²2015, S. 73, der Joh 1,4-5 als über den Begriff φῶς miteinander verbunden ansieht und deshalb einen Einschnitt zwischen diesen beiden Versen ablehnt. Dabei verkennt er jedoch, dass dieser Terminus theologisch-substantial jeweils unterschiedlich definiert wird.

20. Vgl. hierzu A. KAEGI, *Griechische Schulgrammatik*, Berlin, Weidmann, ohne Jahr, §165, S. 156.

21. Vgl. hierzu etwa BECKER, *Johannes* (Anm. 14), S. 73: „Alles Geschaffene verdankt sich nicht nur einmalig dem Logos, sondern hat auch kontinuierlich nur Existenz durch ihn. Er gewährt immerfort Leben".

22. Vgl. hierzu BDR, ¹⁷1990, §327, S. 269, die mit diesem Imperfekt einen Handlungsverlauf transportiert sehen: „Durch das Imp[er]f[ekt]. wird die vergangene Handlung in ihrem Verlauf vorgestellt, sowohl mit näheren Bestimmungen, als auch im Gegensatz zu einem nachfolgenden Verbum der Vollendung".

iterativen Akzent: Der λόγος gewährt das Leben immerfort und immer wieder[23].

Wird der Versuch unternommen, die solchermaßen entwickelte Semantik des Terminus φῶς bzw. des Syntagmas φῶς τῶν ἀνθρώπων, so wie sie in Joh 1,4 erscheinen, in eine umfassendere theologische Systematik einzuordnen, so ergibt sich: Der Begriff φῶς wird in Joh 1,4 theologisch primär bzw. substantial in einen kosmologisch-soteriologischen, sekundär bzw. akzidential, wenn auch nur implizit, in einen christologischen Kontext gestellt und zugleich einerseits inchoativ, andererseits aber auch durativ akzentuiert und damit mit einem temporalen Akzent versehen: Der λόγος „entzündet" – am Anfang bzw. anfänglich und nach einer Zeit der ausschließlichen Dunkelheit, d.h. vor aller Zeit und Geschichte, somit in der protologischen Wirklichkeitsdimension – schöpferisch das φῶς τῶν ἀνθρώπων, das Licht „für die Menschen" und existentialisiert auf diesem Wege den Zustand der andauernden Potentialität des menschlichen Daseins. Ein spatialer Aspekt scheint in dem Joh 1,4 Dargelegten nicht auf –, ein Indiz dafür, dass der im weiteren Verlauf der Darlegungen thematisierte Dualismus zwischen Licht und Finsternis nicht als protologischer und damit auch nicht als ontologischer, sondern als relationaler und zugleich als eschatologischer begriffen werden muss[24].

In Joh 1,5 verlässt die Darstellung die Sphäre der protologischen Dimension von Wirklichkeit und wendet sich, wie schon das nicht mehr im Imperfekt, sondern im Präsens[25] formulierte Prädikat φαίνει Joh 1,5a indiziert[26], nun augenscheinlich der Dimension der Geschichte, konkret den Rezipienten des Joh und ihrer geschichtlichen Gegenwart zu[27].

---

23. Zum iterativen Imperfekt vgl. *ibid.*, §325, S. 268: „Eine wiederholte oder gewohnheitsmäßige Handlung kann durch das Imp[er]f[ekt]. in die Vergangenheit versetzt werden".
24. Vgl. hierzu u. S. 416-419.
25. Vgl. zu dieser Beobachtung BULTMANN, *Johannes* (Anm. 12), S. 26.
26. Vgl. hierzu etwa ZUMSTEIN, *Johannesevangelium* (Anm. 11), S. 78, der mit vielen anderen das Präsens φαίνει entsprechend als ein historisches, nicht jedoch als ein zeitloses Präsens interpretiert: „Oder ist φαίνει ein historisches Präsens …? Dann würde der Text auf den *Logos ensarkos* (den inkarnierten Logos) anspielen".
27. Vgl. hierzu *ibid.*, S. 77: „Während V. 4 den Auftrag des Logos in der Welt definiert hatte und damit schon in den Bereich der Inkarnation gehörte, kommt V. 5 in den Bereich der gelebten Gegenwart des Lesers". Darüber hinaus auch S. 78: „Das Präsens ‚das Licht scheint' beschreibt die gelebte Gegenwart der joh Gemeinde". Im Blick auf eine Zäsur zwischen Joh 1,4 und Joh 1,5 vgl. auch M. THEOBALD, *Im Anfang war das Wort* (SBS, 106), Stuttgart, Katholisches Bibelwerk, 1983, S. 21: „VV. 4a-5a(b) sind zwar nach Art einer Kette miteinander verbunden, bilden aber trotzdem zwei Doppelzeilen, da die Stichwörter zu Beginn der jeweiligen Doppelzeile in V.4a und 5a gegenüber ihrer ersten Erwähnung am Ende der vorangegangenen Zeile leicht variiert sind und so eine gewisse Zäsur anzeigen". An anderer Stelle führt Theobald aus: „Rückblickend bestätigt sich, dass

Beschrieben werden das mit dem Auftreten des inkarnierten λόγος[28] beginnende und bis in die Gegenwart der Abfassung des Joh hineinreichende[29] – und damit offensichtlich auf Dauer angelegte[30] – Scheinen des φῶς in der σκοτία (Joh 1,5a)[31], das von derselben, d.h. von dem mit der Ablehnung des erschienenen φῶς ins Leben gekommenen nicht-christlichen κόσμος[32], in der – bis in die Zeit unmittelbar vor der Rezeption des Joh reichenden – Vergangenheit allerdings geflissentlich ignoriert und eben gerade nicht positiv rezipiert worden ist (Joh 1,5b): καὶ τὸ φῶς ἐν τῇ σκοτίᾳ φαίνει, καὶ ἡ σκοτία αὐτὸ οὐ κατέλαβεν[33].

Jenseits aller mit diesem Vers verbundenen Verstehensprobleme wird unmittelbar erkennbar, dass der Begriff φῶς in Joh 1,5 den ihm noch in Joh 1,4 eignenden substantialen kosmologisch-soteriologischen Verstehenshorizont verlassen hat und nun – allerdings wiederum zunächst nur implizit – substantial als christologische Titulatur erscheint. Das „Licht" metaphorisiert nicht mehr die allen Menschen zugeeignete grundsätzliche

---

V. 5 tatsächlich auf den *Evangelisten* zurückgehe [, somit also nicht ursprünglich zu dem in Joh 1,1-18 verarbeiteten Hymnus zu rechnen sei,] …. In diesem Vers hat er die beiden ersten Strophen des Hymnus … auf die Christologie eingeführt, um die es hier eigentlich geht" (S. 21). Diese Engführung realisiert der „Evangelist" in Sonderheit durch die Ausführungen in Joh 1,5b, die erst den Begriff σκοτία anthropologisch negativ qualifizieren. Es mag daher nicht verwundern, dass die Darlegungen in Joh 1,5b keinerlei Anklänge an diejenigen des ersten Schöpfungsberichtes Gen 1-2 aufweisen. Für die Annahme, hinter dem in Joh 1,5b Ausgeführten stehe die biblische Erzählung vom Sündenfall (vgl. zu dieser in der Forschung vertretenen Annahme referierend THEOBALD, *Johannes* [Anm. 11], S. 115) gibt es im Text keinerlei Signal, das auch nur im Ansatz als ein eine solche Deutung bestätigender Hinweis wahrgenommen werden könnte.

28. Anders hier J. SCHNEIDER, *Das Evangelium nach Johannes* (THKNT, Sonderband), Berlin, Evangelische Verlagsanstalt, 1976, S. 56-57.

29. Vgl. hierzu R. SCHNACKENBURG, *Das Johannesevangelium. 1. Teil: Einleitung und Kommentar zu Kap. 1-4* (HTKNT, 4/1), Freiburg i.Br. – Basel – Wien, Herder, ³1972, S. 223: „Vordergründig hat er [d.h. der Verfasser von Joh 1,5] dabei [d.h. mit seiner Darstellung] das Auftreten des inkarnierten Logos vor Augen (Aorist), verlängert aber durch das φαίνω die Perspektive bis in die Gegenwart".

30. Vgl. hierzu auch THYEN, *Johannesevangelium* (Anm. 19), S. 72: „Das Präsens φαίνει bringt das andauernde und siegreiche *Scheinen* des von Jesus Christus als dem Logos ausstrahlenden Lichtes zur Sprache".

31. Zum Gegensatz zwischen φῶς und σκοτία vgl. ausführlich etwa SCHNACKENBURG, *Johannesevangelium I* (Anm. 29), S. 223-226.

32. Vgl. zu diesem Zusammenhang etwa ZUMSTEIN, *Johannesevangelium* (Anm. 11), S. 78: „‚Die Finsternis' (ἡ σκοτία), als wirkende Kraft der Ablehnung des Logos, ist keine kosmologische Größe, der die Welt seit Anbeginn gehören würde. Die gesamte Welt ist Schöpfung Gottes (vgl. V.3). Das Kommen des Lichtes, und nur dies, löst aus, dass sich Finsternis bildet. Ohne Licht keine Finsternis. Der joh Dualismus ist eine Funktion der Christologie und nicht umgekehrt". In diesem Sinne auch BECKER, *Johannes* (Anm. 14), S. 74.

33. Vgl. hierzu etwa BECKER, *Johannes* (Anm. 14), S. 74, der zu Joh 1,5 anmerkt: „Daß die Menschen sich dem Logos als Licht verweigern und demzufolge der Logos auf Ablehnung stößt, ist einfach als gängige Erfahrung vorausgesetzt".

Möglichkeit des Lebens, sondern die in die σκοτία hineinscheinende und hineinwirkende Figur des λόγος Christus selbst[34], der von derselben und damit natürlich auch von all denen, die in derselben existieren, *bis dato* jedoch eben nicht „geistig und willensmäßig erfaßt" worden ist. Der Terminus φῶς besetzt in Joh 1,5 neben dem christologischen somit akzidential einen, da das in Joh 1,5b beschriebene καταλαμβάνειν schon aufgrund des Joh 1,4b Ausgeführten letzten Endes nur von Menschen geleistet werden kann, im wesentlichen anthropologischen Verstehenshorizont, der aber nicht zuletzt aufgrund der Verwendung des Begriffs σκοτία und eben nicht des Terminus ἄνθρωποι, als Verengung bzw. Konzentration oder Reduktion der kosmologischen Perspektive in Erscheinung tritt. Da das Scheinen des φῶς gegenüber dem Raum der σκοτία ein gänzlich neues, jener letzten Endes diametral entgegenstehendes letztgültiges Zeichensystem als neue letzthinnige Wirklichkeit etabliert, eignet dem Begriff φῶς in Joh 1,5 im Blick auf die von ihm transportierte Dimension von Wirklichkeit ein eschatologisches Momentum. Letzterem sind sowohl eine temporale als auch eine spatiale Komponente zuzuschreiben: Zu einem konkreten Zeitpunkt in der Geschichte begann das φῶς, einen von der σκοτία zu unterscheidenden neuen Raum – im Laufe der weiteren Darstellung des Joh wird dieser Raum dann als Raum der ζωή, somit also als Heilsraum erkennbar – auszuleuchten bzw. zu kreieren[35].

Im Blick auf den im Joh sich abzeichnenden semantischen und theologischen Verstehenshorizont des Terminus φῶς ergibt sich aus dem in Joh 1,4.5 somit folgendes: Dieser Begriff transportiert in Joh 1,4 einen substantialen soteriologischen und zugleich kosmologischen, ins Anthropologische sich ausweitenden, resultativ ausgerichteten Inhalt, ergänzt um ein akzidentiales und zugleich kausatives christologisches Momentum, in Joh 1,5 – *vice versa* nachgerade – einen substantial-kausativen christologischen Inhalt, akzidential bzw. resultativ ergänzt um einen anthropologischen und ins Kosmologische sich erstreckenden Aspekt. Darüber hinaus bezieht sich dieser Begriff – je nach der in Joh 1,4 und 1,5 jeweils unterschiedlichen theologischen Schwerpunktsetzung – entweder auf die protologische oder aber die eschatologische Dimension von Wirklichkeit. Im Unterschied zu der in Joh 1,4 reflektierten protologischen Dimension von Wirklichkeit lässt sich die in Joh 1,5 aufscheinende, der

---

34. Vgl. hierzu SCHNACKENBURG, *Johannesevangelium I* (Anm. 29), S. 222: „Wenn der Evangelist in V 5 die Begegnung des Licht-Logos mit der Menschenwelt meint ...".
35. Vgl. hierzu durchaus mit Recht THYEN, *Johannesevangelium* (Anm. 19), S. 72: „Deshalb muß der ... Aorist οὐ κατέλαβεν wohl als *komplexiver* verstanden werden: Die Finsternis hat das Licht nicht überwältigt und wird es auch in jeder denkbaren Zukunft niemals auslöschen .... Nicht Pessimismus, sondern Siegesgewißheit wird hier laut".

innergeschichtlichen nachgerade aufgepfropfte eschatologische Wirklichkeitsdimension als sowohl temporal als auch spatial geprägt charakterisieren: Das φῶς begann in der σκοτία zu scheinen und entwickelte so einen durch das „Licht" erhellten Raum des „Lichtes", der dem Raum der σκοτία, die dieses Licht ablehnt, diametral entgegensteht.

In Joh 1,9a wird die in der Person Jesu inkarnierte und historisch wahrnehmbare Gestalt des λόγος Christus[36] – offensichtlich im Unterschied zu anderen φῶτα[37] – als „das" φῶς ἀληθινόν bezeichnet, das – ein als eschatologisch zu charakterisierendes Ereignis[38] – in die Welt gekommen und damit in die Geschichte eingetreten ist[39] und jeden Menschen erleuchtet bzw. erleuchten möchte[40]: ἦν τὸ φῶς τὸ ἀληθινόν, ὃ φωτίζει πάντα ἄνθρωπον, ἐρχόμενον εἰς τὸν κόσμον. In Joh 1,9a werden der Terminus φῶς und die durch diesen repräsentierte Realität im Rahmen der theologischen Systematik somit einerseits primär christologisch kontextualisiert: Die Gestalt des λόγος Christus bildet als *definiendum* das definitorische Zentrum der Aussage: λόγος ἦν κτλ., wird einerseits eben durch das *definiens* φῶς ἀληθινόν näher bestimmt und legt seinerseits zugleich den semantischen und den theologischen Verstehenshorizont desselben fest, andererseits zugleich aber auch, wie das von dem Prädikat φωτίζει abhängige Akkusativobjekt πάντα ἄνθρωπον nahelegt, im Lichte des christologischen Verstehenshorizontes ergänzend sowohl soteriologisch als auch anthropologisch – eine nicht ausgesprochene Weitung ins

---

36. Zur umfassenden Diskussion der Frage nach dem Bezugspunkt des diesen Satz einleitenden Prädikats ἦν und damit nach dem Subjekt desselben vgl. THYEN, *Johannesevangelium* (Anm. 19), S. 79; Thyen kommt dabei, angesichts der von ihm referierten alternativen Auslegungen auch durchaus mit Recht zu dem Ergebnis: „Wir bleiben also dabei: Subjekt von V. 9 ist der λόγος". Vgl. hierzu auch BULTMANN, *Johannes* (Anm. 12), S. 31-32.

37. Zu dem mit dem Adjektiv ἀληθινόν gegebenen polemischen Akzent vgl. etwa ZUMSTEIN, *Johannesevangelium* (Anm. 11), S. 81.

38. Vgl. zur Auslegung dieser Ausführungen insgesamt ZUMSTEIN, *Johannesevangelium* (Anm. 11), S. 81: „Daher geschieht die Erleuchtung aller Menschen durch das In-die-Welt-Kommen des Logos .... Dieses Ereignis hat eschatologische Bedeutung: Es betrifft nicht nur die Vergangenheit. Die in der Geschichte eingetretene Inkarnation behält ihre Bedeutung auch für die Gegenwart ..."! Nach SCHNACKENBURG, *Johannesevangelium I* (Anm. 29), S. 229, bezog sich das in Joh 1,9 Gesagte in der ursprünglichen Fassung des im Prolog verarbeiteten Logoshymnus „noch auf die Schöpfungsordnung, d.h. den Logos vor seiner Inkarnation", sei in der jetzigen Fassung jedoch unzweifelhaft auf den inkarnierten λόγος zu beziehen.

39. Zum Bezug der Wendung ἐρχόμενον εἰς τὸν κόσμον auf den Begriff φῶς und damit zugleich auch auf den λόγος vgl. etwa THYEN, *Johannesevangelium* (Anm. 19), S. 79-80. Vgl. zu dem im Rahmen der vorliegenden Studie präferierten Bezug der Ausführungen in Joh 1,9c THEOBALD, *Johannes* (Anm. 11), S. 122.

40. Zum Verständnis des Partizips ἐρχόμενον in modalem Sinne vgl. THEOBALD, *Johannes* (Anm. 11), S. 122.

Kosmologische klingt darüber hinaus zumindest an – konnotiert[41]: „In ihm und nur in ihm ist für die Menschen die Möglichkeit gegeben, sich selbst vor Gott durchsichtig zu werden"[42]. Das in Christus Geschehene realisiert schließlich, wie schon das im Präsens formulierte[43] und auf das Subjekt φῶς ἀληθινόν bezogene Prädikat φωτίζει zeigt, *in actu* eine neue, mit dem Zeitpunkt des Kommens in den κόσμος kreierte letzthinnige Wirklichkeit, die nicht nur die Vergangenheit, sondern augenscheinlich auch die Gegenwart der Rezipienten des Joh umfasst, ein Sachverhalt, der dem durch das Syntagma τὸ φῶς ἀληθινόν Explizierten eine sowohl temporal als auch spatial zu definierende eschatologische Qualität zuschreibt und jenes damit in den Verstehenshorizont der eschatologischen Dimension von Wirklichkeit stellt. In der Summe: Der Terminus φῶς bzw. das von ihm bestimmte Syntagma φῶς ἀληθινόν und die durch dasselbe repräsentierte Realität werden in Joh 1,9a im Kontext der vom Verfasserkreis des Joh entwickelten theologischen Systematik substantial christologisch und akzidential soteriologisch und zugleich anthropologisch definiert und mit einem auf die eschatologische Dimension von Wirklichkeit zielenden raum-zeitlichen Horizont aufgeladen[44].

Nächst Joh 1,9a werden dann in Joh 3,19.20-21[45] die Gestalt des Christus, identifiziert und metaphorisiert wiederum mit dem Begriff τὸ φῶς[46], und dessen Kommen in die Welt zur κρίσις[47], sachlich mit dem Konzept

---

41. Vgl. hierzu ZUMSTEIN, *Johannesevangelium* (Anm. 11), S. 81: „Der Begriff ‚Licht' beschreibt nicht Gott, sondern den Logos in seiner Beziehung zur Welt. Die Symbolik ist anthropologisch und soteriologisch ausgerichtet".

42. BULTMANN, *Johannes* (Anm. 12), S. 33; vgl. darüber hinaus auch S. 32: „Die Exklusivität der in Jesus geschehenen Offenbarung wird noch betont durch den Relativsatz ὃ φωτίζει κτλ.: für alle Menschen ist er, und nur er, der Offenbarer". Vgl. hierzu auch SCHNACKENBURG, *Johannesevangelium I* (Anm. 29), S. 230.

43. Vgl. zu dieser Beobachtung ZUMSTEIN, *Johannesevangelium* (Anm. 11), S. 81.

44. Diesem Dreiklang werden die Ausführungen von RITT, *φῶς* (Anm. 9), Sp. 1074, nur im Ansatz gerecht; durchaus mit Recht spricht er im Blick auf Joh 1,9 von der „christologisch-soteriologische[n] Bedeutung von φῶς", verliert dabei aber den eschatologischen Bezugsrahmen aus dem Blick.

45. Zur Definition einer möglichen theologischen Relation zwischen Joh 3,13-17 und Joh 3,18-21 vgl. etwa THYEN, *Johannesevangelium* (Anm. 19), S. 220-223.

46. Vgl. hierzu *ibid.*, S. 220: „Denn nach dem Vorausgegangenen [, d.h. nach Joh 3,18-19] kann hier ja nicht nur vom ‚*Licht des Tages*' die Rede sein. τὸ φῶς muß vielmehr zugleich den bezeichnen, der in Zeit und Geschichte ‚als das *Licht* in die Welt gekommen ist' (V. 19), den, der später von sich sagen wird: ἐγώ εἰμι τὸ φῶς τοῦ κόσμου κτλ. (8,12)".

47. Zum Verständnis dieses Begriffs vgl. etwa THEOBALD, *Johannes* (Anm. 11), S. 272-273; Theobald interpretiert im Sinne von „Verdammnis": „Aber der Satz endet nicht mit V. 19b, sondern erst mit V. 19c.d: Die Menschen liebten die Finsternis mehr als das Licht, weil sie nicht wollten, dass ihre schlechten Werke aufgedeckt würden. Die Metaphorik hat ihre Pointe also nicht darin, dass die Menschen tatsächlich ins gleißende Licht getaucht wurden und so vor dem alles aufdeckenden Gericht in ihrer Blöße da standen. Vielmehr geht es darum, dass sie in der Dunkelheit der Nacht Schutz vor dem Licht suchten und sich in ihr einschlossen. In der eigenen Dunkelheit verfangen zu sein und in ihr verloren

des Tuns der ἀλήθεια[48] verschränkt: Offensichtlich nur derjenige, der die ἀλήθεια, d.h. „die in Jesus offenbarte Wirklichkeit Gottes"[49] praktiziert, gelangt zum φῶς bzw. erscheint als jemand, der zum φῶς gelangen möchte: αὕτη δέ ἐστιν ἡ κρίσις ὅτι τὸ φῶς ἐλήλυθεν εἰς τὸν κόσμον καὶ ἠγάπησαν οἱ ἄνθρωποι μᾶλλον τὸ σκότος ἢ τὸ φῶς· ἦν γὰρ αὐτῶν πονηρὰ τὰ ἔργα. ²⁰ πᾶς γὰρ ὁ φαῦλα πράσσων μισεῖ τὸ φῶς καὶ οὐκ ἔρχεται πρὸς τὸ φῶς, ἵνα μὴ ἐλεγχθῇ τὰ ἔργα αὐτοῦ· ²¹ ὁ δὲ ποιῶν τὴν ἀλήθειαν ἔρχεται πρὸς τὸ φῶς, ἵνα φανερωθῇ αὐτοῦ τὰ ἔργα ὅτι ἐν[50] θεῷ ἐστιν εἰργασμένα. Die Lektüre von Joh 3,19 lässt zunächst unmittelbar die primäre und substantiale christologische Verankerung des hier ohne jegliche attributive Ergänzung begegnenden Begriffs φῶς erkennen, das in der Gestalt Jesu in den κόσμος gekommen und inkarniert worden[51], von den Menschen *bis dato* jedoch abgelehnt worden ist. Der kausative Aspekt dieser christologischen Verankerung ergibt sich aus dem in Joh 3,19c dokumentierten Sachverhalt, dass das Kommen des φῶς Jesus in diese Welt seitens der ἄνθρωποι eine ablehnende Reaktion provoziert.

Eine Erklärung für diese ablehnende Reaktion liefern nun die Ausführungen in Joh 3,20-21, die – ohne Bezug auf die in Joh 3,19c geschilderte tatsächliche Reaktion der ἄνθρωποι auf das Kommen des λόγος – eine allgemeine und allgemeingültige Regel transportieren und auf der Basis derselben nun den in Joh 3,19 dargestellten Gesamtzusammenhang begründen bzw. explizieren[52]: „Die Menschen lieben die Finsternis mehr

---

zu gehen – das ist dann das Gericht oder die ‚Verdammnis', von der vorweg schon V. 18b.c sprachen".

48. Vgl. zu der Wendung ποιέω τὴν ἀλήθειαν, ZUMSTEIN, *Johannesevangelium* (Anm. 11), S. 150: „Dieser aus dem AT bekannte Ausdruck bezeichnet ein dem Willen Gottes entsprechendes Handeln".

49. *Ibid.*, S. 150.

50. Zum Bedeutungshorizont der Präposition ἐν vgl. etwa *ibid.*, S. 151, Anm. 87; Zumstein scheint für eine instrumentale Bedeutung derselben zu plädieren, was bedeutete, dass hier in Joh 3,21b von Werken die Rede sei, die Gott selbst getan habe. SCHNACKENBURG, *Johannesevangelium I* (Anm. 29), S. 432, hingegen möchte die Wendung ἐν θεῷ im Sinne von „in Übereinstimmung mit Gott bzw. mit seinem Willen" verstanden wissen.

51. Vgl. hierzu ZUMSTEIN, *Johannesevangelium* (Anm. 11), S. 149: „Das Kommen des Lichtes in die Welt – und darunter ist das Ereignis der Inkarnation zu verstehen, das hier mit denselben Worten wie im Prolog angekündigt wird (vgl. 1,9) …".

52. Anders hier THEOBALD, *Johannes* (Anm. 11), S. 273-274, der mit Blick auf Joh 3,20 feststellt: „Das also ist der Grund für das Nein der Menschen zum Wort Jesu: Die eigenen ‚bösen Werke' sollen nicht ans Licht kommen"! (273), und der zu Joh 3,21 ausführt: „Die übergeordnete negative These V. 19c sprach umfassend von ‚*den* Menschen', die die Finsternis mehr liebten als das Licht, und vermittelte damit den Eindruck, die Werke *aller* seien böse. Jetzt richtet sich der Blick auf die Ausnahme, dass jemand ‚die Wahrheit tut und (deshalb) zum Licht drängt, damit seine Werke als in Gott getan offenbar werden'" (S. 274). Wer der in der vorliegenden Studie entwickelten Interpretation von Joh 3,20-21 folgt, muss in Joh 3,21 keine Abweichung von dem Joh 3,19c Ausgeführten erblicken und kann die übergeordnete These auch in ihrer Radikalität und in ihrer

als das Licht, was daran erkannt werden kann[53], daß die Werke der Menschen böse sind. Als allgemeiner Grundsatz nämlich muß gelten: Grundsätzlich ist der φαῦλα πράσσων bestrebt, nicht zum ‚Licht' zu kommen, damit seine Werke nicht aufgedeckt würden, der ποιῶν τὴν ἀλήθειαν ist gerade im Gegenteil andauernd und grundsätzlich bestrebt, zum ‚Licht' zu kommen, damit seine Werke als ἐν θεῷ εἰργασμένα erkennbar würden"[54]. Zugunsten dieser Interpretation lässt sich immerhin in Anschlag bringen, dass die Darstellung in Joh 3,19 durch die Verwendung von Vergangenheitstempora geprägt ist, wohingegen in Joh 3,20-21 das präsentische Tempus dominiert. Um die hier favorisierte Interpretation durchzuhalten, ist es notwendig, eben das präsentische Tempus der in den beiden Hauptsätzen Joh 3,20-21 jeweils vorliegenden Prädikate, zumindest aber das präsentische Tempus des zweimal begegnenden Prädikats ἔρχεται, durativ oder aber auch als Präsens *de conatu*[55], letzten Endes also ein allgemeines Urteil formulierend[56], zu interpretieren, ein allgemeines Urteil, das zunächst bezogen auf das φῶς als ein allgemeines Leucht- und Erhellungsmittel, im Kontext von Joh 3,19 aber auch bezogen auf die Gestalt des inkarnierten λόγος zu verstehen ist.

Der in Joh 3,19b aufscheinende Gegensatz von φῶς und σκότος definiert, hier die in Joh 3,19a formulierte Konzeption der κρίσις und auch die Ausführungen von Joh 3,16-17.18 aufnehmend[57], das Kommen dieses φῶς in die Welt im Blick auf die diesem inhärente qualitative Dimension von Wirklichkeit als ein eschatologisches, als ein als neue letzthinnige Wirklichkeit auch die gegenwärtige geschichtliche Realität der Rezipienten des Joh bestimmendes[58] Ereignis[59]. Eine sekundäre bzw. akzidentiale

---

Eindeutigkeit – denn eine Einschränkung derselben wird in Joh 3,20-21 an keiner Stelle indiziert – beibehalten.

53. Vgl. zu dieser Joh 3,19d als Formulierung des Erkenntnisgrundes qualifizierenden Paraphrase u. S. 422-423.

54. Vgl. hierzu auch SCHNEIDER, *Johannes* (Anm. 28), S. 101.

55. Zur durativen Implikation des Präsens vgl. etwa BDR, §318, S. 264; zum Präsens *de conatu* vgl. §319, S. 264.

56. Vgl. zu dieser Funktion des Präsens KAEGI, *Schulgrammatik* (Anm. 20), §165, S. 136. Durchaus in diesem Sinne augenscheinlich M. THEOBALD, *Die Fleischwerdung des Logos* (NTAbh, 20), Münster, Aschendorff, 1988, S. 323.

57. Zur Kontinuität der Ausführungen in Joh 3,19.20-21 mit denjenigen in 3,16-17.18 vgl. etwa ZUMSTEIN, *Johannesevangelium* (Anm. 11), S. 149: „V.19 nimmt die schon in V.17 und V.18 erscheinende Thematik Gericht/Verurteilung (κρίνειν) auf und definiert sie".

58. Dies indiziert allein schon die Verwendung des Perfekts ἐλήλυθεν (Joh 3,19) in Joh 3,19ba; nach BDR, §340, S. 279, „vereinigt [das Perfekt] gleichsam Präsens und Aorist in sich, indem es die Dauer des *Vollendeten* ausdrückt". D.h.: Das φῶς ist in die Welt gekommen und immer noch da. Vgl. zu diesem Gesichtspunkt auch ZUMSTEIN, *Johannesevangelium* (Anm. 11), S. 149.

59. Vgl. hierzu etwa SCHNACKENBURG, *Johannesevangelium I* (Anm. 29), S. 428: „Ein rein historisches Urteil will der Evangelist in V 19 nicht fällen: die κρίσις erfolgt (ἐστίν,

und resultative soteriologische Konnotation des Begriffs φῶς und der durch denselben repräsentierten Realität in der Weise, wie sie etwa in Joh 1,9a vorliegt, lässt sich in Joh 3,19.20-21 nicht nachweisen[60], dafür aber, in Sonderheit in Joh 3,19c.d.20-21[61], der Ansatz einer resultativen – schon aufgrund des in Joh 3,19a Ausgeführten – letztlich eschatologisch eingefärbten anthropologischen, auf die Reaktion der einzelnen Menschen auf dieses φῶς abhebenden Akzentuierung, die zumindest implizit und im Ansatz eine ekklesiologische Perspektive vorzubereiten vermag[62]: Derjenige, der Böses tut, hasst das Licht, nach Joh 3,19 also nicht nur das „Licht des Tages", sondern nachgerade den inkarnierten λόγος selbst[63], und wird durch das Tun des Bösen erkennbar als jemand, der sich diesem Licht verweigert.

Sachlich durchaus an Joh 3,19.20-21 anknüpfend und die dortigen Ausführungen erinnernd begegnet die Figur des Christus innerhalb des vierten Evangeliums, metaphorisiert als φῶς, etwa noch[64] in Joh 8,12a[65];

---

nicht ἦν) überall dort, wo Menschen die Finsternis dem Licht vorziehen und an den Sohn Gottes nicht glauben".

60. Anders hier jedoch offensichtlich BULTMANN, *Johannes* (Anm. 12), S. 113-115.

61. SCHNACKENBURG, *Johannesevangelium I* (Anm. 29), S. 430, weist mit Recht darauf hin, dass die Ausführungen in Joh 3,20-21 „eine Erläuterung der These, daß die ‚bösen Werke' (V 1c) der schuldhafte Hintergrund des Unglaubens sind", darstellen. Die Joh 3,20 einleitende Konjunktion γάρ ist somit weniger begründend als vielmehr explikativ zu verstehen.

62. Vgl. hierzu etwa K. WENGST, *Bedrängte Gemeinde und verherrlichter Christus: Ein Versuch über das Johannesevangelium*, München, Kaiser, ⁴1992, S. 237; Wengst sieht in Joh 3,19-21 durchaus einen ekklesiologischen Aspekt: „..., dann sind die Aussagen des dritten Teils (19-21) nichts anderes als Ausdruck des notwendigen Kampfgeschehens, in das die bedrängte Gemeinde gestellt ist".

63. Vgl. hierzu etwa THYEN, *Johannesevangelium* (Anm. 19), S. 220: „Das eröffnende πᾶς und der unvermittelte Übergang ins Präsens lassen vermuten, daß das soeben Gesagte jetzt begründet werden soll durch eine jedermann zugängliche Erfahrung etwa dieser Gestalt: ‚Wer Böses im Schilde führt, scheut das Licht und verbirgt sich im Dunkeln, damit seine Untaten nicht entdeckt werden'. Doch über diesen allgemeinen Sinn hinaus hat der Satz fraglos symbolische Obertöne, die nicht überhört werden dürfen. Denn nach dem Vorausgegangenen kann hier ja nicht nur vom ‚Licht des Tages' die Rede sein. τὸ φῶς muß vielmehr zugleich den bezeichnen, der in Zeit und Geschichte ‚als das *Licht* in die Welt gekommen ist' (V.19), den, der später von sich sagen wird: ἐγώ εἰμι τὸ φῶς τοῦ κόσμου κτλ. (8,12)".

64. Der Beleg Joh 5,35 kann im Rahmen der vorliegenden Studie unberücksichtigt bleiben, da sich der hier verwendete Terminus φῶς auf Johannes den Täufer bezieht (vgl. hierzu Joh 5,33). Nicht übersehen werden darf hier allerdings, dass auch in dem Zusammenhang der Begriff ‚Licht' eine personale, nur eben keine substantial christologische Zuspitzung erfährt.

65. Zur Stellung von Joh 8,12 im Gesamtaufriss des Joh vgl. etwa THYEN, *Johannesevangelium* (Anm. 19), S. 420, und ZUMSTEIN, *Johannesevangelium* (Anm. 11), S. 323; zur Verbindung der mit Joh 8,12 einsetzenden Rede mit dem Laubhüttenfest vgl. S. 324-325, THEOBALD, *Johannes* (Anm. 11), S. 568-569, und auch R. SCHNACKENBURG, *Das Johannesevangelium. 2. Teil: Kommentar zu Kap. 5–12* (HTKNT, 4,2), Freiburg i.Br. – Basel – Wien,

in diesem Vers legt der johanneische Jesus von sich selbst Zeugnis ab[66] und formuliert: πάλιν οὖν αὐτοῖς ἐλάλησεν ὁ Ἰησοῦς λέγων· ἐγώ εἰμι τὸ φῶς τοῦ κόσμου[67]; auf diese Offenbarungsformel Joh 8,12aβ folgen in Joh 8,12b.c eine Einladung und eine Verheißung, innerhalb derer der Begriff φῶς dann zusätzlich zu seiner kausativen christologischen Substantialität noch eine akzidentiale bzw. wiederum zugleich auch deutlich resultative soteriologische Färbung, ergänzt um einen impliziten ekklesiologischen Anstrich, gewinnt: ὁ ἀκολουθῶν ἐμοὶ οὐ μὴ περιπατήσῃ ἐν τῇ σκοτίᾳ, ἀλλ᾽ ἕξει τὸ φῶς τῆς ζωῆς[68]. Das von diesem φῶς verliehene Heilsgut firmiert dementsprechend dann als φῶς τῆς ζωῆς[69] (Joh 8,12cβ). Aufgrund der Ausführungen in Joh 8,12a, innerhalb derer der johanneische Christus sich selbst unter Verwendung des bestimmten Artikels τό[70] als „das" φῶς τοῦ κόσμου und sich selbst eben mit diesem identifiziert, legt sich unmittelbar nahe, dass der nun um das Genitivattribut τοῦ κόσμου erweiterte φῶς-Begriff, wie schon in Joh 1,9a, substantial christologisch qualifiziert ist. Diese christologische Primärqualifikation des φῶς τοῦ κόσμου wird in Joh 8,12c dann um eine akzidentiale bzw. resultative soteriologische Konnotation[71] und in Joh 8,12b um ein – allerdings

---

Herder, 1971, S. 239-240. Diesem letzten Gesichtspunkt gegenüber allerdings kritisch SCHNEIDER, *Johannes* (Anm. 28), S. 174.

66. Vgl. zur Problematik des Selbstzeugnisses etwa THEOBALD, *Johannes* (Anm. 11), S. 569-570; dieses Problem wird dann im Anschluss an Joh 8,12 in Joh 8,13-20 thematisiert.

67. Vgl. zu diesem Syntagma etwa auch Joh 9,5. Zu dem in Joh 8,12a Ausgeführten vgl. etwa ZUMSTEIN, *Johannesevangelium* (Anm. 11), S. 324: „Die [mit Joh 8,12 beginnende] Debatte wird mit einer typisch joh christologischen Aussage eröffnet (‚Ich bin das Licht der Welt'); im Evangelium ist dies das zweite Ich-bin-Wort mit Prädikat"; vgl. zu dem Syntagma τὸ φῶς τοῦ κόσμου darüber hinaus S. 325: „Der bestimmte Artikel … gibt dem Prädikat ‚Licht' ausschließenden Charakter: ‚Das' Licht ist Jesus – und sonst keiner. Er ist das Licht der Welt, indem er es gibt, – und er gibt es, weil er es ist". Darüber hinaus macht Zumstein auf den mit diesem Syntagma transportierten universalen Charakter der in Joh 8,12b ausgesprochenen Einladung aufmerksam: „Der Genitiv ‚der Welt' (τοῦ κόσμου) hat universale Tragweite: Die christologische Offenbarung wird ausnahmslos allen Menschen angeboten" (S. 325). Zur traditionsgeschichtlichen Verortung dieses Syntagmas vgl. etwa SCHNACKENBURG, *Johannesevangelium II* (Anm. 65), S. 240-241, darüber hinaus auch THEOBALD, *Johannes* (Anm. 11), S. 567-568, der den alttestamentlichjüdischen und den neutestamentlichen Bedeutungshintergrund des Bildwortes vom φῶς τοῦ κόσμου ausleuchtet.

68. Vgl. zu dieser Struktur von Joh 8,12 etwa ZUMSTEIN, *Johannesevangelium* (Anm. 11), S. 324.

69. Zum traditionsgeschichtlichen Hintergrund dieses Syntagmas vgl. etwa SCHNACKENBURG, *Johannesevangelium II* (Anm. 65), S. 242-243, darüber hinaus SCHNEIDER, *Johannes* (Anm. 28), S. 174, Anm. 6.

70. Vgl. hierzu ZUMSTEIN, *Johannesevangelium* (Anm. 11), S. 325 (vgl. hierzu o. Anm. 67).

71. Vgl. hierzu *ibid.*, S. 325: „Die konsequent soteriologische Ausrichtung der Ichbin-Aussage wird in der Einladung wieder aufgenommen (‚wer mir nachfolgt, wird nicht

via negativa formuliertes – die qualitative Dimension von Wirklichkeit reflektierendes eschatologisches Momentum, bestehend aus einem Hinweis auf die mit dem in spatialer Perspektive wahrnehmbaren Aufscheinen des φῶς τοῦ κόσμου ins Dasein tretende neue schlechthinnige, der bestehenden diametral gegenüberstehende eschatologische Wirklichkeit[72], erweitert. Zu beobachten ist dabei, dass die hier in Joh 8,12 aufscheinende akzidential-resultative soteriologische Konnotation durchaus auch einen – wenn auch impliziten – ekklesiologisch-resultativen Akzent transportiert: Die Summe derer, die dem τὸ φῶς τοῦ κόσμου nachfolgen und dadurch das τὸ φῶς τῆς ζωῆς erhalten werden, bildet – eben aufgrund ihrer Nachfolge und der Gabe des φῶς τῆς ζωῆς – letztendlich die Gemeinschaft der Kirche, die als Quasi-Inkarnation des „‚Raum' des Lichtes" zu dem von der σκοτία definierten[73] Raum[74] in einem diametralen Gegensatz steht[75].

In Joh 12,35.36a.46 – hier ist der Terminus φῶς innerhalb des Joh letztmalig belegt – wird der Zusammenhang zwischen der christologischen und der soteriologischen Dimension des φῶς-Begriffs noch einmal unmissverständlich nachgerade herausgearbeitet: Zunächst spricht der

---

in der Finsternis wandeln'). Die Nachfolgebeziehung (ὁ ἀκολουθῶν ἐμοί), Synonym für den Glauben, ermöglicht eine Befreiung aus der ‚Finsternis'. Diese Befreiung ist mit einer Verheißung versehen: ‚sondern wird das Licht des Lebens haben'". Anders hier THEOBALD, *Fleischwerdung* (Anm. 56), S. 308, der das Syntagma φῶς τοῦ κόσμου als eine „soteriologische Funktionsbestimmung in Form eines Bildwortes" verstehen möchte. In Joh 8,12a liegt eine solche soteriologische Funktionsbestimmung, wenn überhaupt, so allenfalls implizit vor, da die soteriologische Konsequenz des in Joh 8,12a Ausgesagten im eigentlichen Sinne erst in Joh 8,12c thematisiert wird. Gegenüber den Ausführungen Theobalds will es angemessener scheinen, in Joh 8,12a zunächst nur eine rein christologische Zuspitzung wahrzunehmen.

72. Aus diesem Sachverhalt ergibt sich im Blick auf die Interpretation von Joh 8,12c, dass „das Futur ἕξει ... keine ferne Zukunft [bezeichnet], die nach dem natürlichen Tod beginnen würde, sondern ist Gabe, die Gabe der Offenbarung, die hier und jetzt in der Person des Offenbarers anbricht" (ZUMSTEIN, *Johannesevangelium* [Anm. 11], S. 325-326). Vgl. darüber hinaus auch ZUMSTEIN, *ibid.*, S. 325, der die Metapher φῶς hier als „Ausdruck der Finalität der Offenbarung" wahrnehmen möchte.

73. SCHNACKENBURG, *Johannesevangelium II* (Anm. 65), S. 242, charakterisiert den „‚Wandel in der Finsternis'" – weit über ein ethisches Verständnis hinausgehend und wiederum spatial (vgl. hierzu unmittelbar u.) – näherhin als die „Verfallenheit an den Todesbereich", wobei der Begriff σκοτία „die Existenzsituation des Menschen, der ohne das Licht der Heilsoffenbarung ziel- und richtungslos dahinlebt, ‚nicht weiß, wohin er geht' (12,35), und in dieser Gottesferne hoffnungslos dem Todesgeschick preisgegeben ist".

74. Vgl. zu dieser spatialen Dimension etwa *ibid.*, S. 242; vgl. darüber hinaus auch THEOBALD, *Fleischwerdung* (Anm. 56), S. 308.

75. Dieser ekklesiologische Aspekt begegnet, wenn auch nur im Ansatz, in den oben zitierten Ausführungen von J. Zumstein zu dem durch den Artikel τό explizierten ausschließenden Charakter des φῶς (vgl. hierzu o. Anm. 67). Vgl. darüber hinaus auch BULTMANN, *Johannes* (Anm. 12), S. 26.

johanneische Jesus gegenüber dem ὄχλος (Joh 12,34) davon, dass er als das „Licht" noch eine kurze Zeit[76] „bei ihnen", d.h. in der Welt, verweilen wird (Joh 12,35b). Im Anschluss daran fordert er seine Gesprächspartner auf, zu wandeln, so lange sie das „Licht" haben, damit die σκοτία sie nicht überfalle (Joh 12,35c.d). Daran anschließend klärt Jesus seine Zuhörer darüber auf, dass derjenige, der in der Finsternis wandele, nicht wüsste, wo er hinginge (Joh 12,35e): εἶπεν οὖν αὐτοῖς ὁ Ἰησοῦς· ἔτι μικρὸν χρόνον τὸ φῶς ἐν ὑμῖν ἐστιν. περιπατεῖτε ὡς τὸ φῶς ἔχετε, ἵνα μὴ σκοτία ὑμᾶς καταλάβῃ· καὶ ὁ περιπατῶν ἐν τῇ σκοτίᾳ οὐκ οἶδεν ποῦ ὑπάγει. Die Ausführungen in Joh 12,36 knüpfen dann augenscheinlich an das in Joh 12,35c Dargestellte an: Solange sie das „Licht" haben (Joh 12,36aα), sollen sie an dasselbe glauben (Joh 12,36aβ) – d.h. die Möglichkeit nutzen, Glauben an dasselbe zu entwickeln –, damit sie „Söhne" eben jenes „Lichtes" würden: ὡς τὸ φῶς ἔχετε, πιστεύετε εἰς τὸ φῶς, ἵνα υἱοὶ φωτὸς γένησθε. In Joh 12,36aα.β trägt der inkarnierte λόγος als derjenige, der noch eine kurze Zeit Gemeinschaft mit seinen Nachfolgern hat, den hier als Simplex erscheinenden Titel τὸ φῶς[77]; dementsprechend wird die Gemeinschaft der Gläubigen, d.h. die Gemeinschaft der mit dem Joh angeschriebenen Nachfolger Christi folgerichtig dann als υἱοὶ φωτός tituliert (Joh 12,36aγ). Der Terminus φῶς trägt somit hier wiederum in seiner Substantialität eine christologische Perspektive, die um eine sekundär-akzidential zu definierende, wiederum resultativ zu interpretierende soteriologische Konnotation ergänzt wird[78]. Eine ekklesiologische Perspektive, die sich etwa aus der aus dem *bis dato* Ausgeführten gezogenen Konsequenz ergeben hätte, dass etwa die Anzahl derer, die glauben, zugleich auch eine neue Gemeinschaft bildeten, begegnet in Joh 12,35.36a im Rahmen der Konzeption der Glaubenden als υἱοὶ φωτός allenfalls, zugleich aber auch immerhin, implizit[79]. Der in

---

76. Vgl. zu dieser Angabe ZUMSTEIN, *Johannesevangelium* (Anm. 11), S. 463: „Die ‚kurze Zeit', die vor seinem Tod verbleibt …, betont die Dringlichkeit der Situation".

77. Vgl. hierzu *ibid.*, S. 463: „Zunächst definiert er [d.h. der in Jesus inkarnierte λόγος] sich selbst indirekt (in der 3. Pers. Sg.) als ‚das Licht' …, das bei seinen Gesprächspartnern weilt (τὸ φῶς ἐν ὑμῖν) und insistiert auf der Kontingenz seines Wirkens, das einem baldigen Ende geweiht ist".

78. Vgl. hierzu *ibid.*, S. 463-464: „Aber – und dies ist die Folge daraus (ἵνα) – dieser Übergang zum christologischen Glauben bedeutet Veränderung. Er macht aus dem Glaubenden einen ‚Sohn des Lichts'. Anders gesagt stellt er ihn in ein neues Leben, das sich auf eine neue Beziehung gründet (υἱός). Diese letzte Aktion Jesu ist aufs Neue soteriologisch ausgerichtet: Die Priorität liegt für ihn darin, dass die Menschen zum Licht, das heißt zum Heil gelangen".

79. Vgl. hierzu SCHNACKENBURG, *Johannesevangelium II* (Anm. 65), S. 497, der mit Hinweis auf die Qumranschriften formuliert: „In den Qumrantexten ist er [d.h. der Ausdruck υἱοὶ φωτός] (besonders in 1 QS und 1 QM) die bevorzugte Bezeichnung für die

Joh 12,35c.d – nun zum wiederholten Male – thematisierte Gegensatz von φῶς und σκοτία lässt einerseits die spatiale Komponente des hier verwendeten φῶς-Begriffs als der räumlichen Antipode zum *spatium* der σκοτία, ergänzt um einen durch den Hinweis ὡς τὸ φῶς ἔχετε (Joh 12,35c.36aα) vermittelten temporalen Akzent, unmittelbar hervortreten, lässt andererseits erkennen, dass die Inkarnation des λόγος in Jesus gegenüber der Sphäre der σκοτία als eine neue schlechthinnige Wirklichkeit ein letzterer zur Gänze entgegenstehendes letztgültiges Zeichensystem realisiert hat[80], eine Erkenntnis, die unmittelbar dazu führt, den Terminus φῶς und die von ihm repräsentierte Realität an dieser Stelle der eschatologischen Dimension von Wirklichkeit zuzuordnen.

Die in Joh 12,36aγ entwickelte soteriologische Perspektive wird Joh 12,46 in gewisser Weise noch einmal unterstrichen. Hier spricht der johanneische Jesus davon, dass jeder, der an ihn als „ein Licht" glaube, nicht in der σκοτία bleibe, den Unheilsraum derselben somit verlasse und in den durch ihn selber konstituierten Heilsraum eingehen werde[81], eine Aussage, die in dieses Wort neben der substantialen christologischen auch eine akzidentiale soteriologische, über den Gedanken der Gemeinschaft der Glaubenden hinaus zumindest implizit das Momentum des Ekklesiologischen anklingen lassende Akzentuierung injiziert. Dass dieses Wort vor dem Hintergrund der eschatologischen Dimension von Wirklichkeit zu verstehen ist, ergibt sich aus dem in ihm thematisierten Gegensatz von φῶς und σκοτία, dass dieses Wort die Vorstellung eines räumlichen Horizontes mitbringt, aus der Verwendung der Wendung ἐν τῇ σκοτίᾳ μὴ μείνῃ in Joh 12,46bβ.

Fazit: Der Begriff φῶς begegnet im Joh entweder als Simplex oder verknüpft mit – jeweils unterschiedlichen – Genitivattributen. Die übergroße Mehrheit der Belege präsentiert diesen Terminus als Metapher für die in der Gestalt Jesu von Nazareth inkarnierte Figur des λόγος, stellt

---

Angehörigen der Gemeinde, in betontem Gegensatz zu den ‚Söhnen der Finsternis'". Diese Beobachtung lässt die Annahme, dass dieses Syntagma in Joh 12,36aγ auch einen ekklesiologischen Akzent transportiert, keinesfalls unwahrscheinlich erscheinen, auch wenn sich ein unmittelbarer Bezug der Ausführungen in Joh 12,36 auf die Qumranliteratur sicherlich nicht plausibilisieren lässt.

80. Vgl. hierzu ZUMSTEIN, *Johannesevangelium* (Anm. 11), S. 463: „Wer in der Finsternis wandelt, kann seinem Leben keine kohärente Richtung geben; ihm fehlt das Wissen …, das ihm erlauben würde, sein Leben zu verstehen und auszurichten".

81. Vgl. hierzu sehr schön *ibid.*, S. 472: „Die Welt (τὸν κόσμον), in der der Mensch lebt, ist ‚Finsternis' (ἐν τῇ σκοτίᾳ), sodass jedes menschliche Dasein entfremdet ist, der Täuschung und dem Tod anheim gegeben. Allein das Kommen des Lichts in Gestalt des inkarnierten Sohnes (ἐγὼ φῶς …), das die Realität Gottes offenbart, ermöglicht es dem Glaubenden, nicht in der Gefangenschaft der Finsternis zu verbleiben, sondern zum Sinn und dadurch zur Fülle des Lebens zu gelangen".

jenen somit substantial in einen christologischen Kontext, dem in der Regel immer eine verursachende, kausative Wirkung zugebilligt wird. Akzidential werden der Konzeption des inkarnierten λόγος als des φῶς, nicht zuletzt expliziert durch die einzelnen Genitivattribute, jeweils unterschiedliche, resultativ zu fassende theologische (Sekundär-)Kontexte, etwa der soteriologische, der kosmologische, der anthropologische oder aber auch der ekklesiologische Kontext, beigelegt. Der Terminus φῶς bespielt immer das Feld der eschatologischen Dimension von Wirklichkeit und umreißt dabei entweder einen zeitlichen, einen räumlichen oder aber auch einen zeitlichen und räumlichen Horizont.

2. *Der Begriff φῶς κτλ. in den Ignatiusbriefen in seiner Relation zur Verwendung desselben im Joh.*

Diesen im Joh nachweisbaren Benennungen und den dahinterstehenden Konzeptionen zumindest auf den ersten Blick augenscheinlich durchaus vergleichbar charakterisiert der antiochenische Bischof Ignatius in *Phld.* 2.1aα die Glieder der von ihm angeschriebenen Gemeinde in deutlich singulärer, weder im Joh noch in der übrigen johanneischen Literatur belegter Weise[82] als τέκνα φωτὸς ἀληθείας[83]: τέκνα οὖν φωτὸς ἀληθείας, φεύγετε τὸν μερισμὸν καὶ τὰς κακοδιδασκαλίας· ὅπου δὲ ὁ ποιμήν ἐστιν, ἐκεῖ ὡς πρόβατα ἀκολουθεῖτε. Das in *Phld.* 2.1aα belegte Syntagma τέκνα φωτὸς ἀληθείας erinnert einerseits an die Ausführungen in Joh 1,9a – hier wird der inkarnierte λόγος als φῶς ἀληθινόν bezeichnet –, lässt andererseits aber auch die Darstellung in Joh 12,36aγ – hier tragen die Nachfolger eben dieses inkarnierten λόγος den Titel υἱοὶ φωτός – anklingen. Aufgrund seiner Kombination mit dem Terminus τέκνα gewinnt der Begriff φῶς an dieser Stelle einen Bezug auf die unmittelbare gemeindliche Wirklichkeit und somit eine ekklesiologische Dimension; jener bzw. das Syntagma φῶς ἀληθείας bezeichnet diejenige Kategorie, die der Überzeugung des Ignatius zufolge die gemeinsame integrative theologische Basis der angeschriebenen philadelphischen Christen bildet. Die τέκνα φωτὸς ἀληθείας, d.h. die gesamte christliche Gemeinschaft

---

82. Vgl. zu diesem Syntagma etwa W. BAUER, *Die Briefe des Ignatius von Antiochia und der Polykarpbrief* (HNT, Ergänzungs-Band), Tübingen, Mohr Siebeck, 1920, S. 255: „φῶς ἀληθείας aber ist eine Eigentümlichkeit des Ign.".

83. In ihrer Ausgabe der Apostolischen Väter definieren A. Lindemann und H. Paulsen diese Wendung als ein Zitat aus Eph 5,8 (vgl. A. LINDEMANN – H. PAULSEN [Hgg.], *Die Apostolischen Väter: Griechisch-deutsche Parallelausgabe*, Tübingen, Mohr Siebeck, 1992, S. 218), ohne an dieser Stelle jedoch auf eine mögliche johanneische Herkunft derselben zu verweisen.

Philadelphias, wird von dem Bischof Antiochias aufgefordert und ermahnt, sich hinter dem gemeindlichen ἐπίσκοπος zu versammeln und sich an ihm zu orientieren und jeglichen spalterischen Tendenzen (μερισμός) und jeglichen – für die Spaltung bzw. die Spaltungen möglicherweise verantwortlich zeichnenden – falschen Lehren (κακοδιδασκαλίαι) eine Absage zu erteilen[84].

Unklar bleibt, was Ignatius mit dem Terminus ἀλήθεια bzw. dem Syntagma φῶς ἀληθείας an dieser Stelle konkret meint. Bemerkenswert ist allerdings, dass der antiochenische Bischof im Zusammenhang seiner Ausführungen in *Phld.* 2 insgesamt jeglichen Hinweis auf die Person des Christus vermeidet, was dem Begriff ἀλήθεια als dem *nomen rectum* und damit auch dem Syntagma φῶς ἀληθείας bzw. dem Simplex φῶς ein nicht-christologisches, letzten Endes apersonales und rein materiales Gepräge verleiht. Der Begriff ἀλήθεια, der abgesehen von der hier diskutierten Passage noch in Ign. *Eph.* 6.2(bis), *Pol.* 7.3 und *Smyrn.* 5.1 belegt ist, scheint, wie vor allem auch *Eph.* 6.2 wahrscheinlich zu machen vermag, im Kontext der Ignatianen die innerhalb des gemeindlichen Lebens gelebte Verknüpfung von Orthodoxie und Orthopraxie zu bezeichnen. Immerhin nämlich hören die ephesischen Christen auf denjenigen Ἰησοῦς Χριστός, der ἐν ἀληθείᾳ spricht, nicht aber auf einen, der eine falsche, letztlich häretische Botschaft verkündigt[85]: ἀλλ' οὐδὲ ἀκούετέ τινος πλέον, εἴπερ Ἰησοῦ Χριστοῦ λαλοῦντος ἐν ἀληθείᾳ. Der Terminus ἀλήθεια umfasst somit offensichtlich also die rechte Lehre und das daraus resultierende rechte Tun, sämtlich Dinge, die, wie die Ausführungen in Ign. *Phld.* 2 indizieren, von denen korrekt realisiert werden, die sich hinter dem gemeindlichen Bischof versammeln und solidarisch zu ihm stehen; τέκνα φωτὸς ἀληθείας dürften die philadelphischen Christen also deswegen genannt worden sein, weil sie, zumindest der Einschätzung des Ignatius zufolge, als Getreue ihres Bischofs ihre christliche Existenz in ihrer Gesamtheit eben vom „Licht" der Orthodoxie und der Orthopraxie dominieren ließen[86]. Der Begriff φῶς transportiert in *Phld.* 2.1aα demzufolge, anknüpfend an die semantischen Implikationen des Terminus ἀλήθεια, substantial eine räumlich zu denkende

---

84. Vgl. hierzu etwa W.R. SCHOEDEL, *Die Briefe des Ignatius von Antiochien* (Hermeneia), München, Kaiser, 1990, S. 312: „Die Schwierigkeiten in Philadelphia hatten es mit ‚falschen Lehrern' zu tun …, die die Gemeinde spalteten". Vgl. hierzu auch PAULSEN, *Studien* (Anm. 3), S. 145.

85. Vgl. hierzu etwa BAUER, *Briefe* (Anm. 82), S. 206: „Der Schlußsatz kann wohl nur, wie oben versucht wurde, übersetzt werden, wenn εἴπερ (G) zu Recht besteht. Ein Jesus Christus, der ἐν ἀληθείᾳ redet, tritt dann einem häretischen gegenüber, den zu hören die Epheser keine Lust verspüren".

86. Vgl. hierzu auch Ign. *Smyrn.* 5.1a.

ekklesiologische Dimension, die letzten Endes als apersonal und ausschließlich material zu charakterisieren ist: Das „Licht der Wahrheit" leuchtet in dem Raum auf, der durch die durch das Hören auf den gemeindlichen Bischof garantierte Praxis der Orthodoxie und der Orthopraxie abgesteckt wird.

Mit der gegenüber dem Joh charakteristischen semantischen Verschiebung von φῶς ἀληθινόν hin zu φῶς ἀληθείας und der damit einhergehenden Transfiguration des ἀλήθεια-Begriffs – anders als etwa in Joh 14,6 eignet der in Ign. *Phld.* 2.1aα und auch *Eph.* 6.2 aufscheinenden ignatianischen Konzeption von ἀλήθεια keinerlei Bezug auf die Person des Christus – entbehrt dieses von Ignatius verwendete Syntagma der etwa dem annähernd gleichlautenden johanneischen φῶς ἀληθινόν (Joh 1,9a) – noch – innewohnenden personal-christologischen Prägung und damit zugleich dessen eschatologischer Zuspitzung. Vielmehr stellt das ignatianische φῶς ἀληθείας auf der einen Seite eine material-ekklesiologische und damit zugleich auch ausschließlich spatiale, den räumlichen Geltungsbereich des φῶς ἀληθείας bzw. der ἀλήθεια benennende, auf der anderen Seite aber zugleich auch eine in ihrer Spatialität historisierte, letzten Endes eine innerhalb der Geschichte sich realisierende und somit eine innergeschichtliche Realität bezeichnende semantische Neukonstruktion dar, eine Interpretation, die nicht zuletzt auch durch das in Ign. *Phld.* 2.1b, 2 Ausgeführte, dessen ekklesiologisch-spatialen Impetus und dessen innergeschichtliche Akzentuierung gestützt wird[87]. Das aber heißt: In *Phld.* 2.1aα wird der Begriff φῶς substantial – und letzten Endes ausschließlich – ekklesiologisch konnotiert: er transportiert im Blick auf die ihm inhärente qualitative Dimension von Wirklichkeit ein innergeschichtliches, im Blick auf die ihm innewohnende raum-zeitliche Perspektive – hier nun durchaus konsequent – ausschließlich ein spatiales Moment. Das ignatianische Syntagma φῶς ἀληθείας bzw. der ignatianische ἀλήθεια-Begriff kontextualisieren sich, selbst ohne jeglichen erkennbaren personal-christologischen und eschatologischen Bezug, in der Konzeption einer im Rahmen der Geschichte sich realisierenden ἐκκλησία, innerhalb welcher jenes ein Spatium definiert, das sich von demjenigen, in dem die Vorfindlichkeiten des μερισμός und der κακοδιδασκαλίαι (*Phld.* 2.1aβ) Platz greifen, materialiter unterscheidet.

Der Sachverhalt, dass der antiochenische Bischof in Ign. *Phld.* 2.1aα das Syntagma φῶς ἀληθείας in die Diskussion einführt, ohne hier einen

---

87. Vgl. hierzu etwa SCHOEDEL, *Briefe* (Anm. 84), S. 313: „Die Lösung der Schwierigkeiten sieht Ignatius im Gehorsam dem Bischof gegenüber, der als Pastor oder Hirte derartige Spaltungen bekämpft".

christologischen Bezug auch nur anzudeuten, wirft die Frage auf, ob jener innerhalb des Corpus seiner Briefe den Terminus φῶς überhaupt auf die Gestalt des Christus bezogen verstanden wissen wollte. Werden, um diese Frage zu klären, die in den Ignatiusbriefen vorfindlichen Belege für den Begriff φῶς näher untersucht[88], so zeigt sich, dass dieser Terminus jene an keiner Stelle in einer dem Johannesevangelium vergleichbaren Weise repräsentiert. Insgesamt nämlich ist der Begriff φῶς, abgesehen von *Phld.* 2.1, innerhalb des Corpus Ignatianum noch dreimal belegt, zunächst in *Eph.* 19.2(bis)[89], schließlich noch in *Röm.* 6.2. In *Eph.* 19.2[90] verwendet Ignatius diesen Begriff, um – letztlich in theologisch gänzlich unspezifischer Weise und ohne jegliche attributive Ergänzung – das unvergleichliche Leuchten und die überragende Leuchtkraft des Kommen Christi und damit den Beginn einer neuen Weltzeit anzeigenden ἀστήρ zum Ausdruck zu bringen[91]. Weder der in seiner Leuchtkraft hervorstechende ἀστήρ noch dessen Leuchtkraft, dessen φῶς selbst, werden in *Eph.* 19.2 unmittelbar oder explizit mit der Gestalt des Christus identifiziert.

In *Röm.* 6.2-3g bezeichnet der antiochenische Bischof das Heilsgut, bzw. präziser: den Heilsraum, den Ignatius nach seinem Martyrium zu erlangen hofft, verleiht dem Terminus φῶς somit eine substantial soteriologische Konnotation, die durch einen spatialen Akzent erweitert wird. Der antiochenische Bischof strebt an, an den Ort zu gelangen bzw. den Raum zu betreten, in dem das φῶς καθαρόν scheint und an dem er wirklich Mensch[92] sein wird[93]. Ein christologischer Bezug lässt sich für den Begriff φῶς, der in *Röm.* 6.2-3g innerhalb des Syntagmas καθαρὸν φῶς

---

88. Vgl. zu diesen Texten auch VON DER GOLTZ, *Ignatius* (Anm. 5), S. 195.

89. Zur Charakterisierung von Ign. *Eph.* 19.2-3 als eines Hymnus vgl. im Anschluss an R. Deichgräber SCHOEDEL, *Briefe* (Anm. 84), S. 159.

90. H. PAULSEN, *Die Briefe des Ignatius von Antiochia und der Brief des Polykarp von Smyrna* (HNT, 18), Tübingen, Mohr Siebeck, ²1985, S. 44, nimmt im Blick auf die Ausführungen in Ign. *Eph.* 19.2-3 eine ignatianische Herkunft an; ähnlich auch BAUER, *Briefe* (Anm. 82), S. 217.

91. Nicht von ungefähr bezeichnet daher SCHOEDEL, *Briefe* (Anm. 84), S. 166, die Ausführungen in Mt 2,1-12 als „noch immer die wichtigste Parallele zu *Eph.* 19,2".

92. Zu diesem Begriff vgl. BAUER, *Briefe* (Anm. 82), S. 251, darüber hinaus auch ausführlich SCHOEDEL, *Briefe* (Anm. 84), S. 292.

93. Vgl. hierzu etwa BAUER, *Briefe* (Anm. 82), S. 250-251: „Im Gegensatz zur Welt und zur Materie strebt Ign. nach dem reinen Licht (wie zu κόσμῳ und ὕλῃ, so ist auch zu καθαρ. φῶς im Deutschen der Artikel zu setzen), d.h. er will, wie das ἐκεῖ παραγ. zeigt, in das Reich des reinen Lichtes eingehen". Weniger deutlich als Bauer hier SCHOEDEL, *Briefe* (Anm. 84), S. 291; immerhin verweist Schoedel auf Plutarchos, *Pericl.* 39.2; hier benutze jener „die Wendung ‚reinstes Licht' (φῶς καθαρώτατον), um das zu beschreiben, was die Wohnung der Götter erleuchtet" (S. 252), was bedeutet, dass jener dem Begriff φῶς somit ebenfalls einen spatialen Akzent verleiht.

Verwendung findet, nicht namhaft machen; vielmehr wird dasselbe durch den Gegensatz zu den Termini κόσμος und ὕλη definiert.

Diese Diskussion vermag das oben zur Interpretation von Ign. *Phld.* 2.1aα Ausgeführte zu untermauern: Dem in den Ignatianen verwendeten Begriff φῶς eignet bestenfalls ein vom Rezipienten zu postulierender und somit mittelbarer, lediglich auf der rezeptionsästhetischen Ebene verifizierbarer christologischer Bezug; dass der Begriff φῶς an dieser Stelle oder auch sonst in den Ignatiusbriefen, hierin dem Joh auch nur im Ansatz vergleichbar, unmittelbar zur Bezeichnung der Christusgestalt verwendet werde und somit als christologische Titulatur zu verstehen sei, lässt sich allerdings gerade nicht wahrscheinlich machen. Die Analyse der Belege für den Begriff φῶς innerhalb des Corpus Ignatianum zeigt vielmehr, dass der antiochenische Bischof diesen Terminus in keinem seiner Briefe klar inhaltlich definiert, sondern ihn deutlich unspezifischer als im Joh und in jedem Falle ohne jeglichen christologischen Hintergrund gebraucht.

Die Ausführungen in 1 Joh 2,8-9 lassen sich nun als ein konzeptioneller Zwischenschritt zwischen der ausschließlich christologischen Verwendung des Terminus φῶς in Joh und derjenigen in den Ignatiusbriefen lesen. H.-J. Klauck zufolge dürfe das in 1 Joh 2,8 begegnende Syntagma τὸ φῶς τὸ ἀληθινόν nicht als unmittelbare Bezeichnung für Christus gelesen werden, eine Annahme, die durch die Ausführungen in 1 Joh 1,5c – hier wird der Terminus φῶς unmittelbar auf die Gestalt Gottes bezogen – untermauert wird. Vielmehr resultiere zwar das gegenwärtige Scheinen des Lichtes „aus dem zurückliegenden, von Gott in Gang gesetzten Heilsgeschehen in Christus"[94], „den Raum [!] für seine von Gott geschenkte und vom Geist mitgetragene Kontinuität ... [bilde aber] die johanneische Gemeinde"[95]. Das aber heißt letztlich nichts anderes, als dass die bei Ignatius zumindest in *Phld.* 2.1aα beobachtbare, einen substantial ekklesiologisch-spatialen, im Blick auf die qualitative Dimension von Wirklichkeit innergeschichtlich sich orientierenden Akzent transportierende Konzeptionalisierung des Syntagmas φῶς ἀληθείας in der in der johanneischen Tradition, so wie sie in 1 Joh 2,8-9 sichtbar wird, zuhandenen impliziten Transfiguration des johanneischen Syntagmas τὸ φῶς τὸ ἀληθινόν bereits vorgebildet ist. Die bei Ignatius beobachtbare apersonale und ausschließlich materiale Prägung des Begriffs φῶς wird im 1 Joh dadurch vorbereitet,

---

94. H.-J. KLAUCK, *Der erste Johannesbrief* (EKKNT, 23/1), Zürich, Benziger Verlag; Neukirchen-Vluyn, Neukirchener Verlag, 1991, S. 123.

95. *Ibid.*, S. 123; Klauck schreibt weiter: „Insofern kann man sagen, daß die Lichtmetaphorik im Brief historisiert und an die Gemeindegeschichte gebunden wird, ohne daß dies ein negatives Werturteil impliziert".

dass die im Joh noch nachweisbare ausschließlich personal-christologische Ausrichtung desselben durch dessen Ausrichtung auf die Gestalt Gottes ersetzt wird, eine Entwicklung, die innerhalb des Corpus Ignatianum dann mit dem das personale Momentum *ad acta* legenden Bezug desselben auf die in der jeweils angeschriebenen Gemeinde gelebte Summe von Orthodoxie und Orthopraxie weitergeführt wird.

In der Summe: Im Blick auf die Frage nach der Art und Weise der Rezeption des Johannesevangeliums durch Ignatius lassen sich aus diesen Beobachtungen und Erwägungen folgende – zunächst natürlich nur vorläufige und durch weitere Analysen zu bestätigende – Schlussfolgerungen ableiten:

(a) Dass Ignatius zumindest mit dem Syntagma φῶς ἀληθείας johanneisches Traditionsgut aufgenommen und verarbeitet hat, lässt sich angesichts der oben aufgeführten sprachlichen und auch konzeptionell-theologischen Argumente kaum ernsthaft bestreiten[96].

(b) Der antiochenische Bischof löst allerdings den im Joh mit der Person des inkarnierten λόγος verknüpften φῶς-Begriff aus seinem engen christologischen Zusammenhang und bezieht ihn, entpersonalisiert und materialisiert, substantial auf die Ekklesiologie, konkret auf die in der – sofern sie denn den aus der Sicht des Ignatius rechten Weg beschreitet – ἐκκλησία als einzelner Gemeinde geglaubte und gelebte Orthodoxie und Orthopraxie, oder aber auf die Soteriologie, hier konkret auf den nach dem Tod zu gewinnenden Heilsraum[97].

(c) Dies bedeutet theologisch: Ignatius zufolge gewinnt der Mensch das Heil nicht mehr in oder auch aus der unmittelbaren und vor die Entscheidung stellenden Begegnung mit – dem inkarnierten λόγος, – dem eschatologischen Offenbarer als dem φῶς, sondern dann, wenn er einen bestimmten, durch charakteristische Merkmale, konkret durch das Scheinen des nun aber gerade nicht mit der Person etwa des himmlischen Christus zu identifizierenden φῶς gekennzeichneten (Heils- oder Unheils-)Raum entweder betritt oder aber nicht verlässt.

(d) Weitergedacht heißt dies: Wird dem Joh zufolge jemand Christ, wenn er sich für den Offenbarer als das eschatologische φῶς entscheidet

---

[96]. Sowohl die semantische als aber auch die erhebliche konzeptionelle Differenz zwischen den Syntagmata φῶς ἀληθινόν und φῶς ἀληθείας widerraten, für sich betrachtet, der Vermutung, dass Ignatius hier in *Phld.* 2.1aα das Joh zitiert hätte; vgl. hierzu, auf die Ignatianen insgesamt bezogen, etwa PAULSEN, *Studien* (Anm. 3), S. 37 (vgl. hierzu bereits o. S. 430).

[97]. Die hier entwickelte Parallelität zwischen dem Heilsraum, der durch die einzelne Ortsgemeinde konstituiert wird, und dem Heilsraum, in den der Christ nach seinem Sterben hineingelangt, ergibt sich aus dem Sachverhalt, dass sich ignatianischer Anschauung zufolge „die wahre, himmlische ἐκκλησία in den einzelnen Gemeinden" (PAULSEN, *Studien* [Anm. 3], S. 145) repräsentiert.

und in dessen Nachfolge tritt, so Ignatius zufolge, wenn er den Raum des φῶς betritt und die dort geltenden – orthodoxen und orthopraxen – Wahrheiten und Gepflogenheiten akzeptiert und für sich annimmt. Zugespitzt formuliert: Nach Joh vermittelt der Offenbarer das Heil, nach Ignatius die Kirche als eigentlicher Heilsraum. Damit gewinnt die ἐκκλησία eine eigene, wenn auch sicherlich aus dem Christusgeschehen resultierende soteriologische Qualität.

3. *Fazit*

Die hier auf der Basis der Belege Joh 1,4-5.9a; 3,20-21; 8,12a.b.c; 12,35.36a.46 und Ign. *Röm.* 6.2-3g; *Phld.* 2.1aα ergänzt um weitere Belege aus der johanneischen wie auch der ignatianischen Literatur, formulierten, um den Begriff φῶς kreisenden Überlegungen führen im Blick auf die Frage nach der in den Ign sichtbar werdenden Rezeption des Joh zu folgendem – vorläufigen und durch weitere Studien zu erhärtenden oder aber auch zu relativierenden – Ergebnis: Ausgehend vom Joh verändern sich über 1 Joh bis hin zu den Ignatiusbriefen die soteriologischen Gewichtungen: Kommt innerhalb des Joh noch der Gestalt des inkarnierten λόγος die ausschließliche soteriologische „Kompetenz" zu, so verlagert sich diese über 1 Joh bis hin zu den Ignatiusbriefen – zumindest auch – immer mehr auf die ἐκκλησία als denjenigen Raum, innerhalb dessen das Heil in Orthodoxie und Orthopraxie gelebt und weitergegeben wird. Die ausschließliche Begegnung mit dem Offenbarer verliert im Blick auf die ihr inhärente soteriologische Wirksamkeit vom Joh über 1 Joh bis hin zu den Ignatianen immer mehr an Gewicht. An die Stelle des Offenbarers tritt je länger je mehr die ἐκκλησία als heilschaffende Institution, ein Gedanke, der mit der in den Ignatianen entwickelten Konzeption eines monarchischen Episkopates sehr wohl zu korrelieren vermag.

II. Mögliche historische Folgerungen

Aus dem oben formulierten Ergebnis ergibt sich als erste historische Konsequenz zunächst die Annahme, dass zur Zeit der Abfassung der Ignatianen[98] die johanneischen Schriften und auch die diese Schriften unterfütternde johanneische Tradition in der römischen Provinz Asia in jedem Falle – noch – virulent und wirkmächtig gewesen sind. Darüber hinaus ist mehr als denkbar, dass die Ignatiusbriefe von jemandem verfasst

---

98. Vgl. hierzu o. S. 411.

worden sind, der sich bewusst in die johanneische Tradition einzuordnen und diese für seine konkrete historische Situation weiterzuentwickeln beabsichtigte. Das aber heißt: Der Verfasser der Ignatianen ist letzten Endes durchaus vergleichbar mit dem Verfasser oder den Verfassern der Pastoralbriefe, der oder die sich als „Sachverwalter der paulinischen Theologie in Ephesus"[99] darum mühten, das theologische Erbe ihres „Schulhauptes" in ihrer Zeit zu aktualisieren und lebendig zu erhalten. Demzufolge stellten die Ignatianen in ihrer Summe die „Pastoralbriefe des johanneischen Kreises"[100] dar.

Universität Bielefeld   Thomas WITULSKI
Lehrstuhl für Biblische Theologie
Universitätsstrasse 25
DE-33615 Bielefeld
Deutschland
thowit@outlook.de

---

99. SCHNELLE, *Einleitung* (Anm. 2), S. 410.
100. Diesen Ausdruck, der über meinen Kollegen Andreas Lindemann zu mir gekommen ist, verdanke ich Hans Conzelmann. Conzelmann bezog jenen aber auf die Johannesbriefe; die vorliegende Studie geht demgegenüber einen Schritt weiter. Vgl. hierzu auch die instruktive Skizze zur Entwicklung des johanneischen Gemeindeverbandes von J. BECKER (*Johannes* [Anm. 14], S. 46), die durchaus ebenfalls in die in der vorliegenden Studie skizzierte Richtung geht.

THE RECEPTION OF THE *GOSPEL OF PETER* IN LATE ANTIQUITY

In the single most interesting landmark of the material reception of the *Gospel of Peter* – the so-called Akhmîm Codex – the gospel is grouped with another early Christian Petrine apocryphon, the *Apocalypse of Peter*. They are copied by the same hand, yet the two books were sewn upside-down and back-to-front from one another, separated by a blank leaf, forming a curious artefact thought lost a decade ago but recently tracked down in a different Egyptian collection, in the Bibliotheca Alexandrina[1]. The instances where the two apocrypha are mentioned together are equally rare. This contribution revisits and re-evaluates the reception of the *Gospel of Peter* in patristic works and booklists, on the one hand, and the direct reception in the Greek papyri on the other, marking the instances where the two Petrine apocrypha are mentioned in relation to one another.

I. The *Gospel of Peter* in Patristic Literature

The *Gospel of Peter* does not fare well in the booklists of late antiquity that mention it. In *Historia ecclesiastica* 3.25.6, Eusebius lists it with the *Gospel of Thomas* and other titles among the books that are to be completely rejected as νόθα written by heretics under the name of the apostles. However, the *Apocalypse of Peter*, just like the *Shepherd of Hermas*, *Didache*, and Revelation, is listed one level above, among the ἀντιλεγόμενα νόθα (which form a subdivision of the second category, that of disputed books, the ἀντιλεγόμενα, in *Hist. eccl.* 3.25.4): pseudepigraphical works that are known to most Christians, which Eusebius carefully distinguishes from the heretical νόθα like the *Gospel of Peter*. Didymus the Blind, in the *Commentary on Ecclesiastes* 8.3-7[2], mentions the *Gospel of Peter* (together with the *Gospel of Thomas*), adding that the reading of the apocrypha is forbidden, because they are written under false names, and because simple Christians cannot discern what is heretical in

---

1. H.A.G. Houghton – M. Monier, *Greek Manuscripts in Alexandria*, in *JTS* 71 (2020) 119-133, pp. 121-122.
2. The Greek text in G. Binder – L. Liesenborghs, *Didymos der Blinde: Kommentar zum Ecclesiastes. Teil I.1: Kommentar zu Eccl. Kap. 1,1–2,14* (Papyrologische Texte und Abhandlungen, 25), Bonn, Habelt, 1979, p. 22.

them. Similarly, Philip of Side in a fragment of his *Church History*[3] mentions the *Gospel of Peter* (with the *Gospel of Thomas* and the *Gospel of the Hebrews*), reporting that "most of the ancients completely rejected (τελείως ἀπέβαλλον) the gospel according to the Hebrews, that called 'of Peter' and that called 'of Thomas', saying that these were the compositions of heretics".

Jerome stands apart in that he describes the Petrine literature separately, in *De viris illustribus* 1.3-5:

> **3.** *[Simon Petrus]* ... *scripsit duas epistolas quae catholicae nominantur, quarum secunda a plerisque eius esse negatur propter stili cum priore dissonantiam.* **4.** *sed et Euangelium iuxta Marcum, qui auditor eius et interpres fuit, huius dicitur.* **5.** *libri autem e quibus unus Actorum eius inscribitur, alius Euangelii, tertius Praedicationis, quartus Ἀποκαλύψεως, quintus Iudicii, inter apocryphas scripturas repudiantur*[4].

> **3.** He wrote two epistles which are called Catholic, the second of which, on account of its difference from the first in style, is considered by many not to be his. **4.** Then, too, the Gospel according to Mark, who was his disciple and interpreter, is ascribed to him. **5.** On the other hand, the books of which one is entitled his *Acts*, another, his *Gospel*, a third, his *Preaching*, a fourth his *Revelation*, a fifth his *Judgement*, are rejected as apocryphal[5].

From this passage it is clear that Jerome relegates everything beyond 1, 2 Peter and Mark among the *apocryphae scripturae*, but there is reason to doubt that for him this category is one of heretical books[6]. Finally, the *Decretum Gelasianum* 4.5–5.4 of the sixth century[7] lists *Evangelium nomine Petri apostoli* as *apocryphum* (with the *Shepherd*, among other books), which is a category of books entirely to be rejected as compiled or recognised by heretics or schismatics.

Testimonies on the *Gospel of Peter* prior to the *Decretum Gelasianum* can be found in Origen, Serapion of Antioch (*via* Eusebius), Eusebius,

---

3. Greek text in C. DE BOOR, *Neue Fragmente des Papias, Hegesippus und Pierius in bisher unbekannten Excerpten aus der Kirchengeschichte des Philippus Sidetes* (TU, 5), Leipzig, Hinrichs, 1888, p. 169.

4. Latin text in A. CERESA-GASTALDO, *Gerolamo: Gli uomini illustri*, Firenze, Nardini, 1988.

5. Translation from T.P. HALTON, *Jerome: On Illustrious Men* (Fathers of the Church, 100), Washington, DC, Catholic University of America Press, 1999, p. 5.

6. For an assessment of Jerome's concept of apocrypha see T. O'LOUGHLIN, *Inventing the Apocrypha: The Role of Early Latin Canon Lists*, in *Irish Theological Quarterly* 74 (2009) 53-74, and ID., *Jerome's De uiris illustribus and Latin Perceptions of the New Testament's Canon*, in J.E. RUTHERFORD – D. WOODS (eds.), *The Mystery of Christ in the Fathers of the Church: Essays in Honour of D. Vincent Twomey SVD*, Dublin, Four Courts Press, 2012, 55-65.

7. A detailed account of the historical context is available in V. GROSSI, *Il Decretum Gelasianum: Nota in margine all'autorità della Chiesa di Roma alla fine del sec. V*, in *Augustinianum* 41 (2001) 231-255.

Didymus the Blind, Jerome, Rufinus, and Theodoret of Cyrus[8]. Apart from Origen and Serapion, none of these authors says anything about the contents of the *Gospel of Peter*. It is not clear therefore whether or not they know the gospel beyond the name, nor whether they are speaking about the same text as we can reconstruct in our modern editions.

Origen's *Commentary on Matthew* 10.17, for instance, preserves a possible reference to the contents of the *Gospel of Peter*:

> Τοὺς δὲ ἀδελφοὺς ᾽Ιησοῦ φασί τινες εἶναι, ἐκ παραδόσεως ὁρμώμενοι τοῦ ἐπιγεγραμμένου κατὰ Πέτρον εὐαγγελίου ἢ τῆς βίβλου ᾽Ιακώβου, υἱοὺς ᾽Ιωσὴφ ἐκ προτέρας γυναικὸς συνῳκηκυίας αὐτῷ πρὸ τῆς Μαρίας[9].
>
> But on the basis of a tradition contained in the Gospel according to Peter, as it is entitled, or the Book of James, some say the brothers of Jesus are sons of Joseph from a former wife, who was married to him before Mary[10].

This is part of Origen's discussion of Mt 13,54-55, more particularly of Jesus' earthly relatives. In this context, he points out that a tradition found in a *Gospel according to Peter* and/or in a *Book of James* is brought up by those who wish to preserve the purity of Mary. Origen does not dispute the view he is recording here; on the contrary, he seems to adopt it. However, his opinion on the book itself is not explicit. In assessing Origen's implicit claim that he knew the *Gospel of Peter*, a problem would be that there is no account of Jesus' stepbrothers from Joseph in the known text of the gospel. This detail, however, appears in the *Protevangelium of James*, which probably is indicated by the designation *Book of James*. It is not impossible that the *Gospel of Peter* initially contained such an episode; what we have today of its text seems indeed to be fragmentary. However, there is no external evidence to verify this. In any event, if we understand Origen as referring to a longer recension of the *Gospel of Peter* than that found in the so-called Akhmîm Codex, the brief mention in the *Commentary on Matthew* 10.17 is favourable enough to rule out the possibility that for Origen this gospel is to be completely rejected. The question of pseudepigraphy is not brought up for either book and both are said to be used by Christians in debates relating to Jesus.

---

8. Brief surveys are available in T.J. KRAUS – T. NICKLAS, *Hinweise auf ein Petrusevangelium in der antiken christlichen Literatur*, in IID., *Das Petrusevangelium und die Petrusapokalypse: Die griechischen Fragmente mit deutscher und englischer Übersetzung* (GCS NF, 11/Neutestamentliche Apokryphen, 1), Berlin – New York, De Gruyter, 2004, 11-23, and P. FOSTER, *Potential Patristic References to a 'Gospel of Peter'*, in ID., *The Gospel of Peter: Introduction, Critical Edition and Commentary* (TENTS, 4), Leiden – Boston, MA, Brill, 2010, 97-115.

9. Greek text from R. GIROD, *Origène: Commentaire sur l'Évangile selon Matthieu* (SC, 162), Paris, Cerf, 1970, p. 216.

10. Translation from FOSTER, *The Gospel of Peter* (n. 8), p. 102.

Serapion of Antioch's view on this gospel (ca. 200 CE) can only be glimpsed in the few paragraphs devoted to him by Eusebius in *Hist. eccl.* 6.12. It is nonetheless interesting, since he seems to be somewhat better disposed towards the *Gospel of Peter* than Eusebius[11]. Eusebius reports that Serapion wrote a book, apparently named *On the so-called Gospel of Peter*, a refutation of the false statements in the gospel, meant to counter the departure of the Christian community at Rhossus from orthodoxy, explaining that the defection is due to the gospel at issue and to the ἑτερόδοξοι διδασκαλίαι it contains. He then offers a quotation from Serapion, to illustrate the latter's view of the gospel. However, Serapion, as quoted by Eusebius, first states that he himself avoids pseudepigraphical works, knowing that they have not been handed down from earlier times, but then admits that he had not restricted the use of the *Gospel of Peter* in the community from the outset. On the contrary, he had said: "Let it be read", ἀναγινωσκέσθω, considering it harmless, admittedly without having read it. The community, however, had slipped into heresy, which prompted his written reaction. The implication is that their aberration had to do with the *Gospel of Peter* in some way[12], but that is not made explicit. Attempting to address the heresy, Serapion claims then to have studied the gospel, after he had obtained a copy from those who used it (not from those who had produced it), whom he labels as "docetae". Finally, the result of his investigation was that he had established that most of the gospel was "in accordance with the true teaching of the Saviour"[13], with some things added, which he would mention and discuss in the rest of his book, which is now lost. The fact that initially Serapion accepted the *Gospel of Peter* in the community as harmless suggests that before the aggravation of the situation in Rhossus that caused his response, he would not have rejected the book completely. Thus, it would have been to him in a secondary tier of books. Should one take the ἀναγινωσκέσθω to imply that it was read aloud in the church, it would follow that, from the point of view of Serapion, it was not contradictory to have a second tier of pseudepigraphical books read aloud in gatherings of a community.

Theodoret of Cyrus, too, mentions a *Gospel of Peter*, but since he does not refer to any detail of its contents, it is unclear whether he knows it

---

11. *Ibid.*, p. 107.
12. G. BARDY, *Eusèbe de Césarée. Histoire ecclésiastique, livres V–VII* (SC, 41), Paris, Cerf, 1956, pp. 103-104, n. 6, suggests that the formulation makes it likely that the community was of good faith, but "sans grande instruction" and that they allowed themselves to be influenced by the name of the apostle. But Bardy deems it unlikely that the community considered the *Gospel of Peter* to be canonical.
13. Greek text *ibid.*, pp. 102-104; an English translation is available in FOSTER, *The Gospel of Peter* (n. 8), p. 106.

himself or whether he means the same text as the other authors who mention the *Gospel of Peter*. In his *Haereticarum fabularum compendium* 2.2, Theodoret only mentions that the Nazoreans (whom he takes to be Jews) made use of, or proclaimed, the "so-called *Gospel according to Peter*" (τῷ καλουμένῳ κατὰ Πέτρον εὐαγγελίῳ κεχρημένοι)[14]. Since nothing further is said of the gospel, it is not clear whether Theodoret himself disapproves of it.

To conclude, the patristic reception of the *Gospel of Peter* shows that it was deemed to be either in a second tier of books, or properly rejected. The distribution of these views is fairly even: Serapion of Antioch and Jerome would place it on a second level (perhaps also Origen, but the contents he mentions are not in the gospel as we have it today), while Eusebius and Didymus the Blind seem to reject it completely. For the latter group its pseudepigraphical character is clearly a bigger issue than for the former. Moreover, Serapion may attest to its being read publicly in a community. It remains unclear in most cases whether these patristic authors knew the text or only the title, whether they are referring to the same text, or whether they mean a writing reasonably similar to the one we are able to reconstruct today. In a sense, the identity of the book is less clear than that of other early Christian writings, even outside the New Testament, for which there are patristic quotations that match the text we can find in the manuscript tradition (e.g., the *Apocalypse of Peter* and the *Shepherd*).

II. THE DIRECT RECEPTION

The largest witness for the *Gospel of Peter* is the Akhmîm Codex, and from the several papyri that have been suggested to represent this book, only P.Oxy. XLI 2949 is regarded as most likely to do so. It has also been suggested that P.Vindob. G 2325 is a witness of the apocryphon, but this suggestion has not gained acceptance[15]. P.Oxy. LX 4009 is in a more peculiar situation: it is unlikely to be a witness to the *Gospel of Peter*,

---

14. FOSTER, *The Gospel of Peter* (n. 8), p. 112.
15. The arguments pro can be found in D. LÜHRMANN, *Die apokryph gewordenen Evangelien: Studien zu neuen Texten und neuen Fragen* (SupplNT, 112), Leiden, Brill, 2004, pp. 87-90; ID., *Kann es wirklich keine frühe Handschrift des Petrusevangeliums geben? Corrigenda zu einem Aufsatz von Paul Foster*, in *NT* 48 (2006) 379-383; ID., *Die Überlieferung des Petrusevangeliums*, in T.J. KRAUS – T. NICKLAS (eds.), *Das Evangelium nach Petrus: Text, Kontexte, Intertexte*, Berlin, De Gruyter, 2007, 48-51. For the opposite view see KRAUS – NICKLAS, *Das Petrusevangelium und die Petrusapokalypse* (n. 8), p. 68; T.J. KRAUS, *1. P.Vindob.G 2325: The 'Fayûm Fragment'*, in ID. – M.J. KRUGER – T. NICKLAS, *Gospel Fragments* (OECGT), Oxford – New York, OUP, 2009, 219-227,

but since it is a possible instance of reception of the gospel, it is discussed here as well. Moreover, given that the *Gospel of Peter* is combined with the *Apocalypse of Peter* in its main witness, I will also discuss here the Greek papyrus fragments of the latter.

Document	Book / Date / Provenance	Size (cm.) / Format / Hand	*Nomina sacra* / Other abbreviations
P.Oxy. XLI 2949 Sackler Library, Oxford van Haelst 592 LDAB 5111	*The Gospel of Peter* III Oxyrhynchus	4 × 7.5 and 1.7 × 2.6 Papyrus roll, possibly, but not clearly so. Severe style sloping (LDAB).	No extant candidates for abbreviation.

P.Oxy. XLI 2949 consists of two papyrus fragments and was first published by R.A. Coles in 1972[16]. The question of the place of its text in the transmission of the *Gospel of Peter* sparked some debate over the last decades[17]. Of all the papyri that have been proposed as part of this book, 2949 is generally accepted as the most likely to contain a part of the *Gospel of Peter*[18].

Since the verso of the fragment is blank, 2949 is usually considered to be a roll. Bagnall, however, contends that given its very fragmentary condition, "even its identification as a roll is by no means certain ... it is by no means impossible that the text ended not long after the surviving fragment ... and in that case it could come from the end of a codex"[19].

---

pp. 221, 225; P. FOSTER, *Are There Any Early Fragments of the So-called Gospel of Peter?*, in *NTS* 52 (2006) 1-28, pp. 19-22; ID., *The Gospel of Peter* (n. 8), pp. 80-82.

16. In G.M. BROWNE et al., *The Oxyrhynchus Papyri: Volume XLI*, London, Egypt Exploration Society, 1972, 15-16. The fragment has been re-edited a number of times since then, e.g. KRAUS – NICKLAS, *Das Petrusevangelium und die Petrusapokalypse* (n. 8), pp. 55-58; FOSTER, *The Gospel of Peter* (n. 8), p. 206.

17. D. LÜHRMANN, *POx 2949: EvPt 3–5 in einer Handschrift des 2./3. Jahrhunderts*, in *ZNW* 72 (1981) 216-226, p. 225; J.C. TREAT, *The Two Manuscript Witnesses to the Gospel of Peter*, in D.J. LULL (ed.), *Society of Biblical Literature 1990 Seminar Papers*, Atlanta, GA, Scholars, 1990, 391-399; J.D. CROSSAN, *The Cross That Spoke: The Origins of the Passion Narrative*, San Francisco, CA, Harper & Row, 1988, pp. 6-9; LÜHRMANN, *Die apokryph gewordenen Evangelien* (n. 15), pp. 55-104; FOSTER, *Are There Any Early Fragments* (n. 15), pp. 1-28; LÜHRMANN, *Corrigenda zu einem Aufsatz von Paul Foster* (n. 15), pp. 379-383; ID., *Die Überlieferung des Petrusevangeliums* (n. 15), pp. 48-51; T.W. WAYMENT, *A Reexamination of the Text of P. Oxy. 2949*, in *JBL* 128 (2009) 375-382; P. FOSTER, *P.Oxy. 2949 – Its Transcription and Significance: A Response to Thomas Wayment*, in *JBL* 129 (2010) 173-176; ID., *The Gospel of Peter* (n. 8), pp. 58-68.

18. FOSTER, *The Gospel of Peter* (n. 8), p. 57; S.E. PORTER, *Early Apocryphal Gospels and the New Testament Text*, in C.E. HILL – M.J. KRUGER (eds.), *The Early Text of the New Testament*, Oxford, OUP, 2012, 350-369, p. 353, n. 6.

19. R. BAGNALL, *Early Christian Books in Egypt*, Princeton, NJ, Princeton University Press, 2009, pp. 74-75.

Of the two fragments of P.Oxy. XLI 2949, the larger one seems to contain text from the *Gospel of Peter* 2.3-5a. It consists of 13 incomplete lines (maximum 2-3 words per line only starting from line 5), with abraded text and some lack of correspondences between lines 10 to 13 of the P.Oxy. XLI 2949 text and the text of the *Gospel of Peter*[20].

On the other hand, the overlaps (especially for lines 5 to 9) between the P.Oxy. XLI 2949 text and the *Gospel of Peter* made Kraus and Nicklas suggest that P.Oxy. XLI 2949 indicates that such a tradition was in circulation at that time[21]. The smaller fragment consists of the beginnings of 5 lines, with maximum 2-3 letters out of a word. It does not go beyond ten certain letters in total and does not actually contribute much to the discussion, with its very positioning being entirely hypothetical[22].

This papyrus does not preserve marks of punctuation or readings aids, such as middle and high dots, *paragraphoi*, or spaces at the end of sense units.

Document	Book / Date / Provenance	Size (cm.) / Format / Hand	*Nomina sacra* / Other abbreviations
P.Oxy. LX 4009 Sackler Library, Oxford van Haelst add. LDAB 4872	*The Gospel of Peter* (?) IV (first half, on LDAB) Oxyrhynchus	2.9 × 9 extant fragment. 7 × 10 possibly reconstructed leaf. Miniature papyrus codex. Alexandrian stylistic class, sloping to the left (LDAB)	ΚΕ At least a final ν, as a crossbar. No other candidates for abbreviation in the extant text.

P.Oxy. LX 4009 is a fragment of a leaf of a papyrus codex, preserving 21 lines on the → side and 20 lines on the ↓ side[23]. The ↓ side is very fragmentary with only a few identified letters on each line (maximum 6-7 letters). The *editio princeps* argued that it is an early fragment of the *Gospel of Peter*, but that argument failed to convince other scholars, even

---

20. FOSTER, *The Gospel of Peter* (n. 8), p. 65.
21. KRAUS – NICKLAS, *Das Petrusevangelium und die Petrusapokalypse* (n. 8), p. 58. See also FOSTER, *The Gospel of Peter* (n. 8), pp. 65-66. But see WAYMENT, *A Reexamination of the Text of P. Oxy. 2949* (n. 17), pp. 375-382, who suggests that P.Oxy XLI 2949 is a commentary on the *Gospel of Peter*, and that the *Gospel of Peter* preceded the text of P.Oxy XLI 2949.
22. FOSTER, *The Gospel of Peter* (n. 8), pp. 60-62.
23. First published in D. LÜHRMANN, *POx 4009: Ein neues Fragment des Petrusevangeliums?*, in *NT* 35 (1993) 309-410, re-edited one year later: ID. – P.J. PARSONS, in R.A. COLES et al., *The Oxyrhynchus Papyri: Volume LX*, London, Egypt Exploration Society, 1994, pp. 1-5. See also KRAUS – NICKLAS, *Das Petrusevangelium und die Petrusapokalypse* (n. 8), pp. 59-63; FOSTER, *The Gospel of Peter* (n. 8), pp. 207-208.

when they include 4009 in their own editions of the gospel[24]. Since the attribution remains doubtful, the relevance of this papyrus for the reception of the *Gospel of Peter* is negligible – unless it is a reworking of the text of the *Gospel*, in which case it would be a creative case of reception.

Document	Book / Date / Provenance	Size (cm.) / Format / Hand	Nomina sacra / Other abbreviations
Bodl. Ms Gr. th. f. 4 [P] Bodleian Library, Oxford **P.Vindob. G 39756** Nationalbibliothek, Vienna van Haelst 618 and 619 LDAB 5583 (for both)	*The Apocalypse of Peter* V (first half, P. Orsini) Egypt (Oxyrhynchus?)	5.3 × 7.8 codex dimension Parchment miniature codex. Biblical majuscule.	ΘΥ, ΥΥ, ΠΗΡ ΟΥΝΟΙΣ, each once. One instance of final ν written as a horizontal bar above the preceding vowel at the end of line.

With regard to readings aids, the → side displays paragraphing by the means of empty space at the end of a line on line 10, and an *ekthesis* is visible at the beginning of line 10 on the ↓ side. At least one middle point and three blank spaces are visible, but just what they separate is unclear.

Bodl. Ms Gr. th. f. 4 [P][25] and **P.Vindob. G 39756**[26] are two fragments of the *Apocalypse of Peter* of different leaves, remnants of a miniature codex. They contain text from different sections of the *Apocalypse of*

---

24. See, for instance, KRAUS – NICKLAS, *Das Petrusevangelium und die Petrusapokalypse* (n. 8), pp. 62-63, and particularly the discussion in FOSTER, *The Gospel of Peter* (n. 8), 69-80. But see M. MYLLYKOSKI, *The Sinful Woman in the Gospel of Peter: Reconstructing the Other Side of P.Oxy. 4009*, in *NTS* 55 (2009) 104-115.

25. First published by C. WESSELY, *Les plus anciens monuments du christianisme écrits sur papyrus* (PO, 18/II), Paris, Firmin-Didot, 1924; reprint Turnhout, Brepols, 1985, pp. 482-483. Wessely seems to identify it as part of *Acta Petri*, and dated it to the third or fourth century. Subsequent scholarship identified the text as part of the *Apocalypse of Peter*: K. PRÜMM, *De genuino Apoc. Petri textu*, in *Bib* 10 (1929) 62-80, further discussed in M.R. JAMES, *The Rainer Fragment of the Apocalypse of Peter*, in *JTS* 32 (1931) 270-279. The initial dating was also challenged, the current consensus being that it belongs to the second half of the second century: P. VAN MINNEN, *Appendix: The Bodleian and Rainer Fragments*, in J.N. BREMMER – I. CZACHESZ (eds.), *The Apocalypse of Peter* (Studies in Early Christian Apocrypha, 7), Leuven, Peeters, 2003, 34-39. See also T.J. KRAUS, *P. Vindob. G 39756 + Bodl. MS Gr. th. f. 4 [P]: Fragmente eines Codex der griechischen Petrus-Apokalypse*, in *BASP* 40 (2003) 45-61.

26. First published in M.R. JAMES, *Additional Notes on the Apocalypse of Peter*, in *JTS* 12 (1910) 157. However, as James points out, the identification was due to A.E. Cowley and E.O. Winstedt. The latter is also the author of the transcription published by James. Further description is available in VAN MINNEN, *Appendix: The Bodleian and Rainer Fragments* (n. 25), pp. 34-39, and KRAUS, *P. Vindob. G 39756 + Bodl. MS Gr. th. f. 4 [P]*, (n. 25), pp. 45-61.

Peter[27], allowing the possibility that this codex had more than two *bifolia*.

James thinks that at least the Bodleian fragment contains "a shortened text ... by comparison with the Ethiopic"[28]. However, it is now normally considered that these fragments are much closer to the Ethiopic text than to that of the Akhmîm Codex, which is considered to have an expanded, redacted text[29]. In any event, there are altogether six columns of 13 lines adding up to around 150 words.

Regarding readings aids, the scribe uses *diaeresis* over initial ι, breathing marks, and apostrophes between double consonants. Furthermore, the scribe uses low and high points, one instance of a colon (:), blank spaces, and *paragraphoi*; one *paragraphos* marks the end of a sentence and a shift in the narrative, being followed by "Look, Peter, ...".

Document	Book / Date / Provenance	Size (cm.) / Format / Hand	*Nomina sacra* / Other abbreviations
BAAM 0522 P.Cair. 10759 (formerly) Bibliotheca Alexandrina, Alexandria van Haelst 598 and 617 LDAB 1088	The Apocalypse of Peter & the Gospel of Peter VI/VII Panopolis (Akhmîm)	12-12.5 × 15.5-16.5 Parchment codex. Documentary script.	Gospel of Peter: ΘΥ × 3 ΚΣ × 7, ΚΥ × 7, ΚΝ × 2 ΑΝΩΣ, ΑΝΩΝ, each once. θεός is once written in full. κύριος, once in the genitive and once in the accusative, in both cases about Jesus, is written *plene*. The same applies to Ἰσραήλ × 2, οὐρανός × 6 (of heavens, even when it is coordinated by a καί with a *nomen sacrum*, ΑΝΩΣ), and υἱός (always – four times – in the expression "Son of God", *plene*

---

27. A well-known difficulty is that there are several ancient writings that are referred to today as the *Apocalypse of Peter*, whose contents are not related: a) the Coptic *Apocalypse of Peter* found in the Nag Hammadi Codex VII, probably originally composed in Greek; b) the so-called Arabic *Apocalypse of Peter*, otherwise a modern collection named *The Book of Rolls* in manuscript Mingana Syr. 70, written in Syriac script; and c) the early Christian *Apocalypse of Peter*, composed in Greek but surviving for the most part in Ethiopic. The latter is meant here: the apocalyptic text that was composed and was known under this title in early Christianity, sometimes designated as the Greek (Ethiopic) *Apocalypse of Peter*. On the state of the Ethiopic text see A. BAUSI, *Towards a Re-Edition of the Ethiopic Dossier of the Apocalypse of Peter: A Few Remarks on the Ethiopic Manuscript Witnesses*, in Apocrypha 27 (2016) 179-196, and P. MARRASSINI, *Peter, Apocalypse of*, in S. UHLIG – A. BAUSI (eds.), *Encyclopaedia Aethiopica*. Vol. 4: *O-X*, Wiesbaden, Harrassowitz, 2010, 135b-137a.

28. E.g., VAN MINNEN, *Appendix: The Bodleian and Rainer Fragments* (n. 25), p. 35.

29. JAMES, *Additional Notes on the Apocalypse of Peter* (n. 26), p. 157.

| | | | even if in three of these cases θεός is abbreviated as *nomen sacrum*). The same goes for Ἰερουσαλήμ and σωτήρ[30]. Finally, δώδεκα (for the apostles) is not abbreviated either. |
| | | | *Apocalypse of Peter*: ΘΣ × 2, ΘΥ once. ΚΣ × 2; ΚΩ and ΚΝ once. ΑΝΟΥΣ, ΑΝΟΥ, ΑΝΩΝ, ΑΝΟΙ, each once. κύριος is also written once *plene*, about Jesus. θεός is twice written in full. δώδεκα (for the apostles) is not abbreviated. |

The **Akhmîm Codex** (now catalogued as BAAM 0522[31], formerly known as P.Cair. 10759), was found in what was inferred to be a monk's grave near Akhmîm, ancient Panopolis in Upper Egypt, during an archaeological excavation lead by a French team in the winter of 1886/1887. Both the grave and the manuscript were initially dated "anywhere from the sixth to the twelfth centuries CE"[32]. First published in 1892[33], it contains the *Book of Enoch* (*1 Enoch*), the *Gospel of Peter*, the *Apocalypse of Peter*, and a fragment of the *Martyrdom of Julian of Anazarbus*[34].

---

30. KRAUS – NICKLAS, *Das Petrusevangelium und die Petrusapokalypse* (n. 8), p. 30.

31. HOUGHTON – MONIER, *Greek Manuscripts in Alexandria* (n. 1), pp. 121-122: "In February 2018, the authors not only saw two bifolia of this manuscript on display in the Antiquities Museum, but, after telephone permission had been granted from the Ministry of Antiquities, were shown the rest of the codex. This is stored in the metal cabinet immediately under the display case in which the selected leaves are on show, with each bifolium preserved between glass plates. The museum's ownership of the document is confirmed by the database, which includes colour images of four pages". There are now 68 pages available at the web address indicated by the authors: http://antiquities.bibalex.org/Collection/Detail.aspx?lang=en&a=522.

32. D.D. BUCHHOLZ, *Your Eyes Will Be Opened: A Study of the Greek (Ethiopic) Apocalypse of Peter* (SBLDS, 97), Atlanta, GA, Scholars, 1988, p. 83. For a discussion of the scholarly debate raised by this discovery and its subsequent publication in 1892, see *ibid.*, pp. 83-104, with regard to the *Apocalypse of Peter*, and FOSTER, *The Gospel of Peter* (n. 8), pp. 7-38, with regard to the *Gospel of Peter*.

33. U. BOURIANT, *Fragments du texte grec du livre d'Énoch et de quelques écrits attribués à saint Pierre*, in *Mémoires publiés par les membres de la Mission archéologique française au Caire*, t. IX, fasc. 1, Paris, Ernest Leroux, 1892.

34. Images of the *Gospel of Peter* leaves are available in KRAUS – NICKLAS, *Das Petrusevangelium und die Petrusapokalypse* (n. 8); FOSTER, *The Gospel of Peter* (n. 8), pp. 178-194, and online at http://ipap.csad.ox.ac.uk/Apocrypha-Pseudepigrapha.html; only the Kraus – Nicklas volume offers an image of the decorative opening page of the codex. Images of the *Apocalypse of Peter* leaves are available in KRAUS – NICKLAS, *Das Petrusevangelium und*

A thorough analysis of this codex as a composite codex was undertaken by Peter van Minnen, who starts by noting that "the codex is in fact made up of several parchment manuscripts and the leftover of other parchment manuscripts"[35], and eventually dates its various parts to the end of the sixth century (the *Gospel of Peter* and the *Apocalypse of Peter*), and the first half of the seventh century (the other writings)[36]. Van Minnen's dating may have not won the widest acceptance[37], but his essential description (implying that it was a composite codex composed of different initially separate manuscripts) and reconstruction still stand.

The codex is now dismembered and most of the leaves are cut out of their bifolia, seemingly in order "to facilitate photography"[38]. A notable particularity is that the *Apocalypse of Peter* was sewn upside-down and back-to-front after the *Gospel of Peter* (meaning that the last leaf of the gospel was followed, after a blank leaf, by the upside-down last page of the *Apocalypse of Peter*). It is also composed of more than one manuscript, displaying several hands which were eventually dated differently. In all these parts the texts are written in a single column format.

The dimensions of the codex, 12-12.5 × 15.5-16.5, seem somewhat atypical[39]; its 34 leaves would have contained the four works as follows: a decorative front page (three crosses and an α and an ω, in a centred

---

die Petrusapokalypse. The *1 Enoch* leaves are available online at http://ipap.csad.ox.ac.uk/Apocrypha-Pseudepigrapha.html. New color images of the codex are currently available at http://antiquities.bibalex.org/Collection/Detail.aspx?lang=en&a=522.

35. P. VAN MINNEN, *The Greek Apocalypse of Peter*, in BREMMER – CZACHESZ, *The Apocalypse of Peter* (n. 25), 15-39, p. 19.
36. *Ibid.*, pp. 20-24.
37. See, for instance, KRAUS – NICKLAS, *Das Petrusevangelium und die Petrusapokalypse* (n. 8), p. 29, who seem to date it to the early seventh century. Also, FOSTER, *The Gospel of Peter* (n. 8), p. 56: "While without the actual manuscript it is impossible to come to a firm conclusion, it does appear that a date of the late 6th to the early 9th century provides a highly probable period for the composition of the text".
38. FOSTER, *The Gospel of Peter* (n. 8), p. 47.
39. See the discussion in FOSTER, *The Gospel of Peter* (n. 8), pp. 46 and 50, about where this codex fits in the typology of E.G. TURNER, *The Typology of the Early Codex*, Philadelphia, PA, University of Pennsylvania Press, 1977. VAN MINNEN, *The Greek Apocalypse of Peter* (n. 35), p. 25, suggests that this square format "might have been current in the scriptorium where the various components of the codex were written". This would require that this scriptorium was active for the time span between the various dates he assigns to the four initial codices. This would stand against Foster's proposal that "both the quality of hand writing and the amateurish compilation of the codex, lead to the suspicion that the text was not produced in a professional scriptorium, but was rather the product of a relatively unskilled individual"; FOSTER, *The Gospel of Peter* (n. 8), p. 45. Foster's note raises the question as to how we rule out (or in) the possibility of a scriptorium as source for the Akhmîm Codex, professional or otherwise. At any rate, so far as I can tell, Foster does not seem to interact with VAN MINNEN on this particular issue.

rectangle)[40], the *Gospel of Peter* on pages 2-10 followed by a blank leaf or two blank pages (11-12); the *Apocalypse of Peter* on pages 13-19 (although, as said, upside down, so that its first page is on the page 19 of the codex, and its last on page 13 of the codex) followed by another blank page (page 20); two fragments from *1 Enoch* cover pages 21-66, and the recto of the last leaf, page 67; its verso is glued to the cover, as an inside back cover, and contains the *Martyrdom of Julian of Anazarbus*.

The *Gospel of Peter* and the *Apocalypse of Peter* are written by the same scribe, *1 Enoch* by two further scribes, and the *Martyrdom* by a fourth. The *Gospel of Peter* extends over three *bifolia*, of which two were grouped into a *binio* quire, the third being a single *bifolium* quire in the Akhmîm Codex. Given that the second leaf of the third *bifolium* was blank on both sides, van Minnen proposed that it was initially meant as a cover to the initial codex (containing only the *Gospel of Peter*) which would have been initially a single *ternio* quire; in the process of binding it into the Akhmîm Codex, this blank leaf was folded the other way, resulting in two quires; instead of preceding the *Gospel of Peter*, it follows it[41]. The *Apocalypse of Peter*, written by the same hand, extends over a *binio* quire; its first page was left blank[42]. According to van Minnen, three further *quaternion* quires contain fragments of *1 Enoch*, the first two written by one scribe (different from that of the *Gospel of Peter* and the *Apocalypse of Peter*), and the third one written by yet another scribe[43]. The last leaf of the Akhmîm Codex, on which a fourth scribe wrote the *Martyrdom*, was apparently glued to the back cover as an inside back cover.

The possible difference in dating from one part to another of the codex suggests that these were produced independently for their own purposes, and only later bound together to form the Akhmîm Codex[44]. Even in the case of the two pieces written by the same scribe – the *Apocalypse of Peter* and the *Gospel of Peter* – the fact that they were eventually sewn

---

40. The image is available in the illustrations section concluding KRAUS – NICKLAS, *Das Petrusevangelium und die Petrusapokalypse* (n. 8).

41. VAN MINNEN, *The Greek Apocalypse of Peter* (n. 35), p. 20. On the whole, Foster agrees with his reconstruction; FOSTER, *The Gospel of Peter* (n. 8), p. 48.

42. VAN MINNEN, *The Greek Apocalypse of Peter* (n. 35), p. 21, thinks it was intended for a decoration similar to that at the beginning of the *Gospel of Peter*; Foster entertains this possibility as well; FOSTER, *The Gospel of Peter* (n. 8), p. 48.

43. VAN MINNEN, *The Greek Apocalypse of Peter* (n. 35), pp. 22-23. FOSTER, *The Gospel of Peter* (n. 8), pp. 48-49, formulates a number of problems regarding van Minnen's reconstruction, but agrees that "the most likely suggestion is that it [the text of *1 Enoch*] was composed of three quires each originally comprising of sixteen pages", p. 49.

44. VAN MINNEN, *The Greek Apocalypse of Peter* (n. 35), p. 25.

head to toe (and the way the blank leaf between is used) seems to indicate at least the possibility that they might have been independent codices.

As to sense delimitation, there is no page numbering in the Akhmîm Codex, nor are there titles, subtitles, or colophons. The text of the *Gospel of Peter* seems to be the only one to have both its beginning and ending signalled in any way, confined as it is between the decorative front page, and the elaborate decoration at the bottom of its last page. Should one agree with van Minnen and Foster that the blank page before the one on which the *Apocalypse of Peter* starts was meant to bear similar decoration, then this work would also have its beginning signalled; there is nothing comparable to the decoration closing the *Gospel of Peter* at the end of the *Apocalypse of Peter*. Single crosses in the middle of the upper margin are apparent on the first and second pages of the *Gospel of Peter*, similar to one another, and crosses of the same size, but of a second kind on the first and sixth page of the *Apocalypse of Peter*. Given that the text of the *Gospel of Peter* starts on the first verso of the quire, the two in the *Gospel of Peter* are on the same opening; the two in the *Apocalypse of Peter* were not, but they would have been on the same side on the same bifolium.

The text in the *Apocalypse of Peter* and the *Gospel of Peter* – as well as the whole codex – is written in a rather wide block of text, with no apparent paragraphing or any other sense-unit delimitation. The only obvious text divider is provided by the fact that more often than not the words are not split at the end of the line[45]. In the *Gospel of Peter* the number of letters per line can go from 33 to 48[46]. Finishing with complete words was realised by writing either smaller *or* wider than usual letters, at the end of the line. In particular, the *nu* can be drawn as a significantly

---

45. In the *Gospel of Peter*, the ratio of split-words versus number of lines per page is 3/19, 2/18, 6/18, 2/17, 3/17, 3/17, 3/17, 5/17, and 4/14, while in the *Apocalypse of Peter* it is 3/19, 6/19, 5/20, 3/19, 4/18, 9/18, and 3/16. With three exceptions (ὅσ-α, διανοου-μέν-ων, ὁποῖ-ον), the next line starts with a consonant. The word is divided in most cases after a vowel, and in the case of double consonants the scribe puts the break after the first consonant, unless that consonant is σ, in which case the sigma goes on the second line (συνε-σκέπτοντο in the *Gospel of Peter* and κατα-στρεφόμενοι in the *Apocalypse of Peter*), with the exception of ὥσ-περ, divided in its constituent parts. This is not dissimilar to what is described as "rules for the divisions of words in Greek papyri" in F.G. KENYON, *The Palaeography of Greek Papyri*, Oxford, Clarendon, 1899, pp. 31-32. For a recent treatment of similar issues (with similar results) in a different manuscript, see P.M. HEAD, *Some Observations on Various Features of Scribe D in the New Testament of Codex Sinaiticus*, in S. MCKENDRICK et al. (eds.), *Codex Sinaiticus: New Perspectives on the Ancient Biblical Manuscript*, London, British Library, 2015, 127-137.

46. FOSTER, *The Gospel of Peter* (n. 8), p. 52: "the variation seems to be due to the sharpness of the point of the pen".

wider majuscule, somewhat ornamental, so as to fill the remaining space until the end of line, as is the case in the last line of the third page of the *Gospel of Peter*, in the middle of the first page of the *Apocalypse of Peter*; alternatively, the *nu* can be written as a horizontal bar above the preceding letter(s) and extended in the right margin. On the last four positions in the line, most letters tend to be written in a scaled-down manner compared to how they normally are in other positions – unless they fit well in the remaining space. The variation is perhaps most visible for ω, ο, ν, ε, τ.

III. Concluding Remarks

The aim of this contribution was to revisit the question of the reception of the *Gospel of Peter* in patristic literature and among the textual witnesses on papyrus and parchment. The data discussed here suggests that the problem with the *Gospel of Peter* is primarily one of retrievability, perhaps even more than one of textual instability. Is the writing that we reconstruct in modern critical editions the same as the writing mentioned by patristic authors who speak of a "gospel ascribed to Peter"? For instance, the one episode that Origen seems to know as a part τοῦ κατὰ Πέτρον εὐαγγελίου has not been preserved in the Akhmîm Codex, our largest witness. It remains unclear whether Origen is making a mistake, or whether our text is incomplete, or indeed whether he knew an entirely different writing in circulation under that name. The latter possibility raises a related question: are all authors who mention a *Gospel according to Peter* referring to the same writing? Since most late-antique sources only mention the title, it is not even clear whether they know anything more beyond the name, or are simply reporting the notion that there was a writing with that name in circulation.

A certain degree of uncertainty about the shape of this gospel as a book is reflected in the fact that several papyri for which there is little to no firm basis for attribution to the *Gospel of Peter*, have been suggested to preserve parts of it[47]. The only access we have to a *Gospel of Peter* is the text found in the Akhmîm Codex and given the state of the patristic evidence it remains unclear to which extent it resembles (if at all) the writing that the late-antique authors occasionally mention. This is a peculiar situation compared to other early Christian writings that are in a sense

---

47. See the survey and discussion of four such items in Foster, *The Gospel of Peter* (n. 8), pp. 69-91.

more retrievable: for the *Apocalypse of Peter* as well as the *Shepherd* we have patristic quotations that more or less match the text found in the manuscript transmission. In such cases we can verify therefore that at least those late-antique authors are referring to roughly the same writing as that reconstructed in modern editions, whereas for the authors that only mention them by name it remains unclear whether they knew the contents of the book to any meaningful extent. Moreover, the manuscript transmission of both texts is more developed than that of the *Gospel of Peter*. In other words, their shape as identifiable book is significantly more clear (both in manuscripts and in ancient testimonies) than what we can gather from the reception of the *Gospel of Peter*.

KU Leuven
Faculty of Theology and Religious Studies
Sint-Michielsstraat 4/3101
BE-3000 Leuven
Belgium
dan.batovici@kuleuven.be

Dan BATOVICI

UCLouvain
Institut des civilisations, arts et lettres
Place Blaise Pascal 1/L3.03.02
BE-1348 Louvain-la-Neuve
Belgium
daniel.batovici@uclouvain.be

EVANGELIENTRADITIONEN IN DER
OFFENBARUNG DES PETRUS

Vorbemerkung

Joseph Verheyden, geschätzter Kollege, guter Freund, Weggefährte seit vielen Jahren, hat zu nahezu allen Texten und Themen des antiken Christentums und weit darüber hinaus wichtige, substantielle Arbeiten verfasst. Seine Kenntnisse der antiken Welt, ihrer vielfältigen Verflechtungen und ihrer Bedeutung für die Gegenwart übersteigen die meinigen bei weitem. Der folgende Beitrag kann deshalb nicht mehr sein als ein bescheidener Gruß zu seinem Geburtstag. Ich habe meine Zweifel, dass Jos Verheyden viel Neues darin entdecken wird. Eher wird sich fortsetzen, was ich seit längerem als „Hase-und-Igel-Spiel" mit ihm spiele: Wenn ich mich in ein Gebiet der antiken Literatur und Geschichte eingearbeitet habe, sitzt Jos Verheyden meist vergnügt schon dort und ruft „Ick bin allhie". Gleichwohl soll im Folgenden die Aufmerksamkeit auf einen Text gelenkt werden, der zwar bei denen, die sich mit antiken jüdischen und christlichen Apokalypsen befassen, seit längerem bekannt ist und diskutiert wird, im Blick auf seine Rezeption von Evangelientraditionen jedoch bislang weniger beachtet wurde[1]. Die *Petrusoffenbarung* stellt jedoch eine bemerkenswerte und in dieser Form sogar einzigartige Verknüpfung von Jesusüberlieferung und Offenbarungsliteratur dar, was es lohnend erscheinen lässt, dieser Spur etwas genauer nachzugehen. Ich beginne dazu im Folgenden mit einigen generellen Beobachtungen zur Stellung der *Offenbarung des Petrus* innerhalb der antiken christlichen Literatur und gehe im zweiten Teil genauer auf die verarbeiteten Evangelientraditionen ein. Zum Schluss werden die Beobachtungen in einigen Punkten summiert.

I. Die *Petrusoffenbarung* in der antiken christlichen Literatur

Die *Offenbarung des Petrus* ist in der neueren Forschung verstärkt in den Blick getreten. Zwar wird man (noch?) nicht davon sprechen können,

---

1. Die, soweit ich sehe, einzige Arbeit, die sich diesem Thema explizit widmet, ist die unveröffentlichte Dissertation von R.C. HELMER, „*That We May Know and Understand*": *Gospel Tradition in the Apocalypse of Peter*, Ph.D. Diss., Marquette University, 1998. Die Arbeit wurde vor der intensiveren Befassung mit der *Petrusoffenbarung* in den zurückliegenden beiden Jahrzehnten verfasst. Es lohnt deshalb, das Thema erneut aufzugreifen.

dass sie ins Zentrum der Diskussion über die frühchristliche Literatur vorgedrungen wäre, jedoch hat sie bei denen, die sich mit den antiken christlichen Apokryphen – und hier insbesondere mit den apokryphen Apokalypsen – befassen, wieder zunehmend Aufmerksamkeit auf sich gezogen, nachdem sie an der Wende vom 19. zum 20. Jahrhundert schon einmal eine Diskussion hervorgerufen hatte[2]. Wichtig für die erneute Beschäftigung mit der Schrift waren vor allem die diversen Studien von Richard Bauckham[3], denen das Verdienst zukommt, die Bedeutung der *Offenbarung des Petrus* für die frühchristliche Literatur und Geschichte ins Bewusstsein gerückt zu haben. Einen wichtigen Impuls lieferte darüber hinaus die Ausgabe der griechischen Fragmente des *Petrusevangeliums* und der *Petrusapokalypse* durch Thomas Kraus und Tobias Nicklas[4]. Beide Autoren haben zudem einschlägige Beiträge zur *Offenbarung des Petrus* vorgelegt, die die Diskussion angeregt und bereichert haben[5].

2. Die *Offenbarung des Petrus* (hiernach auch *OffbPt*) ist seit der ersten Auflage der Ausgabe *Neutestamentliche Apokryphen in deutscher Übersetzung* (hg. zunächst von E. HENNECKE, seit der dritten Auflage von W. SCHNEEMELCHER), Tübingen, Mohr Siebeck, 1904, vertreten. Die Übersetzung wurde zunächst von H. WEINEL, in der dritten und vierten Auflage von C. MAURER und H. DUENSING (Letzterer war für die Übersetzung des äthiopischen Textes zuständig) und in der fünften und sechsten Auflage von C.D.G. MÜLLER verantwortet, der die Übersetzung von DUENSING einer Durchsicht auf der Grundlage des äthiopischen Textes unterzogen hat (vgl. *ibid*, S. 566, Anm. 1). In der geplanten Neuausgabe C. MARKSCHIES – J. SCHRÖTER (Hgg.), *Antike christliche Apokryphen in deutscher Übersetzung*. Bd. 3: *Antike christliche Apokalypsen*, Tübingen, Mohr Siebeck (in Vorbereitung), wird eine neue Einleitung und Übersetzung durch A. BAUSI vorgelegt werden. Eine englische Übersetzung findet sich bei M.R. JAMES, *The Apocryphal New Testament*, Oxford, Clarendon, 1924 (repr., 1955), S. 505-524 (mit einem Appendix zum zweiten Buch der *Sibyllinischen Orakel*, 521-524). Vgl. J.K. ELLIOTT, *The Apocryphal New Testament: A Collection of Apocryphal Christian Literature in an English Translation Based on M.R. James*, Oxford, Clarendon, 1993 (repr. 2009), S. 593-615. Der äthiopische Text mit einer Einführung und französischen Übersetzung wurde vorgelegt von S. GRÉBAUT, *Littérature éthiopienne pseudo-clémentine*, in *Revue de l'orient chrétien* 12 (1907) 139-151; 15 (1910) 198-214, 307-323, 425-439.

3. Besonders einschlägig ist: R.J. BAUCKHAM, *The Apocalypse of Peter: A Jewish Christian Apocalypse from the Time of Bar Kokhba*, in ID., *The Fate of the Dead: Studies on Jewish and Christian Apocalypses* (SupplNT, 93), Leiden – Boston, MA – Köln, Brill, 1998, S. 160-258. Vgl. weiter R.J. BAUCKHAM, *The Apocalypse of Peter: An Account of Research*, in *ANRW* 2.25.6 (1988) 4712-4750. Darüber hinaus hat Bauckham diverse Studien zu Einzelaspekten der *Offenbarung des Petrus* vorgelegt, auf die im weiteren Verlauf hingewiesen wird.

4. T.J. KRAUS – T. NICKLAS (Hgg.), *Das Petrusevangelium und die Petrusapokalypse: Die griechischen Fragmente mit deutscher und englischer Übersetzung* (GCS, NF 11; Neutestamentliche Apokryphen, 1), Berlin – New York, De Gruyter, 2004.

5. Genannt seien (ohne Anspruch auf Vollständigkeit): T.J. KRAUS, *P.Vindob. G 39756 + Bodl. MS Gr. th. f. 4 [P]: Fragmente eines Codex der griechischen Petrus-Apokalypse*, in *BASP* 40 (2003) 45-61; ID., *Acherousia und Elysion: Anmerkungen im Hinblick auf deren Verwendung auch im christlichen Kontext*, in *Mnemosyne* 56 (2003) 145-163; ID., *Zur näheren Bedeutung der „Götzen(bilder)" in der Apokalypse des Petrus (ApkPetr)*, in *ASE* 24

Hinzuweisen ist weiter auf die diversen Studien von Jan Bremmer[6], einen Sammelband mit wichtigen Beiträgen zur *Offenbarung des Petrus*[7] sowie auf die neuere Arbeit von Eric Beck zum Ort der Schrift in der antiken Literatur, einschließlich einer „composite translation" des äthiopischen Textes und der griechischen Fragmente[8]. Die genannten Untersuchungen haben wichtige Einsichten zur *Offenbarung des Petrus* zutage gefördert und zugleich zentrale Punkte für die weitere Diskussion herausgearbeitet. Diese seien überblicksweise genannt, wobei Einzelheiten im weiteren Verlauf des Beitrags zur Sprache kommen.

Bezüglich der Textüberlieferung sind eine äthiopische Fassung und der bereits zuvor entdeckte griechische Akhmîmtext zu unterscheiden[9].

(2007) 147-176; T. NICKLAS, „*Insider" and „Outsider": Überlegungen zum historischen Kontext der Darstellung „jenseitiger Orte" in der Offenbarung des Petrus*, in W. AMELING (Hg.), *Topographie des Jenseits: Studien zur Geschichte des Todes in Kaiserzeit und Spätantike* (Altertumswissenschaftliches Kolloquium, 21), Stuttgart, Steiner, 2011, 35-48; ID., „*Drink the Cup Which I Promised You!" (Apocalypse of Peter 14.4): The Death of Peter and the End of Times*, in J. KNIGHT – K. SULLIVAN (Hgg.), *The Open Mind: Aspects of Apocalypticism in Second Temple Judaism and Early Christianity. Festschrift for Christopher Rowland* (LNTS, 522), Edinburgh, Bloomsbury T&T Clark, 2015, 183-200; ID., „*Our Righteous Brethren": Some Remarks regarding the Description of the „Righteous Ones" according to the Greek Revelation of Peter*, in A. HOUTMAN – A. DE JONG – M. MISSET-VAN DE WEG (Hgg.), *Empsychoi Logoi: Religious Innovations in Late Antiquity. Studies in Honour of Professor Pieter Willem van der Horst* (AJEC, 73), Leiden – Boston, MA, Brill, 2008, 329-346; ID., *Jewish, Christian, Greek? The Apocalypse of Peter as a Witness of Early 2nd-Cent. Christianity in Alexandria*, in L. ARCARI (Hg.), *Beyond Conflicts: Cultural and Religious Cohabitations in Alexandria and Egypt between the 1st and the 6th Century* CE (STAC, 103), Tübingen, Mohr Siebeck, 2017, 27-46; ID., *Resurrection, Judgment, Punishment: Apocalypse of Peter 4*, in G. VAN OYEN – T. SHEPHERD (Hgg.), *Resurrection of the Dead: Biblical Traditions in Dialogue* (BETL, 249), Leuven – Walpole, MA, Peeters, 2012, 461-474; ID., *Zwei petrinische Apokryphen im Akhmîm-Codex oder eines? Kritische Anmerkungen und Gedanken*, in ID., *Studien zum Petrusevangelium* (WUNT, 453), Tübingen, Mohr Siebeck, 2020, 32-50.

6. J.N. BREMMER, *The Apocalypse of Peter: Jewish or Greek?*, in ID., *Maidens, Magic and Martyrs in Early Christianity: Collected Essays I* (WUNT, 379), Tübingen, Mohr Siebeck, 2017, 269-280; ID., *The Apocalypse of Peter: Place, Date and Punishments*, ibid., 281-293; ID., *Christian Hell: From the Apocalypse of Peter to the Apocalypse of Paul*, ibid., 295-312; ID., *Tours of Hell: Greek, Jewish, Roman and Early Christian*, ibid., 313-328; ID., *Descents to Hell and Ascents to Heaven in Apocalyptic Literature*, ibid., 329-345.

7. J.N. BREMMER – I. CZACHESZ (Hgg.), *The Apocalypse of Peter* (Studies in Early Christian Apocrypha, 7), Leuven, Peeters, 2003.

8. E.J. BECK, *Justice and Mercy in the Apocalypse of Peter: A New Translation and Analysis of the Purpose of the Text* (WUNT, 427), Tübingen, Mohr Siebeck, 2019. Eine Edition des äthiopischen Textes unter Einbeziehung der beiden kürzeren griechischen Fragmente findet sich bei D.D. BUCHHOLZ, *Your Eyes Will Be Opened: A Study of the Greek (Ethiopic) Apocalypse of Peter* (SBLDS, 97), Atlanta, GA, Scholars, 1988.

9. Der Akhmîmtext wurde 1886/87 entdeckt. Der Codex enthält als erste Schrift das *Petrusevangelium*, gefolgt von der *Petrusapokalypse*. Auf den verbleibenden Seiten finden sich Stücke des *Ersten Henochbuches* sowie ein *Martyrium des Julian von Anazarbus*. Der

Darüber hinaus sind die beiden griechischen Fragmente zu beachten, die sich heute in der Bodleian Library in Oxford (Bodl. MS Gr. th. F. 4 4 [P]) bzw. in der Papyrussammlung der Österreichischen Nationalbibliothek in Wien (P.Vindob. G 39756) befinden. Die beiden Fragmente stammen aus demselben Pergamentcodex und sind deutlich älter als der Akhmîmtext[10]. Es ist demnach kein Text erhalten, der das griechische Original der Schrift bewahrt hätte. Gleichwohl können mit Hilfe des äthiopischen Textes und der beiden kürzeren griechischen Fragmente Inhalt und literarischer Charakter, in gewissen Grenzen auch der Text der *Petrusoffenbarung* erschlossen werden.

Der Akhmîmtext stellt dagegen eine gegenüber der äthiopischen Übersetzung selbständige Fassung der *Petrusoffenbarung* dar[11]. Die augenfälligste Differenz, neben dem Umfang (die äthiopische Version ist etwa dreimal so lang wie der Akhmîmtext), ist die abweichende Reihenfolge in der Darstellung der Belohnungen und Strafen für Gerechte und Sünder im Endgericht. Während im äthiopischen Text die Bestrafungen der Sünder voranstehen und als zukünftige Ereignisse geschildert werden, bevor die Jünger die Gerechten im Paradiesgarten sehen, wird im Akhmîmfragment zunächst die Erscheinung der Gerechten im Paradies erzählt, anschließend werden Petrus der gegenüberliegende Ort der Strafe und die dort stattfindenden Bestrafungen der Sünder als bereits vergangenes Geschehen gezeigt. Üblicherweise wird der äthiopischen Fassung der Vorzug gegeben, da sie insgesamt eine zuverlässigere Wiedergabe des ursprünglichen griechischen Textes darstellen dürfte. Dafür sprechen die Passagen im zweiten Buch der *Sibyllinischen Orakel*, die eine enge Berührung mit der *Offenbarung des Petrus* aufweisen[12], die genannten kurzen griechischen Fragmente sowie die Erwähnungen der Schrift bei altkirchlichen Autoren[13]. Eine weitere Differenz betrifft die Rahmenhandlung,

---

äthiopische Text wurde 1910 publiziert. Er ist in zwei eng miteinander verwandten Manuskripten erhalten. Die äthiopische Fassung basiert offenbar auf einer arabischen Übersetzung des griechischen Textes der *Petrusapokalypse*. Die Einteilung des Akhmîmtextes in 34 Abschnitte geht auf A. von Harnack zurück, diejenige des äthiopischen Textes in 17 Kapitel auf H. Weinel.

10. Der Codex wird auf das 5. Jahrhundert datiert. Zu den Fragmenten vgl. M.R. JAMES, *The Rainer Fragment of the Apocalypse of Peter*, in *JTS* 32 (1931) 270-279; KRAUS – NICKLAS, *Petrusevangelium* (Anm. 4), S. 121-130; KRAUS, *P.Vindob. G 39756* (Anm. 5). Auf ihre Bedeutung für die Textrekonstruktion ist zurückzukommen.

11. Vgl. auch die eingehende Beschreibung des Akhmîmcodex durch P. VAN MINNEN, *The Greek Apocalypse of Peter*, in BREMMER – CZACHESZ, *Apocalypse of Peter* (Anm. 7), 15-39.

12. *Or.Sib.* 2.190-338. Diese Passagen sind deshalb bei JAMES und ELLIOTT, *Apocryphal New Testament* (Anm. 2), in englischer Übersetzung mit abgedruckt.

13. Vgl. M.R. JAMES, *A New Text of the Apocalypse of Peter*, in *JTS* 12 (1911) 367-375. Zu den Hinweisen auf die Schrift in der antiken Literatur vgl. unten, Anm. 31.

in die die Offenbarung der endzeitlichen Heils- und Gerichtsorte eingebettet ist. Der äthiopische Text beginnt mit einer Rede des auferweckten Christus auf dem Ölberg über die endzeitlichen Ereignisse, die eine Entsprechung in den synoptischen Endzeitreden besitzt[14]. Er endet mit einer Version der synoptischen Verklärungserzählung, die als Himmelfahrtsszene gestaltet ist. Dazwischen werden die endzeitlichen Bestrafungen geschildert, den Auserwählten und Gerechten wird dagegen das Heil zugesagt.

Der Akhmîmtext setzt mitten in einer Rede Jesu ein, die kurz darauf endet, woraufhin Jesus und seine Jünger ebenfalls auf einen Berg gehen. Dort erscheinen den Jüngern die „gerechten Brüder", anschließend werden Petrus der Ort der Gerechten und anschließend der Ort der Strafen gezeigt. Der Version des Akhmîmtextes liegt demnach eine Zweiteilung zugrunde: Der erste Teil beinhaltet eine Rede Christi, die offenbar nicht auf einem Berg gehalten wird; die Offenbarung selbst findet sodann nach dem Gang auf den Berg statt[15].

Diese Differenzen zeigen, gemeinsam mit zahlreichen sprachlichen Unterschieden, dass der Akhmîmtext eine gegenüber der äthiopischen Fassung sekundäre, vom griechischen Original weiter entfernte Version der *Offenbarung des Petrus* darstellt und für sich zu betrachten ist. Das wird dadurch verstärkt, dass sie sich im Akhmîmcodex gemeinsam mit einer weiteren mit dem Namen des Petrus verbundenen Schrift, nämlich dem *Petrusevangelium*, befindet. Das Verhältnis dieser beiden „petrinischen Apokryphen"[16] ist nicht abschließend geklärt und bedarf weiterer Erörterung. Das soll nicht Gegenstand des vorliegenden Beitrags sein. Es sei jedoch darauf hingewiesen, dass einige Beobachtungen dafür sprechen,

---

14. Dass es sich um eine Rede zwischen Auferweckung und Himmelfahrt handelt, wird zum einen durch das am Schluss erzählte Eingehen in den Himmel von Jesus mit Mose und Elia nahegelegt, zum anderen durch die Offenbarung der endzeitlichen Strafen und des Paradiesgartens. Beides legt die Annahme nahe, dass die synoptische Endzeitrede als narrativer Kontext für die Offenbarung der Endereignisse durch den auferstandenen Christus dient. Damit liegt zugleich eine Verbindung zu anderen Schriften vor, in denen ebenfalls die Situation zwischen Auferweckung und Himmelfahrt Christi zur Mitteilung neuer Offenbarungen verwendet wird. Dies ist vor allem in den sogenannten *Dialogevangelien* der Fall, etwa dem *Mariaevangelium*, der *Epistula Apostolorum*, der *Weisheit Jesu Christi* und dem *Dialog des Erlösers*.
15. Dass die erste Rede, anders als im äthiopischen Text, nicht auf einem Berg gehalten wird, ergibt sich daraus, dass der Akhmîmtext den Szenenwechsel mit der Aufforderung Jesu einleitet, auf „den Berg" zu gehen (4). Im äthiopischen Text ist dagegen die Eingangsszene auf dem Ölberg lokalisiert (1.1), die Schlussszene wird durch die Aufforderung Jesu, auf den „heiligen Berg" zu gehen, eingeleitet (15.1; vgl. 2 Pt 1,18). Vermutlich ist mit dem letzteren der Zionsberg gemeint, wogegen im Akhmîmtext offen bleibt, um welchen Berg es sich handelt.
16. Vgl. NICKLAS, *Zwei petrinische Apokryphen* (Anm. 5).

den Zusammenhang der beiden petrinischen Akhmîmtexte stärker zu berücksichtigen, als dies mitunter geschieht[17]. Die augenfälligste Übereinstimmung ist, dass Petrus in beiden Texten als Ich-Erzähler und Repräsentant der Gruppe der Jünger in Erscheinung tritt[18]. Die Identifizierung des Erzählers als Petrus konnte bereits auf der Basis des Akhmîmtextes vorgenommen werden[19] und wurde durch den äthiopischen Text bestätigt[20]. Daneben gibt es etliche sprachliche Übereinstimmungen, die darauf hinweisen, dass beide Texte aus einer gemeinsamen Perspektive bearbeitet wurden[21]. Schließlich könnte auch der genannte, vom äthiopischen Text abweichende narrative Rahmen dafür sprechen, dass es sich bei der Akhmîmfassung um einen in eine Jesuserzählung integrierten Teil handelt, zu der auch das *Petrusevangelium* gehört[22].

Stellt der Akhmîmtext demnach eine eigene, mit dem voranstehenden Fragment zusammenhängende Fassung der *Petrusoffenbarung* dar, so ist gleichzeitig zu beachten, dass die beiden Petrustexte im Akhmîmcodex nicht einfach aufeinander folgen. Die beiden Seiten nach dem Ende des *Petrusevangeliums* sind vielmehr leer, ebenso wie die erste Seite des zweiten Bogens mit dem Beginn der *Petrusoffenbarung*. Zudem wurde

---

17. In seiner nur wenige Jahre nach der Entdeckung des Akhmîmcodex (und vor Bekanntwerden des äthiopischen Textes) veröffentlichten Untersuchung zur *Petrusoffenbarung* hatte A. Dieterich die Vermutung geäußert, dass es sich bei dieser Schrift um einen ursprünglichen Teil des *Petrusevangeliums* gehandelt habe, aus dem die *Petrusoffenbarung* erst nachträglich erwachsen sei. Vgl. A. DIETERICH, *Nekyia: Beiträge zur Erklärung der neuentdeckten Petrusapokalypse*, Leipzig, Teubner, 1893 (²1913), S. 16-17: „Es wird zu folgern sein, dass wir nicht eine selbständige Apokalypse, nicht *die* Petrusapokalypse vor uns haben, sondern ein Stück eines Evangeliums ... Aus diesem Stück des Petrusevangeliums ist erst die selbständige Petrusapokalypse herausentwickelt". Vgl. weiter M.R. JAMES, *A New Text of the Apocalypse of Peter*, in *JTS* 12 (1911) 573-583, S. 577-582; ID., *Rainer Fragment* (Anm. 10), S. 275-279; T. ZAHN, *Grundriss der Geschichte des neutestamentlichen Kanons: Eine Ergänzung zu der Einleitung in das Neue Testament*, Leipzig, Deichert, ²1901, S. 24-25, Anm. 16. Auch wenn man dieser Annahme nach Bekanntwerden des äthiopischen Textes nicht mehr folgen wird, bleibt der Zusammenhang der beiden „petrinischen" Schriften im Akhmîmcodex zu beachten.

18. *EvPt* 7.26: ἐγὼ δὲ μετὰ τῶν ἑταίρων ἐλυπούμην ... 14.60: ἐγὼ δὲ Σίμων Πέτρος καὶ Ἀνδρέας ὁ ἀδελφός μου ... *OffbPt* 12: καὶ προσελθὼν τῷ κ(υρί)ῳ εἶπον ... (es schließt sich ein Dialog zwischen dem Herrn und dem Ich-Erzähler an); 21: εἶδον δὲ καὶ ἕτερον τόπο(ν) ... (vgl. 25, 26). Die einzige Stelle, an der diese Identifizierung explizit gemacht wird, findet sich im *Petrusevangelium* (14.60), wogegen der Name im zweiten Fragment nicht begegnet.

19. Vgl. DIETERICH, *Nekyia* (Anm. 17), S. 10; ZAHN, *Grundriss* (Anm. 17), S. 25, Anm. 16.

20. *OffbPt* 2.1: „Und ich, Petrus, antwortete ihm und sagte ...".

21. Vgl. JAMES, *A New Text* (Anm. 17), S. 579-580. Als besonders markant hebt er die Wendung ἡμεῖς οἱ δώδεκα μαθηταί hervor.

22. Vgl. NICKLAS, *Zwei petrinische Apokryphen* (Anm. 5), S. 40, mit Verweis auf DIETERICH, *Nekyia* (Anm. 17), S. 18, der bereits auf die narrative Einbettung des Akhmîmfragments verwiesen hatte.

dieser Bogen verkehrt herum eingebunden[23]. Der Schreiber des Codex hatte demnach zwei Texte vor sich, die er auf separaten Bögen kopiert hat. Die Angleichung der beiden petrinischen Fragmente ist somit offensichtlich nicht erst bei der Herstellung des Codex, sondern bereits auf einer früheren Stufe erfolgt. Sie hat zudem nicht dazu geführt, beide Texte miteinander zu vereinen. Gleichwohl dürften dem Schreiber beide Texte gemeinsam vorgelegen haben, als er sie für den von ihm erstellten Codex kopierte[24].

Für die hier verfolgte Fragestellung ist an diesen Beobachtungen vor allem von Interesse, dass in beiden Fassungen der Schrift der narrative Rahmen auf je eigene Weise eine maßgebliche Rolle für die Offenbarung der jenseitigen Bestrafungen und Belohnungen spielt. Dieser wurde zum einen durch eine Erweiterung und narrative Neuplatzierung der apokalyptischen Rede Jesu aus den synoptischen Evangelien entworfen, zum anderen durch eine Neuinterpretation und eigene Einordnung der Verklärungserzählung in die Jesusgeschichte. Die unmittelbare Verbindung der Offenbarung jenseitiger Strafen und Belohnungen mit der (synoptischen) Jesuserzählung ist demnach ein charakteristisches Merkmal der *Petrusoffenbarung*, das sie zugleich von anderen frühchristlichen Apokalypsen unterscheidet[25]. Die narrative Einbettung der Schilderungen endzeitlicher Strafen und des Paradieses in der *Offenbarung des Petrus* zeigt zugleich, dass die Schrift in anderer Weise mit der Figur des Petrus verbunden ist, als dies ansonsten bei frühchristlichen Apokalypsen und ihren – fiktiven oder realen – Verfassern der Fall ist[26]. In der Fassung des Akhmîmtextes ist die Einbindung in die Jesusgeschichte durch die Verknüpfung mit der Passionserzählung des *Petrusevangeliums* zudem offenbar weiter ausgebaut worden.

---

23. Ich folge der Beschreibung des Codex bei KRAUS – NICKLAS, *Petrusevangelium* (Anm. 4), S. 27-28.

24. Dabei kann als wahrscheinlich gelten, dass er nur Fragmente beider Texte vor sich hatte. Die von NICKLAS, *Zwei petrinische Apokryphen* (Anm. 5), S. 43, erwogene Möglichkeit, „dass er bewusst Ausschnitte aus dem Gesamt eines Werks zusammenstellte", erscheint dagegen weniger naheliegend, da sich in diesem Fall die abrupten Anfänge und Schlüsse beider Texte nur schwer erklären ließen.

25. Die Johannesoffenbarung ist als Vision des Sehers Johannes vor dem Thron Gottes gestaltet und hat zudem einen brieflichen Rahmen. Die *Himmelfahrt Jesajas* ist als Verbindung von Martyrium und Vision des Propheten Jesaja gestaltet. Die griechische *Esraapokalypse* und die lateinische *Visio Esdrae* schildern die Entrückung Esras in den Himmel und seinen Gang in den Tartarus. Wie diese wenigen Beispiele zeigen, ist die literarische Bandbreite der frühchristlichen Apokalypsen durchaus groß.

26. Vgl. T. NICKLAS, *Petrusoffenbarung, Christusoffenbarung und ihre Funktion: Autoritätskonstruktion in der Petrusapokalypse*, in J. FREY – M.R. JOST – F. TÓTH (Hgg.), *Autorschaft und Autorisierungsstrategien in apokalyptischen Texten* (WUNT, 426), Tübingen, Mohr Siebeck, 2019, 347-363.

Ein weiterer für die gegenwärtige Diskussion relevanter Aspekt betrifft das Verhältnis der *Offenbarung des Petrus* zum Zweiten Petrusbrief. Ist diesbezüglich in der älteren Forschung die Auffassung vertreten worden, die *Petrusoffenbarung* setze den Zweiten Petrusbrief voraus[27], so wurde in neuerer Zeit gerade umgekehrt dafür argumentiert, dass der Zweite Petrusbrief das jüngere Schreiben sei und seinerseits die *Petrusoffenbarung* benutzt habe[28]. Für die hier verfolgte Fragestellung ist an dieser Diskussion vor allem von Bedeutung, dass sich beide Schriften einem frühchristlichen Diskurs über die Rolle des Petrus als Autoritätsfigur des Jüngerkreises und über sein Geschick zuweisen lassen. Sollten sich die Argumente für eine gegenüber der *Offenbarung des Petrus* spätere Ansetzung des Zweiten Petrusbriefes und seine Abhängigkeit von jener erhärten, könnte dies für die Rekonstruktion eines entsprechenden Diskurses (oder mehrere solcher Diskurse), der (bzw. die) sich in Alexandria lokalisieren lasse(n)[29], wichtige Hinweise liefern. Dabei wäre zunächst eine Erweiterung des Petrusbildes der synoptischen Evangelien bzw. der frühchristlichen Petrustradition durch die nachösterliche Christusoffenbarung an Petrus erfolgt, von dem der Zweite Petrusbrief dann u.a. die Szene der Verklärung auf dem Berg und das Motiv des Weltenbrandes verwendet hätte[30].

Ein letzter Punkt, der in diesem Abschnitt noch angesprochen werden soll, betrifft die Bezeugung der *Petrusoffenbarung* im antiken Christentum[31]. Bekanntlich wird eine Schrift mit dem Namen *Offenbarung des*

---

27. Vgl. R.J. BAUCKHAM, *2 Peter and the Apocalypse of Peter*, in ID., *The Fate of the Dead* (Anm. 3), 290-303.

28. So zuerst W. GRÜNSTÄUDL, *Petrus Alexandrinus: Studien zum historischen und theologischen Ort des Zweiten Petrusbriefes* (WUNT, 2.315), Tübingen, Mohr Siebeck, 2013. Vgl. weiter J. FREY, *Der Brief des Judas und der zweite Brief des Petrus* (THKNT, 15/II), Leipzig, Evangelische Verlagsanstalt, 2015, S. 170-173; J. FREY – M. DEN DULK – J.G. VAN DER WATT (Hgg.), *2 Peter and the Apocalypse of Peter: Towards a New Perspective* (BibInt, 174), Leiden – Boston, MA, Brill, 2019. Von den hier versammelten Autoren folgen die meisten der Annahme einer Abhängigkeit des 2 Pt von der *OffbPt*. Skeptisch bleibt allerdings P. Foster, wogegen Bauckham seine frühere Auffassung revidiert und nunmehr dafür plädiert, beide Schriften als unabhängig voneinander zu betrachten. Vgl. P. FOSTER, *Does the Apocalypse of Peter Help to Determine the Date of 2 Peter*, ibid., 217-260, und R.J. BAUCKHAM, *2 Peter and the Apocalypse of Peter Revisited: A Response to Jörg Frey*, ibid., 261-281.

29. Vgl. die Überlegungen von T. NICKLAS, *Petrus-Diskurse in Alexandria: Eine Fortführung der Gedanken von Jörg Frey*, in FREY et al. (Hgg.), *2 Peter* (Anm. 28), 99-127.

30. Die je eigene Verwendung dieser Traditionen und Motive wäre so gegeben, wenn sich eine direkte literarische Beziehung nicht wahrscheinlich machen ließe. Allerdings ist die Annahme einer solchen Beziehung wohl die näherliegende und damit ökonomischere Hypothese.

31. Vgl. dazu auch die Diskussion der Belege bei KRAUS – NICKLAS, *Petrusevangelium* (Anm. 4), S. 87-99, sowie die Darlegungen bei T. ZAHN, *Geschichte des neutestamentlichen*

Petrus (Ἀποκάλυψις Πέτρου) seit dem Ende des zweiten Jahrhunderts in verschiedenen christlichen Texten erwähnt. Das Muratorische Fragment, das Inhalt und Status diverser Schriften in der christlichen Kirche diskutiert[32], nennt am Ende seiner Ausführungen über die in der Kirche anerkannten Schriften, unmittelbar vor dem *Hirten des Hermas*, die *Offenbarungen des Johannes und des Petrus* (*Apocalypsis etiam Iohannis et Petri*, Z. 71-72) und bemerkt im Blick auf letztere, dass einige sie nicht zur öffentlichen Lektüre zulassen wollen[33]. Die *Offenbarung des Petrus* ist also offenbar eine bekannte Schrift, deren Status jedoch ambivalent ist. Clemens von Alexandria kommt in den *Eclogae propheticae* an zwei Stellen kurz hintereinander auf die *Offenbarung des Petrus* zu sprechen. In der ersten Passage zitiert er „die Schrift", die sage, dass ausgesetzte Säuglinge einem Temelouchosengel (d.h. einem Schutzengel) übergeben würden, durch den sie unterrichtet und aufgezogen werden. Dies wird mit einem Zitat aus der *Offenbarung des Petrus* begründet[34].

Kurz darauf zitiert Clemens ein weiteres Mal aus der *Petrusoffenbarung*, nunmehr um zu demonstrieren, dass sich die göttliche Vorsehung nicht um diejenigen „im Fleisch" (ἐν σαρκί) kümmert[35]. Das wird mit der Aussage des Petrus in seiner Offenbarung begründet, dass im Mutterleib getötete Kinder das bessere Schicksal haben werden, denn sie würden einem Temelouchosengel übergeben, damit sie, nachdem sie Erkenntnis

---

Kanons. Bd. 2: *Zweite Hälfte*, Erlangen – Leipzig, Deichert, 1892, S. 810-820. Die Bezeugung wird auch besprochen bei A. JAKAB, *The Reception of the Apocalypse of Peter in Ancient Christianity*, in BREMMER – CZACHESZ (Hgg.), *The Apocalypse of Peter* (Anm. 7), 174-186.

32. Es handelt sich beim Muratorischen Fragment nicht einfach um eine Auflistung von anerkannten und abgelehnten Büchern, sondern um inhaltliche Ausführungen zu den verschiedenen Schriften. Auf die nach wie vor umstrittene Diskussion über die Datierung des Fragments gehe ich hier nicht eigens ein. Für die Spätdatierung vgl. in jüngerer Zeit L.M. MCDONALD, *The Formation of the Biblical Canon*. Vol. 2: *The New Testament. Its Authority and Canonicity*, London, Bloomsbury, 2017, S. 277-304. Die Datierung um 200 wird dagegen wieder vertreten von J. ORTH, *Das Muratorische Fragment: Die Frage seiner Datierung*, Mainz, Patrimonium, 2020. Neben anderen Aspekten ist zu beachten, dass das Muratorische Fragment die Katholischen Briefe nicht erwähnt, was angesichts der Bedeutung, die der Text der Siebenzahl von Briefen im Fall des Paulus und der Johannesoffenbarung beimisst, dafür spricht, dass diese Sammlung noch nicht existierte oder jedenfalls dem Verfasser nicht bekannt war. Das spricht, neben weiteren Indizien, wie etwa dem Fehlen des Ersten Petrusbriefes und der Zurückweisung des *Hirten des Hermas* als öffentlich in der Kirche zu verlesender Schrift, dafür, dass der Text in das ausgehende zweite oder beginnende dritte Jahrhundert zu datieren ist.

33. *quidam ex nostris legi in ecclesia nolunt* (Z. 72-73).

34. *Ecl.* 41: ἡ γραφή φησι τὰ βρέφη τὰ ἐκτεθέντα τημελούχῳ παραδίδοσθαι ἀγγέλῳ, ὑφ' οὗ παιδεύεσθαί τε καὶ αὔξειν. Διὸ καὶ Πέτρος ἐν τῇ Ἀποκαλύψει φησί· καὶ ἀστραπὴ πυρὸς πηδῶσα ἀπὸ τῶν βρεφῶν ἐκείνων καὶ πλήσσουσα τοὺς ὀφθαλμοὺς τῶν γυναικῶν.

35. *Ecl.* 48–49.

empfangen hätten, eines besseren Geschicks teilhaftig würden, denn sie hätten erlitten, was sie auch im leiblichen Leben erlitten haben würden. Dem folgt kurz darauf ein weiteres Zitat aus der *Petrusoffenbarung*: „Die Milch der Frauen aber, die von den Brüsten herabfließt und gerinnt, wird kleine fleischfressende Tiere erzeugen, die an ihnen hinauflaufen und sie verzehren".

Beide Stellen machen deutlich, dass die *Offenbarung des Petrus* für Clemens eine Autorität als „Schrift" hat und dementsprechend zum Beleg seiner Aussagen herangezogen werden kann. Zu den zitierten Stellen lassen sich dabei Parallelen bzw. Analogien im äthiopischen Text finden. Im Kontext der Schilderung endzeitlicher Strafen für Eltern, die ihre Kinder abgetrieben haben, findet sich eine Passage, die der zuletzt zitierten bei Clemens sehr nahekommt[36]. Die erstgenannte Stelle bei Clemens berührt sich mit dieser Vorstellung, hat allerdings darüber hinaus keine unmittelbare Entsprechung in der *Offenbarung des Petrus*[37].

Bei Methodius von Olympus (um 300) findet sich die Vorstellung, dass die aus Ehebruch hervorgegangenen Kinder Temelouchosengeln übergeben werden, um in Ruhe und Gedeihen aufzuwachsen. Dies sei „in den göttlich inspirierten Schriften" (ἐν θεοπνεύστοις γράμμασιν) bezeugt[38]. Die Stelle bringt die gleiche Vorstellung wie diejenigen bei Clemens zum Ausdruck. Es handelt sich demnach um eine bei frühchristlichen Autoren bekannte Vorstellung, die von Methodius mit den „göttlich inspirierten", also den verbindlichen Schriften in Zusammenhang gebracht wird, auch wenn er nicht angibt, wo sie sich dort befindet.

Euseb ordnet die *Petrusoffenbarung* an zwei Stellen unter die bestrittenen bzw. unechten Schriften ein. An der erstgenannten Stelle äußert er sich über die Schriften des neuen Bundes. Dabei werden zur dritten Kategorie der „unechten Schriften" die *Paulusakten*, der *Hirte*, die *Petrusoffenbarung*, der *Barnabasbrief*, die *Lehren der Apostel* und die Johannesoffenbarung, deren Status allerdings umstritten ist, gerechnet. Letzteres gelte auch für das *Hebräerevangelium*[39]. An der zweiten Stelle referiert

---

36. *OffbPt* 8.8-10. Hier findet sich die Beschreibung der Milch, die aus den Brüsten der Mütter fließt, gerinnt und stinkt, und aus der fleischfressende Tiere hervorgehen, die die Frauen mit ihren Männern in Ewigkeit quälen werden, „weil sie das Gebot Gottes verlassen und ihre Kinder getötet haben. Und ihre Kinder wird man dem Engel Temlakos übergeben". Temelouchos und Temlakos für den Schutzengel dürften dabei Varianten desselben Namens sein.

37. In *OffbPt* 13.5 ist vom „Tartarusengel" (Tatirokos, eine Variante von Tartarouchos) die Rede. Dabei handelt es sich allerdings um einen Strafengel, der die Sünder züchtigt.

38. *Symp.* 2.6, Z. 17-27.

39. *Hist. eccl.* 3.25.4-5: ἐν τοῖς νόθοις κατατετάχθω καὶ τῶν Παύλου Πράξεων ἡ γραφὴ ὅ τε λεγόμενος Ποιμὴν καὶ ἡ Ἀποκάλυψις Πέτρου καὶ πρὸς τούτοις ἡ

Euseb über die *Hypotyposen* des Clemens, der dort kurzgefasste Darlegungen zu den Schriften des Neuen Bundes verfasst und dabei auch die umstrittenen Schriften wie den Judasbrief, die übrigen Katholischen Briefe, den *Barnabasbrief* und die nach Petrus benannte *Offenbarung* nicht übergangen habe[40].

Interessant ist schließlich, dass Sozomenos im 5. Jahrhundert zwar darum weiß, dass die *Petrusoffenbarung* „von den Alten" als unecht (ὡς νόθον) angesehen wurde, bis in seine eigene Zeit hinein jedoch in einigen Gemeinden Palästinas einmal im Jahr (und zwar am Karfreitag) gelesen wird[41].

Wie diese Zeugnisse zeigen, war eine Schrift unter dem Namen *Offenbarung des Petrus* im antiken Christentum bekannt und gehörte zum Kreis der angesehenen oder zumindest diskutierten, mitunter sogar der als verbindlich betrachteten Schriften. Dabei kann die äthiopische Übersetzung nicht unmittelbar mit der griechischen Schrift des zweiten Jahrhunderts gleichgesetzt werden. Es ist jedoch unwahrscheinlich, dass die äthiopische Version eine von dem griechischen Text gänzlich verschiedene Fassung darstellt. Sowohl die genannten Zitate als auch die beiden kürzeren griechischen Fragmente bestätigen vielmehr, dass es sich um eine vertrauenswürdige Übersetzung handelt, die allerdings auch Abweichungen vom griechischen Text aufweist[42]. Dies ist dem Überlieferungsbefund anderer frühchristlicher Schriften, zumal solcher, die nicht ins Neue Testament gelangt sind, vergleichbar.

Die Kenntnis der *Petrusoffenbarung* und ihre Akzeptanz waren vermutlich lokal unterschiedlich und weniger eindeutig als etwa bei den Evangelien und den Paulusbriefen. Das traf auf etliche andere frühchristliche Schriften in analoger Weise zu, wie die Bemerkungen bei Clemens und Euseb zeigen und wie es sich in der Geschichte der Entstehung des Neuen Testaments vielfach belegen lässt. Der Status der *Petrusoffenbarung* ist dabei ähnlich demjenigen der Katholischen Briefe, der Johannesoffenbarung, des *Hebräerevangeliums* und des *Hirten des Hermas*. Die Attraktivität der Schrift dürfte zum einen darauf zurückzuführen sein, dass sie

---

φερομένη Βαρναβᾶ ἐπιστολὴ καὶ τῶν ἀποστόλων αἱ λεγόμεναι Διδαχαὶ ἔτι τε, ὡς ἔφην, ἡ Ἰωάννου Ἀποκάλυψις, εἰ φανείη· ἥν τινες, ὡς ἔφην, ἀθετοῦσιν, ἕτεροι δὲ ἐγκρίνουσιν. τοῖς ὁμολογουμένοις. ἤδη δ᾽ ἐν τούτοις τινὲς καὶ τὸ καθ᾽ Ἑβραίους εὐαγγέλιον κατέλεξαν, ὧι μάλιστα Ἑβραίων οἱ τὸν Χριστόν...

40. *Hist. eccl.* 6.14.1: Ἐν δὲ ταῖς Ὑποτυπώσεσιν ξυνελόντα εἰπεῖν πάσης τῆς ἐνδιαθήκου γραφῆς ἐπιτετμημένας πεποίηται διηγήσεις, μηδὲ τὰς ἀντιλεγομένας παρελθών, τὴν Ἰούδα λέγω καὶ τὰς λοιπὰς καθολικὰς ἐπιστολὰς τήν τε Βαρναβᾶ, καὶ τὴν Πέτρου λεγομένην Ἀποκάλυψιν.
41. Sozomenos, *Hist. eccl.* 7.19.9.
42. Vgl. BAUCKHAM, *Apocalypse of Peter* (Anm. 3), S. 163.

Vorstellungen über die endzeitliche Bestrafung der Sünder und eine Schau des Paradieses enthält. Damit lieferte sie geschichtstheologische Inhalte, die für das entstehende Christentum nicht zuletzt deshalb von Interesse waren, als sie jüdische apokalyptische und griechisch-römische Jenseitsvorstellungen in eigener Weise aufnahm und interpretierte. In der *Petrusoffenbarung* finden sich einerseits der biblische Glaube an die Auferstehung der Toten[43] und das Gericht Gottes nach den Werken[44], andererseits Einflüsse griechisch-römischer Terminologie und Jenseitsvorstellungen[45]. Zu Letzterem dürfte auch der Begriff βόρβορος für den Ort der ewigen Strafe im Akhmîmfragment gehören[46]. Die Beschreibung der Unterwelt und der Orte der ewigen Belohnung und Bestrafung in der *Apokalypse des Petrus* weist demnach Einflüsse griechischer mythologischer Vorstellungen auf[47].

Zum anderen dürfte das Interesse der Schrift mit den bereits genannten „Petrus-Diskursen" im frühen Christentum zusammenhängen[48]. Wenn sich diese in Alexandria lokalisieren ließen und die *Petrusoffenbarung* möglicherweise selbst aus Alexandria stammt, wäre sie sowohl ein Zeugnis

43. In *OffbPt* 4.7-8 findet sich ein an Ez 37,1-4 angelehntes Zitat. BAUCKHAM hat gezeigt, dass die Quelle des Zitates nicht das biblische Ezechielbuch, sondern 4Q385 (4QpsEzek) ist. Vgl. ID., *A Quotation from 4Q Second Ezekiel in the Apocalypse of Peter*, in ID., *The Fate of the Dead* (n. 3), 259-268.

44. Die Vorstellung vom Gericht nach den Werken findet sich in 1.8; 6.3, 6; 13.3, 6.

45. Dazu gehören die bereits genannten Namen Temlakos und Tatirokos für die Engel im Jenseits. Zu nennen sind weiter die Begriffe „Acherusischer See" und „Elysisches Feld", die in 14.1 gemeinsam den Ort bezeichnen, an dem die Berufenen und Erwählten eine „gute Taufe" (oder: ein „gutes Bad", καλὸν βάπτισμα) erhalten werden. Zur Rekonstruktion der Passage ist P.Vindob. G 39756 heranzuziehen. Vgl. KRAUS, *P.Vindob. G 39756* (Anm. 5); ID., *Acherousia und Elysion* (Anm. 5) sowie E. PETERSON, *Die Taufe im Acherusischen See*, in ID., *Frühkirche, Judentum und Gnosis: Studien und Untersuchungen*, Roma – Freiburg i.Br. – Wien, Herder, 1959, 310-332.

46. Der Begriff begegnet im Akhmîmtext in den Abschnitten 23, 24 (zweimal) und 31. In allen Fällen fehlt eine Entsprechung im äthiopischen Text, es kann aber vermutet werden, dass der Begriff im griechischen Text gestanden hat. Der Begriff wird auch in 2 Pt 2,22 sowie einige Male in jüdischer Literatur verwendet (z.B. Jer 45,6^{LXX}, bei Philo und Josephus). Vgl. auch *Die Lehren des Silvanus* (NHC VII,4), p. 85:20. In Plato, *Phaid.* 69c und Diogenes Laertius 6.39 ist βόρβορος auf den Hades als Ort der Bestrafung der Sünder bezogen. Vgl. T.J. KRAUS, *Sprache, Stil und historischer Ort des zweiten Petrusbriefes* (WUNT, 2.136), Tübingen, Mohr Siebeck, 2001, 341-343; ID., *Von Hund und Schwein: Das Doppelsprichwort 2Petr 2,22 und seine Hapax legomena aus linguistischer, textkritischer und motivgeschichtlicher Sicht*, in *ASE* 30 (2013) 37-61, S. 46-49. BREMMER, *Apocalypse of Peter* (n. 6), S. 279, erwähnt zudem Analogien bei Aristophanes und Plato.

47. Das bedeutet nicht, dass die *Petrusoffenbarung* diese Begriffe und Vorstellungen unmittelbar aus griechisch-römischer Tradition übernommen haben muss. Es ist vielmehr durchaus vorstellbar, dass sie über jüdische bzw. frühchristliche Texte vermittelt wurden, wo die entsprechende Terminologie ebenfalls begegnet.

48. Vgl. NICKLAS, *Petrus-Diskurse* (Anm. 29).

für das Christentum Alexandrias im zweiten Jahrhundert[49] als auch eines für die Rezeption des Petrus im antiken Christentum[50]. Wie sich dies in der *Petrusoffenbarung* genauer darstellt, soll im Folgenden etwas näher beleuchtet werden.

II. EVANGELIENTRADITIONEN IN DER *OFFENBARUNG DES PETRUS*

Das Phänomen der Zuschreibung von Apokalypsen an wichtige Gestalten der eigenen Tradition findet sich bereits im Judentum und wird im frühen Christentum fortgeführt. Dabei werden Apokalypsen im Namen zentraler Figuren der Geschichte Israels wie Henoch, Mose, Abraham, Jesaja und Esra verfasst, die jüdischen oder christlichen Ursprungs sein können und bei denen sich das Phänomen der Fortschreibung jüdischer Schriften durch das frühe Christentum findet[51]. Eine Unterscheidung von

---

49. In Auseinandersetzung mit BAUCKHAM, *Apocalypse of Peter* (Anm. 3), und E. NORELLI, *Situation des apocryphes pétriniens*, in *Apocrypha* 2 (1991) 31-83; ID., *L'adversaire eschatologique dans l'Apocalypse de Pierre*, in Y.-M. BLANCHARD – B. POUDERON – M. SCOPELLO (Hgg.), *Les forces du bien et du mal dans les premiers siècles de l'Église* (Théologie historique, 118), Paris, Beauchesne, 2010, 291-317, die den Text mit dem Bar Kochba-Aufstand in Verbindung bringen und seine Entstehung in Palästina bzw. Syrien lokalisieren, haben Nicklas und Bremmer Alexandria als Entstehungsort der *Offenbarung des Petrus* wahrscheinlich gemacht. Vgl. NICKLAS, *Petrus-Diskurse* (Anm. 29); ID., *Jews and Christians? Sketches from Second Century Alexandria*, in J. SCHRÖTER – B.A. EDSALL – J. VERHEYDEN (Hgg.), *Jews and Christians – Parting Ways in the First Two Centuries CE? Reflections on the Gains and Losses of a Model* (BZNW, 253), Berlin – Boston, MA, De Gruyter, 2021, 347-379, S. 363-366. Vgl. weiter J. BREMMER, *The Apocalypse of Peter as the First Christian Martyr Text: Its Date, Provenance and Relationship with 2 Peter*, in FREY – DEN DULK – VAN DER WATT (Hgg.), *2 Peter and the Apocalypse of Peter* (Anm. 28), 75-98. Eine Entstehung in Ägypten wurde bereits von MAURER, *Neutestamentliche Apokryphen* (Anm. 2), S. 469 (3. Auflage); bzw. S. 564 (6. Auflage) vermutet.

50. Die *Petrusoffenbarung* zählt zu denjenigen Schriften, die in verschiedener Weise die Autorität des Petrus in Anspruch nehmen und Schriften in seinem Namen verfassen. Dazu gehören neben den beiden Petrusbriefen des Neuen Testaments auch die koptisch überlieferte *Apokalypse des Petrus* aus Nag Hammadi (NHC VII 3). Wie bereits bemerkt, besteht dabei eine besondere Nähe zwischen der *Petrusoffenbarung* und dem Zweiten Petrusbrief. Es wäre weiter zu diskutieren, ob sich aus diesen und weiteren Schriften ein „Petrus-Diskurs" im frühen Christentum erschließen lässt, in dem die Autorität des Petrus als Offenbarungsträger eine zentrale Rolle spielt und der Beziehungen zur frühchristlichen „Gnosis" aufweist. Vgl. dazu die Überlegungen bei NICKLAS, *Petrus-Diskurse* (Anm. 29). Zu bedenken ist allerdings, dass die an Petrus anknüpfenden Schriften ein breites Spektrum aufweisen (1 Pt und *EvPt* ließen sich in einen solchen Diskurs kaum integrieren), was für die „gnostischen" Schriften (welche zu diesen zu rechnen sind, wäre eigens zu erörtern) in gleicher Weise gilt. Die Einordnung der *Petrusoffenbarung* und des 2 Pt in dieses Spektrum, ebenso wie das Verhältnis zur koptischen *Petrusapokalypse* aus Nag Hammadi, wären deshalb weiter zu präzisieren.

51. Um zwei einschlägige Beispiele zu nennen: Die *Ascensio Isaiae* ist christlichen Ursprungs, schreibt also die Offenbarung der Geburt Jesu Christi, seines Wirkens, seiner

„jüdisch" und „christlich" erweist sich deshalb gerade bei den Apokalypsen als künstlich[52]. Die christliche Fortschreibung jüdischer Apokalypsen und die Zuschreibung christlicher Schriften an jüdische Autoritäten zeigt vielmehr, dass jüdische Geschichte und jüdische Traditionen als genuiner Bestandteil der eigenen, christlichen Tradition aufgefasst wurden. Es handelt sich demnach um ein Analogiephänomen zur Autorisierung jüdischer Schriften und Corpora wie vor allem Tora und Propheten als autoritativer Zeugnisse der eigenen Geschichte im antiken Christentum.

Die Zuweisung apokalyptischer Schriften an Personen der Geschichte des frühen Christentums gehört in diesen Kontext. Die Johannesoffenbarung mag dabei einen gewissen Sonderfall bilden, jedenfalls dann, wenn es sich, wie häufig angenommen wird, um eine orthonyme Schrift handelt. Allerdings wird auch ihre Pseudonymität bis in die Gegenwart mit wichtigen Argumenten erwogen[53]. Bei der *Offenbarung des Petrus* ist dagegen, ebenso wie bei den späteren *Apokalypsen des Paulus und Thomas*, die pseudonyme Autorschaft eindeutig.

In der *Petrusoffenbarung* wird dabei, wie bereits erwähnt, der Inhalt der Vision unmittelbar mit der Geschichte Jesu verbunden. Entsprechend dem oben skizzierten narrativen Rahmen der Schrift[54] spielen dabei die apokalyptische Rede Jesu auf dem Ölberg sowie seine Verklärung eine zentrale Rolle. Die Rezeption der Evangelienüberlieferung bezieht sich vorrangig auf diese beiden Texte, wogegen aus der Jesusüberlieferung ansonsten nur wenige Traditionen begegnen, was insbesondere im Blick auf Petrusüberlieferungen verwundern mag[55].

Kreuzigung und Himmelfahrt einem Propheten der Geschichte Israels zu. Das *4. Esrabuch* ist jüdischen Ursprungs, wurde aber christlich überliefert und fortgeschrieben. Dabei hat sich eine eigene, bis ins Mittelalter reichende Rezeption Esras als Prophet und Visionär herausgebildet.

52. Vgl. BAUCKHAM, *Apocalypse of Peter* (Anm. 3), S. 171: „So far as apocalypses go, this distinction between Old Testament Pseudepigrapha and New Testament Apocrypha is wholly artificial".

53. Vgl. dazu J. FREY, *Das Corpus Johanneum und die Apokalypse des Johannes: Die Johanneslegende, die Probleme der johanneischen Verfasserschaft und die Frage nach der Pseudonymität der Apokalypse*, in S. ALKIER – T. HIEKE – T. NICKLAS (Hgg.), *Poetik und Intertextualität der Johannesapokalypse* (WUNT, 346), Tübingen, Mohr Siebeck, 2015, 71-133, S. 118-133.

54. Aufgrund des beschriebenen Verhältnisses von äthiopischem Text und Akhmîmfragment wird im Folgenden primär dem äthiopischen Text gefolgt. Dabei sind auch die beiden kürzeren griechischen Fragmente zu berücksichtigen.

55. Es hätte sich etwa angeboten, das Wort Jesu an Petrus aus Mt 16,17-19 aufzugreifen, zumal der Verfasser, wie sich noch näher zeigen wird, das MtEv gut zu kennen scheint. Das geschieht jedoch nicht, wenngleich der Verfasser hieraus die Rolle des Petrus als Offenbarungsempfänger abgeleitet haben könnte.

Gleich im ersten Satz[56] wechselt der Text aus der Perspektive des extradiegetischen Erzählers in diejenige der Jünger, die mit dem „Herrn"[57] einen Dialog über die Zeichen des Endes der Welt und seine Parusie führen. In 2.2 gibt es sodann einen weiteren Wechsel der Erzählperspektive, die nunmehr als Dialog zwischen Petrus und Jesus gestaltet ist[58]. Petrus wird damit zur zentralen Figur der Schrift und zum alleinigen Empfänger der Offenbarung, wogegen die übrigen Jünger erst in der Schlussszene wieder auftreten[59]. Auch in dieser begegnet allerdings Petrus als Ich-Erzähler (ab 16.1; Akhmîmtext, Abschnitt 12). Petrus wird demnach in besonderer Weise profiliert, was an seine Bedeutung im frühen Christentum, insbesondere an seine Rolle in den Evangelien, anschließt und diese fortschreibt.

Das Gespräch zwischen den Jüngern und Jesus wird mit der Bitte der Jünger eröffnet, die Zeichen der Parusie und des Endes der Welt zu sehen. Damit wird die entsprechende Eröffnung der eschatologischen Rede in den synoptischen Evangelien aufgegriffen, wobei die engsten Berührungen mit dem MtEv bestehen[60]. Die Begründung für die Bitte

---

56. Der Prolog wird in der Regel als nicht zum ursprünglichen Text gehörig betrachtet. Anders votiert jetzt allerdings BECK, *Justice* (Anm. 8), S. 74-77. Der Prolog lautet in der Übersetzung von H. DUENSING, *Ein Stück der urchristlichen Petrusapokalypse enthaltender Traktat der äthiopischen Pseudo-klementinischen Literatur*, in ZNW 14 (1913) 65-78, S. 66: „Wiederkunft Christi und Auferstehung der Toten, (die er Petrus erzählt hat), welche wegen ihrer Sünde sterben, weil sie das Gebot Gottes, ihres Schöpfers, nicht beobachtet haben. Und darüber dachte er nach, um zu erkennen das Geheimnis des barmherzigen und das Erbarmen liebenden Gottessohnes". Als Argument dafür kann die analoge Einführung der Johannesoffenbarung genannt werden. Zudem führt der Prolog eher in die *Petrusoffenbarung* ein als in den pseudo-klementinischen Kontext der Schrift. Schließlich würde so auch der andernfalls abrupte Beginn der Schrift besser verständlich. Betrachtet man den Prolog als ursprünglichen Bestandteil der Schrift, würden als Inhalt nicht nur das Endgericht, sondern auch das Schicksal der Sünder genannt, was für die Intention des Textes zu beachten wäre.

57. Der Auferstandene wird im äthiopischen Text als „unser Herr" (1.4) bzw. „mein Herr Jesus Christus, unser König" (15.1) bezeichnet. Der Akhmîmtext hat ebenfalls die Bezeichnung „Herr", stets als *nomen sacrum* (4; 12; 15). Der äthiopische Text weist insgesamt eine „hohe" Christologie auf, die vor allem noch in der Bezeichnung Jesu Christi als „Gott" bzw. „mein Herr und Gott" (16.1, 3; der Akhmimtext hat nur „Herr") deutlich wird.

58. Dieser Wechsel ist ein Merkmal der Schrift, das auch im Akhmîmcodex begegnet, und zwar auch beim *Petrusevangelium*. Vgl. dazu den Hinweis bei NICKLAS, *Petrusoffenbarung* (Anm. 26), S. 350 mit Anm. 13.

59. In 15.1 (Akhmîmtext, Abschnitt 4) lautet die Aufforderung des Herrn „Lasst uns auf den (heiligen) Berg gehen".

60. Die entsprechende Formulierung in Mt 24,3 lautet: Καθημένου δὲ αὐτοῦ ἐπὶ τοῦ ὄρους τῶν ἐλαιῶν προσῆλθον αὐτῷ οἱ μαθηταὶ κατ' ἰδίαν λέγοντες· εἰπὲ ἡμῖν, πότε ταῦτα ἔσται καὶ τί τὸ σημεῖον τῆς σῆς παρουσίας καὶ συντελείας τοῦ αἰῶνος; Die Beziehungen zur Eröffnungsbitte der *Petrusoffenbarung* sind offenkundig und enger als zu Mk 13,3-4 und Lk 21,7. Dort wird jeweils nach dem Zeitpunkt und dem Zeichen für

geht allerdings über die synoptischen Evangelien hinaus. Sie lautet: „damit wir erkennen und merken die Zeit deiner Parusie und die nach uns Kommenden unterweisen, denen wir das Wort deines Evangeliums predigen und die wir in deine(r) Kirche (ein)setzen, damit sie, wenn sie es hören, sich in acht nehmen, dass sie merken die Zeit deiner Parusie"[61]. Mit dem Verweis auf die Verkündigung des Evangeliums wird sowohl eine Beziehung zur Bemerkung in der eschatologischen Rede, dass vor dem Ende „allen Völkern" das Evangelium verkündet werden muss, als auch zum Auftrag des Auferstandenen am Ende des Matthäusevangeliums, alle Völker zu lehren[62], hergestellt. Allerdings wird dies in der *Petrusoffenbarung* zum einen von den Jüngern selbst formuliert, zum anderen ist nicht von der Verkündigung an alle Völker die Rede, sondern von der Unterweisung der Personen, die von ihnen in die Kirche eingesetzt werden. Durch die Intensivierung des Hinweises auf die Parusie des Herrn wird zudem die Zeit zwischen seiner Himmelfahrt und seinem Wiederkommen mit einer Warnung zur Wachsamkeit versehen. Auch dieses Thema ist in den synoptischen Evangelien und hier wiederum besonders im MtEv präsent[63].

Die Antwort Jesu auf diese Bitte führt die Bezüge auf die synoptische eschatologische Rede weiter. Die Warnung, sich nicht verführen zu lassen durch solche, die behaupten „Ich bin der Christus", hat dort eine unmittelbare Entsprechung[64], ebenso wie die Ankündigung des Kommens des Gottessohnes wie ein Blitz auf der Wolke des Himmels[65] mit

---

das Ende gefragt, bei Mt und in der *OffbPt* ist das „Zeichen" dagegen auf die Wiederkunft Jesu bezogen, außerdem ist explizit vom „Ende der Welt" (bzw. des Äons) die Rede.

61. Ich folge der Übersetzung von MÜLLER, *Neutestamentliche Apokryphen* (Anm. 2), 6. Auflage, S. 566-578, bzw. DUENSING, *Ein Stück* (Anm. 56), S. 66-74.

62. Mk 13,10; Mt 24,14; 28,20.

63. Vgl. insbesondere den unmittelbar an die eschatologische Rede anschließenden Komplex Mt 24,45–25,46. In diesem wird das Thema der Wiederkunft Jesu und der Warnung vor dem damit verbundenen Gericht in verschiedenen Gleichnissen und schließlich in der großen Rede über das Gericht des Menschensohnes ausgemalt.

64. Mt 24,4-5.11.23-24; Mk 13,5-6.21-22; Lk 21,8. Wiederum besteht die größte Nähe der *OffbPt* zum MtEv. Der Satz „Und viele werden kommen in meinem Namen, indem sie sagen: ‚Ich bin der Christus'" (*OffbPt* 1.5, MÜLLER) hat eine wörtliche Parallele in Mt 24,5: πολλοὶ γὰρ ἐλεύσονται ἐπὶ τῷ ὀνόματί μου λέγοντες· ἐγώ εἰμι ὁ χριστός.

65. *OffbPt* 1.6; vgl. Mt 24,27.30; Mk 13,26; Lk 21,27. In den synoptischen Evangelien ist stets vom Kommen des *Menschensohnes* die Rede, in der *Petrusoffenbarung* dagegen vom *Gottessohn*. Das korrespondiert mit der Rezeption der Jesusüberlieferung in Schriften des zweiten Jahrhunderts, in denen die Bezeichnung „Menschensohn" mehr und mehr in den Hintergrund tritt, vermutlich, weil ihre spezifische Bedeutung in jüdischen apokalyptischen Schriften (Daniel; Bilderreden des *Henochbuches*; *4 Esra* 13) nicht mehr verstanden wurde. Nur bei Lukas ist, wie in *OffbPt*, von *einer* Wolke die Rede. Das ist insofern bemerkenswert, als es sich um ein Zitat aus Dan 7,13 handelt, wo ebenfalls der Plural begegnet.

den Heiligen und den Engeln⁶⁶. Ausdrücklich wird betont, dass Jesus als Gottessohn kommen wird, um die Lebenden und die Toten zu richten und allen nach ihren Taten zu vergelten⁶⁷.

Am Beginn der *Petrusoffenbarung* finden sich demnach Bezüge zum Beginn der synoptischen Rede Jesu über die Endzeit sowie zur Ankündigung des Kommens des Menschensohnes. Letztere steht dort am Übergang zum Gleichnis vom Feigenbaum, das in der *Petrusoffenbarung* ebenfalls folgt. Des Weiteren wird auf das Gericht des Menschensohnes nach den Werken verwiesen, was eine direkte Parallele im MtEv besitzt. Der Verfasser hat dabei auch Bezüge auf die Ankündigung des Kommens des Menschensohnes unmittelbar vor der Verklärungserzählung der synoptischen Evangelien verarbeitet. Er hatte demnach nicht nur allgemeine Kenntnisse synoptischer Überlieferungen, sondern kannte jedenfalls das MtEv literarisch⁶⁸.

Eigene Akzente setzt der Verfasser in der Warnung, nicht Zweifler zu werden und anderen Göttern zu dienen (1.4), sowie in der Formulierung über das Gericht des Gottessohnes⁶⁹. Ersteres erklärt sich aus der Situation der *Petrusoffenbarung*, in der die Warnung vor Götzendienst eine wichtige Rolle spielte⁷⁰. Dieses Thema begegnet auch an späterer Stelle und wird dahingehend präzisiert, dass die Götzendiener sich Bilder von Katzen, Löwen, Reptilien und wilden Tieren angefertigt hatten⁷¹. Das könnte die bereits erwähnte Annahme einer Entstehung der Schrift in Ägypten (vermutlich in Alexandria) verstärken, da sich die Kritik an der Verehrung von Tieren, speziell von Katzen, auch in anderen ägyptischen Texten findet⁷².

---

66. Vgl. Mk 9,38; Mt 16,27; Lk 9,26.
67. *OffbPt* 1.7-8; vgl. Mt 16,27.
68. Vgl. BAUCKHAM, *Apocalypse of Peter* (Anm. 3), S. 176-183, insbesondere die synoptischen Gegenüberstellungen *ibid.*, S. 175-176, sowie ID., *The Two Fig Tree Parables in the Apocalypse of Peter*, in ID., *The Christian World around the New Testament: Collected Essays II* (WUNT, 386), Tübingen, Mohr Siebeck, 2017, 483-501, S. 485-486, und die Ausführungen *ibid.*, S. 487-492. Die Bezüge zum LkEv sind schwach und legen es nicht nahe, dass der Verfasser dieses hier benutzt hat. Gleiches gilt für das MkEv. Eine Analogie zu Lk findet sich im zweiten Feigenbaumgleichnis, aber auch hier sind die Beziehungen eher lose. Vgl. dazu gleich Näheres.
69. Die Formulierung „damit ich richte die Lebendigen und die Toten und jedem vergelte nach seinem Tun" (1.7-8) hat zwar eine sachliche, aber keine genaue sprachliche Parallele in Mt 16,27 (καὶ τότε ἀποδώσει ἑκάστῳ κατὰ τὴν πρᾶξιν αὐτοῦ).
70. Vgl. KRAUS, *Zur näheren Bedeutung der „Götzen(bilder)"* (Anm. 5).
71. *OffbPt* 10.5; vgl. 6.7. Der Akhmîmtext hat hier nur die allgemeine Formulierung, dass sich die Götzendiener „mit eigenen Händen hölzerne Schnitzbilder anstelle Gottes" angefertigt haben (33: οἵτινες ταῖς ἰδίαις χερσὶ ξόανα ἑαυτοῖς ἐποίησαν ἀντὶ θεοῦ).
72. Vgl. BREMMER, *First Christian Martyr Text* (Anm. 49), S. 85-86. Bremmer verweist auf die Weisheit Salomos, den *Aristeasbrief*, die *Sibyllinischen Orakel* und Philo (*ibid.*, S. 86, Anm. 46).

Ein weiteres wichtiges Thema der Schrift ist, wie bereits erwähnt, das Gericht nach den Werken[73]. Die Ausführungen hierzu werden in den weiteren Kapiteln des Eingangsteils ausgebaut, die die Scheidung der Gerechten von den Sündern (3.2) thematisieren, das kommende Gericht Gottes ankündigen und die damit verbundenen kosmischen Ereignisse schildern[74]. Anschließend verweist Jesus noch einmal auf sein Kommen auf einer glänzenden Wolke mit den Engeln Gottes und das Gericht nach dem Tun, bevor der Text in die Darstellung der Strafen im Gericht übergeht.

Der Rede Jesu an die Jünger folgen in Kapitel 2 die beiden Gleichnisse vom Feigenbaum und deren speziell an Petrus gerichtete Auslegung[75]. Der Passus beginnt mit einem einfachen Bild: Vom sprossenden Feigenbaum, dessen Zweige austreiben, sollen die Jünger lernen, dass das Ende der Welt nahe ist. Dieses Gleichnis findet sich auch in den eschatologischen Reden der synoptischen Evangelien[76], dort allerdings mit der Deutung, dass der sprossende Feigenbaum auf den nahen Sommer verweist, gefolgt von dem Hinweis auf das unmittelbar bevorstehende Vergehen von Himmel und Erde. In der *Petrusoffenbarung* erwidert Petrus dagegen, dass der Feigenbaum jedes Jahr Frucht bringt, das Gleichnis deshalb der Auslegung bedürfe. Damit verschiebt sich die Bedeutung des Gleichnisses von dem einmaligen (nämlich dem nächsten) Aufblühen des Feigenbaumes, das auf das nahe Ende verweist, auf die Frage, was dem jährlichen Aufblühen zu entnehmen sei. Die Antwort wird durch ein zweites Feigenbaumgleichnis eingeleitet, das eine Analogie in Lk 13,6-9 besitzt[77]: Ein Gartenbesitzer will einen Feigenbaum, der keine Frucht bringt, ausreißen lassen. Der Gärtner möchte sich jedoch ein weiteres Jahr um den Feigenbaum bemühen; erst wenn auch dies keinen Erfolg zeitigt, soll er ausgerissen und durch einen anderen ersetzt werden[78].

Das zweite Gleichnis wird in der *Petrusoffenbarung* durch die zweimalige rhetorische Frage Jesu an Petrus gerahmt: „Verstehst du nicht

---

73. Vgl. oben, Anm. 44.

74. Vgl. insbesondere den in Kap. 5 beschriebenen Gerichtstag, der eine Vernichtung von Himmel und Erde durch Feuerkatarakte und eine Auflösung der ganzen Schöpfung mit sich bringen wird.

75. *OffbPt* 2.1-13. Vgl. dazu BAUCKHAM, *Fig Tree Parables* (Anm. 68), S. 492-501. Zur Diskussion des äthiopischen Textes und einer Rekonstruktion eines möglichen Ursprungstextes vgl. J.V. HILLS, *Parables, Pretenders, and Prophecies: Translation and Interpretation in the Apocalypse of Peter 2*, in *RB* 98 (1991) 560-573.

76. Mk 13,28-29; Mt 24,32-33; Lk 21,29-30.

77. Für einen detaillierten Vergleich der beiden Fassungen vgl. BAUCKHAM, *Fig Tree Parables* (Anm. 68), S. 494-497. Er kommt zu dem Schluss, dass die beiden Versionen auf „independent gospel tradition" zurückzuführen seien (S. 497).

78. Die Ersetzung durch einen anderen Feigenbaum findet sich nur in der *OffbPt*, nicht im LkEv.

(bzw.: Hast du nicht begriffen), dass der Feigenbaum das Haus Israel ist?" (2.4, 7)[79]. Damit wird eine Bedeutung evoziert, die das Gleichnis auch im LkEv besitzt, nämlich den Aufruf zur Umkehr zu illustrieren, den Jesus unmittelbar zuvor formuliert hatte[80]. Das Thema der Umkehr begegnet im LkEv auch im Ruf des Täufers (Lk 3,7-9/Mt 3,7-10) sowie im Bild vom Baum und seinen Früchten (Lk 6,43-44/Mt 7,16-20; 12,33) in der Metaphorik vom unfruchtbaren Baum. Das Feigenbaumgleichnis gehört in diese Linie[81].

Der spezifische Akzent des lukanischen Gleichnisses ist die Fürsorge, die der Gärtner dem Feigenbaum angedeihen lassen will. Sein Vorschlag, den bereits mehrere Jahre unfruchtbaren Baum[82] noch ein weiteres Jahr stehenzulassen und ihn in besonderer Weise zu pflegen, damit er Frucht bringe, ist das überraschende, „extravagante" Merkmal des Gleichnisses, denn es widerspricht dem gängigen Umgang mit einem über mehrere Jahre unfruchtbaren Baum. Die Pointe des Gleichnisses liegt deshalb auf dem Bemühen um Israel, das sich der Jesusverkündigung öffnen soll. In der bei Lukas vorausgesetzten Situation hat sich dies dahingehend verändert, dass der Feigenbaum für Israel steht, das sich der Umkehr verweigert hat und dem deshalb das Gericht angekündigt wird[83]. In dieser Weise wird das Gleichnis auch in der *Petrusoffenbarung* gedeutet. Neben dem Hinweis auf die Ersetzung des Feigenbaums durch einen anderen verweist darauf der unmittelbare Übergang von der Deutung des Gleichnisses zum Auftreten der „lügnerischen Messiasse" bzw. zu einem „Lügnerischen"[84]. Das Bild vom Feigenbaum wird dabei unmittelbar mit der

---

79. Beim ersten Mal wird damit die Erklärung des zuvor erzählten Gleichnisses eingeleitet, um die Petrus gebeten hatte. Beim zweiten Mal wird zum Auftreten der lügnerischen Messiasse übergeleitet.

80. Lk 13,3: ἐὰν μὴ μετανοῆτε πάντες ὁμοίως ἀπολεῖσθε.

81. Zu nennen ist darüber hinaus die Episode der Verfluchung des unfruchtbaren Feigenbaums, die bei Lk fehlt, bei Mk und Mt dagegen im Kontext der Jerusalemer Ereignisse begegnet (Mk 11,12-14.20-21; Mt 21,18-20).

82. Bei Lk ist von drei Jahren die Rede (13,7), in der *OffbPt* werden „lange Jahre" genannt, die der Besitzer nach der Frucht sucht (2.5).

83. Bereits Lukas stellt den ausbleibenden Erfolg pointiert ans Ende und stellt damit heraus, dass die Zeit zur Umkehr an ihr Ende gelangt ist. Bei Irenäus, *Haer.* 4.36.8, wird das Gleichnis, gemeinsam mit anderen Stellen aus den Schriften des Neuen Testaments, als Beleg dafür angeführt, dass es derselbe Gott ist, der Israel seit langem durch die Propheten zur Umkehr ruft und der schließlich Jesus Christus gesandt hat, dem sich Israel verweigert hat.

84. In *OffbPt* 2.7 ist von „lügnerischen Messiassen" im Plural die Rede, bereits in 2.8 geht der Text jedoch in den Singular über („Ich bin der Christus, der ich einst in die Welt gekommen bin"). In 2.10 heißt es dann: „Dieser Lügnerische ist aber nicht Christus. Und wenn sie ihn verschmähen, wird er mit Schwertern (Dolchen) morden, und es wird viele Märtyrer geben" (DUENSING – MÜLLER [Anm. 2]).

Beschreibung der Situation am Ende der Zeit verknüpft: Die lügnerischen Messiasse werden auftreten, wenn die Zweige des Feigenbaums getrieben haben (2.7); wenn die Zweige des Feigenbaums, nämlich des Hauses Israel, treiben, werden viele zu Märtyrern werden (2.11).

Das Bild vom Feigenbaum geht demnach unmittelbar über in die Situation, die die *Offenbarung des Petrus* voraussetzt. Diese ist offenbar gekennzeichnet von Verfolgungen der Jesusnachfolger, die dabei zu Märtyrern werden[85]. Die Situation von Martyrium, Abfall vom Glauben und Götzendienst begegnet auch anderweitig in der *Petrusoffenbarung* und ist für die zeitliche und lokale Einordnung der Schrift von grundlegender Bedeutung. Für die bereits erwähnte Lokalisierung in Palästina im Kontext des Bar Kochba-Aufstandes durch Bauckham ist die hiesige Passage deshalb wichtig, weil er den „Lügnerischen" mit Bar Kochba identifiziert[86]. Dem wurde allerdings vor allem von Eibert Tigchelaar mit guten Gründen widersprochen[87]. Zunächst ist der äthiopische Text, der in der genannten Passage zwischen Singular und Plural wechselt, nicht eindeutig genug, um eine solche Identifikation zu tragen[88]. Des Weiteren ist die Aussage, dass „viele" Christen Märtyrer werden, kaum mit dem Wirken Bar Kochbas in Verbindung zu bringen. Schließlich ist die Beschreibung des Auftretens des falschen Messias (bzw. der falschen Messiasse) mit traditionellen Motiven und Termini durchsetzt und erlaubt es kaum, auf die spezifische Situation des Bar Kochba-Aufstands bezogen zu werden. Gemeinsam mit den bereits genannten Aspekten, die auf einen ägyptischen Ursprung verweisen, ist eine Entstehung in Alexandria deshalb die näherliegende Annahme.

---

85. „Märtyrer" ist hier offenbar als eine Bezeichnung für diejenigen verstanden, die wegen ihres Bekenntnisses zu Tode kommen. Es handelt sich demnach um eine der frühesten Verwendungen der Bezeichnung in dieser Bedeutung, gewissermaßen als Titel. Vgl. BREMMER, *First Christian Martyr Text* (Anm. 49), S. 77-78. Bremmer verweist dort auf eine Korrespondenz mit Alessandrio Bausi über den äthiopischen Ausdruck für „Märtyrer" (*samā't*), der als Übersetzungsterminus des griechischen μάρτυς verwendet werde. Analoges gelte für den arabischen Text, aus dem der äthiopische Text wahrscheinlich übersetzt wurde. Es kann deshalb davon ausgegangen werden, dass in der griechischen Vorlage der Terminus μάρτυς stand.

86. Die Annahme findet sich bereits bei WEINEL, *Neutestamentliche Apokryphen* (Anm. 2), S. 317.

87. E. TIGCHELAAR, *Is the Liar Bar Kokhba? Considering the Date and Provenance of the Greek (Ethiopic) Apocalypse of Peter*, in BREMMER – CZACHESZ, *Apocalypse of Peter* (Anm. 7), 63-77.

88. Ob überhaupt an eine konkrete Figur gedacht ist, mag offenbleiben. NICKLAS, *Petrusoffenbarung* (Anm. 26), S. 359, erwägt eine Anspielung an einen römischen Kaiser, zumal mit dem „Sohn im Hades" (14.4, im Text von P.Vindob. G 39756) offensichtlich auf Nero angespielt wird. Er konzediert aber, dass eine eindeutige Identifizierung zum Verständnis des Textes nicht notwendig sei (*ibid.*, S. 358).

Das Austreiben der Zweige hat in der *Petrusoffenbarung* eine eigene, von den synoptischen Evangelien verschiedene und konkreter auf die aktuelle Situation bezogene Bedeutung. Da es mit dem Auftreten der lügnerischen Messiasse und dem Sterben der Märtyrer in Zusammenhang gebracht wird, ist es zugleich mit negativen Wirkungen für die Jesusanhänger verbunden. Das könnte auf die Situation in Alexandria nach dem Krieg der Jahre 115-117 hinweisen, in dessen Folge sich die Christen stärker von den Juden distanzierten.[89]

Das Bild vom Feigenbaum wird vom Verfasser der *Petrusoffenbarung* demnach in eigener, die neutestamentlichen Feigenbaumgleichnisse in kreativer Weise aufgreifender Form verwendet und auf die eigene Situation bezogen. Diese ist offenbar durch eine Abgrenzung gegenüber dem Judentum und die Möglichkeit des Martyriums gekennzeichnet. In dieser Lage versichert die *Petrusoffenbarung* den Jesusnachfolgern, dass die „Märtyrer" im kommenden Gericht zu den Guten und Gerechten gezählt und gerettet werden, wogegen die Abgefallenen vernichtet werden.

Der Bezug auf die synoptische Verklärungsszene[90] im letzten Teil der *Petrusoffenbarung* bot sich von daher an, als sie, ebenso wie die eschatologische Rede Jesu und die Abschiedsszene einschließlich der Himmelfahrt[91], auf einem Berg lokalisiert ist. Zudem trägt die Verklärungserzählung deutliche Züge einer Theophanie[92] und legte sich auch von daher für die Gestaltung als Abschiedsszene nahe. Bei der Rezeption der Verklärungserzählung besteht des Weiteren eine interessante Verbindung zwischen der *Petrusoffenbarung* und dem Zweiten Petrusbrief, die auf einer Rezeption des matthäischen Textes basiert[93]. In beiden Fällen ist die Verklärung auf dem „Heiligen Berg" lokalisiert[94], die Gottesstimme

---

89. Zum Aufstand unter Trajan und den Folgen vgl. A.M. SCHWEMER, *Zum Abbruch des jüdischen Lebens in Alexandria – Der Aufstand in der Diaspora unter Trajan (115-117)*, in T. GEORGES – F. ALBRECHT – R. FELDMEIER (Hgg.), *Alexandria* (Civitatum Orbis MEditerranei Studia, 1), Tübingen, Mohr Siebeck, 2013, 381-399. Zur *Petrusoffenbarung* in Alexandria vgl. NICKLAS, *Jewish, Christian, Greek?* (Anm. 5); ID., *Petrus-Diskurse* (Anm. 29), S. 105-108, sowie BREMMER, *First Christian Martyr Text* (Anm. 49).

90. Mk 9,2-9; Mt 17,1-9; Lk 9,28-37.

91. Lk 24,50-52; vgl. Apg 1,6-12.

92. Dazu gehören die Verwandlung Jesu in eine göttliche Gestalt, die Erscheinung von Mose und Elia, die Himmelsstimme aus der Wolke, die Furcht der Jünger, die mit der Aufforderung Jesu, sich nicht zu fürchten, beantwortet wird (Mt 17,6-7). Bei Matthäus sind die theophanen Züge am deutlichsten ausgearbeitet, wie die Verse 6 und 7 zeigen.

93. Zum Vergleich beider Versionen der Verklärungserzählung mit dem synoptischen Befund vgl. GRÜNSTÄUDL, *Petrus Alexandrinus* (Anm. 28), S. 113-123. Besonders wichtig ist die Beobachtung, dass 2 Pt nur dort vom synoptischen Befund abweicht, wo er mit *OffbPt* übereinstimmt.

94. Bei Mk und Mt ist von einem „hohen Berg" die Rede, bei Lk nur von einem „Berg". Wie oben (Anm. 15) erwähnt, nennt der Akhmîmtext ebenfalls nur einen „Berg".

kommt direkt vom Himmel und nicht aus einer Wolke, es wird der Empfang von „Ehre und Herrlichkeit" erwähnt[95]. Die Verklärung Christi spielt demnach für die Rezeption des Petrus im Zweiten Petrusbrief und der *Petrusoffenbarung* eine wichtige Rolle. In der *Petrusoffenbarung* hat sie jedoch noch eine weiterreichende Funktion.

Die in Kapitel 15 einsetzende Schlussszene schildert zunächst die Erscheinung von zwei Männern, die nach ihrer ausführlichen Beschreibung als theophane Gestalten als Mose und Elia identifiziert werden[96]. Auf die Nachfrage von Petrus sehen die Jünger auch die „Scharen der Väter" im Paradiesgarten. Das aus der synoptischen Überlieferung übernommene Ansinnen des Petrus, drei Hütten zu bauen, wird von Jesus mit dem Verweis darauf, dass der himmlische Vater ihm und den Erwählten Hütten nicht von Menschenhand gemacht habe, brüsk zurückgewiesen. Es folgt die Schilderung des geöffneten Himmels, in den Jesus, Mose und Elia hineingehen. Die Verklärungserzählung markiert demnach in der *Petrusoffenbarung* den Abschluss der irdischen Zeit Jesu und zugleich den Übergang in seine himmlische Existenz. Zugleich wird auf diese Weise eine Verbindung zu seiner Rolle als kommender Richter hergestellt, die im Eingangsteil ausführlich dargestellt worden war.

Abschließend sei ein noch kurzer Blick auf die Rezeption der Figur des Petrus in der *Petrusoffenbarung* geworfen[97]. Entscheidende Aspekte des hier begegnenden Petrusbildes sind seine Funktion als Dialogpartner des Auferstandenen in der Endzeitrede und der Verklärungsepisode sowie seine herausgehobene Rolle als Offenbarungsempfänger. Sowohl in der Eingangs- als auch in der Schlussszene tritt Petrus auf diese Weise aus der Gruppe der Jünger hervor. Neben der Autorität des Petrus im frühen Christentum allgemein dürfte dabei speziell die Aussage Jesu, Petrus sei vom Vater im Himmel offenbart worden, dass er der Christus und Sohn des lebendigen Gottes ist (Mt 16,17), im Hintergrund stehen.

Schließlich begegnet in der *Petrusoffenbarung* auch die Weissagung des Todes des Petrus. In Kapitel 14[98] wird den Berufenen und Auserwählten

---

95. 2 Pt 1,17: Jesus empfing von Gott τιμὴ καὶ δόξα; *OffbPt* 16.5: die um der Gerechtigkeit willen verfolgt wurden, empfangen Ehre und Herrlichkeit.

96. Im Akhmîmtext (13) werden anstelle von Mose und Elia „eure gerechten Brüder" genannt. Die anschließende Schilderung des Paradiesgartens ist im Akhmîmtext deutlich ausführlicher als in der äthiopischen Fassung. Vgl. dazu sowie zu Vergleich der Verklärungsepisode im Akhmîmtext mit der äthiopischen Fassung NICKLAS, *„Our Righteous Brethren"* (Anm. 5).

97. Vgl. dazu auch die Beobachtungen von NICKLAS, *Petrusoffenbarung* (Anm. 26), S. 353-354.

98. Die Rekonstruktion dieses Abschnitts ist mit Hilfe von P.Vindob. G 39756 vorzunehmen. Vgl. oben, Anm. 45, sowie BECK, *Justice* (Anm. 8), S. 85-88. Ob dabei die

die „Rettung aus dem Acherusischen See ... im Elysischen Feld" verheißen[99]. Kurz darauf wird Petrus angewiesen, in die Stadt zu gehen, die über den Westen herrscht und den Kelch zu trinken, „den ich dir verheißen habe in der Hand des Sohnes im Hades". Die Stelle ist deshalb bemerkenswert, weil der Verfasser hier über die synoptische Überlieferung, speziell über das von ihm vor allem verwendete MtEv, hinausgeht. Die Metapher vom Trinken des Kelches wird in der Gethsemaneszene der synoptischen Evangelien verwendet[100] und in der *Petrusoffenbarung* auf das dem Verfasser offensichtlich bekannte Martyrium des Petrus in Rom bezogen[101]. Auf den Tod des Petrus wird im Neuen Testament jedoch nur in Joh 21,18-19 Bezug genommen. In der *Petrusoffenbarung* steht jedoch vermutlich nicht diese Stelle, sondern die frühchristliche Tradition über den Tod des Petrus[102] allgemein im Hintergrund.

III. SCHLUSS

Die Verarbeitung von Evangelienüberlieferungen ist ein zentrales Merkmal der *Petrusoffenbarung*, das sie von allen anderen frühchristlichen Apokalypsen unterscheidet. Die Verbindung dieser Überlieferungen ermöglicht es, den Ort dieses Textes innerhalb der frühchristlichen Literatur- und Theologiegeschichte zu präzisieren. Wie gesehen, hat der Verfasser

---

Wendung „Ich werde den Berufenen und Auserwählten den gewähren, den sie aus der Strafe erbitten" dem griechischen Original entspricht und auf eine interzessorische Funktion der Märtyrer schließen lässt (diese Annahme spielt bei Beck eine wichtige Rolle und findet sich auch bei Nicklas und Bremmer), erscheint mir fraglich, und zwar auch dann, wenn die Lesart ὃν ἐὰν ἐτήσωνταί με ἐκ τῆς κολάσεως (Z. 4-6) die ursprüngliche ist (was nach Auskunft von Kraus – Nicklas und van Minnen der Fall ist). VAN MINNEN, *Greek Apocalypse* (Anm. 11), S. 31, hat m.E. zu Recht darauf hingewiesen, dass diese Lesart offensichtlich auf einem Schreibfehler beruht und „completely out of tune with the rest of the text" ist, wogegen nur die Lesart ὃ ἐὰν ἐτήσωνταί με innerhalb der *OffbPt* Sinn ergibt.

99. Übersetzung nach KRAUS – NICKLAS, *Petrusevangelium* (Anm. 4), S. 128.
100. Mk 14,36; Mt 26,39; Lk 22,42. Zur Verwendung der Metapher in weiteren Texten des frühen Christentums vgl. BREMMER, *First Christian Martyr Text* (Anm. 49), S. 83-85, besonders S. 84.
101. Zur Analyse der Passage vgl. T. NICKLAS, *„Drink the Cup Which I Promised You!"* (Anm. 5), S. 184-193. Auf Rom deutet der Hinweis auf „die Stadt, die über den Westen herrscht" (14.4: πορεύου εἰς πόλιν ἀρχούσαν δύσεως) sowie auf den „Sohn im Hades", offenbar ein Verweis auf Nero.
102. Vgl. dazu R. BAUCKHAM, *The Martyrdom of Peter in Early Christian Literature*, in ID., *The Christian World around the New Testament* (Anm. 68), 265-323. Bauckham bespricht die verschiedenen Zeugnisse über den Tod des Petrus, u.a. Joh 13,36-38 und 21,18-19 sowie ausführlich *1 Clem.* 5.4; *AscJes* 4.2-3 und *OffbPt* 14.4-6 (letzteres *ibid.*, S. 297-304).

literarische Kenntnis des MtEv, kennt darüber hinaus aber auch andere Überlieferungen mit synoptischen Analogien. Damit ist die *Petrusoffenbarung* ein Zeugnis für den auch anderweitig bezeugten Befund, dass das MtEv im zweiten Jahrhundert weit verbreitet war und häufig verwendet wurde.

Die Rezeption der Evangelienüberlieferung in der *Petrusoffenbarung* bezieht sich vor allem auf zwei Textbereiche: die eschatologische Rede Jesu auf dem Ölberg sowie die Verklärungserzählung. Daneben begegnen einige weitere Traditionen, die offenbar nicht auf literarische Vermittlung, sondern auf freie, unabhängige Überlieferung zurückzuführen sind. Dazu gehören vor allem das zweite Feigenbaumgleichnis, das einer mit Lk 13,6-9 verwandten Überlieferung entstammt, sowie die Tradition vom Tod des Petrus in Rom. Die *Petrusoffenbarung* gehört damit zu denjenigen Schriften des zweiten Jahrhunderts, die bereits in den Evangelien verschriftlichte Überlieferungen gemeinsam mit weiteren Traditionen in Form einer kreativen „Neuinszenierung" verarbeitet haben[103].

Die Aufnahme der Evangelienüberlieferungen dient in der *Petrusoffenbarung* dazu, die Vision von der Bestrafung der Sünder und der Belohnung der Berufenen und Auserwählten, die ausdrücklich als „Märtyrer" bezeichnet werden, mit dem Wirken Jesu zu verbinden. In einer Vision vom endzeitlichen Gericht werden Petrus die Strafen für diejenigen offenbart, die die Gerechten verfolgen, die Märtyrer töten und Götzen anbeten[104]. Zugleich wird den Gerechten das endzeitliche Heil zugesagt. Die Präsentation der Endzeitereignisse als letzte Rede Jesu vor seiner Himmelfahrt führt dabei dazu, dass die aufgenommenen Evangelientraditionen in einer gegenüber den synoptischen Evangelien deutlich erweiterten und veränderten Form begegnen. Das betrifft sowohl die Eingangsszene auf dem Ölberg als auch die Schlussszene auf dem Zion.

Verschiedene Merkmale des Textes legen eine Entstehung im Alexandria des zweiten Jahrhunderts nahe. Zugleich lässt sich eine enge Verwandtschaft mit dem Zweiten Petrusbrief feststellen. Beide Texte könnten in einen Diskurs des alexandrinischen Christentums des zweiten Jahrhunderts gehören, den sie in je eigener Weise beleuchten. Ein sie

---

103. Den m.E. sehr treffenden Ausdruck „Neuinszenierung" oder auch „kreative Neuschöpfung" für die Verwendung von Jesusüberlieferungen in apokryphen Texten des zweiten und dritten Jahrhunderts übernehme ich von T. Nicklas. Vgl. z.B. T. NICKLAS, *Zwischen Redaktion und „Neuinszenierung": Vom Umgang erzählender Evangelien des 2. Jahrhunderts mit ihren Vorlagen*, in J. SCHRÖTER – T. NICKLAS – J. VERHEYDEN (Hgg.), *Gospels and Gospel Traditions in the Second Century: Experiments in Reception* (BZNW, 235), Berlin – Boston, MA, De Gruyter, 2019, 311-330.

104. Vgl. dazu BREMMER, *The Apocalypse of Peter: Place, Date and Punishments* (Anm. 6).

verbindendes Merkmal ist dabei die Orientierung an der Figur des Petrus, die in beiden Schriften eine wichtige Rolle spielt. Die *Petrusoffenbarung* gehört deshalb in einen Kreis von Schriften mit dem Zweiten Petrusbrief und der koptischen *Petrusapokalypse* aus Nag Hammadi, die auf die Rezeption des Petrus als Autoritätsfigur im antiken Christentum verweisen. Es wäre lohnend, diese Zeugnisse in einer Untersuchung über Petrus im antiken Christentum auszuwerten[105].

Humboldt-Universität zu Berlin Jens SCHRÖTER
Theologische Fakultät
Lehrstuhl für Neues Testament
und antike christliche Apokryphen
Unter den Linden 6
DE-10099 Berlin
Deutschland
schroetj@hu-berlin.de

---

105. M. BOCKMUEHL hat eine Studie vorgelegt, auf der dabei aufgebaut werden kann. Vgl. ID., *The Remembered Peter in Ancient Reception and Modern Debate* (WUNT, 262), Tübingen, Mohr Siebeck, 2010. Vgl. weiter J. LIEU (Hg.), *Peter in the Early Church* (BETL, 325), Leuven – Paris – Bristol, CT, Peeters, 2021. Dieser Band enthält die Vorträge, die 2019 beim 68. Colloquium Biblicum Lovaniense gehalten wurden.

REREADING GOSPEL TRADITIONS IN THE *ACTS OF THECLA*

THE DILEMMA OF THE BEATITUDES

> To Jos Verheyden, an erudite scholar, a critical thinker from whom I have learnt so much (though not enough), a kind and thoughtful man to whom I am deeply indebted.

The *Acts of Paul and Thecla* [*APTh*] promote an ascetic-encratic[1] way of life, connecting eschatological salvation to sexual continence. At the beginning of the Iconian episode, Paul preaches the word of God about continence (ἐγκράτεια) and resurrection (3.5), developed in a series of beatitudes. The eclectic Greek text edited by Richard Lipsius[2] has thirteen macarisms (3.5-6), which quite clearly draw on the Sermon on the Mount. The apostle, solemnly preaching the word of God in macarisms,

---

1. I understand encratism as a form of asceticism that involves rejecting sexuality and marriage. See C. MARKSCHIES, *Das antike Christentum: Frömmigkeit, Lebensformen, Institutionen*, München, Beck, 2006, pp. 160-161; N. KOLTUN-FROMM, *Encratism/Encratites*, in D.G. HUNTER – P.J.J. VAN GEEST – B.J. LIETAERT PEERBOLTE (eds.), *Brill Encyclopedia of Early Christianity Online*, 2018, http://dx.doi.org/10.1163/2589-7993_EECO_SIM_00001065. I argue that the *APTh* promote a strict asceticism and regard sexual continence as a precondition of eternal salvation. Beside the beatitudes, in 3.17, Paul associates ἀκαθαρσία and pleasure with sin, death and corruption. T.H.C. VAN EIJK, *Marriage and Virginity, Death and Immortality*, in J. FONTAINE – C. KANNENGIESSER (eds.), *Epektasis: Mélanges patristiques offerts au Cardinal Jean Daniélou*, Paris, Beauchesne, 1972, 209-235, p. 212; G. SFAMENI GASPARRO, *Gli Atti apocrifi degli Apostoli e la tradizione dell'enkrateia: Discussione di una recente formula interpretativa*, in *Augustinianum* 23 (1983) 287-307; on sexual continence as precondition of the resurrection: A. JENSEN, *Thekla – die Apostolin: Ein apokrypher Text neu entdeckt*, Freiburg i.Br. – Basel – Wien, Herder, 1995, p. 28, n. 35; P.J. LALLEMAN, *The Resurrection in the Acts of Paul*, in J.N. BREMMER, *The Apocryphal Acts of Paul and Thecla* (Studies on the Apocryphal Acts of the Apostles, 2), Kampen, Kok Pharos, 1996, 126-141, pp. 130-131. *Pace* Y. TISSOT, *Encratism and the Apocryphal Acts*, in A. GREGORY – C. TUCKETT (eds.), *The Oxford Handbook of Early Christian Apocrypha*, Oxford, OUP, 2015, 407-423, pp. 414-415; S. HYLEN, *A Modest Apostle: Thecla and the History of Women in the Early Church*, Oxford, OUP, 2015, p. 85.

2. R.A. LIPSIUS – M. BONNET (eds.), *Acta Apostolorum Apocrypha*. Vol. 1: *Acta Petri – Acta Pauli – Acta Petri et Pauli – Acta Pauli et Theclae – Acta Thaddaei*, Leipzig, Hermann Mendelssohn, 1891, pp. 238-239. L. VOUAUX preserves the same text: *Les Actes de Paul et ses lettres apocryphes*, Paris, Letouzey & Ané, 1913, pp. 154, 156, 158. In their translations, J.K. ELLIOTT, *The Apocryphal New Testament: A Collection of Apocryphal Christian Literature in an English Translation*, Oxford, Clarendon, 1993, p. 365, and R.A. PERVO, *The Acts of Paul: A New Translation with Introduction and Commentary*, Cambridge, James Clarke, 2014, p. 4, keep all thirteen beatitudes. J. BARRIER keeps only twelve beatitudes, *The Acts of Paul and Thecla* (WUNT, 270), Tübingen, Mohr Siebeck, 2009, p. 82, an issue to which I shall return in this paper. The critical edition prepared by Willy Rordorf, Pierre Cherix and Peter W. Dunn for the CCSA has not yet appeared.

evokes Jesus introducing his teaching with the programmatic eight beatitudes[3]. Two beatitudes preserved in the Greek manuscript tradition evoke the Gospel of Matthew. The first, on the pure in heart who shall see God, repeats Mt 5,8. The twelfth, on the merciful who shall find mercy, comes from Mt 5,7. The apodosis of the latter is expanded with the promise of eschatological salvation: the merciful shall not see the bitter day of judgement (καὶ οὐκ ὄψονται ἡμέραν κρίσεως πικράν). In addition, the beatitudes have several intertextual references to 1 Corinthians 6 and 7 and some allusions to other gospel traditions.

This paper reassesses the evidence for the reception of the Sermon on the Mount, focusing on the two Matthean beatitudes. For this purpose, I re-examine the evidence provided by the Greek manuscripts, attempting to respond to the question whether gospel traditions were found indeed in the early / "original" Greek text of the beatitudes. Then, to place the question in a broader context, I briefly discuss the (contested) reception of Matthew in the second century, looking for some circumstantial evidence. At the end I review the possible explanations for the lack of Mt 5,7 in a few manuscripts and formulate some conclusions.

I. The Beatitudes: An Ascetic Programme with Matthean References

The beatitudes have an essential function in the *APTh*, as they set the theological-ethical programme of the writing[4]. The series opens with the

---

3. A. Merz, *Die fiktive Selbstauslegung des Paulus: Intertextuelle Studien zur Intention und Rezeption der Pastoralbriefe* (NTOA, 52), Göttingen, Vandenhoeck & Ruprecht, 2004, pp. 326-327; see p. 329, n. 216 (Merz points out the intertextual links with the Sermon on the Mount, which authorise the beatitudes and create a sense of conformity with the teaching of Jesus). The *APTh* assimilate Paul to Jesus in other ways as well, most conspicuously in 3.21. See Pervo, *The Acts of Paul* (n. 2), pp. 65, 100, 102; T. Nicklas, *No Death of Paul in Acts of Paul and Thecla?*, in A. Puig i Tàrrech – J.M.G. Barclay – J. Frey (with O. McFarland) (eds.), *The Last Years of Paul: Essays from the Tarragona Conference, June 2013* (WUNT, 352), Tübingen, Mohr Siebeck, 2015, 333-342, pp. 339-340.

4. For the interpretation of the beatitudes: Merz, *Selbstauslegung* (n. 3), pp. 320-333; M. Ebner, *Paulinische Seligpreisungen à la Thekla: Narrative Relecture der Makarismenreihe in ActThecl 5f.*, in Id., *Aus Liebe zu Paulus? Die Akte Thekla neu aufgerollt* (SBS, 206), Stuttgart, Katholisches Bibelwerk, 2005, 64-79; J.W. Barrier, *The Acts of Paul and Thecla* (WUNT, 2.270), Tübingen, Mohr Siebeck, 2009, pp. 82-85; Id., *Asceticism in the Acts of Paul and Thecla's Beatitudes: The Coptic Heidelberg Papyrus as an Exegetical Test Case*, in H.-U. Weidemann (ed.) – E.A. Clark (introduction), *Asceticism and Exegesis in Early Christianity: The Reception of New Testament Texts in Ancient Ascetic Discourses* (NTOA, 101), Göttingen, Vandenhoeck & Ruprecht, 2013, 163-185; Pervo, *The Acts of Paul* (n. 2), pp. 101-106; T. Nicklas, *Christliche Apokryphen als Spiegel der Vielfalt frühchristlichen Lebens: Schlaglichter, Beispiele und methodische*

praise of the pure in heart. The author thus replaces the macarism of the poor and borrows from Matthew the assertion that suits best the ascetic agenda of the *APTh*. It is no longer the poor (in spirit), but the pure to enjoy a special relationship with God. Just as in Matthew (and in Q/Luke), the first beatitude has a programmatic function. The meaning of the pure heart is illuminated by the following beatitudes[5]. Read in the context, the "pure in heart" are not (simply) the morally irreproachable, whose ethical acts are manifestations of a person's moral integrity (a pure heart/mind). In a work that endorses sexual continence, and in the light of the subsequent beatitudes (notably B2-B5 and B13), the pure in heart are the chaste and continent. Purity is understood as a quality of the body, as (sexual) continence (ἐγκράτεια), as abandoning this world and marital intercourse. From a pure heart comes the chastity of the flesh (B2: οἱ ἁγνὴν τὴν σάρκαν τηρήσαντες)[6]. The pure, those who preserve their chastity will enter in a privileged relationship with God: they shall see God (B1) and they shall become the temple of God (B2[7]). God will speak to the self-restrained (οἱ ἐγκρατεῖς, B3)[8]. Those who forsake this world (B4, a possible allusion to 1 Cor 7,31) and have a wife, but live as if they had none (B5, cf. 1 Cor 7,29) will be pleasing to God[9] and will inherit

---

Probleme, in *ASE* 23 (2006) 27-44; P. HERCZEG, *New Testament Parallels to the Apocryphal Acta Pauli Documents*, in J.N. BREMMER, *The Apocryphal Acts of Paul and Thecla* (Studies on the Apocryphal Acts of the Apostles, 2), Kampen, Kok Pharos, 1996, 142-149, pp. 147-148; K. ZAMFIR, *Asceticism and Otherworlds in the Acts of Paul and Thecla*, in T. NICKLAS – J. VERHEYDEN – E.M.M. EYNIKEL – F. GARCÍA MARTÍNEZ (eds.), *Other Worlds and Their Relation to This World: Early Jewish and Ancient Christian Traditions* (SupplJSJ, 143), Leiden, Brill, 2010, 281-303.

5. The procedure is comparable to that of Q/Luke and Matthew. Q/Luke addresses the destitute, and the second and third expand on it (the poor hunger and weep). All three macarisms proclaim the reversal of the fate of the poor. In the spiritualised reading of Matthew, the poor in spirit are the pious, qualified by further ethical qualities (meek, merciful, pure in heart, peacemakers).

6. F adds the purity of the heart; LIPSIUS – BONNET, *Acta Apostolorum Apocrypha*, 1 (n. 2), p. 238. On the Greek witnesses of the *APTh*, see the third section of this paper, "The Evidence from the Greek Manuscripts".

7. A Pauline idiom, cf. 1 Cor 3,16; 2 Cor 6,16; and 1 Cor 6,19, where "your body" is called the temple of the Holy Spirit. Some Latin translations spiritualise the macarism (*lb*: *anima eorum templa dei erunt*), while others make it more conform to 1 Cor 6,19 (*lcc*: *templum Sancti Spiritus efficientur*). VOUAUX, *Actes* (n. 2), p. 156, n. 1. On the Latin translations: O. VON GEBHARDT, *Die lateinischen Übersetzungen der Acta Pauli et Theclae, nebst Fragmenten, Auszügen und Beilagen* (TU, 22), Leipzig, Hinrichs, 1902; J. KAESTLI, *Les Actes de Paul et Thècle latins: Édition de la version A et de sa réécriture dans le manuscrit de Dublin, Trinity College, 174*, in *Apocrypha* 27 (2016) 9-110.

8. Some Latin manuscripts (*lc*) make it more explicit: *Beati qui abstinuerint se ab omni immunditia*. VOUAUX, *Actes* (n. 2), p. 156, n. 2

9. The selected reading is found in A B G. C E F I K L M have εὐθεῖς κληθήσονται. LIPSIUS – BONNET, *Acta Apostolorum Apocrypha*, 1 (n. 2), p. 238; VOUAUX, *Actes* (n. 2), p. 56, n. 3.

God (probably an allusion to Mt 5,5 and 1 Cor 6,9-10). The inheritance will be God, not the earth (promised to the meek in Mt 5,5) or the kingdom of God (as in 1 Corinthians)[10].

Fearing God[11] and trembling at the word(s) of God[12] (B6-7) has a central place in the list. (The two parallel beatitudes explain each other.) While awe before the divine is a frequently-praised attitude, and, in principle, the sentences could be read as a praise of the pious, in the context, these beatitudes gain a more specific meaning. Trembling at the λόγια τοῦ θεοῦ recalls the introductory λόγος θεοῦ περὶ ἐγκρατείας καὶ ἀναστάσεως (3.5). The words of God remind thus of the relationship between sexual continence, addressed up to this point, and eschatological salvation, promised in B11-13. Those fearing God will become angels of God[13]. The apodosis evokes and surpasses the promise in Mk 12,25. Mark speaks of those living in marriage who will no longer have conjugal relations in the afterlife and will be *like* the angels in heaven. According to the *APTh*, those who give up marriage experience angelism already in this life; in the resurrection they become downright angels of God. Those trembling at the word(s) of God shall be comforted (παρακληθήσονται, see Mt 5,4).

The following three beatitudes seem more loosely connected to the rest of the series. B8 and B10 are essentially synonymous[14]: those receiving the wisdom/understanding of Christ shall be called sons of the Most High (υἱοὶ ὑψίστου κληθήσονται, cf. Mt 5,9, υἱοὶ θεοῦ κληθήσονται, of the peacemakers), and shall be in the light. The two enclose the beatitude of those preserving baptism, who shall find rest by the Father and the Son[15]. Beside the illuminating effect of wisdom and knowledge, being in the light (B10) may also allude to baptism[16], and perhaps to eschatological

---

10. Κληρονομήσουσιν τὸν θεόν evokes nonetheless the apodosis of the beatitude of the meek. Two Syriac mss. (*a* and *c*) and the Latin *la* harmonise the apodosis with Matthew: they will inherit the earth. M has instead βασιλεία τοῦ Χριστοῦ. VOUAUX, *Actes* (n. 2), p. 156, n. 4.

11. E F I K read Χριστοῦ (fear Christ). VOUAUX, *Actes* (n. 2), p. 156, n. 5.

12. E C and *lcd* omit this beatitude, whereas M expands the protasis (καὶ φυλάσσοντες αὐτοῦ τὰς ἐντολάς). VOUAUX, *Actes* (n. 2), p. 156, n. 7.

13. M combines the apodoses of B5 and B6 (ὅτι κληρονομήσουσιν τὸν θεὸν καὶ ἄγγελοι θεοῦ γενήσονται), while E has κληθήσονται, they shall be *called* angels of God (VOUAUX, *Actes* [n. 2], p. 156, nn. 6-7).

14. Unsurprisingly, G switches the order of B8 and B9 and parallels receiving the wisdom of Christ and opening up to the understanding of Christ. C omits B8. VOUAUX, *Actes* (n. 2), p. 156, n. 8.

15. F G and M read "preserving the baptism pure", καθαρόν; M is much longer. See VOUAUX, *Actes* (n. 2), p. 157, n. 9. Purity chimes in with B1.

16. Justin associates baptism, knowledge (ἐπιστήμη) and light (illumination). C.I.K. STORY, *Justin's Apology I,62-64: Its Importance for the Author's Treatment of*

salvation. Receiving the wisdom and knowledge of Christ is not theoretical; it involves a way of life confirmed in baptism. Baptism has a central place in the narrative. As the story of Thecla shows, baptism is not self-evident. It is a reward to the pure, who have preserved their chastity. In the context, keeping baptismal fidelity/purity most likely involves postbaptismal sexual continence[17].

Beatitudes 11 and 12 refer to eschatological salvation; they describe heavenly glorification (ἀγγέλους κρινοῦσιν καὶ ἐν δεξιᾷ τοῦ πατρὸς εὐλογηθήσονται) and escaping judgement (οὐκ ὄψονται ἡμέραν κρίσεως πικράν). Eschatological exaltation rewards those who have left the form of this world[18]. Superiority to angels matches and supersedes B6 (judging angels evokes 1 Cor 6,3). B12 speaks of the reward of the merciful, who will find divine mercy and will not see the bitter day of judgement. The second part of the apodosis explains the first: finding mercy means escaping eternal judgement.

The concluding beatitude has a particular form and a very long apodosis. While all previous beatitudes address persons with a specific merit, B13 speaks of virginity as the quality of the body (τὰ σώματα τῶν παρθένων). The recompense is fourfold: they will be pleasing to God (cf. also B4), they will not miss the reward of their purity (ἁγνεία; cf. B2), the word of God (which they feared, B6) shall be to them a work of salvation of the day of the Son (certainly, the day of judgement, see B12), and they will find eternal rest (cf. B9). Through its distinct form and its links to the previous beatitudes, and its developed apodosis, this final

---

Christian Baptism, in *VC* 16 (1962) 172-178. On the association between baptism and light/fire in the baptism of Thecla: H.J.W. DRIJVERS – G.J. REININK, *Taufe und Licht: Tatian, Ebionäerevangelium und Thomasakten*, in T. BAARDA et al. (eds.), *Text and Testimony: Essays on New Testament and Apocryphal Literature in Honour of A.F.J. Klijn*, Kampen, Kok, 1988, 91-110, p. 94.

17. The interpretation is supported by the variant readings mentioned above. Y. TISSOT, *Encratisme et Actes Apocryphes*, in F. BOVON et al., *Les Actes Apocryphes des Apôtres: Christianisme et monde païen*, Geneva, Labor & Fides, 1981, 109-119, p. 113, referring to Hippolytus, Tertullian and Aphrahat; K. NIEDERWIMMER, *Askese und Mysterium: Über Ehe, Ehescheidung und Eheverzicht in den Anfängen des christlichen Glaubens* (FRLANT, 113), Göttingen, Vandenhoeck & Ruprecht, 1975, pp. 176-186. Giving up conjugal relations after baptism is common in the apocryphal acts (*Acts Thom.* 9–15, 87–103; compare *Acts Andr.* 13–16 and *Acts John* 63, after conversion. See also H.-J. KLAUCK, *Apokryphe Apostelakten*, Stuttgart, Katholisches Bibelwerk, 2005, pp. 66-67; E.M. HOWE, *Interpretations of Paul in the Acts of Paul and Thecla*, in D.A. HAGNER – M.J. HARRIS (eds.), *Pauline Studies: Essays Presented to Professor F.F. Bruce on his 70th Birthday*, Grand Rapids, MI, Eerdmans, 1980, 33-49, pp. 41-42; A.C. RUSH, *Death as Spiritual Marriage: Individual and Ecclesial Eschatology*, in *VC* 26 (1972) 81-101, p. 91.

18. τὸ σχῆμα τοῦ κοσμικοῦ evokes 1 Cor 7,31 (the ephemeral character of τὸ σχῆμα τοῦ κόσμου τούτου). Some manuscripts adopt the latter form.

beatitude summarises the meaning of the series, making it clear that Paul is exhorting sexual continence.

This overview concerns the Greek text of Lipsius and Vouaux, which contains clear quotations of Matthew, and a few other minor allusions. However, the issue is not so straightforward. On the one hand, the number and text of the beatitudes varies in the manuscript tradition (some beatitudes are not found in a number of witnesses). In addition, as we shall see, the Coptic translation, preserved in an early textual witness, omits (at least) one of the two quotations from Matthew.

II. How Many Beatitudes? And Where Is Matthew?

Already the number of the beatitudes in the Greek text seems peculiar, as usually religious texts employ symbolically significant figures[19]. The issue is further complicated by the fact that the Coptic translation and a few Greek manuscripts have different numbers of beatitudes. The fragmentary Coptic Heidelberg papyrus (P.Heid., Cop[1], 6th cent.)[20], which antedates the codices used to reconstruct the Greek text, lacks the Matthean beatitude of the merciful (B12 in the Greek text of Lipsius)[21]. This beatitude is also omitted in some Greek codices[22]. Therefore, Jeremy Barrier does not include this beatitude in his edition of the *APTh*[23].

These observations could suggest that originally the number of beatitudes may have been smaller. In fact, Barrier argues that the Coptic papyrus, which predates the Greek manuscripts by several centuries, not only lacked Mt 5,7 (B12), but most probably did not include the first beatitude

---

19. E.g. 3, 4, 7, 10, 12, or their multiples. In the New Testament there are four beatitudes in Luke, eight in Matthew, seven letters in Revelation, etc. Four, seven and twelve are particularly relevant in Revelation 21. Thirteen appears 14 times in the Hebrew Bible (Gen 17,25; Num 29,13.14; Jos 19,6; 21,4.6.19.33; 1 Kgs 7,1; 1 Chr 6,60.62; 26,11; Ez 40,11). As a number of a calendar unit, 13th is found some more times in the Old Testament, and as a number of items in lists. As numeral, thirteen does not occur in the New Testament. It may be the number of items on vice lists, as in Mk 7,21-22, if one takes οἱ διαλογισμοὶ οἱ κακοί as an umbrella term for the following items.

20. C. Schmidt, *Acta Pauli aus der Heidelberger koptischen Papyrushandschrift Nr. 1*, Leipzig, Hinrichs, 1904; Id., *Acta Pauli: Übersetzung, Untersuchungen und koptischer Text*, Leipzig, Hinrichs, 1905, pp. 5*-6*.

21. Schmidt, *Acta Pauli: Übersetzung* (n. 20), p. 30; Barrier, *Asceticism* (n. 4), p. 169.

22. Lipsius – Bonnet, *Acta Apostolorum Apocrypha*, 1 (n. 2), p. 239 mentions G I (on the translations and mss.: *Acta Apostolorum Apocrypha*, 1, pp. xcix-cvi). Schmidt, *Acta Pauli* (n. 20), p. 30, notes that the mss. A B G I omit it in accordance with the Coptic. In fact, A B do not omit B12, but connect the second part of the apodosis to the previous macarism. Rightly, Vouaux, *Actes* (n. 2), p. 158, n. 4.

23. *Acts* (n. 4), p. 82, with explanation on p. 83, n. 8.

(Mt 5,8), either[24]. (These would have been added by later scribes, to mitigate the encratism of the original text and make the *APTh* more palatable in orthodox circles, by proposing a moderate asceticism[25].) He reaches this conclusion after attempting to reconstruct the missing lines on leaf 4v of Cop[1] (16, as estimated by Schmidt, uncertain according to Barrier), retranslating the Greek text of B1 into Coptic. Barrier speaks of "Greek recensions"[26], suggesting that the Coptic translation reflects an earlier and more original Greek text, which quite probably had no citations from Matthew at all[27]. But other early translations, like the Syriac and the Armenian[28], preserve both Matthean beatitudes. The Syriac translation[29] published by William Wright is based on four manuscripts, of which one is from the sixth century[30]. The translation has all beatitudes, with some rephrasing. B12 reads "Blessed are the merciful, for mercy shall be upon them from God, and on the Day of Judgment they shall receive the Kingdom", with a variant reading adding "and they shall not see the bitter day"[31]. The evidence from the Latin translations is not

---

24. *Asceticism* (n. 4), pp. 165, 168-170. Barrier assumes that one more beatitude was absent in the Coptic (in the missing portion), either the first (the quote from Mt 5,8, misprinted as 5,7) or the fifth, which relies on 1 Cor 7,29.

25. *Ibid.*, pp. 176-178.

26. *Ibid.*, p. 165.

27. *Ibid.*, pp. 170, 178. Preferring the Coptic translation to the Greek extant text reflects the assumption that the Coptic is a faithful rendering of a more original Greek text. The issue is not so obvious, as translations are often rather free renderings of the Greek. See, e.g., the early Syriac translations: C. BURRIS, *The Reception of the Acts of Thecla in Syriac Christianity: Translation, Collection, and Reception*, Dissertation University of North Carolina, Chapel Hill, NC, 2010, pp. 44-45.

28. F.C. CONYBEARE, *The Armenian Apology and Acts of Apollonius and Other Monuments of Early Christianity*, New York, Macmillan, 1896, p. 64. V. CALZOLARI, *Apocrypha Armeniaca*. Vol. 1: *Acta Pauli et Theclae, Prodigia Theclae, Martyrium Pauli* (CCSA, 20), Turnhout, Brepols, 2017, pp. 192-204, lists and describes 26 manuscripts of *APTh* in Armenian, dating from the twelfth to the nineteenth century. The earliest witnesses are three manuscripts dated to the twelfth century. Calzolari's critical edition includes both the quotation of Mt 5,8 ("Blessed those who are pure of heart, for they will see God", p. 248) and that of Mt 5,7 ("Blessed the merciful, for they will find mercy when seeing the Father, and on the day of judgement they will receive the kingdom", p. 254).

29. W. WRIGHT, *Apocryphal Acts of the Apostles Edited from Syriac Manuscripts in the British Museum and Other Libraries*, London, Williams & Norgate, 1871, vol. 1, pp. 128-169: Syriac text; vol. 2, pp. 116-145: English translation; the beatitudes: pp. 118-119.

30. Mss. British Library Add. 14,652 (A, 6th cent.), 14,447 (B, a 10th-cent. fragment), 14,641 (C, 10th/11th cent.); 12,174 (D, 12th cent.). WRIGHT, *Apocryphal Acts* (n. 29), vol. 1, p. xiii, notes that A is significantly older than the Greek mss. used by Tischendorf. More recently used manuscripts are Mss. Deir al-Surian 28 (6th cent.); Deir al-Surian 27 (8th cent.); Mount Sinai Syr. 30 (8th cent.). C. BURRIS – L. VAN ROMPAY, *Thecla in Syriac Christianity: Preliminary Observations*, in *Hugoye: Journal of Syriac Studies* 5 (2002) 225-236; BURRIS, *Reception* (n. 27), pp. 1-5.

31. WRIGHT, *Apocryphal Acts* (n. 29), vol. 2, p. 119 (D).

necessarily relevant, as they probably rely on medieval Greek manuscripts, but it is worth mentioning that all manuscripts preserve the beatitude of the merciful[32].

Barrier's argument for the lack of Mt 5,8 is "the scarcity of quotations of 'New Testament' scripture this early in the history of early Christianity" and the view that "there are no clear instances of Matthew or 1 Corinthians being cited in the *APTh*"[33]. While in principle it is indeed possible that one or more beatitudes were missing in the Coptic, there are some difficulties with the argument. Leaving aside the fact that it is hard to know the number of missing lines (several reconstructions of the lacunae are possible, based on comparable numbers of lines on the preserved pages), the retranslation adds to the uncertainty (a fact he indeed acknowledges). But more problematic seems to be the circular argument, which denies a New Testament citation because of the paucity of New Testament citations.

The question about the reception of Mt 5,7-8 in the beatitudes cannot be answered with certainty, as there are no Greek manuscripts earlier than, or at least contemporary with, the Cop[1] [34]. Any reconstruction of the

---

32. GEBHARDT, *Die lateinischen Übersetzungen* (n. 7), pp. 16-17.

33. BARRIER, *Asceticism* (n. 4), p. 170: "the possibility that one of the first six beatitudes may not have been part of the list of beatitudes that have been preserved in the Greek textual transmission. […] I would propose that either beatitude 1 (which is Matthew 5:7) or beatitude 5 (which quotes 1 Cor 7:29) are the two most likely candidates. I suggest these two as the most likely candidates due to the scarcity of quotations of 'New Testament' scripture this early in the history of early Christianity. If this is the case, we have already reduced the number of beatitudes from 13 down to 12 through mere observation, and then again to a possible 11, if one assumes that Cop[1] leaves out Matthew or 1 Corinthians. I am suggesting that Cop[1] may have been lacking one or both of these particular beatitudes because there are no clear instances of Matthew or 1 Corinthians being cited in the *APTh*".

34. The fourth-fifth-century fragmentary papyri (P.Ant. I 13, Oxford, Sackler Library; P.Oxy. 6), from Egyptian miniature codices, are not helpful, as they contain only short fragments from *APTh* 3.2 and 3.8-9, respectively. For P.Ant. I 13, see C.H. ROBERTS, *The Antinoopolis Papyri*, 1, London, The Egypt Exploration Society, 1950, pp. 26-28; K. HAINES-ETZEN, *The Apocryphal Acts of the Apostles on Papyrus: Revisiting the Question of Readership and Audience*, in T. KRAUS – T. NICKLAS (eds.), *New Testament Manuscripts: Their Texts and Their World* (TENTS, 2), Leiden, Brill, 2006, 293-304, pp. 302-304. Image on the site of the North American Society for the Study of Christian Apocryphal Literature [NASSCAL]: https://www.nasscal.com/e-clavis-christian-apocrypha/acts-of-paul-and-thecla/. For P.Oxy. 6, see B.P. GRENFELL – A.S. HUNT, *The Oxyrhynchus Papyri*, Part 1, London, Egypt Exploration Society, 1898, p. 9. P.Yale 87/P.CtYBR 1376 (4th/5th cent.) may also come from the *APTh* (O. ZWIERLEIN, *Petrus und Paulus in Jerusalem und Rom: Vom Neuen Testament zu den apokryphen Apostelakten*, Berlin – Boston, MA, De Gruyter, 2013, p. 170; see Yale Library: https://findit-uat.library.yale.edu/catalog/digcoll:2758255. The oldest witness, the third-century Fackelmann papyrus (MS 2634/1), is a tiny fragment from Egypt (*APTh* 3.10-11 and 13): Münster Bibelmuseum, P.Schoyen. MS. 2634.1 (Fackelmann 3); https://www.schoyencollection.com/apocryphal-literature/acts-paul-thecla-ms-2634-1;

"original" Greek text of the beatitudes is tentative. However, two lines of continued examination may lead to a provisional answer. On the one hand, re-examining the available Greek manuscripts may point to the tendencies in quoting or omitting one or both Matthean beatitudes. On the other hand, a glance at contemporary sources may show whether "Matthew" was used in the second century.

III. The Evidence from the Greek Manuscripts

The Greek text is edited from mainly tenth-twelfth-century codices. I will discuss them here in some detail, adding links to the digitised manuscripts, because the evidence they provide is relevant to the main question of this paper, the reception of Mt 5,7-8 in the beatitudes.

The first edition of the *APTh* was published by Johann Ernst Grabe in 1698[35] based on the Codex Barocci 180 (11th/12th cent., G in Lipsius)[36]. Constantin von Tischendorf[37] used codices Parisinus gr. 520 (A, 10th/11th cent.)[38], 1454 (B, 10th cent.)[39], 1468 (C, 11th cent.)[40]. To these Lipsius added several other manuscripts: Vaticanus gr. 797 (E, 11th cent.)[41], Vaticanus gr. 866 (F, 11th/12th cent.)[42], Oxon. miscell. gr. 77

M. Gronewald, *Einige Fackelmann-Papyri*, in ZPE 28 (1978) 271-277, pp. 274-275; Haines-Etzen, *Apocryphal Acts*, pp. 301-302.

35. J.E. Grabius, *Spicilegium Ss. Patrum, ut et haereticorum, seculi post Christum natum I. II. & III.*, 1, Oxford, E Theatro Sheldoniano, 1698, ²1700, pp. 81-120, with a Latin translation; the beatitudes on pp. 96-97.

36. Bodleian Library, Barocci 180, fols. 34r-42v, description at NASSCAL, https://www.nasscal.com/manuscripta-apocryphorum/oxford-bodleian-library-barocci-180/. Ms. at DigitalBodleian: https://digital.bodleian.ox.ac.uk/objects/b20e3418-795f-4463-a9a1-76fd060101cd/surfaces/dc293790-dcb9-4230-ae9a-656719d252b3/.

37. C. Tischendorf, *Acta Apostolorum Apocrypha*, Leipzig, Avenarius & Mendelssohn, 1851, pp. xxv-xxvi.

38. Bibliothèque nationale de France [BNF], gr. 520, pp. 39-50; description at NASSCAL, https://www.nasscal.com/manuscripta-apocryphorum/paris-bibliotheque-nationale-de-france-gr-520/ (T. Burke, 2020); link to the digitised manuscript on Gallica (site of the Bibliothèque nationale de France). The beatitudes are found at https://gallica.bnf.fr/ark:/12148/btv1b107225803/f28.item.

39. BNF, gr. 1454, fols. 72r-77v; see NASSCAL, https://www.nasscal.com/manuscripta-apocryphorum/paris-bibliotheque-nationale-de-france-gr-1454/. Ms. on Gallica: https://gallica.bnf.fr/ark:/12148/btv1b10722471r/f77.item.r=1454.zoom.

40. BNF, gr. 1468, fols. 38v-44v; see NASSCAL, https://www.nasscal.com/manuscripta-apocryphorum/paris-bibliotheque-nationale-de-france-gr-1468/; link to the beatitudes on Gallica: https://gallica.bnf.fr/ark:/12148/btv1b107218498/f46.item.zoom.

41. Biblioteca Apostolica Vaticana [BAV], Vat. gr. 797, fols. 94v-105, not yet digitised.

42. BAV, Vat. gr. 866, fols. 27r-30r; see NASSCAL, https://www.nasscal.com/manuscripta-apocryphorum/vatican-biblioteca-apostolica-vaticana-vat-gr-866/, with link to the digitised manuscript on DigiVatLib: https://digi.vatlib.it/view/MSS_Vat.gr.866.

(H, 12th cent.)[43], Parisinus gr. 1506 (I, 11th cent.)[44], Parisinus gr. 769 (K, 13th cent.)[45], Palatinus Vaticanus 68 (L, 13th cent.)[46] and Vaticanus gr. 1190 (M, 1542)[47]. Lipsius regarded E I K L the most reliable.

Several other manuscripts are known today[48]. These include Ohrid, Naroden Muzej, 4 (10th cent.)[49], Mount Sinai gr. 497 (10/11th cent.)[50] and gr. 526 (10th cent.)[51], Jerusalem, Hagios Saba 259 (11th cent.)[52], Milan (Ambrosiana) F 144 sup. (Martini-Bassi 377, 10/11th cent.)[53], Dublin, Trinity College Ms. 185 (early 11th cent.)[54], Rome, Angel. gr. 108

---

43. Earlier Huntingdoni, cf. LIPSIUS – BONNET, *Acta Apostolorum Apocrypha*, 1 (n. 2), C). I could not identify the ms. in the Catalogue of Western manuscripts at the Bodleian Libraries and selected Oxford colleges (incomplete).

44. In the Menologion (September) copied by a monk Antonius: BNF, gr. 1506, https://gallica.bnf.fr/ark:/12148/btv1b10722114g/f71.item.zoom.

45. BNF, gr. 769, https://gallica.bnf.fr/ark:/12148/btv1b10723790m/f149.item.zoom. The beatitudes are found at https://gallica.bnf.fr/ark:/12148/btv1b10723790m/f150.item.zoom.

46. BAV, Pal. gr. 068, fols. 81-87v; the beatitudes at https://digi.vatlib.it/view/MSS_Pal.gr.68.

47. BAV, Vat. gr. 1190, fols. 1215r-1228r (1542, Crete), description at NASSCAL (T. Burke, 2019), https://www.nasscal.com/manuscripta-apocryphorum/vatican-biblioteca-apostolica-vaticana-vat-gr-1190/; ms. on DigiVatLib: https://digi.vatlib.it/view/MSS_Vat.gr.1190.pt.3.

48. See NASSCAL, https://www.nasscal.com/e-clavis-christian-apocrypha/acts-of-paul-and-thecla/ and Biblissima, https://portail.biblissima.fr/fr/ark:/43093/oedata-43e05386a6a8d5477c123f2a27f2846298a1e8a0. I did not have access to the non-digitised mss. listed on Biblissima, notably those in Greece, Russia and Poland.

49. Ohrid, Naroden Muzej, 4, description at NASSCAL: https://www.nasscal.com/manuscripta-apocryphorum/ohrid-naroden-muzej-4/; ms. on the website of G.G. Mitrevski (Professor emeritus, Auburn University): http://pelister.org/manuscripts/pdf/NMOM4-76.pdf. The codex is damaged, but the text is clear.

50. Mount Sinai, Monastery of Saint Catherine, gr. 497, fols. 80v-87v (10th/11th cent.), description on the site of NASSCAL, https://www.nasscal.com/manuscripta-apocryphorum/mount-sinai-mone-tes-hagias-aikaterines-gr-497/; ms. at the Library of Congress: https://www.loc.gov/resource/amedmonastery.00279381798-ms/?sp=86&r=0.309,0.126,0.233,0.159,0. The Mount Sinai ms. gr. 519, 10th cent. (Greek Manuscripts 519. Menologion Sept.-Feb., Library of Congress, fols. 29-34, https://www.loc.gov/resource/amedmonastery.00279380538-ms/?sp=32&r=0.151,0.457,0.828,0.34,0) is damaged at the lower part of the page, but as far as it can be seen, it also has B12.

51. Greek Manuscripts 526 (Panegyrics), fols. 33v-42.; Library of Congress, https://www.loc.gov/item/00279380617-ms/.

52. Jerusalem, Πατριαρχικὴ Βιβλιοθήκη, Hagios Saba 259 (from Vavlas, Cyprus, copied by a monk Gerasimos), fols. 247r-256v, description at NASSCAL, https://www.nasscal.com/manuscripta-apocryphorum/jerusalem-patriarchike-bibliotheke-hagios-saba-259/, with link to the ms.: Library of Congress, https://www.loc.gov/resource/amedmonastery.0027939432A-jo/?sp=251&r=0.194,0.044,0.902,0.37,0.

53. Biblioteca Ambrosiana, F 144 sup. (Martini – Bassi 377), fols. 20r-25r (10th/11th cent.), description at NASSCAL, https://www.nasscal.com/manuscripta-apocryphorum/milan-biblioteca-ambrosiana-f-144-sup/, with link to the digitised ms.: http://213.21.172.25/0b02da828009aa17.

54. Homiliary. IE TCD MS 185, fols. 30-39: https://digitalcollections.tcd.ie/concern/works/g445ck42s?locale=en.

(11th/12th cent.)[55], Vat. gr. 544 (11th cent.)[56]; Vat. Chig. R. VI. 39 (12th cent.)[57] and others[58].

To examine the reception of Mt 5,7 and 5,8, I have investigated 19 digitised manuscripts: most of those mentioned by Lipsius (with two exceptions, E and H, for which I have relied on Lipsius), all the other manuscripts listed on the site of NASSCAL and three more recorded on Biblissima. This adds up to 21 Greek manuscripts, some clearly representing different areas. In all Greek manuscripts, the beatitudes are introduced with that of the pure in heart (B1, cf. Mt 5,8). The reception of Mt 5,7 (the merciful) is less straightforward. This beatitude does not occur in three manuscripts from the eleventh-twelfth century: ms. Barocci 180 (G), Par. gr. 1506 (I), and most likely in Vat. gr. 544. Rescue from the bitter day of judgement is connected to the long apodosis of the previous beatitude (B11, on those who leave this world out of love of God: ἐν δεξιᾷ τοῦ πατρὸς εὐλογηθήσονται καὶ οὐκ ὄψονται ἡμέραν κρίσεως πικράν). In this sense, these manuscripts preserve a Greek text that comes close to the Coptic in P.Heid. It is interesting, nonetheless, that in E (Par. gr. 1506) there is a visible gap in the middle of the line between the end of B11 and the last beatitude (the body of the virgins)[59], not seen anywhere else on the page (or on the adjacent pages). Since the space does not indicate the beginning of a new section, it may suggest (awareness of) an omission.

Fourteen codices ranging from the tenth to the sixteenth century (the bulk from the eleventh-twelfth century) include both Matthean beatitudes in the same way as in the Lipsius-edition: Mount Sinai mss. gr. 497, gr. 526

---

55. Biblioteca Angelica, gr. 108 (B 2.2), fols. 22v-29v, description on the site of NASSCAL (T. Burke, 2019): https://www.nasscal.com/manuscripta-apocryphorum/rome-biblioteca-angelica-gr-108-b-2-2/; link to the ms.: Cataloghi e collezioni digitali delle biblioteche Italiane, http://www.internetculturale.it/jmms/iccuviewer/iccu.jsp?id=oai%3Awww.internetculturale.sbn.it%2FTeca%3A20%3ANT0000%3ACNMD%5C%5C0000151457. F. BOVON – B. BOUVIER, *Miracles additionnels de Thècle dans le manuscrit de Rome, Angelicus graecus 108*, in *Apocrypha* 24 (2013) 91-110.

56. BAV, Vat. gr. 544 (a palimpsest, the *APTh* in underwriting, fols. 97, 194, 1, 32, 39, 46, 43, 34; in overwriting the homilies of Chrysostom to John, twelfth century, description at NASSCAL: https://www.nasscal.com/manuscripta-apocryphorum/vatican-biblioteca-apostolica-vaticana-vat-gr-544/; link to the ms. on DigiVatLib: https://digi.vatlib.it/view/MSS_Vat.gr.544. The beatitudes on fols. 97v and 194r.

57. BAV, Chig. R. VI. 39, fols. 42v-50r, description at NASSCAL (T. Burke, 2019): https://www.nasscal.com/manuscripta-apocryphorum/vatican-biblioteca-apostolica-vaticana-chig-r-vi-39/, with link to the ms. on DigiVatLib: https://digi.vatlib.it/view/MSS_Chig.R.VI.39.

58. *Acta Pauli et Theclae* (grec) at Biblissima.

59. BNF, Gr. 1506, p. 64, on Gallica: https://gallica.bnf.fr/ark:/12148/btv1b10722114g/f72.item.zoom.

and gr. 519 (most likely), the Ambrosiana F 144 sup. (Martini-Bassi 377), the Jerusalem Hagios Saba 259, the Trinity College Ms. 185, Vat. gr. 797 (E), Vat. gr. 866 (F), Angel. gr. 108, Oxon. miscell. gr. 77 (H), Vat. Chig. R. VI. 39, Par. gr. 769 (K), Pal. Vat. 68 (L) and Vat. gr. 1190 (M). The Mount Sinai manuscripts are the earliest (10th/11th cent.). The provenance of most manuscripts is unknown, with a few exceptions: Hagios Saba 259 stems from Cyprus and Vat. gr. 1190 from Crete. The Mount Sinai manuscripts are probably of Egyptian origin.

Four further manuscripts (of unknown provenance) also include both beatitudes, but with some particularities. In three codices – Ohrid, Naroden Muzej, 4, Par. gr. 520 (A) and Par. gr. 1454 (B) – the second part of the apodosis of B12 (καὶ οὐκ ὄψονται ἡμέραν κρίσεως πικράν) is attached to the long apodosis of B11, which means that the macarism of the merciful appears exactly in the Matthean form, without additions. (All these manuscripts are relatively early, from the tenth or the eleventh century at the latest.) In Par. gr. 1468 (C), the beatitude from Mt 5,7 stands alone, followed by the second apodosis (οὐκ ὄψονται ἡμέραν κρίσεως πικράν), which is individualised as a full sentence. These particularities seem to point to a certain independence of the citation from Mt 5,7. (To be sure, in C, which omits B7, B8, B10, B11, keeping only nine beatitudes, B12 is present.)

In sum, of the 21 Greek manuscripts only three lack the beatitude of the merciful. The earliest available witnesses, the Mount Sinai manuscripts and the two Paris-codices (A B), all cite Mt 5,7. Obviously, numbers are not enough to make the point. It would be important to know the provenance of all the manuscripts and their relationship. A multiple attestation in unrelated manuscripts would confirm the wide reception of Mt 5,7. It would also be useful to examine further witnesses that could not be included in this study. What is clear, though, is that no witness omits Mt 5,8, and Mt 5,7 is a rather well-established quote.

The reception of the *APTh* in the fifth-century *Life and Miracles of Saint Thecla* may also provide some sense of the earlier Greek text[60]. The writing retells the story of Thecla, to focus subsequently on the miracles performed at her shrine in Seleucia. The *Life* is a quite free rewriting of the *APTh*, strongly shaped by the doctrinal concerns of the time. Both Paul and Thecla are envisaged as teachers of Nicene and Chalcedonian

---

60. G. DAGRON – M. DUPRÉ LA TOUR, *Vie et miracles de sainte Thècle: Texte grec, traduction et commentaire* (Subsidia hagiographica, 62), Bruxelles, Société des bollandistes, 1978. See also PG 85 (1864), cols. 477-560, 561-618, which prints the 1608 Antwerp edition of Pierre Pantin; here col. 484. S.F. JOHNSON, *The Life and Miracles of Thekla: A Literary Study* (Hellenic Studies Series, 13), Washington, DC, Center for Hellenic Studies, 2006.

Christology and of orthodox trinitarian doctrine. The writing also reflects a shift with respect to marriage: while virginity continues to be the ideal way of life, marriage is treated as a respectable institution, grounded in the divine economy of creation. The speech of Paul in the house of Onesiphorus is much longer, and reflects a strong theological interest, underscoring the reality of the incarnation and its ethical consequences. Instead of enumerating the beatitudes, as in the *APTh*, the author imbedded them in this elaborate speech, paraphrasing and expanding them. Yet, the speech preserves the key ideas and notions of the beatitudes from the *APTh*, even when sometimes designated with different terms. Thus, the first beatitude preserves the connection between purity and the vision of God, although with a different wording. Blessed (μακάριστος) and a contemplator of God (θεοῦ θεωρός) is the one whose soul is pure (εἰλικρινή, ἀμιγή) and free from evils that trouble humans (a free rendering of B1). Blessed is the one who does not deliver his/her body (σάρξ) to shameful pleasures (cf. the protasis of B2), the one who lives a pure and blameless life (καθαρός, ἀκηλίδωτος). The beatitude of those who live in marriage is new and replaces B5. Blessed are those concerned with the reverence and fear of God (viz. B6-B7), with the purity of their soul and body, and virginity (echoing B13), and endeavouring to live the life of angels on earth, those who preserve the grace of baptism (cf. B9), those who care about the destitute and will receive equal mercy (ἔλεος) from God (cf. B12). While there are many differences, the train of thought is largely similar, underscoring the importance of inner purity, purity of the body, including virginity, living as angels, baptismal fidelity and mercy. This latter aspect is the most relevant, as it speaks of God returning mercy on those who are compassionate themselves, a rewording of B12, which, in its turn, relies on Mt 5,7.

The manuscripts of the *Life* come from the tenth-twelfth century[61]; they are thus roughly contemporary with those of the *APTh*. Yet, given the differences between the speech of Paul in the *APTh* and in the *Life*, I find it highly unlikely that the copyists of the latter would have wanted to harmonise the beatitudes with those in the *APTh*, adding an echo of Mt 5,7, which was not found in the original text of the *Life*. The paraphrase of B12 seems to belong to the text of the *Life* itself. If so, it reflects a Greek version of the *APTh* available to Basil of Seleucia in the fifth century, which had the reference to Mt 5,7.

---

61. The earliest is Vat. gr. 1853 (U), a palimpsest whose underwriting dates to the tenth century. Further mss. belonging to the Σ-group are Vat. gr. 796 (11th/12th cent.) and Par. suppl. gr. 240 (11th cent.). DAGRON, *Vie* (n. 60), pp. 141, 166.

IV. Was Matthew Known in the Second Century?

The possible influence of Mt 5,7-8 on the *APTh* is related to the broader question about the reception of Matthew in the second century. As noted, J. Barrier has argued that the beatitude of the pure in heart was probably missing in Cop[1], because "New Testament" citations were scarce at this time. To be sure, the issue with the *APTh* is not to identify possible quotations or allusions to the gospels, as in the case of other contemporary writings. B1 and B12 agree verbatim with two beatitudes of the Sermon on the Mount. The question is whether these quotes, or at least one of them, belonged to the text of the beatitudes from the beginning. However, surveying the reception of Matthew in the second century has certain indirect relevance.

The question of citations or allusions to writings that were to become part of the New Testament is a complicated and controversial matter, fraught with objective and methodological difficulties[62]. I will not discuss here the methodological approaches and responses to this question over the last century[63]. I will only survey some instances that suggest the

---

62. A.F. Gregory and C.M. Tuckett draw attention to the difficulties in establishing references to the New Testament in the Apostolic Fathers. Firstly, we do not know in which form the writings that later became part of the New Testament were available to early Christian writers. Secondly, it is uncertain how accurately the text of the Apostolic Fathers themselves has been transmitted. Methodological issues – e.g., with regard to identifying a citation or allusion, the way to determine whether an author refers to a written gospel, its earlier literary sources, collections of sayings or oral traditions preceding the gospel or circulating in parallel – are also complicated. See their *Reflections on Method: What Constitutes the Use of the Writings That Later Formed the New Testament in the Apostolic Fathers*, in A.F. Gregory – C.M. Tuckett (eds.), *The New Testament and the Apostolic Fathers*. Vol. 1: *The Reception of the New Testament in the Apostolic Fathers*, Oxford, OUP, 2005, 61-82. The Synoptic Gospels coexisted with earlier oral traditions, as well as traditions generated by the written gospels during their transmission, and harmonisations of the gospel material were produced (C.M. Tuckett, *The Didache and the Writings That Later Formed the New Testament*, in the same volume, 83-127, p. 88; H. Koester, *Gospels and Gospel Traditions in the Second Century*, in A.F. Gregory – C.M. Tuckett [eds.], *The New Testament and the Apostolic Fathers*. Vol. 2: *Trajectories through the New Testament and the Apostolic Fathers*, Oxford, OUP, 2005, 27-44, p. 32).

63. For an overview of the history of research and the main tendencies: Gregory – Tuckett, *Reflections* (n. 62), pp. 70-78; S.E. Young, *Jesus Tradition in the Apostolic Fathers: Their Explicit Appeals to the Words of Jesus in Light of Orality Studies* (WUNT, 311), Tübingen, Mohr Siebeck, 2011, pp. 36-69, and the introduction to the papers on each of the Apostolic Fathers in Gregory – Tuckett, *The New Testament and the Apostolic Fathers*, 1 (n. 62). The tendency today is to point to oral traditions rather than to dependence on written gospels. For a brief summary of allusions to, and citations of, Matthew (and 1 Corinthians) in the Apostolic Fathers: B.M. Metzger, *The Canon of the New Testament: Its Origin, Development, and Significance*, Oxford, Clarendon, 1987, pp. 40-73. See also C. Markschies, *Haupteinleitung*, in Id. – J. Schröter (eds.), *Antike christliche Apokryphen*

reception of Matthew and/or oral or written gospel traditions related to the two Matthean beatitudes (5,7 and 5,8) in the Apostolic Fathers and other second-century writings roughly contemporary with the *APTh*[64]. Obviously, even if we can establish with some certainty that an author has used "Matthew", this does not necessarily mean that the *APTh* have done so, too. But it can at least suggest that "Matthew" was known and could be used in that period.

In its landmark 1905 assessment, the Oxford Committee of the Society of Historical Theology was rather hesitant with respect to the use of Matthew (or other gospels), suggesting instead that the Apostolic Fathers may have been familiar with oral or written gospel traditions[65]. With respect to the beatitudes, the first saying in *1 Clem.* 13.2 was thought to come close to Mt 5,7, but the Committee was leaning towards the assumption that Clement was citing from a written or oral Roman "Catechesis" possibly predating the gospels[66]. Mt 5,8 was not mentioned.

The ensuing research oscillated between optimism (Édouard Massaux) and scepticism (Helmut Köster), but the proximity of *1 Clem.* 13.2 and Pol. *Phil.* 2.3a to gospel traditions close to Mt 5,7 was a recurring topic. In his extensive evaluation of the reception of Matthew, Massaux mentioned the (possibly mediated) use of Mt 5,7 in these two passages[67]. Köster argued instead that *1 Clem.* 13.2 was drawing from an oral collection of logia or a local oral catechism, rather than echoing Matthew (a view resembling the position of the Oxford Committee). He believed that

---

in deutscher Übersetzung. Bd. 1: *Evangelien und Verwandtes*, Teilbd. 1, Tübingen, Mohr Siebeck, 2012, 1-180, pp. 38-47.

64. The *APTh* were probably completed in the second half or the last decades of the second century. E. HENNECKE – W. SCHNEEMELCHER (eds.), *Neutestamentliche Apokryphen in deutscher Übersetzung*. Bd. 2: *Apostolisches, Apokalypsen und Verwandtes*, Tübingen, Mohr Siebeck, ³1964, p. 241 (ca. 185-195); KLAUCK, *Apokryphe Apostelakten* (n. 17), p. 64 (ca. 170-180); BARRIER, *Acts* (n. 4). They probably include earlier traditions: D.R. MACDONALD, *The Legend and the Apostle: The Battle for Paul in Story and Canon*, Philadelphia, PA, Westminster, 1983, p. 69.

65. A Committee of the Oxford Society of Historical Theology, *The New Testament in the Apostolic Fathers*, Oxford, Clarendon, 1905, establishing a high degree of probability (B) for Ignatius (pp. 76-77, 79), a reliance on traditions of the Sermon on the Mount in Polycarp (p. 102), but a lower degree of probability (C) for *Hermas* and *2 Clement* (pp. 119, 130, 137). Conversely, the Committee was pretty confident about the use of 1 Corinthians, another pre-text of the beatitudes in the *APTh* (A): certainty for Clement, p. 40, for Ignatius, pp. 64, 67, and Polycarp, pp. 94-95, 137, and a high degree of probability (B) for *Hermas* (p. 105).

66. *The New Testament in the Apostolic Fathers* (n. 65), pp. 58-59, 61.

67. É. MASSAUX, *Influence de l'Évangile de saint Matthieu sur la littérature chrétienne avant saint Irénée* (BETL, 75), Leuven, LUP – Peeters, 1986 (reprint of the 1950-edition with an introduction by F. Neirynck and a bibliography covering the period between 1950-1985 by B. Dehandschutter), pp. 9-13, 166.

while Pol. *Phil.* 2.3a relied on *1 Clem.* 13.2, Polycarp knew Matthew, but used it from memory[68]. Wolf-Dietrich Köhler came closer to Massaux regarding the early reception of Matthew[69], but found the use of Mt 5,7 in *1 Clement* and Polycarp unlikely. (Besides, Köhler was the first to note that the beatitudes in the *APTh* quote Mt 5,7-8[70].) More recently, Andrew Gregory re-examined the evidence for the reception of Matthew in *1 Clement* and reached a similar conclusion as the Oxford Committee a hundred years earlier[71]. With respect to Polycarp, in spite of a number of similarities with the synoptics, and Matthew in particular, Michael W. Holmes argues that the use of the Synoptic Gospels cannot be proved or disproved, and the similarities may be explained by oral traditions. For the beatitudes in Pol. *Phil.* 2.3a and 2.3b, he assumes an oral "sermon material"[72]. The evidence is thus ambivalent, as neither Clement, nor Polycarp provides a clear quotation, but a gospel tradition close to Mt 5,7 is obvious. A better case can be made for Polycarp's knowledge of Matthew.

Others have reached similar, cautiously positive conclusions about the reception of Matthew in the Apostolic Fathers and other second-century writers, even when they did not address the two Matthean beatitudes. Christopher Tuckett is somewhat confident about the mediated use of Matthew in the *Didache*[73]. Paul Foster tends to assume Ignatius' knowledge of Matthew[74]. In his critical review of research concerning the (apparent non-)reception of the New Testament in *Hermas*, Joseph Verheyden goes beyond the *Shepherd*; his essay is significant from a methodological point of view. Verheyden notices the general trend in literature to deny *Hermas*' use of the NT and to argue for common Jewish/oral Christian

---

68. H. KÖSTER, *Synoptische Überlieferung bei den apostolischen Vätern* (TU, 65), Berlin, Akademie-Verlag, 1957, pp. 13-16, 116-118.

69. W.-D. KÖHLER, *Die Rezeption des Matthäusevangeliums in der Zeit vor Irenäus* (WUNT, 24), Tübingen, Mohr Siebeck, 1987.

70. *Ibid.*, pp. 67-71, 106 (unlikely in *1 Clem.* 13.2 and *Pol.* 2.3a); 463-464 (the *APTh* quote Mt 5,7-8, but with a very different agenda).

71. *1 Clement and the Writings That Later Formed the New Testament*, in GREGORY – TUCKETT, *The New Testament and the Apostolic Fathers*, 1 (n. 62), 129-157 (on Mt 5,7: pp. 131-132).

72. *Polycarp's Letter to the Philippians and the Writings That Later Formed the New Testament*, in GREGORY – TUCKETT, *The New Testament and the Apostolic Fathers*, 2 (n. 62), 187-227, pp. 190-194, 197; on Mt 5,7: pp. 190-191.

73. The "dependence is at best very indirect, perhaps several stages removed, and mediated through a process of oral transmission, retelling, and remembering". *Didache* (n. 62), pp. 88, 126-127.

74. *The Epistles of Ignatius of Antioch and the Writings That Later Formed the New Testament*, in GREGORY – TUCKETT, *The New Testament and the Apostolic Fathers*, 1 (n. 62), 159-186.

traditions, often neglecting the evidence[75]. He then persuasively argues for the use of Matthew (and 1 Corinthians) in the *Shepherd*, addressing not only the wording, but also the structure and function of the passages[76]. For *Barnabas*, James Carleton Paget inclines to assume the use of synoptic traditions, notably of passion material, and a possible knowledge of Matthew[77]. Gregory and Tuckett reach a rather positive conclusion about the use of the completed gospels of Matthew and Luke in *2 Clement* (not necessarily in their current form), and the mediated use of these traditions, taken from a harmonisation of the two gospels[78].

In spite of deviations from the canonical text, as now known, and his probable reliance on catechetical harmonisations of Matthew and Luke, Justin knows the Sermon on the Mount (even though he does not cite the beatitudes)[79].

Beyond patristic sources, other early Christian writings should be considered. A significant piece is Valentinus' Fragment 2, preserved by Clement of Alexandria, which provides a paraphrase of Mt 5,8[80]. The passage evokes the beatitude of the pure in heart notably in the concluding line: ἐπειδὰν δὲ ἐπισκέψηται αὐτὴν [the heart] ὁ μόνος ἀγαθὸς πατήρ, ἡγίασται καὶ φωτὶ διαλάμπει, καὶ οὕτω *μακαρίζεται ὁ ἔχων τὴν τοιαύτην καρδίαν* [i.e., the heart purified and sanctified by the visit of the good Father], ὅτι ὄψεται τὸν θεόν[81]. Since this is a secondary citation,

---

75. *The Shepherd of Hermas and the Writings That Later Formed the New Testament*, in GREGORY – TUCKETT, *The New Testament and the Apostolic Fathers*, 1 (n. 62), 293-329, pp. 296-322.

76. *Ibid.*, pp. 323-329.

77. *The Epistle of Barnabas and the Writings That Later Formed the New Testament*, in GREGORY – TUCKETT, *The New Testament and the Apostolic Fathers*, 1 (n. 62), 229-249, pp. 232-239, 249, based on the agreements of *Barn*. 4.14 with Mt 22,14.

78. *2 Clement and the Writings That Later Formed the New Testament*, in GREGORY – TUCKETT, *The New Testament and the Apostolic Fathers*, 1 (n. 62), 251-292, pp. 277, 292.

79. MASSAUX, *Influence* (n. 67), pp. 465-505, 510-556; A.J. BELLINZONI, *The Sayings of Jesus in the Writings of Justin Martyr* (SupplNT, 17), Leiden, Brill, 1967; J. VERHEYDEN, *Assessing Gospel Quotations in Justin Martyr*, in A. DENAUX (ed.), *New Testament Textual Criticism and Exegesis: FS J. Delobel* (BETL, 161), Leuven, LUP – Peeters, 2002, 361-377; KOESTER, *Gospels* (n. 62), p. 33; M. ELLIOTT, *Sermon on the Mount*, in P.M. BLOWERS – P.W. MARTENS (eds.), *The Oxford Handbook of Early Christian Biblical Interpretation*, Oxford, OUP, 2019, 588-601, p. 588.

80. MASSAUX, *Influence* (n. 67), pp. 425-426; KÖHLER, *Rezeption* (n. 69), p. 77 (very possibly). Köhler also noted the possible reference to it in Theophilus of Antioch (*Autol.* 1.2, p. 503); also D.J. BINGHAM, *Irenaeus' Use of Matthew's Gospel in Adversus Haereses* (Traditio Exegetica Graeca, 7), Leuven, Peeters, 1998, p. 211. KÖSTER saw a possible allusion to Mt 5,8 in Hermas, *Sim.* 9.31.2 (*Synoptische Überlieferung* [n. 68], p. 252), but the similarities are rather general.

81. Valentinus, Fr. 2, W. VÖLKER, *Quellen zur Geschichte der christlichen Gnosis*, Tübingen, Mohr, 1932, 58, ll. 16-17, cf. Clem. Alex., *Strom.* 2.20.114.3-6 (Clemens Alexandrinus, 2, *Stromata I-VI*, ed. O. STÄHLIN – L. FRÜCHTEL [GCS, 52; ³1960], pp. 174-175) (emphases

Clement's accuracy in quoting Valentinus could be questioned. Yet, it is unlikely that Clement would have introduced these allusions to Mt 5,8 (and 12,43-44, par. Lk 11,24-26).

Köhler thought it very probable that P.Egerton [inv.] 3 also used Mt 5,8[82]. The authorship and date of the work are debated. But if the papyrus preserves indeed a late second-century writing, and the reconstruction of the passage is accurate, this can be a further example of a quote of Mt 5,8.

The evidence for the reception of Matthew becomes increasingly clear in the last decades of the second century. Irenaeus' use of Matthew is unquestionable. Jeffrey Bingham has discussed extensively the reception of distinct Matthean material in *Adversus haereses*, underscoring the importance of Mt 5,8 in Irenaeus' doctrine. This beatitude allowed him to develop his comprehensive theology of the *visio Dei*, encompassing the themes of revelation and salvation history, incarnation, and resurrection[83]. Incarnation allows believers to see the invisible God in the incarnate Son[84].

Clement of Alexandria is another valuable witness for the reception of the Sermon on the Mount in the late second / early third century. In the *Stromateis*, he reads the virtues praised in the beatitudes as stages of moral

---

added); C. MARKSCHIES, *Valentinus Gnosticus: Untersuchungen zur valentinianischen Gnosis* (WUNT, 65), Tübingen, Mohr Siebeck, 1992, pp. 54-82; Saint Clement of Alexandria, *Stromateis. Books 1–3*, trans. J. Ferguson (Fathers of the Church, 85), Washington, DC, Catholic University of America Press, 2005, p. 232 (emphasising that Clement quotes Valentinus verbatim): "Through him alone can the heart become pure, when every evil spirit has been driven from the heart. [...] (6) [...] But when the Father, the only good being, has visited it, it is sanctified and blazes with light. In this way, the man with a heart like that receives blessings because he will see God". (ANF II, p. 372 translates "*he who possesses such a heart is so blessed, that 'he shall see God'*".) For a literal quote of the beatitude of the pure in heart: *Strom.* 2.11.50.2.

82. KÖHLER, *Rezeption* (n. 69), pp. 453-454. The fragments are usually dated to the early third century, which implies a second-century composition: H.I. BELL – T.C. SKEAT, *Fragments of an Unknown Gospel and Other Early Christian Papyri*, London, Trustees, 1935, pp. 42-46, text; see p. 46, ll. 44-46. On the later debates regarding the date and authorship of the work: R. YUEN-COLLINGRIDGE, *Hunting for Origen in Unidentified Papyri: The Case of P.Egerton 2 (= inv. 3)*, in T.J. KRAUS – T. NICKLAS (eds.), *Early Christian Manuscripts: Examples of Applied Method and Approach* (TENTS, 5), Leiden, Brill, 2010, 39-57.

83. BINGHAM, *Irenaeus* (n. 80), pp. 107, 170-172, 184-185, 207-211, 256-257, 260-261, 310.

84. *Haer.* 4.20.4-6; Irénée de Lyon, *Contre les hérésies: Dénonciation et réfutation de la gnose au nom menteur*, trans. A. ROUSSEAU (SC, 100/2), Paris, Cerf, 1965, pp. 471-473). The chapter develops the theme of seeing. Irenaeus also discusses the meaning of purity: the pure are the spiritual Christians, those who live for God, who are purified by the Spirit of the Father. *Haer.* 5.9.2 (SC, 153, trans. ROUSSEAU [1969], p. 591), compare 5.9.1 on the perfect man. BINGHAM, *Irenaeus* (n. 80), pp. 261-262.

progress. This starts with repentance and mourning over one's earlier life (4.6.37, quoting the beatitude of the mourning). The spiritual journey requires mercy, understood as compassion toward others (as indicated by the macarism of the merciful), the purification of the soul through knowledge (4.6.39, citing the beatitude of the pure in heart), and reaching the peace of the soul (4.6.40, quoting the beatitude of the peacemakers)[85]. Clement is in fact the most important source attesting the reception of the beatitudes from the Sermon on the Mount as a series.

The train of thought cited above shares some similarities with the *Exegesis on the Soul* (*The Expository Treatise of the Soul*), dated to the late second / early third century[86]. The exhortation to repentance (135.5-33) follows the narrative of the restoration and spiritual marriage of the soul. The spiritual journey is similar: it starts with remorse for the previous way of life, leading to confessing sins, weeping for being in darkness and mourning over ourselves that we may find pity; thus the loving Father will send his light over the soul. The hope for finding mercy conjures up the paraphrase of the beatitudes: "Blessed are those who mourn, for it is they who will be pitied; blessed, those who hunger, for it is they who will be filled"[87]. The protasis of Mt 5,4 (the beatitude of the mourning) is combined with the apodosis of Mt 5,7 ("shall find mercy"). (The allusion to the latter is not evoked to underscore compassion for others, as in Clement, but to emphasise the divine mercy received by the repenting sinner.) The beatitude of those who hunger follows (Lk 6,21a, Mt 5,6). (While its form is closer to Luke, the promise of being filled has here a spiritual meaning, closer to Matthew.)

This brief overview points to the increasing use of the Matthean beatitudes in the second half and towards the end of the second century, notably in Irenaeus and Clement.

---

85. *Stromata I-VI*, ed. STÄHLIN – FRÜCHTEL (n. 81), pp. 265-266. See ELLIOTT, *Sermon* (n. 79), p. 589.

86. B. LAYTON – W.C. ROBINSON, JR., *The Expository Treatise on the Soul: Introduction, Critical Edition and Translation*, in B. LAYTON (ed.), *Nag Hammadi Codex II. 2-7. Vol. 2: On the Origin of the World, Expository Treatise on the Soul, Book of Thomas the Contender* (NHS, 21), Leiden, Brill, 1989, 136-169: as early as 200; the biblical quotes possibly secondary, pp. 136, 140; C.-M. FRANKE, *Die Erzählung über die Seele (NHC II,6)*, in H.-M. SCHENKE – H.-G. BETHGE – U.U. KAISER (eds.), *Nag Hammadi Deutsch*. Vol. 1: *NHC I,1–V,1*, Berlin, De Gruyter, 2001, 263-278, p. 266: hardly before the end of the second century.

87. *Exegesis de anima* 135.17; LAYTON – ROBINSON, *Expository Treatise* (n. 86), p. 163.

V. Conclusions

The beatitudes have a programmatic role in the ascetic-encratic agenda of the *APTh*. Setting the ideal of a continent life, they promise a special relationship with Christ and God and eschatological reward to those who renounce marriage and sexuality. For that purpose, they employ a form of speech characteristic to Jesus and propose a *relecture* of the Matthean beatitudes, interwoven with references to 1 Corinthians (which advocates virginity). The macarism of the pure in heart (Mt 5,8) takes the place of that of the poor and has an essential role in summarising the message. It is a saying of Jesus, invested with particular authority, and it may be read as an exhortation to chastity. The subsequent beatitudes explain the meaning of purity, defining it as renunciation to sexuality and leaving this world, leading to eschatological fulfilment. The beatitude of the merciful seems less fitting, but finding divine mercy is synonymous to escaping judgement and reaching eschatological salvation, promised in the other macarisms. The two beatitudes from Matthew, B1 and B12, thus frame the message, matching the précis of Paul's preaching, the λόγος θεοῦ περὶ ἐγκρατείας καὶ ἀναστάσεως. At the end, B13 summarises the series of twelve beatitudes. Except from some echoes, the other Matthean beatitudes are not cited, probably because they would make little sense in the *APTh*[88].

The question I have attempted to address was whether these Matthean references belonged to the "original" text of the *APTh*, given some textual variations and the problems raised by the Coptic translation. The manuscript evidence has shown that all 21 Greek manuscripts reviewed here have the beatitude of the pure in heart (Mt 5,8). Eighteen manuscripts also have the beatitude of the merciful (B12), the majority as in Lipsius, a minority without the second part of the apodosis. To my knowledge, both beatitudes are also present in the Syriac translation, preserved in some manuscripts that are roughly contemporary with P.Heid. or earlier. (The topic deserves further investigation.) They also exist in the Armenian translation.

The absence of Mt 5,7 from some witnesses may be interpreted in several ways. B12 could be regarded as a later addition to the original Greek

---

88. The beatitudes of the poor and of those who hunger (even when for justice) would not suit a writing in which almost all characters belong to the elite, and they would not contribute to the ascetic message either. The beatitude of the mourning would make some sense, if taken to refer to repentance (not deploring one's miserable condition), but the *APTh* are not chiefly concerned with conversion from a sinful life to a decent one. They set a much loftier ideal: reaching chastity and angelism. The beatitude of the meek and the peacemakers would not make much sense.

text. Research on the textual history of the gospels and their reception in the Apostolic Fathers has raised awareness about the fluidity and development of these texts. The same was most likely true for the *APTh*. It is certainly possible that the number and form of the beatitudes varied, and an earlier, shorter form was later supplemented. On this hypothesis, however, the low number of witnesses lacking the beatitude would point to a quite early expansion: I would tentatively say, toward the end of the second century or early in the third century, when the beatitudes of the Sermon on the Mount are clearly quoted. Regarding the reasons of a possible addition, I fail to see how inserting Mt 5,7 (and Mt 5,8) would mitigate the encratism of the beatitudes, expressing an acceptable form of asceticism (Barrier), given that the beatitudes advocate renunciation to sexuality within marriage (B5) and praise the body of the virgins (B13), Thecla gives up marriage after listening this preaching, and Paul connects pleasures to sin, death and corruption (3.17).

Alternatively, the quote of Mt 5,7 could have been dropped, accidentally or intentionally. The latter seems improbable: there is little reason, if any, to delete a saying of Jesus. An accidental omission cannot be ruled out, and a homoioteleuton could be responsible for it[89]. The Syriac translations and the *Life of Thecla* seem to provide some indirect, rather early evidence for the originality of B12. If the work was indeed completed in the second half or the last decades of the second century, the well-established use of the Matthean beatitudes in other writings makes its use plausible. Of course, this evidence is circumstantial, because citations, paraphrases and echoes of the Matthean macarisms in second-century writings do not necessarily mean that the *APTh* also used them.

To conclude, the originality of Mt 5,8 (B1) in *APTh* cannot be lightly questioned and I see no reason to doubt it. The case of Mt 5,7 is indeed special, but the beatitude could also have belonged to the original text. To be sure, reconstructing the "original" Greek text is virtually impossible in the absence of earlier witnesses.

Babeș-Bolyai University
Faculty of Roman Catholic Theology
Iuliu Maniu 5
RO-400095 Cluj
Romania
kori_zamfir@yahoo.com

Korinna ZAMFIR

---

89. BARRIER mentions the possibility of a homoioteleuton but rejects it. *Asceticism* (n. 4), pp. 172-173, n. 43, referring to David Brakke.

DER GÖTTLICHE LEHRER UND SEINE SCHÜLER

EINE ERZÄHLUNG ÜBER PASSION, OSTERN UND DIE ANFÄNGE DER KIRCHE IN TERTULLIANS *APOLOGETICUM*

Die Erforschung von Jesustraditionen hat in den vergangenen Jahren und Jahrzehnten bedeutsame Neuorientierungen erfahren, an denen auch Joseph Verheyden in vielerlei Hinsicht beteiligt war und ist[1]. Weiterhin wichtig ist die Frage nach den ältesten Traditionen und die Diskussion um angemessene, möglichst subtile Methoden, um das literarische Verhältnis zwischen den kanonischen Evangelien (inkl. des Johannesevangeliums) besser als bisher zu beleuchten. Auch wenn etwa die Rekonstruktion von Q heute umstrittener zu sein scheint als noch vor etwa 20 Jahren[2], bleibt es weiterhin sinnvoll und wichtig, sich möglichen Quellen anzunähern, die den Evangelien zugrunde gelegen haben mögen. Daneben, ja damit eng verbunden, zeigt sich ein zunehmendes Interesse an der Entwicklung von Jesustraditionen. Wir erkennen etwa im ausgehenden ersten und dann durchgehend im zweiten Jahrhundert Phänomene der in erster Linie an schriftlichen Texten vollzogenen Redaktion von älterem Material, aber auch solche, in denen Ebenen von Schriftlichkeit und Mündlichkeit kaum voneinander zu trennen sind: Ich habe in diesem Zusammenhängen den Begriff der (mit Phänomenen einer „secondary orality" verbundenen) freien „Neuinszenierung" von Jesus-Material

---

* Wenn ich heute gefragt würde, von wem ich wissenschaftlich am meisten gelernt habe, würde ich sicherlich sehr schnell an Joseph Verheyden denken; vielleicht (aber nur vielleicht) ist er kein göttlicher Lehrer wie der im Text beschriebene, aber doch einer, an dessen übermenschliche Fähigkeiten und dessen Allwissen man manchmal glauben könnte. Vor allem aber bin ich sehr glücklich darüber, in Jos einen sensiblen, humorvollen und ungemein liebenswürdigen Freund zu haben. Alle guten Wünsche, lieber Jos!

1. Zuletzt z.B. J. VERHEYDEN – J.S. KLOPPENBORG (Hgg.), *The Gospels and Their Stories in Anthropological Perspective* (WUNT, 409), Tübingen, Mohr Siebeck, 2018, und J. SCHRÖTER – T. NICKLAS – J. VERHEYDEN (Hgg.), *Gospels and Gospel Traditions in the Second Century: Experiments in Reception* (BZNW, 235), Berlin – Boston, MA, De Gruyter, 2020.

2. Hierzu vgl. z.B. P. FOSTER – A. GREGORY – J.S. KLOPPENBORG – J. VERHEYDEN (Hgg.), *New Studies in the Synoptic Problem: Oxford Conference, April 2008. Essays in Honour of Christopher M. Tuckett* (BETL, 239), Leuven – Paris – Walpole, MA, Peeters, 2011; M. MÜLLER – H. OMERZU (Hgg.), *Gospel Interpretation and the Q-Hypothesis*, London – New York, Continuum, 2018, sowie (für ein breiteres Publikum) der Doppelband 43/44 (2019) der *Zeitschrift für Neues Testament* mit dem Titel *Synoptische Hypothesen*.

gesprochen³. Daneben kann erstaunlich lange das Aufkommen neuer Motive und Traditionen beobachtet werden, welches sich häufig kreativer narrativer Interpretation von Schrifttexten verdankt⁴. Poetische Umsetzungen des Stoffes (wie z.B. die sogenannten *Centones*) entwickeln sich in größerem Umfang erst deutlich später⁵. Wo man sich auf die Entwicklung von Jesustraditionen konzentriert, spielen – auch jenseits ihres möglichen Werts für die unmittelbare Rückfrage nach dem historischen Jesus – apokryphe Evangelien eine zunehmend wichtige Rolle⁶. Leider hat ihre Einordnung als „*neutestamentliche* Apokryphen" immer wieder verhindert, diese Texte als Stimmen im Kontext altkirchlicher Diskurse wahrzunehmen. Dabei könnte eine Verbindungslinie zwischen neutestamentlicher Exegese, apokryphen Evangelien und patristischer Forschung sich bereits darin ergeben, Rezeptionen biblischer Schriften in apokrypher und patristischer Literatur miteinander in Bezug zu bringen, um sie als Teil eines größeren Diskurses um die Bedeutung der Schrift wahrzunehmen⁷. Während sich Ansätze dazu, derartige Verbindungslinien zu knüpfen, wenigstens in den letzten Jahren immer wieder zeigen, ist eine zweite, damit verwandte Möglichkeit bisher weitgehend unbeachtet geblieben. Vielen Expert*innen, die zu apokryphen Evangelien arbeiten, ist kaum bewusst, dass es in patristisch-altkirchlicher Literatur Textpassagen gibt, die sich mit Fragmenten apokrypher Evangelien vergleichen lassen, die jedoch bisher kaum beachtet wurden: Ich denke an Paraphrasen von Passagen der Evangelien, wie wir sie immer wieder zum Beispiel in altkirchlichen Homilien finden. Weder die patristische Forschung noch

---

3. Z.B. T. NICKLAS, *Zwischen Redaktion und ‚Neuinszenierung': Vom Umgang erzählender Evangelien des 2. Jahrhunderts mit ihren Vorlagen*, in SCHRÖTER – NICKLAS – VERHEYDEN (Hgg.), *Gospels and Gospel Traditions* (Anm. 1), 311-330, sowie ID., *Second-Century Gospels as ‚Re-Enactments' of Earlier Writings: Examples from the Gospel of Peter*, in R.M. CALHOUN – D.P. MOESSNER – T. NICKLAS (Hgg.), *Modern and Ancient Literary Criticism of the Gospels: Continuing the Debate on the Gospel Genre(s)* (WUNT, 451), Tübingen, Mohr Siebeck, 2020, 471-486.

4. Schöne, eher späte Beispiele hierzu z.B. in T. NICKLAS, *Weder apokryph noch kanonisch: Eine Passionsgeschichte in Ps-Cyprians* De duobus montibus Sina et Sion, in *Humanitas* 76 (2021) 74-85.

5. Zu den *Centones* vgl. z.B. K.O. SANDNES, *The Gospel ‚According to Homer and Virgil': Cento and Canon* (SupplNT, 138), Leiden – Boston, MA, Brill, 2011.

6. Dass gleichzeitig der Wert fast aller dieser Schriften für die Rückfrage nach dem historischen Jesus höchst begrenzt ist, habe ich in dem Beitrag T. NICKLAS, *Traditions about Jesus in Apocryphal Gospels (with the Exception of the Gospel of Thomas)*, in T. HOLMÉN – S.E. PORTER (Hgg.), *Handbook for the Study of the Historical Jesus*. Vol. 2: *The Study of Jesus*, Leiden – Boston, MA, Brill, 2011, 2081-2118 (inkl. breiter Diskussion relevanter Sekundärliteratur), gezeigt.

7. Dies geschieht immer wieder bei L. ZELYCK, *John among the Other Gospels: The Reception of the Fourth Gospel in the Extra-Canonical Gospels* (WUNT, 2.347), Tübingen, Mohr Siebeck, 2013.

die neutestamentliche Exegese hat sich mit solchen Texten intensiver beschäftigt. Solange man sich in der Exegese einlinig auf die Rückfrage nach dem historischen Jesus konzentrierte, lagen die Gründe dafür klar auf der Hand. Wo die Exegese sich aber auch für die Entwicklung von Jesustraditionen interessiert, sollten auch solche Texte systematischer als bisher in den Blick rücken[8]. Natürlich handelt es sich dabei nicht um apokryphe Evangelien in einem engeren Sinne und sicherlich bieten sie uns kein neues, wertvolles Material zur Rückfrage nach dem historischen Jesus. Doch schon die Tatsache, dass wir in vielen Fällen den Kontext einer solchen Paraphrase kennen, kann uns helfen, besondere narrative Schwerpunkte einer Paraphrase, aber auch die Entwicklung von Motiven, die wir aus kanonischen Evangelien kennen, besser zu verstehen, als dies ohne solche Kontexte der Fall wäre[9].

Der folgende Beitrag möchte Aspekte der hier skizzierten Möglichkeiten an einem konkreten Text illustrieren – und zwar an Kapitel 21.18-25 aus dem *Apologeticum* des Tertullian. Nach einer kurzen Vorstellung und Einordnung des Texts interessiere ich mich für die Frage, wie das Verhältnis der hier vorliegenden Paraphrase wichtiger Aspekte der Passions- und Ostererzählung zu den Parallelen des Neuen Testaments, darüber hinaus aber auch zu apokryphen Schriften und anderen altkirchlichen, wo möglich aber auch gegen das Christentum gerichteten polemischen Texten, präzise zu beschreiben ist und wie sich die Akzentsetzungen Tertullians im Vergleich zu seinen (angenommenen) Vorlagen erklären lassen. Methodisch ist dabei eine Unschärfe in Kauf zu nehmen: Mir ist natürlich bewusst, dass Tertullian kein *Novum Testamentum Graece* wie in unseren heutigen Ausgaben vorlag, sondern dass er mit lateinischen Texten gearbeitet haben muss. So ist, selbst wenn wir heutige (zum Teil ja aus Tertullians Zitaten rekonstruierte) Vetus-Latina-Ausgaben zum Vergleich heranziehen, der Detailvergleich zwischen Tertullians Erzählung im *Apologeticum* und biblischen Passagen immer ein wenig künstlich, da wir Tertullians konkrete Vorlage nicht kennen. Gleichzeitig wird sich

---

8. Ein paralleles Problem ergibt sich mit Jesusmaterial in apokryphen Apostelakten. Hierzu aber (knapp) J.A. SNYDER, *Acts of John, Acts of Peter, Acts of Thecla, Third Corinthians, Martyrdom of Paul*, in J. SCHRÖTER – C. JACOBI (Hgg.), *From Thomas to Tertullian: Christian Literary Receptions of Jesus in the Second and Third Centuries CE* (The Reception of Jesus in the First Three Centuries, 2), London – New York, Bloomsbury, 2020, 363-385.

9. Erste Tiefenbohrungen schon bei NICKLAS, *Weder apokryph noch kanonisch* (Anm. 4) (zu Pseudo-Cyprian, *De duobus montibus Sina et Sion*), sowie ID., *Apocryphal Jesus Stories in the Pseudo-Clementine Homilies: The Syro-Phoenician Woman (H 2,19) and the Dispute with the Sadducees (H 3,50,1 and 3,54,2)*, in B. DE VOS – D. PRAET (Hgg.), *The Pseudoclementine Homilies* (WUNT), Tübingen, Mohr Siebeck, 2022 [im Druck].

schnell zeigen, dass Tertullian wenigstens in dem Abschnitt, der uns im Folgenden interessieren wird, kaum einmal wörtlich Passagen aus den Evangelien übernimmt. Da somit in erster Linie Beobachtungen auf Meso-Ebene möglich sind, es also auf die neue Kombination von umfangreicheren Erzählpassagen und Motiven, und weniger auf Mikro-Ebene (wie die konkrete Verwendung einzelner Termini) ankommt, wird eine solche Randunschärfe das Ergebnis hoffentlich nicht entscheidend verfälschen[10]. Gleichzeitig bin ich mir dessen bewusst, dass ich den Text als Neutestamentler und damit interessiert an Fragen der Darstellung von Jesuserzählungen und nicht als Tertullian-Experte lese.

I. Einführendes zu Text und Textpassage

Das wohl etwa um das Jahr 197 n.Chr. zu datierende *Apologeticum*[11] gehört wahrscheinlich zu den frühesten Werken Tertullians[12] und damit

---

10. Mir ist bewusst, dass T. GEORGES, *Tertullian. Apologeticum* (Kommentar zu frühchristlichen Apologeten, 11), Freiburg i.Br. – Basel – Wien, Herder, 2011, vor nicht allzu langer Zeit eine ausgezeichnete Kommentierung des gesamten *Apologeticums* vorgelegt hat und sich dabei auch ausführlich der hier im Blick stehenden Textpassage gewidmet hat. Ich hoffe aber, mit meinem besonderen Fokus auch über das von Georges Erarbeitete hinaus, das natürlich als Basis meiner Arbeit dient, noch weitere belangvolle Entdeckungen bieten zu können. Da C. BECKER, *Tertullians Apologeticum: Werden und Leistung*, München, Kösel, 1954, und G. ECKERT, *Orator Christianus: Untersuchungen zur Argumentationskunst in Tertullians Apologeticum* (Palingenesia, 46), Stuttgart, Franz Steiner, 1993, die von mir gewählte Passage in ihrer Diskussion des *Apologeticums* kaum berühren, werde ich diese Autoren nur in Einzelfällen heranziehen. Unter den weiteren Ausgaben und Übersetzungen des Texts waren mir C. CASTILLO GARCÍA, *Tertulliano. Apologetico, A los gentiles*, Madrid, Gredos, 2001, sowie P. PODOLAK, *Q.F.S. Tertulliani Apologeticum*, in ID. – C. MORESCHINI (Hgg.), *Q.S.F. Tertulliani Opera apologetica*, Roma, Città Nuova, 2006, 157-377, nicht zugänglich. – Der Beitrag von D. ROTH, *Tertullian*, in SCHRÖTER – JACOBI (Hgg.), *From Thomas to Tertullian* (Anm. 8), 531-538, konzentriert sich vor allem auf *Adv. Marc.*; wichtige Aspekte des im *Apol.* erkennbaren Jesusbilds bleiben damit unberücksichtigt.

11. Argumente hierzu u.a. bei T.D. BARNES, *Pagan Perceptions of Christianity*, in I. HAZLETT (Hg.), *Early Christianity: Origins and Evolution to AD 600*, London, SPCK, 1991, 231-241, S. 236, sowie H.M. ZILLING, *Tertullian: Untertan Gottes und des Kaisers*, Paderborn, Schöningh, 2004, S. 86 (gefolgert aus den Angaben in *Apol.* 37.4 über die Feindschaft der Parther gegen Rom); vorsichtiger ECKERT, *Orator* (Anm. 10), S. 22 („kurz vor Ende des 2. Jahrhunderts"). – Auch der konkrete Anlass zur Niederlegung der *Apologie* ist umstritten; hierzu aber ausführlich (mit Diskussion älterer Sekundärliteratur) GEORGES, *Tertullian* (2011; Anm. 10), S. 23-31.

12. Der vorliegende Beitrag beabsichtigt nicht auf die verschiedenen Fragen zur Biographie des Tertullian oder auch zu seinem Verhältnis zur katholischen Kirche bzw. der montanistischen Bewegung einzugehen. Hierzu besonders wichtig (und gleichzeitig provozierend) ist T.D. BARNES, *Tertullian: A Historical and Literary Study*, Oxford, Clarendon, ²1985 (1971); weiterführend (z.T. kritisch gegenüber Barnes) auch D. RANKIN,

zu den ältesten erhaltenen christlichen Schriften in lateinischer Sprache überhaupt. Zusammen mit seiner Vorgängerschrift *Ad nationes* (*Nat.*) liegt uns hier die älteste christliche Apologie in lateinischer Sprache vor[13]. Mit Tobias Georges gehe ich davon aus, dass die Schrift ein doppeltes Publikum im Auge hat: zunächst einmal Anhänger*innen der römischen Kulte, denen gegenüber zum Ausdruck gebracht wird, dass die christliche Bewegung ungefährlich, ja glaubwürdig ist[14]. Dabei ist jedoch kaum an die explizit angesprochenen Statthalter des Imperium Romanum (*Apol.* 1.1: *romani imperii antistites*; vgl. auch 9.6; 30.7; 44.2 und 50.12) zu denken[15]. Daneben ist es sehr wahrscheinlich, dass Tertullian auch Christinnen und Christen, die Selbstvergewisserung ihres eigenen Denkens in schwieriger Zeit suchten, im Auge hatte. Wahrscheinlich war diese Gruppe gar diejenige, die er tatsächlich am ehesten erreichte. Die dem Text inhärente antijüdische Tendenz wiederum dürfte ausschließen, dass auch Juden sich (in positiver Weise) angesprochen fühlen konnten[16]. Kapitel 21, das im Folgenden im Vordergrund stehen wird, ist Teil eines umfangreicheren Abschnitts, in dem der christliche Glaube positiv dargestellt wird. Georges schreibt:

Tertullian and the Church, Cambridge, CUP, 1995; ZILLING, *Tertullian* (Anm. 11), S. 21-82; D. WRIGHT, *Tertullian*, in P.F. ESLER (Hg.), *The Early Christian World*, New York, Routledge, 2000, 2, 1027-1047; G.W. DUNN, *Tertullian*, London – New York, Routledge, 2004, S. 3-13; und D.E. WILHITE, *Tertullian the African: An Anthropological Reading of Tertullian's Context and Identities* (Millennium-Studien, 14), Berlin – New York, De Gruyter, 2007, S. 17-36, sowie GEORGES, *Tertullian* (2011; Anm. 10), S. 16-21.

13. Zur Diskussion um „Apologetik", ihre Funktion und Entwicklung vgl. z.B. den Überblick bei A. KLOSTERGARD PETERSEN, *The Diversity of Apologetics: From Genre to a Mode of Thinking*, in A.-C. JACOBSEN – J. ULRICH – D. BRAKKE (Hgg.), *Critique and Apologetics: Jews, Christians and Pagans in Antiquity* (Early Christianity in the Context of Antiquity, 4), Frankfurt a.M., Peter Lang, 2009, 15-42, und A.-C. JACOBSEN, *Apologetics and Apologies – Some Definitions*, in ID. – J. ULRICH – M. KAHLOS (Hgg.), *Continuity and Discontinuity in Early Christian Apologetics* (Early Christianity in the Context of Antiquity, 5), Frankfurt a.M., Peter Lang, 2009, 5-22.

14. Grundlegend GEORGES, *Tertullian* (2011; Anm. 10), S. 44-47. – Auch dies wird kontrovers diskutiert (siehe z.B. den knappen Forschungsüberblick bei ZILLING, *Tertullian* (Anm. 11), S. 96-104, die daran denkt, „daß die unmittelbaren Hörer des *Apologeticum* die Gemeindechristen waren"). WILHITE, *Tertullian* (Anm. 12), S. 72-74, differenziert das Publikum des *Apologeticums* von dem in *Ad nationes*: Im *Apologeticum* schreibe Tertullian als Christ und Afrikaner an ein nicht-afrikanisches, römisches Publikum.

15. Eusebius, *Hist. eccl.* 5.5.5 ging davon aus, dass der Text vor dem Senat in Rom vorgetragen wurde. Zur Kritik daran u.a. BARNES, *Tertullian* (Anm. 12), S. 25-26.

16. Zum Verhältnis des Tertullian zum Judentum weiterführend vgl. z.B. BARNES, *Tertullian* (Anm. 12), S. 90-93, 330-331; D.P. EFROYMSON, *Tertullian's Anti-Jewish Rhetoric: Guilt by Association*, in *USQR* 36 (1980) 25-37, sowie (in der Einleitung zu Tertullians Werk *Adversus Iudaeos*) DUNN, *Tertullian* (Anm. 12), S. 47-51, der betont, dass Tertullian in Karthago Kenntnis von Juden gehabt haben dürfte, und der die Israeltheologie Tertullians als „supersessionist" (S. 49) beschreibt.

Vorbereitend wird in Kap. 10–15 die Göttlichkeit der paganen Götter bestritten; in Kap. 16–21 folgt dann die zentrale Darlegung des christlichen Glaubens an den einen Gott, der durch die Entlarvung der Dämonen in Kap. 22f Bestätigung erfährt; in Kap. 24–27 werden einzelne Argumente für die Gottesverehrung der Christen und gegen die der Nichtchristen nachgeliefert[17].

Kapitel 21 setzt, anknüpfend an die Kapitel 18–20, mit einer Variation des Arguments ein, dass die Wurzeln der christlichen Bewegung, obwohl diese erst in der Zeit des Kaisers Tiberius aufgekommen war[18], schon sehr weit zurückgehen. Nach Tertullians Auskunft stützt sich das Christentum auf die uralten *instrumenta* der Juden (21.1)[19]. Gleichzeitig betont er die fundamentale Differenz zwischen Juden und Christen, die für ihn nicht nur darin besteht, dass beide Gruppen sich in vielerlei Teilaspekten wie der Beachtung von Speisegeboten, Feiertagen oder Beschneidung unterscheiden[20]. Der Unterschied geht für ihn gar so weit, dass die Christen nicht dem gleichen Gott wie die Juden zu Eigen seien (21.2: *eidem deo manciparemur*)[21], ohne dass sie deswegen „Anderes über Gott annehmen" (21.3: *neque de deo aliter praesumimus*). Auf das Vorurteil hin, Christus sei einfach irgendein Mensch – und nicht Gott – gewesen (21.3: *hominem utique aliquem*)[22], sieht Tertullian sich gezwungen, „ein wenig über Christus als Gott" zu sprechen (21.3: *pauca de Christo ut deo*). Nach weiteren Auslassungen über die Verstockung der Juden, die trotz

---

17. T. GEORGES, *Tertullian. Apologeticum: Verteidigung des christlichen Glaubens* (Fontes christiani, 62), Freiburg i.Br. – Basel – Wien, Herder, 2015, S. 42.
18. Zur Bedeutung dieses Problems für die christliche Apologetik vgl. A.-C. JACOBSEN, *Main Topic in Early Christian Apologetics*, in ID. – ULRICH – BRAKKE (Hgg.), *Critique and Apologetics* (Anm. 13), 85-110, S. 95-96.
19. Die Übersetzung ist nicht ganz einfach, GEORGES, *Tertullian* (2011; Anm. 10), S. 315, sowie ID., *Tertullian* (2015, Anm. 17), S. 159, übersetzt als „Zeugnisse"; man könnte auch an „Beweismittel" denken.
20. Die Argumentation wird in sich schlüssiger, wenn man bedenkt, dass es Tertullian letztlich nicht auf die gemeinsame Basis im mosaischen Gesetz ankommt, sondern darauf, dass es ein bereits vor dem mosaischen Gesetz existierendes grundlegendes Urgesetz Gottes gibt, das grundsätzlich allen Menschen zugänglich sei und auf dem auch das Gesetz des Mose, und zwar in einer an die speziellen Lebensumstände des jüdischen Volks angepassten Form, basiere (cf. Tertullian, *Adv. Jud.* 2). Hierzu auch knapp M.C. ALBL, *Ancient Christian Authors on Jews and Judaism*, in R. ROUKEMA – H. AMIRAV (Hgg.), *The ‚New Testament' as a Polemical Tool: Studies in Ancient Christian Anti-Jewish Rhetoric and Beliefs* (NTOA, 118), Göttingen, Vandenhoeck & Ruprecht, 2018, 15-56, S. 26.
21. Gleichzeitig finden sich durchaus wertschätzende Aussagen – er spricht vom Judentum als einer „überaus bedeutsamen *religio*", welche, anders als das Christentum gewiss *religio licita* sei (21.1 *certe licitae*).
22. Tertullian verwendet hier den Begriff *uulgus* – Georges übersetzt treffend als „Pöbel" –, der auch später, im Zusammenhang mit der Verbreitung der Auferstehungsbotschaft (*Apol.* 21.22) wieder begegnen wird. Dem Christentum gegenüber kritische Meinungen werden von ihm gerne dem *uulgus* unterstellt, von dem man sich leicht abgrenzen kann.

aller einst von Gott geschenkten Gnade und Größe nun heimatlos und ohne ihren Gott über die Erde irrten (21.4-5)[23], kommt er auf (nicht näher konkretisierte) Prophezeiungen darüber zu sprechen, dass die den Juden übertragene Gnade auf andere Völker übergehen werde (21.6). 21.7-9 beschäftigen sich mit der Frage, wie Christus in die Welt gekommen sei, 21.10-13 mit dem Verhältnis zwischen Gott und Christus, der, wie 21.14 ausführt, als „Gottes Lichtstrahl" (*dei radius*) ... „in eine Jungfrau hinabgestiegen" (*delapsus in uirginem quandam*) und als „ein Mensch, der mit Gott vereinigt[24] ist", geboren wurde (*nascitur homo deo mixtus*)[25]. 21.15-16 betont erneut das Fehlverhalten der Juden, die trotz der Ankündigungen der Propheten die erste Ankunft Christi nicht erkannten. Dies wiederum habe sich auch daran gezeigt, dass sie seine Vollmacht Wunder zu tun, mit Magie verwechselten (21.17)[26]: Es folgt eine Liste von Hinweisen auf Jesu Wunder: Heilung von Blinden, Aussätzigen und Gelähmten, Wiederbelebung von Toten sowie die Bändigung von Stürmen und der Gang auf den Wassern, wie sie sich immer wieder auch in apokryphen Zusammenfassungen des Wirkens Jesu finden (z.B. ausführlich in der *Epistula Apostolorum* 5 [16], im apokryphen *Brief des Pilatus an Claudius*, sehr knapp im *Judasevangelium* CT 33.6-8, auch in der fälschlicherweise Cyrill von Jerusalem zugeschriebenen Homilie *Über Leben und Passion Christi* §§24-29[27] u.a.). Diese Wunder wiederum zeigten, dass „er jener Sohn sei, einst von Gott angekündigt und zum Heil aller geboren, jenes uranfängliche, erstgeborene Gotteswort, von Kraft und Vernunft begleitet und vom Geist getragen" (21.17)[28]. Nachdem, so

---

23. Beispiele für ähnliche Aussagen über das bleibende Schicksal der Juden in antiken antijüdischen Traktaten bei ALBL, *Ancient Christian Authors* (Anm. 20), S. 46-47. Konkret scheint hier auf das nach dem Bar-Kochba-Aufstand (132-135 n.Chr.) geltende Verbot für Juden angespielt, Jerusalem zu betreten; wahrscheinlich bezieht sich die hier erwähnte Heimatlosigkeit aber auch auf den Gedanken, von Gott verlassen zu sein. Hierzu weiterführend GEORGES, *Tertullian* (2011; Anm. 10), S. 321.

24. Möglich wäre auch die Übersetzung „vermischt".

25. All diese Aussagen sind natürlich auch dogmengeschichtlich interessant. Ich lasse ihre Diskussion aber aufgrund des Fokus meines Beitrags für den Moment beiseite. Zur theologiegeschichtlichen Einordnung der Passage 21.13-14 siehe GEORGES, *Tertullian* (2011; Anm. 10), S. 331-332, und ZILLING, *Tertullian* (Anm. 11), S. 119-120, die schreibt: „Die christologische Theorie Tertullians ist wegweisend für die spätere Zwei-Naturen-Lehre" (S. 120).

26. Parallelen hierzu auch bei Justin, *Dial.* 69.7; *1 Apol.* 30.1; Tertullian, *Adv. Marc.* 3.6, 10 (so auch GEORGES, *Tertullian* [2011; Anm. 10], S. 336).

27. Der Text gehört zu der Gruppe der mit Evangelien verwandten *Apostolic Memoirs* der nachchalcedonisch-miaphysitischen Kirche Ägyptens. Zu dieser Gruppe von Schriften weiterführend A. SUCIU, *The Berlin-Strasbourg Apocryphon: A Coptic Apostolic Memoir* (WUNT, 370), Tübingen, Mohr Siebeck, 2017, S. 70-138.

28. Übersetzung adaptiert von GEORGES, *Tertullian* (2015; Anm. 17), S. 16.

zusammengefasst, das Leben Christi als eine einzige Demonstration seiner Vollmacht als göttlicher Gottessohn dargestellt ist, folgen die Passagen über Passion, Auferstehung und Himmelfahrt Christi, die nun genauer vorgestellt und diskutiert werden sollen.

II. Die Abschnitte zu Passion, Auferstehung und Himmelfahrt Christi[29]

Apol. 21.18

Ad doctrinam uero eius, qua reuincebantur, magistri primoresque Iudaeorum ita exasperabantur, maxime quod ingens ad eum multitudo conflueret, ut postremo oblatum Pontio Pilato, Syriam tunc ex parte Romana procuranti, uiolentia suffragiorum in crucem dedi sibi extorserint. Praedixerat et ipse ita facturos; parum hoc, si non et prophetae retro.

Die Lehrer und Vornehmsten der Juden wurden gegenüber seiner Lehre, durch die sie widerlegt wurden, so aufgehetzt – am meisten, weil eine gewaltige Menge zu ihm zusammenströmte –, dass sie schließlich, nachdem er dem Pontius Pilatus, welcher damals von römischer Seite Prokurator in Syrien war, ausgeliefert worden war, diesen mit der Gewalt (ihrer) Stimmen dazu erpressten, ihn ihnen zum Kreuz auszuhändigen. Er hatte selbst vorhergesagt, dass sie es so machen würden; dies nicht genug, wenn nicht auch früher die Propheten (dies getan hätten).

In geraffter Form bietet 21.18 Informationen darüber, unter welchen Umständen es trotz der in 21.17 so betonten Vollmacht Christi zu dessen für die Leserschaft sicherlich anstößiger Kreuzigung gekommen ist. Wie die Evangelisten steht auch Tertullian vor dem Problem, die Gott gegebene Vollmacht Christi und sein Leid zusammenzudenken. Er muss dies zusätzlich in einer Weise tun, die sein intendiertes Publikum nicht vor den Kopf stößt, ja dieses überzeugt. Um dies zu erreichen, betont er einerseits den Gegensatz zu den jüdischen Lehrern und Vornehmen[30], deren Schuld am Tode Jesu er hervorhebt, während die

---

29. Der lateinische Text folgt Georges, *Tertullian* (2015; Anm. 17), ist aber jeweils an H. Hoppe (Hg.), *Tertullianus. Apologeticum* (CSEL, 69), Wien – Leipzig, Österreichische Akademie der Wissenschaften, 1939, sowie E. Dekkers et al. (Hgg.), *Apologeticum*, in *Quinti Septimi Florentis Tertulliani opera* (CCSL, 1-2), Turnhout, Brepols, 1954, S. 77-171, überprüft. – Die folgenden Übersetzungen stammen von mir selbst, sind aber durchgehend mit Georges, *Tertullian* (2011; Anm. 10), und Id., *Tertullian* (2015; Anm. 17), abgeglichen und in Teilen diesen sehr nahe.

30. In der Textwelt des Tertullian erübrigt sich, wer von den im Neuen Testament erkennbaren Charakteren sich denn in den *magistri* und *primores* spiegelt. Die Überlegungen, dass hier Schriftgelehrte einerseits und Priester- wie Laienaristokratie andererseits gemeint sein könnten (vgl. Georges, *Tertullian* [2011, Anm. 10], S. 339, Anm. 754), sind nicht

Beteiligung der römischen Obrigkeit in ein möglichst positives Licht gerückt wird[31]. Andererseits wird er, wie wir schnell sehen werden, besonders demütigend wirkende konkrete Aspekte des Leidens Christi wie z.B. die verschiedenen Foltern, die seinem Tod vorausgingen, den demütigenden Akt, dass er sein Kreuz selbst tragen musste, die in den synoptischen Evangelien so wichtigen Bezugnahmen auf die Klagepsalmen 22 und 69 u.a. vollkommen ausklammern. Gleichzeitig lässt er in 21.18 durchblicken, dass letztendlich ein Lehrstreit zum Tode Jesu führte: So kreiert er das Gegenüber zwischen dem Lehrer (*magister*) Jesus und seiner Lehre (*doctrina*) einerseits sowie den Lehrern und Vornehmsten der Juden (*magistri primoresque Iudaeorum*) andererseits, welche durch die Lehre Jesu widerlegt werden[32]. Vor diesem Hintergrund mag es auch sinnvoll erscheinen, die ab 21.20 wieder erwähnten *discipuli* nicht als „Jünger", sondern als „Schüler" Jesu zu deuten[33]. Das frühe Christentum ist damit wenigstens implizit als Bildungsbewegung charakterisiert, ohne dass deswegen hier die Lehre Jesu konkret illustriert werden müsste (vgl. ähnlich Mk 1,21)[34]. Eine später wichtig werdende Abgrenzung vom *uulgus*, d.h. dem „Pöbel", ist damit umso leichter möglich.

Entscheidend für die Argumentation ist die in Wundern demonstrierte Vollmacht Jesu und seine Überlegenheit gegenüber den jüdischen Lehrern und Vornehmen, die dazu führt, dass eine gewaltige Menge bei ihm

---

falsch, jedoch in der Gefahr, die wichtige Opposition zwischen den verschiedenen „Lehrern", die der Text aufbaut, zu übersehen.

31. So auch GEORGES, *Tertullian* (2011; Anm. 10), S. 339, und ZILLING, *Tertullian* (Anm. 11), S. 121. Die Tendenz, die Römer von aller Schuld am Tode Jesu zu entlasten, ist in frühchristlicher Literatur weniger eindeutig, als häufig angenommen. So ist m.E. weder der Pilatus des Matthäus-, noch der des Johannes- oder auch des apokryphen *Petrusevangeliums* einfach eine positive Figur (oder eine positivere Figur als etwa der Pilatus des Markusevangeliums). In einem wenigstens teilweise an ein nichtchristliches Publikum gerichteten apologetischen Text wie dem hier vorliegenden dagegen ist eine solche Tendenz durchaus gut nachvollziehbar.

32. Dass Tertullian von den „Juden" spricht und nicht verschiedene jüdische Gruppierungen differenziert, wie das die synoptischen Evangelien tun, erinnert natürlich an Entwicklungen in christlicher Literatur, wie sie ab dem Johannesevangelium erkennbar sind. Hintergrund sind Bestrebungen der neuen „christlichen" Bewegung, sich vom Judentum so klar wie möglich abzugrenzen.

33. Dies ist inspiriert durch die Entscheidung bei S. ALKIER – T. PAULSEN, *Die Evangelien nach Markus und Matthäus. Neu übersetzt* (Frankfurter NT, 2), Paderborn, Brill Deutschland, 2021, S. 276 und Anm. 13, das griechische μαθητής durchgehend mit „Schüler" zu übersetzen.

34. Zu dem Gedanken, dass das frühe Christentum als eine Bildungsbewegung verstanden werden *kann*, vgl. U. SCHNELLE, *Das frühe Christentum und die Bildung*, in *NTS* 61 (2015) 113-143, sowie P. GEMEINHARDT, *„Den Heiden eine Torheit"? Bildung im paulinischen Schrifttum und im frühen Christentum*, in *JBTh* 35 (2020) 209-240.

zusammenströmt[35]. An der weiteren Darstellung des Texts ist nicht nur interessant, dass Tertullian Pontius Pilatus als „Prokurator von Syrien" (*Syriam ... procuranti*) bezeichnet[36], sondern dass er *nicht* davon spricht, wer Christus denn an Pilatus ausgehändigt hat – die Worte *oblatum Pontio Pilato* lassen verschiedene Deutungen zu. Auch wenn die kanonischen Evangelien Judas Iskariot nicht mit Pilatus in Verbindung setzen, sondern mit Vertretern der jüdischen Obrigkeit in Jerusalem, mögen christliche Leser*innen hier an die Auslieferung Jesu durch Judas Iskariot denken. Tertullian meidet dieses Motiv sicherlich bewusst[37], verbindet sich mit ihm doch die für Außenstehende anstößige Erinnerung, dass ein engster Vertrauter Jesu diesen zur Verhaftung ausgeliefert hat[38]. Da die Frage nach der Schuld daran, durch wen Jesus an Pilatus ausgeliefert wurde, zumindest nicht explizit beantwortet wird[39], beschränkt sich in der vorliegenden Darstellung die Aktivität der jüdischen Obrigkeit im Grunde darauf, erst *nach der Verhaftung Jesu* Pilatus dazu zu bewegen, ihr Jesus zur Kreuzigung auszuhändigen. Damit aber entfallen alle Aspekte der Darstellung, nach denen jüdische Gegner Jesu dessen Tod beschließen; in den synoptischen Evangelien finden sich diese ja schon sehr früh in der Darstellung des öffentlichen Wirkens Jesu (vgl. z.B. Mk 2,7; 3,6 u.a.); auch die Gründe der Gegner Jesu werden in vielen Fällen nachvollziehbar. Einen Höhepunkt, der auch erlaubt, die Perspektive der jüdischen Obrigkeit nachzuvollziehen, bietet sicherlich die Beschreibung der Ratsversammlung in Joh 11,45-53, bei der der Hohepriester Kajaphas das entscheidende Wort ergreift. Weg fällt damit auch der gesamte Komplex des für alle Evangelien wichtigen jüdischen Verfahrens gegen Jesus (vgl. Mk 14,53-65; Mt 26,57-68; Lk 22,54-55.66-71; Joh 18,13-24). Im Fokus steht, ohne dass dieses explizit beschrieben wird, allein das

---

35. Von großen Menschenmengen, die Jesus wenigstens zeitweise folgen, ist in den Evangelien so regelmäßig die Rede, dass keine Einzelstelle zu identifizieren ist, auf die Tertullian verweisen mag.

36. Vgl. GEORGES, *Tertullian* (2011; Anm. 10), S. 339: „Zu Tertullians Zeit gehörte das von ihm verwaltete Gebiet zur Provinz ‚Syria Palaestina', de facto war Pontius Pilatus aber Statthalter der zu Jesu Zeit noch bestehenden Provinz ‚Iudaea' (vgl. Lk 3,1, Tacitus, ann. 15.44,3, Josephus, a.J. 18,35.177-178)". Ähnlich J.-P. WALTZING, *Tertullien – Apologétique: Commentaire analytique, grammatical et historique*, Paris, Les Belles Lettres, 1929, S. 151.

37. Womöglich fehlte dieses Motiv auch im apokryphen *Petrusevangelium*, das noch im Umfeld des Ostertages problemlos von den „Zwölf" sprechen kann (V. 59).

38. Auch das Motiv, dass alle „Schüler" – zumindest die Männer – Jesus bei seiner Festnahme verlassen haben, aber auch der dreifache Verrat des Petrus entfallen aus sicherlich vergleichbaren Gründen.

39. Nichtchristliche Adressat*innen (ohne Kenntnis der Evangelien) mögen aufgrund des Kontexts dazu geleitet werden, die jüdische Obrigkeit als verantwortlich für Jesu Verhaftung und Auslieferung zu verstehen.

Gerichtsverfahren vor Pilatus. Dabei ist natürlich auch die Szene über die mögliche Paschaamnestie durch Pilatus, in der schreiend die Freilassung eines anderen Häftlings, d.h. des Barabbas, gefordert wird (Mk 15,6-11; Mt 27,15-26; Lk 23,[17].18-25; Joh 18,38-40), für Tertullians Darstellung unwichtig und kann ausgelassen werden. So wie er steht, ist dieser Text sicherlich besser verstehbar für Adressat*innen, die wenigstens eine Grundidee von der Passionserzählung der kanonischen Evangelien haben, in der das Verfahren vor Pilatus zumindest teilweise in der Öffentlichkeit stattfindet.

Für die vorliegende Darstellung ist wichtig, dass der Vertreter Roms durch das Schreien (hier nur) der jüdischen Lehrer und Vornehmen gezwungen ist, Jesus kreuzigen zu lassen. Auch hier zeigen sich kleine Verschiebungen im Gegenüber zu den kanonischen Evangelien: Dort schreit der von den Oberpriestern (sowie den Ältesten [Mt 27,20]) angestachelte Mob (ὄχλος Sg.: Mk 15,8.11.15; ὄχλοι Pl.: Mt 27,20) bzw. „das ganze Volk" (Mt 27,25: πᾶς ὁ λαός) oder der aus Oberpriestern, Führenden und dem Volk bestehende Haufen (παμπληθεί; Lk 23,18; vgl. 23,13) bzw. die „Juden" (Joh 18,38b: οἱ Ἰουδαῖοι). Anders als in den Evangelien, wo es offenbar große Menschenmengen sind, die Pilatus dazu zwingen, Barabbas statt Jesus freizulassen, konzentriert sich Tertullian also auf die jüdische Elite. Seine Darstellung, dass große Menschenmengen Jesus wegen der Zeichen seiner Vollmacht folgten, wird somit konsistenter[40]. Interessant ist auch das Detail, dass Pilatus Christus „ihnen" zur Kreuzigung ausliefern solle – und damit offenbar die Vertreter der „Juden" gemeint sind. Texte, die die jüdische Eliten oder gar „die Juden" als die eigentlichen Henker Jesu verstehen, sind ab dem zweiten Jahrhundert mehrfach belegt: Man könnte hier z.B. an das *Petrusevangelium* (vgl. die Darstellung ab V. 5), den *Brief des Pilatus an Claudius* oder Melitos Homilie *Peri Pascha* (z.B. 73.92-93) denken[41]. Doch auch innerhalb der kanonischen Passionserzählungen bieten sich Anknüpfungspunkte: So lesen wir in Joh 19,16a, dass Pilatus „ihnen" Jesus zur Kreuzigung auslieferte (… παρέδωκεν αὐτὸν αὐτοῖς ἵνα σταυρωθῇ; vgl. auch Lk 23,25 … τὸν δὲ Ἰησοῦν παρέδωκεν τῷ θελήματι αὐτῶν), der Bezug des Pronomens αὐτοῖς aber bleibt unklar. Aufgrund des unmittelbar

---

40. Etwas anders ist die Darstellung der Ereignisse in dem in vielen Motiven verwandten *Brief des Pilatus an Claudius*, der davon spricht, dass das gesamte jüdische Volk Christus als Sohn Gottes erkennt, aber die führenden Priester ihn aus Hass an Pilatus ausliefern; Pilatus wiederum ist alleine für die Geißelung Jesu verantwortlich.

41. Eine Reihe weiterer Beispiele bis ins 5. Jahrhundert hinein bietet ALBL, *Ancient Christian Authors* (Anm. 20), S. 41-43. Immerhin schreckt Tertullian vor der bei Melito, *Pasch.* 96, erstmals erkennbaren Idee zurück, die „Juden" seien Gottesmörder.

Vorhergehenden liegt der Bezug auf die in Joh 19,14 angesprochenen „Juden" bzw. die in 19,15 erwähnten „Oberpriester" nahe. So bleibt unklar, von welchen Texten Tertullian konkret beeinflusst gewesen sein mag – die in vielen Schriften erkennbare Tendenz, alleine den „Juden" oder der jüdischen Obrigkeit die Schuld am Tode Jesu zuzuschieben, dürfte (gerade auch nach dem Diasporakrieg der Jahre 115-117 oder dem Bar-Kochba-Aufstand der Jahre 132-135) für apologetische Zwecke höchst passend gewesen sein. Die von ihm gewählte Art der Darstellung, die Schuld am Tode Christi einseitig Vertretern der „Juden" zuzuschreiben, zeigt Tertullian, wie wohl auch den Verfasser des *Petrusevangeliums*[42], also als Kind seiner Zeit, eines jedoch, das die antijüdischen Motive seiner Darstellung der Passion sicherlich bewusst einsetzt.

Da der Text bisher den Eindruck hätte erwecken können, dass die Gruppe der jüdischen Lehrer und Vornehmen Handlungssouverän des knapp Geschilderten seien, muss der Schlusssatz der kurzen Passage dies widerlegen. Weder die „Juden" noch Pilatus bestimmen frei, was geschieht, Christus selbst wie auch die Propheten hatten vorhergesagt, was geschehen werde. Dass dabei an die Vorhersagen Jesu über sein Leid, seinen Tod und seine Auferstehung, wie wir sie in den synoptischen Evangelien (vgl. Mk 8,31; 9,31; 10,33-34 par.) finden, gedacht ist, ist nicht von der Hand zu weisen[43]. Während das Motiv aber z.B. im Markusevangelium im Dienste einer Christologie steht, die davor warnt, die Dimension des Leidens Christi auszublenden[44], scheint es hier als Zeichen der bleibenden Souveränität dessen, der den Weg ans Kreuz geht, verstanden zu sein. Mit dem Schlusssatz wird all dies schließlich in den breiteren Horizont dessen, was die Propheten angekündigt haben – also eines Schemas der

---

42. In Bezug auf das *Petrusevangelium* vgl. J. VERHEYDEN, *Some Reflections on Determining the Purpose of the ‚Gospel of Peter'*, in T.J. KRAUS – T. NICKLAS (Hgg.), *Das Evangelium nach Petrus: Text, Kontexte, Intertexte* (TU, 158), Berlin, De Gruyter, 2007, 281-299, S. 298: „By having the Jews take part in the trial and death of Jesus in the way as this happens in GP, its author gives witness to what cannot be otherwise described than a general and ‚unreflected' utterance of anti-Jewish sentiments that were probably widely spread throughout all levels of society but that when formulated in a purely narrative way, without any more systematical reflection, as this is the case in GP, rather echoes the voice of somebody living in and addressing a more popular, though perhaps not completely uncultivated, milieu". – Tertullian wiederum kann auf derartigen antijüdischen Vorurteilen aufbauen, setzt die antijüdischen Motive seiner Darstellung der Passion aber sicher nicht einfach nur unbewusst ein.

43. Siehe auch GEORGES, *Tertullian* (2011; Anm. 10), S. 340.

44. Hierzu weiterführend u.a. T. NICKLAS, *The Crucified Christ and the Silence of God: Thoughts on the Christology of the Gospel of Mark*, in C. KARAKOLIS – K.-W. NIEBUHR – S. ROGALSKY (Hgg.), *Gospel Images of Jesus Christ in Church Tradition and in Biblical Scholarship: Fifth International East-West Symposium of New Testament Scholars. Minsk, September 2 to 9, 2010* (WUNT, 288), Tübingen, Mohr Siebeck, 2012, 349-372.

Erfüllung des durch die Propheten Israels Angekündigten –, eingebettet. Dabei mag man natürlich darüber nachdenken, auf welche konkreten prophetischen Schriften Tertullian hier verweisen mag, und vielleicht mögen manch christliche Leser*innen sich aufgefordert gefühlt haben, ihnen bekannte Motive und Texte aus den Schriften Israels einzuspielen[45]. Der Punkt der Argumentation aber scheint mir ein ganz anderer zu sein: Das auf Propheten bezogene Schema von Verheißung und Erfüllung kann auch ohne konkrete Textbezüge funktionieren – und zwar einfach aufgrund der Autorität dessen, der es einführt. Eine Parallele hierzu zeigt sich in den lateinischen *Akten des Petrus*, wie wir sie im Codex Vercelli finden (§24): Gegenüber den Römern erweist Petrus die Vollmacht Christi durch wunderbare Taten „in seinem Namen", verweist aber gleichzeitig darauf, dass er alles, was er lehrt, auch mit Hilfe der Propheten/der Schriften Israels darlegen könne. Für sein Publikum aber, dem diese nicht vertraut seien, verweise er zwar auf diese Argumentationsmöglichkeit, führe sie aber nicht aus[46]. Ohne hier an literarische Abhängigkeit denken zu wollen: Die Parallele in der Argumentation ist interessant, betont doch auch Tertullian zunächst die sich in Wundern zeigende Vollmacht Christi und verweist anschließend knapp auf die Propheten, ohne hier ins Detail zu gehen.

Apol. 21.19

Et tamen suffixus multa mortis illius propria ostendit insignia. Nam spiritum cum uerbo sponte dimisit, praeuento carnificis officio. Eodem momento dies, medium orbem signante sole, subducta est. Deliquium utique putauerunt, qui id quoque super Christo praedicatum non scierunt: ratione non deprehensa, negauerunt, et tamen eum mundi casum relatum in arcanis uestris habetis.

Und dennoch hat er, (ans Kreuz) geschlagen, viele (ausschließlich) für jenen Tod eigentümliche Zeichen getan. Denn er ließ mit einem Wort aus eigenem Antrieb den Geist fahren und kam damit dem Dienst des Henkers zuvor. Im gleichen Moment wurde der Tag, während die Sonne die Mitte (ihrer) Kreisbahn anzeigte, entzogen. Für eine Sonnenfinsternis hielten es jedenfalls die, die nicht wussten, dass auch dies über Christus vorhergesagt war. Was sie mit dem Verstand nicht erfassten, leugneten sie, und doch habt ihr diesen Sturz der Weltordnung festgehalten in euren Archiven.

---

45. GEORGES, *Tertullian* (2011; Anm. 10), S. 340, denkt an Jes 53.
46. Tatsächlich bietet der Text einige Schriftzitate (u.a. Jes 7,14; 53,2.8 u.a.), schließt dann aber mit den Worten des Petrus: „O Männer von Rom, wenn ihr der prophetischen Schriften kundig wäret, würde ich euch alles darlegen; durch sie musste im Geheimnis auch das Reich Gottes vollendet werden. Aber dies wird euch später zugänglich werden". (Übersetzung M. DÖHLER [Hg.], *Acta Petri: Text, Übersetzung und Kommentar zu den Actus Vercellenses* [TU, 171], Berlin – Boston, MA, De Gruyter, 2018, S. 113.)

Die Tendenz des Texts, selbst den gekreuzigten Christus als Handlungssouverän darzustellen, setzt sich hier – z.T. erneut unter Ausblendung wichtiger Motive der kanonischen Evangelien – fort[47]. Wir lesen nichts davon, wie Christus nach Golgotha kommt, wie seine Kleider verlost werden (Mk 15,24 par. Mt 27,35; Lk 23,34; Joh 19,24, aber auch *EvPt* 12 und Justin, *Dial.* 97.3), wie er am Kreuz befestigt wird[48], dass all dies in Abwesenheit der Jünger geschieht, die ihn bei seiner Verhaftung verlassen haben, dass nur noch Frauen aus seiner Begleitung „von weitem" (vgl. Mk 15,40 par. Mt 27,55 und Lk 23,49[49]) zusehen etc. Es entfallen alle Motive der Verspottung des Gekreuzigten (vgl. Mk 15,29-32; Mt 27,39-44; Lk 23,35-37.39) oder auch die Rede über seinen Durst (Joh 19,28)[50]. Nichts von dem, was den Eindruck erwecken könnte, er sei von Gott verlassen (vgl. die Zitate aus Ps 22), ist erkennbar[51] – dies wäre ja auch in höchstem Maße kontraproduktiv für die Argumentation Tertullians. Stattdessen tut der Gekreuzigte Zeichen. Anders als in den kanonischen Evangelien, wo immer wieder Zeichen von Jesus gefordert sind (vgl. Mk 8,11-13 par. Mt 12,38-42; 16,1-4; Lk 11,16.29-32; Joh 2,18, aber auch 1 Kor 1,22), dieser aber nie in der Form reagiert, die von ihm erwartet

---

47. GEORGES, *Tertullian* (2011; Anm. 10), S. 340, hat Recht, dass Tertullian hier „zum großen Teil auf die Erzählungen der kanonischen Evangelien" zurückgreift. Besonders spannend erscheint mir jedoch, was alles er in seiner Darstellung entfallen lässt.

48. Auch das Motiv der „Nägel", mit denen Jesus am Kreuz befestigt wird (z.B. Joh 20,25; *EvPt* 21; Ign., *Smyrn.* 1.2; *Barn.* 5.13; Justin, *Dial.* 97.3; *1 Apol.* 35; Irenäus, *Epid.* 79), entfällt. Wo es ihm angebracht erscheint, kann auch Tertullian selbst (z.B. *Res.* 20.5 und öfter) es erwähnen.

49. Die lukanische Parallele involviert bekanntlich weitere Gruppen; Joh 19,24-27 wiederum widerspricht der Darstellung der Synoptiker, das *Petrusevangelium* schließlich übergeht das Motiv vollständig.

50. Für J. FREY, *Leiblichkeit und Auferstehung im Johannesevangelium*, in ID., *Die Herrlichkeit des Gekreuzigten: Studien zu den johanneischen Schriften I* (WUNT, 307), Tübingen, Mohr Siebeck, 2013, S. 699-738, S. 713, zeigt sich hier eines von vielen Elementen, die die wahre Menschlichkeit des joh. Jesus auch in der Passion darstellen – gerade dieser Aspekt aber würde Tertullians Tendenz der Darstellung natürlich zuwiderlaufen. – Wie problematisch dieses Motiv für die christliche Apologetik gewesen sein muss, zeigt wiederum Origenes, wenn er Celsus mit den Worten zitiert: „Gierig wurde er [Jesus] dazu getrieben, Essig und Galle zu trinken, weil er den Durst nicht ertragen könnte, wie ihn ein jeder beliebige Mensch oft erträgt" (*Cels.* 2.38, Übersetzung von H.E. LONA, *Die ‚Wahre Lehre' des Kelsos* [Kommentar zu den frühchristlichen Apologeten. Ergänzungsband, 1], Freiburg i.Br. – Basel – Wien, Herder, 2005, S. 148).

51. Zur Bedeutung und Entwicklung dieses Motivs für die verschiedenen Darstellungen der Passion Jesu im ersten und zweiten Jahrhundert vgl. T. NICKLAS, *Die Gottverlassenheit des Gottessohns: Funktionen von Psalm 22/21 LXX in frühchristlichen Auseinandersetzungen mit der Passion Jesu*, in W. EISELE – C. SCHÄFER – H.-U. WEIDEMANN (Hgg.), *Aneignung durch Transformation: Beiträge zur Analyse von Überlieferungsprozessen im frühen Christentum. Festschrift für Michael Theobald* (Herders Biblische Studien, 67), Freiburg i.Br. – Basel – Wien, Herder, 2013, 395-415.

würde, versteht Tertullian das im Zusammenhang mit der Kreuzigung Geschehene als beglaubigende Zeichen, wie sie *ausschließlich* bei jenem Tod auftraten. Christus erweist so auch seine Göttlichkeit. Ich halte es für durchaus möglich, dass Tertullian mit der Formulierung *mortis illius propria ostendit insignia* darauf anspielt, dass auch der Tod großer Figuren der Antike – oder deren mit oder nach dem Tode erfolgende Apotheose – mit großen Zeichen in Verbindung gebracht werden konnte. Tertullian selbst spricht an anderer Stelle (*Spect.* 30) von Königen, denen vor angeblichen Zeugen eine Apotheose zuteil geworden sei. Seiner Meinung nach aber verweilten diese nun in der Hölle. Die Zahl der Zeugnisse um Julius Caesar (z.B. im Zusammenhang mit seiner Apotheose im Jahr 44 v.Chr., die mit dem Auftreten eines Kometen in Verbindung gebracht wurde), Augustus, bei dessen Tod ein Adler aufgetreten sei, um seine Seele zum Himmel zu tragen (Sueton, *Aug.* 97.1), Claudius und viele andere ist groß. Zeugnisse christlicher Kritik dieser Vorstellungen lassen sich ab Justin, *1 Apol.* 21.3 und Tatian, *Or. Graec.* 10.3 belegen[52].

Interessanterweise sucht Tertullian nun nicht so viele Zeichen wie möglich zusammenzustellen. Er schweigt etwa von dem bei Mt 27,51 erwähnten Erdbeben[53], das sich womöglich auch auf natürliche Weise erklären ließe, erwähnt nichts von der ebenfalls bei Mt erwähnten Öffnung der Gräber (Mt 27,52-53) oder dem Zerreißen des Tempelvorhangs (Mk 15,38 par. Mt 27,51; Lk 23,45; *EvPt* 20). Stattdessen konzentriert er sich auf zwei Punkte, von denen der erste auf den ersten Blick unscheinbar erscheint. Womöglich inspiriert durch die lukanische Version der letzten Worte Jesu (vgl. Lk 23,46) und vielleicht auch Joh 19,33[54], entwickelt Tertullian das Argument, dass Christus – selbst als Gekreuzigter – anders als andere Menschen Souverän über seinen eigenen Tod war. Der Zusammenhang des Todes Christi mit dem zweiten Zeichen, der in den Evangelien bezeichneten dreistündigen Finsternis von der sechsten bis zur neunten Stunde (Mk 15,33 par. Mt 27,45; Lk 23,44-45; *EvPt* 15, 22)[55], wird durch die Worte „im gleichen Moment" (*eodem*

---

52. Eine ausführliche Übersicht über das Quellenmaterial bis zum Ende des 2. Jahrhunderts bietet J.G. COOK, *Empty Tomb, Resurrection, Apotheosis* (WUNT, 410), Tübingen, Mohr Siebeck, 2018, S. 426-454, von dem ich auch die oben genannten Zeugnisse ausgewählt habe.

53. Eine Parallele hierzu bietet zudem V. 21 des *Petrusevangeliums*, wo die Erde aber erst bebt, als der Leichnam des verstorbenen Herrn auf sie gelegt wird; von Erdbeben (hier als Zeichen des Gotteszorns) spricht auch die Passionserzählung in Ps-Cyprian, *De duobus montibus Sina et Sion* 8.2.

54. Beide Bezüge auch bei GEORGES, *Tertullian* (2011; Anm. 10), S. 340.

55. Weitere apokryphe Parallelen, die zeigen, wie sehr das Motiv sich grundsätzlich im kulturellen Gedächtnis des frühen Christentums „eingegraben" hat, wie sehr es aber

momento) zum Ausdruck gebracht. Tertullian datiert den Beginn der Finsternis wie die Evangelien auf die Mittagsstunde; gleichzeitig aber stellt er sich, vielleicht um den Bezug des Zeichens auf den Zeitpunkt des Todes Jesu klarer zum Ausdruck zu bringen, hier auch *gegen die kanonischen Evangelien*, die den Tod Jesu erst mit dem Ende der Finsternis, also der neunten Stunde, verbinden[56]. Noch die kanonischen Evangelien reflektieren an keiner Stelle über die möglichen Reaktionen der Umstehenden, während das *Petrusevangelium* von ihrer Angst (V. 15) spricht und, wohl inspiriert von Jes 58,2, eine eigenartige Szene einbaut, nach der „viele mit Leuchtern umher" liefen, „weil sie glaubten, es sei Nacht", und hinfielen (V. 18)[57]. Der Gedanke, dass beim Tod Jesu eine Sonnenfinsternis geherrscht habe (vgl. auch Tertullian, *Scap.* 3.3) ist nicht unbedingt „gegenüber den Evangelien neu"[58], sondern kann durchaus durch Lk 23,45a (τοῦ ἡλίου ἐκλιπόντος) inspiriert sein[59]. Gleichzeitig bietet Tertullian, soweit ich sehe, das früheste greifbare Zeugnis einer Debatte, ob sich die Finsternis beim Tode Jesu auf natürliche Weise erklären lasse. Während bereits Hieronymus, *In Matt.* 27.45, gegen „diejenigen, die gegen die Evangelien geschrieben haben", darauf verweist, dass „eine Sonnenfinsternis ausschließlich beim Aufgang des Mondes zu geschehen pflegt" und dabei womöglich auf eine Kritik des Porphyrios reagiert, hält Origenes in Auseinandersetzung mit Celsus an der Deutung fest, dass es sich um eine Sonnenfinsternis gehandelt habe, die zudem auch durch Buch 13 oder 14 der Chronik des Phlegon von Tralleis belegt sei (*Cels.* 2.33). Der Idee, dass dieses Ereignis wunderbar sei, tut dies für Origenes keinen Abbruch[60]. Für Tertullian dagegen wäre es falsch, an eine „natürliche" Erklärung mit Hilfe einer (zufällig zur gleichen Zeit auftretenden) Sonnenfinsternis zu denken. Das Ereignis sei einerseits

---

auch weiterhin variiert werden konnte, finden sich u.a. in den *Sibyllinischen Orakeln* (1.374-375 sowie 8.305-306), in §97 der apokryphen *Johannesakten* und im *Nikodemusevangelium* 11[1].

56. So auch knapp GEORGES, *Tertullian* (2011; Anm. 10), S. 340.
57. Zum Hintergrund der Szene in Jes 58,2 vgl. T. NICKLAS, *Das Petrusevangelium im Rahmen antiker Jesustraditionen*, in ID., *Studien zum Petrusevangelium* (WUNT, 453), Tübingen, Mohr Siebeck, 2020, 63-89, S. 74-75.
58. So GEORGES, *Tertullian* (2011; Anm. 10), S. 340, dem ich auch die Parallele in *Scap.* 3.3 verdanke.
59. So schreibt auch H. KLEIN, *Das Lukasevangelium* (KEK, 1/3), Göttingen, Vandenhoeck & Ruprecht, 2006, S. 713, Anm. 9: „Lk denkt wohl an eine Sonnenfinsternis. Eine solche freilich ist bei Vollmond nicht möglich".
60. Ausführlicher zu diesen Parallelen vgl. auch M. BECKER, *Porphyrios, ‚Contra Christianos': Neue Sammlung der Fragmente, Testimonien und Dubia mit Einleitung, Übersetzung und Anmerkungen* (Texte und Kommentare, 52), Berlin – Boston, MA, De Gruyter, 2016, S. 516-517.

über Christus prophezeit worden – wie bereits oben ist kein konkreter Beleg angegeben[61] –, andererseits aber lasse es sich auch nicht leugnen, denn es sei „in euren Archiven" und somit überprüfbar festgehalten: Welche Quellen damit konkret gemeint sind, bleibt unklar. Doch auch wenn sich ein Bezug auf konkrete Quellen herstellen ließe, würde das Argument weiterhin in erster Linie auf der Autorität Tertullians beruhen, der damit rechnen kann, dass niemand aus seiner Leserschaft konkret überprüfen könnte, in welchen „Archiven" sich dieses Ereignis finde[62]; sehr wahrscheinlich hatte er selbst solche Aufzeichnungen nie gesehen[63]. Tertullians Fazit ist klar: Vor diesem Hintergrund könne an nichts anderes als einen „Sturz der Weltordnung" gedacht werden, der eigentlich allen, die Verstand hätten, einsichtig sein müsse[64]. Damit aber ist – ohne dies explizit erwähnen zu müssen – ein Beweis für die Göttlichkeit Christi erbracht.

Apol. 21.20

Tunc Iudaei detractum et sepulchro conditum magna etiam militaris custodiae diligentia circumsederunt, ne, quia praedixerat tertia die resurrecturum se a morte, discipuli furto amoliti cadauer fallerent suspectos.

Alsdann stellten die Juden, nachdem er abgenommen und in einem Grab bestattet worden war, gar mit großer Sorgfalt ringsherum kriegserfahrene Wachen auf, damit nicht die Schüler, da er ja vorhergesagt hatte, dass er am dritten Tag vom Tod auferstehen werde, durch Diebstahl den Leichnam beseitigten und sie, die Argwöhnischen, betrogen.

Während der Text noch in 21.19 mehrere matthäische Motive „unterschlagen" hat, bietet er nun – zum Erweis dafür, dass der Leichnam Jesu nicht gestohlen worden sein kann – eine knappe Darstellung der nur bei Mt 27,62-66 (vgl. aber auch die Parallele im *EvPt* 30–45)[65] geschilderten

---

61. Erneut ist ein solcher Beleg nicht nötig, das Argument funktioniert über die Autorität des Tertullian alleine (siehe auch oben zu 21.18). Natürlich aber kann man mit GEORGES, *Tertullian* (2011; Anm. 10), S. 340, an Amos 8,9 denken.

62. GEORGES, *Tertullian* (2015; Anm. 17), S. 166, Anm. 290, gibt weitere Informationen, worauf Tertullian anspielen könnte: „Tertullian dürfte hier wie in *apol.* 5,2 an den Bericht des Pontius Pilatus an Tiberius über die Geschichte im Umfeld der Kreuzigung denken, den er in *apol.* 21,24 erwähnt. Schon Justin, 1 *apol.* 35,9 … 48,3 … hat von Akten gesprochen, die unter Pontius Pilatus angefertigt worden seien und Details zur Kreuzigung enthalten hätten. In römischen Quellen aus der Zeit Jesu finden solche Akten aber keine Erwähnung".

63. So auch GEORGES, *Tertullian* (2011, Anm. 10), S. 341.

64. Vgl. hier den Zusammenhang mit 21.10, wo Tertullian davon spricht, dass Gott die Welt durch „Wort, Vernunft und Kraft" (*uerbo et ratione et uirtute*) erschaffen habe.

65. Zudem ist an den *Brief des Pilatus an Claudius* zu denken, der so formuliert ist, als seien „die Juden" allein für die Bewachung des Grabs verantwortlich gewesen.

Bewachung des Grabes. Die Kreuzabnahme, für die sich besonders das *Petrusevangelium* interessiert (V. 21), wie auch die Grablegung durch Josef von Arimathäa (Mk 15,42-47 par. Mt 27,57-61; Lk 23,50-56; *EvPt* 3–5, 24) bzw. durch denselben gemeinsam mit Nikodemus (Joh 19,38-42) werden dagegen nur knapp gestreift. Auch die weitere Erzählung wird in stark geraffter Weise präsentiert: Aus den Lehrern und Vornehmsten der Juden in 21.18 (bzw. den Oberpriestern und Pharisäern bei Mt 27,62) werden nun einfach die *Iudaei*. Die genauen Zeitangaben in Mt 27,62 sind durch einfaches *tunc* ersetzt; die Szene, in der die Priester und Pharisäer Pilatus um eine Grabeswache bitten, welche dieser dann auch gewährt (Mt 27,62-65), fällt vollkommen aus. Pilatus spielt hier überhaupt keine Rolle mehr[66]. Betont wird hier nicht nur die alleinige Initiative der „Juden"[67], sondern – auch im Vergleich zum matthäischen Text – die Tatsache, dass ein Leichenraub nicht möglich ist. Da der Umweg über Pilatus ausfällt, muss betont werden, dass es sich bei der Wache nicht um unerfahrenes Tempelpersonal handelt, sondern echte Soldaten. Dass sie „mit großer Sorgfalt ringsherum" aufgestellt sind, zeigt, dass es sich nicht nur um zwei Mann handeln kann. Gerade deswegen ist interessant, dass Tertullian nicht von einer Versiegelung des Steins, der am Eingang des Grabes liegt, spricht (Mt 27,66; vgl. noch stärker *EvPt* 33) – eigentlich ein Motiv, das seiner Darstellungsabsicht entgegengekommen wäre. Vielleicht ist dies ein Indiz dafür, dass er, der sicherlich die Evangelien des Neuen Testaments kennt (und, wenn es sein muss, auch an ihren Textdetails argumentieren kann)[68], hier so etwas wie eine „virtuelle Erzählung"[69] von Passion und Auferstehung bietet, bei deren Zusammenstellung er nicht konkret schriftliche Texte des Neuen Testaments vor Augen hat. Das Ziel der Darstellung ist klar: Mit ihrem Versuch das Grab gegen einen Leichenraub zu sichern, liefern „die Juden" ungewollt einen Beweis, dass ein Betrug durch die Schüler Jesu unmöglich ist – und stattdessen die erwähnte Vorhersage Christi, er werde am dritten Tage auferstehen (vgl. Mk 8,31; 9,31; 10,34 par.), eingetroffen ist. Wie wichtig es ist, die Erzählung gegen offenbar umgehende Gerüchte von einem Leichenraub

---

66. So auch Georges, *Tertullian* (2011; Anm. 10), S. 341.
67. Ganz ähnlich die Parallele im *Brief des Pilatus an Claudius*.
68. Dies wird bekanntlich überaus deutlich in seiner Schrift gegen Marcion, wo er Marcions Evangelium in der ihm vorliegenden Form zitiert, um damit Marcions Denken zu widerlegen (vgl. *Adv. Marc.* 4.6.1-2).
69. Zur Vorstellung des Neuen Testaments als einer bei antiken Autoren „mentalen" oder „virtuellen Größe" vgl. A. Merkt in Zusammenarbeit mit T. Nicklas – J. Verheyden, *Das Novum Testamentum Patristicum (NTP): Ein Projekt zur Erforschung von Rezeption und Auslegung des Neuen Testaments in frühchristlicher und spätantiker Zeit*, in *Early Christianity* 6 (2015) 573-595, S. 579.

abzusichern, deuten auch Passagen wie Mt 28,15, *EvPt* 30, Justin, *Dial.* 108.2 oder Tertullian, *Spect.* 30.6 an[70].

Apol. 21.21

> *Sed ad tertium diem*[71] *concussa repente terra et mole reuoluta, quae obstruxerat sepulchrum, et custodia pauore disiecta, nullis apparentibus discipulis nihil in sepulcro repertum est praeter exuuias sepulturae*[72].
>
> Doch als am dritten Tag plötzlich die Erde erschüttert, die Felsmasse, die das Grab versperrt hatte, zurückgewälzt und die Wache vor Entsetzen auseinandergejagt wurde, ohne dass einer der Schüler sich gezeigt hätte, wurde im Grab nichts als die abgelegte Kleidung zur Bestattung gefunden.

Entsprechend der in 21.20 erwähnten Vorhersage, dass Christus am dritten Tage auferstehen werde, werden nun, ohne erneut explizit von Jesu Auferstehung sprechen zu müssen[73], äußerlich erkennbare Zeichen geschildert, die auch den zweifelnden Außenstehenden deutlich machen sollen, was im Grab geschieht. Wie in Mt 28,2, allerdings ohne das Kommen der Frauen (Mt 28,1) zu erwähnen, ist von einem überraschenden Erdbeben die Rede, jedoch nichts von einem Engel des Herrn, der den Felsen vor dem Grab weg wälzt und sich auf das Grab setzt. Dieses für ein jüdisches Publikum verstehbare Bild des Handelns Gottes an dem Verstorbenen hätte für das Zielpublikum vielleicht zu „exotisch" und damit schwer akzeptabel gewirkt. Auf welche Weise der das Grab versperrende, auch hier indirekt als „groß" beschriebene Felsen entfernt wird, bleibt in Tertullians Text also offen. Dass sich antike christliche Texte die Szene auch so vorstellen konnten, dass der Stein „von selbst ins Rollen geriet" und „zur Seite rückte", um den Eingang zu öffnen, zeigt die Parallele in V. 37 des *Petrusevangeliums*[74]. Interessant ist vor allem der Umgang mit dem nächsten Motiv: Anders als die matthäische Parallele spricht Tertullian zwar das Entsetzen (*pauor*; vgl. Mt 28,4:

---

70. Das Thema scheint, soweit ich sehe, keine Rolle im *Alethes Logos* des Celsus oder in den erhaltenen Fragmenten des Porphyrios gespielt zu haben. Den vielleicht originellsten Umgang mit dem Problem finden wir in Kapitel 54 der syrischen *Schatzhöhle*, wo Petrus tatsächlich versucht, die Wachen betrunken zu machen und den Leichnam Jesu zu stehlen, ihm der Auferstandene aber zuvorkommt.

71. Der Text ist hier uneindeutig überliefert. Ich folge mit GEORGES, *Tertullian* (2011; Anm. 10) der Ausgabe von DEKKERS (Anm. 29) und damit dem Text des Codex Fuldensis. Anders C. BECKER, *Tertullian. Apologeticum: Lateinisch-deutsch*, München, Kösel, 1952.

72. Der Text ist hier uneindeutig überliefert. Ich folge mit GEORGES, *Tertullian* (2011; Anm. 10) der Ausgabe von DEKKERS (Anm. 29) und damit dem Text des Codex Fuldensis.

73. Diesen Hinweis gibt auch GEORGES, *Tertullian* (2011; Anm. 10), S. 341.

74. GEORGES, *ibid.*, sieht die Szene dagegen alleine aus Mt 28,1-4 entwickelt, eine durchaus plausible Annahme. Die Parallele zum *EvPt* scheint mir jedoch trotzdem nicht irrelevant.

φόβος)⁷⁵ der Wachen an, nicht aber das Motiv, dass diese deswegen „wie tot wurden". Anders als im *Petrusevangelium* wiederum wird der eigentliche Vorgang der Auferweckung Christi (V. 36-42) nicht beschrieben. Somit können die Wachen auch nicht als Zeugen des Ereignisses verstanden werden. Dass Tertullian im Grunde ohne echte Parallele im Matthäusevangelium (eventuell Mt 28,11; vgl. auch *EvPt* 45) als Ergebnis der Ereignisse beschreibt, dass die Wache „auseinandergejagt wurde", führt dazu, dass er noch einmal betonen muss, dass keiner der Schüler Jesu sich bei diesen Ereignissen gezeigt hat. Erneut zeigt sich: Jede Vorstellung davon, dass hier ein Leichenraub vorliegt (und/oder die Soldaten womöglich durch bewaffnete Jesusnachfolger vertrieben wurden), muss verhindert werden. Mit dieser Schwerpunktsetzung allerdings ist Tertullian gezwungen, die in allen Evangelien bezeugte Tradition um die Frauen am Grab Jesu völlig beiseite zu lassen, eine Entscheidung, die ihm vielleicht sogar gelegen kommt⁷⁶: Dem möglichen Gegenargument, dass der Osterglaube der Christen zuallererst auf dem Zeugnis einer „hysterischen Frau" beruhe⁷⁷, wird dadurch schon von vornherein jegliche Grundlage entzogen.

Von der abgelegten Begräbniskleidung Jesu, die natürlich signalisiert, dass er nichts mehr mit dem Tode zu tun hat, ist in Lk 23,12 – Petrus sieht nur die Leinenbinden liegen – und dann ausführlicher im Johannesevangelium die Rede. Beim Wettlauf der Jünger zum Grab (Joh 20,1-10) werden nacheinander mehrere Blicke ins leere Grab geschildert: Maria Magdalena erkennt offenbar, dass der Leichnam Jesu nicht mehr im Grab ist (Joh 20,1.2), der Lieblingsjünger sieht von außen die Leinenbinden (Joh 20,5), Petrus die Leinenbinden und auch das Schweißtuch vom Kopf Jesu (Joh 20,6-7)⁷⁸. Die Tatsache, dass alles einen geordneten Eindruck hinterlässt, zeigt nicht nur, dass nicht an einen Leichenraub zu denken ist, sondern stellt einen deutlichen Kontrast zur Auferweckung des Lazarus her, der erst noch von seinen Binden und dem Schweißtuch, das sein Gesicht verhüllt, befreit werden muss, bevor er weggeht (Joh 11,44). Das

---

75. Anders als bei Tertullian bezieht sich die Furcht der Wachen aber auf die Erscheinung des Engels. In der parallelen Szene im *Petrusevangelium* wiederum werden Wachen und Vertreter der jüdischen Obrigkeit zu Zeugen der Auferweckung Jesu; die Angst der Wachen wird erst später (V. 45: ἀγωνιῶντες μεγάλως) geschildert.

76. Auch GEORGES, *Tertullian* (2011; Anm. 10), S. 342, geht davon aus, dass Tertullian auf die Frauen am Grab bewusst verzichtet.

77. Vgl. hierzu z.B. das Argument des Celsus im *Alethes Logos* (erhalten bei Origenes, *Cels.* 2.55). Porphyrios wiederum scheint nach dem Zeugnis des Petrus Comestor, *Hist. scholast, In evangelia* 185 die Tatsache zu kritisieren, dass die verschiedenen Grabeserzählungen verschiedene Frauen erwähnen. Hierzu BECKER, *Porphyrios* (Anm. 60), S. 355-357.

78. Auch GEORGES, *Tertullian* (2011; Anm. 10), S. 342, hält Joh 20,5-7 für den wahrscheinlichen Hintergrund der Passage.

bei Lukas nur angedeutete und im Johannesevangelium komplex ausgebaute Motiv der „Begräbniskleidung" wird bei Tertullian nur ganz knapp angespielt: Wo die (offenbar von Christus selbst) *abgelegte* Begräbniskleidung gefunden wird, liegt ein weiteres Indiz vor, dass an einen Leichenraub nicht zu denken ist. Wer bei welcher Gelegenheit all dies vorfindet, wird (sicherlich bewusst) nicht erwähnt: Zumindest in der Logik der Tertullian'schen Darstellung können es eigentlich nicht die Schüler sein, im Grunde aber auch nicht die fliehenden Soldaten. Der Text erwartet ein Publikum, das eine solch differenzierte Frage nicht stellt. Selbst mit den Grundlinien der kanonischen Evangelien vertraute Leser*innen können ihm zustimmen, solange ihnen die Erzählungen der Evangelien nicht zu genau vor Augen stehen.

Apol. 21.22

> *Nihilominus tamen primores Iudaeorum, quorum intererat et scelus diuulgare et populum uectigalem et famularem sibi a fide auocare, subreptum a discipulis iactitauerunt. Nam nec ille se in uulgus eduxit, ne impii errore liberantur, sed ut fides, non mediocri praemio destinata, difficultate constaret.*
>
> Nichtsdestotrotz haben die Vornehmsten der Juden, denen daran gelegen war, (unter dem gemeinen Volk) die Rede von einem Verbrechen zu verbreiten und das ihnen gegenüber tributpflichtige und unterworfene Volk vom Glauben abzuhalten, dennoch öffentlich verbreitet, er sei von den Schülern heimlich gestohlen worden. Denn jener verbrachte ja auch keine Zeit im gemeinen Volk, damit die Gottlosen nicht vom Irrtum befreit würden, damit aber der Glaube, dem eine nicht geringe Belohnung festgesetzt ist, auf Beschwerlichkeit gegründet sei.

Das Motiv, dass die Hohenpriester – nun zusammen mit den Ältesten – aufgrund der Berichte der Grabeswache das Gerücht verbreiten, der Leichnam Jesu sei „von den Schülern heimlich gestohlen worden", findet seine Parallele natürlich erneut im Matthäusevangelium (Mt 28,11-15; vgl. auch die Darstellung im *Brief des Pilatus an Claudius*), welches die Szene jedoch deutlich ausführlicher schildert: Die dort zu findenden Motive einer Bestechung der Soldaten (Mt 28,12-13) und der Beschwichtigung des Pilatus (Mt 28,14) spielen für Tertullian allerdings keine Rolle[79]. Während Mt dieses Verhalten als Begründung dafür sieht, dass „bei Judäern" (Mt 28,15: παρὰ Ἰουδαίοις)[80] diese Rede bis heute verbreitet sei,

---

79. GEORGES, *Tertullian* (2011; Anm. 10), S. 342, schreibt: „Wie schon in 21,20 werden die Römer ... aus dem Geschehen gänzlich ausgeschlossen".

80. Das MtEv verwendet das Wort Ἰουδαῖοι außer bei der Rede vom βασιλεὺς τῶν Ἰουδαίων (Mt 2,2; 27,11.29.37) nur hier; anders als im Johannesevangelium halte ich deswegen die hier angegebene Übersetzung für angemessen; sie ist zudem auch sinnvoll, weil das Gerücht sich auch geographisch eindeutig in Judäa verbreitet.

differenziert Tertullian zwischen den *primores Iudaeorum* und dem gemeinen Volk. Letzteres wird sowohl neutral als *populus*, welches den *primores* gegenüber tributpflichtig[81] und unterworfen ist, als auch abschätziger als *uulgus* (vgl. auch die Verwendung des Verbs *diuulgare*) bezeichnet. Dies erinnert zunächst einmal an die Darstellung des *Petrusevangeliums*, wo die Soldaten als Zeugen der Auferstehung gezwungen werden zu schweigen (V. 48-49)[82] – und damit das wenigstens im Ansatz Reue zeigende Volk (V. 28) vom möglichen Glauben abgehalten wird.

Auf mehreren Ebenen spannend ist schließlich der zweite Teil des Abschnitts, der in dieser Form keine Parallele in den kanonischen Evangelien findet: Zunächst einmal distanziert Tertullian den „Lehrer Jesus", seine Lehre und seine Schüler vom allgemeinen Pöbel. Zum zweiten Mal bestätigt sich, dass Tertullian die christliche Bewegung keineswegs als Bewegung *von unten* beschreibt oder als solche, die in erster Linie die einfachsten Leute im Blick hat. Er verbindet den Pöbel stattdessen mit Gottlosigkeit und Irrtum – es hat keinen Wert, bei solchen Leuten etwas zu ändern. Gleichzeitig zeigt sich die Sinnspitze des Abschnitts, nämlich die Antwort auf eine überaus naheliegende Frage: Warum hat sich der Auferstandene nur wenigen Menschen gezeigt? Wäre er in großer Öffentlichkeit aufgetreten, wäre Gerüchten über einen Leichenraub doch sofort der Boden entzogen. Während 1 Kor 15,6 immerhin von einer Erscheinung vor 500 Brüdern zugleich sprechen kann, von denen offenbar viele immer noch als Zeugen befragt werden können, hat Apg 10,40-41 das Problem zumindest im Blick, wenn sie Petrus davon sprechen lässt, dass der Auferweckte nicht dem gesamten Volk (Apg 10,41: οὐ παντὶ τῷ λαῷ), sondern nur den von Gott vorherbestimmten Zeugen erschienen ist[83]. Wie groß das Problem ist, mit dem sich Tertullian auseinanderzusetzen hat, zeigt ein Blick in den *Alethes Logos* des Celsus[84], der schreibt, dass Jesus, wenn er „wirklich seine göttliche Macht offenbaren wollte, ... vor denen, die ihn verachteten, und vor dem, der ihn verurteilte und überhaupt vor allen Menschen hätte erscheinen müssen" (bei Origenes, *Cels.* 2.61; vgl. ähnlich auch *Cels.* 2.70)[85]. Tertullians Argument vermag nur ansatzweise zu überzeugen: Hätte sich der Auferstandene vor allen

---

81. WALTZING, *Commentaire* (Anm. 36), S. 153, hält dies für historisch glaubwürdig; dies ist zumindest in dieser Form wohl kaum zu halten, sondern ein literarisches Mittel Tertullians, um die Gegner Jesu noch einmal negativer zeichnen zu können.

82. Nach dem *Brief des Pilatus an Claudius* schließlich wird den Soldaten befohlen zu schweigen, diese aber halten sich nicht daran.

83. Die Apostelgeschichte hat hier offensichtlich das Volk Israel im Blick.

84. Ich gehe natürlich nicht davon aus, dass Tertullian auf diese Schrift reagiert, vermute aber, dass er mit Argumenten wie denjenigen, die wir bei Celsus finden, konfrontiert gewesen sein mag.

85. Übersetzung LONA, *Wahre Lehre* (Anm. 50), S. 163.

gezeigt, dann wäre der Glaube nicht mehr „auf Beschwerlichkeit gegründet" (*difficultate constaret*). Vor allem wenn man bedenkt, wie viel Mühe er bisher dafür aufgewendet hat, um die Göttlichkeit Christi möglichst zweifelsfrei zu demonstrieren, wirkt dies eher dünn. Der Gedanke schließt jedoch an das Motiv der Verstockung der Juden in 21.16 an[86] und findet seine Logik in der Vorstellung, dass der reiche Lohn, der (von Gott her) für den Glauben festgesetzt ist, in angemessener Weise verdient sein muss. Dies erinnert neben der Diskussion um Lohn und Mühe der Nachfolge in den Evangelien[87] auch an das in Zwei-Wege-Lehren zu findende Motiv, dass der Weg, der zur Gerechtigkeit führt, beschwerlich sei (vgl. das Motiv des Jochs in *Did.* 6.2 oder das der Mühe in *Barn.* 19.1). Ein konkreter literarischer Hintergrund des Gedankens bei Tertullian ist jedoch nicht zu erkennen.

Apol. 21.23

Cum discipulis autem quibusdam apud Galilaeam Iudaeae regionis ad quinquaginta dies egit docens eos quae docerent. Dehinc ordinatis eis ad officium praedicandi per orbem, cicumfusa nube in caelum est ereptus multo uerius quam apud uos asseuerare de Romulis Proculi solent.

Mit einigen Schülern aber verbrachte er an die 50 Tage bei Galiläa in der Region Judäa und lehrte sie, was sie lehren sollten. Nachdem er sie zum Dienst, öffentlich in der ganzen Welt zu sprechen, bestellt hatte, wurde er, von einer Wolke umgeben, in den Himmel entrückt – (und zwar) um vieles wahrer, als es bei euch die Proculusse über die Romulusse zu versichern pflegen.

Anstelle sich vor aller Welt oder gar dem Pöbel zu präsentieren, setzt der Auferstandene die Belehrung seiner Schüler auch nach dem Osterereignis fort. Die Bedeutung des Bildfelds „Lehre", „Lehren", „Schule" hält sich durch: Tertullian inszeniert das Christentum so als Bildungsbewegung, deren Lehre auf den göttlichen Lehrer Christus zurückgeht. Unklar dagegen ist, warum der Text nur von „einigen Schülern" spricht: Ist daran gedacht, dass Judas nicht mehr Teil der Jüngerschar ist? Ich halte dies für unwahrscheinlich. Das Problem löst sich, wenn man bedenkt, dass ein nichtchristliches Publikum wohl, anders als christliche Leser*innen, nichts von der Gruppe der Zwölf wissen kann, sondern – neben dem Hinweis, dass eine große Menschenmenge Christus folgte – nur, dass Christus eine Gruppe von Schülern hatte. So gesehen besagt der Satz nur, dass nicht nur ein Schüler, sondern gleich mehrere

---

86. So auch GEORGES, *Tertullian* (2011; Anm. 10), S. 343.
87. GEORGES, *ibid.*, erinnert hier an Parallelen in den synoptischen Evangelien zu den Themen „Nachfolge" (Mk 8,34-38 par.) und „Lohn" (Mk 10,28-31 par.), die aber an keiner Stelle in vergleichbarer Weise mit dem Motiv der Erscheinung des Auferweckten verbunden sind.

von ihm belehrt wurden[88]. Auch konkrete Namen sind für den Kontext, in dem Tertullian schreibt, unwichtig. Schwer zu beantworten ist allerdings die Frage, warum Tertullian gegen die Angaben der Apostelgeschichte (vgl. Apg 1,2-3) von einer etwa fünfzigtägigen Belehrung der Schüler ausgeht. Apg 1,2 spricht davon, dass er auserwählten Aposteln Gebote gegeben hat, was in Apg 1,3 dadurch illustriert wird, dass er 40 Tage lang erschienen sei und dabei über die Königsherrschaft Gottes gesprochen habe. Ob die Zahl 50 auf einem Versehen Tertullians beruht, ob sie bewusst gegen die Angaben der Apostelgeschichte gesetzt ist oder ob sie aus einem fehlerhaften Text der Apostelgeschichte (oder aus einer apokryphen Tradition) stammt, lässt sich nicht eindeutig entscheiden. Trotz der hier nicht eindeutigen Überlieferung im Text Tertullians scheint sie aber ursprünglich zu sein[89]. Dass die Angaben der Passage insgesamt aber auch nicht einfach auf das lukanische Doppelwerk alleine zurückgehen können, zeigt die Verortung in Galiläa, das zudem unpräzise als Teil der „Region Judäa" bezeichnet wird[90]. Insgesamt jedoch vermischt das Gesagte Angaben aus der Apostelgeschichte mit denen des Markus- und des Matthäusevangeliums[91]: Von einer ausführlichen Belehrung wie der hier genannten ist – innerhalb des Kanons[92] – nur in der Apostelgeschichte die Rede, dort jedoch in Jerusalem. Während das Markusevangelium auf eine Begegnung in Galiläa vorausverweist (vgl. Mk 16,7), ohne von dieser zu berichten, spricht Mt 28,16 von einer Begegnung der Elf mit dem Auferstandenen auf einem Berg in Galiläa. Der bei Tertullian darüber hinaus erwähnte Auftrag an die Schüler[93], öffentlich in der ganzen

---

88. Vielleicht mag Apg 1,2 eine Rolle spielen, wo von den Aposteln, die er auserwählte, die Rede ist.

89. Vgl. hierzu die Diskussion bei GEORGES, *Tertullian* (2011; Anm. 10), S. 343, sowie (zur Textüberlieferung bei Tertullian, bei der nur Codex Fuldensis die Zahl 50 bietet) *ibid.*, S. 343, Anm. 767. Weitere altkirchliche Zeugnisse, die die Himmelfahrt Christi nach 50 Tagen verorten, bietet U. HOLZMEISTER, *Der Tag der Himmelfahrt des Herrn*, in ZKT 55 (1933) 44-82, S. 61-66; besonders wichtig aber erscheint die bei Holzmeister nicht erwähnte, aber bei GEORGES, *Tertullian* (2011; Anm. 10), S. 343, Anm. 767, angegebene Parallele bei Tertullian selbst (*Bapt.* 19.2).

90. Zur Erklärung vgl. aber WALTZING, *Commentaire* (Anm. 36), S. 153.

91. Siehe auch die Angaben bei GEORGES, *Tertullian* (2011; Anm. 10), S. 343.

92. Außerhalb des Kanons ist natürlich an die vielen Dialogevangelien zu erinnern, die von einer besonderen Lehre des Auferstandenen, die nur besonders erwählten Schüler*innen zukommt. Konkret ist an Texte wie die *Sophia Jesu Christi*, das *Apokryphon des Johannes*, die *Epistula Apostolorum*, das *Mariaevangelium* u.a. zu denken. Grundlegend hierzu J. HARTENSTEIN, *Die zweite Lehre: Erscheinungen des Auferstandenen als Rahmenerzählungen frühchristlicher Dialoge* (TU, 146), Berlin, Akademie, 2000.

93. Die Formulierung spricht von der Einsetzung in ein Amt (vgl. auch WALTZING, *Commentaire* [Anm. 36], S. 153) – man könnte im Grunde von einem „Lehramt" sprechen; vgl. aber auch die etwas freiere Deutung bei D. RANKIN, *Tertullian* (Anm. 12), S. 137: „is used to denote Christ's sending out of the disciples after his Resurrection".

Welt zu sprechen, findet sich zwar sinngemäß mehrfach, in der vorliegenden Form aber konkret in keinem der Evangelien des Neuen Testaments. Nach Mt 28,19 sendet der Auferweckte die Elf aus, damit diese alle Völker belehren; Lk 24,47 spricht davon, dass allen Völkern auf seinen Namen hin *Metanoia*[94] zur Vergebung der Sünden verkündet werden solle. Unserer Stelle am nächsten kommt deswegen der sekundäre, lange Schluss des Markusevangeliums, wo der Auferweckte den Elf befiehlt, in die ganze Welt zu gehen und der gesamten Schöpfung die frohe Botschaft zu verkünden (Mk 16,15). Der Gedanke steht zudem als Impuls hinter der kanonischen Apostelgeschichte, die die Apostel bis an die „Grenzen der Erde" führt (vgl. Apg 1,8), aber auch vielen apokryphen Apostelerzählungen, die vor dem Hintergrund des Impulses verfasst sind, dass die verschiedenen Apostel die verschiedenen Teile der Welt als ihre Missionsgebiete aufteilen und dann je eines davon bereisen[95]. Interessant ist wieder, was bei Tertullian im Vergleich zu den möglichen Vorlagen fehlt: Wir lesen nichts von einem Taufauftrag (Mt 28,19; vgl. auch Mk 16,16) noch einem Auftrag zur Lehre (Mt 28,19-20), auch nichts über die Zeichen, die durch die Glaubenden geschehen werden (Mk 16,17-18). Die Szene mündet in einer kurzen Darstellung der Entrückung Christi, die neutestamentliche Parallelen natürlich in Lk 24,50-52 und Apg 1,9-11 (vgl. auch Mk 16,19a) findet. Am nächsten kommt sicherlich Apg 1,9, wo auch das Motiv, dass Jesus von einer Wolke aufgenommen wird, begegnet[96].

Diese Himmelfahrt, so Tertullian, sei „um vieles wahrer, als es bei euch die Proculusse über die Romulusse zu versichern pflegen" und setzt damit Traditionen voraus, wie sie bei Livius 1.16 (zu Iulius Proculus) und Plutarch, *Rom.* 28 (zu Romulus) überliefert und schon im *Octavius* des Minucius Felix (24.1) von christlicher Seite kritisiert werden[97]. Wie auch Minucius Felix, anders aber als Justin, *1 Apol.* 21.3[98], vermeidet

---

94. Ich deute diesen Begriff mit Stefan Alkier als „Umdenken". Hierzu T. NICKLAS, *Buße tun heißt „Um-Denken"! Neutestamentliche Perspektiven*, in S. DEMEL – M. PFLEGER (Hgg.), *Das Sakrament der Barmherzigkeit: Welche Chance hat die Beichte?*, Freiburg i.Br. – Basel – Wien, Herder, 2017, 383-400.

95. Man denke hier z.B. an die *Akten des Thomas* (und Indien), das *Martyrium des Markus* (und Alexandrien) oder selbst die *Akten des Andreas und Matthias* (und die Anthropophagenstadt Myrmidonia).

96. Eine weitere Parallele, die im Kern wohl auf das 2. Jahrhundert zurückgehen dürfte, bietet die apokryphe *Petrusapokalypse*, die in der entsprechenden Passage aber nur in äthiopischer Sprache erhalten ist (Kap. 17 mit besonderer Betonung des Motivs der Wolke) und Elemente der Himmelfahrt Jesu mit solchen seiner Verklärung vermischt.

97. Hinweise auch bei BECKER, *Apologeticum* (Anm. 71), S. 309, und GEORGES, *Tertullian* (2011; Anm. 10), S. 344.

98. Eine ausführlichere Diskussion dieser Passage bietet J. ULRICH, *Justin. Apologien* (Kommentar zu frühchristlichen Apologeten, 4/5), Freiburg i.Br. – Basel – Wien, Herder, 2019, S. 259-260.

Tertullian wohl bewusst die ihm sicherlich bekannten Beispiele römischer Kaiserapotheosen[99] – eine solche Kritik würde in Anbetracht der angezielten Leserschaft vielleicht zu weit gehen[100].

Apol. 21.24

> Et omnia super Christo Pilatus, et ipse iam pro sua conscientia Christianus, Caesari tunc Tiberio nuntiauit. Sed et Caesares credidissent super Christo, si aut Caesares non essent necessarii saeculo, aut si et Christiani potuissent esse Caesares.
> Und alles über Christus hat Pilatus, auch selbst seiner Überzeugung nach ein Christ, dem damaligen Kaiser Tiberius gemeldet. Und auch die Kaiser hätten an Christus geglaubt, wenn die Kaiser nicht für die Weltzeit notwendig wären oder wenn auch Christen Kaiser hätten sein können.

Der Gedanke, dass Pilatus dem Kaiser Tiberius (14-37 n.Chr.) „alles über Christus" gemeldet habe, steht in Zusammenhang mit dem bereits in *Apol.* 5.2 Berichteten[101], Tiberius habe den Senat über die Geschehnisse informiert, die ihm aus Syria Palaestina gemeldet worden waren und „die dort die Wahrheit über die Göttlichkeit von jenem [d.h. Christus] offenbart hatten" (*ueritatem istius diuinitatis reuelauerant*). Obwohl der Kaiser selbst bereits die Sache befürwortet hatte, habe der Senat abgelehnt, weil er die Sache nicht selbst untersucht hatte (*quia non ipse probauerat*)[102]. Trotzdem habe Tiberius verboten, die Christen unter Anklage zu stellen. Solche Gedanken wollen natürlich zum Ausdruck bringen, dass, anders als die jüdische Obrigkeit, die wichtigsten Vertreter Roms das Christentum von Anfang an unterstützt hätten. Damit geht Tertullian natürlich deutlich weiter als die kanonischen Evangelien oder auch die Apostelgeschichte, die die Haltung der verschiedenen Vertreter der römischen Staatsmacht sehr unterschiedlich beschreiben können. Parallelen allerdings finden sich in apokrypher Literatur: Zu denken ist hier v.a. an den womöglich im Kern schon auf das 2. Jahrhundert zurückgehenden, bereits mehrfach erwähnten *Brief des Pilatus an Claudius*, den Tertullian vielleicht gekannt haben mag[103]. Tatsächlich ist dieses Schreiben

---

99. Zur relevanten Passage vgl. C. SCHUBERT, *Minucius Felix ‚Octavius'* (Kommentar zu frühchristlichen Apologeten, 12), Freiburg i.Br. – Basel – Wien, Herder, 2014, S. 441-442, der auf S. 442 die Vermutung äußert, Minucius Felix vermeide in seiner Kritik bewusst „eine Fokussierung auf die Apotheose römischer Kaiser".
100. Beispiele für solche Apotheosen bei COOK, *Empty Tomb* (Anm. 52), S. 426-454.
101. So auch GEORGES, *Tertullian* (2011; Anm. 10), S. 345.
102. Die Übersetzung des Verbs *probare* ist hier nicht ganz einfach: Man könnte auch an eine Deutung in Richtung von „billigen" oder „besichtigen" denken.
103. So auch die Informationen bei M. SCHÄRTL, *Die sonstige Pilatusliteratur*, in C. MARKSCHIES – J. SCHRÖTER (Hgg.), *Antike christliche Apokryphen in deutscher Übersetzung*.

stark antijüdisch geprägt und versucht Pilatus so weit wie möglich von aller Schuld am Tode Jesu zu entlasten; wenigstens implizit könnte dem Text auch der erst in späteren Schriften deutlicher zum Ausdruck kommende Gedanke entnommen werden, dass Pilatus bereits seiner Überzeugung nach Christ gewesen sei[104]. Ganz auf der Linie dieser Argumentation liegt der seltsam wirkende Schlusssatz des Abschnitts. Tobias Georges erklärt ihn überzeugend mit den folgenden Worten: Mit der Behauptung, auch die Kaiser hätten an Christus geglaubt,

> kommt er [Tertullian] dem Einwand zuvor, die christusfreundliche Meinung des Pilatus hätte auch die Kaiser überzeugen müssen. Dass dies nicht geschehen ist, sieht Tertullian begründet in der Unvereinbarkeit der politischen Rolle eines Kaisers einerseits und des Christseins andererseits. Diese Inkompatibilität besteht für ihn zumindest gemäß dem gegenwärtigen Zuschnitt des Kaisertums (vgl. *Apol.* 29–34): Zum einen sind die Kaiser „für die Welt notwendig" … dieser festen Verankerung im saeculum steht aber entgegen, dass die Christen ihre Heimat nicht auf Erden, sondern im Himmel haben …, zum anderen können die Kaiser nicht Christen sein … – wohl eben wegen der gottgleichen Stellung der Kaiser, die von den Christen infrage gestellt wird[105].

Doch damit ist noch nicht alles gesagt. Nachdem er wenigstens Tiberius als einen Christenfreund dargestellt hat, muss er zumindest andeuten, warum es dazu kam, dass sich die Rechtsstellung der Christen seit den Anfängen verändert hat:

Apol. 21.25

Discipuli uero diffusi per orbem et praecepto magistri dei paruerunt, qui et ipsi a Iudaeis persequentibus multa perpessi utique pro fiducia ueritatis libenter Romae postremo per Neronis saeuitiam sanguinem Christianum seminauerunt.

Bd. 1: *Evangelien und Verwandtes*, Teilbd. 1, Tübingen, Mohr Siebeck, 2012, 262-279, S. 263. Ab dem vierten Jahrhundert entstanden dann zudem ein *Briefwechsel zwischen Pilatus und Tiberius* und einer zwischen *Pilatus und Herodes* (Antipas).

104. Vgl. hierzu z.B. der spätere *Briefwechsel zwischen Pilatus und Herodes* (zur Datierung [womöglich] ins 4. Jh. vgl. die Argumentation bei T. NICKLAS, „*An diesem Tag aber wurden Herodes und Pilatus Freunde": Interpretation und Imagination in der Rezeptionsgeschichte von Lk 23,12*, in D. BLAUTH – M. RYDRYCK – M. SCHNEIDER [Hgg.], *Freundschaft in Texten und Kontexten des Neuen Testaments: Eine Festschrift für Stefan Alker zum 60. Geburtstag* [Neutestamentliche Entwürfe zur Theologie, 30], Tübingen – Basel, Francke, 2021, 133-154, S. 142-144) oder spätere Texte vor allem aus Ägypten und Äthiopien, wo Pilatus – entgegen großer Teile der westlichen Tradition – gar als Heiliger verehrt wurde (siehe z.B. Ps-Cyrill von Jerusalem, *Über Leben und Passion Christi*, wo letztendlich Jesus Pilatus davon überzeugen muss, ihn kreuzigen zu lassen).

105. GEORGES, *Tertullian* (2011; Anm. 10), S. 345-346.

> Die Schüler aber verteilten sich über die ganze Welt und gehorchten so dem Auftrag (ihres) göttlichen Lehrers[106]; nachdem auch sie selbst von den Juden, die sie verfolgten, viel ertragen hatten, haben sie gerade kraft ihres Vertrauens auf die Wahrheit schließlich in Rom infolge von Neros Wüten freudig Christenblut gesät.

Von ihrem geographischen Ausgangspunkt in Galiläa (vgl. 21.23) verteilt sich mit den Schülern die Lehre Jesu über die ganze Welt, ein Gedanke, der seinen Ausgangspunkt in Lk 24,48 und Apg 1,8 finden mag[107] – und der in einer Vielzahl apokrypher Apostelakten ausgearbeitet wurde, zu denen hier aber kaum eine literarische Beziehung bestehen dürfte. Erneut wird deutlich: Das Christentum ist als eine Bildungsbewegung verstanden, die eine auf den göttlichen Lehrer Christus selbst zurückgehende und damit letztlich auf die Anfänge der Welt zurückzuführende Lehre, welche für die Wahrheit steht, in die gesamte Welt hinausträgt. Wie auch bereits ihr Lehrer aber sind auch die Schüler selbst „von den Juden" verfolgt, ein Gedanke, der sich, beginnend mit 1 Thess 2,14-16, bereits in vielen Texten des Neuen Testaments andeutet, aber auch in anderen christlichen Schriften der Zeit (vgl. Justin, *Dial.* 17.1-4; Tertullian, *Scorp.* 10.10; *Mart.Pol.* 12.2; 13.1; 17–18) erkennbar ist[108]. Ohne damit zu sagen, dass all diese Aussagen unhistorisch seien, wird gleichzeitig aber deutlich, dass sie zumindest in manchen Kontexten auch der Selbstbestätigung der nach Identität suchenden und sich vom Judentum abgrenzenden Gruppe der Christusanhänger*innen dienen[109]. Ich gehe davon aus, dass auch hier dies die entscheidende Funktion der Aussage ist.

Mit dem Hinweis auf die Verfolgung unter Nero greift Tertullian auf *Apol.* 5.3 zurück, wo er schon einmal Nero als den ersten bezeichnet, der „mit kaiserlichem Schwert" gegen die Christen „gewütet" habe (*Caesariano gladio ferocisse*). Nun kann er wieder daran erinnern: Wenn aber

---

106. Zur Übersetzung des Wortes *deus* in adjektivischer Funktion siehe GEORGES, *Tertullian* (2011; Anm. 10), S. 346, Anm. 777.

107. In beiden Stellen allerdings ist Jerusalem der Ausgangspunkt. Unternimmt Tertullian diese Änderung, weil sein intendiertes Publikum mit Jerusalem – zu seiner Zeit bereits Aelia Capitolina – keine positiven Assoziationen verbinden konnte?

108. Dass die Idee, die Juden seien der Auslöser aller Verfolgung von Christen, bei Tertullian in verschiedenen Schriften wiederkehrt, zeigt DUNN, *Tertullian* (Anm. 12), S. 48-49.

109. Zu den Aussagen im *Martyrium des Polycarp* und ihrer Funktion vgl. z.B. T. NICKLAS, *Jews and Christians? Second Century ‚Christian' Perspectives on the ‚Parting of the Ways'* (Annual Deichmann Lectures, 2013), Tübingen, Mohr Siebeck, 2014, S. 52-61. Allgemeiner zur Funktion von Aussagen über Verfolgungssituationen in den Schriften des Neuen Testaments vgl. die umfangreichen Analysen bei J.A. KELHOFFER, *Persecution, Persuasion and Power: Readiness to Withstand Hardship as a Corrobation of Legitimacy in the New Testament* (WUNT, 270), Tübingen, Mohr Siebeck, 2010.

sich das ursprüngliche kaiserliche Wohlwollen gegen die Christen erst durch Nero (und später Domitian [vgl. 5.4]) verändert hat, dann ist klar, dass menschenfreundliche Herrscher einem solchen Vorbild niemals folgen können[110]. Tertullian, der eben noch vermied, Traditionen über die Apotheosen römischer Kaiser offen zu kritisieren, macht sich hier die Tatsache zunutze, dass Kritik an auch in römischen Augen verdammungswürdigen Kaisern wie Nero oder Domitian nicht als Kritik am römischen Imperium an sich verstanden werden musste[111].

Aus der Tatsache schließlich, dass die von den Schülern verbreitete Lehre Christi für die Wahrheit steht, folgt, dass diese im Vertrauen auf diese Wahrheit in Rom das Martyrium erleiden. Auch wenn Tertullian hier erneut keine Namen nennt, mag es sein, dass in besonderer Weise an Petrus und Paulus gedacht ist, von deren Martyrien in Rom schon frühe Zeugnisse existieren[112]. Doch würde eine solche Engführung dem Ziel der Aussage wohl zuwiderlaufen: Die Tatsache, dass Nero das Blut von Christen vergossen hat, vermag die Verbreitung der Wahrheit nicht zu stoppen. Vielmehr wird es zum Samen (vgl. auch *Apol.* 50.13), aus dem Neues sprießt, ja der missionarische Wirkung entfaltet[113]. Die Frage, ob damit bewusst die Bildwelt des Gleichnisses vom Sämann (und seiner allegorischen, missionstheologischen Deutung) aus den synoptischen Evangelien (Mk 4,1-9.13.20 par.) aufgegriffen ist, ist nicht eindeutig zu beantworten.

---

110. *Apol.* 5.6 bietet als positives Beispiel und Beschützer der Christen den Kaiser Mark Aurel (161-180 n.Chr.). – Vgl. auch die Überlegungen bei C. BECKER, *Tertullians Apologeticum* (Anm. 10), S. 292-293, sowie GEORGES, *Tertullian* (2011; Anm. 10), S. 346, der hierzu schreibt: „Nur ein römischer Machthaber vom Charakter Neros verfolgt die Christen".

111. Ähnliche Argumente im Zusammenhang mit der Frage, inwiefern apokryphe Apostelakten als „anti-imperialistisch" zu verstehen sind, bietet J.A. SNYDER, *Apostles and Politics in the Roman Empire*, in EAD. – K. ZAMFIR (Hgg.), *Reading the Political in Jewish and Christian Texts* (BTS, 38), Leuven – Paris – Bristol, CT, Peeters, 2020, 227-256.

112. Da der vielleicht früheste Hinweis auf das Martyrium des Petrus, Joh 21,18-19, den Ort dieses Martyriums nicht erwähnt, ist hier besonders an die griechische *Petrusapokalypse* 14.4 sowie die *Ascensio Isaiae* 4.1-4 zu denken. Hierzu weiterführend z.B. T. NICKLAS, ‚*Drink the Cup Which I Promised You!*' *(Apocalypse of Peter 14.4): Peter's Death and the End of Times*, in J. KNIGHT – K. SULLIVAN (Hgg.), *The Open Mind: Essays in Honour of Christopher Rowland* (LNTS, 522), London – New York, Continuum, 2015, 183-200, sowie T.D. BARNES, „*Another Shall Gird Thee": Probative Evidence for the Death of Peter*, in H.K. BOND – L.W. HURTADO (Hgg.), *Peter in Early Christianity*, Grand Rapids, MI, Eerdmans, 2015, 76-95. – Im Zusammenhang mit Paulus ist an das (indirekte!) Zeugnis in 2 Tim und der Apostelgeschichte zu denken, womöglich *1 Clem.* 5.7 und dann spätere Texte aus den apokryphen Apostelakten. Hierzu weiterführend die Beiträge in A. PUIG I TARRÈCH – J.M.G. BARCLAY – J. FREY (Hgg.), *The Last Years of Paul: Essays from the Tarragona Conference, June 2013* (WUNT, 352), Tübingen, Mohr Siebeck, 2015.

113. Ähnlich auch GEORGES, *Tertullian* (2011; Anm. 10), S. 346-347.

III. Fazit

Der konkrete Blick auf den Text zeigt, wie frei Tertullian in der Lage ist, für seine sehr geraffte Darstellung von Passion und Auferstehung Christi wie auch der Anfänge der christlichen Bewegung Material aus den heute kanonischen Evangelien heranzuziehen, es neu zu kombinieren, ihm wichtige Aspekte zu betonen und vor allem für seine Sache überflüssig oder anstößig Wirkendes beiseite zu lassen. In einer Reihe von Fällen widerspricht er gar dem, was im Neuen Testament zu finden ist. In anderen zeigte sich, dass Parallelen zu den Tendenzen seiner Darstellung des Jesusmaterials auch in apokryph gewordenen Schriften wie dem *Petrusevangelium* oder auch dem *Brief des Pilatus an Claudius* zu finden sind, ohne dass daraus zwingend gegenseitige literarische Abhängigkeit zu folgern wäre. Tertullian redigiert hier nicht die kanonischen Evangelien (oder auch ein anderes), sondern „inszeniert" für sein angezieltes, vor allem nichtchristliches Publikum Aspekte einer „virtuellen" Jesuserzählung, die sich in entscheidenden Zügen im „kulturellen Gedächtnis" antiker Christinnen und Christen verankert hatte, neu[114]. Dies heißt nicht, dass er schriftliche Evangelien oder auch die Apostelgeschichte nicht kannte oder zur Verfügung hatte. Das heißt aber, dass er diese mit einiger Wahrscheinlichkeit nicht zu Rate ziehen musste, als er seine Erzählung komponierte, die er sicherlich nicht als Redaktion der Evangelien verstand, sondern einfach als „die" Geschichte Jesu, wiedergegeben für ein Publikum, dem er die Wahrheit der christlichen Lehre vorlegen wollte. Zu den Zügen, die er dabei betonte, gehört sicherlich alles, was ihm überzeugend schien, die Göttlichkeit Christi zu betonen. Vielleicht aber noch wichtiger war es ihm, das Christentum als eine auf den göttlichen Lehrer zurückgehende Bildungsbewegung zu beschreiben, die die Wahrheit einer uralten Lehre in der durch Verbum, Ratio und Virtus Gottes erschaffenen Welt (vgl. *Apol.* 21.10) verbreitet und die sich deswegen nicht aufhalten lässt[115]. Die Gegner dieser Lehre sieht er einerseits in den Juden, deren Verstockung er schon in den vorhergehenden Paragraphen beschrieben hat, andererseits in Kaisern wie Nero und Domitian. Gleichzeitig bemüht er sich um die Abgrenzung der christlichen Bewegung vom unverständigen Pöbel, dem der Auferweckte ganz bewusst nicht erschienen sei, um ihn in seiner Gottlosigkeit zu belassen.

---

114. Gleichzeitig deutete sich an, dass ein christliches, informiertes Publikum bestimmte Aspekte des Texts anders lesen konnte als ein nichtchristliches.
115. Dass dieses Thema auch in anderen Schriften Tertullians auftaucht, zeigt BARNES, *Tertullian* (Anm. 12), S. 65-66 (am Beispiel von *Praescr.* 20).

Natürlich ist eine Jesusparaphrase wie die hier diskutierte kein apokryphes Evangelium. Gleichzeitig bieten Texte wie der vorliegende spannendes, bisher, soweit ich sehe, wenig genutztes Material für die Überlieferungsgeschichte der Jesuserzählung. Der Kontext dieser sehr gerafft berichteten „Neuinszenierung" von Passions- und Ostererzählungen und den Anfängen der christlichen Mission in Tertullians *Apologie* hilft einerseits zu verstehen, warum Tertullian bestimmte Motive betont, andere verändert und wieder andere übergeht. In manchen Fällen, z.B. in der von Tertullian so deutlich betonten Schuld der „Juden" am Tode Jesu, aber auch der Verfolgung seiner Schüler, lassen solche Tendenzen auch zu, vorsichtige Schlussfolgerungen im Hinblick auf Darstellungstendenzen in apokryphen Evangelien zu ziehen. Die Überschreitung von Grenzen zwischen kanonischen wie apokryphen Evangelien einerseits wie auch Paraphrasen von Jesusmaterial in anderen Schriften andererseits scheint mir in hohem Maße sinnvoll.

Universität Regensburg   Tobias NICKLAS
Fakultät für Katholische Theologie
DE-93040 Regensburg
Deutschland
tobias.nicklas@theologie.uni-regensburg.de

NEGOTIATING THE PASSION TRADITION

ATHANASIUS AND THE GREAT SETH

Traditional patristic scholarship typically envisages a linear process of doctrinal development that begins with the New Testament and continues with an equally canonical sequence of "church fathers" supposed to articulate with ever-increasing clarity the internal logic of Christian faith. Shadowing this sequence is, of course, a series of "heresies". The present paper seeks to identify unexpected points of convergence as well as divergence between two early treatises on the incarnation, one regarded as impeccably orthodox, the other as manifestly docetic: Athanasius's *De incarnatione* and the *Second Discourse of the Great Seth* from Nag Hammadi Codex VII. The analysis will show that these texts give expression to similar core concerns in spite of differences of idiom. Both authors sketch a Genesis-related background to the divine Word's incarnational initiative, and both authors are anxious to distance the Logos from the suffering and death of his bodily counterpart. Athanasius and his anonymous "heretical" colleague are both concerned to negotiate the fundamental paradox of the gospel tradition, in which the presence of divinity is manifest in works of power yet called into question as the protagonist is subject to suffering and death[1].

External and internal evidence shows that Athanasius's treatise on the incarnation is the second half of a two-part work[2]. The traditional short Latin titles, *Contra gentes* and *De incarnatione*, do not entirely correspond to their most common Greek equivalents, respectively Κατὰ Ἑλλήνων and Περὶ τῆς ἐνανθρωπήσεως τοῦ λόγου καὶ τῆς διὰ σώματος πρὸς ἡμᾶς ἐπιφανείας αὐτοῦ[3]. The titles indicate a broad apologetic strategy of attack and defence, with the defence of distinctively Christian beliefs in the second part prepared by the polemic against "pagan" religious practices in the first. The two parts share a concern with the scandal of

---

1. It is a pleasure to dedicate this paper to Jos Verheyden, in gratitude for his scholarship, friendship, and hospitality.
2. The *De incarnatione* opens with a summary of the *Contra gentes* (1.1, cf. 4.4). Almost all manuscripts include both texts; see R.W. Thomson, *Athanasius: Contra gentes and De incarnatione* (OECT), Oxford, Clarendon, 1971, pp. xxxii-xxxiv.
3. Titles as transmitted by ms. G (10th cent.), with authorship attributions omitted. Witnesses to the secondary Short Recension replace Κατὰ Ἑλλήνων with Κατὰ εἰδώλων or Κατὰ τῆς τῶν εἰδώλων εὑρέσεως.

the cross, which Athanasius (following Paul) sees as the primary target for pagan ridicule[4]. When Greeks mock and laugh at our expense, they have in view "nothing other than the cross of Christ" (*Gent.* 1.3). They must be brought to recognise that "the one who ascended the cross is the Word of God and the Saviour of all" (*Gent.* 1.5)[5]. Athanasius expresses his hope that the faith of his anonymous addressee will be strengthened by the recognition that the Word's humiliation on the cross was only "apparent" or "supposed" (*Inc.* 1.1.2). The appropriateness and necessity of this specific death is the main theme of the *De incarnatione*. Underlying the entire treatise is the assumption that the divine Logos transcends his own embodiment and is unaffected by the suffering inflicted on it: that is the fundamental reason why the humiliation of the cross is more apparent than real. The transcendence of the Logos is already established in the concluding section of the *Contra gentes*, where it is argued that the Logos makes himself known in creation and speaks through the holy scriptures even apart from his embodiment in Jesus Christ. When the Logos assumes flesh he continues to sustain the universe, and his providential rule extends to the crucifixion of his bodily "instrument" (ὄργανον) and the circumstances that accompanied it: the darkening of the sun, the tearing of the temple veil, the earthquake, and the resurrection of the saints.

In an entirely different idiom, the *Second Discourse of the Great Seth* is equally concerned to show that the reality of the cross is quite different from the appearance[6]. The title of this work is widely regarded as problematic. The work consists in a first person discourse of one who identifies himself as "Jesus Christ, the Son of Man, exalted above the heavens" (69.21-22), and there is no explicit reference anywhere to Seth[7]. The

---

4. As K. ANATOLIOS, *Athanasius: The Coherence of His Thought*, London – New York, Routledge, 1998, p. 28, notes: "the *CG-DI* is first and foremost an *apologia crucis*".

5. Translations in this paper are my own unless otherwise specified.

6. The Greek title of this work (ⲇⲉⲩⲧⲉⲣⲟⲥ ⲗⲟⲅⲟⲥ ⲧⲟⲩ ⲙⲉⲅⲁⲗⲟⲩ ⲥⲏⲑ, NHC VII 70.11-12) suggests that the Coptic text is a translation of a Greek original. In rendering this title into English, "discourse" is preferable to "treatise", as the text is presented as direct speech. I have chosen to translate the article ("the Great Seth"), but "Great Seth" is equally valid; so G. RILEY, *NHC VII,2: Second Treatise of the Great Seth*, in B.A. PEARSON (ed.), *Nag Hammadi Codex VII* (Nag Hammadi and Manichaean Studies, 30), Leiden – New York – Köln, Brill, 1996, 129-199; and M.W. MEYER (ed.), *The Nag Hammadi Scriptures*, New York, HarperCollins, 2007, p. 477. Editions: J. ROBINSON (ed.), *The Facsimile Edition of the Nag Hammadi Codices: Codex VII*, Leiden, Brill, 1972, pp. 55-70; L. PAINCHAUD (ed.), *Le Deuxième traité du Grand Seth (NH VII,2)* (Bibliothèque copte de Nag Hammadi. Section "Textes", 6), Québec, Les Presses de l'Université Laval, 1982; B.A. PEARSON (ed.), *Nag Hammadi Codex VII* (Coptic and Gnostic Library), Leiden, Brill, 1972.

7. See the discussion of the title by S. PELLEGRINI, *Der zweite Logos des großen Seth (NHC VII,2)*, in H.-M. SCHENKE – H.G. BETHGE – U.U. KAISER (eds.), *Nag Hammadi*

solution to this problem lies ready to hand, however, in the repeated references to "the Son of Man"[8]. While other early Christian writers take "Son of Man" to refer to Christ's humanity as opposed to his divinity, the Sethian author regards "Man" as a synonym for "the Father", the supreme deity, so that "Son of Man" is functionally equivalent to "Son of God" as employed elsewhere[9]. "The Father of truth" is "the Man of greatness", whose name was usurped by the rulers when they created their inferior imitation and named it Adam, "Man" (53.3-10). Underlying this identification of "the Great One of the heavens" as "the Man of truth" (54.6-8; cf. 53.17) is the assumption that, if man is created in the image of God, then God himself must possess the original human form. If the Father is the primal Adam, then "the Great Seth" is Christ, the Son of Adam. The title of this work matches its contents[10].

It is less clear why it is identified as a "second" discourse. There may once have been a "First Discourse of the Great Seth", now lost, or the title might refer to the other Seth-related work in Codex VII of the Nag Hammadi collection, *The Three Steles of Seth* – although the Seth of that text is the human figure rather than his heavenly original[11]. A more

---

Deutsch. 2. Band: *NHC V,2–XIII,1, BG 1 und 4* (Koptisch-Gnostische Schriften, 3), Berlin, De Gruyter, 2003, 569-590, pp. 570-571. Pellegrini concludes that the title is secondary and that it stems from an identification of Seth and Christ without any relevance to the present text (p. 572).

8. In addition to the passage cited above, the speaker also confirms that "I am Christ, the Son of Man" (65.18-19) and claims that the ignorant will not attain true knowledge "until they know the Son of Man" (64.11-12). David is (oddly) criticised for naming his son "Son of Man" (63.4-7).

9. Other writers reserve "Son of Man" for Jesus's incarnate life. Justin thinks that Jesus called himself the Son of Man because of his birth from Mary or because of her descent from Adam, although as Son of God he existed before all creatures (*Dial.* 100.3-4). The *Treatise on the Resurrection* states that "the Son of God ... was Son of Man, incorporating them both, possessing humanity and divinity" (NHC I 43.21-27).

10. The doctrine that God is Man is attested in Irenaeus, in his account of "the multitude of Gnostics" who have "appeared like mushrooms from the ground" (*Haer.* 1.29.1). Some of these people teach that "the Father of all" is also "the First Man" and that his son, the "Second Man" is therefore "the Son of Man" (1.12.4; 1.30.1), but Irenaeus insists that "the gospel knows of no other Son of Man than the one who was of Mary and who also suffered" (*Haer.* 3.16.5). This motif is elaborated in the *Apocryphon of John* (NHC II 5.4-9; 6.2-4; 8.28–9.17).

11. RILEY, *Nag Hammadi Codex VII* (n. 6), pp. 131-133, suggests that Sethian users of this text regarded it as "second" in relation to the *Paraphrase of Shem*, citing the lack of a subscribed or superscribed title at NHC VII 49.9-10 where the two texts adjoin. While it is true that paired subscriptions and superscriptions occur elsewhere in this codex at 70.11-13 (*The Second Discourse of the Great Seth, Apocalypse of Peter*) and 84.14-15 (*The Apocalypse of Peter, The Teachings of Silvanus*), the latter text concludes with a non-titular subscription at 118.8-9 and there is no superscription for the text that follows, identified only at its conclusion as *The Three Steles of Seth* (127.27). Thus, this codex contains one text with superscribed title only (*The Paraphrase of Shem*), one text with

attractive option is to see this text as "second" in relation to the gospel current in the mainstream church. As we shall see, the author engages extensively with the canonical passion narratives while vehemently rejecting the claim that the divine Christ truly died. As a result, this text is generally assumed to be "docetic", a representative of an aberrant Christology that denies a core feature of mainstream Christian belief[12]. Yet Athanasius too insists that the reality of the cross is far different from the appearance, and that the Logos qua Logos is immune from suffering or death, participating in both as if remotely through the bodily instrument he has assumed. Here the conventional binary divide between "orthodoxy" and "heresy" conceals key concerns shared by two otherwise very different early Christian authors. Each in his own way is concerned to show that the divine protagonist in the passion tradition transcends the suffering of the cross, and to explain why his involvement in this degrading event was appropriate and necessary.

To comprehend this event in its full scope, we must see how it addresses the situation of a lost and fallen humanity. While the two authors draw on different traditions to outline that situation, here too unexpected convergences come to light.

I. Genesis, the Logos, and the Body

For Athanasius, a treatise on incarnation cannot simply follow the fourth evangelist in asserting *that* the Logos became flesh; it must show *why* the Logos became flesh. To do so, it is necessary to turn to the early chapters of Genesis. The scriptural account of human origins is relevant because the incarnation of the Logos is not some random miracle but the logical solution to a problem created by humans that their Maker must address if his work is not to be in vain. Three key Genesis motifs are deployed in Athanasius's attempt to persuade sceptics and unbelievers along with worried fellow-Christians that belief in the incarnation is

---

superscribed title and non-titular subscription (*The Teachings of Silvanus*), one text with both superscribed and subscribed titles (*The Apocalypse of Peter*), and two texts with subscribed title only (*The Second Discourse of the Great Seth, The Three Steles of Seth*). In every case the break between texts is marked by similar patterns of arrowheads and horizontal lines. There is therefore no basis for Riley's claim that *The Second Discourse* is presented as a sequel to *The Paraphrase of Shem*. The different formatting of titles probably stems from the scribe's exemplars.

12. On the origins and limitations of this concept, see J. Verheyden – R. Bieringer – J. Schröter – I. Jäger (eds.), *Docetism in the Early Church: The Quest for an Elusive Phenomenon* (WUNT, 402), Tübingen, Mohr Siebeck, 2018.

reasonable, in spite of appearances to the contrary. His argument may be paraphrased as follows[13].

Plato, so highly regarded among the Greeks, taught that the divine creator shaped the world out of the raw material at his disposal, limited like any human craftsman by the medium in which he worked. In contrast, Moses teaches a radical view of creation that includes the raw material as well as its shaping into the finished product: "In the beginning God created the heaven and the earth" (Gen 1,1). What Moses meant by this is explained by the Shepherd of Hermas (*Mand.* 1.1): in creating the universe, God brought it into being out of non-being (ἐκ τοῦ μὴ ὄντος εἰς τὸ εἶναι)[14].

Creaturely existence is still shadowed and threatened by its origin in non-existence. Creatures are brought into being but left to themselves they sooner or later revert to the non-being from which they derive. Humans, however, have received from their Creator a partial and conditional exemption from this natural law, and here a second Genesis motif comes into play. God created humans not only out of nothing, like every other creature, but also, uniquely, "in his own image" (κατὰ τὴν ἑαυτοῦ εἰκόνα). That is, he imparted to them a share in his own Logos, so that by virtue of this affinity with the divine nature they would enjoy a carefree life in paradise on earth and immortality in heaven. Participation in the Logos also enabled them to know and worship their Creator.

Yet the Creator made this promise of immortality conditional. Athanasius's third Genesis motif is the prohibition that threatened a reversion to the natural creaturely state of non-being if it should be disobeyed[15]. The prohibition brings into focus another crucial aspect of the human

---

13. Cf. *Inc.* 2.3–10.6.

14. On the distinctiveness of Athanasius's emphasis on creation out of nothing, see A. PETTERSEN, *Athanasius*, London, Geoffrey Chapman, 1995, pp. 19-30. This Athanasian theme is translated into modern theological categories by T.F. TORRANCE, *The Trinitarian Faith: The Evangelical Theology of the Ancient Catholic Church*, Edinburgh, T&T Clark, 1988, pp. 95-104. Both authors underplay the role of Genesis exegesis in Athanasius's argument.

15. For Athanasius there is a close connection between his three Genesis motifs – creation out of nothing (Gen 1,1, cited in *Inc.* 3.1), creation in the divine image (Gen 1,27, alluded to in *Inc.* 3.3), the prohibition (Gen 2,16-17, cited in *Inc.* 3.5). The death threatened by the prohibition is seen not as an arbitrary punishment but as an inevitable consequence of creation out of nothing once the incorruptibility bestowed in the gift of the image has been forfeited. *Creatio ex nihilo* is Athanasius's answer to the question why humans were threatened with death. This systematic correlation of Genesis motifs is distinctive to Athanasius, although the fundamental importance of Genesis 1–3 for early Christian theology is already established in Irenaeus; see T. HOLSINGER-FRIESEN, *Irenaeus and Genesis: A Study of Competition in Early Christian Hermeneutics*, Winona Lake, IN, Eisenbrauns, 2009.

condition, the freedom to choose whether to remain in a uniquely privileged relationship to the Creator. Perversely and disastrously, humans chose not to do so, forfeiting the promise of immortality and thereby throwing the whole divine intention for the world into apparent disarray. Athanasius presumably believed that human disobedience was anticipated and already accommodated within the divine providential plan, rather than taking the Lord God by surprise as the Genesis story might suggest to a naive or sceptical reader. Yet Athanasius does not say so, choosing instead to represent the offended deity as deliberating on the appropriate response to an unexpected setback. The divine dilemma and its resolution are outlined in a series of rhetorical questions suggestive of an interior monologue within the common mind of the Father and his Logos[16].

How was a good God to respond to the defection of his prize creatures, participants in his very own Logos? Should he simply leave them to the consequences of their choice, death and corruption? But then what was the point of creating them in the first place? Would they not better have been left uncreated? Would it not be unworthy of God to do nothing and leave his creatures to destruction? Yet, if the warning that "you shall surely die" were to be replaced by a demand for repentance, would that not compromise God's truthfulness, exposing him as changeable and weak-willed? So God cannot either abandon his guilty creatures to death or undermine his own law's demand that they must die. The dilemma seems intractable. Nevertheless, a solution is found: though incapable of dying himself, the Logos must assume a body which, in union with himself, can represent the entire human race in enacting the death required by the law. At this point Pauline themes are perceptible: one has died for all, therefore all have died[17]. Yet the logical necessity for incarnation and cross is conjured out of the first three chapters of Genesis. Athanasius's dramatised rendering of the divine dilemma is presented in third person form, but it reproduces imagined deliberation within the divine mind[18].

---

16. *Inc.* 6.7; 7.2, 4, paraphrased below.

17. 2 Cor 5,14, cited in *Inc.* 10.2 and followed by citations from another text that Athanasius took to be Pauline (Heb 2,9.10.14-15). Especially important for Athanasius is the notion of "fittingness" or appropriateness in Heb 2,10: "It was fitting [ἔπρεπεν] for him, for whom and through whom all things were made ... to make the leader of their salvation perfect through sufferings". Elaborating this, Athanasius argues that the manner of Christ's death was fitting (*Inc.* 21.3, 25.3: ἔπρεπεν; 26.1: πρέπων), and that any other death would have been unfitting (*Inc.* 21.6; 22.1: ἀπρεπές). Synonyms occur at *Inc.* 10.6 (εὐλόγως); 13.6, 37.4 (ἔδει); 25.5 (εἰκότως).

18. In spite of the anthropomorphic representation of the divine thought process, there is no hint here of a dialogue between Father and Son. Athanasius regards the two as

In the *Second Discourse of the Great Seth*, the event of the incarnation is traced back not to an interior monologue but to a proposal made by the Son of Man that finds approval within the heavenly assembly. Speaking in the first person, Jesus recalls how he had said:

> "Let us gather together an Ekklesia! Let us visit that creation of his! Let us send someone forth into it, so as to visit the Ennoias in the regions below!" This is what I said to the whole multitude of the Ekklesia of the Great One, which rejoiced, the whole household of the Father of Truth rejoiced, I being one of them. I recalled the Ennoias that came forth from the undefiled Spirit, the descent upon the water (that is, the regions below). And all were of a single mind, coming from one source: they commissioned me, since I was willing, and I came forth to reveal the glory to my companions and fellow spirits (*2DGSeth* 50.1-24)[19].

The Ennoias are Thoughts issuing from the divine mind that possess a hypostatic existence like the Johannine or Athanasian Logos, but unaccountably distance themselves from the heavenly realms and descend into the depths of materiality, where they are subject to the power of largely hostile rulers[20]. The Ennoias are thus the Elect, addressees of this text, and Jesus the Son of Man proposes to liberate them by entering their world so as to overcome the powers that hold them captive. The chaotic waters of Gen 1,2 now symbolise the material realm into which the Ennoias made their unfortunate descent[21]. Their material embodiment is

---

"intrinsic aspects of one reality or person"; L. AYRES, *Nicaea and Its Legacy: An Approach to Fourth Century Trinitarian Theology*, Oxford, OUP, 2004, p. 46. Only towards the end of his life does Athanasius give qualified acceptance to the proposal of three divine hypostases (*ibid.*, pp. 174-175).

19. PELLEGRINI, *Der zweite Logos* (n. 7), p. 581, takes ⲛ̄ϭⲓ ⲛⲓⲙⲉⲣⲟⲥ ⲉⲧⲥⲁⲡⲉⲥⲏⲧ not as an explanatory clause ("that is, the regions below") but as a genitive dependent on the reference to descent: "... betreffs des Herabkommens dieser unteren Teile auf das Wasser". This seems unlikely on both grammatical and semantic grounds.

20. As PAINCHAUD, *Deuxième traité* (n. 6), p. 80, notes, the descent of the Ennoias represents a "rupture de l'unité primordiale" within the world of the *Pleroma* – an event that its inhabitants appear to have forgotten.

21. The fall of the *Ennoiai* is paralleled in the views of the *Doketai* as summarised in the *Refutation of All Heresies* (mis)attributed to Hippolytus. According to this group, "the Ideas [αἱ ἰδέαι] are called 'souls' [ψυχαί] because cooling [ἀπ(ο)ψυγεῖσαι] <and falling from> the realms above they ended up in darkness, cast from body to body and imprisoned by the Demiurge" (*Ref.* 8.10.1; the insertion derives from M. Marcovich and is accepted by M.D. LITWA [ed.], *Refutation of All Heresies* [Writings from the Greco-Roman World, 40], Atlanta, GA, SBL Press, 2016, p. 591n). Like the *Second Discourse*, the *Doketai* ascribe the incarnation to the Saviour's desire to save the fallen *Ideai* or *Ennoiai*: "The only-begotten Son of the Aeons, seeing the Ideas from above cast into dark bodies, wished to go down to save them [ῥύσασθαι κατέλθων ἠθέλησεν]" (*Ref.* 8.10.3). The "cooling" that brings about the fall is presumably a cooling in the personified Ideas' contemplation of the divine, as in Origen, *Princ.* 2.8.3.

here attributed not to Ialdabaoth the World Ruler but to Sophia, acting on her own initiative. Sophia

> was neither sent nor asked anything from the All or from the Great One of the Ekklesia or the Pleroma. At the first she went forth to prepare dwellings and places for the son of light, and she took fellow workers from the elements below [ⲛ̄ⲛⲓⲥⲧⲟⲓⲭⲉⲓⲟⲛ ⲉⲧⲥⲁⲡⲉⲥⲏⲧ] to build bodily houses through them; but in their vainglory they came to ruin (*2DGSeth* 50.29-51.10).

Sophia's independent action seems to have been motivated by concern for the plight of the fallen Ennoias, and it is for their own protection that she has them enclosed in "bodily houses". This accommodation turns out to be shoddily built, however, in spite of the boastful claims of the personified Stoicheia whom Sophia employs to work for her. Nevertheless, within these semi-derelict properties the Elect live in hope: "In the houses they inhabit, prepared by Sophia, they are ready to receive the life-giving word of the ineffable Oneness" (*2DGSeth* 51.10-16)[22].

The Sethian author shares with Athanasius the assumption that the incarnation of the Logos must be understood against the backdrop of events "at the first" or "in the beginning"[23]. Nevertheless, his brief account of the descent of the Ennoias and Sophia's intervention is largely independent of Genesis, for he considers this text to be fundamentally in error. Genesis knows nothing of Sophia's special creative act, since its author writes from the false perspective of Ialdabaoth, who denies the existence of any divine realm above his own[24]. At this point, the gulf

---

22. The contrast between Sophia's unauthorised action and the commissioning of the Saviour is rightly noted by PAINCHAUD, *Deuxième traité* (n. 6), p. 82. In other versions of the Sophia myth, Sophia's initiative results in the loss of heavenly light-substance, rather than being intended to remedy it (*ApocrJn* NHC II 9.28-10.5; *HypArch* 94.6-8; Irenaeus, *Haer.* 1.2.2; *SophJC* NHC III 114.8-18; *TriTrac* 75.17-77.11, where the Sophia role is taken over by the Logos). On Sophia's fall see A.H.B. LOGAN, *Gnostic Truth and Christian Heresy: A Study in the History of Gnosticism*, Edinburgh, T&T Clark, 1996, pp. 117-128; D. BRAKKE, *The Gnostics: Myth, Ritual, and Diversity in Early Christianity*, Cambridge, MA, Harvard University Press, 2010, pp. 58-61.

23. My references to the author as "Sethian" assume only that the title of this work is related to its contents, as argued above, and need not imply the existence of an ongoing Sethian tradition that can be differentiated from other traditions within the gnostic Christian family. Jean-Daniel Dubois appears to envisage such a model when he writes of the *Second Discourse of the Great Seth* that "nous ne prenons pas ce texte pour séthien, mais basilidien parce qu'il manifeste la plupart des traits de la gnose basilidienne"; J.-D. DUBOIS, *Le docétisme des christologies gnostiques revisité*, in *NTS* 63 (2017) 279-304; see p. 297. The presence of characteristic "Sethian" motifs such as the Ialdabaoth figure (53.13-14; 68.29) and the manifestation of the heavenly Son of Man (51.24-30) does not make this an exclusively Sethian text, any more than it is an exclusively Basilidean one. Motifs with different origins circulate freely in such texts.

24. Ialdabaoth is named twice in this text (53.13; 69.29) and is also referred to as the ⲕⲟⲥⲙⲟⲕⲣⲁⲧⲱⲣ (52.27; 53.28-29) and the ⲁⲣⲭⲱⲛ (54.27; 64.18).

between the Sethian author and Athanasius is at its widest. Athanasius reveres the Old Testament scriptures, their authors, their righteous characters, and their deity. The Sethian author comprehensively rejects them all. In a long, carefully structured passage, he systematically trashes the reputation of key Old Testament figures, beginning with Adam:

> For Adam was laughable, created by the Hebdomad from the outline of an imitation of Man, as if he were greater than me and my brothers. We are blameless towards him, we did not sin (*2DGSeth* 62.27-34)[25].

Adam was manufactured by seven leading rulers who tried to copy the divine-human form that appeared to them in a vision from above but could produce only a grotesque caricature. This is a familiar Sethian subversion of the Genesis image of God, which (as we shall see) the author creatively redeploys in his interpretation of the passion tradition. The creation of Adamic humanity by the Hebdomad is differentiated from Sophia's creation of structures to house the elect. The elect minority derive from above, the unrighteous majority from below. The author's protestation of innocence is a repeated refrain in what follows, perhaps suggesting that his Old Testament criticism has been viewed as blasphemous in mainstream Christian circles.

The catalogue of contempt proceeds to trace the designation of Abraham, Isaac, and Jacob as "the fathers" to Ialdabaoth's Hebdomad, who also inspired the false and arrogant claims of David and Solomon: David is said to have called his son the Son of Man, and Solomon thought himself to be the Christ (63.4-17). In each case a role proper only to the Father and to Jesus is usurped. Similarly, the twelve prophets are hebdomadic counterfeits of true prophets (63.17-26), i.e., those inspired by "the Sophia of hope" (52.21-22)[26]. If the author's repeated protestations

---

25. "Laughable" represents ⲟⲩⲥⲱⲃⲉ, a noun with indefinite article that might be rendered as "a laughingstock" (RILEY, *NHC VII* [n. 6], p. 181) or "a joke" (MEYER [ed.], *The Nag Hammadi Scriptures* [n. 6], p. 483); PAINCHAUD, "Quelle dérision ..." (*Deuxième traité* [n. 6], p. 55); PELLEGRINI, "Zum Lachen ..." (*Der zweite Logos* [n. 7], p. 586). The laughter motif recurs in the *Gospel of Judas* and elsewhere, and may derive ultimately from Psalm 2, where it is said that "the One who dwells in the heavens will laugh at them [ἐκγελάσεται αὐτούς]" (v. 4), i.e., at "the rulers [οἱ ἄρχοντες]" gathered together "against the Lord and against his Christ" (v. 2). Cf. *2DGSeth* 53.31-33; 56.13-21, where the Saviour laughs at the World Ruler and the archons who believe they have crucified him.

26. According to PAINCHAUD, "la mention des vrais prophètes répond à une nécessité logique" and does not imply recognition of specific scriptural prophets (*Deuxième traité* [n. 6], p. 132). Elsewhere, however, it is said of "the Sophia of hope" that she "had earlier given a sign about us and all who are with me", probably a reference to true prophets (52.22-24, cf. 51.11-16). For differentiation between sources of prophetic utterance, see Irenaeus, *Haer.* 1.30.11; an extended and positive account of prophetic diversity is

of innocence respond to the charge of blasphemy, the charge is redirected against Old Testament exemplars and the ignorant rulers who inspired them[27].

Deeply implicated in this systematic falsification is Moses, who is a scriptural author as well as a scriptural character. Moses

> was laughable – the "faithful servant" who was named "the friend"! They bore witness to him falsely, for he never knew me – neither he nor those before him. From Adam to Moses to John the Baptist, none of them knew me or my brothers (*2DGSeth* 63.26–64.1)[28].

Underlying this final summative statement is the saying of the Matthean Jesus:

> Truly I say to you, there has not arisen among those born of women anyone greater than John the Baptist. But whoever is least in the kingdom of heaven is greater than him (Mt 11,11).

Luke makes minor stylistic improvements to this saying (Lk 7,28), but it is Thomas whose version corresponds most closely to its later Sethian form:

> Jesus said: From Adam to John the Baptist, among those born of women there is none higher than John the Baptist so that his eyes would not be broken. But I say that whoever is small among you will know the kingdom and will be higher than John (*Gos. Thom.* 46)[29].

Thomas glosses the phrase "among those born of women" by prefacing it with "from Adam to John the Baptist", and the Sethian author expands the gloss by inserting a reference to Moses and omits the original generic phrase. Thomas replaces "whoever is least in the kingdom of heaven" with "whoever is small among you will know the kingdom", and the Sethian author draws from this the negative conclusion that the major

---

given in *TriTrac* 110.22–114.30. In contrast, the Coptic *ApocPeter* rejects scriptural prophecy entirely (71.6-13).

27. This passage may be intended as an antidote to the sequential catalogues of scriptural exemplars that may have been familiar to many of its early readers. Examples from widely read texts include Ben Sira 44–50, Wisdom 11, Hebrews 11, and *1 Clem.* 4; 7–9; 10–12; 17–18; 31–32; 55. On the use of exemplars in *1 Clement* see C. ROTHSCHILD, *New Essays on the Apostolic Fathers* (WUNT, 375), Tübingen, Mohr Siebeck, 2017, pp. 81-96.

28. "Faithful servant" and "friend" allude respectively to Num 12,7 ("… my servant Moses, who is faithful in all my house", cf. Heb 3,5; *1 Clem.* 43.1) and Ex 33,11 ("Thus the Lord spoke to Moses face to face, as if one were speaking to his own friend"). The author expresses his contempt for the great propagandist of a false deity.

29. On textual and exegetical issues in this passage, see S. GATHERCOLE, *The Gospel of Thomas: Introduction and Commentary* (TENTS, 11), Leiden, Brill, 2014, pp. 394-397.

figures of scriptural history were ignorant of saving truth: "From Adam to Moses to John the Baptist, none of them knew me or my brothers". Also derived from the traditional saying is the repeated reference to comparative greatness: "whoever is least … is greater than him" generates the polemical refrain "… as if he were greater than me and my brothers", suggesting a competitive relation between claim and counter-claim[30].

The most competitive of all the Old Testament characters ridiculed here is the deity himself. Taking up the traditional Sethian motif of Ialdabaoth's boast, the author announces an overwhelming victory over this contemptible figure:

> The Ruler was laughable, for he said: "I am God and there is none greater than me! I alone am the Father, the Lord, and there is no other besides me! I am a jealous God, bringing the sins of the fathers upon the children, for three or four generations" – as if he were greater than me and my brothers! We are blameless towards him, we did not sin … And so through our fellowship we have overthrown his doctrine, he who is arrogant in his vainglory and rejects our Father. For he was laughable with his judgement and false prophecy! (*2DGSeth* 64.17–65.1)[31].

In one sense, an author who can write in this vein inhabits a quite different ideological universe from Athanasius. In another sense, the two authors have much in common. Both of them believe that understanding the incarnation is dependent on a correct interpretation of Genesis but differ as to whether the Mosaic account is true or a distortion of the truth. While their views on this diverge so sharply that each would regard the other as a blasphemer, they are both engaged with the same text. It is co-religionists who are most liable to blasphemy charges, indicators of disrupted community rather than total estrangement.

As we have seen, the Sethian author presents a double account of human origins. Although all humans occupy similar bodies, some originate in Sophia's provision for the fallen Ennoias while others – no doubt the vast majority – are the work of the Hebdomad. Double accounts of human origin are a common feature of early exegesis of the Genesis

---

30. *Gos. Thom.* 46 is a necessary link between the synoptic saying and its extensive Sethian elaboration. Appealing to *Gos. Thom.* 52 in connection with saying 46, Mark Goodacre states that, "[s]ince the author of *Thomas* shows disdain for the Old Testament in the unique material, it is not surprising that his selection and redaction of Synoptic material appears to reflect the same attitude"; M. GOODACRE, *Thomas and the Gospels: The Case for Thomas's Familiarity with the Synoptics*, Grand Rapids, MI, Eerdmans, 2012, p. 189. While this is true, it should be noted that the synoptic saying itself is open to a reading that emphasises the gulf between the situations before and after Jesus.

31. The ellipsis dots at 64.29-33 represent what appears to be a secondary variant of the lines that follow.

creation narratives. This doubling may stem from one or more of several factors that are not necessarily mutually exclusive: the two distinct accounts within Genesis itself, the differentiation of literal from allegorical senses, or the claim to a higher revelation that exposes the Mosaic accounts as falsifications. Common to all three interpretative options is the assumption that human origins lie in the divine realm and that physical embodiment is secondary. The divine origin may be derived from the Genesis motif of creation "according to our image and likeness" (κατ' εἰκόνα ἡμετέραν καὶ καθ' ὁμοίωσιν, Gen 1,26), in which case secondary embodiment may be read from the literal sense of Gen 2,7 (the creation of man from the dust of the ground) or the allegorical sense of Gen 3,21 (the provision of skins). Both interpretations are attested in Philo, who sees no need to choose between them. In answer to a question about the double account of human origins in Genesis 1–2, Philo states that:

> The moulded man is the sense-perceptible man and a likeness of the intelligible type. But the man made according to the image is intelligible and incorporeal and a likeness of the archetype ... And this is the Logos of God, the first principle, the archetypal idea ... (*QG* 1.4)[32].

Later, responding to a question about the garments of skin, Philo distinguishes three stages in the formation of the human person: first there is Mind (Adam), then sense (Eve), then "of necessity he made his body also, calling it symbolically a garment of skin" (*QG* 1.53). Thus the garden or paradise occupied by Mind is not just "a dense place full of all kinds of trees" but

> wisdom or knowledge of the divine and human and of their causes. For it was fitting, after the world had come into being, to establish the contemplative life so that through a vision of the world and the things in it praise of the Father might also be attained (*QG* 1.6).

Philo's account of human origins sees mind as primary and embodiment as secondary, and he reaches this conclusion on the basis both of a double narrative and a double hermeneutic.

Where creation according to the divine image is attributed to hostile rulers, as in Sethian texts, the physical body they create is understood as an inferior copy of a prior divine human who appears to them from above. In the *Second Discourse of the Great Seth*, Genesis is seen to bear witness to the Ennoias' original divinity in its reference to their "descent upon the water, that is, the regions below", a gloss on Gen 1,2. For the Philonic and

---

32. Trans. R. MARCUS (LCL), Cambridge, MA, Harvard University Press; London, Heinemann, 1953, p. 3.

Sethian traditions, Genesis conceals the truth – whether behind the facade of the literal sense or within its ideologically motivated distortions.

Athanasius is familiar with the Philonic hermeneutic, mediated no doubt through Origen and his Alexandrian successors. In the *Contra gentes*, Athanasius interprets the second creation story along Philonic lines as teaching the priority of mind over body. As primarily minds rather than bodies, humans are intended to transcend bodily senses and desires in order to practise the contemplation of the Logos and his Father. This is

> exactly as the first man created, named Adam in Hebrew, is described in the holy scriptures as at the beginning [κατὰ τὴν ἀρχήν] having his mind directed towards God in a freedom unimpaired by shame, and as associating with the holy ones in that contemplation of things perceived by the mind [ἐν τῇ τῶν νοητῶν θεωρίᾳ] which he experienced in the place that the holy Moses figuratively called "Paradise" (*Gent*. 2.4).

Unfortunately that original contemplation of deity did not last, and can now be recovered only by laborious ascetic practice. The recognition of nakedness is understood as a turn to the body:

> They knew that they were naked not so much of clothing as that they had become denuded of the contemplation of divine things and had turned their mind to the opposite. For after turning from the consideration of the one and the true, namely God, and from desire of him, they became entangled in the various desires of the body (*Gent*. 3.3)[33].

Here Athanasius draws on a hermeneutic in which a higher figurative sense eclipses the literal sense, with its slightly embarrassing depiction of the first human couple as naked gardeners who have an unfortunate encounter with a clever talking snake[34]. The double hermeneutic corresponds to its interpretative outcome, according to which the Genesis narrative prioritizes the godlike mind over its lowly material embodiment. There is an exact analogy between the antitheses of spirit and letter, mind and body. While the Sethian author is radically hostile to the ancient scriptural narrative, the same antitheses are at play in his presentation. The relationship between spirit and letter is stretched almost to breaking point, but the violent polemic against the letter confirms that here too the letter retains its role as the spirit's necessary negative counterpart.

---

33. Cf. Philo, *Leg*. 3.55: Moses refers "not to the nakedness of the body but to that by which the mind is found bereft and naked of virtue".

34. Cf. Philo, *Agr*. 96–97, where the absurdity of the literal sense of the Genesis story is acknowledged; the true, non-mythical sense of the text lies beneath the surface of the words. In *Conf*. 2–14, Philo provides an extended account of his demythologizing programme which, like its modern counterpart, makes no attempt to mitigate the implausibility of the literal sense.

II. Incarnation and Its Limits

Athanasius appeals to supernatural events recounted in the gospel passion narratives to demonstrate that the Logos far transcends his own assumed humanity. The same is true of the Sethian author, who is also concerned to reinterpret the traditional passion narrative so as to highlight the divinity of its protagonist. It is intriguing that the great architect of christological orthodoxy and the anonymous "docetist" appear to converge at this point[35].

For both authors, the incarnation is in the first place a singular event, occurring suddenly and without warning at least from the perspective of the human agents it presses into service. This event establishes the dual identity of the protagonist of the gospel story, who transcends his own embodiment and distances himself from the suffering and death narrated in the passion tradition. In the Sethian text the incarnational event is explicitly violent:

> I visited a bodily house, I cast out the one who was in it before, and I entered in. And the whole multitude of the rulers was troubled, and the whole material realm of the rulers and all the earth-born powers trembled, seeing the likeness of the Image, since it was mixed. And it is I who was in it, not resembling him who was in it before. For he was a worldly man, but I, I am from above the heavens! ... I revealed that I am a stranger to the regions below (*2DGSeth* 51.20–52.10)[36].

The "worldly man" ejected from his own body is most probably the individual known as Jesus of Nazareth; his replacement by the heavenly Logos derives from the early tradition of the descent of the Spirit at Jesus's baptism. Attaching the heresiological term "adoptionism" to this Christology conceals its affinity to the Athanasian account, which also entails the commandeering of an existing human body. According to Athanasius, the incorporeal Logos

> takes a body of our kind, and not merely so, but from a spotless and stainless virgin, knowing not a man, a body clean and utterly pure from intercourse of men. For being himself mighty, and Artificer of everything, he prepares the body in the virgin as a temple unto himself, and makes it his very own as an instrument, in it manifested, and in it dwelling (*Inc.* 8.3).

---

35. Contrast the view of Pellegrini, *Der zweite Logos* (n. 7), p. 580, that the "docetism" of *2DGSeth* "zeigt die grundsätzliche weite Entfernung des hier vertretenen gnostischen Denksystems von der anderen christlichen Lehre der 'Großkirche'".

36. As Painchaud, *Deuxième traité* (n. 6), p. 87, notes, the original context of the motif of the troubling of the rulers is anthropogony: thus, "l'incarnation du Sauveur est en quelque sorte la répétition de l'Homme au temps des origines".

While the Logos creates his own body in this account, he must still avail himself of an existing body in order to do so – the intact body of Mary of Nazareth within which he shapes his own "temple" or "instrument". As in the Sethian parallel, this is a unilateral and coercive act. The Lukan annunciation narrative notes Mary's acquiescence in the role imposed on her, but Athanasius is interested only in the creative act of the Logos[37].

Athanasius's preferred term for the body taken by the Logos is ὄργανον, "instrument" or "tool"[38]. The Logos does not *become* flesh, in spite of Athanasius's frequent citation of Jn 1,14, for the Logos is immutable: "While he used the body as his instrument, he participated in none of the properties of the body [οὐδενὸς τῶν τοῦ σώματος μετεῖχεν]" (*Inc.* 43.6)[39]. The Logos *uses* a body to enable him to interact with the world in a new way, while maintaining his ongoing administration of the universe. Thus the Logos far transcends his own embodiment: he "was not enclosed in the body, nor was he in the body and absent elsewhere" (*Inc.* 17.1). There is no kenotic self-limitation to the dimensions of a human soul, confined within and dependent on a bodily counterpart, for that would be to abandon the universe to anarchy.

> Thus, though present in a human body and himself giving it life, he was necessarily giving life to the universe, and was both within all things and outside the universe. So, while known from the body by his works, he was also manifest from his action on the universe (*Inc.* 17.2).

The acts of the Logos within the body are most clearly visible in his miracles. How, Athanasius asks, can anyone fail to perceive that it is divine rather than human power that cleanses lepers, gives sight to the blind, transforms water into wine, walks on the sea, and feeds multitudes out of slender resources? These unambiguous proofs of divine presence indicate that gospel statements are potentially misleading when they represent the Lord as eating and drinking or speak of his birth, suffering, and death. Rightly understood, such statements are of limited scope. They

---

37. In the Lukan account the miraculous conception is preceded by divine-human dialogue, mediated through the angel (Lk 1,28-38). For Athanasius divine action is unilateral, an exercise in sovereign power, and it is the Logos that shapes his own body rather than Mary.

38. This term occurs 14 times in the *De incarnatione*. Another favoured term for the body assumed by the Logos is "temple" (6 times).

39. Paraphrasing Athanasius, PETTERSEN, *Athanasius* (n. 14), p. 118, states that, "although the Logos became very man, he himself is not altered". Pettersen's paraphrase is true to Athanasius, but he does not explain how there can be a becoming without alteration.

refer only to the assumed body and not to the Logos himself, who remains serenely indifferent to these human experiences just as the sun is unaffected by the earthly realities touched by its rays[40].

The gospels also recount some of the Logos's providential actions outside the body, where these are relevant to the story. It was the Logos who caused the star to announce the birth of his body[41]. When his body was that of a small child, the Logos sent his angel to warn Joseph to flee with his family to Egypt[42]. Even as his body suffered and died on the cross, the Logos acted independently of it to ensure that the created order bears witness to his presence. At his death,

> the whole creation confessed that the one known and suffering in the body was not simply a man but the Son of God and the Saviour of all. For the sun turned back and the earth was shaken and the mountains were split, and all were afraid. These things demonstrated that Christ on the cross was God and that all creation was his handmaid ... (*Inc.* 19.3)[43].

Here as elsewhere, the scriptural terms "Son of God" and "Saviour" serve to conceal the *a priori* distinction Athanasius draws between the divine Logos and his own bodily instrument. There is a degree of identification between the Logos and the body, for it remains *his* body: thus, "Christ on the cross was God". Yet, although it is *his* body, the Logos does not share its human experience. In that sense it is *not* his body, for the Logos has taken the place of the experiencing subject while continuing to exercise his primary role of administering the universe he created – for example, in darkening the sun and causing the earthquake. The Logos endured insults yet maintained his impassibility throughout[44]. Athanasius echoes scriptural language when he states that "the common Saviour of all has died for us [ὑπὲρ ἡμῶν]" (*Inc.* 21.1), but he glosses – or rather contradicts – this with the statement that "the Logos, since it was impossible for him to die as he was immortal, took

---

40. Cf. *Inc.* 17.5–18.2. In the post-Athanasian Shorter Recension, the reference in this passage to eating, drinking, and birth is replaced by a statement about the works of the Logos within and without the body: "Being a lover of humanity and only Son of the good Father he left nothing bereft of himself but to invisible beings was invisibly known through his providence towards his own creation, while to humans he was abundantly making the Father known through his own body, by his divine teaching and works showing himself to be Son of God" (Greek text in THOMSON, *Athanasius* [n. 2], p. 278). In this substituted passage, the Athanasian tendency to distance the Logos from ordinary human experiences of hunger, thirst, and suffering is taken still further.

41. *Inc.* 37.4.

42. *Fug.* 12.

43. While created entities are here personified for rhetorical effect, the created order is subject to the direct providential rule of the Logos (cf. *Gent.* 41–44).

44. *Inc.* 54.3.

to himself a body capable of dying so that he might offer it for all as his own" (*Inc.* 20.6)[45].

This distancing of the Logos from the body is important for Athanasius's apologetic strategy, for in his view the figure of the crucified Christ is the main obstacle to Christian faith. Contrary to popular belief, it is not the Logos who suffers and dies, for his divinity makes suffering and death impossible for him. It is his body that has to die in order to satisfy the debt incurred by our sin[46]. It is, however, the body – the embodied human being – who stands in the foreground of the gospel narrative, everywhere except the Johannine prologue which Athanasius cites again and again. Yet the Johannine prologue states that the Logos became flesh and is thus identical to the protagonist of the unfolding narrative. Paradoxically, Athanasius's insistence on the full divinity of the Logos-become-flesh highlights the *remoteness* of the Logos from the flesh-and-blood individual it has fashioned as its "instrument". Athanasius has constructed a hermeneutic in which an immutable and impassible Logos must be preserved from contamination by the events of the gospel narrative. This is implicitly an anti-Arian move, although the apologetic genre of the treatise on the incarnation precludes explicit reference to Arian issues. The threat Athanasius perceives from Arianism and Arian exegesis requires vigilant policing of the boundary between the divine and creaturely realms[47].

The hermeneutical implications of this strategy will come to full expression in the polemical exegesis of the *Orationes adversus Arianos*[48].

---

45. Commenting on a related passage (*Ep. Epict.* 6), where it is said that the Logos suffered yet did not suffer, PETTERSEN, *Athanasius* (n. 14), p. 116, concedes that "[t]his paradox may seem on the edge of slipping into contradiction". The roots of this contradiction lie in Athanasius's rejection of scriptural kenoticism.

46. *Inc.* 20.6.

47. It is unlikely that this work dates from a time when "the Arian heresy has not yet arisen to trouble the Church", during "the few years of confidence that followed the victory of Constantine"; E.R. HARDY (ed.), *Christology of the Later Fathers* (LCC, 3), London, SCM, 1954, p. 44. When the reader is warned "not to think that the Saviour has worn a body in consequence of his nature [φύσεως ἀκολουθίᾳ]" (*Inc.* 1.3), this may be directed against the Arian view that he is "changeable by nature [τῇ φύσει τρεπτός]" (*Orat.* 5.8). The reference to "the works of our blessed teachers" as currently unavailable (*Gent.* 1.3) has been plausibly seen as pointing to composition during Athanasius's exile in Trier (336-337). ANATOLIOS, *Athanasius* (n. 4), pp. 26-30, dates the double work to the early years of Athanasius's episcopate, arguing that the "triumphalistic reasoning" is incompatible with his position as an exiled bishop. Although exiled, however, Athanasius was still the legitimate bishop of Alexandria as Constantine had rejected his deposition by the Council of Tyre; T. BARNES, *Athanasius and Constantius: Theology and Politics in the Constantinian Empire*, Cambridge, MA, Harvard University Press, 1993, pp. 24-25. Enforced leisure in Trier may have provided an opportunity to write, perhaps with a potential sympathetic Western readership in view.

48. For defensive anti-Arian exegesis of gospel passages, see especially *Orat.* 3.26-58.

In Book 3 Athanasius creates an imaginary Arian reader of the gospels who lists acts or experiences they ascribe to Jesus that are incompatible with his full divinity. Whatever power and authority he possesses he has received from his Father. He reveals his ignorance by asking questions. He gives way to fear in the Garden of Gethsemane. He experiences abandonment by his Father on the cross[49]. How can such things be predicated of eternal and omnipotent deity? In opposing this Arian proof-texting Athanasius actually agrees with its fundamental premise, which is that true deity does not and cannot suffer. Once again we are told that the Logos employs a body as his ὄργανον[50]. When the body suffers, the Logos does not and cannot suffer with it, being impassible by nature. Why then do the evangelists invariably fail to make the distinction between the Logos and his body that Athanasius believes to be so crucial? His answer is that sufferings and weaknesses are *ascribed* to the Logos because the body remains *his* body even though he does not share its experiences[51]. The ideal Athanasian reader of the gospels must bear in mind that much of their text speaks only indirectly of their truly divine protagonist, for they contain "a double account of the Saviour" (*Orat.* 3.29). The embodied figure who stands in the foreground is just the instrument and property of a divine counterpart.

Is it Athanasius's view that the Son of God on the cross suffers in appearance only, and not in reality? The answer has to be a qualified yes. There is suffering on the cross but it is not clear who experiences it, for it is inflicted on a body understood as a physical object rather than an embodied subject. That body is animated not by a limited human subject but by the divine Logos who operates within it remotely and non-exclusively. A difference between this view and texts normally regarded as "docetic" is that Athanasius applies a strict *a priori* logic to the gospel story whereas so-called "docetic" texts or passages often take narrative form[52]. Nevertheless there are striking convergences between this founding text of christological orthodoxy and its Sethian opposite number.

Both authors are aware that the scriptural texts current within the mainstream Christian community have the potential to mislead unwary readers. The Sethian author confronts this problem directly, by rejecting

---

49. *Orat.* 3.26. Passages cited or alluded to include Mt 24,36 ("Of that day and hour …"), 26,39 ("Let this cup …"), 27,46 ("My God, my God …"); Jn 11,34 (inquiry about Lazarus), 12,27-28 ("Now is my soul troubled …").

50. *Orat.* 3.31, 35.

51. A typical statement of this disjunction: ὅθεν τῆς σαρκὸς πασχούσης οὐκ ἦν ἐκτὸς ταύτης ὁ λόγος. διὰ τοῦτο γὰρ αὐτοῦ λέγεται καὶ τὸ πάθος (*Orat.* 3.32).

52. Cf. *Acts of John* 87–105; *Apocalypse of Peter* NHC VII 81.3–84.11.

one text and affirming another. Near the start of his discourse, the speaker (Christ, the Logos) states that

> it is slavery to say, "We shall die with Christ", that is, with a Thought imperishable and undefiled, an unthinkable wonder! The scripture about the ineffable water, the word that comes from us, is this: "I in you and you in me, just as the Father is in you ..." (*2DGSeth* 49.25-35)[53].

Here a Pauline baptismal theology is rejected in favour of one derived from Johannine language. In Rom 6,3-4 Paul assumes that his readers will be familiar with an understanding of baptism as participation in Christ's death, yet – without naming him – the Sethian author is almost as forthright in his rejection of the apostle as he is of Moses. The true Christ is "a Thought imperishable and undefiled", and, by definition, the imperishable does not die; that would be an absurdity, "an unthinkable wonder"[54]. Athanasius prefers to speak of Christ as the divine Word rather than a divine Thought, but he would have no reason to object to the attribution of imperishability and undefilement.

Having signalled in advance his opposition to the notion that Christ died, the Sethian author proceeds to tell of the heavenly council that approved the proposed incarnation (50.1-24), the need to which it responded (50.25–51.10), and the event of incarnation itself (51.20–52.10). His primary concern is with the reaction that the incarnate Christ engenders especially among the "rulers":

> There was great disturbance in the whole worldly sphere, with confusion and flight, and in the counsel of the rulers. And some were persuaded when they saw the acts of power I performed, and they all came running – those who derived from the inferior race and from the one who fled from the throne to the Sophia of hope (since she had earlier given a sign about us and all who are with me); those of the race of Adonaios (*2DGSeth* 52.10-25).

It is characteristic of this text that the reaction of the suprahuman powers who have hitherto ruled the world corresponds closely to the

---

53. Criticism of belief in the death of Christ as "slavery" continues later in this text, where those who proclaim "the doctrine of a dead man" are said to promote slavery and fear (60.15-30). This polemic corresponds closely to the view of Basilides as reported by Irenaeus, that "whoever confesses the crucified is still a slave and under the power of those who made the body; but whoever denies is freed from them and knows the plan of the ingenerate Father" (*Haer.* 1.24.4). On Irenaeus's account of Basilides see W. LÖHR, *Basilides und seine Schule: Eine Studie zur Theologie- und Kirchengeschichte des zweiten Jahrhunderts* (WUNT, 83), Tübingen, Mohr Siebeck, 1996, pp. 256-273; on links with *2DGSeth*, see *ibid.*, pp. 269-270.

54. This phrase may however refer to Christ. PAINCHAUD, *Deuxième traité* (n. 6), p. 25, and PELLEGRINI, *Der zweite Logos* (n. 7), p. 580, attach the phrase to the following sentence, but this is grammatically and syntactically problematic.

depiction of human "rulers" in older gospel traditions[55]. As the human Jesus is the bearer of the divine Logos or Thought, so the Jewish and Gentile authorities represent the suprahuman powers whose world-dominion the Logos has come so as to challenge. The analogy is not exact, but it does serve to highlight the unseen spiritual drama behind or above the events that culminate in the passion. In the Gospel of John there is speculation among the crowds about whether "the rulers [οἱ ἄρχοντες] truly believe that he is the Christ" (Jn 7,26). Shortly afterwards the Pharisees deny that "any of the rulers have believed in him, or any of the Pharisees" (7,48), but they are contradicted by the evangelist who reports that "many of the rulers believed in him, but because of the Pharisees they did not confess so as not to be put out of the synagogue" (12,42). Among the rulers who believed is the traditional figure of Joseph of Arimathea (19,38) together with the uniquely Johannine Nicodemus, the "ruler of the Jews" who came to him by night and acknowledged that "no-one could perform the signs that you perform unless God were with him" (3,1-2; cf. 7,50-52; 19,39). Nicodemus fits the profile of those who, according to the Sethian author, "were persuaded when they saw the acts of power I performed, and they all came running ..." (*2DGSeth* 52.14-18). Nevertheless, in spite of the evangelist's claim that there were many other secret believers among the rulers, the Johannine rulers are predominantly hostile, and in conspiring to put Jesus to death they are agents of "the Ruler of the world" (Jn 14,30; 16,11; cf. 12,31), who corresponds to the Sethian Ialdabaoth.

The incarnate Christ is said to cause confusion in "the counsel of the rulers". "Counsel" (ϣⲟϫⲛⲉ) may represent βουλή in the original Greek and alludes to the occasion when the rulers gathered together and "took counsel" (συνεβουλεύσαντο) to put Jesus to death (Mt 26,3-4; cf. Jn 11,53) – with the exception of Joseph of Arimathea, who "did not consent to their counsel [βουλή]" (Lk 23,51), and of Nicodemus. When the Johannine Jesus states that "the Ruler of the world is coming" (Jn 14,30), he views the conspiracy against himself as the work of suprahuman as well as human agency, and here too he is followed by the Sethian author:

> Others also came running as if from the World Ruler [ⲕⲟⲥⲙⲟⲕⲣⲁⲧⲱⲣ] and those with him, bringing every kind of punishment upon me, and they cast around in their mind about how to deal with me, thinking that their greatness is everything and speaking false witness against the Man and the whole greatness of the Ekklesia (*2DGSeth* 52.25–53.1).

---

55. So PAINCHAUD, *Deuxième traité* (n. 6), p. 89.

"Every kind of punishment" includes crucifixion, but the reference to false witness suggests that the author also has in mind Jesus's trials before the Sanhedrin and Pilate, where he is spat upon, struck, insulted, bound, scourged, stripped, and mocked (Mt 26,67; 27,1.26-31). The emphasis on haste ("others also came running") finds a parallel in Melito of Sardis's *On Pascha*, where "Israel" is said to have "hastened to the killing of the Lord", preparing for him "sharp nails and false witnesses and ropes and scourges and vinegar and gall" (79). In the Sethian text the "false witness" seems to consist in an affirmation of the World Ruler and a denial of the true Father ("the Man") and his heavenly entourage ("the Ekklesia"). The false witnesses of the canonical gospel attribute to Jesus a claim about rebuilding the temple after destroying it (Mt 26,60-61), and in Sethian perspective the accusation might be taken to affirm the sanctity of the temple and its resident deity – the World Ruler whose claim to sole divinity Jesus exposes as fraudulent.

In a Sethian tradition that can be traced back to the *Apocryphon of John*, the creation of Adam's body from the dust of the ground is understood as the work of Ialdabaoth and his subordinates in imitation of the heavenly Man who has appeared to them in visionary form from above[56]. Loosely related to this is the motif of Ialdabaoth's boast that there is no other God but he[57]. In a difficult but important passage, the author of the *Second Discourse* appears to extract these traditions from their original Genesis-related context and to transplant them into his version of the passion narrative:

> The rulers of the realm of Ialdabaoth revealed to the sphere of the angels the one whom they sought in the form of humanity, because they did not know the true Man. For Adam, whom they had formed, appeared to them, and there was a fearful commotion throughout their entire domain, in case the angels surrounding them should take a stand against them. For at the hands of those offering praise I died, though not in reality, because their archangel was powerless (*2DGSeth* 53.12-21).

The reference to the speaker's apparent death makes clear that the context here is the passion narrative, in spite of the reference to Adam. "Adam" here is "Man", and his appearance to the angels is evidently based on Pilate's pronouncement, "Behold the Man!" (Jn 19,6), understood now in its cosmic significance[58]. What appears here is not the

---

56. *ApocrJn* NHC II 14.13–15.34.
57. *ApocrJn* 13.5-13.
58. So PAINCHAUD, *Deuxième traité* (n. 6), p. 94. Painchaud also suggests that the threat from "the angels surrounding them" represents the Jewish leaders' anxiety about the Romans coming to destroy their temple (*ibid.*, pp. 94-95).

heavenly Man, however, but "Adam whom they had formed", that is, the body expropriated by the "Stranger from above" at the moment of incarnation. In this passage the rulers' sense that this manifestation of "Adam" somehow poses a threat to their authority over their subordinate angels, yet in the passage that follows the threat seems to have been averted:

> And then the voice of the World Ruler came to the angels: "I am God and there is no other beside me!" But I laughed joyfully when I saw his arrogance. And he kept on saying, "Who is Man?", and the whole host of his angels who saw Adam and his dwelling were laughing at his smallness. This is how far removed their thought is from the Great One of the heavens, the True Man, who saw his name present within the smallness of a dwelling place (*2DGSeth* 53.27–54.10).

The "then" at the start of this passage refers back to the occasion when "I died, but not in reality" (53.24-25). The contemptuous angelic laughter directed against "Adam and his dwelling" reflects the mockery inflicted on the crucified Jesus by the chief priests, scribes, and elders: "He saved others, himself he cannot save!" (Mt 27,41-43). This is the moment of the World Ruler's triumph, when a perceived threat to his authority is exposed as insignificant through Jesus's death. Except that Jesus does not die. He is laughing at those who laugh and mocking those who mock, and he is allowing readers of this discourse to share his enjoyment of their discomfiture. Far from dying, "I suffered only in their eyes and their imagination" (*2DGSeth* 55.17-19). Indeed, "what they thought was my death was actually theirs, in their error and blindness, since they nailed their own man resulting in their own death" (*2DGSeth* 55.30-35). Their own man is Adam, and this substitution of a worldly figure for the heavenly Man is one of several switches of identity that explain how the deception of the rulers was carried out:

> It is I whom they saw and punished, but it was another, their father, who drank the gall and the vinegar, it was not me. They were striking me with the reed, but it was another, Simon, who bore the cross on his shoulder, another on whom they placed the crown of thorns! But I was rejoicing on high over all the wealth of the archons and over the seed of their error and their empty glory. And I was laughing at their ignorance and all their powers I enslaved (*2DGSeth* 56.4-21).

The traditional substitution of Simon of Cyrene for Jesus as bearer of the cross here gives rise to further substitutions[59]. The motif of the vinegar

---

59. The Simon of Cyrene tradition occurs in the synoptics (Mt 27,32; Mk 15,21; Lk 23,26) but is rejected by John (βαστάζων ἑαυτῷ τὸν σταυρόν, Jn 19,17; the variant τὸν σταυρὸν αὐτοῦ tones down the emphatic ἑαυτῷ). The view that Simon of Cyrene was crucified in Jesus's place, attributed to Basilides by Irenaeus (*Haer.* 1.24.5), may have arisen from

and gall is originally Matthean: Jesus is said to have tasted but not consumed this scripturally-derived concoction: "They gave him wine mixed with gall" (Mt 27,34) reflects the psalmist's complaint about enemies who have given him gall for food and vinegar for drink (Ps 68,22 LXX)[60]. The Sethian author has Jesus deny that he even tasted this drink: "It was not me". The speaker distances himself from the one who was crucified, referring to him in the third person: "Having bound him with many ropes, they nailed him to the cross, and they secured him with four bronze nails" (*2DGSeth* 58.23-26)[61]. As for the speaker himself, the cross is "my revealed exaltation" (58.15). Here ϫⲓⲥⲉ ("exaltation") may render a substantive such as ὕψωσις, in clear proximity to the Johannine view of the crucifixion (ὑψοῦν: Jn 3,14; 8,28; 12,32.34)[62]. The supposedly "docetic" denial that Christ truly died articulates the common Christian view that the cross is in reality a victory not a defeat.

This Sethian Jesus acknowledges the gospel miracles as his very own "acts of power" but distances himself from the suffering and death recounted in the gospel passion traditions. Allowing for obvious differences of idiom and ideology, Athanasius's view is remarkably similar. While Athanasius can echo Isaiah 53 and acknowledge that the divine Logos endured ill-treatment for our sake, he hastens to add that "he himself was in no way harmed [ἐβλάπτετο ... οὐδέν], being impassible and imperishable [ἀπαθὴς καὶ ἄφθαρτος]" (*Inc.* 54.3). The evangelists speak of him as eating, drinking, and suffering insofar as they refer to his body, yet the incarnate Logos does not himself eat, drink, or suffer but is the owner of a body that does so as if it were a distinct entity in its own right[63]. For Athanasius as for the Sethian author, the crucifixion is the moment of triumph over the hostile archons:

> Being lifted up [ὑψωθείς] in this way, he cleansed the air from the malice of the devil and all the demons, saying "I saw Satan falling like lightning", and he renewed the way to heaven, saying, "Raise your gates, you rulers [οἱ ἄρχοντες], and be raised, everlasting gates" (*Inc.* 25.6)[64].

Mt 27,32-35 (cf. Mk 15,21-24), where the antecedent of the pronouns in the phrases ἔδωκαν αὐτῷ πιεῖν (v. 34) and σταυρώσαντες δὲ αὐτόν (v. 35) might seem to be Simon (v. 32) rather than Jesus. In *2DGSeth* the substitution motif may derive from Basilides, although in 56.11 Simon is associated only with his conventional role as cross-bearer.

60. This motif recurs in *Gos. Peter* 5.16; Melito, *Peri Pascha* 79, 80, 93.

61. The combination of ropes and nails also occurs in Melito, *Peri Pascha* 79, 93.

62. ὑψοῦν and its derivatives are normally rendered into Coptic by ϫⲓⲥⲉ (M. WILMET, *Concordance du Nouveau Testament sahidique* [CSCO, 185], Louvain, Secrétariat du CorpusSCO, 1959, vol. 2, pp. 1666-1669).

63. *Inc.* 17; cf. *Orat.* 3.31.

64. Citations are from Lk 10,18 and Ps 23,7, and the whole passage is based on Jn 12,32 (cited in *Inc.* 25.4). In the *Life of Antony*, the demonic occupation of the air is a

The analogy between the "orthodox" and the "docetic" text is of course not exact. An Athanasian Christ would never claim that "I did not die in reality but in appearance [ϨⲘ ⲠⲈⲦⲞⲨⲞⲚϨ]"[65], for earlier catholic writers from Ignatius onwards repeatedly attacked appeals to the reality/appearance distinction in christological contexts[66]. Thus Athanasius takes it for granted that what the Logos assumed was "a body in truth and not appearance [ἀληθείᾳ καὶ μὴ φαντασίᾳ]" (*Inc.* 18.1). Yet it is hard to differentiate the Sethian Christ's claim that "I did not suffer anything"[67] from Athanasius's insistence that the divine subject of the crucified body is impassible. And it is equally hard to argue that Athanasius escapes the logic of the proscribed reality/appearance distinction. Unlike the Sethian author he avoids engagement with the gospel passion traditions, preferring to appeal to Pauline texts with a soteriological content and a lack of historical specificity. Yet the hermeneutical principle he would bring to the passion narratives is clear: where the evangelists refer to Jesus as experiencing suffering, a sharp distinction must be drawn between the impassible Logos and the vulnerable body he has appropriated to himself. The paradoxical effect is to distance the divine Logos from the gospel story of the Logos-become-flesh. But that is also the concern of the Sethian author. Binary contrasts between such positions reproduce the assumptions of ancient polemics, but they may serve to conceal what the texts actually say.

Durham University Francis WATSON
Department of Theology and Religion
Abbey House
Palace Green
Durham DH1 3RS
United Kingdom
francis.watson@dur.ac.uk

---

potential problem for the *post mortem* soul as it seeks to ascend but finds itself interrogated by hostile powers (*Vit. Ant.* 65–66; cf. *Gos. Mary* BG 15.1–17.7). See D. BRAKKE, *Athanasius and the Politics of Asceticism*, Baltimore, MD, Johns Hopkins University Press, 1995, pp. 217-226.

65. *2DGSeth* 55.17-19.

66. Ignatius insists that Jesus Christ "truly suffered just as he truly raised himself, not as certain unbelievers say that he only seemed to suffer [τὸ δοκεῖν αὐτὸν πεπονθέναι]" (*Smyrn.* 2.1; cf. 4.2).

67. *2DGSeth* 55.15-16.

RETHINKING THE EARLY CHRISTIAN MISSION

Joseph Verheyden's scholarship is a model of detailed, focused, and rigorous intellectual work. His methodological approaches range from carefully analyzing a single verse or passage in the New Testament, to theorizing compositional patterns among a range of ancient documents, to charting the reception of early Christian ideas into later texts[1]. Thus, my initial goal when invited to contribute to this Festschrift was to emulate this focus and care toward whatever topic I decided to explore. In this methodological spirit, then, this essay thinks systematically about the concept of "mission" in early Christianity[2]. This is a topic that several of Verheyden's publications have touched on in different ways, through, for instance, explorations of Paul's travel and activity, the networks of the first followers of Jesus, and the social forms of early Christ groups[3].

Instead of looking at a particular manifestation of the early Christian mission, I want to employ a wider lens to ask theoretical questions about the phenomenon of mission itself. It has been common in New Testament studies to regard the mission activity of early Christianity as a self-evident phenomenon, and accordingly, scholars have traditionally understood it as intentional traveling to deliberately spread programmatic ideas about Christ to gain converts. I will refer to this framework as the normative understanding of mission. In order to investigate this phenomenon, this essay interrogates the normative use of mission in our discipline, before

---

1. Earlier forms of this essay were presented in the Society of Biblical Literature's Redescribing Christian Origins Seminar, as well as University of Miami's Antiquities Interdisciplinary Research Group. I am grateful for the feedback that I received in both venues.

2. I use "early Christianity" to refer to the collection of texts that center on Jesus and his legacy and the people who engaged with them in different ways. This is obviously an anachronistic and problematic term, not in the least because many of the earliest followers of Jesus were embedded within Judaism. In addition, Christianity was almost certainly not a singular phenomenon. I agree with other scholars who maintain that early Christianity, if it can be distinguished from contemporary Judaism, was really early "Christianities", a series of diverse expressions that roughly orbited around the same set of identities, discourse, and practices.

3. As in J. VERHEYDEN, *Die zweite und dritte Missionsreise*, in F.W. HORN (ed.), *Paulus Handbuch*, Tübingen, Mohr Siebeck, 2013, 109-116; ID. – T. NICKLAS – E. HERNITSCHECK (eds.), *Shadowy Characters and Fragmentary Evidence: The Search for Early Christian Groups and Movements* (WUNT, 388), Tübingen, Mohr Siebeck, 2017; M. GRUNDEKEN – J. VERHEYDEN (eds.), *Early Christian Communities between Ideal and Reality* (WUNT, 342), Tübingen, Mohr Siebeck, 2015.

introducing two complicating factors that destabilize it: the role of competition among religious specialists and the prior existence of social networks among Christ groups. While the essay does not offer a definitive replacement for the category of mission, it complexifies the topic in important ways and shows how some texts in the New Testament appear very differently if we shift our perspective on what the early Christian mission was.

I. The Normative Understanding of the Early Christian Mission

New Testament scholarship is and has long been full of romanticized notions of the earliest followers of Jesus and their activities. As an exemplar par excellence, we can point to Adolf von Harnack's magisterial *The Expansion of Christianity in the First Three Centuries* which described the initial Jewish mission, followed by the later "universal" mission in earliest Christianity[4]. As is well known, Harnack's description of the social processes involved in spreading the elements of the Jesus movement was based largely on Acts of the Apostles. For this reason, his understanding of mission primarily focuses on individual (male) figures in the early church who intentionally sought out potential converts for their new religion. It is rather easy to critique scholars like Harnack for having dated, overly romantic, or idealized notions of the early Christian mission and for relying uncritically on Acts' version of the rise of Christianity, so we need not belabor the point here. However, such undertheorized notions of mission, I maintain, still linger in more recent scholarship, and they are often perpetuated with little question.

To illustrate the extent to which the normative understanding of mission still exists today, we will use Eckhard J. Schnabel's 2004 two-volume study *Early Christian Mission* as a touchstone for the discussion.

Schnabel begins his impressive undertaking by offering a working definition of mission. Mission, in his reckoning, is

> the activity of a community of faith that distinguishes itself from its environment in terms of both religious belief (theology) and social behavior (ethics), that is convinced of the truth claims of its faith, and that actively

---

4. A. von Harnack, *The Mission and Expansion of Christianity in the First Three Centuries*, trans. J. Moffatt, London, Williams & Norgate, 1908; repr. New York, Harper, 1962. The first German edition, *Die Mission und Ausbreitung des Christentums in den ersten drei Jahrhunderten*, appeared in Leipzig, J.C. Hinrichs, 1902; ²1906.

works to win other people to the content of faith and the way of life of whose truth and necessity the members of that community are convinced[5].

This exemplifies what I am deeming the normative understanding of mission and mirrors what Martin Goodman has argued elsewhere to be the characteristic components of a missionary religion: proselytization, universal scope, and an organized/systematic program[6].

Turning to the textual evidence, Schnabel makes an initial distinction between the activity of Jesus and his disciples and Paul's later activities. Partitioning these two "stages" is a common habit among scholars who study the early Christian mission. Drawing evidence from the so-called Missionary Discourse (Mt 10,5-16 and parallels), Schnabel then argues that Jesus instructed the Twelve to take short missionary trips throughout Galilee in pairs. They were restricted to Jewish audiences, to whom they were meant to proclaim Jesus' message about the kingdom of God and to offer services such as healing and exorcism. While they were to take no provisions and accept no money for their services, they relied on the hospitality of those in the villages that they visited[7]. Viewing Jesus' statements about potential rejection as anticipatory warnings (instead of sayings formulated later to reflect the negative responses the missionaries received), Schnabel maintains that Jesus foresaw the rejection that they would encounter.

After a break in missionary activity coinciding with Jesus' last week, Schnabel argues that the events of Pentecost inaugurate the mission that emerged after Jesus' death. While he separates these movements chronologically, we can note that the post-Pentecost mission is depicted essentially as a continuation of the former mission of the Twelve, albeit with some theological developments. Peter's speech in Acts 2,38-40, Schnabel explains, highlights the differences between Jesus' mission and the post-Pentecost mission; the latter centers on Jesus' messianic identity, requires a water baptism, and aims to gather gentiles into the kingdom of God's elect[8]. Part of the overall mission strategy after Jesus' death, Schnabel now contends, is to "establish communities of followers of Jesus"[9].

Paul's missionary activity is discussed in the second volume of his study, and also in the slightly reworked standalone book *Paul the Missionary*[10].

---

5. E.J. SCHNABEL, *Early Christian Mission*. Vol. 1: *Jesus and the Twelve*, Downers Grove, IL, InterVarsity, 2004, p. 11.
6. M. GOODMAN, *Mission and Conversion: Proselytizing in the Religious History of the Roman Empire*, Oxford, Clarendon, 1994, pp. 1-7.
7. SCHNABEL, *Jesus and the Twelve* (n. 5), pp. 293-305.
8. *Ibid.*, pp. 404-405.
9. *Ibid.*, p. 513.
10. E.J. SCHNABEL, *Paul the Missionary: Realities, Strategies, and Methods*, Downers Grove, IL, InterVarsity, 2008.

Schnabel spends a great deal of time looking at how Paul understands his own activity[11], before meticulously outlining his travels and theological development. What is most relevant for our purposes is his discussion of "tactics", for this is where we can see how he is theorizing and systematizing this activity. Paul, he claims, "planned his missionary initiatives in the context of a general strategy that controlled his tactical decisions"[12]. His goal was simply to proclaim ideas of Christ in "areas in which it had not been proclaimed before"[13]. Yet Paul was also adaptable and could easily change plans and tactics if necessary. For instance, Schnabel contends that he deliberately targeted synagogues, because "gentiles who believed in Israel's God were the best candidates for successful evangelism"[14]. He also operated out of private homes, sometimes under the patronage of the householder[15]. In the interest of space, we cannot go into greater detail, but it suffices to say that this is a rather standard (i.e., normative) portrait of the early Christian mission. Schnabel clearly understands Paul's activity as a continuation and expansion upon what Jesus and the disciples had been doing, and Paul's *modus operandi* (preaching in synagogues and private houses) reflects ideas in both Paul's letters and Acts. Admittedly, with Paul, we are on firmer ground because he was a real social agent (as opposed to one that may be a fictitious character in a story) who was actually traveling to urban centers and interacting with other people; yet, as I explore later on in this essay, there are reasons to doubt the systematic, programmatic mission of Paul.

Some final remarks on this normative understanding of mission are necessary, before turning to important critiques. As is probably evident, Schnabel's theory is grounded in particular theological beliefs[16]. This is most obvious when one encounters his efforts to isolate early Christianity from any cultural influence on its activities and when one realizes that he essentially treats the gospel narratives and Acts as historical reports of how the early Christian mission develops[17]. His defense of using Acts especially

---

11. E.J. SCHNABEL, *Early Christian Mission*. Vol. 2: *Paul and the Early Church*, Downers Grove, IL, InterVarsity, 2004, pp. 945-981.
12. *Ibid.*, p. 1293.
13. *Ibid.*, p. 1299.
14. *Ibid.*, p. 1300.
15. *Ibid.*, pp. 1301-1306.
16. Indeed, Schnabel himself was a former missionary to the Philippines (see, https://www.logos.com/product/36465/early-christian-mission-volumes-1-and-2). See also SCHNABEL, *Paul the Missionary* (n. 10), pp. 374-458.
17. SCHNABEL, *Paul and the Early Church* (n. 11), pp. 288-290, 527-545. In order to argue that the early Christian mission was "a shocking innovation in antiquity" (p. 545), he dismisses the following as meaningful *comparanda*: Jewish proselytizing, dissemination of Greco-Roman cults, itinerant philosophers, and Torah teachers.

to reconstruct the early Christian mission merits attention: "The book of Acts is not a work of fiction, nor does it belong in the category of historical fiction"[18]. Moreover, it was "indeed written by an eyewitness (at least of Paul's travels) not long after the events narrated in the account" and as such, "it might be treated as a primary source in any description of earliest Christianity"[19]. We also observe the strategies in which he engages to acknowledge the editorial influences of authors, while still maintaining that the texts are historically accurate. For instance, while he observes that Luke reports things "selectively", such an observation only appears to explain why it is that Luke has not given us a "complete picture"[20] of Paul's missionary activity. He never supposes that, for instance, selective reporting could also imply that Luke *invented* parts of his accounts or had erroneous information about the apostles. There is more overt theological interest in this project as well. When explaining his hermeneutical presuppositions, he follows Ernst Dassmann in treating the early Christian mission as "both a historical and a theological discourse 'that traces how God's salvation was realized in history'"[21]. There is nothing wrong with having this theological interest, of course, provided we understand how it affects the historical study of a particular topic, and in this case, I suggest that there is a significant impact on that historical enterprise.

In short, Schnabel's expansive study often explicitly says what many other scholars of early Christianity have implicitly assumed: that the New Testament texts are more or less accurate reports of the processes involved in spreading early Christianity; that the movement was largely one centered on ideas, which were transferred from community to community by persuasive (male) missionaries, and that the activities of Jesus' disciples before his death should be classed as the same thing (the "mission") as those of Paul and his fellow travelers[22]. We could amass much more data from contemporary scholarship, but their arguments would be largely the same: the early Christian mission was a deliberate, systematic effort to spread a coherent body of ideas about Jesus. By packaging it thus, the scholarly reconstructions have essentially confirmed the stories we have been bequeathed in the canonical gospels and Acts. Yet, as I hope to show, the image of Christianity in these texts has occluded other significant sociological dynamics that were likely influential as well.

18. SCHNABEL, *Jesus and the Twelve* (n. 5), p. 26.
19. *Ibid.*, p. 32.
20. *Ibid.*, p. 522.
21. *Ibid.*, p. 19.
22. Despite my differing viewpoint, Schnabel's wide-ranging study is impressive, comprehensive in scope, and certainly necessary reading for anyone interested in studying the expansion of early Christianity in the first two centuries.

II. Critiquing the Normative Construction of Mission

Since it continues to be common to speak of various stages or moments in the early Christian mission, as well as to regard the early Christian mission as a remarkable, nearly inexplicable success, it is important to unpack what scholars such as Schnabel are actually talking about (and assuming) in their work. Admittedly, one might be reticent to call the concept of mission into question. After all, the ideas about Jesus had to spread *somehow*, and the gospels depict Jesus as actively spreading his teachings with his disciples, while Paul's letters seemingly witness to his supposed missionary activity. For that reason, it has been easy to group all of this data together under the conceptual lens of mission.

But the category is not nearly as simple as it appears, so we turn now to outlining some significant critiques of this category, recalling Schnabel's study at key points to illustrate the discussion. We must keep in mind that all categories do ideological work, and thus, all have problems and blind spots in their own ways. But I maintain that the work done by the category mission has often derailed our historically and sociologically minded attempts to explain the emergence and spread of the Jesus movement throughout the Roman Empire. I will not propose an alternative concept at this point; rather I simply suggest that we disentangle a variety of facets intertwined in the language of mission, so that they can be treated more carefully and appropriately.

We begin with perhaps the most problematic issue with the normative construction of mission: that it regularly engages in mirror readings of texts in the New Testament. By doing so, it treats them as historical reports of early Christian activity instead of idealized, even fabricated, accounts of the movement's origins. Indeed, some scholars have argued that mirror readings of early Christian texts cause numerous problems for historical reconstruction. For instance, this method encourages us to see "persecution" behind every text that claims to be experiencing it[23], and it has also been responsible for the positing of a "Christian community" behind every theologically distinct text[24]. Narrowing our focus to the

---

23. Several scholars have recently aimed to reassess the reality of persecution in early Christianity. See, for instance, C. Moss, *The Myth of Persecution: How Early Christians Invented a Story of Martyrdom*, New York, HarperCollins, 2013; S.E. Rollens, *Persecution in the Social Setting of Q*, in M. Tiwald (ed.), *Q in Context II: Social Setting and Archaeological Background of the Sayings Source* (BBB, 173), Bonn, Bonn University Press, 2015, 149-164.

24. For critiques of the category of community in our field, see S.E. Rollens, *The Kingdom of God Is Among You: Prospects for a Q Community*, in S.E. Porter – A.W. Pitts (eds.), *Christian Origins and the Establishment of the Early Jesus Movement*

bounds of the present discussion, we have already seen above instances of transforming (possibly fictitious) literary accounts about Jesus, his first followers, Paul, and/or Paul's contemporaries into simple records of historical action. Schnabel, for instance, treated Acts as a text that was more or less accurate about how the ideas about Jesus spread: missionaries intentionally shared a systematized body of ideas with audiences who rationally weighed the credibility of the ideas[25]. Yet, when we consider even the most valuable sources for the early Christian mission – namely, the letters of Paul – it is clear that his audiences often barely understood his teachings to begin with; for instance, note the many places where the Corinthians seem to have missed the main points of what he had taught them, such as 1 Corinthians 1 (on baptism), 11 (on the Lord's Supper), and 15 (on the resurrection). The translation of ideas from missionary to recipient was thus not as seamless as the texts would have us believe[26]. In other words, mirror reading of texts on the matter of mission fundamentally glosses over much of the complexity of how people were actually engaging with early Christian texts, ideas, and practices.

In the absence of any other textual accounts of the spread of Christianity in the first century, Acts of the Apostles often becomes the default for what "must have happened" in those hazy years following the death of Jesus. Even if some of it is admitted to be idealized, many scholars see no option but to rely on its basic contours for thinking about the early Christian mission. However, as numerous commentators have long noted, Acts of the Apostles is full of idealizations about the speedy spread of Christianity, the enthusiasm and number of converts, and the size, homogeneity, and visibility of Christ groups in urban centers[27]. It is also increasingly agreed to be a rather late text, at least as late as the

---

(Early Christianity in Its Hellenistic Environment, 4), Leiden, Brill, 2018, 224-241; M.H. SELLEW, *Thomas Christianity: Scholars in Quest of a Community*, in J. BREMMER (ed.), *The Apocryphal Acts of Thomas*, Leuven, Peeters, 2001, 11-35; S.K. STOWERS, *The Concept of 'Community' and the History of Early Christianity*, in *MTSR* 23 (2011) 238-256; H. MÉNDEZ, *Did the Johannine Community Exist?*, in *JSNT* 42 (2020) 350-374; S.E. ROLLENS, *The Anachronism of 'Early Christian Communities'*, in N. P. ROUBEKAS (ed.), *Theorizing "Religion" in Antiquity* (Studies in Ancient Religion and Culture), Sheffield, Equinox, 2019, 307-324.

25. When it comes to the stories about Jesus in the gospels, many commentators ignore or overlook the fact that people appear to have been attracted to Jesus for practical reasons (healing, miracles, etc.), as opposed to doctrinal reasons.

26. ROLLENS, *The Anachronism of 'Early Christian Communities'* (n. 24), pp. 321-322.

27. C.K. ROTHSCHILD, *Luke-Acts and the Rhetoric of History: An Investigation of Early Christian Historiography* (WUNT, 2.175), Tübingen, Mohr Siebeck, 2019; S. MATTHEWS, *Perfect Martyr: The Stoning of Stephen and the Construction of Christian Identity*, Oxford, OUP, 2012; B. WITHERINGTON III, *History, Literature, and Society in the Book of Acts*, Cambridge, CUP, 2007; J.S. KLOPPENBORG, *Christ's Associations: Connecting and*

beginning of the second century[28]. In other words, it stands at a far distance from the history that it purports to recount, and to treat it as an eyewitness to such events is not wise.

Another problem with the normative construction of mission is that it conflates the activities of Paul with the actions of Jesus and his disciples in the gospels. The result gives the impression that there was a singular, unified Christian mission that was inaugurated in the time of Jesus, when it was directed primarily at Jewish audiences, before it gradually targeted gentiles under the auspices of Paul and his fellow missionaries. The very fact that Schnabel has a two-part study on the early Christian mission, featuring Jesus and the disciples in part one and Paul in part two, belies this assumption. However, in my view, to shoehorn both sets of behavior into the common construction of "mission" obfuscates important differences – differences that are critical to a sociologically informed account of the emergence of Christianity.

I would maintain, rather, that it is crucial to separate the so-called mission in the life of Jesus, if such a thing actually existed behind the stories in the gospels, from the activities of Paul and those like him. For one, we are dealing with completely different ideological interests among these groups of people. The early traditions associated with Jesus in Galilee and Judea give voice to a relatively varied group of rural dwellers[29]. These traditions are interested in moralizing discourse, miracles and wonder-working, the bounds of Jewish law, and critiques of the social and political structures. Whether or not there was a real "community" who engaged with these materials, the authors of texts like Q and Mark probably imagined themselves addressing a sort of "constituency" and mobilized traditions that embodied many interests and perspectives that they hoped to target[30].

Belonging in the Ancient City, New Haven, CT, Yale University Press, 2019, pp. 308-309.

28. J.B. TYSON, *Marcion and Luke-Acts: A Defining Struggle*, Columbia, SC, University of South Carolina Press, 2007; M. KLINGHARDT, *The Oldest Gospel and the Formation of the Canonical Gospels* (BTS, 41), Leuven – Paris – Bristol, CT, Peeters, 2021. In the suasive phrasing of one scholar, "Acts is a historical source, no doubt, but it is historical insofar as it offers data about a second-century portrayal of Paul [and other aspects of early Christ groups] which fits with the larger theology and politics of Acts"; L.S. NASRALLAH, *Archaeology and the Letters of Paul*, Oxford, OUP, 2019, p. 84.

29. In his incisive collection of essays on the topic, Douglas E. Oakman explores how many traditions that might preserve the worldview of agrarian dwellers have been "written up" into more elite literary products that we now find in the New Testament; D.E. OAKMAN, *Jesus and the Peasants* (Matrix: The Bible in Mediterranean Context), Eugene, OR, Wipf & Stock, 2008.

30. The Sayings Gospel Q is an excellent example of this framing of ideological concerns; see especially S.E. ROLLENS, *Framing Social Criticism in the Jesus Movement: The Ideological Project in the Sayings Gospel Q* (WUNT, 2.374), Tübingen, Mohr

Paul's target audiences, on the other hand, were urban dwellers, engaging in entirely different modes of production and socialities. Perhaps this is part of the reason that Paul never includes any parables of Jesus: because they evoke an entirely different life world than his audiences were experiencing[31]. In addition to the different ideological perspectives, we are also dealing with disparate social contexts in which the mechanics of constructing social networks diverged. What it means to travel, encounter strangers, and share information with them in rural Galilee was something quite different than when Paul moved throughout dynamic, diverse cities such as Thessalonica or Corinth. Traveling in localized rural space – what is imagined in the gospels – often capitalized on intra-village social and familial networks, whereas travel to major *metropoleis* often required people to rely on occupational or ethnic similarities to make connections in the city[32]. In other words, the social networks in which these movements spread were remarkably different. To conflate them all into "the early Christian mission" occludes their obvious differences.

Furthermore, the normative concept of mission often unintentionally imports modern understandings of missionary activity into the ancient world. Since the eighteenth century, various Christian groups have been systematically going into non-Christian areas to initiate conversions and gain followers. This, I maintain, is a uniquely modern form of activity. As scholars such as Tomoko Masuzawa and Brent Nongbri have shown in their works about the origins of the modern concept of religion, prior to European modernity, Christian encounters with "the Other" initially involved people in their geographical vicinity who had at least heard of Christianity and who had chosen not to adopt it; the Others were thus written off as obstinate heretics instead of targeted as potential converts[33]. With the rise of European (and subsequently American) colonialism, the situation dramatically changed. These Christians suddenly encountered

---

Siebeck, 2014; W.E. ARNAL, *Jesus and the Village Scribes*, Minneapolis, MN, Fortress, 2001; G.B. BAZZANA, *Kingdom of Bureaucracy: The Political Theology of Village Scribes in the Sayings Gospel Q* (BETL, 274), Leuven – Paris – Bristol, CT, Peeters, 2015.

31. Another equally likely possibility is that he simply did not know most of the teachings attributed to Jesus in the gospels, since many of them were no doubt created after Jesus' time and reflect later stages in the development of the movement (e.g., Mk 4,1-20).

32. See, for instance, the important work on ancient associations that highlights the roles of occupations and ethnic backgrounds as the basis for voluntary associations: R.S. ASCOUGH, *1 and 2 Thessalonians: Encountering the Christ Group at Thessalonike*, Sheffield, Sheffield Phoenix Press, 2014; KLOPPENBORG, *Christ's Associations* (n. 27).

33. B. NONGBRI, *Before Religion: A History of a Modern Concept*, New Haven, CT, Yale University Press, 2013; T. MASUZAWA, *The Invention of World Religions: Or, How European Universalism was Preserved in the Language of Pluralism*, Chicago, IL – London, University of Chicago Press, 2005.

peoples in Africa, Latin America, and elsewhere who were entirely unfamiliar with the beliefs, practices, and world views of the Christian tradition. In response, missionaries mounted a systematic effort to spread a nexus of ideas and practices to those peoples who had never encountered them; the goal was to amass converts. What we see, then, is an "official" form of Christianity that is being exported to a new geographical region[34], through word and deed, to people who did not identify with it. In other words, modern missionary activity begins with a systematized, coherent program that can be "spread" easily, in doctrinal sound bites or pamphlets and ritual prescriptions, distributed by self-evidently authoritative representatives of the tradition.

It is no surprise that the normative understanding of the early Christian mission appeared in this period, for it reflects precisely the kind of programmatic and belief-based system that Western missionary activity was promoting. Even paradigms that we consider obvious, like the sequential missionary journeys in Acts, emerge from this particular context. According to John Townsend, before the mid-1700s, no commentator of the New Testament had regarded the journeys in Acts as a series of systematic or deliberate missions:

> What is true of ancient writers is also true of those belonging to a later age. Neither Erasmus (c. 1466-1536) nor John Calvin (1509-64) nor Theodore Beze (1519-1605) nor Cornelius à Lapide (1567-1637) nor Hugo Grotius (1583-1645) interpreted Acts in terms of the traditional [three-fold] missionary journeys. In fact, the earliest reference that I can find to these journeys is in the first edition of J.A. Bengel's *Gnomon Novi Testamenti* ... In the years following the first edition of *Gnomon* most writers on Acts adopted a missionary-journey pattern. It found its way into the major commentaries, including those of J.H. Heinrichs, H.A.W. Meyer, and H. Alford. Thus, by the middle of the century the three-missionary journey system had become firmly established in the exegetical tradition of Acts. Why should a missionary-journey pattern have been imposed on Acts at this time? A likely answer is that commentators were reading their own presuppositions back into apostolic times. The eighteenth and nineteenth centuries saw an escalation of Western missionary activity. It was an era for founding missionary societies ... Since it was standard missionary practice for evangelists to operate out of a home base, one should not be surprised at the exegetical assumption that Paul, the great missionary of the New Testament, had done the same[35].

---

34. Depending on which version of Christianity the missionary adheres to (e.g., a Protestant denomination, Roman Catholicism, Mormonism, etc.), of course, the "official" version will be quite different.

35. J.T. TOWNSEND, *Missionary Journeys in Acts and European Missionary Societies*, in K.H. RICHARDS (ed.), *Society of Biblical Literature 1985 Seminar Papers* (SBLSP, 24), Atlanta, GA, Scholars, 1985, 433-438, pp. 436-437, as cited in L.E. VAAGE, *Ancient*

In other words, even something that is ostensibly "factual" in our field – that Acts is organized around a series of intentional missionary journeys – itself enters the scholarly discourse at a particular time.

In any case, such a systematic project was simply not the *modus operandi* with the Jesus movement in the first century[36]. If we are considering the ideas that Jesus himself taught, the most prominent scholarly opinion was that Jesus was not trying to "start a religion" or "convert" anyone to anything. Rather, Jesus was operating fully within the context of Second Temple Judaism[37]. Thus, it makes little sense to speak of Jesus as having a mission to convert anyone in his environs. In addition, if one tried to systematize the teachings of Jesus, one would end up with an ideological system that was essentially a version of Judaism. Jesus' teaching about God's rule, the finer points of the Jewish law, and the recommended ethical practices all make sense within Second Temple Judaism. Finally, there seems to be no good evidence from the gospel stories that any teachings of Jesus were systematized. To the contrary, his disciples are continually depicted as inquiring about Jesus' teachings and how they fit together or how they should be interpreted, implying that they themselves did not understand their coherency. It is not until we get to Paul that we can imagine something more along the lines of a specific, coherent "body" of tradition being intentionally passed on to others.

Paul's activity is indeed closer to this modern understanding of mission, at least if we assume Paul is accurate in describing his own *modus operandi*, but it still, I contend, falls short. For one, Paul does not appear to have a systematic theology that he is spreading. His ideas are *ad hoc* and are continually amended. One only needs to consider 1 Thessalonians to see how "un-programmatic" his teachings about Jesus may have been. 1 Thessalonians 4–5 suggests that Paul arrived in Thessalonica and, after making some social connections, told them about a Jewish man, known as God's son, who was crucified by the Romans, brought back to life afterwards, and who would return to help safeguard people from the

---

Religious Rivalries and the Struggle for Success: Christians, Jews, and Others in the Early Roman Empire, in ID. (ed.), *Religious Rivalries in the Early Roman Empire and the Rise of Christianity* (Studies in Early Christianity and Judaism, 18), Waterloo, Wilfrid Laurier Press, 2006, 3-19, pp. 16-17. Cf. NASRALLAH, *Archaeology and the Letters of Paul* (n. 28), p. 85.

36. Vaage goes even further to suggest that the first two centuries of Christianity do not evince programmatic persuasive efforts; VAAGE, *Ancient Religious Rivalries and the Struggle for Success* (n. 35), p. 16.

37. See recently, P. FREDRIKSEN, *When Christians Were Jews: The First Generation*, New Haven, CT, Yale University Press, 2018. See also, M. THIESSEN, *Jesus and the Forces of Death: The Gospels' Portrayal of Ritual Impurity within First-Century Judaism*, Grand Rapids, MI, Baker Academic, 2020.

coming wrath of a Jewish deity. Paul seems to have emphasized that Jesus' return would come at literally any moment (1 Thess 4,17; 5,2). He evidently did not tell them what to expect if this return took longer than anticipated, and so they appear to have reached out to ask him about the fate of those who had already died when Jesus returned. His answer is the depiction of Jesus returning in the sky with the archangel's trumpet, ready to rapture first the dead, then the living (1 Thess 4,16-17). Therefore, what we are seeing in Paul's letters is not his promotion of a fully articulated theology, but rather the gradual *creation* of that theology in conversation with his addressees. Furthermore, his travels and his interactions with various Christ groups – what is typically characterized as his mission – is actually what gives him the opportunity to develop these ideas. In that sense, we might say more accurately that mission and theology are *mutually constituting* instead of theology being the basis of mission.

Rodney Stark has offered an important corrective to the idea that missionary work and conversion operate on the basis of belief in doctrines. Stark's account of the rise of Christianity is well known for challenging the often-unstated Protestant bias in scholarship on early Christianity that privileges the centrality of ideas and doctrine in the spread of a religion. As he explains:

> For generations it was assumed that religion conversions were the result of doctrinal appeal – that people embraced a new faith because they found its teachings particularly appealing, especially if these teachings seemed to solve serious problems or dissatisfactions that afflicted new believers. On this, both theologians and social scientists agreed. So much so, that "everyone" was content to "discover" how a particular religious movement gained adherents by inspecting its doctrines and then deducing who converted to this group on the basis of who most needed what was offered[38].

Rather than arguing that Christianity miraculously and enthusiastically spread on the basis of its compelling ideas, Stark argues that there are

---

38. R. STARK, *Cities of God: The Real Story of How Christianity Became an Urban Movement and Conquered Rome*, New York, HarperOne, 2007, p. 8. In an oft-cited part of his research, Stark analyzes conversion in early Christianity through the lens of research done on conversion and missionary work within the Unification Church in the 1960s. He observes that conversion among Unificationists is often brought about by people's social networks, rather than how persuasive an individual finds the Unification Church's theology. As he explains of the church's missionizing activity, "[O]f all the people the Unificationists encountered in their missionary efforts, the only ones who converted were those whose interpersonal ties to members *overbalanced* their ties to nonmembers" (p. 10). He thus concludes, "[C]onversion is primarily about bringing one's religious behavior into alignment with that of one's friends and relatives" (p. 11). Such a view leads him to think through the strategic social relationships that nurtured emerging Christianity, instead of assuming that the theological ideas naturally attracted people to the movement.

other, more mundane social processes at work. Through comparative sociological study, he finds it just as likely that people became affiliated with Christ groups simply because their friends and family members were already in these groups[39]. In this way, Christianity was a social form that spread through social networks, thriving on social pressures and habits of social actors, in some ways disconnected from whether or not those social actors believed or were persuaded by the beliefs.

Yet, despite this important corrective and nuance, Stark still promotes a framework that sees early Christianity as relatively programmatic, more akin to how modern missionary activity takes place, a point that I am trying to push back on deliberately. Missionaries, in his analysis, "are those who seek converts, who attempt to get others to shift from one tradition to another"[40]. In other words, the missionary activity seems to be a deliberate and programmatic operation, despite the fact that he also acknowledges the very ordinary ways that Christianity often could have spread, disconnected from intentional missionizing. With this programmatic statement in place, he then claims that early Christianity was unique in antiquity for having missionary efforts[41]. For critically-minded scholars, such a move is inherently problematic, because it assumes that the social processes in Christianity are entirely unlike those found in Greek and Roman religions.

Bound up in this critique are really two interrelated issues that need to be kept separate. The first issue is that a modern, Protestant understanding of religion lurks behind descriptions of the rise of Christianity in antiquity[42]. This way of looking at religion privileges the ideas that are promoted in the religious discourse and assumes that mission activity and conversion focus almost singularly on the rational communication of ideas. The second issue is that this Protestant bias, in turn, implicitly endorses the idea that early Christianity could be expressed in coherent theology that one could deliberately "spread"[43]. Not only was Christianity

---

39. *Ibid.*
40. *Ibid.*, p. 4.
41. *Ibid.*, p. 7. Stark observes that Judaism had some outreach, but what Christianity uniquely offered was "monotheism stripped of ethnic encumbrances" (p. 7). Martin Goodman encourages a similar view of Christianity's uniqueness. It is only with Christianity, he argues, that we encounter the "shocking novelty" of the deliberate mission; GOODMAN, *Mission and Conversion* (n. 6), p. 109.
42. On the pervasive influence of Protestant assumptions of religion in the academic study of religion, see, of course, J.Z. SMITH, *Drudgery Divine: On the Comparison of Early Christianities and the Religions of Late Antiquity*, Chicago, IL, University of Chicago Press, 1990.
43. Mission is not unknown to Catholicism, of course. One only need to consider the activities of the Jesuits in places like China, Canada, and Latin America. My focus on Protestant missions here is more about how Protestant missionaries have implicitly

not a systematized nexus of beliefs in the first couple of centuries of the Common Era, but also, even people who seem to be sharing some ideas (and practices) with new audiences, such as Paul, appear to be cobbling them together as they go.

A final critique concerns the ways that the language of mission disguises some important nuances and collapses various forms of social and cultural production into the single, problematic category of mission. In so doing, it neglects the *bricolage* aspect of creating Christian discourse and networks, that is, the *ad hoc* ways that cultural producers, intellectuals, and other social actors used whatever cultural resources that they had "on hand" to develop this social and intellectual movement. In my reckoning, there are at least four discrete phenomena that get swept up in the language of mission but that need to be studied separately. The first process involves the *production* of cultural resources about Jesus. Here I am thinking about the cultivation of particular bodies of ideas and practices that came to be identified with Jesus movements – that is, the *content* of what came to be called Christianity[44]. Yet, because the spread of Christianity has been for so long discussed in terms of the "mission" that spread ideas, the vital (albeit ordinary) work of cultural producers writing and engaging with texts has been overlooked as part of the enterprise of mission. A second process to disentangle involves the role of *social networks* in the emergence of Christianity. Textual expressions would be almost entirely impotent if they could not thrive and move through social and intellectual networks. As I show in the final portion of this essay, attention to social networks, especially ones that already existed before people such as Paul arrived on the scene, changes how we imagine the early Christian mission unfolding. A third process in all of this is the *physical travel* involved in moving through social networks, both local and more distant, which in many ways might actually constrain or otherwise affect some of the mission activity of early Christians[45]. A fourth process is the *textual idealization* of these other processes – the

theorized religion as something that can be captured in doctrinal statements and thus exported to non-believers.

44. See the different arguments about the spread development of different kinds of early Christian literature in BAZZANA, *Kingdom of Bureaucracy* (n. 30) (focusing on sub-elite literature produced by scribes) and R.F. WALSH, *The Origins of Early Christian Literature: Contextualizing the New Testament within Greco-Roman Literary Culture*, Cambridge, CUP, 2021 (focusing on elite literature moving through networks of writers).

45. NASRALLAH, *Archaeology and the Letters of Paul* (n. 28), pp. 76-104. Nasrallah offers an excellent case study of how travelers stood to impact the locals in a region, especially when they were expected to provide hospitality for the travelers out of their own pockets. On travel in antiquity more generally, see W.A. MEEKS, *The First Urban Christians: The Social World of the Apostle Paul*, New Haven, CT, Yale University Press,

myth-making, if you will. In other words, even once we have disentangled the cultural production from the social networks in which they thrived and then paid proper attention to the mechanics of spreading a social movement across the Empire, we have to admit that the textual evidence we have for such processes is full of idealizations, fabrications, and reinterpretations. Therefore, part of studying "the early Christian mission", to my mind, should involve thinking about why it ended up being represented as it is and how these textual representations have informed scholars' conclusions about this historical activity.

If we disentangle these features within what is usually called "the mission" and if we do not start from the premise that missionary activity automatically made Christianity distinct from Jewish and Greco-Roman traditions, I would like to suggest that we are in a better position to appreciate how similar the social processes of early Christianity are to other cultic, political, and associative forms in antiquity. Indeed, all four features discussed above (cultural production of ideas and practices, engagement with social networks, travel and mechanics of movement, and myth-making/idealization of these processes) have counterparts elsewhere in antiquity. For instance, in some association inscriptions we can see an early moment in which a "backstory" is crafted for an associative group, which is an excellent analogue to the myth-making practices in early Christianity[46]. Similarly, in the writings of cultural elites like Pliny the Younger, we encounter a window into the social networks that people could build on the local and translocal level, giving us an instance of cultural production and networking practices that can fruitfully be compared to those among Christian writers. And finally, in the widespread practices of religious specialists in antiquity, we see efforts to craft new social networks wherein cultic and divinatory services could be proffered to new audiences, which helps us better understand the movement of early Christianity and the key players involved[47]. In other words, if we

---

1983, pp. 16-23; C. CONCANON, *Economic Aspects of Inter-City Travel in Pauline Assemblies* (Paul and Economics), Minneapolis, MN, Fortress, 2016.

46. For examples of myth-making in early Christianity, see B.L. MACK, *A Myth of Innocence: Mark and Christian Origins*, Minneapolis, MN, Fortress, 1988; S.E. ROLLENS, *Inventing Tradition in Thessalonica: The Appropriation of the Past in 1 Thessalonians 2:14-16*, in *BTB* 46 (2006) 123-132; EAD., *The God Came to Me in a Dream: Epiphanies in Voluntary Associations as a Context for Paul's Vision of Christ*, in *HTR* 111 (2018) 41-65.

47. H. WENDT, *At the Temple Gates: The Religion of Freelance Experts in the Roman Empire*, Oxford, OUP, 2016; J. EYL, *Signs, Wonders, and Gifts: Divination in the Letters of Paul*, Oxford, OUP, 2019; D.C. ULLUCCI, *Toward a Typology of Religious Experts in the Ancient Mediterranean*, in ID. – C. HODGE – S. OLYAN – E. WASSERMAN (eds.), *"The One Who Sows Bountifully": Essays in Honor of Stanley K. Stowers* (Brown Judaic Studies, 356), Providence, RI, Brown University Press, 2013, 89-110.

break "mission" down into its constituent parts, we find that, *contra* the view of Schnabel, Goodman, Stark, and others, what is involved is *not* unique in the Roman Empire. It is only if we uncritically accept the presentation of mission in our ancient texts, that we end up with an unparalleled phenomenon.

III. Complicating Factors for Imagining the Early Christian Mission

In addition to disentangling our unstated assumptions embedded in the normative understanding of mission, it is also the case that we need to *complicate* this basic picture with more recent scholarship on religion and social networks in antiquity, which I briefly do here. Such a discussion will demonstrate that we need new frameworks to think about the spread of early Christianity that are more sociologically nuanced than have hitherto been proposed.

One element that helpfully complicates our studies of the early Christian mission is religious competition[48]. As shown above, scholars have tended to treat the so-called mission activity of early Christianity as active, intentional, and programmatic, but attention to religious competition stands to challenge these features. The existence of religious competition was a regular part of the urban life in antiquity, and when we observe it, it should not necessarily imply an intentional mission[49]. Heidi Wendt has recently examined the widespread phenomenon of religious specialists in the Roman Empire. She demonstrates that Paul was only one among countless religious specialists, often mobile, who proffered their services to people in need[50]. According to Wendt, these "freelance experts" were "any self-authorized purveyor of religious teachings and other practices who drew upon such abilities in pursuit of various social benefits and often more transparent forms of profit"[51]. These experts, moreover, can be found "working actively to regularize their own followings, to form

---

48. Daniel Ullucci offers important cautions about reading too much into the rhetorics of competition in texts: D.C. ULLUCCI, *Competition without Groups: Maintaining a Flat Methodology*, in *Journal of Religious Competition in Antiquity* 1 (2019) 1-17.

49. P.A. HARLAND, *The Declining Polis? Religious Rivalries in the Ancient Civic Context*, in VAAGE (ed.), *Religious Rivalries* (n. 35), 21-49, p. 48.

50. Cf. Andreas Bendlin's important work on the idea of a civic "market" of cults: A. BENDLIN, *Looking beyond the Civic Compromise: Religious Pluralism in Late Republican Rome*, in E. BISPHAM – C. SMITH (eds.), *Religion in Archaic and Republican Rome and Italy*, Edinburgh, Edinburgh University Press, 2000, 115-135.

51. WENDT, *At the Temple Gates* (n. 47), p. 10.

networks with one another, or to develop mutually beneficial relationships with existing religious groups and institutions"[52]. In other words, the practices and habits of these figures might look to scholars like a regularized mission, especially when pressed into the modern understanding discussed above, but more realistically, they were competitive strategies for their survival on the urban landscape.

Indeed, Paul's activities make a great deal of sense in this explanatory framework: like other religious specialists, Paul offers his expertise on teachings of Christ, Judean wisdom, baptism, prophecy, divination, and healing, *inter alia*[53]. Such skills were "hardly unique" among the many other freelance religious experts traversing the Roman Empire[54], and they were deeply embedded in the competitive religious practice on the ancient urban landscape. Terence L. Donaldson has suggested that even the central practice of the Pauline collection was initiated "at least in part" as a consequence of territorial conflicts among rival teachers (i.e., he initiated the collection in order to appease the rival authorities in Jerusalem)[55]. In other words, mainstays of Paul's "program" developed in response to situations of religious competition. They were not fully formed when he set out on his travels, which is what the normative view of mission often assumes. We might wonder something similar about Jesus: did he generate, for instance, some of his central teachings about the Jewish law on the spot, so to speak, through conversation or competition with others? If so, the notion that he had a programmatic mission from the moment he received baptism seems suspect.

Let us consider one textual example that might be interpreted differently if we center on religious competition instead of assuming a programmatic mission. The Letter to the Galatians is the obvious example. What we see in Galatians is the *consequence* of Paul's competition with other religious specialists who differed with him over whether practices of Jewish law were required for Christ followers. Through this competition, Paul has

---

52. *Ibid.*, p. 16. When it comes to developing networks among one another, we can note the significance of the idea of "being sent" among Paul and his fellow travelers, as in M.M. MITCHELL, *New Testament Envoys in the Context of Greco-Roman Diplomatic and Epistolary Conventions: The Example of Timothy and Titus*, in *JBL* 111 (1992) 641-662. The language of "being sent" implies a source for one's authority and accountability to someone beyond oneself; thus, even though Paul might have been a freelance expert (à la Wendt), his rhetoric of subservience to a deity undermines his autonomy.

53. WENDT, *At the Temple Gates* (n. 47), pp. 146-189. On divination in particular, see EYL, *Signs, Wonders, and Gifts* (n. 47).

54. WENDT, *At the Temple Gates* (n. 47), p. 154.

55. T.L. DONALDSON, *'The Field God Has Assigned': Geography and Mission in Paul*, in VAAGE (ed.), *Religious Rivalries* (n. 35), 109-137, p. 133.

the opportunity to voice, perhaps even *generate*, some of the most important theological ideas in early Christianity. In particular, Galatians promotes the necessity of faith over works of the Jewish law (Galatians 3–4), which had hitherto not been discussed in any extant letters. Indeed, it is quite possible that Paul formulated these ideas *precisely for* the situation in Galatia in order to delegitimate his opponents' authority. Or again: consider Paul's apparent competition with Apollos hinted at throughout 1 Corinthians[56]. It is *because* of that conflict that Paul generates some of his more well-known and persuasive statements on the collective identity of Christ groups (e.g., 1 Cor 3,10-23)[57]. My point is that it is often *through* religious competition that what we think of as programmatic features of the Pauline mission are generated, defined, and reproduced. Yet, we have too easily assumed the opposite scenario: that the mission was based on and then exported those fully formed ideas.

In addition to attending to religious competition and the widespread nature of religious specialists, I also maintain that scholars who study mission have not fully appreciated social networks that were already in place before the arrival of Christianity, which offers another important complicating factor for the normative view of the early Christian mission. We are accustomed to thinking of Christianity itself as the social "glue" that holds the Jesus movement and Christ groups together. On this assumption, it follows that before the arrival of Christianity – i.e., before the mission reached a certain locale – there was no "glue" holding such a social formation together. However, there has been important work on social networks that calls such a scenario into question. Recall from earlier Rodney Stark's well-known research on missionaries and conversion, which is often marshalled to encourage us to think differently about the spread of religions; Stark found that conversion was most successful when there were social pressures (friends and family who had already converted) that encouraged conversion, as opposed to merely hoping for conversion in response to doctrinal teaching[58]. Stark's position is helpful, because it centers on social networks as a condition of conversion. But I would like to go even further: in some cases, I would wager that early

---

56. This conflict is hinted at in 1 Cor 1,12; 3,4-22; 4,6; 16,12.

57. Competition was also widespread within the Corinthian association, as members competed with each other for spiritual gifts and authority within the group; see J.S. KLOPPENBORG, *Greco-Roman* Thiasoi, *the* Ekklēsia *at Corinth, and Conflict Management*, in R. CAMERON – M.P. MILLER (eds.), *Redescribing Paul and the Corinthians* (Early Christianity and Its Literature, 50), Atlanta, GA, Society of Biblical Literature, 2011, 187-218. Kloppenborg demonstrates, moreover, that the interpersonal conflicts among the Corinthians were utterly normal in the context of competitive behaviors in ancient associations.

58. STARK, *Cities of God* (n. 38), pp. 8-11.

Christian social networks were almost "parasitical" on other networks that were already in place. Indeed, I would claim that *most* Pauline groups were probably mapped on to social formations that already existed[59]. This suggestion would significantly change how we imagine the spread of Christianity: instead of Christian ideas being the occasion for groups to coalesce, the prior existence of these groups might actually be necessary for the survival of early Christian ideas in the first place. I will consider two examples to illustrate this.

The first example involves the suggestion that the Thessalonian Christ group was built upon a trade association. Richard Ascough has convincingly argued for this case in several publications[60]. Space does not permit us to deeply explore his case, but in short: there are reasons to think that everyone within the group was male and that Paul's rhetoric of work and labor was intentionally deployed to capitalize on behaviors that were already strongly valued among the group. For these reasons, we might suppose that Paul had managed to convince an occupational association to become loyal to Christ, and the result is the Thessalonian group behind 1 Thessalonians. Let us think through the implications of this. We have overwhelming evidence for occupational associations; they could be extensively populated, translocal networks, or merely groups of a handful of members in the same neighborhood[61]. The Thessalonians are probably a locally oriented network with some translocal connections/competitors (see 1 Thess 1,7)[62]. We could suppose that their regular meetings, meal practices, system of self-governance, and even their internal hierarchy were already in place when Paul arrived. Like many associations, they had some challenges and tensions, but in this case, Paul appeals to metaphors of work and labor (e.g., 1 Thess 1,9; 4,11; 5,12.14) in order to

59. Similarly, KLOPPENBORG, *Christ's Associations* (n. 27), pp. 310-312.
60. R.S. ASCOUGH, *Paul's Macedonian Associations: The Social Context of Philippians and 1 Thessalonians* (WUNT, 2.161), Tübingen, Mohr Siebeck, 2013, pp. 169-175; ASCOUGH, *1 and 2 Thessalonians* (n. 32).
61. For excellent treatments of ancient occupational associations, see the following important resources: J.S. KLOPPENBORG – R.S. ASCOUGH, *Greco-Roman Associations: Texts, Translations, and Commentary*. Vol. 1: *Achaia, Central Greece, Macedonia, Thrace* (BZNW, 181), Berlin – New York, De Gruyter, 2011; P.A. HARLAND, *Greco-Roman Associations: Texts, Translations, and Commentary*. Vol. 2: *North Coast of the Black Sea, Asia Minor* (BZNW, 204), Berlin – New York, De Gruyter, 2014; J.S. KLOPPENBORG, *Greco-Roman Associations: Texts, Translations, and Commentary*. Vol. 3: *Ptolemaic and Early Roman Egypt* (BZNW, 246), Berlin – New York, De Gruyter, 2020; S.E. BOND, *Trade and Taboo: Disreputable Professions in the Roman Mediterranean*, Ann Arbor, MI, University of Michigan Press, 2016.
62. R.S. ASCOUGH, *Translocal Relationships among Voluntary Associations and Early Christianity*, in *JECS* 5 (1997) 223-241; ID., *Re-describing the Thessalonians' 'Mission' in Light of Greco-Roman Associations*, in *NTS* 60 (2014) 61-82.

advise them. In doing so, he also continues to develop and communicate his teachings about Christ, as we saw with 1 Thessalonians 4–5. But importantly: it was not these teachings that brought the group together in the first place; *that* was a consequence of their common trade.

We could also consider the group behind Galatians. We know very little about this group, and so the case will be much more speculative. What we do know is that Paul did not intend to visit them and only ended up with them due to circumstances beyond his control (often hypothesized to be an illness; see Gal 4,13-14). Furthermore, it is curious that he does not refer to them as members of a specific city as he does with recipients of other letters; rather, "Galatia" is a regional appellation (a Roman province[63]). That some sort of regional network was in place and could offer Paul a comfortable welcome when he showed up unexpectedly and that he refers to them as inhabitants of a rather large geographical area suggests to me that we might be dealing with an established social network that already existed before Paul arrived[64]. Perhaps this might be some sort of regional social network, regional household network, or even a series of people connected through patronage or translocal civic connections. It is impossible to know, but in any case, it is likely that the Galatian network existed before Paul arrived and was in a position to provide hospitality long enough for him to capitalize on the situation and tell them about Christ[65].

How does the awareness of pre-existing social networks help us reimagine the concept of the Pauline mission? For one, it suggests that Paul himself (and his ideas) are not always responsible for the group formation; many other factors are at play, depending on the particular context. For another, it raises the question of whether Paul may have favored or even targeted social networks that were already in place, because they had a more solid foundation than if he tried to stitch one together anew.

63. The region had a particularly complex political history, and by the first century, it had experienced shifting political boundaries, as well as intentional urbanization efforts that brought more travel to the rural regions; NASRALLAH, *Archaeology and the Letters of Paul* (n. 28), pp. 91-99.
64. On the import of geography in Paul's sense of mission, see DONALDSON, *'The Field God Has Assigned'* (n. 55).
65. One could even marshal a third example with the Letter to the Romans, supposing that at least some portion of the Roman Christ followers was originally part of an established Judean group in the city. As Nasrallah explains, we are probably dealing with a small group of gentiles who affiliated with a "minoritized" network of Jews in Rome, leading to the ethnic tensions in the letter; NASRALLAH, *Archaeology and the Letters of Paul* (n. 28), p. 195.

Focusing on ancient religious competition and the existence of prior social networks strike me as helpful ways to re-describe mission in a way that is more in tune with the real social dynamics in ancient group formation. Both dimensions expose more detailed realities about how religious ideas were generated, how they were sustained, and how they moved through social networks. It is these processes, I maintain, that we should really be interested in when we speak of "the early Christian mission".

IV. Concluding Remarks

Before closing, I would like to highlight one more concern about these normative understandings of mission that was not addressed above: they marginalize figures who are not represented in texts, especially women. Numerous scholars have noted in different ways how important women were to the spread of early Christianity. Joanna Dewey, for instance, has highlighted the fact that many stories about Jesus, even if they were originally composed by educated writers, would have had an oral life among women story-tellers[66]. Somewhat differently, Carolyn Osiek has examined the phenomenon of women leadership in early Christian groups; though our texts have a bias toward official, male leadership positions, she speculates that women played a key role in domestic and other "unofficial" spaces and that many of their activities could be considered leadership[67]. And finally, to return to Stark, he argues that women were instrumental in the swift rise of Christianity in the first two centuries, in part because they were often responsible for the secondary conversion of their spouses[68]. These scholars remind us – in entirely different ways – that women almost certainly helped spread and develop early Christianity. Yet, if we rely on the traditional textual evidence, namely, the canonical gospels, Acts of the Apostles, and Paul's letters, we end up with a "mission" that is largely guided by charismatic *male* figures. Women are not absent in these texts, of course, but they often only figure prominently as

---

66. J. Dewey, *From Storytelling to Written Text: The Loss of Early Christian Women's Voices*, in BTB 26 (1996) 71-78. She imagines how different stories (e.g., Jesus' encounter with the Syrophoenician woman) might be told differently by women speakers and transmitted apart from the textual traditions crafted by literature elites (usually males).

67. C. Osiek, *Leadership Roles and Early Christian Communities*, in B.H. Dunning (ed.), *The Oxford Handbook of New Testament, Gender, and Sexuality*, Oxford, OUP, 2019, 505-520. Numerous other scholars have studied the frequency and import of women's leadership in early Christianity.

68. R. Stark, *The Rise of Christianity*, Princeton, NJ, Princeton University Press, 1996, pp. 95-128.

objects of discussion or objects of male action (such as healings and exorcisms) or when a controversy is present (e.g., 1 Corinthians 11). In other words, they are included when they come to the attention of male authors, and we end up with a skewed picture of how the movement developed.

In closing, I have offered a systematic exploration of the concept of mission and have hopefully shown that the category, as scholars of early Christianity tend to use it, is marked by several theoretical problems. The way that we treat the "early Christian mission" is part of a larger issue in the study of Christian origins, namely, accepting uncritically the depictions and explanations that are given in the textual evidence. At the very least, we need to admit that the matter is far more complicated than we have hitherto acknowledged, and when it comes to mission, we have not yet definitively answered how it is that Christianity spread so quickly and so successfully throughout the Roman Empire. Facets such as religious competition and social networks help us envision these processes more carefully and, indeed, more critically.

Rhodes College Sarah E. Rollens
Religious Studies
Clough Hall
2000 North Parkway
Memphis, TN 38112
USA
rollens@rhodes.edu

INDEX LOCORUM

BIBLICAL REFERENCES

Genesis
1–3	537
1–2	417 544
1,1	537
1,2	414 539 544
1,14-18	109
1,26	544
1,27	537
2,7	544
2,16-17	537
2,23	372
3,21	544
17,1-8	373
17,5	384
18,8	240
19,3	240
22,2	122
27,35-36	333
28,12	297
32,24-29	333
32,29	333
35,10	333
41,33	219
41,39	219
49,11	166

Exodus
2,3-8	368-369
3,14	133
4,10	219
4,22	260
15,20-21	368
22,25-26	31
23,20	99-102 115
23,30	16
25,17-22	279
32,34	99
33,11	542

Numbers
12,2	368
12,5-8	369
12,7	542

Deuteronomy
18,15	296
24,13	31
29,3	106

1 Samuel – 1 Kingdoms
1,18	260
2,21	215
2,26	215
10,10-11	214
16,10	197
16,13	402
20,6	262

2 Samuel – 2 Kingdoms
5,7	262
5,9	262
6,10	262
6,12	262
6,16	262
7,14	163 306
7,15	164
11,43	242

1 Kings – 3 Kingdoms
1,25	242
1,33	166
8,16	197
8,44	197
11,32	197

2 Kings – 4 Kingdoms
2,11-12	283
9,26	192

2 Chronicles
6,5	197
6,34	197

Ezra		*Wisdom*	469
4,12	199	2,13-18	122
4,13	199	5,1	223
5,8	199	6,12	307
		6,13	308
Tobit		6,16	308
6,5	240	7,4-5	260
12,19	240	10,10	308
		11	542
Job			
38,9	260	*Sirach*	
		44–50	542
Psalms		45,3	220
2,2	245 541		
2,4	541	*Isaiah*	
2,7	122-124 142-143 146	5,1-7	164
	162-163 165 306	6,9-10	102-107 115
16 (15),8	201	7,14	253 513
22 (21)	112-113 116 174-175	10,3	115
	178-182 509 514	11,1-9	214
22 (21),2-3	175 177 182	11,2	214
22 (21),2	112 115 171-172 174	13,9-13	109
	182	13,10	109-111 115
22 (21),3	175	29,10	106
22 (21),5	175	34,4	109-111 115
22 (21),6	175 177 181-182	40,3-5	101
22 (21),8-9	113	40,3	101-102
22 (21),8	174 182	42,1	122 143 162
22 (21),9	174 177-178 182	43,1	373
22 (21),19	113 149 174 182	50,6	26
22 (21),25	175 177 181-182	52,13–53,12	161
22 (21),28	174-175 182	53	163 170 555
23,7	555	53,2	513
69	113 509	53,6	161
69 (68),22	173 555	53,8	513
69 (68),10	114	53,12	114 161
94 (93),1	223	56,7	111
110 (109),1	116 131 159 165-166	58,2	516
118 (117),22-23	116	60,1	399
118 (117),22	64-65	61,1-2/58,6	268
		61,1	402
Proverbs		62,1-2	374-375
1,20-28	308	66,24	108-109 115
1,20	223		
8,35-36	415	*Jeremiah*	
8,35	308	5,21	107 115
9,1-6	308	7,11	111
13,5	223	31 (38)	399
20,9	223		

38 (45),6	464	7,27	147-148
		7,33-34	148
Ezekiel		12,6	41
12,2	107	12,39-40	44
16,4	260	12,46	44
36	399	12,58-59	31
37,1-4	464	13,34-35	283
Daniel		*Matthew*	
3,18	199	1–2	254 270
7	285	1,1	252
7,13-14	158-162 167 169-170	1,2-16	252 268
7,13	131 468	1,16	258 362 383
7,14	285	1,17-25	252-253
		1,18	258 362
Hosea		1,20	362
11,1	254	2,1-12	431
		2,1	253
Joel		2,2	521
2,10	110 115	2,5	253
2,28-29	399	2,6	253-254
		2,9	254
Amos		2,11	254 362
8,9	517	2,13-15	254
		2,19-23	254
Micah		3,1-12	255
5,1	253	3,3	101-102
5,3	253	3,7-10	471
		3,7	3 246
Zechariah		3,13-17	255
9,9	149 166	3,15	14 247
12,10-12	159	3,16-17	144
13,7	149	4,1-11	255
		4,13	255 268
Malachi		4,15-16	255
3,1	16 99-102 115 141 147	5–12	16
		5–7	16
4,5 (3,22-23)	141 147	5,4	482 497
		5,5	482
Q		5,6	497
3,2	3	5,7-8	**479-499**
3,7-9	3	5,9	482
3,16-17	3	5,15	106
3,21-22	3 144-145	5,39	24-26
4,1-13	3 145	5,40-41	25
6,23	43	5,41	**32-41** 42
6,27-35	24	6,9-13	53
6,29-30	**23-43**	6,12	53-54
6,38	42	6,14	54

6,15	**53-56** 68-69	16,17	474
6,19-21	54	16,25-28	17
6,20–9,2	57	16,27	469
6,25-34	54	17	17
6,25	**56-58** 68-69	17,1-9	473
6,30	6	17,1-3	6
6,33	56	17,3-4	6
7–12	4	17,5-6	6
7,2	106	17,7-10	6
7,16-20	471	17,14-23	17
8,1-4	15	17,14-21	15
8,5-13	15	17,19-20	5
8,12	59	17,20	**5-7 14-17** 19
8,26	6	17,22	15
9,32-34	59	17,30	6
9,34	**58-59** 68-69	18	16
10,3	325 330	18,1-35	17
10,4	324	18,1-22	14
10,5-16	559	18,6-7	15
10,26	106	18,15	15
10,37	246	18,22	15
10,38	246	19,16-30	7
11,2-19	16	19,21	8
11,5	15	19,27-30	5
11,10	100-102 115	19,27	8 19
11,11	542	19,28	**7-8 17-19**
12,22-32	59	19,29	18-19
12,22-30	251	21,18-20	471
12,33	246 471	21,21	14
12,38-42	514	21,33-46	64 66
12,43-45	255	21,34-37	63
12,43-44	496	21,43	63-64 66
12,46-50	255	21,44	**61-66** 68-69
13–25	16	21,45	63-64 66
13,24	60	22,13	59
13,31-32	106	22,14	495
13,31	60	23,14	65-67
13,33	**60-61** 68-69	23,25	67
13,42	59	23,26	**66-68** 68-69
13,50	59	24–25	4
13,54-58	255	24	17
13,54-55	439	24,3	467
14,28-33	289	24,4-5	468
14,31	6	24,5	468
16	4 15 17	24,11	468
16,1-4	17 514	24,14	468
16,6	107	24,23-24	468
16,8	6	24,27	468
16,17-19	466	24,30	468

INDEX LOCORUM

24,32-33	470	28,4	519
24,36	550	28,6-7	178
24,45–25,46	468	28,6	284
24,51	59	28,7	289
25,29	106	28,8	279
25,30	59	28,9-10	277 279 281 288
25,31	8	28,11-15	277 521
26,3-4	552	28,11	520
26,39	475 550	28,15	277 519
26,57-68	510	28,16-20	274 288
26,60-61	553	28,16	524
26,67	26 553	28,18	285
27,1	553	28,19-20	85 525
27,11	521	28,19	285 525
27,15-26	511	28,20	468
27,17	383		
27,20	511	*Mark*	
27,22	383	1–5	251
27,25	511	1,1–8,29	155
27,26-31	553	1,1-11	**146-148**
27,27-37	338	1,1	81 121 123-124 127-128 130-131 142 153-154 169 249
27,27	338		
27,29	521		
27,30	26	1,2-6	3 20
27,32-35	555	1,2-3	97 **98-102** 114-116 123 149
27,32	38 554		
27,34	555	1,4-8	123 141 268
27,35	50-51 514	1,4-5	143
27,37	337-338 521	1,4	99
27,39-44	514	1,5	3 141
27,41-43	554	1,7-8	3 144 249
27,43	177-178	1,7	122
27,45	515	1,8	142 172
27,46	173 550	1,9-11	3 20 76 81 140 **141-143** 144-145 149 173 249 255 268
27,49	**47-53** 61 68-69		
27,50	173		
27,51	515	1,9	131 **139-150** 255
27,52-53	515	1,10-11	139
27,55	514	1,10	165 401
27,56	376	1,11	81 120 **122-125** 126 136-137 146-147 162-163 175 252
27,57-61	518		
27,57	280		
27,60	280	1,12-13	3 20 76 140 255
27,61	277 376	1,14–8,26	76
27,62-66	277 517-518	1,14–3,12	250
27,8	183	1,14–3,6	76-77
28,1-4	519	1,14-15	268
28,1	277 376 519	1,14	123 318
28,2	277 279 284 519	1,15	137

584 INDEX LOCORUM

1,16-20	76-77 316	4,3-8	106
1,21–3,6	91	4,4	141
1,21-45	125	4,10-20	92
1,21-28	76	4,12	97-98 **102-107** 114-116
1,21	77 91 509		
1,22	77 91	4,13	82 130 529
1,24	80 82 125 130 131	4,17	181
1,25	126	4,20	529
1,27	91 130	4,21-25	106
1,29-31	77	4,21	130
1,32-34	1 77	4,24	106
1,34	125-126	4,25	106
1,35-39	77	4,30-32	106
1,40-45	77	4,30	130
1,40	80	4,33	269
2–3	94	4,35	141
2,1–3,6	125	4,40	130
2,1-12	77	4,41	81-82 130
2,7	130 510	5,1-20	251
2,10	170	5,7	80 82 130-131
2,12	79	5,25-34	80
2,13-17	77	5,28	80
2,13	91	5,34	80
2,15	242	5,35-43	282
2,16	130	5,36	80
2,18-22	77	5,42	215
2,19-20	284	6,1-6	251 255 268-269
2,23-28	77	6,2	91 130
2,28	170	6,3	130 224 362-363
3,1-5	77	6,6	91
3,6	77 129 510	6,12	77
3,7-12	125 154 163	6,14-16	130
3,8	95	6,30	77 92
3,11	80 82 120 **125-127** 131 142	6,32–8,21	107
		6,34	91-92 117
3,12	125	6,35-44	82 92 107
3,13-19	76 250 316	6,38	130
3,18	129 324-325	6,45-52	82
3,20-30	59	6,50	133
3,20-21	250-251 255 269-270	6,52	108
3,22-30	251	7	76 94
3,22	59	7,1–8,10	184
3,31-35	250-251 255 269-270	7,6-7	97 116
3,34-35	269	7,10	97 111
4	76	7,15	94
4,1-20	565	7,17-23	92
4,1-9	529	7,18	130
4,1	91	7,19	94 130
4,3-31	103	7,24	95

7,25-26	95	9,45	115
7,31	95	9,47-49	109
8,1-10	107	9,47	115
8,5	130	9,48	97-98 **108-109** 114-115
8,11-13	514		
8,14-21	107-108	10,1	91
8,18-21	130	10,4	97 116
8,18	97-98 **107-108** 114-116	10,6-8	97 116
		10,7-8	108 111
8,22-26	153	10,13	262
8,27–10,52	76 155	10,17-31	7 17
8,27–10,45	151	10,19	116
8,27–9,1	76 152	10,21	8
8,27-33	128-129 **151-170**	10,23-31	18
8,27-30	74	10,28-31	523
8,27-29	133	10,28	8 19
8,27	82	10,29-31	5
8,29	82-83 120-121 **127-130** 131	10,29-30	181
		10,31	134
8,31	76 82 90-91 116 134 147 177 512 518	10,32-34	76 82 90 147 161 177
		10,32	13 76
8,32	82	10,33-34	512
8,33	82	10,33	170
8,34-38	181-182 523	10,34	518
8,34-37	82	10,41-45	8 17
8,34	158	10,44	132
8,38	169	10,45	155 170
9	15	10,47-48	82
9,2-10	76 81	10,47	166
9,2-9	473	10,48	166
9,7	81 124 143 175	10,52	80
9,9-11	82	11–15	76
9,9-10	180	11,2	149
9,11-13	102 **146-148**	11,7-10	149
9,12	97 106	11,10	166
9,13	97	11,12-14	14 111 471
9,14-29	5	11,15-21	115
9,22-44	80	11,15-19	111
9,24	6-7	11,15-17	14
9,28	5 92	11,17	97 108 111
9,30–10,31	108	11,20-21	471
9,30-32	82	11,20	111
9,31	76 90-91 134 147 161 170 177 512 518	11,23	6
		11,27-33	164
9,38	469	12,1-12	64-65 164
9,42-50	134	12,10-11	97 116
9,42-48	158	12,19	97 111 116
9,42	137	12,25	482
9,43	115	12,26	97 116

12,29-31	111	15,1	135
12,29-30	97 116	15,2-5	134-135
12,30-31	108	15,2	120 130 **134-136** 167
12,31	97	15,6-11	511
12,32-33	97 116	15,8	511
12,35-37	166	15,9	134-135
12,35	91	15,11	511
12,36	83 97 116	15,12	134-135
13	76	15,14	134 180
13,2	179	15,15	511
13,3-27	284	15,16-32	121
13,3-4	467	15,16-20	167 173
13,3	142	15,18	135
13,5-6	468	15,19	26
13,9-13	181	15,20-41	174-175 180-182
13,10	468	15,21-24	555
13,16	142	15,21	38 554
13,17	141	15,24	112-115 149 174 182 514
13,21-22	468		
13,24-30	115	15,26	114 135 337
13,24-25	97-98 **109-111** 114-116	15,29-32	173 514
		15,29-30	112-115
13,24	141	15,29	174 182
13,26-27	158	15,30-32	174 177 182
13,26	110 134 147 155 468	15,32	114 131 168
13,27	117	15,33	515
13,28-29	470	15,34-37	173
13,28	110-111	15,34	97-98 **112-114** 115-116 **171-182**
13,30	134		
14–15	76	15,35-36	172-173
14,14	260	15,36	114 173-174 177 182
14,21	97 161 170	15,37	**171-182**
14,25	8	15,38	142 165 515
14,27	97 114 149	15,39	83 121 131 142 165 172 174 182
14,34	117		
14,36	475	15,40	277 362 376 514
14,41	161 170	15,42-47	518
14,49	149	15,43	280
14,50	149	15,47	277 362 376
14,53-65	510	16,1-8	274-277 283
14,60	130-131	16,1	280 362 376
14,61-62	164 167	16,5	279
14,61	83 120 **130-134**	16,6	281
14,62	83 116-117 131 133 147 154-155 158 165	16,7	277 524
		16,8	121 279
14,65	26 173	[SE]	279
14,66-72	129	16,9-20	276
14,68	128	16,9-11	280
14,70	132	16,9	284 362 376

16,12	291-292	2,41-51	213 217
16,15	525	2,42	265 268
16,16	525	2,43	215
16,17-18	525	2,49	217
16,19	285 287 525	2,51	263 268
		2,52	214-215 220 225
Luke		3	4
1–2	268	3,1-2	268
1,1-4	92-93 258	3,3-20	268
1,3	258	3,4-6	101-102
1,5–2,52	268	3,7-9	471
1,5-25	258	3,7	246
1,11-13	261	3,19-20	14
1,17	101	3,21-22	144 217 268 401
1,26-38	261	3,23-38	268
1,26-27	258	3,23	258
1,27	259	4	4
1,28-38	547	4,1	220
1,28-30	238	4,14-15	3 14 268
1,31	258-259 264	4,16-30	14 217
1,32-33	258	4,16	268
1,34-36	258	4,18-19	268
1,35	271	4,18	401-402
1,39-45	259	4,20-21	268
1,41	262	4,22	249 258 267 269
1,44	262	4,24	269
1,46-55	259	4,29-30	269
1,51	217	4,31–6,19	3
1,56	259	4,31-37	217
1,57-80	258	4,31-32	14
1,57-66	259	4,33-37	14
1,59-66	264	4,38-39	14
1,67-79	259	4,40-41	14
1,80	259 265 268	5,1-11	14
2,1-7	259-260 263	5,29-32	242
2,5	362	6–7	4
2,7	260	6,14	325
2,8-15	261-263	6,15	324
2,10-14	271	6,20-49	4 16
2,16-19	262-263	6,21	497
2,18	267	6,29	24
2,19	267	6,30	42
2,20-21	263-264	6,32	**243-245** 247
2,21-40	264	6,33-34	42
2,22-52	264-267	6,38	106
2,25-38	271	6,43-44	471
2,33	263 267	6,44	246
2,39	265	7,16	217
2,40	214-215 217 220 225	7,18-35	16

587

7,27	100-102 115	15,3-10	242
7,28	542	15,4-7	14 17
7,36-50	14 242	15,11-32	242
8,2	376	16,19-31	239
8,4–9,50	3	16,24-25	266
8,4	269	17	14 17
8,12	7	17,1-19	15-16
8,19-21	269	17,1-10	16
8,21	269	17,5-6	**5-7 14-17**
8,42	215	17,6	19-20
9,9	269	17,11-19	15-17
9,26	469	17,20–18,8	17
9,28-37	473	17,33	16
9,37-43	15	17,35	197
9,41	240	18,15–21,33	3
9,46-48	15	18,15	262
9,51–18,14	4	18,18-30	17
10,1	323	18,18-23	14
10,18	555	18,24-30	5 18
10,23-24	16	18,28	8 19
11,2-4	16	18,34	267
11,14-23	59 251	19,29	106
11,16	514	19,45-46	14
11,24-26	255 496	20,9-19	64
11,27-28	269	20,18	64-66
11,29-32	514	20,26	217-218
11,31	214	21,7	467
11,33	106	21,8	468
12,1	107	21,12-15	223
12,2	106 270	21,15	217-218
12,10	200	21,27	468
12,11-12	217	21,29-30	470
12,12	223	22–24	48
12,28	6 16	22	47
12,35	247	22,1–24,12	3
12,41	4	22,11	260
12,46	240	22,24-30	14 17 19
13,3	471	22,28-30	**7-8 17-19**
13,6-9	470 476	22,29	16 18-20
13,7	471	22,40	8
13,15	261	22,42	475
13,18-19	106	22,46	8
13,26	242	22,54-55	510
13,28	59	22,66-71	510
14,1-14	242	23	245
14,15-24	242	23,6-12	245
14,26	246	23,12	520
14,27	246	23,13	511
15,2	242	23,16	211

23,17-25	511	24,41	292
23,18	511	24,42-43	8 238
23,22	211	24,44-49	289
23,25	511	24,45	267
23,26	38 40 554	24,47	525
23,34	514	24,48	528
23,35-37	514	24,50-53	285
23,38	337	24,50-52	473 525
23,39	514	24,50	273
23,44-48	14		
23,44-45	515	*John*	
23,45	515-516	1	311 320-321
23,46	221 515	1,1-34	301
23,49	514	1,1-18	295
23,50-56	518	1,1-4	407 415
23,50-51	280	1,1-3	413-415
23,51	552	1,1-2	256
23,53	280	1,4-5	**413-428** 434
24	47 52 238-239 245 **273-293**	1,4	413-416
		1,5-13	415
24,1	280	1,9	**413-428** 430 434
24,4	279	1,14	256 258 301 304 308 414 547
24,5-8	279		
24,6-8	280	1,18	256 304
24,10-11	273	1,19–4,3	318
24,10	269 376	1,19-34	296
24,11	240	1,20-51	305
24,12	278 281 286	1,20	306
24,13-15	291	1,21	326
24,15-16	273	1,24-27	326
24,16	291	1,28	316
24,18	324	1,29-34	145
24,19	217 219	1,29	256 395
24,26	282 285-286	1,32-33	304
24,30	8	1,32	317
24,33-43	232-234	1,34	146 307
24,34	275 281	1,35-51	**295-309** 316
24,35	8	1,38-39	317
24,36-53	242	1,38	358
24,36-50	238-242	1,39	317
24,36-49	285	1,41-42	317
24,36-43	238 276 278 289	1,41	317 358
24,36-39	239	1,42	317 333 373 383
24,37-43	273	1,43-44	316-317
24,37	279	1,43	256
24,38	**273-293**	1,44	383
24,39	229 **230-243** 273 279 282 288-289 292	1,45-51	**311-335**
		1,45	256 258 317 323
24,41-43	273	1,46	317 322

1,47-50	317	7,40-44	256
1,47-48	328	7,48	552
1,47	317	7,50-52	552
1,49	317 334	8,12	**413-428** 434
1,51	301 **326-327**	8,13-20	424
2,1-16	256-257	8,28	555
2,1-11	316	8,32	395
2,11	301	9,5	413 424
2,17	257	10,1-16	371
2,18	514	10,4-5	371-372 374
3,1-10	334	10,28-29	395
3,1-2	552	11,1	379-380
3,13-17	420	11,2	379
3,13	286	11,9-10	413
3,14	555	11,16	383
3,16-18	258	11,19	379-380
3,16-17	422	11,20	370 379-380
3,16	256 394	11,28	379-380
3,18-21	420	11,31	379
3,18	256 422	11,32	370 379-380
3,19-21	423	11,34	298 550
3,19	420-422	11,43	374
3,20-21	**413-428** 434	11,44	520
3,21	395	11,45-53	510
3,22	257	11,45	379-380
3,24	318	11,53	552
3,35	258	12,3	379
3,36	318	12,4	383
4,5	384	12,27-28	550
4,6	384	12,31	395 552
4,12	384	12,32	555
4,21	258	12,34	426 555
4,23	258	12,35	**413-428** 434
4,25-26	306	12,36	**413-428** 434
4,29	298	12,42	552
4,42	318	12,46	**413-428** 434
5,25	374	13,2	383
5,33	423	13,13-14	306
5,35	423	13,13	368
5,38	402	13,23	319
5,39-40	333	13,26	383
6,39-40	403	13,34	298 395
6,41-42	257	13,36-38	475
6,42	258	14,5	299
6,44	403	14,6	430
6,71	383	14,7-11	395
7,3-10	257	14,8	299
7,26	552	14,15	298-299 395
7,39	286	14,21	395

14,22	383	20,2	278
14,30	552	20,3-10	278 281
15,4-10	304	20,5-7	520
15,7	402	20,5	278
15,12	395	20,6-7	278
15,17	395	20,6	286
15,26	402	20,11-18	373
15,47	376	20,11-12	278
16,1	376	20,11	365 367 370-371 375 377-378 384
16,8-15	402		
16,11	552	20,12	279
17,1-5	286	20,13	278-280 372
17,3	407	20,14-18	279 281 286 291
17,20-23	304	20,15	278 303 372
17,24	304	20,16-18	374
18,4	303	20,16	306 **361-388**
18,7	303	20,17-18	280 291
18,13-24	510	20,17	286-287
18,22	26	20,18	365 367 371 375 377-378 380-382 384
18,33-38	307		
18,37	395	20,20	240
18,38-40	511	20,21-23	291
18,38	511	20,22	286
19,2-5	307	20,24-28	278
19,3	26	20,24	383
19,6	553	20,25	291 514
19,14	307 512	20,26-29	290-291
19,15	363 512	20,30-31	291 389 399
19,16	511	20,31	306-307 394
19,17	554	21	321-322
19,19	338	21,1-14	291 316
19,20-22	338	21,2	**311-335** 383
19,20	**337-360**	21,15-19	291
19,22	337	21,18-19	475 529
19,24-27	514	21,20-23	291
19,24	51 514	21,24	291
19,25-27	257	22,19	113
19,25	365 370 377-379 383		
19,28	514	*Acts*	
19,33	515	1–15	195 206
19,34	49	1,1-14	242
19,38-42	518	1,2-3	524
19,38	280 552	1,2	189 524
19,39-40	280 334	1,3	204-205 285 289
19,39	552	1,4-14	285
19,41	280	1,4	242
20,1-18	369	1,6-12	473
20,1-10	520	1,6-11	285
20,1	365 377-378 380	1,8	525 528

1,9-11	525	5,12	205 214
1,9	525	5,13	205
1,10	204-205	5,16	205
1,12	206	5,21	214
1,13-14	269	5,25	214
1,13	203 324-325 327 331	5,30-31	285
1,14	205 267 362	5,36	206
1,15	197-198	5,37	259
1,19	183 188 191-192 203 205	6–7	225
		6,1-5	189
1,21-26	289	6,1-2	189
1,23	203 383	6,1	183 187-189 193
1,26	189	6,3	218-220
2,1	197-198 205-206	6,5	189 193 220
2,14-41	85	6,6	201
2,14	199 204	6,7	205
2,18	201	6,8	218-219
2,25	201	6,10	218-219
2,29	222	6,11	200 203-204
2,32-33	285-286	6,13	200
2,33	285	7,2-53	189
2,36	262	7,10	218
2,38-40	559	7,22	211 219 224
2,42	205	7,30	204 219
2,43	205	7,41	201
2,44	197-198	7,45	201 206
2,47	197-198	7,46	201
3,2	200 204	7,47-53	189
3,11	214	7,55	8 220
3,13	204	7,56	203
3,20	206	7,59-60	221
3,25	204-205	8,1	189
3,26	206	8,23	204
4,1-22	223	8,26-39	85
4,5	206	9,15	204
4,8-13	223	9,24-25	87
4,8-12	218	9,26-30	87
4,10	199 201 204	9,27-28	222
4,13-14	224	9,29	188
4,13	217 222 225-226	9,32	206
4,19	201	9,36	203
4,25-28	245	9,37	201 206
4,29	222-223	9,40	203
4,30	205	9,43	206
4,31	222	10,12	202
4,33	205	10,28	202
4,36	193 204	10,30	201
5,3	204-205	10,31	201
5,7	202 205-206	10,33	201

10,38	401-402	20,18-35	205
10,40-41	289 522	20,5–21,18	205-206
10,43	202 206	20,6	206
11,6	202	20,7	204 206
11,11	204 206	21,4	262
11,19-26	193	21,8-9	95
11,19-20	183 193	21,18-25	270
11,19	95	21,37	183 189
11,20	188-189 193	21,40	183 188-192
11,22	193	22,1	192
11,24	220	22,2	183 188-192
11,26	206	22,3	211 214 224-225
11,27	193 200	22,6	206
12,3	202 206	22,10	206
12,4	204-205	22,17-18	206
12,12	363	23,7	239
12,17	269	26,14	190-191
13,1	84-85	26,18	204-205
13,6	203	27,1–28,16	205-206
13,10	204	27,21-26	205
13,24	201 206	27,35	201
13,27-29	277	28,8	206
13,27	205	28,17	206
13,33	143 146	28,28	199 204
13,38	199 204	28,31	222
14,1	206		
14,23	202 205	*Romans*	
15	88 193	1,3	167
15,5	193	6,2-5	86
15,7-11	197	6,3-4	551
15,7	196-197 202 205	6,17	86
15,13-21	270	8,15	192
15,17	204 206	11,8	106
15,20	206	14,14	94
15,21	205-206	14,20	94
15,22	203	16,6	363
16,10-17	205-206		
16,13-15	85	*1 Corinthians*	
16,13	206	1–4	94
16,14	206	1	563
16,16	206	1,12	574
17,16-34	225	1,22	514
18	384	1,26-28	322
18,24–19,1	224	2,3	220
18,24	219	3,4-22	574
18,25-26	222	3,10-23	574
19,1	206	3,16	481
19,4	202 205	4,6	574
19,19	200 204	6	480

6,3	483	4,4	270
6,9-10	482	4,6	192
6,19	481	6,6	85 93
7	480		
7,29	481 485	*Ephesians*	
7,31	481 483	5,8	428
9,1	84		
9,5	270	*Philippians*	
11	563 578	2,9	179
11,23-25	87	3,5	187
12,28	84-85	3,21	292
13,2	7		
14	84	*1 Thessalonians*	
14,10-11	371	1,5-6	402
14,22-25	84	1,7	575
15	563	1,9	575
15,3-5	87	2,14-16	528
15,4-8	283	4–5	567 576
15,5-8	275 283	4,11	575
15,5	234 275	4,16-17	568
15,6	522	4,17	568
15,7	270	5,2	568
15,8	84 276	5,12	575
15,20-22	288	5,14	575
15,35-57	273 288		
15,40-41	292	*2 Thessalonians*	
15,42-49	288	2,1-12	404
15,42-45	282		
15,44	292	*2 Timothy*	
16,12	574	4,13	30
16,22	192		
		Hebrews	
2 Corinthians		1–2	239
1,21-22	401	1,5	143 146
3,15	206	2,9	538
5,14	538	2,10	538
6,16	481	2,14-15	538
11,32-33	87	3,5	542
12,2	162	5,5	143 146
		6,1-2	86
Galatians		9,9-10	86
1,15-17	276	9,14	86
1,17	87	11	542
1,18-19	87	12,23	239
1,19	270		
2,1-10	88	*1 Peter*	
2,9	270	3,19	239
3–4	574		
4,13-14	576	*2 Peter*	
		1,17	474

INDEX LOCORUM 595

1,18	457	3,7-10	396
2,16	371	3,8	396 404
2,22	464	3,11-18	404
		3,11	390 392 394-395
1 John		3,13-15	390
1,1-6	393	3,13	396-397
1,1-5	394	3,14-18	404
1,1-4	390-391 407	3,14-15	390 392
1,1	390 394 408	3,14	393
1,2-3	395	3,24	399-400
1,2	391 398	4,1-4	403
1,3	390 392 394	4,1-3	399
1,4-5	392	4,1	399
1,4	394	4,2	399
1,5-10	395	4,3	390 392 394 399 404
1,5-7	407	4,6	399 404
1,5	390 394-395 432	4,7	392-393
1,6	390	4,8	396
1,8	392	4,9	394
1,10	390 402	4,13	399
2,1-2	397	4,14	395 398
2,1	394	4,16	390 392 396
2,3-6	298	5,3	396
2,4	390	5,6-9	399
2,7-8	394	5,6	146 399-400
2,7	390 392 394	5,8	399
2,8-9	432	5,9-12	398
2,12-14	394	5,10-12	394
2,13-14	392 395	5,11-13	404
2,14	402	5,13	390 392 394
2,18-28	400-403	5,15	392
2,18-27	404	5,18-20	390 393
2,18-22	404	5,18	390 392-393
2,18	390 392 394 404	5,19	390 392-393
2,20-21	390 392	5,20	390-393
2,21	394		
2,22	404	*2 John*	
2,24	392 394 408	1	390
2,26	394	2	402
2,27	390	5	394
2,28–3,4	403	6	390
2,28-29	405	7	404
2,29	390-392		
3,1-3	404-405	*Revelation*	462
3,1	392	1,9-20	285 292
3,2	390 392 405	2,17	374-375
3,5	390 392	12–13	404
3,6	392		

Old Testament Pseudepigrapha

Apocalypse of Ezra	459	13.32	168
Apocalypse of Moses		*Letter of Aristeas*	469
31	287	1–11	191
		3	191
Ascension of Isaiah	459 465	11	191
4.1-4	529		
4.2-3	475	*4 Maccabees*	
		10.5	223
2 Baruch	169		
72	158	*Martyrdom of Isaiah*	
		3.14-19	278
1 Enoch	446-448 455 468	3.16-19	284
22	239	3.16-18	279
27.2-3	108		
37–71	159-160 168-169	*Psalms of Solomon*	166
62.1-9	169	17	169
98.12	199	17.21-22	157
101.6	107		
		Sibylline Oracles	454 456 469
4 Ezra	466	1.374-375	516
11–12	159	2.190-338	456
11.36–12.36	158	8.305-306	516
13	159 169 468		
13.3-11	158	*Vision of Ezra*	459

Dead Sea Scrolls

1QH^a XV 5-6	103	4Q252	163
1QIsa^a	105 109 111	4Q385	464
1QS	198	4Q544	197
4Q174	163	4Q550	199
4Q246	163	11Q10	105

Philo and Josephus

Philo	220 469	*Confusion of Tongues*	
Agriculture		2–14	545
80	364	*Contemplative Life*	
81	364	87	362 364
96–97	545	*Life of Moses*	
Allegorical Interpretation		1.20-23	219
1.76	362 364	*Questions and Answers on Genesis*	
2.66	362 364	1.4	544
3.55	545	1.6	544
3.103	364	1.53	544

INDEX LOCORUM

Josephus	2 150 219	*Jewish War*	
Against Apion		2.280-281	219
2.257	219	2.430-434	157
Jewish Antiquities	227 364	2.441-448	157
2.230	220	4.38	194
2.232-237	219	4.389-395	157
3.13	220	4.510	157
3.252	190-191	5.194	340
11.159	191	6.201	364
11.203	32	7.43-45	193
18.63-64	149	7.154	157
18.116-119	149		

APOSTOLIC FATHERS

Barnabas	462-463	*Mandate*	
4.14	495	1.1	537
5.13	514	*Similitude*	
15.9	285	9.31.2	495
1 Clement	93	Ignatius	**227-248** 493
4	542	*To the Ephesians*	
5.4	475	1.2	246
5.7	529	5.1	290
7–9	542	6.2	429-430
10–12	542	7.2	235
13.2	493-494	11.1	246
17–18	542	14.2	246
31–32	542	19.2-3	431
43.1	542	*To the Magnesians*	
55	542	1.2	235-236
		13.1	235
2 Clement	493 495	13.2	290
13.4	243 247	*To the Romans*	
		6.2-3	431 434
Didache	494	*To the Philadelphians*	
1.3–2.1	25 247	2	429
1.3	244	2.1	**428-434**
1.4	25	2.2	430
6.2	523	*To the Smyrnaeans*	
8.2	83	1.1	236 247
11.1-2	89	1.2	245 514
13.2	89	2	235 237
15.3-4	83	2.1	556
16.1	247	3.1-3	289-290
		3.2-3	232-233
Shepherd of Hermas	239 437-438	3.2	229 **230-243** 245
	441 451 461-		282 289
	463 494	4.2	556

5.1	429	*Martyrdom of Polycarp*	528
12.2	235-236	12.2	528
13.2	236	13.1	528
To Polycarp	231	17–18	528
2.1	229-230 **243-245**		
2.3	494	Polycarp	
7.3	429	*To the Philippians*	
		2.3	493-494

Nag Hammadi Codices

NHC I,4 *Treatise on the Resurrection*
43.21-27   535

NHC I,5 *The Tripartite Tractate*
75.17–77.11   540
110.22–114.30   542

NHC II,1 *Apocryphon of John*
                    288 524 553
1.5-12   287
1.30-32   292
1.31–2.9   292
5.4-9   535
6.2-4   535
8.28–9.17   535
9.28–10.5   540
13.5-13   553
14.13–15.34   553

NHC II,4 *Hypostasis of the Archons*
94.6-8   540

NHC II,6 *Exegesis on the Soul*
135.5-33   497

NHC III,4 *Sophia of Jesus Christ*
                    288 457 524
90.15–91.24   292
114.8-18   540

NHC III,5 *Dialogue of the Saviour*
                    457

NHC VI,1 *Acts of Peter and the Twelve Apostles*
2.10–3.11; cf. 9.1-19   292

NHC VII,1 *Paraphrase of Shem*
                    535-536
49.9-10   535

NHC VII,2 *Second Discourse of the Great Seth*   533-556
49.25-35   551
50.1-24   539 551
50.25–51.10   551
50.29–51.10   540
51.10-16   540
51.11-16   541
51.20–52.10   546 551
51.24-30   540
52.10-25   551
52.14-18   552
52.21-22   541
52.22-24   541
52.25–53.1   552
52.27   540
53.3-10   535
53.12-21   553
53.13-14   540
53.17   535
53.24-25   554
53.27–54.10   554
53.28-29   540
53.31-33   541
54.6-8   535
54.27   540
55.15-16   556
55.17-19   554 556
55.30-35   554
56.4-21   554
56.11   555
56.13-21   541

INDEX LOCORUM

58.15	555	NHC VII,3 *Apocalypse of Peter*	
58.23-26	555		437 441-442 444-
60.15-30	551		451 465 535-536
62.27-34	541	71.6-13	542
63.4-17	541	81.3–84.11	550
63.4-7	535	84.14-15	535
63.17-26	541		
63.26–64.1	542	NHC VII,4 *Teachings of Sylvanus*	
64.11-12	535		536
64.17–65.1	543	85.20	464
64.18	540	118.8-9	535
64.29-33	543		
65.18-19	535	NHC VII,5 *The Three Steles of Seth*	
68.29	540		535-536
69.21-22	534	127.27	535
69.29	540		
70.11-13	535	NHC VIII,2 *Letter of Peter to Philip*	
70.11-12	534	133.17–134.9	292
		134.9-18	292

BERLIN GNOSTIC CODEX

P.Berol. 8502,1 *Gospel of Mary*		10.10-13	292
	457 524	15.1–17.7	556
7.1-9	292		

NEW TESTAMENT APOCRYPHA

Acts of Andrew		3.10-11	486
13–16	483	3.17	479 499
		13	486
Acts of Andrew and Matthias			
	525	*Acts of Peter* (Codex Vercelli)	
		10	7
Acts of John		24	513
63	483		
87–105	550	*Acts of Thomas*	525
93	236	9–15	483
93.10-13	290	87–103	483
97	516		
		Apocalypse of John and Peter	
Acts of Paul	462		461
Acts of Paul and Thecla		*Apocalypse of Paul*	466
3.2	486		
3.5-6	**479-499**	*Apocalypse of Peter*	**453-477**
3.8-9	486	*aet* Prol.	467

1.1	457	*Book of Bartholomew*	326-327
1.4	467		
1.5	468	*Epistle of the Apostles*	320 330 457 524
1.6	468	2 (13)	320
1.7-8	469	5 (16)	507
1.8	464	9.1–11.1	279
2.1-13	470	9.3	280
2.1	458	11.1-2	290
2.2	467	11.6-8	288 290
2.4	471	19.13	290
2.5	471	19.17–26.6	290
2.7	471-472	21.1-3	287
2.8	471	21.1	290
2.10	471	21.3	290
2.11	472	51.1-4	288
3.2	470		
4.7-8	464	*Gospel of the Hebrews*	
5	470		231 289 438 462-463
6.3	464		
6.6	464	fr. 7	279
6.7	469		
8.8-10	462	*Gospel of Judas* (CT)	541
10.5	469	33.6-8	507
13.3	464		
13.5	462	*Gospel of Nicodemus*	
13.6	464	11[1]	516
14	474		
14.1	464	*Gospel of Peter*	245 278 **437-451** 454-455 457-459 465
14.4-6	475		
14.4	472 475 529		
15	474	2.3-5	443
15.1	457 467	3–5	518
16.1	467	5	511
16.3	467	5.16	555
16.5	474	6.21	277
17	525	6.24	280
Akhmîm text		7.26	458
4	457 467	8.29-33	277
12	458 467	9.36	278
13	474	9.37–10.40	284
15	467	9.37	278
21	458	10.38-42	278 282
23	464	10.39-42	287
24	464	10.40	292
25	458	10.42	282
26	458	11.44	279
31	464	11.45-49	278
33	469	12	514
		12.50-52	280
Apocalypse of Thomas	466	13.55	279

13.56	287	52	543
14.60	458	106	7 17
15	515-516	107	17
18	516		
20	515	*History of the Blessed Virgin*	
21	514-515 518		327
22	515		
24	518	*Letter of Peter to Philip*	
28	522		288
30–45	517		
30	519	*Letter of Pilate to Claudius*	
33	518		507 511 517 522
36–42	520		526 530
37	519		
45	520	*Martyrdom of Mark* 525	
48–49	522		
59	510	*Pistis Sophia*	
		1.2	292
Gospel of Thomas	437-438		
9	106	*Protevangelium of James*	
13	239		439
22	17		
46	542-543	*Questions of Bartholomew*	
48	7 17	1.6	326

CLASSICAL, EARLY CHRISTIAN AND PREMODERN WRITINGS

Abu'l Barakat
The Lamp of the Darkness
328

Aeneas Tacticus
Poliorcetica
27.4   199

Aeschylus
Seven against Thebes
18   209

Albert the Great   323

Alcuin   325

Aphrahat   483

Appian
Civil War   9-10
2.117   11

Aristobulus
Fragmenta
frg. 2a, l. 3   187

Aristophanes   464
Clouds
961   209

Aristotle   406
Politics
1338a30   209
Rhetoric
1.5.5, 1360b   389

Arrian   19

Artapanos of Alexandria
3.6-8   219

Asinius Pollio   10-11 13
Histories   9

INDEX LOCORUM

Athanasius of Alexandria
Against the Arians 549
  3.26-58 549
  3.26 550
  3.29 550
  3.31 550 555
  3.32 550
  3.35 550
  5.8 549
Against the Gentiles
  1.3 534 549
  1.5 534
  2.4 545
  3.3 545
  41–44 548
Flight
  12 548
On Incarnation **533-556**
  1.1.2 534
  1.3 549
  2.3–10.6 537
  3.1 537
  3.3 537
  3.5 537
  6.7 538
  7.2 538
  7.4 538
  8.3 546
  10.2 538
  10.6 538
  13.6 538
  17 555
  17.1 547
  17.2 547
  17.5–18.2 548
  18.1 556
  19.3 548
  20.6 549
  21.1 548
  21.3 538
  21.6 538
  22.1 538
  25.3 538
  25.4 555
  25.5 538
  25.6 555
  26.1 538
  37.4 538 548
  43.6 547
  54.3 548 555

Letter to Epictetus
  6 549
Life of Antony
  65–66 556

Augustine 322
Harmony of the Gospels 321
Third Sermon for Easter 322
Tractates on John
  VII 14 322
  VII 16.2–17.2 322

Basil the Great 98

Basilides 551 554

Bede 325

Cassius Dio 9 19

Cave of Treasures
  54 519

Celsus
True Doctrine 519-520 522

Chrysostom 325

Cicero
Orations
  3.205 223

Clement of Alexandria 495 497
Miscellanies
  2.11.50.2 496
  2.20.114.3-6 495
  2.49.1 7
  4.6.37 496-497
  4.6.39 496-497
  4.6.40 496-497
  5.2.6 7
Outlines 463
Prophetic Sayings 461-463
  41 461
  48–49 461

Pseudo-Cyprian
On the Two Mountains Sinai and Zion 503
  8.2 515

Cyril of Alexandria 325

Cyril of Jerusalem
On the Life and Passion of Christ
                   527
  24-29   507

Decretum Gelasianum
4.5–5.4   438

Democritus
180   209

Demosthenes
Against Aristogiton
  1.89.5   107

Didascalia Apostolorum 321 462

Didymus the Blind 439 441
Commentary on Ecclesiastes
  8.3-7   437

Digesta Iustiniani
48.20.6   113

Dio Chrysostom 187

Diodore of Sicily 9

Diogenes Laertius
6.39   464
7.130   406

Dion of Prusa 224
Orations
  72.16   224

Ephrem 323
Commentary on the Diatessaron
  on Jn 1,47   323

Epictetus 187
Discourses   38
  4.1.79   40

Epiphanius 320
Panarion   323
  22.6.5   324
  30.13.2-3   321

  51.7.7-9   318

Erasmus
Novum Instrumentum 365

Eusebius   438 440-441
                      462-463
Chronicon   2
Church History
  3.4   186
  3.11.1-2   325
  3.24.11-12   318
  3.25.4-5   462
  3.25.4   437
  3.25.6   437
  3.36.11   230-231
  3.39.4   319
  5.5.5   505
  6.12   440
  6.14.1   463

Gregory the Great
Commentary on Job
  33.15   322

Herodotus
Histories
  3.126   32
  8.98   32

Hilary of Poitiers
Commentary on Matthew 58

Hippolytus   483
Refutation of All Heresies
  8.10.1   539
  8.10.3   539
Ps.-Hippolytus
On the Seventy Apostles of Christ
                      330

Hugh of Saint Cher 323

Iamblichus
Life of Pythagoras 216

Irenaeus   446-497 537
Against Heresies
  1.2.2   540
  1.12.4   535

1.24.4	551	*2 Apology*	
1.24.5	554	10.8	212
1.29.1	535	*Dialogue with Trypho*	
1.30.1	535	17.1-4	528
1.30.11	541	49	146
3.16.5	535	69.7	507
4.20.4-6	496	97.1	277
4.36.8	471	97.3	514
5.9.1	496	100.3-4	535
5.9.2	496	108	277

Demonstration of the Apostolic Preaching

		108.2	519
1.30.13	236		
79	514	**Life and Miracles of Saint Thecla**	
			490-491 499

Ishodad of Merw 325

Life of Willibald, Bishop of Eichstätt
329

Isocrates 210

		Livy	2 9 11
Jerome	57 231 438-439	1.16	525
	441		

Commentary on Matthew

Lucian of Samosata
The Way to Write History

3.2	99		
27.45	516	48	12

Commentary on Ephesians

2.12	322	**Marcion**	236 238

Commentary on Isaiah

65, prol.	231	**Martyrdom of Julian of Anazarbus**

On Illustrious Men
446 448 455

1.3-5	438	
2	279	**Melito of Sardis**
7	186	*On Pascha*
16	231 289	73.92-93 511
		79 553 555

John Chrysostom

		80	555
Homily on Matthew		93	555
14	318	96	511

Homily on John

20	323	**Methodius of Olympus**
85.4	278	*Symposium*
		2.6 462

Justin Martyr 482 495

		Minucius Felix	526
1 Apology		*Octavius*	
21.1	293	24.1	525
21.3	515 525		
23.1	293	**Musonius**	
29–34	527	*Discourses*	
30.1	507	9.48.14-15	222
35	514		
66	83		

Nicetas Paphlagon 325-326
Oration in Praise of Bartholomew
326

Nicholas of Damascus
Life of Augustus 216

Origen
98 232 325
438-439 441
450

Against Celsus
1.51	277
2.33	516
2.38	514
2.55-56	293
2.55	520
2.61	522
2.70	522
5.58	284

Commentary on John
6.37   287

Commentary on Matthew
10.17   439

Hexapla   2

Letter to Africanus
6   193

On Principles
praef. 8   232
2.8.3   539

Papias of Hierapolis 319-320

Petrus Comestor
Scholastic History on the Gospels
185   520

Philip of Side
Church History fr.   438

Flavius Philostratus 19
Life of Apollonius of Tyana
216

Phlegon of Tralles
Book of Marvels
1   282
Chronicle
13–14   516

Pindar   12 16

Plato   16 210 219 406
537
Gorgias
470e   209
Menexenus
237   389
Phaedo
69c   464
Protagoras
327d   209
Republic
378e   209
519   12
Timaeus
47D–48A   12

Pliny the Younger
Epistles
5.8.12   19

Plutarch   **1-20** 41
Lives   3 10-11 13
  Alexander
  4.2   12
  Anthony   9 10
  13–15   10
  46.2   194
  Brutus   9-11
  7–19   10
  Caesar   9 10
  22.3   11
  62–67   10
  66.4   11
  Cato   9
  51.1   11
  Cicero   9
  42.2   10
  42.3   10
  Crassus   9
  Lucullus   9
  Nicias - Crassus
  4.3   11
  Pericles
  39.2   431
  Pompey   9
  Romulus
  28   525
Moralia   3 11-13
  On Friendship and Flattery
  5 (51BC)

6–8 (51E–52F)	12	**Serapion of Antioch**	438-441
How to Tell a Flatterer from a Friend		**Solomon of Bosra**	
15–16 (58D-F)	12	*Book of the Bee*	324 328 330
On Having Many Friends			
8–9 (96D–97B)	12	**Sozomenos**	
On Superstition		*Church History*	
5	12	7.19.9	463
Tranquility of Mind			
464E–465A	12	**Stephanus (Robert Estienne)**	
12 (472A, 472F)	12		362 365
Table Talk			
1.6	12	**Strabo**	
9.14	12	*Geography*	
That Epicurus Actually Makes a Pleasant Life Impossible		1.2.34	194-195
		7.7.4	41
13–14	12	16.4.27	194-195
Polybius	41		
		Suetonius	9
Porphyry	99	*Augustus*	
		97.1	515
Posidonius	194	*Tiberius*	
		52	34
Quintilian	220 222		
Institutions		**Tacitus**	
1, Pr. 18	221	*Annales*	
1.9	78	2.59–61	34
1.13	221	15.44.2-3	180
2.4	78		
2.5	78	**Tatian**	
4.2	79	*Address to the Greeks*	
5.10.24	389	10.3	515
5.11	79		
8.3.3	221	**Tertullian**	483
8.3.52	221	*Against Marcion*	
9.2.27-28	223	3.6	507
9.4.43	221	3.10	507
10.1.43	223	4.6.1-2	518
		Antidote for the Scorpion's Sting	
Rufinus of Aquileia	232 439	10.10	528
A Commentary on the Apostles' Creed		*Apology*	**501-531**
29	282	1.1	505
		5.3	528
Rupert of Deutz	325	5.4	529
Commentary on John		5.6	529
1.50	326	9.6	505
		18–20	506
Seneca		21.18-25	**501-531**
Epistles		30.7	505
88.32	224	44.2	505

50.12	505	*Compendium of Heretical Accounts*	
50.13	529	2.2	441
On Baptism			
19.2	524	**Theon**	
To the Nations	505	*Progymnasmata*	
On the Prescription of Heretics		5	6
20	530		
On the Resurrection of the Flesh		**Theophilus of Antioch**	
20.5	514	*To Autolycus*	
On Running Away		1.2	495
14.1	7		
To Scapula		**Thomas Aquinas**	323
3.3	516		
On Spectacles		**Thucydides**	
30	515	2.39.1	209
30.6	519		
		Valentinus	
Theodore of Mopsuestia	325	Fragment 2	495
Commentary on John			
2	318	**Xenophon**	
7	278	*Anabasis*	
		3.1.27	107
Theodoret of Cyrus	439-441		

PAPYRI AND OSTRACA

BGU I 140	351	P.Diog. 9	350
BGU I 326	351	P.Diosk. 7	27
BGU III 874	203	P.Egerton 2 [inv. 3]	496
BGU III 1002	344	P.Enteux. 80	27
BGU VI 1247	27	P.Flor. II 278	356
BGU VII 1662	350	P.Gen. I² 30	353
Chrest.Wilck. 439	32	P.Gen. III 92	340
C.Ord.Ptol. 75-76	341	P.Giss. I 36	344
C.Pap.Jud. I 21	27	P.Grenf. I 38	27
CPR XV 1	344	P.Gur. 8	27-29
CPR XV 2	344	P.Harr. I 67	351
CPR XV 3	344	P.Heid. VII 393	30
CPR XV 4	344	P.Heid. VIII 416	27 29
Heidelberg, Institut für Papyrologie P.		P.Hels. 2	27
G434	20	P.Hever 64	357
O.Claud. II 191, 192	355	P.Kellis I 66	188
O.Claud. II 309-336	355	P.Köln VI 272	27
P.Ant. I 13	486	P.Köln VII 313	32 34
P.Berl.Leihg. 2.43	32	P.Lips. I 9	351
P.Bingen 45	32	P.Lond. III 1171	36
P.Cair.Zen. III 59509	32 38	P.Lond. VI 1929	203
P.Col. III 6	27	P.Oxy. I 6	486
P.Dime III 29	353	P.Oxy. II 244	354

P.Oxy. III 1610	9	P.Tor.Choach. 12	344
P.Oxy. IV 735	356	P.Vind. Tand. 26	353
P.Oxy. IX 1201	349	P.Vind.Worp 10	353
P.Oxy. XII 1466	350	P.Vindob. G 2325	441
P.Oxy. XIV 1739	244	P.Vindob. G 39756	444 456 464
P.Oxy. XIX 2231	350		472 474
P.Oxy. XXXI 2606	20	P.Wisc. 33	27
P.Oxy. XXXIV 2710	350	P.Yadin I 14	357
P.Oxy. XXXVI 2772	354	P.Yadin I 15	357
P.Oxy. XLI 2949	441-443	P.Yadin I 20	357
P.Oxy. XLIII 3108	349	P.Yadin I 21	357
P.Oxy. XLV 3214	20	P.Yadin I 22	357
P.Oxy. LI 3617	344	P.Yadin II 52	341 352
P.Oxy. LVII 3904	198	P.Yale 87/P.CtYBR 1376	486
P.Oxy. LVII 3905	198	P.Yale I 56	340
P.Oxy. LVII 3909	198	PSI III 238	203
P.Oxy. LX 4009	441 443-444	PSI IV 332	32
P.Oxy. LXII 4336	198	PSI X 1101	349
P.Oxy. LXIV 4404	62-64	PSI XIV 1401	32
P.Oxy. LXVI 4526	198	SB I 1010	348
P.Oxy. LXXII 4857	198	SB I 3924	32 34
P.Oxy. LXXII 4869	198	SB I 5231	344
P.Oxy. LXXII 4876	198	SB I 5275	344
P.Oxy. LXXII 4878	198	SB III 6304	354
P.Oxy. LXXII 4882	198	SB VI 9068	30
P.Oxy. LXXII 4884	198	SB VI 9298	348-349
P.Petr. I 14	343	SB X 10271	27
P.Petr. II 20	32	SB XII 11041	352
P.Rev. col. ix	345	SB XX 15139	347
P.Rev. col. lxxxvi	344	SB XXVI 16458	20
P.Ross.Georg. II 18	32	UPZ I 108	340
P.Ryl. I 77	27	UPZ II 175a	344
P.Ryl. II 68	27	UPZ II 177	344
P.Schoyen. MS. 2634.1	486	UPZ II 218	345
P.Tebt. I 5	32-34	Wien, Nationalbibliothek G 19999	
P.Tebt. II 383	352		20
P.Tebt. III/2 980	353		

INSCRIPTIONS

OGIS 665   37

WOODEN AND WAX TABLETS

London, British Library, Add MS 37533   20

Paris, Bibliothèque Nationale, Cabinet des Medailles D 2563   20

Codices

Bodl. Ms Gr. th. f. 4 [P]	444 456
Codex Barocci 180	487 489
Codex Palatinus Vaticanus 68	488 490
Codex Parisinus gr. 520	487 490
Codex Parisinus gr. 769	488 490
Codex Parisinus gr. 1454	487 490
Codex Parisinus gr. 1468	487 490
Codex Parisinus gr. 1506	488-489
Dublin, Trinity College Ms. 185	488 490
Jerusalem, Hagios Saba 259	488 490
Milan (Ambrosiana) F 144 sup.	488 490
Mount Sinai gr. 497	488-489
Mount Sinai gr. 519	490
Mount Sinai gr. 526	488-489
MS. British Library Add. 12,174	485
MS. British Library Add. 14,447	485
MS. British Library Add. 14,641	485
MS. British Library Add. 14,652	485
Ohrid, Naroden Muzej, 4	488 490
Oxon. miscell. gr. 77	487 490
P.Cair. 10759 (Akhmîm Codex)	445-446
Rome, Angel. gr. 108	488 490
Vat. Chig. R. VI. 39	489-490
Vaticanus gr. 544	489
Vaticanus gr. 797	487 490
Vaticanus gr. 866	487 490
Vaticanus gr. 1190	488 490

INDEX AUCTORUM

ACHTEMEIER, P.J.   185
ADAMCZEWSKI, B.   181
ADAMS, J.N.   183, 194, 345, 354-357
ADAMS, S.A.   148
ADRIAEN, M.   322
AGUILAR CHIU, J.E.   172
AHEARNE-KROLL, S.P.   112, 119, 123, 176, 178
AKIN, D.L.   400, 403
ALAND, B.   55, 61-62, 67
ALAND, K.   3, 55, 61-62, 67
ALBL, M.C.   506-507, 511
ALBRECHT, F.   473
ALFORD, H.   566
ALKIER, S.   466, 509
ALLEN, W.C.   58
ALLISON, D.C., JR.   50, 59, 274, 276, 278, 282, 284
AMELING, W.   455
AMELOTTI, M.   349
AMIRAV, H.   506
ANATOLIOS, K.   534, 549
ANDRADE, N.J.   194-195
ANDREJEVS, O.   41
ARCARI, L.   455
ARNAL, W.E.   22, 43, 247, 565
ARZT-GRABNER, P.   339, 347
ASCOUGH, R.S.   565, 575
ASGEIRSSON, J.M.   42
ATTRIDGE, H.W.   291
AUFFARTH, C.   210
AUS, R.D.   215
AUVINEN, V.   176
AYRES, L.   539
BAARDA, T.   323, 483
BACKES, J.R.   213
BACKHAUS, K.   140, 143, 145, 212, 221
BAERT, B.   286, 368
BAETENS, G.   31
BAGNALL, R.   442
BALZ, H.   68
BAMMEL, E.   339
BARCLAY, J.M.G.   480, 529
BARDENHEWER, O.   362

BARDY, G.   440
BARNES, T.D.   248, 504-505, 529-530, 549
BARNS, J.W.B.   377-378
BARR, J.   342
BARRETT, C.K.   146, 185, 188-189, 193, 198-200, 203, 206, 269, 286, 304-305, 366
BARRIER, J.W.   479-480, 484-486, 492-493, 499
BARTHES, R.   75, 330
BARTLETT, D.L.   253
BARTON, G.A.   195
BARTON, S.C.   251-252
BASSET, R.   324
BATES, M.   289
BATOVICI, D.   451
BAUCKHAM, R.J.   454, 460, 463-466, 469-470, 472, 475
BAUER, W.   428-429, 431
BAUSI, A.   445, 454, 472
BAUSINGER, H.   73-74
BAYAN, G.   323-324
BAZZANA, G.B.   22, 33, 41, 44, 565, 570
BEARD, M.   353
BEASLEY-MURRAY, G.R.   306
BEATRICE, P.F.   231
BECK, E.J.   455, 467, 474
BECK, M.   11
BECKER, B.   190
BECKER, C.   504, 519, 525, 529
BECKER, E.-M.   75, 81, 94, 249
BECKER, J.   140, 366, 413, 415, 417, 435
BECKER, M.   222, 224-225, 516, 520
BEDENBENDER, A.   177
BELL, H.I.   496
BELLINZONI, A.J.   228, 495
BENDLIN, A.   572
BENGEL, J.A.   365-366, 566
BENNEMA, C.   389, 408
BERGER, K.   74, 274
BERTRAM, G.   209

BETHGE, H.-G. 497, 534
BETZ, H.D. 85
BEUTLER, J. 302, 304, 366, 389
BEYER, K. 194
BEZA, T. 566
BICKERMANN, E. 283
BIELER, L. 156
BIERINGER, R. 273, 276, 278, 286, 295, 368, 385, 536
BIGAOUETTE, F. 177
BIHLMEYER, K. 243
BINDER, G. 437
BINGEN, J. 356
BINGHAM, D.J. 495-496
BISPHAM, E. 572
BLACK, C.C. 131-132
BLACK, M. 198, 200
BLACKBURN, B. 156
BLANCHARD, Y.-M. 465
BLASS, F. 364
BLAUTH, D. 527
BLICKENSTAFF, M. 291
BLOMBERG, C.L. 318
BLOWERS, P.M. 495
BOCKMUEHL, M. 477
BÖHLEMANN, P. 258
BOISMARD, M.-É. 3, 307
BOND, H.K. 529
BOND, S.E. 575
BONNET, M. 479, 481, 484, 488
BONS, E. 112
BORGEN, P. 364
BORING, M.E. 107, 172, 176
BORNKAMM, G. 71
BOSENIUS, B. 250
BOTNER, M. 154, 166-167
BOURIANT, U. 446
BOUVIER, B. 489
BOVON, F. 7, 214-215, 261, 263, 266-267, 269, 281, 483, 489
BOWMAN, A.K. 345, 353
BRAKKE, D. 499, 505-506, 540, 556
BRANDENBURGER, S.H. 8
BRAUNER, U. 8
BRAUNERT, H. 345
BREMMER, J.N. 444, 447, 455-456, 461, 464-465, 469, 472-473, 475-476, 481, 563
BRENT, A. 412
BREYER, F. 344

BREYTENBACH, C. 97-99, 107-108, 111, 116-117, 172, 176, 180
BROCK, S.P. 157
BROCKINGTON, L.H. 158
BROWN, A.J. 365
BROWN, R.E. 213, 257, 279-280, 286-287, 301-304, 307, 309, 358, 364-366, 393, 401, 403, 405, 408-409
BROWN, S. 297
BROWNE, G.M. 442
BRÜNENBERG-BUSSWOLDER, E. 213
BRYAN, C. 152
BUCHHOLZ, D.D. 446, 455
BUCK, C.D. 364
BUCKLEY, M.J. 301-303
BUDGE, E.A.W. 324, 327-328
BÜLOW-JACOBSEN, A. 356
BUITENWERF, R. 181
BULTMANN, R. 71-74, 139, 154, 251, 256-257, 259, 274, 401, 403, 405, 413, 415-416, 419-420, 423, 425
BUNGE, M.J. 253
BURNET, R. 134, 312
BURNS, R.J. 369
BURRIDGE, R.A. 215
BURRIS, C. 485
BUTH, R. 190-191
BYRNE, B. 297, 300, 302, 304-305, 307
BYRSKOG, S. 177
CADBURY, H.J. 195
CALBOLI MONTEFUSCO, L. 78
CALHOUN, R.M. 98-99, 502
CALVIN, J. 566
CALZOLARI, V. 485
CAMERON, R. 574
CAMPBELL, W.S. 176, 205
CANCIK, H. 11
CARLETON PAGET, J. 495
CASTILLO GARCÍA, C. 504
CATCHPOLE, D.R. 239, 242
CERESA-GASTALDO, A. 438
CHAPMAN, D.W. 113
CHARLES, R.H. 158, 313
CHARLESWORTH, M.P. 34
CHARLESWORTH, S.D. 342
CHENNATTU, R. 297, 301-303, 305
CHERIX, P. 479
CHILTON, B.D. 105, 109
CHRISTES, J. 209-211
CLACKSON, J. 346

CLARK, E.A.   480
CLARYSSE, W.   345
CLIVAZ, C.   330
COCKLE, W.E.H.   343
COENEN, L.   209
COLE, R.A.   176, 178
COLES, R.A.   442-443
COLLINS, J.J.   157-158, 160, 163
COLLINS, R.F.   303, 305
COLOE, M.L.   308
COMFORT, P.W.   50-51, 57, 59-60
CONCANON, C.   571
CONNOLLY, R.H.   185-186
CONYBEARE, F.C.   197, 485
CONZELMANN, H.   172, 174, 180, 197, 215, 220-221, 269, 435
COOK, J.G.   113, 283, 285, 288, 339, 515, 526
COOTE, R.B.   74
CORBIER, M.   353
CORNELL, T.   353
CORSTEN, T.   338
COTTON, H.M.   192, 342-343
COWLEY, A.E.   444
CRAFFERT, P.F.   275
CRISCUOLO, L.   28
CROMWELL, J.   345
CROSSAN, J.D.   250-252, 442
CULPEPPER, R.A.   125, 132, 181, 302, 312
CZACHESZ, I.   444, 447, 455-456, 461, 472
DAGRON, G.   490-491
DALMAN, G.   108, 112
DAMM, A.   2
D'ANGELO, M.R.   287, 292
DASSMANN, E.   561
DAVIES, W.D.   50, 59, 284
DE BOOR, C.   438
DEHANDSCHUTTER, B.   493
DEICHGRÄBER, R.   431
DE JONG, A.   149, 455
DE JONG, L.   194
DE JONGE, H.J.   150, 179-181, 214-216, 242, 246, 265-266, 276, 285-286
DE JONGE, M.   143, 147, 178, 401
DEKKERS, E.   508, 519
DE LANG, M.H.   172
DE LA POTTERIE, I.   391-392, 402
DELEHAYE, H.   324

DEMASURE, K.   286, 368
DEMEL, S.   525
DENAUX, A.   145, 184, 187, 190, 194, 196, 200-207, 278, 495
DEN DULK, M.   460, 465
DEPAUW, M.   346
DERRENBACKER, R.A.   2, 19
DERRETT, J.D.M.   361-369, 375, 378
DE TROYER, K.   42
DETTINGER, D.   249
DE VOS, B.   503
DEWEY, J.   577
DIBELIUS, M.   71-74, 79, 113-114, 139
DICKEY, E.   349
DIETERICH, A.   458
DILLON, R.J.   240-241
DO, T.   297-300, 305-306
DOBBELER, A. VON   218
DOCHHORN, J.   316
DODD, C.H.   274, 276
DÖHLER, M.   513
DONAHUE, J.R.   124, 176
DONALDSON, T.L.   573, 576
DORMEYER, D.   81, 173, 177
DOWNING, F.G.   5
DREXHAGE, H.J.   30
DRIJVERS, H.J.W.   483
DSCHULNIGG, P.   176
DUBOIS, J.-D.   540
DUENSING, H.   454, 467-468, 471
DUNN, G.W.   505, 528
DUNN, J.D.G.   139
DUNN, P.W.   479
DUNNING, B.H.   577
DUPRÉ LA TOUR, M.   490
DUQUOC, C.   121
DU TOIT, D.S.   109-110, 117
EBNER, M.   42, 480
ECKERT, G.   504
EDGAR, C.C.   39
EDSALL, B.A.   334, 465
EDWARDS, J.R.   173
EDWARDS, M.J.   248
EDWARDS, R.B.   390
EFROYMSON, D.P.   505
EHORN, S.M.   148
EHRMAN, B.D.   25, 52, 184, 230
EISELE, W.   176, 514
ELBOGEN, I.   190, 192
ELDER, O.   183

ELLIOT, M.   495, 497
ELLIOTT, J.K.   454, 456, 479
ELMER, I.J.   94
ELWOLDE, J.F.   190
ENDSJØ, D.Ø.   283-284
ENGBERG-PEDERSEN, T.   94
ENGEMANN, W.   75
ENSLIN, M.S.   140-141
ERASMUS   365, 566
ERLEMANN, K.   218, 220-223, 225
ERNST, J.   140, 176, 184
ESHEL, E.   190
ESHEL, H.   190
ESLER, P.F.   185, 505
ESTES, D.C.   302
EUBANK, N.   175
EVANS, C.A.   105-106, 185, 342
EVANS, C.F.   284-285
EVANS, T.V.   183, 349
EYL, J.   571, 573
EYNIKEL, E.M.M.   481
FEDER, F.   344
FEISSEL, D.   194
FELDMEIER, R.   473
FELTON, D.   282
FERGUSON, J.   496
FEWSTER, P.   345
FINK, R.O.   356
FINNERN, S.   121
FITZMYER, J.A.   6, 64, 185-186, 190, 192-193, 195-203, 205-207, 240, 286, 342
FLEBBE, J.   179
FLEDDERMANN, H.   27, 31, 41
FLETCHER-LOUIS, C.H.T.   239-240
FLOWERS, M.   173
FLUSSER, D.   25
FOCANT, C.   109, 112, 126, 130-131, 133-134
FÖRSTER, N.   339
FONTAINE, J.   479
FORGET, J.   328
FORNBERG, T.   162
FOSTER, P.   2-3, 59, 70, 228, 243, 245, 247-248, 278, 287, 291, 439-443, 446-450, 460, 494, 501
FRANCE, R.T.   126
FRANKE, C.-M.   497
FREDRIKSEN, P.   567
FREEDMAN, D.N.   141, 195

FREI, H.W.   120
FRENSCHKOWSKI, M.   41
FRETHEIM, T.E.   253
FREY, J.   174, 181, 231, 279, 312, 315-316, 321, 330, 334-335, 459-460, 465-466, 480, 514, 529
FRICKER, D.   179
FRITZEN, W.   176
FRÜCHTEL, E.   220
FRÜCHTEL, L.   495, 497
FÜRST, D.   209
FUGLSETH, K.   364
FUNK, F.X.   243
GADAMER, H.-G.   313
GARCÍA MARTÍNEZ, F.   163, 197, 481
GASQUE, W.W.   196
GATHERCOLE, S.   542
GAVENTA, B.R.   120, 185, 253
GEBHARDT, O. VON   481, 486
GEMEINHARDT, P.   210-212, 509
GEORGES, T.   473, 504-510, 512-521, 523-529
GERBER, C.   141
GESCHÉ, A.   122
GIANNAKIS, G.K.   183
GIBSON, M.D.   325
GIROD, R.   439
GNILKA, J.   105, 141-142, 174, 176-178, 180-181, 250
GÖRGEMANNS, H.   80
GOLTZ, E. VON DER   411-412, 431
GOOD, D.   292
GOODACRE, M.S.   4, 13, 15, 18-19, 143, 274, 543
GOODMAN, D.   240
GOODMAN, M.   559, 569, 572
GOULD, E.P.   176, 178
GOULDER, M.D.   4, 14, 15, 17-19
GRABIUS, J.E.   487
GRÄSSER, E.   86
GRAF, G.   328
GRAFTON, A.   2
GRÉBAUT, S.   454
GREEN, J.B.   185
GREEVEN, H.   3, 87, 142
GREGORY, A.F.   2-3, 227-228, 230-232, 234-235, 243, 412, 479, 492, 494-495, 501
GRENFELL, B.P.   486
GRESSMANN, H.   71

GRIESBACH, J.J.   365
GRINTZ, J.M.   191
GRONEWALD, M.   487
GROSSI, V.   438
GROSSMAN, E.   345
GROTIUS, H.   566
GRÜNSTÄUDL, W.   460, 473
GRUNDEKEN, M.   182, 557
GRUNDMANN, W.   176, 178
GUIDI, I.   324
GUMMERE, R.M.   224
GUNDRY, R.H.   7, 123-124, 126, 132, 176-177, 284
GUNKEL, H.   71-72
GUTTENBERGER, G.   123
HAACKER, K.   209
HAAS, C.   401-402, 405
HAASE, F.   328
HÄGERLAND, T.   177
HÄMMIG, A.   172
HAENCHEN, E.   140, 144, 189, 218
HAENSCH, R.   349
HAGNER, D.A.   56, 228, 232, 483
HAHN, F.   7
HAINES-ETZEN, K.   486-487
HALLA-AHO, H.   347, 357
HALPERN, B.   23
HALTON, T.P.   438
HAMMANN, K.   71-72
HANHART, R.   171
HANSON, A.E.   353
HARDER, R.   210
HARDY, E.R.   549
HARLAND, P.A.   572, 575
HARNACK, A. VON   321, 456, 558
HARRINGTON, D.J.   124, 176
HARRIS, M.J.   483
HARTENSTEIN, J.   274, 524
HARTLEY, D.E.   105
HARTMAN, L.   85, 110, 141
HARTVIGSEN, K.M.   153
HAUFE, G.   284
HAUGE, M.R.   121
HAYS, R.B.   120
HAYWARD, R.   108
HAZLETT, I.   504
HEAD, P.M.   449
HEALY, M.   389
HEIL, C.   144, 221

HEIL, M.   35
HEILIGENTHAL, R.   218, 389
HEININGER, B.   214
HEINRICHS, J.H.   566
HELLER, E.   180
HELLHOLM, D.   162
HELMER, R.C.   453
HENGEL, M.   260, 319
HENNECKE, E.   229, 232, 454, 493
HERCZEG, P.   481
HERDER, J.G.   71, 74
HERNITSCHECK, E.   557
HIEKE, T.   8, 177, 466
HILGENFELD, A.   324
HILL, C.E.   411, 442
HILLS, J.V.   470
HIXSON, E.   65, 68
HOBSON, D.W.   23
HODGE, C.   571
HOFFMANN, P.   8, 24, 26, 31, 35, 40, 42, 144, 169, 244, 246, 283
HOGETERP, A.   184, 187, 190, 194, 196, 198, 200-207
HOLDER-EGGER, O.   329
HOLLADAY, C.R.   156, 285
HOLLANDER, H.W.   181
HOLMÉN, T.   140, 502
HOLMES, M.W.   61, 365, 494
HOLSINGER-FRIESEN, T.   537
HOLTMANN, T.   253
HOLZMEISTER, U.   316, 321, 323-325, 524
HOOKER, M.D.   99, 143, 146, 160, 176
HOPPE, H.   508
HORN, F.W.   75, 87, 557
HORSLEY, G.H.R.   186
HORSLEY, R.A.   21, 153-154
HORT, F.J.A.   45, 47-48, 52-54, 69, 362, 365, 367
HOUGHTON, H.A.G.   57, 345, 437, 446
HOUTMAN, A.   149, 455
HOWARD, W.F.   200, 203-206, 362, 364
HOWE, E.M.   483
HUCK, A.   3
HÜBNER, R.M.   248
HUNT, A.S.   486
HUNT, L.J.   358
HUNTER, D.G.   479
HURTADO, L.W.   152-153, 529

HYLEN, S.   479
IBER, G.   71
IOANNIDOU, G.   20
JACOBI, C.   140, 250, 503-504
JACOBSEN, A.-C.   505-506
JÄGER, I.   536
JAKAB, A.   461
JAMES, M.R.   444-445, 454, 456, 458
JAMES, P.   183, 346
JANOWSKI, B.   174, 177
JANSE, M.   183, 194, 345
JANTSCH, T.   261
JASTROW, M.   190, 191
JENSEN, A.   479
JENSEN, M.H.   23-24
JENSON, R.W.   120
JEREMIAS, J.   104
JERVELL, J.   185, 189
JOHANN, H.-T.   210
JOHANSSON, D.   121
JOHNSON, L.T.   185
JOHNSON, S.E.   154
JOHNSON, S.F.   490
JOHNSON, T.F.   401, 403
JOLLES, A.   73
JONGKIND, D.   65, 68
JOST, M.R.   459
JUDGE, P.J.   295, 302, 304, 309
JÜLICHER, A.   313
JÜNGEL, E.   87
KAEGI, A.   415, 422
KAELIN, O.   344
KÄSEMANN, E.   139
KAESTLI, J.-D.   327, 481
KAHLOS, M.   505
KAISER, U.U.   497, 534
KANNENGIESSER, C.   479
KANY, R.   78
KARAKOLIS, C.   512
KARAVIDOPOULOS, J.   61
KARRER, M.   98, 261
KATZ, F.   141
KATZOFF, R.   349
KECK, L.E.   154-155
KEENAN, J.G.   353
KEENER, C.S.   195, 215, 219-220, 318
KEITH, C.   121
KELHOFFER, J.A.   287, 528
KELLY, B.   23

KENYON, F.G.   449
KIEFFER, R.   145
KIESSLING, E.   353
KIRK, A.   9, 43
KISTEMAKER, S.J.   401-402
KITCHEN, M.   184-185
KLAUCK, H.-J.   101, 391, 400-402, 405, 408, 432, 483, 493
KLEIN, H.   186, 196, 259-260, 262, 264, 266-267, 516
KLEIN, R.   209
KLEINKNECHT, K.T.   178
KLIESCH, K.   219
KLIJN, A.F.J.   230-231
KLINGHARDT, M.   564
KLOPPENBORG, J.S.   2-3, 9 18, 20, 24-25, 27, 29, 41-42, 44, 144-145, 169, 236, 244, 246, 275, 501, 563, 565, 574-575
KLOSTERGARD PETERSEN, A.   505
KLOSTERMANN, E.   58, 103, 172, 176
KLUMBIES, P.-G.   172-173
KNIGGE, C.   344
KNIGHT, J.   455, 529
KNÖPPLER, T.   141
KOCH, D.-A.   75, 80, 87-88, 90, 96, 141, 145
KÖHLER, W.-D.   494-496
KOERRENZ, R.   209
KÖRTNER, U.H.J.   75, 249
KOESTER, C.R.   332
KOESTER, H.   25, 228-229, 233-234, 243-245, 247, 492-495
KOET, B.   130
KOLB, A.   355
KOLTUN-FROMM, N.   479
KONRADT, M.   179, 252, 254, 284
KOPERSKI, V.   273, 276, 278
KRAELING, C.H.   139-140
KRAMER, B.   20
KRAMER, J.   347, 354, 357
KRAUS, T.J.   439, 441-444, 446-448, 454, 456, 459-460, 464, 469, 475, 486, 496, 512
KRAUS, W.   97-98
KREINECKER, C.M.   345, 347, 349, 354, 360
KRELLER, H.   349
KREMER, J.   184, 315

KREUZER, S. 97
KRITZER, R.E. 347
KRÜCKEMEIER, N. 214, 216-217
KRUGER, M.J. 441-442
KÜGLER, J. 262
KÜHNERT, F. 223
KÜNG, H. 121
KUTSCHER, E.Y. 365
LABAHN, M. 44, 295
LÀDA, C.A. 28
LAGRANGE, M.-J. 173, 176
LALLEMAN, P.J. 479
LAMBRECHT, J. 250-251
LAMOUILLE, A. 3
LAMPE, P. 106
LANG, M. 338
LAPIDE, C. À 566
LATAIRE, B. 273, 276, 278
LAYTON, B. 497
LECHNER, T. 248
LEE, D.A. 304
LEE, S.-I. 183, 186
LEHTIPUU, O. 286-288
LELOIR, L. 323
LEVINE, A.-J. 291
LICONA, M.R. 275
LIEBENGOOD, K.D. 42
LIEBESCHÜTZ, W. 78
LIESENBORGHS, L. 437
LIETAERT PEERBOLTE, B.J. 479
LIEU, J.M. 390, 393, 401-402, 405, 477
LINDEMANN, A. 92, 94-95, 145, 172, 174, 180, 228, 248, 254, 271, 428, 435
LIPSIUS, R.A. 479, 481, 484, 487-489, 498
LITWA, M.D. 282-283, 539
LLEWELYN, S.R. 32, 37
LOADER, J. 117
LÖHR, H. 411
LÖHR, W. 551
LOGAN, A.H.B. 540
LOHFINK, G. 285
LOHMEYER, E. 100, 103, 107, 171, 176
LOHSE, E. 86
LONA, H.E. 93, 514, 522
LONGENECKER, B.W. 42
LOUW, J.P. 401

LUCE, T. 11, 19
LÜCKE, F. 318
LÜDEMANN, G. 283
LÜHRMANN, D. 107, 173, 176, 441-443
LÜTH, C. 209-210
LULL, D.J. 43, 442
LUZ, U. 7, 50-51, 85, 277-278, 284, 289, 313-314
MACDONALD, D.R. 493
MACK, B.L. 571
MACRAE, G.W. 292
MAIRS, R. 344-345, 347, 351-352
MALBON, E.S. 119, 122-123, 125, 132-135, 137, 167
MALHERBE, A.J. 391
MALINA, B.J. 389, 404
MANSON, T.W. 104, 106
MARCOVICH, M. 539
MARCUS, J. 94, 100, 120, 130-131, 136, 141-142, 153, 162, 176, 252, 276-277, 280
MARCUS, R. 544
MARGANNE, M.-H. 347
MARGUERAT, D. 196, 198-199, 203
MARKSCHIES, C. 231, 279, 321, 325-326, 454, 479, 496, 526
MARRASSINI, P. 445
MARROU, H.-I. 78, 210
MARSHALL, I.H. 6, 64, 266, 400-401, 403, 405
MARSHALL, J.W. 235, 239
MARTENS, P.W. 495
MARTIN, D.B. 288
MARTIN, M.W. 52
MARTIN, R.A. 196
MARTIN, R.P. 196
MARTIN, V. 377-378
MARTINI, C.M. 61
MARTY, É. 75
MASON, S. 222, 227
MASSAUX, É. 228, 493-495
MASSON, É. 184
MASUZAWA, T. 565
MATERA, F.J. 295
MATTHEWS, S. 228, 234, 274, 280, 289, 563
MATTILA, S.L. 2, 19
MAURER, C. 229, 454, 465
MAYORDOMO, M. 313

McCane, B.R.   280
McDonald, L.M.   461
McFarland, O.   480
McGing, B.C.   29
McGowan, A.B.   143
McHugh, J.F.   302-303, 305, 308
McKendrick, S.   449
Meeks, W.A.   570
Meibauer, J.   75
Meier, J.P.   139, 143-146
Meiser, M.   97-98
Méndez, H.   563
Menken, M.J.J.   99, 390-391, 399, 401-403, 408
Mensching, E.   12
Merk, O.   73
Merkel, H.   318
Merkt, A.   212, 273-274, 312, 518
Merz, A.   480
Metzger, B.M.   49-51, 56-58, 60-61, 65-67, 492
Meyer, E.   140
Meyer, H.A.W.   102, 107, 566
Meyer, M.W.   42, 534, 541
Michaelis, W.   217, 260
Millar, F.G.B.   343
Miller, M.P.   574
Miller, R.C.   283-284
Misset-van de Weg, M.   149, 455
Mitchell, M.M.   573
Mitchell, M.W.   229, 231
Mitteis, L.   36, 340
Moessner, D.P.   99, 502
Moloney, F.J.   297, 301, 304-307, 366
Monier, M.   437, 446
Montanari, F.   11
Moreschini, C.   504
Morgan, T.   395
Morgenthaler, R.   5
Morin, G.   322
Moss, C.   562
Most, G.W.   315
Moule, C.F.D.   339
Moulton, J.H.   200, 202-206, 362, 364
Mount, C.   185
Moyise, S.   99, 148
Müller, C.D.G.   454, 468, 471
Müller, C.G.   214
Müller, M.   4, 18, 94, 228, 501

Müller, P.   141
Mullen, A.P.   183, 346
Muraoka, T.   110, 190
Myers, S.E.   119
Myllykoski, M.   444
Nagel, T.   412
Nasrallah, L.S.   564, 567, 570, 576
Nebe, G.W.   190
Neirynck, F.   1, 5 106, 141-142, 145, 173, 229, 238, 240, 242, 278, 295, 493
Nellessen, E.   254, 263
Nestle, E.   365
Neyrey, J.H.   389, 404
Nickelsburg, G.W.E.   160, 168
Nicklas, T.   99, 176, 228, 273-274, 312, 316, 330, 332, 439, 441-444, 446-448, 454-460, 464-467, 472-476, 480-481, 486, 496, 501-503, 512, 514, 516, 518, 525, 527-529, 531, 557
Nida, E.A.   401
Niebuhr, K.-W.   512
Niederwimmer, K.   25, 89, 483
Nielsen, J.T.   4, 228
Nineham, D.E.   274
Nissen, J.   398
Nolland, J.   7, 50, 60, 64-65, 241
Nongbri, B.   565
Norelli, E.   465
Notley, R.S.   190-191
Novenson, M.V.   151, 169
Oakman, D.E.   24, 564
Oates, J.F.   28, 337
Oatley, K.   121
Obbink, D.D.   183, 349
O'Connell, S.   142
Öhler, M.   338
Oliver, J.H.   34
Olivi, T.   98
O'Loughlin, T.   438
Olson, K.   19
Olsson, B.   398-399, 403
Olyan, S.   571
Omerzu, H.   18, 88, 228
Orth, B.   209
Orth, J.   461
Osiek, C.   577
Overbeck, F.   71, 73

PAINCHAUD, L.   534, 539-541, 546, 551-553
PAINTER, J.   391, 399, 401, 408
PALME, B.   355
PAPACONSTANTINOU, A.   344
PAPATHOMAS, A.   347
PARRY, R.   389
PARSENIOS, G.L.   395
PARSONS, P.J.   443
PASTORE, E.   134
PAULSEN, H.   228, 243, 411, 428-429, 431, 433
PAULSEN, T.   509
PAYNE, D.F.   196-198
PEARSON, B.A.   534
PEDERSEN, S.   398
PELLEGRINI, S.   99, 534-535, 539, 541, 546, 551
PELLETIER, A.   191
PELLING, C.B.   9-11, 13-14
PEPPARD, M.P.   361-366, 369-375, 378, 384
PEREMANS, W.   345
PERRIN, N.   19, 152-155, 159-161, 165
PERVO, R.A.   227, 479-480
PESCH, R.   176, 218-219
PETERS, M.K.H.   98
PETERSON, E.   464
PETERSON, J.   228
PETÖFI, J.S.   98
PETTERSEN, A.   537, 547, 549
PETZKE, G.   184
PETZOLDT, M.   171
PFLEGER, M.   525
PIERCE, C.   190-191
PIERPONT, W.G.   48, 362
PIPER, R.A.   26, 31, 42, 145
PITTS, A.W.   183, 562
PLETT, H.F.   98, 103
PLUMMER, A.   7
PODOLAK, P.   504
POIRIER, J.C.   4-5, 12, 16, 19, 228
POPKES, W.   178
POPLUTZ, U.   209, 226
PORTER, S.E.   140, 183, 342, 442, 502, 562
POUDERON, B.   465
PRAET, D.   503
PRATSCHER, W.   411

PROCTOR, T.W.   235-236
PROSTMEIER, F.R.   212, 220, 389
PROVERA, E.   328
PRÜMM, K.   444
PUECH, É.   199
PUIG I TÀRRECH, A.   480, 529
RABIN, C.   365
RADL, W.   185, 216-217, 260, 263-264, 266-269
RÄISÄNEN, H.   253
RAHLFS, A.   171
RAMON, S.   134
RANKIN, D.   504, 524
REID, D.   2
REINHARTZ, A.   334
REININK, G.J.   483
REITERER, F.V.   273
RENZ, J.   117
RESCH, A.   100-101
RICHARD, E.   195-196
RICHARDS, K.H.   143, 566
RIDDERBOS, H.   366
RIESNER, R.   211
RIGGS, C.   346
RILEY, G.   534-536, 541
RITT, H.   413-414, 420
RITTER, M.A.   210
ROBERTS, C.H.   486
ROBERTSON, A.T.   172, 362, 364
ROBINSON, J.M.   24, 144-145, 169, 244, 246, 292, 534
ROBINSON, M.A.   48, 362
ROBINSON, W.C., JR.   497
ROCHETTE, B.   343, 345, 347
RODGERS, Z.   29
RÖLLEKE, H.   74
ROGALSKY, S.   512
ROHRBAUGH, R.L.   404
ROLLENS, S.E.   22, 562-564, 571, 578
RORDORF, W.   479
ROSKAM, G.   13
ROSKAM, H.N.   179
ROTH, D.T.   44, 504
ROTHSCHILD, C.K.   542, 563
ROUBEKAS, N.P.   563
ROUKEMA, R.   506
ROUSSEAU, A.   496
RUBINCAM, C.R.   9
RÜGER, H.P.   191

RÜGGEMEIER, J.   121
RÜEGGER, H.-U.   172
RÜPKE, J.   211
RUPPERT, L.   178
RUPPRECHT, H.-A.   353
RUSCHMANN, S.   369
RUSH, A.C.   483
RUTHERFORD, J.E.   438
RYDRYCK, M.   527
SÄNGER, D.   112
SALMON, M.   185
SANDAY, W.   2
SANDERS, J.T.   185
SANDNES, K.O.   502
SAUER, J.   40-43
SCHAEFER, C.   176, 514
SCHÄRTL, M.   526
SCHENK, W.   176, 178
SCHENKE, H.-M.   497, 534
SCHENKE, L.   176, 181
SCHERMANN, T.   321, 323-324
SCHILLEBEECKX, E.   121
SCHLERITT, F.   338
SCHLIER, H.   85, 222-223
SCHLIESSER, B.   315
SCHMELLER, T.   389
SCHMIDT, C.   484-485
SCHMIDT, E.D.   88
SCHMIDT, K.L.   71-72
SCHMITHALS, W.   184
SCHNABEL, E.J.   113, 558-564, 572
SCHNACKENBURG, R.   176, 178, 314, 366, 390, 399, 401-403, 408, 417-426
SCHNEEMELCHER, W.   232, 243, 454, 493
SCHNEIDER, G.   68, 93
SCHNEIDER, H.   11
SCHNEIDER, J.   417, 422, 424
SCHNEIDER, M.   527
SCHNEIDER, T.   344
SCHNELLE, U.   81, 94, 211, 366, 411, 435, 509
SCHNIEWIND, J.   139
SCHOEDEL, W.R.   228, 230, 234-236, 243, 245, 429-431
SCHREIBER, J.   177-178
SCHRÖTER, J.   87, 139-140, 143, 228, 231, 250, 279, 321, 325, 334, 454, 465, 476-477, 492, 501-504, 526, 536
SCHUBERT, C.   526
SCHUBERT, P.   345
SCHULZ, S.   6
SCHWEIZER, E.   92, 104, 176, 314
SCHWEMER, A.M.   473
SCHWIEBERT, J.   136
SCOBIE, C.H.H.   140
SCOPELLO, M.   465
SELLEW, M.H.   563
SEVRIN, J.-M.   244, 273
SFAMENI GASPARRO, G.   479
SHEPHERD, T.   176, 178, 455
SHIVELY, E.   133
SIFFER, N.   179
SIM, D.C.   94
SKARSTEN, R.   364
SKEAT, T.C.   496
SKINNER, C.W.   121, 297
SMALL, J.P.   11
SMALLEY, S.S.   400-403, 405
SMITH, C.   572
SMITH, D.A.   229, 238-239, 274, 276-278, 280-281, 283-284, 287-290, 293
SMITH, G.A.   236
SMITH, J.Z.   569
SNODGRASS, K.   58-59, 61, 67
SNYDER, J.A.   503, 529
SÖDING, T.   211
SONNET, J.-P.   137
SPARKS, H.F.D.   157-158, 184, 186, 196, 204
SPENGEL, L.   6
SPICQ, C.   32
STADEL, C.   197
STÄHLIN, O.   495, 497
STANDAERT, B.   175-176
STARK, R.   568-569, 572, 574, 577
STEC, D.M.   112-114
STEIDLE, W.   210
STEIGER, J.A.   332-333
STEIN, A.   347, 355
STEYN, G.J.   98, 117
STICHEL, R.   316, 327-329
STOCK, A.   152-153, 155-156
STOCK, S.G.   197
STONE, M.E.   158, 168

STORY, C.I.K.   482
STOWASSER, M.   171, 174-176
STOWERS, S.K.   563
STRAUSS, M.L.   129-130
STRECKER, G.   401, 403, 405, 408
STREETER, B.H.   19
STRELAN, R.   185
STRUTWOLF, H.   337
STUHLMACHER, P.   313
SUCIU, A.   327, 507
SUHL, A.   112
SULLIVAN, K.   455, 529
SWAIN, S.   183, 194, 345
SWELLENGREBEL, J.L.   401
SWETE, H.B.   100, 102, 107, 110, 112, 152
SYLVA, D.D.   265, 267
TASCHL-ERBER, A.   366
TAYLOR, D.G.K.   194
TAYLOR, V.   104, 107, 143, 152
TCHERIKOVER, V.   39
THEISSEN, G.   42, 72, 74, 80-81, 389
THEOBALD, M.   314, 413-414, 416-417, 419-425
THIESSEN, M.   567
THOMAS, J.D.   63-64
THOMPSON, D.J.   345
THOMPSON, M.M.   185, 302, 366
THOMSON, R.W.   533, 548
THYEN, H.   256, 366, 415, 417-420, 423
TIEDE, D.L.   156
TIGCHELAAR, E.J.C.   163, 197, 472
TISCHENDORF, C. VON   485, 487
TISSOT, Y.   479, 483
TIWALD, M.   562
TOLBERT, M.A.   152, 156
TORALLAS TOVAR, S.   344, 346-347
TORNAU, C.   78
TORRANCE, T.F.   537
TORREY, C.C.   195
TÓTH, F.   459
TOWNSEND, J.T.   566
TREAT, J.C.   442
TREGELLES, S.P.   365
TROMP, J.   149, 181
TROPPER, V.   92, 213-214
TUCKETT, C.M.   4, 109, 121, 142, 145, 153, 160, 170, 181, 228, 244, 247-248, 289, 409, 412, 479, 492, 494-495
TURNAGE, M.   190
TURNER, E.G.   447
TYSON, J.B.   185, 564
UEBERSCHAER, N.   315
UHLIG, S.   445
ULLUCCI, D.C.   571-572
ULRICH, E.   98
ULRICH, J.   83, 505-506, 525
VAAGE, L.E.   566-567, 572-573
VAN BELLE, G.   59, 145, 338
VAN CAPPELLEN, P.   173
VAN DEN HEEDE, P.   213
VANDERKAM, J.C.   160, 168
VAN DER STOCKT, L.   11-13, 16
VAN DER WATT, J.G.   389-390, 399, 406, 409, 460, 465
VAN DE SANDT, H.   25, 273
VANDORPE, K.   28, 346
VAN EIJK, T.H.C.   479
VAN GEEST, P.J.J.   479
VAN IERSEL, B.M.F.   136, 213, 250
VAN MINNEN, P.   444-445, 447-449, 456, 475
VAN OYEN, G.   96-97, 130, 132, 134, 138, 142, 145, 173, 176, 178, 295, 455
VAN ROMPAY, L.   485
VAN SEGBROECK, F.   145
VAN TILBORG, S.   366
VAN UNNIK, W.C.   192, 222, 263
VAN WIERINGEN, A.   130
VASSILIADIS, P.   41
VEGGE, T.   78, 215
VERHEYDEN, J.   1-3, 21, 59, 96-97, 109-111, 145, 209, 228, 250, 273-275, 295, 312, 334, 338, 361, 453, 465, 476, 479, 481, 494-495, 501-502, 512, 518, 533, 536, 557
VERMES, G.   163
VIELHAUER, P.   72, 229-230
VIERROS, M.   346-347
VÖGTLE, A.   140
VÖLKER, W.   495
VÖÖBUS, A.   321
VÖSSING, K.   78
VOLLENWEIDER, S.   210-212
VOUAUX, L.   479, 481-482, 484

Vouga, F.   274
Wahlde, U.C. von   398
Walser, G.   187
Walsh, R.F.   570
Waltzing, J.-P.   510, 522, 524
Wasserman, E.   571
Watson, F.   4, 16-19, 279, 288, 290, 320, 555
Watt, J.M.   183, 187
Wayment, T.W.   442-443
Weeden, T.J.   154-155
Wehen, A.   117
Wehr, L.   412
Weidemann, H.-U.   176, 480, 514
Weinel, H.   454, 456, 472
Weingärtner, D.G.   34
Weiss, B.   102, 107
Weiss, H.Fr.   196
Weissenrieder, A.   74
Wellhausen, J.   151, 155-156, 200
Wendt, H.   571-573
Wengst, K.   83, 423
Wenham, D.   228
Weren, W.J.C.   1, 273, 278
Wessely, C.   444
Westcott, B.F.   45-48, 52-54, 69, 362, 365, 367, 399, 401, 403
Westerhoff, M.   327
Wettstein, J.J.   365
Wibbing, S.   209-210
Wilcken, U.   34, 36, 340-341
Wilckens, U.   220-221
Wilcox, M.   184, 195-203, 205, 207
Wilhite, D.E.   505
Williams, J.G.   154
Williams, M.H.   2
Willis, W.H.   337
Wilmet, M.   555
Wilson, R.McL.   292

Wink, W.   43, 140
Winstedt, E.O.   444
Winter, F.   347
Wischmeyer, O.   94
Witherington III, B.   176, 178, 250, 563
Witulski, T.   435
Wolter, M.   86-87, 93, 106, 214-215, 217-218, 240, 258-261, 263-269, 274, 389
Woods, D.   438
Woolf, G.D.   211, 345
Wrede, W.   121, 151
Wright, B.G.   191
Wright, D.   505
Wright, N.T.   275, 282
Wright, W.   485
Yadin, Y.   365
Yarbro Collins, A.   103, 107, 143, 151-152, 157, 159, 161-167, 170, 172, 176, 250-251, 277
Yardeni, A.   190
Young, S.E.   229, 235, 237, 243, 492
Youtie, H.C.   353
Yuen-Collingridge, R.   496
Zahn, T.   58, 412, 458, 460
Zamfir, K.   481, 499, 529
Zeller, D.   40, 220-221, 274
Zelyck, L.   502
Zerwick, M.   104
Zilling, H.M.   504-505, 507, 509
Zimmermann, A.F.   84
Zimmermann, R.   44
Zmijewski, J.   218-220
Zugmann, M.   343
Zumstein, J.   257, 366, 413-414, 416-417, 419-427
Zwiep, A.W.   285
Zwierlein, O.   486

BIBLIOTHECA EPHEMERIDUM THEOLOGICARUM LOVANIENSIUM

Series III

131. C.M. TUCKETT (ed.), *The Scriptures in the Gospels*, 1997. XXIV-721 p. 60 €
132. J. VAN RUITEN & M. VERVENNE (eds.), *Studies in the Book of Isaiah. Festschrift Willem A.M. Beuken*, 1997. XX-540 p. 75 €
133. M. VERVENNE & J. LUST (eds.), *Deuteronomy and Deuteronomic Literature. Festschrift C.H.W. Brekelmans*, 1997. XI-637 p. 75 €
134. G. VAN BELLE (ed.), *Index Generalis ETL / BETL 1982-1997*, 1999. IX-337 p. 40 €
135. G. DE SCHRIJVER, *Liberation Theologies on Shifting Grounds. A Clash of Socio-Economic and Cultural Paradigms*, 1998. XI-453 p. 53 €
136. A. SCHOORS (ed.), *Qohelet in the Context of Wisdom*, 1998. XI-528 p. 60 €
137. W.A. BIENERT & U. KÜHNEWEG (eds.), *Origeniana Septima. Origenes in den Auseinandersetzungen des 4. Jahrhunderts,* 1999. XXV-848 p. 95 €
138. É. GAZIAUX, *L'autonomie en morale: au croisement de la philosophie et de la théologie*, 1998. XVI-760 p. 75 €
139. J. GROOTAERS, *Actes et acteurs à Vatican II*, 1998. XXIV-602 p. 75 €
140. F. NEIRYNCK, J. VERHEYDEN & R. CORSTJENS, *The Gospel of Matthew and the Sayings Source Q: A Cumulative Bibliography 1950-1995*, 1998. 2 vols., VII-1000-420* p. 95 €
141. E. BRITO, *Heidegger et l'hymne du sacré*, 1999. XV-800 p. 90 €
142. J. VERHEYDEN (ed.), *The Unity of Luke-Acts*, 1999. XXV-828 p. 60 €
143. N. CALDUCH-BENAGES & J. VERMEYLEN (eds.), *Treasures of Wisdom. Studies in Ben Sira and the Book of Wisdom. Festschrift M. Gilbert*, 1999. XXVII-463 p. 75 €
144. J.-M. AUWERS & A. WÉNIN (eds.), *Lectures et relectures de la Bible. Festschrift P.-M. Bogaert*, 1999. XLII-482 p. 75 €
145. C. BEGG, *Josephus' Story of the Later Monarchy (AJ 9,1–10,185)*, 2000. X-650 p. 75 €
146. J.M. ASGEIRSSON, K. DE TROYER & M.W. MEYER (eds.), *From Quest to Q. Festschrift James M. Robinson*, 2000. XLIV-346 p. 60 €
147. T. RÖMER (ed.), *The Future of the Deuteronomistic History*, 2000. XII-265 p. 75 €
148. F.D. VANSINA, *Paul Ricœur: Bibliographie primaire et secondaire - Primary and Secondary Bibliography 1935-2000*, 2000. XXVI-544 p. 75 €
149. G.J. BROOKE & J.-D. KAESTLI (eds.), *Narrativity in Biblical and Related Texts*, 2000. XXI-307 p. 75 €

150. F. NEIRYNCK, *Evangelica III: 1992-2000. Collected Essays*, 2001. XVII-666 p. 60 €
151. B. DOYLE, *The Apocalypse of Isaiah Metaphorically Speaking. A Study of the Use, Function and Significance of Metaphors in Isaiah 24-27*, 2000. XII-453 p. 75 €
152. T. MERRIGAN & J. HAERS (eds.), *The Myriad Christ. Plurality and the Quest for Unity in Contemporary Christology*, 2000. XIV-593 p. 75 €
153. M. SIMON, *Le catéchisme de Jean-Paul II. Genèse et évaluation de son commentaire du Symbole des apôtres*, 2000. XVI-688 p. 75 €
154. J. VERMEYLEN, *La loi du plus fort. Histoire de la rédaction des récits davidiques de 1 Samuel 8 à 1 Rois 2*, 2000. XIII-746 p. 80 €
155. A. WÉNIN (ed.), *Studies in the Book of Genesis. Literature, Redaction and History*, 2001. XXX-643 p. 60 €
156. F. LEDEGANG, *Mysterium Ecclesiae. Images of the Church and its Members in Origen*, 2001. XVII-848 p. 84 €
157. J.S. BOSWELL, F.P. MCHUGH & J. VERSTRAETEN (eds.), *Catholic Social Thought: Twilight of Renaissance*, 2000. XXII-307 p. 60 €
158. A. LINDEMANN (ed.), *The Sayings Source Q and the Historical Jesus*, 2001. XXII-776 p. 60 €
159. C. HEMPEL, A. LANGE & H. LICHTENBERGER (eds.), *The Wisdom Texts from Qumran and the Development of Sapiential Thought*, 2002. XII-502 p. 80 €
160. L. BOEVE & L. LEIJSSEN (eds.), *Sacramental Presence in a Postmodern Context*, 2001. XVI-382 p. 60 €
161. A. DENAUX (ed.), *New Testament Textual Criticism and Exegesis. Festschrift J. Delobel*, 2002. XVIII-391 p. 60 €
162. U. BUSSE, *Das Johannesevangelium. Bildlichkeit, Diskurs und Ritual. Mit einer Bibliographie über den Zeitraum 1986-1998*, 2002. XIII-572 p. 70 €
163. J.-M. AUWERS & H.J. DE JONGE (eds.), *The Biblical Canons*, 2003. LXXXVIII-718 p. 60 €
164. L. PERRONE (ed.), *Origeniana Octava. Origen and the Alexandrian Tradition*, 2003. XXV-X-1406 p. 180 €
165. R. BIERINGER, V. KOPERSKI & B. LATAIRE (eds.), *Resurrection in the New Testament. Festschrift J. Lambrecht*, 2002. XXXI-551 p. 70 €
166. M. LAMBERIGTS & L. KENIS (eds.), *Vatican II and Its Legacy*, 2002. XII-512 p. 65 €
167. P. DIEUDONNÉ, *La Paix clémentine. Défaite et victoire du premier jansénisme français sous le pontificat de Clément IX (1667-1669)*, 2003. XXXIX-302 p. 70 €
168. F. GARCÍA MARTÍNEZ, *Wisdom and Apocalypticism in the Dead Sea Scrolls and in the Biblical Tradition*, 2003. XXXIV-491 p. 60 €
169. D. OGLIARI, *Gratia et Certamen: The Relationship between Grace and Free Will in the Discussion of Augustine with the So-Called Semipelagians*, 2003. LVII-468 p. 75 €
170. G. COOMAN, M. VAN STIPHOUT & B. WAUTERS (eds.), *Zeger-Bernard Van Espen at the Crossroads of Canon Law, History, Theology and Church-State Relations*, 2003. XX-530 p. 80 €
171. B. BOURGINE, *L'herméneutique théologique de Karl Barth. Exégèse et dogmatique dans le quatrième volume de la Kirchliche Dogmatik*, 2003. XXII-548 p. 75 €

172. J. HAERS & P. DE MEY (eds.), *Theology and Conversation: Towards a Relational Theology*, 2003. XIII-923 p. 90 €
173. M.J.J. MENKEN, *Matthew's Bible: The Old Testament Text of the Evangelist*, 2004. XII-336 p. 60 €
174. J.-P. DELVILLE, *L'Europe de l'exégèse au XVIe siècle. Interprétations de la parabole des ouvriers à la vigne (Matthieu 20,1-16)*, 2004. XLII-775 p. 70 €
175. E. BRITO, *J.G. Fichte et la transformation du christianisme*, 2004. XVI-808 p. 90 €
176. J. SCHLOSSER (ed.), *The Catholic Epistles and the Tradition*, 2004. XXIV-569 p. 60 €
177. R. FAESEN (ed.), *Albert Deblaere, S.J. (1916-1994): Essays on Mystical Literature – Essais sur la littérature mystique – Saggi sulla letteratura mistica*, 2004. XX-473 p. 70 €
178. J. LUST, *Messianism and the Septuagint: Collected Essays*. Edited by K. HAUSPIE, 2004. XIV-247 p. 60 €
179. H. GIESEN, *Jesu Heilsbotschaft und die Kirche. Studien zur Eschatologie und Ekklesiologie bei den Synoptikern und im ersten Petrusbrief*, 2004. XX-578 p. 70 €
180. H. LOMBAERTS & D. POLLEFEYT (eds.), *Hermeneutics and Religious Education*, 2004. XIII-427 p. 70 €
181. D. DONNELLY, A. DENAUX & J. FAMERÉE (eds.), *The Holy Spirit, the Church, and Christian Unity. Proceedings of the Consultation Held at the Monastery of Bose, Italy (14-20 October 2002)*, 2005. XII-417 p. 70 €
182. R. BIERINGER, G. VAN BELLE & J. VERHEYDEN (eds.), *Luke and His Readers. Festschrift A. Denaux*, 2005. XXVIII-470 p. 65 €
183. D.F. PILARIO, *Back to the Rough Grounds of Praxis: Exploring Theological Method with Pierre Bourdieu*, 2005. XXXII-584 p. 80 €
184. G. VAN BELLE, J.G. VAN DER WATT & P. MARITZ (eds.), *Theology and Christology in the Fourth Gospel: Essays by the Members of the SNTS Johannine Writings Seminar*, 2005. XII-561 p. 70 €
185. D. LUCIANI, *Sainteté et pardon*. Vol. 1: *Structure littéraire du Lévitique*. Vol. 2: *Guide technique*, 2005. XIV-VII-656 p. 120 €
186. R.A. DERRENBACKER, JR., *Ancient Compositional Practices and the Synoptic Problem*, 2005. XXVIII-290 p. 80 €
187. P. VAN HECKE (ed.), *Metaphor in the Hebrew Bible*, 2005. X-308 p. 65 €
188. L. BOEVE, Y. DEMAESENEER & S. VAN DEN BOSSCHE (eds.), *Religious Experience and Contemporary Theological Epistemology*, 2005. X-335 p. 50 €
189. J.M. ROBINSON, *The Sayings Gospel Q. Collected Essays*, 2005. XVIII-888 p. 90 €
190. C.W. STRÜDER, *Paulus und die Gesinnung Christi. Identität und Entscheidungsfindung aus der Mitte von 1Kor 1-4*, 2005. LII-522 p. 80 €
191. C. FOCANT & A. WÉNIN (eds.), *Analyse narrative et Bible. Deuxième colloque international du RRENAB, Louvain-la-Neuve, avril 2004*, 2005. XVI-593 p. 75 €
192. F. GARCÍA MARTÍNEZ & M. VERVENNE (eds.), in collaboration with B. DOYLE, *Interpreting Translation: Studies on the LXX and Ezekiel in Honour of Johan Lust*, 2005. XVI-464 p. 70 €
193. F. MIES, *L'espérance de Job*, 2006. XXIV-653 p. 87 €

194. C. FOCANT, *Marc, un évangile étonnant*, 2006. XV-402 p. 60 €
195. M.A. KNIBB (ed.), *The Septuagint and Messianism*, 2006. XXXI-560 p. 60 €
196. M. SIMON, *La célébration du mystère chrétien dans le catéchisme de Jean-Paul II*, 2006. XIV-638 p. 85 €
197. A.Y. THOMASSET, *L'ecclésiologie de J.H. Newman Anglican*, 2006. XXX-748 p. 80 €
198. M. LAMBERIGTS – A.A. DEN HOLLANDER (eds.), *Lay Bibles in Europe 1450-1800*, 2006. XI-360 p. 79 €
199. J.Z. SKIRA – M.S. ATTRIDGE, *In God's Hands. Essays on the Church and Ecumenism in Honour of Michael A. Fahey S.J.*, 2006. XXX-314 p. 90 €
200. G. VAN BELLE (ed.), *The Death of Jesus in the Fourth Gospel*, 2007. XXXI-1003 p. 70 €
201. D. POLLEFEYT (ed.), *Interreligious Learning*, 2007. XXV-340 p. 80 €
202. M. LAMBERIGTS – L. BOEVE – T. MERRIGAN, in collaboration with D. CLAES (eds.), *Theology and the Quest for Truth: Historical- and Systematic-Theological Studies*, 2007. X-305 p. 55 €
203. T. RÖMER – K. SCHMID (eds.), *Les dernières rédactions du Pentateuque, de l'Hexateuque et de l'Ennéateuque*, 2007. X-276 p. 65 €
204. J.-M. VAN CANGH, *Les sources judaïques du Nouveau Testament*, 2008. XIV-718 p. 84 €
205. B. DEHANDSCHUTTER, *Polycarpiana: Studies on Martyrdom and Persecution in Early Christianity. Collected Essays*. Edited by J. LEEMANS, 2007. XVI-286 p. 74 €
206. É. GAZIAUX, *Philosophie et Théologie. Festschrift Emilio Brito*, 2007. LVIII-588 p. 84 €
207. G.J. BROOKE – T. RÖMER (eds.), *Ancient and Modern Scriptural Historiography. L'historiographie biblique, ancienne et moderne*, 2007. XXXVIII-372 p. 75 €
208. J. VERSTRAETEN, *Scrutinizing the Signs of the Times in the Light of the Gospel*, 2007. X-334 p. 74 €
209. H. GEYBELS, *Cognitio Dei experimentalis. A Theological Genealogy of Christian Religious Experience*, 2007. LII-457 p. 80 €
210. A.A. DEN HOLLANDER, *Virtuelle Vergangenheit: Die Textrekonstruktion einer verlorenen mittelniederländischen Evangelienharmonie. Die Handschrift Utrecht Universitätsbibliothek 1009*, 2007. XII-168 p. 58 €
211. R. GRYSON, *Scientiam Salutis: Quarante années de recherches sur l'Antiquité Chrétienne. Recueil d'essais*, 2008. XLVI-879 p. 88 €
212. T. VAN DEN DRIESSCHE, *L'altérité, fondement de la personne humaine dans l'œuvre d'Edith Stein*, 2008. XXII-626 p. 85 €
213. H. AUSLOOS – J. COOK – F. GARCÍA MARTÍNEZ – B. LEMMELIJN – M. VERVENNE (eds.), *Translating a Translation: The LXX and its Modern Translations in the Context of Early Judaism*, 2008. X-317 p. 80 €
214. A.C. OSUJI, *Where is the Truth? Narrative Exegesis and the Question of True and False Prophecy in Jer 26–29 (MT)*, 2010. XX-465 p. 76 €
215. T. RÖMER, *The Books of Leviticus and Numbers*, 2008. XXVII-742 p. 85 €
216. D. DONNELLY – J. FAMERÉE – M. LAMBERIGTS – K. SCHELKENS (eds.), *The Belgian Contribution to the Second Vatican Council: International Research Conference at Mechelen, Leuven and Louvain-la-Neuve (September 12-16, 2005)*, 2008. XII-716 p. 85 €

217. J. De Tavernier – J.A. Selling – J. Verstraeten – P. Schotsmans (eds.), *Responsibility, God and Society. Theological Ethics in Dialogue. Festschrift Roger Burggraeve*, 2008. XLVI-413 p. 75 €
218. G. Van Belle – J.G. van der Watt – J. Verheyden (eds.), *Miracles and Imagery in Luke and John. Festschrift Ulrich Busse*, 2008. XVIII-287 p. 78 €
219. L. Boeve – M. Lamberigts – M. Wisse (eds.), *Augustine and Postmodern Thought: A New Alliance against Modernity?*, 2009. XVIII-277 p. 80 €
220. T. Victoria, *Un livre de feu dans un siècle de fer: Les lectures de l'Apocalypse dans la littérature française de la Renaissance*, 2009. XXX-609 p. 85 €
221. A.A. den Hollander – W. François (eds.), *Infant Milk or Hardy Nourishment? The Bible for Lay People and Theologians in the Early Modern Period*, 2009. XVIII-488 p. 80 €
222. F.D. Vansina, *Paul Ricœur. Bibliographie primaire et secondaire. Primary and Secundary Bibliography 1935-2008*, Compiled and updated in collaboration with P. Vandecasteele, 2008. XXX-621 p. 80 €
223. G. Van Belle – M. Labahn – P. Maritz (eds.), *Repetitions and Variations in the Fourth Gospel: Style, Text, Interpretation*, 2009. XII-712 p. 85 €
224. H. Ausloos – B. Lemmelijn – M. Vervenne (eds.), *Florilegium Lovaniense: Studies in Septuagint and Textual Criticism in Honour of Florentino García Martínez*, 2008. XVI-564 p. 80 €
225. E. Brito, *Philosophie moderne et christianisme*, 2010. 2 vol., VIII-1514 p. 130 €
226. U. Schnelle (ed.), *The Letter to the Romans*, 2009. XVIII-894 p. 85 €
227. M. Lamberigts – L. Boeve – T. Merrigan in collaboration with D. Claes – M. Wisse (eds.), *Orthodoxy, Process and Product*, 2009. X-416 p. 74 €
228. G. Heidl – R. Somos (eds.), *Origeniana Nona: Origen and the Religious Practice of His Time*, 2009. XIV-752 p. 95 €
229. D. Marguerat (ed.), *Reception of Paulinism in Acts – Réception du paulinisme dans les Actes des Apôtres*, 2009. VIII-340 p. 74 €
230. A. Dillen – D. Pollefeyt (eds.), *Children's Voices: Children's Perspectives in Ethics, Theology and Religious Education*, 2010. X-450 p. 72 €
231. P. Van Hecke – A. Labahn (eds.), *Metaphors in the Psalms*, 2010. XXXIV-363 p. 76 €
232. G. Auld – E. Eynikel (eds.), *For and Against David: Story and History in the Books of Samuel*, 2010. X-397 p. 76 €
233. C. Vialle, *Une analyse comparée d'Esther TM et LXX: Regard sur deux récits d'une même histoire*, 2010. LVIII-406 p. 76 €
234. T. Merrigan – F. Glorieux (eds.), *"Godhead Here in Hiding": Incarnation and the History of Human Suffering*, 2012. X-327 p. 76 €
235. M. Simon, *La vie dans le Christ dans le catéchisme de Jean-Paul II*, 2010. XX-651 p. 84 €
236. G. De Schrijver, *The Political Ethics of Jean-François Lyotard and Jacques Derrida*, 2010. XXX-422 p. 80 €
237. A. Pasquier – D. Marguerat – A. Wénin (eds.), *L'intrigue dans le récit biblique. Quatrième colloque international du RRENAB, Université Laval, Québec, 29 mai – 1er juin 2008*, 2010. XXX-479 p. 68 €
238. E. Zenger (ed.), *The Composition of the Book of Psalms*, 2010. XII-826 p. 90 €

239. P. Foster – A. Gregory – J.S. Kloppenborg – J. Verheyden (eds.), *New Studies in the Synoptic Problem: Oxford Conference, April 2008*, 2011. XXIV-828 p. 85 €
240. J. Verheyden – T.L. Hettema – P. Vandecasteele (eds.), *Paul Ricœur: Poetics and Religion*, 2011. XX-534 p. 79 €
241. J. Leemans (ed.), *Martyrdom and Persecution in Late Ancient Christianity. Festschrift Boudewijn Dehandschutter*, 2010. XXXIV-430 p. 78 €
242. C. Clivaz – J. Zumstein (eds.), *Reading New Testament Papyri in Context – Lire les papyrus du Nouveau Testament dans leur contexte*, 2011. XIV-446 p. 80 €
243. D. Senior (ed.), *The Gospel of Matthew at the Crossroads of Early Christianity*, 2011. XXVIII-781 p. 88 €
244. H. Pietras – S. Kaczmarek (eds.), *Origeniana Decima: Origen as Writer*, 2011. XVIII-1039 p. 105 €
245. M. Simon, *La prière chrétienne dans le catéchisme de Jean-Paul II*, 2012. XVI-290 p. 70 €
246. H. Ausloos – B. Lemmelijn – J. Trebolle-Barrera (eds.), *After Qumran: Old and Modern Editions of the Biblical Texts – The Historical Books*, 2012. XIV-319 p. 84 €
247. G. Van Oyen – A. Wénin (eds.), *La surprise dans la Bible. Festschrift Camille Focant*, 2012. XLII-474 p. 80 €
248. C. Clivaz – C. Combet-Galland – J.-D. Macchi – C. Nihan (eds.), *Écritures et réécritures: la reprise interprétative des traditions fondatrices par la littérature biblique et extra-biblique. Cinquième colloque international du RRENAB, Universités de Genève et Lausanne, 10-12 juin 2010*, 2012. XXIV-648 p. 90 €
249. G. Van Oyen – T. Shepherd (eds.), *Resurrection of the Dead: Biblical Traditions in Dialogue*, 2012. XVI-632 p. 85 €
250. E. Noort (ed.), *The Book of Joshua*, 2012. XIV-698 p. 90 €
251. R. Faesen – L. Kenis (eds.), *The Jesuits of the Low Countries: Identity and Impact (1540-1773). Proceedings of the International Congress at the Faculty of Theology and Religious Studies, KU Leuven (3-5 December 2009)*, 2012. X-295 p. 65 €
252. A. Damm, *Ancient Rhetoric and the Synoptic Problem: Clarifying Markan Priority*, 2013. XXXVIII-396 p. 85 €
253. A. Denaux – P. De Mey (eds.), *The Ecumenical Legacy of Johannes Cardinal Willebrands (1909-2006)*, 2012. XIV-376 p. 79 €
254. T. Knieps-Port le Roi – G. Mannion – P. De Mey (eds.), *The Household of God and Local Households: Revisiting the Domestic Church*, 2013. XI-407 p. 82 €
255. L. Kenis – E. van der Wall (eds.), *Religious Modernism of the Low Countries*, 2013. X-271 p. 75 €
256. P. Ide, *Une Théo-logique du Don: Le Don dans la* Trilogie *de Hans Urs von Balthasar*, 2013. XXX-759 p. 98 €
257. W. François – A. den Hollander (eds.), *"Wading Lambs and Swimming Elephants": The Bible for the Laity and Theologians in the Late Medieval and Early Modern Era*, 2012. XVI-406 p. 84 €
258. A. Liégois – R. Burggraeve – M. Riemslagh – J. Corveleyn (eds.), *"After You!": Dialogical Ethics and the Pastoral Counselling Process*, 2013. XXII-279 p. 79 €

259. C. KALONJI NKOKESHA, *Penser la tradition avec Walter Kasper: Pertinence d'une catholicité historiquement et culturellement ouverte*, 2013. XXIV-320 p. 79 €
260. J. SCHRÖTER (ed.), *The Apocryphal Gospels within the Context of Early Christian Theology*, 2013. XII-804 p. 90 €
261. P. DE MEY – P. DE WITTE – G. MANNION (eds.), *Believing in Community: Ecumenical Reflections on the Church*, 2013. XIV-608 p. 90 €
262. F. DEPOORTERE – J. HAERS (eds.), *To Discern Creation in a Scattering World*, 2013. XII-597 p. 90 €
263. L. BOEVE – T. MERRIGAN, in collaboration with C. DICKINSON (eds.), *Tradition and the Normativity of History*, 2013. X-215 p. 55 €
264. M. GILBERT, *Ben Sira. Recueil d'études – Collected Essays*, 2014. XIV-402 p. 87 €
265. J. VERHEYDEN – G. VAN OYEN – M. LABAHN – R. BIERINGER (eds.), *Studies in the Gospel of John and Its Christology. Festschrift Gilbert Van Belle*, 2014. XXXVI-656 p. 94 €
266. W. DE PRIL, *Theological Renewal and the Resurgence of Integrism: The René Draguet Case (1942) in Its Context*, 2016. XLIV-333 p. 85 €
267. L.O. JIMÉNEZ-RODRÍGUEZ, *The Articulation between Natural Sciences and Systematic Theology: A Philosophical Mediation Based on Contributions of Jean Ladrière and Xavier Zubiri*, 2015. XXIV-541 p. 94 €
268. E. BIRNBAUM – L. SCHWIENHORST-SCHÖNBERGER (eds.), *Hieronymus als Exeget und Theologe: Interdisziplinäre Zugänge zum Koheletkommentar des Hieronymus*, 2014. XVIII-333 p. 80 €
269. H. AUSLOOS – B. LEMMELIJN (eds.), *A Pillar of Cloud to Guide: Text-critical, Redactional, and Linguistic Perspectives on the Old Testament in Honour of Marc Vervenne*, 2014. XXVIII-636 p. 90 €
270. E. TIGCHELAAR (ed.), *Old Testament Pseudepigrapha and the Scriptures*, 2014. XXVI-526 p. 95 €
271. E. BRITO, *Sur l'homme: Une traversée de la question anthropologique*, 2015. XVI-2045 p. (2 vol.) 215 €
272. P. WATINE CHRISTORY, *Dialogue et Communion: L'itinéraire œcuménique de Jean-Marie R. Tillard*, 2015. XXIV-773 p. 98 €
273. R. BURNET – D. LUCIANI – G. VAN OYEN (eds.), *Le lecteur: Sixième Colloque International du RRENAB, Université Catholique de Louvain, 24-26 mai 2012*, 2015. XIV-530 p. 85 €
274. G.B. BAZZANA, *Kingdom of Bureaucracy: The Political Theology of Village Scribes in the Sayings Gospel Q*, 2015. XII-383 p. 85 €
275. J.-P. GALLEZ, *La théologie comme science herméneutique de la tradition de foi: Une lecture de «Dieu qui vient à l'homme» de Joseph Moingt*, 2015. XIX-476 p. 94 €
276. J. VERMEYLEN, *Métamorphoses: Les rédactions successives du livre de Job*, 2015. XVI-410 p. 84 €
277. C. BREYTENBACH (ed.), *Paul's Graeco-Roman Context*, 2015. XXII-751 p. 94 €
278. J. GELDHOF (ed.), *Mediating Mysteries, Understanding Liturgies: On Bridging the Gap between Liturgy and Systematic Theology*, 2015. X-256 p. 78 €
279. A.-C. JACOBSEN (ed.), *Origeniana Undecima: Origen and Origenism in the History of Western Thought*, 2016. XVI-978 p. 125 €

280. F. Wilk – P. Gemeinhardt (eds.), *Transmission and Interpretation of the Book of Isaiah in the Context of Intra- and Interreligious Debates*, 2016. XII-490 p. 95 €
281. J.-M. Sevrin, *Le quatrième évangile. Recueil d'études*. Édité par G. Van Belle, 2016. XIV-281 p. 86 €
282. L. Boeve – M. Lamberigts – T. Merrigan (eds.), *The Normativity of History: Theological Truth and Tradition in the Tension between Church History and Systematic Theology*, 2016. XII-273 p. 78 €
283. R. Bieringer – B. Baert – K. Demasure (eds.), Noli me tangere *in Interdisciplinary Perspective: Textual, Iconographic and Contemporary Interpretations*, 2016. XXII-508 p. 89 €
284. W. Dietrich (ed.), *The Books of Samuel: Stories – History – Reception History*, 2016. XXIV-650 p. 96 €
285. W.E. Arnal – R.S. Ascough – R.A. Derrenbacker, Jr. – P.A. Harland (eds.), *Scribal Practices and Social Structures among Jesus Adherents: Essays in Honour of John S. Kloppenborg*, 2016. XXIV-630 p. 115 €
286. C.E. Wolfteich – A. Dillen (eds.), *Catholic Approaches in Practical Theology: International and Interdisciplinary Perspectives*, 2016. X-290 p. 85 €
287. W. François – A.A. den Hollander (eds.), *Vernacular Bible and Religious Reform in the Middle Ages and Early Modern Era*, 2017. VIII-305 p. 94 €
288. P. Rodrigues, *C'est ta face que je cherche … La rationalité de la théologie selon Jean Ladrière*, 2017. XIV-453 p. 92 €
289. J. Famerée, *Ecclésiologie et œcuménisme. Recueil d'études*, 2017. XVIII-668 p. 94 €
290. P. Cooper – S. Kikuchi (eds.), *Commitments to Medieval Mysticism within Contemporary Contexts*, 2017. XVI-382 p. 79 €
291. A. Yarbro Collins (ed.), *New Perspectives on the Book of Revelation*, 2017. X-644 p. 98 €
292. J. Famerée – P. Rodrigues (eds.), *The Genesis of Concepts and the Confrontation of Rationalities*, 2018. XIV-245 p. 78 €
293. E. Di Pede – O. Flichy – D. Luciani (eds.), *Le Récit: Thèmes bibliques et variations*, 2018. XIV-412 p. 95 €
294. J. Arblaster – R. Faesen (eds.), *Theosis/Deification: Christian Doctrines of Divinization East and West*, 2018. VII-262 p. 84 €
295. H.-J. Fabry (ed.), *The Books of the Twelve Prophets: Minor Prophets – Major Theologies*, 2018. XXIV-557 p. 105 €
296. H. Ausloos – D. Luciani (eds.), *Temporalité et intrigue. Hommage à André Wénin*, 2018. XL-362 p. 95 €
297. A.C. Mayer (ed.), *The Letter and the Spirit: On the Forgotten Documents of Vatican II*, 2018. X-296 p. 85 €
298. A. Begasse de Dhaem – E. Galli – M. Malaguti – C. Salto Solá (eds.), Deus summe cognoscibilis: *The Current Theological Relevance of Saint Bonaventure International Congress, Rome, November 15-17, 2017*, 2018. XII-716 p. 85 €
299. M. Lamberigts – W. De Pril (eds.), *Louvain, Belgium and Beyond: Studies in Religious History in Honour of Leo Kenis*, 2018. XVIII-517 p. 95 €
300. E. Brito, *De Dieu. Connaissance et inconnaissance*, 2018. LVIII-634 + 635-1255 p. 155 €

301. G. VAN OYEN (ed.), *Reading the Gospel of Mark in the Twenty-first Century: Method and Meaning*, 2019. XXIV-933 p. 105 €
302. B. BITTON-ASHKELONY – O. IRSHAI – A. KOFSKY – H. NEWMAN – L. PERRONE (eds.), *Origeniana Duodecima: Origen's Legacy in the Holy Land – A Tale of Three Cities: Jerusalem, Caesarea and Bethlehem*, 2019. XIV-893 p. 125 €
303. D. BOSSCHAERT, *The Anthropological Turn, Christian Humanism, and Vatican II: Louvain Theologians Preparing the Path for* Gaudium et Spes *(1942-1965)*, 2019. LXVIII-432 p. 89 €
304. I. KOCH – T. RÖMER – O. SERGI (eds.), *Writing, Rewriting, and Overwriting in the Books of Deuteronomy and the Former Prophets. Essays in Honour of Cynthia Edenburg*, 2019. XVI-401 p. 85 €
305. W.A.M. BEUKEN, *From Servant of YHWH to Being Considerate of the Wretched: The Figure David in the Reading Perspective of Psalms 35–41 MT*, 2020. XIV-173 p. 69 €
306. P. DE MEY – W. FRANÇOIS (eds.), *Ecclesia semper reformanda: Renewal and Reform beyond Polemics*, 2020. X-477 p. 94 €
307. D. HÉTIER, *Éléments d'une théologie fondamentale de la création artistique: Les écrits théologiques sur l'art chez Karl Rahner (1954-1983)*, 2020. XXIV-492 p. 94 €
308. P.-M. BOGAERT, *Le livre de Jérémie en perspective: Les deux rédactions conservées et l'addition du supplément sous le nom de Baruch*. Recueil de ses travaux réunis par J.-C. HAELEWYCK – B. KINDT, 2020. LVIII-536 p. 95 €
309. D. VERDE – A. LABAHN (eds.), *Networks of Metaphors in the Hebrew Bible*, 2020. X-395 p. 85 €
310. P. VAN HECKE (ed.), *The Song of Songs in Its Context: Words for Love, Love for Words*, 2020. XXXIV-643 p. 95 €
311. A. WÉNIN (ed.), *La contribution du discours à la caractérisation des personnages bibliques. Neuvième colloque international du RRENAB, Louvain-la-Neuve, 31 mai – 2 juin 2018*, 2020. XX-424 p. 95 €
312. J. VERHEYDEN – D.A.T. MÜLLER (eds.), *Imagining Paganism through the Ages: Studies on the Use of the Labels "Pagan" and "Paganism" in Controversies*, 2020. XIV-343 p. 95 €
313. E. BRITO, *Accès au Christ*, 2020. XVI-1164 p. 165 €
314. B. BOURGINE (ed.), *Le souci de toutes les Églises: Hommage à Joseph Famerée*, 2020. XLIV-399 p. 93 €
315. C.C. APINTILIESEI, *La structure ontologique-communionnelle de la personne: Aux sources théologiques et philosophiques du père Dumitru Stăniloae*, 2020. XXII-441 p. 90 €
316. A. DUPONT – W. FRANÇOIS – J. LEEMANS (eds.), Nos sumus tempora: *Studies on Augustine and His Reception Offered to Mathijs Lamberigts*, 2020. XX-577 p. 98 €
317. D. BOSSCHAERT – J. LEEMANS (eds.), Res opportunae nostrae aetatis: *Studies on the Second Vatican Council Offered to Mathijs Lamberigts*, 2020. XII-578 p. 98 €
318. B. OIRY, *Le Temps qui compte: Construction et qualification du temps de l'histoire dans le récit des livres de Samuel (1 S 1 – 1 R 2)*, 2021. XVI-510 p. 89 €

319. J. VERHEYDEN – J. SCHRÖTER – T. NICKLAS (eds), *Texts in Context: Essays on Dating and Contextualising Christian Writings from the Second and Early Third Centuries*, 2021. VIII-319 p. 98 €
320. N.S. HEEREMAN, *"Behold King Solomon on the Day of His Wedding": A Symbolic-Diachronic Reading of Song 3,6-11 and 4,12–5,1*, 2021. XXVIII-975 p. 144 €
321. S. ARENAS, *Fading Frontiers? A Historical-Theological Investigation into the Notion of the* Elementa Ecclesiae, 2021. XXXII-261 p. 80 €
322. C. KORTEN, *Half-Truths: The Irish College, Rome, and a Select History of the Catholic Church, 1771-1826*, 2021. XII-329 p. 98 €
323. L. DECLERCK, *Vatican II: concile de transition et de renouveau. La contribution des évêques et théologiens belges*, 2021. XVIII-524 p. 97 €
324. F. MIES, *Job ou sortir de la cendre: étude exégétique, littéraire anthropologique et théologique de la mort dans le livre de Job* forthcoming
325. J. LIEU (ed.), *Peter in the Early Church: Apostle – Missionary – Church Leader*, 2021. XXVIII-806 p. 160 €
326. J.Z. SKIRA – P. DE MEY – H.G.B. TEULE (eds.), *The Catholic Church and Its Orthodox Sister Churches Twenty-Five Years after Balamand* forthcoming
327. J. VERHEYDEN – J.S. KLOPPENBORG – G. ROSKAM – S. SCHORN (eds.), *On Using Sources in Graeco-Roman, Jewish and Early Christian Literature* forthcoming
328. J.W. VAN HENTEN (ed.), *The Books of the Maccabees: Literary, Historical and Religious Perspectives* forthcoming
329. J. VERHEYDEN – G. ROSKAM – A. HEIRMAN – J. LEEMANS (eds.), *Reaching for Perfection: Studies on the Means and Goals of Ascetical Practices in an Interreligious Perspective* forthcoming